JUSTICE, PUNISHMENT, TREATMENT

JUSTICE, PUNISHMENT, TREATMENT

The Correctional Process

LEONARD ORLAND
Professor of Law
University of Connecticut School of Law

Introduction by
ABRAHAM S. GOLDSTEIN
Dean, and Cromwell Professor of Law,
Yale Law School

THE FREE PRESS
A Division of Macmillan Publishing Co., Inc.
New York

COLLIER MACMILLAN PUBLISHERS
London

Copyright © 1973 by The Free Press
A Division of Macmillan Publishing Co., Inc.

All rights reserved. No part of this book may be reproduced or transmitted in any form or by any means, electronic or mechanical, including photocopying, recording, or by any information storage and retrieval system, without permission in writing from the Publisher.

The Free Press
A Division of Macmillan Publishing Co., Inc.
866 Third Avenue, New York, N.Y. 10022

Collier–Macmillan Canada Ltd.

Library of Congress Catalog Card Number: 72-94014

Printed in the United States of America

printing number
  2 3 4 5 6 7 8 9 10

For
my children,
Laurin and Paul,
and my parents,
Morris and Sarah,
with love

SUMMARY TABLE OF CONTENTS

PREFACE xxiii

INTRODUCTION by Abraham S. Goldstein xxv

Part I SENTENCING: THE WAY IN

Chapter One INTRODUCTORY PERSPECTIVES 3

Chapter Two LEGISLATIVE CHOICE: DELEGATION OF RESPONSIBILITY TO THE JUDICIARY AND CORRECTIONS 9

Chapter Three BUREAUCRATIC PRECHOICE: PRE-SENTENCE INVESTIGATION AND REPORT 20

Chapter Four JUDICIAL CHOICE: INCARCERATION AND ALTERNATIVES THERETO 33

    A. Alternatives to Incarceration 33
        1. FINES 33
        2. CIVIL COMMITMENT 39
        3. PROBATION AND SUSPENDED SENTENCE 44
        4. THE ALTERNATIVES FAIL: PROBATION REVOCATION 67

    B. Sentences of Imprisonment 78
        1. THE EFFECT OF A GUILTY PLEA: DIFFERENTIAL SENTENCING 78

2. ESTABLISHING MAXIMA AND MINIMA 83
3. EXTENDED INCARCERATION TERMS: THE DANGEROUS OFFENDER AND THE MULTIPLE OFFENDER 89
4. CONSECUTIVE AND CONCURRENT SENTENCES 99
5. SENTENCE REVIEW 102
6. TRAINING THE JUDGE 115

Part II IMPRISONMENT: PUNISHMENT AND TREATMENT

Chapter Five WHAT IS PRISON? 125

  A. Inside Views 125

  B. Empirical Perspectives 133

  C. Historical Perspectives 141

  D. Theoretical Explanations 153

  E. International Perspectives 178

Chapter Six THEORIES OF PUNISHMENT AND CORRECTION: WHAT IS THE FUNCTION OF PRISON? 183

Chapter Seven CLASSIFICATION: HOW SHOULD THE PRISON DIFFERENTIATE AMONG INMATES? 218

Chapter Eight INSTITUTIONAL MISCONDUCT AND RESPONSES THERETO: HOW SHOULD PRISON RULES BE MADE AND ENFORCED? 241

  A. Perspectives 241

    1. HISTORICAL 241

    2. CORRECTIONAL 243

    3. POLITICAL 251

  B. Making "Law": Regulations 254

    1. SETTING POLICY 254

    2. INFORMING THE INMATE 262

  C. Applying "Law": The Misconduct Hearing 272

  D. Judicial Review of Prison Discipline Decisions: The "Hole," the Eighth, and the Fourteenth Amendments 277

    1. THE "HOLE" 277

    2. THE MEANING OF THE EIGHTH AMENDMENT 279

    3. THE "HOLE" AND THE EIGHTH AMENDMENT 290

    4. DISCIPLINARY PROCEEDINGS AND DUE PROCESS OF LAW 309

    5. ADMINISTRATIVE SEGREGATION AND DUE PROCESS OF LAW 317

    6. DAMAGE RECOVERY BY INMATES 319

    7. PROCEDURE IN PRISONER RIGHTS CASES 325

    8. THE INMATE'S RIGHT TO A JUDICIAL HEARING 327

    9. CORPORAL PUNISHMENT AND THE EIGHTH AMENDMENT 330

10. PRISON REGULATIONS AND THE VOID FOR VAGUENESS RULE 333
11. JAIL INMATES 335
12. LEGISLATIVE SPECIFICATIONS OF PRISONER RIGHTS 342

E. Judicial Review of Prison Disciplinary Decisions: Loss of Good Time 355
1. STATUTORY PROVISIONS 355
2. ADMINISTRATIVE INTERPRETATION 355
3. JUDICIAL REVIEW 357
4. GOOD TIME FOR JAIL INMATES 364
5. GOOD TIME AND JOB CLASSIFICATION 366

Chapter Nine THE RULE OF LAW AND PRISON LIFE: THE ROLE OF LAWYER AND JUDGE IN INSTITUTIONAL CONTROL OF THE INMATE POPULATION 368

A. Daily Life 368
B. Sexual Relations 371
C. Medical Treatment 373
D. Racial Discrimination 374
E. Religious Freedom 374
F. Access to Lawyers and Courts 377
G. Inmate Communication 386

Part III RELEASE FROM PRISON: THE WAY OUT (AND IN AGAIN)

Chapter Ten PRERELEASE 401

Chapter Eleven PAROLE: UNFETTERED POWER AND DISCRETIONARY PREDICTION 410

A. Historical Perspectives 410
B. Statutory Structure 413
C. Making "Law": Regulations 418
D. Applying "Law": The Parole Hearing 425
1. THE DECISION-MAKING PROCESS 425
2. EXCERPTS FROM CONNECTICUT PAROLE HEARINGS 437
3. SOME PROBLEM PAROLE CASES 451
4. THE PAROLE HEARING AS PERCEIVED BY THE INMATE 462

E. The Role of Lawyer and Judge 465

F. Parole Supervision 485
1. PAROLE CONDITIONS 485
2. THE PAROLE OFFICER: COP OR CASEWORKER? 494

G. Parole Revocation 499
1. EXCERPTS FROM CONNECTICUT PAROLE REVOCATION PROCEEDINGS 499
2. SOME PROBLEM PAROLE REVOCATION CASES 507

3. THE ROLE OF LAWYER
   AND JUDGE ... 513

H. Problems of Federalism: The
   Parole Compact and Detainers ... 536

I. Mandatory Release ... 541

Chapter Twelve PARDON: THE INSTITUTIONALIZED APPLICATION OF MERCY ... 543

Chapter Thirteen AFTER PRISON: THE HARDEST WAY ... 551

A. Collateral Consequences of
   Conviction ... 551

B. Two Proposals ... 557

TABLE OF CASES ... 561

TABLE OF STATUTES, REGULATIONS, BOOKS, ARTICLES, AND OTHER AUTHORITIES ... 563

INDEX ... 567

TABLE OF CONTENTS

PREFACE   xxiii

INTRODUCTION by Abraham S. Goldstein   xxv

Part I   SENTENCING: THE WAY IN

Chapter One   INTRODUCTORY PERSPECTIVES   3

    LEONARD ORLAND, Perspectives on Prisons   3

    JOHN P. CONRAD, Punishment to Fit Criminals   4

    LESLIE T. WILKINS, The Effectiveness of Punishment   4

    NIGEL WALKER, The Interchangeability of Criminal Sanctions   5

    THE HONORABLE MARVIN E. FRANKEL, Lawlessness in Sentencing   6

Chapter Two   LEGISLATIVE CHOICE: DELEGATION OF RESPONSIBILITY TO THE JUDICIARY AND CORRECTIONS   9

    Sentencing Provisions of the Model Penal Code   9

    Notes   13

       NOTE 1. STATUTORY SENTENCING FRAMEWORK   13

          The President's Commission on Law Enforcement and Administration of Justice, *Task Force Report: The Courts*   13

       NOTE 2. DANIEL GLASER, FRED COHEN, AND VINCENT O'LEARY, THE SENTENCING AND PAROLE PROCESS   17

Chapter Three   BUREAUCRATIC PRECHOICE: PRESENTENCE INVESTIGATION AND REPORT   20

    Williams v. New York   20

    Notes   23

       NOTE 1. THE FREQUENCY OF PRESENTENCE INVESTIGATION   23

The President's Commission on Law Enforcement and Administration of Justice, *Task Force Report: The Courts* ... 23

NOTE 2. THE FUNCTION OF PRESENTENCE INVESTIGATION ... 24

    a. The President's Commission on Law Enforcement and Administration of Justice, *Task Force Report: Corrections* ... 24

    b. Administrative Office of the United States Courts, Division of Probation, *The Presentence Investigation Report* ... 25

NOTE 3: GUIDELINES: AMERICAN BAR ASSOCIATION, *STANDARDS ON PROBATION* ... 25

NOTE 4. ROBERT M. CARTER AND LESLIE T. WILKINS, THE RELATIONSHIP BETWEEN FEDERAL PRESENTENCE RECOMMENDATIONS AND SENTENCES IMPOSED ... 27

NOTE 5. DISCLOSURE OF PRESENTENCE REPORTS ... 30

    a. Conn. Gen. Stat. Sec. 54–109a ... 30
    b. *United States v. Dockery* ... 30
    c. *State v. Kunz* ... 30

NOTE 6. AN ILLUSTRATIVE PRESENTENCE REPORT ... 32

    The Case of Alex Styer ... 32

Chapter Four JUDICIAL CHOICE: INCARCERATION AND ALTERNATIVES THERETO ... 33

A. Alternatives to Incarceration ... 33

  1. FINES ... 33

    Williams v. Illinois ... 34
    Tate v. Short ... 36
    Notes ... 37

    Note 1. Equal Protection and Corrections in Light of Williams *and* Tate ... 37
    Note 2. Robert E. Barrett, *The Frequency of Fines in State Criminal Law Enforcement* ... 38

  2. CIVIL COMMITMENT ... 39

    Specht v. Patterson ... 39
    Notes ... 40

    Note 1. Civil Commitment of "Sexual Psychopaths" ... 41
        CROSS V. HARRIS ... 41

    Note 2. The Difference Between "Civil" and "Penal" Institutions From the Perspective of the Inmate ... 41
        BRIEF OF DONALD MCEWAN, PETITIONER PRO SE ... 41

    Note 3. Federal Civil Commitment of Narcotics Addicts ... 43
        WATSON V. UNITED STATES ... 43

  3. PROBATION AND SUSPENDED SENTENCE ... 44

    United States v. Wiley ... 44
    Notes: Judicial Review of the Grant or Denial of Probation ... 48

    Note 1. Wilson v. United States ... 48
    Note 2. United States v. Daniels ... 49
    Note 3. People v. McAndrew ... 51

    Notes: Perspectives on Probation ... 52

    Note 1. American Correctional Association, The Development of Probation ... 52

    Note 2. An Overview of Probation in the United States, President's Commission on Law Enforcement and Administration of Justice, Task Force Report: Corrections ... 53

    Note 3. Probation Eligibility
    AMERICAN BAR ASSOCIATION, STANDARDS ON PROBATION ... 54

    Note 4. The effectiveness of probation ... 55
        a. J. EDGAR HOOVER, THE

DIRE CONSEQUENCES OF THE PREMATURE RELEASE OF DANGEROUS CRIMINALS THROUGH PROBATION AND PAROLE	55
b. RICHARD F. SPARKS, RESEARCH ON THE USE AND EFFECTIVENESS OF PROBATION	56
Notes: The Conditions of Probation	58
Note 1. Judah Best and Paul I. Birzon, Conditions of Probation: An Analysis	58
Note 2. Illustrative Conditions	61
STATE OF CONNECTICUT DEPT. OF ADULT PROBATION, CONDITIONS OF PROBATION	61
UNITED STATES COURTS, CONDITIONS OF PROBATION	62
Notes: Judicial Review of Probation Conditions	63
Note 1. People v. Mason	63
Note 2. Porth v. United States	64
Note 3. Judah Best and Paul I. Birzon, Judicial Review of Probation Conditions	65
4. THE ALTERNATIVES FAIL: PROBATION REVOCATION	67
Excerpt from Connecticut Probation Revocation Proceeding	67
Report of Violation of Probation	67
Addendum to Probation Violation Report	68
The Hearing	68
MEMPA V. RHAY	70
NOTES: DUE PROCESS IN PROBATION REVOCATION	73
NOTE 1. ESCOE V. ZERBST	73
NOTE 2. HAHN V. BURKE	74
NOTE 3. GOLDBERG V. KELLY	75
GAGNON V. SCARPELLI	77
B. Sentences of Imprisonment	78
1. THE EFFECT OF A GUILTY PLEA: DIFFERENTIAL SENTENCING	78
Introductory Note: The Negotiated Plea of Guilty	78
The President' Commission on Law Enforcement and Administration of Justice, Task Force Report: The Courts	78
From Chief Judge Campbell's Opinion in *United States v. Wiley*	79
From Chief Judge Bazelon's Opinion in *Scott v. United States*	81
2. ESTABLISHING MAXIMA AND MINIMA	83
Notes	83
Note. 1. Responsibility for the Initial Determination of the Term of Imprisonment	83
a. PETER LOW, DETERMINATION OF MAXIMUM AND MINIMUM TERMS	83
b. MEETING OF THE AMERICAN LAW INSTITUTE GROUP IN CONNECTION WITH MODEL PENAL CODE	85
Note 2. National Commission on Causes and Prevention of Violence, Deterrence, Length of Sentence and Recidivism	88
3. EXTENDED INCARCERATION TERMS: THE DANGEROUS OFFENDER AND THE MULTIPLE OFFENDER	89
Spencer v. Texas	89
Notes	92
Note 1. Recidivist Statutes and Constitutional Requirements	92
a. THE RIGHT TO COUNSEL: CHEWNING V. CUNNINGHAM	92
b. DUE PROCESS AND EQUAL PROTECTION: OYLER V. BOLES	92
Note 2. Statutory Innovations for Extended Prison Terms	93

TABLE OF CONTENTS

  a. ORGANIZED CRIME CONTROL ACT OF 1970   93
  b. COMPREHENSIVE DRUG ABUSE, PREVENTION AND CONTROL ACT OF 1970   95

4. CONSECUTIVE AND CONCURRENT SENTENCES   99
 Introductory Notes   99
  Note 1. Gore v. United States   99
  Note 2. Irby v. United States   99
  Note 3. Peter Low, Preliminary Memorandum on Sentencing Structure   100

 Notes: Proposals   101
  Note 1. Advisory Council of Judges of the National Council on Crime and Delinquency, Model Sentencing Act   101
  Note 2. American Bar Association, Standards on Sentencing Procedures and Alternatives   101

5. SENTENCE REVIEW   102
 Introductory Note: Sentence Review in Connecticut   102
  An Empirical Study of Sentence Review in Connecticut   102
 State v. Amiot   104
 Notes   110
  Note 1. The Frequency of Sentence Review   110
  The President's Commission on Law Enforcement and Administration of Justice, Task Force Report: The Courts   110
  Note 2. Guidelines American Bar Association Standards on Appellate Review of Sentences   112

6. TRAINING THE JUDGE   115
 Note 1. Sentencing Institutes   115
  a. Federal   115
  b. State   116
  c. Prevailing Patterns   118
   THE PRESIDENT'S COMMISSION ON LAW ENFORCEMENT AND ADMINISTRATION OF JUSTICE: TASK FORCE REPORT: THE COURTS   118
 Note 2. Sentencing Councils President's Commission on Law Enforcement and Administration of Justice: Task Force Report: The Courts   119
 Note 3. An Evaluation The Honorable Marvin E. Frankel, Lawlessness in Sentencing   121

Part II   IMPRISONMENT: PUNISHMENT AND TREATMENT

Chapter Five   WHAT IS PRISON?   125

A. Inside Views   125

ED TROMANHAUSER, First Day in Prison   125

ELDRIDGE CLEAVER, A Day in Folsom Prison   128

GEORGE JACKSON, A Letter from Soledad Prison   130

HO CHI MINH, At the End of Four Months   132

B. Empirical Perspectives   133

AUSTIN MACCORMICK, Adult Correctional Institutions in the United States   133

A Survey of American Corrections   139

C. Historical Perspectives   141

DAVID J. ROTHMAN, The Invention of the Penitentiary   141

D. Theoretical Explanations   153

ERVING GOFFMAN, Characteristics of Total Institutions ... 153

DONALD CLEMMER, The Prison Community ... 158

GRESHAM M. SYKES, The Society of Captives ... 160

Notes: Prison Theory ... 167

    NOTE 1. RICHARD A. CLOWARD, *SOCIAL CONTROL IN THE PRISON* ... 167

    NOTE 2. LLOYD OHLIN, *MODIFICATION OF THE CRIMINAL VALUE SYSTEM* ... 168

    NOTE 3. CLARENCE SCHRAG, *SOME FOUNDATIONS FOR A THEORY OF CORRECTION* ... 169

    NOTE 4. GRESHAM M. SYKES AND SHELDON MESSINGER, *THE INMATE SOCIAL SYSTEM* ... 172

    NOTE 5. STANTON WHEELER, *SOCIALIZATION IN CORRECTIONAL INSTITUTIONS* ... 174

E. International Perspectives ... 178

JOHN P. CONRAD, Trends in European Corrections ... 178

NORVAL MORRIS, Lessons from the Adult Correctional System of Sweden ... 181

Chapter Six THEORIES OF PUNISHMENT AND CORRECTION: WHAT IS THE FUNCTION OF PRISON? ... 183

    HERBERT L. PACKER, The Justification for Punishment ... 183

    JOHN P. CONRAD, The Irrational Equilibrium ... 189

    FRANCIS A. ALLEN, Criminal Justice, Legal Values, and the Rehabilitative Ideal ... 193

THE HONORABLE MARVIN E. FRANKEL, Indeterminate Sentencing, Punishment, and the Rehabilitative Ideal ... 196

The Fallacy of the Individualized Treatment Model ... 197

Notes: The Effectiveness of Penal Treatment ... 202

    NOTE 1. LESLIE T. WILKINS, *THE MEANING OF TREATMENT* ... 202

    NOTE 2. R. HOOD, *RESEARCH ON THE EFFECTIVENESS OF PUNISHMENTS AND TREATMENTS* ... 203

    NOTE 3. WALTER C. BAILEY, *CORRECTIONAL OUTCOME: AN EVALUATION OF 100 REPORTS* ... 203

    NOTE 4. RALPH SCHWITZGEBEL, *DEVELOPMENT AND LEGAL REGULATION OF COERCIVE BEHAVIOR MODIFICATION TECHNIQUES WITH OFFENDERS* ... 205

    NOTE 5. COMMUNITY TREATMENT ... 207

        a. Special Community Programs ... 207
        b. Community Reintegration ... 215

Chapter Seven CLASSIFICATION: HOW SHOULD THE PRISON DIFFERENTIATE AMONG INMATES? ... 218

American Correctional Association, Essential Features of Classification ... 218

The Results of Classification ... 223

    THE DIAGNOSTIC SUMMARY The Case of Gerald T. Merrill ... 223

Inmates' View of Classification ... 224

    MIKE MISENHEIMER, *CLASSIFICATION* ... 224

JOE MARTINEZ, *REHABILI-
TATION AND TREATMENT*   225

Morris v. Travisono   225

Chapter Eight INSTITUTIONAL MISCONDUCT AND RESPONSES THERETO: HOW SHOULD PRISON RULES BE MADE AND ENFORCED?   241

A. Perspectives   241

   1. HISTORICAL   241

     First Annual Report of the Board of Managers of the Prison Discipline Society   241

   2. CORRECTIONAL   243

     American Correctional Association, Essential Elements of Correctional Discipline   243

   3. POLITICAL   251

     Richard H. McCleery, Authoritarianism and the Belief System of Incorrigibles   251

B. Making "Law": Regulations   254

   1. SETTING POLICY   254

     Connecticut Department of Correction, Policy Directive on Discipline Procedures   254

     Notes

       Note 1. Connecticut Department of Correction, Policy Directive on Use of Force   260

       Note 2. Federal Bureau of Prisons, Policy Statement on Inmate Discipline   262

   2. INFORMING THE INMATE   262

     Rules and Regulations of the Connecticut State Prison (1830)   262

     South Dakota Prison Rules and Regulations   263

     Connecticut Department of Correction, Inmate Handbook of Regulations (1970)   270

     Note: The Frequency of Institutional Misconduct   271

     Vernon Fox, Analysis of Prison Disciplinary Problems   271

C. Applying "Law": The Misconduct Hearing   272

     FRANK B. COCHRAN, THE FORMAL DISCIPLINE SYSTEM IN CONNECTICUT PENAL INSTITUTIONS   272

D. Judicial Review of Prison Discipline Decisions: The "Hole," the Eighth, and the Fourteenth Amendments   277

   1. THE "HOLE"   277

     Notes

       Note 1. Leonard Orland, On Being Incarcerated   277

       Note 2. Brooks v. Florida   278

   2. THE MEANING OF THE EIGHTH AMENDMENT   279

     Furman v. Georgia   279

   3. THE "HOLE" AND THE EIGHTH AMENDMENT   290

     Notes

       Note 1. Wright v. McMann   290

       Note 2. Hancock v. Avery   291

       Note 3. LaReau v. MacDougall   292

       Note 4. Landman v. Royster   294

     Sostre v. Rockefeller   294

   4. DISCIPLINARY PROCEEDINGS AND DUE PROCESS OF LAW   309

     Notes

       Note 1. Wright v. McMann   309

       Note 2. Clutchette v. Procunier   310

       Note 3. Nolan v. Scafati   313

       Note 4. Kritsky v. McGinnis   314

       Note 5. Bundy v. Cannon   314

   5. ADMINISTRATIVE SEGREGATION AND DUE PROCESS OF LAW   317

Notes
- *Note 1.* Young v. Wainwright 317
- *Note 2.* Urbano v. McCorkle 317
- *Note 3.* Walker v. Mancusi 318

6. DAMAGE RECOVERY BY INMATES 319
   Notes
   - *Note 1.* United States v. Muniz 319
   - *Note 2.* United States v. Demko 320
   - *Note 3.* a. Sostre v. Rockefeller 320
     b. Sostre v. McGinnis 321
   - *Note 4.* Wright v. McMann 322
   - *Note 5.* Liles v. South Carolina Department of Corrections 323
   - *Note 6.* Logue v. United States 324

7. PROCEDURE IN PRISONER RIGHTS CASES 325
   Notes
   - *Note 1.* William Bennett Turner, Establishing the Role of Law in Prisons: A Manual for Prisoner's Rights Litigation 325
   - *Note 2.* Ronald Goldfarb and Linda Singer, Redressing Prisoners' Grievances 326

8. THE INMATE'S RIGHT TO A JUDICIAL HEARING 327
   Notes
   - *Note 1.* Haines v. Kerner 327
   - *Note 2.* Cruz v. Beto 328

9. CORPORAL PUNISHMENT AND THE EIGHTH AMENDMENT 330
   Note: Jackson v. Bishop 330

10. PRISON REGULATIONS AND THE VOID FOR VAGUENESS RULE 333
    Note: Landman v. Royster 333

11. JAIL INMATES 335
    Notes
    - *Note 1.* On Jails 335
    - *Note 2.* Jail Conditions and the Eighth Amendment 336
      JONES V. WITTENBERG 336
    - *Note 3.* Jail Conditions and the Fourteenth Amendment 339
      HAMILTON V. LOVE 339
    - *Note 4.* Administrative Segregation of Jail Inmates 340
      DAVIS V. LINDSAY 340

12. LEGISLATIVE SPECIFICATIONS OF PRISONER RIGHTS 342
    - Note 1. Leonard Orland, Human Rights for Prisoners 342
    - Note 2. United Nations Standard Minimum Rules for the Treatment of Prisoners 342
    - Note 3. Robert Cotzbauer, Bill of Rights Posted for State Prisoners 352
    - Note 4. An Act to Provide for Minimum Standards for the Protection of Rights of Prisoners 352

E. Judicial Review of Prison Disciplinary Decisions: Loss of Good Time 355

1. STATUTORY PROVISIONS 355
   Notes 355
   - Note 1. Conn. Gen. Stat. § 18-7 355
   - Note 2. 18 U.S.C. § 4161 355

2. ADMINISTRATIVE INTERPRETATION 355
   U.S. Bureau of Prisons, Policy Statement on Withholding, Forfeiture, and Restoration of Good Time 355

3. JUDICIAL REVIEW 357
   Rodriguez v. McGinnis 357
   Wright v. McMann 362

4. GOOD TIME FOR JAIL INMATES 364
   Royster v. McGinnis 364

5. GOOD TIME AND JOB CLASSIFICATION 366
   Colen v. Norton 366

Chapter Nine THE RULE OF LAW AND PRISON LIFE: THE ROLE OF LAWYER AND JUDGE IN INSTITUTIONAL CONTROL OF THE INMATE POPULATION ... 368

A. Daily Life ... 368

    UNITED STATES EX REL POPE V. WILLIAMS ... 368
    RHODES V. SIGLER ... 369
    SEALE V. MANSON ... 369

B. Sexual Relations ... 371

    PAYNE V. DISTRICT OF COLUMBIA ... 371
    TARLTON V. CLARK ... 371
    COLUMBUS B. HOPPER, THE CONJUGAL VISIT ... 371
    PIRI THOMAS, SEX IN PRISON ... 372

C. Medical Treatment ... 373

    MARTINEZ V. MANCUSI ... 373

D. Racial Discrimination ... 374

    LEE V. WASHINGTON ... 374

E. Religious Freedom ... 374

    COOPER V. PATE ... 374
    BARNETT V. RODGERS ... 375

F. Access to Lawyers and Courts ... 377

    EX PARTE HULL ... 377
    JOHNSON V. AVERY ... 378
    Notes
        Note 1. Implementing Johnson v. Avery ... 383
            CROSS V. POWERS ... 383
        Note 2. Inmates' Views of Johnson v. Avery ... 384
            A PRISONER LOOKS AT WRIT WRITING ... 384
            HO CHI MINH, WRITING A PETITION FOR A JAIL-MATE ... 385

G. Inmate Communications ... 386

    NOLAN V. FITZPATRICK ... 386
    NOTES
        Note 1. *Sostre v. McGinnis* ... 389
        Note 2. *Smith v. Robbins* ... 391
        Note 3. *Washington Post v. Kleindienst* ... 392
        Note 4. *Carothers v. Follette* ... 393
        Note 5. *Berrigan v. Norton* ... 394
        Note 6. *Fortune Society v. McGinnis* ... 394
        Note 7. *Sostre v. Otis* ... 395

Part III RELEASE FROM PRISON: THE WAY OUT (AND IN AGAIN)

Chapter Ten PRERELEASE ... 401

Connecticut Department of Correction, Community Release Programs ... 401

Notes

    NOTE 1. REDUCING ISOLATION FROM THE COMMUNITY AS A CORRECTIONAL OBJECTIVE ... 406

        The President's Commission on Law Enforcement and Administration of Justice Task Force Report: Corrections ... 406

    NOTE 2. THE FREQUENCY OF WORK-RELEASE ... 408

        Elmer H. Johnson, Report on an Innovation—State Work-Release Programs ... 408

    NOTE 3. INTERNATIONAL PERSPECTIVES ... 409

        Stanley E. Grupp, Work Release in Other Countries ... 409

TABLE OF CONTENTS

Chapter Eleven PAROLE: UNFETTERED POWER AND DISCRETIONARY PREDICTION   410

A. Historical Perspectives   410

FREDERICK A. MORAN, The Origins of Parole   410

B. Statutory Structure   413

An Illustrative Statute: Connecticut   413

Notes: The Model Penal Code and Prevailing American Statutory Structure   414

    NOTE 1. LEONARD ORLAND, ON PAROLE   414

    NOTE 2. DONALD GLASER, FRED COHEN, AND VINCENT O'LEARY, THE SENTENCING AND PAROLE PROCESS   415

    NOTE 3. PREVAILING PAROLE PATTERNS   415

        The President's Commission on Law Enforcement and Administration of Justice, Task Force Report: Corrections   415

C. Making Law: Regulations   418

    CONNECTICUT BOARD OF PAROLE, STATEMENT OF ORGANIZATION AND PROCEDURES   418

    NOTES: FEDERAL PAROLE   421

        Note 1. Kenneth Culp Davis, Discretion and the U.S. Parole Board   421

        Note 2. United States Board of Parole Rules   422

        Note 3. Leonard Orland, The United States Board of Parole   423

        Note 4. Relative Responsibility of Prison and Parole Officials to Decide When the Inmate is Eligible for a Parole Hearing   423

            People Ex Rel Abner v. Kinney   423

D. Applying "Law": The Parole Hearing   425

1. THE DECISION-MAKING PROCESS   425

    Introductory Notes   425

        Note 1. Leonard Orland, Politics and Parole   425

        Note 2. Leonard Orland, Parole Board Structure   425

        Note 3. The Decision-Making Process   426

            THE PRESIDENT'S COMMISSION ON LAW ENFORCEMENT AND ADMINISTRATION OF JUSTICE, TASK FORCE REPORT: CORRECTIONS

    Criteria for Decision   427

        Advisory Council on Parole, National Council on Crime and Delinquency, Guides for Parole Selection   427

    Basic Data for Parole Prediction   430

        Uniform Parole Reports of the National Probation and Parole Institutes   430

    Notes: Parole Prediction   436

        Note 1. Victor J. Evjen, Current Thinking on Parole Prediction Tables   436

        Note 2. Georg K. Sturup, Will This Man Be Dangerous?   436

2. EXCERPTS FROM CONNECTICUT PAROLE HEARINGS

    The Case of Alex Styer   437

        Parole Hearing Progress Report   437

        Admission Summary   438

        Prior Institutional Adjustment at Conn. State Prison   438

        Presentence Investigation Report   439

        Psychiatric Evaluations   443

        Parole Application   445

        The Hearing   448

3. SOME PROBLEM PAROLE CASES   451

    a. The Case of Jason Tinger   451

        Parole Hearing Progress Report   451

        Information Summary   452

TABLE OF CONTENTS

United States Department of Justice, Federal Bureau of Investigation, Criminal Record ... 453
b. The Case of Thomas Mean ... 454
Parole Hearing Progress Report ... 454
Misconduct Reports ... 455
A Psychiatric Evaluation ... 456
c. The Case of John Alling ... 457
Parole Hearing Progress Report ... 457
Misconduct Reports ... 458
d. The Case of Ronald Grimes ... 458
Psychiatric Evaluation ... 458
e. The Case of Gerald Merrill ... 459
Parole Hearing Progress Report ... 459
Diagnostic Summary ... 460
Reception and Diagnostic Center Recommendations ... 461
Vocational Evaluation ... 461

4. THE PAROLE HEARING AS PERCEIVED BY THE INMATE ... 462
Ed Tromanhauser, Parole ... 462
George Jackson, Soledad Brother: The Prison Letters of George Jackson ... 464

E. The Role of Lawyer and Judge ... 465
VINCENT O'LEARY AND JOAN NUFFIELD, PAROLE DECISION-MAKING CHARACTERISTICS: REPORT OF A NATIONAL SURVEY ... 465
Menechino v. Oswald ... 468
Monks v. New Jersey Parole Board ... 477
Scarpa v. United States Parole Board ... 481

F. Parole Supervision ... 485
1. PAROLE CONDITIONS ... 485
Certificates of parole ... 485
State of Connecticut, Board of Parole, Parole and Conditions of Parole ... 485
Certificate of Parole, United States Board of Parole ... 487
United Kingdom Home Office, Probation and Aftercare Department, License, Criminal Justice Act 1967 ... 489
Notes: The Theory of Imposing Conditions of Parole ... 489
Note 1. Leonard Orland, Politics and Parole ... 489
Note 2. Leonard Orland, Conditions of Parole ... 489
Note: The Prevailing Conditions of Parole ... 490
Nat R. Arluke, A Summary of Parole Rules—Thirteen Years Later ... 490
ARCINIEGA V. FREEMAN ... 492
SOBELL V. REED ... 492

2. THE PAROLE OFFICER: COP OR CASEWORKER? ... 494
Notes
Note 1. Introductory Note ... 494
OBSERVATIONS ON THE ADMINISTRATION OF PAROLE ... 494
Note 2. The Use of Unlawfully Seized Evidence in Parole Revocation Proceedings ... 496
UNITED STATES EX. REL. SPERLING V. FITZPATRICK ... 496
Note 3. The Use of Evidence Unlawfully Seized by a Parole Officer in a Subsequent Trial ... 497
UNITED STATES EX. REL. SANTOS V. NEW YORK STATE BOARD OF PAROLE ... 497

G. Parole Revocation ... 499
1. EXCERPTS FROM CONNECTICUT PAROLE REVOCATION PROCEEDINGS ... 499
The Case of Mark Ronald ... 499
Parole Violation Report ... 499
Police Report to Prosecutor ... 500
Addendum to Parole Violation Report ... 501
Parole Hearing Progress Report ... 502

Admission Summary	502
Prior Institutional Adjustment at Conn. State Prison	503
Criminal History	504
The Revocation Hearing	505

2. SOME PROBLEM PAROLE REVOCATION CASES — 507
- The Case of Sherman Leonard — 507
  - *Parole Violation Report* — 507
  - *Addendum to Parole Violation Report* — 509
- The Case of Charles Golden — 510
  - *Parole Violation Report* — 510
- The Case of Kevin West — 511
  - *Parole Violation Report* — 511

3. THE ROLE OF LAWYER AND JUDGE — 513
- *United States Ex. Rel. Bey v. Connecticut State Board of Parole* — 513
- *Morrissey v. Brewer* — 518
- *Gagnon v. Scarpelli* — 527
- Note: Prevailing American Parole Revocation Practices Prior to *Morrissey v. Brewer* — 532
- Note: The Relationship between Proof of Revocation Charges and Self-Incrimination on New Criminal Charges — 534
- *Melson v. Sard* — 534
- Notes: "Street Time" — 535
  - Note 1. *Freedom or Incarceration Pending Disposition of Parole Revocation Charges* — 535
    - ROSE V. NICKESON — 535
  - Note 2. *"Credit" for "Clean" Street Time* — 535
    - BONOMO V. NEW JERSEY STATE PAROLE BOARD — 535
  - Note 3. *Establishing Release Date After Revocation* — 536
    - GIORDANO V. HENDERSON — 536

H. Problems of Federalism: The Parole Compact and Detainers — 536

THE PAROLE COMPACT — 536
NOTE: IMPLEMENTATION OF THE PAROLE COMPACT — 538
Ralph C. Brendes, Interstate Supervision of Parole and Probation — 538

NOTES: DETAINERS — 539
- Note 1. Ralph C. Brendes, The Detainer Agreement — 539
- Note 2. *Smith v. Hooey* — 539
- Note 3. *Cooks v. United States Board of Parole* — 540

I. Mandatory Release — 541
HANSEN V. SCHMIDT — 541

Chapter Twelve PARDON: THE INSTITUTIONALIZED APPLICATION OF MERCY — 543

CHRISTEN JENSEN, Pardon — 543
MARVIN E. WOLFGANG, The Relation between Judicial and Prosecutorial Recommendations and Pardon Board Action — 544
REED COZART, The Benefits of Executive Clemency — 545
RICHARD BANBURY, The Pardoning Authority in the Several States: Structures Used and Trends in the Makeup of the Decision-Making Bodies — 546
Conn. Gen. Stat. § 18–24a *et. seq.* — 546
WILLIAM F. STONE, Pardons in Virginia: An Empirical Study — 547
The Role of Counsel in Pardon Proceedings — 549

Chapter Thirteen AFTER PRISON: THE HARDEST WAY — 551

A. Collateral Consequences of Conviction — 551

THE PRESIDENT'S COMMISSION ON LAW ENFORCEMENT AND ADMINISTRATION OF JUSTICE, TASK FORCE REPORT: CORRECTIONS — 551

B. Two Proposals — 557

1. THE CRIMINAL OFFENDER, WHAT SHOULD BE DONE? — 557
2. NATIONAL COUNCIL ON CRIME AND DELINQUENCY, ANNULMENT OF CONVICTION OF CRIME: A MODEL ACT — 557

TABLE OF CASES — 561

TABLE OF STATUTES, REGULATIONS, BOOKS, ARTICLES, AND OTHER AUTHORITIES — 563

INDEX — 567

PREFACE

This volume explores neglected and vaguely obscure aspects of criminal justice—the "correctional" process, which encompasses sentencing, incarceration, and release from prison. The book sequentially traces the events which befall the convicted felon *after* determination of guilt—the stage where many criminal law courses have ended.

The book is divided into three major parts: Sentencing, Imprisonment, and Release from Prison. Successive chapters deal with legislative structure; presentence investigation; sentencing; theoretical, historical, and empirical bases for imprisonment; punishment and correction; prison classification; prison life and procedures; judicial review of prison administration; discipline and inmate rights; work and education release; parole and parole revocation; pardon and postconviction disabilities.

In addition to more traditional legal materials, such as statutes and judicial decisions, the volume has extensive excerpts from the rich theoretical and empirical social science literature on sentencing, incarceration, and release from prison. In addition, correction department data have been utilized extensively; these include regulations and material derived from prisoner files and transcriptions of various stages of the correctional process taken from files of the Federal Bureau of Prisons and the Connecticut Department of Correction.

Much of the prison and parole material has never before been published and is data to which I was given access only because of my position as a member of the Connecticut Parole Board. In setting forth inmate correctional files, I have endeavored to protect the confidentiality of both inmate and professional worker by fictionalizing names and changing dates. In all other respects, however, these files accurately reflect their original counterparts.

The conventions adopted in the organization of this book follow those initiated in *Criminal Law**: "The NOTES omit string citations and references to other materials easily located through standard indices. Because they raise important issues, NOTES are printed in the same type as the major problem material." Footnotes in reprinted materials, for the most part, have been

* Richard C. Donnelly, Joseph Goldstein, and Richard D. Schwartz, *Criminal Law,* New York: The Free Press (1962).

omitted. In addition to the conventional Table of Cases, there is also an expanded Table of Statutes, Regulations, Books, Articles, and Other Authorities, broken down by major categories, as well as a subject index.

Acknowledgements

The development of this book has been supported, in its inception, by grants from the Ford Foundation and the Connecticut Research Foundation. This volume would not have been possible without the aid and cooperation of many people. I must particularly thank two Connecticut Correction Commissioners, Ellis MacDougal and John Manson. Also, thanks to Robert Brooks, Director of Planning for the Connecticut Department of Correction; Larry Albert, Director of Rehabilitative Services for the Connecticut Department of Correction; my colleagues on the Connecticut Parole Board, including, in particular, its Chairman, J. Bernard Gates. I have had the benefit of comment and evaluation from A. S. Goldstein and Stanton Wheeler, who taught from a preliminary version of these materials at Yale Law School, and from Federal Judges Marvin Frankel and Harold Tyler, who reviewed the materials in connection with their courses at Columbia and New York University Law Schools. Joseph Goldstein of Yale Law School provided invaluable encouragement and insight. I have had the benefit of two superb research assistants: David Smith and Andrew Wittstein. Tom Belote, while a student at the University of Connecticut, provided sustained assistance and support without which completion of this book would have been impossible. My secretary, Florence Souney, labored patiently with innumerable drafts, while Connie Lee was most helpful in duplicating.

INTRODUCTION
Abraham S. Goldstein*

The nearly exclusive concern of lawyers and of criminal law courses has been with the elements of criminal liability and the procedures of adjudication. Yet most offenders have little or no contact with the formal law. For them, criminal law is made up of informal discretionary processes dominated by police and prosecutor, or a brief court appearance to plead guilty—followed by a presentence investigation and report, supervision by a probation officer, work assignments in prison, rules on prison conduct and disciplinary proceedings, parole and parole supervision.

Until very recently, these informal processes were regarded largely as beyond judicial supervision, and therefore, by a curious sleight-of-hand, outside the range of law studies. This has made the study and administration of criminal law surprisingly lifeless. What actually happened to the offender —on the street or in his dealings with police and prosecutor, the years of stigma or supervision or imprisonment—was treated as secondary and incidental to doctrinal purity in fixing criminal liability.

This neglect has been substantially repaired where police and prosecutor are concerned, particularly since the Supreme Court entered the field by expanding judicial supervision of the police; and it has been further repaired in the new attention being paid to the plea of guilty, which accounts for the overwhelming proportion of convictions. But it has taken prison riots and unusually aggressive efforts to draw the attention of lawyers to sentencing and to correctional processes. And that attention is as yet relatively undirected and unformed.

The fact that lawyers were neglecting correctional processes did not mean that corrections lacked a literature of its own. The field of corrections—informed by criminology and practiced by social workers, mental health workers, former policemen, and prison guards—has developed a detailed set of attitudes and practices towards inmates, their care, and their treatment. Unfortunately, however, neither the literature nor the emergence of a conscientious "profession" has brought with it notable improvement in the rate of genuine rehabilitation.

---

* Dean, and Cromwell Professor of Law, Yale Law School

Our criminal justice system remains one in which the recidivism rate is very high, even when, as is often the case, it is marked by more humane supervision and custody and by a rich mix of vocational, recreational, and treatment programs. Whatever improvement occurs seems as much attributable to maturation or to spiritual rebirth as to what is "done" to or for the inmate.

These grim results of even the most generous intentions have been both confusing and dangerous. Offenders have been taught to expect they would be made better by forces external to themselves. Like the rest of us, they have heard a great deal of talk about treatment and rehabilitation, about supervision and help. Acting on the assumption that we could really "correct," we have revamped sentencing structures so that officials could decide just when the offender was getting better or worse, and do something about it—by releasing or detaining within the confines of a relatively indeterminate sentence, or by granting or denying a wide variety of benefits and privileges.

Under the circumstances, it was almost inevitable that we would soon witness the collision of forces which had been developing great momentum, without much notice of each other. The promise of correction, which had become an article of faith for corrections officials, could not keep pace with the expectations generated by that promise in offenders newly conscious of their "rights" and expecting those rights to be recognized. The newest round of prison riots illustrates all too dramatically the consequences of overselling the rehabilitative ideal. The riots and protests have increasingly taken the form of a demand for the "treatment" which had been promised; in the alternative, they have demanded either complete freedom or relief from the myriad restrictions while in custody or under supervision on the outside. Overall, they have been fired by a deep resentment of widely disparate sentences built on what may well be illusory assumptions about "treatment."

In the abrasive contacts between disappointed expectations and what may inevitably be a custodial prison system, the law is being presented with unparalleled challenges. Courts and legislatures will have to develop standards and patterns of accommodation for the roles to be played by judges, administrators, and by the inmates themselves. Among the issues which will dominate the debate are the extent to which custody is necessary at all and how total the custody need be; the part to be played by the lawyer and his adversary culture in making critical decisions in correctional processes; the fateful choice to be made between relying upon the charge of crime or the conviction as the occasion for correction; and the risk that a new preoccupation with procedures and "rights" and judicial intervention may divert attention and resources from the harder job of providing more effective treatment and supervision.

The publication of this casebook is especially timely because it joins currents social concerns with a newly defined field of study. Correction demands a deep understanding of people and institutions. It requires the interweaving of many disciplines and professions in order to fashion theories of sentencing and treatment which are more than wish fulfillment. Not only has Professor Orland anticipated the major themes which will form the law and practice of sentencing and corrections, but also, in instance after instance, he has selected cases and readings which are richly suggestive of what might better be done if we are to build on theoretically valid foundations. His book breaks important new ground in providing students of law, criminology, and penal administration with the materials from which such understanding and theory may evolve.

Part I

SENTENCING: THE WAY IN

Chapter One

INTRODUCTORY PERSPECTIVES

LEONARD ORLAND

Perspectives on Prisons*

In the beginning, prisons housed the untried who, if found guilty, were beheaded or hanged or, if more fortunate, whipped or maimed and then set free. One hundred and fifty years ago, the reformers, principally Quakers, urged prison as an alternative to death to enable the wicked in solitude to see the error of their ways and to reform.

Since that time, we have been dehumanizing, brutalizing and punishing, all in the name of "treatment." A century ago, the leaders of American penology assembled in Cincinnati and issued a declaration of principles. It stated that the objective of imprisonment was "the reformation of criminals, not the infliction of suffering," that the "prisoner's self-respect should be cultivated to the utmost," that "every effort be made to give back to him his manhood." The Cincinnati congress concluded that "there is no greater mistake than the studied imposition of degradation as a part of punishment."

But then, as today, the divergence between

---

* Leonard Orland, "Human Rights for Prisoners," *The New York Times,* Sept. 24, 1971, p. 41. Reprinted by permission of the author.

objectives and reality is gross. A survey of American prisons by the Prison Discipline Society in 1826 concluded that the prevailing mode of prison punishment was "stripes [whipping], chains and solitary confinement, with hunger."

Relatively little has changed. It is true that much of the whipping and mutilation is now gone from the American prison scene. (Even so, a Federal court, in 1970, found beatings and torture prevalent in the entire Arkansas prison system.)

American prisons continue to function as warehouses for long-term storage of human refuse. In 1967, a consultant to the President's Crime Commission found that most American prisons are "mediocre at best." More recently, a Ford Foundation observer of foreign prisons found only a handful of penal institutions in the world which claim to be designed for "rehabilitation," let alone be effective in reaching that objective. In 1967, the President's Crime Commission found that of the one half billion dollars spent annually on prisons, ninety-five cents out of each dollar went to "custody," with only a nickel for "treatment."

In point of fact, we are not even sure of how to go about the task of rehabilitation.

The scope of the problem has been spelled out in a series of commission recommendations, including, most notably, the task force report on corrections of the crime commission, the final report of the joint commission on correctional manpower and training and the report of the President's task force on prisoner rehabilitation.

JOHN P. CONRAD

Punishment to Fit Criminals*

The indeterminate sentence was introduced as a feature of American and some Continental correctional systems as a device to relate the length of confinement to the problem to be solved. Somehow, we have been aware for many generations that punishments must fit criminals. This object has never been reached. The time served *is* the punishment. When practical penologists say that prisoners are sent to prison *as* punishment rather than *for* punishment, they are skirting the reality that the punishment occurs day by day and hour by hour; it does not cease with the clang of the reception door in the sallyport. It goes on with differing degrees of severity with differing inmates, but the passage of time punishes, and changes as it punishes. How long it goes on is of overwhelming importance. A system for rationally deciding the length of term in advance has never been devised. In England and some Continental countries it has been impossible to divest the sentencing function from the courts. Essentially the punishment is fitted to the crime by the judge, and minor adjustments, usually in favor of the criminal, are made by the prison administration through the remission of time for good behavior. Some judges are to some extent guided by presentence investigations, but these are never more than an optional source of information.

To a considerable extent, American courts have been removed from the complex and social considerations of sentencing. In the United States the parole boards and commissions have been assigned a share in the sentencing process which determines the punishment on the basis of an appraisal of the success of treatment adjusted to an impression of the tolerance of the community. Both considerations are subjective and based on assumptions which derive little from theory or principle.

* John P. Conrad, *Crime and Its Correction: An International Survey of Attitudes and Practices,* 52–53 (1967). Originally published by the University of California Press. Reprinted by permission of the Regents of the University of California.

LESLIE T. WILKINS

The Effectiveness of Punishment*

There would seem to be no feature of the criminal justice system of any country throughout the world which is not open to challenge. In the majority of countries, it is not possible to say what is actually happening to offenders. True, it is possible to count those who are incarcerated in one form or another of correctional establishment. This is possible mainly because prisoners are fed, and the counting of

* Leslie T. Wilkins, "Variety, Conformity, Control and Research: Some Dilemmas of Social Defense," *International Review of Criminal Policy,* No. 28, United Nations, New York, 1970, p. 18. Reprinted with permission.

them is part of the security system without which the prison would not be a prison at all. There is, however, little more information on correctional systems that is comparable among different countries. It is known that the proportions of the population removed from the open society vary widely between countries, but no reasons for the different incarceration rates can be supported by any sound evidence.

It is reasonable to postulate that the different incarceration rates are not explained to any major degree by differences in the rates of crime, nor by differences in the types of crime known to the police. Duration of the period of detention seems to be one of the major factors giving rise to variations in the incarceration rates, but even this explains little of the differences.

If prison were successful in reforming offenders, or if long periods of detention of offenders were a sound preventive measure to deter others from committing crimes, it might be expected that those countries where penalties are more severe would show relatively lower crime rates. This is not so; indeed, in terms of very general data, the inverse is the case. Clearly, the relationship between measures taken to deal with offenders and the outcome for society presents a most complex problem.

It might be thought by laymen that those involved with the correctional system would be concerned to obtain measures of the successes and failures of the processes so that changes could be made with reference to a valid data base. Again, such is not the case. There are no satisfactory measures of the success of correctional methods and of the treatment of offenders. If one asked to what factors those changes in the correctional system which have taken place within the advanced countries in recent years are mainly related, it would have to be confessed that one of the important factors has been prison riots. This is most unfortunate. To make desirable changes when forced to do so by pressures which, in themselves, have undesirable features is a most unsatisfactory process. Perhaps the second most important factor in changes in correctional systems has been the humanitarian approach. The consideration that even prisoners have some claim to "human rights" is, of course, a valid ethical factor. Indeed, the riot would not be a means of reform if there were not some support for the claims made by the rioters, in terms of ethical arguments.

NIGEL WALKER

The Interchangeability of Criminal Sanctions*

Reconviction studies have shown that at least five "hard" variables are strongly associated with the probability of reconviction:

(a) other things being equal, females are less likely than males to be reconvicted after a given penal measure has been applied;

(b) other things being equal, the older an offender the less likely he is to be reconvicted after any given penal measure;

(c) other things being equal, the more previous convictions an offender has the more likely he is to be reconvicted;

(d) other things being equal, the more time he has spent in penal institutions on previous occasions the more likely he is to be reconvicted;

(e) other things being equal, the reconviction rate is higher for some types of offence (e.g. house-breaking) than for others (e.g. sexual offences), although this may well reflect little more than differences in the probability that an offence of the type in question will be reported and traced to the offender.

Any investigation, therefore, which aims at a comparison of the "success rates" of penal measures must ensure that these rates are not distorted by uneven proportions of females, first offenders, older offenders and so on amongst the samples being compared. Fortunately there are statistical methods for coping with this difficulty. The most satisfactory

* Excerpted from *Sentencing in a Rational Society*, pp. 93–94 by Nigel Walker. Copyright © 1969 by Nigel Walker. Appendix A copyright © 1969 by Nigel Walker, Michael Wilmer and Roy Carr-Hill. Basic Books, Inc. Publishers, New York, and Allen Lane, The Penguin Press, London.

investigation from this point of view (and from several other points of view) ... found that:

(a) in general, *fines* are followed by fewer reconvictions than other measures;
(b) *heavy fines* are followed by fewer reconvictions than light fines;
(c) in general, next to fines, the measure followed by fewer reconvictions seemed to be *discharge* (absolute or conditional). The exceptions were the older "first offenders" aged thirty or more who received a discharge; these tended to have an abnormally *high* reconviction rate;
(d) *imprisonment* was followed by more reconvictions than fines or discharges;
(e) but *imprisonment* compared better with other measures when applied to offenders with previous convictions than when applied to "first offenders";
(f) *probation* was followed by more reconvictions than imprisonment;
(g) *probation* compared rather better with the other measures when it was applied not to "first offenders" but to offenders with previous convictions (but was still the least often effective);
(h) for some reason, however, "first offenders" convicted of house-breaking showed lower reconviction rates than any other kind of probationer when placed on *probation*.

THE HONORABLE MARVIN E. FRANKEL

Lawlessness in Sentencing*

The common form of criminal penalty provision confers upon the sentencing judge an enormous range of choice. The scope of what we call "discretion" permits imprisonment for anything from a day to one, five, 10, 20, or more years. All would presumably join in denouncing a statute that said "the judge may impose any sentence he pleases." Given the mortality of men, the power to set a man free or confine him for up to 30 years is not sharply distinguishable.

The statutes granting such powers characteristically say nothing about the factors to be weighed in moving to either end of the spectrum or to some place between. It might be supposed by some stranger arrived in our midst that the criteria for measuring a particular sentence would be discoverable outside the narrow limits of the statutes and would be known to the judicial experts rendering the judgments. But the supposition would lack substantial foundation. Even the most basic sentencing principles are not prescribed or stated with persuasive authority. There is, to be sure, a familiar litany in the literature of sentencing "purposes": retribution, deterrence ("special" and "general"), "denunciation," incapacitation, rehabilitation. Nothing tells us, however, when or whether any of these several goals are to be sought, or how to resolve such evident conflicts as that likely to arise in the effort to punish and rehabilitate all at once. It has for some time been part of our proclaimed virtue that vengeance or retribution is a disfavored motive for punishment. But there is reason to doubt that either judges or the public are effectively abreast of this advanced position. And there is no law—certainly none that anybody pretends to have enforced—telling the judge he must refrain, expressly or otherwise, from trespassing against higher claims to wreak vengeance.

Moving upward from what should be the philosophical axioms of a rational scheme of sentencing law, we have no structure of rules, or even guidelines, affecting other elements arguably pertinent to the nature or severity of the sentence. Should it be a mitigating factor that the defendant is being sentenced upon a plea of guilty rather than a verdict against him? Should it count in his favor that he spared the public "trouble" and expense by waiving a jury? Should the sentence be more severe because the judge is convinced that the defendant perjured himself on the witness stand? Should churchgoing be considered to reflect favorably? Consistently with the first amendment, should it be considered at all? What factors should be assessed—and where, if anywhere, are comparisons to be sought—in gauging the relative seriousness of the specific offense and offender as against the spectrum of offenses by others in the same legal

* 41 *Cin. L. Rev.*, 4–10; 15–16; 29–31 (1972).

category? The list of such questions could be lengthened. Each is capable of being answered, and is answered by sentencing judges, in contradictory or conflicting, or at least differing, ways. There is no controlling requirement that any particular view be followed on any such subject by the sentencing judge.

With the delegation of power so unchanneled, it is surely no overstatement to say that "the new penology has resulted in vesting in judges and parole and probation agencies the greatest degree of uncontrolled power over the liberty of human beings that one can find in the legal system." The process would be totally unruly even if judges were superbly and uniformly trained for the solemn work of sentencing. As everyone knows, however, they are not trained at all.

Viewed as a group, the people who enter upon service as trial judges are somewhat elderly, more experienced than most lawyers in litigation, almost totally unencumbered by learning or experience relevant to sentencing, and inclined by temperament and circumstance toward the major orthodoxies. Nothing they studied in law school touched our subject more than remotely....

Because the sentence is not appealable except on rare and extraordinary grounds, there is little occasion for the kind of relatively organized reflection instigated by the reading of advance sheets. The experienced trial judge, then, is one who has imposed many sentences, improving, we would hope, from a course of solitary brooding and conversations with probation officers, consulting in the end himself as the final authority, and perhaps sinking deeper each year the footings of premises that have never been tested by detached scrutiny or by open debate.

Given the sure combination of substantially unbounded discretion and decision-makers unrestrained by shared professional standards, it is not astonishing that the commonplace worry in any discussion of sentencing concerns "disparity." The factual basis for the worry is clear and huge; nobody doubts that essentially similar people in large numbers receive widely divergent sentences for essentially similar or identical crimes. The causes of the problem are equally clear: judges vary widely in their explicit views and "principles" affecting sentencing; they vary, too, in the accidents of birth and biography generating the guilts, the fears, and the rages that affect almost all of us at times and in ways we often cannot know. The judge who reports there is no surge of emotion when he imposes a stiff sentence is likely to be mistaken, unperceptive, or a person of alarmingly flat affect. It is unnecessary, though not irrelevant, to frighten ourselves with the statistical probability and direct personal knowledge that some percentage of judges may be psychotic. It is disturbing enough that a charged encounter like the sentencing proceeding, while it is the gravest of legal matters, should turn so arbitrarily upon the variegated passions and prejudices of individual judges....

We learned long ago that the giving of reasons helps the decision-maker himself in the effort to be fair and rational, and makes it possible for others to judge whether he has succeeded. And so we require our federal district judges and many others to explain themselves when they rule whether a postal truck driver was at fault in crumpling a fender and, if so, how much must be paid to right the wrong.

There is no such requirement in the announcement of a prison sentence. Sometimes judges give reasons anyway, or reveal in colloquy the springs of their action. The explanations or revelations sometimes disclose reasoning so perverse or mistaken that the sentence, normally unreviewable, must be invalidated on appeal. Most trial judges (to my impressionistic and conversational knowledge, at least) say little or nothing, certainly far less than a connected "explanation" or rationale of the sentence. Many, aware of their unreviewable powers, and sharing a common aversion to being reversed, are perhaps motivated by the view (not unknown on trial benches) that there is safety in silence. It is likely that the judge, not expected to explain, has never organized a full and coherent explanation even for himself. Some judges use the occasion of sentencing to flaunt or justify themselves by moral pronunciamentos and excoriations of the defendant. This has no relation to the serious and substantial idea that the community's "denunciation" is a—possibly the—chief aim of sentencing. It is, in any event, not kin to the reasoned decisions for which judges are commissioned....

Parole officials carry on for the most part the motif of Kafka's nightmares. It has been expressed by the United States Board of Parole almost as a matter of pride that the judgment whether or when a prisoner will be released is inscrutable. Describing itself and its functions, the Board has written:

> Voting is done on an individual basis by each member and the Board does not sit as a group for this purpose. Each member studies the prisoner's file and places his

name on the official order form to signify whether he wishes to grant or deny parole. The reasoning and thought which lead to his vote are not made a part of the order, and it is therefore impossible to state precisely why a particular prisoner was or was not granted parole.

Viewing this oracular style of unexplained edict as an article of doctrine, parole boards meet demands for explanations with stout resistance, usually successful. The New Jersey Supreme Court has lately denounced and altered for its State this imperious tradition. The change reflects a growing body of thoughtful opinion. As things stand in most jurisdictions, however, and have long stood, parole boards, subject to no precise criteria and offering no explicit clues as to why particular decisions go as they do, exercise secretly the power to decide within broad ranges the actual number of years of confinement. . . .

Among the changes in the law of punishments over the last 100 years or so has been the movement toward what may be loosely referred to as "indeterminate sentences." The quoted term is widely used. But it has a somewhat indeterminate meaning. As I use it here, it refers generally to any sentence of confinement in which the actual term to be served is not known on the day of judgment but will be subject, within a substantial range, to the later decision of a board of parole or some comparable agency. In this sense there are varying degrees of indeterminacy, ranging from places like California, where the Adult Authority is empowered to set a maximum term of anywhere from a year to life, to, say, our federal system where, as a general matter, the Board of Parole has discretion to grant parole at any point between completion of one-third and two-thirds of the stated sentence.

The basic premise of the indeterminate sentence is the modern conception that rehabilitation is the paramount goal in sentencing. The idea is to avoid the Procrustean mold of uniform sentences to fit crimes in the abstract and to focus upon the progress over time of the unique individual in order to determine when it may be safe for society and good for him to set him free, at least within the limits of parole supervision. At the same time, the power given to a single parole agency may be expected to mitigate the disparities in sentencing caused by the unregulated vagaries of individual judges. While it has not been advanced as a primary justification for the indeterminate sentence, this seeming power of equalization appears to be at least one among the conceptions of their functions entertained by parole boards.

The goals of flexibility and even-handedness seem compellingly worthy. While they do not state the whole case, they go far to explain why the movement toward indeterminacy in sentencing is a powerful and continuing one. Recognizing that the shift means a transfer of much power and responsibility from the sentencing judge to the parole board, many judges have warmly endorsed this development. Troubled by the weight of the burden, authoritatively aware of their limited qualifications, and committed to the principle that sentencing is for rehabilitation, concerned judges are often eager to hand the task on to the supposedly more expert and full-time attention of parole officials. The principle of at least substantial indeterminacy has acquired potent support through adoption in such august products as the Model Penal Code, the proposed Federal Criminal Code of the National Commission on Reform of Federal Criminal Laws, and the Model Sentencing Act proposed in 1963 by the National Council on Crime and Delinquency. The impact of these models in State revisions of their criminal codes has been, and continues to be, substantial.

In short, the trend toward indeterminate sentences seems irresistible at the moment. I think, however, that it should be resisted. . . .

I do not argue that the indeterminate sentence is always and everywhere inappropriate. I believe, however, that its unqualified use rests upon undemonstrated premises; that the premises, even if sound, should not have the sweeping application they are given; and that the excessive extension of indeterminacy has probably resulted in much cruelty and injustice, rather than the great goods its proponents envisage.

Chapter Two

LEGISLATIVE CHOICE: DELEGATION OF RESPONSIBILITY TO THE JUDICIARY AND CORRECTIONS

Sentencing Provisions of the Model Penal Code*

The Model Penal Code, the product of nearly a decade's labor by the distinguished co-reporters and criminal law advisory committee of the American Law Institute, is generally acknowledged as the single most influential legislative drafting undertaking in criminal law in the twentieth century. Completion of the "Proposed Official Draft" in 1962 coincided with a movement toward criminal law codification in the states, which tended to borrow heavily from the Model Code.

In brief, the distinctive features of the adult felony sentencing and correction provisions of the Model Code are as follows:

1. *Three degrees of felonies* (first, second, and third degree, § 6.01)
2. *Sentencing alternatives* (§ 6.02)
   a. suspended sentence
   b. civil commitment in lieu of sentence
   c. fine
   d. probation
   e. imprisonment
   f. fine and probation or fine and imprisonment
3. *Maximum fines* (§ 6.03)
   a. $10,000 for first or second degree felonies
   b. $5,000 for third degree felonies
4. *Criteria for imposing of fines* (§ 7.02)
   (1) The Court shall not sentence a defendant only to pay a fine, when any other disposition is authorized by law, unless having regard to the nature and circumstances of the crime and to the history and character of the defendant, it is of the opinion that the fine alone suffices for protection of the public.
   (2) The Court shall not sentence a defendant to pay a fine in addition to a sentence of imprisonment or probation unless:
       (a) the defendant has derived a pecuniary gain from the crime; or
       (b) the Court is of opinion that a fine is specially adapted to de-

* Proposed Official Draft. Copyright 1966. Reprinted with the permission of the American Law Institute.

terrence of the crime involved or to the correction of the offender.

(3) The Court shall not sentence a defendant to pay a fine unless:

(a) the defendant is or will be able to pay the fine; and

(b) the fine will not prevent the defendant from making restitution or reparation to the victim of the crime.

(4) In determining the amount and method of payment of a fine, the Court shall take into account the financial resources of the defendant and the nature of the burden that its payment will impose.

5. *Criteria for probation* (§ 7.01)

(1) The Court shall deal with a person who has been convicted of a crime without imposing sentence of imprisonment unless, having regard to the nature and circumstances of the crime and the history, character and condition of the defendant, it is of the opinion that his imprisonment is necessary for protection of the public because:

(a) there is undue risk that during the period of a suspended sentence or probation the defendant will commit another crime; or

(b) the defendant is in need of correctional treatment that can be provided most effectively by his commitment to an institution; or

(c) a lesser sentence will depreciate the seriousness of the defendant's crime.

(2) The following grounds, while not controlling the discretion of the Court, shall be accorded weight in favor of withholding sentence of imprisonment:

(a) the defendant's criminal conduct neither caused nor threatened serious harm;

(b) the defendant did not contemplate that his criminal conduct would cause or threaten serious harm;

(c) the defendant acted under a strong provocation;

(d) there were substantial grounds tending to excuse or justify the defendant's criminal conduct, though failing to establish a defense;

(e) the victim of the defendant's criminal conduct induced or facilitated its commission;

(f) the defendant has compensated or will compensate the victim of his criminal conduct for the damage or injury that he sustained;

(g) the defendant has no history of prior delinquency or criminal activity or has led a law-abiding life for a substantial period of time before the commission of the present crime;

(h) the defendant's criminal conduct was the result of circumstances unlikely to recur;

(i) the character and attitudes of the defendant indicate that he is unlikely to commit another crime;

(j) the defendant is particularly likely to respond affirmatively to probationary treatment;

(k) the imprisonment of the defendant would entail excessive hardship to himself or his dependents.

(3) When a person who has been convicted of a crime is not sentenced to imprisonment, the Court shall place him on probation if he is in need of the supervision, guidance, assistance or direction that the probation service can provide.

6. *Minima and maxima for degrees of felonies* (§ 6.06)

Degree	Minimum	Maximum
1st	1 to 10 yrs.	life
2nd	1 to 3 yrs.	10 yrs.
3rd	1 to 2 yrs.	5 yrs.

7. *Extended terms of imprisonment*

a. *For whom authorized* (§ 7.03)

The Court may sentence a person who has been convicted of a felony to an extended term of imprisonment if it finds:

(1) The defendant is a persistent offender whose commitment for an extended term is necessary for protection of the public.

The Court shall not make such a finding unless the defendant is over twenty-one years of age and has previously been convicted of two felonies or of one felony and two misdemeanors, committed at different times when he was over [insert Juvenile Court age] years of age.

(2) The defendant is a professional criminal whose commitment for an extended term is necessary for protection of the public.

The Court shall not make such a finding unless the defendant is over twenty-one years of age and:

(a) the circumstances of the crime show that the defendant has knowingly devoted himself to criminal activity as a major source of livelihood; or

(b) the defendant has substantial income or resources not explained to be derived from a source other than criminal activity.

(3) The defendant is a dangerous, mentally abnormal person whose commitment for an extended term is necessary for protection of the public.

The Court shall not make such a finding unless the defendant has been subjected to a psychiatric examination resulting in the conclusions that his mental condition is gravely abnormal; that his criminal conduct has been characterized by a pattern of repetitive or compulsive behavior or by persistent aggressive behavior with heedless indifference to consequences; and that such condition makes him a serious danger to others.

(4) The defendant is a multiple offender whose criminality was so extensive that a sentence of imprisonment for an extended term is warranted.

The Court shall not make such a finding unless:

(a) the defendant is being sentenced for two or more felonies, or is already under sentence of imprisonment for felony, and the sentences of imprisonment involved will run concurrently ... or

(b) the defendant admits in open court the commission of one or more other felonies and asks that they be taken into account when he is sentenced; and

(c) the longest sentences of imprisonment authorized for each of the defendant's crimes, including admitted crimes taken into account, if made to run consecutively would exceed in length the minimum and maximum of the extended term imposed.

b. *Authorized extended terms* (§ 6.07)

Degree	Minimum	Maximum
1st	6 to 10 yrs.	life
2nd	1 to 5 yrs.	10 to 20 yrs.
3rd	1 to 3 yrs.	5 to 10 yrs.

8. *Parole* (§ 6.10)

(1) *First Release of All Offenders on Parole.* An offender sentenced to an indefinite term of imprisonment in excess of one year ... shall be released conditionally on parole at or before the expiration of the maximum of such term. ...

(2) *Sentence of Imprisonment Includes Separate Parole Term: Length of Parole Term.* A sentence to an indefinite term of imprisonment in excess of one year includes as a separate portion of the sentence a term of parole or of recommitment for violation of the conditions of parole which governs the duration of parole or recommitment after

the offender's first conditional release on parole. The minimum of such term is one year and the maximum is five years....

(3) *Length of Recommitment and Reparole after Revocation of Parole*. If an offender is recommitted upon revocation of his parole, the term of further imprisonment upon such recommitment and of any subsequent reparole or recommitment under the same sentence shall be fixed by the Board of Parole but shall not exceed in aggregate length the unserved balance of the maximum parole term provided by Subsection (2) of this Section.

(4) *Final Unconditional Release*. When the maximum of his parole term has expired or he has been sooner discharged from parole under Section 305.12, an offender shall be deemed to have served his sentence and shall be released unconditionally.

9. *Pre-sentence Investigation* (§ 7.07)

(1) The Court shall not impose sentence without first ordering a pre-sentence investigation of the defendant and according due consideration to a written report of such investigation where:

(a) the defendant has been convicted of a felony; or

(b) the defendant is less than twenty-two years of age and has been convicted of a crime; or

(c) the defendant will be [placed on probation or] sentenced to imprisonment for an extended term.

(2) The Court may order a pre-sentence investigation in any other case.

(3) The pre-sentence investigation shall include an analysis of the circumstances attending the commission of the crime, the defendant's history of delinquency or criminality, physical and mental condition, family situation and background, economic status, education, occupation and personal habits and any other matters that the probation officer deems relevant or the Court directs to be included.

(4) Before imposing sentence, the Court may order the defendant to submit to psychiatric observation and examination for a period of not exceeding sixty days or such longer period as the Court determines to be necessary for the purpose. The defendant may be remanded for this purpose to any available clinic or mental hospital or the Court may appoint a qualified psychiatrist to make the examination. The report of the examination shall be submitted to the Court.

(5) Before imposing sentence, the Court shall advise the defendant or his counsel of the factual contents and the conclusions of any pre-sentence investigation or psychiatric examination and afford fair opportunity, if the defendant so requests, to controvert them. The sources of confidential information need not, however, be disclosed.

(6) The Court shall not impose a sentence of imprisonment for an extended term unless the ground therefor has been established at a hearing after the conviction of the defendant and on written notice to him of the ground proposed. Subject to the limitation of Subsection (5) of this Section, the defendant shall have the right to hear and controvert the evidence against him and to offer evidence upon the issue.

(7) If the defendant is sentenced to imprisonment, a copy of the report of any pre-sentence investigation or psychiatric examination shall be transmitted forthwith to the Department of Correction [or other state department or agency] or, when the defendant is committed to the custody of a specific institution, to such institution.

10. *Diagnostic Commitment* (§ 7.08)

(1) If, after pre-sentence investigation, the Court desires additional in-

formation concerning an offender convicted of a felony or misdemeanor before imposing sentence, it may order that he be committed, for a period not exceeding ninety days, to the custody of the Department of Correction, or, in the case of a young adult offender, to the custody of the Division of Young Adult Correction, for observation and study at an appropriate reception or classification center. The Department and the Board of Parole, or the Young Adult Divisions thereof, shall advise the Court of their findings and recommendations on or before the expiration of such ninety-day period. If the offender is thereafter sentenced to imprisonment, the period of such commitment for observation shall be deducted from the maximum term and from the minimum, if any, of such sentence.

(2) When a person has been sentenced to imprisonment upon conviction of a felony, whether for an ordinary or extended term, the sentence shall be deemed tentative, to the extent provided in this Section, for the period of one year following the date when the offender is received in custody by the Department of Correction [or other state department or agency].

(3) If, as a result of the examination and classification by the Department of Correction [or other state department or agency] of a person under sentence of imprisonment upon conviction of a felony, the Commissioner of Correction [or other department head] is satisfied that the sentence of the Court may have been based upon a misapprehension as to the history, character or physical or mental condition of the offender, the Commissioner, during the period when the offender's sentence is deemed tentative under Subsection (2) of this Section shall file in the sentencing Court a petition to re-sentence the offender. The petition shall set forth the information as to the offender that is deemed to warrant his re-sentence and may include a recommendation as to the sentence to be imposed.

(4) The Court may dismiss a petition filed under Subsection (3) of this Section without a hearing if it deems the information set forth insufficient to warrant reconsideration of the sentence. If the Court is of the view that the petition warrants such reconsideration, a copy of the petition shall be served on the offender, who shall have the right to be heard on the issue and to be represented by counsel.

(5) When the Court grants a petition filed under Subsection (3) of this Section, it shall re-sentence the offender and may impose any sentence that might have been imposed originally for the felony of which the defendant was convicted. The period of his imprisonment prior to re-sentence and any reduction for good behavior to which he is entitled shall be applied in satisfaction of the final sentence.

(6) For all purposes other than this Section, a sentence of imprisonment has the same finality when it is imposed that it would have if this Section were not in force.

(7) Nothing in this Section shall alter the remedies provided by law for vacating or correcting an illegal sentence.

NOTES

Note 1. Statutory Sentencing Framework

THE PRESIDENT'S COMMISSION ON LAW ENFORCEMENT AND ADMINISTRATION OF JUSTICE, *Task Force Report: The Courts* 14–18 (1967)

Over half the States are now engaged in penal law revision, including reconsideration of their sentencing codes, and in October 1966 Congress, at the request of President Johnson, established a special commission to study and propose revisions of Federal penal laws and sentencing statutes. These revision efforts emphasize the importance of considering the problems in existing sentencing codes.

Statutory provisions affect sentencing decisions in individual cases in two primary ways. The statutes distribute sentencing authority among the legislature, the court, and the correctional agencies. They also determine the criteria used by the courts and correctional agencies to make the decisions delegated to them and place limits on their authority.

The influence of the statutory sentencing framework may be illustrated by the case of a hypothetical adult offender who stands convicted of armed robbery and who previously has been imprisoned for a felony: Under typical American penal codes, at the time of sentence the court might impose imprisonment, probation, or a fine. In a few jurisdictions the death penalty is available for armed robbery, but it is rarely imposed.

If the offender is sentenced to prison, the two most important decisions are how long he may be kept there and when he will first become eligible for release on parole. In all jurisdictions the legislature fixes the maximum length of imprisonment for an offense, but in most States the courts are permitted to select a sentence for each offender within a range provided by the statute, such as "any term up to 20 years" or "any term between 10 and 20 years." In a few States, however, the judge is limited to the imposition of a fixed statutory maximum term, with all other aspects of the actual length of imprisonment later set administratively by correctional authorities.

The laws of many States would impose further limitations on the judge's authority. A number of States provide a mandatory minimum sentence of imprisonment, sometimes 10 years or more, for particularly dangerous crimes, such as armed robbery. In addition a majority of States require heavier punishment for repeated offenders by a mandatory provision applicable to all recidivists. In most of the remaining States heavier punishment is permitted at the judge's discretion.

Few prisoners serve their maximum terms of imprisonment. After serving a fraction of their maximum sentences most are released on parole or on conditional release earned because of good time credit. In many States prisoners are eligible for parole when they serve a fixed part, typically one-third or one-half, of their maximum sentences. In most, the courts have authority to impose a specific minimum sentence that an offender must serve in prison before he becomes eligible for parole. The date of parole eligibility is determined solely by the correctional authorities in a few States.

In all States the court may sentence an offender to serve a period of probation up to a maximum fixed by statute. But statutes in a number of States would prohibit probation for an armed robber with a prior felony conviction because of the seriousness of the offense or because of his criminal record.

The maximum amount of the fine which the court may impose is also fixed by statute. It is unlikely that the court would sentence an armed robber to pay a fine, since few judges would consider a fine adequate punishment for a violent offense, and in any event, few felons have the money to pay a substantial fine. . . .

Imprisonment

Because of its severity as compared with fine or probation, imprisonment is believed to have a greater deterrent effect on potential offenders and on the prisoner himself. It isolates from society persons who are likely to commit further criminal acts, and it may provide a type of discipline and training in an institutional setting that would be helpful in beginning certain programs of rehabilitation.

Imprisonment is not without its costs, however. It is financially the most expensive way of dealing with a convicted offender, not only in terms of custodial costs but also in the loss of the prisoner's productive capacity and support for his dependents. The Commission's nationwide survey of correctional operations revealed that the average cost of probation supervision for an adult felony offender is $200 per year, while the average yearly cost of imprisoning such an offender is almost $2,000. Moreover, removing a man completely from the community may impede his successful reintegration later, and the atmosphere, associations, and stigma of imprisonment may reinforce his criminality.

An enlightened sentencing code, therefore, should provide for a more selective use of imprisonment. It should ensure that long prison terms are available for habitual, dangerous, and professional criminals who present a substantial threat to the public safety and that it is possible for the less serious offender to be released to community supervision without being subjected to the potentially destructive effects of lengthy imprisonment. Moreover, it should provide the courts and correctional authorities with sufficient flexibility to fix lengths of imprisonment which are appropriate on the facts of each case.

The statutory sentencing provisions in many jurisdictions, however, prevent the courts from making discriminating use of imprisonment. The clearest instances of restrictive provisions are those which require the courts to impose a specific prison sentence on certain offenders. These mandatory prison sentences are of three basic types. The most prevalent requires the court to impose increased prison terms on recidivists. The second type specifies for a particular offense either the minimum period which an offender must serve before he becomes eligible for parole or the maximum period he may be required to serve before he must be released. Finally, in a few States the court must impose consecutive sentences on an offender who is convicted of several offenses at one trial.

Mandatory prison sentences often are extremely severe. The habitual offender laws in about one-third of the States make life imprisonment mandatory on the third or fourth conviction of a felony, and in more than one-half of the States the courts are required to impose increased terms on second offenders. Under certain sections of the Federal narcotics laws the court must sentence an offender to a prescribed mandatory 10-year prison sentence without eligibility for parole.

Because of the need to deter potential offenders and to isolate dangerous persons from the community, it is necessary that long prison sentences be available for those who have committed the most serious offenses or for those who are likely to commit further crimes. Mandatory sentences, however, prevent the courts from basing their sentences on the relative importance of these factors in each case. Judges and prosecutors often regard punishment by long mandatory terms as unreasonably harsh, and they are faced with the dilemma of adhering to the statutory requirement or avoiding it to produce results that seem to be just in individual cases. Furthermore, the avoidance of mandatory sentences may be almost a practical necessity, since an undermanned prosecutor's office depends on the possibility of leniency to obtain guilty pleas. An office which does not reduce charges for offenses carrying long mandatory terms or which routinely seeks to obtain convictions under mandatory habitual offender laws would become overwhelmed with trials because defendants would have no incentive to plead guilty.

There is persuasive evidence of nonenforcement of these mandatory sentencing provisions by the coutrs and prosecutors. . . .

* * *

The nullification of mandatory sentencing provisions suggests the need for a more flexible means of effectuating legislative sentencing policy. This need might be satisfied by repealing mandatory sentences which have proved unworkable and by enacting statutory standards to guide the courts and correctional authorities in the exercise of their discretion.

The enactment of statutory criteria also would tend to ensure that a consistent and rational sentencing policy is applied in the many cases in which mandatory sentences presently are not required. In most jurisdictions the length of prison sentences which a trial judge may impose is restricted only by broad statutory limits; he may be authorized to sentence an offender to any term of years not exceeding a specified maximum or to any term of years between an upper and lower limit designated by the statute, for example, 15 to 5 years. The trial judge generally must make this decision without guidance from the legislature and without the opportunity for a defendant to have his sentence reviewed by an appellate court. Furthermore, a common characteristic of American penal codes is the severity of sentences available for almost all felony offenses. In the Illinois penal code, for example, there are more than 20 offenses for which the court may impose any sentence from one year to life imprisonment.

The statutory lengths of sentences are reflected in the sentencing practices of the courts. More than one-half of the adult felony offenders sentenced to State prisons in 1960 were committed for maximum terms of 5 years or more; almost one-third were sentenced to terms of at least 10 years. And more than one-half of the prisoners confined in State institutions in 1960 had been sentenced to maximum terms of at least 10 years. There is a substantial question whether sentences of this length are desirable or necessary for the majority of felony offenders. The experience of a number of other countries throughout the world that rely on relatively short prison sentences for most offenders supports the view that long sentences properly may be reserved for the special case. In addition there are indications that despite the long sentences initially imposed, the administrators of penal systems in this country in practice have relied on shorter periods of confinement. Of the approximately 80,000 felony prisoners released in 1960 from State institutions, the median time actually served before first release was about 21 months; only 8.7 percent of the prisoners released actually served five years or more.

The enactment of statutory criteria provides a way of directing the judge's attention to those factors which the legislature has determined to be relevant to the sentencing decision. Both the Model Penal Code and the Model Sentencing Act employ statutory criteria in conjunction with separate sentencing provisions which attempt to discriminate between offenders who require lengthy imprisonment and those who are likely to be released after relatively brief periods of custody. For each offense the Code and the Act provide an ordinary term, which is generally shorter than authorized under present statutes, and an extended term, which the court may impose when certain factors are present. Under the Code, for example, the court may impose an extended term only if it finds that lengthy imprisonment is necessary for the protection of the public because the defendant is a persistent offender; a professional criminal; a dangerous, mentally abnormal person; or a multiple offender whose criminality was so extensive that an extended term is warranted.

Developing proper standards to guide the courts in determining the length of prison sentences is only in the elementary stages. Standards such as the Code's "dangerous, mentally abnormal person," or the Act's "severe personality disorder indicating a propensity toward criminal activity" are subject to many interpretations, and there is a risk that they may be used improperly by the courts. They are the most definite criteria, however, which have been formulated on the basis of limited ability to predict behavior. These standards will be revised should the behavioral sciences develop improved ways of identifying dangerous offenders. The advantage of the approach taken by the Model Penal Code and the Model Sentencing Act is that it provides a vehicle for incorporating improved criteria into the basic sentencing structure.

Probation

The ... central advantages of probation as an alternative to imprisonment are that it facilitates the reintegration of the offender into the community, avoids the negative aspects of imprisonment, and reduces the financial burden on the State. Despite these important benefits many courts still view probation only in its historical context, that is, as "an act of grace and clemency to be granted in a proper case."

The statutory provisions authorizing the use of probation do little to dispel this image. Legislatures in almost all jurisdictions have restricted the courts' power to grant probation by limitations based on such factors as the type of offense, the length of prison sentence which could be imposed, and the offender's prior criminal record. Moreover, the criteria for granting probation to eligible offenders are often so highly abstract that they provide very limited guidance to the courts. In California, for example, the court is authorized to grant probation when it determines "that there are circumstances in mitigation of punishment prescribed by law, or that the ends of justice would be subserved."

Restrictions on the courts' power to grant probation have produced the same practice of avoidance by courts and prosecutors discussed in the context of mandatory prison terms. The absence of meaningful legislative standards for granting probation aggravates the problem of disparity of sentences because each judge is left virtually unrestrained in applying his own theories of probation to individual cases. And it may decrease the use of probation, because the court may be more reluctant to risk public criticism in the event of further criminality by a probationer when it is unable to justify its action at least in part by legislative direction.

To enable the courts to utilize probation effectively, legislatures should reduce the number of restrictions on the courts' power to grant probation and provide statutory standards to guide courts in the exercise of their discretion. This is the approach taken by the drafters of the Model Penal Code and adopted by the New York Legislature in revising the State's penal law. Both the Code and the New York statute permit courts to grant probation in all cases except murder and, in New York, kidnaping. The reason for enlarging the courts' discretion, as expressed by the drafters of the Model Penal Code, is that:

> However right it may be to take the gravest view of an offense in general, there will be cases comprehended in the definition where the circumstances were so unusual, or the mitigations so extreme, that a suspended sentence or probation would be proper. We see no reason to distrust the courts upon this matter or to fear that such authority will be abused.

The Code establishes a preference against imprisonment by directing the court to suspend sentence or grant probation unless it finds that imprisonment is necessary for the protection of the public....

The New York statute ... enumerates similar criteria as affirmative grounds for probation and directs the court to grant probation only where these affirmative grounds are present. Although the standards of the Code and the New York Penal Law are quite general, they are an improvement over current statutes because they direct the courts' attention to the correctional purposes of probation.

Fines

Two unfortunate characteristics of sentencing practices in many lower courts are the routine imposition of fines on the great majority of misdemeanants and petty offenders and the routine imprisonment of offenders who default in paying fines. These practices result in unequal punishment of offenders and in the needless imprisonment of many persons because of their financial condition.

Thirty years ago the National Commission on Law Observance and Enforcement called attention to the inordinate number of offenders who were imprisoned for failure to pay fines. A more recent study of the Philadelphia County jail showed that 60 percent of the inmates had been committed for nonpayment. And in 1960 there were over 26,000 prisoners in New York City jails who had been imprisoned for default in payment of fines.

The consequences of the failure to pay a fine are extremely severe in many States. The New York Court of Appeals only last year ruled unconstitutional a statute which permitted the court to imprison a defendant for one day for each dollar of a fine which he had not paid. However, other jurisdictions still retain comparably harsh sanctions for nonpayment.

Legislative action should impose limitations on the common practice of imposing sentences which offer the offender a choice of paying the fine or serving a stated period of imprisonment, such as "$10 or 10 days." This type of sentence is inherently discriminatory because it determines the severity of punishment solely on the basis of a defendant's wealth. Statutes which authorize the imposition of fines should provide that if the court concludes that the public would be adequately protected by the payment of a fine, the fine itself is the appropriate sentence.

It is unlikely that all of the discriminatory consequences of fines will ever be eliminated. There will continue to be many instances in which offenders are deserving of punishment but the judges' realistic alternatives are limited to fines or jail. The fact that our society has not devised suitable alternative punishments gives rise to a vexing dilemma in the use of fines. For so long as jail is the routine alternative to a fine, those unable to pay will be punished more severely than those of greater means. Putting all offenders in jail is a wholly unacceptable alternative, as is relieving those unable to pay a fine of all penalties.

A reduction in the number of offenders imprisoned for nonpayment might be achieved through legislation providing the courts with more flexible methods for collecting fines. Under the Model Penal Code, for example, the court may grant permission for the fine to be paid within a specified period of time or in several installments, and the court may grant the defendant additional time to pay the fine if necessary; a method of civil attachment and execution for the collection of unpaid fines is also available. In addition a defendant may not be imprisoned unless his default is due to a willful refusal to pay or to make a good faith effort to obtain the money. The difficulty with provisions of this type, however, is that they may make it possible for defendants to escape all penalties and thus make judges more hesitant to impose fines.

Note 2.

DANIEL GLASER, FRED COHEN,
AND VINCENT O'LEARY

The Sentencing and Parole Process
9–15 (1966)

The Traditional Dichotomy

The most commonly made distinction between systems for specifying parole board authority is that between the definite and the indeterminate sentence. These labels provide a useful starting point for further distinctions, but they are somewhat misleading, since parole can occur even under a definite sentence, and thus the effects of the sentence are not fully definite or determinate when it is imposed.

An indeterminate sentence, as the term is ordinarily used, is one in which the court specifies two periods of confinement for each case, one being the minimum and the other the maximum. Thus, indeterminate sentences may be for 1 year to life, for 1 to 5 years, for 10 to 20 years, or for any other combination of a minimum and a maximum. A prisoner with an indeterminate sentence is eligible for parole at any time after completion of the minimum, and he must be discharged from his sentence at completion of the maximum. In some jurisdictions, time may be taken off the minimum sentence for good behavior, elsewhere it may be taken off the maximum, and sometimes it is taken from both. In some systems, the statutes specify what the minimum and maximum shall be for each offense, and in others they give discretion to the judge, in fixing one or both of these limits.

* * *

Under a definite sentence system, the court imposes a sentence for a given number of years, within statutory limits, but the parole board may release a prisoner on parole after a portion of this sentence has been served in prison. Usually this portion is set as a fraction of the sentence, such as one-third, but it may be a given number of months or years. This system is also referred to as a "fixed," "flat," or "general" sentence system.

Because the freedom of the parole board to alter the period of confinement often is greater under definite, than under indeterminate sentencing, these traditional labels are not very useful. When the judge has authority to fix both minimum and maximum for each offender, he can make the difference between the two very small, for example, an 8 to 10 year sentence. The indeterminate sentence then becomes much more rigidly fixed than a definite sentence of 8, 9, or 10 years, on which parole can occur when one-third is completed.

The bargaining process in the courts frequently takes parole possibilities into account. An experienced criminal usually likes to have his term as predictable as possible, and will bargain for a low maximum sentence, rather than accept a low minimum with a high maximum and take his chances on early parole. Conversely, the prosecutor may persuade a novice offender that if he cooperates by pleading guilty he will get a low minimum sentence and will have good prospects for an early parole.

Varieties of Sentencing Structure

Because of the diversity of practice under both the indeterminate and the definite sentence systems, other types of classification may define more clearly the various ways in which length of imprisonment is determined.

We shall indicate here the most distinctive combinations of statutory arrangement, and the judicial systems in which they are employed. It should be noted, however, that many jurisdictions have different types of sentencing structures for different offenses, or even give the court a choice of alternative types of sentencing in a given case. Therefore, our reference to a particular pattern existing in a jurisdiction may not mean that it is the only pattern found there. The following attempt at a classification within these limits is an expansion of categories developed in a previous survey by the *Columbia Law Review*.*

1. *Both Maximum and Minimum Term Fixed by the Court* (*Within Upper Limit for Maximum and Lower Limit for Minimum Set by the Law for Each Offense*). Parole eligibility under this system occurs at completion of the minimum term, or the minimum less time off for good behavior. With this system, there usually is great disparity—within the range permitted by statute—in the minimum, in the maximum, and in the span between the two, since judges have much discretion in varying each. This system is found in 14 States, and is used exclusively or almost exclusively in 9 States....

2. *Both Maximum and Minimum Term Fixed by the Court* (*Within Limits Set by Law*), *But Minimum Not To Exceed a Fraction of Maximum*. This system guarantees the possibility of a certain maximum relationship of the parole period to the term of confinement....

3. *Maximum Term Fixed by the Court* (*Within Limits Set by Law*), *Minimum Fixed by Law*. This is the court-imposed variety of the definite sentence system. Effectively, the minimum is the period before parole eligibility, although it is not called a minimum sentence. Sometimes this period is a fraction of the sentence, sometimes it is a specific period of time such as 1 year, and sometimes it is either a fraction or a given number of years, whichever is least. There has been some contention that prison terms tend to be shortest in jurisdictions having this definite sentence system. However, the differences are not consistent or extreme, and it has been argued that these differences

---

* Note, "Statutory Structures for Sentencing Felons to Prison," *Columbia Law Review*, vol. 60, No. 8 (December 1960), pp. 1134–1172. We have found a few apparent discrepancies in this and in every other compilation we have encountered, and some errors may also exist in our compilation, but it has been checked with statutes, cases, articles, and personal reports by parole board members.

occur because the jurisdictions with this system least often use probation; they impose short prison terms in cases which elsewhere would receive probation.

This system is used exclusively or almost exclusively in 12 States. . . .

4. *Maximum Term Fixed by Law for Each Offense, But Minimum Term Fixed by the Court.* This is the system in Hawaii and Michigan. . . .

5. *Maximum and Minimum Sentence Fixed by Law for Each Offense.* Under this system, the court has no formal part in selecting a sentence once it finds a man guilty, although informally, the court's interest in the sentence may determine the charge on which a man is convicted. This system is used exclusively or predominantly in eight States. . . .

6. *Maximum Terms Fixed by Law for Each Offense, No Minimum Sentence, But Minimum Term Set by Parole Board at an Early Hearing Is Equivalent to Minimum Sentence.* This is known as the "administrative sentencing" or "sentencing tribunal" system. It is used in California, Washington, Utah, and Iowa, and is optional in the Federal system. . . .

7. *Maximum Sentence Fixed by Court, No Minimum Sentence.* When the court sets a high maximum sentence, such as almost guarantees that the first release will be by parole, this system approximates administrative sentencing in the extent to which the parole board determines the effective sentence. This system is found exclusively in Oregon, Missouri, and Minnesota, and it predominates in Idaho. . . .

8. *Law Fixes Minimum Sentence, Maximin Period Before First Parole, and Maximum Sentence.* This describes the Youth Correction Act sentencing option in Federal courts, under which offenders below age 26 may receive a 6-year sentence from which they are eligible for parole after 60 days, and from which they must be paroled once before 4 years. The parole board also may discharge them from their sentence before 6 years. This is modeled on the British Borstal sentence. This system guarantees that all first releases are by parole.

9. *Law Prescribes That Inmate Shall Be Under Correctional Supervision Until He Reaches a Given Age, Unless Discharged from the Sentence Earlier, and May Be Paroled at Any Time.* The California Youth Authority and the Minnesota Youth Conservation Commission may receive any offender under 21 years of age and subject to more than 90 days' confinement, and they maintain authority over these persons until age 25. Such inmates may be paroled immediately, but in practice, 60 days or more is likely to elapse before they have been observed adequately to permit a decision to parole them, and almost all have their first release by parole. Therefore, this sentence, in its effects, is very similar to the Federal Youth Correction Act. . . .

Chapter Three

BUREAUCRATIC PRECHOICE: PRESENTENCE INVESTIGATION AND REPORT

WILLIAMS V. NEW YORK
337 U.S. 241 (1949)
Supreme Court of the United States

MR. JUSTICE BLACK delivered the opinion of the Court.

A jury in a New York state court found appellant guilty of murder in the first degree. The jury recommended life imprisonment, but the trial judge imposed sentence of death. In giving his reason for imposing the death sentence the judge discussed in open court the evidence upon which the jury had convicted stating that this evidence had been considered in the light of additional information obtained through the court's "Probation Department, and through other sources." Consideration of this additional information was pursuant to § 482 of New York Criminal Code which provides:

> ... Before rendering judgment or pronouncing sentence the court shall cause the defendant's previous criminal record to be submitted to it, including any reports that may have been made as a result of a mental, phychiatric [sic] or physical examination of such person, and may seek any information that will aid the court in determining the proper treatment of such defendant.

The Court of Appeals of New York affirmed the conviction and sentence over the contention that as construed and applied the controlling penal statutes are in violation of the due process clause of the Fourteenth Amendment of the Constitution of the United States "in that the sentence of death was based upon information supplied by witnesses with whom the accused had not been confronted and as to whom he had no opportunity for cross-examination or rebuttal . . . ." 298 N.Y. 803, 804, 83 N.E. 2d 698, 699. Because the statutes were sustained over this constitutional challenge the case is here on appeal under 28 U.S.C. § 1257 (2).

The narrow contention here makes it unnecessary to set out the facts at length. The record shows a carefully conducted trial lasting more than two weeks in which appellant was represented by three appointed lawyers who conducted his defense with fidelity and zeal. The evidence proved a wholly indefensible murder committed by a person engaged in a burglary. The judge instructed the jury that if it returned a verdict of guilty as charged, without recommendation for life sentence, "The Court must impose the death penalty," but if such recommendation was made, "the Court may impose a life sentence." The judge went on to emphasize that "the Court is not bound to accept your recommendation."

About five weeks after the verdict of guilty with recommendation of life imprisonment, and after a statutory pre-sentence investigation report to the judge, the defendant was brought to court to be sentenced. Asked what he had to say, appellant protested his innocence. After each of his three lawyers had appealed to court to accept the jury's recommendation of a life sentence, the judge gave reasons why he felt that the death sentence should be imposed. He narrated the shocking details of the crime as shown by the trial evidence, expressing his own complete belief in appellant's guilt. He stated that the pre-sentence investigation revealed many material facts concerning appellant's background which though relevant to the question of punishment could not properly have been brought to the attention of the jury in its consideration of the question of guilt. He referred to the experience appellant "had had on thirty other burglaries in and about the same vicinity" where the murder had been committed. The appellant had not been convicted of these burglaries although the judge had information that he had confessed to some and had been identified as the perpetrator of some of the others. The judge also referred to certain activities of appellant as shown by the probation report that indicated appellant possessed "a morbid sexuality" and classified him as a "menace to society." The accuracy of the statements made by the judge as to appellant's background and past practices was not challenged by appellant or his counsel, nor was the judge asked to disregard any of them or to afford appellant a chance to refute or discredit any of them by cross-examination or otherwise.

The case presents a serious and difficult question. The question relates to the rules of evidence applicable to the manner in which a judge may obtain information to guide him in the imposition of sentence upon an already convicted defendant. Within limits fixed by statutes, New York judges are given a broad discretion to decide the type and extent of punishment for convicted defendants. Here, for example, the judge's discretion was to sentence to life imprisonment or death. To aid a judge in exercising this discretion intelligently the New York procedural policy encourages him to consider information about the convicted person's past life, health, habits, conduct, and mental and moral propensities. The sentencing judge may consider such information even though obtained outside the courtroom from persons whom a defendant has not been permitted to confront or cross-examine. It is the consideration of information obtained by a sentencing judge in this manner that is the basis for appellant's broad constitutional challenge to the New York statutory policy.

Appellant urges that the New York statutory policy is in irreconcilable conflict with the underlying philosophy of a second procedural policy grounded in the due process of law clause of the Fourteenth Amendment. That policy as stated in *In re Oliver*, 333 U.S. 257, 273, is in part that no person shall be tried and convicted of an offense unless he is given reasonable notice of the charges against him and is afforded an opportunity to examine adverse witnesses. That the due process clause does provide these salutary and time-tested protections where the question for consideration is the guilt of a defendant seems entirely clear from the genesis and historical evolution of the clause. . . .

Tribunals passing on the guilt of a defendant always have been hedged in by strict evidentiary procedural limitations. But both before and since the American colonies became a nation, courts in this country and in England practiced a policy under which a sentencing judge could exercise a wide discretion in the sources and types of evidence used to assist him in determining the kind and extent of punishment to be imposed within limits fixed by law. Out-of-court affidavits have been used frequently, and of course in the smaller communities sentencing judges naturally have in mind their knowledge of the personalities and backgrounds of convicted offenders. A recent manifestation of the historical latitude allowed sentencing judges appears in Rule 32 of the Federal Rules of Criminal Procedure. That rule provides for consideration by federal judges of reports made by probation officers containing information about a convicted defendant, including such information "as may be helpful in imposing sentence or in granting probation or in the correctional treatment of the defendant. . . ."

In addition to the historical basis for different evidentiary rules governing trial and sentencing procedures there are sound practical reasons for the distinction. In a trial before verdict the issue is whether a defendant is guilty of having engaged in certain criminal conduct of which he has been specifically accused. Rules of evidence have been fashioned for criminal trials which narrowly confine the trial contest to evidence that is strictly relevant to the particular offense charged. These rules rest in part on a necessity to prevent a time-consuming and confusing trial of collateral issues. They were also designed to prevent tribunals concerned solely with the issue of guilt of a particular offense from being influenced to convict for that offense by evidence that the defendant had habitually engaged in other misconduct. A sentencing judge, however, is not confined to the narrow issue of guilt. His task within fixed statutory or constitutional limits is to determine the type and extent of punishment after the issue of guilt has been determined. Highly relevant—if not essential—to his selection of an appropriate sentence is the possession of the fullest information possible concerning the defendant's life and characteristics. And modern concepts individualizing punishment have made it all the more necessary that a sentencing judge not be denied an opportunity to obtain pertinent information by a requirement of rigid adherence to restrictive rules of evidence properly applicable to the trial.

Undoubtedly the New York statutes emphasize a prevalent modern philosophy of penology that the punishment should fit the offender and not merely the crime. . . . The belief no longer prevails that every offense in a like legal category calls for an identical punishment without regard to the past life and habits of a particular offender. This whole country has traveled far from the period in which the death sentence was an automatic and commonplace result of convictions—even for offenses today deemed trivial. Today's philosophy of individualizing sentences makes sharp distinctions for example between first and repeated offenders. Indeterminate sentences the ultimate termination of which are sometimes decided by non-judicial agencies have to a large extent taken the place of the old rigidly fixed punishments. The practice of probation which relies heavily on non-judicial implementation has been accepted as a wise policy. Execution of the United States parole system rests on the discretion of an administrative parole board. . . . Retribution is no longer the dominant objective of the criminal law. Reformation and rehabilitation of offenders have become important goals of criminal jurisprudence.

Modern changes in the treatment of offenders makes it more necessary now than a century ago for observance of the distinctions in the evidential procedure in the trial and sentencing processes. For indeterminate sentences and probation have resulted in an increase in the discretionary powers exercised in fixing punishments. In general, these modern changes have not resulted in making the lot of offenders harder. On the contrary a strong motivating force for the changes has been the belief that by careful study of the lives and personalities of convicted offenders many could be less severely punished and restored sooner to complete freedom and useful citizenship. This belief to a large extent has been justified.

Under the practice of individualizing punishments, investigational techniques have been given an important role. Probation workers making reports of their investigations have not been trained to prosecute but to aid offenders. Their reports have been given a high value by conscientious judges who want to sentence persons on the best available information rather than on guesswork and inadequate information. To deprive sentencing judges of this kind of information would undermine modern penological procedural policies that have been cautiously adopted throughout the nation after careful consideration and experimentation. We must recognize that most of the information now relied upon by judges to guide them in the intelligent imposition of sentences would be unavailable if information were restricted to that given in open court by witnesses subject to cross-examination. And the modern probation report draws on information concerning every aspect of a defendant's life. The type and extent of this information make totally impractical if not impossible open court testimony with cross-examination. Such a procedure could endlessly delay criminal administration in a retrial of collateral issues.

The considerations we have set out admonish us against treating the due process clause as a uniform command that courts throughout the Nation abandon their age-old practice of seeking information from out-of-court sources to guide their judgment toward a more enlightened and just sentence. New York criminal statutes set wide limits for maximum and minimum sentences. Under New York statutes a state judge cannot escape his grave responsibility of fixing sentence. In determining whether a defendant shall receive a one-year minimum or a twenty-year maximum sentence, we do not think the Federal Constitution restricts the view of the sentencing judge to the information received in open court. The due process clause should not be treated as a device for freezing the evidential procedure of sentencing in the mold of trial procedure. So to treat the due process clause would hinder if not preclude all courts—state and federal—from making progressive efforts to improve the administration of criminal justice.

It is urged, however, that we should draw a constitutional distinction as to the procedure for obtaining information where the death sentence is imposed. We cannot accept the contention. Leaving a sentencing judge free to avail himself of out-of-court information in making such a fateful choice of sentences does secure to him a broad discretionary power, one susceptible of abuse. But in considering whether a rigid constitutional barrier should be created, it must be remembered that there is possibility of abuse wherever a judge must choose between life imprisonment and death. And it is conceded that no federal constitutional objection would have been possible if the judge here had sentenced appellant to death because appellant's trial manner impressed the judge that appellant was a bad risk for society, or if the judge had sentenced him to death giving no reason at all. We cannot say that the due process clause renders a sentence void merely because a judge gets additional out-of-court information to assist him in the exercise of this awesome power of imposing the death sentence.

Appellant was found guilty after a fairly conducted trial. His sentence followed a hearing conducted by the judge. Upon the judge's inquiry as to why sentence should not be imposed, the defendant made statements. His counsel made extended arguments. The case went to the highest court in the state, and that court had power to reverse for abuse of discretion or legal error in the imposition of the sentence. That court affirmed. We hold that appellant was not denied due process of law.

Affirmed.

MR. JUSTICE MURPHY, dissenting.

A combination of factors in this case impels me to dissent.

Petitioner was convicted of murder by a jury, and sentenced to death by the judge. The jury which heard the trial unanimously recommended life imprisonment as a suitable punishment for the defendant. They had observed him throughout the trial, had heard all the evidence adduced against him, and in spite of the shocking character of the crime of which they found him guilty, were unwilling to decree that his life should be taken. In our criminal courts the jury sits as the representative of the community; its voice is that of the society against which the crime was committed. A judge, even though vested with statutory authority to do so, should hesitate indeed to increase the severity of such a community expression.

He should be willing to increase it, moreover, only with the most scrupulous regard for the rights of the defendant. The record before us indicates that the judge exercised his discretion to deprive a man of his life, in reliance on material made available to him in a probation report, consisting almost entirely of evidence that would have been inadmissible at the trial. Some, such as allegations of prior crimes, was irrelevant. Much was incompetent as hearsay. All was damaging, and none was subject to scrutiny by the defendant.

Due process of law includes at least the idea that a person accused of crime shall be accorded a fair hearing through all the stages of the proceedings against him. I agree with the Court as to the value and humaneness of liberal use of probation reports as developed by modern penologists, but, in a capital case, against the unanimous recommendation of a jury, where the report would concededly not have been admissible at the trial, and was not subject to examination by the defendant, I am forced to conclude that the high commands of due process were not obeyed.

NOTES

Note 1. The Frequency of Presentence Investigation

THE PRESIDENT'S COMMISSION ON LAW ENFORCEMENT AND ADMINISTRATION OF JUSTICE, *Task Force Report: The Courts* 18–19 (1967)

The statutes or rules of court in about one-quarter of the States make a presentence report mandatory for certain classes of offenses, generally those punishable by imprisonment in excess of one year. In the great majority of States and in the Federal system a request for a presentence report is discretionary with the trial judge, although in some of these States probation may not be granted unless a presentence report has been prepared.

Little information is available on the extent to which presentence reports are actually used in those jurisdictions where they are not mandatory. Data for the Federal courts show that presentence investigations were made in 88 percent of all felony convictions in 1963, and it has been estimated that some form of presentence report is prepared in most felony cases in the country. Studies of individual court systems, however, show that wide variations exist in the thoroughness of the investigation.

Systematic gathering of sentence information is virtually nonexistent in many misdemeanor courts. In Detroit, for example, where probation facilities are available in misdemeanor cases, presentence reports were ordered in only 400 out of more than 12,000 misdemeanor convictions in 1965. The Commission's national corrections survey showed that few misdemeanor courts have probation services available to prepare reports. Whatever background information lower court judges receive before imposing sentence is generally furnished by the police or prosecutor or is elicited from the defendant through a few brief questions. The dangers of incomplete, inaccurate, and misleading presentation is great when this method is used.

The importance of adequate presentence investigation has long been recognized. The National Commission on Law Observance and Enforcement and many of the State crime commissions chartered in the 1920's recommended increased use of presentence reports. More recently the drafters of the Model Penal Code stated that the use and full development of the presentence investigation and report offer the "greatest hope for the improvement of judicial sentencing."

Note 2. *The Function of Presentence Investigation*

a. THE PRESIDENT'S COMMISSION ON LAW ENFORCEMENT AND ADMINISTRATION OF JUSTICE, *Task Force Report: Corrections* 18–19 (1967)

At present, the main tool for providing background information for sentencing is the presentence report. This report is prepared in most cases by the probation staff of a court on the basis of investigation and interviews. It seeks to assess the offender's background and present circumstances and to suggest a correctional disposition.

A fully developed presentence investigation usually includes, among other items, an analysis of the offender's motivations, his identification with delinquent values, and his residential, educational, employment, and emotional history. It relates these factors to alternative plans of treatment and explores the resources available to carry out the suggested treatment.

The compilation of the standard presentence report is extremely time-consuming. In addition to the offender himself, numerous persons must be located and interviewed. Records must be secured and verified. The information collected must be discussed and analyzed and recommendations formulated. The Special Committee on Correctional Standards formed to advise the Commission's staff in connection with the National Survey of Corrections concluded that a probation officer could adequately prepare no more than 10 such reports during a month—and that exclusive of any other duties. In fact, in most cases the staff who carry on presentence investigations are also engaged in supervising probationers. Since presentence investigations usually take precedence, the officer may have so little time left that "supervision" may take the form of receiving monthly reports filed by probationers.

The high manpower levels required to complete reports have caused some authorities to raise questions as to the need for the kind and quantity of information that is typically gathered and presented. These questions are raised particularly with respect to the misdemeanant system, where millions of cases are disposed of each year and relatively few presentence investigations made.

In order to evaluate the information needed in a presentence report, it is important first to take account of the variety of decisions that depend upon it. Besides helping the judge to decide between probation and prison, it also assists him to fix the length and conditions of probation or the term of imprisonment. Beyond these functions, the report is usually the major information source in all significant decisions that follow—in probation programing or institutional handling, in eventual parole decision and supervision, and in any probation and parole revocation.

Not all of these decisions are involved, of course, in every case. Particularly in many misdemeanant cases, where correctional alternatives are usually limited, less information may suffice. Bail projects have developed reporting forms that can be completed and verified in a matter of a few hours and have proven reliable for decisions on release pending trial, which often involve considerations similar to those of ultimate disposition. These forms cover such factors as education and employment status, family and situation, and residential stability. In many lesser cases, these and similar easily obtainable facts may help at least to determine whether more detailed investigation or diagnostic processes are needed. Much information of this kind can also be collected by non-professional personnel under the supervision of trained correctional staff. There is also a need for development of information systems that can provide more rapid and reliable access to records.

Experimentation with new and simpler forms of presentence investigation is important for reasons beyond the conservation of scarce resources of probation offices. Presentence reports in many cases have come to include a great deal of material of doubtful relevance to disposition in most cases. The terminology and approach of reports vary widely with the training and outlook of the persons preparing them. The orientation of many probation officers is often reflected in, for example, attempts to provide in all presentence reports comprehensive analyses of offenders, including extensive descriptions of their childhood experiences. In many cases this kind of information is of marginal relevance to the kinds of correctional treatment actually available or called for. Not only is preparation time-consuming, but its inclusion may confuse decision-making.

b. ADMINISTRATIVE OFFICE OF THE UNITED STATES COURTS, DIVISION OF PROBATION, *The Presentence Investigation Report* 1 (1965)

The presentence investigation report is a basic working document in judicial and correctional administration. It performs five functions: (1) to aid the court in determining the appropriate sentence, (2) to assist Bureau of Prisons institutions in their classification and treatment programs and also in their release planning, (3) to furnish the Board of Parole with information pertinent to its consideration of parole, (4) to aid the probation officer in his rehabilitative efforts during probation and parole supervision, and (5) to serve as a source of pertinent information for systematic research.

The primary objective of the presentence report is to focus light on the character and personality of the defendant, to offer insight into his problems and needs, to help understand the world in which he lives, to learn about his relationships with people, and to discover those salient factors that underlie his specific offense and his conduct in general. It is not the purpose of the report to demonstrate the guilt or the innocence of the defendant.

Authorities in the judicial and correctional fields assert that a presentence investigation should be made in every case. With the aid of a presentence report the court may avoid committing a defendant to an institution who merits probation instead, or may avoid granting probation when confinement is appropriate.

Probation cannot succeed unless care is exercised in selecting those who are to receive its benefits. The presentence report is an essential aid in this selective process.

Where the defendant is committed to the custody of the Attorney General, copies of the presentence report are sent to the institution. The institution relies on the report for pertinent data relating to the kind and degree of custody required by the defendant, needed medical attention, and the needs, capacities, and problems of the individual. These data will aid the institution in making its preliminary diagnostic study and in promptly formulating a treatment and training program. Moreover, the presentence report not only saves the time and effort of the institution in procuring essential community and family information about the defendant, but also gives this necessary information more completely and accurately than can be obtained by the institution through correspondence and questionnaires.

In considering whether to grant or deny parole, the Board of Parole finds in the presentence report helpful information not only about the offender's personal and social adjustment prior to commitment, but also about his relationships within the community to which he may return.

Note 3. Guidelines

AMERICAN BAR ASSOCIATION *Standards on Probation* 9–12 (1970)*

The Presentence Report

2.1 *Availability and use.*

(a) All courts trying criminal cases should be supplied with the resources and supporting staff to permit a presentence investigation and a written report of its results in every case.

(b) The court should explicitly be authorized by statute to call for such

---

* Quoted with permission of the American Bar Association, 1155 East 60th Street, Chicago, Illinois 60637. The ABA Standards are printed in individual volumes. They may be ordered from the American Bar Association, Circulation Department, American Bar Center, 1155 East 60th Street, Chicago, Illinois 60637, telephone (312) 493-0533. Cost is $2 per volume, or $1 each in lots of ten or more, whether the same or assorted titles.

an investigation and report in every case. The statute should also provide that such an investigation and report should be made in every case where incarceration for one year or more is a possible disposition, where the defendant is less than [21] years old, or where the defendant is a first offender, unless the court specifically orders to the contrary in a particular case.

2.2 *Purpose of report.*

The primary purpose of presentence report is to provide the sentencing court with succinct and precise information upon which to base a rational sentencing decision. Potential use of the report by other agencies in the correctional process should be recognized as a factor in determining the content and length of the report, but should be subordinated to its primary purpose. Where the presentence investigation discloses information useful to other correctional agencies, methods should be developed to assure that this data is made available for their use.

2.3 *Content, scope and length of report.*

Presentence reports should be flexible in format, reflecting differences in the background of different offenders and making the best use of available resources and probation department capabilities. Each probation department should develop gradations of reports between:

(i) a short-form report for primary use in screening offenders in order to assist in a determination of when additional and more complete information is desirable. Short-form reports could also be useful in courts which do not have adequate probation services;

(ii) a full report, which normally should contain the following items:

(A) a complete description of the offense and the circumstances surrounding it, not limited to aspects developed for the record as part of the determination of guilt;

(B) a full description of any prior criminal record of the offender;

(C) a description of the educational background of the offender;

(D) a description of the employment background of the offender, including any military record and including his present employment status and capabilities;

(E) the social history of the offender, including family relationships, marital status, interests and activities, residence history, and religious affiliations;

(F) the offender's medical history and, if desirable, a psychological or psychiatric report;

(G) information about environments to which the offender might return or to which he could be sent should probation be granted;

(H) supplementary reports from clinics, institutions and other social agencies with which the offender has been involved;

(I) information about special resources which might be available to assist the offender, such as treatment centers, residential facilities, vocational training services, special educational facilities, rehabilitative programs of various institutions to which the offender might be committed, special programs in the probation department, and other similar programs which are particularly relevant to the offender's situation;

(J) a summary of the most significant aspect of the report, including specific recommendations as to the sentence if the sentencing court has so requested.

A special effort should be made in the preparation of presentence reports not to burden the court with irrelevant and unconnected details.

Note 4.

ROBERT M. CARTER AND LESLIE T. WILKINS

The Relationship Between Federal Presentence Recommendations and Sentences Imposed*

The following discussion relates mainly to the federal probation system, and we are indebted to the Administrative Office of the United States Courts for furnishing pertinent data. Information has also been drawn from the San Francisco Project, a study of the federal probation system, supported by the National Institute of Mental Health. It should be noted that these data cover different populations over different periods of time, and are not to be seen as interesting in themselves, but as throwing light on the presentence report recommendation and court disposition.

Recommendations and Dispositions:

The Relationship

The presentence report is a document basic to the functioning of both judicial and correctional administrations. The contents of the report, including the recommendation, assist the court in making a judgment consistent with its dual responsibilities to society and the defendant. Within the federal system the report aids the institutions within the Bureau of Prisons in determining classification and treatment programs and also in planning for subsequent release. The report provides information to the Board of Parole, furnishing information believed to be pertinent to its deliberations. Furthermore, the report contributes to the probation officer's rehabilitative efforts while an offender is under his supervision.

In February, 1965, with the publication of a 39 page monograph entitled *The Presentence Investigation Report*, a standard outline and format was adopted for the preparation of presentence reports in the federal courts. The final paragraph headings of the report are "Evaluative Summary" and "Recommendation". The importance of these paragraphs is recognized by the American Correctional Association which includes among its standards for the preparation of presentence reports a "recommendation for or against probation, or for other disposition according to court policy."

The fact that there is a substantial number of sentencing alternatives available to federal judges also means that an equal number of possible recommendations may be considered by the probation officer. The selection ranges, of course, from probation with or without a fine or restitution, and/or a jail sentence, and imprisonment under various statutes which determine parole eligibility, to other dispositions which include commitment for observation and study and continuances for community observation.

Because of this variety of available disposals, the relationship between a recommendation and a disposition may be more simply considered from one of two directions. The first method would be to contrast recommendations for probation made by probation officers with actual court dispositions resulting in probation. The second would be from an opposite direction, viewing recommendations against probation (or for imprisonment) with actual court dispositions for probation.

Data developed during the San Francisco Project contrast recommendations and dispositions for 500 consecutive cases processed through the United States District Court in the Northern District of California between September 1964 and August 1965. These data indicate that:

> there is a close relationship between the recommendation of probation and the actual granting of probation. Probation was recommended in 227 cases and was granted in 212 of those cases. If the 7 cases of "observation and study" are not included, probation was granted, when recommended, in 212 of the 220 cases or in 96 percent of the cases. In only 2 of the 227 cases was there a substantial difference between the probation officer's recommendation and the court's disposition of the cases. In these instances, prison sentences were ordered where probation had been recommended.

These data closely parallel the California data. The percentages of probation officer recommendations for probation followed by California Superior Courts, for the years cited, are shown in Table I.

Data on the federal system, arranged by the ten judicial circuits, indicate the relation-

---

* Robert M. Carter and Leslie T. Wilkins, "Some Factors in Sentencing Policy," 58 *Journal of Criminal Law, Criminology and Police Science*, No. 4, 504–06; 513–14 (1967). Reprinted by special permission of the Journal of Criminal Law, Criminology and Police Science. Copyright © 1967 by Northwestern University School of Law, Vol. 58, No. 4.

TABLE I.—PERCENTAGE OF PROBATION OFFICER RECOMMENDATIONS FOR PROBATION FOLLOWED BY CALIFORNIA SUPERIOR COURTS

1959	95.6%
1960	96.4%
1961	96.0%
1962	96.5%
1963	97.2%
1964	97.3%
1965	96.7%

Source: State of California, Department of Justice. *Delinquency and Probation in California,* 1964, p. 168; and *Crime and Delinquency in California,* 1965, pp. 98–99.

TABLE III.—PERCENTAGE OF PROBATION OFFICER RECOMMENDATIONS AGAINST PROBATION NOT FOLLOWED BY CALIFORNIA SUPERIOR COURTS

1959	13.5%
1960	12.8%
1961	14.8%
1962	17.4%
1963	21.6%
1964	21.1%
1965	19.9%

Source: State of California, Department of Justice. *Delinquency and Probation in California,* 1964, p. 168; and *Crime and Delinquency in California,* 1965, pp. 98–99.

ship, shown in Table II, between probation officer recommendations for probation and such dispositions in court for Fiscal Year 1964.

The patterns in these first two tables exhibit almost total agreement between a probation officer's recommendation for probation and an actual disposition of probation. However, this trend appears less stable when viewed from the opposite perspective—the relationship between recommendations against probation (or for imprisonment) and court dispositions of probation. California data reveal, in Table III, the percentages of "against probation" recommendations and probation dispositions in court.

It is noteworthy that California authorities indicate the "superior court judges are more lenient than probation officers as to who should be granted probation." This pattern has already been observed by one of the authors, and by others, in respect to the federal probation officer. Further confirmation of this pattern is found throughout the federal system as indicated by a review, in Table IV, of "against probation" recommendations and probation dispositions according to the ten judicial circuits for Fiscal Year 1964.

As already indicated, the probation officer has a wide latitude in his choice of a recommendation. Table V presents data on the specific recommendations of probation officers in the Northern District of California between September 1964 and February 1967, and shows the wide variety of possible recommendations.

Table VI* presents overall data on the relationship between recommendations and dispositions of 1,232 cases processed through the District Court in Northern California. The reader will note that of 601 cases recommended for probation, 15 were ordered imprisoned; of 334 cases recommended for imprisonment, 31 were placed on probation.

These data seem to support certain gener-

TABLE II.—PERCENTAGE OF PROBATION OFFICER RECOMMENDATIONS FOR PROBATION FOLLOWED BY TEN JUDICIAL CIRCUITS, FISCAL YEAR 1964

First Circuit	99.4%
Second Circuit	96.0%
Third Circuit	93.2%
Fourth Circuit	93.3%
Fifth Circuit	95.2%
Sixth Circuit	93.9%
Seventh Circuit	89.9%
Eighth Circuit	95.0%
Ninth Circuit	93.5%
Tenth Circuit	97.8%
Overall	94.1%

Source: Data furnished by the Administrative Office of the United States Courts.

TABLE IV.—PERCENTAGE OF PROBATION OFFICER RECOMMENDATIONS AGAINST PROBATION NOT FOLLOWED BY TEN JUDICIAL CIRCUITS, FISCAL YEAR 1964

First Circuit	7.3%
Second Circuit	9.5%
Third Circuit	27.4%
Fourth Circuit	31.8%
Fifth Circuit	11.5%
Sixth Circuit	19.3%
Seventh Circuit	15.9%
Eighth Circuit	16.5%
Ninth Circuit	23.3%
Tenth Circuit	9.2%
Overall	19.7%

Source: Data furnished by the Administrative Office of the United States Courts.

* [Omitted in this edition.—Ed.]

alizations about the nature of the relationship between probation officer recommendations and court dispositions. We have seen that there is a very strong relationship between recommendations *for probation* and court dispositions of probation, an average agreement of about ninety-five percent. It has also been observed that the strength of the relationship diminishes slightly when recommendations *against probation* (or for imprisonment) are contrasted with court dispositions of probation. Thus, it may be concluded that where disagreements exist between recommendations and dispositions, they occur when the officer recommends imprisonment. In a sense, if this relationship measures "punitiveness" then it may be concluded that the probation officer is more punitive than the judge.

* * *

TABLE V.—PROBATION OFFICERS'
RECOMMENDATIONS AS TO SENTENCE
Northern District of California
September 1964 to February 1967

Recommendation	Total	Percent of Total
All Cases	1,232	100.0
No recommendation	67	5.4
Mandatory sentence (Under certain narcotic law violations)	45	3.6
Probation	601	48.9
Regular	(284)	(23.1)
With Fine and/or Restitution	(197)	(16.0)
Split Sentence (Imprisonment up to Six Months Followed by Probation)	(49)	(4.0)
Under Youth Corrections Act	(71)	(5.8)
Fine only	38	3.1
Jail only	35	2.8
Imprisonment	334	27.1
Parole Eligibility After 1/3 Sentence	(234)	(19.0)
Parole Eligibility At Any Time	(64)	(5.2)
Under Youth Corrections Act	(36)	(2.9)
Observation and study	51	4.2
Adult	(39)	(3.2)
Youth	(12)	(1.0)
Continuance for 90 days observation	16	1.3
Deferred prosecution	3	.2
Commitment under federal juvenile delinquency act	2	.2
Other recommendations	40	3.3

Source: Unpublished San Francisco Project data.

In this paper, some of the dangers of continued reliance on tradition and the development of a body of correctional folklore have been pointed out. It has been determined that the relationship between recommendations for and dispositions of probation are high and that the relationship diminishes when viewed from the recommendations against and the subsequent grant of probation perspective. Limited data on the outcome of supervision by recommendation and by percentage use of probation are provided. We have inquired into the reasons for the close agreement between recommendation and disposition and suggest that four factors, in varying degrees, account for it. We have observed that the overall relationship between recommendation and disposition does not vary from District Court to District Court, but rather remains relatively constant, regardless of the percentage use of probation. We suggest that disparities in sentencing are supported by the probation officer and it appears that these differences, in part, are a reflection of the officer's individual academic training and experience. Length of service brings about a trend toward conformity with colleagues and the development of a more conservative perspective toward the use of probation.

There are other segments of the presentence report process to which questions should be addressed. These include operational and administrative considerations, the decision-making processes of probation officers, and an examination of the nature and impact of the social system of correctional agencies. Within the operational considerations would be inquiries as to the role of subprofessionals in presentence investigations, the rearrangement of the standard presentence format to provide a developmental sketch instead of the current segmented report, a determination as to the appropriateness of "confidential" presentence reports, the collection of presentence data in a fashion which allows computer analysis, and the separation of the investigation and supervision functions. Although some examination has been made of the decision-making process, we need additional information about the sequence of data collection, the relative importance of certain kinds of data, and the eventual use of the data for decision-making within the correctional system. We find almost a complete void in knowledge on the social systems of correctional agencies, although available data indicate that the system itself has a profound influence on job behavior, beliefs, values, and the definition and achievement of correctional goals. Indeed, we know more about the social systems of the offenders with whom we deal than about the systems of the agencies which provide correctional services.

There are vast gaps in our knowledge about the entire correctional process, but these gaps may be closed by imaginative, innovative, and creative research and operational designs and programs. This requires a willingness to subject our current traditional, correctional models to scrutiny and a willingness to set aside those features, cherished though they may be, which are inefficient and ineffective.

Note 5. Disclosure of Presentence Reports

a. CONN. GEN. STAT. SEC. 54–109a

In any case, without a showing of good cause, upon the request of defendant or his attorney, prior to sentencing, the court shall provide the defendant or his attorney with a copy of his record of prior convictions and in any case wherein a presentence investigation is ordered, without a showing of good cause, the court shall provide the defendant or his attorney with a copy of the presentence investigation report at least twenty-four hours prior to the date set for sentencing and in both such cases shall hear motions addressed to the accuracy of any part of such record or report.

b. UNITED STATES v. DOCKERY
447 F.2d 1178 (1971), cert. den. 404 U.S. 950 (1971)
United States Court of Appeals, District of Columbia Circuit

PER CURIAM:

We here decide, consistently with the great weight of authority, that it was not a denial of due process of law for the trial judge in sentencing to rely upon the presentence investigative report without disclosing its entire contents to appellant. The longstanding and uniform understanding of the requirements of due process makes the contrary argument one "more properly to be made to the Supreme Court," Castle v. United States, 120 U.S.App. D.C. 398, 401, 347 F.2d 492, 495 (1964), cert. denied, 381 U.S. 929 (1965), and to the rulemaking authority. . . .

Having thus determined that it was not a violation of the constitutional rights of defendants appearing for sentence for Rule 32(c) (2) to vest discretion in the judge to disclose all or part of the presentence report, we next consider whether that discretion was properly exercised in this case. . . .

In the instant case we find that the trial judge when requested willingly offered to go over appellant's "alleged prior record, to see whether or not there are any discrepancies with you, and with the defendant." She also indicated her receptiveness "to hear any mitigating circumstances * * * that would be helpful in imposing sentence" and offered "to go down the list of the offenses for which she was found guilty so that we will know whether we are talking about the same things or not." The judge then did just that and disclosed the prior convictions from the presentence report that she was considering in connection with her sentence. She also indicated that she was aware of certain juvenile offenses, but was not interested in them or in anything by way of possible offenses except the "offenses for which she was found guilty," thus eliminating arrests where no conviction resulted. Thereafter, appellant's counsel made a lengthy plea for leniency from which it cannot be said that his assistance was ineffective in protecting those rights of appellant which were entitled to protection. Also the transcript here does not show that the court's decision with respect to disclosure of the report conformed to a set pattern it invariably followed in all cases which would negate the exercise of an individual discretion in this case. We accordingly find from the face of the record that the court properly exercised the discretion vested in it by Rule 32(c) (2) and that the rights of appellant were adequately protected.

We are not unmindful that the Committee on Rules of Practice and Procedure of the Judicial Conference of the United States is tentatively suggesting a change in Rule 32(c) to give defendants and their counsel an expanded opportunity in more cases to be advised of a larger portion of the material set forth in the presentence investigative reports, and that such suggested amendment also has the support of many members of the organized bar. However, it is our observation that the opinion of those who have had familiarity with presentence reports is preponderantly opposed to increasing the degree of disclosure.

c. STATE v. KUNZ
55 N.J. 128, 259 A.2d 895, 903–04 (1969)
Supreme Court of New Jersey

The situation in the . . . case at hand furnishes an . . . apt illustration of the need for disclosure and meaningful representation at sentencing time as well as on appeal. The defendant was charged with having purchased the Degenshein Cadillac with knowledge that it was stolen. He denied knowledge but the jury found against him. When the probation officer spoke to him before sentencing the defendant persisted in his denial. At sentencing time the defendant had not seen the presentence report and his counsel, having specifically been denied opportunity to examine it, made his argument to the trial judge on the basis of the trial proceedings which contained nothing to indicate any involvement beyond the single purchase of the Degenshein Cadillac. But the probation report which the trial judge had before him stated flatly that there was other involvement and that the defendant was the New Jersey "contact" for a stolen vehicle ring and had been involved with several other identified purchases of stolen vehicles. This charge, much more sweeping than the one on which the defendant was tried, was never preferred against him and is now vigorously denied by him. As a matter of fundamental fairness he is entitled to be heard on it before it can properly form the basis of increasing the severity of his punishment.

The report did not suggest that the probation officer had discussed this untried charge with the defendant or his counsel. It did contain a statement to the effect that although the defendant had earlier been confronted with the evidence of his larger involvement he "would not plead guilty" and thereafter went to trial resulting in his present conviction under N.J.S.A. 2A:139–1. Just where the probation officer received his information does not appear in the report. In any event, there is nothing to suggest that either the aforementioned statement or anything else in the report was called to the attention of the defendant or his counsel in connection with the sentencing or indeed at any time prior to the argument on the appeal. Counsel for the defendant was in the dark and his participation in the sentencing hearing was largely meaningless. He based his stand on the open record of the trial whereas the judge based his sentence on the closed presentence report. Surely this type of hearing with its cross bases does not fit within any rational concept of the sound administration of justice. It is entirely clear to us that the trial judge should have acceded to the request by defense counsel at sentencing for an opportunity to review the presentence report; accordingly the matter will be remanded for resentencing after the defendant has been furnished with a copy of the report and has been afforded fair opportunity to meet any prejudicial material which may play a part in the sentencing.

Furthermore, we take this occasion to announce that in all future sentencing proceedings, defendants will be entitled to disclosure of the presentence report with fair opportunity to be heard on any adverse matters relevant to the sentencing. Although persuasive constitutional arguments have been advanced (*cf.* Sentencing Alternatives and Procedures, *supra,* at 223–24) this step is not being taken as a matter of constitutional compulsion for the Supreme Court holdings to date do not dictate it (*see* Gregg v. United States, 394 U.S. 489, 89 S.Ct. 1134, 22 L.Ed.2d 442, 446 (1969); Williams v. New York, *supra,* 337 U.S. 241, 69 S.Ct. 1079, 93 L.Ed. 1337) and we are not now prepared to find that it is of constitutional dimension under our State Constitution. It is being taken as a matter of rudimentary fairness and though it may entail some administrative difficulties they can readily be minimized by proper handling. Thus the presentence report may first be examined by the trial judge so that matters which will actually play no part in the sentencing process may be excluded. In this fashion irrelevances may be eliminated, confidential sources may be protected, and disclosure may be avoided of diagnostic matters which would be harmful to the defendant's rehabilitation if he were told about them. The report, as thus edited and furnished to the defendant, must of course contain in toto the presentence material which will have any bearing whatever on the sentencing and the trial judge must so recognize in his deliberation and determination.

In Putt v. United States, 363 F.2d 369 (5 Cir. 1966) a sentence was attacked on the ground that the presentence report contained false charges. The trial judge certified that the allegedly false charges played no part in the sentencing and accordingly the sentence was upheld. In Rex v. Campbell, 6 Crim.App.R. 131, 132 (1911) the court described the English practice which permits the police officers to furnish the trial judge, after the defendant has been convicted, with a statement as to the defendant's record, background and present condition. The defendant may challenge any part of the statement, in which event the judge may put it to proof "or he may ignore it, and if he does so he should state that he is not taking it into consideration." *See* Rex v. Van Pelz [1943] 1 All Eng. 36 (Ct.Crim.App.); Note, *supra,* 49 Colum.L. Rev. at 572. The ability of trained judges to exclude from their consideration irrelevant or improper evidence and materials which have come to their attention and to so certify for appellate purposes, has been recognized throughout our law. We have no reason to doubt that it may properly be applied in the field of sentencing.

The sentencing hearing, as we have outlined it, will fairly protect the rights of the defendant as well as the State and, conducted in commonsensible and flexible fashion, will not entail any undue delays or undue burdens on the judicial system. The probation report, when accurate and adequate, will as a practical matter generally remain unchallenged. Even where it is challenged, inquiry may quickly disclose that the challenge relates to matter of insufficient importance to warrant the taking of proof and, in such event, the trial judge may disregard the challenged matter and so declare. It is only in the occasional instance where the challenged matter is crucial to the sentencing process that any further step will be called for but, clearly, here the risk of injustice is far too great to proceed without proof. There may be additional incidental procedural questions but they can readily be dealt with as they arise from time to time. In the meantime and as in *Wingler, supra,* 25 N.J. at 179, 135 A.2d 468, a suitable administrative directive dealing with disclosure of presentence reports will be prepared and distributed. The judgment of conviction against the defendant Kunz stands as rendered but his sentence is set aside and the cause is:

Remanded to the trial court for resentencing.

Note 6. *An Illustrative Presentence Report*

THE CASE OF ALEX STYER [REPRINTED INFRA., *PAGE* 437].

Chapter Four

JUDICIAL CHOICE: INCARCERATION AND ALTERNATIVES THERETO

A. Alternatives to Incarceration

1. FINES

WILLIAMS V. ILLINOIS
399 U.S. 235 (1970)
Supreme Court of the United States

MR. CHIEF JUSTICE BURGER delivered the opinion of the Court.

This appeal from Illinois presents an important question involving a claim of discriminatory treatment based upon financial inability to pay a fine and court costs imposed in a criminal case. The narrow issue raised is whether an indigent may be continued in confinement beyond the maximum term specified by statute because of his failure to satisfy the monetary provisions of the sentence. . . .

On August 16, 1967, appellant was convicted of petty theft and received the maximum sentence provided by state law: one year imprisonment and a $500 fine. Appellant was also taxed $5 in court costs. The judgment directed, as permitted by statute, that if appellant was in default of the payment of the fine and court costs at the expiration of the one year sentence, he should remain in jail pursuant to § 1–7 (k) of the Illinois Criminal Code to "work off" the monetary obligations at the rate of $5 per day. Thus, whereas the maximum term of imprisonment for petty theft was one year, the effect of the sentence imposed here required appellant to be confined for 101 days beyond the maximum period of confinement fixed by the statute since he could not pay the fine and costs of $505.

On November 29, 1967, appellant, while still an inmate in the county jail, petitioned the sentencing judge to vacate that portion of the order requiring that he remain imprisoned upon expiration of his one year sentence because of nonpayment of the fine and court costs. Appellant alleged that he was indigent at all stages of the proceedings, was without funds or property to satisfy the money portion of the sentence, and that he would "be able to get a job and earn funds to pay the fine and costs, if . . . released from jail upon expiration of his one year sentence." The State did not dispute the factual allegations and the trial court granted the State's motion to dismiss the petition

> for the reason that [appellant] was not legally entitled at that time to the relief re-

quested ... because he still has time to serve on his jail sentence, and when that sentence has been served his financial ability to pay a fine might not be the same as it is of the date [of sentencing].

Appeal was taken directly to the Supreme Court of Illinois, which appears to have rejected any suggestion by the trial court that the petition was premature and went on to decide appellant's constitutional claim on the merits. It held that "there is no denial of equal protection of the law when an indigent defendant is imprisoned to satisfy payment of the fine." *People* v. *Williams*, 41 Ill. 2d 511, 517, 244 N.E. 2d 197, 200 (1969).

In addition to renewing the constitutional argument rejected by the state courts, appellant advances a host of other claims which, in light of our disposition, we find unnecessary to reach or decide. Appellant challenges the constitutionality of § 1–7 (k) of the Illinois Criminal Code and argues primarily that the Equal Protection Clause of the Fourteenth Amendment prohibits imprisonment of an indigent beyond the maximum term authorized by the statute governing the substantive offense when that imprisonment flows directly from his present inability to pay a fine and court costs. In response the State asserts its interest in the collection of revenues produced by payment of fines and contends that a "work off" system, as provided by § 1–7 (k), is a rational means of implementing that policy. That interest is substantial and legitimate but for present purposes it is not unlike the State's interest in collecting a fine from an indigent person in circumstances where no imprisonment is included in the judgment. The State argues further that the statute is not constitutionally infirm simply because the legislature could have achieved the same result by some other means. With that general proposition we have no quarrel but that generality does not resolve the issue.

As noted earlier, appellant's incarceration beyond the statutory maximum stems from separate albeit related reasons: nonpayment of a fine and nonpayment of court costs. We find that neither of those grounds can constitutionally support the type of imprisonment imposed here, but we treat the fine and costs together because disposition of the claim on fines governs our disposition on costs.

The custom of imprisoning a convicted defendant for nonpayment of fines dates back to medieval England and has long been practiced in this country. At the present time almost all States and the Federal Government have statutes authorizing incarceration under such circumstances. Most States permit imprisonment beyond the maximum term allowed by law, and in some there is no limit on the length of time one may serve for nonpayment. While neither the antiquity of a practice nor the fact of steadfast legislative and judicial adherence to it through the centuries insulates it from constitutional attack, these factors should be weighed in the balance. Indeed, in prior cases this Court seems to have tacitly approved incarceration to "work off" unpaid fines. See *Hill* v. *Wampler*, 298 U.S. 460 (1936); *Ex parte Jackson*, 96 U.S. 727 (1878).

The need to be open to reassessment of ancient practices other than those explicitly mandated by the Constitution is illustrated by the present case since the greatly increased use of fines as a criminal sanction has made nonpayment a major cause of incarceration in this country. Default imprisonment has traditionally been justified on the ground that it is a coercive device to ensure obedience to the judgment of the court. Thus, commitment for failure to pay has not been viewed as a part of the punishment or as an increase in the penalty; rather, it has been viewed as a means of enabling the court to enforce collection of money that a convicted defendant was obligated by the sentence to pay. The additional imprisonment, it has been said, may always be avoided by payment of the fine.

We conclude that when the aggregate imprisonment exceeds the maximum period fixed by the statute and results directly from an involuntary nonpayment of a fine or court costs we are confronted with an impermissible discrimination that rests on ability to pay, and accordingly, we vacate the judgment below....

A State has wide latitude in fixing the punishment for state crimes. Thus, appellant does not assert that Illinois could not have appropriately fixed the penalty, in the first instance, at one year and 101 days. Nor has the claim been advanced that the sentence imposed was excessive in light of the circumstances of the commission of this particular offense. However, once the State has defined the outer limits of incarceration necessary to satisfy its penological interests and policies, it may not then subject a certain class of convicted defendants to a period of imprisonment beyond the statutory maximum solely by reason of their indigency.

It is clear, of course, that the sentence was not imposed upon appellant because of his indigency but because he had committed a crime....

On its face the statute extends to all deendants an apparently equal opportunity for limiting confinement to the statutory maximum imply by satisfying a money judgment. In fact, this is an illusory choice for Williams or any indigent who, by definition, is without funds. Since only a convicted person with access to funds can avoid the increased imprisonment, the Illinois statute in operative effect exposes only indigents to the risk of imprisonment beyond the statutory maximum. By making the maximum confinement contingent upon one's ability to pay, the State has visited different consequences on two categories of persons since the result is to make incarceration in excess of the statutory maximum applicable only to those without the requisite resources to satisfy the money portion of the judgment.

The mere fact that an indigent in a particular case may be imprisoned for a longer time than a non-indigent convicted of the same offense does not, of course, give rise to a violation of the Equal Protection Clause. Sentencing judges are vested with wide discretion in the exceedingly difficult task of determining the appropriate punishment in the countless variety of situations that appear. The Constitution permits qualitative differences in meting out punishment and there is no requirement that two persons convicted of the same offense receive identical sentences. Thus it was that in *Williams* v. *New York*, 337 U.S. 241, 247 (1949), we said: "The belief no longer prevails that every offense in a like legal category calls for an identical punishment without regard to the past life and habits of a particular offender."

Nothing in today's decision curtails the sentencing prerogative of a judge because, as noted previously, the sovereign's purpose in confining an indigent beyond the statutory maximum is to provide a coercive means of collecting or "working out" a fine. After having taken into consideration the wide range of factors underlying the exercise of his sentencing function, nothing we now hold precludes a judge from imposing on an indigent, as on any defendant, the maximum penalty prescribed by law.

It bears emphasis that our holding does not deal with a judgment of confinement for nonpayment of a fine in the familiar pattern of alternative sentence of "$30 or 30 days." We hold only that a State may not constitutionally imprison beyond the maximum duration fixed by statute a defendant who is financially unable to pay a fine. A statute permitting a sentence of both imprisonment and fine cannot be parlayed into a longer term of imprisonment than is fixed by the statute since to do so would be to accomplish indirectly as to an indigent that which cannot be done directly. We have no occasion to reach the question whether a State is precluded in any other circumstances from holding an indigent accountable for a fine by use of a penal sanction. We hold only that the Equal Protection Clause of the Fourteenth Amendment requires that the statutory ceiling placed on imprisonment for any substantive offense be the same for all defendants irrespective of their economic status.

The State is not powerless to enforce judgments against those financially unable to pay a fine; indeed, a different result would amount to inverse discrimination since it would enable an indigent to avoid both the fine and imprisonment for nonpayment whereas other defendants must always suffer one or the other conviction.

It is unnecessary for us to canvass the numerous alternatives to which the State by legislative enactment—or judges within the scope of their authority—may resort in order to avoid imprisoning an indigent beyond the statutory maximum for involuntary nonpayment of a fine or court costs. Appellant has suggested several plans, some of which are already utilized in some States, while others resemble those proposed by various studies. The State is free to choose from among the variety of solutions already proposed and, of course, it may devise new ones.

We are not unaware that today's holding may place a further burden on States in administering criminal justice. Perhaps a fairer and more accurate statement would be that new cases expose old infirmities which apathy or absence of challenge has permitted to stand. But the constitutional imperatives of the Equal Protection Clause must have priority over the comfortable convenience of the status quo. "Any supposed administrative inconvenience would be minimal, since . . . [the unpaid portion of the judgment] could be reached through the ordinary processes of garnishment in the event of default." *Rinaldi* v. *Yeager*, 384 U.S. 305, 310 (1966).

Nothing we hold today limits the power of the sentencing judge to impose alternative sanctions permitted by Illinois law; the definition of such alternatives, if any, lies with the Illinois courts. We therefore vacate the judgment appealed from and remand to the Supreme Court of Illinois for further proceedings not inconsistent with this opinion.

MR. JUSTICE BLACKMUN took no part in the consideration or decision of this case.

Appendix to Opinion of the Court

State Statutory Provisions Concerning Incarceration for Failure to Pay Fine

California

Judgment that defendant pay a fine may also direct that he be imprisoned until the fine is satisfied. Rate of credit: not less than $2 per day. When the defendant is convicted of a misdemeanor, the judgment may provide for payment of the fine in installments with imprisonment in the event of default. Cal. Pen. Code Sec. 1205 (1968).

But imprisonment for nonpayment of a fine may not exceed in any case the term for which the defendant might be sentenced for the offense of which he has been convicted. *Id.* . . .

Connecticut

If a convict fails to pay a fine lawfully imposed, he shall be committed to jail until the fine is paid. Conn. Gen. Stat. Ann. Sec. 18–63 (1968).

Rate of credit: $3 per day. *Id.* Sec. 18–50.

When a person is convicted of a crime punishable by a fine or imprisonment, the court may impose upon the offender a conditional sentence and order him to pay a fine within a limited time and in default of so doing, to be imprisoned. *Id.* Sec. 54–119.

Massachusetts

When a person convicted is sentenced to pay a fine, he may also be sentenced to be committed until it is paid. Mass. Ann. Laws, ch. 279, Sec. 1; ch. 127, Sec. 144 (1969).

Rate of credit: $1 per day. *Id.* ch. 127, Sec. 144.

The execution of the sentence of confinement may be suspended and the defendant placed on probation on condition that he pay the fine within a certain time, either in one payment or in installments. In case of default, the court may revoke the suspension of the execution of the sentence. *Id.* ch. 279, Sec. 1.

Discharge of the poor prisoners incarcerated for failure to pay fines. *Id.* ch. 127, Sec. 145, (when fine is less than ten dollars); Sec. 146, (when the prisoner has been confined for three months).

Michigan

The court may impose upon the offender a conditional sentence and order him to pay a fine within a limited time and in default of so doing to be imprisoned. The court may also place the offender on probation with a condition that he pay a fine in installments and in default of such payments be imprisoned. Mich. Comp. Laws Ann. Sec. 769.3 (1968).

Execution may issue for the collection of fines in cases where no alternative sentence or judgment of imprisonment has been rendered, but no one may be imprisoned under such execution for longer than 90 days. *Id.* Sec. 600.4815.

New York

In the event the defendant fails to pay a fine as directed, the court may direct that he be imprisoned until the fine is satisfied (limitations: for a felony, the imprisonment may not exceed one year; for a misdemeanor, it may not exceed one third of the maximum authorized sentence.) N.Y. Code Crim. Proc. Sec. 470–d (Supp. 1969).

Sec. 470–d has been limited by *People* v. *Saffore*, 18 N.Y. 2d 101, 218 N.E. 2d 686 (1966).

Mr. Justice Harlan, concurring in the result.

I concur in today's judgment, but in doing so wish to dissociate myself from the "equal protection" rationale employed by the Court to justify its conclusions.

The "equal protection" analysis of the Court is, I submit, a "wolf in sheep's clothing," for that rationale is no more than a masquerade of a supposedly objective standard for *subjective* judicial judgment as to what state legislation offends notions of "fundamental fairness." . . .

Tate v. Short
401 U.S. 395 (1971)
Supreme Court of the United States

Mr. Justice Brennan delivered the opinion of the Court.

Petitioner accumulated fines of $425 on nine convictions in the Corporation Court of Houston, Texas, for traffic offenses. He was unable to pay the fines because of indigency and the Corporation Court, which otherwise has no jurisdiction to impose prison sentences, committed him to the municipal prison farm according to the provisions of a state statute and municipal ordinance which required that he remain there a sufficient time to satisfy the fines at the rate of five dollars for each day; this required that he serve 85 days at the prison farm. After 21 days in custody, petitioner was released on bond when he applied to the County Criminal Court of Harris County for a writ of habeas corpus. He alleged that: "Because I am too poor, I am, therefore, unable to pay the accumulated fine of $425." The county court held that "legal cause has been shown for the imprisonment," and denied the application. The Court of Criminal Appeals of Texas affirmed, stating: "We overrule appellant's contention that because he is too poor to pay the fines his imprisonment is unconstitutional." 445 S.W. 2d 210 (1969). We granted certiorari, 399 U.S. 925 (1970). We reverse on the authority of our decision in *Williams* v. *Illinois*, 399 U.S. 235 (1970).

The Illinois statute involved in *Williams* authorized both a fine and imprisonment. Williams was given the maximum sentence for petty theft of one year's imprisonment and a $500 fine, plus $5 in court costs. The judgment, as permitted by the Illinois statute, provided that if, when the one-year sentence expired, Williams did not pay the fine and court costs, he was to remain in jail a sufficient length of time to satisfy the total amount at the rate of $5 per day. We held that the Illinois statute as applied to Williams worked an invidious discrimination solely because he was too poor to pay the fine, and therefore violated the Equal Protection Clause.

Although the instant case involves offenses punishable by fines only, petitioner's imprisonment for nonpayment constitutes precisely the same unconstitutional discrimination since, like Williams, petitioner was subjected to imprisonment solely because of his indigency. In *Morris* v. *Schoonfield*, 399 U.S. 508, 509 (1970), four members of the Court anticipated the problem of this case and stated the view, which we now adopt, that

> the same constitutional defect condemned in *Williams* also inheres in jailing an indigent for failing to make immediate payment of any fine, whether or not the fine is accompanied by a jail term and whether or not the jail term of the indigent extends beyond the maximum term that may be imposed on a person willing and able to pay a fine. In each case, the Constitution prohibits the State from imposing a fine as a sentence and then automatically converting it into a jail term solely because the defendant is indigent and cannot forthwith pay the fine in full.

Our opinion in *Williams* stated the premise of this conclusion in saying that "the Equal Protection Clause of the Fourteenth Amendment requires that the statutory ceiling placed on imprisonment for any substantive offense be the same for all defendants irrespective of their economic status." 399 U.S. at 244. Since Texas has legislated a "fines only" policy for traffic offenses, that statutory ceiling cannot, consistently with the Equal Protection Clause, limit the punishment to payment of the fine if one is able to pay it, yet convert the fine into a prison term for an indigent defendant without the means to pay his fine. Imprisonment in such a case is not imposed to further any penal objective of the State. It is imposed to augment the State's revenues but obviously does not serve that purpose; the defendant cannot pay because he is indigent and his imprisonment, rather than aiding collection of the revenue, saddles the State with the cost of feeding and housing him for the period of his imprisonment....

We emphasize that our holding today does not suggest any constitutional infirmity in imprisonment of a defendant with the means to pay a fine who refuses or neglects to do so. Nor is our decision to be understood as precluding imprisonment as an enforcement method when alternative means are unsuccessful despite the defendant's reasonable efforts to satisfy the fines by those means; the determination of the constitutionality of imprisonment in that circumstance must await the presentation of a concrete case.

The judgment of the Court of Criminal Appeals of Texas is reversed and the case is remanded for further proceedings not inconsistent with this opinion.

It is so ordered.

MR. JUSTICE BLACKMUN, concurring.

The Court's opinion is couched in terms of being constitutionally protective of the indigent defendant. I merely add the observation that the reversal of this Texas judgment may well encourage state and municipal legislatures to do away with the fine and to have the jail term as the only punishment for a broad range of traffic offenses....

NOTES

Note 1. Equal Protection and Corrections in Light of Williams and Tate

Queries

1. Can a parole board deny parole until an inmate pays a $1,000 imposed fine or "works it off" at $5 a day? See *State* v. *Lavelle*, 54 N.J. 315, 255 A.2d 223 (1969).

2. Can a state require prison inmates to pay for the cost of their incarceration? See *Auditor General* v. *Olezniczak*, 302 Mich. 336, 4 N.W. 2d 679 (1942); Michigan Prison Reimbursement Act, 28 Mich. Stat. Ann. § 1701 *et. seq.*

3. Can a state statute permit prison inmates to earn an additional 5 days a month "good time" for each month of work without compensation? See *Baldwin* v. *Smith*, 446 F.2d 1043 (2d Cir. 1971).

4. Can a state deny state prisoners, who have been refused bail, "good time" credit for the period of their pre-sentence county jail incarceration, while granting full credit for the entire period of prison confinement to those released on bail prior to sentence? See *McGinnis* v. *Royster*, 12 Cr.L. 3143 (U.S., 1973).

Note 2.

ROBERT E. BARRETT

The Frequency of Fines in State Criminal Law Enforcement*

Fines have always been an accepted part of punishment in most societies. The practice of fining antisocial behavior in feudal England probably began to help the overlord pay for the expenses of the trial. Often he would be asked to judge a dispute between two parties, and to pay for the expenses of arbitrating he would exact a fee from the party judged guilty. This fee then was easily assimilated into the criminal law as a direct charge by the state against one who has caused the state's protective and judiciary systems to be used.

Other cultures early in their development have also extracted fines from members of the community who committed offenses which were contrary to the accepted law in the society. The Tlingil Indians of Northwest America assessed fines for our equivalent of an assault. The Bantu tribe of Africa fines anyone committing assault, adultery, and theft, and it's interesting to notice that the amount of the fine varies according to the rank of the offender and the gravity of the offense.

The more civilized society of Massachusetts is no different from these societies. Massachusetts imposes fines on a variety of offenses ranging all the way from walkathons, Mass. Ann. Laws ch. 272 sec. 103 (1959), to attempted murder, Mass. Ann. Laws ch. 265, sec. 103 (1959). Recently some archaic sections were eliminated, but three hundred fifty-six sections will remain in the criminal section of the Massachusetts General Laws in which fines are the accepted sanction, either solely, in the alternative, or cumulative. . . .

Just as there are many different kinds of crimes punished by the imposition of a fine, so there are many different levels of fines. They range all the way from $1.00 for detention of library books or cursing (Mass. Ann. Laws ch. 266, sec. 100 (1959) and Mass. Ann. Laws ch. 272, sec. 37 (1959)) to $10,000.00 for untruthfully swearing allegiance to the U.S. government or for misconduct as a bank official (Mass. Ann. Laws ch. 264, sec. 15 (1959) and Mass. Ann. Laws ch. 266, sec. 53 (1959)). . . .

Whatever the reason, there are only forty-five different levels of fines currently in use in Massachusetts for the three hundred fifty-six sections of the code which authorize the imposition of a fine for their violation. Of these levels, only twenty-two are used just once or twice. Only four are used just three or four times. Two hundred eighty-seven or the offenses listed (80% of the total) are punished by only fifteen different levels of fines. Even more surprising, 57% of the offenses punished by fines (or two hundred three sections) are punished by only *four* different levels of fines, viz., $50.00, $100.00, $500.00, and $1,000.00. . . .

Criminals suffer fines as punishment for breaking a law rather than some other punishment approximately 75% of the time in the United States. When this figure is given, it is usually prefaced by a comment that this is only conjecture since no statistics on this matter are kept. Nevertheless, this figure coincides remarkably with the figures discovered by analyzing the statistics published on Massachusetts disposition of cases. There is some empirical basis for accepting the figure as true, then, since there is nothing in the criminal code of Massachusetts or in the attitude of its judges or public that would make its figures much different from the figures in the country as a whole.

---

* Robert E. Barrett, "The Role of Fines in the Administration of Criminal Justice in Massachusetts," 48 *Massachusetts Law Quarterly* 435–37; 440–42 (1963). Copyright by, and reprinted with the permission of, The Massachusetts Bar Association, 1 Center Plaza, Boston 02108.

2. CIVIL COMMITMENT

SPECHT V. PATTERSON
386 U.S. 605 (1967)
Supreme Court of the United States

MR. JUSTICE DOUGLAS delivered the opinion of the Court.

We held in *Williams* v. *New York,* 337 U.S. 241, that the Due Process Clause of the Fourteenth Amendment did not require a judge to have hearings and to give a convicted person an opportunity to participate in those hearings when he came to determine the sentence to be imposed. . . .

That was a case where at the end of the trial and in the same proceeding the fixing of the penalty for first degree murder was involved—whether life imprisonment or death.

The question is whether the rule of the *Williams* case applies to this Colorado case where petitioner, having been convicted for indecent liberties under one Colorado statute that carries a maximum sentence of 10 years (Colo. Rev. Stat. Ann. § 40–2–32 (1963)) but not sentenced under it, may be sentenced under the Sex Offenders Act, Colo. Rev. Stat. Ann. §§ 39–19–1 to 10 (1963), for an indeterminate term of from one day to life without notice and full hearing. The Colorado Supreme Court approved the procedure, when it was challenged by habeas corpus (153 Colo. 235, 385 P. 2d 423) and on motion to set aside the judgment. 156 Colo. 12, 396 P. 2d 838. This federal habeas corpus proceeding resulted, the Court of Appeals affirming dismissal of the writ, 357 F. 2d 325. The case is here on a petition for certiorari, 385 U.S. 968.

The Sex Offenders Act may be brought into play if the trial court "is of the opinion that any . . . person [convicted of specified sex offenses], if at large, constitutes a threat of bodily harm to members of the public, or is an habitual offender and mentally ill." § 1. He then becomes punishable for an indeterminate term of from one day to life on the following conditions as specified in § 2:

(2) A complete psychiatric examination shall have been made of him by the psychiatrists of the Colorado psychopathic hospital or by psychiatrists designated by the district court; and

(3) A complete written report thereof submitted to the district Court. Such report shall contain all facts and findings, together with recommendations as to whether or not the person is treatable under the provisions of this article; whether or not the person should be committed to the Colorado state hospital or to the state home and training schools as mentally ill or mentally deficient. Such report shall also contain the psychiatrist's opinion as to whether or not the person could be adequately supervised on probation.

This procedure was followed in petitioner's case; he was examined as required and a psychiatric report prepared and given to the trial judge prior to the sentencing. But there was no hearing in the normal sense, no right of confrontation and so on.

Petitioner insists that this procedure does not satisfy due process because it allows the critical finding to be made under § 1 of the Sex Offenders Act (1) without a hearing at which the person so convicted may confront and cross-examine adverse witnesses and present evidence of his own by use of compulsory process, if necessary; and (2) on the basis of hearsay evidence to which the person involved is not allowed access.

We adhere to *Williams* v. *New York, supra;* but we decline the invitation to extend it to this radically different situation. These commitment proceedings whether denominated civil or criminal are subject both to the Equal Protection Clause of the Fourteenth Amendment as we held in *Baxstrom* v. *Herold,* 383 U.S. 107, and to the Due Process Clause. We hold that the requirements of due process were not satisfied here.

The Sex Offenders Act does not make the commission of a specified crime the basis for sentencing. It makes one conviction the basis for commencing another proceeding under another Act to determine whether a person constitutes a threat of bodily harm to the public, or is an habitual offender and mentally ill. That is a new finding of fact (*Vanderhoof* v. *People,* 152 Colo. 147, 149, 380 P. 2d 903, 904) that was not an ingredient of the offense charged. The punishment under the second Act is criminal punishment even though it is designed not so much as retribution as it is to keep individuals from inflicting future harm. *United States* v. *Brown,* 381 U.S. 437, 458.

The Court of Appeals for the Third Circuit in speaking of a comparable Pennsylvania statute said:

It is a separate criminal proceeding which

may be invoked after conviction of one of the specified crimes. Petitioner therefore was entitled to a full judicial hearing before the magnified sentence was imposed. At such a hearing the requirements of due process cannot be satisfied by partial or niggardly procedural protections. A defendant in such a proceeding is entitled to the full panoply of the relevant protections which due process guarantees in state criminal proceedings. He must be afforded all those safeguards which are fundamental rights and essential to a fair trial, including the right to confront and cross-examine the witnesses against him. *Gerchman* v. *Maroney,* 355 F. 2d 302, 312.

We agree with that view. Under Colorado's criminal procedure, here challenged, the invocation of the Sex Offenders Act means the making of a new charge leading to criminal punishment. The case is not unlike those under recidivist statutes where an habitual criminal issue is "a distinct issue" (*Graham* v. *West Virginia,* 224 U.S. 616, 625) on which a defendant "must receive reasonable notice and an opportunity to be heard." *Oyler* v. *Boles,* 368 U.S. 448, 452; *Chandler* v. *Fretag,* 348 U.S. 3, 8. Due process, in other words, requires that he be present with counsel, have an opportunity to be heard, be confronted with witnesses against him, have the right to cross-examine, and to offer evidence of his own. And there must be findings adequate to make meaningful any appeal that is allowed. The case is therefore quite unlike the Minnesota statute we considered in *Minnesota* v. *Probate Court,* 309 U.S. 270, where in a proceeding to have a person adjudged a "psychopathic personality" there was a hearing where he was represented by counsel and could compel the production of witnesses on his behalf. *Id.,* at 275. None of these procedural safeguards we have mentioned is present under Colorado's Sex Offenders Act. We therefore hold that it is deficient in due process as measured by the requirements of the Fourteenth Amendment. *Pointer* v. *Texas,* 380 U.S. 400.

Reversed.

NOTES

Note 1. Civil Commitment of "Sexual Psychopaths"

CROSS V. HARRIS
418 F.2d 1095 (1969)
United States Court of Appeals, District of Columbia Circuit

BAZELON, J.

The 1948 Sexual Psychopath Act now applies only to those who are *not* "mentally ill," while compulsory treatment of those who *are* "mentally ill" is governed by the 1964 Act. This construction restores the original relationship of mutual exclusivity between sexual psychopath commitments and other civil commitments.... It remains for future cases to show whether there are in fact any dangerous sexual recidivists who are not "mentally ill" within the broad meaning of the 1964 Act....

To be "dangerous" for the purposes of the Sexual Psychopath Act, one must be

> *likely* to attack or otherwise *inflict injury,* loss, pain, or other evil on the objects of his desire.

The focus of the statute is not on expected conduct, but on the harm that may flow from that conduct. Commitment cannot be based simply on the determination that a person is likely to engage in particular acts. The court must also determine the harm, if any, that is likely to flow from these acts. A mere possibility of injury is not enough; the statute requires that the harm be *likely.* For no matter how certain one can be that a person will engage in particular acts, it cannot be said that he is "likely to * * * inflict injury" unless it can also be said that the acts, if engaged in, are likely to result in injury.

These determinations must be made on the basis of the record in the particular case before the court. The expert testimony will therefore be relevant to three questions of fact: (1) the likelihood of recurrence of sexual misconduct; (2) the likely frequency of any such behavior; and (3) the magnitude of harm to other persons that is likely to result.

Having found the facts, the court must then determine as a matter of law—in this case, as a matter of statutory construction—whether those facts provide a legal basis for commitment. Two questions must be answered in making this determination. The first is what *magnitude of harm* will justify commitment....

The second question is what *likelihood of harm* will justify commitment. It may well be impossible to provide a precise definition of "likely" as the term is used in the statute. The degree of likelihood necessary to support commitment may depend on many factors. Among the particularly relevant considerations are the seriousness of the expected harm, the availability of inpatient and outpatient treatment for the individual concerned, and the expected length of confinement required for in-patient treatment....

We have not ... decided any constitutional questions. But when a determination of "dangerousness" will result in a deprivation of liberty, no court can afford to ignore the very real constitutional problems surrounding incarceration predicated only upon a supposed propensity to commit criminal acts. Incarceration may not seem "punishment" to the jailors, but it is punishment to the jailed. Incarceration for a mere propensity is punishment not for acts, but for status, and punishment for status is hardly favored in our society. In essence, detention for status is preventive detention.

Only a "blind court" could ignore the intense debate, in and out of Congress, over the extent to which the Constitution can tolerate prevention detention. Similar questions have been raised sporadically for years, but the problem has rarely been analyzed. It may be that in some circumstances preventive detention is in fact permissible. If so, such detention would have to be based on a record that clearly documented a high probability of serious harm, and circumscribed by procedural protections as comprehensive as those afforded criminal suspects. Detention for any significant period of time would have to be attended by periodic review as well as continuing assurance of bona fide efforts at treatment suited to the particular individual detained.

Unquestionably, Congress may prohibit acts of exhibitionism even if such acts are unlikely to do serious harm; and Congress may punish willful violations of laws forbidding indecent behavior. But the test of what anticipated conduct may justify preventive detention cannot be simply whether the legislature has power to prohibit such conduct or to attack the evil it portends. Congress may legislate to protect many different interests—psychic and esthetic as well as physical and economic. But while it may prohibit ugly billboards because they give offense, it may not lock up ugly people for the same reason. The power to control an evil does not remove all restrictions on the means that may be employed for that purpose. This principle is fundamental to the constitutional order.

On the present record, confinement of appellant under the Sexual Psychopath Act would deprive him of his liberty indefinitely—and perhaps permanently—for a propensity to commit acts punishable by a fixed jail sentence. Moreover, confinement would ignore, and apparently frustrate, his treatment needs. Confinement for a mere propensity is preventive detention. Particularly when the act in question is commonly punishable only by a short jail sentence, indefinite confinement, even though labeled "civil," is preventive detention with a vengeance. If required by the Sexual Psychopath Act, it would raise not only one but many difficult constitutional issues:

(1) Is the harm threatened by a potential exhibitionist sufficiently serious to provide a constitutional justification for indefinite deprivation of liberty?

(2) Is the possibility that no harm will in fact result from appellant's future conduct sufficiently large to make incarceration based on possible harm arbitrary and capricious and therefore in violation of the due process clause?

(3) Does the Sexual Psychopath Act provide adequate procedural due process to permit indefinite detention?

(4) Is the absence in the Sexual Psychopath Act of the procedural protections accorded those sought to be committed under the 1964 Act a denial of equal protection?

(5) In view of 1964 Act, does the equal protection clause require consideration of the adequacy of less restrictive alternatives to hospital confinement for a "sexual psychopath"?

(6) If less restrictive alternatives would in fact adequately protect the public while best promoting appellant's rehabilitation, is confinement a deprivation of his liberty without the justification required by the due process clause?

(7) If appellant's need for treatment requires that he not be confined, is indefinite confinement because of his condition cruel and unusual punishment?

These hard questions may be avoided if appellant is not a "sexual psychopath." If he is not, he is either not committable at all, or committable only under the 1964 Act, which requires the consideration of alternatives he seeks in the instant petition....

Note 2. The Difference Between "Civil" and "Penal" Institutions From the Perspective of the Inmate

BRIEF OF DONALD McEWAN, PETITIONER PRO SE

By means of the following chart the petitioner proposes to show in detail the penal nature of his confinement [at Bridgewater Treatment Center]. Any one item taken separately is trivial, but together they reflect an attitude, so difficult to represent in any other way, which is even more punitive than that of the administration of the state prison at Walpole.

Though institutional officials may allege otherwise, the only rationale behind the more restrictive rules and regulations of the treatment center is punishment—punishment of those persons whom the commonwealth has declared to be sick. Such treatment is totally destructive of the supposed rehabilitative purpose of the statute.

COMPARISON OF PUNITIVE MEASURES

Item	Treatment Center	State Prison at Walpole
Personal clothing	Limited to 3 pairs white underwear, 6 pairs white or gray socks, 1 pair shoes without steel shank. May be ordered only at specified times.	Allowed any color underwear, socks, sweatshirts, bathrobe, pajamas, slippers, shoes without regard to shank, black or blue sweater. No limit, many items available in canteen.
Institutional clothing	Always wrinkled, usually ill-fitting, frequently worn out. All marked by messy stencil with "T.C." and name. Can change only at specified times and places. Cannot have institutional underwear if have personal.	One pair pressed each week; proper size; replaced when worn-out. Shirt only marked, neatly, with name. Change as required in own cell. Underwear issued to everyone.
Punishment (lock-up)	No semblance of trial. Any guard may order.	Only disciplinary Board (composed of deputy supt., a guard, and a civilian employee).
Rules and procedures	Different for night and day.	Same all the time.
Free time	Required to be either in yard or rec. room (no choice) or locked in cell.	Choice of yard, TV rooms, gym, chapel, own cell (which is open), other cell-block rec. areas.
Avocational area (free time)	Can enter and leave shops at only one specified time each night.	Can enter and leave whenever shops are open.
Library	Cannot browse; no catalog available.	Open daily for browsing; catalog available.
Visiting	1 hour once a week across table with wire fence underneath.	All morning or afternoon (2½ hours) twice a week, in chairs side by side.
Lawyer visit	In presence of guard.	Private.
Guards	Always "standing over your shoulder," causing tension. Harassment common.	Discreetly apart. Leave well-behaved inmates alone.
Rules	Continually being added.	Infrequent changes.
State job	Assigned arbitrarily; just work under threat; little variety.	Inmate's preference consulted in assignment and job changes. Greater variety of jobs.
Pay	More than 50% make lowest wages. Little opportunity for increase.	Only 25% make lowest wage. Easy to move to better paying job.
Marching	To work, evening recreation, church, entertainments, meals.	Only to meals and entertainments.
Entertainments	Sometimes forced to attend.	Always optional.
Common medications (aspirin, cold pills, etc.)	Handed out a dose at a time.	3 days supply or more given at once.
Food and menu	Frequently insipid and unimaginative.	Good quality, good preparation and imagination.
Time to eat	Frequently rushed at night.	Can remain until finished.
Meal schedule	Too close for digestion. (18 hour fast at night.)	Well spaced. (13 hour fast at night.)
Silverware	Frequently only a spoon. Always counted.	Always have appropriate utensils. Not counted.
Cells	No lockers; no control of light from inside; no lamps allowed. No smoking. Arrangements of furniture, blankets, etc. specified in detail. No glass objects or food allowed.	Wall locker provided; light switch inside; lamps allowed. Smoking allowed. No specification on arrangement. Glass objects and food allowed.
Institutional radio	None.	Two stations on earphone in cell.

Item	Treatment Center	State Prison at Walpole
Sleep at night	Frequently disturbed by guards.	Rarely disturbed.
Corridors	No smoking (though guards may).	Smoking allowed.
Personal safety razor	Not allowed.	Issued by institution and available in canteen.
Personal appearance	Told when to get haircut, shave. No beards allowed.	Left to individual. Beards allowed.
Canteen orders	Must be made 4 days in advance. One order per week.	Six times a week by order (same day delivery). A summer canteen in yard daily for purchases in person.
Canteen	Operated by civilians. High prices, low profits.	Operated by inmates. Low prices, high profits.
Cigarette lighters, nail clippers, metal ballpoint refills, stingers	Not allowed.	Available for purchase in canteen.
National slick magazines (Life, Newsweek, etc.)	Censored and sometimes multilated.	Not censored; delivered intact.
Sanitary facilities	Primitive, no running water in cell; showers available only at specified times; frequently only 1 toilet for entire population (100+).	Modern toilet and basin in cell; showers available any free time.
Minimum security section	None.	Yes.
Trustee status	None.	Opportunities to work outside the wall. Special passes inside.
Mail	Frequently delayed by being passed to various persons. Outgoing certified mail may take weeks. Supt. includes apology in all mail to public officials. Censor stamp used on all mail.	Prompt delivery both incoming and outgoing. No unauthorized missives enclosed. Censor stamp not ordinarily used.
Inmate Council	Appointed by staff.	Elected by inmates.

Note 3. Federal Civil Commitment of Narcotics Addicts

WATSON v. UNITED STATES
408 F.2d 1290 (1969)
United States Court of Appeals, District of Columbia Circuit

BAZELON, Chief Judge:

This appeal challenges the legality of a sentence to treatment under Title II of the Narcotic Addict Rehabilitation Act of 1966, 80 Stat. 1442–1444 (1966), 18 U.S.C. §§ 4251–4255 (Supp. III, 1968).

Appellant Ida Watson was indicted three times within seven weeks in the spring of 1967—first on four counts of forgery and uttering, then on a count each of larceny and housebreaking, then on four more counts of larceny and housebreaking. In September, 1967, she entered guilty pleas to one count of uttering and to the housebreaking count of the second indictment. Apparently in exchange, the Government promised to dismiss the third indictment and the remaining counts in the other two indictments at the time of sentencing. The bargain was kept, and appellant expressly concedes that her guilty pleas were voluntarily and intelligently made.

When she appeared for sentencing, the court granted her request for preliminary commitment for examination under the Rehabilitation Act, to determine whether she was a treatable addict. See 18 U.S.C. § 4252. Her probation report revealed that she had no criminal record prior to her involvement with narcotics, but had been driven to theft in order to support her $75 per day habit. As the 24-year-old mother of four children, she seemed an obvious candidate for the therapeutic disposition she sought. When the Chief of the National Institute of Mental Health Clinical Research Center in Lexington, Kentucky, reported her likely to be rehabilitated through treatment, the stage was set for a happy conjunction of societal and humanitarian interests.

This rare harmony was shattered when appellant announced that she no longer wished to be committed for treatment. Though she could have been sentenced to as many as 25 years in prison for her two convictions, whereas the maximum commitment term under the Rehabilitation Act is 10 years (and the minimum term of confinement only 6 months), she said she would rather take her chances on a short jail sentence (or, presumably, probation) than go to Lexington for treatment; she did not want to be so far from her children for so long. Her attorney attempted to dissuade her, to no avail. But the court saw no advantage to her or to her children, either in sending her to jail or in releasing her, fully addicted, on probation. Accordingly, he ordered her committed. Appellant now seeks vacation of this order and a remand for sentencing under the appropriate criminal statutes, arguing that the court could not commit her over her objection and that, in any event, she was not an "eligible offender" within the meaning of the Act.

Appellant's contention that commitment under Title II requires her consent is without merit. Unlike Title I of the Act, which permits some addicted defendants to opt for commitment in lieu of prosecution, Title II makes no provision for an election by the defendant. It provides unqualifiedly that the court "may place" in the custody of the Attorney General for examination an eligible convicted offender believed to be an addict. 18 U.S.C. § 4252. The section which defines an "eligible offender" makes no mention of a request by, or the consent of, the defendant. 18 U.S.C. § 4251(f). If after examination the court finds him addicted and treatable, and provided appropriate facilities are available, section 4253(a) says the court "shall commit him" for treatment. The legislative history likewise makes abundantly clear the congressional intent to establish such commitment as a sentencing alternative available in the discretion of the court. We need not now decide whether there are limits to the court's discretion to refuse an eligible offender's request for post-conviction commitment or whether a court may ever honor an objection to commitment once an eligible offender has been found treatable. But that the court is not obliged to honor such an objection is not open to doubt. In this respect, a sentence to treatment is like any other sentence....

Affirmed.

3. PROBATION AND SUSPENDED SENTENCE

UNITED STATES V. WILEY
184 F. SUPP. 679 (1960)
United States District Court,
Northern District of Illinois

CAMPBELL, Chief Judge.

There have been countless studies made, and articles written, about the various considerations, such as reformation, deterrence and retribution, which motivate a criminal sentence. There are no rigid rules, no formulas and each case stands on its own particular facts as they are evaluated by the trial judge who is assisted only by general principles and his own conscience. I am sure that I speak for my many colleagues when I state that the imposition of a criminal sentence is the most delicate, difficult and distasteful task for the trial judge.

In the cause before me, after defendant's conviction on Count II of an indictment charging him and four other defendants with unlawfully, willfully, knowingly and feloniously having in their possession certain goods, unlawfully stolen while moving in an interstate shipment and known by them to have been stolen in violation of Title 18 U.S.C. Section 659, I sentenced defendant, after full consideration of all the evidence introduced during his trial, as well as the reports of the government investigators, to imprisonment for a period of three years. After full consideration of the reports of the government investigators, I sentenced the other four defendants, who had previously pled guilty as follows: Ulysses McGhee, 2 years; Joseph Helen, 1 year and 1 day; Joseph M. Kelley, 1 year and 1 day; and Roman Jackson, 1 year and 1 day. McGhee had four prior felony convictions and was more or less the ringleader insofar as the actual stealing operations of this particular gang were concerned. Helen, Kelley and Jackson likewise had records of prior convictions.

Defendant Wiley, prior to the imposition of sentence moved for a presentence investigation after which the following colloquy took place:

> "THE COURT: No, I ordinarily don't do that when I hear the evidence in the case. I ordinarily do where there is no prior record.

Where the defendant stands trial it is well-known in this Court I proceed to sentence immediately after the trial. I will hear anything you care to say as to his family situation and his background and his prior history."

(Thereupon, defendant testified as to his residence, marriage, family, employment and that he had never served any time in any penal institution.)

"THE COURT: Any questions of the defendant?

"MR. GRADY: No.

"THE COURT: Is there anything you want to say before the imposition of sentence?

"MR. EVINS: (Defendant's counsel) Yes, Judge. I would like to say this, that you have offered here in mitigation and in view of the fact that this defendant has no previous record of any kind and that in view of the further fact that he is married and he has a family and he is living with his wife, supporting his family, and he has a good job out of which he is supporting his family, I feel that justice could be served in this case if the Court sees fit to put him on probation for a period of time, and I am asking the Court to show him some leniency and consideration because of those facts, because of his family and because of the fact he just got a new-born baby and as I understand it, he is the main and only support of that family.

"I am asking the Court at this time if he wouldn't consider granting probation.

"THE COURT: Those are the facts the defendant should have considered prior to committing the offense.

* * * * *

"THE COURT: In view of the fact that the trial was expedited by waiving a jury and by stipulation of the various items that expedited the proof I make the sentence less than I otherwise would. *It is, however a serious crime, and it is a case for the imposition of a sentence, either on a plea of guilty or on a trial.* Had there been a plea of guilty in this case probably probation might have been *considered* under certain terms, but you are all well aware of the standing policy here that once a defendant stands trial that element of grace is removed from the consideration of the Court in the imposition of sentence.

"Taking into consideration the various factors that you have referred to—and that I have referred to, I make the sentence less than I otherwise would, but a sentence must be imposed.

"On the judgment of guilty heretofore, rendered the defendant is sentenced to the custody of the Attorney General of the United States to be incarcerated in a penitentiary of the United States for a term of three years." (Emphasis supplied.)

Upon appeal, the judgment insofar as it adjudged defendant guilty was affirmed though the cause was remanded, Chief Judge Hastings dissenting, for consideration of defendant's application for probation because, as the Court stated, of my "standing policy" to the effect that "that element of grace is removed from the consideration of the court" once a defendant stands trial. United States v. Wiley, 7 Cir., 267 F.2d 453, 455, 456.

When the mandate was filed, I proceeded to hearing on the motion of Wiley for probation and after full consideration of all the factors before me I reimposed the sentence of imprisonment for a period of three years.

Upon further appeal, the sentence was set aside and the cause remanded with directions because, as the Court of Appeals stated:

"(t)he district court has, without any justification, arbitrarily singled out a minor defendant for the imposition of a more severe sentence than that imposed upon the co-defendants * * *" United States v. Wiley, 7 Cir., 278 F.2d 500, 503.

The cause is now before me pursuant to this mandate.

The maximum penalty for violation of Title 18 U.S.C. Section 659 is imprisonment for a period of ten years together with a fine of $5,000. Any sentence within this limit is, of course, discretionary with the trial judge. It has now been determined by the Court of Appeals that I have abused this discretion by imposing a three years' sentence on Wiley. This determination by the Court of Appeals is apparently based upon a comparison of the sentences imposed upon the several defendants in this cause; my statements regarding probation for a defendant who has exercised his constitutional right of trial; my statement of November 7, 1958 where, during an unrelated hearing upon the motion of McGhee to vacate an order setting his appeal bond. I described Wiley as "a minor participant"; and finally, a comparison of the criminal records and general background of each of the defendants as revealed in the record before the Court of Appeals.

Prior to these two Wiley decisions by the Court of Appeals, there were serious doubts as to whether or not appellate review of a trial judge's discretion under the Federal Probation Act, 18 U.S.C. § 3651 et seq. or his discretion to determine a criminal sentence was in fact possible....

However, since our Court of Appeals has now determined that appellate review of a judge's discretion with regard to probation and sentencing does exist, this question has been resolved and I am so bound.

In addition to this question, heretofore unresolved, there was and is another reason why, though there has been a great deal of discussion and debate about appellate review of sentencing, and though England and some of our states have invoked varying systems of review, there has been no great movement in the federal system to review sentencing. I believe that reviewing courts have recognized many of the practical problems involved, in a few of which are clearly exemplified by the effect the Wiley decisions will have upon the present administration of the Federal Probation Act. First, I believe these decisions will have a coercive effect on the use of presentence investigation and consideration for probation even in cases where this privilege should clearly be denied. This is a waste of valuable time, effort and money. Second, the information contained in the reports of government investigators, which is not in the record, is highly confidential since otherwise it would be impossible for government investigators to continue certain investigations or gain confidential information about a defendant. If the trial judge is in part motivated by the reports of the government investigators in denying probation in a given case, he cannot in good conscience divulge this information and yet, risks having the cause remanded because of appellate review of the record. Third, there is likewise the danger that the secrecy of the presentence investigation will also yield to the pressure of appellate review and this, I need not add, would undermine seriously, the Federal Probation Act since it would become nearly impossible to secure confidential information about a defendant. Fourth, there have already been a number of frivolous appeals based upon the denial of consideration of probation or probation and I feel that now that the floodgates have been opened, there will be many more. Fifth, our already overworked appellate courts will be unable to bear the heavy burden tht review of discretion under the Federal Probation Act entails.

These practical problems which impede a proper appellate review of a trial judge's discretion under the Federal Probation Act, are by analogy, the same, and in my opinion, more pronounced under our system of appellate review now that it has been determined that appellate courts can review the discretion of a trial judge in his determination of a criminal sentence.

Finally, there is one other important reason why appellate courts have refused to review the discretion of a trial judge with regard to probation and sentencing. Those factors which motivate the trial judge in either granting or denying probation, or which motivate a sentence are, for the most part, difficult to determine by a reviewing court because of their obvious subjective qualities. A reviewing court cannot say with any degree of certainty what motivated the trial judge in his determination that probation should be refused or a particular sentence imposed. The trial judge may have been influenced by factors contained in the reports of government investigators or the presentence investigation report which are not set forth in the record and which are not before the reviewing court. It is generally accepted that these factors should be considered carefully in the determination of a criminal sentence, Williams v. People of State of New York, 337 U.S. 241, 69 S.Ct. 1079, 93 L.Ed. 1337. A reviewing court also does not have the opportunity to observe the defendant or his witnesses which may in part, motivate the trial judge especially where rehabilitation is concerned. In other words, a court reviewing the discretion of a trial judge with regard to probation or sentencing is limited to those factors which appear of record or to statements made by the trial judge with regard to his consideration of probation or his determination of a sentence which can easily be misconstrued or misinterpreted. In short, it is generally recognized that under our present system of appellate review, it is impossible to intelligently, or correctly review sentencing. I sincerely believe that these defects in appellate review of sentencing to which I have referred, are to some degree exemplified in the cause before me now.

Generally speaking, the same factors that prompted the determination of the Court of Appeals that I have abused my discretion under the Federal Probation Act, also prompted the determination that I have abused my sentencing discretion.

I should first like to discuss my statement that it is my "standing policy" not to consider probation where a defendant has exercised his constitutional right to trial....

It is true that my denial of Wiley's application for probation, as well as the three year sentence I imposed upon him were, for the reasons here given, in my opinion, rightfully motivated in part by the fact that he stood trial. However, there were other factors present in this cause, though not in the record, which I considered and which also, in part, motivated my denial of his application for probation and his sentence. That is why, when denying Wiley's application for probation I stated, as Chief Judge Hastings pointed out, dissenting, that this was "a serious crime, and it is a case for the imposition of a sentence, either on a plea of guilty or on a trial." [267 F.2d 458]

For example, the Court of Appeals found that Wiley's criminal record was not so "serious" as that of his co-defendants. It is true that on its face his criminal record does not compare equally to the criminal records of his co-defendants McGhee and Helen, though it is comparable to the criminal records of Jackson and Kelley. He was arrested in December of 1956 on a charge of receiving stolen property and placed on probation for a period of six months and also has been arrested several times for gambling. However, there is ample evidence in the reports of the government investigators, which are not a part of this record, but which I thoroughly considered before the imposition of sentence, that Wiley was involved in a similar offense, the burglary of the Chicago Terminal of Super Service Motor Freight Company on October 15, 1957 for which he was not indicted because of the pendency of the cause now before me. I think it is clear from the reports of the government investigators that Wiley perjured himself when he testified that he had never helped to dispose of any other stolen merchandise.

I should like now to refer to another factor I considered in sentencing Wiley which is covered fully in the reports of the government investigators though only hinted at in the record. Wiley has a political position with the City of Chicago, Bureau of Sanitation. His foreman at the time these offenses here mentioned were committed, was a man named Charles B. Vaughn. There is evidence in the reports of the government investigators which shows that Vaughn was the actual immediate contact for a number of "fences" for stolen property and that it was Vaughn who actually made the deliveries to these several "fences" after taking over the movement of a load from someone who had stolen merchandise, such as, in the present cause, McGhee. It is clear from the reports of the government investigators that it was Wiley who had originally put McGhee in contact with Vaughn, as a man who would dispose of stolen merchandise. It is also clear from the reports that Vaughn was an associate of individuals known to be members of the organized crime syndicate in Chicago. Thus, Wiley was a "chaser" for Vaughn and actually induced the commission of crimes such as these, since he, in the first instance provided the means of disposal for stolen merchandise to men like McGhee, Helen, Kelley and Jackson.

I cannot say with certainty that this crime would never have occurred if Wiley had not put McGhee in contact with Vaughn, but certainly, his part as a "chaser" is an important factor to be considered, especially, where as here, there are strong overtones of organized crime and political influence.

Since the "fencing" operation of Vaughn appeared to be on rather a large scale and since government investigators were in the midst of their investigation of Vaughn and his various outlets for the disposal of stolen merchandise, it was impossible for me to describe for the record, Wiley's major part in the operations of Vaughn at the time I was dealing with Wiley. I feel that I can now in good conscience reveal the Wiley-Vaughn operation because just recently, shortly after the release of the latest decision of the Court of Appeals in United States v. Wiley, supra, Charles B. Vaughn was brutally murdered.

When I described Wiley as a "minor participant" in this crime some weeks subsequent to the time I imposed sentence upon him, it was at a hearing upon a motion of McGhee to vacate an order setting his appeal bond. I was at this time particularly concerned with McGhee who was, as I stated "somewhat of a ringleader" insofar as the actual stealing operations of McGhee, Kelley, Jackson and Helen were concerned. Without question, Wiley was a "minor participant" in regard to the actual theft by these defendants but he was a major participant in the operation of Vaughn which was not reported in the record of this cause and which, for reasons of confidence, I could not refer to. Furthermore, since I was only concerned with McGhee at this time, it does not seem logical to me to refer to my out of context statements about Wiley to determine that the sentence I imposed upon him several weeks prior was arbitrary and "without justification."

In sentencing Wiley, I seriously considered his prospects for rehabilitation. When he originally changed his plea from guilty to not guilty, there was no remorse in this man. McGhee, Kelley, Jackson, and Helen pled guilty and did stand conscience-stricken in repentance before the Court. Wiley did not cooperate with the government investigators. McGhee, Kelley, Jackson and Helen gave them their full cooperation and, I might here add, that this is especially true of McGhee. Wiley's demeanor during all of these proceedings does not indicate repentance nor am I impressed by the testimony of his aunt or the Reverend Davis since the total effect of everything said leaves little doubt in my mind that Wiley was, is, and will remain, far removed from their guidance. Despite their records, I see McGhee, Kelley, Helen and Jackson as men who can be helped. They are not particularly bright men or men of strong, moral character and this has, in part, led to their downfall because they are always subject to the temptations presented by men like Wiley. These men can be helped because they have indicated that they want to be helped. Wiley, on the other hand, does not want to be helped. He is, by all outward manifestations, the self-assured "smart guy." From what I have learned about Wiley, I am convinced that he is not only contemptuous of law and order and those people who attempt to live their lives according to law and the moral standards of the community, but he is also contemptuous of men like McGhee, Kelley, Helen and Jackson who are not as "smart" as he thinks he is. Wiley, I feel will go back to his underworld friends without remorse and will continue to infect and disease our society.

In short, as far as I am motivated by reformation in my sentences of these co-defendants, I feel that McGhee, Kelley, Jackson and Helen have greater prospects of rehabilitation than Wiley.

Deterrence also motivated the sentence I imposed upon Wiley. First, Wiley induced the commission of crimes by "chasing" for Vaughn. It is my opinion that deterrence best serves the interest of society when it is used effectively against "fences," men like Vaughn or their "chasers" such as Wiley because these men are far more responsible for most burglaries than the men like McGhee, Kelley, Jackson and Helen who actually perform the act. Like many other trial judges I believe that if "fences" are eliminated, crime will be effectively reduced and to this end, I advocate deterrence as a greater motivating factor in the sentence of a man like Wiley than I would in the case of McGhee, Kelley, Jackson or Helen. Furthermore, Wiley is an employee of the City of Chicago and therefore represents the people of Chicago. I feel in the instant cause, for these and other reasons, that deterrence is far more important as a sentencing factor in the case of Wiley rather than in the case of any of the other co-defendants.

Though during my entire twenty years as a Federal Judge I have never been motivated in any criminal sentence to any great degree by a consideration of retribution, I again suggest that Wiley as an employee of the City of Chicago is far more vulnerable to this particular philosophy of sentencing then any of the other co-defendants.

I of course take no issue with the Court of Appeals. It has acted with apparent justification to correct what it feels to be an unjust sentence. With great respect, I do feel however, for the reasons stated herein, that until provision is made in law for appellate review of a trial judge's discretion under the Federal Probation Act and his discretion to determine a criminal sentence, based upon all the factors considered by the trial judge, it is an uncertain and dangerous precedent that is now advanced by the Seventh Circuit Court of Appeals in the two Wiley decisions.

In good conscience and with due regard to my oath of office I cannot conclude that any sentence less than three years is either just or proper in the case of Wiley now before me. Accordingly, I hereby now again reimpose my original sentence of three years. However, out of my deep respect for the Court of Appeals, and in obedience to its mandate, I also hereby suspend the execution of the said sentence.

The defendant Wiley may go hence without delay.

NOTES

Judicial Review of the Grant or Denial of Probation

Note 1.

WILSON V. UNITED STATES
278 A.2d 461 (1971)
Court of Appeals for the District of Columbia

KERN, Associate Judge:

Appellant entered a plea of guilty to the charge of possessing heroin and was sentenced to six months imprisonment. On appeal his challenge goes only to his sentence....

One aspect of the sentencing proceeding does call for comment. The trial court before imposing sentence demanded that appellant reveal in open court the name of his drug supplier.* However much we may agree with the trial court's understandable concern over the present traffic in narcotics in the District of Columbia, we believe it is inappropriate for a judge in the act of sentencing to badger and threaten a defendant in open court to reveal information to the prosecutor. Moreover, under our system of government the investigation and development of a criminal case is entrusted primarily to the executive branch and it is hardly likely that any defendant would be willing to trumpet publicly the information which the trial court here sought so avidly.

Appellant argues that the trial court imposed a sentence of imprisonment rather than granted probation solely to penalize him for his failure to name his supplier. While the trial court's words were threatening, we note that his ultimate sentence was in fact but one-half what he could have imposed for this particular offense and that appellant had three prior convictions, including a narcotics felony for which he had received a five-year sentence. Miler v. United States, D.C.App., 255 A.2d 497 (1969), relied upon by appellant, in inapposite because there we held that requiring remorse from the defendant to avoid a heavier sentence was in effect forcing him to acknowledge guilt, thereby waiving his rights to appeal and to move for a new trial. Here, appellant has acknowledged his guilt. Given the circumstances outlined above appellant's challenge to his sentence cannot be upheld and the judgment is

Affirmed.

Note 2.

UNITED STATES V. DANIELS
446 F.2d 967 (1971)
United States Court of Appeals, Sixth Circuit

CELEBREZZE, Circuit Judge.

This is the second time this case has come before this Court. In July, 1970, we affirmed the conviction of Appellant—a member of the Jehovah's witness faith and a conscientious objector—for failing to comply with an order of his local selective service board to report to said board for instructions to commence with civilian employment, as alternate service, in violation of 50 U.S.C. App. § 462. United States v. Daniels, 429 F.2d 1273 (6th Cir. 1970). In affirming Appellant's conviction, however, we remanded this cause to the District Court to permit reconsideration of the five year sentence of imprisonment which the District Court imposed upon the Appellant. United States v. Daniels, *supra* at 1273.

Our remand order was based in large part on the peculiar facts of the instant case: Appellant is a young man whose sole motivation for refusing to obey an order of his local selective service board was a devout adherence to his religious beliefs. Further, he is of "good character" and apparently stood willing at all times to comply with a judicial order to present himself for civilian employment as required by federal law. And finally, other young men in different districts within our jurisdiction were not being disciplined by imprisonment for their religious beliefs so long as they were willing to comply with a judicial order to do the exact conscientious objector work which they had refused to perform when ordered by the local draft board. United States v. Daniels, *supra*. See United States v. Griffin, 434 F.2d 740, 742 (6th Cir. 1970). Cf. United States v. Dudley, 436 F.2d 1057 (6th Cir. 1971).

Upon remand, the District Court refused to reduce or suspend its original five year sentence of Appellant. Indeed, the trial court judge observed that for the over thirty years that he had been on the federal bench he has "felt that in cases of this kind [a refusal to obey an order of a local draft board] that

---

* The transcript reads in pertinent part:

THE COURT: Do the police know who the man is you bought the stuff from?
Well, let's find out. What's his name?
OFFICER STRONG: He wouldn't give us any information sir.
THE COURT: That's why I've got him now. That's why I asked him the question.
MR. WILSON [appellant]: Well, I don't really know his name myself.
THE COURT: Oh, you don't know his name?
MR. WILSON: I know him.
THE COURT: How do you get ahold of him? How do you describe him? Are you willing to get in a police car and go out and ride around and point him out?
MR. WILSON: Well, does it pertain to the case?
THE COURT: No, you don't want to squeal on your friendly junk dealer, do you?
MR. WILSON: It's not that I don't want to squeal.

* * * * *

THE COURT: It comes down to this in the ultimate: Unless I get the name of the man who supplied you so that I can give it to the police, you've got no chance of making probation with me; you're going right straight to jail for a good long stretch today. I want a name, and I want a description.

*** [those who violate that order] deserve a five year sentence; and I think almost without exception I have given a five year sentence * * *." In so holding, the District Court noted that the law Appellant violated "strikes at the very foundation and fundamentals * * * of our whole governmental system." Finally, the District Court indicated that it was "qualified by experience, temperament [and] knowledge of law * * * in giving this sentence [of five years]" and that the Court used such experience and the record of this case in determining the challenged sentence. This appeal followed.

The sole issue on appeal is whether the District Court properly discharged its duty to impose an appropriate sentence. Williams v. Oklahoma, 358 U.S. 576, 585, (1959). *See* Livers v. United States, 185 F.2d 807, 809 (6th Cir. 1950). . . .

. . . We are gravely concerned—in at least three respects—about the manner in which the District Court exercised its discretion in discharging its duty to impose an appropriate sentence.

First, we are seriously perturbed about the trial judge's avowal that since 1938 or 1939, his court has—to the best of his memory—sentenced to five years in the penitentiary every young man who has refused to obey an order of a draft board. That statement, taken along with the observations of the United States attorney at oral argument, suggests a general practice in at least one federal district in Kentucky of imposing a sentence without particular reference to the circumstances surrounding the commission of the crime or of the background of the criminal defendant.

A trial court which fashions an inflexible practice in sentencing contradicts the judicially approved policy in favor of "individualizing sentences." Williams v. New York, 337 U.S. at 248.

We are unable to understand how the trial judge could have fairly considered all of the circumstances surrounding the commission of the crime and the past life and habits of the Appellant that he is obliged to consider and impose the identical punishment he has been handing down for thirty years in "cases of this kind." Williams v. Oklahoma, *supra,* Williams v. New York, *supra.*

Second, the District Court may not wholly justify its seemingly mechanical imposition of five year sentences on all those who violate the provisions of 50 U.S.C. App. § 462, by stating that the law violated is "a very serious law that strikes at the very foundations and fundamentals * * * of our whole governmental system." The United States Congress has expressly provided that offenders of 50 U.S.C. App. § 462 shall upon conviction "be punished by imprisonment for not more than five years or a fine of not more than $10,000, or by both such fine and imprisonment. * * *" The United States Congress did not provide that every violation of 50 U.S.C. App. § 462 shall be punishable by a term of imprisonment of no less than five years. Hence, 50 U.S.C. App. § 462 is an express legislative sanction of the practice of meting out sentences substantially less than five years in prison for willful and knowing refusals to obey an order of a local selective service board in situations where there are appropriate mitigating circumstances.

In the instant case, the Appellant is conceded to have been motivated to commit the offense charged solely in order to adhere to his religious beliefs. He was found to be of "good character" and of "apparent model behavior." The crime he committed was not an act of violence. It did not invade the privacy of others or endanger the property or person of others. The Appellant was willing to serve his country in a civilian capacity if required to do so under judicial orders. We believe that under the mitigating circumstances present here the District Court's mechanical sentencing of the Appellant to five years in the penitentiary defies the United States Congress' implied legislative will to impose a lesser sentence where appropriate.

Third, we are disturbed by the District Court's failure to conceive of the sentencing procedure in terms of the modern penological philosophy praised by the United States Supreme Court in Williams v. New York, *supra*. In Williams v. New York, *supra* at 248 n13, the United States Supreme Court cited with approval certain basic considerations to be used in determining an appropriate sentence: (a) the reformation of the offender, (b) the protection of society, (c) the disciplining of the wrongdoer, and (d) the deterrence of others from committing like offenses.

The imprisonment of Appellant can hardly be deemed helpful in reforming a young man of concededly "good character" and "model behaviour." Imprisonment cannot serve as protection for society because the immediate release of Appellant poses no risk to society's safety. Moreover, disciplining or punishing the Appellant by imprisonment would seem to be an inappropriate rationale for sentencing where, as here, a young man has devoutly adhered to his religious beliefs without impeding the rights of others. Finally, under the limited factual circumstances of this case, the issuance of an order probating the Appellant subject to his performance of the identical work demanded of him by the Selective Service is not the kind of sentencing which would induce widespread disobedience of the orders of local Selective Service boards. *Cf.* Gillette v. United States, 401 U.S. 437 (1971). In summary, there is no evidence in the record that the District Court evaluated the information in the record in the light of any of the basic factors relevant to the sentencing of a criminal offender.

In our judgment, the District Court pursuant to our first remand of this case failed to exercise its sound discretion, but instead sought merely to justify its original sentence which it had been imposing as a "minimum" sentence in similar cases for over thirty years. Yates v. United States, 356 U.S. 363, 366–367 (1958). We find that under the circumstances of this case the District Court plainly failed to discharge its duty to impose a proper sentence when it sentenced Appellant to five years in the penitentiary....

Note 3.

PEOPLE V. MCANDREW
96 Ill. App. 2d 441, 239 N.E.2d 314 (1968)
Illinois Court of Appeals

DAVIS, Justice.

The defendant, John Clifford McAndrew, was charged with unauthorized possession of narcotic drugs, in violation of section 22–3 of the Criminal Code (Ill.Rev.Stat. 1967, ch. 38, par. 22–3). He entered a plea of guilty, was denied probation and was sentenced to a minimum of two years and a maximum of three years in a state penitentiary. He appealed.

While courts have held that refusal to grant probation is not subject to review, the granting or revoking of probation is normally within the discretion of the trial court, but is subject to review to the extent of determining whether the trial court did, in fact, exercise discretion in its determination on probation or whether it abused such discretion and acted in an arbitrary manner.

* * *

It is not within our discretion to determine whether or not the trial court should have granted probation. It is only for us to determine the narrow question of whether the trial court abused its discretion in denying probation. In considering the defendant's contention, we will examine the remarks of the court....

Following the arguments by counsel, the court stated: "I have spent a lot of time thinking about this case. * * * The State's Attorney didn't have much to say here today, he left it entirely up to the Court. I guess that's right, that's my responsibility. There are a few things I might disagree with the attorney for the defendant. Principally when he gets up here and says to this Court the court should bear in mind that this young man hasn't damaged anybody but himself. I take exception to that, Mr. Merrick, I think he has damaged everybody that he has associated with. I certainly think that he damaged or was certainly in a position possibly of damaging little youngsters who were in a State mental institution placed under this man's care where everybody now decides he is so sick. I think he was damaging somebody there. He has damaged a thousand students out at Sauk Valley College, he has damaged the possibility of a thousand students at Dixon High School because anyone of them could have been exposed to his potential sale which he and this young lady had made very careful plans and by his own admission was about to be in the business of selling. I don't believe it was the intention whatsoever that these packets, all of which were very carefully prepared, all of which were very carefully filled, all of which were very handy, with intention of taking these packets back to Antioch College to sell them because we have got testimony here this young man became acquainted with the individual who has the distribution of this type of thing in this particular area. * * * I don't think that he needed to take it back to Antioch because, by his own testimony, 75 percent of the student body at Antioch College were marihuana users. This to me is a shameful reflection on an educational institution and an educational institution which knew that this boy was using marihuana and did absolutely nothing about it and apparently hasn't done anything about it yet. I would hate to think I had a son or daughter of mine attending a school like Antioch College and I am not going to let Sauk Valley College become an Antioch College, I will tell you that. * * *

"I might point out to you, * * * I am reading from the Statute of the Laws of the State of Illinois—'before someone can be admitted to probation it must appear that the defendant is not likely to commit another offense.' There hasn't been a question asked by anybody, when this young man was on the stand or from anybody else, that would indicate to this Court whether or not this young man was likely to commit another offense. I * * * observed this young man testifying; the Court is not convinced that this young man, at the present time, has any intentions of changing his type of life that he has been leading. It's going to take a long time to change his philosophy of life because by his own admission, whether it was in a report to me or on the witness stand, he doesn't like the middle class society, none of the hippies like the middle class society, yet what is society generally composed of? Most of us are middle class. * * * I hope when you have the time that maybe you will try to understand this middle class of society which is the class of society which has made this the greatest country in the world, but unless something is done pretty soon by the Courts or by law enforcement agencies or somebody else to see that the laws are enforced and to see that the laws are carried out, we are not going to have a very strong society because it is getting weaker every day and it is the hippies and it is a few other people who have a complete disregard for laws that are tearing down the very basis of this country. * * *

"The second basis on which you must establish in order to have probation is that the public interest does not require that the defendant receive a penalty. Well, I think the public interest does require that, because I think it is time the public and everybody in it understands we do have laws and if we don't live and abide by them then this country is going to be completely demoralized. * * * I feel it is this Court's responsibility to see that the law is upheld. * * * By doing what I am going to do today on the pretense that this young man needs psychiatric help, well I think I can find you about 1500 people in the next hour and a half that need a little psychiatric help, and he will get psychiatric help where he is going because they have plenty of psychiatrists. I have nothing here in evidence that establishes whatsoever that he is not likely to commit another offense, even by his own testimony, except he says he is starting getting off the smoking. * * *

"THE COURT: Please stand up here, young man. You have filed a petition for probation. The court is not satisfied—Alright, if you wish to say something I will be glad to hear it.

"DEFENDANT: First of all, Diana and I never had sexual intercourse.

"THE COURT: I didn't say that. I said you slept together.

"DEFENDANT: We couldn't afford to do it any other way.

"THE COURT: I don't understand you when you say to me you couldn't afford to do it any other way when your stepfather is a doctor.

"DEFENDANT: We didn't want to come to our parents.

"THE COURT: Well, that's tough. Then somebody missed some place along the road about who should see who and who to talk to.

"Stand up like a man. For once in your life be a man for your mother's sake, because up to this time you haven't established or shown too much manhood so I expect at this time for you to be a man. * * *"

In view of the foregoing statements, we cannot but believe that the court brought to this hearing for probation, its own prejudices and predilections as to the behavior of hippies as a class, and that the court had such a strong feeling on this subject that it could not accord to the defendant, who had sought to be identified as a hippie, the full and fair consideration of the factors which should be given careful thought in connection with the application for probation....

Under the power vested in us by Supreme Court Rule 366(a) (5) (Ill.Rev.Stat.1967, ch. 110A, par. 366(a) (5)), we affirm the judgment of guilty and for the purpose of affording the defendant a new hearing on his petition for probation, we vacate the sentence which was imposed, reverse the denial of the application for probation and remand the cause to the trial court with directions to procure a probationary report and thereupon cause the action to be assigned to another judge of the 15th Judicial Circuit for a new hearing upon the application for probation....

NOTES

Perspectives on Probation

Note 1.

AMERICAN CORRECTIONAL ASSOCIATION
The Development of Probation*

Probation is not wholly an American invention, although it was first legally established in the United States and has been developed in

* American Correctional Association, *Manual of Correctional Standards* 20–21 (3d Ed. 1966). Reprinted with the permission of the American Correctional Association.

this country to a fuller extent than in any other. The "direct ancestor of probation" was the procedure used in early English courts of suspending or deferring judgment and releasing the offender on his own recognizance. This procedure was based on an ancient practice developed in England in the 14th century. A person before the court but not yet convicted was released on his sworn promise that he would "keep the peace" and "be of good behavior." Surety or bail was usually required, and the person providing surety had the power and the duty to return the offender to court if he did not live up to the conditions of his release. The practice of recognizance was employed by the courts in all countries adopting English common law.

In the American colonies instances of this and another early English practice, judicial reprieve or respite, were common. Precedents were thus set for the courts of American states to develop the practice of suspension of sentence, which was written into law in many states and preceded the enactment of probation laws.

Massachusetts in the early 19th century was the birthplace of probation. As Chute and Bell point out, "The first practical demonstration of probation, the first use of the term as a court service, and the enactment of the first probation law occurred in Massachusetts." Judge Peter Thacher used the method of recognizance, or release on bail for good behavior, extensively in the Municipal Court of Boston during his term of office (1823–43) and in 1831 rendered a judgment which laid the foundation for the legal enforcement of the conditions of probation. It was during this period, in 1841, that a philanthropic shoemaker named John Augustus began in the Boston police court to render the volunteer and informal services which a century later caused him to be termed "The Father of American Probation."

Although he was without training and lacked the social resources available now, "John Augustus originated in rudimentary form many of the techniques used by probation officers and other social workers today, including preliminary social investigation, tactful interviewing, family casework, foster-home placement, protective work for women and children, detention, and cooperation with schools, employers, institutions and social agencies. As far as he was able he investigated every case before recommending probation." His reference to persons he had "bailed on probation" is believed to be the first recorded use of the term probation anywhere in the world as applying to the court release and supervision of an offender.

The first probation law, limited to Boston, was passed by the Massachusetts Legislature in 1878, and in 1880 it enacted a statute permitting the appointment of a probation officer for adult offenders in every city and town in the state. In 1898 the Massachusetts Superior Courts were authorized to appoint and fix the salaries of probation officers to serve in all districts, and the power of the court to grant probation to any person charged with a criminal offense was confirmed. Thus Massachusetts became the first state to provide mandatory statewide salaried probation service, and to make probation available to all persons, regardless of the crimes with which they were charged.

The success of probation in Massachusetts gradually became known in other English-speaking countries, but no other American state passed a probation law until Vermont did so in 1898. The enactment, in 1899, of the first American juvenile court law in Cook County (Chicago), Illinois, stimulated similar action by other states. By 1921, forty-six states and the District of Columbia had enacted juvenile court laws, with provisions for probation, and today every state has such a law. The idea of adult or general probation spread much less rapidly than that of juvenile probation, but has now been written into law by all states and the Federal government.

Note 2. An Overview of Probation in the United States

PRESIDENT'S COMMISSION ON LAW ENFORCEMENT AND ADMINISTRATION OF JUSTICE, *Task Force Report: Corrections* 27–28 (1967)

Slightly more than half of the offenders sentenced to correctional treatment in 1965 were placed on probation—supervision in the community subject to the authority of the court. Table 1 sets forth data from the National Survey of Corrections and the Federal corrections system on the number of persons under probation on an average day in 1965 and the number in institutions or on parole. Also shown are estimates of what these populations are likely to be in 1975 on the basis of assumptions detailed in Appendix B. As the table indicates, probation is the correctional treatment used for most offenders today and is likely to be used increasingly in the future.

The estimates for probation shown in the above table project a growth in the number

TABLE 1.—NUMBER OF OFFENDERS ON PROBATION, AND ON PAROLE OR IN INSTITUTIONS, 1965; PROJECTIONS FOR 1975

Location of Offender	1965 Number	1965 Percent	1975 Number	1975 Percent
Probation	684,088	53	1,071,000	58
Parole or institution	598,298	47	770,000	42
Total	1,282,386	100	1,841,000	100

Sources: 1965 data from National Survey of Corrections and special tabulations provided by the Federal Bureau of Prisons and the Administrative Office of the U.S. Courts; 1975 projections by R. Christensen, of the Commission's Task Force on Science and Technology, as described in Appendix B of this report.

of adults on probation almost 2½ times greater than the growth in institutional and parole populations. . . .

The best data available indicate that probation offers one of the most significant prospects for effective programs in corrections. It is also clear that at least two components are needed to make it operate well. The first is a system that facilitates effective decision-making as to who should receive probation; the second is the existence of good community programs to which offenders can be assigned. Probation services now available in most jurisdictions fall far short of meeting either of these needs.

Table 2 shows the number of delinquents and adult felons on probation at the end of 1965 and the annual costs of these services. It is quickly apparent in terms of the number of persons served and of total operating costs that the juvenile system has relatively greater resources than the adult. Cost comparisons, however, require qualification. The juvenile total includes the cost of many foster homes and some private and public institutional costs. Furthermore, juvenile probation in some jurisdictions has a substantial responsibility for orphaned or other non-delinquent dependent children.

Probation in the United States is administered by hundreds of independent agencies operating under a different law in each State and under widely varying philosophies, often within the same State. They serve juvenile, misdemeanant, and felony offenders. In one city, a single State or local agency might be responsible for handling all three kinds of probation cases; in another, three separate agencies may be operating, each responsible for a different type of probationer. All of these probation programs must contend with similar issues.

Note 3. Probation Eligibility

AMERICAN BAR ASSOCIATION, *Standards on Probation* 9–10 (1970)*

General Principles

1.1 *Nature of sentence to probation.*

(a) The legislature should authorize the sentencing court in every case to impose a sentence of probation. Exceptions to this principle are not favored and, if made, should be limited to the most serious offenses.

(b) In this report the term "probation" means a sentence not involving confinement which imposes conditions and retains authority in the sentencing court to modify the conditions of the sentence or to resentence the offender if he violates the conditions. Such a sentence should not involve or require suspension of the imposition or the execution of any other sentence.

(c) Upon a sentence to probation, the court should not be required to attach a condition of supervision by the probation department if in its judgment supervision is not appropriate for the particular case.

(d) The court should specify at the time of sentencing the length of any

TABLE 2.—NUMBER OF FELONS AND JUVENILES ON PROBATION, 1965, AND ANNUAL COSTS OF SERVICES FOR EACH GROUP

Type of Probation	Number on Probation	Annual Costs
Felony	257,755	$ 37,937,808
Juvenile	224,948	75,019,441
Total	482,703	112,957,249

Sources: National Survey of Corrections and special tabulations provided by the Federal Bureau of Prisons and the Administrative Office of the U.S. Courts.

* Quoted with permission of the American Bar Association, 1155 East 60th Street, Chicago, Illinois 60637.

term during which the defendant is to be supervised and during which the court will retain power to revoke the sentence for the violation of specified conditions. Neither supervision nor the power to revoke should be permitted to extend beyond a legislatively fixed time, which should in no event exceed two years for a misdemeanor or five years for a felony.

(e) A sentence to probation should be treated as a final judgment for purposes of appeal and similar procedural purposes.

(f) Upon revocation of probation the court should have available the same sentencing alternatives that were available at the time of initial sentencing. The court should not foreclose any of these alternatives before revocation.

1.2 *Desirability of probation.*
Probation is a desirable disposition in appropriate cases because:

(i) it maximizes the liberty of the individual while at the same time vindicating the authority of the law and effectively protecting the public from further violations of law;

(ii) it affirmatively promotes the rehabilitation of the offender by continuing normal community contacts;

(iii) it avoids the negative and frequently stultifying effects of confinement which often severely and unnecessarily complicate the reintegration of the offender into the community;

(iv) it greatly reduces the financial costs to the public treasury of an effective correctional system;

(v) it minimizes the impact of the conviction upon innocent dependents of the offender.

1.3 *Criteria for granting probation.*
(a) The probation decision should not turn upon generalizations about types of offenses or the existence of a prior criminal record, but should be rooted in the facts and circumstances of each case. The court should consider the nature and circumstances of the crime, the history and character of the offender, and available institutional and community resources. Probation should be the sentence unless the sentencing court finds that:

(i) confinement is necessary to protect the public from further criminal activity by the offender; or

(ii) the offender is in need of correctional treatment which can most effectively be provided if he is confined; or

(iii) it would unduly depreciate the seriousness of the offense if a sentence of probation were imposed.

(b) Whether the defendant pleads guilty, pleads not guilty or intends to appeal is not relevant to the issue of whether probation is an appropriate sentence.

Note 4. The Effectiveness of Probation

a. J. EDGAR HOOVER

The Dire Consequences of the Premature Release of Dangerous Criminals Through Probation and Parole*

The premature release of dangerous criminals through frequently occurring abuses in our system of parole, probation, and other forms of clemency demands the serious attention of police and public alike. Law enforcement is a vast machinery of criminal justice established for the protection of society. The shortcomings of any part in this mechanism not only impede the police profession but also imperil the safety of the Nation's citizens. It is therefore imperative that law enforcement and the general public recognize and re-evaluate the rehabilitation procedures which allow ill-advised leniency to criminals.

The dire consequences of maladministration of the parole and probation programs, daily paraded before the public in the newspaper headlines across the land, can no longer be ignored. No less than 92 of the 109 dangerous criminals listed among the FBI's "Ten Most Wanted Fugitives" since March, 1950, had been the recipients of parole, probation,

* Statement of Director J. Edgar Hoover, *F.B.I. Law Enforcement Bulletin* Vol. 27, No. 11, pp. 1, 2 (1958). Reprinted with permission.

or other forms of clemency. The service martyr plaques of the Nation's police agencies are filled with the names of dedicated men slain at the hands of gunmen who were the recipients of ill-advised clemency.

The validity of the principle of parole, probation, and other forms of clemency is not a question in issue. What must be sought is not the abolition of the systems of rehabilitation but the improvement in their administration to assure that the welfare of the public, as well as the criminal, is served. To achieve this objective, a critical self-analysis of present procedures and results is essential.

The failures of "easy freedom" policies cannot be attributed to any one solitary cause. Certainly, the handicaps of the parole and probation systems resulting from insufficient manpower, paltry budgets, and excessive workloads must be removed. In addition, moreover, soft-hearted leniency, coddling of juvenile criminals, cheap solutions to overcrowded prison facilities, and other unrealistic techniques are potent factors which should be brought out in the open. An ostrich-like attitude, apologetic statements, and unwarranted resentment of concern for the abuses threatening the public upon the part of not only penologists but also a small segment of the judiciary can only aggravate an already serious problem.

The remarkable progress gained by law enforcement in recent years is due in no small degree to the intelligent evaluation of procedures and the ardent solicitation of public assistance in overcoming handicaps. In like manner, the parole and probation failures of yesterday and today can be the bases for the successes of tomorrow. In dealing with human failings, there can be no guarantee of 100% success. Each failure, however, presents a challenge and should be objectively analyzed in an effort to avoid recurrence.

The primary obligation for making the parole and probation systems serve their rightful purpose naturally lies with the established agencies and authorities in this field. In the light of current experience, the law-abiding public and the rest of law enforcement are entitled to a frank evaluation of past results, an honest appraisal of present policies, and a carefully planned program for future operation to halt the unleashing of unreformed criminals upon American communities.

In the rehabilitation phase of law enforcement, parole and probation authorities, police officials, the judiciary, and the citizenry share grave interests and responsibilities. With united and cooperative effort, success can be achieved.

The only alternative is surrender to lawlessness and social disorder.

b. RICHARD F. SPARKS

Research on the Use and Effectiveness of Probation*

The object of this report is to summarize the results of research to date on the use and effectiveness of probation, parole and certain measures of after-care.

I have reviewed, in preparing the report, all of the relevant research studies available to me: and I believe that these cover all of the important work done in this field in the past twenty years. Not all of these projects are described in the report, since a number are inconclusive or of doubtful value on methodological grounds. But I have described briefly a few research projects which are still in progress, and which seem likely to produce important results within the next few years.

Almost all of the research described in the report was carried out either in England or in the United States. This is so, for two reasons. The first is that, at least until very recently, those two countries have accounted for almost all of the empirical research in all areas of criminology and penology, and in particular have had, between them, a virtual monopoly on research on the effectiveness of treatment. The second is that they have—again, until very recently—made by far the most extensive use of probation, parole and the kinds of after-care considered in this report. . . .

Virtually every study of the after-conduct of offenders placed on probation has found that the majority are not reconvicted within the chosen follow-up period. In England, the Cambridge study published in 1958 found that no less than 79% of the adults included in the research, and 73% of the juveniles, successfully completed their periods of probation. Even when the offenders were followed up for a three-year period after the end of supervision, 70% of the adults, and 58% of the juveniles, could still be said to have succeeded. Similar results are reported from the United States. R. W. England found that 82.3% of a group of 490 offenders placed on probation in Pennsylvania were not reconvicted within a period of 6 to 12 years after completion of probation. . . .

* Richard Sparks, "Research on the Use and Effectiveness of Probation, Parole and Measures of After-care," Council of Europe, European Committee on Crime Problems, III *Collected Studies in Criminological Research* 129 (1968).

These figures are, of course, much higher than the overall success rates typically reported for institutional treatment. (For example, Glaser found evidence that less than two thirds of those discharged from US prisons are "successes" in the sense that they are not reimprisoned.) But this crude comparison actually reveals nothing about the relative effectiveness of probation and imprisonment, since it takes no account of the differences in the offenders who are dealt with in each way, and their different liability to reconviction independent of the treatment they receive. Most of the surveys just cited have found that certain types of offender are more likely to be reconvicted during or after probation than others: the Cambridge study, for example, found higher reconviction rates among juveniles, males, and recidivists than among adults, females and first offenders. The majority of the factors associated with reconviction on probation have also been found to be associated with reconviction following other forms of treatment; and any differences in these respects between offenders placed on probation and offenders dealt with in other ways must be taken into account when comparing the success rates of probation and other forms of treatment.

The few studies which have done this strongly suggest that probation is in general at least as effective (in terms of reconviction rates) as imprisonment or other forms of custodial treatment. Wilkins found no significant difference in the reconviction rates (in a three-year follow-up period) of a group of 31 offenders placed on probation at an English higher court, and a group of 31 individually matched controls dealt with in other ways (mostly prison and Borstal). Babst and Mannering followed up 5,274 adult male offenders in Wisconsin, and compared the reconviction rates (in a two-year period) of those placed on probation with those sent to prison and paroled. When type of current offence, criminal record and marital status (the factors most highly predictive of recidivism in this group) were held constant, it was found that the success rate of probation was about the same as that of imprisonment for recidivists, and was significantly better for first offenders. According to Martin a similar result was found in a demonstration project carried out in Saginaw, Michigan. Finally, in a study carried out by the Home Office Research Unit, Hammond found that the observed reconviction rates of offenders placed on probation in 1956 were broadly comparable with those of offenders given institutional treatment, in relation to expected reconviction rates computed from the characteristics of the offenders involved. In a reassessment of the earlier Cambridge study of probation, Hammond suggested that it showed that when expected reconviction rates were taken into account, the effectiveness of probation was about the same as that of other treatments for first offenders, but slightly better than expected for recidivists; in his own sample recidivists also did relatively better on probation than first offenders. (It should be noted, however, that the most significant finding of the Home Office study was that fines and discharges were relatively much more effective, overall, than either imprisonment or probation.)

Two recent studies of receptions into California penal institutions also support the view that probation might well be used more liberally instead of institutional treatment. In the first, Mueller estimated that 20% of all new adult male admissions to the California Department of Corrections could have been recommended for probation instead of imprisonment, since the risk of their being reconvicted (as determined by base expectancy tables regularly in use in California) under minimum supervision was relatively low. In the second, Roberts and Secket found evidence that about 40% of California Youth Authority wards could be released immediately to the community without serious risk of reconviction, compared with the 16–17% who are at present released immediately in this way.

The general conclusions that probation is at least as effective as institutional treatment also receives some support from a group of studies of experimental community treatment programmes carried out in the United States in recent years. These studies—the Provo project in Utah, the Silverlake experiment in Los Angeles, the Essexfields project in New Jersey and the Community Treatment Project in Sacramento and Stockton, California—all found that the reconviction rates of offenders placed on probation were markedly lower than those of control groups sent to penal institutions. However, it is probable that for present purposes not too much weight should be placed on these studies. None was specifically designed to evaluate probation; in two (the Community Treatment Project, and Silverlake) the delinquents dealt with in the community did not receive regular probation, while three (the Community Treatment Project, Essexfields and Provo) suffer from methodological limitations concerning the matching of treatment and control groups and the supervision of each during the follow-up period.

It is important to bear in mind that the main conclusion to be drawn from the research discussed so far is really a negative one: namely, that institutional treatment is *not* more effective (in terms of preventing reconvictions) than treatment in the community. In the light of this conclusion, it would obviously be reasonable on grounds of cost alone to place on probation a proportion of those offenders now sent to prisons or other institutions. But it may also be that for some offenders who are now placed on probation, a nominal measure not involving supervision (for example, a fine or discharge) would be at least as effective as probation.

NOTES

Note 1.

JUDAH BEST AND PAUL I. BIRZON

Conditions of Probation: An Analysis*

As has been indicated earlier, the trial court must initially determine the nature of the condition to be imposed upon the would-be probationer. In some jurisdictions, statutes require the imposition of certain conditions in all cases where probation is to be granted. These may require that the probationer shall not violate the criminal laws of any state or the federal government, shall not leave the state without the court's consent, shall comply with the rules and regulations prescribed by the court or by the agency designated for his supervision, shall report periodically with regard to his whereabouts, conduct and employment, shall post bond with or without sureties for the performance of the conditions imposed, or shall pay costs to the court.

With respect to these conditions, no discretion is lodged in the trial court; they must be incorporated within every order of probation. But this does not prevent the court from imposing conditions in addition to those made mandatory by statute. Certain typical conditions found authorized but not required by statutes in most states, are *inter alia*, support

* 51 *Georgetown Law Journal* 817–19; 821; 823–24; 826–30 (1963). Reprinted with permission of Georgetown Law Journal.

of dependents (which generally comprises the largest single category of probationers), the making of restitution to the victim of the crime committed, and initiation of a course of vocational training.

This legislative enumeration is by no means exhaustive of the conditions that can or have been imposed as an incident to a conditional release. In the somewhat less conventional cases conditions have been imposed which run the gamut of every conceivable human relationship; *e.g.,* take care of mother and father, do not make remarks against the sheriff, join the Navy, insure a third party's car against accident and casualty loss, disclose names of associates in crime and shore up an adjacent building. These latter conditions result from powers conferred upon the courts through statutes permitting a defendant to be admitted to probation upon such terms and conditions as the court deems best, proper, or the like. In some jurisdictions there is no preliminary enumeration, and the sole direction given the court is that it should affix terms and conditions as the court in its discretion shall determine, fix, prescribe, or see fit to impose.

This then is the authority under which the courts operate. Let us now consider those conditions which commonly result from the exercise of that authority and the circumstances and rationale attending their imposition.

Costs

Frequently the payment of costs is imposed as a condition of probation. Ordinarily the amount of such payment is equivalent to the cost of the judicial proceeding involved, though the measure imposed may be the expenses of the ensuing probation. On occasion the exaction may be gauged by some extrinsic factor, as for instance, the cost of utilizing a private prosecutor.

Like the other pecuniary conditions involving payment to the state rather than to a private party, the rationale for the condition of costs is supposedly the rehabilitation of the defendant. By making the defendant pay, the argument runs, his sense of obligation to society is awakened. This approach to rehabilitation, namely, that the defendant is returned to complete freedom in society only through undergoing some tangible sacrifice, has its counterpart in psychoanalysis, where the sacrifice undergone through payment of substantial fees plays a significant role in treatment. However, the rationale is rarely articulated in the "costs" cases, and it would seem from the enormous range of offenses in which the condition has been imposed that rehabilitation of the offender is a secondary consideration. . . .

Fines

The same rationale used to justfy the imposition of costs as a condition to probation is applicable to imposition of the condition of fines: it quickens the sense of social responsibility in the offender. A fine, nevertheless, is clearly punitive in character, usually varying in amount with the gravity of the offense for which the defendant has been convicted, and is payment to the state in expiation for the defendant's offense. Sometimes the sum exacted as a fine is diverted for the "use of the county," or in rare instances, for the use of a private individual. In these circumstances, the money exacted cannot properly be termed a fine, for the primary purpose appears to have been some form of *restitution* rather than punishment of the defendant. What has occurred is that a statutory measure is being utilized as a rough gauge to satisfy other ends of the criminal law. . . .

Bonds

The posting of bond either for appearance or for assurance that the probationer will faithfully observe the conditions of probation also seems inconsistent with the premise that the erstwhile probationer is worth salvaging. The rationale of individual treatment of the offender can retain very little vitality in the states where a statute requires the posting of bond as a condition of probation. A suggestion has been made that the omnipresent bond is a vestige of an early, unsupervised probation or suspension of sentence. In any event, the net result of this requirement is that those capable of obtaining bonds most easily are those professional criminals who have a reputation for not bolting. . . .

Support

The support of dependents remains the one most common condition imposed upon probationers, since even states which had no other adult probation law created a somewhat analogous system with regard to persons convicted of nonsupport. Generally the condition is handled by payment to the probation officer of a monthly installment for remittance to the child, wife or indigent parents. The support of dependents cannot be predicated upon a rehabilitation of the offender, save as compulsory payment may awaken a sense of responsibility. However, this is never seriously raised as the purpose of the condition of support. In effect, the legislature has taken a position that this is the only way remaining to provide for dependents other than by the state itself assuming the burden. . . .

Restitution

Restitution to aggrieved parties for loss or damage caused by the defendant's unlawful act is frequently made a condition of probation, and authority to impose such a condition is granted to the courts either expressly by statute or is sanctioned by practice pursuant to a broad grant of authority relating to the terms and conditions of probation. A distinction will be drawn, for the purposes of the present analysis, between restitution and reparation. Restitution normally consists of reimbursement of that sum of money which the defendant appropriated in the commission of his criminal act. The imposition of such a condition occurs commonly in the area of embezzlement, income tax evasion and larceny. Reparation is generally considered to be synonymous with tort damages; *i.e.*, a sum of money paid to an injured party that is roughly commensurate with special and general damages. The amount of such reparation may be set by the sentencing court, the probation officer or it may be deferred until a subsequent civil hearing is held on the issue. When the last is the case, the sentencing court may require as a condition of probation that the defendant "should have the financial ability to pay any judgment rendered against him in a civil action for damages."

The rationale articulated for the imposition of the restitution and reparation conditions is the reformative effect the imposition of such a responsibility will have upon the probationer's character. To be clearly consonant with such a purpose, it is necessary that the defendant be closely supervised during the period of the condition's existence. Such supervision of course should not entail harassment, but rather an examination into the financial situation of each defendant in order to work out a system of payment which most effectively accomplishes reimbursement, and yet does not interfere with the defendant's family and other responsibilities. However, it is difficult to tell in circumstances whether the best interests of the *probationer* are uppermost. Restitution has been utilized so often to achieve its own admittedly desirable goal that the courts fail to articulate any real concern as to reformation and rehabilitation of the probationer. . . .

Banishment

Normal probation procedure requires the probationer to remain within the jurisdiction and to keep the probation officer informed at all times of his whereabouts. A condition of probation that the offender leave the state, United States, county, town, village, or neighborhood would be inconsistent with such procedure. Nevertheless it has been imposed from time to time by a sentencing court—and quite as readily the condition is struck down as invalid by the reviewing court.

The condition of banishment suffers from the same opprobrium that attaches to the sentence of banishment: It is contrary to public policy to allow one state to foist its undesirables onto sister states. There sometimes appears to be an attempt to justify the imposition of such a condition (especially where the condition consists merely of removal from one nearby village to another) upon the ground that the offender can be rehabilitated only by removing him from an environment which prompted commission of the offense. Granting some merit to this thesis, it seems anachronistic and as a practical matter, unusable today.

Imprisonment

A condition of imprisonment as one of a number of conditions imposed with probation is theoretically inconsistent with the rationale of probation. Probation is based upon the premise that the offender has been found fit to re-enter society, supervised to some degree, but otherwise enjoying the same freedom as anyone else. There is simply no way to reconcile incarceration with this premise. However, there are cases where a condition of imprisonment has been imposed upon the offender as a part of his probation requiring as long or longer a term in prison that the maximum that could be imposed as a sentence. California, in particular, consistently utilizes a period of incarceration as a condition precedent to probation. This is sometimes justified by the interesting assertion that "a taste of punishment" will not harm the probationer. Because the condition of imprisonment is not subject to the statutory and customary limitations of a sentence, the danger of unfairness increases. As has been pointed out above, the condition may impose a longer term than a sentence; in addition, the term of imprisonment imposed as a condition precedent to probation may be harsher than the sentence.

Moreover, since discretion remains vested in the trial judge, he retains the power to modify this condition before it is completely discharged so as to lengthen the period of incarceration. While California, in particular, consistently upholds such mid-term modification, it would seem that such maintenance of control over the offender once he has entered prison should be struck down as an unwarranted extension of the trial court's jurisdiction.

JUDICIAL CHOICE: INCARCERATION AND ALTERNATIVES THERETO

The Conditions of Probation

Note 2. Illustrative Conditions

STATE OF CONNECTICUT
DEPARTMENT OF ADULT PROBATION

CONDITIONS OF PROBATION

In accordance with the authority conferred by the State of Connecticut Probation Law, you ...
....
have on this date .... been placed on probation for a period of ....
by the Honorable ...., Judge of the ....
Court, holding in ...., Connecticut.
         County, City, Town

You are hereby advised that the Court may at any time revoke or modify any condition of the probation, impose any special condition it deems proper and may at any time within the period of your probation, if it sees fit, impose the judgment and sentence it might have imposed in the first instance.

During the probationary term herein fixed, you shall abide by the following terms and conditions:

FIRST,   You shall not during the term of this probation violate any criminal law of the United States, the State of Connecticut, any ordinance of a municipality of said state or the criminal law of any other state in the United States.

SECOND,   You shall not leave the state of Connecticut without the permission of the Court.

THIRD,   You agree to waive extradition from any state in the United States.

FOURTH,   You shall report to the probation officer as he directs.

FIFTH,   You shall keep your probation officer informed of your whereabouts at all times and immediately notify him of any change of address or employment.

SIXTH,   You shall make all payment of monies as directed by the Court and/or the probation officer.

SEVENTH,   You shall make every effort to keep yourself steadily employed and shall support those dependent upon you.

EIGHTH,   You shall not engage in any anti-social conduct which shall furnish good cause for the Court to believe the probationary order should be revoked in the public interest.

NINTH,   You shall not partake in the use of alcoholic beverages or narcotics.

I have read the foregoing conditions of probation. I understand the conditions herein set forth and will abide by the conditions and terms thereof.

....
  (Date)   Probationer

Witness:

....
 Probation Officer

UNITED STATES COURTS
CONDITIONS OF PROBATION

Probation Form No. 7   Conditions of Probation

UNITED STATES DISTRICT COURT

For The ....

TO ....   Docket No. ....

Address ....

In accordance with authority conferred by the United States Probation Law, you have been placed on probation this date.   for a period of   by the Hon.
United States District Judge, sitting in and for this District Court at

CONDITIONS OF PROBATION

It is the order of the Court that you shall comply with the following conditions of probation.

(1) You shall refrain from violation of any law (federal, state and local). You shall get in touch immediately with your probation officer if arrested or questioned by a law-enforcement officer.

(2) You shall associate only with law-abiding persons and maintain reasonable hours.

(3) You shall work regularly at a lawful occupation and support your legal dependents, if any, to the best of your ability. When out of work you shall notify your probation officer at once. You shall consult him prior to job change.

(4) You shall not leave the judicial district without permission of the probation officer.

(5) You shall notify your probation officer immediately of any change in your place of residence.

(6) You shall follow the probation officer's instructions and advice.

(7) You shall report to the probation officer as directed.

The special conditions ordered by the Court are as follows:

I understand that the Court may change the conditions of probation, reduce or extend the period of probation, and at any time during the probation period or within the maximum probation period of 5 years permitted by law, may issue a warrant and revoke probation for a violation occurring during the probation period.

I have read or had read to me the above conditions of probation. I fully understand them and I will abide by them.

(Signed)
                    Probationer .... Date ......

You will report as follows:
                    U.S. Probation Officer .... Date ......

NOTES

Judicial Review of Probation Conditions

Note 1.

PEOPLE V. MASON
5 Cal. 3d 759, 488 P.2d 630 (1971)
California Supreme Court

BURKE, Justice.

This case involves the legality of a search conducted pursuant to the terms of a condition of defendant's probation requiring him to submit to a search by police officers at any time without the necessity of a search warrant. . . . Defendant moved to suppress certain evidence on the ground that it was the product of an illegal search. The court granted the motion to suppress and, since the People had no further evidence against defendant, dismissed the charges against him. The People appeal from the order of dismissal.

We have concluded that the search was proper and that the order of dismissal must be set aside and the case remanded for trial.

The facts leading to defendant's arrest are as follows: In January 1970 burglars broke into the Alvarado Medical Center in San Diego and stole money, stamps, retail sales items, a radio, 4,000 hypodermic needles and over 30,000 pills and capsules, mostly barbiturates and amphetamines. At the time of the burglary, a hospital employee observed suspicious activity by two men in the parking lot; a second employee noted the license number of their car, and reported it to the police. The officers traced the car to defendant, living at 2124 Reed Street in San Diego, and discovered that defendant had registered as a narcotics offender and was on probation for possessing marijuana in 1969. The officers noted that one of the conditions of defendant's probation required him to "submit his person, place of residence, vehicle, to search and seizure at any time of the day or night, with or without a search warrant, whenever requested to do so by the Probation Officer or any law enforcement officer."

The officers went to defendant's residence and saw his car parked in front. One of the officers knocked on the door of the house, loudly identified himself and announced that he wanted to search the apartment. Defendant opened the door and an officer informed him that he had reason to believe defendant had participated in a burglary and was subject to search and seizure by court order as a condition of his probation. According to the officer, defendant replied that he was subject to such a condition. Thereupon, without giving defendant the opportunity to refuse or grant permission for a search, the officers entered the house, searched and found in the kitchen a radio which resembled the one stolen from the Medical Center. They arrested defendant, took him away, and subsequently searched defendant's car and house, uncovering further items of contraband.

The foregoing search was conducted without a warrant and, at least in part, extended in scope beyond the limits of a reasonable search incidental to arrest, as set forth in Chimel v. California, 395 U.S. 752. The People contend, however, that the warrantless search was justified by the terms of the defendant's condition of probation that he submit to a search, with or without a warrant, whenever requested by police officers. We agree that under the circumstances in the instant case, the probation condition authorized the search of defendant's residence and car. . . .

Turning to the question of the validity of the condition as we have interpreted it, we are guided by the principles set forth in In re Bushman, *supra*, 1 Cal. 3d 767, 776–777, 83 Cal.Rptr. 375, 381, 463 P.2d 727, 733, as follows: "When granting probation, courts have broad discretion to impose restrictive conditions to foster rehabilitation and to protect public safety. Penal Code section 1203.1 authorizes the court to impose any 'reasonable conditions, as it may determine are fitting and proper to the end that justice may be done, * * * and specifically for the reformation and rehabilitation of the probationer.' If the defendant considers the conditions of probation more harsh than the sentence the court would otherwise impose, he has the right to refuse probation and undergo the sentence. [Citations.] In such case he may challenge the legality of any proposed conditions of probation on an appeal from the judgment or on habeas corpus. [Citations.] . . .

Defendant contends that a probation condition which requires submission to a warrantless search constitutes an unreasonable invasion of his Fourth Amendment rights. We have heretofore suggested, however, that persons conditionally released to society, such as parolees, may have a reduced expectation of privacy, thereby rendering certain intrusions by governmental authorities "reasonable" which otherwise would be invalid under traditional constitutional concepts, at least to the extent that such intrusions are necessitated by legitimate governmental demands. Thus, a probationer who has been granted the privilege of probation on condition that he submit at any time to a warrantless search may have no reasonable expectation of traditional Fourth Amendment protection. . . .

We conclude that the search conducted by the officers herein was reasonable and proper, and that the order of dismissal entered following the court's granting of defendant's motion to suppress should be vacated.

The order of dismissal is hereby vacated and the cause remanded to the Superior Court of San Diego County for further proceedings not inconsistent with this opinion.

PETERS, Justice (dissenting).

I dissent.

It is clear that the protection afforded by the Fourth Amendment extends to probationers. The question is to what extent the state may deny or condition governmental benefits upon a waiver of Fourth Amendment rights. Our cases make clear that probationers may have a reduced right to Fourth Amendment protections, but that restrictions upon those rights must be narrowly drawn to meet needs for reformation and rehabilitation of the offender. . . . A probationer may be entitled to a diminished expectation of privacy because of the necessities of the correctional system, but his expectation may be diminished *only* to the extent necessary for his reformation and rehabilitation.

I cannot believe that such a total denial of Fourth Amendment rights is necessary or even desirable in rehabilitating a criminal offender. . . .

The majority appear to assert that prior consent to search by *any* law enforcement officer is necessary to the discovery of future offenses. We do not conditionally release a man because we wish to trap him in future offenses. Nor do we provide a probation officer for the purpose of being a one-man shadow of the probationer. Surely it is a proper purpose of the probation officer to ascertain whether the probationer is obeying all laws and the terms of his probation. But this function is undertaken with the goal of rehabilitating the offender. Law enforcement officers generally, on the other hand, do not have such goals in mind. It must be neither their role nor their prerogative to treat probationers as a specially suspect class of citizens. I can see no justification for extending the waiver of all Fourth Amendment rights to all law enforcement officers. I would hold the condition overbroad.

Moreover, there is no necessity for law enforcement officers to have such a privilege, given their lack of involvement in the rehabilitative process. Law enforcement officers investigating commission of a crime may properly question or search a probationer or parolee. And in considering the propriety of searches without warrants, one's status as a probationer or parolee may be of weight in giving officers probable cause to search. . . .

Note 2.

PORTH V. UNITED STATES
453 F.2d 330 (1971)
United States Court of Appeals, Tenth Circuit

Appellant here seeks an order voiding certain conditions of probation prohibiting him from circulating materials questioning the constitutionality of the Federal Reserve system and the Federal Income Tax laws and requiring him to abstain from speaking or writing activities questioning the constitutionality of the Federal Reserve System and the Federal Income Tax laws and requiring him to obtain authorization in writing in order to leave the jurisdiction of the court.

In 1967 appellant was convicted in the Kansas District Court on five counts charging him with failure to file withholding tax returns and failure to file an individual income tax return for the year 1963. The defendant was sentenced to the maximum period. . . .

Appellant has a long history of personal disagreement with the income tax laws dating back to 1954 at least. * * * It was undoubtedly this antipathy to income taxes on the part of the appellant which led to his 1967 conviction, and on the occasion of the review of the case in this court his belief was described as fanatical. . . .

Obviously, the years have not resulted in any modification or mellowing of appellant's viewpoints, for seemingly he continues unabated to conduct his personal vendetta against the money system and the income tax laws. . . .

It is, of course, questionable whether special conditions are appealable as such. See Judicial Review of Probation Conditions, 67 Colum. L. Rev. 181, 188–196 (1967). Inasmuch as this uncertainty exists, we deem it proper to review the matter as a Sec. 2255 case. Probation does impose substantial restraints and thus good reason exists for reviewing the restraints pursuant to 28 U.S.C. Sec. 2255. . . .

The sentencing judge has a broad power to impose conditions designed to serve the accused and the community. The only limitation is that the conditions have a reasonable relationship to the treatment of the accused and the protection of the public. . . .

At the same time, not all conditions which have been imposed have been upheld by courts. Some have been ruled unnecessarily restrictive.

We glean from the record in this case and from previous cases that the judge in imposing the conditions which are here questioned was seeking to prevent the defendant from carrying out a campaign, the effect of which would not only call into question the constitutionality of the laws, but would directly or indirectly, expressly or impliedly, urge people to disregard them. . . . To muzzle the appellant to this extent is on its face a violation of his First Amendment freedom of expression. This is not to say that one on probation has the rights of citizens who are not on probation. He forfeits much of his freedom of action and even freedom of expression to the extent necessary to successful rehabilitation and protection of the public programs. We see no basis for criticizing a condition which prohibits the violation of any public law or which prohibits the inducing of others to violate the law, and we hold the instant condition invalid only to the extent that it prohibits the expression of opinions as to invalidity or unconstitutionality of the laws in question. Insofar as it prohibits public speeches designed to urge or encourage others to violate the laws, the condition is valid.

Note 3.

JUDAH BEST AND PAUL I. BIRZON

Judicial Review of Probation Conditions*

Administrative in nature, affecting vast areas of everyday life, the conditions imposed under probation tend to cut across a whole range of possible legal safeguards in order to get a job done. Moreover, although it has been said that the proper exercise of such authority is guaranteed through strict supervision by the appellate courts, unhappily this view has not been borne out in practice. Indeed, it may be said that the reviewing courts are reluctant to overturn any conditions once they have been imposed. Such reluctance is generally based upon one of several grounds: (1) the broad discretion accorded the trial court; (2) the am-

* 51 *Georgetown Law Journal* 831-36 (1963). Reprinted with permission of Georgetown Law Journal.

biguity in the "reasonable condition" test; and (3) the consent theory.

As to the first of these grounds, a condition of probation generally can be sanctioned by statutory language which authorizes the trial judge to impose as an incident of probation any condition he may deem best. Such conditions may be declared invalid only where the trial court has clearly abused its discretion, and in order for an appellate court to arrive at such a conclusion, it must decide whether the condition imposed is consistent with the ultimate aims of probation. The problem, then, should become one of statutory interpretation, both as to the express and implied purposes of the Probation Act. Rarely, however, does such an analysis take place.

As to the second ground for upholding the trial court's imposition of a condition of probation, the statement that the condition is "reasonable" is a rubric which in practice is seldom subjected to careful analysis. Normally all a reviewing court signifies by this term is that the imposition of the condition is within the discretion of the trial court, or that the condition does not appear to be immoral, impossible to perform, or the like. On occasion the appellate court will inquire into the relationship between the condition and the crime committed by the offender; such relevance then becomes a factor in assaying the reasonableness of the condition. However, since the discretion of the trial court is broad, and conditions imposed normally are not such as would shock the conscience, invariably all manner of conditions are termed reasonable. The case of *State v. Smith* presents a striking instance of the tendency. In a conviction for the larcenous taking of grain, the condition imposed was that the defendant shall refrain from driving a car upon the highways. While the condition is *reasonable* enough in the sense that it is not horrendous, the appellate decision does not satisfactorily spell out the especial relevance between the offense and the condition.

In many cases, however, the reasonableness of the condition upon which sentence is suspended is never even at issue. Particularly in the revocation hearing, where the defendant, accused of failure to live up to the condition, is pleading the unreasonableness or illegality of the condition, courts have found it convenient to avoid the issue by resort to a theory of waiver: the defendant has consented to the condition in the trial court and therefore cannot raise the issue of its illegality. Some courts have gone one step beyond, and have analogized the transaction between the defendant and the trial court to a *contract* and at least one court has gone so far as to criticize the defendant for "welching."

Difficulty arises with such reasoning, however, because the analogy is not complete. The law of contract is posited upon the notion of an equality of bargaining position between parties which culminates in a voluntary agreement. However, defendants are not in a position to bargain with a court because virtually any condition is preferable to jail. The nonfederal narcotics cases are perhaps the best instance of the inequality of positions. In these cases the offender is faced with Hobson's choice, for the alternative to accepting probation and its concomitant conditions is to endure the effects of narcotic withdrawal in a county jail. In apparent recognition of the defects in the consent theory, within recent times at least one jurisdiction has held with consistency that acceptance of an unreasonable or illegal condition is no bar to a later objection. It would seem that this holding may even be explained upon the strict contract theory that a person cannot consent to an illegal contract.

Aside from the "contract analogy" the reviewing courts generally hold that there is no necessity to inquire into the consonance of the condition with the aims of probation on the grounds that the defendant is free not to accept the State's offer, and that the offer is being made by the state as a matter of grace and clemency. It is submitted, however, that this approach taken by the courts to the problem is misleading. The conduct of the defendant is largely irrelevant if the real question is the legality or illegality of a condition. The duty of the reviewing court is to interpret the laws and to ensure that the trial court does not exceed its jurisdiction. Indeed, aside from this strictly statutory consideration the public policy of the state should mark such transactions as invalid regardless of any consent of the parties.

On the basis of the above material, it becomes apparent that one of the principal deficiencies in the present use of conditions of probation is a need for more definite legislative control over the use of probation by the courts. This control should take the form of a specific enumeration of permissible conditions which the sentencing courts may impose as an incident of probation.

The presence of such a legislative enumeration would act as a guide to the sentencing court, and establish a standard for review as well. At the same time however, it is recognized, albeit reluctantly, that the fullest realization of the objectives of probation requires the sentencing court to be vested with some discretion to impose other conditions when necessary for reformation of the offender. The problem then becomes one of determining the permissible limits of judicial discretion, and, hence, the validity of the conditions imposed. In this regard it is suggested that the following standards be employed by the reviewing courts.

Is the Condition Validly Authorized by Statute?

Where a jurisdiction already has a legislative enumeration of permissible conditions, there is a ready-made standard by which to judge the validity of the contested condition. In such a jurisdiction, if restitution, for example, is limited by statute to an amount actually lost by an aggrieved party, a condition imposing a greater payment is clearly illegal.

Does the Condition Come Into Conflict With One of the General Aims of Probation?

A condition that the would-be probationer be sterilized cannot be reconciled with the avowedly corrective aims of probation. Granting some leeway to the discretion of the trial judge, there must nevertheless be some discernible relationship between the condition imposed and the reformation of the offender. If such relationship does not exist the condition is unnecessary to the probation process and is therefore invalid. This test is easily enough applied when the conditions imposed are harsh and punitive; in such circumstances one may readily enough discern no reasonable relationship between, say, sterilization and reformation. The difficulty arises where the condition is not itself onerous. Thus, the condition that a probationer not allow people to congregate in her home after the hours of darkness is not in itself a difficult condition to perform—but is it reasonably related to the probationer's reformation?

Does the Condition Conflict With Some Right of the Defendant?

The defendant, despite his conviction, nevertheless retains certain basic, personal rights. On occasion, a condition will be imposed which violates such rights. In one such case, the United States Court of Appeals for the Ninth Circuit held invalid as an unwarranted intrusion into the privacy of the person, a condition that the defendant donate a pint of blood to the Red Cross. There is no difficulty in concluding that such a condition is an unwarranted violation of the personal rights of the defendant, and is therefore invalid. Much less clear are the conditions which place limitations upon the offender where the activity limited may not be legally protected as a right. For example, in those cases where the sentencing court has imposed as a condition of probation that the defendant shall not engage in a specific course of employment, what sometimes happens is that a defendant is effectively deprived of the means of securing a livelihood, particularly when through age or lack of training he is unable to adapt to his change of circumstances. In such a case, it is suggested that the condition would be invalid as offending against the individual's basic right to work.

Does the Condition Come into Conflict With a Basic Tenet of Our Society? Is it Fair?

This standard is the most elusive of all: it is clear that a condition offends against our concept of fair play and is therefore invalid where the condition imposed upon a defendant totals up to a harsher punishment than the maximum sentence available pursuant to statute. Similarly, the courts should find invalid the support condition imposed where no prior adjudication of responsibility has been made, or the situation where the trial court imposes a condition that a probationer enter a sanitarium when the record fails to demonstrate evidence of insanity. What has happened in these circumstances is that the sentencing court has performed functions which are normally assigned to other mechanisms of our society. In the support case, the criminal court has undertaken to determine paternity, a function assigned to the civil forum; in the other illustration, the court has functioned without regard to the commitment procedures designed for involuntary treatment of the mentally ill. And in both cases the criminal court has by-passed the safeguards that custom, time and practice have incorporated into these other processes of our society. In these circumstances, quite clearly the conditions imposed are unfair, are invalid, and the imposition is an abuse of judicial discretion.

4. THE ALTERNATIVES FAIL: PROBATION REVOCATION

Excerpt from Connecticut Probation Revocation Proceeding

D.N. 21905　　　　HARTFORD COUNTY
　　　50921　　　　SUPERIOR COURT
STATE
　VS.　　　　　　　JULY 19, 1970
JACK SHARP

Report of Violation of Probation

At a criminal session of the Superior Court held in Hartford County on September 25, 1967, Jack Sharp was convicted of the crime of Pool Selling and was sentenced by the Court to be confined in the County Jail for the period of one (1) year, but execution of said sentence was suspended, and he was placed on probation for two (2) years, sentence to take effect at the expiration of sentence in Docket Number 34112.

Sharp's probation took effect August 8, 1968, the date of his release from the Hartford County Jail. On July 13, 1969, in the Hartford Police Court, a charge of Breach of Peace against Jack Sharp was Nolled. This charge concerned an argument that occurred on the street in front of Sharp's residence between Sharp and his girl friend on July 10, 1969. In Court, the girl would not testify against him and the nolle resulted.

On December 15, 1969, in the Town of Manchester, Connecticut, Jack Sharp was arrested on a charge of Breach of Peace and, again, this concerned an argument with his girl friend. The whole situation was observed by a Manchester police officer who made the arrest. On December 21, 1969 in the Manchester Town Court, the charges against Sharp were Nolled.

On January 5, 1970, Sharp was arrested by officers of the Manchester Police Department at the home of his girl friend, in Manchester, Connecticut. It had been thoroughly explained to Sharp by his Probation Officer, Mr. Clark, on December 14, 1969, that he was to stay away from this girl since she had been in the probation office and had lodged a formal complaint about his constant harassment and continuous abuse. On January 25, 1970, in the Manchester Town Court, the charge of Breach of Peace against Jack Sharp was Nolled. On this same date, January 25, 1970, Sharp was in the probation office with his attorney, Harry

Gale of Manchester, and was again told to refrain from any contact or communication with this girl.

Since that time, this girl has attempted to lead a life of her own and go out with other men. This man has followed her, and has made threats to men who have dated her, and has also continued to call her at her job during the day.

On June 18, 1970, in Misquamicut, Rhode Island, Jack Sharp, was arrested by officers of the Westerly, Rhode Island Police Department and charged with Assault. This offense involved the same girl, who had been spending the weekend in Westerly, and about whom Sharp had been warned on previous occasions. At this time, Sharp was staying in the Andrea Hotel, under an assumed name, and was driving a Ford automobile with Florida registration. It should also be noted, that on the evening of June 17, 1970, Sharp had been observed in the vicinity of this girl's home in Manchester, snooping around the house and the police were notified. At the time of this last arrest, Sharp was outside the State of Connecticut, without the permission of the probation officer, and was further in violation of his probation by again bothering this woman.

Therefore, in the judgment of the undersigned Probation Officer, Jack Sharp has violated the terms of this Probation and said Officer has arrested Jack Sharp and has him before the Court for further disposition.

Respectfully submitted,

Terrance Clarke
Chief Probation Officer

Addendum to Probation Violation Report

An additional complaint was received by the Probation Department in regard to this man's activities on July 18, 1970, and, as a result, the area in the vicinity of this girl's home was placed under surveillance. On Wednesday, July 20, 1970, at 7:45 p.m., Jack Sharp was observed on North Main Street, in the Buckland area of Manchester, approximately a half-block from this girl's residence. He was operating a 1960 Ford Thunderbird, color white, Connecticut Dealer's registration FX308.

At 8:08 p.m., he again drove by the same location and, at this time, was followed briefly by the undersigned officer. He was not stopped and questioned at this time in regard to his activities, but his presence in such close proximity to this girl's home would indicate that he is continuing in the same pattern of behavior as previously described in this report.

Respectfully submitted,

Terrance Clarke
Chief Probation Officer
July 21, 1970

The Hearing

No. 50912
STATE   :   SUPERIOR COURT
V.   :   HARTFORD COUNTY
JACK SHARP   :   JULY 29, 1970

Before Hon. Charles J. Hone, Judge

Appearances:

John D. Level, Esq. . . . . . . For the State
David D. Barnes, Esq. . . . . For the Defendant

MR. LEVEL: Your Honor please, in 50912, Jack Sharp, another report of violation of probation. He is represented by Mr. Barnes.

THE COURT: You are familiar with the contents of the report I take it, Counsel?

MR. BARNES: Yes, I am, Your Honor, and it is because of the contents of this report and two other circumstances that I would like to request a continuance. You see, Your Honor, this man was picked up and arrested this week. After he was released on bond I immediately contacted the Probation Department in order to discuss and find out what the contents of this report would be in order to prepare myself for today. I have found there have been some glaring inaccuracies which the Probation Department agrees with me in this report. For example, an allegation in there that he was arrested in Misquamicut, Rhode Island, and charged with assault. None of this is true, and I have begun an investigation which would make me believe I could produce other evidence which would show further inaccuracies as far as this report is concerned, and for that reason, Your Honor, I ask Your Honor's indulgence for a continuance in order to complete my investigation in order to get a full and accurate account of this situation.

MR. LEVEL: The report had many inaccuracies?

MR. CAHIL: On page two, referring to an arrest for assault in Misquamicut, there is an error. The reports from the Westerly police indicate this girl involved made a complaint of assault and as a result of this complaint the accused here was apprehended by the police as he was leaving the area, and at that time the complainant and the accused gave statements to the police and he was arrested. He was not charged with assault as such.

MR. LEVEL: That is the only error?

MR. CAHIL: That I know of. Does Mr. Barnes wish to point out the errors?

MR. BARNES: The only one I know of now, Your Honor. Frankly, there is a common denominator in the other three basic allegations involving the specific woman as far as the breach of peace is concerned, and for that reason I am asking for an opportunity to complete my investigation. I feel if there was room for error in one area in this report it is possible there might have been error elsewhere.

THE COURT: Of course, it is only a possibility, but should this be continued what assurance does the Court have that there wouldn't be a repetition of the annoyance of this young lady?

MR. BARNES: Well, Your Honor, basically I have learned in the last two or three days that there is a serious question as to whether or not this lady has been annoyed. There has been a reliance upon some telephone calls which I don't think are too conclusive. The only assurance I could give the Court is that he has stated to me, and I am inclined to believe him, that if I am given the opportunity for a reasonable amount of time, Mr. Sharp has told me he won't be near the neighborhood or near the individual in question.

THE COURT: Mr. Level, do you have any comment on this request?

MR. LEVEL: Well, Your Honor, this conduct referred to in the probation report apparently is not denied. There is no question he was in Rhode Island which is out of the state without permission, and there is no question of the arrest that had taken place in Manchester, and apparently has been going on since it started last December.

MR. BARNES: May it please Your Honor, I might also point out as to the matter of the Rhode Island incident, given the amount of time that you would consider reasonable, I hope to be able to establish there was a consent for the Rhode Island trip.

THE COURT: From the Probation Department?

MR. BARNES: Yes.

MR. CAHIL: I would be glad to answer any questions Mr. Barnes has. Of the earlier things in the report the case was nolled in the Manchester Court. The accused was shown consideration at that time in as much as he was not brought before this Court for violation of probation. On January 25th he appeared in the Manchester Court and was represented by Harold Grayson of Manchester, and that is the time Mr. Grayson and the defendant came to my office. At that time he was again cautioned and told and warned to stay away from the complainant, and in front of Mr. Grayson this information was passed out so that he knew he was not to be in that area.

Now, the question that Mr. Barnes may have in his mind as far as Rhode Island is concerned, many times the probation officer gives permission to a probationer to leave the state if it is for some emergency and can't contact the probation officer. However, prior to the day that he went to Rhode Island this officer was in his office every day and there was no request made to go to Rhode Island.

Now, after his return from Rhode Island he stated he had gone there to look for a cottage for his wife and for his children. Well, I don't deny that he might have gone for that purpose. However, he happened to go to the Andrea Hotel where this complainant again was staying. He went—what he tells me in his own words—he went to the cocktail lounge, saw the girl there. He left and returned, saw her again. He later gave a note to two youngsters to notify this complainant that Mr. Such-and-Such would be in room four, not using his own name. Now, it was after that that the alleged altercation took place there.

THE COURT: This man is married?

MR. BARNES: Divorced, Your Honor.

MR. CAHIL: At that time I had considered again bringing him before the Court because of the series of things that had happened. We had other calls from Mr. Kay in Farmington that Jack Sharp had been making several calls to his wife stating he had been out with her. We don't have proof of this. That is why it is not in the report. That was also made to Captain Dome of the State Police Department. The complaining witness in this case has also complained to Captain Dome of the State Police Department.

I had recently gone away to school for a month and upon my return Mr. Clark had noted that he had received a complaint from somebody else who had gone out with this girl; he was being bothered by Mr. Sharp. Therefore, on the evening of July 18th, I believe, it is stated in the report Mr. Clark, our senior probation officer here, drove to the area in which this complainant lives, the girl involved, and he saw Mr. Sharp on two occasions in the area.

MR. BARNES: If it pleases Your Honor, I am not arguing now, but in requesting this continuance I should like to point this out also; in the brief time, two or three days, since I've been acquainted with the situation I have been given enough information now so that if given an opportunity to pursue it, it is reasonable to assume we will be able to show the complaints that have been made by this woman as well as the breaches of the peace which are referred to herein all involving this woman, all of which were nolled, involve very possibly and very probably malicious conduct on her part in an effort to get this man into trouble with the Probation Department. For that reason also I ask for a continuance, Your Honor.

THE COURT: Well, it certainly appears to be on this report there has been a violation of his probation. Now, I am not going to foreclose you from an opportunity to call it to the Court's attention if you think this report is erroneous as indicated; otherwise, he had admitted error with respect to the situation of assault at Misquamicut. I am not going to turn this man free at this point in view of this indication here.

It is the order of the Court that the execution of the sentence as imposed, that the probation be revoked and the execution be put in effect, and it may appear on the record that counsel may apply to the Court at any time for a review of this order of the Court in the event that you find the situation as reported by the probation officer with the exception indicated is inaccurate.

MR. BARNES: Well, Your Honor, I wonder if it is possible, this man is divorced but he is supporting his wife and two children who are living in New Britain, and he has been in business ever since he's been on probation. I wonder if it is possible for a twenty-four hour stay of the execution in order that he might have that time to straighten out his business affairs.

MR. LEVEL: This has been pending for about ten days, Your Honor. He's been aware of the situation. He's been in jail and made bond. I don't see that this twenty-four hour continuance is required.

MR. BARNES: I beg to differ, Mr. Level, but this matter came up Tuesday of this week.

THE COURT: He has known since Tuesday. What sort of business is he in that requires—

MR. BARNES: He is in the automobile business, Your Honor. He has an apartment. He has furnishings, clothing to dispose of.

MR. LEVEL: He posted a $5,000 bond, Your Honor, for his appearance in this hearing. His bondsman is here.

THE COURT: This is Friday; I have in mind granting a stay until Monday at 12 o'clock in view of the bond, $5,000 bond.

MR. LEVEL: I want to be sure the bond is in effect. The bondsman is here.

THE COURT: The bondsman, may he come forward. May I have your name for the record?

MR. RASSO: Silvio Rasso.

THE COURT: You are the bondsman in this matter?

MR. RASSO: Yes, Your Honor.

THE COURT: $5,000 bond?

MR. RASSO: Yes, Your Honor.

THE COURT: You heard what has gone on here in Court, the request of counsel for this accused, that the accused have a stay of execution on this matter until Monday at twelve o'clock at which time he is to report to the County Jail, and if the case is continued for execution, well, we are suspending execution since we are revoking the probation, if this matter be continued with that understanding he will report to the County Jail at twelve o'clock, that that same $5,000 bond stay in effect for carrying out that order and his appearance either at the jail at that time or in this court at that time. Are you agreeable to that?

MR. RASSO: Yes, Your Honor.

THE COURT: Very well. Then I will grant a stay of the order of the Court with respect to revocation of probation until Monday at twelve o'clock, at which time the accused is to report to the County Jail under this same bond, and of course it is a definite condition of this continuance there be no attempt whatsoever to communicate with the young lady involved in the situation.

MR. BARNES: Thank you very much, Your Honor.

MEMPA V. RHAY
389 U.S. 128 (1967)
Supreme Court of the United States

MR. JUSTICE MARSHALL delivered the opinion of the Court.

These consolidated cases raise the question of the extent of the right to counsel at the time of sentencing where the sentencing has been deferred subject to probation.

Petitioner Jerry Douglas Mempa was convicted in the Spokane County Superior Court on June 17, 1959, of the offense of "joyriding," Wash. Rev. Code § 9.54.020. This conviction was based on his plea of guilty entered with the advice of court-appointed counsel. He was then placed on probation for two years on the condition, *inter alia*, that he first spend 30 days in the county jail, and the imposition of sentence was deferred pursuant to Wash. Rev. Code §§ 9.95.200, 9.95.210.[1]

About four months later the Spokane County prosecuting attorney moved to have petitioner's probation revoked on the ground that he had been involved in a burglary on September 15, 1959. A hearing was held in the Spokane County Superior Court on October 23, 1959. Petitioner Mempa, who was 17 years old at the time, was accompanied to the hearing by his stepfather. He was represented by counsel and was not asked whether he wished to have counsel appointed for him. Nor was any inquiry made concerning the appointed counsel who had previously represented him.

At the hearing Mempa was asked if it was true that he had been involved in the alleged burglary and he answered in the affirmative. A probation officer testified without cross-examination that according to his information petitioner had been involved in the burglary and had previously denied participation in it. Without asking petitioner if he had anything to say or any evidence to supply, the court immediately entered an order revoking petitioner's probation and then sentenced him to 10 years in the penitentiary, but stated that it would recommend to the parole board that Mempa be required to serve only a year.[2]

In 1965 Mempa filed a *pro se* petition for a writ of habeas corpus with the Washington Supreme Court, claiming that he had been deprived of his right to counsel at the proceeding at which his probation was revoked and sentence imposed. The Washington Supreme Court denied the petition on June 23, 1966, by a vote of six to three. *Mempa* v. *Rhay*, 68 Wash. 2d 882, 416 P. 2d 104. We granted certiorari to consider the questions raised. 386 U.S. 907 (1967).

Petitioner William Earl Walkling was convicted in the Thurston County Superior Court on October 29, 1962, of burglary in the second degree on the basis of his plea of guilty entered with the advice of his retained counsel. He was placed on probation for three years and the imposition of sentence was deferred. As conditions of his probation he was required to serve 90 days in the county jail and make restitution. On May 2, 1963, a bench warrant for his arrest was issued based on a report that he had violated the terms of his probation and had left the State.

On February 24, 1964, Walkling was arrested and charged with forgery and grand larceny. After being transferred back to Thurston County he was brought before the court on May 12, 1964, for a hearing on the petition by the prosecuting attorney to revoke his probation. Petitioner then requested a continuance to enable him to retain counsel and was granted a week. On May 18, 1964, the hearing was called and Walkling appeared without a lawyer. He informed the court that he had retained an attorney who was supposed to be present. After waiting for 15 minutes the court went ahead with the hearing in the absence of petitioner's counsel. He was not offered appointed counsel and would not have had counsel appointed for him had he requested it. Whether he made such a request does not appear from the record.

At the hearing a probation officer presented hearsay testimony to the effect that petitioner had committed the acts alleged in the 14 separate counts of forgery and 14 separate counts of grand larceny that had been charged against petitioner previously at the time of his arrest. The court thereupon revoked probation and imposed the maximum sentence of 15 years on Walkling on his prior second degree burglary conviction. Because of the failure of the State to keep a record of the proceeding, nothing is known as to whether Walkling was advised of his right to appeal. He did not, however, take an appeal.

In May 1966 Walkling filed a habeas corpus petition with the Washington Supreme Court, claiming denial of his right to counsel at the combined probation revocation and sentencing proceeding. The petition was denied on the authority of the prior decision in *Mempa* v. *Rhay, supra*. We granted certiorari, 386 U.S. 907 (1967), and the cases were consolidated for argument.

---

[1] The State suggests that the Supreme Court of Washington was in error in stating that Mempa received a deferred rather than a suspended sentence, but we accept that court's characterization of the sentence as supported by the record.

[2] Under Washington procedure the trial judge is required by statute to impose the maximum sentence provided by law for the offense, Wash. Rev. Code § 9.95.010, but is also required, along with the prosecuting attorney, to make a recommendation to the parole board of the time that the defendant should serve accompanied by a statement of the facts concerning the crime and any other information about the defendant deemed relevant. Wash. Rev. Code § 9.95.030. However, it is the parole board that actually determines the time to be served. Wash. Rev. Code § 9.95.040.

In 1948 this Court held in *Townsend* v. *Burke,* 334 U.S. 736, that the absence of counsel during sentencing after a plea of guilty coupled with "assumptions concerning his criminal record which were materially untrue" deprived the defendant in that case of due process. Mr. Justice Jackson there stated in conclusion, "In this case, counsel might not have changed the sentence, but he could have taken steps to see that the conviction and sentence were not predicated on misinformation or misreading of court records, a requirement of fair play which absence of counsel withheld from this prisoner." *Id.*, at 741. Then in *Moore* v. *Michigan,* 355 U.S. 155 (1957), where a denial of due process was found when the defendant did not intelligently and understandingly waive counsel before entering a plea of guilty, this Court emphasized the prejudice stemming from the absence of counsel at the hearing on the degree of the crime following entry of the guilty plea and stated, "The right to counsel is not a right confined to representation during the trial on the merits." *Id.*, at 160.

In *Hamilton* v. *Alabama,* 368 U.S. 52 (1961), it was held that failure to appoint counsel at arraignment deprived the petitioner of due process, notwithstanding the fact that he simply pleaded not guilty at that time, because under Alabama law certain defenses had to be raised then or be abandoned. See also *Reece* v. *Georgia,* 350 U.S. 85 (1955), and *White* v. *Maryland,* 373 U.S. 59 (1963).

All the foregoing cases, with the exception of *White,* were decided during the reign of *Betts* v. *Brady,* 316 U.S. 455 (1942), and accordingly relied on various "special circumstances" to make the right to counsel applicable. In *Gideon* v. *Wainwright,* 372 U.S. 335 (1963), however, *Betts* was overruled and this Court held that the Sixth Amendment as applied through the Due Process Clause of the Fourteenth Amendment was applicable to the States and, accordingly, that there was an absolute right to appointment of counsel in felony cases.

There was no occasion in *Gideon* to enumerate the various stages in a criminal proceeding at which counsel was required, but *Townsend, Moore,* and *Hamilton,* when the *Betts* requirement of special circumstances is stripped away by *Gideon,* clearly stand for the proposition that appointment of counsel for an indigent is required at every stage of a criminal proceeding where substantial rights of a criminal accused may be affected. In particular, *Townsend* v. *Burke, supra,* illustrates the critical nature of sentencing in a criminal case and might well be considered to support by itself a holding that the right to counsel applies at sentencing.[3] Many lower courts have concluded that the Sixth Amendment right to counsel extends to sentencing in federal cases.

The State, however, argues that the petitioners were sentenced at the time they were originally placed on probation and that the imposition of sentence following probation revocation is, in effect, a mere formality constituting part of the probation revocation proceeding. It is true that sentencing in Washington offers fewer opportunities for the exercise of judicial discretion than in many other jurisdictions. The applicable statute requires the trial judge in all cases to sentence the convicted person to the maximum term provided by law for the offense of which he was convicted. Wash. Rev. Code § 9.95.010. The actual determination of the length of time to be served is to be made by the Board of Prison Terms and Paroles within six months after the convicted person is admitted to prison. Wash. Rev. Code § 9.95.040.

On the other hand, the sentencing judge is required by statute, together with the prosecutor, to furnish the Board with a recommendation as to the length of time that the person should serve, in addition to supplying it with various information about the circumstances of the crime and the character of the individual. Wash. Rev. Code § 9.95.030. We were informed during oral argument that the Board places considerable weight on these recommendations, although it is in no way bound by them. Obviously to the extent such recommendations are influential in determining the resulting sentence, the necessity for the aid of counsel in marshaling the facts, introducing evidence of mitigating circumstances and in general aiding and assisting the defendant to present his case as to sentence is apparent.

Even more important in a case such as this is the fact that certain legal rights may be lost if not exercised at this stage. For one, Washington law provides that an appeal in a case involving a plea of guilty followed by probation can only be taken after sentence is imposed following revocation of probation. *State* v. *Farmer,* 39 Wash. 2d 675, 237 P. 2d 734 (1951). Therefore in a case where an accused agreed to plead guilty, although he had a valid defense, because he was offered probation, ab-

---

[3] See Kadish, The Advocate and the Expert—Counsel in the Peno-Correctional Process, 45 Minn. L. Rev. 803, 806 (1961).

sence of counsel at the imposition of the deferred sentence might well result in loss of the right to appeal. While ordinarily appeals from a plea of guilty are less frequent than those following a trial on the merits, the incidence of improperly obtained guilty pleas is not so slight as to be capable of being characterized as *de minimis*.

Likewise the Washington statutes provide that a plea of guilty can be withdrawn at any time prior to the imposition of sentence, Wash. Rev. Code § 10.40.175, *State* v. *Farmer, supra,* if the trial judge in his discretion finds that the ends of justice will be served, *State* v. *Shannon,* 60 Wash. 2d 883, 376 P. 2d 646 (1962). Without undertaking to catalog the various situations in which a lawyer could be of substantial assistance to a defendant in such a case, it can be reiterated that a plea of guilty might well be improperly obtained by the promise to have a defendant placed on the very probation the revocation of which furnishes the occasion for desiring to withdraw the plea. An uncounseled defendant might very likely be unaware of this opportunity.

The two foregoing factors assume increased significance when it is considered that, as happened in these two cases, the eventual imposition of sentence on the prior plea of guilty is based on the alleged commission of offenses for which the accused is never tried.

In sum, we do not question the authority of the State of Washington to provide for a deferred sentencing procedure coupled with its probation provisions. Indeed, it appears to be an enlightened step forward. All we decide here is that a lawyer must be afforded at this proceeding whether it be labeled a revocation of probation or a deferred sentencing. We assume that counsel appointed for the purpose of the trial or guilty plea would not be unduly burdened by being requested to follow through at the deferred sentencing stage of the proceeding.

The judgments below are reversed and the cases are remanded for further proceedings not inconsistent with this opinion.

Reversed and remanded.

NOTES

Due Process in Probation Revocation

Note 1.

ESCOE V. ZERBST
295 U.S. 490 (1935)
Supreme Court of the United States

MR. JUSTICE CARDOZO delivered the opinion of the Court.

Petitioner was convicted of a crime in the United States District Court for the Eastern District of Texas after indictment and a plea of guilty. He was sentenced, October 10, 1932, to imprisonment for four and a half years in the Penitentiary at Leavenworth, Kansas. On the same day the sentence was suspended for five years upon conditions of probation, and the defendant (the petitioner in this court) was placed in charge of the District Probation Officer for that length of time. One of the conditions was that the probationer would refrain from the violation of any state or federal penal laws. Another was that he would live "a clean, honest and temperate life."

In July, 1933, information was conveyed to the District Probation Officer that petitioner had broken these conditions. In a letter written by his father he was charged with drunkenness and the forgery of two checks. The officer made report of this information to the District Judge and requested a revocation of the order for suspension of sentence. On July 29, 1933, the District Judge issued a mandate for a warrant of arrest. On August 5, he signed an order that the suspension be revoked and that the defendant be committed to prison to serve the stated term. Upon arrest under the warrant the defendant was not brought by his custodian before any court or judge. He was transported at once to the penitentiary at Leavenworth, Kansas, and there imprisoned. Later, in December, 1933, he filed a petition for a writ of *habeas corpus* in the United States District Court for the District of Kansas, contending that his imprisonment was unlawful for the reason that probation had been ended without the opportunity for a hearing made necessary by statute. The District Judge dismissed the application for the writ, and the Circuit Court of Appeals for the Tenth Circuit affirmed his order. 74 F. (2d) 924. A writ of certiorari issued from this court. . . .

Under the statute as amended as well as in its original form, the probationer "shall forthwith be taken before the court." This mandate was disobeyed. The probationer, instead of being brought before the court which had imposed the sentence, was taken to a prison beyond the territorial limits of that court and kept there in confinement without the opportunity for a hearing. For this denial of a legal privilege the commitment may not stand.

In thus holding we do not accept the petitioner's contention that the privilege has a basis in the Constitution, apart from any statute. Probation or suspension of sentence comes as an act of grace to one convicted of a crime, and may be coupled with such conditions in respect of its duration as Congress may impose. *Burns* v. *United States,* 287 U.S. 216. But the power of the lawmakers to dispense with notice or a hearing as part of the procedure of probation does not mean that a like dispensing power, in opposition to the will of Congress, has been confided to the courts. The privilege is no less real because its source is in the statute rather than in the Fifth Amendment. If the statement of the Congress that the probationer shall be brought before the court is command and not advice, it defines and conditions power. *French* v. *Edwards,* 13 Wall. 506, 511. The revocation is invalid unless the command has been obeyed. . . .

The judgment is reversed and the cause remanded with instructions that the writ must be sustained and the prisoner discharged.

Reversed.

Note 2.

HAHN v. BURKE
430 F.2d 100 (1970) *cert. den.* 402 U.S. 933 (1971)
United States Court of Appeals, Seventh Circuit

KERNER, Circuit Judge.

This is an appeal from the district court's denial of a petition, pursuant to 28 U.S.C. § 2254 attacking petitioner's Wisconsin incarceration. Petitioner Frank Hahn pled guilty to a charge of burglary on September 12, 1964, and was sentenced to five years in the state prison for the burglary charge and an additional offense of trying to escape from the County Jail. The execution of petitioner's sentence was stayed, however, and he was placed on probation for a five-year period. Petitioner's probation was revoked without a hearing on December 4, 1964, on the basis that he had violated its terms by absconding to California, and upon his return to Wisconsin in September of 1965, petitioner was confined to the Wisconsin State prison. . . .

Petitioner's final contention is that the failure to provide a hearing upon revocation of his probation violated his constitutional rights. The conditions of petitioner's probation were not clear. It appears that petitioner was to return to Illinois, where his mother lived, and practice his trade of barbering. Illinois, however, would not accept petitioner as a probationer, and petitioner claims that because he interpreted his probation as being contingent on staying out of Wisconsin, he believed he could not return to Wisconsin and left for California. The State Department of Public Welfare, without a hearing or without giving petitioner any opportunity to be heard, revoked his probation.

We hold the revocation of petitioner's probation was violative of the basic requirements of due process. While we are mindful that probation is a privilege and not a right and is subject to the conditions of the court, *see* Escoe v. Zerbst, 295 U.S. 490, (1935), essential procedural due process no longer turns on the distinction between a privilege and a right. *See* Goldberg v. Kelly, 397 U.S. 254, (May 23, 1970); Shapiro v. Thompson, 394 U.S. 618, (1969); Sherbert v. Verner, 374 U.S. 398, (1963); Slochower v. Board of Higher Education, 350 U.S. 551, (1956). *See also* Von Alstyne, The Demise of the Right-Privilege Distinction in Constitutional Law, 81 Harv. L. Rev. 1439 (1967–8).

The United States Supreme Court in a recent decision holding that welfare recipients were entitled to a hearing before termination of public assistance payments stated:

> The extent to which procedural due process must be afforded the recipient is influenced by the extent to which he may be "condemned to suffer grievous loss" Joint Anti-Fascist Refugee Committee v. McGrath, 341 U.S. 123, 168, 71 S.Ct. 624, 95 L.Ed. 817 (1951) (Frankfurter, J., concurring) and depends upon whether the recipient's interest in avoiding that loss outweighs the governmental interest in summary adjudication. Goldberg v. Kelly, *supra,* 90 S.Ct. at 1017–1018. . . .

The immediacy of desperation is at the very least equally as strong in the case of a probationer who is literally being denied his freedom. Weighing the "extent to which he [the petitioner] may be condemned to grievous loss'" against "the governmental interest in summary adjudication" we find the petitioner's loss of freedom to outweigh the added state burden of providing a limited hearing to allow petitioner to be confronted with his probation violation and to be heard.

The state need not grant probation, but if it does so, it should not be able to arbitrarily revoke such probation without giving petitioner a reasonable opportunity to explain away the accusation that he had violated the conditions upon which his probation was granted. *See*

Fleenor v. Hammond, 116 F.2d 982 (6th Cir. 1941); *see also* ALI Model Penal Code § 301.4 (1962); ABA Sentencing Alternatives and Procedures § 5.5(c); Study Draft of a New Federal Criminal Code, published June 8, 1970, by the National Commission on Reform of Federal Criminal Laws, § 3104(2) at 277–78; 1 Davis Administrative Law Treatise § 716, pp. 174–81 (1965 Supp.). When the state created conditions of probation it impliedly agreed to continue petitioner's probation as long as the conditions were satisfied. To allow the state to summarily revoke the petitioner's probation without a hearing to determine if the conditions upon which the probation was granted have been violated, is state action inconsistent with the due process guarantees of the fourteenth amendment.

In addition to the right-privilege dichotomy, some courts have based their denial of a hearing on the theory that probation is a form of contract. Consequently, if one condition of the probation contract is the possibility of summary revocation, the probationer or parolee cannot complain if that action is taken. We find this theory unpersuasive. Probation is in fact not a contract. The probationer does not enter into the agreement on an equal status with the state. As Judge Celebrezze stated in his excellent dissenting opinion in Rose v. Haskins, 388 F.2d at 100, finding that due process required a hearing in the case of a parole revocation:

> [I]f the negative pregnant that is implicit in the contract theory is true (that if the parolee had not agreed to summary revocation he would have had the right to hearing), then that theory has recognized that a right to a hearing is inherent in the revocation situation. Waiver of such a valuable right is not to be lightly determined, and when the "choice" of the parolee is to remain in prison or accept such a burdensome provision, the "choice" to accept parole can hardly be termed a voluntary waiver of a hearing.

We agree.

We are cognizant of the Supreme Court's opinion in Escoe v. Zerbst, 295 U.S. 490, (1935), holding that there is no constitutional right to a hearing in the case of probation revocation. . . .

The Court in *Escoe*, however, did in fact grant petitioner a hearing pursuant to a Congressional statute. We interpret the dicta in *Escoe* to indicate only that the Court's opinion was not based on a constitutional right to a hearing and not as a binding precedented rejection of such a constitutional right. Our interpretation of the *Escoe* dicta coupled with the fact that the basis of the dicta—privilege-right distinction—has all but been obliterated by recent Supreme Court opinions, see page 103 *supra,* moves us to hold that fundamental constitutional requirements of due process necessitate a limited hearing prior to a probation revocation.

> No society is free when the government makes one person's liberty depend upon the arbitrary will of another. Shaughnessy v. United States ex rel. Mezei, 345 U.S. 206, 217, (1953). Black, J., dissenting. . . .

For the foregoing reasons, we hold petitioner's probation revocation to be a nullity and therefore reverse and remand to the district court with directions to expunge the revocation from petitioner's record. The Wisconsin court may, however, hold a probation revocation hearing at this time if it has jurisdiction over probationer.

Reversed and remanded.

Note 3.

GOLDBERG V. KELLY
397 U.S. 254 (1970)
Supreme Court of the United States

MR. JUSTICE BRENNAN delivered the opinion of the Court.

The question for decision is whether a State that terminates public assistance payments to a particular recipient without affording him the opportunity for an evidentiary hearing prior to termination denies the recipient procedural due process in violation of the Due Process Clause of the Fourteenth Amendment. . . .

The constitutional issue to be decided, therefore, is the narrow one whether the Due Process Clause requires that the recipient be afforded an evidentiary hearing *before* the termination of benefits. The District Court held that only a pre-termination evidentiary hearing would satisfy the constitutional command, and rejected the argument of the state and city officials that the combination of the post-termination "fair hearing" with the informal pre-termination review disposed of all due process claims.

. . . We affirm.

Appellant does not contend that procedural due process is not applicable to the termination of welfare benefits. Such benefits are a matter of statutory entitlement for persons qualified to receive them. Their termination involves state action that adjudicates important rights. The constitutional challenge cannot be answered by an argument that public assistance benefits are "a 'privilege' and not a 'right.'" *Shapiro* v. *Thompson,* 394 U.S. 618, 627 n. 6 (1969). Relevant constitutional restraints apply as much to the withdrawal of public assistance benefits as to disqualification for unemployment compensation, *Sherbert* v. *Verner,* 374 U.S. 398 (1963); or to denial of a tax exemption, *Speiser* v. *Randall,* 357 U.S. 513 (1958); or to discharge from public employment, *Slochower* v. *Board of Higher Education,* 350 U.S. 551 (1956). The extent to which procedural due process must be afforded the recipient is influenced by the extent to which he may be "condemned to suffer grievous loss," *Joint Anti-Fascist Refugee Committee* v. *McGrath,* 341 U.S. 123, 168 (1951) (Frankfurter, J., concurring), and depends upon whether the recipient's interest in avoiding that loss outweighs the governmental interest in summary adjudication. Accordingly, as we said in *Cafeteria & Restaurant Workers Union* v. *McElroy,* 367 U.S. 886, 895 (1961), "consideration of what procedures due process may require under any given set of circumstances must begin with a determination of the precise nature of the government function involved as well as of the private interest that has been affected by governmental action." See also *Hannah* v. *Larche,* 363 U.S. 420, 440, 442 (1960). . . .

We also agree with the District Court, however, that the pre-termination hearing need not take the form of a judicial or quasi-judicial trial. We bear in mind that the statutory "fair hearing" will provide the recipient with a full administrative review. Accordingly, the pre-termination hearing has one function only: to produce an initial determination of the validity of the welfare department's grounds for discontinuance of payments in order to protect a recipient against an erroneous termination of his benefits. Cf. *Sniadach* v. *Family Finance Corp.,* 395 U.S. 337, 343 (1969) (HARLAN, J., concurring). Thus, a complete record and a comprehensive opinion, which would serve primarily to facilitate judicial review and to guide future decisions, need not be provided at the pre-termination stage. We recognize, too, that both welfare authorities and recipients have an interest in relatively speedy resolution of questions of eligibility, that they are used to dealing with one another informally, and that some welfare departments have very burdensome caseloads. These considerations justify the limitation of the pre-termination hearing to minimum procedural safeguards, adapted to the particular characteristics of welfare recipients, and to the limited nature of the controversies to be resolved. We wish to add that we, no less than the dissenters, recognize the importance of not imposing upon the States or the Federal Government in this developing field of law any procedural requirements beyond those demanded by rudimentary due process.

"The fundamental requisite of due process of law is the opportunity to be heard." *Grannis* v. *Ordean,* 234 U.S. 385, 394 (1914). The hearing must be "at a meaningful time and in a meaningful manner." *Armstrong* v. *Manzo,* 380 U.S. 545, 552 (1965). In the present context these principles require that a recipient have timely and adequate notice detailing the reasons for a proposed termination, and an effective opportunity to defend by confronting any adverse witnesses and by presenting his own arguments and evidence orally. These rights are important in cases such as those before us, where recipients have challenged proposed terminations as resting on incorrect or misleading factual premises or on misapplication of rules or policies to the facts of particular cases. . . .

The city's procedures presently do not permit recipients to appear personally with or without counsel before the official who finally determines continued eligibility. Thus a recipient is not permitted to present evidence to that official orally, or to confront or cross-examine adverse witnesses. These omissions are fatal to the constitutional adequacy of the procedures.

The opportunity to be heard must be tailored to the capacities and circumstances of those who are to be heard. It is not enough that a welfare recipient may present his position to the decision maker in writing or secondhand through his caseworker. Written submissions are an unrealistic option for most recipients, who lack the educational attainment necessary to write effectively and who cannot obtain professional assistance. Moreover, written submissions do not afford the flexibility of oral presentations; they do not permit the recipient to mold his argument to the issues the decision maker appears to regard as important. Particularly where credibility and veracity are at issue, as they must be in many termination proceedings, written submissions are a wholly unsatisfactory basis for decision.

The secondhand presentation to the decisionmaker by the caseworker has its own deficiencies; since the caseworker usually gathers the facts upon which the charge of ineligibility rests, the presentation of the recipient's side of the controversy cannot safely be left to him. Therefore a recipient must be allowed to state his position orally. Informal procedures will suffice; in this context due process does not require a particular order of proof or mode of offering evidence. Cf. HEW Handbook, pt. IV, § 6400 (a).

In almost every setting where important decisions turn on questions of fact, due process requires an opportunity to confront and cross-examine adverse witnesses. *E.g., ICC* v. *Louisville & N. R. Co.*, 227 U.S. 88, 93–94 (1913); *Willner* v. *Committee on Character & Fitness*, 373 U.S. 96, 103–104 (1963). What we said in *Greene* v. *McElroy*, 360 U.S. 474, 496–497 (1959), is particularly pertinent here:

> Certain principles have remained relatively immutable in our jurisprudence. One of these is that where governmental action seriously injures an individual, and the reasonableness of the action depends on fact findings, the evidence used to prove the Government's case must be disclosed to the individual so that he has an opportunity to show that it is untrue. While this is important in the case of documentary evidence, it is even more important where the evidence consists of the testimony of individuals whose memory might be faulty or who, in fact, might be perjurers or persons motivated by malice, vindictiveness, intolerance, prejudice, or jealousy. We have formalized these protections in the requirements of confrontation and cross-examination. They have ancient roots. They find expression in the Sixth Amendment. . . . This Court has been zealous to protect these rights from erosion. It has spoken out not only in criminal cases, . . . but also in all types of cases where administrative . . . actions were under scrutiny.

Welfare recipients must therefore be given an opportunity to confront and cross-examine the witnesses relied on by the department.

"The right to be heard would be, in many cases, of little avail if it did not comprehend the right to be heard by counsel." *Powell* v. *Alabama*, 287 U.S. 45, 68–69 (1932). We do not say that counsel must be provided at the pre-termination hearing, but only that the recipient must be allowed to retain an attorney if he so desires. Counsel can help delineate the issues, present the factual contentions in an orderly manner, conduct cross-examination and generally safeguard the interests of the recipient. We do not anticipate that this assistance will unduly prolong or otherwise encumber the hearing. Evidently HEW has reached the same conclusion. See 45 CFR § 205.10, 34 Fed. Reg. 1144 (1969); 45 CFR § 220.25, 34 Fed. Reg. 13595 (1969).

Finally, the decisionmaker's conclusion as to a recipient's eligibility must rely solely on the legal rules and evidence adduced at the hearing. *Ohio Bell Tel. Co.* v. *PUC*, 301 U.S. 292 (1937); *United States* v. *Abilene & S. R. Co.*, 265 U.S. 274, 288–289 (1924). To demonstrate compliance with this elementary requirement, the decision maker should state the reasons for his determination and indicate the evidence he relied on, cf. *Wichita R. & Light Co.* v. *PUC*, 260 U.S. 48, 57–59 (1922), though his statement need not amount to a full opinion on even formal findings of fact and conclusions of law. And, of course, an impartial decision maker is essential. Cf. *In re Murchison*, 349 U.S. 133 (1955); *Wong Yang Sung* v. *McGrath*, 339 U.S. 33, 45–46 (1950). We agree with the District Court that prior involvement in some aspects of a case will not necessarily bar a welfare official from acting as a decision maker. He should not, however, have participated in making the determination under review.

Affirmed.

GAGNON V. SCARPELLI
41 U.S.L. WEEK (1973)
Supreme Court of the United States

[REPRINTED INFRA., PAGE 527].

B. Sentences of Imprisonment

1. THE EFFECT OF A GUILTY PLEA: DIFFERENTIAL SENTENCING

Introductory Note:
The Negotiated Plea of Guilty

THE PRESIDENT'S COMMISSION ON LAW ENFORCEMENT AND ADMINISTRATION OF JUSTICE: *Task Force Report: The Courts* 9–10 (1967)

The question of guilt or innocence is not contested in the overwhelming majority of criminal cases. A recent estimate is that guilty pleas account for 90 percent of all convictions; and perhaps as high as 95 percent of misdemeanor convictions. But the Commission has found it difficult to calculate with any degree of certainty the percentage of cases disposed of by guilty plea, since reliable statistical information is limited. Clearly it is very high. The following statistics indicate the number and percentage of guilty plea convictions in trial courts of general jurisdiction in States in which such information was available.

A substantial percentage of guilty pleas are the product of negotiations between the prosecutor and defense counsel or the accused, although again precise data are unavailable. Commonly known as "plea bargaining," this is a process very much like the pretrial settlement of civil cases. It involves discussions looking toward an agreement under which the accused will enter a plea of guilty in exchange for a reduced charge or a favorable sentence recommendation by the prosecutor. Even when there have been no explicit negotiations, defendants relying on prevailing practices often act on the justifiable assumption that those who plead guilty will be sentenced more leniently.

Few practices in the system of criminal justice create a greater sense of unease and suspicion than the negotiated plea of guilty. The correctional needs of the offender and legislative policies reflected in the criminal law appear to be sacrificed to the need for tactical accommodations between the prosecutor and defense counsel. The offense for which guilt is acknowledged and for which the sentence is imposed often appears almost incidental to keeping the business of the courts moving.

The system usually operates in an informal, invisible manner. There is ordinarily no formal recognition that the defendant has been offered an inducement to plead guilty. Although the participants and frequently the judge know that negotiation has taken place, the prosecutor and defendant must ordinarily go through a courtroom ritual in which they deny that the guilty plea is the result of any threat or promise. As a result there is no judicial review of the propriety of the bargain—no check on the amount of pressure put on the defendant to plead guilty. The judge, the public, and sometimes the defendant himself cannot know for certain who got what from whom in exchange for what. The process comes to look less rational, more subject to change factors, to undue pressures, and sometimes to the hint of corruption. Moreover, the defendant may not get the benefit he bargained for. There is no guarantee that the judge will follow the prosecutor's recommendations for lenient sentence. In most instances the defendant does not know what sentence he will receive until he has pleaded

State (1964 statistics unless otherwise indicated)	Total Convictions	Guilty Pleas Number	Percent of Total
California (1965)	30,840	22,817	74.0
Connecticut	1,596	1,494	93.9
District of Columbia (year ending June 30, 1964)	1,115	817	73.3
Hawaii	393	360	91.5
Illinois	5,591	4,768	85.2
Kansas	3,025	2,727	90.2
Massachusetts (1963)	7,790	6,642	85.2
Minnesota (1965)	1,567	1,437	91.7
New York	17,249	16,464	95.5
Pennsylvania (1960)	25,632	17,108	66.8
U.S. District Courts	29,170	26,273	90.2
Average [excluding Pennsylvania][1]			87.0

[1] The Pennsylvania figures have been excluded from the average because they were from an earlier year, and the types of cases included did not appear fully comparable with the others.

guilty and sentence has been imposed. If the defendant is disappointed, he may move to withdraw his plea, but there is no assurance that the motion will be granted, particularly since at the time he tendered his guilty plea, he probably denied the very negotiations he now alleges.

A more fundamental problem with plea bargaining is the propriety of offering the defendant an inducement to surrender his right to trial. This problem becomes increasingly substantial as the prospective reward increases, because the concessions to the defendant become harder to justify on grounds other than expediency. There is always the danger that a defendant who would be found not guilty if he insisted on his right to trial will be induced to plead guilty. The defendant has an absolute right to put the prosecution to its proof, and if too much pressure is brought to discourage the exercise of this right, the integrity of the system, which the court trial is relied upon to vindicate, will not be demonstrated. When the prosecution is not put to its proof and all the evidence is not brought out in open court, the public is not assured that illegalities in law enforcement are revealed and corrected or that the seriousness of the defendant's crimes are shown and adequate punishment imposed. Prosecutors who are overburdened or are insufficiently energetic may compromise cases that call for severe sanctions.

Despite the serious questions raised by a system of negotiated pleas, there are important arguments for preserving it. Our system of criminal justice has come to depend upon a steady flow of guilty pleas. There are simply not enough judges, prosecutors, or defense counsel to operate a system in which most defendants go to trial. Many of the Commission's proposals, such as the recommendation to expand appointment of counsel for the indigent, will strain the available resources for many years. If reliance on trial were increased at this time, it would undoubtedly lower the quality of justice throughout the system. Even were the resources available, there is some question whether a just system would require that they be allocated to providing all defendants with a full trial. Trial as we know it is an elaborate mechanism for finding facts. To use this process in cases where the facts are not really in dispute seems wasteful.

The plea agreement, if carried out, eliminates the risk inherent in all adversary litigation. No matter how strong the evidence may appear and how well prepared and conducted a trial may be, each side must realistically consider the possibility of an unfavorable outcome. At its best the trial process is an imperfect method of factfinding; factors such as the attorney's skill, the availability of witnesses, the judge's attitude, jury vagaries, and luck will influence the result. Each side is interested in limiting these inherent litigation risks. In addition, the concessions of a negotiated plea are also commonly used by prosecutors when a defendant cooperates wth law enforcement agencies by furnishing information or testimony against other offenders.

Confining trials to cases involving substantial issues may also help to preserve the significance of the presumption of innocence and the requirement of proof beyond a reasonable doubt. If trial were to become routine even in cases in which there is no substantial issue of guilt, the overwhelming statistical probability of guilt might incline judges and jurors to be more skeptical of the defense than at present.

Because of the invisibility of the plea bargaining system, the essential issues involved have generally not received adequate consideration by the courts. Some courts have, however, begun to look at the system for what it is and to focus on the need to regulate it to assure that neither public nor private interests are sacrificed. As a Federal Court of Appeals noted in a recent case:

> In a sense, it can be said that most guilty pleas are the result of a "bargain" with the prosecutor. But this, standing alone, does not vitiate such pleas. A guilty defendant must always weigh the possibility of his conviction on all counts, and the possibility of his getting the maximum sentence, against the possibility that he can plead to fewer, or lesser, offenses, and perhaps receive a lighter sentence. The latter possibility exists if he pleads guilty...
>
> No competent lawyer, discussing a possible guilty plea with a client, could fail to canvass these possible alternatives with him. Nor would he fail to ascertain the willingness of the prosecution to "go along."...
>
> The important thing is not that there shall be no "deal" or "bargain," but that the plea shall be a genuine one, by a defendant who is guilty; one who understands his situation, his rights, and the consequences of the plea, and is neither deceived nor coerced.

FROM CHIEF JUDGE CAMPBELL'S
OPINION IN UNITED STATES V. WILEY
184 F. SUPP 679 (1960)
United States District Court,
Northern District of Illinois

I should first like to discuss my statement that it is my "standing policy" not to consider probation where a defendant has exercised his constitutional right to trial. I cannot agree with the construction placed upon this statement by the Court of Appeals for several reasons. While this statement is of course immediately relevant to the question of whether or not it was an abuse of discretion on my part to deny Wiley's application for consideration of probation, it is irrelevant to the actual sentence imposed upon Wiley except as it is subject to the deduction that if a defendant does stand trial in my Court and is found guilty, he will not ordinarily be afforded the same leniency he would have received if he had pled guilty.

I readily admit the truth of this deduction. I think that almost any trial judge in the United States will take into consideration a plea of guilty when imposing sentence and, in fact, most judges usually state for the record words to the effect that "since the defendant has saved the government the time and expense of trial, the sentence is less than it ordinarily would be." What is deducted from my statement is merely the reverse side of the coin and is subject to the same justification.

As Justice Lummus of the Supreme Judicial Court of Massachusetts has pointed out in his book, "The Trial Judge" at pages 46–47:

> If all the defendants should combine to refuse to plead guilty, and should dare to hold out, they could break down the administration of criminal justice in any state in the Union. But they dare not hold out, for such as were tried and convicted could hope for no leniency. The prosecutor is like a man armed with a revolver who is cornered by a mob. A concerted rush would overwhelm him, but each individual in the mob fears that he might be one of those shot during the rush. When defendants plead guilty, they expect more leniency than when convicted by a jury, and must receive it, or there will be no such pleas. The truth is, that a criminal court can operate only by inducing the great mass of actually guilty defendants to plead guilty, paying in leniency the price for the plea.
>
> This, I agree, is a stark reality, not the ideal. In an ideal judicial system, leniency would be a free gift from the sovereign people to an erring citizen. The criminal would have no voice in the decision, much less barter for it with his sovereign. But courts are not free, and never have been free, from the pressure in favor of criminals that the very volume of criminal business exerts. The defenders of criminals know this perfectly. It is their principal asset. The actual trial of criminal cases is only a small part of the work of a criminal lawyer. Since his clients are usually guilty, and a good part of them would be found guilty by a jury, he seeks to turn to their advantage some defect in the machinery of public justice.

Besides the need for exchanging some degree of leniency in return for a plea of guilty because, as Justice Lummus indicates, of our overwhelming volume of criminal cases, I should also like to point out as an additional reason, the great saving of expense and time to the government that is possible and that is achieved by properly inducing defendants to plead guilty. For example, in the cause before me, the official total cost to the government for the complete investigation up to the time of sentencing was $11,250. The Assistant United States Attorney, upon representation spent three days in preparation for Wiley's trial and one day on trial. Several investigators likewise spent three days in preparation for trial and one day at the trial. I myself spent one half day in preparation for trial and then one day on trial and accordingly the Court was totally occupied for a day and a half. Though the expense and time that would have been saved the government if Wiley had pled guilty is fairly obvious, I suggest that, if this had been a criminal trial lasting weeks or months as many of our trials actually do, then the saving of time and expense to the government would have been far more striking.

Finally, there is one more reason for affording some degree of leniency in exchange for a plea of guilty. One of the principal considerations in the imposition of a criminal sentence is reformation. Where, as here, the defendant first pleads guilty and then, with the permission of the Court, withdraws his plea of guilty, enters a plea of not guilty and exercises his constitutional right to trial despite the fact that the evidence of his guilt is overwhelming, I find it difficult to believe that the defendant is actually repentant and seriously concerned with rehabilitation which is generally true when a defendant pleads guilty.

For these reasons, I believe, and it is generally accepted by trial judges throughout the United States, that it is entirely proper and logical to grant some defendants some degree of leniency in exchange for pleas of guilty. If then, a trial judge grants leniency in exchange for a plea of guilty, it follows, as the reverse side of the same coin, that he must necessarily forego leniency, generally speaking, where the defendant stands trial and is found guilty. This is especially true where there are several co-defendants indicted for the same offense and some plead guilty while others stand trial and are found guilty. In such a case, again generally speaking, the trial judge should grant leniency to those who plead guilty and refuse leniency to those who choose to stand trial. Usually, the result is, as would be expected, a disparity in the sentences imposed on the various defendants. However, it is incorrect, in my opinion, to say, as the Court of Appeals has termed by sentence of Wiley, that a "more severe sentence" is imposed on a defendant who stands trial. Rather, it seems more correct to me to say that the defendant who stands trial is sentenced without leniency according to law.

When I referred to my "standing policy," I meant nothing more than that which is already established for the reasons stated above, as a valid principle of sentencing. In addition to these reasons, I should also like to point out that throughout the United States there were a total of 35,517 defendants in criminal proceedings commenced during the fiscal year 1959. Since each of these defendants must be dealt with by one of the 248 district judges in the United States with the great majority of defendants falling within the jurisdiction of the greater metropolitan districts such as the Northern District of Illinois, it is perhaps easier to understand why, in accord with the thinking of Justice Lummus, I might make general reference to a "standing policy" not to consider probation where a defendant stands trial even though I do not in fact strictly adhere to such a policy. However, if in one year, 248 judges are to deal with 35,517 defendants, the district courts must encourage pleas of guilty. One way to encourage pleas of guilty is to establish or announce a policy that, in the ordinary case, leniency will not be granted to a defendant who stands trial.

FROM CHIEF JUDGE BAZELON'S OPINION
IN SCOTT V. UNITED STATES
419 F.2D 264 (1969)
United States Court of Appeals,
District of Columbia Circuit

Vincent Scott was convicted of robbery under 22 D.C. Code § 2901 (1967) and sentenced to prison for five to fifteen years. The proceedings preceding his conviction were, we conclude, free from error. The events surrounding his sentencing, however, present thorny questions concerning what factors the trial judge may properly consider at that stage. We affirm the conviction, but remand for a resentencing in accordance with the principles announced in this opinion. . . .

The trial judge also stated at the sentencing hearing, "If you had pleaded guilty to this offense, I might have been more lenient with you." The stark import of this comment is that the defendant paid a price for demanding a trial. In view of the prohibitions the Supreme Court has laid down against making the exercise of Fourth, Fifth, and Sixth Amendment rights costly, the pricetag thus placed on the right to a fair trial which these amendments guarantee would, on first impression, seem clearly impermissible.

And yet, despite the startling incongruity, empirical evidence supports the proposition that judges do sentence defendants who have demanded a trial more severely. At least one Court of Appeals has taken approving "judicial notice of the fact that trial courts quite generally impose a lighter sentence on pleas of guilty than in cases where the accused pleaded not guilty but has been found guilty by a jury." An advisory committee of the American Bar Association has concluded that "it is proper for the court to grant charge and sentence concessions to defendants who enter a plea of guilty * * * when the interest of the public in the effective administration of criminal justice would thereby be served."

Much of this adulation for differential sentencing has been rationalized without frank recognition of the fact that whatever its advantages, the practice does exact a price from those who insist upon a trial. But the arguments in favor of differential sentencing cannot be dismissed by a wooden insistence that the exercise of constitutional rights can never be made costly. Some rights may be so vital that no deterrence to their free exercise can be tolerated. The Supreme Court has accorded such preeminent status to the self-incrimination privilege. But in other areas the Court has suggested the need for a less truncated analysis. In United States v. Jackson, the Court held that Congress could not provide for a death penalty "applicable only to those defendants who assert the right to contest their guilt before a jury." But in doing so the majority did not dely upon the summary argument that the exercise of such a right could in no way be made costly. The Court rather asked "whether that effect is unnecessary and therefore excessive." . . .

The Supreme Court has offered little guidance concerning which constitutional rights can tolerate some chilling effect and which cannot. Perhaps the right to a trial, like the self-incrimination privilege but apparently unlike the right to a jury, belongs in the latter camp. But until the Supreme Court speaks, the practice of differential sentencing should be evaluated with some attention paid to the nature of the price exacted from those who plead innocent and why it is exacted.

Two arguments inevitably appear whenever differential sentencing is discussed. The first is that the defendant's choice of plea shows whether he recognizes and repents his crime. One difficulty with this argument is that no court or commentator has explained why a defendant's insistence upon his self-incrimination privilege is not also evidence of a lack of repentance. Or his insistence that evidence unconstitutionally seized should not be admitted.

Repentance has a role in penology. But the premise of our criminal jurisprudence has always been that the time for repentance comes after trial. The adversary process is a fact-finding engine, not a drama of contrition in which a prejudged defendant is expected to knit up his lacerated bonds to society.

There is a tension between the right of the accused to assert his innocence and the interest of society in his repentance. But we could consider resolving this conflict in favor of the latter interest only if the trial offered an unparalleled opportunity to test the repentance of the accused. It does not. There is other, and better, evidence of such repentance. The sort of information collected in presentence reports provides a far more finely brushed portrait of the man than do a few hours or days at trial. And the offender while on probation or in prison after trial can demonstrate his insight into his problems far better than a trial.

If the defendant were unaware that a proper display of remorse might affect his sentence, his willingness to admit the crime might offer the sentencing judge some guidance. But with the inducement of a lighter sentence dangled before him, the sincerity of any cries of *mea culpa* becomes questionable. Moreover, the refusal of a defendant to plead guilty is not necessarily indicative of a lack of repentance. A man may regret his crime but wish desperately to avoid the stigma of a criminal conviction.

The Supreme Court was careful to point out in Sherbert v. Verner that "no showing merely of a rational relationship to some colorable state interest would suffice" to justify an infringement of First Amendment rights. Even if we assume that the right to a fair trial may in some circumstances be made costly, the required justification here also must be a paramount goal achievable in no other way. The supposed value of a guilty plea in demonstrating repentance does not meet this test.

The second argument for differential sentencing is necessity. Most convictions, perhaps as many as 90 per cent in some jurisdictions, are the product of guilty pleas. Unless a large proportion of defendants plead guilty, the argument runs, the already crowded dockets in many jurisdictions would collapse into chaos. Since most defendants are indigent, the only price they can be forced to pay for pleading innocent is time in jail. Ergo, differential sentences are justified for those who plead guilty and those who plead innocent.

When approached from this perspective, the problem inevitably becomes entwined with that of plea bargaining. And the difficulties that practice presents are exceeded only by its pervasiveness. In many areas such bargaining dominates the criminal process. Its format may vary. The prosecutor may agree to reduce the charge in exchange for a guilty plea, or he may agree to recommend a lighter sentence. The judge may be aware of the agreement or he may not. If aware that a bargain has been struck, the court may or may not ratify the agreement before a plea is offered and accepted.

When a defendant pleads guilty in exchange for the promise of the prosecutor or court, a subsequent challenge to the voluntariness of his plea raises a recognized constitutional issue. When the accused refuses to plead guilty and subsequently receives a heavier sentence, the invisibility with which the system operates in indivdual cases too often conceals the constitutional issue. But the problem is the same in both contexts. Whether the defendant surrenders his right to a trial because of a bargain with court or prosecutor, or exercises his right at the cost of a stiffer sentence, a price has been put on the right.

The two sides of this coin are related in a practical sense as well. At least when only a single charge is involved, the effectiveness of plea bargaining depends upon the willingness of the court to impose a lighter sentence when a defendant pleads guilty. If such is the custom within a jurisdiction, the prosecutor enjoys credibility. Indeed, if the custom is sufficiently well known, actual bargaining may be unnecessary: enough defendants will be cowed into guilty pleas simply by the force of their lawyers' warnings that defendants convicted after demanding a trial receive long sentences.

Thus, to the extent that the appellant here received a longer sentence because he pleaded innocent, he was a pawn sacrificed to induce other defendants to plead guilty. Since this is so, to consider the price he paid for the exercise of his right without regard for the process of which it is but one instance would be to ignore reality. . . .

2. ESTABLISHING MAXIMA AND MINIMA

NOTES

Note 1. Responsibility for the Initial Determination of the Term of Imprisonment

a. PETER LOW

Determination of Maximum and Minimum Terms*

In terms of current practice in this country, opinion is nearly unanimous that determination of the maximum sentence is properly a decision for the trial court. The overwhelming majority of Federal sentences are determined in this manner, for example, by authorizing a sentence of imprisonment "for not more than 5 years" and by permitting the judge to select any term which does not exceed the stated limit. A few Federal statutes, on the other hand, attempt to control the discretion of the court in a limited fashion by providing that a sentence to prison shall be for a term, for example, of "not less than 2 nor more than 5 years" (as in 18 U.S.C. § 140) and by permitting the judge to select an actual maximum in a specific case at some point within the stated range. And finally, there is at least one provision (18 U.S.C. § 2114) which states that an offender who is sentenced to prison "shall be imprisoned for 25 years," thus denying to the sentencing court authority to fix any other maximum than the stated term. Again, it should be noted that the issues of parole and probation are separate problems that are not necessarily affected, that certainly need not be affected, and that are not in fact affected as the Federal structure now exists, by any of these three formulas for stating the maximum sentence levels and the extent of judicial control. . . .

The arguments of those who prefer the type of sentence which gives complete discretion to the sentencing court over the maximum term to be imposed, that is, the form of sentence illustrated above by the language imprisonment "for not more than 5 years," proceed as follows:

(a) The legislature necessarily speaks in generalities when it makes the essentially moral judgment that an offense should under no circumstances be punished for a period in excess of a specified maximum term. Particular cases do not fit these generalizations all of the time, and there is thus the need for someone to be able to express such a judgment rooted in the facts of the particular case. The best person to do this—the person who is closest to the offense and to the community in which it was committed—is the trial judge. He should thus be given control over the length of the maximum term when he imposes a prison sentence.

(b) The second argument is an attack on the argument advanced in favor of no judicial control based on the timing of the parole decision. As stated in the ABA Report:

> The proposition that parole authorities are in a better position than judges to assess the readiness of the defendant to return to society needs more support than merely the advantage of more favorable timing. In particular, such a system would seem to call on more highly developed and more adequately funded correctional and parole facilities than many states have to date provided. In addition, the fact that judicial sentencing occurs in open court following an opportunity to present a case with the assistance of an attorney affords a visibility to the process which is normally absent before parole authorities, as well as greater procedural protection.

There is also the point that minor transgressions within the prison are likely to impair parole consideration of the inmate, and though not really serious, may result in service of a long term more for his reaction to prison discipline than for the nature of his original offense or how he would be likely to conduct himself if he were released.

(c) The third argument begins from the premise that sentences are already too long in this country, and that the effect of a system which denies judicial control over the maximum is to make them longer. Whatever the theoretical soundness of this argument, the best that can be said for it statistically is that the results of comparisons of the two systems seem to be inconclusive.

(d) The fourth argument is an expression of concern over the effect of no judicial control on the well-entrenched process of plea bargaining. If the judge does not have the power to control the length of a maximum term, the result will inevitably be, so the argument goes, an increased pressure on the prosecution to grant charge concessions in return for guilty pleas. On the other hand, if the judge

---

* Peter Low, "Preliminary Memorandum on Sentencing Structure," I. *Working Papers of the National Commission on Reform of Federal Criminal Laws* 1274–81 (1970).

does have control over the length of the maximum, then the prosecutor has the additional offer of a sentencing recommendation to make in exchange for a guilty plea. Retention of judicial control over the maximum thus has the twofold advantage of increasing the visibility of the plea-bargaining process and of retaining for the judge a more important role in keeping it within proper bounds.

(e) Finally, it should be noted that judicial control is firmly entrenched in the present Federal system and that the judges can be expected strongly to favor it. There is great question whether the arguments in favor of a change are persuasive enough to justify the political battle that would have to be waged in order to produce it. . . .

In considering how the minimum term should be imposed, it is helpful to consider the legislative and the judicial roles separately.

There is a clear consensus among the Model Penal Code, the Model Sentencing Act and the ABA Report to the effect that it is inappropriate for the legislature to fix a minimum term for any offense. . . .

It remains to consider the judicial role in the determination of a minimum term. At least two issues are posed in this connection: (a) whether there should be a minimum term at all, *i.e.*, whether the judge should be authorized to impose a minimum sentence; and (b) if so, the extent to which his discretion to do so should be limited by legislative bounds. Each of these issues will be separately considered.

(a) There is a significant split between the Model Penal Code and the Model Sentencing Act on the first issue. The Model Sentencing Act permits no minimum terms; the Model Penal Code does within a specified range. The American Bar Association sides with the Model Penal Code on the issue, with emphasis, however, on the need for careful consideration of the legislative limitations which should be placed on the judicial discretion to impose a minimum term and on the need for an outlet in the case of error.

There are four basic arguments advanced by the opponents of the minimum term:

(i) The most fundamental is that the minimum term freezes mistakes. The court at the time of sentencing is not in a particularly good position to know what the status of the offender will be 5 years hence. The provision of a high minimum unduly shackles the parole authorities from releasing the offender at the optimum time.

(ii) Closely related is the point that the issue in most cases is not whether an offender is ever going to be released, but when. And that question should be resolved by bringing our best resources to a determination of the best time for release in terms of protection of the public from future offenses by the defendant and in terms of the best judgments of which we are capable as to the most likely time when he will successfully reintegrate himself into the community. A minimum sentence which requires the continued detention of an offender beyond this time—and neither judge nor legislature can accurately predict in advance when, or indeed whether, it is going to occur in a given case—can substantially impede the offender's progress, can embitter him, and can reinforce the tendencies toward crime which led him to prison in the first place. Put more directly, a misplaced minimum term can increase the danger of a new and serious offense by the defendant rather than decrease it.

(iii) One of the most difficult problems that exists in sentencing as it is practiced at present is the much-discussed problem of disparity. Too many defendants who ought to get similar sentences are treated in vastly different ways by the present system. One way to attack the problem is to give parole authorities the power to even off disproportionate sentences by treating similarly situated offenders in the same way with respect to release on parole. The power to impose a high minimum sentence, in other words, is the power to freeze a disparate sentence in a manner which cannot later be undone.

(iv) Finally, proponents of minimum terms argue that parole board conservatism will be induced by leaving the release decision entirely in the hands of the parole board. It is more likely that a proper release decision will be made if both judge and parole board participate in the decision. Whatever the merits of this argument, those who oppose the minimum term answer that its thrust would not seem to require that the judge be empowered to make a binding decision on when release should first be considered. A recommendation by the judge would give the parole authorities the benefit of his perspective and at the same time not carry with it the disadvantages of freezing an error into the sentence should the judge turn out to have been too severe.

The proponents of the minimum term respond in the following manner:

(i) A judicially fixed minimum is a desirable means of sharing the release responsibility between the judge—with his roots in the community where the offense occurred—and the parole authority—which tends to be somewhat removed from the context in which the crime was committed. For reasons of general deterrence and in order to maintain community respect for law, there needs to be a method by which the judge can assure the public that a particular defendant will be imprisoned for at least a minimum period of time.

(ii) Clearly the worst of all possible worlds is the legislatively prescribed minimum. To advocate that the opposite extreme be embraced, however—that the legislature prohibit minima—is likely to be self-defeating. The motives which have produced so many legislatively prescribed minima are not going to disappear easily. But they can for the most part be accommodated by a system which permits the judge to impose a minimum. Since this is a far better alternative, it is politically more realistic to strive for the intermediate position of judicially imposed minima than it is to strive for the complete abolition of minimum terms. The California experience illustrates the difficulty: the original conception was that complete discretion over release date be given to the Adult Authority, that the judge have no control over the length of the sentence. Since then, however, numerous ad hoc enactments have specified minimum terms which must be served before the Adult Authority could act. This might not have happened if the pattern had permitted judicial imposition of minimum sentences in appropriate cases.

(b) As was noted above, there are two issues which must be considered in connection with the judicial role in fixing minimum terms. The first—whether there should be any minimum terms—has been discussed. The second—what statutory controls there should be if the judge is to be authorized to impose a minimum—remains for consideration.

There is a clear consensus on at least one point: the court should not be permitted to destroy the principle of indeterminacy through use of the power to impose a minimum term. In one State case, for example, a judge imposed an "indeterminate" term with a minimum of 199 years and a maximum of life. The judge should not be permitted to destroy the operation of the parole concept through the imposition of a minimum term which so nearly approaches the maximum in length. There should always be a significant spread between the time when the offender must be released and the time when he may be released.

For this reason, the Model Penal Code, the ABA Report and practically every jurisdiction which permits the imposition of minimum terms provide that the minimum should in no case be permitted to exceed a specified percentage of the maximum. One-third is the most common provision and is the present Federal limit.

In addition, the ABA Report contains five further recommendations which should also be considered:

(i) Minimum sentences should be considered to be rarely appropriate and should be reasonably short, never to exceed 10 to 15 years (and of course never to exceed one-third of the maximum actually imposed). The present Federal limit of 15 years conforms to this recommendation.

(ii) Imposition of a minimum sentence should require the affirmative action of the sentencing court. This is exactly the reverse of the present Federal practice, where affirmative action is required in order for the sentence not to contain a minimum.

(iii) A minimum sentence should not be permitted without detailed study of the defendant through a presentence report and a further diagnostic study under a provision similar to present section 4208(c) of Title 18.

(iv) The court should be required to consider prior to the imposition of a minimum term whether a nonbinding recommendation would adequately serve the purposes which would be served by a minimum term.

(v) The court should be authorized to reduce an imposed minimum term at any time on motion of the corrections or parole authorities. The District of Columbia presently has a statute to this effect. . . .

b. *MEETING OF THE AMERICAN LAW INSTITUTE GROUP IN CONNECTION WITH MODEL PENAL CODE, DECEMBER 21, 1956* (*Extracts From Mimeograph Transcript*)*

> MR. WECHSLER: . . . Now, on the first question of whether the court in the ordinary term should have power to reduce the maximum, I think I am correct that the prime consideration with those of us who considered it in taking the view that we took, was that if you give the court power to control the maximum, you were inescapably going to get right back into the anarchy that you are trying to avoid. That is, ines-

---

* Reprinted in Monrad Paulsen, *The Problem of Sentencing* 18-27 (1962). Copyright 1962. Reprinted with the permission of the American Law Institute.

capably then, you will have men sentenced for the same offense under different maxima, with, therefore, different eligibilities for release, and comparing their situations in prison, the whole matter relating back to the action of the judge at the time of sentence, relating not to the correctional experience or to response to the correctional experience or to the judgment of the Board of Parole as to when release is appropriate.

JUDGE EDWARDS: If this be anarchy, I am afraid this is the point where we must say, let's make the most of it.... Because at least I ... feel that one of the problems dealing with this type of situation . . . , in terms of logic, is that you lose sight of the prisoner in the courtroom, who never looks like any other prisoner who comes in the courtroom. Every single one of them is an individual. Every single one of them has a different background, and every offense is different . . . [I]f you take from the sentencing judge control over the maximum, then you are really saying, when you set these crimes up, that they are all the same thing when a person has been convicted. . . .

MR. WECHSLER: No, I don't think we are saying that, and I think this is a fundamental point, Judge. I think that we are addressing ourselves to a problem in the distribution of authority, and the problem is whether in distributing authority for this very difficult matter of sentencing and correction, it is more desirable at this point to have control in the court, or whether it is more desirable to have control passed on to the organs of correctional administration who govern release. . . . Our judgment was that given the nature of the problem, given the relative advantage of time which the correctional organs have and the court has not got, because the court must act at the time of sentence, given also the differences in the residual prison situation, if you are dealing with inequalities that they think they feel which is based on release, the wisdom or justice of which they can't understand, that you make a better attack and don't pay too much for it if you have everybody sentenced for the maximum provided by law. . . .

MR. RUBIN: . . . I think there is a certain anarchy in the fixing of sentences by judges, because of the differences in judges and their attitudes and their philosophies of correctional treatment. I think, however, that it is also true and may be truer that the disparity in sentencing is governed by the difference in the individuals. In any event, this is also an element, and if what you do is try to overcome the anarchy and the differences among judges by equating all defendants, you are substituting another anarchy, because what you are saying is that the sentence for each defendant should be the same. . . . The second point in this connection is that . . . if you look at the practical effect of the automatic maximum, you find that it operates to lengthen the time the individual spends in the institution. It is a point that has been made several times already, and this is one of the ways in which it operates. If the parole board is faced with a ten-year maximum, it governs itself accordingly and the individual is held in longer. . . .

MR. PAUL TAPPAN: . . . As [Mr. Rubin] has made the point that boards are inclined to look towards the excessive maxima and to retain in prison offenders who are under very long terms, I think that there is such a tendency where maxima vary widely from one prisoner to another. If you have a standardized maximum for a given crime or a given grade of felony, on the other hand, you have specifically allocated responsibility to your board to determine when the person is ready for release, after appropriate response to correctional treatment, and their concern then becomes one of getting him out after he has served his minimum, if he has responded adequately to the correctional process. . . .

HONORABLE LEARNED HAND: If I understand you, what you mean is the sentence is not the exercise of a judicial judgment itself. The Board will have less reluctance to deal with it if, in so doing, they [don't?] have to overrule the judge. Is that correct?

MR. TAPPAN: That is correct. . . .

JUDGE OTIS: . . . If we extend the concept that has been proposed here, you would deprive us of all right to probation or suspended sentence.

MR. WECHSLER: No, no.

JUDGE OTIS: Let me finish. If you say there should be uniformity and hence the judge shouldn't restrict the maximum, then there should be uniformity, and every prisoner should be committed according to law, and only the parole board can put the man on probation or suspend the sentence. . . .

JUDGE HILL: Professor Wechsler, I think the general public would be utterly dismayed at the sentences which result in the various cases if there were no individualization made. Let it be a sentence not to exceed five years for one offender, a sentence not to exceed eight years for another, but don't make us make it a mandatory ten-year sentence for everybody. The public just doesn't understand that. . . . I mean, for the same grade of offense where two boys go out and do about the same thing. One of them has been in the reformatory, never been worth anything, he won't hold a job. The other boy is a rather ideal kind of boy all of his life, and yet the judge sentences them both to a mandatory

JUDICIAL CHOICE: INCARCERATION AND ALTERNATIVES THERETO

ten-year period. Of course, I understand that you then put the burden on the parole board to do something about it.

MR. WECHSLER: That's right.

JUDGE HILL: But I don't think that is the answer. It makes the spirit and wording of the Penal Code in the first place trend toward the longness of the sentence....

MR. WECHSLER: Well, Mr. President, I think we should now pass to the next topic, which is really a problem of judicial control over a minimum sentence. Here again I am tempted to say what I have already said to Judge Edwards, that it is remarkable in this area how men, having the same sense for the data and, in a sense, really the same values, can come out with diametrically opposite conclusions as to what the practical course to follow is, because we have here in each of these three grades introduced and defended some judicial power over a minimum sentence.

Our view was that it was in relation to the minimum rather than the maximum that it is more significant to speak of the judge as representing the conscience of the community; that where a terrible thing has happened there is great community feeling if the sentence is only to a maximum, whether a judicially determined maximum or a statutorily determined maximum, but with freedom in the paroling authorities to release at any time, that the community is not accorded that sense of immediate security that it perceives in a judicially imposed minimum.

On the other hand, we were completely in accord with what I am sure are the views of our guests as to the abuses that are incident to the judicial power to fix the minimum. I would state them in this way: First, and most important, that if you believe in the indeterminate sentence, as we do, then the spread between minimum and maximum must be a very substantial spread. This was the first criterion that we set ourselves. Second, we were concerned that in the heat of the moment or at the time when the crime was recent and the community was inflamed, the temptation to impose an unduly onerous minimum, even the temptation that a court would feel, is at its height, and that if there are to be minima, those minima must be relatively modest....

Now, with respect to the first degree of felony, we have run into a tougher problem, and here to attempt to state in just a few words the thinking that went into this, it has been part of our hope that we might be able to move the Institute to take a position against capital punishment, and that therefore, if that should prevail, this first category would be the substitute for a present capital category of crimes....

Now, you will observe the minimum is not mandatory upon the court, except that it is fixed at a year. That involved a different judgment. That involved the judgment that there was no use sending people to state as distinct from local correctional institutions under regimes that involve less than a duration of eight to nine months.... [T]his was really, in our view, a matter of giving the correction organs enough time to go to work. That was the judgment in any event, right or wrong, that that minima time is indicated if the correctional process is to be meaningful or even get substantially beyond the diagnostic stage.

Now, as far as minima are concerned, I ask you to consider one other point. You gentlemen in the correctional world are losing this fight, just about as badly as any fight is being lost. You are not only losing the fight against judicially imposed minima. What is being piled up on you are legislatively imposed minima.

I call your attention to the narcotic areas. I call your attention to the sex area. How effective have you been in controlling the legislative impulse to pile up statutorily prescribed minima?

Now, I don't regard this, in my humble view, as an ephemeral legislative impulse. I think this is a stable legislative condition, and I think that even a model for 50 years has got to take into account that there is this sense, and that if not even the court may impose a minimum, if the position that you take is that this is all up to the Parole Board, on the one hand you are inducing or forcing the Parole Board to focus far more on questions of community attitude than on questions of individual rehabilitation and potentialities than you ought to, but, on the other hand, you have no answer to legislatures. The whole world is moving against you on this point, I submit, and I think it is very important, therefore, that a model, and I have said this in the Institute, and I say it to you, should represent a middle position that is defensible in principle and interposes some barrier to the legislative extremism that is unfortunately characteristic of our time in this field....

JUDGE MURRAH: Well, I will ask my colleagues to respond briefly, but before they do I should say that in our conferences we have had differences about matters. Some of them involved concepts and principles, but not a single judge or parole authority in our conference has advocated a minimum sentence....

JUDGE EDWARDS: ... [W]e are not now dealing with the Michigan legislature. We are not dealing with the legislature of any state. We are stating what we think ought to be, and if we start to revise the Michigan criminal code, I would prefer for this document to analyze the best thought on this, to represent just what Judge Murrah has stated to you: No minimum sentences, either mandatory by law or at the discretion of the judge.

MR. WECHSLER: Well, would you state for us, either Judge Edwards or Judge Murrah, or anybody, ... what in principle is the argument against judicial control over the maximum [minimum?]?

JUDGE EDWARDS: ... It is my feeling that the judge, after he has heard the evidence in relation to what happened, is better able to say what the outside limit of the punishment should be than he is able to say when this person can best be returned to the community. Now, this in a capsule is the whole of my argument. I would be willing to see us live with a situation where we set the maximum within the discretion we talked about, and left to the parole board, who had the opportunity to live institutionally with this person, the opportunity to judge when he should be returned to the community. ...

MR. BATES: Why does the judge at the time of trial know more about the maximum than he does about the minimum possibilities?

JUDGE EDWARDS: It seems to me that the judge has an opportunity to make some judgment of the offense, some judgment of the person, and came closer to determining the maximum which should be set in relation to that disposition than he has an opportunity to make a judgment as to how quickly that person will respond to rehabilitation inside the institution.

MR. WECHSLER: Well, these were precisely the reasons that explain the formulation as it stands. We thought the maximum was much more related to what Sanford [Bates] is talking about, what you find out after you get to know the individual about what his future may be, but that the minimum was, on the other hand, primarily related to the community's need for some sense of assurance at the time of conviction. To put it another way, if you like, that if there is a punitive element in the sense by which I would mean an element primarily oriented to its effect on the general imagination to the general deterrence of crime, that it inheres in the minimum, that this the judge is better able to think about than the parole board. The judge is in the community in which the offense occurred. He has a sense for the community's needs. The parole board is removed. The whole theory of these provisions was to vest in the parole board as much as possible that which appertains to the individual, and to vest in the court as much as possible that which appertains to the offense and to the needs of the community in relation to the reaction to the offense. ...

JUDGE FLOOD: What little I know about it has indicated to me that somebody is going to fix a minimum, and if the court does not fix the minimum after the man has been in the institution for a while, somebody else will. In California, the youth authority or the adult authority does after the man is in some months. They call him up and say, "You are going to be eligible for parole in 24 months or 36 months." We have a completely uncontrolled, completely indeterminate sentence for some prisoners in Pennsylvania, to youthful prisoners. There they call them up after a few months and say, "In 13 months you will be eligible for parole." ... You have an imposition if within a relatively short period after the man arrives he doesn't know when he is going to be eligible to be considered for parole, and practical experience up till now would indicate to me that if we take that away from the judges, we are going to hand it over to somebody else, and that is the place where I come to just the opposite conclusion on this from some of my brother judges. That is the place where I think the judge who has the community behind him, who is there representing the community, is the one to say what that minimum should be rather than a parole board.

Note 2.

NATIONAL COMMISSION ON CAUSES AND PREVENTION OF VIOLENCE

Deterrence, Length of Sentence and Recidivism*

The question of the "deterrent" effects of different lengths of sentence has been greatly debated. Will longer sentences serve as a deterrent against recidivism? Will they make no difference? Will they increase the likelihood of recidivism?

One study has shown that, in the first 2 to 5 years after incarceration, only one-third of all persons released returned to prison. The reasons for not recidivating vary from case to case. Some individuals are successful in positively rehabilitating themselves. Others may have simply matured, "burning off" the greater volitility and impulsiveness characteristic of youth. Many more factors are involved.

It is probable that only a small proportion

* National Commission on the Causes and Prevention of Violence, Staff Report, *Crimes of Violence,* Vol. 12 at 561, 569 (1969).

of those who "go straight" do so because prison life is so repugnant that the risk of being reincarcerated is not worth taking. These are the only offenders who are really "deterred" from recidivating. By "average level of deterrence" we mean the average percentage of all offenders incarcerated over different periods of time and then released who do not recividate primarily as a result of making this kind of rational, cost-benefit decision—and not for some other reason, such as the effectiveness of the rehabilitation process.

No valid conclusions can be drawn from the current data on the average level of deterrence, even though it has always been assumed to be significant by those justifying correctional restraint on the basis of deterrence. This lack of critical information should not continue; there is a need for careful research to determine the average percentage of prisoners in specified cohorts who do not recidivate because they are "deterred" in the manner specified. . . .

Length of sentence seems to bear no regular relationship to likelihood of recidivism for violent offenders. If anything, there may be a tendency for violent offenders who have served longer sentences to recidivate more often than those who have served shorter sentences. Although longer sentences may satisfy the desire to punish the violent offender, they do not unequivocally deter him from further crimes.

3. EXTENDED INCARCERATION TERMS: THE DANGEROUS OFFENDER AND THE MULTIPLE OFFENDER

SPENCER V. TEXAS
385 U.S. 554 (1967)
Supreme Court of the United States

MR. JUSTICE HARLAN delivered the opinion of the Court.

Texas, reflecting widely established policies in the criminal law of this country, has long had on its books so-called recidivist or habitual-criminal statutes. Their effect is to enhance the punishment of those found guilty of crime who are also shown to have been convicted of other crimes in the past. The three cases at hand challenge the procedures employed by Texas in the enforcement of such statutes.

Until recently, and at the time of the convictions before us, the essence of those procedures was that, through allegations in the indictment and the introduction of proof respecting a defendant's past convictions, the jury trying the pending criminal charge was fully informed of such previous derelictions, but was also charged by the court that such matters were not to be taken into account in assessing the defendant's guilt or innocence under the current indictment. . . .

The common and sole constitutional claim made in these cases is that Texas' use of prior convictions in the current criminal trial of each petitioner was so egregiously unfair upon the issue of guilt or innocence as to offend the provisions of the Fourteenth Amendment that no State shall "deprive any person of life, liberty, or property, without due process of law. . . ." We took these cases for review, 382 U.S. 1022, 1023, 1025, because the courts of appeals have divided on the issue. For reasons now to follow we affirm the judgments below. . . .

Petitioners do not even appear to be arguing that the Constitution is infringed if a jury is told of a defendant's prior crimes. The rules concerning evidence of prior offenses are complex, and vary from jurisdiction to jurisdiction, but they can be summarized broadly. Because such evidence is generally recognized to have potentiality for prejudice, it is usually excluded except when it is particularly probative in showing such things as intent, *Nye & Nissen* v. *United States,* 366 U.S. 613, *Ellisor* v. *State,* 162 Tex. Cr. R. 117, 282 S. W. 2d 393; an element in the crime, *Doyle* v. *State,* 59 Tex. Cr. R. 39, 126 S. W. 1131; identity, *Chavira* v. *State,* 167 Tex. Cr. R. 197, 319 S. W. 2d 115; malice, *Moss* v. *State,* 364 S. W. 2d 389; motive, *Moses* v. *State,* 168 Tex. Cr. R. 409, 328 S. W. 2d 885; a system of criminal activity, *Haley* v. *State,* 87 Tex. Cr. R. 519, 223 S. W. 202; or when the defendant has raised the issue of his character, *Michelson* v. *United States,* 335 U.S. 469, *Perkins* v. *State,* 152 Tex. Cr. R. 321, 213 S. W. 2d 681; or when the defendant has testified and the State seeks to impeach his credibility, *Giacone* v. *State,* 124 Tex. Cr. 141, 62 S. W. 2d 986.

Under Texas law the prior convictions of the defendants in the three cases before the Court today might have been admissible for any one or more of these universally accepted reasons. In all these situations, as under the recidivist statutes, the jury learns of prior crimes committed by the defendant, but the conceded possibility of prejudice is believed to be outweighed by the validity of the State's purpose in permitting introduction of the evidence. The defendants' interests are protected by limiting instructions, see *Giacone* v. *State, supra,* and by the discretion residing with the trial judge to limit or forbid the admission of particularly prejudicial evidence even though admissible under an accepted rule of evidence. . . .

It is contended nonetheless that in this instance the Due Process Clause of the Fourteenth Amendment requires the exclusion of prejudicial evidence of prior convictions even though limiting instructions are given and even though a valid state purpose—enforcement of the habitual-offender statute—is served. We recognize that the use of prior-crime evidence in a one-stage recidivist trial may be thought to represent a less cogent state interest than does its use for other purposes, in that other procedures for applying enhancement-of-sentence statutes may be available to the State that are not suited in the other situations in which such evidence is introduced. We do not think that this distinction should lead to a different constitutional result.

Cases in this Court have long proceeded on the premise that the Due Process Clause guarantees the fundamental elements of fairness in a criminal trial. But it has never been thought that such cases establish this Court as a rule-making organ for the promulgation of state rules of criminal procedure. And none of the specific provisions of the Constitution ordains this Court with such authority. In the face of the legitimate state purpose and the long-standing and widespread use that attend the procedure under attack here, we find it impossible to say that because of the possibility of some collateral prejudice the Texas procedure is rendered unconstitutional under the Due Process Clause as it has been interpreted and applied in our past cases. As Mr. Justice Cardozo had occasion to remark, a state rule of law "does not run foul of the Fourteenth Amendment because another method may seem to our thinking to be fairer or wiser or to give a surer promise of protection to the prisoner at bar."

. . . Tolerance for a spectrum of state procedures dealing with a common problem of law enforcement is especially appropriate here. The rate of recidivism is acknowledged to be high, a wide variety of methods of dealing with the problem exists, and experimentation is in progress. The common-law procedure for applying recidivist statutes, used by Texas in the cases before us, which requires allegations and proof of past convictions in the current trial, is, of course, the simplest and best known procedure. Some jurisdictions deal with the recidivist issue in a totally separate proceeding, see, *e.g., Oyler* v. *Boles,* 368 U.S. 448, and as already observed (n. 2, *supra*) Texas to some extent has recently changed to that course. In some States such a proceeding can be instituted even after conviction on the new substantive offense, see Ore. Rev. Stat. § 168.040 (1959); *Graham* v. *West Virginia,* 224 U.S. 616. The method for determining prior convictions varies also between jurisdictions affording a jury trial on this issue, *e.g.,* Fla. Stat. Ann. § 775.11 (1965); and those leaving that question to the court, see, *e.g.,* Fed. Rule Crim. Proc. 32(a); Mo. Rev. Stat. § 556.280(2) (1959). Another procedure, used in Great Britain and Connecticut, see Coinage Offences Act, 1861, 24 & 25 Vict., c. 99; *State* v. *Ferrone,* 96 Conn. 160, 113 A. 452, requires that the indictment allege both the substantive crime and the prior conviction, that both parts be read to the defendant prior to trial, but that only the allegations relating to the substantive crime be read to the jury. If the defendant is convicted, the prior-offense elements are then read to the jury which considers any factual issues raised. Yet another system relies upon the parole authorities to withhold parole in accordance with their findings as to prior convictions. See, *e.g.,* N.J. Stat. Ann. § 30.4–123.12 (1964). And within each broad approach described, other variations occur.

A determination of the "best" recidivist trial procedure necessarily involves a consideration of a wide variety of criteria, such as which method provides most adequate notice to the defendant and an opportunity to challenge the accuracy and validity of the alleged prior convictions, which method best meets the particular jurisdiction's allocation of responsibility between court and jury, which method is best accommodated to the State's established trial procedures, and of course which method is apt to be the least prejudicial in terms of the effect of prior-crime evidence on the ultimate issue of guilt or innocence. To say that the two-stage jury trial in the English-Connecticut style is probably the fairest, as some commentators and courts have suggested, and with which we might well agree were the matter before us in a legislative or rule-making context, is a far cry from a constitutional determination that this method of handling the problem is compelled by the Fourteenth Amendment. Two-part jury trials are rare in our jurisprudence; they have never been compelled by this Court as a matter of constitutional law, or even as a matter of federal procedure. With recidivism the major problem that it is, substantial changes in trial procedure in countless local courts around the country would be required were this Court to sustain the contentions made by these petitioners. This we are unwilling to do. To take such a step would be quite beyond the pale of this Court's proper function in our federal system. It would be a wholly unjustifiable encroachment by this Court upon the constitutional power of States to promulgate their own rules of evidence to try their own state-created crimes in their own state courts, so long as their rules are not prohibited by any provision of the United States Constitution, which these rules are not. The judgments in these cases are

Affirmed.

Mr. Justice Stewart, concurring.

If the Constitution gave me a roving commission to impose upon the criminal courts of Texas my own notions of enlightened policy, I would not join the Court's opinion. For it is clear to me that the recidivist procedures adopted in recent years by many other States—and by Texas herself since January 1 of last year—are far superior to those utilized in the cases now before us. But the question for decision is not whether we applaud or even whether we personally approve the procedures followed in these recidivist cases. The question is whether those procedures fall below the minimum level the Fourteenth Amendment will tolerate. Upon that question I am constrained to join the opinion and judgment of the Court.

Mr. Chief Justice Warren, with whom Mr. Justice Fortas concurs, dissenting and concurring. . . .

It seems to me that the use of prior-convictions evidence in these cases is fundamentally at odds with traditional notions of due process, not because this procedure is not the nicest resolution of conflicting but legitimate interests of the State and the accused, but because it needlessly prejudices the accused without advancing any legitimate interest of the State. If I am wrong in thinking that the introduction of prior-convictions evidence serves no valid purpose I am not alone, for the Court never states what interest of the State is advanced by this procedure. And this failure, in my view, undermines the logic of the Court's opinion.

There is much said about the valid purpose of enhanced punishment for repeating offenders, with which I agree, and about the variety of occasions in criminal trials in which prior-crimes evidence is admitted as having some relevance to the question of guilt or innocence. But I cannot find support for this procedure in either the purposes of recidivist statutes or by analogy to the traditional occasions where prior-crimes evidence is admitted. And the Court never faces up to the problem of trying to justify this recidivist procedure on the ground that the State would not violate due process if it used prior convictions simply as evidence of guilt because it showed criminal propensity. . . .

Whether or not a State has recidivist statutes on its books, it is well established that evidence of prior convictions may not be used by the State to show that the accused has a criminal disposition and that the probability that he committed the crime currently charged is increased. While this Court has never held that the use of prior convictions to show nothing more than a disposition to commit crime would violate the Due Process Clause of the Fourteenth Amendment, our decisions exercising supervisory power over criminal trials in federal courts, as well as decisions by courts of appeals and of state courts, suggest that evidence of prior crimes introduced for no purpose other than to show criminal disposition would violate the Due Process Clause. . . .

The majority of States have adopted procedures which cure the prejudice inherent in the procedure in the cases at bar. In all, some 31 States have recidivist procedures which postpone the introduction of prior convictions until after the jury has found the defendant guilty of the crime currently charged. And at least three others have substantially mitigated the prejudice of the single-stage recidivist procedure by affording the defendant the right to stipulate to his prior crimes to prevent their introduction at the trial. Thus, only 16 States still maintain the needlessly prejudicial procedure exemplified in these three cases. The decision I propose would require only a small number of States to make a relatively minor adjustment in their criminal procedure to avoid the manifest unfairness and prejudice which have already been eliminated in England and in 34 of the United States.

NOTES

Note 1. Recidivist Statutes and Constitutional Requirements

a. *The Right to Counsel*

CHEWNING V. CUNNINGHAM
368 U.S. 443 (1962)
Supreme Court of the United States

Petitioner, then imprisoned in Virginia, was charged with having been three times convicted of and sentenced for a felony. He was accordingly tried under the recidivist statute; and he is now serving the sentence imposed at that trial. He brought this habeas corpus proceeding in the Virginia courts to challenge the legality of that sentence. The crux of his complaint was that he was tried and convicted without having had the benefit and aid of counsel, though he had requested one....

We conclude that a trial on a charge of being a habitual criminal is such a serious one ... the issues presented under Virginia's statute so complex, and the potential prejudice resulting from the absence of counsel so great that the rule we have followed concerning the appointment of counsel in other types of criminal trials is equally applicable here....

b. *Due Process and Equal Protection*

OYLER V. BOLES
368 U.S. 448 (1962)
Supreme Court of the United States

It is petitioners' position that procedural due process under the Fourteenth Amendment requires notice of the habitual criminal accusation *before* the trial on the third offense or at least in time to afford a reasonable opportunity to meet the recidivist charge....

As interpreted by its highest court, West Virginia's recidivist statute does not require the State to notify the defendant prior to trial on the substantive offense that information of his prior convictions will be presented in the event he is found guilty. Thus notice of the State's invocation of the statute is first brought home to the accused when, after conviction on the substantive offense but before sentencing, the information is read to him in open court as was done here. At this point petitioners were required to plead to the information. The statute expressly provides for a jury trial on the issue of identity if the accused either denies he is the person named in the information or just remains silent....

The petitioners' claim that they were deprived of due process because of inadequate opportunity to contest the habitual criminal accusation must be rejected in these cases. Each of the petitioners had a lawyer at his side, and neither the petitioners nor their counsel sought in any way to raise any matters in defense or intimated that a continuance was needed to investigate the existence of any possible defense. On the contrary, the record clearly shows that both petitioners personally and through their lawyers conceded the applicability of the law's sanctions to the circumstances of their cases.

Petitioners also claim they were denied the equal protection of law guaranteed by the Fourteenth Amendment....

Thus petitioners' contention is that the habitual criminal statute imposes a mandatory duty on the prosecuting authorities to seek the severer penalty against all persons coming within the statutory standards but that it is done only in a minority of cases. This, petitioners argue, denies equal protection to those persons against whom the heavier penalty is enforced. We note that it is not stated whether the failure to proceed against other three-time offenders was due to lack of knowledge of the prior offenses on the part of the prosecutors or was the result of a deliberate policy of proceeding only in a certain class of cases or against specific persons. The statistics merely show that according to penitentiary records a high percentage of those subject to the law have not been proceeded against. There is no indication that these records of previous convictions, which may not have been compiled until after the three-time offenders had reached the penitentiary, were available to the prosecutors. Hence the allegations set out no more than a failure to prosecute others because of a lack of knowledge of their prior offenses. This does not deny equal protection due petitioners under the Fourteenth Amendment....

Moreover, the conscious exercise of some selectivity in enforcement is not in itself a federal constitutional violation. Even though the statistics in this case might imply a policy of selective enforcement, it was not stated that the selection was deliberately based upon an unjustifiable standard such as race, religion, or other abitrary classification. Therefore grounds supporting a finding of a denial of equal protection were not alleged....

Note 2. Statutory Innovations for Extended Prison Terms

a. ORGANIZED CRIME CONTROL ACT OF 1970*

§ 3575. Increased sentence for dangerous special offenders

(a) Whenever an attorney charged with the prosecution of a defendant in a court of the United States for an alleged felony committed when the defendant was over the age of twenty-one years has reason to believe that the defendant is a dangerous special offender such attorney, a reasonable time before trial or acceptance by the court of a plea of guilty or nolo contendere, may sign and file with the court, and may amend, a notice (1) specifying that the defendant is a dangerous special offender who upon conviction for such felony is subject to the imposition of a sentence under subsection (b) of this section, and (2) setting out with particularity the reasons why such attorney believes the defendant to be a dangerous special offender. In no case shall the fact that the defendant is alleged to be a dangerous special offender be an issue upon the trial of such felony, be disclosed to the jury, or be disclosed before any plea of guilty or nolo contendere or verdict or finding of guilty to the presiding judge without the consent of the parties. If the court finds that the filing of the notice as a public record may prejudice fair consideration of a pending criminal matter, it may order the notice sealed and the notice shall not be subject to subpoena or public inspection during the pendency of such criminal matter, except on order of the court, but shall be subject to inspection by the defendant alleged to be a dangerous special offender and his counsel.

(b) Upon any plea of guilty or nolo contendere or verdict or finding of guilty of the defendant of such felony, a hearing shall be held, before sentence is imposed, by the court sitting without a jury. The court shall fix a time for the hearing, and notice thereof shall be given to the defendant and the United States at least ten days prior thereto. The court shall permit the United States and counsel for the defendant, or the defendant if he is not represented by counsel, to inspect the presentence report sufficiently prior to the hearing as to afford a reasonable opportunity for verification. In extraordinary cases, the court may withhold material not relevant to a proper sentence,

*18 U.S.C.A. § 3575 *et seq.*

diagnostic opinion which might seriously disrupt a program of rehabilitation, any source of information obtained on a promise of confidentiality, and material previously disclosed in open court. A court withholding all or part of a presentence report shall inform the parties of its action and place in the record the reasons therefor. The court may require parties inspecting all or part of a presentence report to give notice of any part thereof intended to be controverted. In connection with the hearing, the defendant and the United States shall be entitled to assistance of counsel, compulsory process, and cross-examination of such witnesses as appear at the hearing. A duly authenticated copy of a former judgment or commitment shall be prima facie evidence of such former judgment or commitment. If it appears by a preponderance of the information, including information submitted during the trial of such felony and the sentencing hearing and so much of the presentence report as the court relies upon, that the defendant is a dangerous special offender, the court shall sentence the defendant to imprisonment for an appropriate term not to exceed twenty-five years and not disproportionate in severity to the maximum term otherwise authorized by law for such felony. Otherwise it shall sentence the defendant in accordance with the law prescribing penalties for such felony. The court shall place in the record its findings, including an identification of the information relied upon in making such findings, and its reasons for the sentence imposed.

(c) This section shall not prevent the imposition and execution of a sentence of death or of imprisonment for life or for a term exceeding twenty-five years upon any person convicted of an offense so punishable.

(d) Notwithstanding any other provision of this section, the court shall not sentence a dangerous special offender to less than any mandatory minimum penalty prescribed by law for such felony. This section shall not be construed as creating any mandatory minimum penalty.

(e) A defendant is a special offender for purposes of this section if—

(1) the defendant has previously been convicted in courts of the United States, a State, the District of Columbia, the Commonwealth of Puerto Rico, a territory or possession of the United States, any political subdivision, or any department, agency, or instrumentality thereof for two or more offenses committed on occasions different from one another and from such felony and

punishable in such courts by death or imprisonment in excess of one year for one or more of such convictions the defendant has been imprisoned prior to the commission of such felony, and less than five years have elapsed between the commission of such felony and either the defendant's release, on parole or otherwise, from imprisonment for one such conviction or his commission of the last such previous offense or another offense punishable by death or imprisonment in excess of one year under applicable laws of the United States, a State, the District of Columbia, the Commonwealth of Puerto Rico, a territory or possession of the United States, any political subdivision, or any department, agency or instrumentality thereof; or

(2) the defendant committed such felony as part of a pattern of conduct which was criminal under applicable laws of any jurisdiction, which constituted a substantial source of his income and in which he manifested special skill or expertise; or

(3) such felony was, or the defendant committed such felony in furtherance of, a conspiracy with three or more other persons to engage in a pattern of conduct criminal under applicable laws of any jurisdiction, and the defendant did, or agreed that he would, initiate, organize, plan, finance, direct, manage, or supervise all or part of such conspiracy or conduct, or give or receive a bribe or use force as all or part of such conduct.

A conviction shown on direct or collateral review or at the hearing to be invalid or for which the defendant has been pardoned on the ground of innocence shall be disregarded for purposes of paragraph (1) of this subsection. In support of findings under paragraph (2) of this subsection, it may be shown that the defendant has had in his own name or under his control income or property not explained as derived from a source other than such conduct. For purposes of paragraph (2) of this subsection, a substantial source of income means a source of income which for any period of one year or more exceeds the minimum wage, determined on the basis of a forty-hour week and a fifty-week year, without reference to exceptions, under section 6(a) (1) of the Fair Labor Standards Act of 1938 (52 Stat. 1602, as amended 80 Stat. 838), and as hereafter amended, for an employee engaged in commerce or in the production of goods for commerce, and which for the same period exceeds fifty percent of the defendant's declared adjusted gross income under section 62 of the Internal Revenue Act of 1954 (68A Stat. 17, as amended 83 Stat. 655), and as hereafter amended. For purposes of paragraph (2) of this subsection, special skill or expertise in criminal conduct includes unusual knowledge, judgment or ability, including manual dexterity, facilitating the initiation, organizing, planning, financing, direction, management, supervision, execution or concealment of criminal conduct, the enlistment of accomplices in such conduct, the escape from detection or apprehension for such conduct, or the disposition of the fruits or proceeds of such conduct. For purposes of paragraphs (2) and (3) of this subsection, criminal conduct forms a pattern if it embraces criminal acts that have the same or similar purposes, results, participants, victims, or methods of commission, or otherwise are interrelated by distinguishing characteristics and are not isolated events.

(f) A defendant is dangerous for purposes of this section if a period of confinement longer than that provided for such felony is required for the protection of the public from further criminal conduct by the defendant.

(g) The time for taking an appeal from a conviction for which sentence is imposed after proceedings under this section shall be measured from imposition of the original sentence.

§ 3576. Review of sentence

With respect to the imposition, correction, or reduction of a sentence after proceedings under section 3575 of this chapter, a review of the sentence on the record of the sentencing court may be taken by the defendant or the United States to a court of appeals. Any review of the sentence taken by the United States shall be taken at least five days before expiration of the time for taking a review of the sentence or appeal of the conviction by the defendant and shall be diligently prosecuted. The sentencing court may, with or without motion and notice, extend the time for taking a review of the sentence for a period not to exceed thirty days from the expiration of the time otherwise prescribed by law. The court shall not extend the time for taking a review of the sentence by the United States after the time has expired. A court extending the time for taking a review of the sentence by the United States shall extend the time for taking a review of the sentence or appeal of the conviction by the defendant for the same period. The taking of a review of the sentence by the United States shall be deemed the taking of a review of the sentence and an appeal of the conviction by the defendant. Review of the sentence shall include review of whether the procedure employed was lawful, the findings made were clearly erroneous, or the sentencing court's discretion was abused. The court of appeals on review of the sentence may, after considering the record, including the entire presentence report information submitted during the trial of such felony and the sentencing hearing, and the findings and reasons of the sentencing court, affirm the sentence, impose or direct the imposition of any sentence which the sentencing court could originally have imposed, or remand for further sentencing proceedings and imposition of sentence, except that a sentence may be made more severe only on review of the sentence taken by the United States and after hearing. Failure of the United States to take a review of the imposition of the sentence shall, upon review taken by the United States of the correction or reduction of the sentence, foreclose imposition of a sentence more severe than that previously imposed. Any withdrawal or dismissal of review of the sentence taken by the United States shall foreclose imposition of a sentence more severe than that reviewed but shall not otherwise foreclose the review of the sentence or the appeal of the conviction. The court of appeals shall state in writing the reasons for its disposition of the review of the sentence. Any review of the sentence taken by the United States may be dismissed on a showing of abuse of the right of the United States to take such review.

§ 3577. Use of information for sentencing

No limitation shall be placed on the information concerning the background, character, and conduct of a person convicted of an offense which a court of the United States may receive and consider for the purpose of imposing an appropriate sentence.

b. **COMPREHENSIVE DRUG ABUSE, PREVENTION AND CONTROL ACT OF 1970***

§ 841. Prohibited acts A—Unlawful acts

(a) Except as authorized by this subchapter, it shall be unlawful for any person knowingly or intentionally—

(1) to manufacture, distribute, or dispense, or possess with intent to manufacture, distribute, or dispense, a controlled substance; or

(2) to create, distribute, or dispense, or possess with intent to distribute or dispense, a counterfeit substance.

* 21 U.S.C.A. §§ 841 et seq.

Penalties

(b) Except as otherwise provided in section 845 of this title, any person who violates subsection (a) of this section shall be sentenced as follows:

(1) (A) In the case of a controlled substance in schedule I or II which is a narcotic drug, such person shall be sentenced to a term of imprisonment of not more than 15 years, a fine of not more than $25,000, or both. If any person commits such a violation after one or more prior convictions of him for an offense punishable under this paragraph, or for a felony under any other provision of this subchapter or subchapter II of this chapter or other law of the United States relating to narcotic drugs, marihuana, or depressant or stimulant substances, have become final, such person shall be sentenced to a term of imprisonment of not more than 30 years, a fine of not more than $50,000, or both. Any sentence imposing a term of imprisonment under this paragraph shall, in the absence of such a prior conviction, impose a special parole term of at least 3 years in addition to such term of imprisonment and shall, if there was such a prior conviction, impose a special parole term of at least 6 years in addition to such term of imprisonment. . . .

Special Parole Term

(c) A special parole term imposed under this section or section 845 of this title may be revoked if its terms and conditions are violated. In such circumstances the original term of imprisonment shall be increased by the period of the special parole term and the resulting new term of imprisonment shall not be diminished by the time which was spent on special parole. A person whose special term has been revoked may be required to serve all or part of the remainder of the new term of imprisonment. A special parole term provided for in this section or section 845 of this title shall be in addition to, and not in lieu of, any other parole provided for by law.

§ 845. Distribution to persons under age twenty-one

(a) Any person at least eighteen years of age who violates section 841(a) (1) of this title by distributing a controlled substance to a person under twenty-one years of age is (except as provided in subsection (b) of this section) punishable by (1) a term of imprisonment, or a fine, or both, up to twice that authorized by section 841(b) of this title, and (2) at least twice any special parole term authorized by section 841(b) of this title, for a first offense involving the same controlled substance and schedule.

(b) Any person at least eighteen years of age who violates section 841(a) (1) of this title by distributing a controlled substance to a person under twenty-one years of age after a prior conviction or convictions under subsection (a) of this section . . . have become final, is punishable by (1) a term of imprisonment, or a fine, or both, up to three times that authorized by section 841(b) of this title, and (2) at least three times any special parole term authorized by section 841(b) of this title, for a second or subsequent offense involving the same controlled substance and schedule.

§ 848. Continuing criminal enterprise—Penalties; forfeitures

(a) (1) Any person who engages in a continuing criminal enterprise shall be sentenced to a term of imprisonment which may not be less than 10 years and which may be up to life imprisonment, to a fine of not more than $100,000, and to the forfeiture prescribed in paragraph (2); except that if any person engages in such activity after one or more prior convictions of him under this section have become final, he shall be sentenced to a term of imprisonment which may not be less than 20 years and which may be up to a life imprisonment, to a fine of not more than $200,000, and to the forfeiture prescribed in paragraph (2).

(2) Any person who is convicted under paragraph (1) of engaging in a continuing criminal enterprise shall forfeit to the United States—

(A) the profits obtained by him in such enterprise, and
(B) any of his interest in, claim against, or property or contractual rights of any kind affording a source of influence over, such enterprise.

Continuing Criminal Enterprise Defined

(b) For purposes of subsection (a) of this section, a person is engaged in a continuing criminal enterprise if—

(1) he violates any provision of this subchapter or subchapter II of this chapter the punishment for which is a felony, and
(2) such violation is a part of a continuing series of violations of this subchapter or subchapter II of this chapter—

(A) which are undertaken by such person in concert with five or more other persons with respect to whom such person occupies a position of organizer, a supervisory position, or any other position of management, and
(B) from which such person obtains substantial income or resources.

Suspension of Sentence and Probation Prohibited

(c) In the case of any sentence imposed under this section, imposition or execution of such sentence shall not be suspended, probation shall not be granted. . . .

Jurisdiction of Courts

(d) The district courts of the United States (including courts in the territories or possessions of the United States having jurisdiction under subsection (a) of this section) shall have jurisdiction to enter such restraining orders or probations, or to take such other actions, including the acceptance of satisfactory performance bonds, in connection with any property or other interest subject to forfeiture under this section, as they shall deem proper.

§ 849. Dangerous special drug offender sentencing—Notice to court by United States Attorney

(a) Whenever a United States attorney charged with the prosecution of a defendant in a court of the United States for an alleged felonious violation of any provision of this subchapter or subchapter II of this chapter committed when the defendant was over the age of twenty-one years has reasons to believe that the defendant is a dangerous special drug offender such United States attorney, a reasonable time before trial or acceptance by the court of a plea of guilty or nolo contendere, may sign and file with the court, and may amend, a notice (1) specifying that the defendant is a dangerous special drug offender who upon conviction for such felonious violation is subject to the imposition of a sentence under subsection (b) of this section, and (2) setting out with particularity the reasons why such attorney believes the defendant to be a dangerous special drug offender. In no case shall the fact that the defendant is alleged to be a dangerous special drug offender be an issue upon the trial of such felonious violation, be disclosed to the jury, or be disclosed before any plea of guilty or nolo contendere or verdict or finding of guilty to the presiding judge without the consent of the parties. If the court finds that the filing of the notice as a public record may prejudice fair consideration of a pending criminal matter, it may order the notice sealed and the notice shall not be subject to subpena or public inspection during the pendency of such criminal matter, except on order of the court, but shall be subject to inspection by the defendant alleged to be a dangerous special drug offender and his counsel.

Hearing; Inspection of Presentence Report; Counsel; Process; Examination of Witnesses; Penalty; Sentence

(b) Upon any plea of guilty or nolo contendere or verdict or finding of guilty of the defendant of such felonious violation, a hearing shall be held, before sentence is imposed, by the court sitting without a jury. The court shall fix a time for the hearing, and notice thereof shall be given to the defendant and the United States at least ten days prior thereto. The court shall permit the United States and counsel for the defendant, or the defendant if he is not represented by counsel, to inspect the presentence report sufficiently prior to the hearing as to afford a reasonable opportunity for verification. In extraordinary cases, the court may withhold material not relevant to a proper sentence, diagnostic opinion which might seriously disrupt a program of rehabilitation, any source of information obtained on a promise of confidentiality, and material previously disclosed in open court. A court withholding all or part of a presentence report shall inform the parties of its action and place in the record the reasons therefor. The court may require parties inspecting all or part of a presentence report to give notice of any part thereof intended to be controverted. In connection with the hearing, the defendant and the United States shall be entitled to assistance of counsel, compulsory process, and cross-examination of such witnesses as appear at the hearing. A duly authenticated copy of a former judgment or commitment shall be prima facie evidence of such former judgment or commitment. If it appears by a preponderance of the information, including information submitted during the trial of such felonious violation and the sentencing hearing and so much of the presentence report as the court relies upon, that the defendant is a dangerous special drug offender, the court shall sentence the defendant to imprisonment for an appropriate term not to exceed twenty-five years and not disproportionate in severity to the maximum term otherwise authorized by law for such felonious violation. Otherwise it shall sentence the defendant in accordance with the law prescribing penalties for such felonious violation. The court shall place in the record its findings, including an identification of the information relied upon in making such findings, and its reasons for the sentence imposed.

Sentences for Life or for a Term Exceeding Twenty-Five Years

(c) This section shall not prevent the imposition and execution of a sentence of imprisonment for life or for a term exceeding twenty-five years upon any person convicted of an offense so punishable.

Mandatory Minimum Penalties

(d) Notwithstanding any other provision of this section, the court shall not sentence a dangerous special drug offender to less than any mandatory minimum penalty prescribed by law for such felonious violation. This section shall not be construed as creating any mandatory minimum penalty.

Special Drug Offender Defined

(e) A defendant is a special drug offender for purposes of this section if—

(1) the defendant has previously been convicted in courts of the United States or a State or any political subdivision thereof for two or more offenses involving dealing in controlled substances, committed on occasions different from one another and different from such felonious violation, and punishable in such courts by death or imprisonment in excess of one year, for one or more of such convictions the defendant has been imprisoned prior to the commission of such felonious violation, and less than five years have elapsed between the commission of such felonious violation and either the defendant's release, or parole or otherwise, from imprisonment for one such conviction or his commission of the last such previous offense or another offense involving dealing

in controlled substances and punishable by death or imprisonment in excess of one year under applicable laws of the United States or a State or any political subdivision thereof; or

(2) the defendant committed such felonious violation as part of a pattern of dealing in controlled substances which was criminal under applicable laws of any jurisdiction, which constituted a substantial source of his income, and in which he manifested special skill or expertise; or

(3) such felonious violation was, or the defendant committed such felonious violation in furtherance of, a conspiracy with three or more other persons to engage in a pattern of dealing in controlled substances which was criminal under applicable laws of any jurisdiction, and the defendant did, or agreed that he would, initiate, organize, plan, finance, direct, manage, or supervise all or part of such conspiracy or dealing, or give or receive a bribe or use force in connection with such dealing.

A conviction shown on direct or collateral review or at the hearing to be invalid or for which the defendant has been pardoned on the ground of innocence shall be disregarded for purposes of paragraph (1) of this subsection. In support of findings under paragraph (2) of this subsection, it may be shown that the defendant has had in his own name or under his control income or property not explained as derived from a source other than such dealing. For purposes of paragraph (2) of this subsection, a substantial source of income means a source of income which for any period of one year or more exceeds the minimum wage, determined on the basis of a forty-hour week and fifty-week year, without reference to exceptions, under section 206(a)(1) of Title 29 for an employee engaged in commerce or in the production of goods for commerce, and which for the same period exceeds fifty percent of the defendant's declared adjusted gross income under section 62 of Title 26, Internal Revenue Code of 1954. For purposes of paragraph (2) of this subsection, special skill or expertise in such dealing includes unusual knowledge, judgment or ability, including manual dexterity, facilitating the initiation, organizing, planning, financing, direction, management, supervision, execution or concealment of such dealing, the enlistment of accomplices in such dealing, the escape from detection or apprehension for such dealing, or the disposition of the fruits or proceeds of such dealing. For purposes of paragraphs (2) and (3) of this subsection, such dealing forms a pattern if it embraces criminal acts that have the same or similar purposes, results, participants, victims, or methods of commission, or otherwise are interrelated by distinguishing characteristics and are not isolated events.

Dangerous Defendants

(f) A defendant is dangerous for purposes of this section if a period of confinement longer than that provided for such felonious violation is required for the protection of the public from further criminal conduct by the defendant.

Appeal

(g) The time for taking an appeal from a conviction for which sentence is imposed after proceedings under this section shall be measured from imposition of the original sentence.

Review of Sentence

(h) With respect to the imposition, correction, or reduction of a sentence after proceedings under this section, a review of the sentence on the record of the sentencing court may be taken by the defendant or the United States to a court of appeals. Any review of the sentence taken by the United States shall be taken at least five days before expiration of the time for taking a review of the sentence or appeal of the conviction by the defendant and shall be diligently prosecuted. The sentencing court may, with or without motion and notice, extend the time for taking a review of the sentence for a period not to exceed thirty days from the expiration of the time otherwise prescribed by law. The court shall not extend the time for taking a review of the sentence by the United States after the time has expired. A court extending the time for taking a review of the sentence by the United States shall extend the time for taking a review of the sentence or appeal of the conviction by the defendant for the same period. The taking of a review of the sentence by the United States shall be deemed the taking of a review of the sentence and an appeal of the conviction by the defendant. Review of the sentence shall include review of whether the procedure employed was lawful, the findings made were clearly erroneous, or the sentencing court's discretion was abused. The court of appeals on review of the sentence may, after considering the record, including the entire presentence report, information submitted during the trial of such felonious violation and the sentencing hearing, and the findings and reasons of the sentencing court, affirm the sentence, impose or direct the imposition of any sentence which the sentencing court could originally have imposed, or remand for further sentencing proceedings and imposition of sentence, except that a sentence may be made more severe only on review of the sentence taken by the United States and after hearing. Failure of the United States to take a review of the imposition of the sentence shall, upon review taken by the United States of the correction or reduction of the sentence, foreclose imposition of a sentence more severe than that previously imposed. Any withdrawal or dismissal of review of the sentence taken by the United States shall foreclose imposition of a sentence more severe than that reviewed but shall not otherwise foreclose the review of the sentence or the appeal of the conviction. The court of appeals shall state in writing the reasons for its disposition of the review of the sentence. Any review of the sentence taken by the United States may be dismissed on a showing of the abuse of the right of the United States to take such review.

4. CONSECUTIVE AND CONCURRENT SENTENCES

INTRODUCTORY NOTES

Note 1.

GORE V. UNITED STATES
357 U.S. 386, 395–97 (1958)
Supreme Court of the United States

Mr. Justice Douglas, with whom Mr. Justice Black concurs, dissenting.

The first three counts of this indictment cover one sale of narcotics made on February 26, 1955. The one sale was broken down for purposes of the three counts into three crimes:

(1) petitioner made the sale "not in pursuance of a written order" which is contrary to the requirement of 68A Stat 551, 26 USC (Supp V) § 4705 (a);

(2) the narcotics were sold "not in the original stamped package" which is contrary to the requirements of 68A Stat 550, 26 USC (Supp V) § 4704 (a);

(3) petitioner "facilitated the concealment and sale" which is in violation of 65 Stat 767, 21 USC § 174.

Another single sale, one made on February 28, 1955, was likewise broken down into three separate and distinct crimes.

Consecutive sentences were imposed for the three crimes resulting from the first sale. Sentences imposed for the three crimes resulting from the second sale were made to run concurrently with each other and with the sentences imposed for the three offenses resulting from the first sale.

Plainly, Congress defined three distinct crimes, giving the prosecutor on these facts a choice. But I do not think the courts were warranted in punishing petitioner three times for the same transaction....

... I would hold that the prosecutor was given the choice of one of three prosecutions for this single sale. I would resist a reading which inferred that Congress intended multiple offenses from the same sale, for that would not make the statutes square with the Constitution.

Note 2.

IRBY V. UNITED STATES
390 F.2d 432, 439, 444 (1967)
United States Court of Appeals, District of Columbia Circuit

Chief Judge Bazelon, with whom Circuit Judge Wright concurs, dissenting.

There are two questions before us. The first is whether, in some cases, the D. C. housebreaking and robbery statutes prohibit cumulative punishment. The second is whether Irby's is one of those cases.

The answer to the first question depends entirely upon statutory construction. The issue is whether Congress authorized cumulative punishment not whether the trial judge properly exercised judicial sentencing discretion. No doubt, the process of statutory construction, which entails examining the history of these common law crimes, the legislative history of the statutes, the words of each statute, and the relationship between them is very difficult. But the process is not necessarily more difficult here than in many other contexts in which we must construe statutes. In any event, the difficulty of the process does not excuse us from our duty.

We depend upon statutory construction because the authority to punish resides in the legislature, not in the courts, and we cannot arrogate to ourselves authority which has not been granted. Neither can we assume that Congress wanted separate punishment simply because it created separate crimes. To do so would be to allow the prosecutor and the trial judge almost unfettered discretion to multiply punishment since often it takes nothing more than a fertile imagination to spin several crimes out of a single transaction. The cases are perfectly clear that the legality of cumulative punishment depends on more than a finding that separate crimes have been committed. Indeed, the Supreme Court has established a "rule of lenity" which requires courts to forego cumulative punishment when there is a doubt about what Congress intended. . . .

We think the record sufficiently shows that defendant entered the dwelling with the objective of stealing property, by force if necessary, and that he carried out this objective. Since there is substantial doubt that Congress intended cumulative punishment in this situation, the rule of lenity must be applied. Irby should have been punished for either housebreaking or robbery but not both consecutively.

Note 3.

PETER LOW

Preliminary Memorandum on Sentencing Structure*

Consecutive Sentences. —There is a consensus between the Model Penal Code, the ABA Report and the New York statute to the effect that it is desirable that a penal Code place an upper limit on the extent to which consecutive sentences may be cumulated. All agree that within such a limit, whether prison terms for multiple offenses should be served consecutively or concurrently should be a matter for the discretion of the court.

A related problem must first be noticed. In *Gore* v. *United States,* 357 U.S. 386 (1958), the defendant made a single sale of drugs on a given date, and was charged with a sale not pursuant to a written order on a prescribed Treasury form, with a sale of drugs not in the original stamped package, and with a sale of drugs with knowledge that they had been illegally imported. The defendant was convicted of all three counts and given consecutive sentences, even though each count was in fact a different method of reaching by criminal prosecution exactly the same sale.

Some recent proposals would strike at this by providing as does section 22 of the Model Sentencing Act, for example, that "separate sentences of commitment imposed on a defendant for two or more crimes constituting a single criminal episode shall run concurrently." In New York, the related provision is more narrowly phrased: sentences must run concurrently if "more than one sentence of imprisonment is imposed on a person for two or more offenses committed through a single act or omission, or through an act or omission which in itself constituted one of the offenses and also was a material element of the other . . ." The Model Penal Code, on the other hand, does not contain a similar provision, nor does the ABA Report; but both, as will be discussed, would place limits on the extent to which consecutive sentences could be cumulated.

There are basically two ways to deal with a case such as *Gore*. The first is through provisions in the law defining offenses which in effect prohibit conviction of more than one offense in such a situation. Whether the robbery of two people on a single occasion or the theft of money and of jewelry during a single burglary should constitute one or two offenses is at the first instance a question of interpretation of the statute defining the offenses of robbery and of larceny. The second is through such a provision as the Model Sentencing Act or the New York proposals quoted above—a provision which, even though it is determined that there can be two convictions in such an instance, prohibits the cumulation of sentences. A choice between these two methods—or perhaps the adoption of some combination of them—should be part of a new Federal Criminal Code. It is clearly indefensible to permit the fragmentation of a single offense so that a sentence in excess of the legislative maximum can be imposed.

This still leaves for resolution the major problem with consecutive sentences, namely whether—given a case where there clearly are two separately punishable criminal acts—consecutive punishment should be permitted and if so under what circumstances. Each of the recent proposals has concluded that there should be no limits on cumulation where the second offense is an escape or where it is committed

* National Commission on Reform of Federal Criminal Laws, *Working Papers,* Vol. I at 1282–83 (1970).

while the offender is in prison. For other cases, there have been several suggestions.

The solution of the new proposal in Michigan is a simple one. Multiple sentences imposed upon an offender "shall be served concurrently." The solution in New York, on the other hand, is to adopt a stated term of years as the limit to which consecutive sentences can reach: if one of the offenses was a Class B felony, the limit is 30 years; if all of the offenses are less than Class B, the limit is 20 years; in the case of misdemeanors, the limit is two years; there is also a provision prohibiting the cumulation of fines in certain circumstances. The Model Penal Code has adopted still a third alternative. As was developed in the section on "Length of Sentences; Extended Terms," *supra*, the Model Penal Code suggests an extended term for use in the case of certain types of particularly dangerous offenders. It also suggests that the extended term should serve as the limit on the extent to which consecutive sentences may be cumulated. The cumulated sentence may not exceed the extended term for the most serious of the offenses of which the defendant stands convicted.

It is fairly clear that a new Federal Code should contain at least a limitation of the sort contained either in the New York statute or the Model Penal Code. In the past, ridiculously cumulated sentences have been a major source of unjustified disparities and have produced some of the clearest injustices among the Federal prison population. It is rare indeed when multiple criminality will justify a sentence beyond limits such as those stated in either the New York statute or the Model Penal Code.

NOTES
Proposals
Note 1.

ADVISORY COUNCIL OF JUDGES OF THE NATIONAL COUNCIL ON CRIME AND DELINQUENCY, MODEL SENTENCING ACT § 22 (1963)*

§22. Concurrent or Consecutive Service of Terms

Separate sentences of commitment imposed on a defendant for two or more crimes constituting a single criminal episode shall run concurrently. Sentences for two or more crimes not constituting a single criminal episode shall run concurrently unless the judge otherwise orders.

Comment

A therapeutic penology is supported by a unified sentence rather than a multiplicity of sentences against a defendant who has committed more than one crime. A treatment plan is one which works toward the offender's return to the community for another start. But if the termination of one sentence serves only as the beginning of another, perhaps in another institution, no plan of treatment can be said to exist. So existing law favors concurrent rather than consecutive terms; and section 22 provides for concurrent terms in preference to consecutive terms, subject to judicial discretion. The words "not constituting a single criminal episode" are included so that the many indictments of more than one count will not lead to consecutive sentences where only a single criminal episode was involved.

Note 2.

AMERICAN BAR ASSOCIATION STANDARDS ON SENTENCING PROCEDURES AND ALTERNATIVES (APPROVED DRAFT, 1968) 171–172*

    3.4 *Multiple offenses: same state; concurrent and consecutive terms.*

        (a) After convictions of multiple offenses which are separately punishable or in cases where the defendant is serving a prison sentence at the time of conviction, the question of whether to impose concurrent or consecutive sentences should be a matter for the discretion of the sentencing court.

        (b) Consecutive sentences are rarely appropriate. Authority to impose a consecutive sentence should be circumscribed by the following statutory limitations:

            (i) The aggregate maximum of consecutive terms should not be permitted to exceed the term authorized for an habitual offender . . . for the most serious of the of-

---

* Reprinted, with permission of the National Council on Crime and Delinquency, from *Crime and Delinquency,* October 1963, p. 368, § 22.

* Quoted with permission of the American Bar Association, 1155 East 60th Street, Chicago, Illinois 60637.

fenses involved. If there is no provision for an habitual offender for the offenses involved, there should be a ceiling on the aggregate of consecutive terms which is related to the severity of the offenses involved; and

(ii) The aggregate minimum of consecutive terms should be governed by the limitations stated in section 3.2; and

(iii) The court should not be authorized to impose a consecutive sentence until a presentence report . . . , supplemented by a report of the examination of the defendant's mental, emotional and physical condition . . . , has been obtained and considered; and

(iv) Imposition of a consecutive sentence should require the affirmative action of the sentencing court. The court should be authorized to impose a consecutive sentence only after a finding that confinement for such a term is necessary in order to protect the public from further criminal conduct by the defendant.

These limitations should also apply to any sentence for an offense committed prior to the imposition of sentence for another offense, whether the previous sentence for the other offense has been served or remains to be served.

(c) Corrections and parole authorities should be directed to consider an offender committed under multiple sentences as though he had been committed for a single term the limits of which were defined by the cumulative effect of the multiple sentences.

5. SENTENCE REVIEW

Introductory Note:
Sentence Review in Connecticut

An Empirical Study of Sentence Review in Connecticut*

Tribunals empowered to review criminal sentences imposed by trial judges and other primary sentencing authorities can contribute significantly to the improved use of criminal sanctions. Review affords a second look at the sentence in light of the social aims which such sanctions should achieve. More important, the body of decisions made by the reviewing tribunal may provide meaningful criteria for the guidance of sentencing authorities. Although in thirty-nine states and the federal courts no sentence within the statutory limits for a proven offense may be modified by a higher court, eleven states now have some system of appellate review. Of these eleven, nine vest the power to affirm or reduce sentence in their existing appellate courts. . . .

* Note, "Appellate Review of Primary Sentencing Decisions: A Connecticut Case Study." Reprinted by permission of The Yale Law Journal Company and Fred B. Rothman Company from *The Yale Law Journal*, Vol. 69, pp. 1453, 1462–64, 1466, 1475–77 (1960).

By statute, the Connecticut Sentence Review Division is composed of three Superior Court trial judges and is empowered to review sentences which direct incarceration for one year or more in the state prison, and to substitute any sentence that the trial judge could have imposed, including an increased term. Upon imposition of sentence, the clerk of the sentencing court must give the offender written notice of his right to appeal to the Review Division within thirty days, and notice of the possibility that his sentence will be increased on appeal. While the Division has construed the statute to prevent it from considering evidence which was not before the trial judge, such as post-sentence rehabilitation and "cooperation," the statute allows the Division to require the production of presentence reports and "any other records, documents, or exhibits connected with such review proceedings." The trial judge may submit a statement of his reasons for a particular sentence to the Division and the Division may require the submission of such a statement. The most important change from the Massachusetts procedure is the requirement that the Division hand down a written opinion stating the reasons for the disposition of each appeal.

In practice, the Division's panel of judges

has been rotated among the judges of the Superior Court. Every appellant is permitted to appear before the Division and is allowed representation by counsel. The State's Attorney from the county in which the offender was prosecuted appears at the hearing for the state. In lieu of requiring the trial judge to prepare a statement of reasons for a particular sentence, the Division sends for the transcript of the arguments of the State's Attorney and the defense counsel together with the comments of the trial judge in open court on sentencing day. Thus the Division has before it the presentence report, the transcript of sentencing day proceedings, and other documents, such as psychiatric studies, which were before the primary sentencing authority. In addition, the Secretary of the Division prepares a synopsis of these documents for each judge of the Division. Normally the Division will hand down its written opinion within a month after the hearing. The Division sits as its business requires, meeting approximately one day every two months to dispose of less than twenty-five cases. To date, the Division has heard two-hundred-fifty-six appeals, reducing fifteen sentences and increasing seven. In only one case was the type of punishment imposed by the trial judge changed....

To improve sentencing decisions, the Review Division must write opinions which clearly describe the relationship between the factors involved in a specific case and the aim or aims of the criminal law that should be emphasized in that case. With relatively few exceptions, the opinions of the Connecticut panel have not satisfied this requirement. Some opinions give relatively clear directions to trial judges. Others, if supplemented by a tentative process of extrapolating principles from the facts apparently considered significant in the opinion, may furnish limited guidance in future cases. But in a substantial number, it is extremely difficult if not impossible to deduce what aim or aims of the criminal law are being emphasized and, a fortiori, to abstract any sentencing principles....

As a result of the few sentence modifications made and the Division's reluctance to articulate sentencing policies, the Division has not aroused the interest of bench, bar, and public. Originally, the legislature provided for publication of the Division's opinions in the *Connecticut Supplement,* presumably making them available to all lawyers and judges in the state. But the Connecticut judges interviewed have stated that, except when called upon to serve on the Review Division they read only those opinions reviewing cases in which they were the trial judge. The bench, in fact, tends to view the Division not as an affirmative policy-creating body, but only as a restraint on palpably unreasonable sentencing decisions. The Division has occasionally indicated that the sentence imposed by the trial judge will be affirmed so long as it meets a "reasonable judge" test, a statement of little assistance to a trial judge seeking a positive statement of principles for future application. To compound this problem, the 1959 Session of the Connecticut General Assembly has removed the mandatory publication requirement. Instead, it instructed the Recorder of Judicial Decisions to "select ... for publication such decisions as he deems will be useful as precedents or will serve the public interest." Now, even those opinions which should be of interest to the judiciary may be unavailable.

The Connecticut bar shares the judiciary's disinterest in the work of the Division. Prosecutors and defense counsel alike have stated that they did not read the opinions even when all were published. The appearances of defense counsel before the Division have been relatively few. They feel that the practical value of such appearances is minimal, since the vast majority of opinions affirm the sentence imposed. State's Attorneys tend to view their required appearances before the Division as an unnecessary burden. Like defense counsel, they feel that the Division's only function is to apply the "reasonable judge" test and that the use of presentence reports by trial judges reduces the likelihood that the Division will find many palpably unreasonable sentences. Thus it is not uncommon to find State's Attorneys offering little or no comment at the review hearing. This disinterested attitude has increased the difficulty of realizing the potentialities of the Review Division. Considering the present quality of Division opinions, greater scrutiny and criticism by the bar of such sentencing principles as are proposed would contribute substantially to the improvement of future opinions and, ultimately, to the improvement of the sentencing process itself.

Since criminal sentencing and, indeed, the criminal process as a whole are oriented toward effectuating community objectives, informed public criticism is also essential. For example, if the Division's opinions, stressing the aim of rehabilitation, revealed that certain types of offenders were being committed to state prison only because better rehabilitative facilities did not exist, the public might urge the legislature to provide the needed facilities.

Similarly, if the public felt that the Division was not sufficiently emphasizing the deterrent aim in certain types of offenses, it might prevail upon its representatives to enact mandatory minimum penalties for these offenses. Before it can suggest policy decisions, however, the public must be informed of the standards proposed by the Division. The press is the logical source of such information. It should realize, therefore, that not only the results of a particular case must be reported, but also the sentencing goals which formed the basis of the Division's opinion.

To date, the most serious drawback to the Division's effectiveness has been the idea that it's primary function is to prevent "horrible sentencing examples." By seldom attempting to supply generally applicable sentencing criteria, the Division has overlooked its most significant potentialities and has lost the interest of other participants and decision-makers of the criminal process. Unless it assumes the role of an affirmative policy-maker, *ad hoc,* instinctive decisions will continue to impede development in the field of sentencing.

STATE V. AMIOT
CONNECTICUT SENTENCE REVIEW
DIVISION, JUNE 27, 1968*

BY THE DIVISION. The defendant, age forty, pleaded guilty to both counts of an information charging him in the first count with the crime of robbery with violence in violation of § 53–14 of the 1958 Revision of the General Statutes and in the second count with the crime of breaking and entering with criminal intent in violation of § 53–76 of the 1958 Revision of the General Statutes. The penalty prescribed by § 53–14 is imprisonment for not more than twenty-five years and that prescribed by § 53–76 is imprisonment for not more than four years. On the first count the defendant was sentenced to the state prison for not less than five years and no more than eight years and on the second count to one year, making an effective sentence of not less than five years and not more than nine years.

On January 16, 1967 at approximately seven o'clock in the morning the defendant came upon a house in the rural section of Ashford which was the home of a Mr. and Mrs. Lovell. He noted that the home was in darkness, without any vehicles and apparently unoccupied. After driving past this house several times he parked his car in a field some distance

* "Not approved for publication by the Sentence Review Division." The case is unreported.

south of the Lovell house and parked it out of sight between some trees. He then walked to the Lovell house and went around the building looking into windows. Thereafter he returned to his car and removed from the trunk a small crowbar, a roll of two-inch wide adhesive tape, a mask fashioned from red cloth, cotton work gloves and a headless wooden hammer handle. His purpose in breaking into this house was to steal any money he could find there. Using the crowbar he forced the rear door open by prying the molding strip away from the door jamb. He entered the house and walked into the kitchen and living room. Upon entering a bedroom he observed the victim, Mrs. Lovell, asleep in bed. The defendant placed his hand over her mouth, whereupon Mrs. Lovell awakened and saw the defendant standing over her wearing a red mask. She attempted to scream. The defendant said "Don't scream or I'll cut your heart out." She then observed that he had a knife in his hand with a blade approximately five inches in length. He then struck her twice in the back of her head with the hammer handle, causing lacerations and heavy bleeding. Thirteen sutures were required to close these wounds. He placed a piece of the adhesive tape over her mouth so that she could not scream. After he pulled the cover off her he tied her wrists and ankles with some nylon stockings which he took from a nearby chair. With another stocking the defendant tied her wrists to her ankles and then covered Mrs. Lovell with the blanket. Leaving her thus bound and bleeding the defendant then proceeded to ransack the Lovell home. He took two chrome-plated pistols from a dresser drawer and some coins he found in a jar. Thereafter he left the house through the same door he had forced open, went to his car and placed the stolen items in the trunk of his car. After Mrs. Lovell heard the defendant leave the house she managed to free herself and called the police. Subsequent investigation led to the apprehension of the defendant for the instant offenses and he was arrested on January 19, 1967. The defendant admitted the offenses. He told the police he threw the pistols from a bridge into the Connecticut River. He burned the roll of adhesive tape and the hammer handle so they would not be discovered by the police. He said that the hammer handle had a couple of blood spots on it.

The defendant is married and has five children, and resided with his wife and family in East Hartford. He received an honorable discharge from the United States Navy after service in the second World War. For about fifteen years prior to July 1966 he had been employed as a freight handler by a large grocery chain corporation. In July 1966 he was laid off because of excessive absenteeism which the defendant said was due to his illnesses and mental problems. He has a history of mental problems. In 1963 he went to the outpatient clinic in Hartford and in that year he was admitted to the Institute of Living where he stayed for ten weeks. In 1965 he was readmitted for a period of four weeks. According to reports, depression was his problem at the time of both admissions. However, at the time of the second admission it was learned that the defendant had been taking drugs (barbiturates) since 1957 and his diagnosis at that time was passive-aggressive personality (passive-aggressive type) and drug addiction (amphetamine). On January 20, 1967, shortly after his arrest for the instant offenses, the defendant was admitted to the Norwich Hospital on an emergency commitment after he felt depressed and medicated himself in a suicide gesture. The hospital reports there indicate that he has been experiencing fugue-like states during which he would drift around aimlessly and not be able to remember his actions. Such states have been noticed and described when he had been a patient at the Institute of Living and Hartford Hospital. It is significant to note that with regard to the instant crimes the hospital record states "At this time, it is difficult to judge if this is a real amnesic period or if patient does not want to remember this episode." He was also found at this time to be without psychosis. It would appear that the defendant's total indebtedness at the time of the instant offenses, excluding payments on his home, was about six thousand dollars, the major portion of which is owed for medical expenses.

The defendantt's only previous offense is a conviction for speeding in 1965.

The function of this Division is a limited one governed entirely by the statutes which created it. General Statutes §§ 51-194 to 51-197. Its limited function is to determine upon review whether a particular sentence is appropriate considering the offenses involved, the defendant, and the public interest. See *State* v. *Carpenter*, 25 Conn. Sup. 149, 152. "The sentencing problem does not yield to exact analysis. It deals with human beings with differing qualities, and is still the product essentially of a process requiring the analytical skill, competence and judgment of human wisdom." *State* v. *Johnson*, 21 Conn. Sup. 381, 383. In reviewing a penalty, the opinion of the trial judge deserves great weight and careful consideration. *State* v. *Hackley*, 21 Conn. Sup. 412, 414. The Review Division cannot substitute its discretion for that of the sentencing Court. *State* v. *Carpenter*, supra.

The fifty-eight year old victim in this case was brutally struck by this defendant causing lacerations and profuse bleeding. He threatened her and she saw the knife he held. The defendant had broken into her home after surveying the premises, returning to his car and procuring the tools and equipment he had brought to effect his illegal entry. Mrs. Lovell's nearest neighbor was three-tenths of a mile away. Her husband was away at work. She was entitled to be secure not only that her bodily integrity would not be invaded by brutal blows such as she received, but also that her home not be ransacked and property in it stolen as it was. The terrifying events of the morning hours of January 16, 1967 proved otherwise. The gravity with which robbery with violence is regarded by our law finds expression in the penalty permissible under the statute. See *State* v. *Black*, 21 Conn. Sup. 384, 386. The right of the community to be safe not only in the streets from such a crime but certainly in the privacy of one's own home is one required to be guarded wisely with both justice and zeal. The integrity of property and its possessors is recognized by our law which provides sanctions for breaking and entering in violation of our law. The crime of robbery with violence is fraught with danger to human life. That is shockingly patent in this case.

It is true that sentences are not to be measured solely on the basis of the crime committed, for to do so would effectuate fixed punishment and defeat the fundamental of individualized punishment and the purpose of the indeterminate sentence provided by statute. The defendant and his background, the crimes involved and the public interest are to be carefully considered in passing upon an application for sentence review. With reference to the mental make-up of this defendant, this Division has stated that the objective of the prevention of the repetition of the crime by an offender is the same whether its commission has its source and basis in a normal or abnormal personality. See *State* v. *O'Connor*, 21 Conn. Sup. 474, 476. The element of the protection of the public through the segregation of the offender should have at least equal weight with the consideration of the return of an offender to society as a useful and law-abiding member of the community. See *State* v. *Johnson*, 21 Conn. Sup. 381, 384.

Under all the circumstances the sentences imposed both as to minimum and maximum in this case are fair and just and should stand.

Healey and Wall, Js. participated in this decision.

Rubinow, J. (dissenting). In my view, the sentence imposed in this case should be modified.

To set forth in detail the basis for that view will, I believe, further the purpose of the Sentence Review legislation, which was enacted to "achieve more rational sentences and greater equality of treatment between offenders." *State v. Harris*, 21 Conn. Supp. 448, 151, 159 A2d 188, 190 (1958). The published opinions of the Division can help the attaining of these objectives by articulating specific sentencing principles that may provide "significant guidance in determining the next sentence." The development of such principles, through the published opinions of the Division, was an important aim of the Governor's Committee that recommended the creation of the Sentence Review Division. If the published opinions of the Division do not attempt the formulation of such principles, the sentence-review process may give the appearance of being "no more than the substitution of one guess about the proper disposition for another."

There are, of course, limitations on the extent of the guidance that the opinions of the Division can provide. One obvious limitation results from the unique quality of the conglomeration of facts relevant to a sentence. "As has been well stated, 'Although a robbery is always a robbery, not all robbers are alike in the harm actually done by them, in the motivation of their crime, and their mental and emotional make-up and social background . . . These facts in a sense make each crime a unique event and each criminal a unique individual.' "

Another limitation results from the lack of empirical data about the consequences of incarceration and its alternatives. "We know even less about the effect of what we try to do about crimes and criminals than we do about the facts concerning crime itself." This lack of data has, in turn, produced a "contrariety of expert opinion about sentencing procedures and their effect" and a wide disparity in sentences, reflecting the "individual philosophies of the judges and their different attitudes toward particular kinds of offenses." Until convincing data homogenize these disparate philosophies and attitudes, they will continue to play a substantial role in the sentencing process.

These comments on disparity should not be interpreted, however, as implying that "equality of treatment between offenders" means that the sentence should always be the same whenever the same statute has been violated. As has been previously noted, differences in facts relevant to a sentence tend to make each offense unique. "No advocate of sentence reform argues for uniformity where there are reasonable grounds for differentiation. What is sought, on the other hand, is reasonable, as opposed to arbitrary, differentiation: an approach to the sentence that not only recognizes the justice of individualized sentences, but also demands their rational use."

In spite of the foregoing limitations on the general applicability of sentencing principles, such principles, "even if relatively imprecise," are a necessity to ensure that the sentencing process, like the civil adjudication process, represents a judgment based on rational standards, and not the exercise of a discretion unfettered save for the maximum statutory penalty.

The statutory maximum, however, does more than set a legal limit on the sentence; it is one of the guide-lines to a proper sentence, for the statutory maximum reflects the degree of community condemnation that society, speaking through the legislature, attaches to the offense and that degree of condemnation is a proper consideration for the court in imposing sentence. On the other hand, where the statutes (like the statutes in the present case) do not fix a minimum penalty, the legislature implicitly recognizes that there may be circumstances where a small or minimal penalty would constitute the proper penalty for the offense, notwithstanding a high statutory maximum.

This conjunction of a high-statutory-maximum and no-minimum-penalty does not mean, however, that the legislature has gone no further than that in formulating sentencing policies. Rather, it means that those policies must be sought in declarations by the General Assembly in statutes other than in the statutes defining the range of the penalty, for in matters of sentencing, as in all other matters of adjudication, the public policy of the state, as declared by the General Assembly, is always of paramount relevance.

The basic public policy of this state, with respect to sentencing to the State Prison, is the policy expressed in the Indeterminate Sentence Act and its adjunct, the Parole Statute. The Indeterminate Sentence, in its original form, was conceived of as a "term without a maximum or minimum length." The theory of such a term was that the defendant would be released only when he was deemed suitable for release, thus "protecting society by controlling the offender for a period of unlimited duration." This form of "complete indeterminacy" was, however, converted in many jurisdictions, including Connecticut, in a modified form, employing both minimum and maximum terms. "The purpose of the (Connecticut modified form) . . . doubtless was to encourage and hold out hope to the convict that by good conduct and reform he may secure his liberty after the expiration of the minimum term, or at most before he has served the maximum sentence." *State* v. *McGuire*, 84 Conn. 470, 477 80 A 761, 764 (1911).

The parole system, likewise, emphasizes "reform" of the defendant, not so much, however, as an inducement to the defendant but as a means of protecting society. "The new feature of this act is that providing and discipline of prisoners, whether serving under fixed or indeterminate sentences. It is evidently prompted by a desire to reform, as well as to punish, to make better those under sentence, as well as to protect society . . . The paramount object is the welfare of society, hence the sentence to imprisonment of those convicted, and hence, also, the effort to educate and reform the convict, so that he may, if possible, become a good member of society when he is released or his term expires." *State* v. *Peters*, 43 Ohio 629, 646, 4 N. E. 81, 82 (1885).

Our Indeterminate Sentence Act requires that the minimum term of a State Prison sentence "shall not be less than one year." This minimum period of one year is regarded as "an institutional necessity for any constructive program." Under the Parole Act, after a person has served his minimum term (less "earned time"), he "may be allowed to go at large on parole in the discretion of a quorum of the board of parole if (1) it appears . . . that there is reasonable probability that such inmate will live and remain at liberty without violating the law and (2) such release is not incompatible with the welfare of society"; after release, the parolee while on parole remains "in the legal custody and control of the board of parole until the expiration of the maximum term." The Parole Act thus, on the one hand, requires that a defendant committed to State Prison serve the minimum term (less "earned time") fixed by the court. On the other hand, the board of parole is under no duty to release the defendant at the expiration of the minimum term; on the contrary, regardless of the expiration of the minimum term, the board of parole is under a duty to keep the defendant confined until, subject to the maximum term, there is a "reasonable probability" that he can, to paraphrase, be a law-abiding member of society.

In 1967, the foregoing statutory provisions were supplemented by legislation of far-reaching significance with respect to the public policy of this state in sentencing. This legislation is the Department of Corrections Act, which gives jurisdiction over jails and prisons to a new agency, the Department of Corrections. 1967 P. A. No. 152, Sec. 1. The act also establishes a Council of Correction, which is charged with the duty of "formulating policies for the administration of a sound correctional program" and recommending to the Governor and the General Assembly "such legislation as will in its judgment provide effective and humane correctional and rehabilitative custody and treatment of offenders." *Id*. Sec. 2. The Commissioner of Corrections is charged with the duty of establishing rules "for the administrative practices and custodial and rehabilitative methods . . . in accordance with recognized correctional standards." *Id*. Sec. 4. He is responsible for "establishing disciplinary, diagnostic, classification, treatment, vocational and academic education, research and statistics, training and development services and programs throughout the department" *Id*. Sec. 5. Section 9 of the act repeals the definition of "penal institutions" in Conn. Gen. Stat. Sec. 1–1 and provides that the term "penal institutions" shall be construed to mean "correctional institutions." The new sections of the act use the word "inmate" instead of "prisoner," although the latter word remains in some of the sections that modify existing legislation. Section 10 provides, " 'Correctional institutions' means the State Prison, the State Prison for Women, the jails, the Connecticut Reformatory, and the Connecticut State Farm for Women."

These three acts—the Indeterminate Sentence Act, the Parole Statute, and the Department of Corrections Act—formulate a consistent and well-defined sentencing policy for this state. That policy holds that the protection of society, rather than retribution against the offender, is the principal purpose of incarceration, and that incarceration can best protect society by reforming the offender, rather than by punishing him. The furtherance of this purpose should be the lodestar that guides the court in the sentencing process and the correctional and parole agencies in performing their statutory duties.

Essential to the proper performance by the parole agency of its duties is that it "have a large measure of discretion as to the actual time of the offender's release from confinement." This discretion is interfered with if the defendant is committed under a minimum sentence of excessive length. "It must be recognized that a high minimum term limits parole flexibility and handicaps the entire correctional process. Parole boards need the power to release the offender when his adjustment seems to them to warrant it. If the parole board does not have this power, then the commitment is obviously one of sheer punishment, depriving not only the individual, but the parole board—and, hence, the community—of the opportunity of applying what may be the most appropriate form of rehabilitation."

On a mathematically logical basis, this principle of reliance on the discretion of the board of parole would lead to the conclusion that the court should not fix any minimum sentence. This is, indeed, the position taken by the Model Sentencing Act. The Model Penal Code, on the other hand, takes the position that the commitment must be for a period of at least one year. The American Bar Association Project on Minimum Standards for Criminal Justice adopts an intermediate position: it deems it "unsound for the legislature to require that the court impose a minimum period of imprisonment... or for the legislature to prescribe such a minimum term... (A) majority of the Advisory Committee would support a statute which authorizes but does not require the sentencing court to impose, within carefully prescribed legislative limits, a minimum sentence..." Although these three authorities evidence the same differences in views that prevail throughout the literature on sentencing, the difference does not involve the question whether a minimum term should be short, but whether there should be any minimum at all. In sum, these authorities favor either no minimum or a minimum that is "reasonably short." In this state, a minimum sentence must be fixed, and, to carry out the public policy expressed in our Parole Statute and Department of Corrections Act, I would adopt the principle that the minimum sentence should be "reasonably short."

In determining what is a "reasonably short" minimum, of special significance are those statutory provisions that limit the power of the court to reduce a minimum sentence after commitment, but empower the parole agency to keep the defendant incarcerated beyond the minimum term if he does not meet the statutory requirements for release. The consequence of these provisions is that there is greater potential harm from a minimum that is too long than from a minimum that is too short. If the minimum is too long, the rehabilitation process is completed before the expiration of the minimum term, the defendant remains purposelessly incarcerated, and the aims of our sentencing, parole, and correctional statutes may be frustrated. On the other hand, if the minimum term imposed by the court is shorter than turns out to be necessary for the rehabilitation of the defendant, the parole agency has the duty to protect society by continuing the incarceration for the necessary duration of the correctional program.

Both the American Bar Association Project on Minimum Standards for Criminal Justice and the Model Penal Code make specific suggestions for guide-lines to a "reasonably short" minimum. The former says, "In considering the debate between the Model Penal Code and the Model Sentencing Act, there is a danger that their points of disagreement will obscure the points where they are in full accord. One such area of agreement is that the courts should not be authorized to impose a sentence in which the parole eligibility is fixed at a point approximating the maximum sentence. The Advisory Committee concurs in this view, and would propose that the figure of one-third be set as the point beyond which this principle is endangered. This percentage is representative of the provision now in effect in many states." The Model Penal Code, in an alternative to Section 6.06, proposes that the minimum may not be longer than one-half of the maximum term imposed, and the Connecticut Commission to Revise the Criminal Statutes makes a similar proposal.

In referring to these proposals, I do not suggest that there should be a rigid mathematical ratio between the minimum and the maximum sentence imposed. "The spread between minimum and maximum terms should be determined... by considerations appropriate to each, rather than by an inflexible formula that controls one through the other." The value of these proposals lies in their emphasizing that the correctional function of the indeterminate sentence and the parole system may be thwarted if the minimum bears too high a ratio to the maximum.

As a working guide-line that recognizes the unsuitability of a minimum sentence that too closely approximates the maximum sentence imposed, I would adopt the principle that, in the absence of strong and compelling considerations, a minimum sentence that exceeds one-half of the total maximum effective sentence is not "reasonably short." By this, I do not mean to imply that any sentence that falls within that ratio meets, *ipso facto,* the "reasonably short" standard. A minimum does not become "reasonably short" solely by comparison with the maximum and, conversely, when "strong and compelling considerations" warrant a high minimum, the minimum should not be modified solely because of its approximation to the maximum. The standard I would apply, in all cases, is this: is the minimum "reasonably short," taking into consideration the facts of the case and the public policy inherent in our sentencing and correctional legislation.

Although, in suggesting this principle, I am emphasizing the correctional function of incarceration as a basis for formulating sentencing policies, I am mindful that incarceration has a punitive function, also, and that punishment is a recognized means of regulating human behavior. Modern penal theory, however, does not regard punishment as the most numerous " 'medicines' or devices that are more and more being put at the disposal of trained experts." The task of these experts is to have incarceration function as both punishment and correction. "If the administration of the institution is resourceful and humane, a convicted person can understand that he is deprived of his liberty because he voluntarily committted a harm proscribed by penal law, that he must eat simple food and so on because he deserves that sort of privation; and at the same time he can also understand that he was not entirely at fault, that he has various impairments and that, in any case, he is not subjected to abuse or indignity. Doctors, vocational guidance personnel, chaplains and others are employed in eloquent testimony of public recognition of his human claims and of the desire to assist him, not least by curing him, if possible, of defects caused by lack of education, poor environment, traumatic experience and the like."

The purpose of this punishment is deterrence, not retribution, for the latter "does not achieve any purpose of value to society and, ethically, is not a worthy motive for an enlightened age." Deterrence, of course, is a desirable objective, whether from the standpoint of deterring the person incarcerated or deterring others by the threat of incarceration. "The efficacy of criminal punishment as a deterrent has often been doubted," but eminent students of the processes of the criminal law hold that there is a sound psychological basis for believing that punishment does have this double-barrelled deterrent effect.

Whatever may be the deterrent effect of incarceration, applying the principle of the "reasonably short" minimum sentence does not diminish that effect. The person sentenced remains on parole if released prior to the expiration of the maximum, so that, even if released immediately after the "reasonably short" minimum, he is still subject to whatever deterrent force there may be in the threat of further incarceration. With respect to persons who may be contemplating the commission of wrongful acts, it is the "threat of criminal condemnation and punishment" that is the deterrent force, rather than the severity of that punishment. Even if severity of punishment were to be regarded as an element in the effect of that threat, the prospective offender has no way of knowing how severe his punishment will be, for regardless of the minimum, he has no way of knowing when the parole board will consider him a good risk for release. In sum, the principle of the "reasonably short" minimum is compatible with the theory of deterrence by punishment.

As a further guide to determining a "reasonably short" minimum, the Model Penal Code provides that the minimum term shall not exceed three years except in the case of a conviction for a "felony of the first degree," which carries a proposed minimum between one year and ten years. These provisions of the Model Penal Code are cited, with approval by both the President's Commission on Law Enforcement and Administration of Justice and the American Bar Association Project on Minimum Standards for Criminal Justice. The offense now under consideration falls within the classification of a "felony of the first degree," for that classification includes "robbery coupled with infliction or attempted infliction of serious bodily injury or attempt to kill." That classification also provides for a maximum sentence of life imprisonment. This is significant for its bearing on the interpretation of "reasonably short," since it would limit the minimum sentence to no more than ten years even though the offense is of such nature and the offender of such character as to warrant the imposition on him of a life sentence.

Applying the standard of the "reasonably short" minimum in this case I would hold that the minimum sentence in this case should be three years. There are two principal reasons for not making it any longer. First, the defendant is a first offender. He has no history of fixed or ingrained anti-social behavior patterns demonstrating the need for an extended correctional period. Second, a minimum term of three years adequately expresses, in my opinion, the community's condemnation of this serious offense, "since any loss of liberty measured by years is a substantial deprivation." Further, with respect to this point, it is significant that the State's Attorney recommended a minimum sentence of three years. This recommendation I accept as evidence of the degree of condemnation the community wishes to express, for the State's Attorney represents "the people of the State" and the "public interest," *State* v. *Ferrone* 96 Conn. 160, 168, 169, 113 A. 452, 455 (1921).

As previously noted, this three-year minimum does not mean that this defendant will be automatically released on parole upon the expiration of that sentence. It does mean, however, that he may be so released if, at that time, there is a reasonable probability that he can be "at liberty without violating the law" and "such release is not incompatible with the welfare of society." It means, also, that he will remain incarcerated beyond the expiration of the minimum term if, in the judgment of the parole agency, he is not then ready for release on parole.

Although the public policy of this state with respect to incarceration is concerned more with the nature of the offender than the nature of the offense, the latter is always a relevant consideration, not only because the sentence contains an expression of the degree of community condemnation, but also because the nature of the offense may be a measure of the defendant's anti-social capability. This does not mean that every offender who commits an offense that is often committed by dangerous people is a dangerous person. Nevertheless, an offense disclosing a high measure of anti-social capability is an indication that the offender may "require more control than the average offender."

Where, as in the present case, a first offender commits such an offense, it is difficult to predict how the offender will respond to the correctional process and what length of time will be required for it. In such circumstances, the flexibility of the indeterminate sentence system makes that system an especially useful tool. That flexibility requires in a case such as this, where the defendant has shown himself capable of aggravated anti-social behavior, that the correction authorities have the power, for the protection of society as well as for the rehabilitation of the defendant, to keep the defendant incarcerated, or under parole supervision, for an extended period.

In the light of these considerations, I find no basis for modifying the effective maximum sentence of nine years.

In a letter dated April 28, 1967, to Paul M. Palten, Esq., Executive Secretary of the Sentence Review Division, Warden Frederick G. Reincke of the State Prison stated, in substance, that it would be helpful to the prison authorities if they were informed of those cases where the sentencing authority desires that a sentenced defendant should have psychiatric treatment. In view of this communication and the previously-recited history of the defendant's mental illness, I believe it would be appropriate to state in this opinion that this defendant should have professional treatment for that illness.

NOTES

Note 1. The Frequency of Sentence Review

THE PRESIDENT'S COMMISSION ON LAW ENFORCEMENT AND ADMINISTRATION OF JUSTICE: *Task Force Report: The Courts* 25–26 (1967)

One of the most serious aspects of the disparity problem is the imposition of sentences which are grossly excessive in relation to the seriousness of the crime or the character of the offender. As James V. Bennett, former Director of the Federal Bureau of Prisons, observed:

> In one of our institutions a middle-aged credit union treasurer is serving 117 days for embezzling $24,000 in order to cover his gambling debts. On the other hand, another middle-aged embezzler with a fine past record and a fine family is serving 20 years, with 5 years probation to follow. At the same institution is a war veteran, a 39-year-old attorney who has never been in trouble before, serving 11 years for illegally importing parrots into this country. Another who is destined for the same institution is a middle-aged tax accountant who on tax fraud charges received 31 years and 31 days in consecutive sentences. In stark contrast, at the same institution last year an unstable young man served out his 98-day sentence for armed bank robbery.

In all Western countries except the United States, grossly excessive sentences are subject to routine review and correction by appellate tribunals. The great majority of jurisdictions in the United States, however, vest sentencing power solely within the discretion of the trial judge, with appellate review available only to correct sentences which do not conform to the statutory limits. Authority for appellate review of the merits of sentences has been expressly granted by the legislatures of about one-quarter of the States and by Congress for military courts. In addition the appellate courts of a few States have construed general review statutes as including such authority.

Among the States which have adopted appellate review of sentences there are two major variations in procedure. In most of these States sentences are reviewed by the regular appellate courts, and the appellate court has the power to review the merits of the sentences in any case over which it otherwise has jurisdiction. In four States, however, a specially created court staffed by experienced trial judges is convened solely for the purpose of reviewing the merits of sentences; only sentences of imprisonment in the penitentiary may be appealed, and the review division is empowered to increase as well as to reduce sentences.

In recent years adoption of appellate review of sentences has substantially increased. Since 1964 three States have enacted legislation to permit appellate review. The Council of State Governments recommended the adoption of procedures for appellate review and proposed model legislation in 1962. Bills introduced in Congress to authorize appellate review of sentences in the Federal system have received the support of the Department of Justice and the Judicial Conference of the United States. And this year the Advisory Committee on Sentencing of the American Bar Association's minimum standards project urged the enactment of appellate review legislation in all States. The committee's report carefully considers the important procedural issues involved in appellate review, such as the type and length of sentences which may be appealed, the desirability of opinions by the reviewing court, the authority of the reviewing court to increase sentences, and the right of the prosecution to appeal sentences.

The most important contribution of appellate review is the opportunity it provides for the correction of grossly excessive sentences. Although appellate review will not totally eliminate the problem of disparity of sentences, by reducing the peaks of disparity, it would narrow the range in which individual differences among judges can affect the length and type of sentences.

Moreover, appellate review aids the development of a uniform sentencing policy within a jurisdiction. It tends to cause both trial and appellate courts to give sustained consideration to the justification for particular sentences. And the opinions of appellate courts in modifying excessive sentences can provide a body of law to guide trial courts in all cases.

Finally, appellate review would tend to reduce the number of anomalous decisions on procedural and substantive law which appellate courts have made in order to reverse cases involving unusually harsh sentences. As former Chief Judge Simon E. Sobeloff of the Fourth Circuit Court of Appeals has stated:

> Many appeals are docketed today only because of the severity of the sentence pronounced in the district court and since the appellate tribunal cannot tackle the real issue in a forthright manner, it may, and often does, in its endeavor to strike down a harsh penalty, give the law a strained construction liable to work havoc in future cases.

The primary objection to appellate review is that it might greatly increase litigation because review would become available for all those defendants who plead guilty—between 70 and 90 percent of all convicted offenders—and who are generally unable to obtain direct review of their convictions. And it is possible that the expanded availability of counsel would encourage many of these defendants to appeal their sentences. Jurisdictions permitting appellate review, however, have not experienced an unreasonable burden on the reviewing court. From 1960 through 1965 in Massachusetts, for example, there was an average of about 300 sentence appeals per year, and the review division sat for an average of 15 days a year. Judge Charles D. Breitel of the New York State Court of Appeals has estimated that although excessiveness of sentence is mentioned in about three-fourths of the criminal appeals heard in the Appellate Division of the Supreme Court, "this issue is seriously argued in very few, and ... even then, little additional work is involved."

A second objection to appelate review is that sentencing is a discretionary matter involving questions of judgment and not of law such as appellate courts are used to handling. In view of the importance of sentencing to the defendant and to the effectiveness of the criminal processes it is unreasonable to consider sentencing as a matter of such exceptional discretion that it should be immune from appellate review. Appellate courts routinely are called upon to review discretionary rulings by trial judges in both civil and criminal cases. Appellate review is not an occasion for the appellate court to resentence the defendant to a punishment which it would have imposed had it been the trial court. The policy of the English Court of Criminal Appeal is that a sentence will be altered only when it represents such a substantial departure from the norm that the court is satisfied that the trial judge failed to apply the correct principles. Experience with appellate review of sentences indicates that appellate judges in this country have not substituted their discretion for that of the trial court.

A third objection is that appellate judges are less able to assess an appropriate sentence because of their inability to observe the defendant. But inability to observe the defendant, although relevant in determining the latitude of appellate review, does not place the reviewing court at a great disadvantage. In the majority of cases the trial court's confrontation of the defendant is extremely brief because no trial is held. And even when conviction follows a trial, the unusual and difficult circumstances facing a criminal defendant are not the most favorable for a fair assessment of his character.

Note 2. Guidelines

AMERICAN BAR ASSOCIATION STANDARDS ON APPELLATE REVIEW OF SENTENCES 7–12 (1968)*

1.1 *Principle of review.*
  (a) In principle, judicial review should be available for all sentences imposed in cases where provision is made for review of the conviction. This is specifically meant to include
    (i) review of a sentence imposed after a guilty plea or the equivalent, if the case is one in which review of the conviction would be available had the case gone to trial;
    (ii) review of a sentence imposed by a trial judge, a trial jury, or the two in combination; and
    (iii) review of a re-sentence in the same class of cases.
  (b) Although review of every such sentence ought to be available, it is recognized that it may be desirable, at least for an initial experimental period, to place a reasonable limit on the length and kind of sentence that should be subject to review.

1.2 *Purposes of review.*
The general objectives of sentence review are:
  (i) to correct the sentence which is excessive in length, having regard to the nature of the offense, the character of the offender, and the protection of the public interest;
  (ii) to facilitate the rehabilitation of the offender by affording him an opportunity to assert grievances he may have regarding his sentence;
  (iii) to promote respect for law by correcting abuses of the sentencing power and by increasing the fairness of the sentencing process; and
  (iv) to promote the development and application of criteria for sentencing which are both rational and just.

Availability of Review

2.1 *Reviewing court.*
  In general, each court which is empowered to review the conviction should also be empowered to review the disposition following conviction. It may be advisable to depart from this principle in some context, as, for example, where intermediate appellate courts are available to review sentences and it is deemed unwise to involve the highest court in such matters. In any event, specialized courts should not be created to review the sentence only.

2.2 *Procedure and conditions.*
  (a) In all cases where sentence is imposed after a trial on the question of guilt, review of the sentence should be available on the same basis as review of the conviction.
  (b) In all cases where a sentence is imposed after a guilty plea or the equivalent, review of the sentence, as

---

* Quoted with permission of the American Bar Association, 1155 East 60th Street, Chicago, Illinois 60637.

well as review of other matters which can be raised, could appropriately be governed by a procedure patterned after the following:

(i) Notice of appeal should be required of the defendant within [15] days of the imposition of sentence. The court should advise the defendant at the time of sentencing of his right to appeal and of the time limit, and should at the same time afford him the opportunity to comply orally with the notice requirement. It should be the responsibility of the attorney who represented the defendant at the sentencing stage to advise him with respect to the filing of the notice of appeal, and to assure that his rights in this respect are protected. Both the sentencing court and the reviewing court should be authorized to enlarge the time for filing the notice of appeal for good cause;

(ii) The sentence appeal should be of right, except to courts where appeal from a conviction after trial would be by leave of court. In cases where leave is required, it may be preferable to follow normal procedures instead of a special procedure patterned after this subsection;

(iii) Unless the defendant is able to retain his own legal assistance or elects not to be represented, an attorney should be appointed as soon as the notice of appeal is filed. Unless it appears inappropriate in a particular instance, it is desirable that the same attorney who represented the defendant at the trial level be appointed to prosecute the sentence appeal;

(iv) The clerk or other responsible official should be required to secure a transcript of the record within [10] days of the filing of the notice of appeal. He should also be required to provide a copy as soon as it is available to the defendant's attorney, to the defendant if he has no attorney, to the state, and to the reviewing court;

(v) All papers in support of the merits of the appeal should be required to be filed within [15] days from the time the attorney, or the defendant if he has no attorney, receives the record, unless the time is enlarged upon application to the reviewing court;

(vi) Any response which the state desires to make should be required to be filed within [10] days of the filing of the defendant's papers, unless the time is enlarged upon application to the reviewing court. The state should promptly notify the court if it has decided not to file a response;

(vii) All writtten submissions may be typed rather than printed;

(viii) In courts of more than three judges, panels of three may be designated to hear the sentence appeal, without a hearing en banc unless the court sua sponte so orders. The appeal should be decided as expeditiously as is consistent with a fair hearing of the defendant's claims. If possible, time should be allocated each week for the hearing of all appeals which are then ready for disposition, and a decision should be rendered as promptly as the case permits. It may be appropriate in some cases, as where the appeal is patently without merit, to decide the case summarily without a hearing;

(ix) The defendant should commence service of a prison term upon imposition of the sentence, unless bail or the equivalent is granted by the sentencing court or the reviewing court upon special application, or unless either the sentencing court or the reviewing court specifies upon application that the defendant should be detained in a local facility until the sentence appeal has been concluded.

If such a procedure is developed for guilty plea cases, it may also be appropriate to use it in all cases where matters relating to the sentence are the only questions which can be appealed.

2.3 *Record on appeal; statement explaining sentence.*

(a) The following items should be available for inclusion in the record on appeal:

(i) a verbatim record of the entire sentencing proceeding, including a record of any statements in aggravation or mitigation made by the defendant, the defense attorney and the prosecuting attorney, together with any testimony received of witnesses on matters relevant to the sentence, any instructions or comments by the court to the jury in cases where the jury participated in the sentencing decision, and any statements by the court explaining the sentence;

(ii) a verbatim record of such parts of the trial on the issue of guilt, or the proceedings leading to the acceptance of a plea, as are relevant to the sentencing decision;

(iii) copies of the presentence report, the report of a diagnostic facility, or any other reports or documents available to the sentencing court as an aid in passing sentence. The part of the record containing such reports or documents should be subject to examination by the parties only to the extent that such examination was permitted prior to the imposition of sentence.

(b) The record normally should be prepared in each case in the same manner as would any other record to be presented to the court involved.

(c) The sentencing judge should be required in every case to state his reasons for selecting the particular sentence imposed. Normally, this should be done for the record in the presence of the defendant at the time of sentence. In cases in which the sentencing judge deems it in the interest of the defendant not to state fully the reasons for the sentence in the presence of the defendant, he should prepare such a statement for transmission to the reviewing court as a part of the record.

Scope of Review

3.1 *Duties of reviewing court.*

(a) It should be the obligation of the reviewing court to make its own examination of the record designed to effect the objectives of sentence review as stated in section 1.2.

(b) In those cases in which it would substantially contribute to the achievement of the objectives of sentence review as stated in section 1.2, the reviewing court should set forth the basis for its disposition in a written opinion. Normally, this should be done in every case in which the sentence is modified or set aside by the reviewing court.

3.2 *Powers of reviewing court: scope of review.*

The authority of the reviewing court with respect to the sentence should specifically extend to review of:

(i) the excessiveness of the sentence, having regard to the nature of the offense, the character of the offender, and the protection of the public interest; and

(ii) the manner in which the sentence was imposed, including the sufficiency and accuracy of the information on which it was based.

3.3 *Powers of reviewing court: available dispositions.*

Every reviewing court should be specifically empowered to:

(i) affirm the sentence under review;

(ii) with the exception stated

in section 3.4, substitute for the sentence under review any other disposition that was open to the sentencing court; or

(iii) remand the case for any further proceedings that could have been conducted prior to the imposition of the sentence under review and, with the exception stated in section 3.4, for re-sentencing on the basis of such further proceedings.

3.4 *Limitation on available dispositions.*

(a) No reviewing court should be empowered to impose, or direct the imposition of, a sentence which results in an increase over the sentence imposed at the trial level.

(b) On a remand for the purpose of re-sentencing an offender, no sentencing court should be empowered to impose a sentence which results in an increase over the sentence originally imposed.

6. TRAINING THE JUDGE

Note 1. Sentencing Institutes

a. *Federal*

28 U.S.C.A. provides:

§ 334. Institutes and joint councils on sentencing

(a) In the interest of uniformity in sentencing procedures, there is hereby authorized to be established under the auspices of the Judicial Conference of the United States, institutes and joint councils on sentencing. The Attorney General and/or the chief judge of each circuit may at any time request, through the Director of the Administrative Office of the United States Courts, the Judicial Conference to convene such institutes and joint councils for the purpose of studying, discussing, and formulating the objectives, policies, standards, and criteria for sentencing those convicted of crimes and offenses in the courts of the United States. The agenda of the institutes and joint councils may include but shall not be limited to: (1) The development of standards for the content and utilization of presentence reports; (2) the establishment of factors to be used in selecting cases for special study and observation in prescribed diagnostic clinics; (3) the determination of the importance of psychiatric, emotional, sociological and psysiological factors involved in crime and their bearing upon sentences; (4) the discussion of special sentencing problems in unusual cases such as treason, violation of public trust, subversion, or involving abnormal sex behavior, addiction to drugs or alcohol, and mental or physical handicaps; (5) the formulation of sentencing principles and criteria which will assist in promoting the equitable administration of the criminal laws of the United States.

(b) After the Judicial Conference has approved the time, place, participants, agenda, and other arrangements for such institutes and joint councils, the chief judge of each circuit is authorized to invite the attendance of district judges under conditions which he thinks proper and which will not unduly delay the work of the courts.

(c) The Attorney General is authorized to select and direct the attendance at such institutes and meetings of United States attorneys and other officials of the Department of Justice and may invite the participation of other interested Federal officers. He may also invite specialists in sentencing methods, criminologists, psychiatrists, penologists, and others to participate in the proceedings.

(d) The expenses of attendance of judges shall be paid from applicable appropriations for the judiciary of the United States. The expenses connected with the preparation of the plans and agenda for the conference and for the travel and other expenses incident to the attendance of officials and other participants invited by the Attorney General shall be paid from applicable appropriations of the Department of Justice.

In response, most of the federal judicial circuits have conducted sentencing institutes of one kind or another. See, *e.g.,*

Pilot Institute on Sentencing, 26 F.R.D. 231 (1959)

Ninth Circuit Sentencing Institute, 27 F.R.D. 287 (1960)

Fifth Circuit Sentencing Institute, 30 F.R.D. 185 (1961)

Second Circuit: Appellate Review of Sentences, 32 F.R.D. 249 (1962)

Third Circuit Sentencing Institute, 37 F.R.D. 111 (1964)

Ninth Circuit Sentencing Institute, 39 F.R.D. 523 (1965)

Eighth and Tenth Circuit Sentencing Institute, 42 F.R.D. 175 (1966)

Fourth and Fifth Circuit Sentencing Institute, 45 F.R.D. 149 (1967)

There have also been several sentencing institutes for new district judges. See, *e.g.,*

District Judges Sentencing Institute, 35 F.R.D. 381 (1964)

District Judges Sentencing Institute, 37 F.R.D. 111 (1964)

b. *State*

Illustrative of the approach of a state judicial sentencing institute is the following extract from the 1967 California Sentencing Institute, 62 Cal. Rep. Appendix at 14–19:

> JUDGE WALTER R. EVANS, Mono Superior Court, who served as panel moderator, introduced the panelists, Judge Richard F. C. Hayden, Los Angeles Superior Court, Judge Redmond C. Staats, Jr., Alameda Superior Court, and Judge Warren K. Taylor, Yolo Superior Court.
>
> After reading aloud Case No. 1, Judge Evans asked the judges in the audience to indicate the sentence they would impose on a "straw vote" ballot form. After the ballots were collected, Judge Hayden discussed the first case.
>
> CASE #1
> OFFENSE: BATTERY. Victim left home to go to see sister. In front of the house, Defendant was in car with two other men. Victim knew one of the men and accepted offer to ride. However, they did not drive to sister; instead they cruised around, picked up another woman and stopped at a park. Defendant forced himself on victim, and when she refused to have sex relations, struck her on side of face with a chain. Victim then submitted to Defendant and when they drove to a liquor store she ran away and hid until she called police. Defendant pled guilty to charge of battery.
>
> **PRIOR CRIMINAL HISTORY:**
>
> | | | | | |
> |---|---|---|---|---|
> | 6/58 | County X | Auto theft | One year county jail |
> | 4/63 | County X | Petty theft | Thirty days county jail |
> | 2/67 | County X | PRESENT OFFENSE | |
>
> CASE HISTORY INFORMATION: This is a 32-year-old, single Negro man, the third of six children born to sharecropper parents from Mississippi. During World War II parents and family moved to California where father was intermittently employed in industrial plants as a laborer. Father exerted strict discipline in home, but Defendant says he never was able to form satisfying relationship with father. Family had limited income, and was raised in impoverished economic circumstances. Mother died of TB in 1949, when Defendant was 14 years old. After the mother's death, first of a series of minor offenses occurred, which culminated in 1958 in auto theft, for which he received one year county jail term.
>
> Defendant achieved 10th grade in high school, but actually is barely literate. His I.Q. tests are 72, far below normal. He was constant behavioral problem in school. He has no marketable skills, and has not had steady employment. Sporadically employed at house cleaning, car washing, and unskilled labor.
>
> MILITARY HISTORY: Has never been a member of Armed Services because of prior criminal record.
>
> CASE EVALUATION: This is an uncommunicative, socially unattached person who has few available resources in community, and apparently has several liabilities. From a deprived social background, he is borderline in intelligence, estranged from his family, and seemingly unmoved and unmotivated. While he doesn't have an extensive history of criminality, it is obvious that from time to time he does not seem to exert adequate control over his behavior.
>
> He does not accept any responsibility for this particular offense, implying that the victim had cooperated in the sex act, and became fearful later that this fact would be known, and therefore started acting frightened and hysterical. According to Defendant, he struck her to keep her quiet.
>
> JUDGE RICHARD F. C. HAYDEN (Los Angeles County): Since this is a felony reduced to a misdemeanor, I would give him six months in the county jail and no probation which is the maximum sentence.
>
> This is my evaluation of the social, psychological and criminal factors in the case: The principal mitigating social factor was that he was a poor Negro from a rural southern culture. His conduct is not as strange as it might be if he were a graduate of one of the law schools that you attended. A negative factor was his very low social and psychological resources: tenth grade education, but not really tenth grade achievement, low I. Q., no steady employment, unattached, estranged from his family, a single person. Speaking of psychological factors, once again the I. Q. is important and his having been a behaviorial problem in school also gives you difficulties. His un-

communicativeness, his lack of concern about his guilt and his denial of responsibility are also troublesome.

To speak to the criminal factors: If there were any facts in this case other than what I have here, I would be very strongly interested in the fact that it was a sexual offense of violence. But since I come from Los Angeles County and know the policy of the District Attorney I can't believe that a plea to battery would have been taken on these facts unless that was really all that he thought he had. I think the District Attorney in our county would rather lose a marginal rape case than take a battery plea. So, I must assume that the District Attorney didn't believe that he had a rape case here at all and that he had, indeed, a woman who started to complain out of some kind of anxiety after sexual relations, and was hit on the side of the face with a chain. I am sentencing with these assumptions. If I had other assumptions, I would be making a quite different disposition of this case.

But the violence is bad and the use of a chain which I am assuming was of some substance, is troublesome. The absence of any previous history of sexual or violent behavior is in his favor because he's a 32 year old man and this behavior hasn't manifested itself before. Finally, the fact that the whole event occurred in the presence of another woman and two other men, once again makes you wonder about its nature.

Now, what are my sentencing options? I could fine him up to $1,000 and impose an additional fine under Section 11211 of the Welfare and Institutions Code to support other victims of violence, but a fine seems to me quite irrational in this case. The man can't pay a fine, and to impose one would be kind of silly. I can give him up to six months in the county jail and that is what I indicated I would do. I could place him on three years' probation with various conditions, or I could commence proceedings to commit him as a mentally disordered sex offender. That's what I was alluding to when I said if I had any really serious belief that there were significant sexual overtones in this assault I would do that. I did so on one occasion after finding a man guilty of battery in a statutory rape case, and after two years he is still in Atascadero State Hospital. So even though it is not a sex offense, you are not without resources if you really think you have a sex case.

You can talk about a number of theories for sentencing: retribution, social deterrence, rehabilitation by treatment, rehabilitation just by aging a man, rehabilitation by teaching him what happens if you do these things, and isolation. I don't ordinarily do so, but in this instance I think I am basing my sentence on a combination of retribution and social deterrence. It is an awfully mean act to hit a woman on the side of the face with a chain, and such conduct brings out the meanness in me. Assuming that the man comes from a culture where behavior like this might have a certain kind of acceptability, then I am interested in modifying that culture by indicating through my sentence that society as a whole seriously disapproves of this conduct.

JUDGE WALTER R. EVANS (Mono County): Thank you for an excellent job. Now the matter is open to discussion and questions.

JUDGE PETER ANELLO (Santa Clara County): I would like to ask Judge Hayden why you did not impose probation?

JUDGE HAYDEN: He's obviously a very poor probation risk. He has very few resources to call upon and has very little stability. He's unaccepting of the idea of punishment so that you can expect a probation violation. If I were really angry with him, I'd give him 120 days in the county jail and put him on probation for three years, because I know I'd have him back for more jail time.

Once in a while, I will put a person who's that marginal on probation. But to do so I usually have to have some goal for the man. I'm not trying to educate this man; I'm not working to have him support his dependents (he doesn't have any dependents); and I'm not trying to get him vocationally trained (he's not trainable at age 32 with a 72 I. Q., if he has not been trained by now). He doesn't have an active criminal pattern. By the standards in our county, this is not a bad record. So he is not someone who scares you to death. Those were the principal considerations in rejecting probation.

JUDGE FRANK W. ROSE (San Mateo County): I agreed with you except that I would give him probation along with his six months jail term. I would do so because it wasn't obvious that jail time would give him the message which he needs. Only through some counseling in probation would he get the message that society does not condone such behavior.

JUDGE WILLIAM J. McGUINESS (Alameda County): I would accept every basis of the judge's comment in support of his sentence. Psychologically, I think probation would serve his purpose, however. The man will be back, as the judge concedes, but psychologically, the supervision of the probation officer would serve a purpose. I would have given him the maximum sentence he would have accepted as a term of probation. I would have given him jail for about four months as a term of probation and then maintained jurisdiction over him for about three years. I don't view this sentence as punitive; I'm thinking of the psychological approach. I believe it would serve a constructive purpose to place the man on three years' probation.

JUDGE SAMUEL GREENFIELD (Los Angeles County): I felt that here is a man who didn't profit from previous confinements. He comes from a family of poor economic resources and society played some role in shaping this individual. He has never had any identification with a figure of authority, so I would give this man straight probation, no jail, no fine. I would do so because I thought here was an opportunity to give the man an identification with an authority figure, a probation officer, and not breed additional resentment. In my mind he doesn't have the capacity to conclude anything other than additional resentment because of confinement.

JUDGE RICHARD A. SCHOENIG (Yuba County): I think we are overlooking one factor. I would assume he would either have had a Public Defender or a defense counsel appointed because he can't afford his own counsel. No Public Defender or defense counsel is going to accept the terms of probation that you gentlemen are talking about. If you offer him 120 days and probation for 3 years he has the right to turn down probation. Then he'll only get 60 more days and obviously this person is going to take that rather than accept probation.

JUDGE SHERMAN W. SMITH (Los Angeles County): It seems to me that once you sentence this man to the maximum, considering his background you have finalized the situation. I would assume that he has not been able to make bail, and has been in custody from the time that he was arrested until the day of sentence. Taking that into consideration, I would give him six months' suspended which would be the maximum suspended sentence, letting him know that you mean business, and at the same time put him on three years of probation, with an additional 60 days in jail because he struck this lady with a chain, a very serious act of violence. It may well be that the probation officer can do something to get this man on the right track. If he violates probation, then you can give him the maximum sentence, which would be six months in jail. In other words, you will have given him a chance to do something with himself, whereas if you give him the six months in jail at that time you finalize the situation.

JUDGE EVANS: In view of the statement made by the judge speaking just prior to you, do you feel that 60 days would be within the area that the defendant might accept rather than the full six months?

JUDGE SMITH: I think that the 60 days would be enough to impress him that you do not think lightly of this offense. And I would also let him know that you are referring him to the probation officer for his benefit to rehabilitate him and make him a good citizen. Then if he does not comply, the probation officer could cite him for violation of terms of the probation, and at that time you could impose the maximum sentence.

JUDGE FRANCIS McCARTY (San Francisco County): If we are to accept the facts as stated here then the defendant has received all the consideration to which he is entitled by being permitted to plead to a misdemeanor, and therefore should be given the maximum sentence of the term in jail.

JUDGE EVANS: What are the results of the poll?

MR. SHAIN: Here are the results of the straw poll taken before the discussion commenced: Out of 74 ballots, 41, which is 55 percent, voted for some time in jail and/or road camp with probation; 27 of the 74, about 36 percent, voted for straight jail sentence with no probation; 3 voted for straight probation with no additional jail time added to that which he served while waiting for trial; and 3 voted for referral to the Department of Corrections under Penal Code Section 1203.03.

c. *Prevailing Patterns*

THE PRESIDENT'S COMMISSION ON LAW ENFORCEMENT AND ADMINISTRATION OF JUSTICE: *Task Force Report: the Courts* 22–23 (1967)

The sentencing decision demands considerable expertise on the part of the trial judge. He must have a thorough knowledge of the whole range of sentencing alternatives and of their usefulness in dealing with the many types of offenders appearing before him. And he must develop sophisticated skills for interpreting presentence and psychiatric evaluations.

A number of programs have been developed to improve judicial sentencing proficiency. During the last five years the Joint Committee for the Effective Administration of Justice assisted in the organization of over 40 regional seminars which were available to almost every trial judge sitting in a State court of general jurisdiction. Most of these seminars included discussion of sentencing theories and alternatives and the development of uniform sentencing criteria.

The National College of State Trial Judges, founded in 1964, annually conducts a four-week program of intensive study, primarily for judges who have recently assumed the bench. In its first two years, 200 judges from 49 States attended classes at the College. A case method of instruction is used in the course on sentencing. The judges are given a set of presentence reports, and the sentence which each judge selects is discussed and evaluated by the other judges in the class.

Another technique for improving the sentencing skills of judges is through institutes devoted entirely to sentencing, which are presently conducted in the Federal system and in California, New York, and Pennsylvania. Since the Federal sentencing institute program was inaugurated in 1959, 16 institutes have been held, and the judges of all circuits have had an opportunity to participate in at least 1 institute.

The content of the programs of the Federal institutes has varied. For example, at the most recent institute, held in July 1966 for the judges of the 8th and 10th Circuits, papers were delivered on the identification and treatment of dangerous offenders and on the Model Sentencing Act's provisions for sentencing dangerous and nondangerous offenders. After each topic was introduced, the judges were divided into panels to discuss particular problems in sentencing and treatment for the two classes of offenders. Other institutes have used the same format to consider the problems presented by the mentally disordered offender and to develop standards for sentencing in certain types of cases, such as income tax evasion and interstate transportation of stolen automobiles.

At the Federal Institute on Disparity of Sentences each judge selected a sentence on the basis of a presentence report, and a discussion of relevant sentencing principles followed. This method, which revealed widely disparate sentencing philosophies among the judges, has been used in subsequent institutes where the problem of disparity was considered.

One important feature of the Federal sentencing institutes is that several have been held in the vicinity of Federal correctional institutions. This provides an opportunity for the judges to visit these facilities and to observe the type of rehabilitative programs which are available.

The California sentencing institutes have followed the procedures used in the Federal system. The first California institute, held in 1964, explored standards for commitment to local correctional facilities and to State penal institutions, and the judges were informed of the adult authority's policies on term setting and parole eligibility.

It would be highly desirable for all jurisdictions to conduct sentencing institutes on a regular basis. They provide a forum for judges to discuss the causes of disparity within their courts and to formulate uniform policies to be applied in individual cases. They open valuable channels of communication between the courts and correctional authorities on the most effective use of sentencing alternatives and on the content of correctional programs. And judges are given expert guidance on the characteristics and problems of certain types of defendants, such as the dangerous or mentally disordered offender.

In addition, the development of new opportunities for judges to meet and discuss the problems of sentencing should be studied. One type of program might be a summer session at a university, at which judges, correctional authorities, social scientists, law professors, and other interested specialists could meet in seminars to discuss the theories and practical problems of sentencing and treatment of offenders. Through such a program judges could enlarge their own knowledge while providing perspectives from which to evaluate the sentencing process.

Note 2. Sentencing Councils

PRESIDENT'S COMMISSION ON LAW ENFORCEMENT AND ADMINISTRATION OF JUSTICE: *Task Force Report: The Courts* 24–25 (1967)

The sentencing council is a procedure by which several judges of a multijudge court meet periodically to consider what sentences should be imposed in pending cases. Sentencing councils have been instituted on a regular basis in three U.S. district courts; no evidence of their systematic use in State courts has been found. The basic operation of a sentencing council as it is employed in the Eastern District of Michigan, the first district court to develop the procedure, is described in the following comments:

> Under the practice of our district, these meetings are held at an hour in the morning, before the commencement of the day's routine, when the judges may give the matters their undivided attention. The judges meet in panels of three, each judge having the presentence investigation report from the

probation department and having prepared a study sheet, not only for the offenders he must sentence, but also for those who are the primary responsibility of the other two judges. Customarily, the one judge will call his first case, merely stating the name of the offender and giving a brief statement of the offense. He will then state to his brother judges the factors, in his judgment, believed to be controlling as to disposition, and will recommend a disposition to be made. Each of the other two judges will then give, in turn, the factors believed by him to be controlling, together with his recommended sentence. The sentences will normally vary, although I have observed with a great deal of interest that the sentences of judges working together in this manner tend, as times goes on, to approach a common ground. It is in the discussion following the recommendation as to sentencing that the Council performs its most useful function. ... The weights assigned the various factors thought to be controlling as to disposition of the case are sometimes modified by the sentencing judge in the light of the experience of his brother judges with their own previous sentences.

Under the practice followed in the Northern District of Illinois the 10 district court judges are equally divided into two panels. The first panel meets each week to consider the cases in which the judges of the panel must impose sentence during the following week. The second panel of judges devotes its full attention to reviewing cases certified to it by the other panel.

Although the ultimate responsibility for determining sentence in both jurisdictions rests with the judge to whom the case is assigned, the interplay among judges has tended to repress the imposition of excessively severe or lenient sentences. The Michigan council produced changes from the sentencing judge's initial recommendation in slightly over 40 percent of the cases considered during its first five months of operation. Among the cases in which the judges altered their original disposition, the number in which sentence was made more severe was approximately equal to the number in which it was reduced.

Foremost among the advantages of the sentencing council is that it reveals to the participating judges their differences in sentencing philosophies, and it provides a forum in which these differences may be debated in the context of particular cases and from which a consensus on sentencing standards may emerge. It also promotes fuller consideration of the sentencing alternatives available to the court. Finally, where the sentencing council procedure is accomplished by the collection of data on the initial recommendations and final sentencing decisions, as in Michigan and Illinois, it provides a mechanism for periodic evaluation of the sentencing practices of the court.

One troublesome aspect of existing sentencing council procedures is that the judges meet prior to the sentencing hearing. The sentencing judge thus presides over the hearing after having heard the views of his colleagues about the case and after having taken a position himself within the sentencing council. This may impair the judge's ability to give openminded consideration to the arguments and information presented at the sentencing hearing. At the same time the judges participating in the council do not have the benefit of the facts and insights presented by the prosecutor, defense counsel, or the defendant himself. Particularly where there is disclosure of the presentence report, the hearing may reveal that the deliberations in the sentencing council were based on inaccurate or incomplete information.

Some of these difficulties might be avoided by permitting defense counsel and the prosecutor to make a presentation at the sentencing council. However, this would greatly encumber the procedure and perhaps make it impractical for busy urban courts. A preferable solution would be to hold the sentencing council after the hearing, at which time the sentencing judge could inform his colleagues of the arguments and information presented at the hearing and of his resolution of disputed factual questions. Although this would require a separate proceeding for the imposition of sentence, it is likely that the additional burden on the courts could be minimized by careful scheduling.

The relationship between the sentencing council, and appellate review of sentences, . . . also presents questions of economy of effort. Although a sentencing council should eliminate to some extent the grossly excessive sentences which appellate review is designed primarily to correct, appellate review would still be desirable to ensure that the council was applying the proper standards and to correct cases in which grossly disparate sentences were imposed despite the council procedure. It would be wasteful, however, for reviewing courts to give full consideration to all cases in which an appeal was taken from a sentence considered by a sentencing council. This problem might be alleviated if reviewing courts used summary procedures or other devices to dispose of appeals which do not raise substantial questions.

Note 3. An Evaluation

THE HONORABLE MARVIN E. FRANKEL

Lawlessness in Sentencing*

Sentencing Institutes

Sentencing institutes have been, as was foretellable, fairly limited enterprises. They are occasional gatherings for a day or so of judges and, frequently, others (probation officers, parole officials, lawyers, and scholars) from a single Circuit or group of Circuits. Selected topics may include problems of sentencing in particular kinds of cases (tax, auto theft, etc.), general forms of sentence and sentencing procedure (*e.g.,* parole eligibility, commitments for study, motions to reduce sentence), or actual cases in which presentence reports are distributed, the assembled judges formulate tentative sentences, and there is discussion of the predictably divergent views.

The institutes are of some utility. But their worth could easily be overstated. They serve to inform the judges of sentencing options and alternatives that might otherwise be overlooked (at least in the absence of a competent probation officer). They supply occasions for deliberate, connected exchanges of differing premises and attitudes. While that much is worthwhile, it is a small thing after all. The sharp limitations include the infrequency and brevity of these convocations. Without knowing exactly how typical it is, I imagine my own experience cannot be utterly atypical. In six years on the largest of our federal district courts I have spent two afternoons at sentencing institutes, one within my own Circuit, the other at a national seminar for "new" judges to which I was invited after two and one-half years on the bench and some hundreds of years of prison sentences imposed.

The subjects treated in the institutes are somewhat random and disconnected. The results of the discussions are quaintly inconclusive. The goals of the statute providing for the institutes include the hope of achieving "a desirable degree of consensus" among the judges. If this has happened, it is not patent. Sometimes the institutes produce "majority support" for one view or another—supposedly assuring a defendant that something is more likely to happen to him than the opposite if he is sentenced by one of the judges voting. Sometimes it is recorded that there is "no consensus,"

* 41 Cin. L. Rev. 17–22 (1972).

which may or may not be less reassuring to a defendant. Some judges may change their views after discussion—perhaps adopting or abandoning positions such as (1) that draft law offenders should all get maximum (five-year) sentences to balance the service of those who comply or (2) that draft law offenders should never be imprisoned if their resistance is principled. For the most part the judges tend to record their differences, reassure each other of their independence, and go home to do their disparate things as before.

The imperfections may not be grounds for abandoning the institutes. If they are to be meaningful, however, they must become significantly broader and deeper. Recalling that most federal district judges are more or less thoroughly ignorant of the criminal law when they come to the bench, I would suggest there is need for a serious, carefully planned and organized course of initial study, perhaps for a month or so, devoted to this area, and largely to problems of sentencing. There should be reading, lecturing, and discussion about the fundamental questions of philosophy and penology. Prisons should be visited and studied. Professional scholars should be the main faculty, not older judges too much given to anecdotal wisdom. How much else might be desirable is a question best postponed while we determine the degree to which individual judges are to be left, as they are now, with wide-ranging autonomy.

Sentencing Councils

Despite the enthusiasm of the participants, the sentencing council has not spread among the multijudge federal courts. The Ninth Circuit, in a 1964 sentencing institute, adopted a resolution calling for creation of such councils. As of 1966, no district court within the Circuit had followed it. The arguments against the procedure are, first, that it is too time-consuming, and, second, that it is a threat or an affront to the independence of the sentencing judge. These are, with utmost deference to their proponents, not among the most inspiring theses for federal judges. As to the question of time, it is hard to take seriously the matter of a couple of hours a week measured against (a) the hours federal district judges spend deciding copyright claims on plastic flowers or similar objects, questions of "fault" in auto accident cases that should certainly be handled elsewhere, issues as to whether the shipper's or the carrier's insurance company should pay for spoiled vegetables, and other subjects not necessarily momentous; and (b) the possibility that years of people's lives in or out of prison may turn on the time thus invested.

As to the question of "independence," this conception, in this context, is among the most basic confusions afflicting judges and their friends. It is one thing to worry lest extraneous influences or pressures be exerted in ways that might impair judicial integrity by deflecting the decisional process from the course of law. It is quite another thing, and an error, to suppose that the same subversion might follow from subjecting judges to procedures for study, deliberation, and the exercise of reason. The supporters of sentencing councils have been at pains to emphasize that the sentencing judge remains unfettered in any event. The concern seems excessive; no value worth preserving would be bruised, and solid ends would be furthered, by modifying the absolute authority of the single, unpredictable, possibly unwise district judge. The professed concern about "independence" in sentencing should be compared with the responsible observation of a group by no means revolutionary "that in no other area of our law does one man exercise such unrestricted power. No other country in the free world permits this condition to exist."

What may be the most characteristic, and perhaps the most troublesome, aspect of this subject is the fact that each multijudge court has been left to decide independently whether its time and its integrity will permit the use of sentencing councils. Perhaps a period of 11 years or so is not long enough to warrant acting, either way, upon the experiment. But this does not appear to be the real reason, or a good one, for inaction. We are back once again to the kind of national indifference to "criminals" that leaves to individual judges a sweeping autonomy lacking rational justification in principle. There has been time enough and evidence enough to know whether sentencing councils are valuable. If the answer is yes, they should be required by law.

Part II

IMPRISONMENT: PUNISHMENT AND TREATMENT

Chapter Five

WHAT IS PRISON?

A. Inside Views

ED TROMANHAUSER

First Day in Prison*

The walls, about forty feet high, were on three sides. Directly in front of us was a dirty limestone three-story building with bars on all the windows. A sign over the building entrance said: Illinois State Penitentiary—Joliet Branch, and just below this: Diagnostic Depot.

A couple of the guys started whispering, and one of the men in brown yelled out, "Knock off that talking!" Now the courtyard was still. They clanged the gates shut behind us and walked down the rows, unlocking our handcuffs, letting them fall with a clank on the concrete at our feet. As soon as our hands were free they motioned us toward the entrance to the limestone building.

I looked up at the wall as I walked toward the building and saw a guard in the gun tower over my head. He had a carbine pointed at me. I looked down quickly and stepped through the doors into a wide light-green corridor with benches along the walls. None of the men ahead of me sat down so I didn't either.

Two more men in brown uniforms stepped out of a door about midway down the corridor and stood staring at us, shoulders together. One was tall, about fifty, with a set of silver bars on his shoulders. The other was short, fat, and was wearing sergeant's stripes on the sleeve of his badly rumpled shirt. When the last of the busload straggled in the door, the sergeant tugged on his pants and stepped forward. "Empty yer pockets an' put all yer belongin's in these here envelopes," he yelled as he waved a batch of brown manila envelopes.

We lined up and got our envelopes. I put my watch, comb, wallet, belt, and handkerchief in the envelope. As each of us turned in his personal property, the sergeant handed us a pencil stub and told us to write our name on the front of the envelope.

---

* From H. Jack Griswold, Mike Misenheimer, Art Powers, and Ed Tromanhauser, *An Eye for an Eye* 7–22 (1970). Copyright © by H. Jack Griswold, Mike Misenheimer, Art Powers, and Ed Tromanhauser. Reprinted with permission of Holt, Rinehart and Winston, Inc. and Curtis Brown Ltd.

An old convict in faded blue denims, his number stenciled in black ink on the front and back of his shirt and pants, shuffled down the corridor toward us, dragging two heavy gray canvas bags. These were for our shoes and clothes.

"Everybody strip bare-ass!" yelled the sergeant. We all stripped standing up and stuffed our belongings in the bags, which the old convict dragged off down the corridor.

The fat sergeant bellowed again and jabbed his thumb in the direction of a gate halfway down the corridor. We lined up along the wall by the gate. As we stepped one at a time through the gate, the one with the silver bars greeted us with a flashlight. He looked in our hands, under our arms, at the soles of our feet, and then in our mouths and anuses for "contraband." When he had finished this routine he sent us down the hall to stand in front of a door marked SHOWER ROOM.

After we had been standing bare-assed on the concrete for about half an hour the sergeant strutted down the corridor and unlocked the door. It was a large square-shaped room with shower heads jutting out from the walls at four-foot intervals. The floor sloped toward a large drain in the center, and a small concrete rim ran around the room three feet from the wall.

"In and out," the fat sergeant shouted. "Two minutes."

There were about twenty shower heads. A man got under each one, and the rest stood milling about in the center of the room.

"*Everyone* in," the sergeant screamed. "Two men to a shower . . . three men to a shower. *Everyone* in."

The rest of the men jammed into the space under the shower heads until we all stood elbow to ass waiting for the water to come on.

A Negro con in a blue denim jacket passed down the line giving out one-inch cubes of yellow soap to every other man. When he reached the end of the row he reached above his head and turned a wheel.

Ice cold water spat from the shower heads and struck us about the shoulders. I jumped forward out of reach of the jet of water and stood shivering by the drain. Now the old Negro was turning another wheel and hot water began to mix with the cold.

I stepped over the trough and waited for the man with the cube of soap to finish lathering. He stepped aside and handed me the soap. I stepped under the water just as the sergeant shouted, "Rinse off and get out!"

I looked up in disbelief. The man next to me said, "Hurry up," so I stepped aside to let him under the water.

"Water off!" announced the sergeant, and the convict whipped the wheels, shutting down the shower. A few men stood under the heads with soap covering their bodies.

"Out of the showers," said the sergeant. We moved like a herd of cattle into the middle of the room, dripping soap and water.

The convict picked up a Campbell's Soup carton and ambled into the group. The box contained small hand towels, about the size and texture of dish rags. We dried ourselves, if you can call it that, and stood in a shivering mass of nakedness watching the fat sergeant, who was obviously enjoying his work.

He herded us out into the hall and lined us up before a door marked CLOTHING ROOM. We stood in front of this door for another half-hour before a con came down the hall and entered the door. He gave us all brownish gray overalls and gray canvas slippers. My coveralls were too small and I asked for a larger size. The con laughed and said, "Tough shit man."

I started to argue with him when one of the guys behind me tugged on my arm and pulled me away from the door.

"You crazy?" he asked. "Argue with that rat and you'll wind up in the hole." He grinned. "Nobody gets the right size anything in this joint."

I nodded and leaned against the wall, back hunched because I couldn't straighten up in the small coveralls. The sergeant and the one with the silver bars, who I later learned was a captain, walked down the hall toward us. As they came abreast of me I said, "Excuse me, but I'd like to get another pair of coveralls. These are too small."

The fat sergeant stared at me for a moment, slowly shifting the snuff in his mouth with his tongue. Then he grinned and walked on. The captain said, "Where do you think you are, the Ritz?"

I flushed. "No, but I . . ."

"Awright, you'll get another pair of coveralls on laundry day." He walked off down the hall.

"See," said the guy who had pulled me away from the clothing room door.

I jammed my hands in the pockets of the coveralls.

"Better get your hands out of them pockets."

"I can't put my hands in my pockets?"

"Nope," he replied. "From now on you can't do *nothing* without permission. They tell you when to eat, drink, piss, wash, go to bed, get up, pray, and breathe."

"You been here before?"

"Yah." He bobbed his head up and down. "Three times." I shook my head.

"You'll get used to it," he said. "Just keep your mouth shut and your eyes open. Learn the ropes."

"Hey you!" someone shouted in my ear. I turned and looked into the face of the fat sergeant, which was growing uglier with each passing moment. "I done tol' you about talkin'. Catch you again and you git the hole, unnerstan'?"

I nodded.

"What?" he shouted again, his face beet red. "What?"

"Yes," I said. "I understand."

"Yes what!" he screamed. "Yes what?"

The guy behind me poked me in the back. "Yes *sir*," I said.

"That's better," he said, and turned away with a grin on his face. I watched him strut off down the hall and stop in front of another man to begin the same routine all over again.

I turned to the little guy behind me.

"They're gonna rehab-ill-tate your ass." He grinned. "It's all part of the *treatment* program."

I stared glumly at the floor.

"Aw, don't worry about it," he said. "He just seen you was a cherry. He knows you ain't been in no joint before." He leaned closer and spoke almost without moving his lips. "I know how to handle these dumb rednecks. You got to go into a little act is all. You say 'yes *sir*, cap'n,' and 'right away, cap'n,' and he'll leave you alone. All screws are 'cap'n sir,' and you hate their guts *inside*." . . .

Now the sergeant and the captain paced back and forth in front of us, looking us over. "Aw right," snarled the sergeant, "pay attention now. Cap'n's gonna talk to yo'll."

The captain cleared his throat. "You're now *inmates* of the Illinois State Penitentiary. We didn't send for you. We didn't bring you here. You brought yourselves. But we're gonna see that you stay here until your sentence is complete or you are paroled."

He scratched his buttock and continued. "We don't stand for any crap from no *inmate* here, so get that through your heads right now. Step out of line and we'll come down on you hard. My advice to you is to do your own time, mind your own business, and obey all the rules. That'll make your time easier and our job easier."

He spoke in a dull, flat monotone, with a slow, southern Illinois accent. He had obviously given this little speech a thousand times before and knew every word by rote.

"You'll find some *inmates* who'll try to lead you astray. Don't listen to 'em. You'll find some *inmates* who'll tell you how to beat the system and get around the rules. Don't listen to 'em. You'll find some *inmates* who'll try to escape. They won't make it. We ain't had no escapes in twenty years. Remember what I said. Do your own time. Obey all the rules. You'll find a rule book in your cells. Study it. Memorize them rules. You got no excuses if you break one. We got a place for rulebreakers and troublemakers in here, and it ain't pleasant."

He coughed and shifted his weight. "OK, Sarge," he said, and walked away.

"Aw right," said the sergeant, "Stand here till yer name is called by the clerk. He'll give you a doorcard and assign ya to a cell." He started to walk away, then paused and yelled over his shoulder, "An keep yer mouths shut!" . . .

I entered the cell and the door slammed, the key grating in the lock. I heard him trudge away.

The cell was about nine feet long and seven feet wide. Directly opposite the door was a heavily barred window which overlooked a yard. A toilet was mounted on the wall near the door, and just above it was a wash basin and single faucet. Two metal slabs jutted out from the wall, each fitted with what could pass for a mattress. A thin gray blanket and a sheet were folded at the foot of the top bunk. On the bottom one lay a boy of about twenty with blue eyes and a slight build. He had a blond stubble on his chin, and of course he had been shaved bald. . . .

I looked out the barred window at the yard below. It was just after Halloween, but a light snow was coming down, partially obscuring the distant wall and gun towers.

Sounds at the door made me turn my head. I got up to receive a bowl of whatever was thrust through the opening. I looked at it. I smelled it. The bottom of the metal bowl was filled with watery navy beans on the surface of which floated a solitary piece of fat with hairs sticking out of it like the chuck of a hairbrush. Two pieces of bread were jammed down the side of the bowl halfway into the watery beans. I took the bowl over to the window and placed it on the sill. . . .

I climbed into the bunk, kicking off the canvas slippers. The mattress cover was stuffed with straw. It was old straw, lumpy and hard in places, loose as sawdust in others. I beat the lumps, trying to smooth out the mattress, but quickly gave up the idea when a huge cloud of dust, dirt, and lint swirled around my face. I folded the blanket and using it as a pillow, stretched out on the hills and valleys beneath me. The steel plate behind my head chattered and hummed as someone flushed a toilet, and the clanking of keys and buckets and steel doors resounded through the cellhouse.

There was no reading material, not even the ubiquitous Bible. I gazed at the ceiling and began counting the cracks and lines in the plaster. Well, I thought, just about got my first day in. Only fifteen-hundred to go.

ELDRIDGE CLEAVER

A Day in Folsom Prison*

Folsom Prison,
September 19, 1965

My day begins officially at 7:00, when all inmates are required to get out of bed and stand before their cell doors to be counted by guards who walk along the tier saying, "1, 2, 3 . . ." However, I never remain in bed until 7. I'm usually up by 5:30. The first thing I do is make up my bed. Then I pick up all my books, newspapers, etc., off the floor of my cell and spread them over my bed to clear the floor for calisthenics. In my cell, I have a little stool on which I lay a large plywood board, about 2½ by 3 feet, which I use as a typing and writing table. At night, I load this makeshift table down with books and papers, and when I read at night I spill things all over the floor. When I leave my cell, I set this board, loaded down, on my bed, so that if a guard comes into my cell to search it, he will not knock the board off the stool, as has happened before. Still in the nude, the way I sleep, I go through my routine: kneebends, butterflies, touching my toes, squats, windmills. I continue for about half an hour.

Sometimes, if I have something I want to write or type so that I can mail it that morning, I forgo my calisthenics. But this is unusual. (We are required, if we want our mail to go out on a certain day, to have it in the mailbox by about 8:00. When we leave our cells at 7:30 to go to breakfast, we pass right by the mailbox and drop in our mail on the way to mess hall.)

* From *Soul on Ice* by Eldridge Cleaver, pp. 40–45. Copyright © 1968 by Eldridge Cleaver. Used by permission of McGraw-Hill Book Company and Jonathan Cape Ltd.

Usually, by the time I finish my calisthenics, the trustee (we call him tiertender, or keyman) comes by and fills my little bucket with hot water. We don't have hot running water ourselves. Each cell has a small sink with a cold-water tap, a bed, a locker, a shelf or two along the wall, and a commode. The trustee has a big bucket, with a long spout like the ones people use to water their flowers, only without the sprinkler. He pokes the spout through the bars and pours you about a gallon of hot water. My cell door doesn't have bars on it; it is a solid slab of steel with fifty-eight holes in it about the size of a half dollar, and a slot in the center, at eye level, about an inch wide and five inches long. The trustee sticks the spout through one of the little holes and pours my hot water, and in the evenings the guard slides my mail in to me through the slot. Through the same slot the convicts pass newspapers, books, candy, and cigarettes to one another.

When the guard has mail for me he stops at the cell door and calls my name, and I recite my number—A-29498—to verify that I am the right Cleaver. When I get mail I avert my eyes so I can't see who it's from. Then I sit down on my bed and peep at it real slowly, like a poker player peeping at his cards. I can feel when I've got a letter from you, and when I peep up on your name on the envelope I let out a big yell. It's like having four aces. But if the letter is not from you, it's like having two deuces, a three, a four, and a five, all in scrambled suits. A bum kick. Nothing. What is worse is when the guard passes my door without pausing. I can hear his keys jingling. If he stops at my door the keys sound like Christmas bells ringing, but if he keeps going they just sound like—keys.

I live in the honor block. In the other blocks, the fronts of the cells consist of nothing but bars. When I first moved into the honor block, I didn't like it at all. The cells seemed made for a dungeon. The heavy steel doors slammed shut with a clang of finality that chilled my soul. The first time that door closed on me I had the same wild, hysterical sensation I'd felt years ago at San Quentin when they first locked me in solitary. For the briefest moment I felt like yelling out for help, and it seemed that in no circumstances would I be able to endure that cell. All in that split second I felt like calling out to the guards, pleading with them to let me out of the cell, begging them to let me go, promising them that I would be a good boy in the future.

But just as quickly as the feeling came, it went, dissolved, and I felt at peace with myself. I felt that I could endure anything, everything, even the test of being broken on the rack. I've been in every type of cell they have in the prisons of California, and the door to my present cell seems the most cruel and ugly of all. However, I have grown to like this door. When I go out of my cell, I can hardly wait to get back in, to slam that cumbersome door, and hear the sharp click as the trustee snaps the lock behind me. The trustees keep the keys to the cells of the honor block all day, relinquishing them at night, and to get into your cell, all you have to do is round up the trustee in charge of your tier. Once inside my cell, I feel safe: I don't have to watch the other convicts any more or the guards in the gun towers. If you live in a cell with nothing but bars on the front, you cannot afford to relax; someone can walk along the tier and throw a Molotov cocktail in on you before you know it, something I've seen happen in San Quentin. Whenever I live in one of those barred cells, I keep a blanket within easy reach in case of emergency, to smother a fire if need be. Paranoia? Yes, but it's the least one can do for oneself. In my present cell, with its impregnable door, I don't worry about sabotage—although if someone wanted to badly enough, they could figure something out.

Well... after I've finished my calisthenics and the hot water has arrived, I take me a bird (jailbird) bath in the little sink. It's usually about 6:00 by then. From then until 7:30, when we are let out for breakfast, I clean up my cell and try to catch a little news over the radio. Radio?—each cell has a pair of earphones!—with only two channels on it. The programs are monitored from the radio room. The radio schedule is made up by the radio committee, of which I am a member.

At 7:30, breakfast. From the mess hall, every day except Saturday, my day off, I go straight to the bakery, change into my white working clothes, and that's me until about noon. From noon, I am "free" until 3:20, the evening mandatory lockup, when we are required, again, to stand before our cell doors and be counted. There is another count at 6:30 P.M.—three times every day without fail.

When I'm through working in the bakery, I have the choice of (1) going to my cell; (2) staying in the dining room to watch TV; (3) going down to the library; or (4) going out to the yard to walk around, sit in the sun, lift weights, play some funny game—like checkers, chess, marbles, horseshoes, handball, baseball, shuffleboard, beating on the punching bag, basketball, talk, TV, paddle-tennis, watching the other convicts who are watching other convicts. When I first came to Folsom, I was astonished to see the old grizzled cons playing marbles. The marble players of Folsom are legendary throughout the prison system: I first heard about them years ago. There is a sense of ultimate defeat about them. Some guy might boast about how he is going to get out next time and stay out, and someone will put him down by saying he'll soon be back, playing marbles like a hasbeen, a neverwas, blasted back into childhood by a crushing defeat to his final dream. The marble players have the game down to an art, and they play all day long, fanatically absorbed in what they are doing.

If I have a cell partner who knows the game, I play him chess now and then, maybe a game each night. I have a chess set of my own and sometimes when I feel like doing nothing else, I take out a little envelope in which I keep a collection of chess problems clipped from newspapers, and run off one or two. But I have never been able to give all my time to one of these games. I am seldom able to play a game of chess out on the yard. Whenever I go out on the yard these days, I'm usually on my way to the library.

On the yard there is a little shack off to one corner which is the office of the Inmates Advisory Council (IAC). Sometimes I visit the shack to shoot the bull and get the latest drawings (news). And sometimes I go out to the weight-lifting area, strip down to a pair of trunks, and push a little iron for a while and soak up the sun.

At 3:20, lockup. Stand for count. After count, off to the evening meal. Back to the cell. Stand for count at 6:30. After the 6:30 count, we are all let out of our cells, one tier at a time, for showers, to exchange dirty socks and towels for clean ones, a haircut, then back to the cell. I duck this crush by taking my showers in the bakery. At night, I only go to exchange my linen. In the honor block, we are allowed to come out after the 6:30 count every Saturday, Sunday, and Wednesday night to watch TV until 10:00, before we are locked up for the night. The only time I went out for TV was to dig the broads on Shindig and Hollywood-A-Go-Go, but those programs don't come on anymore. We recently got the rule changed so that, on TV nights, those in the honor block can type until 10:00. It used to be that no typing was allowed after 8:00. I am very pleased to be able to get in that extra typing time: I can write you more letters.

On Thursday I go out of my cell after the 6:30 count to attend the weekly IAC meetings. These meetings adjourn promptly at 9:00. On Saturday mornings, my day off, I usually attend the meetings of the Gavel Club, but this past Saturday I was in the middle of my last letter to you and I stole away to my cell. I enjoyed it so much that I am tempted to put the Gavel Club down, but I hope that I don't because that's where I'm gaining some valuable experience and technique in public speaking.

On the average I spend approximately seventeen hours a day in my cell. I enjoy the solitude. The only drawback is that I am unable to get the type of reading material I want, and there is hardly anyone with a level head to talk to. . . .

GEORGE JACKSON

A Letter from Soledad Prison*

This is George Jackson speaking from Dachau, Soledad, California. This message was smuggled out on roll-your-own cigarette paper at great risk to the prison's one sympathetic guard. Its intent is to make it impossible for you to claim ignorance later on, after the war, when the world sits down to judge you, Amerikan society, Anglo-Saxon law. "We didn't know those things were going on" will not save you from the condemnation of history and the world's people. Accountability for the actions of your government will not be avoided so easily this time. After you have read this message and others to follow, you will investigate, and if your investigation is thorough you will have discovered that the inevitable round-the-corner fascist repression, secret police and their secret files, concentration camps, government by assassination are no longer around the corner but upon us now.

There is the possibility that you will not investigate, or that your investigation will be a perfunctory one, then you will be put off, placated, beguiled by the apparent instead of shocked by the reality of what is happening in the center of the ghetto, the barrio, the university, behind prison walls.

* *The Village Voice*, Sept. 10, 1970. Reprinted with permission of Julian Bach Literary Agency, Inc. Copyright © 1970, by World Entertainers Ltd.

Behind prison walls, that's where I've been for 10 years now. Seven years at "the end of the world, San Quentin" (that spot on the social map where one falls over the edge, into infinity), three years of being shuttled back and forth between the other concentration centers instituted to confine the most desperate victims of the Amerikan corporate nightmare; I have spent the last year and a half here in Soledad.

. . . Prisons, concentration camps, and similar places of exile and detention are often the starting and, almost equally often, the finishing point of the revolutionary mind. No other experience, no other social phenomenon, can equal the traumatic effect of imprisonment, the total loss of all liberty. Any further downward movement takes one out of this existence. Because a small body of men cannot govern a larger body without either the consent of the larger body or force (the submission of the larger body), the prisoner has an opportunity to see his society and some of its products at its worst. All pretenses and disguises are abandoned; the guard is there to hold you, there is no need for him to fake the idea that he is a public servant. He is there to kill you if you touch the wall or resist his heavy hand too strongly. Reducing men to dormancy and trembling in his trade. There is no other method to successfully hold a man inside an Amerikan prison. Very few men forced into economic crimes by so impersonal a society as this one actually feel guilty enough to remain inside one of the walled prisons two days. Were it not for the gun towers, the only occupants would be the rats (four- and two-leg varieties). Consider now that anyone who has handled guns knows they are far from perfect tools. Further consider that the guards who think for the other guards are aware that concrete and steel being inorganic and lacking intelligence are also far from foolproof. It isn't altogether impossible for men with imagination to overcome the problems presented by both holding devices, cage and gun. Terror becomes an absolute necessity. The wall is thus given a symbolic fatal quality of its own; the wall and barbed wire fences must never even be touched. Lines are painted in front of them, a misstep across this line could bring the blow that kills. Even if no one dies the fact of being shot at for so small a indiscretion has a permanent emotional effect on all who witness it.

The spiral of ill-will, fear, and dread starts right there with this thing concerning the wall and grows by feeding upon the consequent erratic behavior of both guard and victim.

Great significance is attached to the sentiment that to deprive another of his freedom can also mean a concomitant loss for the man who is depriving. The obvious loss suffered by the guard is the time spent watching the victim, but within the atrocious Amerikan prison systems the whole intent is to trap, hold, and isolate its victims. It shouldn't be hard to imagine what side effects this sort of activity will have on the mind of the guard. Most of the men attracted to concentration camp work do not have a great deal of tenderness left in them to begin with. The pre-conceived notions regarding prison rationale in general are enough to dissuade any really healthy person from ever voluntarily signing on as guard. Consider what types are usually drawn to gunslinger jobs. Any who may enter this work with his feelings, his sensibilities intact must lose them or lose his job. Most prefer to keep the wage. We have then all of the ingredients of an extremely explosive exchange. The relations, on all levels, between keeper and kept will be defensive and antagonistic. One senses immediately the reasons that underlie a defensive, counter-active attitude on the part of the man who is trapped, but the reasons for a similar attitude assumed by the guard call for a little more elaboration. Since the guard controls the gate and may call on the organized violence of his and other government forces on up to the U.S. Airborne Army, it may seem odd for him to feel insecure. This is the case, however, in fact (and I speak here as objectively as is possible—I never underestimate the intelligence of the people), it is a matter of *fact* that the guard is *less* psychologically secure than the man he has trapped. He is more defensive, counter-active, "hostile," than his victim. Although he does control the greater violence he still feels that he can never relax. This is understandable when you consider that he knows how offending and disgusting his actions are. He knows that a man can die in seconds and although he does have help they are almost always too far away to save him from a determined attacker. He knows he is one of 40 men whose function is to suppress thousands and, although he can bring into play a superior arm, any one of the thousands streaming past him on normal errands could be armed with a crude but lethal knife, club, zip gun with silencer. Among the men he is commissioned to watch are probably hundreds of schizophrenic-reaction cases. He knows this and he is trying to remember the faces of those he's kicked or clubbed recently, but he senses he can never remember them all or watch all directions. And he is also aware that he looks a great deal like all the rest of the guards, meaning he must also bear their guilt. He has been told the schizoid will react to the uniform principally. Add to all of this the mechanics of control: aren't the 40 who control the thousands the most hated of men? How else can they maintain internal control of the prison except through fear, terror tactics? Look around the world, this country. How does an unpopular government retain control, by sheer brutality? The equation goes like this: the greater the dissent of the governed, the greater will be the violence of government. If it occurred to you that these prisons can be, for sake of understanding, considered as simply other Yankee towns and its inmates a sort of slave class (this convict class is much larger than say the upper class, the real owners and rulers of Fascist Amerika, the 60 to 100 families), then you are following my theme as I intended it.

In these California prisons the usual set-up is for several riflemen to take positions in towers or on cat-walks over the heads of the entrapped and the rest of the guards. The cat-walks are attached to the inside and outside walls of the connected cell-blocks in San Quentin. Gun cover over the general population of Soledad comes from outside a centrally located "window-gun post" in each of the wings. The guards are generally rotated so that every one of them enjoys the opportunity to man a tower or cat-walk. But the days and months that a guard has to spend on the ground (sometimes locked in a wing or cell-block with no gun guard) are what destroy anything at all that was good, healthy, or social about him before. Fear begets fear. And we come out with two groups of schizoids, one guarding the other. The spiral extends outward and up.

The guards who think for the others do not come into close contact with the prisoner but their responses are governed by some of the same fears that are driving the lowliest of turn-keys. Their wage depends on control "without incident." The people who appoint wardens and superintendents, and the people who read newspapers, don't like to hear of stirrings and discontent from behind the walls. It implies a lack of control over the men that the system has turned against itself, victims of the nightmare who have been made to seem, and in some cases are, a threat to its continued existence. These older and sometimes intelligent guards are actually the initial source of the organized violence, the planned terror. They're at the top of the pecking order. When Sacramento is forced to wield its axe to satisfy political demands for stronger control (less killing and escape), the cuts will be aimed at the captains and wardens. These men entered into concentration camp work in many cases because they could do nothing else. To protect themselves, a rigid program of psychological and physical violence is tied into the humiliating work assignments and "missionary school" type educational projects (what to think lessons).

For what worked out to be a second degree robbery I received a sentence of from one year to life. In other words, I may do life for the same economic offense I could do one year for. . . .

In prison with a "to life" sentence—it's the worst way "to be." Eventual release depends upon pleasing the guard, all of them with whom you come in contact. Any one of them has the power to write formal reports concerning your behavior of which you may or may not be informed. There are the "bad conduct" reports for which you must account before a panel of higher keepers with punishment ranging from a few days in "the hole" or two years in "the hole," and if they elect, you could be referred to the district attorney for a regular prosecution in a court of law if your conduct was or can be made to seem deserving of that much correction.

HO CHI MINH

At the End of Four Months*

"One day in jail is equal to a thousand years outside
   it . . ."
How right were the ancients, expressing it in those
   words!
Four months leading a life in which there is nothing
   human
Have aged me more than ten years.
Yes: in a whole four months I have never eaten my fill,
In four months I have never had a comfortable night's
   sleep,
In four months I have never changed my clothes, and
   in four months
I have never taken a bath.
So: I have lost a tooth, my hair has grown grey,
And, lean and black as a demon gnawed by hunger,
I am covered with scabies.
                                         Fortunately
Being stubborn and patient, never yielding an inch,
Though physically I suffer, my spirit is unshaken.

* Ho Chi Minh, *The Prison Diary of Ho Chi Minh* 85 (New York: Bantam Books, Bantam Edition, 1971).

B. Empirical Perspectives

AUSTIN MacCORMICK

Adult Correctional Institutions in the United States*

The actual situation today is that there are very few very good correctional systems in the country and very few bad ones. Those in between include a few fairly good ones at the upper edge of the middle bracket and a few at the lower edge that are bad but not among the worst ones. The rest of the middle bracket, which is a large one, is composed of systems that must be classed as mediocre, at best. . . . It is dangerous to rate a few correctional systems as very good. The personnel of other systems may resent their exclusion from the highest rated group, and that feeling may be justified. In the American correctional field there is general recognition, however, of the preeminent position shared by the adult institutional systems operated by the United States Bureau of Prisons and the California Department of Corrections. Both have risen from positions of exceedingly low estate.

The Federal System

The federal system began its upward climb in 1929, when Sanford Bates was appointed to head it and was charged with the task of bringing about a complete reorganization of an institutional system long bedeviled by political domination, official incompetence and, at times, corruption. The Bureau of Prisons was established in 1930, and since then the system's progress to a position where it commands national and international respect has been steady under three outstanding Directors: Mr. Bates (1929–37), James V. Bennett (1937–64) and Myrl E. Alexander (1965–).

In 1929 there were only five federal institutions: three penitentiaries, a reformatory for men, and one for women. Today, as stated previously, there is a system of 34 diversified institutions and facilities for adults and youths, of which 29 are of the medium or minimum security type. Notable among them are several new reformatories and camps, the Medical Center for physically and mentally ill prisoners, and the unique Pre-Release Guidance Centers in six large cities for youthful offenders in a "trial parole" status.

All personnel are under civil service, salaries are good, and tenure is on merit alone. Medical services and personnel are provided by the U.S. Public Health Service. Academic and vocational training personnel are certificated. The number and quality of professional and technical personnel are higher than in most state systems. Correctional officers have the morale and self-respect that come from being in a career service.

Programs of rehabilitative training and treatment are varied and well-staffed. The prison industries manufacture products for government use, pay wages to prisoners assigned to them, support the extensive vocational training programs, and return substantial profits to the Treasury.

The Bureau of Prisons has initiated several innovative projects under recent Congressional legislation: the Work Release Program, begun in 1966; the six Pre-Release Guidance Centers cited above, opened since 1961; and the implementation of a bill which permits the Attorney General to designate any place he chooses as the place of confinement of a prisoner. Under this bill a prisoner, while still serving his sentence, can be allowed to attend a University, or to go to a distant hospital for highly specialized medical treatment.

The California System

The correctional system operated by the California Department of Corrections, in common with the federal system, has made remarkable progress in a comparatively short span of years, has applied its philosophy of rehabilitation with practical efficiency, has brought the standards of its administration,

* President's Commission on Law Enforcement and Administration of Justice, *Consultant's Paper* 36–53 (1967).

personnel, plants and programs to a high level, and has had the courage to try innovative methods and the ability to make them succeed.

When the Department was established in 1944 there were only 5,700 prisoners in four institutions and a few camps. With the rapid growth in the state's population, the number of prisoners in 1966 reached 27,500 and the facilities numbered ten institutions, two Reception-Guidance Centers and over 40 forest conservation centers and camps. Of the original four institutions, the open institution for men at Chino has long been world famous, the institution for women at Tehachapi has been replaced by a new one at Corona, and the policies and programs of the maximum-security prisons at San Quentin and Folsom have been thoroughly modernized.

All of the new facilities are classed as medium or minimum security. Notable among them are the 1,450-bed Medical Facility at Vacaville; the Vocational Institution for older youths and young adults at Tracy; the so-called satellite institutions, composed of several comparatively small and semi-autonomous units under a central administration and using central facilities, at Soledad and San Luis Obispo; and the 2,300-capacity Rehabilitation Center for civilly committed narcotic addicts.

The institutions' programs of rehabilitative training and treatment are extensive, varied and well staffed. Over half the prisoners are voluntarily enrolled in academic education and vocational training under certified personnel. The outstanding group counseling and conservation camp programs have been previously described. The program for the control and treatment of narcotic addicts is the most extensive, and thus far the most successful, to be found anywhere is the United States. Parole supervision, which is under the Department of Corrections, is an important factor in this program.

The excellence of the California system is due in large part to the quality of its personnel on all levels, and especially to the superior leadership the Department of Corrections has had since its establishment in 1944. Its first Director was Richard A. McGee, a career man of great ability and vision. In 1961 he was appointed Administrator of the Youth and Adult Corrections Agency, newly established to combine the Department, Youth Authority, Adult Authority, and related boards. Walter Dunbar, Deputy Director of Corrections, a career man who entered the service in 1941 as a counselor at Chino, was appointed Director.

The Texas System

The Texas Department of Corrections deserves a high rating for the spectacular progress made in its institutional system since 1947, when it consisted of one prison ("The Walls") and a far-flung string of prison farms. To get away from the brutal discipline, work in the fields in broiling heat from sun-up to sun-down, and life in the vice-ridden dormitories known as "tanks," dozens of prisoners each year maimed themselves by cutting their "heel-strings" (the tendon of Achilles), breaking an arm, or cutting off the fingers of their left hands.

Following an exposé of these conditions by the Osborne Association, the late O. B. Ellis was made head of the system and made sweeping reforms with Herculean vigor. Under this remarkable man and his successor, Dr. George Beto, efficiency and humanity have worked wonders. Modern institutions have been constructed by prisoners at a third of the usual cost. Personnel standards have been raised, and professionally and technically trained people now man medical, educational, vocational and other training and treatment programs.

Industries have been added to reduce the over-emphasis on farm work. Farm production, however, has been increased many times over the production achieved in the old days. University trained agricultural experts have introduced modern methods, and the improvement in personnel of all types, in living conditions at the farms, and in disciplinary methods is also reflected in the farm production record. This is particularly important in Texas because the average tax-payer understands improvements that result in increased state revenue, and the legislature is ready to grant funds for personnel of all types and not merely for new physical facilities. Other facts that the public comprehends are that self-maiming has all but vanished and the escape rate on the farms is negligible.

Other State Systems

By virtue of their size and importance, and the good features to be found in individual institutions or programs if not uniformly throughout the system, the correctional systems of such populous states as Illinois, Michigan, New York, New Jersey, Ohio and Pennsylvania deserve favorable mention in spite of the fact that the correctional administrations in some of these states have allowed concern for custody to retard progress.

To cite only a few examples of progress in these states, administration of the Illinois system has recently passed from the hands of a custody-oriented official to those of one who is training-and-treatment minded. The reconstruction of the old Joliet Prison under the former administrator reflects his practical efficiency. Michigan has come a long way since the Jackson Prison riots of 1952. The improvements at Jackson, including the reduction of its population by greater use of probation and parole, the establishment of a Reception-Diagnostic Center there, the new Training Unit (a 600-capacity educational facility for youthful felons) at Ionia, the Department's Youth Division, and its Corrections-Conservation Camps are notable advances.

The New York State Department of Correction has recently opened the modern and well-staffed $1,300,000 educational plant at Auburn Prison already cited and has funds for similar plants, to cost a million dollars each, at Napanoch (which will no longer receive mentally defective delinquents) and at the Westfield Reformatory for Women. Authorization and funds have been provided for projected halfway houses throughout the state. The medium-security Wallkill Prison has been for 34 years, and still is, an outstanding credit to the state. There is currently a trend toward lessening the emphasis on maximum custody which has prevailed in the Department for many decades, and is reflected in the five large maximum-security prisons, two over 100 and one 150 years old, which house about 9,000 of the Department's prisoners.

New Jersey too has come far from its 1952 riots, but the old prison at Trenton where these riots started and swept across the country still stands as one of the most archaic institutions in America. The Department of Institutions and Agencies, fortunately, can also point to the Reformatory for Women at Clinton, considered by many authorities the best institution of its kind in the country. Its rating is not based primarily on its buildings and attractive open campus, but on the quality of its administration, philosophy and program. The new Youth Reception and Correction Center at Yardville, a constellation of reception and special treatment units for all reformatory commitments, now under construction, is worthy of special note.

Ohio is still saddled with its old (1834), large and over-crowded penitentiary at Columbus and its 70-year-old, over-large Reformatory for Men. It has relieved the bad conditions at both somewhat by establishing honor camps for prisoners transferred from them and from four other institutions. Three correctional institutions opened since 1925 (two of them since 1955) also receive transfers from the Penitentiary and the Reformatory.

Pennsylvania also has an ancient relic, the Eastern State Penitentiary at Philadelphia, opened in 1829. As has been noted, it is about to be demolished. The State Correctional Institution at Graterford, opened in 1928 as a branch of the Eastern Penitentiary, is a 2,000-man prison described by the State Bureau of Correction as medium-security. Actually, a wall 35 feet high and running well below the surface of the ground encloses an area of 65 acres, the largest prison enclosure in the United States. The Pennsylvania institutional system has been diversified somewhat by the opening of an institution for youths at Camp Hill and one for defective delinquents at Dallas; both these institutions also accept juveniles. The Bureau's only significant step in the direction of minimum security is the establishment of mobile forestry camps.

Among the states having middle-sized and small institutions or systems, there are some that also deserve special mention, if only for a single point of excellence or item of progress. Only a few will be cited, and they will be taken in alphabetical sequence.

The Alabama system, less than 20 years ago notoriously bad, has achieved respectability under an able, honest and progressive Commissioner of Corrections. The valuable land on which its old prison stands has been sold, and the prison will be demolished. Modern institutions of smaller size will be built with the proceeds of the sale. The system includes a minimum-security Youth Center for the 16–21 age group and a Correctional Center for elder youths and young adults. The latter has a remarkable educational program financed by a federal grant.

Colorado opened a medium security Penitentiary at Canon City in 1962 and an Honor Farm at Pueblo in 1964 as subsidiary units of the State Penitentiary. Connecticut, as noted earlier, has combined its nine county jails in a State Jail Administration, headed by a career man from the federal system. Delaware has recently established a Department of Corrections, including probation and parole services as well as the four institutions for adults. Florida now has four Correctional Institutions for felons to supplement its State Prison and road-camps. Hawaii went to the mainland for the Administrator of its Correction Division and selected a California correctional career man who has made progress under difficult conditions. Indiana operates three Youth Camps and a Receiving and Diagnostic Center for youthful felons. Kansas in 1962 established a State Reception and Diagnostic Center at Topeka for male felons; it has the blessing and assistance of the Menninger Foundation.

In Kentucky, under a well-qualified Commissioner of Corrections, improvements were made at the old (1888) Penitentiary, and a start was made at bringing the State Reformatory (for male felons) up from the low level to which it had fallen. Late in 1966, politics swept the Commissioner out of office. Maryland has established five Correctional Camps and a work release program. Massachusetts, having demolished the old Charlestown Prison, has only two old institutions left: the former Concord Reformatory, now with no age limits; and the Reformatory for Women at Framingham. At both there have been new additions and reconstruction of old buildings, and both have a new name: Correctional Institution. Four institutions with that title were opened in the 1950's: the one at Walpole and three camps.

Nebraska in 1963 combined its Penitentiary and its Reformatory for Men into the State Penal and Correctional Complex. Nevada, which has one of the smallest prisons in the country, has abolished gambling at the institution, and the prison has received funds for a few medium and minimum security buildings and for additional and better qualified personnel. New Hampshire has the smallest prison and one of the ablest and most respected wardens in the United States.

North Carolina, under a former Director of Prisons and his successor, a university professor who was the author of the state's progressive correctional legislation, is operating the most extensive work release program to be found anywhere in the country. The Prison Department, as stated before, receives both felons and misdemeanants. The 1,600 prisoners in the work release program are divided about equally between the two categories. The Department has constructed a new hospital and other modern facilities at the Central Prison, transformed the Women's Prison into an excellent Correctional Center for Women, converted a large Prison Farm into a Youth Center emphasizing vocational training, and has opened two smaller Youth Centers with the same emphasis.

South Carolina has made great progress in the past five years under a vigorous and capable Director of Corrections. The Correctional Institution for Women was moved into a small college obtained from a religious organization. A new Correctional Institution for men operates a huge modern laundry and does work for a large number of state departments and institutions. Another new facility is a Pre-Release Center through which all male prisoners are processed during the last 30 days of their sentences.

In Washington, where the State Department of Institutions includes state hospitals and juvenile institutions as well as adult correctional institutions, old institutions have been improved, and a Correction Center was opened in 1964 to serve as the Reception and Diagnostic Center for all prisoners received in the system, and to provide a reformatory-type program accentuating education for an in-resident population. The Wisconsin Division of Corrections is widely respected because of the quality of its Director, the improvements made at the State Prison and State Reformatory, and the new Correctional Center at Fox Lake which receives transfers from both these institutions.

Systems With Low Rating

Although no great harm may be done if a rating that is too high is given an institution or system and publicized, great injustice and harm may be done by giving a rating that is too low, especially if it is very low in comparison with those given others. It therefore seems unwise and unfair to say what, in one's opinion, are the worst correctional institutions or systems in the United States. It should suffice to lump those that seem to fall at the bottom of the rating list with those in the lower half of the middle bracket, and to discuss them under the general heading "mediocre or worse". Finally, it seems wise and fair not to identify those in this category by the name of the institution, department or state. To do so may bring sharp criticism on department or institution heads who are powerless to change conditions and practices which they deplore.

Close to the bottom of the rating list one would find three state systems which, among other bad practices, use a custodial method generally condemned by the correctional profession: the guarding of prisoners at work and in living quarters by other prisoners armed with pistols, shotguns, rifles and sometimes with machine-guns. In one state's Penitentiary, which is actually a huge plantation, the prisoner-guards are known as "shooters" and female as well as male prisoners have that title and duty. All prisoners, including the "shooters", are required by the rules to wear at least one striped garment. Flogging with a heavy leather strap up to seven strokes is permitted by law, but was banned by the present governor during his administration, and has not been used since October, 1963.

Heavy emphasis, of necessity, is placed on "making a crop". Appropriations are cut to the bone, and the farm operations are expected to raise cash crops, principally cotton, that will put money in the state treasury in addition to meeting practically all the institution's food needs. Even such rudimentary training programs as education and vocational training have been almost non-existent until recently. Since October, 1965, two notable steps have been taken by the Superintendent and the Penitentiary Board with the backing of the Governor. A vocational school with courses in five skilled trades and the institution's first industry, a public school textbook repair plant, have been established. Both the school and the industry are under the supervision of the State Department of Vocational Education, which furnishes equipment and instructors for the school. It is hoped to increase its capacity to 200 men in the near future.

These steps, limited as they may seem, have special significance: they are the first breakthrough in the Penitentiary's policy and practice of assigning all types of prisoners—young first offenders and hardened criminals, educated and ignorant—to work as field hands. That progress is not easily achieved in this state is indicated by the fact that a bill introduced in the last legislative session to make flogging illegal, establish a program of rehabilitation, and make other improvements at the Penitentiary died in committee in the lower house without consideration.

The Penitentiary of another of the three states has extensive farm operations and places even greater emphasis on raising cash crops. Not only is it expected to be self-supporting but also to make a substantial profit. It sells farm products in its own state and ships them to out-of-state markets as far away as is practicable. Rehabilitation is given little attention, although the Superintendent who resigned early in 1966 is credited with having built the first chapel the institution ever had and a modern hospital. His successor is attempting to improve the Penitentiary and, among other things, has extended the educational classes. They still meet only two nights a week and are taught by inmates. Some prisoners take high school courses by correspondence.

The State Penitentiary Board's idea of rehabilitation is expressed in the new rules and regulations which it adopted in January, 1966. The reference to rehabilitation is as follows:

> The State Board and the Superintendent, acting in compliance with law, have established a rehabilitation system which largely occupies the time of prisoners by engaging in farm enterprise. This system is based on the theory that certain crops must be planted, cultivated, harvested, stored and sold and this work must be performed by all inmates physically able. No one shall be permitted to shirk the work that they are capable of doing. Your prison commitment reads that you shall be confined "at hard labor" and you are expected to perform labor that you are capable of in a diligent and proper manner.

Although the prisoners number 2,000 men and 50 to 60 women, the paid personnel number only 34. Of these, 10 are designated as custodial but the actual guarding is done by armed prisoners. Flogging is legal and was practiced freely until late in 1965, when several prisoners sought relief in the United States District Court. The Penitentiary Board then adopted the rules and regulations referred to above, and they were approved by the Court. They provide that corporal punishment may be inflicted for certain offenses, but that it shall not exceed ten lashes with the strap, that the number shall be determined by a board of Penitentiary officials, that no inmate shall ever be authorized to inflict corporal punishment on another inmate, and that it shall not be administered in the field.

The newly elected Governor * * * in January, 1967, released the report of a State Police investigation made in September, 1966, and withheld from the public by the previous administration. The report's allegations of extortion, neglect, brutality and other extreme abuses will now be investigated by a commission established by the Legislature.

The third farm-type state penitentiary that has the prisoner-guard system does not use prisoners exclusively, and was gradually replacing them with correctional officers prior to 1962. In that year a crippling cut of a million dollars in the Department of Institutions budget, most of it falling on the Penitentiary, made it necessary to eliminate most of the educational and other rehabilitation personnel and 68 correctional officers. To replace these officers, guns were put in the hands of additional prisoner-guards.

In 1952 a competent authority had labeled this institution "the worst prison in the country". Constantly recurring scandals at that time aroused the state. A new penitentiary was built, experienced personnel for key positions were made available by the U.S. Bureau of Prisons, and the institution progressed rapidly until the 1962 budget cut. In 1964, following a survey made by an out-of-state expert, it appeared for a time that the climb back to its former level had begun. The upturn was short-lived, and the institution soon slipped back into a morass of politics and legislative apathy. The new penitentiary buildings are filled and the crude, unsanitary, overcrowded barracks known as "jungle camps", which they were built to replace, are again being used to house prisoners. The only bright spot in the picture is that, with funds derived from a transfer of land to the State University, a new institution may be constructed for the Women's Division of the Penitentiary, now badly located in inadequate buildings on the grounds of a farm camp for male prisoners.

Systems Rated "Mediocre or Worse"

In the broad category of "mediocre or worse" systems there are large and small ones: some systems with many institutions and some with only one or two. Some of those mentioned previously because of a few points of excellence are mediocre when judged on an overall basis. Mediocre systems are usually spotty: they may have one or two good institutions, a few good programs, and good personnel in some categories. More often than not, they are influenced and handicapped by politics, if not under constant political domination.

A mediocre institution, on the other hand, often has no good spots and is mediocre or worse on every count and in total. A typical institution in this category can usually be described in these general terms. It is headed by a warden or superintendent of limited ability and vision, with no department head or other state official over him who is capable of giving him strong leadership and guidance. There is no merit system, or only a partial one, salaries and personnel qualifications are low, and politics enters into getting and retaining jobs. Personnel are inadequate in numbers as well as quality in all categories, including the custodial force. Such an institution receives all types of adults and youths from age 16 up. Rehabilitative programs and activities are limited and under-staffed or virtually non-existent. There is not enough work for the prisoners and idleness is rampant. Discipline is lax, and prison-wise inmates have special privileges and exercise "con boss" control over the other prisoners.

An institution of this type offers little or nothing of value to the prisoners, and demands little of them beyond surface conformity to loosely enforced rules. They are locked in their cells for about 14 hours a day, from 5:00 P.M. to 7:00 A.M., except during the months when a longer evening exercise period in the yard is permitted. Their life is for the most part monotonous and meaningless, and only those with mental and moral stamina can escape the deteriorating and often degenerating effects of the long days, months and years of their incarceration.

This is not merely a picture of the situation one will find in a number of institutions in states with a small population, few prisoners, and limited resources. In part or all of its details it is also an accurate picture of some large institutions in populous states with ample resources. One may find such an institution in a large correctional system which as a whole has a good reputation in the correctional field. Political influences that affect the lone institution in a small state are usually not as strongly felt by the individual institutions in a large system, but they are potent influences, nevertheless.

A Survey of American Corrections*

The old stone walls have refused to crumble. Prison buildings were built most sturdily, and it has been difficult to secure their replacement. Today there are 25 prisons in the United States over 100 years old. These institutions perpetuate the old theories around which they were constructed. As an example, the Bureau of Prisons operates a federal prison in Sandstone, Minn., in a virtual wilderness between Minneapolis and Duluth. The institution was authorized in 1933, when northern Minnesota was a center for the activities of bottleggers. Sanford Bates, who was at that time the Director of the Bureau of Prisons, decided to "put one up there where they are coming from." But by the time the prison had been built, prohibition had been repealed, and, according to the present Director, "there we had an institution 16 miles from anywhere, where it gets pretty cold in the winter."

No less appalling than the physical structure and condition of our nation's prisons is the number and caliber of employees on their staffs, and worse yet is the unbalanced allocation of staff personnel to offenders. Approximately 1.3 million people are under correctional authority in the United States. Of these, only one-third are in institutions; the other two-thirds are supervised in the community on probation or parole. But the ratios of staff and costs are inverse to these proportions: only one-fifth of the money and one-seventh of the staff are engaged with the two-thirds of the offenders who are in the community.

Of the more than 121,000 people employed in corrections in 1965, only 24,000, or 20 percent of the staff, had any connection with rehabilitation. The other 80 percent merely guarded the 426,000 incarcerated offenders. A glance at the ratios of the 20 percent of the staff—supposedly charged with the objective of rehabilitation—to offenders is suggestive of the reason for their difficulties. The following statistics were compiled as a result of a special study conducted by the Joint Commission on Correctional Manpower and Training.

* Task Force on Law Enforcement, National Commission on Causes and Prevention of Violence, James P. Campbell, *et al.*, *Law and Order Reconsidered* 623-26 (1969).

Position	Number of Inmates per Staff Person
Classification worker	365
Counselor	758
Psychiatrist	1,140
Psychologist	803
Physician, surgeon	986
Social worker	295
Teacher:	
Academic	104
Vocational	181
Vocational rehabilitation counselor	2,172

Clearly these figures reveal the almost impossible task facing rehabilitative personnel: their caseload is simply overwhelming.

The lopsided allocation of funds budgeted to correctional institutions also reveals our outdated approach to the handling of prisoners. In 1965, $435 million was expended for the operation of institutions for adult offenders. According to the President's Crime Commission, "The bulk of this . . . was spent to feed, clothe and guard prisoners." Of every dollar, 95¢ is for custody; 5¢ is for rehabilitation.

The Corrections Task Force of the President's Crime Commission in 1967 tabulated the numbers of persons actually employed by correctional authorities in various job categories and estimated how many additional such personnel would be required if improvement in our nation's prisons was to become a reality. The Corrections Task Force reported that 63,184 custodial personnel and group supervisors were employed, but that 89,600 were needed; 2,685 caseworkers in prisons were employed, but that 10,200 were needed; 14,731 caseworkers in community based corrections were employed, but that 44,800 were needed; 6,657 specialists such as vocational and academic teachers, psychologists, and psychiatrists were employed, but that 20,400 were needed. The Corrections Task Force then projected manpower requirements for 1975 which amounted to a total of 304,000 correctional personnel, an increase of 172,837 when compared to the

121,163 actually employed in 1965. These jobs presently are not being filled to within even a fraction of requirements.

These prison statistics, depressing as they are, are nowhere near so deplorable as those associated with our nation's jails, local workhouses and other facilities for detaining accused persons before and during trial and for short misdemeanor sentences. As one Crime Commission consultant put it:

> Most counties and cities persist in operating their own jails, nearly all of which are nothing more than steel cages in which people stay for periods of time up to a year. Most of the jails are custody-oriented and supervised by ill-trained, underpaid personnel. In some cases, the institution is not manned except when a police officer on duty can look in once during his eight hour shift.

It is rare to find any rehabilitative program being conducted by our jails. In fact, less than three percent of the total staff of our nation's 3,500 jails have any rehabilitative responsibilities. Those few persons who are engaged in such programs are preposterously overloaded with case assignments. A Crime Commission study revealed these ratios between rehabilitative staff and inmates in jails and other local misdemeanant institutions:

Position	Number	Ratio of Staff to Inmates
Social workers	167	1:846
Psychologists	33	1:4,282
Psychiatrists	58	1:2,436
Academic teachers	106	1:1,333
Vocational teachers	137	1:1,031
Custodial officers	14,993	1:9

Not only are our Nation's prisons and jails understaffed, but the existing staffs are undertrained both before acceptance for employment and after reporting for work. With respect to custodial workers alone, the Corrections Task Force of the President's Crime Commission found that they are—

> undereducated, untrained and unversed in the goals of corrections. Unless salaries are raised, substantial improvements cannot be expected in the kind of people who can be recruited.

The average prison guard is paid only between $3000–$4000 a year. Parole and probation officers, on the average, are paid as little as $5000–$6000 a year. With respect to management and other rehabilitation specialists, the Corrections Task Force asserted, their "salaries fail to attract and retain enough capable personnel and act as a ceiling on the salaries of all subordinates."

One might think that intensive inservice training programs would be in existence to attempt to bridge the gap between educational requirements and actual educational attainment of correctional personnel. Surveys, however, have shown that this is not the case. The following data reflect that less than half of our correctional systems have any inservice training programs at all.

Type of System	Systems Reporting Programs		Systems Reporting no Programs	
	Number	Percent	Number	Percent
Probation and parole systems	359	44	448	56
Correctional institutions	197	59	137	41
Total	556	....	585	....

C. Historical Perspectives

DAVID J. ROTHMAN

The Invention of the Penitentiary*

Americans' understanding of the causes of deviant behavior led directly to the invention of the penitentiary as a solution. It was an ambitious program. Its design—external appearance, internal arrangement, and daily routine—attempted to eliminate the specific influences that were breeding crime in the community, and to demonstrate the fundamentals of proper social organization. Rather than stand as places of last resort, hidden and ignored, these institutions became the pride of the nation. A structure designed to join practicality to humanitarianism, reform the criminal, stabilize American society, and demonstrate how to improve the condition of mankind, deserved full publicity and close study.

In the 1820's New York and Pennsylvania began a movement that soon spread through the Northeast, and then over the next decades to many midwestern states. New York devised the Auburn or congregate system of penitentiary organization, establishing it first at the Auburn state prison between 1819 and 1823, and then in 1825 at the Ossining institution, familiarly known as Sing-Sing. Pennsylvania officials worked out the details of a rival plan, the separate system, applying it to the penitentiary at Pittsburgh in 1826 and to the prison at Philadelphia in 1829. In short order, the Connecticut legislature stopped using an abandoned copper mine to incarcerate offenders, and in 1827 built a new structure at Wethersfield. Massachusetts reorganized its state prison at Charlestown in 1829; that same year, Maryland erected a penitentiary, and one year later New Jersey followed suit. Ohio and Michigan built penitentiaries in the 1830's, and so did Indiana, Wisconsin, and Minnesota in the 1840's.

The results of all this activity deeply concerned Americans, so that annual reports to state legislators and popular journals as well contained long and detailed discussions and arguments on the merits of various enterprises. Europeans came to evaluate the experiment and the major powers appointed official investigators. France in 1831 dispatched the most famous pair, Alexis de Tocqueville and Gustave Auguste de Beaumont; in 1832 England sent William Crawford, and in 1834, Prussia dispatched Nicholas Julius. Tourists with no special interest in penology made sure to visit the institutions. Harriet Martineau, Frederick Marryat, and Basil Hall would no more have omitted this stop from their itinerary than they would have a southern plantation, a Lowell textile mill, or a frontier town. By the 1830's, the American penitentiary had become world famous.

The focus of attention was not simply on whether the penitentiary accomplished its goals, but on the merits of the two competing modes of organization. The debate raged with an incredible intensity during these decades, and the fact that most prisons in the United States were modeled after the Auburn system did not diminish it. Even more startling, neither did the basic similarity of the two programs. In retrospect they seem very much alike, but nevertheless an extraordinary amount of intellectual and emotional energy entered the argument. The fervor brought many of the leading reformers of the period to frequently bitter recriminations, and often set one benevolent society against another. Periodicals regularly polled foreign visitors for their judgment or printed a vigorous defense by one school and then a critical rejoinder by the other. The roster of participants in this contest was impressive, pitting Samuel Gridley Howe (a Pennsylvania advocate) against Matthew Carey (for Auburn), Dorothea Dix against Louis Dwight, Francis Lieber against Francis Wayland. Every report from the New York and Pennsylvania penitentiaries was an explicit apology for its procedures and an implicit attack on its opponents. And as soon as a state committed its prison organization to one side or the other

---

* From David J. Rothman, *The Discovery of the Asylum: Social Order and Disorder in the New Republic* (Boston: Little, Brown and Co., 1971), Ch. 4, pp. 79–108. Copyright © 1971 by David J. Rothman. Reprinted by permission of Little, Brown and Co.

then it too entered the controversy with the zeal of a recent convert.

The content of the debate between the Auburn and Pennsylvania camps points to the significance of the ideas on the causes of crime to the creation of the penitentiary, and the zeal reflects the expectations held about the innovation. To understand why men became so passionate about internal questions of design is to begin to comprehend the origins and popularity of institutionalization in this era. Under the Auburn scheme, prisoners were to sleep alone in a cell at night and labor together in a workshop during the day for the course of their fixed sentences in the penitentiary. They were forbidden to converse with fellow inmates or even exchange glances while on the job, at meals, or in their cells. The Pennsylvania system, on the other hand, isolated each prisoner for the entire period of his confinement. According to its blueprint, convicts were to eat, work, and sleep in individual cells, seeing and talking with only a handful of responsible guards and selected visitors. They were to leave the institution as ignorant of the identity of other convicts as on the day they entered. As both schemes placed maximum emphasis on preventing the prisoners from communicating with anyone else, the point of dispute was whether convicts should work silently in large groups or individually within solitary cells.

To both the advocates of the congregate and the separate systems, the promise of institutionalization depended upon the isolation of the prisoner and the establishment of a disciplined routine. Convinced that deviancy was primarily the result of the corruptions pervading the community, and that organizations like the family and the church were not counterbalancing them, they believed that a setting which removed the offender from all temptations and substituted a steady and regular regimen would reform him. Since the convict was not inherently depraved, but the victim of an upbringing that had failed to provide protection against the vices at loose in society, a well-ordered institution could successfully re-educate and rehabilitate him. The penitentiary, free of corruptions and dedicated to the proper training of the inmate, would inculcate the discipline that negligent parents, evil companions, taverns, houses of prostitution, theaters, and gambling halls had destroyed. Just as the criminal's environment had led him into crime, the institutional environment would lead him out of it.

The duty of the penitentiary was to separate the offender from *all* contact with corruption, both within and without its walls. There was obviously no sense to removing a criminal from the depravity of his surroundings only to have him mix freely with other convicts within the prison. Or, as Samuel Gridley Howe put it when composing a prisoner prayer: "In the name of justice, do not surround me with bad associates and with evil influences, do not subject me to unnecessary temptation, do not expose me to further degradation. . . . Remove me from my old companions, and surround me with virtuous associates." Sharing this perspective, officials in the 1830's argued that the great mistake of the prisons of the 1790's had been their failure to separate inmates. Lacking an understanding of the forces of the environment and still caught up with the idea that humane and certain punishment would eradicate deviancy, they had neglected to organize or supervise the prisoners' immediate surroundings. Consequently their institutions became seminaries of vice. Now, however, reformers understood the need to guard the criminal against corruption and teach him the habits of order and regularity. Isolation and steady habits, the right organization and routine, would yield unprecedented benefits.

As a result of this thinking, prison architecture and arrangements became the central concern of reformers of the period. Unlike their predecessors, they turned all their attention inward, to the divisions of time and space within the institution. The layout of cells, the methods of labor, and the manner of eating and sleeping within the penitentiary were the crucial issues. The most influential benevolent organization devoted to criminal reform, the Boston Prison Discipline Society, appropriately considered architecture one of the most important of the *moral* sciences. "There are," the society announced, "principles in architecture, by the observance of which great moral changes can be more easily produced among the most abandoned of our race. . . . There is such a thing as architecture adapted to morals; that other things being equal, the prospect of improvement, in morals, depends, in some degree, upon the construction of buildings." Those who would rehabilitate the deviant had better cultivate this science.

As with any other science, the advocates of moral architecture anticipated that the principles which emerged from the penitentiary experiment would have clear and important applications to the wider society. An arrangement which helped to reform vicious and depraved men would also be effective in regulating the behavior of ordinary citizens in other situations. The penitentiary, by its example, by its discovery and verification of proper principles of social organization, would serve as a model for the entire society. Reformers fully anticipated that their work behind prison walls would have a critical significance beyond them. Since crime was symptomatic of a breakdown in traditional community practices, the penitentiary solution would point the way to a reconstitution of the social structure.

Tocqueville and Beaumont appreciated how significant both of these purposes were to the first penologists. The institutions, Americans believed, would radically reform the criminal and the society. "Philanthropy has become for them seems the remedy for all the evils of profession, and they have caught the *monomanie* of the penitentiary system, which to them," observed the two visitors, "a kind of society." Proponents described the penitentiary as "a grand theatre, for the trial of all new plans in hygiene and education, in physical and moral reform." The convict "surrendered body and soul, to be experimented upon," and the results, as the Boston Prison Discipline Society insisted, would benefit not only other custodial institutions like alms-houses and houses of refuge, but also "would greatly promote order, seriousness, and purity in large families, male and female boarding schools, and colleges." Perhaps the most dramatic and unabashed statement of these views appeared in a memoir by the Reverend James B. Finley, chaplain at the Ohio penitentiary. "Never, no never shall we see the triumph of peace, of right, of Christianity, until the daily habits of mankind shall undergo a thorough revolution," declared Finley. And in what ways were we to achieve such a reform? "Could we all be put on prison fare, for the space of two or three generations, the world would ultimately be the better for it. Indeed, should society change places with the prisoners, so far as habits are concerned, taking to itself the regularity, and temperance, and sobriety of a good prison," then the grandiose goals of peace, right, and Christianity would be furthered. "As it is," concluded Finley, "taking this world and the next together . . . the prisoner has the advantage."

It is no wonder, then, that Auburn and Pennsylvania supporters held their positions staunchly, eager to defend every detail. With the stakes so high and the results almost entirely dependent upon physical design, every element in penitentiary organization assumed overwhelming importance. Nothing less than the safety and future stability of the republic was at issue, the triumph of good over evil, of order over chaos. Intense partisanship was natural where the right program would reform the criminal and reorder the society, and the wrong one would encourage vice and crime.

The Pennsylvania camp had no doubt of its superiority, defining in countless pamphlets, articles, and reports its conception of the model institution. It aggressively insisted that the separate design carried the doctrine of isolation to a logical and appropriate conclusion. The arrangements at the Philadelphia prison, as partisans described them, guaranteed that convicts would avoid all contamination and follow a path to reform. Inmates remained in solitary cells for eating, sleeping, and working, and entered private yards for exercise; they saw and spoke with only carefully selected visitors, and read only morally uplifting literature—the Bible. No precaution against contamination was excessive. Officials placed hoods over the head of a new prisoner when marching him to his cell so he would not see or be seen by other inmates.

Once isolated, the prisoner began the process of reform. "Each individual," explained Pennsylvania's supporters, "will necessarily be made the instrument of his own punishment; his conscience will be the avenger of society." Left in total solitude, separated from "evil society . . . the progress of corruption is arrested; no additional contamination can be received or communicated." At the same time the convict "will be compelled to reflect on the error of his ways, to listen to the reproaches of conscience, to the expostulations of religion." Thrown upon his own innate sentiments, with no evil example to lead him astray, and with kindness and proper instruction at hand to bolster his resolutions, the criminal would start his rehabilitation. Then, after a period of total isolation, without companions, books, or tools, officials would allow the inmate to work in his cell. Introduced at this moment, labor would become not an oppressive task for punishment, but a welcome diversion, a delight rather than a burden. The convict would sit in his cell and work with his tools daily, so that over the course of his sentence regularity and discipline would become habitual. He would return to the community cured of vice and idleness, to take his place as a responsible citizen.

The separate system of penitentiary organization promised to accomplish these ends with a minimum of distraction and complication. The ordinary guards would not have to be well-trained, for their contact with the inmates would be slight and superficial; prisoners continuously confined to their cells would not have to be herded to meals or supervised in workshops and common exercise yards. Security would be easily maintained, since escape plans would be difficult to plot and to fulfill. There would be little recourse to the whip—cruel punishment would be rare, since men in isolation would have little occasion to violate regulations. Finally, these arrangements would permit officials to treat prisoners as individuals, rewarding some with more frequent visitors and books for good behavior, depriving recalcitrant others of these privileges. The Pennsylvania penitentiary promised to be a secure, quiet, efficient, humane, well-ordered, and ultimately reformatory institution.

Advocates of the separate system dismissed the competing congregate program as an incomplete and inconsistent version of the Pennsylvania scheme. The basic imperfection of Auburn, insisted critics like Samuel Gridley Howe, was a failure to maintain a thorough isolation of inmates. New York knew enough to separate prisoners at night, but for misguided motives allowed them to work together during the day. One result was that convicts came to recognize the other inmates, making it that much more likely that they would meet after release to resume a life in crime. They would also influence one another while still within the penitentiary walls. So many possibilities for conversation occurred during work and meals and exercise that guards could not eliminate all communication. Auburn's procedures diabolically tempted the convicts. They were to sit together at mess tables and workbenches, and yet abstain from talking—an unnecessarily painful situation. Officials, compelled to enforce rules that were too easily broken, inevitably meted out frequent and harsh punishments without solving the problem. These basic defects, Pennsylvania's partisans concluded, made cruelty and corruption endemic to the congregate plan.

For its part, the Auburn school vigorously defended the principle of separation and the reformatory promise of the penitentiary, fully sharing the axioms and optimism of its rival. But in reply to criticism, Auburn was necessarily on the defensive, for its arrangements did not so totally isolate the inmates or so studiously aim to prevent all chance of contamination. Auburn's supporters, therefore, spent more time picking fault with their opponents than advancing the superiority of their own procedures. Whenever possible they moved the debate from the ideal to the real, insisting that New York had the more practical scheme, a balanced combination of commitment and flexibility. They argued that Pennsylvania did not carry out its program perfectly, and then went on to contend that the very consistency of the separate design was itself a grave fault. Auburn's partisans answered complaints of frequent inmate communication in congregate prisons by contending that the walls of the Philadelphia prison were not thick enough and its sewer pipes not arranged well enough to prevent convict conversations. Charge, of course, prompted countercharge and before long intricate measurements of institutional walls and elaborate diagrams of the layout of pipes filled much of the penitentiary pamphlet literature.

One main thrust, however, of the congregate school came on the issue of the effects of constant and unrelieved isolation of prisoners. It was unnatural, the New York camp insisted, to leave men in solitary, day after day, year after year; indeed, it was so unnatural that it bred insanity. The organization of the Philadelphia institution, argued Francis Wayland, was "at variance with the human constitution," and his supporters tried to marshall appropriate statistics. The comparative mental health of prisoners under the two arrangements, the causes and rates of death, the physical health of the convicts entered the debate. No accurate data allowed precise calculations of these phenomena and partisans did little more than set down subjective judgments in the guise of absolute numbers. But the Auburn attack did manage to cast some doubt on the wisdom of Pennsylvania's routine.

After asserting that the separate system was no more effective or perfect than the congregate one, the New York school presented what proved to be its most persuasive point: the added expenses of establishing the Pennsylvania program were unnecessary. Auburn-type institutions, their defenders flatly, and accurately, declared, cost less to construct and brought in greater returns from convict labor. Since the two systems were more or less equal, with faults and advantages fairly evenly distributed, states ought not to incur the greater costs of the separate plan. By having prisoners work together in shops, Auburn's cells did not have to be as large as those at Philadelphia; also, a greater variety of goods could be efficiently manufactured in congregate prisons. The New York program provided the best of both worlds, economy and reform.

The pamphlet warfare between the two

camps dominated practically all thinking and writing about the problem of crime and correction. The advantages and disadvantages of Pennsylvania as against Auburn blocked out any other consideration. No one thought to venture beyond the bounds of defining the best possible prison arrangements, and this narrowness of focus was clear testimony to the widespread faith in institutionalization. People argued whether solitary should be continuous and how ducts ought to be arranged, but no one questioned the shared premise of both systems, that incarceration was the only proper social response to criminal behavior. To ponder alternatives was unnecessary when the promise of the penitentiary seemed unlimited.

The ideas on the origins of deviant behavior led directly to the formulation of the Auburn and Pennsylvania programs, and these in turn became the blueprints for constructing and arranging new prisons. The pamphlet literature exerted a critical influence on legislators' resolves to erect penitentiaries and officials' decisions on how to administer them. As the inspectors of the Auburn penitentiary aptly concluded in 1835: "The founders of this system relied almost entirely upon theory for the groundwork on the plan."

There was a clear value and import to a program of incarceration that removed the deviant from one town without sending him to another. In a physically mobile society, the prison was a useful form of control. And undoubtedly some supporters were drawn to the program only because they believed that the terrors of isolation and silence would decrease crime. But the appeal of institutionalization was still broader. Its functionalism was part of the story of its origins but not all of it. If incarceration had been nothing more than a practical alternative to expulsion or to whippings, then a minimum of effort and expenditure would have been made on these institutions. The penitentiaries, however, in first appearance were elaborate and expensive structures, with peculiar and idiosyncratic routines that had no obvious functional quality. To understand why thick walls and individual cells and the isolation of convicts became standard one must look beyond the immediate needs of the community to broader considerations, to reform, to model-building, to an almost utopian program.

Earlier structures, erected soon after the Revolution, had operated in a very ad hoc fashion, providing few lessons worth following. By the 1820's there had hardly been any advances in prison design in the United States, and only scattered ones in Europe. In the 1790's, reformers anticipating the benefits of statutory revisions had devoted little energy to internal prison arrangements. Since laws, and not blueprints, captured their attention, the prisons erected at the end of the eighteenth century usually only minor or confused departures from colonial arrangements. As a result, they did not provide the next generation with tested principles. "Reform in prison discipline," declared one participant, "was an experiment. They had no model prison to visit; no pioneers in the march of reform, to warn them of errors or guide them to truth." The first encounter with institutions was so disappointing, in fact, that many observers considered them positively harmful and dangerous.

Officials in the 1790's avoided the problems critical to making a prison the basic form of criminal correction, and the consequences, to judge by frequency of riots, escapes, and statements of public displeasure, were disastrous. The architecture of the institutions still commonly followed the model of the household. The Walnut Street jail in Philadelphia, built in 1790 and quickly copied in such cities as New York, resembled an ordinary, if somewhat large, frame house, indistinguishable from other sizable dwellings. The New Jersey prison at Trenton, opened in 1798, was a typical two-storied home complete with a columned doorway, and set apart only by a low wall enclosing a courtyard. One departure from this pattern occurred in Massachusetts, where architects in 1800 carefully constructed a building to provide maximum security. The Board of Visitors to the Charlestown prison was pleased with the results, especially with the high wall of hard flint stone that surrounded the structure and an arrangement that fronted two sides of the building on water. "Competent judges," it happily reported, "pronounce this to be among the strongest and best built prisons in the world. . . . It can neither be set on fire by prisoners, nor be undermined." But for all this confidence, sixteen inmates soon escaped. In fact, sensitivity to prison structures was so blunted during this period that the Connecticut legislature in 1790 decided to use an abandoned copper mine for a state prison. Prisoners served their sentences in slime-covered caverns with water dripping from the ceilings. Fortunately, no other state took over this model.

The first prisons also failed to devise an alternative design to the household for their internal organization. Prisoners still lived together in large rooms and took their meals in one common dining area; they mingled freely, without restrictions. Institutional life remained casual, undisciplined, and irregular. Occasionally, prison officers instituted a new procedure intending to buttress the security of the institution. Thus in the 1790's, convicts for the first time began to wear uniforms in order to render it more difficult for an escaped inmate to disappear into a town. Maryland and New Jersey prisons relied upon a coarse brown suit; Massachusetts, among the more security conscious of systems, devised a more bizarre one, half red and half blue. New York compromised with coarse brown for the first offender, red and blue for the second. The focus on recapture pointed to the expectation as well as reality of frequent escapes. The uniform did not signal the routinization of prison life but an effort to keep the convicts from leaving the institution at will.

In the same spirit, wardens confronted the problem of coping with a refractory prisoner. The dilemma had not been acute when jails confined offenders only temporarily; but once convicts became more or less permanent residents, keepers had to search for additional powers of coercion. Most of them reverted to eighteenth-century practices, whipping or chaining an unruly inmate, as they once had the violent insane. Some officials, however, tried to devise solutions more in accord with republican ideals, seeking to avoid corporal punishment within as well as without the institution. Pennsylvania, New York, and Massachusetts corrected disobedient convicts by placing them alone in single rooms on a limited diet. This punishment was to strike terror in the heart of inmates, compel them to abide by the rules, yet not require bloodletting or a basic rearrangement of the style of penitentiary life. The confinement of a prisoner to a cell was convenient. Wardens did not intend for it to reform or elevate the criminal, or to have general applicability among all convicts.

Prison officials in the post-Revolution period met other difficulties. By its very nature, a lengthy sentence entailed unprecedented expenses; feeding and clothing convicts for a period of years would swell costs. Then, some kind of daily activity was necessary, for otherwise inmates might come to suffer physical or perhaps emotional disability. The common solution in the 1790's was the most obvious one, as well as the least disruptive to the structure of the institution: to set aside several rooms and a garden for convicts to labor in. This tactic appeared to be an apt way to keep prisoners busy while reimbursing the state for the growing costs of confinement. And it would help to differentiate the prison from the almshouse, making it something else than a rest home between arrests. Some students of crime declared that the routine of labor might serve to rehabilitate the offender, transforming him into a hard-working citizen. Quaker reformers in Pennsylvania especially held out this prospect. But most officials were simply trying to save the state some money, to occupy the inmates, and to make clear that incarceration was a punishment.

The results were not impressive. Officials made some of the adjustments necessary to carry out the logic of the decision, ending, for example, the colonial practice of having prisoners pay the jailer for their board, and deciding that even inmates with property would have to work while serving their sentences. But still they came up against unanticipated difficulties not easily resolved. The household model was not as appropriate to the organization of labor as they had believed. Prisoners were not kinfolk, and the institution was unable to order their actions effectively. Convicts worked slowly and sloppily, shirking whatever tasks they could. Lacking incentive and close supervision, they were neither reliable nor efficient.

Officials were ill-prepared to manage their side of the enterprise. They lacked experience in bulk purchasing of raw materials and in marketing procedures; they were uncertain as to whether the state should provide all the necessary goods or lease the entire operation to private contractors. Their ignorance together with prisoners' ill will made almost every prison ledger show a loss. Most institutions, rather than abandon convict labor, increasingly used it as a method of punishment. New Jersey legislators, concerned more with correction than with profit, instructed prison officials to institute "labor of the hardest and most servile kind, in which the work is least liable to be spoiled by ignorance, neglect or obstinacy." New York experimented with a treadmill, the prisoners turning it to exhaust and discipline themselves. But no one considered the introduction of labor a success.

By 1820, the viability of the entire prison system was in doubt, and its most dedicated supporters conceded a near total failure. Institutionalization had not only failed to pay its own way, but had also encouraged and educated the criminal to a life in crime. "Our favorite scheme of substituting a state prison for the gallows," concluded one New York lawyer, "is a prolific mother of crime. . . . Our state prisons, as at present constituted, are grand demoralizers of our people." Other critics issued harsh verdicts. A Massachusetts investigatory body and a group of Philadelphia reformers both labeled the prison "a school for vice," while a New York philanthropic society declared that it "operates with alarming efficacy to increase, diffuse, and extend the love of vice, and a knowledge of the arts and practices of criminality." Practically no one would have estimated that within fifteen years American penitentiaries would become the object of national acclaim and international study.

The key to this transformation was the Auburn and Pennsylvania programs. Their concepts restructured the penitentiary, changing the popular verdict from failure to success. Little distance separated the ideas and the reality of the new penitentiaries; construction and organization to a considerable degree followed reformers' blueprints. The match, to be sure, was by no means perfect, and by the 1850's, abuses were undermining the system. But the states made an energetic and not unsuccessful attempt to put the programs into effect. These latest institutions were not the logical end of a development that began with the seventeenth-century house of correction, continued in the eighteenth-century workhouse, and improved in the post-Revolution prison. Of course various components in the system had roots in older ideas and practices, but the sum of the penitentiary was qualitatively different from its several parts. Europeans traveled to the new world to examine an American creation, not to see a minor variant on an old world theme. The antebellum generation could rightly claim to have made a major innovation in criminal punishment.

The new principle of separation was as central to penitentiary practices as it was to reformers' pamphlets. Officials repeatedly looked to it to solve specific problems (the rules governing letter-writing, how visitors should be treated), as well as to shape general policies (the inmates' daily routine, the overall design of the structure). It was never the only guideline—wardens and agents had financial obligations to fulfill, since state legislators anticipated that prisons would contribute substantially to their own upkeep. But the ledgers alone were not determinative.

The institutions rigorously attempted to isolate the prisoner both from the general community and from his fellow inmates. To fulfill the first charge, they severed almost every tie between the prisoner and his family and friends, and even attempted with some degree of success to block out reports of outside events. Pennsylvania went to the furthest extremes. The prison at Philadelphia prohibited any relative or friend from visiting the inmate and allowed only a handful of carefully screened persons, of whose virtue there could be no doubt, to see the convict in his cell. It banned all exchanges of correspondence and excluded newspapers to insure convicts' ignorance of external affairs. Partisans accurately boasted that a Pennsylvania inmate was "perfectly secluded from the world . . . hopelessly separated from one's family, and from all communication with and knowledge of them for the whole term of imprisonment." Throughout the pre–Civil War period, penitentiaries organized on the separate system made almost no compromises with these regulations.

New York's practices were hardly less rigid. The state penitentiary rules in the 1830's declared that convicts were to "receive no letters or intelligence from or concerning their friends, or any information on any subject out of prison." Relatives were not permitted to visit with an inmate and he, in turn, was not allowed to correspond with them. "The prisoner," a Sing-Sing chaplain of this period recalled, "was taught to consider himself dead to all without the prison walls." And the warden himself repeated this analogy when instructing new convicts on their situation. "It is true," he told them in 1826, "that while confined here you can have no intelligence concerning relatives or friends. . . . You are to be literally buried from the world." Officials somewhat relaxed these regulations in the 1840's, but the concessions were minimal. At Sing-Sing convicts were then allowed to send one letter every six months, and at the new prison at Clinton, one every four months—subject of course to the chaplain writing and the warden censoring it. They could also receive a single visit from relatives, in the presence of guards, during the course of their sentence. Throughout these decades the penitentiaries prohibited newspapers and books. The results were mixed, but if convicts often managed to smuggle these materials in, periodic cell inspections ferreted them out.

Institutions in other states adhered to similar standards, all attempting, with varying degrees of success, to isolated the convict from society. New Jersey officials, for example, complained bitterly in 1830 that prisoners knew too much about public events. Convinced that "discipline is interrupted by a knowledge in the prison, among the convicts, of almost everything that is done abroad," they unhappily reported that inmates were learning through newspapers and conversations what was happening at the state capital, especially in regard to prison matters. The administrative reaction was predictable: more stringent isolation of the inmates from each other, from the guards, and from the community. Indeed, New Jersey soon decided to follow the more stringent procedures of the Pennsylvania system rather than the Auburn plan. Maine's prison commissioner in this period, future presidential candidate James Blaine, was also certain that "information upon events of current interest, and glimpses of the outer world, have a tendency to unsettle the convict's mind and render him restless and uneasy." Distressed to find magazines and newspapers circulating in the state's congregate prison, Blaine charged officials to work still harder at "separating the convict from all association with the world at large," at banishing external influences from the penitentiary. The thick walls that surrounded the penitentiary were not only to keep inmates in, but the rest of the world out.

Just as critical to the organization of the penitentiary was the isolation of inmates from each other. The program was formidable, far more difficult than excluding visitors; still, wardens and keepers, especially before 1840, enjoyed a fair measure of success. The obstacles were greater in congregate than in separate institutions and the congregate system swept the states. But the popularity of Auburn was no less a triumph for the principle of separation. The prestigious Boston Prison Discipline Society announced that since congregate systems operated just as effectively as separate ones, it was senseless and wasteful to appropriate the extra funds. An influential pamphleteer like Matthew Carey also urged officials to adopt the New York plan, convinced that the separate system had no monopoly on proper discipline. Pennsylvania's defenders in rebuttal argued that no one ought to prescribe a particular medicine for the patient simply because it was cheaper. But their contentions carried little weight against the voluminous literature that legitimated the Auburn plan as a reform enterprise. Legislators deeply concerned with the issues of social control and rehabilitation, and yet tax-conscious, could honestly conclude that the New York plan promised success equal to that of its rival.

In practice, Pennsylvania's institutions effectively prevented communication between convicts. The Philadelphia prison, for example, despite charges of faulty ducts and thin walls, did eliminate almost all inmate contact. Visitors' impressions, wardens' reports, and state investigations commonly testified to its success. "It is incontestable," wrote Tocqueville and Beaumont, "that this perfect isolation [at Philadelphia] secures the prisoner from all fatal contamination."

The performance of Auburn-type institutions varied, more dependent than its competitor on skillful administration. Some prisons kept communication between convicts to an absolute minimum, with a single cell for every inmate at night and effective policing of workshops and exercise yards during the day. Others were more lax, understaffed, and overcrowded, operating with too small a budget or incompetent administrators. Prisoners lived two, three, or more to a cell, mingled freely in exercise yards, conversed openly at work. Still others enforced a silence but with such repressive and cruel tactics that even the most ardent defenders of the system had their doubts. Discipline also changed over time. The penitentiaries organized in the 1820's and 1830's largely satisfied the criterion of separation, particularly in New York, Massachusetts, and Connecticut. But in later decades control weakened. Older prisons became less rigorous while newer institutions in midwestern states frequently relaxed standards.

The early years at Auburn, the model for congregate prisons everywhere, were its most disciplined. The stillness that pervaded this prison was hardly less complete than that at Philadelphia. "Everything passes," Tocqueville and Beaumont noted after their 1831 visit, "in the most profound silence, and nothing is heard in the whole prison but the steps of those who march, or sounds proceeding from the workshops." After the convicts returned to their cells, "the silence within these vast walls . . . is that of death. . . . We felt as if we traversed catacombs; there were a thousand living beings, and yet it was a desert solitude."

Officials were able to maintain this silence by preventing overcrowding. As soon as swelling numbers imperiled the one-man-to-a-cell principle, they persuaded the legislature to appropriate funds to correct the situation. The state, rather than simply erecting higher walls and more strictly enforcing internal security, responded by adding cells to Sing-Sing in 1832, and to Auburn in 1833. Consequently, Auburn was able to satisfy the most basic prerequisite of the system and isolate inmates at night.

Its wardens also policed convicts effectively during the day. The state-appointed prison inspectors were fully satisfied with Auburn's performance in the 1830's. Although the inspectors were not disinterested parties—having themselves selected the prison's top administrators—their reports were usually honest, candid, and to the point. When Auburn faced a crisis of over-crowding in 1830, they gave the legislature every grim detail; later, in the 1850's, when administrative diligence declined, their judgments were harsh and critical. But in these first years, they were ecstatic with Auburn's operations, convinced that internal regulation was effective. "The system of discipline which regulates this prison," they declared in 1835, "has advanced to a degree of perfection as desirable as it is difficult of attainment. . . . Our penitentiary system . . . has now become a model which the philanthropists of neighboring states, as well as of foreign countries, find it an object to follow. . . . It may now be said, without the charge of vanity, to be the best system of prison discipline in the world." Even the Pennsylvania camp tacitly conceded Auburn's effectiveness. It criticized the frequency and severity of punishments and the temptations placed before the convicts, but did not contend that the prisoners were without discipline. From every indication, Auburn, like Pennsylvania, conformed to the principles of separation.

Success in the model institution did not guarantee faithful emulation, and Auburn's imitators often fell short of the program's goals. Still, they fully accepted the system's premises, and with different degrees of skill and concern enacted them. The Massachusetts and Connecticut institutions came closest to achieving Auburn's standards, rigorously enforcing the rule of silence and the separation of prisoners. Massachusetts moved quickly in the 1820's to adapt its prison at Charlestown to the congregate system, and for much of the next several decades, the solitary cell and the close supervision of inmates prevented most communication. Connecticut transferred prisoners from the wretched copper mine to a newly built congregate penitentiary at Wethersfield. Its wardens during this period, Amos Pilsbury and then his son Moses, were not without faults. But frequent state prison investigations usually agreed that Wethersfield was preserving silence and separation and was certainly no seminary for vice.

Conditions degenerated as one moved westward. The Ohio penitentiary was intellectually committed to maintaining rules of silence with one prisoner to a cell. "The whole system of discipline," announced the directors in the prison rules, "depends upon non-intercourse between convicts." To this end, the legislature in the 1830's appropriated funds for a new institution that would not soon become overcrowded. But the structure proved superior to the administration and solitary cells did not insure an effective program. In the 1840's, convicts enjoyed an almost free run of the place, communicating at will and controlling much of their routine. Guards bribed inmates with food and clothing to secure compliance—a development that seems endemic to all prisons where administration is lax and permissive, and the convicts well organized. "At the start of my duties here," declared an entering warden in the 1850's with probably only slight exaggeration, "nearly all convicts were clamorous for what *they* claimed were their rights. . . . They acted as though they were martyrs. . . . Indeed the prison seemed a perfect bedlam." So, while the principles and the physical organization of the Auburn plan reached Ohio, the end product was hardly a triumph for it.

The congregate ideology made headway at Illinois, but again the final result was mixed. Iowa's officials also spread the congregate program. They erected a penitentiary in 1852 and then immediately dispatched a member eastward to survey the current methods of discipline, certain that "the subject of prison construction and discipline is a specialty . . . which mechanics and architects . . . generally do not understand." Impressed with what they learned, they set out to make the state institution "as perfect" as the ones in New York and Massachusetts. But although the institution was new, and the number of convicts was small, Iowa confronted disciplinary problems. The outbreak of the Civil War, however, turned attention elsewhere, putting to rest these ambitions for at least another decade.

The problem of enforcement in the congregate system raised the dilemma of whether obedience was worth any price. Did the end of discipline justify every means of punishment? Was the cure more dangerous than the disease? The question had obvious relevance to an institution like Sing-Sing, which on the whole managed to curtail communication between convicts but with a type and frequency of correction that public investigators found cruel and sadistic. The issue, however, was not confined to one penitentiary or notorious warden. Prisons everywhere had to decide what punishments were proper for enforcing the system. Were the regular use of the whip, the yoke, the ball and chain, cold showers, or curtailed rations appropriate weapons in the battle to preserve order? Were offenders against prison law without rights, without protection from their keepers? The answer to this question offers evidence not only of the special administrative needs of penal institutions but also of the strength and implications of the concepts of deviancy and the reformatory program.

Sing-Sing officials in the 1830's were prepared to use every possible form of correction to enforce order, and justified their behavior by denigrating the whole notion of rehabilitation. Guards relied freely upon the whip, unhesitantly using it for the smallest infraction, and their superiors defended this behavior vigorously. As Robert Wiltse, assistant to the warden, informed the state legislature in 1834: convicts "must be made to know, that *here* they must submit to every regulation, and obey every command of their keepers." Perversely insisting that most reformers had already abandoned the notion of a "general and radical reformation of offenders through a penitentiary system," Wiltse contended that a prison "should not be governed in such a manner as to induce rogues to consider it as a comfortable home. They must be *made* to *submit* to its rules, and this by the most energetic means; corporeal punishments for transgression, which to be effectual must be certain, and inflicted with as little delay as possible."

Other institutions too were commonly far more intent on securing absolute obedience than on protecting convicts from cruel or unusual punishments. The whip was commonplace in Auburn and in Charlestown, in Columbus and in Wethersfield. Pennsylvania had recourse to the iron gag, Maine to the ball and chain, Connecticut to the cold shower. And officials wholeheartedly defended these punishments. Auburn's chaplain insisted that it would be "most unfortunate . . . if the public mind were to settle down into repugnance to the use of such coercive means." To isolate and rehabilitate convicts, corporal punishment was unquestionably proper and legitimate. "Only relax the reins of discipline . . . and a chaplain's labors would be of no more use here than in a drunken mob." A Pennsylvania investigatory body justified using an iron gag on refractory prisoners. Convicts were "men of idle habits, vicious propensities, and depraved passions," who had to be taught obedience as the first step to reformation. Ohio's warden also considered the whip vital to a prison system. "For whenever the Penitentiary becomes a pleasant place of residence," he declared, "whenever a relaxation of discipline . . . converts it into something like an *Asylum* for the wicked, then it loses all its influence for good upon the minds of men disposed to do evil."

Penal institutions' widespread and unembarrassed reliance on harsh disciplinary measures was due in part to the newness of the experiment. It reflected too a nagging concern that convicts might possibly join together to overpower their few keepers—no one was yet altogether confident that forty men could control eight hundred. Yet even more fundamental was the close fit between the punitive measures and the reform perspective. The prevailing concepts of deviancy put a premium on rigorous discipline. The premises underlying the penitentiary movement placed an extraordinary emphasis on an orderly routine. Confident that the deviant would learn the lessons of discipline in a properly arranged environment, everyone agreed that prison life had to be strict and unrelenting. And with regularity a prerequisite for success, practically any method that enforced discipline became appropriate.

Reformers and prison officials agreed on the need for inmates to obey authority. Criminals, in their view, had never learned to respect limits. To correct this, the penitentiary had to secure absolute obedience, bending the convicts' behavior to fit its own rigid rules. Should wayward inmates resist, their obstinacy would have to be "broken," and as the word itself implied, the means were not nearly so important as the ends. Perhaps the most striking, testimony to the influence of these ideas in legitimating disciplinary procedures came from Tocqueville and Beaumont. The visitors were under no illusions as to the nature or the extent of penitentiary punishments. "We have no doubt," they concluded, "but that the habits of order to which the prisoner is subjected for several years . . . the obedience of every moment to inflexible rules, the regularity of a uniform life, in a word, all the circumstances belonging to this severe system, are calculated to produce a deep impression upon his mind. Perhaps, leaving the prison he is not an honest man, but he has contracted honest habits . . . and if he is not more virtuous, he had become at least more judicious." Sing-Sing officials quoted these findings at length, and with obvious satisfaction.

The commitment to a daily routine of hard and constant labor also pointed to the close correspondence between the ideas on the causes of crime and the structure of the penitentiary. Idleness was part symptom and part cause of deviant behavior. Those unwilling to work were prone to commit all types of offenses; idleness gave time for the corrupted to encourage and instruct one another in a life of crime. Proponents of a penitentiary training believed that the tougher the course, the more favorable the results. As one spokesman, Francis Gray, declared: "The object of prison discipline is to induce [the convict] not merely to form good resolutions . . . but to support himself by honest industry. The only effectual mode of leading him to do this, is to train him . . . to accustom him to work steadily and diligently from 8 to 10 hours a day, with no other respite. . . . The discipline best adapted to such men, is that which inures them to constant and vigorous toil."

State legislators and wardens found these notions attractive and were eager to implement them. Secure in the knowledge that they were acting in the best interests of taxpayers and inmates alike, that they were simultaneously furthering financial and reformist goals, they had no objection to making some contracts with private manufacturers to lease convict labor or to establishing a prison routine of long hours with little relief. Hoping in this way to make the penitentiary a self-supporting, even profitable venture while rehabilitating the offender, they favored a schedule that maximized work. The results in New York were not unusual: convicts were up at five o'clock for two hours of work before breakfast, then back to it for three hours and forty-five minutes; lunch was at noon for one hour and fifteen minutes, then a return to the shop for another four hours and forty-five minutes. The weekly workday averaged ten hours, from sunup to sunset six days a week. A Christian Sunday and the lack of artificial lighting prevented a lengthening of the schedule.

But prison labor never brought great returns and in many instances was unable to meet the daily expenses of operation, let alone cover the costs of construction. Some of the first prisons did claim a profit in their annual reports, but often the figures were more testimony to the jugglings of the warden than to actual returns. Officials gleefully cited a "profit" of ten thousand dollars at the end of the year, neglecting to mention that the costs of the institution's construction was two hundred thousand dollars. It would be decades before such a small return paid off the debt. Other agents published a favorable balance by not including officials' salaries or the cost of repairs. The figures in the annual reports are generally too untrustworthy to allow firm conclusions, but it seems clear that if profit alone preoccupied the states, they could have found a better return on their investment elsewhere.

External difficulties also arose constantly. Free labor bitterly and effectively protested against prison competition, and frequently secured the passage of restrictive legislation. In some states convicts were not permitted to practice a trade that they had not already learned and followed before confinement; in others the institution could not produce goods already being manufactured within the state's borders. Under these circumstances legislatures not only had to make up the deficits but bear the brunt of political protest as well. The widespread organization of convict labor was, therefore, not simply testimony to its economic rewards, any more than the persistence of penal institutions reflected their financial prowess. The idea of labor, even more than the calculations of profit and loss, made it central to the penitentiary.

The doctrines of separation, obedience, and labor became the trinity around which officials organized the penitentiary. They carefully instructed inmates that their duties could be "comprised in a few words"; they were "to *labor diligently*, to *obey all orders*, and preserve an *unbroken silence*." Yet to achieve these goals, officers had to establish a total routine, to administer every aspect of the institution in accord with the three guidelines, from inmates' dress to their walk, from the cells' furnishing to the guards' deportment. The common solution was to follow primarily a quasi-military model. The regulations based on this model promised to preserve isolation, to make labor efficient, and to teach men lacking discipline to abide by rules; this regimented style of life would inculcate strict discipline, precision, and instantaneous adherence to commands. Furthermore, a military model in a correctional institution seemed especially suitable for demonstrating to the society at large the right principles of organization. Here was an appropriate example for a community suffering a crisis of order.

The first designers of the prison had few other useful models to emulate. In fact, the penitentiary was not the only institution in the 1820's and 1830's facing the dilemma of organization. Such a novel economic unit as the factory was also beginning to use rigorous procedures to bring an unprecedented discipline to workers' lives. Prison designers could find the factory an interesting but limited source of inspiration, appropriating that part of it which was most regulatory and precise. Both organizations were among the first to try to take people from casual routines to rigid ones.

Regimentation became the standard mode of prison life. Convicts did not walk from place to place; rather, they went in close order and single file, each looking over the shoulder of the man in front, faces inclined to the right, feet moving in unison, in lockstep. The lockstep became the trademark of American prisons in these years, a curious combination of march and shuffle that remained standard procedure well into the 1930's. Its invention and adoption exemplified the problems and responses of the first penitentiary officials. How were they to move inmates about? Prison officials with fixed ideas on convict communication and obedience, had to reject informal movement. Searching for greater discipline, they turned to the military march, crossed it with a shuffle to lessen its dignity, and pointed heads to the right, rather than facing straight ahead, to prevent conversation. The result, the lockstep, was an immediate success and became the common practice.

Wardens organized the convicts' daily schedule in military style. At the sound of a horn or bell, keepers opened the cells, prisoners stepped onto the deck, and then in lockstep marched into the yard. In formation they emptied their night pails, moved on and washed them, took a few more steps, and placed them on a rack to dry. Still in line they marched to the shops. There they worked at their tasks in rows on long benches until the bell rang for breakfast. They grouped again in single file, passed into the kitchen, picked up their rations (regulations admonished them not to break step), and continued on to their cells, or in some institutions, to a common messroom where they ate their meal. (Regulations again instructed them to sit erect with backs straight.) At the bell they stood, reentered formation, and marched back to the shops. They repeated this routine at noon, and again at six o'clock; then they returned to their cells for the night and at nine o'clock lights went out, as at a barracks. Although some institutions were more exacting than others in enforcing these procedures, almost all of them tried to impose a degree of military routine on their prisoners.

The furnishings of convicts' cells also indicates the relevance of the military model. A cot and pail and tin utensils were the basic objects. Prisoners now wore uniforms of a simple, coarse, striped fabric, and all had their hair cut short to increase uniformity. The military example affected keepers as well as convicts. Several wardens came to their positions directly from an army or navy career, legislators obviously eager to have them apply their former training to this setting. Guards wore uniforms, mustered at specific hours, and kept watch like sentries. Regulations ordered them to behave in a "gentlemanly manner," like officers, without laughter, ribaldry, or unnecessary conversation while on duty. As Sing-Sing's rules put it, in only a slight overstatement of a general sentiment: "They were to require from the convicts the greatest deference, and never suffer them to approach but in respectful manner; they are not to allow them the least degree of familiarity, nor exercise any towards them; they should be extremely careful to *command* as well as to compel their respect."

The military style also influenced the construction and appearance of the institutions. Some were modeled after medieval fortresses. An adaptation of a structure from the Middle Ages was necessarily monumental, appropriate in size to a noble experiment like the penitentiary, capable of stimulating a citizen's pride and a visitor's respect. It also had functional qualities, for thick walls promised security against prison breaks, and turrets became posts for guarding an enclosed space. Another popular alternative was to construct the prison along factory lines—a long and low building, symmetrically arranged with closely spaced windows, all very regular and methodical. Whatever it lacked in grandeur it tried to make up in fixity and order.

The functioning of the penitentiary—convicts passing their sentences in physically imposing and highly regimented settings, moving in lockstep from bare and solitary cells to workshops, clothed in common dress, and forced into standard routines—was designed to carry a message to the community. The prison would train the most notable victims of social disorder to discipline, teaching them to resist corruption. And success in this particular task should inspire a general reformation of manners and habits. The institution would become a laboratory for social improvement. By demonstrating how regularity and discipline transformed the most corrupt persons, it would reawaken the public to these virtues. The penitentiary would promote a new respect for order and authority.

Reformers never spelled out the precise nature and balance of this reformation. They hoped that families, instead of overindulging or neglecting their children, would more conscientiously teach limits and the need for obedience to them. Assuming that social stability could not be achieved without a very personal and keen respect for authority, they looked first to a firm family discipline to inculcate it. Reformers also anticipated that society would rid itself of corruptions. In a narrow sense this meant getting rid of such blatant centers of vice as taverns, theaters, and houses of prostitution. In a broader sense, it meant reviving a social order in which men knew their place. Here sentimentality took over, and critics in the Jacksonian period often assumed that their forefathers had lived together without social strain, in secure, placid, stable, and cohesive communities. In fact, the designers of the penitentiary set out to re-create these conditions. But the results, it is not surprising to discover, were startlingly different from anything that the colonial period had known. A conscious effort to instill discipline through an institutional routine led to a set work pattern, a rationalization of movement, a precise organization of time, a general uniformity. Hence, for all the reformers' nostalgia, the reality of the penitentiary was much closer to the values of the nineteenth than the eighteenth century.

D. Theoretical Explanations

ERVING GOFFMAN

Characteristics of Total Institutions*

The total institutions of our society can be listed for convenience in five rough groupings. First, there are institutions established to care for persons thought to be both incapable and harmless; these are the homes for the blind, the aged, the orphaned, and the indigent. Second, there are places established to care for persons thought to be at once incapable of looking after themselves and a threat to the community, albeit an unintended one: TB sanitariums, mental hospitals, and leprosoriums. Third, another type of total institution is organized to protect the community against what are thought to be intentional dangers to it; here the welfare of the persons thus sequestered is not the immediate issue. Examples are: Jails, penitentiaries, POW camps, and concentration camps. Fourth, we find institutions purportedly established the better to pursue some technical task and justify themselves only on these instrumental grounds: Army barracks, shops, boarding schools, work camps, colonial compounds, large mansions from the point of view of those who live in the servants' quarters, and so forth. Finally, there are those establishments designed as retreats from the world or as training stations for the religion: Abbeys, monasteries, convents, and other cloisters. This sub-listing of total institutions is neither neat nor exhaustive, but the listing itself provides an empirical starting point for a purely denotative definition of the category. By anchoring the initial definition of total institutions in this way, I hope to be able to discuss the general characteristics of the type without becoming tautological. . . .

In total institutions, . . . there is a basic split between a large class of individuals who live in and who have restricted contact with the world outside the walls, conveniently called *inmates,* and the small class that supervises them, conveniently called *staff,* who often operate on an eight-hour day and are socially integrated into the outside world. Each grouping tends to conceive of members of the other in terms of narrow hostile stereotypes, staff often seeing inmates as bitter, secretive, and untrustworthy, while inmates often see staff as condescending, high-handed, and mean. Staff tends to feel superior and righteous, inmates tend, in some ways at least, to feel inferior, weak, blameworthy, and guilty. Social mobility between the two strata is grossly restricted; social distance is typically great and often formally prescribed; even talk across the boundaries may be conducted in a special tone of voice. These restrictions on contact presumably help to maintain the antagonistic stereotypes. In any case, two different social and cultural worlds develops, tending to jog along beside each other, with points of official contact but little mutual penetration. It is important to add that the institutional plant and

* Symposium on Preventive and Social Psychiatry, Walter Reed Army Institute of Research, U.S. Gov't. Printing Office (1958).

name comes to be identified by both staff and inmates as somehow belonging to staff, so that when either grouping refers to the views or interests of "the institution," by implication they are referring (as I shall also) to the views and concerns of the staff....

It is characteristic of inmates that they come to the institution as members, already full-fledged, of a home world, that is, a way of life and a round of activities taken for granted up to the point of admission to the institution. It is useful to look at this culture that the recruit brings with him to the institution's door—his presenting culture, to modify a psychiatric phrase—in terms especially designed to highlight what it is the total institution will do to him. Whatever the stability of his personal organization, we can assume it was part of a wider supporting framework lodged in his current social environment, a round of experience that somewhat confirms a conception of self that is somewhat acceptable to him and a set of defensive maneuvers exercisable at his own discretion as a means of coping with conflicts, discreditings and failures.

Now it appears that total institutions do not substitute their own unique culture for something already formed. We do not deal with acculturation or assimilation but with something more restricted than these. In a sense, total institutions do not look for cultural victory. They effectively create and sustain a particular kind of tension between the home world and the institutional world and use this persistent tension as strategic leverage in the management of men. The full meaning for the inmate of being "in" or "on the inside" does not exist apart from the special meaning to him of "getting out" or "getting on the outside."

The recruit comes into the institution with a self and with attachments to supports which had allowed this self to survive. Upon entrance, he is immediately stripped of his wonted supports, and his self is systematically, if often unintentionally, mortified. In the accurate language of some of our oldest total institutions, he is led into a series of abasements, degradations, humiliations, and profanations of self. He begins, in other words, some radical shifts in his moral career, a career laying out the progressive changes tht occur in the beliefs that he has concerning himself and significant others.

The stripping processes through which mortification of the self occurs are fairly standard in our total institutions. Personal identity equipment is removed, as well as other possessions with which the inmate may have identified himself, there typically being a system of nonaccessible storage from which the inmate can only reobtain his effects should he leave the institution. As a substitute for what has been taken away, institutional issue is provided, but this will be the same for large categories of inmates and will be regularly repossessed by the institution. In brief, standardized defacement will occur. In addition, ego-invested separateness from fellow inmates is significantly diminished in many areas of activity, and tasks are prescribed that are infra dignitatem. Family, occupational, and educational career lines are chopped off, and a stigmatized status is submitted. Sources of fantasy materials which had meant momentary releases from stress in the home world are denied. Areas of autonomous decision are eliminated through the process of collective scheduling of daily activity. Many channels of communication with the outside are restricted or closed off completely. Verbal discreditings occur in many forms as a matter of course. Expressive signs of respect for the staff are coercively and continuously demanded. And the effect of each of these conditions is multiplied by having to witness the mortification of one's fellow inmates.

We must expect to find different official reasons given for these assaults upon the self. In mental hospitals there is the matter of protecting the patient from himself and from other patients. In jails there is the issue of "security" and frank punishment. In religious institutions we may find sociologically sophisticated theories about the soul's need for purification and penance through disciplining of the flesh. What all of these rationales share is the extent to which they are merely rationalizations, for the underlying force in many cases is unwittingly generated by efforts to manage the daily activity of a large number of persons in a small space with a small expenditure of resources.

In the background of the sociological stripping process, we find a characteristic authority system with three distinctive elements, each basic to total institutions.

First, to a degree, authority is of the echelon kind. Any member of the staff class has certain rights to discipline any member of the inmate class. This arrangement, it may be noted, is similar to the one which gives any adult in some small American towns certain rights to correct and demand small services from any child not in the immediate presence of his parents. In our society, the adult himself, however, is typically under the authority of a *single* immediate superior in connection with his work or under authority of one spouse in connection with domestic duties. The only echelon authority he must face—the police—typically are neither constantly nor relevantly present, except perhaps in the case of traffic-law enforcement.

Second, the authority of corrective sanctions is directed to a great multitude of items of conduct of the kind that are constantly occuring and constantly coming up for judgment; in brief, authority is directed to matters of dress, deportment, social intercourse, manners, and the like. In prisons these regulations regarding situational properties may even extend to a point where silence during mealtime is enforced, while in some convents explicit demands may be made concerning the custody of the eyes during prayer.

The third feature of authority in total institutions is that misbehaviors in one sphere of life are held against one's standing in other spheres. Thus, an individual who fails to participate with proper enthusiasm in sports may be brought to the attention of the person who determines where he will sleep and what kind of work task will be accorded to him.

When we combine these three aspects of authority in total institutions, we see that the inmate cannot easily escape from the press of judgmental officials and from the enveloping tissue of constraint. The system of authority undermines the basis for control that adults in our society expect to exert over their interpersonal environment and may produce the terror of feeling that one is being radically demoted in the age-grading system. On the outside, rules are sufficiently lax and the individual sufficiently agreeable to required self-discipline to insure that others will rarely have cause for pouncing on him. He need not constantly look over his shoulder to see if criticism and other sanctions are coming. On the inside, however, rulings are abundant, novel, and closely enforced so that, quite characteristically, inmates live with chronic anxiety about breaking the rules and chronic worry about the consequences of breaking them. The desire to "stay out of trouble" in a total institution is likely to require persistent conscious effort and may lead the inmate to abjure certain levels of sociability with his fellows in order to avoid the incidents that may occur in these circumstances.

It should be noted finally that the mortifications to be suffered by the inmate may be purposely brought home to him in an exaggerated way during the first few days after entrance, in a form of initiation that has been called the welcome. Both staff and fellow inmates may go out of their way to give the neophyte a clear notion of where he stands. As part of this rite de passage, he may find himself called by a term such as "fish," "swab," etc., through which older inmates tell him that he is not only merely an inmate but that even within this lowly group he has a low status.

While the process of mortification is in progress, the inmate begins to receive formal and informal instruction in what will here be called the privilege system. Insofar as the inmate's self has been unsettled a little by the stripping action of the institution, it is largely around this framework that pressures are exerted, making for a reorganization of self. Three basic elements of the system may be mentioned.

First, there are the house rules, a relatively explicit and formal set of prescriptions and proscriptions which lay out the main requirements of inmate conduct. These regulations spell out the austere round of life in which the inmate will operate. Thus, the admission procedures through which the recruit is initially stripped of his self-supporting context can be seen as the institution's way of getting him in the position to start living by the house rules.

Second, against the stark background, a small number of clearly defined rewards or privileges are held out in exchange for obedience to staff in action and spirit. It is important to see that these potential gratifications are not unique to the institution but rather are ones carved out of the flow of support that the inmate previously had quite taken for granted. On the outside, for example, the inmate was likely to be able to unthinkingly exercise autonomy by deciding how much sugar and milk he wanted in his coffee, if any, or when to light up a cigarette; on the inside, this right may become quite problematic and a matter of a great deal of conscious concern. Held up to the inmate as possibilities, these few recapturings seem to have a reintegrative effect, reestablishing relationships with the whole lost world and assuaging withdrawal symptoms from it and from one's lost self.

The inmate's run of attention, then, especially at first, comes to be fixated on these supplies and obsessed with them. In the most fanatic way, he can spend the day in devoted thoughts concerning the possibility of acquiring these gratifications or the approach of the hour at which they are scheduled to be granted. The building of a world around these minor privileges is perhaps the most important feature of inmate culture and yet is something that cannot easily be appreciated by an outsider, even one who has lived through the experience himself. This situation sometimes leads to generous sharing and almost always to a willingness to beg for things such as cigarettes, candy, and newspapers. It will be understandable, then, that a constant feature of inmate discussion is the release binge fantasy, namely, recitals of what one will do during leave or upon release from the institution.

House rules and privileges provide the functional requirements of the third element in the privilege system: punishments. These are designated as the consequence of breaking the rules. One set of these punishments consists of the temporary or permanent withdrawal of privileges or abrogation of the right to try to earn them. In general, the punishments meted out in total institutions are of an order more severe than anything encountered by the inmate in his home world. An institutional arrangement which causes a small number of easily controlled privileges to have a massive significance is the same arrangement which lends a terrible significance to their withdrawal.

There are some special features of the privilege system which should be noted.

First, punishments and privileges are themselves modes of organization peculiar to total institutions. Whatever their severity, punishments are largely known in the inmate's home world as something applied to animals and children. For adults this conditioning, behavioristic model is actually not widely applied, since failure to maintain required standards typically leads to indirect disadvantageous consequences and not to specific immediate punishment at all. And privileges, it should be emphasized, are not the same as perquisites, indulgences, or values, but merely the absence of deprivations one ordinarily expects one would not have to sustain. The very notions, then, of punishments and privileges are not ones that are cut from civilian cloth.

Second, it is important to see that the question of release from the total institution is elaborated into the privilege system. Some acts will become known as ones that mean an increase or no decrease in length of stay, while others become known as means for lessening the sentence.

Third, we should also note that punishments and privileges come to be geared into a residential work system. Places to work and places to sleep become clearly defined as places where certain kinds and levels of privilege obtain, and inmates are shifted very rapidly and visibly from one place to another as the mechanisms for giving them the punishment or privilege their co-operativeness has warranted. The inmates are moved, the system is not.

This, then, is the privilege system: a relatively few components put together with some rational intent and clearly proclaimed to the participants. The over-all consequence is that co-operativeness is obtained from persons who often have cause to be unco-operative. . . .

The mortifying processes that have been discussed and the privilege system represent the conditions that the inmate must adapt to in some way, but however pressing, these conditions allow for different ways of meeting them. We find, in fact, that the same inmate will employ different lines of adaptation or tacks at different phases in his moral career and may even fluctuate between different tacks at the same time.

First, there is the process of situational withdrawal. The inmate withdraws apparent attention from everything except events immediately around his body and sees these in a perspective not employed by others present. This drastic curtailment of involvement in interactional events is best known, of course, in mental hospitals, under the title of "regression." Aspects of "prison psychosis" or "stir simpleness" represent the same adjustment, as do some forms of "acute depersonalization" described in concentration camps. I do not think it is known whether this line of adaptation forms a single continuum of varying degrees of withdrawal or whether there are standard discontinuous plateaus of disinvolvement. It does seem to be the case, however, that, given the pressures apparently required to dislodge an inmate from this status, as well as the currently limited facilities for doing so, we frequently find here, effectively speaking, an irreversible line of adaptation.

Second, there is the rebellious line. The inmate intentionally challenges the institution by flagrantly refusing to co-operate with staff in almost any way. The result is a constantly communicated intransigency and sometimes high rebel-morale. Most large mental hospitals, for example, seem to have wards where this spirit strongly prevails. Interestingly enough, there are many circumstances in which sustained rejection of a total institution requires sustained orientation to its formal organization and hence, paradoxically, a deep kind of commitment to the establishment. Similarly, when total institutions take the line (as they sometimes do in the case of mental hospitals prescribing lobotomy or army barracks prescribing the stockade) that the recalcitrant inmate must be broken, then, in their way, they must show as much special devotion to the rebel as he has shown to them. It should be added, finally, that while prisoners of war have been known staunchly to take a rebellious stance throughout their incarceration, this stance is typically a temporary and initial phase of reaction, emerging from this to situational withdrawal or some other line of adaptation.

Third, another standard alignment in the institutional world takes the form of a kind of colonization. The sampling of the outside world provided by the establishment is taken by the inmate as the whole, and a stable, relatively contented existence is built up out of the maximum satisfactions procurable within the institution. Experience of the outside world is used as a point of reference to demonstrate the desirability of life on the inside; and the usual tension between the two worlds collapses, thwarting the social arrangements based upon this felt discrepancy. Characteristically, the individual who too obviously takes this line may be accused by his fellow inmates of "having found a home" or of "never having had it so good." Staff itself may become vaguely embarrassed by this use that is being made of the institution, sensing that the benign possibilities in the situation are somehow being misused. Colonizers themselves may feel obliged to deny their satisfaction with the institution, if only in the interest of sustaining the counter-mores supporting inmate solidarity. They may find it necessary to mess up just prior to their slated discharge, thereby allowing themselves to present involuntary reasons for continued incarceration. It should be incidentally noted that any humanistic effort to make life in total institutions more bearable must face the possibility that doing so may increase the attractiveness and likelihood of colonization.

Fourth, one mode of adaptation to the setting of a total institution is that of *conversion*. The inmate appears to take over completely the official or staff view of himself and tries to act out the role of the perfect inmate. While the colonized inmate builds as much of a free community as possible for himself by using the limited facilities available, the convert takes a more disciplined, moralistic, monochromatic line, presenting himself as someone whose institutional enthusiasm is always at the disposal of the staff. In Chinese POW camps, we find Americans who became "pros" and fully espoused the Communist view of the world. In army barracks there are enlisted men who give the impression that they are always "sucking around" and always "bucking for promotion." In prison there are "square johns." In German concentration camps, longtime prisoners sometimes came to adapt the vocabulary, recreation, posture, expressions of aggression, and clothing style of the Gestapo, executing their role of straw-boss with military strictness. Some mental hospitals have the distinction of providing two quite different conversion possibilities—one for the new admission who can see the light after an appropriate struggle and adapt the psychiatric view of himself, and another for the chronic ward patient who adopts the manner and dress of attendants while helping them to manage the other ward patients with a stringency excelling that of the attendants themselves....

Total institutions frequently claim to be concerned with rehabilitation, that is, with resetting the inmate's self-regulatory mechanisms so that he will maintain the standards of the establishment of his own accord after he leaves the setting. In fact, it seems this claim is seldom realized and even when permanent alteration occurs, these changes are often not of the kind intended by the staff. With the possible exception presented by the great resocialization efficiency of religious institutions, neither the stripping processes nor the reorganizing ones seem to have a lasting effect. No doubt the availability of secondary adjustments helps to account for this, as do the presence of counter-mores and the tendency for inmates to combine all strategies and "play it cool." In any case, it seems that shortly after release, the ex-inmate will have forgotten a great deal of what life was like on the inside and will have once again begun to take for granted the privileges around which life in the institution was organized. The sense of injustice, bitterness, and alienation, so typically engendered by the inmate's experience and so definitely marking a stage in his moral career, seems to weaken upon graduation, even in those cases where a permanent stigma has resulted.

But what the ex-inmate does retain of his institutional experience tells us important things about total institutions. Often entrance will mean for the recruit that he has taken on what might be called a *proactive status*. Not only is his relative social position within the walls radically different from what it was on the outside, but, as he comes to learn, if and when he gets out, his social position on the outside will never again be quite what it was prior to entrance. Where the proactive status is a relatively favorable one, as it is for those who graduate from officers' training schools, elite boarding schools, ranking monasteries, etc., then the permanent alteration will be favorable, and jubilant official reunions announcing pride in one's "school" can be expected. When, as seems usually the case, the proactive status is unfavorable, as it is for those in prisons or mental hospitals, we popularly employ the term "stigmatization" and expect that the ex-inmate may make an effort to conceal his past and try to "pass." . . .

DONALD CLEMMER

The Prison Community*

When a person or group of ingress penetrates and fuses with another group, assimilation may be said to have taken place. The concept is most profitably applied to immigrant groups and perhaps it is not the best term by which to designate similar processes which occur in prison. Assimilation implies that a process of acculturation occurs in one group whose members originally were quite different from those of the group with whom they mix. It implies that the assimilated come to share the sentiments, memories, and traditions of the static group. It is evident that the men who come to prison are not greatly different from the ones already there so far as broad culture influences are concerned: All speak the same language, all have a similar national heritage, all have been stigmatized, and so on. While the differences of regional conditioning are not to be overlooked, it is doubtful if the interactions which lead the professional offender to have a "we-feeling" with the naive offender from Coalville can be referred to as assimilation—although the processes furnishing the development of such an understanding are similar to it. The term assimilation describes a slow, gradual, more or less unconscious process during which a person learns enough of the culture of a social unit into which he is placed to make him characteristic of it. While we shall continue to use this general meaning, we recognize that in the strictest sense assimilation is not the correct term. So as we use the term Americanization to describe a greater or less degree of the immigrant's integration into the American scheme of life, we may use the term *prisonization* to indicate the taking on in greater or less degree of the folkways, mores, customs, and general culture of the penitentiary. Prisonization is similar to assimilation, and its meaning will become clearer as we proceed.

Every man who enters the penitentiary undergoes prisonization to some extent. The first and most obvious integrative step concerns his status. He becomes at once an anonymous figure in a subordinate group. A number replaces a name. He wears the clothes of the other members of the subordinate group. He is questioned and admonished. He soon learns that the warden is all-powerful. He soon learns the ranks, titles, and authority of various officials. And whether he uses the prison slang and argot or not, he comes to know its meanings. Even though a new man may hold himself aloof from other inmates and remain a solitary figure, he finds himself within a few months referring to or thinking of keepers as "screws," the physician as the "croaker" and using the local nicknames to designate persons. He follows the examples already set in wearing his cap. He learns to eat in haste and in obtaining food he imitates the tricks of those near him.

After the new arrival recovers from the effects of the swallowing-up process, he assigns a new meaning to conditions he had previously taken for granted. The fact that food, shelter, clothing, and a work activity had been given him originally made no especial impression. It is only after some weeks or months that there comes to him a new interpretation of these necessities of life. This new conception results from mingling with other men and it places emphasis on the fact that the environment *should* administer to him. This point is intangible and difficult to describe in so far as it is only a subtle and minute change in attitude from the taken-for-granted perception. Exhaustive questioning of hundreds of men reveals that this slight change in attitude is a fundamental step in the process we are calling prisonization. Supplemental to it is the almost universal desire on the part of the man, after

* Pp. 298–302. From *The Prison Community* by Donald Clemmer. Copyright 1940, © 1958, by Donald Clemmer. Reprinted by permission of Holt, Rinehart and Winston, Inc.

a period of some months, to get a good job so, as he says, "I can do my time without any trouble and get out of here." A good job usually means a comfortable job of a more or less isolated kind in which conflicts with other men are not likely to develop. The desire for a comfortable job is not peculiar to the prison community, to be sure, but it seems to be a phase of prisonization in the following way. When men have served time before entering the penitentiary they look the situation over and almost immediately express a desire for a certain kind of work. When strictly first offenders come to prison, however, they seldom express a desire for a particular kind of work, but are willing to do anything and frequently say, "I'll do any kind of work they put me at and you won't have any trouble from me." Within a period of a few months, however, these same men, who had no choice of work, develop preferences and make their desires known. They "wise up," as the inmates say, or in other words, by association they become prisonized.

In various other ways men new to prison slip into the existing patterns. They learn to gamble or learn new ways to gamble. Some, for the first time in their lives, take to abnormal sex behavior. Many of them learn to distrust and hate the officers, the parole board, and sometimes each other, and they become acquainted with the dogmas and mores existing in the community. But these changes do not occur in every man. However, every man is subject to certain influences which we may call the *universal factors of prisonization.*

Acceptance of an inferior rôle, accumulation of facts concerning the organization of the prison, the development of somewhat new habits of eating, dressing, working, sleeping, the adoption of local language, the recognition that nothing is owed to the environment for the supplying needs, and the eventual desire for a good job are aspects of prisonization which are operative for all inmates. It is not these aspects, however, which concern us most but they are important because of their universality, especially among men who have served many years. That is, even if no other factor of the prison culture touches the personality of an inmate of many years residence, the influences of these universal factors are sufficient to make a man characteristic of the penal community and probably so disrupt his personality that a happy adjustment in any community becomes next to impossible. On the other hand, if inmates who are incarcerated for only short periods, such as a year or so, do not become integrated into the culture except in so far as these universal factors of prisonization are concerned, they do not seem to be so characteristic of the penal community and are able when released to take up a new mode of life without much difficulty.

The phases of prisonization which concern us most are the influences which breed or deepen criminality and antisociality and make the inmate characteristic of the criminalistic ideology in the prison community. As has been said, every man feels the influences of what we have called the universal factors, but not every man becomes prisonized in and by other phases of the culture. Whether or not complete prisonization takes place depends first on the man himself, that is, his susceptibility to a culture which depends, we think, primarily on the type of relationships he had before imprisonment, i.e., his personality. A second determinant effecting complete prisonization refers to the kind and extent of relationships which an inmate has with persons outside the walls. A third determinant refers to whether or not a man becomes affiliated in prison primary or semi-primary groups and this is related to the two points already mentioned. Yet a fourth determinant depends simply on chance, a chance placement in work gang, cellhouse, and with cellmate. A fifth determinant pertains to whether or not a man accepts the dogmas or codes of the prison culture. Other determinants depend on age, criminality, nationality, race, regional conditioning, and every determinant is more or less interrelated with every other one.

With knowledge of these determinants we can hypothetically construct schemata of prisonization which may serve to illustrate its extremes. In the least or lowest degree of prisonization the following factors may be enumerated:

1. A short sentence, thus a brief subjection to the universal factors of prisonization.
2. A fairly stable personality made stable by an adequacy of positive and "socialized" relationships during pre-penal life.
3. The continuance of positive relationships with persons outside the walls.
4. Refusal or inability to integrate into a prison primary group or semiprimary group, while yet maintaining a symbiotic balance in relations with other men.
5. Refusal to accept blindly the dogmas and codes of the population, and a willingness, under certain situations, to aid officials, thus making for identification with the free community.
6. A chance placement with a cellmate and

workmates who do not possess leadership qualities and who are also not completely integrated into the prison culture.

7. Refraining from abnormal sex behavior, and excessive gambling, and a ready willingness to engage seriously in work and recreative activities.

Other factors no doubt have an influencing force in obstructing the process of prisonization, but the seven points mentioned seem outstanding.

In the highest or greatest degree of prisonization the following factors may be enumerated:

1. A sentence of many years, thus a long subjection to the universal factors of prisonization.
2. A somewhat unstable personality made unstable by an inadequacy of "socialized" relations before commitment, but possessing, none the less, a capacity for strong convictions and a particular kind of loyalty.
3. A dearth of positive relations with persons outside the walls.
4. A readiness and a capacity for integration into a prison-primary group.
5. A blind, or almost blind, acceptance of the dogmas and mores of the primary group and the general penal population.
6. A chance placement with other persons of a similar orientation.
7. A readiness to participate in gambling and abnormal sex behavior.

We can see in these two extremes the degrees with which the prisonization process operates. No suggestion is intended that a high correlation exists between either extreme of prisonization and criminality. It is quite possible that the inmate who fails to integrate in the prison culture may be and may continue to be much more criminalistic than the inmate who becomes completely prisonized. The trends are probably otherwise, however, as our study of group life suggests. To determine prisonization, every case must be appraised for itself. Of the two degrees presented in the schemas it is probable that more men approach the complete degree than the least degree of prisonization, but it is also probable that the majority of inmates become prisonized in some respects and not in others. It is the varying degrees of prisonization among the 2,300 men that contribute to the disassociation which is so common. The culture is made complex, not only by the constantly changing population, but by these differences in the tempo and degree of prisonization.

Assimilation, as the concept is customarily applied, is always a slow, gradual process, but prisonization, as we use the term here is usually slow, but not necessarily so. The speed with which prisonization occurs depends on the personality of the man involved, his crime, age, home neighborhood, intelligence, the situation into which he is placed in prison and other less obvious influences. The process does not necessarily proceed in an orderly or measured fashion but tends to be irregular. In some cases we have found the process working in a cycle. The amount and speed of prisonization can be judged only by the behavior and attitudes of the men, and these vary from man to man and in the same man from time to time. It is the excessive number of changes in orientation which the men undergo which makes generalizations about the process so difficult.

GRESHAM M. SYKES

The Society of Captives*

The Task of Custody

There seems little doubt that the task of custody looms largest in the eyes of the officials of the New Jersey State Prison and in this they differ but little from most if not all of the administrators who are charged with the responsibility for maximum security institu-

* Selections from Gresham M. Sykes, *The Society of Captives: A Study of Minimum Security Prison* (copyright © 1958 by Princeton University Press; Princeton Paperback, 1971), pp. 18–34 and entire Chapter II, "The Pains of Imprisonment," pp. 65–78. Reprinted, with footnotes omitted by permission of Princeton University Press.

tions in the United States. The prison exists as a dramatic symbol of society's desire to segregate the criminal, whatever reasons may lie behind that desire; and the prison wall, that line between the pure and impure, has all the emotional overtones of a woman's maidenhead. One escape from the maximum security prison is sufficient to arouse public opinion to a fever pitch and an organization which stands or falls on a single case moves with understandable caution. The officials, in short, know on which side their bread is buttered. Their continued employment is tied up with the successful performance of custody and if society is not sure of the priority to be attached to the tasks assigned the prison, the overriding importance of custody is perfectly clear to the officials. . . .

The Task of Internal Order

If custody is elevated to the first rank in the list of tasks to be accomplished by the prison, the objective of maintaining internal order is a close second. And it must be admitted that under the best of circumstances the maintenance of order among a group of men such as those who are confined in the New Jersey State Prison would present formidable problems. . . .

Whatever may be the personal traits possessed by these men which helped bring them to the institution, it is certain that the conditions of prison life itself create strong pressures pointed toward behavior defined as criminal in the free community. Subjected to prolonged material deprivation, lacking heterosexual relationships, and rubbed raw by the irritants of life under compression, the inmate population is pushed in the direction of deviation from, rather than adherence to, the legal norms. . . .

The custodians' task of maintaining order within the prison is acerbrated by the conditions of life which it is their duty to impose on their captives. The prison official, then, is caught up in a vicious circle where he must suppress the very activity that he helps cause. It is not surprising that he should overlook his part in the process, that he should tend to view the prisoner as innately vicious or depraved. The conduct of the inmate is used to justify further repressive measures and the antagonisms between the guard and his prisoner spiral upward. . . .

The Task of Punishment

It is sometimes said that criminals are placed in prison not *for* punishment but *as* punishment; presumably, stress is being placed on the idea that the officials of the custodial institution are determined not to hurt their captives either physically or mentally beyond the pain involved in confinement itself. And, in a certain sense, it would certainly appear to be true that the administrators of the New Jersey State Prison have no great interest in inflicting punishments on their prisoners for the crimes which they committed in the free community, as paradoxical as it may seem. There is no indication in the day-to-day operation of the prison that the officials have any desire to act as avenging angels; nor do the officials exhibit much attachment to the idea that a painful period of imprisonment is likely to deter the criminal who has been confined—the reappearance of discharged prisoners has made them grow cynical on that score. . . .

The Task of Reform

If the officials of the New Jersey State Prison are relatively indifferent when it comes to punishing their prisoners for their past sins, so also are they relatively indifferent when it comes to saving their prisoners from sins in the future. It is true that there is frequent mention of "individualization of treatment," "correction," "self-discipline," "a favorable change in attitudes," and so on, by the Department of Institutions and Agencies. And it is true that within the prison itself a number of counsellors, a chaplain, a psychologist, and several teachers for the inmate school have the duty of somehow implanting that inner conviction in the offender which will keep him from the path of crime when he is released. But allegiance to the goal of rehabilitation tends to remain at the verbal level, an expression of hope for public consumption rather than a coherent program with an integrated, professional staff. . . .

The Deprivation of Liberty

Of all the painful conditions imposed on the inmates of the New Jersey State Prison, none is more immediately obvious than the loss of liberty. The prisoner must live in a world shrunk to thirteen and a half acres and within this restricted area his freedom of movement is further confined by a strict system of passes, the military formations in moving from one point within the institution to another, and the demand that he remain in his cell until given permission to do otherwise. In short, the prisoner's loss of liberty is a double one—first, by confinement to the institution and second, by confinement within the institution.

The mere fact that the individual's movements are restricted, however, is far less serious than the fact that imprisonment means that the inmate is cut off from family, relatives, and friends, not in the self-isolation of the hermit or the misanthrope, but in the involuntary seclusion of the outlaw. It is true that visiting and mailing privileges partially relieve the prisoner's isolation—if he can find someone to visit him or write to him and who will be approved as a visitor or correspondent by the prison officials. Many inmates, however, have found their links with persons in the free community weakening as the months and years pass by. This may explain in part the fact that an examination of the visiting records of a random sample of the inmate population, covering approximately a one-year period, indicated that 41 percent of the prisoners in the New Jersey State Prison had received no visits from the outside world.

It is not difficult to see this isolation as painfully depriving or frustrating in terms of lost emotional relationships, of loneliness and boredom. But what makes this pain of imprisonment bite most deeply is the fact that the confinement of the criminal represents a deliberate, moral rejection of the criminal by the free community. Indeed, as Reckless has pointed out, it is the moral condemnation of the criminal—however it may be symbolized—that converts hurt into punishment, i.e. the just consequence of committing an offense, and it is this condemnation that confronts the inmate by the fact of his seclusion.

Now it is sometimes claimed that many criminals are so alienated from conforming society and so identified with a criminal subculture that the moral condemnation, rejection, or disapproval of legitimate society does not touch them; they are, it is said, indifferent to the penal sanctions of the free community, at least as far as the moral stigma of being defined as a criminal is concerned. Possibly this is true for a small number of offenders such as the professional thief described by Sutherland or the psychopathic personality delineated by William and Joan McCord. For the great majority of criminals in prison, however, the evidence suggests that neither alienation from the ranks of the law-abiding nor involvement in a system of criminal value is sufficient to eliminate the threat to the prisoner's ego posed by society's rejection. The signs pointing to the prisoner's degradation are many—the anonymity of a uniform and a number rather than a name, the shaven head, the insistence on gestures of respect and subordination when addressing officials, and so on. The prisoner is never allowed to forget that, by committing a crime, he has foregone his claim to the status of a full-fledged, *trusted* member of society. The status lost by the prisoner is, in fact, similar to what Marshall has called the status of citizenship—that basic acceptance of the individual as a functioning member of the society in which he lives. It is true that in the past the imprisoned criminal literally suffered civil death and that although the doctrines of attainder and corruption of blood were largely abandoned in the 18th and 19th Centuries, the inmate is still stripped of many of his civil rights such as the right to vote, to hold office, to sue in court, and so on. But as important as the loss of these civil rights may be, the loss of that more diffuse status which defines the individual as someone to be trusted or as morally acceptable is the loss which hurts most.

In short, the wall which seals off the criminal, the contaminated man, is a constant threat to the prisoner's self-conception and the threat is continually repeated in the many daily reminders that he must be kept apart from "decent" men. Somehow this rejection or degradation by the free community must be warded off, turned aside, rendered harmless. Somehow the imprisoned criminal must find a device for rejecting his rejectors, if he is to endure psychologically.

The Deprivation of Goods and Services

There are admittedly many problems in attempting to compare the standard of living existing in the free community and the standard of living which is supposed to be the lot of the inmate in prison. How, for example, do we interpret the fact that a covering for the floor of a cell usually consists of a scrap from a discarded blanket and that even this possession is forbidden by the prison authorities? What meaning do we attach to the fact that no inmate owns a common piece of furniture, such as a chair, but only a homemade stool? What is the value of a suit of clothing which is also a convict's uniform with a stripe and a stencilled number? The answers are far from simple although there are a number of prison officials who will argue that some inmates are better off in prison, in strictly material terms, than they could ever hope to be in the rough-and-tumble economic life of the free community. Possibly this is so, but at least it has never been claimed by the inmates that the goods and services provided the prisoner are equal to or better than the goods and services which the prisoner could obtain if he were left to his own devices outside the walls. The average inmate finds himself in a harshly Spartan environment which he defines as painfully depriving.

Now it is true that the prisoner's basic material needs are met—in the sense that he does not go hungry, cold, or wet. He receives adequate medical care and he has the opportunity for exercise. But a standard of living constructed in terms of so many calories per day, so many hours of recreation, so many cubic yards of space per individual, and so on, misses the central point when we are discussing the individual's feeling of deprivation, however useful it may be in setting minimum levels of consumption for the maintenance of health. A standard of living can be hopelessly inadequate, from the individual's viewpoint, because it bores him to death or fails to provide those subtle symbolic overtones which we invest in the world of possessions. And this is the core of the prisoner's problem in the area of goods and services. He wants—or needs, if you will —not just the so-called necessities of life but also the amenities: cigarettes and liquor as well as calories, interesting foods as well as sheer bulk, individual clothing as well as adequate clothing, individual furnishings for his living quarters as well as shelter, privacy as well as space. The "rightfulness" of the prisoner's feeling of deprivation can be questioned. And the objective reality of the prisoner's deprivation—in the sense that he has actually suffered a fall from his economic position in the free community—can be viewed with skepticism, as we have indicated above. But these criticisms are irrelevant to the significant issue, namely that legitimately or illegitimately, rationally or irrationally, the inmate population defines its present material impoverishment as a painful loss.

Now in modern Western culture, material possessions are so large a part of the individual's conception of himself that to be stripped of them is to be attacked at the deepest layers of personality. This is particularly true when poverty cannot be excused as a blind stroke of fate or a universal calamity. Poverty due to one's own mistakes or misdeeds represents an indictment against one's basic value or personal worth and there are few men who can philosophically bear the want caused by their own actions. It is true some prisoners in the New Jersey State Prison atttempt to interpret their low position in the scale of goods and services as an effort by the State to exploit them economically. Thus, in the eyes of some inmates, the prisoner is poor not because of an offense which he has committed in the past but because the State is a tyrant which uses its captive criminals as slave labor under the hypocritical guise of reformation. Penology, it is said, is a racket. Their poverty, then, is not punishment as we have used the word before, i.e. the just consequence of criminal behavior; rather, it is an unjust hurt or pain inflicted without legitimate cause. This attitude, however, does not appear to be particularly widespread in the inmate population and the great majority of prisoners must face their privation without the aid of the wronged man's sense of injustice. Furthermore, most prisoners are unable to fortify themselves in their low level of material existence by seeing it as a means to some high or worthy end. They are unable to attach any significant meaning to their need to make it more bearable, such as present pleasures foregone for pleasures in the future, self-sacrifice in the interests of the community, or material asceticism for the purpose of spiritual salvation.

The inmate, then, sees himself as having been made poor by reason of his own acts and without the rationale of compensating benefits. The failure is *his* failure in a world where control and possession of the material environment are commonly taken as sure indicators of a man's worth. It is true that our society, as materialistic as it may be, does not rely exclusively on goods and services as a criterion of an individual's value; and, as we shall see shortly, the inmate population defends itself by stressing alternative or supplementary measures of merit. But impoverishment remains as one of the most bitter attacks on the individual's self-image that our society has to offer and the prisoner cannot ignore the implications of his straitened circumstances. Whatever the discomforts and irritations of the prisoner's Spartan existence may be, he must carry the additional burden of social definitions which equate his material deprivation with personal inadequacy.

The Deprivation of Heterosexual Relationships

Unlike the prisoner in many Latin-American countries, the inmate of the maximum security prison in New Jersey does not enjoy the privilege of so-called conjugal visits. And in those brief times when the prisoner is allowed to see his wife, mistress, or "female friend," the woman must sit on one side of a plate glass window and the prisoner on the other, communicating by means of a phone under the scrutiny of a guard. If the inmate, then, is rejected and impoverished by the facts of his imprisonment, he is also figuratively castrated by his involuntary celibacy.

Now a number of writers have suggested that men in prison undergo a reduction of the sexual drive and that the sexual frustrations of prisoners are therefore less than they might appear to be at first glance. The reports of reduced sexual interest have, however, been largely confined to accounts of men imprisoned in concentration camps or similar extreme situations where starvation, torture, and physical exhaustion have reduced life to a simple struggle for survival or left the captive sunk in apathy. But in the American prison these factors are not at work to any significant extent and Linder has noted that the prisoner's access to mass media, pornography circulated among inmate, and similar stimuli serve to keep alive the prisoner's sexual impulses. The same thought is expressed more crudely by the inmates of the New Jersey State Prison in a variety of obscene expressions and it is clear that the lack of heterosexual intercourse is a frustrating experience for the imprisoned criminal and that it is frustration which weighs heavily and painfuly on his mind during his prolonged confinement. There are, of course, some "habitual" homosexuals in the prison—men who were homosexuals before their arrival and who continue their particular form of deviant behavior within the all-male society of the custodial institution. For these inmates, perhaps, the deprivation of heterosexual intercourse cannot be counted as one of the pains of imprisonment. They are few in number, however, and are only too apt to be victimized or raped by aggressive prisoners who have turned to homosexuality as a temporary means of relieving their frustration.

Yet as important as frustration in the sexual sphere may be in physiological terms, the psychological problems created by the lack of heterosexual relationships can be even more serious. A society composed exclusively of men tends to generate anxieties in its members concerning their masculinity regardless of whether or not they are coerced, bribed, or seduced into an overt homosexual liaison. Latent homosexual tendencies may be activated in the individual without being translated into open behavior and yet still arouse strong guilt feelings at either the conscious or unconscious level. In the tense atmosphere of the prison with its known perversions, its importunities of admitted homosexuals, and its constant references to the problem of sexual frustration by guards and inmates alike, there are few prisoners who can escape the fact that an essential component of a man's self conception—his status of male—is called into question. And if an inmate has in fact engaged in homosexual behavior within the walls, not as a continuation of an habitual pattern but as a rare act of sexual deviance under the intolerable pressure of mounting physical desire, the psychological onslaughts on his ego image will be particularly acute.

In addition to these problems stemming from sexual frustration per se, the deprivation of heterosexual relationships carries with it another threat to the prisoner's image of himself —more diffuse, perhaps, and more difficult to state precisely and yet no less disturbing. The inmate is shut off from the world of women which by its very polarity gives the male world much of its meaning. Like most men, the inmate must search for his identity not simply within himself but also in the picture of himself which he finds reflected in the eyes of others; and since a significant half of his audience is denied him, the inmate's self image is in danger of becoming half complete, fractured, a monochrome without the hues of reality. The prisoner's looking-glass self, in short—to use Cooley's fine phrase—is only that portion of the prisoner's personality which is recognized or appreciated by men and this partial identity is made hazy by the lack of contrast.

The Deprivation of Autonomy

We have noted before that the inmate suffers from what we have called a loss of autonomy in that he is subjected to a vast body of rules and commands which are designed to control his behavior in minute detail. To the casual observer, however, it might seem that the many areas of life in which self-determination is withheld, such as the language used in a letter, the hours of sleeping and eating, or the route to work, are relatively unimportant. Perhaps it might be argued, as in the case of material deprivation, tht the inmate in prison is not much worse off than the individual in the free community who is regulated in a great many aspects of his life by the iron fist of custom. It could even be argued, as some writers have done, that for a number of imprisoned criminals the extensive control of the custodians provides a welcome escape from freedom and that the prison officials thus supply an external Super-Ego which serves to reduce the anxieties arising from an awareness of deviant impulses. But from the viewpoint of the inmate population, it is precisely the triviality of much of the officials' control which often proves to be most galling. Regulation by a bureaucratic staff is felt far differently than regulation by custom. And even though a few prisoners do welcome the strict regime of the custodians as a means of checking their own aberrant behavior which they would like to curb but cannot, most prisoners look on the matter in a different light. Most prisoners, in fact, express an intense hostility against their far-reaching dependence on the decisions of their captors and the restricted ability to make choices must be included among the pains of imprisonment along with restrictions of physical liberty, the possession of goods and services, and heterosexual relationships.

Now the loss of autonomy experienced by the inmates of the prison does not represent a grant of power freely given by the ruled to the rulers for a limited and specific end. Rather, it is total and it is imposed—and for these reasons it is less endurable. The nominal objectives of the custodians are not, in general, the objectives of the prisoners. Yet regardless of whether or not the inmate population shares some aims with the custodial bureaucracy, the many regulations and orders of the New Jersey State Prison's official regime often arouse the prisoner's hostility because they don't "make sense" from the prisoner's point of view. Indeed, the incomprehensible order or rule is a basic feature of life in prison. Inmates, for example, are forbidden to take food from the messhall to their cells. Some prisoners see this as a move designed to promote cleanliness; others are convinced that the regulation is for the purpose of preventing inmates from obtaining anything that might be used in the *sub rosa* system of barter. Most, however, simply see the measure as another irritating, pointless gesture of authoritarianism. Similarly, prisoners are denied parole but are left in ignorance of the reasons for the decision. Prisoners are informed that the delivery of mail will be delayed—but they are not told why.

Now some of the inmate population's ignorance might be described as "accidental"; it arises from what we can call the principle of bureaucratic indifference, i.e., events which seem important or vital to those at the bottom of the heap are viewed with an increasing lack of concern with each step upward. The rules, the commands, the decisions which flow down to those who are controlled are not accompanied by explanations on the grounds that it is "impractical" or "too much trouble." Some of the inmate population's ignorance, however, is deliberately fostered by the prison officials in that explanations are often withheld as a matter of calculated policy. Providing explanations carries an implication that those who are ruled have a right to know—and this in turn suggests that if the explanations are not satisfactory, the rule or order will be changed. But this is in direct contradiction to the theoretical power relationship of the inmates and the prison officials. Imprisoned criminals are individuals who are being punished by society and they must be brought to their knees. If the inmate population maintains the right to argue with its captors, it takes on the appearance of an enemy nation with its own sovereignty; and in so doing it raises disturbing questions about the nature of the offender's deviance. The criminal is no longer simply a man who has broken the law; he has become a part of a group with an alternative viewpoint and thus attacks the validity of the law itself. The custodians' refusal to give reasons for many aspects of their regime can be seen in part of an attempt to avoid such an intolerable situation.

The indignation aroused by the "bargaining inmate" or the necessity of justifying the custodial regime is particularly evident during a riot when prisoners have the "impudence" to present a list of demands. In discussing the disturbances at the New Jersey State Prison in the Spring of 1952, for example, a newspaper editorial angrily noted that "the storm, like a nightmarish April Fool's dream, has passed, leaving in its wake a partially wrecked State Prison as a debasing monument to the ignominious rage of desperate men."

The important point, however, is that the frustration of the prisoner's ability to make choices and the frequent refusals to provide an explanation for the regulations and commands descending from the bureaucratic staff involve a profound threat to the prisoner's self image because they reduce the prisoner to the weak, helpless, dependent status of childhood. As Bettelheim has tellingly noted in his comments on the concentration camp, men under guard stand in constant danger of losing their identification with the normal definition of an adult and the imprisoned criminal finds his picture of himself as a self-determining individual being destroyed by the regime of the custodians. It is possible that this psychological attack is particularly painful in American culture because of the deep-lying insecurities produced by the delays, the conditionality and the uneven progress so often observed in the granting of adulthood. It is also possible that the criminal is frequently an individual who has experienced great difficulty in adjusting himself to figures of authority and who finds the many restraints of prison life particularly threatening in so far as earlier struggles over the establishment of self are reactivated in a more virulent form. But without asserting that Americans in general or criminals in particular are notably ill-equipped to deal with the problems posed by the deprivation of autonomy, the helpless or dependent status of the prisoner clearly represents a serious threat to the prisoner's self image as a fully accredited member of adult society. And of the many threats which may confront the individual, either in or out of prison, there are few better calculated to arouse acute anxieties than the attempt to reimpose the subservience of youth. Public humiliation, enforced respect and deference, the finality of authoritarian decisions, the demands for a specfied course of conduct because, in the judgment of another, it is in the individual's best interest—all are features of childhood's helplessness in the face of a superior adult world. Such things may be both irksome and disturbing for a child, especially if the child envisions himself as having outgrown such servitude. But for the adult who has escaped such helplessness with the passage of years, to be thrust back into childhood's helplessness is even more painful, and the inmate of the prison must somehow find a means of coping with the issue.

The Deprivation of Security

However strange it may appear that society has chosen to reduce the criminality of the offender by forcing him to associate with more than a thousand other criminals for years on end, there is one meaning of this involuntary union which is obvious—the individual prisoner is thrown into prolonged intimacy with other men who in many cases have a long history of violent, aggressive behavior. It is a situation which can prove to be anxiety-provoking even for the hardened recidivist and it is in this light that we can understand the comment of an inmate of the New Jersey State Prison who said, "The worst thing about prison is you have to live with other prisoners."

The fact that the imprisoned criminal sometimes views his fellow prisoners as "vicious" or "dangerous" may seem a trifle unreasonable. Other inmates, after all, are men like himself, bearing the legal stigma of conviction. But even if the individual prisoner believes that he himself is not the sort of person who is likely to attack or exploit weaker and less resourceful fellow captives, he is apt to view others with more suspicion. And if he himself is prepared to commit crimes while in prison, he is likely to feel that many others will be at least equally ready.... Regardless of the patterns of mutual aid and support which may flourish in the inmate population, there are a sufficient number of outlaws within this group of outlaws to deprive the average prisoner of that sense of security which comes from living among men who can be reasonably expected to abide by the rules of society. While it is true that every prisoner does not live in the constant fear of being robbed or beaten, the constant companionship of thieves, rapists, murderers, and aggressive homosexuals is far from reassuring.

An important aspect of this disturbingly problematical world is the fact that the inmate is acutely aware that sooner or later he will be "tested"—that someone will "push" him to see how far they can go and that he must be prepared to fight for the safety of his person and his possessions. If he should fail, he will thereafter be an object of contempt, constantly in danger of being attacked by other inmates who view him as an obvious victim, as a man who cannot or will not defend his rights. And yet if he succeeds, he may well become a target for the prisoner who wishes to prove himself, who seeks to enhance his own prestige by defeating the man with a reputation for toughness. Thus both success and failure in defending one's self against the aggressions of fellow captives may serve to provoke fresh attacks and no man stands assured of the future.

The prisoner's loss of security arouses acute anxiety, in short, not just because violent acts of aggression and exploitation occur but also because such behavior constantly calls into question the individual's ability to cope with it, in terms of his own inner resources, his courage, his "nerve." Can he stand up and take it? Will he prove to be tough enough? These uncertainties constitute an ego threat for the individual forced to live in prolonged intimacy with criminals, regardless of the nature or extent of his own criminality; and we can catch a glimpse of this tense and fearful existence in the comment of one prisoner who said, "It takes a pretty good man to be able to stand on an equal plane with a guy that's in for rape, with a guy that's in for murder, with a man who's well respected in the institution because he's a real tough cookie. . . ." His expectations concerning the conforming behavior of others destroyed, unable and unwilling to rely on the officials for protection, uncertain of whether or not today's joke will be tomorrow's bitter insult, the prison inmate can never feel safe. And at a deeper level lies the anxiety about his reactions to this unstable world, for then his manhood will be evaluated in the public view.

NOTES

Prison Theory

Note 1.

RICHARD A. CLOWARD

Social Control in the Prison*

From the prisoner's point of view the administration of criminal justice may be understood as a series of "status degradation ceremonies," which begin at the time of contact with the police and end with the expiration of one's sentence. These ceremonies have important consequences for the emergence of deviant behavior in the prison. Two aspects of the ceremonies are crucial. First, status degradation entails the ritual destruction of the individual's identity. As Garfinkel observes, the work of "denunciation effects the recasting of the objective character of the perceived other: The other person becomes in the eyes of his condemners literally a different and *new* person. . . . He is not changed, he is reconstituted. . . . In the social calculus of reality representations and test, the former identity stands as accidental; the new identity is the 'basic reality.' What he is now is what, 'after all,' he was all along." Second, the new identity assigned to the individual is always of a lower order in the social scheme; he is defined as having been all along "*in essence* of a lower species."

In a stable society most institutions succeed in converting force into authority. People conform not so much because they must as because they feel they should; that is, most institutions succesfully motivate individuals to want to do what they have to do. But this conversion does not take place in the penal environment. Prisoners are less likely to impute legitimacy to the bases of social control in the prison than is typical of persons in other spheres of the society. Having been denounced, degraded, segregated and confined, many renounce the legitimacy of the invidious definitions to which they are subjected, and thus further pressure toward deviance is created. This socially induced strain toward deviance, above all else, sets the stage for a major problem of social control in the prison.

The acute sense of status degradation that prisoners experience generates powerful pressures to evolve means of restoring status. Principal among the mechanisms that emerge is an inmate culture—a system of social relationships governed by norms that are largely at odds with those espoused by the officials and the conventional society. In other words, prisoners are led to seek from within their own numbers what the outside world so fully withholds: prestige. But a lofty state for some presupposes that the many in lowly states will accord legitimacy to these invidious distinctions; if eminence is to be enjoyed by some, then deference and homage must be secured from the lesser ranks. But deference is not so easily secured, especially in the prison. If, as Veblen said, prestige is always in short supply, is is the more so in the prison because so many are deprived of it. Consequently, these disenchanted individuals are forced into bitterly competitive relationships through which the essential superiority of one or another criminal status over other criminal statuses is asserted. Thus it is hardly surprising to find that the upper echelons of the inmate world come to be occupied by those whose past behavior best symbolizes that which society rejects and who have most fully repudiated institutional norms. For those who succeed in asserting the superiority of their particular criminal status, a sense of worth and dignity is the reward. According to McCorkle and Korn, "Observation suggests that the major problems with which the inmate social system attempts to cope center about the theme of social rejection. In many ways, the inmate social system may be viewed as providing a way of life which enables the inmate to avoid the devastating psychological effects of internalizing and converting social rejection into self-rejection. In effect, it permits the inmate to reject his rejectors."

---

* Richard A. Cloward, *et al.*, *Theoretical Studies in Social Organization of the Prison* 20–21 (1960). Reprinted with permission of Social Science Research Council.

Note 2.

LLOYD OHLIN

Modification of the Criminal Value System*

The central task of penal administration is to effect changes in the criminal value system of the imprisoned inmates. This task involves the addition problem of devising methods for giving equal or greater legitimacy to the conventional system represented by the administrative staff. It is doubtful whether it is possible to make much progress in modifying the criminal value system of the inmates until those inmates who express a willingness to control their prison behavior in terms of a conventional value system feel safe in doing so. This requires reorganization of the formal and informal social structure of the prison system. The solidarity of conventionally oriented inmates must be encouraged and protected. Opposition to the criminal value system must be both feasible and successful from the standpoint of informal prestige relations. It would also require a marked reduction in social distance between the administrative staff and the inmate body so that the prison situation would personalize the normative conflict for the inmate and provide motivation for a shift in value identification.

In most prisons today the inmate spends a major part of his time in close contact with his inmate fellows. The situation places a premium on getting along with one's fellows so that prison time may be passed as comfortably as possible. To structure the prison organization to protect those inmates striving for a conventional value orientation, it would appear necessary to employ classification and segregation procedures whose major operating criteria are based on the susceptibility of the inmate to a shift in value orientation. The administrative manipulation of rewards, favors, privileges, and punishments with a view to promoting changes in value identification would be a central administrative objective. The thorough involvement of inmates in interest-provoking and educative activities has proved beneficial in restricting the dissemination of the criminally oriented prison culture by limiting the amount of time spent in idleness and prison chatter.

In a number of prison systems recent humanitarian reforms designed to alleviate the punitive aspects of prison life have become improperly identified as rehabilitation programs. Such humanitarian reforms appear desirable, for they set the framework within which successful treatment programs may be instituted. These reforms in themselves, however, do not create changes in criminal value systems. In that such reforms give evidence of good intentions and the desire of the prison authorities to interest themselves in the inmate's welfare, they create the possibility of establishing relationships of trust, rapport, and loyalty between the administration and certain conventionally motivated inmates. It is not enough, however, to set such a framework and to expect that changes in value system will follow as a matter of course. It is necessary also to deal directly with the normative conflict involved by systematically frustrating behavioral expressions of the criminal value system and promoting, rewarding, and encouraging behavioral expressions consistent with a conventional value orientation. It is likely that marked personal conflict will take place before an individual inmate is prepared to make a major shift in value identification. It must become clear to the inmates that adherence to a criminal value system is a defeating and frustrating experience; whereas behavior controlled in terms of conventional norms not only will receive the support of the administration and a majority of the inmate body, but will lead to the satisfaction of personal needs, to status and prestige rewards, and to the achievement of goals which are culturally supported and sanctioned.

The achievement of such shifts in value orientation is a most difficult and subtle task. It is not yet apparent what methods are most appropriate for achieving these ends. There has been no systematic evaluation of the effects of different types of treatment efforts in producing such value shifts. In fact, little is actually known about the culture of the prisoner community. Very few studies by sociologists have addressed themselves to this problem. The insights that are available come in large part from the autobiographies of convicted offenders. And these accounts are primarily descriptive in nature. Relatively little analytical work has been done on the social and cultural processes operating within the prisoner community to effect or retard shifts in criminal value orientations.

This central task of prison administration poses an extremely challenging problem for sociologists. The problem of changing criminal

---

* Lloyd Ohlin, *Sociology and the Field of Corrections* 29–32 (New York: Russell Sage Foundation, 1956). Reprinted with permission of Russell Sage Foundation.

value orientations in a conventional direction is posed under conditions that afford almost complete control over the lives of individual inmates. The challenge occurs under conditions where the conflict in cultural values is clearly drawn. The situation does not require that sociologists simply invent certain administrative formulas for effecting change, since it is doubtful how successful such prescriptions would be in the present state of our knowledge of these problems. Instead, it calls for exploitation of the opportunity for prison research along sociological lines. There is great need for studies dealing with problems of cultural conflict, diffusion, accommodation, and change. It is possible that research within the prison system could provide a more rapid development of theory and knowledge concerning the relationship between personality and culture and the relationship between culture and social organization that can be secured with comparable effort in other situations in our society.

Note 3.

CLARENCE SCHRAG

*Some Foundations for a Theory of Correction**

Sources of Contemporary Criminological Theory

Tracing the histories and interdependencies of ideas is always hazardous. This is especially the case in a relatively new field such as correctional research. We therefore cautiously venture the opinion that contemporary correctional research reflects the influence of three major theoretical sources. Specifically, we refer to Sutherland's arguments regarding differential association, Durkheim's views on anomie, Weber's analyses of bureaucratic organizations, and to the works of students of these authors. Let us very briefly outline some of the chief arguments involved in these theories.

Differential Association

The theory of differential association develops the idea that criminal values and attitudes are transmitted through social contacts.

* Pp. 315–21. From *The Prison: Studies in Institutional Organization and Change*, edited by Donald R. Cressey. Copyright © 1961 by Holt, Rinehart and Winston, Inc. Reprinted by permission of Holt, Rinehart and Winston, Inc.

It does not explain the origin or genesis of criminal behavior. Rather, it assumes the existence of a criminal culture that contradicts the norms of the broader community and commands the allegiance of criminals and other law violators. This criminalistic element within our culture is viewed as being highly organized and possessing its own values, codes, and enforcement methods.

Those persons who have the closest contacts with patterns of crime and the most tenuous contacts with anticriminal patterns are regarded as most likely to exhibit criminal behavior. Although early formulations of the theory stressed frequency and consistency of contact as the main causal factors, later adaptations of it placed greater emphasis on a number of contact variables, including priority, duration, and intensity. The most recent reformulations have given the theory a more interactionist orientation by taking into account the self-conceptions of criminal offenders and the degree to which different persons identify with criminal behavior patterns.

Anomie

Durkheim's theory of deviant behavior assumes that methods used in the attainment of social goals, although they ordinarily are effectively regulated by tradition and convention, are sometimes freed from social restraints. Restraints are likely to be ineffective in times of crisis, under rapidly changing social conditions, and when great discrepancies occur between goals or aspirations and prospects for their attainment.

Disparities between goals and means of attainment, for example, are common during periods of economic depression or extraordinary prosperity. Again, the attainment of aspirations may be very difficult in rapidly expanding technologies or under social philosophies calling for perpetual progress. Durkheim also noted that relative emancipation from conventional regulations is characteristic of persons occupying certain social positions.

The result of social disruptions and incongruities such as those mentioned is a state of de-regulation, normlessness, or anomie in which deviant behavior is greatly encouraged. Thus, the theory of anomie considers deviant behavior as a product of social influences, and it minimizes the causal role of personal predilections.

Disparities between culturally prescribed goals and alternative means for their attainment are utilized by Merton in classifying several types of deviant behavior. Goals and means may be accepted or rejected by different cultures, societies, groups, or individuals. For example, emphasis on goals may be so great that the means for acquiring them are virtually disregarded. The consequence in this instance is innovation, or the employment of unconventional methods for the achievement of goals. Conversely, devotion to conventional means may be such that goals are assigned relatively insignificant values. Ritualistic conformance to custom is then observed. Rejection of both goals and means results in retreatist behavior, such as isolation, withdrawal, or psychosis. Rebellion, according to Merton, entails the substitution of unconventional goals and means for more traditional objectives and methods.

Since access to alternative means of goal attainment varies among the members of a society, the above scheme provides a basis for predicting observed forms of deviant behavior. This is more apparent if it is assumed that in our culture both legitimate and illegitimate means have been institutionalized, an assumption that can well be justified in terms of Sutherland's account of criminal culture. Thus, Cloward argues that our ordinary criminals are persons who have been deprived of access to legitimate means for achieving success but who have regular access to illegitimate avenues towards success goals. He further maintains that persons who are bereft of both legitimate and illegitimate success routes are likely to engage in drug addiction, alcoholism, and other forms of retreatist behavior. Consolidation of the conceptions of Sutherland, Durkheim, and Merton offers some promise for the prediction of specific types of deviance and criminality.

Perhaps the fullest extension of the notions of differential association and anomie, along with certain psychogenic arguments, is found in the theory of working-class delinquency as propounded by Albert Cohen. The theory holds that juvenile members of the lower classes are systematically frustrated in their efforts to gain security and stature in conventional middle-class society. However, instead of succumbing to de-regulation and anomie, these persons develop a subculture that provides opportunities for mutual strivings toward unconventional goals.

Youths of the lower classes find sympathetic understanding in delinquent gangs composed largely of others who share similar problems of adjustment. Interaction among gang members encourages innovation and rebellion, helps to establish norms for innovative behavior organized around officially proscribed goals, and promotes self-conceptions that facilitate identification with deviant norms and nonconformist groups. The psychological process of reaction-formation results in the inversion of conventional goals and values. Assignment of negative values to middle-class practices enables gang members to reject the society from which they have been rejected. Hence, the culture of delinquent gangs encourages, and provides opportunities for, the expression of malicious, negativistic, and non-utilitarian conduct.

Bureaucracy and Formal Organization

The above cursory review indicates that for several decades criminology has been greatly influenced by the works of Sutherland and Durkheim. In contrast, the impact of Weber seems to have been more recent and less direct. Nevertheless, the problems of concern to Weber have special significance for the field of correction, and it appears likely that they will receive closer attention in the immediate future.

Weber studied the rise of bureaucracy in modern society, its typical structures and procedures, its widespread social ramifications, and its effects on individual freedom. Modern bureaucracy is fostered by the employment of science and technical knowledge in the management of human affairs. With the advancement of science, tradition gives way to formal or legal organizations in which human efforts are deliberately and rationally coordinated in the pursuit of explicitly-stated objectives. These are the general topics with which Weber's theory of formal organization is concerned.

Achievement of the goals of an organization depends upon the difficulties inherent in the asigned task and the availability of necessary knowledge, skills, and other resources. These factors may be regarded as external to the organization in question. But even more important, in the long run, are factors operating within the organization. Foremost among the internal determinants of organizational efficiency are member consensus with respect to goals and objectives, coordination of member activities, and relative utilization of available skills and resources.

Bureaucratic mobilization of human and material resources, as Weber saw it, calls for the employment of a special class of administrators who are responsible for the policies of the organization. It also calls for a hierarchical arrangement of staff positions in order to provide clear and consistent lines of communication and authority. In addition, bureaucracy demands a finely graded system of member rewards based on assigned duties and responsibilities.

The blueprint of bureaucracy is that of a machine. The role played by each member is geared to the activities of other members by means of official rules and regulations. So long as all members perform according to instructions, the organization operates with clock-like precision.

However, there are many things that can go wrong with the bureaucratic machine. For example, there is a notable tendency for the organization to lose sight of its avowed objectives. Once an organization is established, it seems to acquire the primary function of perpetuating itself. Activities aimed at maintaining the organization may overshadow the efforts directed at the original goals and objectives. In such a case regulations acquire a sacred character, blind obedience gains recognition as a virtue, and loyalty to staff members is interpreted as evidence of personal integrity. Procedures that were formerly employed for the achievement of external objectives come to be regarded as ends in themselves.

As a result of the pressures mentioned above, there frequently evolves a system of unofficial controls that may have little similarity to the original, rationally planned, official program.

Many corollaries concerning Weber's theory of bureaucracy can be observed in correctional research, especially in studies of the "informal" society of prisoners,[1] the conflicts between "formal" and "informal" prison social systems,[2] the role of communication in the establishment and maintenance of staff authority,[3] the effects of divergent administrative policies on staff and inmate behavior,[4] the causes of prison riots,[5] and the impact of custodial emphasis versus treatment emphasis on staff-

[1] Donald Clemmer, *The Prison Community*, New Edition (New York: Rinehart, 1958); and Gresham M. Sykes, *The Society of Captives* (Princeton: Princeton University Press, 1958). See also Gresham M. Sykes, "Men, Merchants, and Toughs: A Study of Reactions to Imprisonment," *Social Problems*, 4 (1956), 130–138; Norman S. Hayner and Ellis Ash, "The Prison Community as a Social Group," *American Sociological Review*, 4 (1939), 362–369; Hans Reimer, "Socialization in the Prison Community," *Proceedings of the American Prison Association*, 1937, 151–155.

[2] Erving Goffman, "On the Characteristics of Total Institutions," in *Symposium on Preventive and Social Psychiatry* (Washington: Government Printing Office, 1957), 43–84; Lloyd W. McCorkle and Richard Korn, "Resocialization Within Walls," *Annals of the American Academy of Political and Social Science*, 293 (1954), 88–98; Richard R. Korn and Lloyd W. McCorkle, *Criminology and Penology* (New York: Henry Holt and Company, 1959), chapters 21 and 22; Frank Tannenbaum, *Crime and the Community* (New York: Ginn and Company, 1938), especially ch. 27; Donald R. Cressey, "Achievement of an Unstated Organizational Goal: An Observation on Prisons," *Pacific Sociological Review*, 1 (1958), 43–49; Donald R. Cressey and Witold Krassowski, "Inmate Organization and Anomie in American Prisons and Soviet Labor Camps," *Social Problems*, 5 (1957–8), 217–230; Johan Galtung, "The Functions of a Prison," *Social Problems*, 6 (1958), 127–140; Norman Polansky, "The Prison as an Autocracy," *Journal of Criminal Law and Criminology*, 33 (1942), 16–22.

[3] Richard H. McCleery, *Policy Change in Prison Management* (East Lansing: Michigan State University Governmental Research Bureau, 1957).

[4] S. Kirsen Weinberg, "Aspects of the Prison's Social Structure," *American Journal of Sociology*, 47 (1942), 717–726; Harvey Powelson and Reinhart Bendix, "Psychiatry in Prison," *Psychiatry*, 14 (1951), 73–86; Gresham M. Sykes, "The Corruption of Authority and Rehabilitation," *Social Forces*, 34 (1956), 257–262; S. B. Peizer, E. B. Lewis, and R. W. Scollon, "Correctional Rehabilitation as a Function of Interpersonal Relations," *Journal of Criminal Law, Criminology, and Police Science*, 46 (1956), 632–640; L. E. Ohlin, H. Piven, and D. M. Pappenfort, "Major Dilemmas of the Social Worker in Probation and Parole," *National Probation and Parole Journal*, 2 (1956), 211–225; George H. Weber, "Conflicts Between Professional and Nonprofessional Personnel in Institutional Delinquency Treatment," *Journal of Criminal Law, Criminology, and Police Science*, 48 (1957), 26–43.

[5] F. E. Hartung and M. Floch, "A Socio-Psychological Analysis of Prison Riots," *Journal of Criminal Law, Criminology, and Police Science*, 47 (1956), 51–57; G. M. Sykes, *op. cit.*, ch. 6; J. B. Martin, *Break Down the Walls* (New York: Ballantine Books, 1954); Lloyd E. Ohlin, *Sociology and the Field of Corrections* (New York: Russell Sage Foundation, 1956), 22–26; *Prison Riots and Disturbances* (New York: American Prison Association, 1953); "Aftermath of Riot," *The Prison Journal*, 34 (1954), entire issue; Austin H. MacCormick, "Behind the Prison Riots," *Annals of the American Academy of Political and Social Science*, 293 (1954), 17–27; Vernon Fox, *Violence Behind Bars* (New York: Vantage Press, 1956; P. McGraw and W. McGraw, *Assignment: Prison Riots* (New York: Henry Holt and Company, 1954).

inmate relations and on inmate leadership phenomena.[6] These studies indicate some of the advantages to be gained from the consolidation of organization theory and criminological theory in correctional research.

Now the various theories mentioned have serious logical and empirical defects. Indeed, none of them appears to meet even minimal standards for balance, boundaries, claims, and congruence. Differential association, for example, does not clearly specify the kinds of crime that fall within its scope. It does not provide satisfactory definitions or empirical measures for frequency, duration, priority, or intensity of contact. Moreover, it does not claim any observable interconnections among these contact variables....

Note 4.

GRESHAM M. SYKES AND SHELDON L. MESSINGER

The Inmate Social System*

The loss of liberty is but one of the many deprivations or frustrations inflicted on imprisoned criminals, although it is fundamental to all the rest. As Hayner and Ash have pointed out, inmates are deprived of goods and services that are more or less taken for granted even at the lowest socioeconomic levels in the free community. Inmates must live in austerity as a mater of public policy. Barnes and Teeters have discussed the constraints imposed by the mass of institutional regulations under which prisoners are required to live. Clemmer, Fishman, and others have stressed the severe frustrations imposed on prisoners by the denial of heterosexual relationships. Numerous other writers have described the various pains of confinement in conditions of prolonged physical and psychological compression.

Although the inmate population may no longer suffer the brutality and neglect that in the past aroused the anger of John Howard and similar critics of penal institutions, prisoners still must undergo a variety of deprivations and frustrations which flow either by accident or intent from the fact of imprisonment. Furthermore, it is of greatest significance that the rigors imposed on the inmate by the prison officials do not represent relatively minor irritants which he can somehow endure; instead, the conditions of custody involve profound attacks on the prisoner's self-image or sense of personal worth, and these psychological pains may be far more threatening than physical maltreatment. Brief analysis of the nature of these attacks on the inmate's personality is necessary, for it is as a response to them that we can begin to grasp the rtaionale of the inmate social system.

The isolation of the prisoner from the free community means that he has been rejected by society. His rejection is underscored in some prisons by his shaven head; in almost all, by his uniform and the degradation of no longer having a name but a number. The prisoner is confronted daily with the fact that he has been stripped of his membership in society at large, and now stands condemned as an outcast, an outlaw, a deviant so dangerous that he must be kept behind closely guarded walls and watched both day and night. He has lost the privilege of being *trusted* and his every act is viewed with suspicion by the guards, the surrogates of the conforming social order. Constantly aware of lawful society's disapproval, his picture of himself challenged by frequent reminders of his moral unworthiness, the inmate must find some way to ward off these attacks and avoid their introjection.

In addition, it should be remembered that the offender has been drawn from a society in which personal possessions and material achievement are closely linked with concepts of personal worth by numerous cultural definitions. In the prison, however, the inmate finds himself reduced to a level of living near bare subsistence, and whatever physical discomforts this deprivation may entail, it apparently has deeper psychological significance as a basic attack on the prisoner's conception of his own personal adequacy.

No less important, perhaps, is the ego threat that is created by the deprivation of heterosexual relationships. In the tense atmosphere of the prison, with its perversions and constant references to the problems of sexual frustration, even those inmates who do not engage in overt homosexuality suffer acute attacks of anxiety about their own masculinity. These anxieties may arise from a prisoner's unconscious fear of latent homosexual tenden-

---

[6] Oscar Grusky, "Organizational Goals and the Behavior of Informal Leaders," *American Journal of Sociology,* 65 (1959), 59–67; Clarence Schrag, "Leadership Among Prison Inmates," *American Sociological Review,* 19 (1954), 37–42.

* From Richard A. Cloward, *et al., Theoretical Studies in Social Organization of the Prison* 13–17 (1960). Reprinted with permission of Social Science Research Council.

cies in himself, which might be activated by his prolonged heterosexual deprivation and the importunity of others; or at a more conscious level he may feel that his masculinity is threatened because he can see himself as a man—in the full sense—only in a world that also contains women. In either case the inmate is confronted with the fact that the celibacy imposed on him by society means more than simple physiological frustration: an essential component of his self-conception, his status as male, is called into question.

Rejected, impoverished, and figuratively castrated, the prisoner must face still further indignity in the extensive social control exercised by the custodians. The many details of the inmate's life, ranging from the hours of sleeping to the route to work and the job itself, are subject to a vast number of regulations made by prison officials. The inmate is stripped of his autonomy; hence, to the other pains of imprisonment we must add the pressure to define himself as weak, helpless, and dependent. Individuals under guard are exposed to the bitter ego threat of losing their identification with the normal adult role.

The remaining significant feature of the inmate's social environment is the presence of other imprisoned criminals. Murderers, rapists, thieves, confidence men, and sexual deviants are the inmate's constant companions, and this enforced intimacy may prove to be disquieting even for the hardened recidivist. As an inmate has said, "The worst thing about prison is you have to live with other prisoners." Crowded into a small area with men who have long records of physical assaults, thievery, and so on (and who may be expected to continue in the path of deviant social behavior in the future), the inmate is deprived of the sense of security that we more or less take for granted in the free community. Although the anxieties created by such a situation do not necessarily involve an attack on the individual's sense of personal worth—as we are using the concept—the problems of self-protection in a society composed exclusively of criminals constitute one of the inadvertent rigors of confinement.

In short, imprisonment "punishes" the offender in a variety of ways extending far beyond the simple fact of incarceration. However just or necessary such punishments may be, their importance for our present analysis lies in the fact that they form a set of harsh social conditions to which the population of prisoners must respond or *adapt itself*. The inmate feels that the deprivations and frustrations of prison life, with their implications for the destruction of his self-esteem, somehow must be alleviated. It is, we suggest, as an answer to this need that the functional significance of the inmate code or system of values exhibited so frequently by men in prison can best be understood.

The dominant theme of the inmate code is group cohesion, with a "war of all against all" —in which each man seeks his own gain without considering the rights or claims of others— as the theoretical antipode. But if a war of all against all is likely to make life "solitary, poor, nasty, brutish, and short" for men with freedom, as Hobbes suggested, it is doubly so for men in custody. Even those who are most successful in exploiting their fellow prisoners will find it a dangerous and nerve-wracking game, for they cannot escape the company of their victims. No man can assure the safety of either his person or his possessions, and eventually the winner is certain to lose to a more powerful or more skilled exploiter. Furthermore, the victims hold the trump card, since a word to the officials is frequently all that is required to ruin the most dominating figure in the inmate population. A large share of the "extra" goods that enter the inmate social system must do so as the result of illicit conniving against the officials, which often requires lengthy and extensive cooperation and trust; in a state of complete conflict the resources of the system will be diminished. Mutual abhorrence or indifference will feed the emotional frictions arising from interaction under compression. And as rejection by others is a fundamental problem, a state of mutual alienation is worse than useless as a solution to the threats created by the inmate's status as an outcast.

As a population of prisoners moves toward a state of mutual antagonism, then, the many problems of prison life become more acute. On the other hand, *as a population of prisoners moves in the direction of solidarity, as demanded by the inmate code, the pains of imprisonment become less severe.* They cannot be eliminated, it is true, but their consequences at least can be partially neutralized. A cohesive inmate society provides the prisoner with a meaningful social group with which he can identify himself and which will support him in his struggles against his condemners. Thus it permits him to escape at least in part the fearful isolation of the convicted offender. Inmate solidarity, in the form of toleration of the many irritants of life in confinement, helps to solve the problems of personal security posed by the involuntary intimacy of men noteworthy for their seriously antisocial behavior in the past.

Similarly, group cohesion in the form of a reciprocity of favors undermines one of the most potent sources of aggression among prisoners, the drive for personal aggrandizement through exploitation by force and fraud. Furthermore, although goods in scarce supply will remain scarce even if they are shared rather than monopolized, such goods will be distributed more equitably in a social system marked by solidarity, and this may be of profound significance in enabling the prisoner to endure better the psychological burden of impoverishment. A cohesive population of prisoners has another advantage in that it supports a system of shared beliefs that explicitly deny the traditional link between merit and achievement. Material success, according to this system, is a matter of "connections" rather than skill or hard work, and thus the imprisoned criminal is partially freed from the necessity of defining his material want as a sign of personal inadequacy.

Finally, a cohesive inmate social system institutionalizes the value of "dignity" and the ability to "take it" in a number of norms and reinforces these norms with informal social controls. In effect, the prisoner is called on to endure manfully what he cannot avoid. At first glance this might seem to be simply the counsel of despair; but if the elevation of fortitude into a primary virtue is the last refuge of the powerless, it also serves to shift the criteria of the individual's worth from conditions that cannot be altered to his ability to maintain some degree of personal integration; and the latter, at least, can be partially controlled. By creating an ideal of endurance in the face of harsh social conditions, then, the society of prisoners opens a path to the restoration of self-respect and a sense of independence that can exist despite prior criminality, present subjugation, and the free community's denial of the offender's moral worthiness. Significantly, this path to virtue is recognized by the prison officials as well as the prisoners.

One further point should be noted with regard to the emphasis placed on the maintenance of self as defined by the value system of prisoners. Dignity, composure, courage, the ability to "take it" and "hand it out" when necessary—these are the traits affirmed by the inmate code. They are also traits that are commonly defined as masculine by the inmate population. As a consequence, the prisoner finds himself in a situation where he can recapture his male role, not in terms of its sexual aspects, but in terms of behavior that is accepted as a good indicator of virility.

Note 5.

STANTON WHEELER

*Socialization in Correctional Institutions**

Until the decade of the 1950's the most serious effort to understand the process of socialization in prison was that of Donald Clemmer. Clemmer was a sociologist with many years of experience behind the walls of prisons and he produced the first book-length study of a prison as a community. Clemmer described the culture and social organization of the prison, and noted that most of the characteristics he found suggested a system distinctly harmful to anything that might be regarded as a process of rehabilitation: The norms and codes of the inmate world appear to be organized in opposition to those of conventional society. He then turned his attention to the process by which inmates become a part of that world. He used the concept of *prisonization* as a summarizing concept revealing the consequences of exposure to inmate society. He defined prisonization as "the taking on, in greater or lesser degree, of the folkways, mores, customs and general culture of the penitentiary." And while he felt that no inmate could remain completely "unprisonized," he devoted a good deal of attention to variables that he thought probably influenced both the speed and the degree of prisonization. Some of these variables reflected the inmates' participation in conventional society. Thus prisonization would be lowest, he felt, for inmates who had positive relationships during pre-penal life, and for those who continued their positive relationships with persons outside the walls during the time they were in prison. But the feature that he thought was most important in determining the degree of prisonization was simply the degree of close interpersonal contact that inmates had with other inmates within the institution. Those who became affiliated with inmate primary groups and those whose work and cell assignments placed them in very close contact with other inmates were likely to show the greatest degree of prisonization.

It was possible to put these ideas to a fairly direct empirical test in a survey research study of Washington State Reformatory. An attitude

* Stanton Wheeler, "Socialization in Correctional Institutions," in David A. Goslin (Ed.), *Handbook of Socialization Theory and Research,* © 1969 by Rand McNally and Company, Chicago, pp. 1006–1010, 1018–1019. Reprinted with permission of the publisher.

measure of attitudinal conformity versus nonconformity to the values of the staff (and presumably, those of the conventional world) was developed to serve as an empirical indicator reflecting Clemmer's concept of prisonization. And although the study utilized a cross-sectional design rather than a panel design in which we could actually trace changes in attitudes over time, we could at least approximate the temporal aspect of imprisonment by comparing inmates who had been in the institution for varying lengths of time in order to test Clemmer's hypothesis that the longer the duration of stay, the more likely one was to become "prisonized."

The result of this analysis provided strong support for Clemmer's hypotheses. There was a general trend toward greater nonconformity to staff values with increase in length of time in the prison. And the trend was much stronger for those inmates who had made many friends in the institution than for those who were relatively isolated.

But one of the interesting features of Clemmer's account is that he had little to say about what happens to inmates as they prepare to leave the institutions. Many of his ideas about the socialization process in prison were drawn from studies of assimilation of ethnic groups into American life, and since by and large those groups were here to stay, the problem of what happens to them as they prepare to return to a former way of life does not arise. Perhaps for this reason, Clemmer's account has much to say about the early stages of imprisonment and about the general effects of being in prison, with no systematic attention devoted to the process of leaving the prison, and particularly to the possibility that the impact of prison culture is short-lived.

These concerns led us to consider the time measure in studies of prisonization in a manner different from that conceived by Clemmer. Very simply, we divided inmates into three groups: those who had been in only a short time, those who had only a short time remaining to serve, and those who were near neither entry nor release. The general results of this analysis suggested important modifications in Clemmer's original hypotheses. While we found a larger percentage of inmates who were strongly opposed to staff norms during the last stage of their confinement than during the first, we also found a U-shaped distribution of high conformity responses over the three time periods: there were fewer than half as many high conformity respondents during the middle phase than during the early and later phases of imprisonment. These findings suggest that while some inmates might become increasingly alienated during the course of their stay, an even larger number may exhibit the process of prisonization until the middle of their stay, when it is replaced by a process of resocialization to the more conventional values of the outside world. And there was further evidence in support of the latter pattern: The U-shaped pattern of conforming responses was found both for inmates who had developed many friends in the institution and for those who had not, though it was stronger for the former group. It was also found both for first offenders and for recidivists. The clear suggestion from the evidence, then, was that this may well be a systematic feature of response to imprisonment, and not simply a minor deviation from the prisonization theme.

It would be simple enough to add the idea of "anticipatory socialization" to that of prisonization in an effort to make sense of both patterns of data. Indeed, Robert K. Merton had already written about the process of anticipatory socialization, and in retrospect, there was good reason to assume that such a process would operate, even though it had not been formally incorporated into Clemmer's scheme. But while this would have given us two descriptive labels for two different patterns of empirical results, it would not have moved us very far toward understanding the conditions under which one or the other pattern would be expected to occur. In attempting to move toward the latter aim we were forced to ask questions about the nature of the inmate culture itself, and particularly about the sources that give rise to it.

Almost all accounts of close custody prisons in the United States are in agreement on the fundamental qualities of the inmate world in such institutions. Very briefly, three features seem most important:

1. There is a normative order defined largely in opposition to the staff and placing great emphasis on loyalty to other inmates.

2. There is a system of informal social differentiation that is reflected in the series of social types or argot roles noted by Sykes, Schrag and many others. Special labels are assigned to inmates depending on their mode of response to prison life and expressing the quality of their interaction with staff and inmates. The system of informally defined social types gives evidence both of the dominant values of the inmate world—for the pejoratives always apply to those inmates who support the staff or

who exploit other inmates for their own benefit—and of the range of subcultures that form within the walls of the institutions.

3. Accounts of everyday life in American prisons point to numerous struggles for power, frequent involvement in illicit activities, and a fair amount of violence behind the walls. Every institution has its share of fist-fights and occasional knifings, with force used as a means of social control. Though it would be easy to exaggerate such matters, it seems clear that the American prison is not a particularly warm, tolerant or congenial cultural setting. Almost every institution finds that it needs, in addition to the unit designed to hold the assault-minded or escape-risk inmates, a special segregation unit to protect some inmates from others who are out to get them.

Why does the prison so typically show these patterns of inmate response? Two conflicting views can be found. One interpretation is along the lines of "cultural diffusion" theories in anthropology. Very briefly, inmate society is what it is because inmates have imported their antagonism toward law and order from the outside world. The single trait held in common by all inmates is participation in criminal activity. The capacity to engage in criminal acts suggests at least some degree of withdrawal of support from conventional values, and indeed can be viewed as indicating an opposition to conventional norms and values. By bringing together in a twenty-four-hour living establishment individuals who have deviated from conventional norms, the prison offers opportunities for mutual reinforcement of criminal values. Those inmates who occupy prominent positions within the inmate hierarchy and who spend the most time in interaction with their fellows should be the ones whose values are most likely to serve as the basis for the organization and culture of inmate life. And these same inmates, we know from other sources, are those who are likely to be most committed to a criminal value system —those who have followed systematic criminal careers, those who are most hostile and aggressive in their expression of opposition to the staff. And if the culture is viewed as an outgrowth of the dominant sort of attitudes entering inmates bring with them, it is reasonable to expect a reinforcement process operating throughout the duration of their confinement. This is consistent with the image of correctional institutions as "crime schools" and with a theory that accounts for the socialization processes in prison largely in terms of a concept such as "prisonization." And this is very much the sort of process hinted at by Clemmer, although he very largely took the values of the inmate system for granted, and did not set out to explain them.

An alternative interpretation of the sources for the inmate culture emerged in the years following Clemmer's work, and received its fullest expression in an analysis of the inmate's social system presented by Gresham Sykes and Sheldon Messinger. Instead of viewing inmate culture as a simple expression, and perhaps extension, of the individual values inmates may bring to the prison, Sykes and Messinger saw the inmate culture as a response to the adjustment problems posed by imprisonment itself, with all of its frustrations and deprivations. Among the important deprivations include the low and rejected status of being an inmate, the material and sexual deprivations of imprisonment, the constant social control exercised by the custodians of the prison, and the presence of other offenders who may be perceived as dangerous and threatening. The normative order and the system of social differentiation discussed above can be seen as responses to the series of deprivations. The normative order may reinstate self-esteem by providing a meaningful reference group that will support an inmate's attack on the staff, and it may lessen the dangers of exploitation on the part of other inmates. Further, the system of social differentiation itself reflects the variety of individual adaptations to the deprivations in question. In short, an alternative to the cultural diffusion scheme is a functional theory in which inmate culture is seen as a response to the conditions of imprisonment rather than an extension of the values men bring to prison.

If this interpretation is valid, we might expect that inmate culture would exert its major impact on inmates during the middle of their stay in prison, at the point in time when they are farthest removed from the outside world. And if the inmate value system is a response to the deprivations of imprisonment, it would seem only natural that as men prepare to leave the prison, those deprivations begin to wane in their significance. Thus they move away from adherence to the inmate value system and toward the values of the conventional society to which they are soon returning. Furthermore, the deprivations themselves may be objectively less severe as men approach release, when they are likely to be allowed more freedom within the walls, and somewhat more of the few amenities prison life may offer.

This provides us with a more substantial

theoretical underpinning for the empirical finding of a U-shaped socialization and resocialization cycle within the prison. We are left, then, with two different patterns of change over time in the prison, and with two different and conflicting ideas regarding the sources of inmate culture itself, ideas that might possibly explain one or another of the patterns of adjustment to the prison over time.... The concept of socialization, like so many of the concepts in behavioral science, has been subject to a wide variety of definitions and interpretations. The definition suggested in the introduction to this volume, "the process by which individuals acquire the knowledge, skills and dispositions that enable them to participate as more or less effective members of groups and the society" can be given either a narrow or a broad interpretation. As applied to the prison, for example, it can be taken to refer to the ways in which inmates learn how to manage their lives within the institution at some minimal level of effectiveness. A substantive focus on this concern would lead to an effort to answer the questions: What does an inmate need to know, in addition to what he already knows, that will enable him to make a minimal adjustment to the prison? What skills must he develop that he does not already have? What attitudinal or behavioral dispositions will be needed?

There are abundant documentary materials to suggest that, in terms of these questions, adaptation to the prison is not greatly different from adaptation to any other setting. The inmate will learn from others what the guards expect of him as a routine matter, what the inmates expect, and how he can successfully negotiate between these two conflicting sets of expectations. He may also learn how to achieve those minimum creature comforts tht make life tolerable within the institution. What is learned will depend upon the local culture of the institution in question, and on the degree to which an individual inmate becomes involved in that culture. The chief difference between the prison and many other social settings in this connection is that, as a "total institution," the pains resulting from failure to become socialized are particularly severe for there is literally no escape from the norms and role demands of the setting. As Goffman has pointed out, the prison shares this quality with many other forms of organization, including the ship, the mental hospital, the private boys' school, and the monastery. But aside from the "total" character of such settings, and the special importance that attaches to getting along, there is not a lot that distinguishes the total institution from other settings where socialization, in this narrow sense, goes on.

A more inclusive view of the socialization process would place less emphasis on problems of surface adjustment, more emphasis on deeper, more fundamental changes. It would emphasize the internalization of norms, rather than overt compliance with the setting in question. It might give less attention to external features of adjustment, more to possible changes in one's basic conception of himself, his sense of worth and dignity. Many who speak of socialization within the prison indeed have these latter qualities in mind. The typical assumption has been that the harsh and dramatic circumstances of imprisonment as a form of human existence are likely to lead to deep-seated and fundamental changes in values, ideologies and personal styles. And the assumption has typically been that these changes will have long-lasting effects. Similarly, when persons have talked about "rehabilitation" or "resocialization" they have been concerned with more than establishing a new surface adaptation to conventional ways of life. They have had in mind some relatively basic reconstruction or reconstitution of one's values, beliefs, and way of life....

It is this broader meaning of socialization that has been implicit in the matters discussed in this chapter. The prison is often viewed as a setting within which fundamental changes in attitudes and values are likely to take place. A growing body of both evidence and thought suggests that this view may be incorrect. Indeed, the central argument of this chapter may be put as follows:

1. Persons do not enter prison motivated to seek a basically new and different vision of themselves.

2. To the extent that they do change, the change is produced as much by the reaction to being confined and separated from the free community as it is by the dynamics of life within the institution.

3. The values and attitudes expressed by prison inmates are shaped in important ways by the circumstances to which inmates have been exposed prior to their period of incarceration.

4. In addition to its impact on the values held by entering inmates, the external world influences the kind of culture and social organization that is formed within the prison, and which serves as the social context within which adaptation to imprisonment takes place.

5. As a result of these conditions, whatever

impact the experience of imprisonment itself might have on inmates, either positive or negative, is sharply attenuated. *It is the social definition of the prison in society, rather than the social status of the inmate within the prison, that appears to be most relevant for the future life and career of prison inmates.*

6. It follows from all of the above that a full understanding of processes of socialization and resocialization within the prison requires much greater attention than has heretofore been given to the relationship of both the prison and the prisoner to the external world....

E. International Perspectives

JOHN P. CONRAD

Trends in European Corrections*

To understand innovation and change in European correctional practice, some account must be taken of certain regularities which hold generally true of all continental countries west of the Communist bloc. Although some of the generalizations which follow are open to exception as to some countries, they establish boundaries of practice beyond which little development is to be expected. It is the writer's belief that the following propositions are significant for both juvenile and adult practice.

1. The correctional apparatus in all European countries is an instrument of the national government. There is no locally administered correctional system or facility corresponding to the county jails and probation departments in the United States. This statement holds true for the Iron Curtain countries as well as for Western Europe. The result is that correctional organization tends to conform to uniform standards of administration with well-defined bureaucratic controls. Such innovation as may be encountered will be centrally initiated or sanctioned.

2. Except in the United Kingdom, administration of correctional programs tends to be in the hands of juridically trained personnel. These people are ordinarily successful competitors for positions in the higher civil service. Their experience in operational contact with offenders is limited. The promotion of probation officers or custodial officers to administrative posts is rare....

Most of the European correctional leadership is in the hands of people who are trained for the maintenance of the systems over which they preside. There are distinguished exceptions, but they are handicapped by bureaucratic structures whose efficiency is obvious but whose approach to duty leaves little room for imagination.

3. Innovation is most feasible within the established administrative structure at the level of inmate-staff interaction. Institution management is open to some initiatives, particularly in the areas of classification and counseling. So long as a prison manager or approved school headmaster does not violate some centrally established directive, he is free to do what he can with the resources provided. It is reasonable, however, to say that relatively few take advantage of this freedom.

4. Correctional facilities throughout Europe tend to be much smaller than their American counterparts. An institutional population in excess of 500 is unusual. Where it occurs, it is usually a facility receiving inmates for short-term confinement or detention pending trial. Most institution heads place considerable stress on their need to maintain personal contact with all inmates under their control as a requirement for institutional effectiveness. This approach necessarily limits optimal size of institutions to a figure of less than 300.

5. Except in the United Kingdom, the use of probation has been of relatively recent establishment. There is some disposition in the Scandinavian countries and the Netherlands to use the English probation service as a model. In these countries, probation is still in transition from volunteer services performed under private auspices to publicly controlled and pro-

---

* President's Commission on Law Enforcement and Administration of Justice, *Consultant's Paper* 1–29; 48–50 (1967).

fessionalized agencies. In France and Italy, probation service is limited, new, and more in the nature of leniency under surveillance than a form of treatment. Probation has yet to be introduced in Spain or Portugal. It is not used in any of the Eastern European countries.

6. Parole and aftercare services are generally in the hands of probation officers. There is an important exception. In Denmark some initiative has been taken by institution management to undertake aftercare services with casework personnel employed by the institution.

7. Probation personnel are generally trained in social work, either prior to employment or as a part of inservice training. An important, if curious, exception exists in France, where two kinds of probation personnel are employed. The *agent de probation,* usually a man, is intended to represent authority and is required to carry out surveillance functions. The *assistant social,* usually a woman, will be trained as a social worker and will play the part of a counselor and will deal with personal problems of adjustment. This division of labor is new. Both of these roles are under the supervision of the *juge d'application des peines,* who is responsible for assuring that the sentence of the court is effectively carried out in treatment. A somewhat similar organization of probation functions has been introduced in Italy.

8. Although reported crime rates in several European countries have markedly increased in the last decade, in all countries they are much lower than in the urban industrial sections of the United States. The increase in England and Sweden has been of great concern to policy-makers and to the general public. In some countries, notably Italy and Denmark, crime rates seem to have declined significantly. It is fair to say that innovations tend to occur in the countries in which the control of increasing criminal populations has borne most heavily on existing correctional resources. There are some notable exceptions, especially in the Netherlands and Denmark, where social and economic planning in other areas of national life are well advanced.

9. The assumptions of practice customary in the helping professions are not ordinarily modified when introduced into correctional settings. Although distinguished exceptions exist, some of which will be described in later sections of this paper, psychiatrists, psychologists, social workers, and educators tend to follow the conventional procedures and base their practice on the assumptions prevailing in the community at large. This tendency is significant in that diagnoses, expectations, and treatment methods developed for use in general practice are usually quite explicit in the assumption that offenders are not treatable.

10. Correctional practice is seldom grounded on theoretical premises regarding intervention and its consequences. Although the volume of criminological literature is large, little attention has been given to the effectiveness of given intervention patterns. Statistical analyses of programs are rare outside the United Kingdom. Under the circumstances, such program development as takes place is either based on *a priori* syntheses or on sheer intuition. . . .

From these generalizations some interpretations may be derived regarding the place of corrections in the social fabric. To begin with, although there are many differences in practice from country to country in Western Europe, there are some common factors which distinguish European correctional work from the American counterpart. As will be shown later, it is reasonable to expect that considerable change in European correctional policy will occur in the coming 10 to 20 years. It is doubtful that these changes will closely parallel the resocialization model which is widely accepted among advanced correctional leaders in the United States. It seems more likely that the use of probation will be extended in Europe, but that treatment strategies based on offender typologies will be a long time in gaining influence.

The role of the offender in the correctional apparatus is for the most part based on the expectation that his social and psychological handicaps will render him a dependent on the system for the indefinite rather than forming the basis for planned change aimed at social restoration. To the extent that this analysis is correct, it must be reasonable to suppose that the relationship of the system to the client is paternal rather than change-oriented.

It is consistent with the foregoing that in the field of adult corrections, the apparatus is a system of social control whose objective has been to execute the sentence of the court. Whatever can be done within the time to be served in prison or on probation to render the client less likely to return to criminal activity, will be provided for. At best, however, he will be counseled and educated; at least he will be kept busy. To the extent that he brings to the correctional experience a set of attitudes of deference toward authority, he is most likely to benefit from the experience.

Significantly, the concept of the indeterminate sentence has never taken hold, in the United Kingdom or on the continent. There are exceptions. Juvenile offenders in institutions patterned after the British approved schools and borstals are under the long-term control of a correctional system in which release and recall may alternate over a fairly extended period of time. (It is important to note that the Model Youth Corrections Authority Act of the American Law Institute was influenced by observation of the borstal system.)

Another exception is the concept of preventive detention which is used in several northern European countries. As administered in England, this is a system for the long-term confinement of the chronic recidivist, with some provision for flexibility in the remission of between one-third and one-sixth of the sentence of the court. But the administration of justice is generally tied firmly to the prerogatives of the court in determining the disposition of the offender. In fixing a term, the courts dispose of the offender in the interests of justice, not considering the requirements for the offender's potential return to society as a contributing member. The frequently repeated maxim of the English bench, "Justice must not only be done, but it must be seen to be done," clearly points to the sentencing function as an instrument for maintaining an equitable balance of crime and punishment as the foundation of an orderly society. There is a possible reconciliation between retributive justice and the resocialization of the offender, but it does not appear that European jurists have sought it with zeal.

A bureaucratic system with powerful judicial support seems characteristic of European corrections. It is a stable and conservative structure with a high resistance to change. Most upper-level staff come to their work with skill and training in the management of an administrative system. They are not educated in the behavioral sciences, and the techniques which they use in dealing with offenders are derived from training in command. The uniformed staff are trained with care in the execution of routines. But until recently, and even now only exceptionally, were given no duties which expect of them any influence over inmates or offenders. The American vogue for group counseling has attracted much interest in Europe, but its practice is most often in the hands of psychologists and social workers rather than prison or borstal officers. It is a paradox that the highly flexible role system established in the Social Rehabilitation Unit at Henderson Hospital in England by Dr. Maxwell Jones has been infrequently emulated in England or on the continent, whereas it has been so popular in the United States as to be considered by some a fad which has been far too uncritically imported.

What has been described here is an administrative approach to correctional practice. Though its stability and resistance to change are great, there are at least three important, if peripheral forces, which challenge the present regime. None of them are irresistible, but their existence makes development probable in systems which have been long standardized. These forces are:

1. The influence of psychiatry.
2. The influence of probation.
3. The tendency to believe that a correctional system should have some criteria for success beyond the mere maintenance of order.

Psychiatry and Corrections

Throughout Europe, including the Marxist countries, there is a consensus that the psychologically damaged offender, such as the schizophrenic or the brain-damaged, should be removed entirely from the correctional apparatus and placed in specialized psychiatric facilities. What is in dispute, both conceptually and operationally, is the role of the psychiatrist with the offender who is not diagnosed as psychotic or brain-damaged. Some of the most famous and interesting correctional developments in Europe have been based on the hypothesis that psychotherapy is an appropriate intervention with problem classes of offender. Such institutional facilities as Herstedvester in Denmark, Roxtuna in Sweden, the van der Hoeven Kliniek in the Netherlands, and the Grendon Underwood psychiatric prison in England attest to the interest and resourcefulness of a handful of psychiatrists in the treatment of violent offenders, sexual offenders, and certain recidivists who display classic psychoneurotic syndromes. It must be said, however, that the methods of treatment are adaptations from the general practice of psychiatry rather than innovations generated by the nature of the correctional problem and a conceptualization of its solution.

NORVAL MORRIS

Lessons from the Adult Correctional System of Sweden*

Not only do the Swedish courts try to avoid committing offenders to penal institutions but when imprisonment is the sentence, the terms of years imposed also are short in comparison with those obtaining in the United States. The prison administrators further try to minimize both the actual terms served and the amount of social isolation and separation that is involved in a prison sentence. For example, of the 5,000 prisoners, over one-third are at any one time held in completely open conditions. . . .

Pervading the Swedish social and political system is a high level of respect for individual human rights. It is also a very polite society in which citizen treats citizen and the state treats its citizens with punctilious respect. These attitudes lie deep in Swedish social organization and are in no way abandoned when the citizen becomes a criminal or a prisoner. Thus, section 23 of the law on Treatment in Correctional Institutions, 1964, the first general provision on the conditions of imprisonment, provides that "An inmate shall be treated with firmness and determination and with respect . . . injurious effects of the loss of freedom shall be prevented as far as possible."

This humanitarian and egalitarian attitude is indeed the mainspring of the whole correctional system, an explanation of both the low incidence of imprisonment and of many of the conditions and practices within the prison system. This attitude is both its strength and a key to some of its weaknesses. . . . The prison administrator and the prison officer in Sweden has this advantage over his colleague in many other countries: Swedish citizens generally are intensely proud of their social welfare system. More and more they take their very high standard of living for granted and express pride in their country in relation to its care for the sick, incompetent and discordant elements within it. When they turn to the international field their national amour-propre is likewise expressed in terms of extensive technical and financial contributions to the developing countries and to the United Nations. The Swedish citizen not connected with prison work will, at the dinner table, express pride in the Swedish correctional system; this is hardly a common experience at the American dinner table. And his satisfaction is not in any clinical skills that the system mobilizes or in its effect on recidivist rates, but rather in the fact that the Swedish criminal or prisoner still remains a Swedish citizen meriting respect, continuing properly to enjoy a quite high standard of living, and remaining a part of the community.

Examples of this attitude are frequently to be found in the press, where the prisoners' complaints to the Ombudsman often receive considerable press attention. The community appears to be interested in and to take seriously complaints by prisoners which would not in this country merit protracted attention within the walls and certainly would receive no consideration whatsoever outside.

. . . For the 5,000 prisoners in Sweden there are at present 88 prisons. With a range and diversity of small prisons and with an institutional staff in excess of one member of staff for every two prisoners, with small institutions and small groups of prisoners, it has proved possible to set up a correctional institutional system which avoids the mass anonymity characteristic of the penal system in this country, and which largely avoids the hot-house growth of the evil subculture which has characterized our correctional efforts. . . .

Women are found to be working not only in institutions for younger offenders in Sweden but also throughout their adult correctional system. I do not mean working only in the front offices outside the security perimeter; I mean within the walls and within the cell blocks. And there are women governors of prisons for male prisoners. Only in Långholmen, of the institutions I visited, is there the sense of an exclusively male society. Monasticism is avoided even in the main long term institution of Hall which is the central prison for the internment group, who are the persis-

---

* 30 *Federal Probation* No. 4, pp. 4–8 (1966). Reprinted with permission.

tent and professional criminals; it is likewise avoided for the 18- to-21-year-old group of vigorous males, and indeed when I visited the institution of Mariefred, holding such offenders, the warden was a woman. The advantages of our learning this lesson from Sweden are obvious; women bring a softening influence to the prison society, assisting men by their presence, to strengthen their inner controls, through a variety of deeply entrenched processes of psychosocial growth.

What are the disadvantages or risks involved in emulating this sensible plan, which would be sensible even did we not face chronic staff shortages? I suppose the risks or disadvantages are four-fold: Loss of discipline, a barrage of obscenity, sexual assaults, and successful courtship by those we too often see as pariahs. The first I doubt, the second is a matter of staff training, the third is not a serious threat, and the fourth is to be occasionally expected and welcomed.

. . . Conditional and final release under the indeterminate commitment is under the control of an internment board presided over by a judge or retired judge of the Supreme Court, and with four other members, including a senior lawyer, a member of parliament, usually a psychiatrist, and the director general of the Correctional Administration.

Considerable effort is made to delegate powers to the five regional correctional systems, and substantial authority in relation to the date of conditional and final release of inmates is given to local supervisory boards. There are 47 supervisory boards in Sweden, each serving one or more trial court districts, and responsible for recommending the parole of prisoners in its district. Parole is for 1 year or the unexpired portion of the sentence, whichever is longer. . . .

An aphorism frequently heard in the prison administration of Sweden concerning their work program is: "First build a factory, then add a prison to it." Prisoners work a 45-hour, 5-day week from 7 in the morning to 5 in the evening with 1½ hours for lunch; the able-bodied idle prisoner is rare in Sweden. A few inmates, of course, are employed on maintenance work, but the atmosphere of all the industrial prisons is close to that of a factory. And even many of their very small open institutions are also industrial. One finds institutions of 40 inmates living in lightly built and unlocked and unfenced facilities in which about half the inmates will be engaged in farm work and half will be running a small timber-yard or carpentry workshop. The industries range from small, almost village industries, to substantial mass-production factories. The machine shop industry provides 500 jobs, the wood industry 850, and the garment industry 850. These are the major products, but there are also large laundries and substantial boat-building and prefabricated house building activities (200). Indeed, for the 5,000 prisoners, 2,500 jobs are available within various types of industry, while roughly 1,000 are employed in farming and forestry activities.

The correctional administration is one of Sweden's largest rural land owners, with 6,500 acres of farm land. The building industry is of importance, prison labor having recently been used to build several open institutions. There still remain tensions between employers and trade union organizations as to the extent to which prison building should be done by prison inmates for the larger closed and complex institution, but for the smaller open institutions the battle is won and they are largely the product of inmate labour.

Chapter Six

THEORIES OF PUNISHMENT AND CORRECTION: WHAT IS THE FUNCTION OF PRISON?

HERBERT L. PACKER

The Justification for Punishment*

Today as always the criminal law is caught between two fires. On the one hand, there is the view that punishment of the morally derelict is its own justification. On the other, there is the view that the only proper goal of the criminal process is the prevention of antisocial behavior. As if the problem of reconciling these views were not enough, the second has lately given rise to a new formulation that threatens the very foundations of the criminal law. This new formulation seemingly creates a dilemma for those who do not accept the retributive position yet who do not want to reject the whole concept of the criminal law.

. . . The retributive position is an old one, and its content has not changed much over the centuries. It holds, very simply, that man is a responsible moral agent to whom rewards are due when he makes right moral choices and to whom punishment is due when he makes wrong ones. According to this view, these imperatives flow from the nature of man and do not require—indeed do not permit—any pragmatic justification. There is a per-

* Pp. 9-14; 36-37; 39-40; 45-46; 48-49; 53-56. Reprinted, with footnotes omitted, from *The Limits of the Criminal Sanction* by Herbert L. Packer with the permission of the publishers, Stanford University Press. © 1968 by Herbert L. Packer.

ceived sense of fitness in the sight of wrongdoers being made to suffer for their misdeeds. As individuals we have a wholly proper desire to seek revenge when wrongs are inflicted on us; as a society we demand that constituted authority punish those who unjustifiably inflict injury on others or otherwise act in ways we think are wrong. If other benefits are incidentally derived from making the wicked suffer, well and good; but those benefits must not be sought for their own sake. The purpose of punishment is to inflict deserved suffering, and the purpose of the criminal law is to provide an acceptable basis within the social framework for doing so.

The retributive position does not command much assent in intellectual circles, but there seems little reason to suppose that it does not continue to retain a strong hold on the popular mind. The language of punishment is full of its traces. We talk about a criminal "paying his debt to society"; we express satisfaction or dissatisfaction when a criminal "gets what is coming to him" or "gets off lightly." The language of capital punishment is especially rich in examples. The condemned murderer is said to be "paying" for his crime, thereby providing one of the rare instances our law affords of a perfect proportion between crime and punishment. More expressively, if the doomed man dies or commits suicide before he can be executed, he is said to have "cheated the gallows."

Public prosecutors often see themselves as the voice of the community's demand for retribution. The closing argument to the jury in any important criminal trial is heavy with the rhetoric of revenge. And many judges—more openly, it is true, in England than here—conceive of their sentencing function as the expression of society's demand that the criminal expiate his crime. The police use a different set of metaphors: they speak of the criminal sometimes as an animal, sometimes simply as "the enemy." He is seen as a "rat" or a "vermin"—whatever his position in the animal kingdom, he is something to be exterminated. As an enemy he becomes the target in the "war on crime," and the public pronouncements of law enforcement officials leave no doubt that it is a Holy War. The retributive view is summed up in the great Victorian jurist Sir James Stephen's powerful and compelling image: "the sentence of the law is to the moral sentiment of the public in relation to any offense what a seal is to hot wax." . . . In the same passage Stephen says that the criminal law stands in the same relation to the passion for revenge as marriage does to the sexual passion. Oddly enough, we are more euphemistic today, but the idea is not an unfamiliar one.

To the retributive view there has always been opposed one that we may characterize as utilitarian: it holds that the purpose of the criminal law is to prevent or reduce the incidence of behavior that is viewed as antisocial. This view rejects retribution as a basis for punishment on the ground that suffering is always an evil and that there is no justification for making people suffer unless some secular good can be shown to flow from doing so. The retributive view is essentially backward-looking; it regards the offense committed by the criminal as crucial, and adjusts the punishment to it. The utilitarian view is forward-looking; it assesses punishment in terms of its propensity to modify the future behavior of the criminal and (especially, in the classic view) of others who might be tempted to commit crimes. In its essence, it sees man as a rational, pleasure-seeking creature who can be prevented from engaging in antisocial behavior by the prospect that the pain it brings him will more than cancel out the pleasure. It relies, in a word, on deterrence.

I shall come back to the classic utilitarian view, because it remains, with all its defects, the most useful starting point for an integrated rationale of crime and punishment; but for the moment I want to consider a variant of it that has taken a firm hold in recent years and that seems in a fair way to supplanting the classic utilitarian position in the minds of those most disposed to hold that position. This view, which for convenience I shall call the behavioral, is in complete opposition to the retributive view, and provides the other horn of the seeming dilemma that threatens the existence of criminal law today. Its adherents are vocal and influential. They have or appear to have on their side the lessons of the new learning about human behavior. Their challenge is a simple one: either the criminal law must stand on the retributive position—in which event it will become in time a kind of fossilized remain of a departed era—or it must abandon any attempt to ascribe responsibility for criminal conduct. Crime, guilt, and punishment are meaningless concepts to one who holds this view. He sees the occurrence of the kind of disturbing event that we naïvely call a crime as simply an occasion for social intervention, not the reason for it. Moreover, that occurrence is only one of several possible such occasions, having no characteristic that uniquely compels society to treat it differently from other such occasions. The "commission" of a "crime" is simply one signal among many that a person needs to be dealt with. If this view is right, inquiry into the rational basis for ascribing behavior content to the criminal law is bound to fail. There can be no such basis. Much of this essay is given over to considering whether and to what extent the behavioral view is right.

The behavioral position is considerably more complex than the retributive position. Its four principal bases can, however, be generally stated here. First, free will is an illusion, because human conduct is determined by forces that lie beyond the power of the individual to modify. Second, moral responsibility, accordingly, is an illusion, because blame cannot be ascribed for behavior that is ineluctably conditioned. Third, human conduct, being causally determined, can and should be scientifically studied and controlled. Fourth, the function of the criminal law should be purely and simply to bring into play processes for modifying the personality, and hence the behavior, of people who commit antisocial acts, so that they will not commit them in the future; or, if all else fails, to restrain them from committing offenses by the use of external compulsion (e.g., confinement).

The behavioral view has gained substantial ascendancy in recent years, not so much from the number of its adherents as from their strategic placement for affecting the opinions of others and for modifying public policies. It is a view subscribed to by many if not most psychiatrists, by most practitioners of the behavioral sciences who think about problems of the criminal law, by the overwhelming majority of "professionalized" workers in the correctional field—probation officers, case workers, and the like—and by an increasing number of those popular writers who perform the extremely important function of translating the ideas of the intellectually advanced into current popular terms. Its catchwords—"treat the criminal, not the crime," "punishment is obsolete," "criminals are sick," and the like—are standard fare in large-circulation magazines, and show that the popular culture has absorbed, even if it has not yielded to, the behavioral approach to crime. . . .

The retributive position holds that punishment must be proportioned to the offense. The graver the offense (on some kind of scale of moral outrage), the more severe the punishment. Nonsense, say the proponents of the behavioral view. Punishment (or treatment, as they usually prefer to call it) should be suited to the needs of the offender and of the rest of the community rather than to the nature of his offense. That is the only way it can look forward to those needs rather than backward to the expiation of his crime. Legislatures can decide in advance on the range of punishment that should be allowable for a given offense, e.g., a minimum of one year of imprisonment and a maximum of ten for, say, burglary. (Even that much in the way of *a priori* limitation would offend hard-core adherents to the behavioral view, who would want to see the correctional authorities left entirely free.) But legislatures have no way of determining how much punishment should be allowable for a given offender. If punishment (or treatment) is to be individualized, there should be large if not complete discretion in the sentencing authority to decide the kind and length of treatment for each offender. In the allocation of sentencing authority, then, the judge should simply turn the offender over to the correctional experts for a completely indeterminate sentence, as opposed to the conventional and traditional procedure by which the judge says to the defendant "Five years" (or whatever), or as opposed to any modification of this procedure whereby limits are placed on the discretion of correctional authorities. To proponents of the behavioral position, any sentence that invokes the nature of the offense rather than the situation of the offender is a throwback to retributive ideas or, at best, to classic utilitarian ideas of deterrence, which these proponents see simply as retribution thinly disguised. Another alleged dilemma, then, which we will have to examine in considerable detail at a later point, is this one: must one either support completely indeterminate sentences or be thought of as a retributionist?

In my view, there are two and only two ultimate purposes to be served by criminal punishment: the deserved infliction of suffering on evildoers and the prevention of crime. It is possible to distinguish a host of more specific purposes, but in the end all of them are simply intermediate modes of one or the other of the two ultimate purposes. These two purposes are almost universally thought of as being incompatible; and until recently, moral philosophers, who are the arbiters as well as the combatants in this struggle, have tended to assume that one or the other of these purposes must be justifiable to the exclusion of the other. My main point here is that, not simply as a description of existing reality but as a normative prescription for legal action, the institution of criminal punishment draws substance from both of these ultimate purposes; it would be socially damaging in the extreme to discard either. Before arguing this point, however, it may be desirable to elaborate somewhat the description of the two ultimate purposes of punishment.

Retribution

The retributive view rests on the idea that it is right for the wicked to be punished: because man is responsible for his actions, he ought to receive his just deserts. The view can take either of two main versions: the revenge theory or the expiation theory. Revenge as a justification for punishment is deeply ingrained in human experience, and goes back at least as far as the *lex talionis*: an eye for an eye, a tooth for a tooth, and, we might add, a life for a life. . . .

Utilitarian Prevention: Deterrence

The utilitarian or preventive position, by contrast, has considerable appeal although, as we shall see, it does not suffice as a justification for punishment. Its premise is that punishment, as an infliction of pain, is unjustifiable unless it can be shown that more good is likely to result from inflicting than from withholding it. The good that is thought to result from punishing criminals is the prevention or reduction of a greater evil, crime. There are many different, and often inconsistent, ways in which punishment may prevent the commision of crimes, but the inconsistencies should not be allowed to obscure the fact that the desired result is the same in every case.

The classic theory of prevention is what is usually described as deterrence: the inhibiting effect that punishment, either actual or threatened, will have on the actions of those who are otherwise disposed to commit crimes. Deterrence, in turn, involves a complex of notions. It is sometimes described as having two aspects: after-the-fact inhibition of the person being punished, special deterrence; and inhibition in advance by threat or example, general deterrence. These two are quite different although they are often confused in discussion of problems of punishment. For example, it is sometimes said that a high rate of repeat offenses, or recidivism as it is technically known, among persons who have already been once subjected to criminal punishment shows that deterrence does not work. The fact of recidivism may throw some doubt on the efficacy of *special* deterrence, but a moment's reflection will show that it says nothing about the effect of *general* deterrence.* An even more preposterous argument is sometimes heard to the effect that the very existence of crime or (more moderately but equally fallaciously) the increase in crime rates is evidence that deterrence does not work. Unless we know what the crime rate would be if we did not punish criminals, the conclusion is unfounded. It may well be that some forms of punishment, through their excessive severity, produce a net increase in the amount of crime, but that is a very different issue (although one often confusingly invoked by people skeptical of the deterrent efficacy of punishment). Since these same people are typically proponents of rehabilitation as a goal of punishment (also, be it noted, in the interest of prevention) and since punishment is not the less punishment for being rehabilitative in purpose, it is evident that the argument is beside the point. As so often in debates on this issue, the problem of how severe given forms of punishment should be is confused with the problem of whether punishment is itself justifiable. It cannot be too often emphasized that the severity of punishment is a question entirely separate from that of whether punishment in any form is justifiable. . . .

Special Deterrence or Intimidation

A second utilitarian justification for punishment is its asserted propensity to reduce or eliminate the commission of future crimes by the person being punished. Again, the concept rests primarily on a rational, hedonistic model of behavior. Once subjected to the pain of punishment, so the theory runs, the individual is conditioned to avoid in the future conduct that he knows is likely to result again in the infliction of pain through punishment.

No aspect of preventive theory has been subjected to such a barrage of criticism in recent years as has the idea of intimidation. The criticism centers on what is thought to be a conclusion emerging from empirical study of recidivism among offenders. Although there is much disagreement over specific figures and even more over their significance, it is universally recognized that persons who have served prison sentences have a high rate of

---

* In the interest of clarity, I shall reserve the term "deterrence" for general deterrence and shall use "intimidation" for special deterrence.

reconviction, perhaps as much as fifty per cent. Superficially, this well-documented fact does appear to raise substantial questions about the efficacy of intimidation. Yet, as we shall see, there are reasons not to reject out of hand its usefulness in crime prevention.

First, there is the obvious but frequently overlooked fact that we do not know how much higher the recidivism rate would be if there had been no criminal punishment in the first place. It is not unreasonable to suppose that the rate would probably be somewhat higher if persons who committed crimes were free to continue committing them without being punished. Second, the argument against intimidation often confuses the severity of punishment with the fact of punishment. By singling out those who have been subjected to the relatively severe sanction of imprisonment, the generalization ignores the effect of such punishment measures as probation and suspended sentences on persons who commit crimes. As we have previously pointed out, the very fact of criminal conviction is itself a form of punishment, particularly to the relatively law-abiding citizen. To be detected in the commission of crime and then subjected to the stigma of a criminal conviction may in itself have a strong impact on the future behavior of the offender. The studies we have on the subject seem to demonstrate that those subjected to the relatively less severe sanctions of probation or of early release from prison on parole have a lower rate of recidivism than do persons subjected to more severe punishment. A related point is that by and large those who are selected for severe punishment are less likely to conform with standards of law-abidingness. They are the more experienced, more hardened criminals who are for one reason or another not amenable to intimidation. . . .

Behavioral Prevention: Incapacitation

The simplest jurisdiction for any punishment that involves the use of physical restraint is that for its duration the person on whom it is being inflicted loses entirely or nearly so the capacity to commit further crimes. By contrast with the idea of general deterrence, about whose empirical basis there is continuing disagreement, the empirical basis for incapacitation is clear beyond argument. So long as we keep a man in prison he will have no opportunity at all to commit certain kinds of crimes —burglary, obtaining property by false pretenses, and tax fraud are three of the many types precluded in this way. And his opportunities to commit certain other kinds—such as assault or murder—are greatly diminished by confinement. Of course, such extreme forms of punishment as execution and solitary confinement for life can assure total and near total incapacitation. In a society that was single-mindedly devoted to the repression of crime as a paramount objective of social life, incapacitation would be the most immediately plausible utilitarian justification for the punishment of offenders. On further inspection, however, its plausibility diminishes.

We may start by noting that incapacitation differs radically from general deterrence as a mode of crime prevention and that, in consequence, it must be justified on different bases. Deterrence operates according to the nature of the offense. The personal characteristics of the numerous people who are every day punished for committing crimes cannot be known by the public, to whom the deterrent threat is addressed. The threat of punishment or the spectacle of its imposition creates general awareness that people who do certain kinds of things will be punished if they are caught, no matter what their personal characteristics are. Incapacitation has a much subtler and more attenuated relationship to the nature of the offense. To the extent that there is any connection at all, it rests on a prediction that a person who commits a certain kind of crime is likely to commit either more crimes of the same sort or other crimes of other sorts. This latter prediction does not seem to figure largely in the justification for incapacitation as a mode of prevention. To the extent that we lock up burglars because we fear that they will commit further offenses, our prediction is not that they will if left unchecked violate the antitrust laws, or cheat on their income taxes, or embezzle money from their employers; it is that they will commit further burglaries, or other crimes associated with burglary, such as homicide or bodily injury. The premise is that the person may have a tendency to commit further crimes like the one for which he is now being punished and that punishing him will restrain him from doing so.

Incapacitation, then, is a mode of punishment that uses the fact that a person has committed a crime of a particular sort as the basis for assessing his personality and then predicting that he will commit further crimes of that sort. It is an empirical question in every case whether the prediction is a valid one. To the extent that the prediction is valid, utilitarian ethics can approve the use of punishment for incapacitative purposes, on the view that the pain inflicted on persons who are punished is less than the pain that would be inflicted on their putative victims and on society at large if those same persons were left free to commit further offenses. . . .

Behavioral Prevention: Rehabilitation

The most immediately appealing justification for punishment is the claim that it may be used to prevent crime by so changing the personality of the offender that he will conform to the dictates of law; in a word, by reforming him. In that ideal many have seen the means for resolving the moral paradox of the utilitarian position: that punishment is an instrumental use of one man for the benefit of other men. Perhaps "resolving" is too strong a word. After all, the goal sought by the rehabilitative ideal is not reform for its own sake or even for the sake of enabling its object to live a better and a happier life. We hope that he will do so, but the justification is a social one: we want to reform him so that he will cease to offend. He is still being made use of. Whatever moral truth inheres in Kant's famous imperative—"One man ought never to be dealt with merely as a means of subservient to the purpose of another. . . . Against such treatment his inborn personality has a right to protect him"—is not made inapplicable by the benevolence of the reformer. Perhaps all we can say is that the ideal of reform mitigates the harshness of the paradox. We are helping society, true. But we are doing so by helping the offender.

It has become fashionable to reject the unpleasant word "punishment" when talking about rehabilitation. For reasons I have given in some detail, this emerging linguistic convention is a misleading one. However benevolent the purpose of reform, however better off we expect its object to be, there is no blinking the fact that what we do to the offender in the name of reform is being done to him by compulsion and for *our* sake, not for his. Rehabilitation may be the most humane goal of punishment, but it is a goal of *punishment* so long as its invocation depends upon finding that an offense has been committed, and so long as its object is to prevent the commission of offenses.

What are the significant characteristics of a system of punishment based on the goal of rehabilitation? Principally, such a system is—like incapacitation—offender-oriented rather than offense-oriented. If rehabilitation is the goal, the nature of the offense is relevant only for what it tells us about what is needed to rehabilitate the offender. To be sure, that relevance is greater than is commonly supposed. In the present state of our knowledge about the human personality and the springs of human action we cannot afford to ignore what a man has done as an index of the kind of man he is and, consequently, of what measures are required to make him better. Still, what he has done is only one measure, and a rough one at that, of what he is. The rehabilitative ideal teaches us that we must treat each offender as an individual whose special needs and problems must be known as fully as possible in order to enable us to deal effectively with him. Punishment, in this view, must be forward-looking. The gravity of the offense, however measured, may give us a clue to the intensity and duration of the measures needed to rehabilitate; but it is only a clue, not a prescription. There is, then, no generally postulated equivalence between the offense and the punishment, as there would be in the case of the retributive or even the deterrent theory of punishment.

It follows from this offender-oriented aspect of the rehabilitative ideal that the intensity and duration of punishment are to be measured by what is thought to be required in order to change the offender's personality. Unlike the related goal of incapacitation, the inquiry is not into how dangerous the offender is but rather into how amenable to treatment he is. If a writer of bad checks can be cured of his underlying disorder only by five years of intensive psychotherapy, then that is what he is to receive. And, of course, no one knows at the outset how much of what kind of therapy will be needed in his or anyone else's case, so it cannot be said in advance what the duration of his punishment will be. It ends whenever those in authority decide that he has been rehabilitated. Of course, if he does not yield to treatment and is thought to present a danger, he will not be released. The two goals always go hand in hand. No rehabilitationist has ever been heard to say that offenders whom we are incapable of reforming should be released when this incapacity becomes manifest. Indeed, some of them eagerly embrace the view that incorrigible offenders must be kept in custody for life, if necessary. They have not been concerned to inquire too closely into the criteria of necessity. In its pure form, the ideology seems to call for cure or continued restraint in every case. Incapacitation, then, is the other side of the rehabilitative coin. It may well seem a dark underside.

There are two major objections to making rehabilitation the primary justification for punishment. The first probably comes very close to settling the matter for present purposes. It is, very simply, that we do not know how to rehabilitate offenders, at least within the limit of the resources that are now or might reasonably be expected to be devoted to the task. The more we learn about the roots of crime, the clearer it is that they are non-specific, that the social and psychic spring lie deep within the human condition. To create on a large scale the essentials of a society that produced no crime would be to remake society itself. To say this is not to suggest that the goal of so improving society is not worthwhile, or that there is any superior social goal. It is merely to suggest that this is a task to be undertaken in the name of objectives and using techniques that far transcend the prevention of undesirable behavior. One trouble with the rehabilitative ideal is that it makes the criminal law the vehicle for tasks that are far beyond its competence. Surely the point does not require laboring that a general amelioration of the conditions of social living is not a task that can be very well advanced in the context of the institutions and processes that we devote to apprehending, trying, and dealing with persons who commit offenses.

Rehabilitation after the fact, which is all we can realistically propose, suffers simply from a lack of appropriate means. The measures that we can take are so dubiously connected with the goal that it is hard to justify their employment. We can use our prisons to educate the illiterate, to teach men a useful trade, and to accomplish similar benevolent purposes. The plain disheartening fact is that we have very little reason to suppose that there is a general connection between these measures and the prevention of future criminal behavior. What is involved primarily is a leap of faith, by which we suppose that people who have certain social advantages will be less likely to commit certain kinds of crimes. It is hard to make a good argument for restraining a man of his liberty on the assumption that this connection will be operative in his case. It is harder still if he already possesses the advantages that we assume will make people less likely to offend.

We know little about who is likely to commit crimes and less about what makes them apt to do so. So long as our ignorance in these matters persists, punishment in the name of rehabilitation is gratuitous cruelty. In truth, the threat of punishment for future offenses as extrapolated from the experience of suffering punishment for a present offense may be the strongest rehabilitative force that we now possess. To the extent that a man is rendered more prudent about committing offenses in the future by reason of unpleasantness suffered on account of offenses past, he may be said to be rehabilitated in as meaningful a sense of the term as we can generate from present-day experience. For the gross purposes of the criminal law, a man is better when he knows better. As already suggested, intimidation and rehabilitation have more affinities than present fashions in penal thought accord them.

JOHN P. CONRAD

The Irrational Equilibrium*

In the correctional world the standards set by policy makers and their day-to-day execution almost never coincide. Goals are described, but the roads to reach them are less

* From John P. Conrad, *Crime and Its Correction: An International Survey of Attitudes and Practices* 11–14; 55–57 (1967). Originally published by the University of California Press; reprinted by permission of The Regents of the University of California.

easily charted. With graceful magnanimity and high purpose, Rule Six of the British Prison Commission prescribes: "The purpose of training and treatment of convicted prisoners shall be to establish in them the will to lead a good and useful life on discharge, and to fit them to do so" (1949).

Only an apologist could maintain that the mailbag shops and the coil-mattress renovation sheds, which are staples of British prison programs, are means consistent with these purposes. In every country there are similar contrasts between stated aims and actual means. The *Manual of Correctional Standards* (1959) provides perhaps the most elaborate statement of aims and courageous prescription of means. But though these are standards to which most correctional administrations profess to adhere, examination of practice will uncover few institutions or agencies in which they are met. It would be wrong to draw invidious conclusions from this situation. The reasons for the cleavage between practice and prescription are not hard to find, and some of them will be studied in detail in this chapter. But the setting of standards spurs change, as the last two or three decades of correctional progress have shown. Throughout our correctional pilgrimage we encountered no administrators who did not sincerely express their whole-hearted adherence to the standards, written or unwritten, of the prevailing correctional consensus. Not all their subordinates were as sure of the rightness of the aims or means; indeed there were few administrators who touched on their problems without frankly admitting difficulties in persuading personnel of the social truth and value of the new correctional philosophy.

A look at this philosophy and the uneasy balance of forces which it strikes accounts for the difficulties of its execution. The philosophy, as nearly as we can distill it from observations in eighteen countries, condenses into five postulates, taken literally by policy makers wherever we went.

Postulate 1: Offenders are social deviates; something is wrong with them.

Comment: We cannot generalize as to what is "wrong." In some cultures, notably in the United States, the notion is easily accepted that the offender is sick. By furthest contrast, in the Soviet Union, the offender learns that he cannot possibly be sick, but rather he is lacking in the moral education he needs for honest participation in a Socialist community. In the United States, the offender is likely to be an unfortunate person needing "treatment." In the Soviet Union he is, an unfortunate person needing opportunities to learn. Either way, something is wrong with the offender.

Postulate 2: Punishment exacted by the system is futile. Commitment to the system is punishment enough.

Comment: Whenever correctional practice has emerged from the age of legitimated sadism, this axiom has been accepted as self-evident. Whether the commitment is to prison or to probation, the punishment takes place in the court room where new conditions of existence are assigned. The aphorism of Sanford Bates, that offenders are sent to prison *as* punishment, not *for* punishment, is basic doctrine. However, formidable elements of the general public are not in agreement; the enlightened principles of the new philosophy are still in jeopardy from the forces of darkness.

We were impressed, in this connection, with the aversion of correctional practitioners against the administration of any of the more obviously inhumane practices. In England, where corporal punishment is perhaps a more lively issue than in any other Western country, its reintroduction is massively blocked by the unwillingness of any public agency, especially the Prison Commission, to administer it. It is as though the correctional administrator, having shed the role of turnkey, finds his new role too attractive to return to old ways.

Postulate 3: During the period of commitment the correctional agency has an obligation to administer a regime which will equip offenders to "lead a good and useful life on discharge."

Comment: The regime consists of anything from analytic psychotherapy to supervised athletics; it is purposefully related to an idea about change in attitudes or behavior. The obligation to treat implies an obligation to adopt a rationale for change. Though the rationales varied widely in sophistication, all administrators had one or more ready to hand. Few were tested in any way; there was general regret that neither method nor resources were available to evaluate and refine methods of treatment. Only in the Soviet Union, where a completed theoretical system is being applied, is the correctness of the treatment rationale considered certain. Data for conventional methods of analysis are not, however, made available to the foreign observer.

Postulate 4: Because the treatment required by the offender varies from individual to individual in accordance with what is "wrong" with each, the duration and circumstances of the commitment must also vary.

Comment: This principle is universally accepted, but opinions differ on how to apply it. Correctional thought is far from agreement as to who should prescribe treatment and when it should be prescribed. Concern for equity in sentencing and the state of public opinion heavily influences the nature of the treatment, whatever may have been prescribed.

Postulate 5: All correctional agencies have the obligation to maintain control over committed offenders.

Comment: Although obvious for correctional institutions, which must prevent escape, the obligation is not so clear-cut with the field agencies. But even if, as in England, the field agencies have been divested of all direct control requirements, many indirect obligations survive and are likely to continue to survive for a long time. The real nature of the relationship between probation officer and probationer cannot be evaded; whatever else goes on between them, control is the basic issue. Similarly, in the welfare schools of the four Scandinavian countries, though punishment is abjured and help is imaginatively proffered, control remains the essence of the relationship between the child and the school. The means of control may be more subtle than walls and surveillance—and in all observed institutions the direction of program was toward a parental quality of control—but, where necessary, walls, surveillance, and even physical isolation were made part of the control.

The obligation of the correctional apparatus to provide control of its clients is reflected in every phase of its operations. The probation officer may be an examplar of casework skill, but he still has his reports to the court to make. The chances are—in the United States at least—that he has a pair of handcuffs in his briefcase. The dilemma between control and change is at the bottom of the correctional muddle. It is often taken to be insoluble, and on that account many professionals are diverted from practice in the field.

This series of postulates constitutes a correctional philosophy from which all sorts of applications flow. These postulates constitute a revolutionary change in the human race's notion of the obligations of the majority toward those who stray beyond the limits of its tolerance. Within much less than a century the administration of justice has shifted from its crude philosophy of individual and collective deterrence of criminals and crime. Throughout the world, those who administer the correctional apparatus assume control and change to be their proper task. We must credit this revolution to the educators and physicians who have seen crime as a problem to be solved rather than as a *casus belli* against those who prey upon their fellows. If the clergyman and the reformer put a floor under the depths of misery which the law could inflict, it remained for the social sciences to open doors through which the offender could emerge from the structure of misery altogether.

But, having congratulated civilization on the increasing disuses of barbarism as a means of combating barbarism, we must appraise the application of these changes. Though these postulates may be taken for granted by correctional leadership, though judges may espouse them and push for their implementation, practice falls dismally short of the humanitarian standards promulgated in model statutes and manuals, and the spirit of the rules and regulations governing official agencies. We can therefore define the standard practice of corrections as the *application (through the medium of the correctional apparatus) of individualized methods of change, under standardized means of control.*

* * *

It must be repeated that the word "irrationality" in describing the correctional apparatus is not used here in a maligning sense. Thousands of sincere and professional workers, including ourselves, are committed to careers in the discouraging work of corrections. We do what we can with the means at hand, hoping for the best and always fearing the worst. It is an equilibrium we maintain, whether in a probation office, a county jail, a training school, or a prison. Apathy surrounds us from the outside and the inside. What little change for the better occurs is almost invariably generated from the inside.

We accommodate to an equilibrium which balances an endless series of personal dilemmas presented by the offenders with whom we deal. These dilemmas can be traced back to the great internal conflicts of standard correctional practice reflecting in turn the conflicted values of the social order around it. This is the place in which these conflicts can be summarized; we hope that support for their existence is sufficiently explicit in this chapter.

The Conflict of Control and Change

If the role of the prison staff is to control ultimately through force, how can the permissiveness and the individualization required for change be safely introduced? The resolution of standard practice is in favor of control—control through surveillance by the field agency, and control through the traditional limiting characteristics of the total institution in both juvenile and adult institutions.

The Conflict of Objectives and Capabilities

There is little disagreement on the official goals of correction, but the capabilities of the apparatus to reach them are restricted by ignorance. We do not know what we must know in order to perform the tasks which we have to do. Research is unevenly but with increased momentum pushing back the frontier. The practice of control is rooted in tradition and unexamined doctrine. It is only incidentally related to propositions developed from scientific method. Traditional methods of control cannot be supplanted until validated theory supports a change. Similarly, the methods of planned change and therapy are only moderately reliable in the field of conventional psychiatry. For the clients of the correctional apparatus we cannot yet point to a procedure which can be reliably applied to any group in any typology yet conceptualized.

The Conflict of Standard and Actual Practice

We discussed the assumptions of standard practice as found in manuals and other official statements; and we examined the framework of the three elements of the correctional apparatus in some relatively advanced communities. The gap between assumptions and the means provided is so wide that the question arises whether assumptions are meant to be acted upon. They are assumptions which have been the sources of correctional goals for generations. The Declaration of Principles of the American Prison Association in 1870 only brought together postulates about humanity and human nature which had inspired reformers and enlightened penologists for many previous generations. As principles to affirm they are comforting to the social order in general and specially to those of us who must work within the field. As guides to action they are impeded by the same obstacles which block the practical application of any great ethical system. Money is lacking, and the lack is eloquently bewailed. Even more evident is the lack of goodwill and the irrationality which is born of ill-will. Concern and care for the thieving, violent, and mendacious men and women who are our clients is difficult to engender and even more difficult to sustain. It is much easier, much less bruising to construct and justify systems which will do justice and protect the public than to provide for change and to create systems and communities which facilitate change.

The Conflict of Tradition and Reason

Resistance to organizational change in any field of group activity is always in part rooted in traditional and custom. Tradition and custom are particularly influential in correctional services. Methods and procedures are sometimes the fruits of hard-won resolutions of long forgotten crises; sometimes they are meaningless rites installed on a caprice. Whatever the reason, they are known and understood—they may not be very effective, but they fit into a system which holds together. Some methods and procedures have to do with the protection of staff, inmates, and the community at large from obvious hazards. It is no light matter to remove the baton from the prison officer or the gun tower from the wall. Equally and even more effective controls may be thought of but confidence in reason will be superseded by the weight of tradition until reason is overwhelmingly reinforced by experimental evidence. Under the circumstances, such evidence is rarely acquired in reinforcing volume.

With these conflicts pervading its structure, the correctional apparatus is in uneasy and irrational equilibrium. Where it is under the pressure of numbers, as in the Anglo-Saxon countries and as in Sweden, changes occur because they are required by circumstance. In the administrative and official climate of the times, organizational change tends to be guided by recourse to analysis and the rule of reason. The consequence has been a considerable amount of conceptualization, experimentation, and re-formulation of principles. The next chapter will examine these consequences as the basis for a rational organization of correctional services.

The present equilibrium *processes* its hapless clientele. A ponderous mechanism receives the offender, collects relevant and irrelevant information, tabulates data, maintains activity, and releases him. Some offenders are the better for the experience, some have at least suffered no harm, and some are incomparably the worse. To contain this motley segment of humanity is achievement enough for some; not to increase criminality is the goal of others. To achieve the favorable modification of the behavior of as many offenders as possible is the rational goal which emerges before us and which encompasses the lesser objectives.

FRANCIS A. ALLEN

Criminal Justice, Legal Values, and the Rehabilitative Ideal*

Although one is sometimes inclined to despair of any constructive changes in the administration of criminal justice, a glance at the history of the past half-century reveals a succession of the most significant developments. Thus, the last fifty years have seen the widespread acceptance of three legal inventions of great importance: the juvenile court, systems of probation and of parole. During the same period, under the inspiration of continental research and writing, scientific criminology became an established field of instruction and inquiry in American universities and in other research agencies. At the same time, psychiatry made its remarkable contributions to the theory of human behavior and, more specifically, of that form of human behavior described as criminal. These developments have been accompanied by nothing less than a revolution in public conceptions of the nature of crime and the criminal, and in public attitudes toward the proper treatment of the convicted offender.

This history with its complex developments of thought, institutional behavior, and public attitudes must be approached gingerly; for in dealing with it we are in peril of committing the sin of oversimplification. Nevertheless, despite the presence of contradictions and paradox, it seems possible to detect one common element in much of this thought and activity which goes far to characterize the history we are considering. This common element or theme I shall describe, for want of a better phrase, as the rise of rehabilitative ideal.

The rehabilitative ideal is itself a complex of ideas which, perhaps, defies completely precise statement. The essential points, however, can be articulated. It is assumed, first, that human behavior is the product of antecedent causes. These causes can be identified as part of the physical universe, and it is the obligation of the scientist to discover and to describe them with all possible exactitude. Knowledge of the antecedents of human behavior makes possible an approach to the scientific control of human behavior. Finally, and of primary significance for the purposes at hand, it is assumed that measures employed to treat the convicted offender should serve a therapeutic function, that such measures should be designed to effect changes in the behavior of the convicted person in the interests of his own happiness, health, and satisfactions and in the interest of social defense.

Although these ideas are capable of rather simple statement, they have provided the arena for some of the modern world's most acrimonious controversy. And the disagreements among those who adhere in general to these propositions have been hardly less intense than those prompted by the dissenters. This is true, in part, because these ideas possess a delusive simplicity. No idea is more pervaded with ambiguity than the notion of reform or rehabilitation. Assuming, for example, that we have the techniques to accomplish our ends of rehabilitation, are we striving to produce in the convicted offender something called "adjustment" to his social environment or is our objective something different from or more than this? By what scale of values do we determine the ends of therapy?

These are intriguing questions, well worth extended consideration. But it is not my purpose to pursue them in this paper. Rather, I am concerned with describing some of the dilemmas and conflicts of values that have resulted from efforts to impose the rehabilitative ideal on the system of criminal justice. I know of no area in which a more effective demonstration can be made of the necessity for greater mutual understanding between the law and the behavioral disciplines.

There is, of course, nothing new in the notion of reform or rehabilitation of the offender as one objective of the penal process. This idea is given important emphasis, for example, in the thought of the medieval churchmen. The church's position, as described by Sir Francis Palgrave, was that punishment was not to be "thundered in vengeance for the

---

* 50 *Journal of Criminal Law, Criminology and Police Science*, No. 3, 226–30 (1959). Reprinted, with footnotes omitted, with permission.

satisfaction of the state, but imposed for the good of the offender: in order to afford the means of amendment and to lead the transgressor to repentance, and to mercy." Even Jeremy Bentham, whose views modern criminology has often scorned and more often ignored, is found saying: "It is a great merit in a punishment to contribute to the *reformation of the offender*, not only through fear of being punished again, but by a change in his character and habits." But this is far from saying that the modern expression of the rehabilitative ideal is not to be sharply distinguished from earlier expressions. The most important differences, I believe, are two. First, the modern statement of the rehabilitative ideal is accompanied by, and largely stems from, the development of scientific disciplines concerned with human behavior, a development not remotely approximated in earlier periods when notions of reform of the offender were advanced. Second, and of equal importance for the purposes at hand, in no other period has the rehabilitative ideal so completely dominated theoretical and scholarly inquiry, to such an extent that in some quarters it is almost assumed that matters of treatment and reform of the offender are the only questions worthy of serious attention in the whole field of criminal justice and corrections.

The Narrowing of Scientific Interests

This narrowing of interests prompted by the rise of the rehabilitative ideal during the past half-century should put us on our guard. No social institutions as complex as those involved in the administration of criminal justice serve a single function or purpose. Social institutions are multi-valued and multi-purposed. Values and purposes are likely on occasion to prove inconsistent and to produce internal conflict and tension. A theoretical orientation that evinces concern for only one or a limited number of purposes served by the institution must inevitably prove partial and unsatisfactory. In certain situations it may prove positively dangerous. This stress on the unfortunate consequences of the rise of the rehabilitative ideal need not involve failure to recognize the substantial benefits that have also accompanied its emergence. Its emphasis on the fundamental problems of human behavior, its numerous contributions to the decency of the criminal-law processes are of vital importance. But the limitations and dangers of modern trends of thought need clearly to be identified in the interest, among others, of the rehabilitative ideal, itself.

My first proposition is that the rise of the rehabilitative ideal has dictated what questions are to be investigated, with the result that many matters of equal or even greater importance have been ignored or cursorily examined. This tendency can be abundantly illustrated. Thus, the concentration of interest on the nature and needs of the criminal has resulted in a remarkable absence of interest in the nature of crime. This is, indeed, surprising, for on reflection it must be apparent that the question of what is a crime is logically the prior issue: how crime is defined determines in large measure who the criminal is who becomes eligible for treatment and therapy. . . .

Another example of the narrowing of interests that has accompanied the rise of the rehabilitative ideal is the lack of concern with the idea of deterrence—indeed the hostility evinced by many modern criminologists toward it. This, again, is a most surprising development. It must surely be apparent that the criminal law has a general preventive function to perform in the interests of public order and of security of life, limb, and possessions. Indeed, there is reason to assert that the influence of criminal sanctions on the millions who never engage in serious criminality is of greater social importance than their impact on the hundreds of thousands who do. Certainly, the assumption of those who make our laws is that the denouncing of conduct as criminal and providing the means for the enforcement of the legislative prohibitions will generally have a tendency to prevent or minimize such behavior. Just what the precise mechanisms of deterrence are is not well understood. Perhaps it results, on occasion, from the naked threat of punishment. Perhaps, more frequently, it derives from a more subtle process wherein the mores and moral sense of the community are recruited to advance the attainment of the criminal law's objectives. The point is that we know very little about these vital matters, and the resources of the behavioral sciences have rarely been employed to contribute knowledge and insight in their investigation. Not only have the criminologists displayed little interest in these matters, some have suggested that the whole idea of general prevention is invalid or worse. Thus, speaking of the deterrent theory of punishment, the authors of a leading textbook in criminology assert: "This is simply a derived rationalization of revenge. Though social revenge is the actual psychological basis of punishment today, the apologists for the punitive regime are likely to bring forward in their defense the more sophisticated, but equally futile, contention that punishment deers from [sic] crime." We are thus confronted by a situation in which the dominance of the rehabilitative ideal not only diverts attention from many serious issues, but leads to a denial that these issues even exist.

Debasement of the Rehabilitative Ideal

Now permit me to turn to another sort of difficulty that has accompanied the rise of the rehabilitative ideal in the areas of corrections and criminal justice. It is a familiar observation that an idea once propagated and introduced into the active affairs of life undergoes change. The real significance of an idea as it evolves in actual practice may be quite different from that intended by those who conceived it and gave it initial support. An idea tends to lead a life of its own; and modern history is full of unintended consequences of seminal ideas. The application of the rehabilitative ideal to the institutions of criminal justice presents a striking example of such a development. My second proposition, then, is that the rehabilitative ideal has been debased in practice and that the consequences resulting from this debasement are serious and, at times, dangerous.

This proposition may be supported, first, by the observation that, under the dominance of the rehabilitative ideal, the language of therapy is frequently employed, wittingly or unwittingly, to disguise the true state of affairs that prevails in our custodial institutions and at other points in the correctional process. Certain measures, like the sexual psychopath laws, have been advanced and supported as therapeutic in nature when, in fact, such a characterization seems highly dubious. Too often the vocabulary of therapy has been exploited to serve a public-relations function. Recently, I visited an institution devoted to the diagnosis and treatment of disturbed children. The institution had been established with high hopes and, for once, with the enthusiastic support of the state legislature. Nevertheless, fifty minutes of an hour's lecture, delivered by a supervising psychiatrist before we toured the building, were devoted to custodial problems. This fixation on problems of custody was reflected in the institutional arrangements which included, under a properly euphemistic label, a cell for solitary confinement. Even more disturbing was the tendency of the staff to justify these custodial measures in therapeutic terms. Perhaps on occasion the requirements of institutional security and treatment coincide. But the inducements to self-deception in such situations are strong and all too apparent. In short, the language of therapy has frequently provided a formidable obstacle to a realistic analysis of the conditions that confront us. And realism in considering these problems is the one quality that we require above all others.

There is a second sort of unintended consequence that has resulted from the application of the rehabilitative ideal to the practical administration of criminal justice. Surprisingly enough, the rehabilitative ideal has often led to increased severity of penal measures. This tendency may be seen in the operation of the juvenile court. Although frequently condemned by the popular press as a device of leniency, the juvenile court, is authorized to intervene punitively in many situations in which the conduct, were it committed by an adult, would be wholly ignored by the law or would subject the adult to the mildest of sanctions. The tendency of proposals for wholly indeterminate sentences, a clearly identifiable fruit of the rehabilitative ideal, is unmistakably in the direction of lengthened periods of imprisonment. A large variety of statutes authorizing what is called "civil" commitment of persons, but which except for the reduced protections afforded the parties proceeded against, are essentially criminal in nature, provide for absolutely indeterminate preiods of confinement. Experience has demonstrated that, in practice, there is a strong tendency for the rehabilitative ideal to serve purposes that are essentially incapacitative rather than therapeutic in character.

The Rehabilitative Ideal and Individual Liberty

The reference to the tendency of the rehabilitative ideal to encourage increasingly long periods of incarceration brings me to my final proposition. It is that the rise of the rehabilitative ideal has often been accompanied by attitudes and measures that conflict, sometimes seriously, with the values of individual liberty and volition. . . . We are concerned here with the perennial issue of political authority: Under what circumstances is the state justified in bringing its force to bear on the individual human being? These issues, of course, are not confined to the criminal law, but it is in the area of penal regulation that they are most dramatically manifested. The criminal law, then, is located somewhere near the center of the political problem, as the history of the twentieth century abundantly reveals. It is no accident, after all, that the cies of criminal justice and law enforcement are those first seized by an emerging totalitarian regime. In short, a study of criminal justice is most fundamentally a study in the exercise of political power. No such study can properly avoid the problem of the abuse of power.

The obligation of containing power within the limits suggested by a community's political values has been considerably complicated by the rise of the rehabilitative ideal. For the problem today is one of regulating the exercise of power by men of good will, whose motivations are to help not to injure, and whose ambitions are quite different from those of the political adventurer so familiar to history. There is a tendency for such persons to claim immunity from the usual forms of restraint and to insist that professionalism and a devotion to science provide sufficient protections against unwarranted invasion of individual right. This attitude is subjected to mordant criticism by Aldous Huxley in his recent book, "Brave New World Revisited." Mr. Huxley observes: "There seems to be a touching belief among certain Ph.D's in sociology that Ph.D's in sociology will never be corrupted by power. Like Sir Galahad's, their strength is the strength of ten because their heart is pure—and their heart is pure because they are scientists and have taken six thousand hours of social studies." I suspect that Mr. Huxley would be willing to extend his point to include professional groups other than the sociologists. There is one proposition which, if generally understood, would contribute more to clear thinking on these matters than any other. It is not a new insight. Seventy years ago the Italian criminologist, Garafalo, asserted: "The mere deprivation of liberty, however benign the administration of the place of confinement, is undeniably punishment." This proposition may be rephrased as follows: Measures which subject individuals to the substantial and involuntary deprivation of their liberty are essentially punitive in character, and this reality is not altered by the facts that the motivations that prompt incarceration are to provide therapy or otherwise contribute to the person's well-being or reform. As such, these measures must be closely scrutinized to insure that power is being applied consistently with those values of the community that justify interferences with liberty for only the most clear and compelling reasons.

But the point I am making requires more specific and concrete application to be entirely meaningful. It should be pointed out, first, that the values of individual liberty may be imperiled by claims to knowledge and therapeutic technique that we, in fact, do not possess and by failure candidly to concede what we do not know. At times, practitioners of the behavioral sciences have been guilty of these faults. At other times, such errors have supplied the assumptions on which legislators, lawyers and lay people generally have proceeded. Ignorance, in itself, is not disgraceful so long as it is unavoidable. But when we rush to measures affecting human liberty and human dignity on the assumption that we know what we do not know or can do what we cannot do, then the problem of ignorance takes on a more sinister hue.

THE HONORABLE MARVIN E. FRANKEL

Indeterminate Sentencing, Punishment, and the Rehabilitative Ideal*

1. The case for the indeterminate sentence rests upon what a perceptive scholar has called, and skeptically appraised as, the "rehabilitative ideal." The offender is "sick," runs the humanitarian thought, and/or dangerous. He needs to be treated and cured. Nobody, certainly not the sentencing judge, can know when he will be well or safe. Hence, those charged with treating and observing him must be left to decide the time for release.

The theory is flawed in the vagueness and overbreadth of its first premise, the idea of "sickness" calling for medical or quasi-medical "treatment." Many convicted people are not

*From Marvin E. Frankel, "Lawlessness in Sentencing," 41 *Cin. L. Rev.* 31–34 (1971). Reprinted with permission.

n need of any known form of therapy or rehabilitation. We sentence large numbers of people who probably fall within the class tagged in a lively, psychoanalytically oriented book as "normal criminals" (in contrast with those driven to crime by neurotic or psychotic drives)—that is, people who have coldly and deliberately appraised the risks and rewards, taken their stand against received morality, but then had the misfortune to be caught. Whatever else such defendants may need or deserve, they are not promising candidates for any sort of useful "treatment" available in either our prisons or our hospitals.

Many defendants, especially among those passing through the federal courts, are clearly outside the reach of the indeterminate sentence theory; they are, that is, neither in need of nor amenable to any known form of rehabilitation. One thinks, for example, of the doctor who evaded taxes, the corrupt public official, the antitrust violator. The sentences of at least many such defendants may be thought to serve the ends of deterrence, of "denunciation," or, if we face what many judges are openly doing, of retribution. Again, however, only a somewhat thoughtless lack of discrimination would subject them to the horror of indeterminacy—to wait while a parole board, with no pertinent criteria for judgment, decides that release should be ordered.

Yet notable advocates of indeterminacy and parole board discretion make no distinctions. The Model Penal Code makes *all* sentences indeterminate, leaving to the parole board in all cases a broad range of discretion to determine the eventual length of the sentence. . . . The National Council on Crime and Delinquency, in its Model Sentencing Act, [does] the same. A number of the States have similar provisions. None of these several codes says what the parole board is supposed to do —what standards it is to follow, what kinds of judgments it is to make—in deciding when to release those who are neither sick nor dangerous.

2. The essentially medical model is employed crudely and simple-mindedly by the proponents of indeterminate sentences—ignoring how little is known about rehabilitation and misconceiving the medical analogy in the process. . . .

Because we commonly do not know for sure what we mean by treatment, it is a corollary that we cannot know how long it will take. It follows for the indeterminate sentencers, on beneficent grounds, that the prisoner must live with the torture of "one year to life" or some similar atrocity. . . .

The naive faith in the presumed expertise of penologists and parole officials effectively blots out some of the stark and familiar realities of prisons as they actually function. The notion that the unrehabilitated prisoner should be denied parole because he needs more treatment is not merely unsupported; it runs counter to considerable evidence and opinion concerning the effects of confinement. Taking prisons as they are, and as they are likely to be for some time, it is powerfully arguable that their net achievement is to make their inhabitants worse, not better. It may be bracing doctrine to insist that the prisons must be improved to make rehabilitation a reality. Passing now the question whether we know how to do this, the ideal is worthy beyond question. And I hope nothing said here suggests any cavil about that. My central point, however, entails a firm view about the proper order of things: we have no right to keep people confined ostensibly to rehabilitate them when we lack the means of rehabilitation. Until or unless we have some reasonable hope of effective treatment, it is a cruel fraud to have parole boards solemnly order men back to their cages because cures that do not exist are found not to have been achieved.

The Fallacy of the Individualized Treatment Model*

The underlying rationale of this treatment model is deceptively simple. It rejects inherited concepts of criminal punishment as the payment of a debt owed to society, a debt proportioned to magnitude of the offender's wrong. Instead it would save the offender through constructive measures of reformation, protect society by keeping the offender locked up until that reformation is accomplished, and reduce the crime rate not only by using cure-or-deten-

* Reprinted with the permission of Hill and Wang, a division of Farrar, Straus & Giroux, Inc. from *Struggle for Justice, A Report on Crime and Punishment in America* (pp. 34–47), prepared for the American Friends Service Committee. Copyright © 1971 by Hill and Wang, Inc.

tion to eliminate recidivism, but hopefully also by the identification of potential criminals in advance so that they can be rendered harmless by preventive treatment. Thus the dispassionate behavioral expert displaces judge and theologian. The particular criminal act becomes irrelevant except insofar as it has diagnostic significance in classifying and treating the actor's particular criminal typology. Carried to an extreme, the sentence for all crimes would be the same: an indeterminate commitment to imprisonment, probation, or parole, whichever was dictated at any particular time by the treatment program. Any sentence would be the time required to bring about rehabilitation, a period which might be a few weeks or a lifetime.

The treatment model's judicious blend of humanitarian, practical welfare, and scientific ancestry was nicely illustrated sixty years ago by the Elmira Reformatory's Zebulon R. Brockway:

> The common notion of a moral responsibility based on freedom should no longer be made a foundation principle for criminal laws, court procedure, and prison treatment. The claim of such responsibility need neither be denied nor affirmed, but put aside as being out of place in a system of treatment of offenders for the purpose of public protection. Together with abrogation of this responsibility goes, too, any awesome regard for individual liberty of choice and action by imprisoned criminals. Their habitual conduct and indeed their related character must needs be directed and really determined by their legalized custodians...
>
> The perfected reformatory will be the receptacle and refinery of antisocial humans who are held in custody under discretional indeterminateness for the purpose of the public protection. Legal and sentimental inhibitions of necessary coercion for the obdurate, intractable element of the institution population will be removed and freedom given for the wide use of unimpassioned useful, forceful measures. Frequent relapses to crime of prisoners discharged from these reformatories will be visited upon the management as are penalties for official malfeasance. The change will be, in short, a change from the reign of sentiment swerved by the feelings to a passionless scientific procedure pursuing welfare.

As with any model, of course, its implementation has been uneven, often halting, and seldom complete. Perhaps the closest approximation to the ideal is in certain so-called sexual psychopath statutes under which an indeterminate and potentially lifelong incarceration can be ordered as a civil commitment without conviction of any crime. Judicial power is yielded grudgingly, however, and legislators cling to the notion that maximum penalties should be graded according to their ideas of relative blameworthiness, so that the result is a patchwork quilt of inconsistent rationales. Overall, however, the movement toward the individualized treatment model is unmistakable. Every state has some form of parole, which provides a core indeterminacy. Compared to the median time served, the maximum possible sentence for most crimes is so excessive that the disposition of almost any conviction utilizes the treatment process in some manner.

While opposition to "mollycoddling" prisoners still exists, the basic thrust of the model has been accepted by almost all liberals, reformers of all persuasions, the scientific community, probably a majority of judges, and those of law-and-order persuasion who perceive the model's repressive potential.

How has the model united such a motley collection of supporters? Its conceptual simplicity and scientific aura appeal to the pragmatism of a society confident that American know-how can reduce any social problem to manageable proportions. Its professed repudiation of retribution adds moral uplift and an inspirational aura. At the same time, the treatment model is sufficiently vague in concept and flexible in practice to accommodate both the traditional and utilitarian objectives of criminal law administration. It claims to protect society by incapacitating the prisoner in an institution until pronounced sufficiently reformed. This prospect is unpalatable enough and sufficiently threatening in its uncertainty to provide at least as effective a deterrent to potential offenders as that of the traditional eye-for-an-eye model. Maximum flexibility is required to achieve the model's goal, that of treatment individualized to each offender's unique needs, so the system's administrators are granted broad discretionary powers. Whatever the effect on offenders, these powers have secured the support of a growing body of administrators, prosecutors, and judges, for it facilitates the discharge of their managerial duties and frees them from irksome legal controls. Even the proponents of retribution, although denied entry through the front door, soon discovered that harsh sentences could be accommodated within the treatment model as long as they were rationalized in terms of public protection or the necessity for prolonged regimes of reeducation.

The treatment model tends to be all things to all people. This partially accounts for the paradox that while the model's ideological command has become ever more secure, its implementation has tended to form rather than substance. In fact, the model has never commanded more than lip service from most of its more powerful adherents. The authority given those who manage the system, a power more absolute than that found in any other sphere of law, has concealed the practices carried on in the name of the treatment model. At every level—from prosecutor to parole-board member—the concept of individualization has been used to justify secret procedures, unreviewable decision making, and an unwillingness to formulate anything other than the most general rules or policy. Whatever else may be credited to a century of individualized-treatment reform effort, there has been a steady expansion of the scope of the criminal justice system and a consolidation of the state's absolute power over the lives of those caught in the net.

The irony of this outcome emphasizes the importance of a searching examination of the assumptions underlying the individualized treatment model. Hopefully such an analysis will illuminate efforts to delineate the proper role of criminal justice in a free and democratic society. It may also help us to understand what factors have perpetuated our present criminal justice system decade after decade in the face of compelling evidence of its systematic malfunctioning.

Unexamined Assumptions

When one probes beneath the surface of the treatment model, one finds not only untenable factual assumptions, but also disturbing value judgments that pose serious policy questions for our society. Here are some of the more perplexing of these problems with which we will be concerned:

1. A model of criminal justice that rests on the proposition that at least in large measure crime is a problem of individual pathology; that is, the model assumes that crime rates can be reduced by the treatment and cure of individual criminals and that future crimes can be prevented by the incapacitation of those predicted to be dangerous until they are cured. The difficulty of identifying the characteristics of such a pathology, if indeed it exists at all, will be noted below. To the extent that it is also acknowledged that social and environmental factors, such as slums, poverty, unemployment, and parental guidance or the lack of it, also "cause" crime, a program of individualized treatment is inadequate. If social factors cannot be controlled or predicted, the relevance of individualized treatment is decreased and may be negligible. If the social pathology assumed to encourage a criminal culture is not being changed, is there ethical justification for individualized preventive detention? A prisoner detained to prevent crimes that could be avoided by social reforms may bear a greater resemblance to a scapegoat than to either a patient or a public enemy. We do not and probably cannot know the relative contributions of individual and social pathology to criminality; to the extent that social causation is relevant, the rationale for individualization is undercut. To date, our society has largely ignored this dilemma.

2. At the level of individual pathology, treatment ideology assumes that we know something about the individual causes of crime. If it is to have any scientific basis, such knowledge must be based on the study of representative samples both of criminals and of control groups of noncriminals. Comparison of the two may reveal factors that distinguish the criminals from the control groups; whether such differences have any causal significances poses additional research problems which, in this context, we have no occasion to face. We have libraries full of criminological research on the etiology of crime, but most of it has been conducted without control groups and therefore tells us nothing about causation (and usually not much else, either). In all this research, moreover, the data about criminals are derived from those who have been subject to correctional regimes and therefore identified and made available for study. But only a small proportion of those who commit criminal acts are caught, convicted, and subjected to correctional treatment. The criminals who are the subjects of all our research are almost certainly not representative. Our available sample is heavily biased toward criminals from the poor and outcaste classes and away from the white middle and upper classes. Bias is also introduced by selective enforcement of criminal law. Welfare fraud or manslaughter in a ghetto barroom brawl is likely to land the perpetrator on the rolls of diagnosed criminals; business fraud or manslaughter by automobile on the freeway goes largely unprosecuted and unstudied. Therefore, even if we had a body of adequately controlled research findings it

would merely describe the kinds of persons subjected to criminal treatment in a society where race and poverty are major determinants for the application of the criminal label. Such data might afford revealing insights about the administration of criminal justice in such a society, but would hardly provide the basis for a usable science of individual criminal pathology. We think it is important to ask why treatment ideology was embraced with such enthusiasm without bothering to inquire about the validity of the science on which it depends.

3. Even if the existence, significance, and characteristics of an individual criminal pathology are unknown, one might in theory still evolve treatment methods that turned criminals into noncriminals. It has been a frequent occurrence in medicine to stumble upon treatments that worked despite ignorance about the cause of the disease or the reasons for the treatment's success. The minimum methodological standards for investigating this possibility as to any particular treatment are (a) comparison with control groups of similar subjects who are not treated; (b) control of other variables, such as maturation or changed environmental or social conditions, to negate the possibility that factors other than the treatment process were responsible for the outcome; and (c) reasonably reliable criteria for determining success or failure. Most research fails the first and second tests. Control groups are conspicuous by their rarity in treatment evaluation investigations. But the apparently insoluble problem of such research is the third requirement: the necessity of establishing indicators to distinguish success from failure. This is true even if one proceeds at the most superficial level, defining failure as recidivism, the commission of another crime following treatment. We have no way of determining the real rate of recidivism because most criminals are undetected and most suspected criminals do not end up being convicted. Recidivism rates are also subject to both deliberate manipulation and unconscious bias. Parole revocation (failure) rates can be manipulated for public relations or other purposes. Documented examples of such research falsification are known and the practice is probably not uncommon. Unconscious bias is introduced by the tendency of predictive and diagnostic judgments to become self-fulfilling prophecies. For example, those released on parole from a treatment program are likely to be formally or informally classified for the purpose of parole supervision into good risks (responded favorably to treatment) and poor risks (resisted treatment). The "poor risks" are likely to be subjected to tighter surveillance; their violations are therefore much more likely to be detected; their parole is more likely to be revoked; and the resulting differences in recidivism rates emerge as a "research finding" validating the efficacy of the particular treatment program.

4. In the absence of credible scientific data on the causation or treatment of crime, the content of the correctional treatment program rests largely on speculation or on assumptions unrelated to criminality. Thus one finds that accepted correctional practice is dominated by indoctrination in white Anglo-Saxon middle-class values. In institutions this means learning a trade, establishing work habits through the therapy of labor, keeping clean and clean-shaven, minding your own business, and acquiring such basic or supplemental educational skills and religious training as the institution might provide and the parole board might think relevant. On probation or parole, in addition to abstaining from crime, the ingredients for success are similar: sticking at a job, staying where you belong, supporting your family, avoiding bad companionship and bad habits, and abiding by the spoken ideals of conventional sexual morality. Without debating the merits of these ingredients of the good life—those of us not being corrected are free to take them or leave them—the fact that the correlation between such Puritan virtues and crime causation is speculative or nonexistent would, one might suppose, have raised some troubling questions. If the treatment has no proven (or likely) relationship to criminal pathology, what is its purpose? In the absence of such evidence, what is the propriety of coerced cultural indoctrination?

The closest parallel we can think of in American history, which developed at the same time as the correctional treatment model in response to the same kinds of reform pressures, was the policy of compulsory assimilation of American Indians, which the Indian Bureau attempted to carry out from 1849 through the end of the century. The deliberate discrediting of Indian cultural values, compulsory proselytizing, and the destruction of the tribal economic base were supplemented by government boarding schools, which Indian children were forced to attend throughout their formative years. The program and style of these schools bore striking resemblance to the correctional treatment model. There are other similarities as well. The correctional system also draws most of its clients from subcultures; perhaps half are from racial minorities (including some

Indians on their second round of "treatment") and more than half from cultures of poverty or near-poverty. We do not suggest that the parallel is complete or that it follows that the motivation and purpose of the correctional system's treatment program is necessarily the same as the policy of the nineteenth-century Indian Bureau. But we are disturbed both by the similarities and by the absence of any probing dialogue that might explore the whole purpose and philosophy of correctional treatment.

5. Using rates of recidivism as the criterion for evaluating the success or failure of criminal justice programs poses more fundamental problems than the unreliability of the statistics. Surely it is ironic that although treatment ideology purports to look beyond the criminal's crime to the whole personality, and bases its claims to sweeping discretionary power on this rationale, it measures its success against the single factor of an absence of reconviction for a criminal act. Whether or not the subject of the treatment process has acquired greater self-understanding, a sense of purpose and power in his own destiny, or a new awareness of his relatedness to man and the universe is not subject to statistical study and so is omitted from the evaluation.

It will make a critical difference for the future of democracy whether our institutional and noninstitutional environments encourage the creation of morally autonomous, self-disciplined people who exercise independent judgment and purposefulness from their own inner strength, or whether instead they tend to stunt the human potential by training programs that, as with animals, condition their subjects to an unthinking conformity to inflexible, externally imposed rules. In studying the criminal justice system we have found few things to be thankful for, but the ineffectiveness of correctional treatment may well be one of those few. The only kind of morality the sticks-and-carrots regime of indeterminate treatment in correctional institutions can teach is the externally imposed variety. If such correctional methods really did work, it might be more success than a free society could endure.

6. Remaking people is an educational function. What, then, of prison education? We typically find an inadequate staff in a depressing environment with minimal facilities and equipment (no field studies here) operating an adult educational program across class, race, cultural, and status barriers for inmates whose chief motivation is to chalk up attendance marks so as to satisfy The Man on the Parole Board. From this soil we expect to reap the miracle—the maturation of a unique human being. At least that is what one would conclude from the uncritical acceptance of prison education as a "good thing" and a hallmark of society's humanity to prisoners.

7. The discretionary power granted to prosecutors, judges, and administrators in an individualized treatment system is unique in the legal system, awesome in scope and by its nature uncontrollable. If the theory posits that any one of many variables can be determinative of any individual decision, standards are necessarily nonexistent or so vague as to be meaningless, and review by any sort of court or appellate process is impossible. Yet it is evidently accepted without question that absolute power does not corrupt when exercised by government agents upon criminals. The chronicles of criminology and jurisprudence are filled with paeans celebrating the wise discretion of humble and contrite judges and administrative agencies. Their authors, however, would not for one moment surrender to the discretion of those same judges and agencies the assessment of their income and property taxes in accordance with the official's individualized determination of the subject's value to his country and his ability to pay. Indeed, the best antidote to being swept off one's feet by the claims made for the necessity and importance of the discretion that permeates criminal justice administration is to engage in a comparative examination of criminal law and the laws governing taxation, corporations, and commercial transactions. One will speedily discover that when it comes to matters concerning their vested interests, the men who have the power to write the law in this country give short shrift to discretion. They are not about to delegate the determination of the size of the oil depletion allowance to the discretion of the local internal revenue agent. If discretion is written into major law, it is because legislators are confident from the outset that they will be able to control its exercise.

Criminal justice is the surviving bastion of absolute legal discretion. The last of its colleagues, of which it is reputed to be the heir, was the Office for the Administration of Colonial Affairs.

8. In coming finally to the end of this preliminary enumeration of problem areas, we reach the area that is the most perplexing and the culmination of what has gone before. We have sketched a number of problematic features of a correctional treatment model of criminal justice. Most of the problems and defects that have been posed are not very difficult

to understand; one might even categorize a number of them as obvious. How is one to account, then, for the enthusiastic and uncritical acceptance by most of the liberal and progressive elements in our society of reformative, indeterminate, individualized treatment as the ideal goal of a criminal justice system?

There is something about this phenomenon akin to religious conversion, an acceptance of what appears to be true and valuable, what we want to be true, even though it cannot be reduced to anything more precise than vague generalities. It seems obvious that extremely complex forces lie behind liberal treatment ideology's mission to control not just the crimes but the way of life of others. Guilt about the gulf that separates our material well-being from poverty and oppression may account for some of the prejudice against and irrational fear of the poor and the oppressed; or it may help to account for our eagerness to hand over the problem to specialists as a way of relieving our anxiety. Once you have delegated a problem to an expert, you are off the hook.

If we could make some sense out of this extraordinary willingness to believe unreasonable things about criminal justice and corrections, we might begin to have some understanding of the forces that perpetuate so unjust a system. We explore this problem further below; it is hardly necessary to state here, however, that we cannot provide a satisfactory solution to this major puzzle. We do, however, hope to promote its analysis and encourage its study. Such an inquiry seems to us to be prerequisite to effectuating basic changes in our concepts and practices of criminal justice. The most stubborn obstacles to such change are not, in our opinion, the growing problem of violent crime or the hard-line advocates of punitive law-and-order repression or the rigidity and increasingly conservative polarization of our law enforcement and correctional bureaucracies or the perversity of adverse public opinion. Serious as they are, such forces can be contained if adequate options are developed and promoted. We suspect that much of the current strength of these conservative forces derives from the fact that there is no tenable alternative model of a criminal justice system that affords accommodation of such competing values as equality, respect for individual dignity and autonomy, encouragement of cultural diversity, and the need for a reasonably orderly society. The corectional treatment model does not begin to meet this need.

NOTES

The Effectiveness of Penal Treatment

Note 1.

LESLIE T. WILKINS

*The Meaning of Treatment**

In many countries, the term "treatment" as it relates to offenders is taken as being closely analogous with the term "treatment" as applied to disorders of the physical or mental make-up of an individual. The prevalence of this analogy does not justify it. It is, in fact, most unsatisfactory on several counts. In medical treatment, it is possible to state when the person is no longer suffering from the condition and, hence, when treatment is no longer required. But the question is when does a criminal cease to be a criminal. The finding of guilt by a court is the especial characteristic that defines a person as a criminal. There is, however, no similar procedure whereby that person is defined as no longer a criminal, except in very rare cases of royal pardons and retrials. Medical treatment is applied not so much to a person as to a condition of the person. In the majority of cases of criminal behaviour, there is no identified condition that is independent of the person. Corrections is a means of dealing with the whole person, rather than with an identified element or extraneous factor associated with the disorder or dysfunctioning of that person's system....

It can ... be recorded that the net outcome of many hundreds of researches into recidivism may be summarized as showing that the best that can be done with offenders is as little as is considered possible. The shorter the period spent in correctional institutions, the less the risk of reconviction; the smaller the degree of surveillance, the better the chances for rehabilitation. It must be mentioned, however, that all these studies have been made within the limitations of the existing legal codes of the countries concerned, and the range of variation has therefore been very restricted. Persons placed on probation show no greater likelihood of recidivism than similar persons otherwise disposed of, even in countries where there is no legislated limitation upon who may be placed

* From Leslie T. Wilkins, "Variety, Conformity, Control and Research: Some Dilemmas of Social Defense," *International Review of Criminal Policy*, No. 28, United Nations, New York, 1970, pp. 19, 22. Reprinted with permission.

on probation. It is also clear that the more humanitarian the disposition of the court, the less, in general, the cost to the taxpayer is; and the recidivism rate again reveals no significant change from that of the more severe penalties. The security provisions of all correctional institutions are most costly and are by no means as necessary as is usually believed. It is also agreed, as a result of many studies, that only a small proportion of offenders present a security risk; but little is known of means for identification of this small percentage.

Note 2.

R. HOOD

*Research on the Effectiveness of Punishments and Treatments**

Let us first consider the main conclusions:

(1) There are indications that fines are more successful than probation or institutional treatment with both first offenders and those with previous conviction in all age groups...

(2) Most studies show that lengthy institutional sentences are no more successful than shorter alternatives...

(3) Open institutions, particularly for the "better type of offender," appear at least as effective as closed treatments...

(4) That overall results are not much different as between different treatments...

(5) Even if overall success rates for different treatments are much the same they have a different effect on different types of offenders...

Note 3.

WALTER C. BAILEY

*Correctional Outcome: An Evaluation of 100 Reports***

This article presents selected results of a content analysis of 100 reports of empirical evaluations of correctional treatment. The reports, which are listed at the end of the article, were systematically selected primarily from those correctional outcome studies published between 1940 and 1960. Within these broad limits, actual selection of reports was guided by three principles: (1) the report must have been based upon empirical data; (2) the treatment evaluated must have been dependent upon the manipulation of some form of interpersonal relations as the independent variable, and (3) the behavior to be corrected must have had a negative value in the sense of being actually or potentially subject to legal sanctions.

Five preliminary questions are explored: (1) What is the relative frequency of various types of correctional outcome reports in terms of research design? (2) What is the relative frequency of various forms of *group* treatment approaches as compared with *individual* forms such as *individual counseling, psychotherapy*, etc.? (3) What is the relative frequency of occurrence of study reports dealing with outcomes of treatment carried out in correctionally administered settings (forced treatment or "treatment at the point of a gun") as compared with treatment carried out in noncorrectional settings such as private practice, outpatient clinics, etc. (voluntary treatment)? (4) What kinds of persons, in terms of training and background, conduct correctional outcome research projects? and (5) What kinds of theories of causation of criminal behavior are implicit or explicit in the treatment programs evaluated? Finally, the main question is considered, namely, how effective is correctional treatment?...

Effectiveness of Treatment

How corrective is correctional treatment? Of the total sample of correctional outcome reports evaluated, 10% described effects of the treatment as resulting in either "harm" or "no change" in behavior. Thirty-eight percent of the studies reported "some improvement." Thirty-seven percent reported a statistically significant difference in the direction of improvement for the group treated. Five percent of the reported results weer classified as "not relevant" to the outcome problem posed by the study.

Thus, roughly one-half of the outcome reports evaluated concluded considerable improvement in the treatment group. Almost one-fourth of the reports concluded either harmful results or "no change." These results, based upon the reported findings themselves, raise some serious questions regarding the efficacy of correctional treatment.

---

* Council of Europe, European Committee on Crime Problems, I *Collected Studies in Criminological Research* 73, 79–83 (1967).

** Reprinted, with footnotes omitted, by special permission of the *Journal of Criminal Law, Criminology and Police Science*. Copyright © 1966 by Northwestern University School of Law, Vol. 57, No. 2, pp. 153; 155–57.

Reports Describing Experimental Designs

Five of the 22 correctional outcome reports classified as experimental indicated either harmful results or "no change" in the treatment group. This amounts to roughly 23% of the sample of experimental studies. Four (17%) reported "some improvement"; four reported "marked improvement." Nine of these studies (43%) reported a "positive" statistically significant change in indices of the dependent variable applied to the treatment group.

Again, positive and negative findings are about equal. Roughly 60% ("marked improvement" plus statistically significant) may be classified as reporting successful outcomes. However, only 43% provided statistical evidence that the changes which occurred in the experimental group were not due to chance. On the other hand, roughly one-fourth of the experimental reports concluded that the treatment group either became worse, or, there was no statistically significant change in the index of the dependent variable employed.

Reports Describing Systematic-Empirical Designs

Only 3 of the 26 systematic-empirical studies reported harmful results or "no change" (12%). Ten reported "some improvement" (38%). Eleven reported "marked improvement" (42%). Only one reported a statistically significant positive change in the treatment group (4%). Finally, one study finding was considered "not relevant."

Reports Describing Non-Systematic Empirical Designs

At the level of the least rigorously designed correctional outcome studies only 2 of the 52 studies evaluated reported harmful results or "no change" (4%). Twenty-four (46%) reported "some improvement" in the treatment group. Twenty-two (42%) reported "marked improvement." No studies in this category used tests of statistical significance. Finally, 4 (8%) cited findings considered to be irrelevant to the question posed.

Summary

A sample of 100 correctional outcome reports was subjected to a content analysis in an effort to obtain provisional answers to a number of questions relevant to an evaluation of the status of correctional treatment. Results of the analysis indicated that a slight majority of the correctional treatment programs evaluated in the reports was carried out in "forced treatment" settings (prison, parole or probation situations) as compared with correctional treatment programs carried out in "voluntary treatment" settings (private practice, private agencies, etc.). It was also found that psychologists and sociologists seem to have something of a monopoly on conducting this type of evaluative study. In addition, despite the fact that well over one-half of the reports were concerned with some form of group treatment, only a few described treatment procedures conceptually based upon the group relations premise. The most popular approach to explaining criminal or delinquent behavior and conceputualizing treatment goals and procedures involves some form of the sick premise regardless of whether the treatment deals with groups or individuals.

Over one-half of these reports described research designs of questionable rigor (classified as nonsystematic empirical). Roughly one-fourth of the reports dealt with more rigorous designs (systematic empirical). The remaining one-fourth of the reports described experimental designs. However, variations in research design seemed to have exerted little influence on frequency of reported successful treatment outcome. As the rigor of design increases, the frequency of reported treatment success increases (nonsystematic empirical—42%, systematic-empirical—46%, experimental—60%). Although the differences are not marked, the trend is in the unexpected direction. This is clarified somewhat when we note that as the rigor of design increases, the frequency of irrelevant conclusions markedly decreases; and that as the rigor of the design decreases, there is a marked decrease in the frequency of reported "harm" or "no change" in the treatment group (experimental—23%, systematic-empirical—12%, nonsystematic-empirical—4%). In this sample of reports apparently wishful thinking, when not subject to appropriate design controls, tends to be expressed in a resistance to negative results and indulgence in obscure generalities.

Since positive results were indicated in roughly one-half of the total sample of 100 reports analyzed, the problem of interpretation is not unrelated to that of determining "whether the cup is half empty or half full." But, when one recalls that these results, in terms of success or failure of the treatment used, are based upon the conclusions of the authors of the reports, themselves, then the implications of these findings regarding the effectiveness of correctional treatment become rather discouraging. A critical evaluation of the actual design and the specific research procedures described in each instance would substantially decrease the relative frequency of successful outcomes based upon reliably valid evidence. Therefore, it seems quite clear that, on the basis of this sample of outcome reports with all of its limitations, evidence supporting the efficacy of correctional treatment is slight, inconsistent, and of questionable reliability.

This negative conclusion regarding correctional treatment is in general agreement with those drawn from several reviews of the correctional outcome literature. For example, in 1952 Dalton reported his fairly pessimistic impression of the value of counseling techniques in probation work. In 1954, Kirby reviewed the literature on the effects of treating criminals and delinquents and concluded that "most treatment programs are based on hope and perhaps informed speculation rather than on verified information." Two years later, Witmer and Tufts reviewed the literature on the effectiveness of delinquency prevention programs and concluded that such programs had not been notably effective.

On the positive side there is impressive evidence of an increasing concern with correctional outcome research and progressive improvement in the calibre of the scientific investigations conducted. This is shown in the increasing numbers of experimental and systematic-empirical investigations, the greater involvement of professionally trained researchers and the resulting increase in sophistication and rigor of research designs, and in the growing efforts to more explicitly relate treatment practice to behavioral science theory.

But how can we account for the apparent fact that although the operational means and resources of correctional outcome research have substantially improved, there has been no apparent progress in the actual demonstration of the validity of various types of correctional treatment? There probably could be no one answer to this question which, at least for a period, must remain unanswered. However, one or more of the following "explanations" may be suggestive: (1) there is the possibility that reformative treatment is "really" ineffectual either in its own right or as a consequence of the ambivalence of the "crime and punishment" setting in which it takes place; (2) one may hazard that much of the correctional treatment currently practiced is not corrective and that little of the rehabilitation work being done should be dignified by the term *treatment*; (3) it may be that some types of correctional treatment are "really" effective with some types of individuals under certain conditions, but so far we have been unable to operationally describe the independent variable (treatment), reliably identify in terms of treatment response the type of behavioral patterns being treated, adequately control the conditions under which such treatment takes place, or reliably delineate and measure relevant indices of the dependent variable; (4) perhaps much of the reformative treatment currently practiced is based upon the "wrong" theories of delinquent and criminal behavior.

Note 4.

RALPH SCHWITZGEBEL

Development and Legal Regulation of Coercive Behavior Modification Techniques with Offenders 1–5 (1971).

Within the past few years there has been a rapid growth in the experimental study and application of behavior modification techniques derived from the principles of learning and technology. These techniques, which have been used primarily in clinical and experimental setting thus far, create the potential for major changes in the area of corrections. It may be helpful to compare briefly these techniques with other techniques that have been used historically to modify the behavior of offenders. . . . Failures have been noted for group counseling in prison, group counseling outside of prison, and individual counseling. In some studies, the group receiving the treatment has shown even more maladaptive behavior, psychoneurotic symptoms, or recidivism than the control group not receiving the treatment.

The general picture is not promising. In a review of 100 outcome reports on correctional programs, Baily reported that those studies based upon rigorous research designs usually showed statistically nonsignificant improvement, no change, or a worsening in regard to the outcome criteria used by the study. It is these often disappointing results that have led, at least in part, to an increased emphasis on treatment procedures derived from certain principles of learning theory. These procedures are usually developed in psychology laboratories on a small scale and then applied to institutionalized or outpatient populations.

A. General Characteristics of Behavior Modification Programs

A major characteristic of behavior modification programs is their emphasis upon overt behaviors and the systematic manipulation of the environment to change these behaviors. Some of the techniques that can be included within the category of behavior modification are operant and classical conditioning, aversive suppression, and electronic monitoring and intervention. These techniques are only a few of many behavior modification techniques that may also include imitation, progressive relaxation, and sensitivity training.

... Behavior modification, as a separate area of study, began to emerge clearly in the early 1950's. Its direction as a new discipline is still not clear. The emphasis upon the treatment of overt behaviors and the measurement of observable events in the patient's environment gives the discipline a great heuristic value over some of the more traditional, psychoanalytically oriented treatment procedures. Its theoretical bases are, however, still in the process of being formulated.

Although behavior modification procedures are often oriented toward operant or classical conditioning theories, they are not necessarily so oriented and there is much diversity. Regardless of orientation, the basic underlying theory usually involves carefully specified changes in the environment of the person whose behavior is to be changed. A procedure for changing behavior that relies upon unique, nontransferable characteristics of a therapist or change agent lies outside of the domain of scientific behavior modification.

B. Specific Programs and Research

The following programs and related research are briefly described to give a general purview of behavior modification studies that have been completed or those that are now being conducted. The studies that have been selected are those that are generally related to present or potential treatment programs for offenders.

1. Operant Conditioning

In operant conditioning studies, a reinforcer (popularly called a "reward") is given to a subject after he produces the required behavior once or several times. In terms of operant conditioning, it is said that the reinforcer is made contingent upon the emission of the correct response. This response is known as an operant. If the response is not emitted by the individual, no reinforcer is given. In a sense, the person must voluntarily "operate" upon his environment to receive reinforcement. A reinforcer such as food, money, or time out from a task is known to be a reinforcer when it increases the rate, or changes the form of the behavior it follows. One of the most familiar examples of operant conditioning at the infrahuman level is the early work of B. F. Skinner in which he trained pigeons to peck at lights for many hours at a time to receive small pellets of food. . . .

One rapidly emerging area of research in operant conditioning should perhaps be mentioned before discussing classical conditioning programs. It is the operant conditioning of responses which have been traditionally associated with the autonomic nervous system. Some studies, though not all, have been able to operantly change human skin potential, heart rate, and salivation. Animal studies have an advantage over human studies in that the animals can be temporarily paralyzed by curare to remove artifacts caused by movement. Under these conditions, animals have been taught to increase or decrease heart rate, intestinal contractions, stomach contractions, urine formation, and electrical brain waves. Either direct electrical stimulation of the brain or escape from mild electrical shock has been used as a primary reinforcer. In some instances, clear and extreme physiological changes can be produced using this process. Some success has also been obtained in training epileptic patients to suppress abnormal paroxysmal spikes in their electroencephalograms. As Miller notes, "While it is far too early to promise any cures, it certainly will be worthwhile to investigate thoroughly the therapeutic possibilities of improved instrumental training techniques."

2. Classical Conditioning

Another type of conditioning frequently used to change behavior is classical conditioning as demonstrated by the work of Ivan Pavlov. If a stimulus such as food or an electric shock is presented to a person, it can generally elicit an involuntary response (or "reflex") such as salivation or muscle contraction. This eliciting stimulus is called the unconditioned stimulus. In a typical classical conditioning experiment, a neutral stimulus such as a bell is presented to the person and this stimulus is followed shortly (from a few tenths of a second to 3 or 4 seconds) by the presentation of the unconditioned stimulus and the response. Sometimes the neutral stimulus and the unconditioned stimulus overlap each other briefly. When these stimuli are repeatedly paired with each other in this manner, the neutral stimulus eventually becomes able to elicit the response even when the unconditioned stimulus is no longer present. The neutral stimulus is then labeled a conditioned stimulus and the response is known as a conditioned response.

In Pavlov's early experiments, dogs were presented with the sound of a metronome followed by meat powder until the presentation of the sound alone elicited salivation. Similar conditioning procedures have been used with humans to produce salivation as a conditioned response....

Classical conditioning procedures have been used primarily with two major categories of offenders—alcoholics and homosexuals. The central objective is to produce an unpleasant reaction in the patient to alcohol or to homosexual activity. In the case of alcoholism, the patient is given an emetic such as emetine hydrochloride (the unconditioned stimulus) and just before the onset of nausea he is required to look at, smell, or taste the alcohol (the conditioned stimulus). The results of this procedure appear to be as effective as the usual psychotherapeutic approaches.

... The procedures used in the treatment of alcoholism have also been used in substantially the same form in the treatment of sexual disorders, particularly homosexuality. The underlying assumption is that, except for very basic physiological responses, sexual behavior is learned. As Kinsey and his associates have noted, "The variations which exist in adult sexual behavior probably depend more upon conditioning than upon variations in the gross anatomy or physiology of the sexual mechanisms." Traditionally, behavior modification techniques have attempted to pair the stimulus that elicits the homosexual behavior, e.g., a picture of a nude male, with an aversive stimulus such as an electric shock or nausea....

Similar conditioning procedures employing aversive stimuli have also been used to treat transvestism, fetishism, and sadism....

3. Aversive Suppression

The aversive suppression of behavior corresponds in common usage with the concept of punishment. But the term "punishment" as it is ordinarily used has several conflicting meanings when examined from the viewpoint of learning theory. Most customarily, punishment refers to the presentation of an aversive stimulus after the person has emitted the behavior which is to be reduced in frequency or eliminated. Thus, the child is slapped on the hand (aversive stimulation) after he has reached into the cookie jar or even after he has started to eat the cookie....

The application of aversive stimuli following the prohibited behavior is surely not new. Whippings, mutilations, and duckings in cold water have had a long history of use.

Behavioral modification techniques closely pair the prohibited behavior, or precursors of it, with the subsequent aversive stimuli. Considerable experimentation of this nature has been conducted in the past few years with sexually deviant persons. In one well known early study of the treatment of transvestism, the patient received painful electric shocks on his feet from a grid on which he was standing while dressing in women's clothes. Over a period of 8 days, the patient received a total of 200 shocks during the frequent treatment sessions. A follow-up study 14 months later indicated only one subsequent relapse of cross-dressing by this patient.

The use of aversive stimuli in the suppression of homosexual behavior or other deviant sexual behavior has been reported in over 26 studies. These studies, generally using electric shock or an emetic to induce vomiting, often do not clearly distinguish between classical conditioning procedures and aversive suppression procedures. The studies tend to show an effectiveness in changing behavior which is at least equal to or better than the traditional, psychoanalytic treatment of these disorders. Greater attention, however, needs to be given to the design of these treatment methods to incorporate learning theory paradigms to assess more accurately their therapeutic potential.

Note 5. Community Treatment

a. SPECIAL COMMUNITY PROGRAMS*

In recent years a number of experimental community programs have been set up in various parts of the country, differing substantially in content and structure but all offering greater supervision and guidance than the traditional probation and parole programs. The new pro-

---

* President's Commission on Law Enforcement and Administration of Justice, *Task Force Report: Corrections* 38–44 (1967).

grams take many forms, ranging from the more familiar foster homes and group homes to halfway houses, "guided group interaction" programs, and intensive community treatment. As such, they offer a set of alternatives between regular probation supervision and incarceration, providing more guidance than probation services commonly offer without the various disruptive effects of total confinement. They also greatly enrich the alternatives available in parole supervision. The advent of these programs in the postwar decades and their recent growth in numbers and prominence are perhaps the most promising developments in corrections today.

These programs are by and large less costly, often far less costly, than incarceration in an institution. Evaluation has indicated that they are usually at least as effective in reducing recidivism and in some cases significantly more so. They therefore represent an important means for coping with the mounting volume of offenders that will be pouring into corrections in the next decade. Although populations forecasts indicate that the number of adult criminals who will be incarcerated in the next 10 years will increase only slightly, the projections for juveniles on the basis of present trends are alarming. It is estimated that by 1975 the number of juveniles who would be confined would increase by 70 percent; whereas in 1965, there were about 44,000 juveniles in State and Federal correctional institutions, by 1975 this number would reach about 74,000. Such an increase would place a burden on the correctional system that increased community programming could go far to alleviate.

Among the special community programs at least five types are important enough to warrant special discussion: guided group interaction programs; foster homes and group homes; prerelease guidance centers; intensive treatment programs; and reception center parole. These programs are reviewed here as examples of approaches that are capable of, and deserve, widespread application in a variety of modifications.

Guided Group Interaction Programs

Underlying one of the newer programs for treating the young delinquent in the community is the premise that juvenile delinquency is commonly a group experience and that therefore efforts to change delinquent behavior should focus primarily on a group like that within which the individual operates. A number of group counseling methods have been employed but the method called guided group interaction has been used most extensively in those programs which involved a research component.

The general strategy of guided group interaction calls for involving the offenders in frequent, prolonged, and intensive discussions of the behavior of individuals in the group and the motivations underlying it. Concentrating on participants' current experiences and problems, the approach attempts to develop a group "culture" that encourages those involved to assume responsibility for helping and controlling each other. The theory is that the offender-participants will be more responsive to the influence of their fellow offenders, their peers, than to the admonitions of staff, and less likely to succeed in hood-winking and manipulating each other.

As the culture develops and the group begins to act responsibly, the group leader, a staff member, seeks to encourage a broader sharing of power between the offenders and the staff. At first, group decisions will be limited to routine matters, such as the schedule of the day, but over time they may extend to disciplinary measures against a group member or even to decisions concerning readiness for release from the program.

Highfields

The Highfields project in New Jersey was the pioneer effort in guided group interaction. Initiated in 1950, it has been duplicated in communities and also in institutions and used with both juveniles and adults. Highfields limits its population to 20 boys aged 16 and 17, who are assigned directly to it from the juvenile court. Boys with former commitments to correctional schools are not accepted, nor are deeply disturbed or mentally retarded youths. The goal is to effect rehabilitation within 3 to 4 months, about half the average period of incarceration in the State training school.

The youths are housed in the old Lindbergh mansion. They work during the day at a mental institution immediately adjacent to their residence. In the evening they participate in the group counseling sessions. On Saturdays, they clean up the residence. Saturday afternoon is free, and Sunday is reserved for receiving visitors and going to religious services. Formal rules are few.

Early efforts to evaluate the effects of the project on recidivism, as compared with those of the State reformatory, are still the subject of academic dispute. However, it is clear that Highfields was at least as effective as the reformatory, perhaps more effective, and that it accomplished its results in a much shorter period of time at greatly reduced monthly costs.

Pinehills and Other Developments

Important variations on the Highfields project developed at Essexfields, also in New Jersey, and at Pinehills in Provo, Utah. As at Highfields, program content at Essexfields and Pinehills centered around gainful employment in the community, school, and daily group meetings. The most significant difference was that, in the Essexfields and Pinehills experiments, the offenders continued to live at home.

The regimen at both Essexfields and Pinehills was rigorous. At Pinehills, for example, all boys were employed by the city. They put in a full day's work on the city streets, on the golf course, in the cemetery, wherever they were needed. They were paid 50 cents an hour. During the late afternoon, after the day's work was finished, all boys returned to the program headquarters where they met in daily group sessions. About 7 p.m. they were free to return home. They were also free on Sundays.

In the daily group sessions all group members, not just adult staff, were responsible for defining problems and finding solutions to them. By making the program operations to some extent the work of all involved, both offenders and staff, it was possible to make a better estimate of just how much responsibility for his own life a given offender could take.

The fact that these guided group interaction programs are located in the community means that the problems with which the group struggles are those that confront them daily in contacts with their families, friends, teachers, and employers. This is one great strength of a community program over an institutional program. The artificiality of institutional life is avoided, and concentration can be placed upon the issues with which every offender eventually has to deal.

The Pinehills experiment was one of the first to set up an experimental design by which to assess the effectiveness of the project. Offenders assigned to the program were compared with two control groups: One group which was placed on probation, and another which was committed to a training school. The initial design was such that all three groups could be drawn randomly from a common population of persistent offenders living in the same county. Although there was some difficulty in exactly maintaining the research design, the data appear significant. The results, as measured in terms of recidivism, are shown in table 1.

Other variations of guided group interaction projects have been developed in the Parkland project in Louisville, Ky., in the GUIDE (Girls Unit for Intensive Daytime Education) program in Richmond, Calif., and in another girls' program in San Mateo, Calif. All three of these projects entail the daily gathering of the group in a center for participation in a combination of educational activities, craft projects, center development and beautification, and group and individual counseling. The Parkland project took its name from its location in two portable classrooms on the grounds of the Parkland Junior High School. In addition to morning classes in the school, the program entails afternoon work in and about the Louisville Zoo and terminates with group counseling sessions and dinner.

Contributions of Guided Group Programs

These projects, like Highfields, represent an authentic departure from traditional community programs for delinquents. The Highfields type of program is unique in that the group process itself shapes the culture and social system of the total program. The key element

TABLE 1.—EFFECTIVENESS OF THREE PROGRAMS FOR JUVENILE DELINQUENTS, UTAH, 1964, AS MEASURED BY PERCENTAGES OF RELEASEES NOT ARRESTED WITHIN 6 MONTHS OF RELEASE.

Program	Percentage of Releasees Not Arrested Within 6 Months	
	All Boys Assigned to Program	All boys Completing Program
Pinehills (experimental)	73	84
Probation (controls)	73	77
State school (controls)	42	42

Source: Adapted from LaMar T. Empey, "Alternatives to Incarceration," Office of Juvenile Delinquency and Youth Development Studies in Delinquency (Washington: U.S. Government Printing Office, 1967), pp. 38–39.

seems to be the amount of decision-making authority permitted the group, which has considerably more authority to decide than in traditional group therapy programs. J. Robert Weber, who made a study of promising programs for delinquents, said of the Highfields type of program:

> If one asks a youth in most conventional institutions, "How do you get out?" one invariably hears some version of, "Be good. Do what you are told. Behave yourself." If one asks a youth in a group treatment program, "How do you get out?" one hears, "I have to help myself with my problems," or "When my group thinks I have been helped." This implies a basic difference in the social system of the organization, including staff roles and functions.

In the large institution, Weber concluded, the youth perceives getting out in terms of the problem of meeting the institutional need for conformity. In the group treatment program the youth sees getting out in terms of his solution to his own problems, or how that is perceived by other youths in the group.

Foster Homes and Group Homes

Foster-home placement has long been one of the most commonly used alternatives to institutionalization for juvenile probationers. The National Survey of Corrections reported that 42 percent of the 233 probation departments surveyed utilized this resource. A sizable proportion of juvenile aftercare programs also make foster placements a routine part of their work.

The utilization of foster homes or group homes in lieu of institutional confinement has several obvious advantages, provided the offender does not require the controls of an institution. Such placements keep the offender in the community where he must eventually work out his future. They carry less stigma and less sense of criminal identity, and they are far less expensive than incarceration.

Weber reported in 1966:

> Discussions with State administrators would seem to indicate that foster care is in an eclipse. Reception center staffs report disillusionment with foster care for delinquents. Yet a look at actual placement practices of the State agencies and local courts indicates an unabated use of foster care.

The opinions encountered by Weber may be a reflection of the long and controversial history of foster-home placement for delinquents. The decision to sever family ties, even temporarily, is a hard one to make for the youth who might otherwise be placed on probation at home. And more difficult juveniles who might be sent to institutions are often beyond the capacity of the usual foster home to manage. It is obvious, however, that many delinquent youngsters come from badly deteriorated family situations and that such conditions are significant, perhaps critical, factors in generating delinquent behavior. When the delinquency-inducing impact of a slum neighborhood is added to a destructive family setting, placement of the delinquent away from home becomes increasingly necessary.

A number of States have begun to develop group homes as a variant to traditional foster-home care for youths who need a somewhat more institutional setting or cannot adjust to family life. The Youth Commission of Minnesota, for example, reported using seven group homes under arrangements with the home operator or with an intermediate agency. A nominal retaining fee was paid for each bed licensed; and, when a youth actually was placed in the home, the rate of pay was increased.

The Wisconsin Division of Corrections in 1966 was operating an even more ambitious program. Thirty-three homes for boys or girls were in use under a payment plan similar to that employed in Minnesota. With four to eight adolescents in each home, the total population handled was equivalent to that of at least one institution, but operating costs were one-third to one-fourth less.

In both States the adolescents placed in group homes were those who had been received on court commitment as candidates for institutional placement. In Wisconsin, approximately one-fourth of the group had been released from institutions for placement in a foster home. Other jurisdictions are experimenting with the group-home technique. Michigan, for example, reported a plan to use larger homes operated by State employees for parolees from their institutions.

There is some doubt about the wisdom of committing offenders to State agencies for placement in foster homes or group homes, when this function could as readily be performed by the courts through associated probation and welfare services. It is far less expensive for a local court to commit a youth to the State, even though that commitment entails some additional stigmatization, than to undertake the development and operation of local resources of the same kind. This problem derives from the fragmented administrative structure of American corrections, and could be overcome by a carefully planned program of subsidies from State to local governments. Such a plan was developed in California in 1965. Under its terms subsidies are given to those county probation departments which are successful in reducing commitments to State institutions by the development of improved community-based programs.

Halfway Programs: The Prerelease Guidance Center

In corrections as in related fields, the "halfway house" is an increasingly familiar program. Initially, such programs were conceived for offenders "halfway out" of institutions, as a means of easing the stresses involved in transition from rigid control to freedom in the community. The prerelease guidance centers of the Federal Bureau of Prisons are the best-known halfway-out programs in the United States. Recently the halfway house has come to be viewed as a potential alternative to institutionalization, and thus a program for those "half-way in" between probation and institutional control.

Federal Prerelease Guidance Centers

The first prerelease guidance centers of the Federal Bureau of Prisons were opened in 1961 in New York, Chicago, and Los Angeles, and others were established subsequently in Detroit, Washington, and Kansas City. Each center accommodates about 20 Federal prisoners who are transferred to it several months before their expected parole date. Thus they complete their terms in the community but under careful control.

Some of the centers are located in what were large, single-family houses; some occupy a small section or scattered rooms in a YMCA hotel; and one is located in a building once operated as a small home for needy boys. All are in neighborhoods with mixed land usage, racial integration, and nearby transportation.

Offenders transferred to these centers wear civilian clothes. They generally move from prison to the centers by public transportation without escort. For a day or two they are restricted to the building, although they may receive visitors there. In the YMCA's they eat in a public cafeteria in the building and use the public recreation areas, taking out YMCA memberships. Following a day or two of orientation and counseling, they go out to look for jobs. After they are on a job, they are gradually given more extensive leaves for recreational purposes and for visits with their families. As their parole date approaches, some may even be permitted to move out of the center, although they are still required to return to the center for conferences several times a week.

These centers are staffed in large part by persons rotated from regular institution staff who are highly oriented to counseling. One full-time employee is an employment counseling specialist. Several others, such as college students in the behavioral sciences, are employed on a part-time basis and provide the only staff coverage during the late night hours and part of the weekend. In addition to individual counseling, there are several group sessions a week. Federal probation officers, who will supervise the offenders when they go on parole, participate in the center's counseling activities. By the time a resident is ready to begin his parole, almost all of his individual counseling has been assumed by his parole supervision officer.

A major function of these temporary release programs has been to augment the information available to correctional staff. This information includes both diagnostic data on the individuals temporarily released and information on the assets and deficiencies of correctional programs and personnel. In addition, they provide optimum circumstances for counseling, since the counseling can deal with immediate realities as they are encountered, rather than with the abstract and hypothetical visions of the past and the future or the purely institutional problems to which counseling in institutions is largely restricted.

Inmate misbehavior while on work release or in prerelease guidance centers is not a rare thing, particularly for youthful offenders. Although a majority adjust quite satisfactorily, some get drunk, some get involved in fights and auto accidents when out with old or new friends, and some are late in returning to the center. An appreciable number of the youth have difficulty in holding jobs, some fail to go to work or to school when they are supposed to be there, a few abscond, and a few get involved in further crime. The important point is that they would be doing these things in any case, and probably more extensively, if they had been released more completely on their own through parole or discharge. Under the latter circumstances, however, correctional staff would know of the releasee's difficulties, if at all, not nearly so promptly as is possible with temporary release measures.

When an individual returns from a temporary release to home, work, or school, his experience can be discussed with him by staff, to try to assess his probable adjustment and to note incipient problems. Many difficulties can be anticipated in this way. The inmate's anxieties can be relieved by discussion, and discussion may also help him develop realistic plans for coping with prospective problems. When persistent or serious misbehavior occurs, sanctions are available to staff, ranging from restriction of further leaves or temporary incarceration to renewed institutionalization, with a recommendation to the parole board that the date of parole be deferred.

A number of offenders on work release, ... live in prerelease guidance centers. Some of them attend school part- or full-time, in addition to or instead of working; this sometimes is called "study release." It is particularly appropriate for juvenile and youthful offenders and is highly developed at several State establishments resembling the Federal prerelease guidance centers.

State Prerelease Centers

The Kentucky Department of Corrections, under a grant from the Office of Economic Opportunity, has a series of vocational training courses in its State reformatory which are identical with courses established at several centers in the State under the Department of Labor. Prerelease guidance centers were established near these centers in three cities, so that reformatory inmates could continue their institution courses in the community, where as trainees they receive a small stipend, in addition to highly developed job placement services.

The Federal Bureau of Prisons assisted in establishing these centers and sends Federal inmates from these cities to the centers. Conversely, State correctional agencies share in the operation of the Federal prerelease guidance centers in Detroit and Kansas City, assigning some State inmates there, and the District of Columbia Department of Corrections plays a major role in the operation of the center in Washington. This State-Federal collaboration could well serve as a model for many types of correctional undertaking.

Intensive Community Treatment

Perhaps the best known of the country's efforts at controlled experimentation in the correctional field is the California Youth Authority's Community Treatment Project, now in its sixth year. Operating within a rigorous evaluative design, it offers an excellent illustration of the profitable partnership which can develop when carefully devised program innovations are combined with sound research.

The subjects of the project consist of boys and girls committed to the Youth Authority from two adjacent counties, Sacramento and San Joaquin. While under study in a reception center, each new group is subjected to a screening process which excludes some 25 percent of the boys and 5 to 10 percent of the girls because of the serious nature of their offenses, the presence of mental abnormality, or strenuous community objections to their direct release. The remaining youngsters are then either assigned randomly to the community project—in which case they form part of the experimental group—or are channeled routinely into an institution and eventually paroled.

An interview by a member of the research staff provides the basis for classification of the offender subgroups. This categorization is made in terms of the maturity of the youth, as reflected in his relationships with others, in the manner in which he perceives the world, and in the way he goes about gaining satisfaction of his needs. A variety of standardized tests seeks to measure the extent of his identification with delinquent values as well as his general personality characteristics.

The program provided for the experimental group offers singly or in combination most of the techniques of treatment and control which are in use in corrections today: individual counseling, group counseling, group therapy, family therapy, involvement in various other group activities, and school tutoring services by a certificated teacher with long experience in working with delinquents. The goal is to develop a treatment plan which is tailored to the needs of each type of offender. The resulting plan is then implemented at a level of high intensity, made possible by the availability of carefully selected and experienced staff on a ratio of 1 staff member for each 12 youths.

A program center serves as the hub of activity; it houses the staff and provides a recreation area, classrooms, and a musicroom. A limited outdoor sports activities area also is available. In the late afternoon and some evenings, the center resembles a small settlement house operation as the wards come in after school for counseling, tutoring, and recreational activity.

An unusual and controversial feature of the experiment is the frequent use of short-term detention at the agency's reception center to assure compliance with program requirements and to "set limits" on the behavior of the participants. The detention may vary from a few hours to a few days.

Results have been measured in several ways. A repetition of the psychological test battery seeks to determine what movement has occurred in the socialization of the individual offender. The responses of the various categories of youth have revealed greater success with some than with others, and may eventually provide a more reliable indicator of who should be institutionalized. Finally, the "failure rate," as measured by the proportion who are later institutionalized because they have committed additional offenses, is carefully compared with similar information on members of the control group who have been institutionalized and then returned to the community under regular parole supervision.

The latest report of the project activity available to the Commission revealed that checks of parolees, at the end of 15 months of parole exposure, showed that 28 percent of the experimental group had been subject to revocation of parole, as compared to 52 percent of the control group which was afforded regular institution and parole handling.

After several years of pilot work, the California Youth Authority decided in 1964 to extend the community treatment format to the Watts area of Los Angeles and to a neighborhood in west Oakland. Both are high-delinquency areas; both are heavily Negro in population. Essentially duplications of the original experiment, the two new program units do not have a research component. Instead of random assignment of the subject, the youths committed from a given area are screened by project staff for direct release from the reception center.

In the absence of a control group, the success of the program has been measured by comparing the failure rate of the youth assigned to it with equivalent statewide rates for youths of the same middle to older adolescent age range. At the end of 15 months of parole exposure, 39 percent of project wards had been subject to parole revocation as compared to a statewide revocation rate of 48 percent for youths of the same age bracket.

The Los Angeles and Oakland adaptations of the original demonstration were initiated, in part, to alleviate acute population pressures in the institutions. With caseloads of 15 youths per officer, the $150 per month cost per boy is three to four times as much as that of regular parole. But it is less than half the average monthly cost of institutionalizing an offender. These experiments are now handling a group that is larger than the capacity of one of the new institutions that the Youth Authority is building. Thus they obviate the investment of $6 to $8 million.

Reception Center Parole and Short-Term Treatment Programs

Diagnostic parole is a program whereby all commitments from the juvenile court are referred to a reception center where they can be screened for eligibility for parole, either immediately or after a short period of treatment. This program has reached significant proportions in an increasing number of States.

While most State systems have long had some informal arrangements for returning a few cases to the community at an early date, more organized procedures developed almost simultaneously in New York, Washington, Kentucky, and California in the early 1960's. These programs were conceived in part as a response to acute population pressures in overcrowded institutions. The seemingly successful results have led to a substantial increase in the volume of cases diverted from the training school to short, intensive treatment programs followed by parole in the comunity.

In New York the screening is undertaken by special aftercare staff while the youngsters are in New York City's Youth House awaiting delivery to the State school system. The youths selected to return to the community are those who are thought to be amenable to conventional casework procedures. Those selected are placed in an intensive casework program. The apparent success of the original unit in New York City has led to an expansion of the program and to the practice of returning still other youngsters to the community after the intake studies carried on in the State schools.

Washington, another State with a central reception center for juvenile offenders, is also screening those committed. A significant percentage of cases are assigned to immediate placement in foster homes or other community-based programs, including four halfway houses.

The California Youth Authority apparently is making the greatest use of the reception center release procedure. Currently some 20 percent of the boys and 35 percent of the girls processed are being released to regular parole or to foster-home placement at the termination of reception period. This is typically a month long, but in some instances release may be postponed for another 30 to 90 days.

The California Youth Authority's Marshall Program represents an interesting variation in the practices discussed above. The program was initiated 3 years ago as a device for easing population pressures in the institutions. It provides for the selection of cases by the clinical staff and the project director for a 3-month intensive treatment program at the reception center at Norwalk.

Based on "therapeutic community" concepts, the project involves the youths in a half-day work program in institution operation and maintenance, some specialized education classes, and daily group counseling. Active participation is rewarded by progressively longer and more frequent home furloughs. Parents provide the transportation, and furloughs are scheduled so that parents can participate in group counseling activities as they return their sons to the center. Parental involvement is seen as a significant program component.

While the performance of the project graduates has not been subjected to comparison with a control group, agency research staff have sought to match the subjects with youths possessed of the same characteristics who have been processed through the regular institution programs. With 15 months of parole exposure time, 44 percent of the Marshall youths, as against 47 percent of the matched group, were subject to parole revocation. Moreover, the relatively short program period of 3 months, as compared against the average stay of 8 to 9 months in the State schools, means a significant saving of public funds.

The success of reception center parole has been encouraging. Other States will undoubtedly develop reception centers that feature sophisticated screening techniques and intensive treatment for those offenders who are deemed most susceptible. To date, parole from reception centers has been confined to the juvenile field. However, there is no inherent reason why this approach should not be taken with adults, and hopefully it will be so used in the near future.

* * *

Problems to be Confronted

Extensive development of alternatives to institutions requires that several problems be solved, and solved simultaneously. First is the need to make administrators and legislators aware of these programs and thus create conditions favorable for developing them. Demonstration projects which duplicate successful alternatives to institutionalization will have to be set up in various parts of the country. Such a process would require changes in the funding policies of many Federal and private agencies, which usually will support only a new type of program and not a duplication of one already proved successful. Such duplication is essential if correctional personnel and citizens are to become aware of the potentials of alternatives to institutions.

A second major problem is the familiar one of manpower. Most of these programs require skills which many correctional personnel do not have. Several centers should be established at sites of successful programs of all kinds, to train workers in the skills involved. This proposal would have particular application to training personnel for the special community programs described here.

The variety among correctional administrative structures in the country makes it difficult to determine how the new community programs could best be administered. The limited history of the prototypes indicates that the State itself will have to play a major and continuing role in order to coordinate services.

In some jurisdictions, the State may well operate virtually all of the alternative programs; in others, only part of them. For example, it is anticipated that the State will usually operate community programs for parolees. For probationers the situation is different, since a number of counties will continue to operate probation services. Where the State does not operate all community programs, it should at least supply leadership and subsidies in order to promote their development.

Whatever the administrative arrangement, it is essential that all elements of corrections should be involved. Special community programs must be perceived by all parts of the correctional apparatus as legitimate and integral parts of the system. There is a great tendency for each part of the system to push forward with its own existing programs. For example, institutional managers are apt to urge new institutions rather than looking at the possibility of alternative programs. Failure to involve important elements of the correctional community can jeopardize not only the creation of new community programs but the survival of those which prove successful. The Pinehills project in Provo, Utah, described earlier in this chapter as exciting both in its operation and in its research design, does not exist today. This project and other successful ones were not picked up by a correctional agency once the initial grant moneys were exhausted. It is clear that new community programs must be integrated into the main line of corrections if they are to succeed and survive.

It is also essential that representatives of allied service agencies, such as welfare and mental health, be involved in planning for community programs. Correctional foster-home placements, for example, are closely involved with such placements by welfare agencies, and consideration must be given to the needs of both systems. Many of the specialized community programs in corrections will lay demands on the same resources as mental health agencies. It is essential that corrections and the mental health field work out accommodations, so that there is a functional relationship.

Finally, one of the most critical problems in developing new community programs is to secure the involvement and participation of the community itself. Too often, promising programs such as halfway houses have failed simply because the community was not prepared to tolerate them. Thus it is essential that the public be brought into planning early and that correctional managers make intense efforts to insure citizen understanding and support.

b. *COMMUNITY REINTEGRATION**

Partly out of despair with the ineffectiveness of institution-based programs, partly out of humane considerations, and partly out of the notion that the best place to learn how to live in the normal world is the normal world itself, the advocacy of offender rehabilitation in the free community has increased. This position is sensitive to the likelihood that protection of the community will probably always require that a certain percentage of offenders be restrained within institutional confines and that continuing scrutiny will have to be exercised over those who are released into the community. It is also believed that community treatment may result in more rapid and effective adjustment to normative life by the offenders. The basic theoretical notion here is that law-abiding lives require integration into the normal round of life, involving ties to work, family, recreation, church, friendship, and general community institutions. The lack of such ties, it is felt, frees men to commit criminal acts, and hence their reintegration into these group bonds is required if they are to resume normal life.

Although some may see this suggestion as outlandishly "permissive" and dangerous, such community-based treatment has in fact been going on for a long time now, mainly in the form of probation (release without institutionalization) and parole (release after serving part of a sentence). About two-thirds of the present correctional caseload is under probation and parole supervision.

The evidence on rates of recidivism of men probated or paroled is variable, but none suggests that men on probation and parole commit more new offenses than men who have been confined for longer periods in institutions. Some of the studies suggest, indeed, that men who have been probated or paroled may commit fewer new crimes—although this is not certain. Insofar as safety of the community is concerned, little difference exists between institutional versus community treatment as both are now practiced. But community-based treatment is obviously less expensive; it reduces the number of men who must be treated in institutions; and, in theory, it thereby releases funds and other resources badly needed for adequate treatment both in and outside of institutions. Presumably, too, community-based treatment is at least as effective for rehabilitation as institutional treatment, and may, given greater knowledge and resources, prove more effective. Because comunity-based treatment also permits men to resume normal life more fully, it is both more humane and more promising of possible reintegration.

Thus, the Crime Commission found that programs placing the offender in the actual community seemed more promising than those operating within confining institutions. Similarly, those programs which have done most to individualize treatment appear promising. One such effort, the California Treatment Program, seems to have had considerably more success than others. Offenders are studied to secure an understanding of their perceptions and personalities, and treatments are then prescribed accordingly.

Community-based programs may therefore be justifiably advocated on the grounds of

---

* National Commission on the Causes and Prevention of Violence, *Staff Report, Crimes of Violence,* Vol. 12 at 586–89 (1969).

safety, economy, humaneness, and their contribution to rehabilitation.

Existing programs are, of course, quite variable. They range from minimal supervision by parole officers (who are usually loaded with far too many cases to keep effective contact and supervision of released offenders, much less provide any treatment or counsel) to closely supervised facilities such as halfway houses, where full-scale treatment programs may be offered, along with vocational counseling, continuing education, financial support and the like—all aimed at easing and facilitating the return of the offender to the community.

Other activities that take the institutionalized offender a step closer to normal community life include allowing conjugal and other sex-partner visits; reinstating certain civil rights (e.g., the right to vote); permitting short furloughs with families; initiating vocational and academic training where participants leave prison during the day; establishing houses on institution grounds where men eat and sleep at night, but work in the community during the day; and providing temporary release periods for specific recreational, religious, and civic activities.

Much interest and enthusiasm have lately been centered around the programs of halfway houses—seen as social "decompression" chambers that provide for a graduated transition to normal life. An early innovation was the experimental Highfields project. Young offenders were released by the court directly to a treatment home, where they did regular work, participated in group-therapy sessions, and could choose, if they wished, to return to more traditional treatment. Evaluation of the program suggests that it has had no less and perhaps significantly more success than more traditional forms of response to offenders.

Partly under the impetus of the Highfields model and partly out of the perceived need for realistic integration, halfway houses have begun to spring up throughout the country. They have characteristically been able to recruit more highly trained personnel and have often benefited from the active interest and involvement of professional criminologists, penologists, and clinical psychological personnel. The ratio of personnel to inmates has almost always been much higher than is found in normal incarcerative institutions and, overall, the program and resources tend to be both more innovative and more ample. At the moment, the evidence regarding their impact on the rate of recidivism is not substantial or clear enough to permit any generalizations, other than that they seem to have no worse results than full-scale institutional treatment and no better results than probation or parole directly into the community.

Compared to the costs of direct release into the community, halfway houses tend to be relatively expensive, although they are probably less expensive than incarceration in custodial institutions. This suggests that further exploration of alternative designs of halfway-house programs is warranted on grounds of economy, efficiency, and humaneness.

Perhaps the most promising possibilities here lie in the combination of normal work and normal sexual experiences, with continuing opportunities to explore the emerging problems of adjustment to these experiences in therapeutic sessions, either individual or group. In short, the theraputic sessions can be attuned to the realistic problems of adjustment in the normative community, whereas when therapy is administered in institutions of incarceration, no such continuing guided evaluation of actual normative experiences and difficulties is possible.

Among the most important of community experiences that the release offender encounters—aside from work and sex—is the confrontation of the usual negative attitudes of the public who regard him as an ex-offender. Numerous observers have commented on the difficulties that face the "ex-con" at his job, if he has been lucky enough to secure employment. Although many efforts have been made to establish bridges of acceptance by employers and others through whom the ex-offender can find his way into normal community life, the general public attitude toward ex-offenders tends to remain dominantly one of suspicion, distrust, and unwillingness to extend normal opportunities. Nor is private industry alone at fault. The U.S. Civil Service Commission, for instance, requires that 2 years elapse after discharge from a felony sentence before a person may be considered for a position requiring a high degree of integrity. If private industry exhibits comparable reluctance, it is no surprise; and is it easy, under the circumstances, for government officials to urge that private industry extend more understanding and assistance than is granted by official government policy.

In the reformulation of existing programs in halfway houses and in the design of new ones, the need for job preparation and placement would seem paramount. Yet because employment is so hard to find for released offenders, and because financial needs press down upon them immediately after release. various students have suggested the importance of providing such assistance, either through grants or loans, so that the individual would not feel forced to resort to criminal activity simply to provide the necessities of life. In this regard, the terms of the Social Security Act are most ill-fitting for released offenders. To secure such unemployment insurance, one must have been previously employed at a firm covered by the act and earned a specific amount in a designated period of the preceding year. Only the smallest number of released offenders can possibly meet these criteria.

Such evaluations of halfway houses and other community release programs call attention to the quality of the environment into which the ex-offender is reintegrated. If he moves directly back into a community saturated with criminogenic influences, the likelihood of his recidivism is, of course, enhanced. Yet, in more cases than not, it is precisely communities of this type to which ex-offenders return, if they have any place to go back to at all. Some have suggested in such cases a policy of deliberate relocation in other communities, hoping thereby to avoid the probable criminogenic impact of the "old neighborhood." But where families are involved, this idea presents serious difficulties. And again, more often than not, young offenders have no other "home" to return to. It will, therefore, be of the utmost importance in the design of future programs to take these problems into account.

In the same vein, persons released on parole are continually subject to rather stringent restrictions on their behavior. They are not normally permitted the ordinary free man's range of choices and decisions regarding job, residence, companions, and sexual activities. Typically, too, they can be forcibly returned to incarceration if these regulations are violated. Thus, for example, failure to secure permission to change jobs may result in reincarceration, when such an act by a free person would not normally even be considered irregular, much less worthy of being judged criminal. Because the whole theory of rehabilitation is premised on the notion that the released offender is in the process of relearning how to live in the community, and because such persons should expectably make more ordinary mistakes than others, it would seem excessively shortsighted to be more stringent with them. No community-based program can expect to work if it continues to place upon the offender more severe standards of conduct than those expected of the non-offender citizen.

Chapter Seven

CLASSIFICATION: HOW SHOULD THE PRISON DIFFERENTIATE AMONG INMATES?

AMERICAN CORRECTIONAL ASSOCIATION

Essential Features of Classification*

1. *The Classification Process*. The classification process consists of organized procedures by which diagnosis, treatment-planning, and the carrying out of the component parts of the general treatment program are coordinated and focused *on the individual* in prison and on parole.
2. *The Reception Program*. The reception program includes the instruction of orientation of the newly-received inmate regarding the institutional and parole programs during his stay in reception facility while the initial diagnostic case studies are being made.
3. *The Admission Summary*. The admission summary consists of the compilation, first, of information from all phases of the diagnostic study during the reception period; and, second, of the listing of recommendations issuing from this diagnosis for the treatment of each individual. The Admission Summary is the cornerstone upon which a cumulative case history is developed, as information about the inmate is

* American Correctional Association, *Manual of Correctional Standards* 352–56; 358–61; 364–65 (3d Ed. 1966). Reprinted with permission of the American Correctional Association.

added to it systematically during his time in prison and on parole.
4. *The Records Office.* A records office, conveniently located and well organized, is essential for the classification program. The cumulative case histories are the primary sources of information about the inmates' programs and all other aspects of their cases.
5. *The Institutional Classification Committee.* The institutional classification committee consists of personnel representing all institutional departments having contact with individual inmates. They meet together as a whole or in subgroups to consider and to direct the care and treatment program of each individual inmate.
6. *The Initial Classification Meeting.* The initial classification meeting occurs shortly after an inmate's assignment to an institution. All diagnostic factors available in the case are studied, and a realistic program of custodial care and constructive treatment is formulated.
7. *Reclassification.* Reclassification meetings are held at regular intervals, and whenever a major change in an inmate's program appears indicated. Such reviews of an individual's case help insure continuity in the treatment program and expedite necessary program revisions to meet the changing needs of the inmate.
8. *Classification Procedures Immediately Prior to Parole or Release.* Prior to a parole hearing, the classification committtee may prepare a special summary or preparole report which represents the coordinated staff thinking about an inmate's adjustment and readiness for release so important in the deliberations of a paroling authority. It may also include relevant suggestions as to the most satisfactory treatment program for the individual after release on parole. . . .

The Classification Process

The primary objective of classification as a systematic process is the development and administration of an integrated and realistic program of treatment for the individual, with procedures for changing the program when indicated. This primary objective is attained through five general approaches: (a) The analysis of the individual's problems through the use of every available diagnostic technique, including social investigation, medical, psychological, psychiatric examinations, educational, vocational, religious, and recreational studies. The observations of custodial officers offer data of value. (b) A treatment and training program is evolved in staff conference during or after the inmate's personal appearance before them, based upon these analyses and a frank discussion of its purposes with the inmate. (c) The program decided upon must be placed into operation. (d) It may be revised when indicated. Classification, a dynamic process, cannot be effective unless program modifications are made in accordance with the changing needs of the individual inmate. (e) What is done for the inmate in the institution needs to be correlated with his program on parole.

Classification, therefore, is neither specific training nor general treatment, but rather the process through which the resources of the correctional institution can be applied effectively to the individual case. Classification is more than labeling inmates in categories or types, or the segregation of similar groups of offenders in separate institutions. Yet the classification program becomes more effective when separate, specialized facilities are available for the treatment of different types of offenders. Classification may be conceived of as the process of pooling all relevant knowledge about the inmate so that important decisions and activities affecting him may be better coordinated. It serves also as the means of directing toward him the individualized and group treatment he needs.

Classification is part of the program of the correctional system as a whole. Upon the basis of classification findings, the planning of the correctional system is assisted through knowledge of what types of programs and institutions are needed. Every state correctional department should employ a high-ranking member of the staff to be responsible for supervising classification in the correctional system as a whole, and for coordinating the institutional program with parole planning and treatment. Standards should be set for the system-wide classification program with provision for necessary variations in details in the several facilities.

For the operation of a classification program, adequate facilities, the necessary diagnostic and treatment personnel and the understanding and cooperation of management personnel are essential. However, the principles of classification may be applied even when personnel and facilities are minimal. A classification program is, therefore, not entirely dependent upon a full staff of professional personnel, well-trained management people, and extensive treatment facilities, although the program can be more effective to the extent that these conditions exist. The correctional system with little by way of professional staff or facilities, if it still attempts to apply the principles of classification, may achieve thereby a more effective use of its resources in individualized treatment.

The Reception Program

No time may be more important to the prisoner, in determining his later attitudes and patterns of behavior, than when he enters the institution. He may entertain the layman's concept of the prison as a place of punishment. He may be in the throes of emotions, such as guilt, anxiety, resentment, self-pity, depression, remorse, and hostility. Few prisoners bring with them any reality-based understanding of the correctional program or any real hope of profiting from this experience. Most have erroneous preconceptions gained from other prisoners while in jail awaiting trial and commitment. The reception period immediately following admission to prison is, therefore, of great significance. Intimate and skilled counseling is especially necessary to help the inmate start his efforts to gain insight into his situation and to accept what he, himself, must do about it.

A. *Advantages of a Separate Reception Process.* The segregation of new inmates for medical or custodial reasons is provided. Some authorities believe that the medical quarantine period need be no longer than five days. The total period of separate housing for inmate orientation and case study varies in practice from four to eight weeks. It is desirable that the reception or admission-orientation unit have its own facilities for interviews, group testing, educational classes, discussion groups, and recreation. A period of segregation insures that the new inmate will be readily available for diagnostic studies. An orientation program for inmates may be carried out advantageously. In this situation orientation means informing the inmate not only regarding the details of everyday life in prison, but also the broader purposes of treatment in the institution and thereafter on parole. To the man who has never before been in prison, there is much he needs to know, not only about prison regulations, practices and organization, but also about the treatment and training opportunities available. To the man who has been confined previously, his past institutional experiences may have established uncooperative attitudes which must be changed before he will accept assistance or enter into a constructive program.

In most jurisdictions, inmates are still committed by the courts directly to a particular institution, for example, to one of the state prisons or the state reformatory. It is far more desirable to provide by law that offenders be committed by the courts to the state correctional system and the custody of the Director or Commissioner of Corrections, or the equivalent official or board. This central authority should then be empowered to determine the institution to which the individual will be committed. Upon the basis of the admission classification study it can be determined to what particular type of program and institution the inmate properly belongs. When this is done, it may be said that the classification procedure in a state or federal correctional system begins when the offender is committed to prison.

B. *Staff Role in Reception Processing.* If resources permit, specialized staff conduct the diagnostic-classification process. The staff soon becomes skilled in the case-conference method and in the preparation of brief, yet comprehensive, case summaries. Moreover, opportunity is given in the reception unit for careful observation of the newly-received prisoners by correctional officers and other staff members. The staff may recognize and plan for those inmates who are likely to present institutional problems by virtue of mental illness or defectiveness or acted-out hostility toward authority. Likewise, those who may try to escape may be noted as would be true also of others who need to be handled carefully by virtue of some special features of their cases, such as newspaper notoriety or political implications. Inmates with special problems such as these may be recognized and recommendations for their disposition prepared in accordance with the policies and procedures of the prison system.

To accomplish the important objectives of orientation mentioned above, staff members from the various departments meet with groups of inmates and not only give them information, but also through discussion encourage the new men to raise the innumerable questions which are in their minds. Inmate speakers, representing organizations like Alcoholics Anonymous, may also assist in the program. Orientation is most effective if spaced throughout the period of classification study. Some correctional systems provide initial group psychotherapy or group counseling during this period.

Other techniques currently being used include guided tours through the institution, motion pictures and slides showing the institutional activities, facilities and programs, and distribution of brochures describing the institutional programs as well as its rules and regulations. Such "rule books" should contain clear, concise statements as to the "do's" as well as the "don'ts." They should be informative and explanatory in tone rather than harsh and threatening, true guidelines for conduct rather than detailed listing of all the possible infractions. Group discussion of "the rules" is a valuable means of increasing understanding of them and may at the same time elicit information about individual inmate's difficulties in conforming.

C. *Inmate Activity Program During the Reception Period.* There is great need for a well-organized activity program during the reception period. Most persons committed to correctional institutions have already spent considerable time in idleness in jail awaiting trial, sentence, and commitment. Further idleness during the reception period tends to increase tensions and hostilities. The reception program should provide reading material, regular recreational activities, including exercise periods, religious services, and special work assignments either in the reception unit or outside it. The reception inmate should be kept separate from the general population at all times.

The Admission Summary

The compilation of the results of the diagnostic study has been called commonly the admission summary. It forms the first document of the cumulative case history. The admission summary should consist of the following: (1) account of the legal aspects of the case. In addition to citations from the summaries of the reports of law enforcement, judicial, and other officials, this may contain an explanation by the inmate of how he got into trouble; (2) summary of the man's earlier criminal history. If he has previously been in a juvenile or an adult correctional institution, reports from these places contain information regarding his program therein and related facts about his attitudes and behavior; (3) Social history, or the man's biography as a person, based upon the probation report or field investigation, staff interviews, tests, examinations, and other staff observations. This may also be provided or amplified by his family or friends, former employers, and others who may assist through interviews or answers to questionnaires; (4) physical condition; (5) vocational interests, competence and experience; (6) educational status; (7) religious background and interest; (8) recreational interest; (9) psychological characteristics evaluated by the psychiatrist and the psychologist; (10) behavior in the reception center, reported by the custodial staff; and (11) initial reaction to group psychotherapy or group counseling, or other forms of treatment. From the above interview and counseling situations, data are obtained from the inmate's standpoint, that is, the man's own story, as well as from other persons. The admission summary becomes a practical document when the final page is devoted to a listing of recommendations in the above areas of diagnostic study for the inmate's institutional and parole program. . . .

The Institutional Classification Committee

The key element of the classification process is the Classification Committee, or, as it is sometimes called, the Classification Board. Because of its functions in coordinating the activities concerning the inmate in the institution, the classification committee should be composed of those staff members who most represent the diagnostic, treatment, and security responsibilities of the institution. These are usually department heads or their designees. The membership will vary as between institutions, depending upon size and the extent to which diagnostic, training and treatment services have been developed. In the more adequately staffed institutions, the committee may include the warden or superintendent, as chairman, (usually ex officio) and as alternate chairman, an associate or deputy warden in charge of classification and treatment activities. The presence of the Warden or Superintendent emphasizes the importance of the Classification Committee functions, and in institutions where classification is not yet thoroughly "sold" insures that committee actions carry his full support and authority. In larger institutions, it is usually impossible for the Warden or Superintendent to attend all Classification Committee meetings or to devote the time effective classification demands. In these cases, the chairman is usually an associate warden (treatment) or a supervisor of classification. In addition, any of the following may be included, the supervisor of education, the vocational supervisor or counselor, the industries supervisor, the chaplains, the chief medical officer, the psychiatrist, the psychologist, and the correctional officer in charge of the admission unit.

For effective and economical service in the large prison, the committee may be subdivided into smaller working units. This trend toward smaller committees is believed by many to be most desirable, especially for purposes of reclassification. Some even believe the classification process should be completely decentralized and placed in the hands of individual caseworkers. The committee, then, would serve as a classification and treatment council where principles and policies, rather than individual cases, can be discussed.

The institution supervisor of classification is responsible for the development of procedures which will permit smooth and efficient operation of the program. He schedules cases for the meetings, notifies committee members of the dates when reports are required, and supervises their assembly into the various classification reports. He reviews the material submitted, noting discrepancies, incompleteness and repetition, and takes the steps necessary to eliminate deficiencies and maintain classification standards at a high level. Finally, he has the important responsibility of seeing that the recommendations are referred to the proper persons and to check thereafter to note whether or not they have been carried out. In the parole agency, there is a simplified form of the classification process. The study of the man's case is carried on largely by the field parole agent alone or sometimes with a supervisor present.

The Initial Classification Meeting

The purpose of the initial classification meeting held after the reception period is to develop a program for and with the inmate which will be realistically directed toward his rehabilitation. At initial classification, it is necessary to coordinate the diagnostic material prepared by the staff, to weigh the various factors contributing to his delinquent behavior, and to evaluate his potentialities and limitations. This is accomplished through the staff conference method. . . .

The inmate should participate in the planning of his own program since one which is imposed upon him will not be as well accepted as one in whose development he feels he has had a part. The time during his personal appearance should be conducted so as to put the inmate immediately at ease. The way has been prepared for inmate participation by discussions of the inmate's future during interviews held during the reception period. At the meeting, he is free to express his frank opinion of the values of the proposed program as he views it. In some cases, conflicts and misunderstandings may be assuaged by interpreting to him the meaning and purpose of his program, and, when indicated, adjusting it according to his own expressed needs.

Committee recommendations should cover all important aspects of the inmate's institutional life. Some recommendations at initial classification will be tentative and dependent upon further information and observation. The first decision to be made by the classification committee, if a reception center is not available in the prison system, may be the inmate's assignment to a suitable institution. Such recommendations will be limited by the number and variety of institutions in the correctional system and the statutory provisions permitting transfers. In the main, transfers are made (a) to place the inmate in an institution better suited to his training and treatment needs; (b) to separate recidivists and vicious offenders from the unsophisticated; (c) to place inmates who are in need of special medical or psychiatric treatment in institutions affording the appropriate facilities; (d) to separate informers from persons against whom they have informed; and (e) to separate an inmate from a co-defendant or an associate who has an adverse influence on him. Also, transfers may be made on occasion to adjust populations by relieving overcrowding or for other administrative reasons.

The second consideration is the degree of custody required for the inmate. It is obvious that mental defectives, known homosexuals, escape risks and others likely to present management problems need to be classified custodially so as to try to protect them from exploitation and the institution from avoidable management problems.

A third phase of classification concerns work assignments. Recommendations are based upon physical condition, the inmate's mental and mechanical aptitudes, his past work history, occupational interests, his needs and opportunities upon release, and last but not least, the jobs and the training available within the institution. If possible, work assignments are made on a training basis. In order to insure that a specific program of vocational training not be changed without committee action, work assignments should be classified into two groups. The first group consists of jobs which may be changed only on recommendation of the classification committee, such as vocational training and specific occupational or industrial assignments. The second groups consist of those which may be changed by the administrative officer in charge of work assignments. Ordinarily, inmates assigned at institutional convenience to general labor or maintenance may be changed from one of these assignments to another without committee action.

The fourth area, recommendations relating to the academic program, must be realistic and coordinated with the rest of the program, especially work and vocational assignments. Academic placements will, of course, depend upon the policies and facilities of the institution together with the inmate's mental ability, educational record and his interests. This is another phase of the program which rests exclusively with the committee. No single officer should have the authority to remove an inmate from such an assignment. Many other types of recommendations may be mentioned briefly. Medical and psychiatric recommendations are considered in themselves as well as in connection with assignments to other aspects of the program. Social service recommendations may include requests for additional information or the desirability of arrangements with community agencies to provide assistance and other social services to the inmate's family during his confinement. Provision for regular casework contacts with the inmate or his family may also be outlined in collaboration with local private and public agencies.

The recommendations of the chaplain may include attendance at church services, enrollment in religious-education classes, and religious counseling. Provisions for church services and a program of religious education classes add much to the institutional climate and to the treatment program. It is in the area of personal religious counseling, however, that the chaplain may make his greatest contribution to the individualized treatment.

A good recreational program may raise the general institutional morale and reduce the amount of time devoted by inmates to the discussion of criminal activities. Socially acceptable avocational interests may be suggested for the use of leisure time.

... In general, classification contributes to an efficiently operated correctional program from reception to discharge from parole. This it does by the cumulative recording of all relevant information concerning the individual offender, by continuous development and revision of the program for the individual based upon this information, and by trying to keep the program realistically in line with the individual's welfare. Classification furnishes an orderly method by which the varied needs of each prisoner may be followed through from commitment to discharge from parole. Through its diagnostic and coordinating functions, it not only contributes to the objective of rehabilitation, but also to more efficient institutional management and morale and more effectively directed supervision on parole.

Informal discussions, during classification meetings or thereafter, of questions of policy or procedure raised by staff members, are important for the advancement of the correctional program. Suggestions from these discussions may assist in the long-range planning of needed local or system-wide facilities and in developing policies and procedures, both in the individual institution and in the correctional system as a whole.

The Results of Classification

The Diagnostic Summary

The Case of Gerald T. Merrill
[Reprinted *infra.*, page 459.]

Inmates' Views of Classification

MIKE MISENHEIMER

Classification*

When I came to the Indiana State Prison, with a life sentence in 1959, . . . I received the full benefit of the prison's treatment personnel. I was given a battery of tests which occupied a week of my time. Then I lay in a cell in the Admission & Orientation section for three months waiting for the results of the tests to be determined so the classification committee could assign me to a job.

The only break in that confinement came the day my counselor interviewed me. After referring to my past record and present charge, he told me I probably needed psychiatric help; but he added that it was doubtful that I would receive any such help unless I got into some kind of trouble. I must admit that he summed the situation up very accurately. And so far, since I have managed to avoid any serious trouble, I have also avoided the psychiatric help I allegedly needed. I keep promising myself though that someday I will try to get into enough trouble to deserve help.

When the big day finally came and I was called before the Classification Committee, they told me I was going to be assigned to the Education Department. I had a high school diploma and the eighth grade was the highest level offered at that time, I asked them what I would be doing there. The Classification Director seemed to take affront at my question, grumpily pointed at Mr. Buck, the school principal, who was also on the committee, and told me to report to him when I was assigned.

A week later, when I was released from A&O, I did as I had been told. Mr. Buck seemed uncertain as to what my duties were to be, and he finally referred me to his assistant, Mr. Winn, who openly admitted that he didn't know where to place me. He asked if I wanted to be a teacher. I certainly didn't feel qualified to teach. I couldn't type, so that eliminated being a clerk. Finally, Mr. Winn told me to look around for a few days and find something I wanted to do. After three days of "looking" I selected the drafting class because there was a window fan in the classroom. I spent a lot of time in that room wondering just what it was that indicated to the Classification Committee that the Education Department was where I belonged.

After serving ten years here, I still can't explain how they determined what a man's job assignment should be. There is one factor in their behavior though that has remained fairly constant. Every time I have requested a job change I have been met with resistance or a flat denial. At one point I had been assigned to the shoe shop after being returned from escape. The foreman and I didn't get along. We rubbed each other wrong from the first day I entered the shop. I controlled my feelings for several months, but I eventually found myself thinking more and more of smacking him right in the mouth. This is an unhealthy attitude, in any prison.

I sent the Classification Committee an interview slip requesting a transfer, and I had the supervisor of the medical lab write a request asking for me to be assigned there. The Classification Director, Mr. Dave Sweet, told me I was needed in the shoe shop. (I worked fifteen minutes daily there.) I explained that I wanted a transfer to avoid trouble, but I didn't tell them with whom. Mr. Sweet told me to try harder to get along and sent me back to the shoe shop. I went instead to my cell, packed my toothbrush, and went to a cell on the Idle Gang. A week later I appeared before the Classification Committee from the Idle Gang. This time I asked to be assigned anywhere in the prison except the shoe shop. Mr. Sweet reminded me that I was in prison and I had to work where I was told to work. (Hell, Bull could have told me that!) He again

* From H. Jack Griswold, Mike Misenheimer, Art Powers, and Ed Tromanhauser, *An Eye for an Eye* 31–34 (1970). Copyright © 1970 by H. Jack Griswold, Mike Misenheimer, Art Powers, and Ed Tromanhauser. Reprinted with permission of Holt, Rinehart and Winston Inc. and Curtis Brown Ltd.

assigned me to the shoe shop. When I refused this time, it constituted a violation of the rules, and my next appearance was before the institutional court. They found me guilty of refusing to work and gave me ten days in lockup, but they also transferred me to the tag shop, where I got along fine. It might have been simpler to have smacked the foreman.

Within six months the shoe shop foreman had been fired because he had trouble with so many men, and Mr. Sweet was reassigned when it was discovered that he had only three hours of college credits instead of the degree in sociology he had claimed when applying for his job. I can't take any credit for those dismissals, but I shed not a tear.

Once, while still assigned to the drafting class, I heard my name called over the recreation loudspeaker with instructions to report to the cannery right away. I walked over there, wondering who could possibly want me at the cannery. The foreman met me at the gate and told me I was now assigned to the cannery. I protested that I hadn't requested a job change and certainly hadn't appeared before the Classification Committee.

"You been to Classification," he said, "You just didn't know it." . . .

JOE MARTINEZ

Rehabilitation and Treatment*

The convict strolled into the prison administration building to get assistance and counseling for his personal problems. Just inside the main door were several other doors, proclaiming: *Parole, Counselor, Chaplain, Doctor, Teacher, Correction,* and *Therapist.* The convict chose the door marked *Correction,* inside of which were two other doors: *Custody* and *Treatment.* He chose *Treatment,* and was confronted with two more doors, *Juvenile* and *Adult.* He chose the proper door and again was faced with two doors: *Previous Offender* and *First Offender.* Once more he walked through the proper door, and, again, two doors: *Democrat* and *Republican.* He was a Democrat; and so he hurried through the appropriate door and ran smack into two more doors; *Black* and *White.* He was black; and so he walked through that door—and fell nine stories to the street.

MORRIS V. TRAVISONO
310 F. SUPP. 857 (1970)
United States District Court,
District of Rhode Island

PETTINE, District Judge.

This is a civil rights suit pursuant to 42 U.S.C. § 1983, in which several issues are raised relating to the constitutionality and statutory permissibility of certain rules, practices, and conditions of life at the Adult Correctional Institution.

The history of this litigation will first be recited in order to establish the background against which this court is ruling. On Saturday, October 11, 1969 and ex parte temporary restraining order was sought by Rhode Island Legal Services on behalf of their clients, a group of prisoners who had allegedly been arbitrarily and discriminatorily segregated out from the general prison population and placed in a so-called Behavioral Control Unit where many of the more ordinary facets of their daily prison life, such as the opportunity to work, the opportunity to engage in regular prison activities, the opportunity to attend chapel, and the like, were denied them. Additionally, it was alleged that health conditions, in part created by the prisoners, and in part permitted to continue by the prison administration, were so seriously deteriorated in the B.C.U. as to amount to a serious health hazard and a violation of the Eighth Amendment to the United States Constitution. After some lengthy discussions with counsel for the plaintiffs, counsel for the prison administration and others, the court entered a temporary order requiring the defendants to provide the plaintiffs with minimal maintenance of personal hygiene and to permit plaintiffs outdoor exercise and access to religious services. The court further indicated that a physician should im-

* From Etheridge Knight, *Black Voices from Prison* 63 (1970). Reprinted by permission of Pathfinder Press. Copyright © 1970 by Pathfinder Press, Inc.

mediately examine the B.C.U. to determine the nature of any health hazard there present.

Commencing Monday, October 13, 1969 the court both heard in-court testimony and engaged in in-chambers negotiations in an attempt to break the impasse that had developed between the plaintiff prisoners and the defendant prison administration. For the entire week of October 13, 1969 the court and counsel labored virtually around the clock both in the adversarial atmosphere of the courtroom, where expert testimony met head on and clashed on the issue of the B.C.U. health hazard, and in the negotiation climate of court chambers where segregation and classification were the real bargaining points.

On Wednesday, October 15, 1969 the testimony of Mr. Anthony P. Travisono, the Director of the Department of Social Welfare, set the stage for two crucial developments. The first was the realization that the underlying issue in the case was that of the correctness, legally and penologically, of the classification and segregation concepts and operations. The second was the agreement of the plaintiff prisoners, predicated upon the court's indications that the underlying procedural issues would be considered, to break the impasse by cleaning up the food and excrement which caused the health hazard in the B.C.U.

On Thursday, October 16, 1969 negotiations in private between the parties continued. On Friday, October 17, 1969 several further developments came to light. First, the plaintiffs sought a continuance in order to prepare their case, believed by them then to have been considerably broadened into the area of due process of law in prison life. Second, the plaintiffs' chief counsel, Mr. John Donahue, indicated more than adequate personal health factors as an additional reason for continuance. The court, faced with the still to be tried and still then being negotiated classification matters, entered a temporary order regarding the classification matters. Prior to the entry of that order, the court stated at Transcript 354:

> . . . I will tell you what I am thinking perhaps should be done: These men be placed in a B classification and remain in that classification with whatever rights and privileges go with it until this case is ultimately determined, that the warden will have the right to change this classification down to C or D, but that would have to be based on their conduct, their conduct from this day forward and not for past conduct . . . .

Following a brief recess, the defendants offered a counter-proposal by which all prisoners then remaining in the B.C.U. would be placed into B classification, immediately heard in reclassification proceedings, and thence reclassified as either remaining in B or returned to C or restored to A. No prisoner was to be returned to D status. All classifications were to be predicated upon conduct from October 17, 1969 forward and past prison history, excluding the events between September 27, 1969 and October 17, 1969, except insofar as to consider favorably the cleanup of October 15, 1969. This proposal then was accepted, was entered on the record on Tuesday, October 21, 1969 and the case was continued to November 7, 1969 with certain suggestions by the court as to future proceedings. On October 30, 1969 a motion for further continuance was filed and on October 31, 1969 a continuance to December 5, 1969 was granted so that expert counsel might be found to try this case.

On December 8, 1969 Mr. Cary Coen of Rhode Island Legal Services and Mr. William Bennett Turner of the NAACP Legal Defense Fund entered their appearances on the record as counsel for the plaintiffs. On December 12, 1969 plaintiffs filed a motion to amend their complaint which was argued on December 15, 1969 and granted as of that date. On December 16, 1969 an amended complaint was filed alleging a class action on behalf of all the prisoners at the Adult Correctional Institution and a separate sub-class action on behalf of those prisoners in the B.C.U. The complaint was a broad-ranging one addressed principally to the constitutionality of the classification and disciplinary procedures and also to certain qualities of prison life at the Institution. From early in December until early January the parties conferred and negotiated to reach settlement of their differences. From the commencement of negotiations the court indicated its willingness to abide by settlement, subject, however, to its own review of the settlement proposal and to its determination of the nature of the decree to be entered. Early in January the parties submitted a draft of the proposed "Regulations Governing Disciplinary and Classification Procedures at the Adult Correctional Institutions, State of Rhode Island" to the court. See Appendix A. This draft represented the arms-length, good-faith bargaining product of the parties.

The court can state unequivocally to those prisoners who may be in doubt that there was no outside influence whatsoever placed upon your counsel who represented you skillfully throughout these difficult and tough bargaining sessions. The court read the proposed Regulations carefully and conferred with counsel. At one such conference it was brought to the court's attention that certain of the plaintiffs, particularly those confined in the B.C.U., were not satisfied with the proposed Regulations and wanted to go to trial. The court then determined to hear the views of these prisoners, all of whom were at this time confined in the B.C.U.

On January 16, 1970 six prisoners, including the named party plaintiff, stated their generalized objections to the Regulations and to certain facets of life at the prison. The court then ordered that the Regulations be prepared and distributed to the prisoners under an order of notice permissible under Fed.R.Civ.P. 23(d)(2) and perhaps mandatory under Fed.R.Civ.P. 23(e). The procedures for preparation and distribution were carried out. The court has received and read with utmost care the responses of the prisoners.

By stipulation of February 2, 1970 it was agreed that new classification proceedings in accordance with the Regulations would commence for all those prisoners who had originally been placed in the B.C.U. on or about September 27, 1969 and who still remained in B, C, or D status. It was further agreed that the court would receive and review all such classification hearings. The court notes that the Regulations are now in effect at the Adult Correctional Institution.

On its own initiative but with the concurrence of the parties the court, moreover, consulted with certain penologists of national experience who pointed out that in their opinion these Regulations are far more precise and provide for much more extended procedures in disciplining and classifying than the Federal regulations. As a matter of fact, it seemed to them that the Regulations in question go well beyond most States systems. The court notes that one expert felt that the organization of classification and disciplinary boards was too highly structured and precluded necessary flexibility, that the role for the warden should be general administrator rather than clinical director, that the procedures were too formalized, rigid and detailed, and that an undue amount of time would be spent at the expense of goals and programs. However, there was not complete agreement in this regard, for others felt that the institutions could live with the Regulations recognizing that they would require a great deal of time and attention. To quote directly as to another portion of the comments received, "The tone of the regulations may be a bit unfortunate because they seem to equate classification and disciplinary procedures to criminal trials. The use of the term 'conviction' of a disciplinary offense along with the term 'evidence' seems to imply a quantum and kind of proof required which is beyond the needs of an administrative determination. It might also place an impossible burden upon the administrator who is not learned in the law or the rules of evidence."

As to the classification, the statement was made that, "The breakdown of classifications seems to be logical and desirable."

The following decision, predicated jurisdictionally upon 28 U.S.C. § 1343, and grounded procedurally upon both the court's broad settlement discretion as an Article III court and its settlement and supervisory discretion under Fed.R.Civ.P. 23, gives due weight to the justifiable criticisms of the plaintiff class, to the very real interests of the defendant prison administration in an ordered prison environment, and to the commentary received from the aforementioned penologists.

The responses of the prisoners in both the minimum-medium security section and the maximum security section were quantitatively limited. Certain of the prisoners indicated that this was due to the difficulty many of the prisoners had understanding the Regulations. Many requested the court to come personally to the prison to explain the Regulations and answer questions. After consideration the court cannot think of any means within its control, other than that which has already been carried out, to convey the meaning of the Regulations and their significance to the prisoners, without seriously jeopardizing the judicial function. In addition, the serious grievances raised by the prisoners were generalized and cumulative. The court was able to grasp the real problems by a careful reading of the letters actually sent. Quantitatively, they may not be a statistically sufficient sample. One hundred thirteen answers were received out of a total sentenced prison population of three hundred sixty. Qualitatively, they more than adequately convey the important messages. . . .

The grievances submitted which the court thinks to be inappropriate to this action at this time concern the absence of standards. In particular it has been contended that standards of substantive wrong for which an inmate can be classified into a lower category are either non-existent or so vague as to be meaningless. In essence, this grievance seeks a code of conduct setting out clear but fair categories of intra-prison anti-social behavior for which punishment can be given. While the court has decided to place this grievance beyond the reach of this case, it is one which should be given serious consideration.

A second class of grievances concerns the subject matter of this action but can be explained by this court. There is first the claim that arbitrary and punitive action is a commonplace at the Adult Correctional Institution. The court merely points out that this is one reason for the existence of these Regulations—they are designed to bind prison officials to the rule of law.

It has been contended that those who perform classification functions do not even know the inmate. These Regulations require that the classification officials be thoroughly acquainted with the files of inmates to be classified.

There has been recurrent serious inmate opposition to the final two pages of the Regulations entitled "Emergency or Temporary Provisions." The court, while it can appreciate that opposition, is mindful of the administrative need of the prison officials. The key to the final two pages, as it may be to the whole, is the way in which they are carried out; it would behoove the administration to construe the "Emergency or Temporary Provisions" as narrowly as their language suggests.

It has been complained that no specified penalties are enumerated for particular offenses, and that punitive segregation often extends for indeterminate periods of time. Part B of The Procedural Outline of Disciplinary Action specifies to an extent sufficient, at least on its face and unless shown to be abused, the penalties which may be imposed on an inmate for a violation. Part A(2) of Classification Procedures establishes outer limits for periods of review of inmates in punitive segregation. It too seems sufficient on its face and acceptable unless shown to be abused.

Finally, it has been most seriously and most frequently asserted that the Regulations will not be followed. This is simply not so; these Regulations establish rules of law which *must* be followed. If they are not, enforcement rights may be sought in this court for at least an eighteen-month period from the date of entry of this decision. This retention of jurisdiction will offer the opportunity to revise and improve these Regulations as their practical application may require or appear desirable.

Before passing on to the final and most difficult grievance, the court notes that in general the inmates in their responses did particularize grievances but did not specifically reject the Regulations and seemed to recognize that there has to be a beginning somewhere; utopia is not upon us. Additionally, certain of the inmates specifically disavowed any desire for membership in the plaintiff class; they were in an exceedingly small minority. Moreover, insofar as this class action involves relief which will apply to the whole institution, it would serve no fruitful purpose now to excise the few dissenting inmates.

The court now turns to that grievance which goes to certain conditions of life at the Adult Correctional Institution and which may, after further study and investigation by the parties, require adjudication in some other action. It is hoped a solution satisfactory to both the prisoners and the prison administration can be reached. See Holt v. Sarver, 300 F. Supp. 825 (E.D.Ark.1969). The Regulations establish classification C which covers "* * * inmates whose conduct indicates chronic inability to adjust to general prison population or who require maximum protection for themselves or others who constitute a serious threat to the security of the institution." The Regulations establish classification D which covers "* * * inmates who because of their course of conduct while classified within Category C require closer control than provided with C Category." Many inmates have complained that the punitive aspects of segregation are basically unfair, destructive of the human person and not reasonably related to any legitimate prison purpose. There is deep-seated inmate resentment at the conditions of life in categories C and D. Many inmates, while conceding the necessity for segregation of prisoners rightfully determined to be dangerous to the prison community, are nevertheless morally offended by the deprivations imposed in the B.C.U.

Faced with this situation, where there appears to be some satisfaction with the Regulations but where there is substantial dissatisfaction with the conditions of life in the B.C.U., the court has decided upon the following course of procedure.

(1) The Regulations, which are now in force at the Adult Correctional Institution in any event, are to become an interim decree of this court and are to be entered on the record forthwith.

(2) For an eighteen-month period from the date of entry of this decision the court will retain jurisdiction over the perviously described interim decree. At that time a final decree will be entered. Such retention will allow the parties to get into a working scheme of enforcement of the Regulations but will also

permit enough flexibility for necessary rule changes.

(3) Sitting as a single-judge, in accordance with the stipulation of February 2, 1970, this court will receive and consider the reclassifications of all those prisoners who were retained in the B.C.U. after the reclassification hearings which followed the proceedings in this court from October 11, 1969 to October 17, 1969. In short, the court will hear up to date the status of all those inmates who were originally segregated in the B.C.U. on September 27, 1969.

(4) The court will send a standard-form letter to all prisoners requesting their permission to turn over to counsel for the plaintiffs the letters confidentially sent to the court in response to its order of notice. See Appendix B. Any prisoner may deny such permission and his letter will then be retained by this court and entered into the record, under seal. This procedure is done because the plaintiffs' counsel will need those letters to prepare for possible further legal proceedings with respect to the conditions of life in the B.C.U. The policy implicit in the court's previous grant of confidentiality obviously precludes a revelation of the letters to the prison administration.

(5) Upon receipt of the prisoners' responses to the court's request, all letters permitted by their writers to be turned over to plaintiffs' counsel will be so turned over.

APPENDIX A
STATE OF RHODE ISLAND AND PROVIDENCE PLANTATIONS
DEPARTMENT OF SOCIAL WELFARE
ADULT CORRECTIONAL INSTITUTIONS
HOWARD, RHODE ISLAND 02834
February 9, 1970

In accordance with the powers invested in me by Section 13–1–2 of the General Laws of Rhode Island, 1956, I herewith promulgate the attached rules and regulations governing the discipline and classification of the inmates of the Adult Correctional Institutions.

John F. Sharkey
Assistant Director for
Correctional Services

Notice

A civil action has been commenced in the United States District Court on behalf of Joseph Morris and all other inmates of the Adult Correctional Institutions, raising legal questions concerning the existing classification and disciplinary procedures at the ACI. As a result of said action, attorneys representing the plaintiff inmates and attorneys representing the defendant administrators of the ACI have drafted and submitted to the Court a proposal for new classification and disciplinary procedures to be put into effect as the rules and regulations of the ACI. In order to properly rule on the proposed procedures, the Court has ordered that each inmate affected by them shall be allowed to write to Judge Pettine by sealed, uncensored and unopened letter, his comments, objections or approval, if any, of such proposed procedures.

Agreement was also reached by counsel for all parties, that within fifteen days from the Court order putting the new classification and disciplinary rules into effect, new classification hearings in accordance with the new rules would be held for those inmates placed in the BCU on or about September 27, 1969 and who remain in B C or D status. It was further agreed that Defendants would report the details of each hearing, including records thereof both to the Court and to counsel for the plaintiffs. Because of the time involved in to the Court, it has been further agreed allowing you to make your views known that these hearings may be held prior to a decision by the Court.

It has also been agreed that upon final approval of the proposed rules and regulations, copies shall be made available to all inmates and officials and said rules and regulations shall be published in a revised inmate guide as soon as possible.

Enclosed you should find:

(1) a copy of the pertinent Court order.
(2) a copy of the proposed rules and regulations.
(3) an envelope and writing paper.

You may read the rules at your convenience during the next five days and if you have any comments you should write them on the paper provided. You are to place your comments in the envelope, seal it and address the envelope to Judge Raymond J. Pettine.

On Monday, February 9th, following the 9 p.m. count, correctional officers will come to each cell with a locked box and you will have the opportunity to place the envelope in the box. The box will be taken with its contents uncensored and unopened to Judge Pettine the next day. He will open it and review your comments.

While awaiting trial men are not involved in the case, ten copies of the proposed rules and accompanying materials will be available for their use in the library. Ten additional copies will be available at the awaiting trial dormitory in the Medium-Minimum Security Section.

IN THE UNITED STATES DISTRICT COURT
FOR THE DISTRICT OF RHODE ISLAND

JOSEPH MORRIS, on behalf of himself and all other inmates of the Adult Correctional Institutions, Cranston, Rhode Island,

Plaintiffs,

—against—

ANTHONY T. TRAVISONO, individually and as Commissioner of the Department of Social Welfare of Rhode Island, and JOHN SHARKEY, individually and as Acting Warden of the Adult Correctional Institutions at Cranston, Rhode Island,

Defendants.

CIVIL ACTION
NO. 4192

Order

Upon the report of counsel for all parties to the Court on January 16, 1970 and upon all other papers or proceedings heretofore filed or had herein, it is hereby ordered that Defendants shall promptly distribute to each inmate incarcerated at the Adult Correctional Institutions, excepting those only awaiting trial, one copy of the proposed classificaion and disciplinary procedures submitted by counsel to the Court on January 16, 1970, including provisions governing:

(A) Hearings to be given to inmates presently in B, C or D status, who were among those moved to the BCU on or about September 27, 1969, (B) the publishing of all rules in a new "Inmate Guide."

Each copy of the proposed classification and disciplinary procedures distributed in the above manner shall be accompanied by written notice to each inmate that he may write to the Court by sealed, uncensored and unopened letter his comments, objections, or approval if any, of such proposed procedures within five days after receipt thereof.

Defendants shall promptly provide all materials necessary to carry out this order and shall insure that all responses from the inmates will be received by the Court within twenty-one (21) days from the date of this order.

Defendant Travisono shall file an affidavit with the Court detailing the manner of effecting the provisions of this order.

It is so ordered.

Dated January 21 1970

(S) Raymond J. Pettine
Raymond J. Pettine
United States District Judge

(S) Neale Murphy
Clerk

REGULATIONS GOVERNING DISCIPLINARY AND CLASSIFICATION PROCEDURES AT THE ADULT CORRECTIONAL INSTITUTIONS, STATE OF RHODE ISLAND

I. *General Information*

A. Definition

Classification . . . contributes to a smoothly, efficiently-operated correctional program by the pooling of all relevant information concerning the offender, by devising a program for the indivdual based upon that information, and by keeping the program realistically in line with the individual's requirements. It furnishes an orderly method to the institution administrator by which the varied needs and requirements of each inmate may be followed from commitment through discharge. Through its diagnostic and coordinating functions, classification not only contributes to the objective of rehabilitation but also to custody, discipline, work assignments, officer and inmate morale, and the effective use of training opportunities. Through the data it develops, it assists in long-range planning and development, both in the correctional system as a whole and in the individual institution.

B. Objectives

The Classification Process

The primary objective of classification as a systematic process is the development and administration of an integrated and realistic program of treatment for the individual, with procedures for changing the program when indicated. This primary objective is attained through five general approaches: (a) The analysis of the individual's problems through the use of every available diagnostic technique, including social investigation, medical, psychological, psychiatric examinations, educational, vocational, religious, and recreational studies. The observations of custodial officers offer data of value. (b) A treatment and training program is evolved in staff conference during or after the inmate's personal appearance before the Board, based upon these analyses and a frank discussion of its purposes with the inmate. (c) The program decided upon must be placed into operation. (d) It may be revised when indicated. Classification, a dynamic process, cannot be effective unless program modifications are made in accordance with the changing needs of the individual inmate. (e) What is done for the inmate in the institution needs to be correlated with his program on parole.

C. Essential Features of Classification

1. *The Classification Process.* The classification process consists of organized procedures by which the diagnosis, treatment-planning, and the carrying out of the component parts of the general treatment program are coordinated and focused on the individual in prison and on parole. Procedures shall be as indicated in the General Laws of Rhode Island, § 13–3–1.

2. *The Reception Program.* The reception program includes the instruction or orientation of the newly-received inmate regarding the institutional and parole programs during his stay in reception facility while the initial diagnostic case studies are being made.

3. *The Admission Summary.* The admission summary consists of the compilation, first, of information from all phases of the diagnostic study during the reception period; and, second, of the listing of recommendations issuing from this diagnosis for treatment of each individual. The admission summary is the cornerstone upon which a cumulative case history is developed, as information about the inmate is added to it systematically during his time in prison.

4. *The Records Office.* A records office, conveniently located and well organized, is essential for the classification program. The cumulative case histories are the primary sources of information about the inmates' programs and all other aspects of their cases.

5. *The Institutional Classification Board.* The Institutional Classifica-

tion Board consists of personnel as indicated in the General Laws of Rhode Island, § 13–3–2. They meet together as a whole or in subgroups to consider and to direct the care and treatment program of each individual inmate.

6. *The Initial Classification Meeting.* The initial classification meeting occurs shortly after an inmate's assignment to an institution. All diagnostic factors available in the case are studied, and a realistic program of custodial care and constructive treatment is formulated.

7. *Reclassification.* Reclassification meetings are held at regular intervals, and whenever a major change in an inmate's program appears indicated. Such reviews of an individual's case help insure continuity in the treatment program and expedite necessary program revisions to meet the changing needs of the inmate.

8. *Classification Procedures Immediately Prior to Parole or Release.* These classification procedures shall be as indicated in the General Laws of Rhode Island.

D. Applicable Statutes, Rhode Island General Laws

13–3–1. Receiving and orientation unit—Study of incoming prisoners. —To establish security standards which will safeguard society and which will provide for the most efficient possible rehabilitation of individual prisoners there shall be established within the division of correctional services a receiving and orientation unit which shall receive all male persons sentenced to the adult correctional institutions for a term of imprisonment of more than one (1) year. Every such person so sentenced shall be segregated for a period not to exceed thirty (30) days during which period such person shall be studied and evaluated to determine whether such person shall be a maximum, medium or minimum security risk, and to develop a program of rehabilitation, education and medical and other care as shall be deemed necessary and appropriate to prepare such person to become a useful member of society. During such period medical, psychometric and psychological examinations shall be made of such person and the results thereof, together with the nature of the offense for which such person has been committed, the previous criminal history, if any, the recommendations of the department of the attorney-general and of the sentencing court and the social history of such person shall be studied and evaluated in determining the degree of custodial care of such person, the rehabilitation program for such person, such medical or other care as may be necessary and such spiritual and religious guidance as shall be indicated by the preference of such person.

13–3–2. Classification board. —For the purpose of such study, there shall be a classification board which shall consist of the warden who shall be chairman, the supervisor of classification, the supervisor of vocational training and education, the deputy warden in charge of custody, and the prison physician. Minutes shall be kept of all meetings and actions and recommendations of the board.

13–3–3. Determination of classification and rehabilitation programs of prisoners. —It shall be the duty of said classification board to review all studies made of each prisoner during the period of his reception and from time to time thereafter as shall be necessary to further the purposes of this chapter; and to recommend to the assistant director the security classification and rehabilitation program for such person. Said assistant director shall review said recommendation and if he shall approve the same he shall cause said recommendation to be put into effect. In the event he shall disapprove the same he shall request said board to make further study and review. In the event thereafter the assistant director shall disapprove such further recommendation the matter shall be resolved by the director of social welfare whose decision shall be final.

13–3–4. **Classification unit.** —Within said division of correctional services there shall be a classification unit which shall collect and record all the data concerning each person sentenced to the adult correctional institutions. Said unit shall periodically review the file of each male person and shall report to the board its findings and recommendations for such persons as shall have been sentenced to imprisonment for more than one (1) year for such action as the board may deem necessary and appropriate. The classification unit shall furnish the parole board for its consideration in every case the file of each person under consideration for parole.

13–8–22. **Manner of obtaining information by board.** —The parole board in the discharge of its duties under this chapter shall not be required to receive or consider any petition, and it may secure the information upon which it exercises its authority, or upon which it makes its findings in any case, in such manner and by such means as it may consider most fitting to carry out the purpose of this chapter; provided, however, it shall be the duty of the clerks of the several courts of the state, the sheriffs and their deputies, the police officers of the several cities and towns of the state, the probation officers, the officers of the adult correctional institutions, and every person having charge of any other place where prisoners are confined or detained, to furnish to the parole board and to any member thereof, whenever requested by the board or by any member thereof, any and all information they may have relating to the character and history of any prisoner whose sentence is placed under the control of the board by this chapter.

13–8–23. **Agencies required to give reports to parole board.** —Information concerning applicants for parole shall be provided by (a) the warden of the adult correctional institutions who shall submit a list of all prisoners under his control who will be eligible for parole in a given month not later than the tenth day of the second month preceding. Such list shall identify the prisoner by name, offense, date of commitment; (b) the warden of the adult correctional institutions who shall secure reports from prison officials who have had direct contact with the prisoner including the deputy warden, the chaplain, the work detail officer, the prison physician and the classification officer. He shall transmit such reports, together with all pertinent classification information, such as social history, etc., and any actions or recommendations made by a classification board or committee in the institution, to the office of the parole board not later than the twentieth day of the month next preceding the month in which the individual is eligible to appear before the board; (c) the attorney-general's department who shall supply to the office of the parole board a report of any recommendation which it may care to make, and shall consult the trial judge in the case to determine if he may wish to make any comment or recommendation; (d) the state psychiatrist who shall examine the prison upon notice from the office of the parole board and shall submit his findings and recommendations to the office of the parole board not later than the twentieth day of the month next preceding the month in which the prisoner is eligible to appear before the board; (e) the state division of psychological services who shall upon notice from the office of the parole board examine the prisoner and report their findings and recommendations to the office of the parole board not later than the twentieth day of the month next preceding the month in which the prisoner is eligible to appear before the board; (f) the state division of correctional services which shall submit a transcript of the previous criminal record of the prisoner including the date of offenses, nature of offenses, and the disposition of each; a copy of the presentence investigation; a full summary of the contact of this division with the prisoner during any prior period under supervision, either probation or parole or both; and any recommendations concerning the current application for parole.

II. *Classification Categories*
   Receiving Status
   A. Category of all inmates remanded to institution by court after disposition of charge. Receiving status is not to exceed thirty (30) days during which period all procedures outlined in § 13-3-1 of the General Laws of Rhode Island will be observed.
   B. *Category "A"*
   General prison population. Normal category of referral from receiving unit and normal category of inmate during term at Adult Correctional Institutions.

   Inmate may be removed from category for the following reasons:
   1. Temporary removal for stated period by Disciplinary Board after conviction of disciplinary offense.
   2. Reclassification by Classification Board shall be predicated on conduct of inmate which indicates inability to adjust in general prison population for the protection of inmates or others and for the security of the institution.

   All inmates within category shall be eligible for all work and educational rehabilitative and recreational programs of the institution. They shall be afforded full visiting privileges in regular institution visiting area together with regular mail privileges and normal category living location.

   C. *Category "B"*
   Category of inmates who because of their pattern or conduct require close restrictive movement and closer supervision than Category "A" population on a temporary basis. Work eligibility is suspended in this category; the inmate shall have use of educational materials recommended by education department. The inmates in this category shall be subject to the following controls:
   1. Living location to be determined by administration.
   2. Unemployed.
   3. Meals in cells—subject to administrative decision.
   4. No televisions. Radios are permitted.
   5. No institutional activities.
   6. Normal visiting and mail privileges. No visits unless clean shaven and proper haircut.
   7. May attend religious services.
   8. Limited yard privileges.
   9. Routine health services—normal toilet articles allowed.
   10. Regular store orders.
   11. Usual clothing regulations.
   12. Requests to staff via "pink slip."
   13. Reading material—subject to administrative control.
   14. Weekly change of linen and laundry service.

   D. *Category "C"*
   Category of inmates whose conduct indicates chronic inability to adjust to general prison population or who require maximum protection for themselves or others or who constitute a serious threat to the security of the institution. The inmates shall have use of educational materials and services recommended by the education department and approved by the Deputy Warden. Hobby activity shall be allowed subject to the control of the Deputy Warden. Inmates in this category shall be subject to the following controls:
   1. Separate living location—to be determined by the administration.
   2. Visiting to be held in an area other than the regular visiting room to be approved by a member of the administrative staff with the position of Deputy or above. Inmates to be cleanly shaven and with proper haircuts before being allowed out for visits.
   3. All regular store orders except glass.
   4. Normal toilet articles
   5. Meals—in cell.
   6. Work—routine housekeeping duties within the unit only.
   7. Spiritual needs—chaplains to visit regularly or on request.

8. Request to see staff via "pink slip."
9. Health
    a) Showers—minimum of two a week in the unit.
    b) Physician—submit to officer at breakfast time.
    c) Dentist—submit request to officer at breakfast time.
    d) Exercise—one hour a day indoors and outdoors alternate dates Monday through Friday. Outdoor exercise will not be given in inclement weather. Weekends and holidays excluded.
    e) Medical—emergencies to be attended to immediately.
10. Travel—all inmates leaving and entering the unit shall be searched and shall be escorted to and from their destinations.
11. A reasonable amount of reading material will be allowed. Type of material subject to institutional control.
12. No televisions or phonographs.
13. Radios—with earphones only.
14. Weekly change of linen. Weekly laundry privileges.
15. Mail—usual mail privileges.
16. Clothing—regulation shirt and trousers.
17. No institutional activities.

E. *Category "D"*

Category for inmates who because of their course of conduct while classified within Category "C" require closer control than provided with "C" category. In this category the inmates shall have use of educational materials and services recommended by the education department and approved by the Deputy Warden. Hobby activity shall be allowed subject to the control of the Deputy Warden. Inmates in this category shall be subject to the following controls:

1. Separate living location to be determined by the administration.
2. Unemployed, except housekeeping details in the unit.
3. Meals in.
4. Spiritual needs—chaplains to visit regularly and upon request.
5. Health—same as "C."
   Exercise—same as "C."
6. Visits—same as "C."
7. Mail—same as "C."
8. Request to see staff—"pink slip."
9. Normal toilet articles except razors.
10. Store orders—toilet articles and tobacco products only.
11. Reading material—current newspaper and not more than six approved publications of any other kind.
12. No institutional activities.
13. No televisions—no radios.
14. Travel—same as "C."
15. Weekly change of linen. Weekly change of laundry.

Inmates in Categories "C" and "D" will reside in the Behavioral Correctional Unit. They shall earn all privileges that can be earned by the general population that are consistent with Behavioral Correctional Unit custody.

III. *Classification Procedures*

A. The Classification Board

1. The Classification Board shall consist of: the warden who shall be chairman, the supervisor of classification, the supervisor of vocational training and education, the deputy warden in charge of custody, and the prison physician. They will meet together as a whole or in subgroups. It shall be the duty of the chairman of the Board to preside at the classification meeting. He shall determine the order of proceeding in each hearing and shall be responsible for determining the relevancy of information presented to the Board. No subgroup shall consist of less than three persons.
2. The Classification Board shall re-

view the status of every inmate in "B" and "C" classifications at least once every 90 days. An inmate placed in "C" classification shall be entitled to review upon his request in writing giving the reason for such request, after 30 days in such classification; and thereafter he shall be entitled to review if either (a) his request is supported by a statement from any institution officer, chaplain, teacher, classification counselor, physician, or employee, or (b) his request includes new information or circumstances not previously called to the attention of the Classification Board. Inmates in "D" classification shall be entitled to review every 30 days.

B. Notice

An inmate shall receive timely written notice of the subject and purpose of a classification meeting at which he is to appear. In cases where downgrading of classification grade is to be considered, said notice shall also inform the inmate of his right to be assisted by a classification counselor at the classification meeting. If an inmate requests assistance of a classification counselor, such assistance will be rendered a reasonable time in advance of the hearing.

C. The Classification Meeting

1. No decision of the Classification Board considering a possible change of status shall be made without consulting the inmate's central file.

2. The chairman of the Board shall explain the purpose of the meeting and the particular aspects of the inmate's record which may result in a classification change.

3. No misconduct shall be considered by the Classification Board unless the Disciplinary Board has made a finding unfavorable to the inmate.

4. The findings of the Disciplinary Board as to a particular infraction shall be conclusive and not subject to review at the classification hearing.

5. The inmate's file shall not be available to the inmate but may be reviewed by the classification counselor representing the inmate.

6. The inmate shall present pertinent information in relation to the classification procedure.

7. The Board shall discuss with the inmate any contemplation of classification change and the reasons therefor.

8. Upon completion of the discussion, the Board shall take the matter under advisement.

9. After decision is reached the inmate shall be called before the Board to hear the decision and to be advised of its rationale and meaning.

10. A decision of the Classification Board must be based upon substantial evidence and reflect consideration of an inmate's entire record.

11. A record of the classification meeting shall include:

a) A summary of the proceedings and matters considered.

b) The classification decision manifesting a consideration of an inmate's total record and based upon substantial evidence therein.

12. All recommendations of the Classification Board shall be subject to the review of the assistant director pursuant to the provisions of § 13–3–3 of the General Laws of Rhode Island.

IV. *Records*

The central file of each inmate committed to the Adult Correctional Institutions for more than one year must include the following:

A) A copy of a cumulative case summary.

B) Probation officer's report and other diagnostic summaries from other agencies.

C) Up-to-date progress reports in the areas of work assignments, vocational training, education, psychiatry, and medical treatment.

D) Records of Disciplinary Board determinations.

E) Any correspondence relating to the inmate.

F) Identification material, including a recent picture.

G) A record of all classification transactions.

Procedural Outline of Disciplinary Action

Five Mandatory Steps

1. Written charge by reporting officer or employee.

2. Investigation and review by superior officer.

3. Hearing before Disciplinary Board.

4. Administrative review.

5. Record.

Part A. Rules and Regulations

I. Charge by Reporting Officer or Employee

   A. An officer or employee observing minor violations should handle such incidents tactfully and firmly by warning and counseling.

   B. When an employee or officer considers a written charge necessary for proper discipline and control, he must show in writing on an inmate violation report form: inmate's name, housing, work assignment, if applicable, time, date, place and charge; give known details concerning the alleged violation, and sign the report.

   C. The inmate is to be released or sent to his housing unit pending further action by a superior officer (rank of Lieutenant or above) unless the alleged violation could constitute a threat to institution order or the physical safety of inmates or personnel.

   D. An officer may take immediate custody of the inmate being charged if such action is deemed by the officer to be necessary in order to avoid grave assault or serious disorder.

   E. When a threat to order or safety is, in an officer's opinion, present as a result of the alleged violation, a superior officer shall determine whether the inmate should be released or held pending further investigation.

II. Investigation by Superior Officer

   A. The reporting officer or employee must submit a written report to a superior officer as soon as possible after the alleged violation occurs.

   B. The superior officer shall orally inform the inmate of the charge against him.

   C. The superior officer shall conduct a preliminary investigation of the matter without unnecessary delay. The investigation will include interviews with the reporting employee, the inmate charged, and any other employee or inmates indicated.

   D. The superior officer shall make written summary of his investigation including the results of his interviews and a notation of notice to the inmate. He shall sign and submit the full report to the Deputy Warden of the facility in which the infraction occurs.

   E. The Deputy Warden shall transmit notice of the hearing to the senior classification counselor who shall in turn assign responsibility for the notice and subsequent procedures to a classification counselor. Said notice shall be timely and shall include the time and place of the hearing, the charge, including the time, place, and other persons involved, if any.

   F. The assigned classification officer will provide the inmate with a copy of the notice he has received concerning the hearing. Notice of the hearing must be transmitted to the inmate a sufficient period of time prior to the hearing to give the inmate an opportunity to prepare his defense, if any.

   G. The inmate being charged shall

have the right to be assisted by a classification officer at the disciplinary hearing. The inmate shall be informed of this right as part of the notice provided of the hearing itself.

H. Only a superior officer shall have authority to order an inmate locked up pending a Disciplinary Board hearing. If this is done, it must not be in accordance with punitive segregation regulations, and the inmate must be furnished a bed and regular diet, which will be subject to change only if abused.

I. Only a duly-authorized Disciplinary Board has power to issue punishment to inmates, including those in the Behavioral Correctional Unit.

III. The Hearing Before the Disciplinary Board

A. The Disciplinary Board shall consist of three members. The Deputy Warden of the facility in which the alleged infraction occurred shall be the chairman. The two remaining members shall be selected from the custody and treatment departments.

B. Any officer or employee who initiates a violation report or who investigates and reviews the initiating officer's report is not eligible to sit on the Disciplinary Board to hear that case.

C. The hearing shall be conducted in the following manner:

1. The circumstances of the charge will be read and fully explained by the chairman of the Board.

2. The inmate shall admit or deny the charges.

3. The Board members may interrogate the inmate and others as necessary.

4. If the inmate thinks the charge against him is untrue (in whole or in part), he may present information available to him and others.

5. If the inmate has requested the assistance of a classification counselor, the classification counselor shall assist him in the presentation of the case.

6. Upon completion of the hearing, the Disciplinary Board shall take the matter under advisement.

7. After decision is reached by the Board, the inmate shall be called before the Board to hear the decision and to be advised of its rationale and consequences.

8. A board decision must be based upon substantial evidence.

9. The inmate will be informed that the Board decision will be formally reviewed by the Warden.

10. It is to be made clear to the inmate that he may request assistance from his classification counselor in framing what he believes is wrong with the decision. The inmate shall be allowed to have his objection, if any, incorporated in the case record submitted for review.

IV. Review

A. Within three days of the Disciplinary Board's decision (Sundays and holidays excluded), the record of any proceedings shall be forwarded to the Warden who shall review the record of any proceeding which shall result in an unfavorable decision for the inmate.

B. If the Warden is in agreement with the Disciplinary Board decision, the decision is approved and ordered.

C. If the Warden does not agree with the Disciplinary Board decision, he may order further proceedings or he may reduce or suspend any result of a Disciplinary Board hearing unfavorable to the inmate.

D. The inmate will be notified of any change resulting from the review process.

V. The Disciplinary Record
   A. A record shall be maintained of all disciplinary proceedings including review by the Warden.
   B. The disciplinary record shall include:
      1. An appropriate summary of all information produced at a hearing plus the written summary investigation referred to in II (D) above.
      2. Physical evidence viewed.
      3. A brief explanation of the rationale of the Board's determination.
   C. Substantial Evidence

   A determination of the Disciplinary Board must be based upon substantial evidence manifested in the record of the disciplinary proceeding. If any of the facts establishing a Board determination are derived from an unidentified informant: (1) the record must contain some underlying factual information from which the Board can reasonably conclude that the informant was credible or his information reliable; (2) the record must contain the informant's statement in language that is factual rather than conclusionary and must establish by its specificity that the informant spoke with personal knowledge of the matters contained in such statement.
   D. A complete record of all disciplinary proceedings shall be maintained in the inmate's permanent file.

Part B. Actions Taken by a Disciplinary Board May be as follows:
1. Dismissal of charge.
2. Reprimand.
3. Recommendation to Classification Board for change of status.
4. Temporary loss of specified privileges within inmate classification not to exceed thirty days.
5. One to thirty days placement in punitive segregation.
6. 5 above plus referral to Classification Board with recommendation of reclassification.
7. Loss of good time as prescribed by law under § 13-2-44 of the General Laws.
8. Any combination of 3 through 7 above and/or suspended action on any or all of 3 through 7 above.

Wherever individuals are named in their position of authority, it is permissible in their absence for their lawful substitutes to replace them.

Emergency or Temporary Provisions

When faced with an immediate threat to the security or safety of the Adult Correctional Institutions or any of its employees or inmates, officials of the institution may temporarily reassign inmates in accordance with the following regulations.

I. Reassignment by a correctional officer on approval of his immediate supervisor:

A. When correctional officer or other employee witnesses an inmate commit a serious wrongdoing.

B. When other inmates state that they saw an inmate commit a serious wrongdoing.

C. When inmate seeks safety or protection from others.

II. By supervisory officials of rank of Lieutenant or above, pending investigation:

A. When inmate is suspected of serious wrongdoing, either committed or planned.

B. When inmate is suspected of being a witness to overt acts which constitute a serious violation of institution regulations or a violation of state law.

C. When requested by prosecuting attorney or Superintendent of State Police.

1. When inmate is suspected as perpetrator of a crime.

2. When inmate is a material witness to a criminal act.

Requests under C will be honored upon oral request but shall not be observed beyond 72 hours in absence of receipt by Warden of a written confirmation by requesting authority.

III. All inmates assigned temporarily under the preceding provisions will, as soon as security permits, be informed in writing of the reason for their assignment and will be afforded all other rights due them under institution disciplinary and classification procedures.

IV. A written record of all temporary reassignments shall be forwarded to the Deputy Warden for his concurrence or nonconcurrence, and he shall forward the record to the Warden for approval or disapproval. The report showing review of each is to be placed in the inmate's permanent classification file.

V. All temporary assignments shall be reviewed at the next regular meeting of the Classification Board, which in any case will not exceed one week, and final action by that Board will be ordered without unnecessary delay.

Appendix B

March 11, 1970

Dear Inmate:

Each of you received recently a copy of the proposed Regulations for the Adult Correctional Institution in connection with a civil action pending in the United States District Court in Providence. After careful consideration, the Regulations have been put in force at the A.C.I. However, a number of inmates have raised strong objection to the conditions of punitive segregation. Accordingly, there may be some further legal proceedings in the case.

When you previously wrote to me about the Regulations, you did so under a promise of complete confidentiality. I am now asking those of you who expressed yourselves to me to give me permission to turn your letters over to the attorneys for the plaintiff-prisoners in order to help them prepare for the possible further proceedings. In no case, by no means will these letters be turned over to the prison administration. Of course, if you do not want me to do this, I will honor your request and will preserve your letter in complete confidence under seal. Below you will see two boxes: check the one you wish, put your checked letter into an envelope, seal, and return it to me. These envelopes will be opened only by me.

Very truly yours,

RAYMOND J. PETTINE
United States District Judge

☐ I do not want my previous letter revealed to the attorneys for the plaintiffs.

☐ I hereby give my permission for the court to turn over my previous letter to the attorneys for the plaintiffs.

Signed_____

Chapter Eight

INSTITUTIONAL MISCONDUCT AND RESPONSES THERETO: HOW SHOULD PRISON RULES BE MADE AND ENFORCED?

A. Perspectives

1. HISTORICAL

FIRST ANNUAL REPORT OF THE BOARD OF MANAGERS OF THE PRISON DISCIPLINE SOCIETY 17–19 (1826)

Mode of Punishment

The punishments used in these institutions, now claim our attention. These are stripes [whipping], chains, and solitary confinement, with hunger. In regard to these different modes of punishment, there is a considerable diversity of opinion and practice, in this country. In some extensive establishments, chains and stripes are dispensed with altogether. In others, both are used severely. In others still, stripes alone are used. At Auburn, stripes are almost the only mode of punishment. In Richmond, Baltimore, Philadelphia, New York city, Charlestown, and Concord, solitary confinement mostly, with a small allowance of bread and water. In Connecticut, stripes, chains, solitary confinement, and severe hunger. If the efficacy of these different modes of punishment were to be judged of, by the discipline of the respective institutions, punishment by stripes, as at Auburn, would be preferred. The difference, in the order, industry, and subdued feeling, as exhibited by the prisoners, is greatly in favor of the Prison at Auburn. This difference, however, is to be attributed, not so much to the mode of punishment, as to the separation of the convicts, at night, and several other salutary regulations, which are not adopted elsewhere. At the same time, a part of the difference is supposed by the friends of this system, to arise from the mode of punishment. In favor of this mode, the advocates of it urge the following reasons: it requires less time; the mind of the prisoner does not brood over it, and settle down in deliberate resentment and malignity; it is in some cases more effectual; it is less severe; it can be more easily proportioned to the offence.

That it requires less time, there can be no doubt; and if in other respects, it is as good or better, it is for this reason to be preferred.

That the mind of the prisoner does not brood over it, as over solitary confinement and hunger, there can be no doubt. But then it would be said by the advocates of solitary confinement, that this is an argument against stripes, because the effect is not so permanent. It may be said in reply, that if the effect of punishment is bad, it ought not to be permanent, and men often appear subdued by solitary confinement and hunger, merely for the sake of being relieved, while in their hearts, there is a rankling enmity against the mode of punishment, and the person inflicting it. If this effect is produced, the punishment, so far as the convict is concerned, is injurious. That this is the fact, in many instances, those who have been conversant with prisoners have melancholy evidence.

But while this is admitted, it is also true, that the instances are numerous, in which solitary confinement, with low diet, have not failed to subdue men, who appeared to be hardened against every other mode of punishment. The officers of the New Hampshire and Philadelphia Penitentiaries, bear testimony to this. And moreover, that the end is often gained, in much less time, than it was supposed would be necessary.

It is objected, however to solitary confinement, that it is a mode of punishment which operates unequally. If a man has been fond of society; if his mind has been cultivated; if his sensibility is acute; solitary confinement is a terrible punishment. If, on the contrary, the man is a mere animal; if he is stupid, and ignorant, and carnal; if the operations of his mind are dull and sleepy; if, in one word, he is like the torpid animals, (and there are men of this description,) solitary confinement is much less severe than stripes.

Nor is solitary confinement, in the former case, a more severe and effectual mode of punishment, especially if the convict is a proud man; nor is it as much so, as stripes. A man in a narrow cell, which was almost a dungeon, where he had been in heavy chains, on a small allowance of food, three months, was asked whether he had rather remain three months longer, in the same situation, than receive a small number of stripes on his bare back. He said he had rather remain.

It should be stated, however, that his allowance of food had not been so much diminished, as greatly to reduce his body, as is sometimes the case. In those cases, where the allowance of food is six or eight ounces of bread per day, with water only; and in those cells, which in winter are warmed by no fire, solitary confinement produces the most intense and aggravated suffering. In such cases, there is nothing but death, which the most obdurate villain would not endure to be relieved from it, after a confinement generally of less than thirty days. In these cases, it is difficult to tell, whether the cold, the hunger, the pangs of a guilty conscience, the fear of death, the wretchedness of being subject to revenge and malignity, is the greatest cause of suffering, and whether each of them is not equal to the pain of solitary confinement. Stripes, in comparison with solitary confinement, in such circumstances are not severe.

It is obvious, from these remarks, that the severity, and effect, and adaptation of punishment to crime, depends more on the manner, than on the kind of punishment. Stripes may be made, and it is believed in more instances than one in our Penitentiaries, have been made, to result in death. Solitary confinement has brought the men to a state of insensibility, and in some cases produced diseases, which have terminated in death. Chains so heavy have been used, and for so long a time, as to mar the flesh, and produce most painful wounds. It is perfectly obvious from these remarks, that punishment, of whatever kind, should be committed to persons of discretion, and that there should be some checks to prevent abuses.

It is, also, obvious, that different modes may be adapted to different individuals and circumstances, and that discretionary power, as to the mode, as well as the manner, ought to be left with the government of the Prison.

It is obvious, too, that the best security, which society can have, that suitable punishments will be inflicted in a siutable manner; MUST *arise from the character of the men to whom the government of the Prison is entrusted.* There are men, whom no laws would restrain from indiscretion and cruelty, if not barbarity, in punishment. There are others, whose humanity is excessive, and they would never punish at all. To men of either class, the power of punishment, and the management of penitentiaries, should not be entrusted.

2. CORRECTIONAL

AMERICAN CORRECTIONAL ASSOCIATION

Essential Elements of Correctional Discipline*

Discipline is . . . "treatment . . . oriented toward enabling the (inmate) to clarify his self-concept and toward enabling him to practice new methods of adjustment in a protected setting." It is recognized that "people need security in the group before they can afford to look at the underlying basis for their actions."

"Everyone connected with prisons, including inmates, agrees that there must be 'discipline' among the inmates and among staff members." Even the "incorrigibles," the recurrent maximum security section inmates, are . . . "especially concerned that there be known limits established and maintained," expressing a . . . "strong desire for certainty," believing that . . . "punishment is necessary in order to maintain conformity," and wanting to know . . . "what the limits were in their relationship to authority."

Even more important than imposed discipline and rules, however, is the necessary development of self-discipline and self-controls within the inmate: not merely the ability to conform to institutional rules and regulations, but the ability and the *desire* to conform to accepted standards for individual and community life in free society.

Essential Elements of Correctional Discipline

1. *Good morale.* The only sound basis for good discipline is good morale. Conversely, proper discipline builds morale.
2. *Custody and control.* Custodial care is the supervision of inmates designed to prevent escapes or incidents. It does not mean that it is necessary that all prisoners be under close supervision at all times.
3. *Contributing disciplines.* The staff and all phases of the institutional program in their special ways contribute to the general discipline and morale of the institution.

* American Correctional Association, *Manual of Correctional Standards* 402–03; 408–20 (3d Ed. 1966). Reprinted with the permission of the American Correctional Association.

4. *Individualized discipline.* Not only should discipline be consistent, reasonable, objective, firm, and prompt, but it must be appropriately varied in terms of an understanding of the personalities of the inmates.
5. *Preventive discipline.* It is desirable to forestall punitive disciplinary practices with a workable program of preventive discipline.
6. *Good communication.* A good system of communication will replace mutual suspicion and other disturbed feelings between inmates and staff by greater mutual acceptance. It is particularly imperative to have good communication when instituting any change of program which affects masses of the inmate body.
7. *Program and procedures for maintaining proper standards of institutional control.* Since discipline in its broadest sense is one of the most important factors in institutional life, primary responsibility must rest with the senior officials who will develop good disciplinary practices and prevent undesirable disciplinary practices which are now considered archaic.

Discipline, with the immediate aim of good order and good conduct, looks beyond the limits of the inmate's term of confinement. It must seek to insure carry-over value by inculcating standards which the inmate will maintain after release. It must always be objective and must develop in the inmate personal responsibility to that social community to which he will return. . . .

Programs and Procedures for Maintaining Proper Standards of Institutional Control

Disciplinary and punitive action is ordinarily the responsibility of the deputy or associate warden or assistant superintendent in larger institutions; in smaller ones the warden or superintendent often exercises that function. When anyone other than the two senior officials is in charge of disciplinary matters, it is usually a person on the next lower administrative level (assistant deputy warden, for example) and the responsibility is only partially delegated, along with the authority. Since discipline in its broadest sense is one of the most important factors in institutional life, primary responsibility for maintaining it should not be delegated any further down the administrative scale than is absolutely necessary, taking into account the many demands on the senior official's time.

It is a common, although too limited concept of discipline that it consists of holding hearings on the cases of inmates reported for infractions of the rules, and prescribing punishment for them. This is only a part of discipline, sometimes the least important part. Nevertheless, infractions occur and must be dealt with promptly and justly.

Reports. Correctional employees as a part of their function in a treatment process, must recognize that the writing of reports need not always be concerned with misconduct. Many institutions use behavior reports, incident reports, or monthly work and conduct reports as separate from misconduct reports. These are designed to call attention to inmate acts and attitudes which might otherwise be erroneously classified as misconduct. Such compulsive behavior as suspiciousness, withdrawal symptoms, incessant talkativeness, indifference to surroundings, persistent failure to understand simple commands and to follow orders, lack of self-control, etc., should be called to the attention of staff members who are responsible for classification and treatment. To label all such acts, especially where unintentional, as misbehavior, under-emphasizes the officer's role in discipline. The officer who must make a decision as to which kind of report is best suited in the handling of minor infractions of rules has the opportunity to express his judgment, and he is more likely to recognize the importance of reports in the treatment of offenders.

Behavior reports, incident reports, and monthly work and conduct reports are also used to indicate exceptionally good work habits and attitudes which might not be recorded in the usual routine progress reports. This positive function can help every employee to recognize the importance of his role in correction.

Every infraction of discipline should be reported and the inmate given a hearing before any punishment is administered. The report should be in writing on a form prescribed for that purpose and should include the name of the inmate and other identifying data, the offense charged, a brief description of the circumstances, the names of the complainant and of witnesses, if any, and the signature of the staff member making the report. It should then be forwarded for review concerning its completeness and accuracy or for additional action before it is filed with the Disciplinary Committee.

Hearings. A hearing should take place as soon as practicable after the offense is reported, but it is customary to schedule routine hearings at an hour that interferes as little as possible with work, sickline, etc. If the offense needs immediate investigation, it should be initiated at once and the hearing on the offense may be postponed as long as necessary to complete the investigation. If the offense is serious enough to warrant it or there is a danger that the offender will try to influence witnesses, he may be placed in segregation pending investigation and hearing, but should not be in a punishment status. In some cases inmates should be brought at once to the officials in charge of discipline for questioning.

It is desirable that the more serious or repetitious types of misconduct and offenses be thoroughly investigated. This procedure reduces the incidence of violations through the discovery and correction of bad practices or unreasonable conditions or rules which contributed to the misconduct or offense and reassures the inmate that any hearings will be impartially and fairly conducted.

At the hearing the inmate reported should be given a full opportunity to state his case and, if the offense is a serious one and he claims that witnesses could establish his innocence or bring out important mitigating factors, such claims should be carefully investigated. It is usually not wise or practical to have staff members or inmates appear as witnesses at hearings. The administrative problems involved in having staff members and inmates at the hearing and the possibility of feeling of hate and resentment by the inmate against those testifying makes this practice undesirable in most cases. The soundest practice is to have a staff member investigate and report his findings to the disciplinary officer, including statements of witnesses, where applicable, for use at the time of hearings. In short, the hearing should be an orderly attempt to arrive at the truth and is not a formal court proceeding. As much of the inmate's case history and record of adjustment as is pertinent should be taken into account and not merely his criminal history and previous infractions.

Offenders shall be provided and advised of a regular channel of appeal from the finding made or the penalty assessed at any disciplinary hearing. For example, where a subordinate officer handles routine matters, disposition may be appealed to the Disciplinary Committee. Provision should be made for the inmate to send sealed uncensored letters to the Governor, the Director or Commissioner, or his deputy, and members of the paroling authority.

Records. A written record should be made of every infraction reported and how it is disposed of, even when it is dismissed or disposed of by mild reprimand. An entry should be made on the inmate's disciplinary card, in the classification committee's progress report files, and wherever else individual data are entered. In many institutions entries are also made on a bound disciplinary record book kept in chronological form, so that an inspecting official can see for any particular day what offenses were reported, what ones disposed of and how, what punishments were imposed, the inmate's physical condition, etc. These records can also be used for statistical purposes including frequency and type of incidents, budgetary justifications, program planning, research, etc. It is a practice in some institutions to place in the employee's file a copy of the citation when he makes a report to the Disciplinary Committee. The number of such citations in the file could be considered a factor in analyzing his effectiveness on an assignment.

Disciplinary Committee. It is better to have a three-person Disciplinary Committee conduct hearings rather than a single official and that this should be a regular and established practice. The Federal Prison System, the Army Correctional System, and many states have such committees in operation. They have proven to be practicable and desirable, especially in the cases of repeated petty offenders, those charged with serious misconduct and chronic trouble makers of the agitator type.

The composition of a Disciplinary Committee will differ according to the size of the institution and personnel available. The person in charge of disciplinary matters (associate warden, assistant superintendent, etc.) should preside. A psychiatrist or psychologist may be used as a resource consultant in the handling of the complicated or aggravated cases. In selecting members of the Disciplinary Committee, weight should be given to personality, judgment, training, and experience, as well as to the position occupied. The Committee must be fair and just in its decisions and recognized by the inmates as being so.

The manner in which disciplinary hearings are conducted is all-important. The Disciplinary Officer or Committee can further or destroy the treatment process, since discipline is a vital element of treatment. By calm, dispassionate hearings which seek to find and correct the causes of misconduct, and which avoid a punitive, legalistic, or courtroom type atmosphere, the disciplinary proceedings can be effectively utilized for correction.

Accepted Disciplinary Practices

Good disciplinary practices are dependent upon a wholesome treatment program. In any institution where inmates are only serving time, persistent efforts of the administration and the upper management staff will be required to prevent and hold in check the spread of bad disciplinary practices. In those institutions which have a constructive correctional program, good or positive disciplinary practices can be created. It is not enough to have discipline consistent, reasonable, objective, firm and prompt. From an historical point of view, it is significant that the mitigation of severe punishments has accompanied the increase of reformative influences within the prison community.

The exercise of disciplinary authority is so vital to administration of institutions, both from the standpoint of public relations and treatment of inmates, that the types of disciplinary measures authorized should be established and strictly controlled by the central office or governing board of the state correctional system.

The routine use of severe disciplinary measures usually serves to embitter inmates rather than deter them. Except for serious offenses or chronic violators, more moderate controls can serve as effective deterrents.

Types of disciplinary measures which may be used constructively in the control of prisoners' behavior are as follows:

Counsel and reprimand. A written report of misconduct which is filed in an inmate's case record may serve as an adequate warning for his future behavior. Inmates who recognize that a clean institutional record may help influence their earlier release from prison usually conform to rules. When such an inmate commits an occasional infraction, counsel and reprimand may be sufficient to discourage future misconduct.

Loss of privileges. One of the most effective controls of prisoners' behavior is the possibility of losing valued privileges through misconduct. Recreation time, canteen purchases, package privileges, movies and other organized leisure time activities are privileges which may be taken away for the violation of institutional rules. It is not advisable to restrict inmates' letter writing or visiting privileges unless the offense is in violation of the regulations relating to these practices.

Loss of good time. In some jurisdictions, legislation provides for inmates to accrue "good time" or receive a partial remission of sentence as a reward for good conduct and industry. In such cases, it has become a practice to assess unruly prisoners a portion or all of their good time for institutional misconduct. It is good disciplinary practice to be cautious in the imposition of penalties which remove the possible incentive for future good behavior. It is desirable to have, at some future date, a review of "lost time" penalties in order to insure against over-severity and to provide for restoration of time lost when subsequent good conduct of the inmate merits such restoration.

Suspended sentence. While a variety of penalties may be imposed upon an inmate such imposition of penalty may be suspended contingent upon his future good conduct, the suspension usually being for a specified probationary period. The suspension of a stronger penalty may serve to reinforce a reprimand or temporary loss of privileges and discourage future misconduct. To be most effective, this type of penalty must be followed by reward or appropriate recognition of the ensuing conduct of the inmate involved during or at the conclusion of the stipulated period of suspension. The basic and essential element of good disciplinary practice is the development of a good system of incentives for inmates.

Close confinement. It is necessary to segregate some inmates from the main population and provide close confinement for varied periods of time for the purposes of punishment, for the protection of themselves or others, or because of their inability to get along in the general population. But to use this as a standard disciplinary action for almost the entire range of offenses is hardly a sensible solution to disciplinary problems.

When inmates are restricted to close confinement it is necessary that they be closely supervised by experienced, competent personnel and that they be closely and regularly observed by the official exercising disciplinary responsibility and other key staff members. Procedures and requirements governing the equipment of close confinement quarters, and the care, treatment and supervision of inmates in close confinement, should be carefully prescribed in detail by the warden or superintendent and every precaution taken against abuses or laxity. Segregation is sometimes subject to serious abuse but if proper safeguards are provided and are carefully enforced, it can be safely used by a competent Committee.

Segregation when used as a type of punishment has been variously called isolation, segregation, punitive segregation, solitary confinement, etc. For this discussion the terms punitive segregation (punishment) and administrative segregation (restriction) will replace those formerly employed.

The deterrent values of punitive segregation lie not only in the amount of time served, which may be relatively short in duration, but also in the influence upon the actions of the paroling authorities. In some penal systems, such a disposition of disciplinary charges may affect an inmate's calendar status or may result in revoking of a parole hearing date.

Punitive and administrative segregation are not synonymous. If space permits, the quarters for punitive segregation should be detached from the administrative segregation area. Those sent to punitive segregation go there as punitive action, usually for a definite period of time. An administrative segregation unit for men with serious problems of maladjustment, such as homosexuality, should be used as a place for confinement and treatment of those who are unable to adjust to the ordinary routine of the institutional program until evidence of adjustment warrants return to the general population.

Punitive segregation is ordinarily used as punishment when reprimands, loss of privileges, suspended sentences, and similar measures have been tried without satisfactory results and when the infractions are not serious enough to warrant bringing the inmate to trial in a criminal court. In some cases it accompanies one or more of those other forms of punishment. It is a major disciplinary measure, which can have damaging effect upon some inmates, and should be used judiciously when other forms of action prove inadequate or where the safety of others or the serious nature of the offense makes it necessary. Perhaps we have been too dependent on isolation or solitary confinement as the principle methods of handling the violators of institutional rules. Isolation may bring short-term conformity for some, but brings increased disturbances and deeper grained hostility to more.

We need continually to analyze our institutional programs, regulations and practices to determine whether we are not causing rather than preventing the development of severely recalcitrant inmates. It is essential that we abandon the purely punitive approach in the handling of such inmates and work towards solving the fundamental problems which make them "severely recalcitrant." If punitive segregation is indicated, it should be of as short duration as possible and there should be intensive therapeutic follow-up to the basic problems.

When an inmate is tried in an outside court and receives an additional sentence, it is not considered double punishment to segregate him on normal diet while awaiting action, or after conviction, as a precautionary safeguard. The distinction between administrative segregation and punitive segregation is occasionally confused when an inmate is segregated for a comparatively short period of punishment (for an assault with a knife on another inmate, for example) and is then placed in administrative segregation for an indefinite period for the general good of the institution. It may be said the latter type protection of the inmate and the institution is for mutual convenience rather than punishment of the individual. It is essential that inmates transferred to administrative segregation fully understand their new status and the purpose behind it.

Segregation may take any one of the following forms:

a) *Restriction to cell or room*. This may be with full equipment of furniture, regular diet, reading and mail privileges, etc., or on restricted diet, with one's furniture removed during the working hours, and with no privileges. Restriction to quarters is used for short periods for infractions that call for loss of yard, movies and other privileges, but do not require transfer to a punishment section. This type of restriction may also be used for sexual deviates who do not need to be completely segregated, inmates who cannot control their tempers and are perpetually in trouble but are well-meaning and do not need to be confined in a separate section or building, and inmates who are not insane but are so defective that they cannot get along, or are easily taken advantage of, in the general inmate population.

b) *Segregation in a section of ordinary cells or rooms*. These are sometimes separated from the rest of the tier or corridor to prevent introduction of contraband. The restriction of diet, deprivation of privileges, etc., vary as above. A section of this type in an institution with cell blocks is often referred to as a segregation section and is properly located on a tier where few inmates or visitors are allowed access. In any location it is customary to extend wire screening from the edge of the gallery in front of the cells to the gallery above and to install a partition and door on the gallery. In an institution with rooms instead of cells the corridor is similarly cut off by wire screening or a solid partition.

Only one inmate should occupy each cell while confined in segregation.

There is ordinarily a small special yard where prisoners in this type of segregation are permitted to exercise under supervision. They should either be fed in their cells, seated at special tables separated from the other prisoners in the mess hall, or have a separate mess hall.

c) *Punitive segregation in a special punishment section or building*. This section is usually not a part of the regular living quarters. Inmates confined in this area usually receive a restricted diet and a loss of privileges. They should be in a punishment status and kept there for comparatively brief periods. Ordinarily no inmate should be retained in punitive segregation on restrictive diet more than fifteen days, and normally a shorter period is sufficient. Those who fail to make an adjustment under such conditions can often be treated more effectively in special administrative segregation facilities. The punitive segregation section should not be utilized for indefinite or permanent segregation. The not uncommon practice of confining insane inmates there is indefensible; *all* insane inmates should be transferred to a mental hospital or medical-psychiatric treatment facility.

The punitive segregation section and all the cells in it should be evenly heated and adequately lighted and ventilated. Artificial ventilation is usually necessary. High sanitary standards should be maintained, bathing facilities should be provided in the section and inmates permitted to bathe frequently. Most of the cells should contain a washbowl and toilet. It is necessary to omit this equipment from a few cells and assign them to inmates who persist in misusing the plumbing facilities. A few cells may have toilets that can be flushed only by the officer from outside the cell; these are either ordinary seat toilets or "Oriental type" toilets, which are openings level with the floor. Toilets which the occupant of the cell cannot flush need constant supervision by the officer. Wholly dark cells should not be used and if there is a solid door on the cell, it should be so designed that it does not exclude all light. Natural or artificial lighting should be provided during normal hours of the day or evening in keeping with standards for regular living quarters.

Punitive segregation cells should be so constructed that all parts are visible to the patrolling officer from the corridor. Such cells or at least some of them should be soundproofed for obvious reasons. Doors may be hollow with insulation in the hollow spaces. All efforts possible should be made to prevent the transmission of sound to the outside through ventilating shafts, ducts, etc.

Normally, inmates are not confined in cells with solid doors or placed on restricted diet unless they have created a disturbance while confined in standard cells in the segregation section. Occasionally they are put in cells of this type to prevent communication with other prisoners or to minimize noise from disturbances. Some institutions have solid fronts on all punishment cells, using wire glass or glass brick to admit some natural light and providing ample mechanical ventilation. The use of double doors with open grill gates supplemented by solid front doors, makes it possible to maintain better observation by leaving solid doors open except when necessary to control the noise of a disturbed or unruly inmate for temporary periods. View ports or windows of tempered glass should be provided in such cells to permit good supervision and to prevent mutilation or suicide.

d) *Adjustment Center.* "An important index of the true humanitarian character and rehabilitative purpose of a prison system is its policies and procedures regarding the treatment of severely recalcitrant inmates."

An Adjustment Center is an area of the institution designed solely for the intensive treatment of problem inmates. It represents a progressive development of the ordinary administrative segregation. In addition to drawing upon existing treatment facilities in an institution, such as education, library and chaplains' services, etc., this Center is designed to provide for occupational therapy, recreational therapy and individual and group counseling and psychotherapy. An appropriate staff is necessary.

Since most of the inmates confined in the Adjustment Center may be potentially dangerous, adequate provision must be made in both structural design and equipment to enable the staff to maintain control without exposure to unnecessary hazards. The limitations of physical facilities and the differing characteristics of their inmate residents, as would be expected, have considerable bearing upon the operation of adjustment centers. However, staff morale and competency to deal effectively with the expected problems as they arise are of greater importance.

Transfer. In any penal system embracing several institutions, transfer from one to another is often an effective disciplinary procedure as well as an administrative necessity. When all possible treatment and disciplinary resources of any one institution have been exhausted on a problem inmate without success in terms of his effecting a satisfactory adjustment, or if he constitutes a major threat to the welfare or security of that institution, transfer to an institution which affords greater custodial control or specialized treatment may be indicated. A chronic offender in one institution often adjusts surprisingly well when transferred to another institution where he is no longer compelled to keep up the "tough guy-big shot" pretense and can start anew in a changed environment. Special problem cases or chronic recalcitrants may need to be moved to an institution having an available administrative segregation unit or adjustment center when general population housing in institutions not equipped with such facilities ceases to be practical or safe.

Undesirable Disciplinary Practices

Most capable and experienced officials in the correctional field condemn certain forms of punishment and discipline as inhumane and because experience has shown them to be less effective than more progressive methods. They are frequently destructive to the good discipline they are designed to establish and maintain.

Over-severity. Restrictions, imposed chiefly to remind inmates that they are doing time, defeat work and training programs, put a premium on scheming and are the poorest sort of preparation for release. Rules and regulations that cover every minute detail of a prisoner's daily activities, specifically prohibiting everything that any inmate in the whole history of the institution has ever thought of doing, are certain to produce infractions, followed by punishments and more infractions in a vicious circle.

Punishments out of all proportion to the offense, employing inhumane and archaic methods and dictated by brutality coupled with ignorance, incompetence, fear and weakness, are demoralizing to both inmates and staff. Such punishments substantially increase the chances that the inmates will continue to be disciplinary problems in the institution and will return to crime after release.

Physical punishment. Corporal punishment should never be used under any circumstances.

This includes such practices as flogging, strapping, beating with fists or clubs, spraying with a stream of water, stringing up by the wrists, exposure to extremes of heat or cold or to electric shock, confinement in the stocks or in cramped sweatboxes, handcuffing to cell doors or posts, shackling so as to enforce cramped position or to cut off circulation, standing for excessive periods "on the line" or barrel-heads, painted circles, etc., deprivation of sufficient light, ventilation, food or exercise to maintain physical and mental health, forcing a prisoner to remain awake until he is mentally exhausted, etc.

Use of force. "Moral forces, organized persuasion and scientific treatment should be relied upon in the control and management of offenders, with as little dependence upon physical force as possible." *The regulations of well-run prisons usually provide, in effect, that force may be used only when necessary to protect one's self or others from injury, or to prevent escape, or serious injury to property.* Only as much force is authorized as is necessary to control the person against whom it is directed. The use of force is never justified as punishment. If a certain amount of unjustified force is permitted or condoned it is not long before it gets out of hand and rises to dangerous proportions.

Officers should not be permitted to carry clubs, partly for the practical reason that inmates almost always seize them in case of serious trouble, and partly because experience has shown that clubs cause more trouble than they prevent. The threat of public scandal must also be considered, for it is demoralizing to the entire system to have a good record of constructive effort destroyed by one incident of the use of unwarranted force.

Laxity. Laxity in discipline, permitting unearned privileges, and other mistaken practices are indefensible. Most prisoners of normal mentality do not like an overly permissive institution.

> The prisoner who wants to do his time and get it over with has little liking for a prison where he can find no sense of direction in a maze of favoritism, prison politics, variable rules, indefinite procedures in discipline, and the hypocrisies that underlie weak administration.

This is particularly true in new institutions or in those under new management. If one must err in a new institution, it would be better in the direction of too great strictness for a while. It is easier to relax discipline that is too strict after an institution has been operating for a while than to tighten up discipline after the prisoners have become conditioned to laxity.

Use of rock piles. Useless made-work for purposes of punishment or humiliation has no place in present day practices. Even though the work is often less arduous than that being performed by many prisoners in good status, it is degrading and viewed by all prisoners as having punishment as its primary object. However, the production of gravel for roads, using proper equipment, does not fall in this category.

To assign some prisoners to especially hard work or disagreeable work with definite production value such as digging ditches that are actually needed, building dikes or levees to prevent the flooding of farm land, or clearing a piece of land of stumps and roots is an accepted practice. Usually enough useful work may be found to make the rock pile unnecessary.

Authority and Responsibility for Disciplinary Matters

Definite precautions must be taken in the use of administrative segregation or punitive segregation.

Authority. Authority to segregate prisoners should be delegated by the warden or superintendent only to authorize committees such as the Disciplinary Committee or the Adjustment Center Committee. Subordinate personnel should only have authority to lock up an inmate when it is necessary to restrain him. They should be required to make an immediate report of their action to their superior officer. The latter should make an immediate investigation and report to the associate warden (associate superintendent) or to the senior official designated to deal with disciplinary matters.

Time limits. Segregation for punishment should be for the shortest period that will accomplish the desired result of a favorable adjustment, and in any event not over thirty days. With most inmates and for most infractions a period of a few days proves sufficient. In other cases, a few days in punitive segregation followed by thirty to ninety days in administrative segregation, or in some other status that involves continued control or loss of privileges, is sufficient. Excessively long periods of punishment defeat treatment goals by embittering and demoralizing the inmate. If he needs to be segregated for a long period, it should be in administrative segregation rather than punitive segregation.

The associate warden (assistant superintendent), or whoever is in charge of discipline, should visit inmates in punitive segregation daily, and more often if possible. He may make recommendations to the Disciplinary Committee for release of inmates from punitive segregation whenever he feels the desired results have been accomplished. The cases of those placed in indefinite segregation should be brought before the Classification Committee or Disciplinary Committee at regular intervals, or should be considered periodically by the official in charge of discipline if no such committee or board has been established.

Supervision. In addition to the visits of the official in charge of discipline, the captain and watch commanders should visit segregation sections frequently and at varying times of the day and night. The officers in charge of the segregation sections should observe every prisoner carefully at least every thirty minutes and give particular attention to prisoners in solitary confinement. A card should be on the door of each segregation cell or a tier roster posted giving the name of the occupant and stating when he was confined and for how long. Additionally a log-sheet should be maintained for each man. Whenever a senior official visits the isolation or the segregation group, he should make a notation on the log-sheet of the date and time of his visit and should initial it. The officer in charge should make appropriate entries such as medications, general behavior and attitudes or detail operations such as baths, shaves, or any unusual occurrences. When the prisoner is released from isolation or segregation, his card or log-sheet should be placed in the central file.

Health. A medical officer should visit every prisoner in segregation at least once a day. If there is a psychiatrist on the staff he should also make at least one daily visit. If only a visiting psychiatrist is available, he should be required to visit segregated inmates as often as possible and should give general advice as well as advice on specific cases. All such visits should be recorded on log-sheets in the manner specified above.

Punitive segregation must not occur under conditions or continue for periods which produce a detrimental effect on the physical or mental health of those segregated. If the medical staff recommends that a particular inmate should not be placed in segregation or recommends release, this advice should be carefully considered. Particular care should be exercised in cases of segregation with restricted diet. Mental and emotional health are as important as physical health; therefore, attention should be given to a program of therapy and/or group or individual counseling for men in segregation. It is not enough to provide the other things mentioned unless some attempt is made to change the attitudes which bring about the cases of the assignments to these sections.

Clothing. It is advisable to strip and search inmates placed in segregation for punishment and give them felt slippers and loose-fitting clothing. A cover-all is a satisfactory type of garment. Underwear without an outer garment should not be used for this purpose.

Exercise. Inmates in segregation should be given a daily exercised period, preferable in a special yard or in the main yard at a time when not occupied by other inmates.

Diet. A fundamental rule of good custodial management is that the diet should always be sufficient in calories and properly balanced as to food elements. Therefore, prisoners who have been segregated should be on a regular diet, but with the amounts reduced because they are not working. 2,100 calories per day have been determined to be sufficient to maintain health and vigor in a person so confined. If they misbehave while in segregation, inmates may be placed on a restricted diet of a special type, such as the "monotonous diet" prescribed by the United States Bureau of Prisons for prisoners undergoing punishment in federal institutions. After experimenting with the monotonous diet, some states have eliminated it entirely and the regular institution diet is fed in all segregation sections. In any event, the menu must be adequately prepared and consist of sufficient calories and properly balanced as to food elements so that the health of those undergoing segregation will not be impaired.

No inmate should be placed on a restricted diet without approval of the institution physician. A regular menu every third day, at least, should be provided. To make the diet more unpalatable, some institution officials mix several types of food together in a dish so that the prisoner's fare closely resembles a meal set out for an animal to eat. There is no justification for this undesirable practice. . . .

3. POLITICAL

RICHARD H. McCLEERY

Authoritarianism and the Belief System of Incorrigibles*

The prison, even in its larger dimensions, is a world of steel, concrete and shadows—a society of gray and lonely men in which love and laughter remain as hollow echoes of the past. Yet within that larger pattern of punishment and control, there are patches where its hard, sharp lines are softened by a plot of grass. There are times when the hardened world of social relationships is lightened by moods of affection or respect, and hours when the metallic clang of grated doors fades into the background of an old song, softly played. Even prison rules, which regiment the day with lines of sullen, silent men, relax at evening time. Then the outcasts from the larger world mingle in what is called the "freedom of the yard," exchange pictures, form private cliques and petty conspiracies, trade from an always surprising accumulation of private goods, and order their affairs in terms of patterns that constitute the prison community. The yard is the forum and the market place of the prison community.

In the prison world, however, there is still another degree of extreme constraint—a corner in which the steel, the concrete, and the shadows converge into a massive and gloomy cell block. Its walls are thicker, its bars more closely spaced, and its regimentation more exacting. This most heavily guarded section is the incorrigible unit. Confined in individual cells within that unit are rows of men removed from contact with free society and the prison community by every device available to the management of the institution. For months or, in some cases, even years, these isolated men live in a perceptual universe which consists of the steel walls of their cells and the more barren wall beyond the grated cell door. The stark simplicity of life in the incorrigible unit combines the qualities of a nightmare with those of an extremely rational, and artificial, logic. In the ordered squares of steel, restriction and a denial of individuality reach an extreme that cannot be extended, even in one's imagination. The governing of men within this unit becomes in part a prototype and in part a fantastic caricature of the authoritarian situation.

It is not so much in the ordered knowledge of social science as in the farthest flights of the imagination that suggestions for understanding the social psychology of the incorrigible unit may be found. One of the most perceptive of these flights is Plato's allegory of the cave. He creates an image of prisoners chained so that they see nothing but shadows on a distant wall, and hear only the echoes of other voices. This is almost a description of incorrigible prisoners who in reality are prevented from seeing one another, but whose shadows are projected outward from their cells. To them, like Plato's imaginary prisoners, the truth can be nothing but the shadow of images. These are men who live on a level of reality different from that of the world outside, men whose life in the shadows gives them a most uncertain contact with reality at best. . . .

In neither of the prisons studied was the incorrigible unit the primary punitive sanction. Each institution had its row of block cells adjacent to the incorrigible section, and additional facilities in which a man could be broken by the withdrawal of food and other privileges. . . . The American Prison Association officially [states]:

> It may seem like hairsplitting to those who have no experience in institutional work to differentiate between administrative segregation and punitive segregation . . . It may be said that [administrative] segregation is also punitive segregation in its effect, but its intent is protection of the inmate and the institution rather than punishment of the individual. It is essential that inmates understand their new status and the purpose behind it.

---

* Pp. 263–64; 266–68; 271–72; 304–06; 315–21. From *The Prison: Studies in Institutional Organization and Change*, edited by Donald R. Cressey. Copyright © 1961 by Holt, Rinehart and Winston, Inc. Reprinted by permission of Holt, Rinehart and Winston, Inc.

Whatever distinctions may officially be made, and whatever the distinctions made by administrators of the prisons studied, the inmates understood only that they were being punished. Neither of the units provided the facilities for recreation, education, religion, work, supervision, or counseling which standards prescribe for "administrative segregation." Yet both units also compromised absolute conditions of punishment in view of the length of time for which men were confined. Reading, writing, smoking were permitted, within limits. Thus, unit confinement was, in fact, punishment. However, when confinement was prolonged over many months and into years, it became a way of life rather than just a special experience of punishment.

Authoritarian Qualities

As a way of life, the incorrigible unit displays some of the characteristics of authoritarian social systems in an extreme degree. One of these characteristics is the use of force. This does not mean that the inmates were systematically flogged or physically tortured. The force used is not the dynamic energy of the whip: it is the static power of tool-proof steel cells. The inflexible restraint of a square of steel is a directly-felt physical experience. As time turns the thumbscrew of that square down closer on the mind, the pain may express itself in a physical sensation. When, as often happens, the isolated inmate beats his own head and hands against the walls, the bloody results cannot be easily distinguished from brutality.

A second characteristic of authoritarian systems is regimentation and depersonalization, both of which mark the incorrigible unit. Life goes on in absolutely unchanging routines. The guard pads by the cells with clocklike regularity, and all but the most elementary physical processes are ordered in complete detail. Unlike life in some fantastically "ideal" authoritarian state, however, regimentation does not take the form of a variety of disciplined behaviors. Its form is the removal of alternatives for behavior. There is no type of work or social activity which will enable the prisoner to create an experiential product and give expression to his own individuality. Only thought and a small selection of carefully screened reading matter are available to give a man a vehicle for achievement or the development of personality. Absolute conformity is the only type of behavior that gains official approval, and such approval can be expressed only by a promise, stated or implied, that deprivations will be reduced at some distant future time. The system of government is geared to compel a vegetable-like level of existence.

An additional characteristic of the incorrigible unit is the ever present eye of authority. Advertisements in the trade magazines of penology have featured an invention which smacks of fiction and fantasy—a television device that produces, on a central control panel, a picture of the activities in every cell. An identical device and the psychology of those on whom it was turned provide a central theme in George Orwell's imaginative story of an absolute dictatorship. In neither of the incorrigible units studied was absolutism equipped with such a technical convenience. In its place, there were rules which required the guard to look into each individual cell at frequent intervals. The constant presence of repressive authority was a dominant fact in the experience of the men.

An equally important characteristic is the unresponsiveness of the governing authority. Guards in the incorrigible units are only slightly less bound by regimentation and regulations than the men they watch. It is not within the guard's discretion to answer the requests of the men, and the rules of his post prohibit him from approaching the front of the cells close enough that he can be seized. Few requests made by inmates could be granted under such circumstances, but even those that were possible to grant gain little response. The units are detached from the communication and the habit patterns of the main prison to essentially the same degree that they are segregated physically. Requests for writing paper, interviews, medicine, or a new light bulb often fail to enter into the communication channels of the larger prison, and hence bring no response. Factors of social and physical distance, convenience, and security combine to lower the degree of responsiveness to men in the units even below that applying to men in the prison yard.

A final authoritarian characteristic of the units is uncertainty and indefiniteness. However personally responsible the men of the units may be for the situation in which they are placed, their future is removed from their effective control. Particularly in the case of Central Prison, the period of men's confinement in the unit depended on the will of persons on whom they had no influence and was decided on the basis of factors which they did not understand. . . .

Other Extremes

There is a small body of literature available on the individual and social behaviors which appear in the type of extreme authoritarian situation represented by incorrigible units. This material is drawn primarily from observations of Nazi concentration camps. An article by Theodore Abel supports the basic assumption of the present study, namely that the nature of the governing process, at least in extreme cases, determines basic social relationships in the group governed:

> One of the more interesting observations is the fact that in every one of the more than two hundred large concentration camps, identical patterns of reaction developed among inmates in spite of the virtual absence of contact between them as well as the heterogeneity of their populations....

The Nazi concentration camps included a number of intellectuals in their populations, and that fact has produced some sociological study of inmate behavior by inmates themselves. Bruno Bettelheim's reports on the behavior of leaders, the processes of adjustment, the brutalization of social relationships, mass fantasy, and regressive phenomena are perhaps the most extensive of these. Curt Bondy, another ex-inmate, has written on the spread of rumor, emotional epidemics, and the drive for dominance resulting from calculated degradation. Bondy admits to an approval of the indeterminate sentence in his earlier days as a criminologist. His conclusion after experience in the camp was that the indefinite sentence, like all forms of uncertainty, exercises a "depraving effect on the personality of the internees."

The dominant characteristics of the incorrigible units studied were expressed in the presence of force, authority, regimentation, and uncertainty in the relations of the subjects to the governing officials. These, plus the factor of isolation, gave the units a number of qualities in common with concentration camps; both types of institution represent extreme instances of an authoritarian system of social control....

Certain general conclusions may be drawn from study of the most extreme authoritarian situations in prisons, and these conclusions seem to apply to the culture of entire prisons as well. In cases where men are governed with repression, restriction, and regimentation, both the social system and the belief system seem to become extremely rigid. Neither ambiguity nor nonconformity can be tolerated by the social group. The social structure is sharply defined as a rigid hierarchy. The belief system is equally rigid and dogmatic. It is protected from criticism by a withdrawal of communication processes, in a kind of informal system of censorship against hostile ideas, from those who do not conform to the group belief.

When this authoritarian situation becomes uncertain and ill-defined, the hostility and aggression of the group become extreme. It appears that rigidity of belief and social structure are fiercely defended as a means of providing the sense of certainty and emotional security which is missing in the formal situation. Men are only slowly admitted into the fellowship of the group, and leadership falls to those who prove their strength in relation to the dominant power governing the men. Yet such proof of strength is not active rebellion. One proves himself by adjusting to the situation on the best possible terms and draining off the hostility of the group by verbalizations which give satisfaction. The authoritarian situation produces a group which feels that it is made up of men who are select, especially important, and better than others who have not suffered the same trials. The leader exemplifies this conception and gives it expression. When any person behaves in a way that challenges the group's conception of itself, his action is defined as betrayal. Because the leader is the figure who mediates between the group and power, and is consequently extended a greater freedom of action, his position is unstable. He is expected to manipulate power, but he is rejected if his manipulations are not satisfying.

The belief system of incorrigible groups is conservative and conventional. The thinking is moralistic rather than pragmatic, probably because a function of the belief system is to provide self-justification to a group that is being condemned. The belief system is not tempered by practical considerations or the need successfully to seek physical objectives. A sense of rightness and justification can be achieved in a psychologically intolerable situation if the men believe that others are more evil than they are. They seize every scrap of evidence suggesting that those responsible for their confinement were, and are, motivated by a desire to persecute them for personal gain. In the environment in which they are placed, justice is represented by power and force. As they come to the conviction that justice is with them, they are prepared to exercise force in the defense of what they believe to be right.

These aspects in the social life of incorrigible units may offer insights into the occasional eruptions of collective violence in such units, and in prisons generally. The sequence leading to violence may take the following course. Men are placed in a rigid and repressive situation in which power is the dominant element, and their society becomes an adjustment to power. Power is formally identified with justice and right, so that the men respect both inmates and officials who exercise it. At the same time, the men use highly idealized conventional values to erect a belief system that characterizes them as a select and persecuted minority. As a consequence of formal isolation and informal censorship of criticism, nothing challenges this belief system, and it becomes a theoretical basis for revolt. In a stable situation, both the belief system and the social system are relatively satisfying means of adjustment—the group has a conservative rather than a revolutionary foundation. However, in an arbitrary and undefined situation, an extreme amount of hostility is created, and it serves to defend and reaffirm both the social system based on power and the belief system. If an unstable and aggressive individual rises to power or to a position of leadership on the wave of that hostility, the group is ready for open rebellion.

There seems to be a close relationship between maximal external constraint and the internalized values which complete the system of social control in incorrigible units. The extreme authoritarian system does not lead to the complete personal demoralization which might logically be expected. In a majority of individuals, the counterpart of authoritarian controls appears to be a rigid, moral idealism and a compulsive conformity. Such behavior patterns protect and justify the individual's personality in the face of hostile forces. Neither the idealism nor the conformity seem to be useful devices for adjusting to the demands of the broader society. Thus, the over-all impact of the incorrigible unit in penal practice probably is one that intensifies tendencies to criminal attitudes and behavior.

B. Making "Law": Regulations

1. SETTING POLICY

Connecticut Department of Correction, Policy Directive on Discipline Procedures

Goals and Purposes of Discipline

The dictionary defines discipline as training that corrects, molds, or perfects the mental faculties or moral character of a person. Most people conform to acceptable behavior standards willingly and without external constraints. However, individuals whose conduct is unacceptable must be controlled by outside pressures. Inmates, as a result of undisciplined, unacceptable behavior, have been placed in a correctional institution where they must learn to conform to acceptable behavior standards.

In a correctional setting, disciplining assumes even greater importance for two reasons. First, incarcerating large numbers of relatively young people around the clock for long periods of time in compact and close quarters tends to exaggerate reactions and at the same time makes misconduct even more disruptive. Thus, rule violation is more serious than in the outside world. Second, discipline is important because learning self control is one of the central goals of the correctional process. While this long term objective cannot be clearly separated from the necessity of maintaining immediate control and order within the institution, the general purpose of discipline is directed toward the development of patterns of behavior which will be of help to the inmate in his future adjustment in the free community.

In the Connecticut Department of Correction, each Superintendent or Warden shall be responsible to the Commissioner for the discipline of inmates confined to the institution for which he is responsible. All inmates shall adhere to the orders and discipline of the daily life and routine of the institution, shall carry out all instructions given them by the institutional authorities and they shall conform to the rules and regulations prescribed for the government of inmates in the correctional institutions of Connecticut.

Preventive Discipline

Preventive discipline consists of effective initial orientation and continuing group and individual instruction with a view to obviating the necessity of taking punitive action. These corrective techniques should be employed when trivial deviations occur due to ignorance or lack of understanding or when resulting from carelessness or faulty habits. The expression of genuine interest in the conduct of an inmate may show the subject how to avoid future errors.

Training Programs

The goals and purposes of discipline and preventive discipline, terms used, and the procedures outlined in this directive should be incorporated into the staff training program.

Reporting Infractions

When an officer witnesses or has knowledge of an act by an inmate which is in violation of the rules and regulations or good order, and if the infraction cannot be properly handled by the observing officer, he will take the action necessary to bring the inmate before the supervising officer on duty. If the supervising officer is not able to properly dispose of the infraction, the report of infraction will be processed as provided in the section below.

The supervising officer may, in his discretion, place the inmate in detention where he will remain for action by the Disciplinary Committee. The inmate should be placed in detention if not doing so would present a danger to himself or any other inmate or staff person, or would be detrimental to the welfare of the institution. A report should be made by the witnessing or reporting officer following each significant corrective consultation with an inmate. This report should go through appropriate channels, be presented to the supervising captain, and finally placed in the inmate's file.

Disciplinary Committee

Each institution shall have a Disciplinary Committee. In the institutions where staff size will permit, the committee will be comprised of a Supervising Captain, a Lieutenant, a member of the Classification Committee, and a Counselor or a member of the Medical Staff. In the remaining institutions, the committee will be comprised of the Warden or designated representative, one supervising officer and a number of the treatment staff where possible or a line officer. A line correctional officer is to be included on every board, rotating same after several weeks so that many officers will be exposed to board activity. The Disciplinary Committee may invite other institution staff into the committee meeting for consultation as needed for specific cases.

Disciplinary Report

A Disciplinary Report (Form COR-2A, Rev. 7/71) will be prepared and processed as outlined below:

Section I—Self explanatory.

Section II—

A. Nature and time of *offense*—obtain from codification of charges which appears on back of page 1 of COR-2A.

B. Reporting officer's name and time of *report*.

C. Delivery of charges and officer's signature.

D. Officer's statement of charges—upon completion of the above, the officer will deliver page 3 to the inmate and will ascertain that the inmate understands the charge. If the inmate cannot read, the officer will read the charge to him.

E. *Advocates*.
Each institution will, after soliciting volunteers from interested staff, name a *minimum* of three staff members, including both custodial and treatment personnel, to serve as advocates. They should be assigned to the same shift that the disciplinary board meets.
The names of the advocates are to be made known to all staff and inmates through appropriate publications.

When an officer gives an inmate his copy of the Disciplinary Report, he will ask the inmate if he desires to have an advocate for his disciplinary hearing. If the inmate declines advocate, the officer will indicate "advocate declined" on the reverse side of the original. If the inmate desires an advocate, he will advise the officer, in order of choice, which advocate he prefers and the officer will list the names in the priority ranking indicated.

Section III—

Investigation.

The Warden or Superintendent will investigate, or cause to be investigated, the charges against the inmate if deemed necessary. A full and complete report of the findings of the investigation should be set forth in Section III.

Upon receipt of the Disciplinary Report, the Supervising Captain or Supervising Officer responsible for disciplinary board action will assign an advocate to the case based on the preference of the inmate but consistent with the work schedule of the advocate. The advocate will discuss the Disciplinary Report with the inmate and gather whatever information necessary to represent the viewpoint of the inmate at the disciplinary hearing.

Section IV—

A member or delegate of the Disciplinary Committee will complete Section IV from the inmate's file.

Section V—

The Disciplinary Committee will meet as often as required to provide a speedy and fair trial on the charges that have been referred for hearing. Hearings are to be conducted in the following manner, within one week of the offense or at the next scheduled Disciplinary Board meeting.

The inmate is to be brought before the committee and the charge and offense read to him.

The advocate will be present at the disciplinary hearing to make whatever representations he feels desirable in the interest of the inmate. However, if the inmate desires to plead guilty to the charge, the inmate must so state and may *not* plead guilty through the advocate.

If an advocate assigned to a given case becomes ill or otherwise is unable to be present for the disciplinary hearing, a substitute advocate will be provided for the hearing. However, the inmate may elect to continue the hearing to the next disciplinary hearing date so that the substitute advocate can familiarize himself with the case.

The inmate will be given an opportunity to state his case and to enter a plea of guilty or not guilty.

The inmate will be asked to give his version of the offense.

The inmate may be questioned by members of the committee.

The reporting officer, the officer who investigated the offense, and any other person having knowledge of the violation, may state the facts and circumstances of the violation.

The committee will make its findings and actions known to the inmate including any recommended loss of good time.

If necessary, in addition to entering the findings and actions on the Disciplinary Report, the Committee may also give a brief explanation on the back of pages 1 and 2 as to why that action was taken for the benefit of the reviewers.

(See Section below for information on the Disciplinary Alternatives available to the committee.)

Superintendents and Wardens act as approving authorities and may approve, modify, return with comments for reconsideration, or disapprove of the institutional recommendation.

Section VI will be completed only on page 2 which is forwarded to the Central Office.

Disciplinary Alternatives

At any stage in the disciplinary proceedings where it becomes evident that the inmate is innocent or he is to be given a reprimand and warning, probation, or suspended sentence, and a judgment is made that no further processing of the Disciplinary Report is necessary, appropriate notations should be made on the report and it should be placed in the inmate's file for future reference. Such reports should be forwarded to the Central Office. All disciplinary cases handled should be reported in the "Weekly Disciplinary Report" (Form COR-2 10/68).

If the inmate is found guilty, the Disciplinary Committee shall take such action as may be appropriate on an individual basis, as follows:

A. Reprimand, probation, suspended sentence;
B. Loss of any other privileges (movie, canteen, etc.) as the committee feels justifiable including extra duty assignments during leisure hours;
C. Loss of visiting privileges or restriction of mail privileges for such period as the committee feels justifiable;
D. Place in punitive segregation;
E. Place in maximum punitive segregation;
F. Recommend loss of an amount of good time or jail time credit as the committee may feel is justified in each case;
G. Recommend reassignment;
H. Monetary fine, under following conditions:
   1. The money is deducted from State-paid wages only. Monies from families, friends or any other source cannot be used to pay fines.
   2. The deductions from State-paid wages to inmates cannot exceed 40% of his daily wage. For example, an inmate earning 25¢ per day can have only 10¢ per day deducted until his fine is paid; if he earns 74¢ per day, 29¢ per day can be deducted; if he earns $1.48 per day, 59¢ can be deducted.
   3. All monies collected from fines must be deposited in the institution's Inmate Welfare Fund.
   4. Monies from State wages which have been put in a banking account cannot be utilized to pay fines.
   5. An inmate can pay a fine in its entirety from accrued State wages.
   6. When an inmate is transferred from the institution in which he has incurred a fine, be it parole, another institution or program, any balance owed shall be cancelled and cannot be reinstituted in the event he is transferred back to the original institution.

The Disciplinary Committee should take into account the seriousness of the offense and the period of time the inmate may be in a confinement status when making its recommendation for the forfeiture of good time.

Transfers

(A) If an inmate is undergoing disciplinary treatment and a transfer to another institution is indicated, every effort should be made to complete the disciplinary action prior to the transfer.

(B) If it becomes necessary to transfer an inmate to another institution, who is awaiting action by the Disciplinary Committee, the committee hearing should be held at the sending institution prior to transfer.

The only exception to this would be in extremely unusual circumstances such as strikes or disturbances involving many inmates where the situation dictates immediate transfer before the Disciplinary Committee has time to act. In cases such as this, the Disciplinary Committee of the receiving institution may hold the hearing. However, the sending institution should complete the "Charges" and "Report of Investigation" sections of the Disciplinary Report for the receiving institution and, if possible, an investigating officer or officers from the sending institution should personally go to the receiving institution to present the information at the hearing. Full and complete information should be furnished to the receiving institution.

(C) If it becomes necessary to transfer an inmate to another institution, who is undergoing disciplinary action, and the sending institution feels this disciplinary action should continue at the receiving institution, the following actions should be taken:

1. If page 2 of the Disciplinary Report (Form COR-2A Ref. 7/71) has already been forwarded to the Central Office, the sending institution should attach to the inmate file an extra copy of the Disciplinary Report if available, or a complete memorandum outlining the infraction for the information of the Disciplinary Committee at the receiving institution.

2. If page 2 of the original Disciplinary Report has not been forwarded to the Central Office, both pages 1 and 2 should be completed through Section IV and attached to the inmate file for the information of the Disciplinary Committee at the receiving institution. A Disciplinary Committee hearing must be held before additional disciplinary measures may be taken at the receiving institution. If additional disciplinary measures are taken, this action should be endorsed on the Disciplinary Report furnished by the sending institution or a new Disciplinary Report should be prepared based on the information provided by the sending institution.

Types of Segregation

Administrative Detention

Inmates may be placed in administrative detention for any of the following reasons:
(A) Awaiting Disciplinary Committee action;
(B) For investigation;
(C) Pending trial for a crime committed in the institution;
(D) Awaiting approval from Central Office to continue an inmate in administrative segregation.

Administrative Segregation

Inmates may be placed in administrative segregation for any of the following reasons:

(A) For protection of self or others or for the welfare of the institution community;
(B) At the inmate's own request;
(C) Inmates who after punitive treatment still cannot reasonably and safely be returned to the regular inmate population.

Inmates in administrative segregation will be frequently reviewed by the Warden or his delegate(s) for possible release from this status.

Maximum Punitive Segregation

Inmates may be placed in maximum punitive segregation by the Warden or Superintendent upon the recommendation of the Disciplinary Committee for a maximum of eight (8) consecutive days, all such sentences to be indeterminate. The actual time is to be dependent on the inmate's attitude and behavior. Successive commitments will be made only with the approval of the Commissioner's Office. In maximum punitive segregation, no privileges other than those specified in this policy statement will be permitted.

Punitive Segregation

Inmates may be placed in punitive segregation by the Warden or Superintendent upon recommendation of the Disciplinary Committee for a maximum of thirty days, the actual time to be dependent on the inmate's behavior and attitude. In punitive segregation the granting of privileges is the responsibility of the Warden and the Disciplinary Committee.

Segregation Facilities

A. Cells—Facilities

All inmates in punitive and administrative segregation cells will be provided with lights, toilet facilities and running water for drinking and other sanitary purposes. Running water facilities should have their ultimate control outside the cell. In the event it is impossible to provide these facilities in the cell, the occupant will be furnished an adequate supply of drinking water by other means and given access to toilet facilities upon his request, so long as it is reasonable.

B. Cells—Design

Cells should meet the criteria set forth in the *Manual of Correctional Standards* and the *Handbook of Correctional Institution Design and Construction*. The location of punitive segregation cells should be remote from the general population.

Segregation Procedures

A. Diet

Inmates in administrative segregation and detention should receive the same diet as the regular population. Inmates in punitive or maximum punitive segregation should receive a minimum of 2,300 calories for males and 2,000 for females. They should receive the regular diet except for:

1. No additional seasoning.
2. No liquid other than water and a glass of fruit juice or an equivalent drink high in Vitamin C in the morning.
3. No dessert.
4. No bread or butter.

B. Mail

Inmates in maximum punitive segregation will not be permitted mail privileges. Inmates in punitive segregation will receive mail privileges at the discretion of the Warden or Superintendent. Inmates in administrative segregation will receive regular mail privileges. In any case, letters to and from attorneys or courts will be permitted.

C. Clothing and Bedding

The standard issue of clothing for male inmates in both types of punitive segregation, administrative segregation and administrative detention should consist of either of the following: undershorts and coveralls; or tee-shirt, undershorts, and a pair of regulation trousers (knee-length trousers may be substituted). Socks will be provided as footwear. Change of clothing shall be effected at least once per week.

The standard issue of clothing for female inmates in punitive segregation shall consist of night clothes and shower slides.

The issue in administrative segregation will be regular state daytime issue unless otherwise ordered.

In punitive segregation, bedding shall consist of adequate blankets and a mattress that will be provided for a minimum of eight continuous hours per night.

In administrative segregation, bedding shall consist of adequate linens, blankets, and a mattress.

D. Comfort Items

Certain comfort items should be afforded inmates in punitive segregation. These items should consist of a toothbrush, toothpaste, and small bars of soap as a minimum.

E. Showers and Shaves

Each inmate in segregation should be required to shower a minimum of two times per week. Male inmates should be permitted to shave at least two times per week.

F. Haircuts

Male inmates in segregation shall receive haircuts pursuant to grooming policy.

If it is necessary to restrict any privilege or item listed in this section, the deviations should be noted on the "Daily Inspection of Segregation Record."

Release from Segregation

Disciplinary Committee members will frequently review the case of each inmate in punitive segregation, determine the inmate's attitude, and return the inmate to the regular population when, in the committee's opinion, he may reasonably be expected to adequately adjust and conform to the rules and regulations. Segregation for punishment should always be for the shortest period of time that will accomplish the desired results of favorable adjustment. No inmate is to be held in maximum punitive segregation in excess of eight (8) consecutive days without permission of the Commissioner.

Visits to Segregation

Prisoners in segregation shall be visited a minimum of:

(A) Every two hours by a correctional officer.

(B) Daily by officer-in-charge of each shift.

(C) Every twenty-four hours by a representative of the medical staff. Where full-time medical staff is available, these visits should be made by the physician, but where the physician is not available every day, by a medic and every four days by a physician.

(D) As frequently as necessary by Disciplinary Committee members to assure inmate's welfare is properly provided for and to determine the time and method of release.

(E) Chaplains and Treatment staff may provide spiritual guidance and counsel to inmates in segregation.

Daily Segregation Inspection Log

A "Daily Segregation Inspection Log" will be maintained on each individual person housed in any area away from the general population.

All persons performing the regular visits to segregation as required in section above, including the Chaplain and Treatment staff, will sign this form at the time of each inspection. By signing this form, the officer is certifying that he checked all inmates located in the housing area. Instructions on the form should be followed.

The officers-in-charge of the day and evening shift, representatives of the Medical staff, and Disciplinary Committee members, will sign the forms whenever they make visits to an inmate as required. Full and complete remarks are to be made in the following situations:

(A) *Custodial Department—Officer-in-Charge*
1. Unusual occurrence in inmate's behavior.
2. It becomes necessary to notify the medical department.
3. It becomes necessary to restrict any privilege or remove any clothing, bedding or comfort items for the inmate's own protection or to prevent destruction.
4. If inmate refuses food.
5. Cell changes.
6. Release to population.
7. To further explain a notation made under "Physical Appearance" or "Attitude".

(B) *Medical Department*
1. Inmate is ordered removed from segregation and where removed to.
2. Diet is ordered changed.
3. Changes of clothing, bedding, or other restrictions are ordered.
4. Complaints received and treatment given.
5. Any unusual circumstances.

(C) *Disciplinary Committee*
1. At each review of the case.
2. On release from segregation.

When the inmate is released, all copies of the Log (Form COR-55) and the completed copy of the fact sheet (Form COR-54) should be sent to the Warden's Office for his examination and for filing.

NOTES

Note 1.

CONNECTICUT DEPARTMENT OF CORRECTION, POLICY DIRECTIVE ON USE OF FORCE

July 11, 1969

The use of force on inmates will be allowed only in the following situations:

1. When an inmate is attempting to escape jurisdiction.
2. When an inmate is physically resisting the authority of the Department of Correction.
3. When an inmate has first attempted to strike or has attacked an employee or other person, including other inmates.

Only such force as is necessary to contain or stop the actions of an inmate in the above situations will be authorized.

The employee of the Department will be held responsible when it is found that excessive force was used in such situations.

The Use of Force Report shall be completed in all cases where any force, regardless of degree, is used on an inmate of a correctional center or institution. With regard to distribution of said report, correctional centers shall make two (2) copies. The original shall be forwarded to Deputy Commissioner Manson and a copy to the Warden or supervisor of the correctional center. All other institutions shall complete (2) copies, with the original forwarded to Deputy Commissioner Eubanks and the copies to the warden or supervisor of the institution.

INSTITUTIONAL MISCONDUCT AND RESPONSES THERETO

Use-of-Force Report
Connecticut Department of Correction

4/14/69
Cor 38

I. IDENTIFICATION

Institution	Inmate Name: Last	First	Middle Initial	Inmate No.

II. OFFICER'S REPORT

A. Circumstances Leading to Use of Force: *Time   Mo.   Day   Yr. of Incident*

_____
_____
_____
_____

B. *Type and Extent of Forceful Action: Include Equipment Employed, if any:*

_____
_____
_____
_____

REPORTING OFFICER'S SIGNATURE _____

Was inmate or inmates injured ☐ Yes ☐ No.

C. *Name(s) of Witness(es) to Incident:*

  1. Officer(s) _____   Inmate(s) _____
     _____   _____
     _____   _____

D. Officer who Applied Force: _____   Signature _____
                                                Time   Mo.   Day   Yr. of Report

  1. Was Correctional Officer injured ☐ Yes ☐ No.
     (See Use of Force Medical Report for detailed Information.)

E. Shift Supervisor at Time of Incident: Signature _____

III. INMATE DATA

Mo. Day & Yr. of Admission	Work Detail	Specific Assignment	Custody Classification	Living Quarters	Age

IV. WARDEN'S INVESTIGATION

A. Findings: _____
_____
_____
_____

B. Conducted By: _____   TITLE _____   Date _____

C. Warden's Comments: _____

Note 2.

FEDERAL BUREAU OF PRISONS, POLICY STATEMENT ON INMATE DISCIPLINE

It is the policy of the Bureau of Prisons that inmates shall be subjected to disciplinary action only ... in accordance with basic requirements listed below. This is in recognition that disciplinary sanction is but one factor in correctional treatment and control and that, as applied to an inmate who has misbehaved, the sole objective is his future voluntary acceptance of certain limitations which are being imposed upon him.

Essential Principles

(1) Disciplinary action shall be taken only at such times and in such measures and degree as is necessary to regulate an inmate's behavior within acceptable limits.
(2) Inmate behavior must be controlled in a completely impersonal, impartial and consistent manner.
(3) Disciplinary action shall not be capricious nor in the nature of retaliation or revenge.
(4) Program assignment and changes are made to achieve treatment goals not as punishment or reward.
(5) Corporal punishment of any kind is strictly prohibited.
(6) The initiation of disciplinary measures against any inmate is the province only of the Adjustment Committee (a subcommittee of the classification committee) or, for minor infractions, as may be defined and delegated by the head of the institution and controlled by the Adjustment Committee.
(7) Disciplinary action shall be taken as soon after the occurence of misconduct as circumstances permit.
(8) Inmate case records shall reflect misconducts, dispositions and shall include interpretive and evaluative statements regarding them.

2. INFORMING THE INMATE

Rules and Regulations of The Connecticut State Prison (1830)*

Duties of the Convicts

1] Every convict shall be industrious, submissive, and obedient, and shall labor diligently and in silence.

2] No convict shall secrete, hide, or carry about his person, any instrument or thing with intent to make his escape.

3] No convict shall write or receive a letter to or from any person whatsoever, nor have intercourse with persons without the prison, except by leave of the warden.

4] No convict shall burn, waste, injure, or destroy any raw materials or article of public property, nor deface or injure the prison building.

5] Convicts shall always conduct themselves toward the officers with deference and respect; and cleanliness in their person, dress, and bedding, is required. When they go to their meals or labor, they shall proceed in regular order and in silence, marching in the lock step.

6] No convict shall converse with another prisoner, or leave his work without permission of an officer. He shall not speak to, or look at visitors, nor leave the hospital when ordered there, nor shall he make any unnecessary noise in his labor, or do any thing either in the shops or cells, which is subversive of the good order of the institution.

* Reprinted in G. deBeaumont and A. de Tocqueville, *On the Penitentiary System in the United States and Its Application in France* 166–67 (1964).

South Dakota Prison Rules and Regulations

Following is a list of rules and regulations of the institution. These apply generally, and to specific places and activities. They are clear and concise. Study them carefully. Only by strict adherence to each and every rule can you do your time the most easily and earn the maximum time off your sentence in accordance with the law. Keep in mind that the inmate who does not cooperate will pay by loss of good time and | or disciplinary action on the part of the prison authorities in a court established for that purpose. You can never win by violating the rules. Remember too, if you violate a law of the State while in prison, you can be indicted and tried in the local court. Of course, the violation of any State law is also a violation of the prison rules.

It would be well to remember that under the law, men confined in the prisons of the State are clothed, fed, housed, and given what medical attention is deemed necessary only. All other concessions are privileges granted by the Officials of the institution and the Board of Charities and Corrections, and these will only be granted if your conduct warrants them. Therefore, it will pay you dividends to live within the rules.

If you fail to ask questions about the rules and regulations during your stay in quarantine or soon after transfer to one of the cell halls where you will serve your time, it will be understood by the Officials that you have a full knowledge of the rules.

The rules, regulations, and instructions listed under each of the following subjects and assignments must be strictly observed. Failure to do so will be considered a violation. Those who violate rules can expect one or more of the following disciplinary actions: Reprimand, denial of privileges, segregation, isolation, and loss of good time and | or prosecution.

On the whole, most of the inmates who are received here want to do their time in the best possible way, and gain their release either by parole or discharge, as soon as possible. Some, because of an erroneous concept, feel that the rules and regulations do not apply to them. They attempt to lay out their own way of operation by agitating, creating unrest and inciting trouble. This is to inform you that if at any time a disturbance or mass assault is started, and you desire to avoid trouble and keep your record good, you are to go to your cell or cell hall, or any other place when directed by an officer of the institution, in an orderly manner and remain there. Those who take part in, or encourage conduct of this type will find themselves dealt with severely. You should make sure that you avoid any contact that might indicate your connection with the trouble in any way.

We will not compromise or accede to any demands made through any group pressure or duress. If you have a complaint, you will be given an individual hearing. Groups or committees will not be recognized at any time.

Any inmate who participates in a riot or mass disturbance, can and will be subject to prosecution and sentence in the State Penitentiary. Such sentence imposed will run consecutive to the sentence being served.

Title I

General Conduct

1. Orders will be obeyed promptly and proper respect shown for all Officers at all times. Officers shall be addressed and answered by the use of the word "Sir" or "Mister" (Yes Sir; No Sir; Mr. Jones). This shall be done in a gentlemanly manner.
2. Inmates shall not gaze at, or in any way signal or give recognition to any person visiting or passing through the institution. No contact between inmates and outsiders shall be permitted at any time except by permission of the Deputy Warden's Office.
3. Caps shall be removed upon entering cell halls and administration building and when appearing before an administrative Officer.
4. Any inmate or group that shall carelessly or willfully damage State property or that of another person shall be required to make restitution for same.
5. Inmates shall keep their person, clothing and quarters in a clean and neat condition at all times.
6. If repairs are needed on your shoes or clothing notify the Officer in charge, do not wear them beyond repair. Altering of clothing will not be permitted.
7. When outside of cell, shirts shall be tucked into pants. Your shirt sleeves may be rolled no

higher than the elbows. Shirts may be removed during the summer months; weather permitting, during the recreation period, but when put back on shall be buttoned and tucked into trousers. The Deputy Warden will make the determination as to when the weather is suitable for the removal of shirts.

8. Long sleeved sweat shirts or underwear will not be worn under a short sleeved shirt.

9. Unless specifically excepted, all inmates shall rise promptly on given signal each morning, wash, dress, make up bed neatly as instructed and be in readiness to march out. If you wish to remain in your cell you will still be expected to rise and dress and be prepared to leave your cell in the event you are called. You may then lay on your bunk with shoes removed and you may use your blanket as a cover if desired. At the signal to leave your cell you will open the cell door, step out in line and march to proper destination. Inmates who are sick or otherwise disabled, shall report the fact to the cell hall Officer. On sheet day, bed may be left unmade for the purpose of airing until noon time. Fold blankets neatly and place at head of bunk. Beds must be made by afternoon ring down.

10. Inmates shall retire at night promptly upon signal. You will be expected to be undressed and in your bed by 9:00 P.M.

11. When leaving or going to your cell you will not stop on the way to visit, talk, or make contact with any other inmate. Go directly to your cell and remain there, immediately closing the door behind you. If in a two man cell you will enter your cell and remain in your cell while waiting the return of your cell partner. Stand in front of your cell door and step in or out as the case may be, maintaining cell formation when leaving cell at all times.

12. Gambling or games of chance are prohibited. Any article used in violation hereof shall be confiscated. Dice, homemade or otherwise, are contraband items.

13. Transfer of property between inmates is prohibited except upon specific approval of the Warden. Any items transferred without the permission of the Warden will be confiscated.

14. Unnecessary or loud noises are prohibited. Inmates will refrain from the use of profane, vulgar or obscene language.

15. Smoking will be permitted in the cell houses, dormitories and yard and such other places as may be designated by the Warden. Cigar and cigarette butts shall be deposited in receptacles provided and not thrown on floor and stairs, or in the yard.

16. There will be no talking from cell to cell.

17. You or your quarters are subject to search at any time.

18. You may write to the Warden, Deputy Warden, Assistant Deputy Wardens, Captains, Record Clerk or Business Administrator and deposit same in a box provided for that purpose in the cell house, using the prescribed "kite" form sheet obtainable in the cell hall.

19. Sealed letters may be written to the following: Governor, Attorney General, Executive Director of the Board of Pardons and Paroles, and Executive Director of the Board of Charities and Corrections.

20. All money taken upon entrance and all received from any source after arrival shall be retained in an account for each inmate. Possession of money at any time is a violation of rules and all found in your possession will be confiscated and the violator punished.

21. Fighting is prohibited.

22. You will be held responsible for contraband articles found in your cell or on your person. On occupying a cell make certain that no contraband articles are contained in it. If in doubt, contact the cell hall Officer to make certain that items are not contraband.

23. Tattooing or altering of any tattoos is strictly prohibited. Possession of materials to be used for the purpose of tattooing is sufficient evidence of intent to tattoo.

24. When desiring an interview on personal problems, outside orders or extra letters, you will submit a request to the Deputy's or Reformatory Office.

25. Requests to see the doctor, Dentist or Chaplain shall be made through your cell house Officer. . . .

Title III

Cell

1. You are housed in a cell that is equipped with toilet, lavatory and all facilities necessary for your comfort. You are expected to keep this equipment in good condition. Under no circumstances is refuse such as large pieces of paper, fruit peelings, rags, or debris which may cause clogging, to be thrown into the toilet. Water is of great value and is not to be wasted. Leaking faucets and defective toilets are to be reported to your cell house keeper, and toilets flushed only when necessary. Turn out cell lights when not in use or when leaving cell.

2. Keep your cell walls, bars, bed, sink, toilet, floor, and furnishings in the cleanest and most orderly condition possible.

3. When signal is given for count, immediately stand in front of your cell with a hand on the bars, remaining in this position until the all clear signal is given.
4. When in cell, the door shall be closed and locked unless exception be authorized by the Officer in charge.
5. When lying on bunk, shoes must be removed and the head shall be visible from the gallery.
6. Do not open or close cell doors by jerking or with violence. Operate it with a firm but gentle motion.
7. Locking devices will not be tampered with. To do so is considered a serious violation.

Permitted Per Cell

8. Broom (short handle).
9. Mop and dust rags (must be kept clean).
10. Thread (small quantity).
11. Toilet paper (1 roll per toilet).

Not Permitted

12. More than prescribed furniture.
13. More than designated number of blankets.
14. Mattresses other than issued by the institution.
15. To scratch or mark the walls and furnishings in your cell.
16. Obstruction or darkening of light bulb or having larger or smaller than is issued by the cell hall Officer.
17. Throwing refuse or cigarette butts on the floor, the gallery or the cell hall floor. It must be deposited in the waste receptacles or places provided for that purpose.
18. Spitting on the floor, either in your cell or elsewhere in the institution.
19. Sweeping dirt or dust or refuse from your cell out on to the galleries.
20. To accumulate medicine even though originally authorized. Empty bottles and medicine no longer needed are to be given to the cell hall Officer for disposal.
21. Accumulation of old newspapers, magazines and other literature. They may, however, be forwarded to another inmate providing they have been marked thereon with the cell number of the man to whom you wish them sent and that they are placed in the box provided for the exchange of such items. They are not to be transferred from one cell hall to another. There need be no limit to the number of inmates who may have a newspaper or magazine, provided, they are kept in reasonably good condition.
22. Singing, whistling, dancing, shouting or talking from one cell to another, booing and all forms of boisterous conduct.
23. Pasting or nailing pictures or other articles on the wall or cabinets.
24. Entering cell other than your own.
25. Depositing any article in cell other than your own.
26. State issue bath towel in cell.

Permitted Per Man

27. Blankets as allotted.
28. Bed sheets, 2.
29. Belt, State issue only.
30. Caps, State issue 1, Baseball, personal 1, Black or navy blue only.
31. Cards, 2 regular decks and 2 pinochle decks.
32. Can Opener, 1.
33. Checker board, 1.
34. Checkers, 2 sets.
35. Chair, 1.
36. Chess, 2 sets.
37. Cigarettes, 13 packs.
38. Chewing tobacco, 1, State issue.
39. Church card (1 denomination).
40. Cribbage board, 1.
41. Cup, shaving, 1.
42. Comb, 1.
43. Denim jacket, 2 (1 lined, 1 unlined, numbered).
44. Dominoes, 2 sets.
45. Ear phones, 1 set per man (must be worn when in use and not to be tinkered with. When not in use radio equipment is to be disconnected and hung or placed so as to prevent damage.)
46. Glass, 1.
47. Handkerchiefs, 6 personal.
48. Handkerchiefs, (State issue as allotted).
49. Hair brush, 1.
50. Mattress, 1.
51. Magazines (not to accumulate).
52. Matches, 3 packages.
53. Nail clippers, 1.
54. Newspapers (not to accumulate).
55. Pants, State issue as allotted and numbered.
56. Pillow, 1.
57. Pillow slip, 1.
58. Pen and pencil set, 1.
59. Pipes, 3.
60. Pictures (family, framed and on shelf).
61. Paper, 1 ream.

62. Razors, double edge safety type 1, Electric 1, registered.
63. Rule book.
64. Razor Blades, 10.
65. Shirts, State issue as allotted and numbered.
66. Soap, commissary, 3 bars.
67. Soap, State issue, 1 bar.
68. Shoes, State issue 2 pairs, personal 2 pairs, baseball 1 pair, tennis 1 pair.
69. Socks, State issue as allotted.
70. Slippers, 1 pair.
71. Sweat shirts, white, 2 numbered.
72. Tooth paste or powder, 2 tubes or 2 tins.
73. Towels, hand, State issue as allotted.
74. Towels, hand, 6 personal, numbered, colored.
75. Underwear, State issue as allotted, numbered.
76. Underwear, personal, numbered, white only, 6 tops, 6 bottoms.
77. Watch, 1 registered.
78. Wash cloths, 6 colored only, numbered.

Title IV

Marching Formations

1. When your line is being formed, quietly take your place. At the order to fall in, form a double column line, cease all activity and stand at attention. When ordered to forward march, step forward maintaining your paired formation, keep at arms length behind the man ahead of you. You are to walk with eyes to the front and remain paired with the inmate beside you when marching or when line has stopped. Remain in line until the order is given to fall out.
2. When in formation, no talking, whistling, or smoking is permitted. There shall be no crowding, pushing or shoving and hands shall be out of pockets and at the sides. Stepping to one side to pass other inmates or allowing others to pass you is forbidden.

Title V

Dining Room

1. At ring down for meals, inmates shall march in a single file line to the lobby of the mess hall, remaining quite so that men at serving tables can hear the requests of inmates as they are served. Each man shall take a tray and a full complement of the silverware provided for that meal.
2. Your hands and face must be clean, hair combed, and your clothes as clean as possible at all meals.
3. Take only the amount that you feel you can eat. You may indicate small, medium or large portion when served, with the exception of meats and desserts.
4. After receiving food, you will proceed to the dining hall and take the next seat in line or as directed by an officer. Do not skip a seat.
5. Beverages will be served at the table and seconds will be passed on beverages and bread only. Cups are not to be passed across aisle or from end to end for the purpose of receiving extra servings.
6. Silence need not be observed during the meal. Loud or excessive talking or turning around in seat will not be tolerated.
7. Inmates will leave the dining room when the bell indicates the end of the meal. The row or rows indicated by an Officer will rise and face the aisle awaiting your turn to march out. While standing you will remain between the tables. Do not crowd into the aisle. After you are standing all talking is to cease. Men seated in other rows will remain seated until the second signal is given when you will march out in the same order as the first group.
8. On leaving, silverware will be placed in the proper receptacles which are located near the entrance to the dining hall, everyone must make certain that he checks in one of each type of utensil provided for the meal.
9. It is strictly against the rules to carry food or furnishings out of the dining room except unpeeled fruits or ice cream. Any other exceptions will be posted on the bulletin board in the dining room.

Not Permitted

10. Reaching into food containers. You must accept what is given you by the waiter, however, if waiter does serve you a larger portion of food than you can eat, have the waiter remove a portion of the food item in question from your tray at the time of serving.
11. Asking for or receiving any special part of the food on the steam table.
12. Taking more food than you can eat. Edibles are not to be left on your tray.
13. Smoking.
14. Loud talking or boisterous behavior.
15. Arguing with waiters at any time.
16. SILVERWARE, SALT AND PEPPER SHAKERS, CUPS OR ANY OTHER FURNISHINGS shall not be taken from the dining room nor in any way damaged.
17. Throwing food or beverage on the floor....

Title VIII

Correspondence, Paper, Books and Packages

1. Upon admission to the institution, and before permission is given to receive and to send mail, you will be required to sign an order authorizing the Warden or his representative to open and read all of your mail, and to withhold such as he may deem improper.
2. Inmates shall not send out or receive any packages, letters, papers, or other reading matter except through the mail department.
3. Letters written by an inmate shall be confined to a permissible list established at the time of entrance which generally includes immediate family and two (2) designated friends. For exceptional reasons changes may be granted by the Deputy Warden or Assistant Deputy Warden. Special letters may be granted by the Deputy Warden or Assistant Deputy Warden in exceptional cases for urgent business matters and in reference to paroles, pardons or legal questions.
4. You will not write notes to other inmates nor carry the same from one inmate to another.
5. Inmates are not permitted to correspond with inmates of other institutions except by special permission.
6. All letters must be written on regulation paper furnished by the institution unless special permission is given by the Warden to the contrary. All paper or envelopes not used by an inmate shall be returned to the Officer in charge, and under no circumstances shall such paper be given by one inmate to another. Letters are not to be typewritten except by special permission.
7. Inmates shall write their own letters and sign their names in full, together with their registration number. If for any reason an inmate is unable to write, special permission by the Officer in Charge may be obtained for another inmate to write for him, in which case the letter shall designate "Written by No. _____."
8. Inmates shall confine their correspondence to matters concerning themselves without mentioning the affairs or names of other inmates. Letters containing statements derogatory to any Officer or other person connected with the institution, or letters questioning matters of regulations or policies of the institution, or details of claimed grievances, will subject the entire letter to rejection.
9. Inmates shall arrange their correspondence so as to keep the same within the allowed number and not make continual requests for extra letters.
10. Rules governing library books will be found in front of the library catalogue.
11. Books, magazines and papers will not be delivered unless they come directly from the publisher thereof, and are on the approved magazine list which is posted on the bulletin board.
12. Packages from friends or relatives are not allowed except that double edge or electric razors, white T-shirts, shorts and socks are permissible.
13. Money received will be credited to the inmate's account, and he will be so notified.
14. Should it be desired to transfer a paper or magazine which you have finished, scratch your number, and mark the number of the cell to which you wish the paper or periodical sent, and drop in the exchange box. No paper, book, or magazine will be taken to or from the cell hall.
15. No magazine that has been defaced by writing, drawing or otherwise shall be eligible for exchange.
16. Discussion of subjects that are controversial are not permitted.
17. You will not be permitted to write to former inmates of this or any other penal institution, including your relatives, except by permission.
18. Do not mention another inmate's name or number or anything pertaining to another inmate.
19. Do not use vulgar, profane or malicious expressions.
20. Never write untruths or false accusations.
21. Because of the type of institution and the men who live within its boundaries, the officials reserve the right to reject any merchandise, packages, messages or mail, either incoming or outgoing.
22. All letters, incoming and outgoing must be written in the English language. Any exceptions to this rule must have the approval of the Warden.

Title IX

Visits

1. Inmates are allowed visits from relatives who are on their correspondence list. These relatives may visit for One-half hour every Fourteen (14) days. Visiting hours are from 8:30 A.M. to 3:30 P.M. week days; and from 8:00 A.M. to 3:00 P.M. on Saturdays.
2. No visits on Sundays or Holidays.

3. Take the seat in the visiting room to which you are directed. Do not pass things through the bars, embrace, or shake hands with the visitor.

4. Speak the English language when having a visit.

5. Refrain from discussing other inmates or their problems, the institution, State Government, law enforcement or any of the officials of these agencies.

6. Suggestive or profane language or loud arguments will result in termination of the visit. Remember others may be present including women and children.

7. An inmate may accumulate visiting time, but the maximum amount to be accumulated will not exceed a total of six (6) hours in any one year. Any exception to this visiting time must have the approval of the Warden. The rate of accumulated visiting time shall be based on the rate of one-half (½) hour each two (2) weeks of un-used visiting time. The maximum time which may be accumulated is six (6) hours. The maximum amount of accumulated visiting which can be used in any one years time is six (6) hours. When the six (6) hours time has been used during a year, the remainder of the years visits will be at the usual rate of one-half (½) hour each two weeks (14) days.

8. The maximum amount of time of any one visit, shall not exceed one and one-half (1½) hours, and no more than three (3) hours in any one day.

Title X

Commissary

1. One of the privileges granted is that of trading at the Commissary. Here you may purchase tobacco, candy, foodstuffs and other permitted articles.

2. You will be permitted to spend a maximum of $7.00 per week at the Commissary.

3. In lining up for Commissary, have your store order with you and properly filled out.

4. On certain articles you will be required to turn in used or empty containers before additional purchase of the same item will be allowed.

5. All items are sold at prices as near or below current retail prices as possible. Profits are placed in the Commissary Fund which pays for Chapel supplies, athletic equipment, library books, school and educational supplies, motion pictures and other items directly connected with inmate recreation and rehabilitation, both mental and physical. The Commissary is not the concession of any employee or Official. Profits are used only to pay for such items listed or in behalf of the mentioned activities.

6. Go to the Commissary only and when designated by your Officer.

7. Having more than one week's supply of commissary purchased items, edibles and tobaccos in your cell, trading or trafficking or holding property for others is not allowed or having others "hold personal property for you."

8. Forging or any irregularity in connection with commissary order will result in disciplinary action.

9. Commissary items in your possession not purchased by you may be declared contraband and confiscated.

Title XI

Shops and Assignments

1. Inmates assigned to shops or other assignments shall report to the Officer or foreman in charge and carry out instructions.

2. Work shall be performed in accordance with such rules as may be posted or as instructed and in accordance with orders given by the person in charge. Assignments to work will be made by the Deputy Warden. Wages, if any, will be determined by the Warden. A change from regular clothing may be approved by the Warden for any department, shop or assignment.

3. Inmates shall not enter a work assignment, other than the one to which they have been regularly assigned except on a duly executed pass in writing, signed by the proper Officer, and shall immediately present such pass to the Officer or Foreman in charge, transact his business promptly, have his pass countersigned, and return to his proper station immediately. An inmate shall not leave a work assignment without permission, and then only upon a written pass as herein before outlined, or in the company of an Officer.

4. Cooperation and application to the task at hand are demanded at all times on all assignments.

5. Wages will, as far as possible, be based upon importance of the job and skill required, together with interest and application shown by the individual.

6. Care in avoiding accidents shall have constant attention and any danger observed shall be reported to the person in charge immediately.

7. Care shall be constantly given to all machines, tools and property at any given assignment and neglect in this respect will call for appropriate punishment. Inmates will be

held responsible for a proper accounting of all tools and materials placed in their hands on any assignment.

8. In case of injury or illness, the fact shall be reported to the Officer in charge at once.

9. Inmates working on assignments may contact the Warden, Deputy Warden or Captain on personal matters if urgent only. All other matters shall be taken up on a written request.

10. A refusal to work or carry out an order promptly shall constitute a serious violation.

11. An employee is responsible for the operation of all assignments. He will help to lay out your work if you are in doubt as to the procedures. The employee in charge of all assignments will pick qualified inmate leaders to help the less skilled men, and to teach the various vocations, etc.

12. Men having been temporarily laid in from work because of a shortage of material, break down etc., will be sent for by the Officer in charge of shop or work assignment when the man is needed or wanted. He will not be coming out of his cell at the work ring down unless he has been notified to do so. Regular lay-ins will not be leaving their cells for any purpose at the work line ring down.

13. Under shop and other work assignments a progress report is submitted by the Officer in charge of each inmate assigned to him. This report will be submitted each week and will include the following: Personal appearance, Behavior, Attitude, Industry, Reliability, Progress.

This report becomes a part of your permanent record here at the institution and is made available to the Board of Pardons and Paroles, as well as to the sentencing Judge if requested, if and when he may be giving consideration to you for a suspended sentence. A good record can do you no harm and is highly desirable. . . .

Title XV

Recreation

1. Yard recreation will vary both as to time and place, due to weather conditions and program involved, but attempts will be made to have recreation on all days that are at all possible. You will follow the Officer's instructions in all instances.

2. You will be required to confine your various activities to certain areas.

3. If you go down to recreation you will not be permitted to return to your cell or dormitory except in emergency cases and then only with permission from the Officer in charge.

4. Abuse of recreation or athletic equipment will not be tolerated, and can result in disciplinary action.

Title XVI

Punishment and Loss of Privileges

1. Any inmate violating these rules and regulations will be subject to punishment. The penalty will be at the direction of the Warden or the Deputy Warden. All violations will be recorded on the inmate's record and this record will be available to the Board of Pardons and Parole. This record will have an effect on your pardon or parole, and may even result in the loss of good time.

2. Punishment may range from a reprimand to isolation. Things that are in the nature of privileges can and will be taken away for violation of these rules and the more serious your offense or the repetition of offenses will evoke more stringent punishment.

3. Officials of this institution are not responsible for your being here, but are required to keep you. To make it possible for you to live a reasonable and well ordered life with the rest of the population, rules are laid down. These rules will be enforced impartially in so far as it is humanly possible. You will find it to your advantage to avoid infraction of these rules. REMEMBER YOU ARE BUILDING YOUR OWN RECORD WHILE HERE. Keep it clean and shorten your time. In the long run you will find that compliance with the rules pays off—a defiant attitude—smart aleck deportment—will get you exactly what you are looking for. . . .

Connecticut Department of Correction, Inmate Handbook of Regulations (1970)

This handbook has been prepared for your information and guidance. If you use it frequently and wisely, it may prove very helpful to you during your stay with the DEPARTMENT OF CORRECTION.

A court of this state has remanded you to the care and custody of the Commissioner of Correction who is charged with the overall responsibility for all institutions, facilities, and programs within the Department. In turn, he will endeavor to see that these institutions and programs are geared to helping you return yourself to your community as a self-sustaining, self-respecting member.

Let us put first things first! The many services and programs which are available to you must be used by you. Many staff members and specialists counsel you and assist you in making wise choices, but you must take full responsibility for your own progress, work, education, and social growth. The Department will provide the opportunities; you must provide the willingness and effort to take advantage of them. . . .

Transfers of money, personal property, or clothing between inmates is not allowed.

Clothing

Adequate and suitable clothing will be issued to you. These clothes are State property, and must not be altered or mutilated in any way. You may not trade or sell clothing issued to you, and all clothing must be worn as directed. You may not have unauthorized clothing in your possession, and upon leaving the Institution must return all issued clothing.

Personal Property and Contraband

Items not issued by the State are considered personal property. No one shall have such items in his possession unless they are authorized or registered in his name. Such approved items shall be produced upon demand.

Any article not issued to you, or through commissary, or otherwise authorized for your possession, is considered contraband. Possession of contraband may lead to disciplinary action.

Care of Quarters and Personal Cleanliness

Living quarters must be kept neat and clean. Clothing should be stored neatly and beds made up when not in use. Personal letters and other unofficial articles, in reasonable quantities, shall be carefully stored. Additions or alterations to quarters are not allowed without proper permission.

Personal cleanliness is a safeguard against disease and a courtesy to others. Take full advantage of your institution's hygienic facilities.

Visits

Visiting privileges are available to all authorized members of your immediate family. Other visitors must be approved in writing by the appropriate staff member.

Visiting hours, visiting days, length of visits and number of visits, vary from institution to institution. . . .

Commissary

A store, or commissary, is maintained for you at all facilities of the Department. You will be informed as to what the store hours are, what is on sale, the prices, and the method by which you pay from your account for the items selected. Any commissary profits go to the Inmate Welfare Fund. . . .

Food

Through a carefully planned twenty-eight day menu operated throughout all institutional facilities of the Department, you will be provided with healthful, well-balanced meals, featuring a variety of foods. You may not exchange food with others. Take only the amount you can eat. Waste of food may result in disciplinary action.

Discipline

Good order is the foundation and keystone of a good society. Without rules and regulations, groups of people would find it extremely difficult to live together and maintain any semblance of proper respect for the property and privileges of others. The specific rules of the Department of Correction are based on fair, reasonable standards of behavior, and frequently are the result of years of experience in our system. The rules and regulations are systematically reviewed and approved by the State Council of Correction. Adherence to published rules eases the way through your stay, indicates a willingness to accept the laws of the State, and may be a factor in determining your parole eligibility.

Violation of rules and regulations may result in disciplinary action. Violators are reported to the proper officials, after which they are turned over to a Disciplinary Committee for such action as it may take. Punishment may range from a reprimand to segregation, from loss of privileges, to loss of good-time, or in the case of an unsentenced inmate, loss of "jail time" credit.

Note: The Frequency of Institutional Misconduct

VERNON FOX

Analysis of Prison Disciplinary Problems*

The persons in solitary confinement are those who have been found guilty of violation of the prison rules. It is this group and this relationship, then, to which many people refer as "disciplinary procedures." It is this relationship which is the ultimate manifestation of the general levels and quality of the custodial relationship. Consequently, any analysis of prison disciplinary problems must include an anlaysis of the specific violations of institutional rules and regulations and how they are handled.

Rules and regulations are drawn by custody in order to set standards of behavior and to define to inmates and to officers the kinds of behavior for which an officer should arrest and report an inmate. The rules are fairly standard in most prisons, although some rule books are thicker than others. The offenses most frequently reported in custodial summary courts are:

Fighting
Gambling
Homosexual Practices
Stealing (from cells, kitchen, library, work assignments, and "high-jacking")
Smuggling in contraband or possession of contraband
Skating (being in an unauthorized area without a pass)
Disobedience
Refusal to work
Making alcoholic beverages (spud-juice, cane-buck, raisin-jack, etc.)
Bartering with other inmates without permission
Escapes, planned or attempted escapes

These offenses appear fairly frequently in all institutions. The types of offenses committed by each individual may be psychiatrically diagnosed according to the area in which the individual finds conformity most difficulty. The specific nature of the offenses committed by each individual is partially dependent upon the personality structure of the offender. There is a tendency for each offender, outside prisons and within prisons, to repeat the same type of offenses, some to a greater extent than others.

The motivation for misconduct appears to lie within the personality, since the sanctions in society and prison culture from guards, administration, and inmate colleagues, are to "get along" with a minimum of friction. Further, a relatively small percentage of the inmate body has a record of misconduct reports. The average prison in 1957 had approximately one inmate in punishment status per one hundred prisoners.

Approximately three percent of the inmate population is involved in misconduct reports in any given year. This means that there is a high incidence of repeating, an indication which is confirmed by the observation of experienced prison personnel and an examination of the records of inmates who have accumulated misconduct reports.

The three most common major disciplinary problems in prison are gambling, sex, and fighting. The fighting frequently results from the gambling and sex problems. Inability to pay a gambling debt or disagreement as to the quality and quantity of the debt may lead to fighting, as may also the "eternal triangle" in a homosexual relationship. Consequently, many prison people hold that gambling, fighting, and sex are the three major disciplinary problems.

* Reprinted by special permission of the *Journal of Criminal Law, Criminology and Police Science.* Copyright © 1958 by Northwestern University School of Law, Vol. 49, No. 4, p. 324.

C. Applying "Law": The Misconduct Hearing

FRANK B. COCHRAN

The Formal Discipline System in Connecticut Penal Institutions 8–8; 24–36 (1969)*

What follows is the author's impressions of formal discipline systems in two Connecticut penal institutions: The State Prison Maximum Security Division at Somers, Connecticut, and the State Reformatory at Cheshire. For the most part, the raw material used comes from observations of the disciplinary hearings themselves. I attended approximately 120 such hearings at Cheshire and 35 at Somers. Both institutions were visited regularly in the months of February through April 1969. These direct observations are supplemented by various prison records. Because I agreed to keep specific records confidential, no single inmate will be discussed in any detail....

Both of these institutions are currently undergoing rapid change, primarily as a result of the introduction of a unified State Department of Corrections. Because of this rapid change, the conclusions drawn here are limited by the time at which the observations were made....

This study of prison discipline systems took place in two Connecticut institutions: The Connecticut State Prison (Somers), Maximum Security Division, and the Connecticut State Reformatory (Cheshire). Somers is the maximum security division of the State Prison. The State Prison receives all prisoners serving sentences of more than one year except those under the age of twenty-one, most of whom are sent to Cheshire. There is also a minimum security division of the State Prison, the Osborn Division....

The Somers division contains about 800 inmates. Since it has several cell blocks, considerable subdividing of the inmate population is possible. There is, for example, one cell block which is "maximum security" for troublemakers, one which is explicitly for homosexuals, and so on. It is a modern building and has a double chain link fence rather than a masonry wall. It has a modern and quite elaborate security system. There is a school, and, for those not eligible or those who prefer something else, there are various jobs of differing social status and relevance to potential jobs on the outside.

Cheshire is nominally a "reformatory," but if that connotes a school for minors who are disciplinary problems the term is somewhat misleading. It is better viewed as a prison for young offenders, and most of the inmates have substantial records of criminal convictions before they are sentenced to the Reformatory. It has a program in most respects similar to that of Somers. The major physical differences are age and size. Cheshire is an old stone building; about 300 of its 380 inmates live in one cell block. The larger cell block is about 100 yards long and consists of 8 galleries, two sets each four tiers high, constructed back to back in the center of the building. The other block is considerably pleasanter and, like the Osborn division of the State Prison, is used as an incentive for good behavior....

Cheshire

At Cheshire, hearings are heard on disciplinary reports every Monday, Wednesday and Friday immediately following the noon meal. The Assistant Superintendent of the Reformatory presides (his position is analogous to that of the Deputy Warden at Somers), and the other members include his assistant, the shift captain on duty, the Director of Industries, and the Educational Director. The average length of time a hearing takes is slightly less than three minutes, though there is considerable variation, dependent primarily on the complexity of the facts of the case and the

---

* Reprinted with permission of the author.

possibility of some specialized disposition. Until April 21, the inmate had no formal notice of the charge against him, and unless the reporting guard had told him, he might not even have known that there was a charge against him until immediately before the hearings, when he would have been called out of the noon meal. Since April 21 (which was after the last hearings observed), the inmate has been served with a copy of part of the report at the same time it is filed with the Assistant Superintendent's office. His copy contains the general charge but not the officer's statement of fact.

The hearings are held in the office of the Shift Captain, a room about thirty feet square with two desks and several chairs in it. It is also an anteroom for the Assistant Superintendent's office. Lining the walls are several file cabinets, an assignment board showing the work assignments of each inmate, and several clipboards with various documents on them hung up on hooks.

> Example A. The inmate, who has been waiting in a line outside the hearing room, is ushered in. He has been waiting there with the others on report for about twenty minutes. Five inmates have come in and gone out before him during this twenty minute period. Present are the members of the committee (minus the Director of Industries who is in Hartford attending a meeting), an officer who is in charge of records, the records clerk, and the officer in charge of the segregation cells, which are entered through this office. The officer who gave the report is not present.
>
> As the inmate is ushered in, the officer nearest the door asks him to state his name and number to the Board. He looks around the room (probably notices me and doesn't know who I am, and no explanation is proffered), walks slowly to the center of the room directly in front of the Captain's desk facing all members of the Committee. In a low but level tone of voice, he gives his last name and his prison number. "_____," Officer _____ gives you a report for talking in the corridor near the shower room." Captain D., the Assistant Superintendent's Assistant, reads the report, giving the date and time of the offense, and the officer's statement as to what he saw. According to this statement, the officer warned the inmate several times to stop talking, but the inmate continued to do so. The inmate listens, head cocked to one side, and says nothing. Captain D. finishes reading the statement which consists of 3 or 4 brief, explanatory sentences.
>
> "Well, how about it," asks the Assistant Superintendent after the inmate says nothing in response to the report. The inmate replies that he wanted to yell at the guard, who had been riding him, but managed to restrain himself to the point of mumbling beneath his breath. He answers readily enough, but it is clear he will not volunteer any more than seems necessary. "The officer says he warned you repeatedly to stop talking." "Once, he only told me once." "He says he warned you several times. Not once but *repeatedly*," says the Shift Captain. As the inmate seems not to have any further reply to make, the Assistant Superintendent directs him to go back out to the hall, while the committee decides what to do with him. Several of them seem to know him well. The Assistant Superintendent calls him by his first name. The Assistant Superintendent says that he has been under arrest constantly since last October (meaning that he has had no recreation privileges since then). Furthermore, he has recently been granted a parole. The Assistant Superintendent thinks he needs recreation, even though this would normally be an offense punished by a brief period under arrest. There is a brief discussion, but all agree, either silently or aloud, that this is a minor offense. "Lets give him a break;" there is no dissent. The inmate is returned to the room, and once more stands before the desk. The Assistant Superintendent assumes a worried, sincere stance. "Did you do anything wrong, John?" The inmate simply says, "Yes." He is given a brief lecture, reciting his record of many trivial offenses, and concluding "You haven't tried hard enough to avoid them." The "break" turns out to be that he will have to miss two movies, but will have his recreation privileges returned. He is impassive; "Thank you, sir," and walks out without looking at the other people present in the room. The hearing lasted seven minutes.

There was no serious dispute over the facts in this case, the only issue being the number of times the guard warned him before deciding to issue the report. This type of dispute is common, and as the example indicates, is normally not explicitly resolved by the committee. The only substantial question is one of disposition. . . .

> Example B. The setting is the same, but neither the Director of Industries nor the Shift Captain is present. This is the first hearing of the day. The inmate enters, gives name and number, stands, hands clasped behind back, feet apart, looking from one face to another as if to decide upon an at-

tractive tactic. The charge is contraband. A search of the inmate's cell turned up a copy of a novel which had never been authorized and which did not come from the Library. The rule on books is rather complicated; essentially any book which is approved may be given to the inmate by an authorized visitor. A notation is made that this has occurred, and after reading it, the inmate may either donate it to the Reformatory Library or keep it, but he may not lend it to another inmate. The book in question had never been authorized for anyone, this inmate or any other. The officer's report continues that when the book was found, the inmate threatened to tell the committee the officer had given it to him, and to write the Commissioner of Corrections about it. The inmate readily admits that he didn't get the book from the officer, and says the "threat" was really just "fooling around." The Assistant Superintendent gives him a brief lecture about not fooling around in this way, and particularly not to use a threat to write the Commissioner as a jest. Contraband is always considered a serious charge. Without sending the inmate out of the room or consulting the other members present, the sentence of 30 days arrest is pronounced. As the inmate turns to go, the Education Director asks who gave him the book. He hesitates and says he doesn't want to get anyone in trouble. He is prodded with a promise that no action will be taken against the other inmate, the committee just wants to know who it was. The inmate names a name, and exits. The hearing lasted three minutes.

There was no claim by anyone that the book in question was in any sense inappropriate. It might have been approved had it come in through the regular channel. Nor was it claimed that this particular piece of contraband posed a danger either to institutional order or to the individual's rehabilitation. Again, there is no dispute as to the facts....

Example C. Three hearings, all the same day, considered Fighting charges. Each was heard separately, though two stemmed from the same fight. Boy One is a white boy. He says the background of the fight is that the other boy accused him of stealing his soap. Both work in the powerhouse boiling room, a prestigious job, and among other privileges are allowed to take showers daily. This boy was taken to detention, which consists of segregation cells with a different name for those who have not yet had the charges against them formally heard. These are used only for what the guard considers a serious offense. While there, One wrote a letter to the Assistant Superintendent explaining the fight as he saw it, which explanation by no means exonerated himself, but did state he was not the soap thief. He has been a trustee, and if he goes into segregation for any reason, he would lose his job. For that reason, and because all see the fight as "foolishness," he is given 30 days arrest. Boy Two is black. He too has been in detention, and he too is a trustee working in the powerhouse. His soap had been stolen several times, and he was attempting to find out who had done it. He had asked all of the boys on the shift after the one which he worked, and One protested at the accusation. As Two was showing the other boy his locker, One hit him. "The fight was stupid, but it was unavoidable." Both One and Two receive a stern lecture on their responsibilities as trustees, threatening loss of that status if there should be any repetition. Both solemnly promise that there would be none, with seeming sincerity. As best as one can tell, the trustee status does mean something to them, and that rather than the threat of segregation is their assumed motivation. Both are given 30 days arrest. Boy Three was involved in a different fight, this one at his place of work, the cabinet shop. The officer's statement does not give any explanation of who started the fight or why, probably because he didn't see the start. He does praise Three for breaking off immediately when the officer shouted at them. Nonetheless, both were hustled off to detention. Three, at the hearing, protests several times that he had not even defended himself from the other inmate's assault. There is no direct evidence in the officer's report which bears upon this contention. It is quite evident from his tone of voice that Three was thoroughly miserable in detention, and the committee notes that his motivation to prevent a recurrence appeared good. Unlike One and Two, both of whose emotions seemed well under control, Three was preventing an emotional scene with considerable difficulty. Three is sent back to the segregation unit for an indefinite period. (The boy with whom Three was fighting was also sent to segregation.) Each hearing took 4 minutes....

Example D. The inmate was reported for Dilatoriness and Disobedience of Orders. From the Officer's statement, it appears that he had refused to move down the gallery from his cell rapidly enough to suit the Officer, and that this report had come about after a series of warnings. The inmate's explanation is that he was still putting his clothes on when the incident occurred, but he has to be prodded before it is proffered. The Shift Captain, adopting a very gentle attitude, points out this is the third report the inmate has had in one month, and asks what is wrong. The inmate seems more dejected yet, his head sinks lower and no reply is forthcoming. Is it that his parole was turned down yesterday? Still no response. He is given 16 days arrest, exactly the "normal" penalty. The hearing took 3 minutes....

Somers

At Somers, the hearings are held in the morning on Tuesdays and Fridays. The membership of the Disciplinary Board was considerably more fluid than it was at Cheshire, and there was a distinct difference of style depending upon whether the Deputy Warden or the Shift Captain was in charge. The most obvious manner in which this can be shown is the average amount of time spent in hearings. While the overall average was about 9 minutes, the average when the Shift Captain was in charge was 3 minutes 49 seconds, and the average when the Deputy Warden was in charge was 18 minutes 33 seconds.

> Example E. The hearing room is a virtually empty 20 foot by 30 foot rectangle. It contains only a chair bolted to the floor facing a table around which the Board members sit.
> The Board includes the Deputy Warden, a Captain, and a Correctional Counselor. The inmate is brought in by about five guards who arrange themselves in informal poses around the door. The charge is possession of contraband; it is read by the Deputy. On a routine shakedown of the inmate's cell, two pictures of the female organist of the Protestant Chapel were discovered. As they didn't contain a stamp affixed by the censor permitting the pictures in, they are considered contraband. The inmate is black, the woman is white. Whether this is of any relevance is not known. The inmate pleads not guilty, and is asked matter of factly for an explanation. The explanation is that the pictures were sent to him by mail, recently, by the organist. When the letter was returned because she was not on his approved correspondence list, she sent them to his girl friend who included them with a letter and some pictures of her own. The organist had been friendly with the inmate, and the inmate says after they had been friendly for a while he had asked for the pictures and she sent them in. When they arrived, he was called in by his Correctional Counselor (not the one present on the Board), who sent the pictures back. The members of the Board are agreed that pictures do sometimes pass through censorship without receiving the stamp. The inmate continues; he has helped the organist on with her coat on occasion. This brings up another possible explanation of the incident which the Deputy had received from the chaplain earlier that morning: that the pictures had been brought for the chaplain and had fallen out of the pocket of her coat as the inmate helped her on with it. The inmate says this isn't so. He does admit helping the woman on with her coat, and is reminded he shouldn't do that. The Correctional Counselor who supposedly sent the pictures back enters the room, having been summoned for the purpose. He sits at another chair behind the table, with the Board, and for all practical purposes becomes a member of the Board. The inmate repeats his story without changing it. The Counselor doesn't recall the incident. When pressed on his relationship with the organist, the inmate says he likes her because she is one of the few people he has met while in prison who will help if they can. He says their conversation was chiefly about music. A check with the records department by telephone shows that three requests to have her put on the approved correspondence list had been sent to her for approval, but had not been returned. It appears that she would not have been eligible for inclusion both because he already was corresponding with another female not a member of his family, and because of her position in the prison. The Correctional Counselor did not know of the latter when he preliminarily approved the request. The prisoner and guards leave the room. A check with the inmate's complete file reveals that he has had several previous reports, one of them for attempting to smuggle out a letter to a girl with whom he was not authorized to correspond. There is nothing otherwise extraordinary about the record, and the Board is in agreement that the only issue is simply one of fact. It further agrees that no satisfactory answer to several key questions has been presented. They decide to hold the report without disposition until a more thorough check can be made of the correspondence records and the principals other than the inmate can be interviewed again. The inmate is brought back in and informed that he will remain in lockup (without privilege to go to recreation) until such investigation is concluded and that some other disposition is possible then. The hearing lasted 24 minutes.

The hearing touched on virtually nothing but the facts of the case, and yet took up 24 minutes, making it the longest hearing observed. The facts were quite complicated, and became more so as the Board tried to probe more deeply, leaving the Board convinced they had not learned the truth. . . .

Example F. Before the inmate entered the hearing room, the Deputy Warden informed the Board that he is a transferred jail inmate. He is ushered in, sits down; he appears somewhat withdrawn. The charge is refusing to accept a job assignment. After being transferred from the state jail and being referred to the classification committee, he declined to go to his assigned job. He is asked, is this true? Yes, it is. He is sick and weak from 8 months in jail doing nothing. He is waiting for a chance to see the doctor for x-rays on his head and perhaps a special diet to make up for the considerable weight he has lost in jail. In response to further questioning by the Deputy Warden he says he wasn't asked for his preference regarding transfer, but was transferred directly from the segregation unit in his old jail (he had been in because of possession of narcotics in the jail). He has no desire to mix with other inmates at all. His sentence has about 2 months to go unless he loses good time (regular) which he has already accumulated. He is informed that inmates work in the prison, and that other programs are available to help him to be able to adjust to the "outside." Then he is sent out of the room. The Board discusses what the prison can do for him; all agree that his narcotics addiction will not change either there or anywhere else. A memo is made to give him a psychiatric interview. The Shift Captain expresses the opinion that segregation will not convince him to accept a job, and that putting him in the regular population might not be a good idea either. The others agree to this analysis without further discussion. The decision to agree with his desire to stay out of the general inmate population seems to be based primarily on concern for the particular inmate's welfare rather than for the stability of the prison, but the point is not discussed in detail. The result, since other options are not available, is a decision to keep him in a holding cell pending psychiatric evaluation. If, following that and without some "psychiatric justification," he continues to refuse work, he will be referred to the Commissioner of Corrections for a hearing on administrative segregation. He is brought back, informed of this decision (which he accepts with slight relief) and asked whether he has gone to recreation in the past. Yes, he did go to recreation but all he did was to talk with other inmates and watch TV. The hearing lasted 13 minutes.

* * *

Example G. The Board for this hearing consists of the Shift Captain, a different Captain, and a Correctional Counselor. The inmate is charged with disturbing the cell block. The officer's statement is that the block was in a considerable uproar on the night in question, much of it abuse directed at him personally (and racially, since he is black). The inmate is one of five charged with playing a prominent role in the disturbance. The inmate concedes that a disturbance took place on the evening in question, but says he was not taking part in it. This is in direct conflict with the officer's testimony that he observed the inmate shouting insults from close range. The inmate says no, he was sleeping in his cell at the time. The officer woke him up and marched him down to the isolation block (where he has been a day and a half) without telling him what the report was for. He is sent out briefly, while all agree with the Shift Captain's first response; the inmate is lying. He is brought back in, and the Shift Captain tells him he will be assigned to isolation indefinitely and will be assigned to a different cell block upon release. The hearing lasted 4 minutes.

D. Judicial Review of Prison Discipline Decisions: The "Hole," the Eighth, and the Fourteenth Amendments

1. THE "HOLE"

NOTES

Note 1.

LEONARD ORLAND

On Being Incarcerated*

As a Parole Board member charged with the obligation to decide when felons should be released from prison, I had an intense desire to understand how it feels to be incarcerated. At 3:00 p.m., on a blustery gray Friday in January, I had an opportunity to find out, when I boarded a dirty blue Connecticut Department of Correction transportation van with 18 of my University of Connecticut law students and, two hours later, arrived at the Haddam Jail to begin a weekend simulated prison experience.

During the next 48 hours, no one was beaten by a guard; no one was attacked by an inmate; everyone was adequately, if simply, fed and clothed. Yet everyone emerged from the experience deeply shaken. A month went by before I could bring myself to write about the incarceration. Even now, I am not sure I can convey to others what happened to us during that weekend. Were it not for the fact that I had transcribed a psychological debriefing session which the group underwent in jail on Sunday afternoon, I think the task would have been impossible.**

A central feature of the Haddam training program for correctional personnel is the simulation of the first 48 hours of an actual prison experience. At the outset, I was skeptical about the desirability of simulating a prison experience, viewing it as a pale imitation of the "real thing." I have since been persuaded that as a matter of theory as well as actual impact, the simulated experience resulted in a deeper and more meaningful experience than actual incarceration for the same period of time. . . .

The simulation process became quite real for me when, five minutes before my arrival in Haddam, one of the two uniformed guards on the correctional bus "reported" me (falsely) for creating a disturbance on the bus.

At Haddam, I was forcibly removed from the bus, and less than five minutes later, thrown, nude, into "the hole," a 4 x 8 steel box with no windows, a bare light bulb, a small peep hole (which only the guards could control and which was kept closed most of the time), a sink (occupied by three cockroaches), a toilet, and one steel "shelf" on which, if the guards so desired, a mattress could be placed for sleeping. The effect was much like being forced into a very small stalled elevator:

> I don't know who did the initial processing, but he scared the shit out of me. When he told me to move it, I moved it; when he told me to get those mattresses out of the hole, I moved them. My recollection is that it was about 2½ minutes from the time I walked in the front door to the time I was locked in the hole. My immediate response was all right, that's very interesting, here I am in the hole in the Haddam Jail, and then I thought, how do you get out of the hole? Sooner or later, I realized that I was going to spend the night here and that I'd better start getting adjusted." I ended up spending 18 consecutive hours in the hole, one of the most painful experiences of my life.

The initial experience of being thrown in the hole had great impact, not only on me, but on the entire group. As Jim, one student, put it:

> The whole situation became very real to me by the rapidity with which Leonard was rushed off the bus. By the time we got inside he was nowhere in sight and the only thing that we thought of was that he was already in the hole. I was one of the first ones to

---

* Connecticut Department of Correction, 1971.

** The quotations in this article are transcribed verbatim from this debriefing session. However, the liberty of changing student names to preserve anonymity has been taken.

come in the main door, and whoever was there pointed to a seat and said 'put your ass there,' and if he had said put it on the ceiling I would have. And he said strip, and I did strip and I think I took off everything in about three strokes.

I was in the hole from the time of our arrival at Haddam at 5:00 p.m. on Friday until noon on Saturday....

Ken, Greg, and I spent 18 hours in the hole; at least half the others spent at least an hour in that steel box.

Ken

I think the most important thing I learned was that when I was first thrown in, I thought that well, here I am in jail, and I didn't distinguish between the different levels in jail and being outside. There are two levels in my mind and they were being outside and being inside. The next morning I got my green slip and my hearing. Then, they put me in a different cell and they were going to take away my food. I couldn't have any books. Somebody said if you don't knock it off you go in the hole. I said, what's the difference? Well, I found out. You learn that there are a thousand different levels of freedom: Having a mattress and not having a mattress; having a blanket or not, having a pillow or not, toilet paper or not. All these things are just as important as our initial jump from freedom to going inside.

Greg

We were in there the longest. I guess it was the morning after we were put in when we were given a three page sheet to fill out, my first reaction was to fill everything out completely wrong and make jokes on it. I started doing that and about the second page I erased it and I figured that was going to keep me in there if they found out that some of the stuff was wrong, I started filling it out really straight. At first just talking wasn't too bad, then we started singing but the lights started pulsing and I had a hard time keeping my eyes off the light. I think if I were in there for much longer it would have really started to get to me. When I was going up for my hearing, I thought, I'm going to say anything that I want to say and they're not going to intimidate me. When they started talking to me and I realized there was a good chance I would go back to the hole if I didn't play along, I decided to play it a little more humble than I expected I would.

Len

You know, it's funny, when I came into the hole I didn't have toilet paper and I wasn't sure if I was going to get any and I didn't think it would make any difference if I asked for it or not, if I was going to get it I was going to get it, and if I wasn't and I started making contingency plans and I noticed there was an old paper bag. I was cursing in the hole. Cursing anybody whose name came to mind. And I really got some kicks out of it. Some satisfaction. And I think it was when I really started getting colder and colder and I really thought that they might really not give me a uniform or blanket that I stopped being a brave wise guy and knocked it off. At some point in time that is, I thought that I really might not get a blanket, and it was at that point and no sooner that I stopped cursing.

The second thing that was very important was that I carefully measured the length and width of the hole, and then when I got out I measured the length and the width of the cell by paces and they were exactly the same, but they were worlds apart and I was overwhelmed with how beautiful it is to be in a cell as opposed to being in the hole. The cell is really a wonderful place to be, wonderful in contrast to the hole. And the luxuries that were heaped upon me. I could see in front of me and I had a blanket and I had a mattress. All this incredible luxury.

Note 2.

BROOKS v. FLORIDA
389 U.S. 413 (1967)
Supreme Court of the United States

The disturbance in the prison occurred on May 27, 1965. The same day Brooks was ordered confined in a punishment cell for 35 days with two other prisoners also accused of the rioting. Brooks says the cell was 7 feet long and 6½ feet wide.... The parties agree that the punishment cell had no external window, that it contained no bed or other furnishings or facilities except a hole flush with the floor which served as a commode, and that during the first 14 days he lived in this cell Brooks' only contact with the outside was an unspecified number of interviews with the prison's investigating officer. It is also agreed that while so confined Brooks was fed a "restricted diet" consisting, according to the testimony of the investigating officer, of "peas and carrots in a soup form" three times daily.

Brooks' more detailed description of this concoction—"they fed us four ounces of soup three times a day and eight ounces of water"—was not controverted, nor was his testimony that he was stripped naked before being thrown into the cell. . . . For two weeks this man's home was a barren cage fitted only with a hole in one corner into which he and his cell mates could defecate. For two weeks he subsisted on a daily fare of 12 ounces of thin soup and eight ounces of water. For two full weeks he saw not one friendly face from outside the prison, but was completely under the control and domination of his jailers. . . .

The record in this case documents a shocking display of barbarism which should not escape the remedial action of this Court.

2. THE MEANING OF THE EIGHTH AMENDMENT

FURMAN V. GEORGIA
408 U.S. 238 (1972)
Supreme Court of the United States

Per Curiam.*

Petitioner in No. 69–5003 was convicted of murder in Georgia and was sentenced to death. . . . Petitioner in No. 69–5030 was convicted of rape in Georgia and was sentenced to death. . . . Petitioner in No. 69–5031 was convicted of rape in Texas and was sentenced to death. . . . Certiorari was granted limited to the following question: "Does the imposition and carrying out of the death penalty in [these cases] constitute cruel and unusual punishment in violation of the Eighth and Fourteenth Amendments?" 403 U.S. 952 (1971). The Court holds that the imposition and carrying out of the death penalty in these cases constitutes cruel and unusual punishment in violation of the Eighth and Fourteenth Amendments. The judgment in each case is therefore reversed insofar as it leaves undisturbed the death sentence imposed, and the cases are remanded for further proceedings.

So ordered.

* Mr. Justice Douglas, Mr. Justice Brennan, Mr. Justice Stewart, Mr. Justice White, and Mr. Justice Marshall filed separate opinions in support of the judgments. The Chief Justice, Mr. Justice Blackmun, Mr. Justice Powell, and Mr. Justice Rehnquist filed separate dissenting opinions.

Mr. JUSTICE BRENNAN, concurring.

The question presented in these cases is whether death is today a punishment for crime that is "cruel and unusual" and consequently, by virtue of the Eighth and Fourteenth Amendments, beyond the power of the State to inflict.

Almost a century ago, this Court observed that "[d]ifficulty would attend the effort to define with exactness the extent of the constitutional provision which provides that cruel and unusual punishments shall not be inflicted." *Wilkerson* v. *Utah,* 99 U.S. 130, 135–136 (1879). Less than 15 years ago, it was again noted that "[t]he exact scope of the constitutional phrase 'cruel and unusual' has not been detailed by this Court." *Trop* v. *Dulles,* 356 U.S. 86, 99 (1958). Those statements remain true today. The Cruel and Unusual Punishments Clause, like the other great clauses of the Constitution, is not susceptible of precise definition. Yet we know that the values and ideals it embodies are basic to our scheme of government. And we know also that the Clause imposes upon this Court the duty, when the issue is properly presented, to determine the constitutional validity of a challenged punishment, whatever that punishment may be. In these cases, "[t]hat issue confronts us, and the task of resolving it is inescapably ours." *Id.,* at 103.

I

We have very little evidence of the Framer's intent in including the Cruel and Unusual Punishments Clause among those restraints upon the new Government enumerated in the Bill of Rights. The absence of such a restraint from the body of the Constitution was alluded to, so far as we now know, in the debates of only two of the state ratifying conventions. In the Massachusetts convention, Mr. Holmes protested:

> What gives an additional glare of horror to these gloomy circumstances is the consideration, that Congress have to ascertain, point out, and determine, what kind of punishments shall be inflicted on persons convicted of crimes. They are nowhere restrained from inventing the most cruel and unheard-of punishments, and annexing them to crimes; and there is no constitutional check on them, but that *racks* and *gibbets* may be amongst the most mild instruments of their discipline. 2 J. Elliot's Debates 111 (2d ed. 1876).

Holmes' fear that Congress would have unlimited power to prescribe punishments for crimes was echoed by Patrick Henry at the Virginia convention:

> ... Congress, from their general powers, may fully go into business of human legislation. They may legislate, in criminal cases, from treason to the lowest offense—petty larceny. They may define crimes and prescribe punishments. In the definition of crimes, I trust they will be directed by what wise representative ought to be governed by. But when we come to punishments, no latitude ought to be left, nor dependence put on the virtue of representatives. What says our [Virginia] bill of rights?—'that excessive bail ought not to be required, nor excessive fines imposed, nor cruel and unusual punishments inflicted.' Are you not, therefore, now calling on those gentlemen who are to compose Congress, to ... define punishments without this control? Will they find sentiments there similar to this bill of rights? You let them loose; you do more—you depart from the genius of your country....
>
> In this business of legislation, your members of Congress will loose the restriction of not imposing excessive fines, demanding excessive bail, and inflicting cruel and unusual punishments. These are prohibited by your [Virginia] declaration of rights....

These two statements shed some light on what the Framers meant by "cruel and unusual punishments." Holmes referred to "the most cruel and unheard-of punishments," Henry to "tortures, or cruel and barbarous punishment." It does not follow, however, that the Framers were exclusively concerned with prohibiting torturous punishments. Holmes and Henry were objecting to the absence of a Bill of Rights, and they cited to support their objections the unrestrained legislative power to prescribe punishments for crimes. Certainly we may suppose that they invoked the specter of the most drastic punishments a legislature might devise.

In addition, it is quite clear that Holmes and Henry focused wholly upon the necessity to restrain the legislative power. Because they recognized "that Congress have to ascertain, point out, and determine, what kinds of punishments shall be inflicted on persons convicted of crimes," they insisted that Congress must be limited in its power to punish. Accordingly, they called for a "constitutonal check" that would ensure that "when we come to punishments, no latitude ought to be left, nor dependence put on the virtue of representatives."

The only further evidence of the Framers' intent appears from the debates in the First Congress on the adoption of the Bill of Rights. As the Court noted in *Weems* v. *United States*, 217 U.S. 349, 368 (1910), the Cruel and Unusual Punishments Clause "received very little debate." The extent of the discussion, by two opponents of the Clause in the House of Representatives, was this:

> Mr. Smith, of South Carolina, objected to the words 'nor cruel and unusual punishments;' the import of them being too indefinite.
>
> Mr. Livermore.—The [Eighth Amendment] seems to express a great deal of humanity, on which account I have no objection to it; but as it seems to have no meaning in it, I do not think it necessary.... No cruel and unusual punishment is to be inflicted; it is sometimes necessary to hang a man, villains often deserve whipping, and perhaps having their ears cut off; but are we in future to be prevented from inflicting these punishments because they are cruel? If a more lenient mode of correcting vice and deterring others from the commission of it could be invented, it would be very prudent in the Legislature to adopt it; but until we have some security that this will be done, we ought not to be restrained from making necessary laws by any declaration of this kind.
>
> The question was put on the [Eighth Amendment], and it was agreed to by a considerable majority." 1 Annals of Cong. 754 (1789).

Livermore thus agreed with Holmes and Henry that the Cruel and Unusual Punishments Clause imposed a limitation upon the legislative power to prescribe punishments. However, in contrast to Holmes and Henry, who were supporting the Clause, Livermore, opposing it, did not refer to punishments that were considered barbarous and torturous. Instead, he objected that the Clause might someday prevent the legislature from inflicting what were then quite common and, in his view, "necessary" punishment—death, whipping, and earcropping. The only inference to be drawn from Livermore's statement is that the "considerable majority" was prepared to run that risk. No member of the House rose to reply that the Clause was intended merely to prohibit torture.

Several conclusions thus emerge from the history of the adoption of the Clause. We know that the Framers' concern was directed specifically at the exercise of legislative power.

They included in the Bill of Rights a prohibition upon "cruel and unusual punishments" precisely because the legislature would otherwise have had the unfettered power to prescribe punishments for crimes. Yet we cannot now know exactly what the Framers thought "cruel and unusual punishments" were. Certainly they intended to ban torturous punishments, but the available evidence does not support the further conclusion that *only* torturous punishments were to be outlawed. As Livermore's comments demonstrate, the Framers were well aware that the reach of the Clause was not limited to the proscription of unspeakable atrocities. Nor did they intend simply to forbid punishments considered "cruel and unusual" at the time. The "import" of the Clause is, indeed, "indefinite," and for good reason. A constitutional provision "is enacted, it is true, from an experience of evils, but its general language should not, therefore, be necessarily confined to the form that evil had theretofore taken. Time works changes, brings into existence new conditions and purposes. Therefore a principle to be vital must be capable of wider application than the mischief which gave it birth." *Weems* v. *United States,* 217 U.S., at 373.

It was almost 80 years before this Court had occasion to refer to the Clause. See *Pervear* v. *The Commonwealth,* 5 Wall. 475, 479–480 (1867). These early cases, as the Court pointed out in *Weems* v. *United States, supra,* at 369, did not undertake to provide "an exhaustive definition" of "cruel and unusual punishments." Most of them proceeded primarily by "looking backwards for examples by which to fix the meaning of the clause," *id.,* at 377, concluding simply that a punishment would be "cruel and unusual" if it were similar to punishments considered "cruel and unusual" at the time the Bill of Rights was adopted. In *Wilkerson* v. *Utah,* 99 U.S., at 136, for instance, the Court found it "safe to affirm that punishments of torture ... and all others in the same line of unnecessary cruelty, are forbidden." The "punishments of torture," which the Court labeled "atrocities," were cases where the criminal "was embowelled alive, beheaded, and quartered," and cases "of public dissection ... and burning alive." *Id.,* at 135. Similarly, in *In re Kemmler,* 136 U.S. 436, 446 (1890), the Court declared that "if the punishment prescribed for an offence against the laws of the State were manifestly cruel and unusual, as burning at the stake, crucifixion, breaking on the wheel, or the like, it would be the duty of the courts to adjudge such penalties to be within the constitutional prohibition." The Court then observed, commenting upon the passage just quoted from *Wilkerson* v. *Utah, supra,* and applying the "manifestly cruel and unusual" test, that "[p]unishments are cruel when they involve torture or a lingering death; but the punishment of death is not cruel, within the meaning of that word as used in the Constitution. It implies there something inhuman and barbarous, something more than the mere extinguishment of life." 136 U.S., at 447.

Had this "historical" interpretation of the Cruel and Unusual Punishments Clause prevailed, the Clause would have been effectively read out of the Bill of Rights. As the Court noted in *Weems* v. *United States, supra,* at 371, this interpretation led Story to conclude "that the provision 'would seem to be wholly unnecessary in a free government, since it is scarcely possible that any department of such a government should authorize or justify such atrocious conduct.'" And Cooley in his book, Constitutional Limitations, said the Court, "apparently in a struggle between the effect to be given to ancient examples and the inconsequence of a dread of them in these enlightened times, ... hesitate[d] to advance definite views." *Id.,* at 375. The result of a judicial application of this interpretation was not surprising. A state court, for example, upheld the constitutionality of the whipping post: "In comparison with the 'barbarities of quartering, hanging in chains, castration, etc.,' it was easily reduced to insignificance." *Id.,* at 377.

But this Court in *Weems* decisively repudiated the "historical" interpretation of the Clause. The Court, returning to the intention of the Framers, "rel[ied] on the conditions which existed when the Constitution was adopted." And the Framers knew "that government by the people instituted by the Constitution would not imitate the conduct of arbitrary monarchs. The abuse of power might, indeed, be apprehended, but not that it would be manifested in provisions or practices which would shock the sensibilities of men." *Id.,* at 375. The Clause, then, guards against "[t]he abuse of power"; contrary to the implications in *Wilkerson* v. *Utah, supra,* and *In re Kemmler, supra,* the prohibition of the Clause is not "confine[d] ... to such penalties and punishment as were inflicted by the Stuarts." 217 U.S., at 372. Although opponents of the Bill of Rights "felt sure that the spirit of liberty could be trusted, and that its ideals would be represented, not debased, by legislation," *ibid.,* the Framers disagreed:

[Patrick] Henry and those who believed as he did would take no chances. Their predominant political impulse was distrust of power, and they insisted on constitutional limitations against its abuse. But surely they intended more than to register a fear of the forms of abuse that went out of practice with the Stuarts. Surely, their [jealousy] of power had a saner justification than that. They were men of action, practical and sagacious, not beset with vain imagining, and it must have come to them that there could be exercises of cruelty by laws other than those which inflicted bodily pain or mutilation. With power in a legislature great, if not unlimited, to give criminal character to the actions of men, with power unlimited to fix terms of imprisonment with what accompaniments they might, what more potent instrument of cruelty could be put into the hands of power? And it was believed that power might be tempted to cruelty. This was the motive of the clause, and if we are to attribute an intelligent providence to its advocates we cannot think that it was intended to prohibit only practices like the [Stuarts',] or to prevent only an exact repetition of history. We cannot think that the possibility of a coercive cruelty being exercised through other forms of punishment was overlooked. *Id.,* at 372–373.

The Court in *Weems* thus recognized that this "restraint upon legislatures" possesses an "expansive and vital character" that is " 'essential . . . to the rule of law and the maintenance of individual freedom.' " *Id.,* at 376–377. Accordingly, the responsibility lies with the courts to make certain that the prohibition of the Clause is enforced. Referring to cases in which "prominence [was] given to the power of the legislature to define crimes and their punishment," the Court said:

> We concede the power in most of its exercises. We disclaim the right to assert a judgment against that of the legislature of the expediency of the laws or the right to oppose the judicial power to the legislative power to define crimes and fix their punishment, unless that power encounters in its exercise a constitutional prohibition. In such case not our discretion but our legal duty, strictly defined and imperative in its direction, is invoked. *Id.,* at 378.

In short, this Court finally adopted the Framers' view of the Clause as a "constitutional check" to ensure that "when we come to punishments, no latitude ought to be left, nor dependence put on the virtue of representatives." That, indeed, is the only view consonant with our constitutional form of government. If the judicial conclusion that a punishment is "cruel and unusual" "depend[ed] upon virtually unanimous condemnation of the penalty at issue," then, "[l]ike no other constitutional provision, [the Clause's] only function would be to legitimize advances already made by the other departments and opinions already the conventional wisdom." We know that the Framers did not envision "so narrow a role for this basic guaranty of human rights." Goldberg & Dershowitz, Declaring the Death Penalty Unconstitutional, 83 Harv. L. Rev. 1773, 1782 (1970). The right to be free of cruel and unusual punishments, like the other guarantees of the Bill of Rights, "may not be submitted to vote; [it] depend[s] on the outcome of no elections." "The very purpose of a Bill of Rights was to withdraw certain subjects from the vicissitudes of political controversy, to place them beyond the reach of majorities and officials and to establish them as legal principles to be applied by the courts." *Board of Education* v. *Barnette,* 319 U.S. 624, 638 (1943).

Judicial enforcement of the Clause, then, cannot be evaded by invoking the obvious truth that legislatures have the power to prescribe punishments for crimes. That is precisely the reason the Clause appears in the Bill of Rights. The difficulty arises, rather, in formulating the "legal principles to be applied by the courts" when a legislatively prescribed punishment is challenged as "cruel and unusual." In formulating those constitutional principles, we must avoid the insertion of "judicial conception[s] of . . . wisdom or propriety," *Weems* v. *United States,* 217 U.S., at 379, yet we must not, in the guise of "judicial restraint," abdicate our fundamental responsibility to enforce the Bill of Rights. Were we to do so, the "constitution would indeed be as easy of application as it would be deficient in efficacy and power. Its general principles would have little value and be converted by precedent into impotent and lifeless formulas. Rights declared in words might be lost in reality." *Id.,* at 373. The Cruel and Unusual Punishments Clause would become, in short, "little more than good advice." *Trop* v. *Dulles,* 356 U.S., at 104.

II

Ours would indeed be a simple task were we required merely to measure a challenged punishment against those that history has long condemned. That narrow and unwarranted view of the Clause, however, was left behind with the 19th century. Our task today is more complex. We know "that the words of the [Clause] are not precise, and that their scope is not static." We know, therefore, that the Clause "must draw its meaning from the evolving standards of decency tht mark the progress of a maturing society." *Trop* v. *Dulles, supra*, at 100–101. That knowledge, of course, is but the beginning of the inquiry.

In *Trop* v. *Dulles, supra*, at 99, it was said that "[t]he question is whether [a] penalty subjects the individual to a fate forbidden by the principle of civilized treatment guaranteed by the [Clause]." It was also said that a challenged punishment must be examined "in light of the basic prohibition against inhuman treatment" embodied in the Clause. *Id.*, at 100 n. 32. It was said, finally, that:

> The basic concept underlying the [Clause] is nothing less than the dignity of man. While the State has the power to punish, the [Clause] stands to assure that this power be exercised within the limits of civilized standards. *Id.*, at 100.

At bottom, then, the Cruel and Unusual Punishments Clause prohibits the infliction of uncivilized and inhuman punishments. The State, even as it punishes, must treat its members with respect for their intrinsic worth as human beings. A punishment is "cruel and unusual," therefore, if it does not comport with human dignity.

This formulation, of course, does not of itself yield principles for assessing the constitutional validity of particular punishments. Nevertheless, even though "[t]his Court has had little occasion to give precise content to the [Clause]," *ibid.*, there are principles recognized in our cases and inherent in the Clause sufficient to permit a judicial determination whether a challenged punishment comports with human dignity.

The primary principle is that a punishment must not be so severe as to be degrading to the dignity of human beings. Pain, certainly, may be a factor in the judgment. The infliction of an extremely severe punishment will often entail physical suffering. See *Weems* v. *United States*, 217 U.S., at 366. Yet the Framers also knew "that there could be exercises of cruelty by laws other than those which inflicted bodily pain or mutilation." *Id.*, at 372. Even though "[t]here may be involved no physical mistreatment, no primitive torture," *Trop* v. *Dulles, supra*, at 101, severe mental pain may be inherent in the infliction of a particular punishment. See *Weems* v. *United States, supra*, at 366. That, indeed, was one of the conclusions underlying the holding of the plurality in *Trop* v. *Dulles* that the punishment of expatriation violates the Clause. And the physical and mental suffering inherent in the punishment of *cadena temporal*, see nn. 11–12, *supra*, was an obvious basis for the Court's decision in *Weems* v. *United States* that the punishment was "cruel and unusual."

More than the presence of pain, however, is comprehended in the judgment that the extreme severity of a punishment makes it degrading to the dignity of human beings. The barbaric punishments condemned by history, "punishments which inflict torture, such as the rack, the thumbscrew, the iron boot, the stretching of limbs and the like," are, of course, "attended with acute pain and suffering." *O'Neil* v. *Vermont*, 144 U.S. 323, 339 (1892) (Field, J., dissenting). When we consider why they have been condemned, however, we realize that the pain involved is not the only reason. The true significance of these punishments is that they treat members of the human race as nonhumans, as objects to be toyed with and discarded. They are thus inconsistent with the fundamental premise of the Clause that even the vilest criminal remains a human being possessed of common human dignity.

The infliction of an extremely severe punishment, then, like the one before the Court in *Weems* v. *United States*, from which "[n]o circumstance of degradation [was] omitted," 217 U.S., at 366, may reflect the attitude that the person punished is not entitled to recognition as a fellow human being. That attitude may be apparent apart from the severity of the punishment itself. In *Louisiana ex rel. Francis* v. *Resweber*, 329 U.S. 459, 464 (1947), for example, the unsuccessful electrocution, although it caused "mental anguish and physical pain," was the result of "an unforeseeable accident." Had the failure been intentional, however, the punishment would have been, like torture, so degrading and indecent as to amount to a refusal to accord the criminal human status. Indeed, a punishment may be degrading to human dignity solely because it *is* a punishment. A State may not punish a person for being "mentally ill, or a leper, or...afflicted with a venereal disease," or for being addicted to narcotics. *Robinson* v. *California*, 370 U.S. 660, 666 (1962). To inflict punishment for having a disease is to treat the individual as a diseased thing rather than as a sick human being. That the punishment is not severe, "in the abstract," is irrelevant; "[e]ven one day in prison would be a cruel and unusual punishment for the 'crime' of having a common cold." *Id.,* at 667. Finally, of course, a punishment may be degrading simply by reason of its enormity. A prime example is expatriation, a "punishment more primitive than torture," *Trop* v. *Dulles,* 356 U.S., at 101, for it necessarily involves a denial by society of the individual's existence as a member of the human community.

In determining whether a punishment comports with human dignity, we are aided also by a second principle inherent in the Clause—that the State must not arbitrarily inflict a severe punishment. This principle derives from the notion that the State does not respect human dignity when, without reason, it inflicts upon some people a severe punishment that it does not inflict upon others. Indeed, the very words "cruel and unusual punishments" imply condemnation of the arbitrary infliction of severe punishments. And, as we now know, the English history of the Clause reveals a particular concern with the establishment of a safeguard against arbitrary punishments. See Granucci, "Nor Cruel and Unusual Punishments Inflicted:" The Original Meaning, 57 Calif. L. Rev. 839, 857–860 (1969).

This principle has been recognized in our cases. In *Wilkerson* v. *Utah,* 99 U.S., at 133–134, the Court reviewed various treatises on military law in order to demonstrate that under "the custom of war" shooting was a common method of inflicting the punishment of death. On that basis, the Court concluded:

> Cruel and unusual punishments are forbidden by the Constitution, but the authorities referred to [treatises on military law] are quite sufficient to show that the punishment of shooting as a mode of executing the death penalty for the crime of murder in the first degree is not included in that category, within the meaning of the [Clause]. Soldiers convicted of desertion or other capital military offenses are in the great majority of cases sentenced to be shot, and the ceremony for such occasions is given in great fulness by the writers upon the subject of courts-martial. *Id.,* at 134–135.

The Court thus upheld death by shooting, so far as appears, solely on the ground that it was common method of execution.

As *Wilkerson* v. *Utah* suggests, when a severe punishment is inflicted "in the great majority of cases" in which it is legally available, there is little likelihood that the State is inflicting it arbitrarily. If, however, the infliction of a severe punishment is "something different from that which is generally done" in such cases, *Trop* v. *Dulles,* 356 U.S., at 101 n. 32, there is a substantial likelihood that the State, contrary to the requirements of regularity and fairness embodied in the Clause, is inflicting the punishment arbitrarily. This principle is especially important today. There is scant danger, given the political processes "in an enlightened democracy such as ours," *id.,* at 100, that extremely severe punishments will be widely applied. The more significant function of the Clause, therefore, is to protect against the danger of their arbitrary infliction.

A third principle inherent in the Clause is that a severe punishment must not be unacceptable to contemporary society. Rejection by society, of course, is a strong indication that a severe punishment does not comport with human dignity. In applying this principle, however, we must make certain that the judicial determination is as objective as possible. Thus, for example, *Weems* v. *United States,* 217 U.S., at 380, and *Trop* v. *Dulles,* 356 U.S., at 102–103, suggest that one factor that may be considered is the existence of the punishment in jurisdictions other than those before the Court. *Wilkerson* v. *Utah, supra,* suggests that another factor to be considered is the historic usage of the punishment. *Trop* v. *Dulles, supra,* at 99, combined present acceptance with past usage by observing that "the death penalty has been employed throughout our history, and, in a day when it is still widely accepted, it cannot be said to violate the constitutional concept of cruelty." In *Robinson* v. *California,* 370 U.S., at 666, which involved the infliction of punishment for narcotics addiction, the Court went a step further, concluding simply that "in the light of contemporary human knowledge, a law which made a criminal offense of such a disease would doubtless be universally thought to be an infliction of cruel and unusual punishment."

The question under this principle, then, is whether there are objective indicators from which a court can conclude that contemporary society considers a severe punishment unacceptable. Accordingly, the judicial task is to review the history of a challenged punishment and to examine society's present practices with respect to its use. Legislative authorization, of course, does not establish acceptance. The acceptability of a severe punishment is measured, not by its availability, for it might become so offensive to society as never to be inflicted, but by its use.

The final principle inherent in the Clause is that a severe punishment must not be excessive. A punishment is excessive under this principle if it is unnecessary: The infliction of a severe punishment by the State cannot comport with human dignity when it is nothing more than the pointless infliction of suffering. If there is a significantly less severe punishment adequate to achieve the purposes for which the punishment is inflicted, cf. *Robinson* v. *California, supra,* at 666; *id.,* at 677 (Douglas, J., concurring); *Trop* v. *Dulles, supra,* at 114 (Brennan, J., concurring), the punishment inflicted is unnecessary and therefore excessive.

This principle first appeared in our cases in Mr. Justice Field's dissent in *O'Neil* v. *Vermont,* 144 U.S., at 337. He there took the position that:

> [The Clause] is directed, not only against punishments of the character mentioned [torturous punishments], but against all punishments which by their excessive length or severity are greatly disproportioned to the offences charged. The whole inhibition is against that which is excessive either in the bail required, or fine imposed, or punishment inflicted. *Id.,* at 339–340.

Although the determination that a severe punishment is excessive may be grounded in a judgment that it is disproportionate to the crime, the more significant basis is that the punishment serves no penal purpose more effectively than a less severe punishment. This view of the principle was explicitly recognized by the Court in *Weems* v. *United States, supra.* There the Court, reviewing a severe punishment inflicted for the falsification of an official record, found that "the highest punishment possible for a crime which may cause the loss of many thousand[s] of dollars, and to prevent which the duty of the State should be as eager as to prevent the perversion of truth in a public document, is not greater than that which may be imposed for falsifying a single item of a public account." *Id.,* at 381. Stating that "this contrast shows more than different exercises of legislative judgment," the Court concluded that the punishment was unnecessarily severe in view of the purposes for which it was imposed. *Ibid.* See also *Trop* v. *Dulles,* 356 U.S., at 111–112 (Brennan, J., concurring).

There are, then, four principles by which we may determine whether a particular punishment is "cruel and unusual." The primary principle, which I believe supplies the essential predicate fo rthe application of the others, is that a punishment must not by its severity be degrading to human dignity. The paradigm violation of this principle would be the infliction of a torturous punishment of the type that the Clause has always prohibited. Yet "[i]t is unlikely that any State at this moment in history," *Robinson* v. *California,* 370 U.S., at 666, would pass a law providing for the infliction of such a punishment. Indeed, no such punishment has ever been before this Court. The same may be said of the other principles. It is unlikely that this Court will confront a severe punishment that is obviously inflicted in wholly arbitrary fashion; no State would engage in a reign of blind terror. Nor is it likely that this Court will be called upon to review a severe punishment that is clearly and totally rejected throughout society; no legislature would be able even to authorize the infliction of such a punishment. Nor, finally, is it likely that this Court will have to consider a severe punishment that is patently unnecessary; no State today would inflict a severe punishment knowing that there was no reason whatever for doing so. In short, we are unlikely to have occasion to determine that a punishment is fatally offensive under any one principle.

Since the Bill of Rights was adopted, this Court has adjudged only three punishments to be within the prohibition of the Clause. See *Weems* v. *United States,* 217 U.S. 349 (1910) (12 years in chains at hard and painful labor); *Trop* v. *Dulles,* 356 U.S. 86 (1958) (expatriation); *Robinson* v. *California,* 370 U.S. 660 (1962) (imprisonment for narcotics addiction). Each punishment, of course, was degrading to human dignity, but of none could it be said conclusively that it was fatally offensive under one or the other of the principles. Rather, these "cruel and unusual punishments" seriously implicated several of the principles, and it was the application of the principles in combination that supported the judgment. That, indeed, is not surprising. The function of these principles, after all, is simply to provide means by which a court can determine whether a challenged punishment comports with human dignity. They are, therefore, interrelated, and in most cases it will be their convergence that will justify the conclusion that a punishment is "cruel and unusual." The test, then, will ordinarily be a cumulative one: If a punishment is unusually severe, if there is a strong probability that it is inflicted arbitrarily, if it is substantially rejected by contemporary society, and if there is no reason to believe that it serves any penal purpose more effectively than some less severe punishment, then the continued infliction of that punishment violates the command of the Clause that the State may not inflict inhuman and uncivilized punishments upon those convicted of crimes.

III

The punishment challenged in these cases is death. Death, of course, is a "traditional" punishment, *Trop* v. *Dulles, supra,* at 100, one that "has been employed throughout our history," *id.,* at 99, and its constitutional background is accordingly an appropriate subject of inquiry....

The punishment of death is inconsistent with all four principles: Death is an unusually severe and degrading punishment; there is a strong probability that it is inflicted arbitrarily; its rejection by contemporary society is virtually total; and there is no reason to believe that it serves any penal purpose more effectively than the less severe punishment of imprisonment. The function of these principles is to enable a court to determine whether a punishment comports with human dignity. Death, quite simply, does not....

I

MARSHALL, J., concurring:

The Eighth Amendment's ban against cruel and unusual punishments derives from English law. In 1583, John Whitgift, Archbishop of Canterbury, turned the High Commission into a permanent ecclesiastical court, and the Commission began to use torture to extract confessions from persons suspected of various offenses. Sir Robert Beale protested that cruel and barbarous torture violated Magna Carta, but his protests were made in vain.

Cruel punishments were not confined to those accused of crimes, but were notoriously applied with even greater relish to those who were convicted. Blackstone described in ghastly detail the myriad of inhumane forms of punishment imposed on persons found guilty of any of a large number of offenses. Death, of course, was the usual result.

The treason trials of 1685—the "Bloody Assizes"—which followed an abortive rebellion by the Duke of Monmouth, marked the culmination of the parade of horrors, and most historians believe that it was this event that finally spurred the adoption of the English Bill of Rights containing the progenitor of our prohibition against cruel and unusual punishments. The conduct of Lord Chief Justice Jeffreys at those trials has been described as an "insane lust for cruelty" which was "stimulated by orders from the King" (James II). The assizes received wide publicity from Puritan pamphleteers and doubtless had some influence on the adoption of a cruel and unusual punishments clause. But, the legislative history of the English Bill of Rights of 1689 indicates that the assizes may not have been as critical to the adoption of the clause as is widely thought. After William and Mary of Orange crossed the channel to invade England, James II fled. Parliament was summoned into session and a committee was appointed to draft general statements containing "such things as are absolutely necessary to be considered for the better securing of our religion, laws and liberties." An initial draft of the Bill of Rights prohibited "illegal" punishments, but a later draft referred to the infliction by James II of "illegal and cruel" punishments, and declared "cruel and unusual" punishments to be prohibited. The use of the word "unusual" in the final draft appears to be inadvertent.

This legislative history has led at least one legal historian to conclude "that the cruel and unusual punishments clause of the Bill of Rights of 1689 was, first, an objection to the imposition of punishments that were unauthorized by statute and outside the jurisdiction of the sentencing court, and second a reiteration of the English policy against disproportionate penalties," and not primarily a reaction to the torture of the High Commission, harsh sentences, or the assizes.

Whether the English Bill of Rights prohibition against cruel and unusual punishments is properly read as a response to excessive or illegal punishments, as a reaction to barbaric and objectionable modes of punishment, or as both, there is no doubt whatever that in borrowing the language and in including it in the Eighth Amendment, our Founding Fathers intended to outlaw torture and other cruel punishments.

The precise language used in the Eighth Amendment first appeared in America on June 12, 1776, in Virginia's "Declaration of Rights," § 9 of which read: "That excessive bail ought not to be required, nor excessive fines imposed, nor cruel and unusual punishments inflicted." This language was drawn verbatim from the English Bill of Rights of 1689. Other States adopted similar clauses, and there is evidence in the debates of the various state conventions that were called upon to ratify the Constitution of great concern for the omission of any prohibition against torture or other cruel punishments.

The Virginia Convention offers some clues as to what the Founding Fathers had in mind in prohibiting cruel and unusual punishments. At one point George Mason advocated the adoption of a Bill of Rights, and Patrick Henry concurred, stating:

> By this Constitution, some of the best barriers of human rights are thrown away. Is there not an additional reason to have a bill of rights? ... Congress, from their general powers, may fully go into business of human legislation. They may legislate, in criminal cases, from treason to the lowest offence—petty larceny. They may define crimes and prescribe punishments. In the definition of crimes, I trust they will be directed by what wise representatives ought to be governed by. But when we come to punishments, no latitude ought to be left, nor dependence put on the virtue of representatives. What says our bill of rights?—'that excessive bail ought not to be required, nor excessive fines imposed, nor cruel and unusual punishments inflicted.' Are you not, therefore, now calling on those gentlemen who are to compose Congress, to prescribe trials and define punishments without this control? Will they find sentiments there similar to this bill of rights? You let them loose; you do more—you depart from the genius of your country....
>
> In this business of legislation, your members of Congress will loose the restriction of not imposing excessive fines, demanding excessive bail, and inflicting cruel and unusual punishments. These are prohibited by your declaration of rights. What has distinguished our ancestors?—That they would not admit of tortures, or cruel and barbarous punishment. But Congress may introduce the practice of the civil law, in preference to that of the common law. They may introduce the practice of France, Spain, and Germany—of torturing, to extort a confession of the crime. They will say that they might as well draw examples from those countries as from Great Britain, and they will tell you that there is such a necessity of strengthening the arm of government, that they must have a criminal equity, and extort confession by torture, in order to punish with still more relentless severity. We are then lost and undone.

Henry's statement indicates that he wished to insure that "relentless severity" would be prohibited by the Constitution. Other expressions with respect to the proposed Eighth Amendment by Members of the First Congress indicate that they shared Henry's view of the need for and purpose of the Cruel and Unusual Punishments Clause.

Thus, the history of the clause clearly establishes that it was intended to prohibit cruel punishments. We must now turn to the case law to discover the manner in which courts have given meaning to the term "cruel."

II

This Court did not squarely face the task of interpreting the cruel and unusual punishments language for the first time until *Wilkerson* v. *Utah*, 99 U.S. 130 (1879), although the language received a cursory examination in several prior cases. See, *e. g.*, *Pervear* v. *Commonwealth*, 5 Wall. 475 (1867). In *Wilkerson*, the Court unanimously upheld a sentence of public execution by shooting imposed pursuant to a conviction for premediated murder. In his opinion for the Court, Mr. Justice Clifford wrote:

> Difficulty would attend the effort to define with exactness the extent of the constitutional provision which provides that cruel and unusual punishments shall not be inflicted; but it is safe to affirm that punishments of torture, ... and all others in the same line of unnecessary cruelty, are forbidden by that amendment to the Constitution. 99 U.S., at 135–136.

Thus, the Court found that unnecessary cruelty was no more permissible than torture. To determine whether the punishment under attack was unnecessarily cruel, the Court examined the history of the Utah Territory and the then-current writings on capital punishment, and compared this Nation's practices with those of other countries. It is apparent that the Court felt it could not dispose of the question simply by referring to traditional practices; instead, it felt bound to examine developing thought.

Eleven years passed before the Court again faced a challenge to a specific punishment under the Eighth Amendment. In the case of *In re Kemmler*, 136 U.S. 436 (1890), Chief Justice Fuller wrote an opinion for a unanimous Court upholding electrocution as a permissible mode of punishment. While the Court ostensibly held that the Eighth Amendment did not apply to the States, it is very apparent that the nature of the punishment involved was examined under the Due Process Clause of the Fourteenth Amendment. The Court held that the punishment was not objectionable. Today, *Kemmler* stands primarily for the proposition that a punishment is not necessarily unconstitutional simply because it is unusual, so long as the legislature has a humane purpose in selecting it.

Two years later in *O'Neil* v. *Vermont*, 144 U.S. 323 (1892), the Court reaffirmed that the Eighth Amendment was not applicable to the States. O'Neil was found guilty on 307 counts of selling liquor in violation of Vermont law. A fine of $6,140 ($20 for each offense) and the costs of prosecution ($497.96) were imposed. O'Neil was committed to prison until the fine and the costs were paid; and the Court provided that if they were not paid before a specified date, O'Neil was to be confined in the house of corrections for 19,914 days (approximately 54 years) at hard labor. Three Justices—Field, Harlan, and Brewer—dissented. They maintained not only that the Cruel and Unusual Punishments Clause was applicable to the States, but that in O'Neil's case it had been violated. Mr. Justice Field wrote:

> That designation [cruel and unusual], it is true, is usually applied to punishments which inflict torture, such as the rack, the thumbscrew, the iron boot, the stretching of limbs and the like, which are attended with acute pain and suffering.... The inhibition is directed, not only against punishments of the character mentioned, but against all punishments which by their excessive length or severity are greatly disproportioned to the offences charged. The whole inhibition is against that which is excessive.... *Id.,* at 339–340.

In *Howard* v. *Fleming*, 191 U.S. 126 (1903), the Court, in essence, followed the approach advocated by the dissenters in *O'Neil*. In rejecting the claim that 10-year sentences for conspiracy to defraud were cruel and unusual, the Court (per Mr. Justice Brewer) considered the nature of the crime, the purpose of the law, and the length of the sentence imposed.

The Court used the same approach seven years later in the landmark case of *Weems* v. *United States*, 217 U.S. 349 (1910). Weems, an officer of the Bureau of Coast Guard and Transportation of the United States Government of the Philippine Islands, was convicted of falsifying a "public and official document." He was sentenced to 15 years' incarceration at hard labor with chains on his ankles, to an unusual loss of his civil rights, and to perpetual surveillance. Called upon to determine whether this was a cruel and unusual punishment, the Court found that it was. The Court emphasized that the Constitution was not an "ephemeral" enactment, or one "designed to meet passing occasions." Recognizing that "[t]ime works changes, [and] brings into existence new conditions and purposes," the Court commented that "[i]n the application of a constitution ... our contemplation cannot be only of what has been but of what may be."

In striking down the penalty imposed on Weems, the Court examined the punishment in relation to the offense, compared the punishment to those inflicted for other crimes and to those imposed in other jurisdictions, and concluded that the punishment was excessive. Justices White and Holmes dissented and argued that the cruel and unusual prohibition was meant to prohibit only those things that were objectionable at the time the Constitution was adopted.

Weems is a landmark case because it represents the first time that the Court invalidated a penalty prescribed by a legislature for a particular offense. The Court made it plain beyond any reasonable doubt that excessive punishments were as objectionable as those that were inherently cruel. Thus, it is apparent that the dissenters' position in *O'Neil* had become the opinion of the Court in *Weems*.

Weems was followed by two cases that added little to our knowledge of the scope of the cruel and unusual language, *Badders* v. *United States*, 240 U.S. 391 (1916), and *United States ex rel. Milwaukee Social Democratic Publishing Co.* v. *Burleson*, 255 U.S. 407 (1921). Then came another landmark case, *Louisiana ex rel. Francis* v. *Resweber*, 329 U.S. 459 (1947).

Francis had been convicted of murder and sentenced to be electrocuted. The first time the current passed through him, there was a mechanical failure and he did not die. Thereafter, Francis sought to prevent a second electrocution on the ground that it would be a cruel and unusual punishment. Eight members of the Court assumed the applicability of the Eighth Amendment to the States. The Court was virtually unanimous in agreeing that "[t]he traditional humanity of modern Anglo-American law forbids the infliction of unnecessary pain," but split 5–4 on whether Francis would, under the circumstances, be forced to undergo any excessive pain. Five members of the Court treated the case like *In re Kemmler* and held that the legislature adopted electrocution for a humane purpose, and that its will should not be thwarted because, in its desire to reduce pain and suffering in most cases, it may have inadvertently increased suffering in one particular case. The four dissenters felt that the case should be remanded for futher facts.

As in *Weems,* the Court was concerned with excessive punishments. *Resweber* is perhaps most significant because the analysis of cruel and unusual punishment questions first advocated by the dissenters in *O'Neil* was at last firmly entrenched in the minds of an entire Court.

Trop v. *Dulles,* 356 U.S. 86 (1958), marked the next major cruel and unusual punishment case in this Court. Trop, a native-born American, was declared to have lost his citizenship by reason of a conviction by court-martial for wartime desertion. Writing for himself and Justices Black, Douglas, and Whittaker, Chief Justice Warren concluded that loss of citizenship amounted to a cruel and unusual punishment that violated the Eighth Amendment.

Emphasizing the flexibility inherent in the words "cruel and unusual," the Chief Justice wrote that "[t]he Amendment must draw its meaning from the evolving standards of decency that mark the progress of a maturing society." His approach to the problem was that utilized by the Court in *Weems:* he scrutinized the severity of the penalty in relation to the offense, examined the practices of other civilized nations of the world, and concluded that involuntary statelessness was an excessive and, therefore, an unconstitutional punishment. Justice Frankfurter, dissenting, urged that expatriation was not punishment, and that even if it were, it was not excessive. While he criticized the conclusion arrived at by the Chief Justice, his approach to the Eighth Amendment question was identical.

Whereas in *Trop* a majority of the Court failed to agree on whether loss of citizenship was a cruel and unusual punishment, four years later a majority did agree in *Robinson* v. *California,* 370 U.S. 660 (1962), that a sentence of 90 days' imprisonment for violation of a California statute making it a crime to "be addicted to the use of narcotics" was cruel and unusual. Mr. Justice Stewart, writing the opinion of the Court, reiterated what the Court had said in *Weems* and what Chief Justice Warren wrote in *Trop*—that the cruel and unusual punishment clause was not a static concept, but one that must be continually re-examined "in the light of contemporary human knowledge." The fact that the penalty under attack was only 90 days evidences the Court's willingness to carefully examine the possible excessiveness of punishment in a given case even where what is involved is a penalty that is familiar and widely accepted.

We distinguished *Robinson* in *Powell* v. *Texas,* 392 U.S. 514 (1968), where we sustained a conviction for drunkenness in a public place and a fine of $20. Four Justices dissented on the ground that *Robinson* was controlling. The analysis in both cases was the same; only the conclusion as to whether or not the punishment was excessive differed. *Powell* marked the last time prior to today's decision that the Court has had occasion to construe the meaning of the term "cruel and unusual" punishment.

Several principles emerge from these prior cases and serve as a beacon to an enlightened decision in the instant cases.... A punishment may be deemed cruel and unusual for any one of four distinct reasons.

First, there are certain punishments that inherently involve so much physical pain and suffering that civilized people cannot tolerate them—*e. g.,* use of the rack, the thumbscrew, or other modes of torture. See *O'Neil* v. *Vermont,* 144 U.S., at 339 (Field, J., dissenting). Regardless of public sentiment with respect to imposition of one of these punishments in a particular case or at any one moment in history, the Constitution prohibits it. These are punishments that have been barred since the adoption of the Bill of Rights.

Second, there are punishments that are unusual, signifying that they were previously unknown as penalties for a given offense. Cf. *Unitde States ex rel. Milwaukee Social Democratic Publishing Co.* v. *Burleson,* 255 U.S., at 435 (Brandeis, J., dissenting). If these punishments are intended to serve a humane purpose, they may be constitutionally permissible. *In re Kemmler,* 136 U.S., at 447; *Louisiana ex rel. Francis* v. *Resweber,* 329 U.S., at 464. Prior decisions leave open the question of just how much the word "unusual" adds to the word "cruel." I have previously indicated that use of the word "unusual" in the English Bill of Rights of 1689 was inadvertent, and there is nothing in the history of the Eighth Amendment to give flesh to its intended meaning. In light of the meager history that does exist, one would suppose that an innovative punishment would probably be constitutional if no more cruel than that punishment which is superseded. We need not decide this question here, however, for capital punishment is certainly not a recent phenomenon.

Third, a penalty may be cruel and unusual

because it is excessive and serves no valid legislative purpose. *Weems* v. *United States, supra*. The decisions previously discussed are replete with assertions that one of the primary functions of the cruel and unusual punishments clause is to prevent excessive or unnecessary penalties, *e. g., Wilkerson* v. *Utah*, 99 U.S., at 134; *O'Neil* v. *Vermont*, 144 U.S., at 339–340 (Field, J., dissenting); *Weems* v. *United States*, 217 U.S., at 381; *Louisiana ex rel. Francis* v. *Resweber, supra;* these punishments are unconstitutional even though popular sentiment may favor them....

Fourth, where a punishment is not excessive and serves a valid legislative purpose, it still may be invalid if popular sentiment abhors it. For example, if the evidence clearly demonstrated that capital punishment served valid legislative purposes, such punishment would, nevertheless, be unconstitutional if citizens found it to be morally unacceptable. A general abhorrence on the part of the public would, in effect, equate a modern punishment with those barred since the adoption of the Eighth Amendment. There are no prior cases in this Court striking down a penalty on this ground, but the very notion of changing values requires that we recognize its existence....

3. THE "HOLE" AND THE EIGHTH AMENDMENT

NOTES

Note 1.

WRIGHT v. McMANN
387 F.2d 519 (1967)
United States Court of Appeals, Second Circuit

Lawrence William Wright, an inmate of Clinton State Prison at Dannemora, New York, appeals from a dismissal of his complaint without a hearing by the District Court for the Northern District of New York, Brennan, J., 257 F.Supp. 739 (N.D.N.Y.1966). The complaint, brought under the Civil Rights Act and seeking an injunction and $10,000 damages for alleged violations of rights secured to Wright by the Constitution of the United States, was dismissed on the grounds that it failed to make a sufficient showing of the denial of Wright's constitutional rights, or, alternatively, that Wright's remedy, if any, lay in the New York courts. We reverse and remand to the District Court....

The core of Wright's charge seems to be based on the claim that upon reception in solitary confinement, he was placed first in what is known in prison jargon as a "strip cell," where all sorts of cruelties were visited upon him. The conditions to which Wright allegedly was subjected in this cell are best described in his language:

> [T]he said solitary confinement cell wherein plaintiff was placed was dirty, filthy and unsanitary, without adequate heat and virtually barren; the toilet and sink were encrusted with slime, dirt and human excremental residue superimposed thereon; plaintiff was without clothing and entirely nude for several days [elsewhere said to be 11 days] until he was given a thin pair of underwear to put on; plaintiff was unable to keep himself clean or perform normal hygienic functions as he was denied the use of soap, towel, toilet paper, tooth brush, comb, and other hygienic implements and utensils therefore; plaintiff was compelled under threat of violence, assault or other increased punishments to remain standing at military attention in front of his cell door each time an officer appeared from 7:30 A.M. to 10:00 P.M. every day, and he was not permitted to sleep during the said hours under the pain and threat of being beaten or otherwise disciplined therefore; the windows in front of his confinement cell were opened wide throughout the evening and night hours of each day during subfreezing temperatures causing plaintiff to be exposed to the cold air and winter weather without clothing or other means of protecting himself or to escape the detrimental effects thereof; and the said solitary confinement cell was used as a means of subjecting plaintiff to oppression, excessively harsh, cruel and inhuman treatment specifically forbidden by the Eighth Amendment to the United States Constitution. (Complaint, ¶ 12.)

In other filed papers Wright states that this "strip cell" was completely barren of furniture with the exception of a sink and toilet. He goes on to state that he was forced to sleep completely nude on the cold rough concrete floor and that the cell was so cold and uncomfortable that it was impossible for him to sleep for more than an hour or two without having to stand and move about in order to keep warm. He adds that food was served to him in bowls placed on the floor of his cell and that he was forced to handle and eat his rations without even the semblance of cleanliness. He describes the cell as fetid and reeking from the stench of the bodily wastes of previous occupants which he says covered the floor, the sink, and the toilet.

Wright was continuously kept in this cell until March 23, 1965—a total of 33 days. A year later, he again was placed in a "strip cell," this time for 21 consecutive days, for violating a prison rule.

Until recently the federal courts refused to review charges instituted under the Civil Rights Act and arising out of state prison disciplinary procedures. The prisoners, instead, were left to pursue whatever remedies were available in the state courts. The oft repeated reasons used to justify this result were (a) that the Eighth Amendment's prohibition against cruel and unusual punishment did not apply to the states, (b) a reluctance to interfere in the internal discipline of state prisons, and (c) the need to utilize state remedies in the first instance. See Redding v. Pate, 220 F.Supp. 124, 126 (N.D. Ill.1963).

Recent decisions, however, have demonstrated a sharp alteration in the judicial attitude toward these rationales and today the older cases retain little vitality. Indeed, there is no longer any question that a state prisoner may bring an action under the Civil Rights Act. Cooper v. Pate, 378 U.S. 546, 84 S.Ct. 1733, 12 L.Ed.2d 1030 (1964). Any lingering uncertainty over the applicability of the Eighth Amendment to the States was laid to rest by Robinson v. State of California, 370 U.S. 660, 82 S.Ct. 1417, 8 L.Ed.2d 758 (1962). And, while federal courts are sensitive to the problems created by judicial interference in the internal discipline of state prisons, in appropriate cases they will not hesitate to intervene.

The harshest blow to the old "hands-off" doctrine was struck by Monroe v. Pape, 365 U.S. 167, 81 S.Ct. 473, 5 L.Ed.2d 492 (1961). There, in an action under the Civil Rights Act to recover money damages against city police officers for violating rights secured by the fourteenth Amendment, the Court held that exhaustion of state remedies was not a condition precedent to accepting jurisdiction....

We have no hesitancy in holding that the debasing conditions to which Wright claims to have been subjected, would, if established, constitute cruel and unusual punishment in violation of the Eighth Amendment. They offend more than "some fastidious squeamishness or private sentimentalism." Rochin v. People of California, 342 U.S. 165, 172, 72 S.Ct. 205, 209, 96 L.Ed. 183 (1952). Indeed, the Assistant Attorney General of New York with commendable candor conceded during argument before us that the conditions, if they were as Wright alleged, were "terrible" and should not be permitted to exist."...

We are of the view that civilized standards of humane decency simply do not permit a man for a substantial period of time to be denuded and exposed to the bitter cold of winter in northern New York State and to be deprived of the basic elements of hygiene such as soap and toilet paper.[1] The subhuman conditions alleged by Wright to exist in the "strip cell" at Dannemora could only serve to destroy completely the spirit and undermine the sanity of the prisoner. The Eighth Amendment forbids treatment so foul, so inhuman and so violative of basic concepts of decency. Trop v. Dulles, 356 U.S. 86, 100, 101, 78 S.Ct. 590, 597, 598, 2 L.Ed.2d 596 (1958).

Note 2.

HANCOCK v. AVERY
301 F. Supp. 786 (1969)
United States District Court, Middle District of Tennessee

Countering the contentions of plaintiff that he is being subjected to cruel and unusual punishment, defendants argue that plaintiff's confinement in the dry cell was necessary to protect the safety of prison personnel and plaintiff's own safety. They contend that confinement of plaintiff without clothing in the totally barren cell was necessary to prevent his access to any material from which a weapon could be fashioned for use against himself or

[1] The Warden's answer states that "A strip cell is a necessary part of prison discipline owing to the fact that a prisoner when being punished for breach of prison discipline is placed in solitary confinement or segregation, he often becomes violent and destroys property, tears the cell up, sets fires and otherwise conducts himself as to be dangerous to himself and others. The strip cell is only used to avoid the dangerous consequences of placing a prisoner in a segregated area immediately upon his being sentenced to such punishment." But apparently no determination was made that this *particular* prisoner was or would have become violent. Indeed, the Warden's answer admits that "The treatment of Wright was strictly routine treatment for a violation of prison discipline. * * *"

We do not rule out the possibility that in exceptional circumstances it might be necessary to take from a prisoner all objects with which he could harm himself or others. If such circumstances were present in this case, they may, of course, be brought to the attention of the District Court to which this case is being remanded.

prison personnel. They further contend that articles of clothing, plumbing fixtures and furnishings could all provide raw material for such a weapon and thus must be denied to the plaintiff. Defendants argue that plaintiff's health was not seriously endangered by such practices because he had daily opportunity to make medical complaints to prison medical personnel. Defendants' concern with these matters arises out of the fact that plaintiff has twice attempted suicide and is suspected of involvement in the serious stabbing of a prison guard. Furthermore, plaintiff has twice attempted to escape from cells less secure than the dry cell. It is defendants' contention that dry cells are employed for the housing of those inmates who are so incorrigible as to be beyond the reach of normal methods of confinement. Finally, it is defendants' basic position that the determination as to the methods of dealing with such incorrigible persons is a matter of internal management of state prisons and should be left to the discretion of prison administrators....

...the Court finds that the effect of confining plaintiff in the dry cell under the conditions shown to have existed was to subject him to cruel and unusual punishment in violation of the Eighth Amendment. The conditions of his dry cell confinement are such as to make it evident that fundamental concepts of decency did not prevail. Particularly barbaric are the facts that plaintiff is forced to sleep in the nude on a bare concrete floor without even the comfort of a blanket and that he is deprived at all times of adequate light and ventilation. Equally offensive is the fact that he is provided with no means by which he can maintain his personal cleanliness, with the result that he is forced to live and eat under animal-like conditions. The debasing conditions to which plaintiff is subjected offend more than some mere "fastidious squeamishness or private sentimentalism." Rochin v. People of California, 342 U.S. 165, 172 (1952). It is clear that requiring a prisoner to live, eat and sleep in such degrading circumstances does violence to civilized standards of human decency. Wright v. McMann, *supra;* Jordan v. Fitzharris, *supra.*

It is also apparent that the dry cell punishment, as administered in the instant case, is unnecessarily cruel in view of the purpose for which it is used. The stated aims in confining plaintiff in the dry cell were to protect him from self-inflicted injury, to protect the general prison population and personnel from violent acts on his part, and to prevent his escape. Solitary confinement for the purpose of achieving such goals is not per se an unconstitutional form of punishment. Graham v. Willingham, *supra.* However, the Court is of the opinion that such goals can be attained without requiring a prisoner to live in the exacerbated conditions of filfth and discomfort demonstrated in the instant case. Where prison officials impose such deplorable living conditions in conjunction with solitary confinement, the Court is compelled to find that cruel and unusual punishment has been imposed in violation of the Constitution.

While it is true, as the defendants assert, that all imprisonment is to an extent inhumane, this fact does not excuse the imposition of forms of punishment so harsh as to violate basic standards of human decency.

The conclusion here reached is not altered because the dry cell confinement under prison regulations could not exceed 15 days (15 days less than the maximum allowed by the state statute). Confinement under the conditions of harshness and cruelty reflected by the present record should not be tolerated for any length of time, however brief.

Note 3.

LaReau v. MacDougall
_____F. Supp._____(1971)
United States District Court, District of Connecticut

The third count alleges that the petitioner was subject to cruel and unusual punishment by reason of his confinement in a stripped or barren cell, in violation of the eighth amendment to the United States Constitution. He represents that this confinement in a stripped cell was cruel per se and that the punishment meted out to him was disproportionate to the violations which he was found to have committed. Another phase of his claim was that his long confinement in administrative segregation without adequate exercise, also constituted cruel and inhuman punishment.

There are three general categories of segregation which deprive an inmate of the general privileges, which are afforded to all those in the open prison population. The first grouping is administrative segregation; the second, punitive segregation; and the third is the stripped cell, now called maximum punitive segregation. The first category requires a continuous 24-hour cell confinement, except for one hour of recreation each day. Prisoners so confined are provided three full meals, a bed with mattress, a desk, writing utensils with writing supplies, toilet facilities, a lavatory and general toiletries. They are allowed the use of a radio, newspapers, magazines, and general commissary items, except that they are not free like those in the general prison population to go to the store to make their own purchases. They are also permitted to have reasonable visitation privileges to the prison law library.

Punitive segregation, on the other hand, is limited to not more than 30 days (Tr. 30, 308), and it is imposed only after a formal notice of charges and the holding of a hearing before the disciplinary committee. Those in punitive segregation are provided with three meals a day, but without dessert or condiments. They are furnished a mattress, but only between the hours of 3:00 P.M. and 8:00 A.M.; there are toilet and lavatory facilities; sheets and blankets are provided; radios and reading materials are not permitted, but a bible will be furnished if requested.

Maximum punitive segregation is limited to no more than eight days, except with the special approval of the Commissioner of Corrections or his deputy. The average period for this type of punitive incarceration is five days. This punishment is imposed only after a formal written notice, followed by a hearing before the disciplinary committee. Three meals per day are provided, but with no condiments, desserts or coffee with cream and sugar (Tr. 316); a mattress is provided between 3:00 P.M. and 8:00 A.M., and a blanket is furnished when the room temperature so requires. The size of the cell is approximately 6' x 10' x 8'; it contains a regular commode with a sink; the inmates are permitted toothpaste and a toothbrush on request and they may have a bible.

Since the original construction of the prison, there has been specially constructed in addition to the regular maximum punitive cells, an addition series of stripped cells, so-called, that are barren of any commode or sink. These units are substantially the same as the maximum punitive cells (Tr. 321), except that they have what is called a Chinese toilet. These latter facilities are built into the floor by providing a hole with a grill (Tr. 371) in a corner of the cell. This toilet may be flushed by a manually controlled valve outside the cell. There is no built-in ledge in these units on which to sleep (Tr. 388); lighting is provided by a fixture located outside the cell, which shines through a glass in the rear cell wall. General prison policy requires that no dark cells should exist (Tr. 312), however, the Commissioner was unable to say with certainty, that any written policy existed, which directed guard personnel to provide lighting when requested by a cell occupant. Prison guard Waldo testified that the light in the strip cell was lighted during feeding time, thus inferring it was not otherwise lighted (Tr. 215).

This stripped cell (maximum punitive) was the same size as the ordinary regulation cell, except that after one enters through the steel access door, there is a space or entryway of approximately two feet, before one reaches the exterior cell bars fronting on the cell. Each unit is completely separated and isolated from the adjoining cell units by walls of solid cement. When the exterior steel door is closed, the opening in the door may be covered by a metal plate, so that inmate noise and disturbance is eliminated. Such cells are primarily used to isolate an inmate who has made himself generally obnoxious in the maximum punitive area by yelling, screaming, and causing general annoyance. Such conduct, of course, cannot be permitted to go unchecked, because the noise is carried into other areas through the ventilation duct work and is likely to invite violent response from other inmates in the same cell block or even spread throughout the entire institution. These isolated stripped cells provide a complete solitary confinement area for those who become incorrigible. It also assures the existence of a facility where physical damage to fixtures or prison property cannot occur.

A regulation was promulgated by the Corrections Commissioner on March 2, 1970, which prescribed that inmates in punitive segregation must receive a daily minimum of 2300 calories of food per day. The prison officials misinterpreted this to mean, that if the minimum food service was provided in one meal, that would fulfill the rule requirements. This error was discovered by the administration and corrected by a directive in August 1970. Contrary to LaReau's testimony, the prison records do not indicate that he had served time in punitive segregation during this specific period between March 2, 1970 and August 1970, thus he could not claim to have been subjected to the misapplication of this regulation. . . .

It is the petitioner's claim that the stripped cell and the conditions of confinement therein constituted cruel and unusual punishment per se. The Court personally viewed these cells on May 18, 1970, accompanied by counsel for both parties. The Court saw the physical facilities provided for the various categories of segregation as hereinbefore described. It finds that these cells, when properly used for limited periods according to the existing rules, do not constitute cruel and abusive punishment per se; and that their use did not become such in the manner in which punishment was administered in LaReau's case. In reaching this conclusion, this Court concurs in the findings of the state court.

Note 4.

LANDMAN V. ROYSTER
1 Prison L. Rptr. 13 (1971)
United States District Court, Eastern District of Virginia

MERHIGE, J.

Order

For the reasons stated in the memorandum of the Court this day filed, and deeming it proper so to do, it is ADJUDGED, ORDERED and DECREED as follows:

The defendants, their successors, agents, servants, employees, and all acting in concert therewith, be, and they are hereby, enjoined and restrained from performing, causing to perform, or permitting the performance of any acts found in the memorandum of the Court to be violative of the prohibition against cruel and unusual punishment, and specifically:

1. The imposition of a bread and water diet on any inmate of the Virginia State Penitentiary System, or
2. The use of such force as chains, handcuffs, tape or tear gas, except when necessary or required to protect a person from imminent physical harm, or to prevent escape or serious injury to property. In no event shall the use of any of the foregoing be for a longer period than is necessary to isolate any prisoner against whom said actions may have been taken. In no event shall *any* physical force be used against any inmate for purposes of punishment.
3. No inmate shall be kept nude, or restrained, for any period longer than it shall be reasonably necessary to secure the services of a doctor, to the end that said doctor may determine whether or not [2] said inmate's health will be affected thereby, and further whether or not such nudity or restraints are required by reason of a substantial risk of said inmate injuring himself. No inmate shall be so confined or restrained except in those cases wherein a doctor affirmatively states, in writing, that the health of the inmate will not be affected thereby, and that the inmate presents a substantial risk of injuring himself unless said steps are taken. Any such statement shall contain reasons upon which the doctor's conclusions are based.

4. No inmate shall be put in a solitary cell with any other inmate except by reason of an emergency and in no event for longer than it shall be reasonably necessary to make other arrangements.

5. The defendants will cause to be put into full force and effect, forthwith, those minimum due process standards referred to in detail in the Court's memorandum, and they are enjoined from the imposition of penalties prior thereto except as may be necessary to maintain order within the State Prison System until such time as arrangements have been made for the orderly implementation of the requirements of due process referred to in the Court's memorandum.

SOSTRE V. ROCKEFELLER
312 F. Supp. 863 (1970), *aff'd. in part, reversed in part, sub. nom.*
SOSTRE V. MCGINNIS
422 F. 2d 178 (1971), cert. den. 404 U.S. 1049 (1972)
United States District Court, Southern District of New York

MOTLEY, District Judge.

This is a civil rights action, 42 U.S.C. § 1983, 28 U.S.C. § 1343(3), brought by plaintiff, Martin Sostre, an "Afro-American citizen of the United States" and resident of Green Haven Prison against the Governor of New York, the Commissioner of Corrections and the Wardens of two New York State prisons.

Mr. Sostre is no stranger to the New York State prison system, having already served twelve years, 1952–1964, four of which were spent in solitary confinement at Attica State Prison for Black Muslim activity. (T. 3, 7, 160–166). He is also no stranger to the federal courts with his civil rights complaints against New York prison officials. (T. 4). He secured for Black Muslim prisoners their rights to certain unrestricted religious liberties during his prior incarceration. Pierce, Sostre, Sa Marion

v. La Vallee, 293 F.2d 233 (2d Cir. 1961) and Sostre v. McGinnis, 334 F.2d 906 (2d Cir.), cert. den., 379 U.S. 892, 85 S.Ct. 168, 13 L.Ed. 2d 96 (1964). His earlier legal activity also resulted in the elimination of some of the more outrageously inhumane aspects of solitary confinement in some of the state's prisons. (T. 163, 167).

Martin Sostre is again in prison. This time he is there pursuant to a sentence of 30–40 years, to be followed by a one year sentence and a sentence of 30 days for contempt of court, imposed upon him by the Supreme Court of New York, Erie County, on March 18, 1968. (Def. Proposed Finding of Fact No. 1 and Exh. A).

On the day of his sentence, he was immediately taken to Attica Prison where he remained overnight in a cell block which contained no other prisoners. (T. 5–6, 157–158). The next morning, he was taken in a "one-man draft" to Green Haven Prison. (T. 6, 538). According to the Deputy Warden in charge of Attica (the warden, a defendant here, being on vacation), he sought Sostre's removal from that prison as soon as possible. (T. 520). He, therefore, called the office of the Commissioner of Corrections of the State of New York and spoke to the Deputy Commissioner who approved the transfer. (T. 520–521; Def. Proposed Finding of Fact No. 11). The Deputy Warden of Attica testified vaguely and without substantiation as follows: "I thought it was best for the interests of the inmate and for the state that this man be transferred to another institution." (T. 521).

Immediately after his arrival at Attica, Sostre began a legal battle for reversal of his conviction. He sought to mail an application for a certificate of reasonable doubt to the state court which he had prepared prior to sentence, but the guard at Attica refused to mail the application. (T. 181–182, 638–640).

The next day, Sostre found himself in solitary confinement in Green Haven where he remained for several days. (T. 8–9, 11; Pl. Exh. 37 at 2; Def. Proposed Finding of Fact No. 13). He was then permitted to join the general population and to mail his application for a certificate of reasonable doubt. (T. 259–260).

However, shortly thereafter, on June 25, 1968, Sostre was back in solitary confinement (now called "punitive segregation" by defendants). He remained in such confinement until July 2, 1969, when he was returned to the general population pursuant to a temporary restraining order issued by this court in the present action, followed by a preliminary injunction. 309 F.Supp. 611 (S.D.N.Y. Sept. 4, 1969). A trial followed upon which were established the facts found herein and upon which the relief granted in this opinion is based.

On June 25, 1968, Sostre placed in the prison mail box for mailing to his attorney a letter with handwritten legal motions and other papers attached. One of these was a motion for change of venue of the trial of his codefendant, Mrs. Geraldine Robinson, who had not yet been tried, from Erie County (Buffalo). (T. 50, 53; Pl. Exh. 17). He was called to the office of defendant Follette, Warden of Green Haven Prison, who had the papers on his desk. The Warden asked Sostre whether he had a license to practice law, to which he replied in the negative. (T. 51). The Warden admittedly denied Sostre the right to prepare legal papers for his codefendant, since he was not a licensed attorney, and flatly refused to mail out the motion papers. (Def. Proposed Finding of Facts No. 24–25; T. 1240–1241).

At the same time, Warden Follette questioned Sostre about a reference in his letter to his attorney about an organization known as R.N.A. (Republic of New Africa) "because defendant Follette was concerned about a statement in plaintiff's May 19, 1968 letter to his sister." (Def. Proposed Finding of Fact No. 28; T. 1241–1242; Pl. Exh. 29F). This statement reads:

> As for me, there is no doubt in my mind whatsoever that I will be out soon, either by having my appeal reversed in the courts or by being liberated by the Universal Forces of Liberation. The fact that the militarists of this country are being defeated in Viet Nam and are already engaged with an escalating rebellion in this country by the oppressed Afro-American people and their white allies are sure signs that the power structure is on its way out. They are now in their last days and soon they won't be able to oppress anybody because they themselves will be before the People's courts to be punished for their crimes against humanity as were the German war criminals at Nuremberg. (Pl. Exh. 19; Def. Proposed Finding of Fact No. 28).

It is undisputed that as a result of plaintiff's refusal to cease and desist from "practicing law" in the institution, and his refusal to answer questions about R.N.A., and because of the statement in plaintiff's letter to his sister that "he would be leaving the institution soon," defendant Follette decided to place plaintiff in the punitive segregation unit. (Def. Proposed Finding of Fact No. 31; T. 1248–1249).

The proof also established: 1) plaintiff received no prior written notice of the above charges which resulted in his segregation; 2) there was no record made of the discussion with the Warden; 3) defendant McGinnis, the Commissioner of Corrections, was notified of plaintiff's confinement and the reasons therefor but took no action (T. 692–700; Pl. Exh. 29, 29A–F); 4) plaintiff was not charged with violence, attempting to escape, incitement to riot or any similar charge; and 5) plaintiff remained in segregation from June 25, 1968 until released by order of this court, more than a year later, on July 2, 1969.

The parties have stipulated that as a result of solitary confinement for more than a year, Sostre has lost 124⅓ days of "good time" credit, since under the rules a prisoner in solitary cannot earn good time. [N.Y.Correction Law §§ 230, 234 (McKinney's Consol.Laws c. 43, 1968); Pl. Exh. 1 at 5, Pl. Exh. 31; Reply Brief of Def. at 20].

There is also no real dispute as to the conditions which obtained in punitive segregation during plaintiff's yearlong stay. There was only one other person incarcerated in the same group of cells as plaintiff (about four out of thirteen months) from August 14, 1968 to December 20, 1968. (Def. Proposed Finding of Fact No. 55; T. 97–98). One prisoner brought to solitary and placed in another group of cells committed suicide the next day. (T. 127–131, 400–406, 793, 839, 895–896, 905–906). Plaintiff was deprived of second portions of food (T. 887–888) and all desserts as a punishment for the entire time. (Def. Proposed Finding of Fact No. 41). He remained in his cell 24 hours per day. He was allowed one hour per day of recreation in a small, completely enclosed yard. Sostre refused this privilege because it was conditioned upon submission, each day to a mandatory "strip frisk" (completely naked) which included a rectal examination. (Def. Proposed Finding of Facts No. 37–38; T. 88–90). He was permitted to shower and shave with *hot* water only once a week. (Def. Proposed Finding of Fact No. 34). He was not permitted to use the prison library, read newspapers, see movies, or attend school or training programs. (T. 91–93, 96–97). He was not allowed to work. (T. 91). Prisoners in the general population who work are able to earn money with which they may purchase items from the prison commissary, or purchase books, or subscribe to newspapers. (T. 93). Prisoners in punitive segregation have access to only a few novels and "shoot-'em ups" selected for them. (T. 92–93). But, as plaintiff and defendants' counsel put it, the crux of the matter is human isolation—the loss of "group privileges." (T. 87–88, 165–166). Release from segregation is wholly within the discretion of the Warden. However, a recommendation from a non-professional, so-called, group therapy counsellor might help. (T. 134–136, 388, 773–774, 917, 921).

This court finds that punitive segregation under the conditions to which plaintiff was subjected at Green Haven is physically harsh, destructive of morale, dehumanizing in the sense that it is needlessly degrading, and dangerous to the maintenance of sanity when continued for more than a short period of time which should certainly not exceed 15 days. (T. 300, 317–320).

After plaintiff was sent to solitary confinement on June 25, 1968, his cell was searched. The Warden alleged in an affidavit filed on July 3, 1969 that the search revealed contraband. This consisted of: 1) a letter from a court belonging to another inmate (which plaintiff was translating into Spanish for that other inmate (T. 66–67; Pl. Exh. 21); and 2) two small pieces of emery paper. (Pl. Exh. 37, at 2; T. 683–684.) A Disciplinary Report dated June 25, 1968 (Pl. Exh. 22–C) records that plaintiff was reprimanded for possessing the letter. There is no similar report regarding the emery paper, although the Warden alleged both items were found at the same time. (Pl. Exh. 37, at 2). The Warden claims that the emery paper was "adaptable for the fashioning of a key or lock picking tool." (Pl. Exh. 37, at 2). Plaintiff denied ever having seen the emery paper before trial. (T. 65–67). The court believes plaintiff's testimony for the following reasons: 1) plaintiff was already in punitive segregation when the emery paper was allegedly found in his cell; 2) the Disciplinary Report of June 25, 1968 does not contain this charge (Pl. Exh. 22–C); 3) the first written recordation of any such charge against Sostre does not appear until October 29, 1968, shortly after Sostre filed his *pro se* complaint in this action on October 15, 1968 (Pl. Exh. 29–F); 4) defendants have not requested this court to make any finding with respect to the emery paper in their proposed findings of fact. On June 25, 1968, search of Sostre's cell also revealed that he was lending his law books to other inmates, after removing therefrom a stamp identifying these books (which turned out to be copies of the Harvard Law Review) as belonging to Sostre. (Follette Dep. 62–64, 117). This along with the two preceding charges was one of the charges originally put forth by defendants as a reason for Sostre's confinement but dropped upon the trial (T. 1248–1249, 683–684).

The day after plaintiff's court-ordered release from segregation, July 3, 1969, he was again disciplined. This time he was charged with having dust on his cell bars. The punishment was to confine him to his cell for several days. Again, plaintiff denied this charge, claiming he was so charged and punished in order that he would miss the regular July 4th celebration. This celebration would have brought Sostre in contact with prisoners from another part of the prison. Such contact is permitted only once a year on July 4. (T. 78–79). This court finds that this charge and punishment were imposed upon Sostre in retaliation for his legal success.

On or about August 3, 1969, plaintiff was again disciplined for having "inflammatory racist literature" in his cell. The punishment was deprivation of yard and movie privileges for 60 days. (T. 74–77, 1071–1073). The so-called "inflammatory racist literature" consisted of handwritten political articles by Sostre, some of which contained excerpts from articles printed in newspapers and magazines in general circulation in the prison (T. 72–77; Pl. Exh. 23) and lists of officers of the Black Panther Party and the Republic of New Africa, copied from similar articles in *Esquire* and other magazines. (T. 72).

All of plaintiff's letters to and from his attorney, Joan Franklin, were censored by the Warden. He excised therefrom everything which he believed was not directly related to Sostre's immediate case. (Pl. Exh. 3, 4, 7, 8, 10, 12, 13, 14, 19–23, 29–30, 33–38; Follette Dep. at 69, 70, 136, 139). And a letter to the Postal Inspector of the United States Post Office complaining about plaintiff's failure to receive receipts for certified mail was also not mailed by the Warden. (Pl. Exh. 11; T. 35).

This court finds from all of the facts and circumstances of this case, as set forth above, that Sostre was sent to punitive segregation and kept there until released by court order not because of any serious infraction of the rules of prison discipline, or even for any minor infraction, but because Sostre was being punished specially by the Warden because of his legal and Black Muslim activities during his 1952–1964 incarceration, because of his threat to file a law suit against the Warden to secure his right to unrestricted correspondence with his attorney and to aid his codefendant (T. 52; Def. Post Trial Brief at 20, 32) and because he is, unquestionably, a black militant who persists in writing and expressing his militant and radical ideas in prison. (T. 71–77, 1316–1319; Pl. Exh. 23).

I. Cruel and Unusual Punishment

Plaintiff claims that his confinement to punitive segregation for an indefinite period of time amounted to cruel and unusual punishment forbidden by the Eighth and Fourteenth Amendments to the Constitution, arising not only from the reasons for his confinement and the length of his confinement, but also from the conditions of his confinement. This court agrees and so holds. See Wright v. McMann, 387 F.2d 519 (2d Cir. 1967). . . . This court holds that the punishment imposed upon Sostre for this offense, which was indefinite confinement to punitive segregation, was so disproportionate to the offense committed as to amount to cruel and unusual punishment. Weems v. United States, 217 U.S. 349 (1910); Fulwood v. Clemmer, 206 F.Supp. 370 (D.C. D.C.1962). It is clear from all of the facts in this case that but for the intervention of this court (which released Sostre from confinement after more than a year) Sostre would, in all likelihood, still be in punitive segregation for this alleged offense.

The Warden claimed that he assigned Sostre to punitive segregation because Sostre refused to answer "fully and truthfully" questions put to him by the Warden about the meaning of the letters R.N.A. (Pl. Exh. 1, Rule 12, Inmates' Rule Book). The court disbelieves that ambiguous claim. But even if this were true, assignment to punitive segregation for an indefinite period of time for this infraction of the rules is likewise so disproportionate to the charge, as to be clearly barred by the Eighth Amendment's prohibition against disproportionate punishment.

The court also holds that the totality of the circumstances to which Sostre was subjected for more than a year was cruel and unusual punishment when tested against "the evolving standards of decency that mark the progress of a maturing society." Trop. v. Dulles, 356 U.S. 86, 101 (1958) (Opinion of Warren, C. J.).

"[T]his condemnation of segregation is the experience years ago of people going stir crazy, especially in segregation." (T. 320). The conditions which undeniably existed in punitive segregation at Green Haven, this court finds, "could only serve to destroy completely the spirit and undermine the sanity of the prisoner," Wright v. McMann, *supra,* 387 F.2d at 526, when imposed for more than fifteen days. Subjecting a prisoner to the demonstrated risk of the loss of his sanity as punishment for any offense in prison is plainly cruel and unusual punishment as judged by present standards of decency. *Cf.* Ex parte Medley, 134 U.S. 160, 167–170, 10 S.Ct. 384, 33 L.Ed. 835 (1890). In order to be constitutional, punitive segregation as practiced in Green Haven must be limited to no more than fifteen days and may be imposed only for serious infractions of the rules.

II. Procedural Due Process

Plaintiff claims that his confinement to segregation for more than a year was effected in violation of his right not to be deprived of his liberty without due process of law as guaranteed by the Fifth and Fourteenth Amendments to the Federal Constitution, in that: 1) he was sentenced to such confinement for offenses which under the rules of the prison did not constitute offenses; 2) with respect to the charge involving the emery paper there was no proof that he had such paper in his possession; 3) he did not receive advance written notice of the charges; 4) he was denied the right to assistance of counsel or a counsel substitute; 5) he was denied the right to call witnesses in rebuttal of the charges; 6) he was denied the right to confront or cross-examine witnesses; 7) there were no written records of the disciplinary proceedings against him other than a notation of the charges, plaintiff's plea, and defendants' summary determination of guilt; 8) the right of appeal and the ability to make a meaningful appeal were denied as a result of the omission of his right to counsel, to call and cross-examine witnesses, and to have a written record.

As a result of his confinement, plaintiff lost 124⅓ days of good time which might otherwise have been applied both to hasten consideration of his eligibility for parole and in mandating his release on parole N.Y.Correction Law §§ 230, 803 (McKinney 1968).

Very recently, the Supreme Court reiterated the firmly established due process principle that where governmental action may seriously injure an individual, and the reasonableness of that action depends on fact findings, the evidence used to prove the government's case must be disclosed to the individual so that he has an opportunity to show that it is untrue. The individual must also have the right to retain counsel. The decision-maker's conclusion must rest solely on the legal rules and evidence adduced at the hearing. In this connection, the decision-maker should state the reasons for his determination and indicate the evidence upon which he relied. Finally, in such cases, the high Court ruled, an impartial decision-maker is essential. Goldberg v. Kelly, 397 U.S. 254, 90 S.Ct. 1011, 25 L.Ed.2d 287 (1970); *accord,* Escalera v. New York City Housing Authority, 425 F.2d 853 (2d Cir. 1970).

This court holds that plaintiff was, in effect, "sentenced" to more than a year in punitive segregation without the minimal procedural safeguards required for the imposition of such drastic punishment upon a prisoner. This punishment not only caused plaintiff physical deprivation, needless degradation, loss of work, training and self improvement opportunities, and mental suffering, but materially affected the length of time he must serve under his court-imposed sentence.

Before plaintiff could have been constitutionally "sentenced" to punitive segregation, he was entitled to: 1) written notice of the charges against him (in advance of a hearing) which designated the prison rule violated; 2) a hearing before an impartial official at which he had the right to cross-examine his accusers and call witnesses in rebuttal; 3) a written record of the hearing, decision, reasons therefor and evidence relied upon; and 4) retain counsel or a counsel substitute.

A prisoner carries with him to prison his right to procedural due process which applies to charges for which he may receive punitive segregation or any other punishment for which earned good time credit may be revoked or the opportunity to earn good time credit is denied. There is no place in our system of law for reaching the result which occurred here without the safeguards listed above. . . .

United States Court of Appeals, Second Circuit

Before Lumbard, Chief Judge, Waterman, Senior Circuit Judge, and Moore, Friendly, Smith, Kaufman, Hays, Anderson and Feinberg, Circuit Judges.

KAUFMAN, Circuit Judge:

We voted to hear the initial argument of this appeal *en banc,* a procedure we reserve for extraordinary circumstances, so that we might give plenary review to a complex of urgent social and political conflicts persistently seeking solution in the courts as legal problems, a phenomenon de Tocqueville commented upon many years ago. Democracy in America, vol. I at 290 (Vintage ed. 1945). The elaborate opinion and order below raise important questions concerning the federal constitutional rights of state prisoners which neither Supreme Court precedent nor our own past decisions have answered. The sparse authority from other courts is for the most part either inconclusive or conflicting.

This is an appeal from an order entered May 14, 1970, by Judge Motley, sitting in the Southern District of New York, 312 F.Supp. 863, which granted plaintiff Martin Sostre punitive and compensatory damages against defendants Follette and McGinnis as well as a wide variety of injunctive relief in his action pursuant to the Civil Rights Act of 1871, 42 U.S.C. § 1983, and 28 U.S.C. §§ 1331, 1343(3). . . .

Judge Motley on May 14, 1970, entered the following order, which because of its complexity and importance to the questions we must decide, we reproduce in full. The district court subsequently granted a stay of its order pending appeal as to the bracketed portions. A stay as to the remainder of the order was denied.

> It is now ordered, that defendants Follette, McGinnis and Mancusi, their employees, agents, successors, and all persons in active concert and participation with them be, and they are hereby, perpetually enjoined and restrained from:
>
> 1) Returning plaintiff to punitive segregation for charges previously preferred against him;
> 2) Placing plaintiff in punitive segregation or subjecting him to any other punishment as a result of which he loses accrued good time credit or is unable to earn good time credit, without:
>   a. giving him, in advance of a hearing, a written copy of any charges made against him, citing the written rule or regulation which it is charged he has violated;
>   b. granting him a recorded hearing before a disinterested official where he will be entitled to cross-examine his accusers and to call witnesses on his own behalf;
>   c. granting him the right to retain counsel or to appoint a counsel substitute;
>   d. giving him, in writing, the decision of the hearing officer in which is briefly set forth the evidence upon which it is based, the reasons for the decision, and the legal basis for the punishment imposed.
> 3) Censoring, refusing to mail or refusing to give to Sostre: 1) Any communication between Sostre and the following—(a) any court; (b) any public official or agency; (c) any lawyer; (d) his co-defendant in the criminal matter pending against him; and, 2) Any letter relating to any legal matter to or from any other inmate who requests the assistance of Sostre in translating that letter into English.
> 4) Punishing Sostre for sharing with other inmates his law books, law reviews, and other legal materials, and from refusing to permit Sostre to assist any other inmate in any legal matter as long as defendants have not provided any court approved alternative means of legal assistance for such inmates.
> 5) Punishing Sostre for having in his possession political literature and for setting forth his political views orally or in writing, except for violation of reasonable rules approved by the court regulating freedom of speech.
>
> [It is further ordered that the above named defendants submit, within 90 days from the date of this order, for approval by this court, proposed rules and regulations governing the following:
> 1) the receipt, distribution, discussion and writing of political literature;
> 2) all future disciplinary charges and hearings with respect thereto where the possible punishments include solitary confinement, punitive segregation or any other segregation, and any other punishment in connection with which there is loss of, or inability to earn, good time credit.]
>
> It is further ordered that the above named defendants and their agents credit plaintiff with the 124⅓ days of good time credit which he was unable to earn while wrongfully incarcerated in punitive segregation from June 25, 1968 to July 2, 1969.
>
> [It is further ordered that the plaintiff, Martin Sostre, recover of the defendants, Warden Follette, and Commissioner McGinnis the sum of $13,020.00.]

Punishment for Political Beliefs and Legal Activities

The question as to the propriety of withdrawing from incarcerated individuals constitutional privileges enjoyed by citizens of the community, although troublesome, is not new to the courts. It is clear that in many respects the constitutionally protected freedoms enjoyed by citizens-at-large may be withdrawn or constricted as to state prisoners, so far as "justified by the considerations underlying our penal system," Price v. Johnston, 334 U.S. 266, 285,

68 S.Ct. 1049, 1060, 92 L.Ed. 1356 (1948). Federal courts have been reluctant to intrude themselves into the complex and delicate problems of prison administration. E.g., United States ex rel. Knight v. Ragen, 337 F.2d 425 (7th Cir.), cert. denied, 380 U.S. 985, 85 S.Ct. 1355, 14 L.Ed.2d 277 (1964); Hatfield v. Bailleaux, 290 F.2d 632, 640 (9th Cir. 1961); Childs v. Pegelow, 321 F.2d 487 (4th Cir. 1963). The time is long since past, however, when a court might describe a prisoner as temporarily "a slave of the state," Ruffin v. Commonwealth, 62 Va. (21 Gratt.) 790, 796, or treat him as such. Among those rights *not* taken from Sostre when he entered Attica, either "expressly or by necessary implication," Coffin v. Reichard, 143 F.2d 443, 445 (6th Cir. 1944), is freedom from discriminatory punishment inflicted solely because of his beliefs, whether religious or secular. Cooper v. Pate, 378 U.S. 546, 84 S.Ct. 1733, 12 L.Ed.2d 1030 (1964) (per curiam) (unlawful to withdraw prison privileges because of inmate's religious faith); see Lee v. Washington, 390 U.S. 333, 88 S.Ct. 994, 19 L.Ed.2d 1212 (1968) (per curiam) (racial segregation); Fulwood v. Clemmer, 206 F.Supp. 370, 373–374 (D.C.D.C.1962) (religious discrimination). Moreover, the Constitution protects with special solicitude, a prisoner's access to the courts. Ex parte Hull, 312 U.S. 546, 61 S.Ct. 640, 85 L.Ed. 1034 (1941); Johnson v. Avery, 393 U.S. 483, 89 S.Ct. 747, 21 L.Ed.2d 718 (1969). Accordingly, Sostre's lengthy confinement to segregation violated due process of law if, as the district court found, Warden Follette inflicted the punishment either because of Sostre's militant political ideas or his litigation, past or threatened, against Follette or other state officials.

Sostre does not shrink from characterizing himself as a "jailhouse lawyer" and the record before us does justice to this label, as does the history of Sostre's earlier period of confinement in New York prisons from 1952–64 following his first conviction for selling narcotics. It is not unreasonable to suppose, as the district court apparently did, that Warden Follette was aware of Sostre's Black Muslim activities during that period; of his solitary confinement in Attica Prison for four years, resulting from his religious activism; and of his success in securing through earlier litigation before this court the recognition of certain constitutional liberties for state prisoners. See Pierce v. LaVallee, 293 F.2d 233 (2d Cir. 1961); Sostre v. McGinnis, 334 F.2d 906 (2d Cir.), cert. denied, 379 U.S. 892, 85 S.Ct. 168, 13 L.Ed.2d 96 (1964). Sostre's version of his June 25, 1968, interview with Follette, if believed, was a proper basis for Judge Motley's conclusion that Follette committed Sostre to segregation, if not in retaliation for his black militancy or past litigation, then at least to squelch Sostre's threat to take Follette to court over his censorship of Sostre's correspondence. Some substantiation for Sostre's account might be inferred from Follette's summary commitment of Sostre, without following the practice described in the New York Department of Correction's Employees' Rule Book (Rule 8.4), requiring trial by a "disciplinary officer or court."

On this evidence, we cannot conclude that the district judge was "clearly erroneous" in attributing improper motives to Follette, affording as we must "due regard * * * to the opportunity of the trial court to judge of the credibility" of Sostre and Follette, F.R.Civ.P. 52(a). See Zenith Radio Corp. v. Hazeltine Research, Inc., 395 U.S. 100, 89 S.Ct. 1562, 23 L.Ed.2d 129 (1969) (reviewing court may overturn finding if on the entire evidence it is left with the definite and firm conviction that a mistake has been made). On the other hand, McGinnis was not privy to Follette's interview with Sostre. The record is barren of any justification for attributing to him, in sanctioning Sostre's continued confinement, any more sinister motive than appropriate deference to the judgment of Warden Follette. McGinnis on the record before us, had no reason to suspect Follette of other than proper motivation.

Cruel and Unusual Punishment

A reflection of maturing sensitivity in this country to the condition of some of our prisons may be seen in the district court's finding that deprivations such as Sostre endured for a year may not again be inflicted on New York State prisoners for longer than fifteen days, and only then for serious violations of prison rules. Otherwise, Judge Motley held, such punishment would run ashoal of the Eighth Amendment prohibition of cruel and unusual punishment, as applied to the states through the due process guarantee of the Fourteenth Amendment, Robinson v. California, 370 U.S. 660, 82 S.Ct. 1417, 8 L.Ed.2d 758 (1962).

We respect the outrage, given form and content by scholarly research and reflection, that underlay the expert testimony at trial of Sol Rubin, for many years Counsel for the National Council on Crime and Delinquency, and Dr. Seymour Halleck, a psychiatrist at the

University of Wisconsin with long experience in state correctional practices. Mr. Rubin testified that Sostre's segregated environment was degrading, dehumanizing, conducive to mental derangement, and for these reasons "a gross departure" from enlightened and progressive contemporary standards for the proper treatment of prison inmates. Dr. Halleck feared that the isolation from human contact in punitive segregation might cause prisoners to hallucinate and to distort reality. Long-term isolation might have so serious an impact, in fact, as to "destroy" a person's "mentality." Dr. Halleck singled out for particular censure Green Haven's "group therapy" program, whose compulsory aspects he found repugnant to effective treatment of participants and indeed inconsistent with minimal standards of professionalism among trained group counsellors.

Nor would candor permit us to dismiss these opinions as aberrational among those views revealed in relevant sources referred to us by counsel or known to us through our own research. To the contrary, it would not be misleading to characterize many of the opinions of plaintiff's experts as fairly representative of the perspective of adherents to the "new penology," see Knuckles v. Prasse, 302 F.Supp. 1036, 1047–1048 (E.D.Pa.1969), the thrust of whose doctrine may be gauged by the preference for the adjective "correctional" rather than "penal" as more accurately indicating the proper function of a prison system. The rapidly rising standards in the field of penology and corrections that Mr. Rubin referred to in his testimony are reflected in a growing preoccupation with institutional strictures and techniques designed to "reintegrate" prisoners with society or, in the jargon of the experts, to "provide * * * motivation for acquiring a conventional role in a non-delinquent setting." Conjugal visiting, daytime work or educational-release programs, vocational training, half-way houses, and inmate publication of prison newspapers are some of the vanguard weapons in the "modern" approach to prison administration. The key concepts are access and involvement of prisoners with the free society "on the outside." Anathema to this perspective are perhaps more traditional practices which subject prisoners to deprivation, degradation, subservience, and isolation, in an attempt to "break" them and make them see the error of their ways. It is suggested by many observers that such techniques are counter-productive, tending only to instill in most prisoners attitudes hostile to rehabilitation, summarized by one author as "doubt, guilt, inadequacy, diffusion, self-absorption, apathy [and] despair."

We do not question, either, the relevance to an inquiry under the Eighth Amendment of opinions which may represent a progressing sense of humaneness as well as a new calculation as to the efficacy of penal practices. See Trop v. Dulles, 356 U.S. 86, 101, 78 S.Ct. 590, 2 L.Ed.2d 630 (1958) (Eighth Amendment invokes "the evolving standards of decency that mark the progress of a maturing society").

For a federal court, however, to place a punishment beyond the power of a state to impose on an inmate is a drastic interference with the state's free political and administrative processes. It is not only that we, trained as judges, lack expertise in prison administration. Even a lifetime of study in prison administration and several advanced degrees in the field would not qualify us *as a federal court* to command state officials to shun a policy that they have decided is suitable because to us the choice may seem unsound or *personally* repugnant. As judges we are obliged to school ourselves in such objective sources as historical usage, see Wilkerson v. Utah, 99 U.S. 130, 25 L.Ed. 345 (1870), practices in other jurisdictions, see Weems v. United States, 217 U.S. 349, 30 S.Ct. 544, 54 L.Ed. 793 (1910), and public opinion, see Robinson v. California, 370 U.S. 660, 666, 82 S.Ct. 1417, 8 L.Ed.2d 758 (1962), before we may responsibly exercise the power of judicial review to declare a punishment unconstitutional under the Eighth Amendment.

Accordingly, we have in the past declined to find an Eighth Amendment violation unless the punishment can properly be termed "barbarous" or "shocking to the conscience." See Church v. Hegstrom, 416 F.2d 449, 451 (2d Cir. 1969). Although the conditions Sostre endured were severe, we cannot agree with the district court that they were "so foul, so inhuman, and so violative of basic concepts of decency," Wright v. McMann, 387 F.2d 519 (2d Cir. 1967) as to require that similar punishments be limited in the future to any particular length of time. Nor can we agree that Sostre's own long confinement—however contrary such prolonged segregation may be to the views of some experts—would have been "cruel and unusual" had Sostre in fact been confined for the reasons asserted by Warden Follette, rather than on account of his beliefs and litigiousness.

It is undisputed on this appeal that segregated confinement does not itself violate the Constitution. Indeed, we learn that a similar form of confinement is probably used in almost every jurisdiction in this country and has been described as one of "the main traditional disciplinary tools" of our prison systems. President's Commission on Law Enforcement and Administration of Justice, Task Force Report: Corrections 50–51 (1967); S. Rubin, et al., The Law of Criminal Corrections 293 (1963). Plaintiff has directed our attention to currently operative rules in other jurisdictions which limit the duration of segregated confinement, and to several commentaries recommending or approving such rules. In several states, however, incarceration in segregated cells seems to be for an indefinite period, as it is in New York. The federal practice appears to be that prisoners shall be retained in solitary "for as long as necessary to achieve the purposes intended," sometimes "indefinitely." Furthermore, "willful refusal to obey an order or demonstrated defiance of personnel acting in line of duty may constitute sufficient basis for placing an inmate in segregation." Such analogous practices do not impel us to the conclusion that the Eighth Amendment forbids indefinite confinement under the conditions endured by Sostre for all the reasons asserted by Warden Follette until such time as the prisoner agrees to abide by prison rules—however counter-productive as a correctional measure or however personally abhorrent the practice may seem to some of us.

In arriving at this conclusion,[1] we have considered Sostre's diet, the availability in his cell of at least rudimentary implements of personal hygiene,[2] the opportunity for exercise and for participation in group therapy, the provision of at least some general reading matter from the prison library and of unlimited numbers of law books, and the constant possibility of communication with other segregated prisoners. These factors in combination raised the quality of Sostre's segregated environment several notches above those truly barbarous and inhumane conditions heretofore condemned by

---

[1] Judge Feinberg expresses the view in his dissent, that 'isolation of an adult prisoner for a sharply limited period as punishment for a serious breach of prison discipline" would be constitutional. But then he goes on to ask rhetorically whether solitary or segregated confinement "for two years instead of one, or for five years, or for ten, or more," would be constitutional. We have made an effort to suggest the impracticality of setting any specific time period for segregated confinement, beyond which the punishment would be "cruel and unusual." In some instances, depending upon the conditions of the segregation, and the mental and physical health of the inmate, five days or even one day might prove to be constitutionally intolerable. We would ask our dissenting brother in turn, would nine months, six months, or three months of segregated confinement be unconstitutional, without reference to the circumstances of confinement?

Judge Feinberg is also properly concerned with "endless solitary confinement * * * unless the prisoner 'gives in.'" Our response is that we are concerned also. But one must ask on what was it that Sostre was expected to "give in." He was asked to show a change in his intransigent defiance of several prison regulations, defiance which posed a credible threat to the security of the prison, by attending group therapy sessions. Does it violate principles of fundamental decency to insist that a prisoner comply with reasonable rules applicable to all similarly situated?

[2] In response to Judge Feinberg's dissent, we emphasize that no one testified that based on his observation or as the result of a physical or psychological examination of Sostre, he concluded that Sostre was being adversely affected or that his physical or mental health was threatened. We note that the record shows that a prison physician visited Sostre's segregation unit daily, and at no time did the physician observe, or did Sostre call to his attention, any such effects.

Indeed, the experts before the district court were in conflict even over the hypothetical question whether the conditions that Sostre experienced in segregation would be dangerous to the sanity of "a prisoner." See p. 190 and fn. 11, *supra*. On the basis of these conflicting expert opinions, Judge Feinberg observes that the district court found as a fact that these conditions "could only serve to * * * undermine the sanity of the prisoner" * * * when imposed for more than fifteen days. We do not agree with our brother that we are required to declare this "finding" to be either right or wrong, either "clearly erroneous" or adequately supported by the record and therefore correct. We are not concerned here with conflicting testimony of witnesses to the same *unique* historical event. The question, rather, is a *general* one: whether the Eighth Amendment absolutely forbids a state to use a means of discipline when there is no evidence of any physical or psychological injury to the health of the prisoner who complains of the measure, and also when the opinions of the experts as to the effects of the *type* of discipline are in conflict. To hold the district court either right or wrong would be tantamount to ruling that either Dr. Halleck or Dr. Johnston is right, and the other is wrong. That is not our function, nor was it the function of the district court. It is a judgment among competing, rational policies, a judgment therefore properly reserved for decision by state political and administrative processes. . . .

ourselves and by other courts as "cruel and unusual." See Ford v. Board of Managers, 407 F.2d 937 (3rd Cir. 1969) (no running water or wash bowl; bread and water diet except one regular meal each third day; held constitutional); Landman v. Peyton, 370 F.2d 135 (4th Cir. 1966), cert. denied, 388 U.S. 920, 87 S.Ct. 2142, 18 L.Ed.2d 1367 (1967); Knuckles v. Prasse, 302 F.Supp. 1036 (E.D. Pa.1969) (400 days segregation held constitutional).

Finally, we cannot agree with Judge Motley that even if New York might in an appropriate case subject a prisoner to the conditions of Sostre's segregated confinement, had Follette's motives been as he described them, the punishment would in any event have been unconstitutionally disproportionate to the offense. Were we to rule otherwise, we would deny to prison authorities the power to use an entirely constitutional means of discipline in response not only to a credible threat to the security of the prison, but in response to a prisoner's refusal to answer appropriate questions put by prison authorities and to obey valid prison regulations.

Procedural Due Process

A divergence of perspectives similar to those we have seen in considering the Eighth Amendment issue is presented in another form by the district court's order that Sostre may not be punished in the future in such a way as to forfeit earned "good time" credit or to lose the chance to earn such credit unless he has (a) written notice of the charges against him; (b) a recorded hearing before a disinterested official with a chance to cross-examine adverse witnesses and call witnesses in his own behalf; (c) the right to retain counsel or counsel substitute; and unless (d) a written decision is rendered.

Sostre presses upon us a variety of cases, relied upon by the district court and said to be analogous to this case, in which federal courts have required states to square corners before exacting a penalty by following procedures similar to those mandated by Judge Motley. Particular importance is attached to Goldberg v. Kelly, 397 U.S. 254, 90 S.Ct. 1011, 25 L.Ed.2d 287 (1970), where the Supreme Court announced that before states may terminate welfare payments they must adopt "minimum procedural safeguards" and afford those who are to suffer loss "rudimentary due process," including advance written notice and a hearing at which the welfare recipient may cross-examine adverse witnesses and be represented by counsel. In addition, there must be a written statement of reasons for any termination, including some indication of the evidence supporting the adverse decision.

Our recent decision in Escalera v. New York City Housing Authority, 425 F.2d 853 (2d Cir. 1970), instructed that a state's withdrawal of the "privilege" of residing in a public housing project was onerous enough to require it to provide those affected with adequate advance notice, a hearing, access to adverse evidence, cross-examination of adverse witnesses, full disclosure of rules governing the hearing, and a reasoned decision based solely on the evidence adduced at the hearing.

Somewhat closer in point to the present case is Mempa v. Rhay, 389 U.S. 128, 88 S.Ct. 254, 19 L.Ed.2d 336 (1967). The court held that representation of petitioners by counsel was essential to the fairness of their deferred sentencing proceedings. The imposition of sentence had been suspended and the petitioners placed on probation. In the proceedings under review, defendants were faced with both sentencing and imprisonment on the first convictions for committing second offenses while out on probation. The Supreme Court determined that defendants should have been represented by counsel. Legal skills, the Court reasoned, would have aided petitioners in "marshalling the facts" and might have ensured that important legal rights were not lost because unexercised at that stage.

Federal courts disagree as to the reach of *Mempa* to probation revocation proceedings generally. *See* the extensive citation of cases in Hewett v. North Carolina, 415 F.2d 1316, 1322 (4th Cir. 1969). In *Hewett* the court decided that counsel was a necessary component of fundamental fairness at a probation revocation hearing, "the event which makes operative the loss of liberty," because a trained lawyer might have prevented the admission against defendant of improper evidence, and, through appropriate objections, exceptions, and assignments of error, have preserved defendant's right to appeal.

Escalera and *Goldberg* are persuasive recent authority that states may not avoid the rigors of due process by labelling an action which has serious and onerous consequences as a withdrawal of a "privilege" rather than a "right." *Mempa* warns us that procedural formality may be required in the operation of the criminalization and incarceration process beyond the determination of guilt at trial.

Thus, we do not doubt that Sostre was entitled to "due process of law" before he was punished for an infraction of prison rules. The exaction of segregated confinement was onerous indeed, and the distinction between a "right" and a "privilege"—or between "liberty" and a "privilege" for that matter—is nowhere more meaningless than behind prison walls. The difficult question, as always, is what process was due. In answering that question, we may not uncritically adopt the holdings of decisions that take color from contexts where the shadings are as different from the instant case as the cases we have discussed:

> [A]s a generalization, it can be said that due process embodies the differing rules of fair play, which through the years, have become associated with differing types of proceedings. Whether the Constitution requires that a particular right obtain in a specific proceeding depends upon a complexity of factors. The nature of the alleged right involved, the nature of the proceeding, and the possible burden on that proceeding, are all considerations which must be taken into account.

Hannah v. Larche, 363 U.S. 420, 442, 80 S.Ct. 1502, 1515, 4 L.Ed.2d 1307 (1960).

Beyond the process of guilt determination and initial incarceration, courts have displayed greater reluctance to import all the trappings of formal due process. Thus, a panel of this court has recently held that formal trial-type due process is not a requirement in connection with a parole *release* determination. Menechino v. Oswald, 430 F.2d 403 (1970). Like the relationship between Menechino and the parole board, Follette's relation to Sostre should not be viewed as adversarial in the same sense that a criminal trial is adversarial. Certainly, formal rules of evidence would be entirely inappropriate at a disciplinary proceeding. To dispose sensitively and carefully of each prisoner's unique case with due regard for the effect of each decision on the total fabric of the prison community, prison authorities must have wide access to relevant information. Since, in addition, there is no likelihood that substantial rights would be sacrificed if a prisoner failed, for example, to raise a proper objection or to take a timely appeal, the need for legal skills is less acute here than in *Mempa, Townsend,* or *Hewett.* Moreover, the evidence as to whether the prisoner has violated a prison regulation is likely to be simpler, more precise, and more readily at hand, than, for example, the evidence bearing on the question whether welfare payments should be terminated. There is correspondingly less need for cross-examination and calling of witnesses.

Most important, we think it inadvisable for a federal court to pass judgment one way or another as to the truly decisive consideration, whether formal due process requirements would be likely to help or to hinder in the state's endeavor to preserve order and discipline in its prisons and to return a rehabilitated individual to society. It would be too simplistic to dissociate the impact of punishment meted out after a disciplinary hearing from the method by which the hearing itself is conducted. As one court has observed: "The association between men in correction institutions is closer and more fraught with physical danger and psychological pressures than is almost any other kind of association between human beings." Edwards v. Sard, 250 F.Supp. 977, 981 (D.D.C. 1966). It is sad but true that the study of the prison subculture by psychologists and sociologists has until recently been largely neglected. Those who have looked into the problem, however, do not gainsay the volatility of relationships among prisoners and prison officials. See, e. g., Corrections 46–47; Gibbons, Changing the Law Breaker 200–12 (1965). We would not presume to fashion a constitutional harness of nothing more than our guesses. It would be mere speculation for us to decree that the effect of equipping prisoners with more elaborate constitutional weapons against the administration of discipline by prison authorities would be more soothing to the prison atmosphere and rehabilitative of the prisoner or, on the other hand, more disquieting and destructive of remedial ends. This is a judgment entrusted to state officials, not federal judges.

We are particularly unwilling to interfere with state administrative processes when reliable, detailed information or empirical studies are as scanty as they are on the subject of prison disciplinary procedures. See Corrections at 16; D. Glaser, The Effectiveness of a Prison and Parole System 172 (1964) ("prison discipline * * * has not received extensive objective research by anyone"). Judge Learned Hand wisely instructed us "[c]onstitutions are deliberately made difficult of amendment; mistaken readings of them cannot easily be corrected. Moreover, if they could be, constitutions must not degenerate into *vade mecums* or codes; when they begin to do so, it is a sign of a community unsure of itself and seeking protection against its own misgivings." The Spirit of Liberty 179 (1952).

Analogies and recommendations called to our attention do not go far to advance Sostre's position. Neither the Model Penal Code nor the Manual of the American Correctional Association would require confrontation and cross-examination, calling of witnesses by the prisoner, counsel or counsel substitute, or a written statement of evidence and rationale. Similarly, Rhode Island has voluntarily adopted new disciplinary procedures for its prisons, under court supervision, Morris v. Travisono, 310 F.Supp. 857 (D.R.I.1970), which include provisions for a hearing, advance written notice, and assistance by a prison officer, but no other of the formal safeguards required by Judge Motley's injunction. Sostre has referred us to rules adopted for the Missouri State Penitentiary, under which prisoners are assisted during a disciplinary proceeding by a member of the prison staff and where there must be a written summary of the disciplinary proceeding, including a statement of relevant evidence. Personnel Information Pamphlet: Rules and Procedures 3–4 (Sept.1967). Again, however, there is no provision for calling witnesses or cross-examination.

Indeed, it appears that, among those practices known to us, only in the federal correctional system must a formal proceeding, including each of the elements in the district court's mandate, precede *forfeiture* of good time allowances. Bureau of Prisons, Policy Statement: Withholding, Forfeiture, and Restoration of Good Time (No. 7400.6 Dec. 1, 1966). Notably, however, these formalities need *not* accompany discipline that results in the *withholding* of good time credit, as Judge Motley would require.

We therefore find ourselves in disagreement with Judge Motley's conclusion that each of the procedural elements incorporated in her mandatory injunction are necessary constitutional ingredients of every proceeding resulting in serious discipline of a prisoner. In thus rejecting Judge Motley's conclusions, however, we are not to be understood as disapproving the judgment of many courts that our constitutional scheme does not contemplate that society may commit lawbreakers to the capricious and arbitrary actions of prison officials. If substantial deprivations are to be visited upon a prisoner, it is wise that such action should at least be premised on facts rationally determined. This is not a concept without meaning. In most cases it would probably be difficult to find an inquiry minimally fair and rational unless the prisoner were confronted with the accusation, informed of the evidence against him, see Armstrong v. Manzo, 380 U.S. 545, 552, 85 S.Ct. 1187, 14 L.Ed.2d 62 (1965); Mullane v. Central Hanover Bank & Trust Co., 339 U.S. 306, 70 S.Ct. 652, 94 L.Ed. 865 (1950), and afforded a reasonable opportunity to explain his actions. See Nolan v. Scafati, 306 F.Supp. 1 (D.Mass.1969) (Wyzanski, J.). . . .

Conclusion

Because of the nature of this case, the multitude and complexity of claims raised and the extent of Judge Motley's considered opinion and the injunctive and other relief granted, we have been compelled to engage in this protracted exegesis. In light of what we have set forth, our conclusions follow.

A. Injunctive

1. Although not necessary to the disposition of Sostre's complaint, the district court held that several elements of trial-type procedure, enumerated in its order, were required by due process in every instance of prisoner discipline resulting in withholding of good time credit to the prisoner or loss of his opportunity to earn good time. Because of the importance of the question to the state of New York, and the frequency with which similar questions are being litigated in district courts of this jurisdiction, we are compelled to say that the district court was in error. All of the elements of due process recited by the district court are not necessary to the constitutionality of every disciplinary action taken against a prisoner. In light of this, we reverse the district court insofar as it enjoined defendants and others from so disciplining Sostre that he loses accrued good time credit or is unable to earn good time credit without full compliance with all the procedural steps set forth in Judge Motley's injunction. We do not thereby imply that discipline in New York prisons may be administered arbitrarily or capriciously. We would not lightly condone the absence of such basic safeguards against arbitrariness as adequate notice, an opportunity for the prisoner to reply to charges lodged against him, and a reasonable investigation into the relevant facts —at least in cases of substantial discipline. However, as consideration of Sostre's case

does not properly raise any question whether New York prisons regularly or systematically ignore minimal due process requirements, we must reverse the order of the district court that defendants submit for its approval, proposed rules and regulations governing future disciplinary actions. In this connection, we note that New York State has recently promulgated rules and regulations governing prison discipline which appear to give inmates new procedural protections. . . .

LUMBARD, Chief Judge (concurring):

I concur in Judge Kaufman's thorough opinion except as to Section VI regarding Procedural Due Process. While I agree in reversing those provisions of paragraph 2 of the order of the district court, I see no need to express any opinion on what the New York State authorities should do when determining whether or not to withhold or withdraw good time credit, or the general principles which should govern such situations.

WATERMAN, Circuit Judge (concurring):

I concur in each of the results reached in the majority opinion. Nevertheless, I am concerned that the discussion there with reference to Due Process rights of a state prisoner who is threatened with loss of good time or with a loss of the chance to earn such credit because of an alleged infraction of prison rules would seem inaccurately to portray the obligation of a federal court asked to "interfere with state administrative processes" on constitutional grounds. I submit that it is our duty, mandated by the U. S. Constitution, authorized by Congress, and demanded by conscience, to strike down any practice sanctioned by a State which does not conform to at least minimally acceptable levels of due process. The court, aptly noting that appellant has asked us to determine what process is constitutionally due him, a convicted and imprisoned felon, declines to determine the "truly decisive issue" because it lacks empiric information. While I most assuredly agree that studies and surveys and the presentation thereof to us might provide further information of value in balancing competing interests, their absence should never mean that the federal courts will ignore or condone state activity obviously violative of individual rights when that activity is indulged in under the guise of preserving order.

SMITH, Circuit Judge (concurring in part and dissenting in part):

I agree with most of Judge Kaufman's thoughtful and thorough opinion, but disagree in two respects and therefore dissent in part.

I agree with Judge Feinberg that the district court's finding that Sostre's segregation for more than one year was cruel and unusual punishment is supported by the record. Punishment of a nature found likely to bring about an inmate's insanity should be proscribed whether or not it is shown to have succeeded in doing so in the particular case, and whether or not it could be alleviated by "submission." . . .

FEINBERG, Circuit Judge (dissenting and concurring):

Because I agree with most of the exhaustive majority opinion, I regret that I find it necessary to dissent from the treatment of the cruel and unusual punishment point and from the reversal as to defendant McGinnis. As to the former, the majority opinion reaches three results, from each of which I dissent. The most important of these is the refusal to hold that there must be a definite limit on how long a prisoner may be kept in punitive segregation, or solitary confinement.[1] The majority holds that for "serious" offenses, the Constitution requires no limit so long as the prisoner has the option of submitting to prison discipline. Second, the majority holds that Sostre's alleged offenses considered together would have been "serious," if Warden Follette had acted for proper motives. Third, even though the warden's motives were "improper," the majority refuses to rule that Sostre's punishment was cruel and unusual.

Before considering these three aspects of the majority opinion, it must be emphasized that Sostre was segregated for over a year and, as Judge Motley noted, would in all likelihood still be effectively isolated but for the intervention of the district court. There is an intimation in the majority opinion that Sostre was not effectively cut off from usual day to day

---

[1] See, e. g., "[W]e cannot agree [that the conditions Sostre endured] require that similar punishments be limited in the future to any particular length of time," p. 191, *supra;* "[T]he Eighth Amendment [does not forbid] indefinite confinement under the conditions endured by Sostre for all the reasons asserted by Warden Follette until such time as the prisoner agrees to abide by prison rules," p. 193, *supra.*

contact with other human beings,[2] but the district judge's opinion makes clear that he was. The district judge and the majority both agree that "the crux of the matter is human isolation," and the district court opinion sets forth in melancholy detail the conditions that were imposed upon Sostre and the reasons why. I will not repeat them here except to note that the full vindictive flavor of defendants' treatment of Sostre is indicated by one incident, relegated to a footnote in the majority opinion. The day after Judge Motley ordered Sostre's release from over a year of segregation, he was again disciplined for having "dust on his cell bars." This caused him to miss the regular July 4th celebration, which would have brought him in contact with prisoners from another part of the prison, such contact being permitted only once a year on July 4. Judge Motley found that the punishment was imposed upon Sostre in retaliation for his legal success before her.

The district judge found that the isolation imposed on Sostre was "dangerous to the maintenance of sanity" and " 'could only serve to destroy completely the spirit and undermine the sanity of the prisoner.' " 312 F.Supp. 863, 868, 871 (S.D.N.Y.1970), quoting Wright v. McMann, 387 F.2d 519, 526 (2d Cir. 1967). This was a finding of fact. The judge also concluded as a matter of law that "subjecting a prisoner to the demonstrated risk of the loss of his sanity as punishment for any offense in prison is plainly cruel and unusual punishment as judged by the present standards of decency." *Id.* at 871. The majority opinion does not make explicit whether it overrules the judge's finding of fact, although it hints that it does. But in order to reverse the district court on this issue the majority must hold either that Judge Motley's finding of fact is clearly erroneous or that, even if true, the punishment imposed on Sostre did not amount to cruel and unusual punishment as a matter of law. Neither holding would be justified.

As to the first, it is difficult to see how Judge Motley's factual finding that Sostre's isolation threatened sanity could be characterized as clearly erroneous. Testimony at trial from experts with impressive credentials clearly supported that finding. Dr. Halleck, in response to a hypothetical question outlining the conditions of Sostre's punishment, stated that they could undermine the prisoner's sanity. Sol Rubin supported that view. It is true that Dr. Johnston, testifying for the State, disagreed. But while the district judge, as trier of fact, was free to believe the experts for plaintiff or for defendants, we may do neither. The trial judge chose to believe the former, and I do not see how her finding on this evidence can be characterized as clearly erroneous.

On the second assumption, what the majority does is to hold that Sostre's lengthy, unlimited isolation, which was "dangerous" to his sanity, does not violate the eighth amendment. With deference, I disagree. The standard for determining "cruel and unusual punishment" has been expressed in a number of ways, all imprecise; e. g., "the wanton infliction of pain," Louisiana ex rel. Francis v. Resweber, 329 U.S. 459, 463, 67 S.Ct. 374, 91 L.Ed. 422 (1947); conduct which "shocks the most fundamental instincts of civilized man," *id.* at 473, 67 S.Ct. at 381 (dissenting opinion); a method of punishment which violates the "evolving standards of decency that mark the progress of a maturing society," Trop v. Dulles, 356 U.S. 86, 101, 78 S.Ct. 590, 598, 2 L.Ed.2d 630 (1958). These notions are, of course, subjective to some extent. What may be safely said is that the amendment prohibits "a hard core of inhuman conduct," see 84 Harv.L.Rev. 456, 457 (1970). There is no doubt, as the majority concedes, that a prisoner is not a constitutional pariah. Were that not the case, there would be no basis for the holding that the first amendment was violated here. But the eighth amendment, no less than the first, protects Sostre. Its command is both spacious and changing.

The fact that solitary confinement for an indefinite period has historically been accepted as a viable instrument of prison discipline does not prevent us from finding that it violates the eighth amendment. What might once have been acceptable does not necessarily determine what is "cruel and unusual" today. Recently, the Eighth Circuit has held that whipping by strap is proscribed, although it had once been a familiar practice. Jackson v. Bishop, 404 F.2d 571 (8th Cir. 1968). Indeed, this court emphasized only a few years ago that the eighth amendment "is not fastened to the obsolete." See Wright v. McMann, *supra*, 387 F.2d at 525, quoting Weems v. United States, 217 U.S. 349, 378, 30 S.Ct. 544, 54 L.Ed. 793 (1910). In this Orwellian age, punishment that endangers sanity, no less than physical injury by the strap, is prohibited by the Constitution. Indeed, we have learned to our sorrow in the last few decades that true inhumanity seeks to destroy the psyche rather than merely the

---

[2] "[H]e was not as isolated in his segregation as 'solitary' would imply," see p. 183, *supra*.

body. The majority opinion emphasizes that after all Sostre could have obtained release from isolation at any time by agreeing to abide by the rules and to cooperate. Perhaps that is so, but that does not change the case. That response could be made were a prisoner kept in solitary for two years instead of one, or for five years, or for ten, or more. The possibility of endless solitary confinement is still there, unless the prisoner "gives in." The same observation could be made if Sostre were tortured until he so agreed, but no one would argue that torture is therefore permitted. The point is that the means used to exact submission must be constitutionally acceptable, and the threat of virtually endless isolation that endangers sanity is not.

The crucial holding of the majority opinion is the refusal to put any limit upon the period of solitary confinement. It is the unusual duration and the open-ended nature of the isolation that the district court and the experts regarded as inflicting the worst psychological harm. Accordingly, as we did in Wright v. McMann, *supra*, 387 F.2d at 526, I would hold that the punishment here, "which could only serve to destroy completely the spirit and undermine the sanity of the prisoner," runs afoul of the eighth amendment.

The second fundamental reason why I differ with the majority opinion stems from the contrast between what it finds necessary to decide and what it refuses to decide. As indicated above, the majority states in an extended dictum that if the warden's motives had been proper, the combined effect of Sostre's alleged violations would have been "serious" enough to justify the harsh punishment he received. Thus, the majority stresses "the seriousness of the multiple offenses charged against Sostre" and expresses "no view as to the constitutionality of such segregated confinement if it had been imposed on account of any one or any combination of the offenses charged against Sostre other than all of them." But the fact is that two of the allegedly serious "multiple offenses" were Sostre's refusal to desist from preparing legal papers for a codefendant and his possession of six tables of contents torn from issues of the Harvard Law Review. I would not hold unconstitutional the isolation of an adult prisoner for a sharply limited period as punishment for a serious breach of prison discipline, e. g., what the majority calls "a credible threat to the security of the prison," see p. 194, *supra*. But these two offenses were simply not grave enough to justify the extremely severe punishment visited upon Sostre.

Accordingly, the excessiveness of the penalty for these two alleged transgressions would alone violate the eighth amendment's proscription of cruel and unusual punishment, and I would say so.

Finally, while the majority reaches out to decide that Sostre's confinement would have been constitutional under a hypothetical set of facts, it refuses to rule that his punishment was cruel and unusual even though it was actually meted out for improper reasons. It is true that the majority also leaves open the constitutionality of such "confinement as Sostre experienced," if imposed for "lesser offenses." The inconsistency of this approach is apparent since if such confinement, in the majority's view, could ever be so excessive a penalty as to be unconstitutional, it should be declared so when there was no basis for the confinement at all.

In sum, keeping Sostre in solitary for over a year was "cruel and unusual punishment" because (1) the length and open-ended nature of his confinement threatened sanity; (2) two of the alleged offenses were so minor as to make the penalty constitutionally disproportionate; and (3) the ostensible reasons were a pretext for vindictive action. I also agree with Judge Smith's opinion with regard to defendant McGinnis. For the reasons and to the extent set forth above, I dissent.

HAYS, Circuit Judge, dissenting (with whom MOORE, Circuit Judge, concurs):

I dissent from the affirmance of any grant of injunctive relief or damages.

In deciding this case the majority have overlooked two fundamental guiding principles. The first is that although persons serving sentences in prison for crime are not to be denied all constitutional protections, there are significant differences between the constitutional rights such prisoners may assert and the constitutional rights of those who are free from prison restraints. For example, although the majority holds that Sostre is protected by the Constitution in his right orally to set forth his political opinions to his fellow prisoners, it may be that even they would balk at a claim that the Constitution gave Sostre the right, similar to the right which he would have if he were free, to assemble the inmates and harangue them with revolutionary political doctrines. As the Court of Appeals of the Fourth Circuit said in McCloskey v. Maryland, 337 F.2d 72, 74 (4th Cir. 1964), persons in prison have "no judicially enforceable right to propagandize within the prison walls * * *." The other fundamental principle which receives short shrift at the hands of the majority is that the federal courts should be extremely hesitant to take over the administration of state prisons. We have said that the federal courts should refuse to interfere with the internal affairs of state prisons except in the most extreme case involving " 'conduct that shocks the conscience' " or where the acts of prison officials are " 'barbarous.' " Church v. Hegstrom, 416 F.2d 449, 450–451 (2d Cir. 1969) (citations omitted). Correction authorities must have wide discretion in matters of internal prison administration. Their decisions in matters of prison discipline should not be disturbed when they are supported by evidence and do not result in shocking deprivations of fundamental human rights. See Wright v. McMann, supra.

In the present case Warden Follette testified that Sostre's punishment was based upon (1) defiance of Follette's order to desist from preparing legal papers, (2) refusal to answer proper questions, (3) statements about his impending liberation, and (4) possession of several items of contraband in his cell. Sostre did not even deny the truth of the first three of these accusations and the fourth was supported by ample evidence. Nevertheless Judge Motley disregarded Follette's findings and testimony and found that Sostre was not punished for any of these infractions.

Observance of the correct legal principles would lead in this case to reversing the trial court with respect to all relief granted.

4. DISCIPLINARY PROCEEDINGS AND DUE PROCESS OF LAW

NOTES

Note 1.

WRIGHT V. MCMANN
460 F.2d 126 (1972)
United States Court of Appeals, Second Circuit

LUMBARD, J.

For the reasons set out below, we reverse those portions of the district court's orders requiring trial-type procedures (para. c) or the promulgation of rules and regulations either regarding trial-type procedures in prison disciplinary hearings (para. b) . . .

Our disposition is largely controlled by Sostre v. McGinnis, 442 F.2d 178 (2d Cir. 1971), cert. denied sub nom. Oswald v. Sostre, 405 U.S. 978, 92 S.Ct. 1190, 31 L.Ed.2d 254 (1972) decided subsequent to the lower court ruling herein. In *Sostre* this court sitting *in banc* considered, *inter alia,* the delicate balance between the due process rights of state prisoners charged with infractions of prison rules and the necessity for the maintenance of prison order and security. The district court's order that trial-type procedures accompany prison disciplinary hearings was reversed, in the main because the federal courts are inappropriate to the task of weighing the effect of elaborate procedural safeguards on either the outcome of a particular hearing or prison morale in general, *id.* at 194–199. *Sostre* thus mandates reversal of Judge Foley's requirement that appellants promulgate and adhere to rules and regulations regarding either trial-type procedures in prison disciplinary hearings or procedures to be used in determining whether an inmate should be confined to a psychiatric observation cell. *Sostre* also indicated, however, that a "minimally fair and rational" inquiry would require observation of "such basic safeguards against arbitrariness as adequate notice, an opportunity for the prisoner to reply to charges lodged against him, and a reasonable investigation into the relevant facts—at least in cases of substantial discipline." *Id.* at 198, 203. In short, because we are loathe to graft onto state prison disciplinary hearings a broad panoply of procedural requirements does not mean that rudimentary due process can be ignored at the caprice of prison officials.*

OAKES, Circuit Judge (concurring):

I concur both in the result and in so much of Judge Lumbard's opinion that this opinion would be superfluous if I did not rather fundamentally disagree with the language of two parts of that opinion.

First, I believe it would be entirely appropriate—indeed mandated by the due process clause—for a federal court, absent state action,

---

* The rules and regulations of the New York State Department of Correctional Services have been changed since the decision below, in an attempt, according to appellants, to bring prison disciplinary hearing procedures at least to the minimum recognized in *Sostre. See* 7 N.Y.C.R.R. §§ 250–270. As with recent State efforts regarding cell conditions and treatment of inmates, *infra,* we commend the state for its responsiveness but say nothing, of course, as to the constitutionality of the new rules.

to require basic procedural safeguards in connection with prison disciplinary proceedings or to regulate conditions under which inmates are held in segregation or observation cells. Sostre v. McGinnis, 442 F.2d 178 (2d Cir. 1971), cert. denied, 405 U.S. 978 (1972), does not go so far as to hold otherwise although it rejected the orders made in that case. 442 F.2d at 194, 198. Since *Sostre* was decided, other courts have exercised under varying circumstances rather broad supervision of particular prison systems to assure—with rules by court order—that prisoners not be subjected to the "capricious and arbitrary actions of prison officials," as decried by *Sostre, supra* at 198. Holt v. Sarver, 442 F.2d 304 (8th Cir. 1971; Landman v. Royster, 333 F.Supp. 621 (E.D.Va.1971). The case is so old, however, and so much has transpired since it was initiated—including but not limited to the adoption of new rules by the New York Department of Correctional Services and amendment of the New York Correctional Law, as set forth in Judge Lumbard's opinion—that it does not seem to me to be an appropriate vehicle for federal court promulgation of minimal correctional standards. Under appropriate circumstances, however, judicial intervention may be clearly warranted—nay, required—and this it seems to me Judge Lumbard's opinion does not make sufficiently clear. Thus, my own views as to federal judicial power accord closely with those of Judges Waterman, Smith and Feinberg, respectively concurring or concurring and dissenting in *Sostre, supra*, 442 F.2d at 206 and 207, although I do not believe this to be the appropriate case for its exercise.

Note 2.

CLUTCHETTE V. PROCUNIER
328 F. Supp. 767 (1971)
United States District Court, Northern District of California

Procedural due process must obtain whenever the individual is subject to "grievous loss" at the hands of the state or its instrumentalities. Goldberg v. Kelly, 397 U.S. 254, 90 S.Ct. 1011, 25 L.Ed.2d 287 (1969). This cannot be judged after the fact, in light of the punishment actually ordered, but must be based on the potential punishment that the disciplinary committee can require. Cf., Duncan v. Louisiana, 391 U.S. 145, 159–160, 88 S.Ct. 1444, 20 L.Ed.2d 491 (1968). The rules presently permit the disciplinary committee or a single hearing officer to impose the full range of potential punishments for violation of any prison rule. Thus, since some of those punishments are serious enough, as defined by *Goldberg*, to require the imposition of procedural due process, these requirements must obtain in all disciplinary committee or hearing officer proceedings. This is not to say that prison officials could not develop specific criteria for imposing various punishments; for example, they might choose to establish a schedule of potential punishments for every offense, so as to know in advance whether or not the hearing may result in punishment which will require these due process safeguards.

With this thought in mind, and without attempting to be either exhaustive or binding, the following situations are offered as instances in which the loss to the prisoner is sufficiently serious so as to require the imposition of procedural due process as delineated below:

(a) Violations punishable by indefinite confinement in the adjustment center or segregation;

(b) Violations, the punishment for which may tend to increase a prisoner's sentence; *i. e.,* those which must be referred to the Adult Authority;

(c) Violations which may result in a fine or forfeiture;

(d) Violations which may result in any type of isolation confinement longer than ten days;

(e) Violations which may be referred to the district attorney for criminal prosecution.

Should respondent prison officials choose to adopt this or some similar schedule rather than afford all prisoners charged with any violation the due process safeguards set out below, this court would of course expect to review the schedule prior to its promulgation and for this purpose retains jurisdiction over this aspect of the proceedings. . . .

"[C]onsideration of what procedures due process may require under any given set of circumstances must begin with a determination of the precise nature of the government function involved as well as of the private interest that has been affected by governmental action." Cafeteria & Restaurant Workers Union, etc. v. McElroy, 367 U.S. 886, 895, [81 S.Ct. 1743, 6 L.Ed.2d 1230] (1961) * * *. We wish to add that we, no less than the dissenters, recognize the importance of not imposing upon the States or the Federal Government in this developing field of law any procedural requirements beyond those demanded by rudimentary due process. Goldberg v. Kelly, 397 U.S. 254, 263, 267, 90 S.Ct. 1011, 1018, 1020, 25 L.Ed.2d 287 (1969).

With this introduction, the Supreme Court proceeded to clearly establish what is demanded by rudimentary due process.

A. Notice

In *Goldberg*, the Court said that rudimentary principles of due process "require that a recipient have *timely* and adequate notice *detailing the reasons* for a proposed termination * * *." *Goldberg, supra* at 267–268, 90 S.Ct. at 1020 (emphasis supplied). Specifically, it approved the 7 day notice requirement and the substance of the notice which "inform(s) a recipient of the *precise questions* raised about his continued eligibility." *Goldberg, supra* at 268, 90 S.Ct. at 1020 (emphasis added).

In the present context, both the form and procedure of the notice given are constitutionally infirm. Those cases currently heard and decided by the hearing officer have no real provision for notice. The procedure simply requires that several days after the alleged offense the hearing officer shall approach the prisoner, advise him of the charge, take his statement and plea and adjudicate the case. While this may be adequate in some cases, it is clearly inadequate when serious punishment may result.

If the hearing officer concludes that the case is a proper one for the disciplinary committee to hear, he subsequently "serves" the prisoner with a Form 263 Notice of Complaint. This notice is constitutionally defective in two ways. First, since all that is required to state is a rule number and name, it does not adequately apprise the prisoner of what he is accused of having done. Second, hearings are held every week at which time all cases arising during the week are heard. Thus, the maximum amount of time a prisoner would have to prepare his case is 7 days; the minimum is overnight.

While *Goldberg* did not establish constitutional minimums, it seems clear that to satisfy constitutional requirements, notice of at least 7 days of any charge requiring procedural due process, whether heard by a hearing officer or disciplinary committee, is the minimum acceptable period. Furthermore, to constitute meaningful notice, at least a brief statement of the facts upon which the charge is based, as well as the name and number of the rule allegedly broken must be included. Absent these, an accused prisoner is without sufficient time or information to prepare any defense on the merits.

B. Witnesses

In almost every setting where important decisions turn on questions of fact, due process requires an opportunity to confront and cross-examine adverse witnesses. E. g., I.C.C. v. Louisville & N.R. Co., 227 U.S. 88, 93–94, [33 S.Ct. 185, 57 L.Ed. 431] (1913); Willner v. Committee on Character and Fitness, 373 U.S. 96, 103–104, [83 S.Ct. 1175, 10 L.Ed.2d 224] (1963). Goldberg v. Kelly, *supra* at 269, 90 S.Ct. at 1021.

The San Quentin Prison Rules provide that all "testimony" take the form of written reports by witnesses. Not only are the authors of these reports unavailable for personal examination, the reports themselves are not shown to or even read to the accused. This clearly misses, by a wide mark, the fundamental principles of due process required in *Goldberg*. Prisoners must be given the right to call witnesses in their own behalf and cross-examine witnesses against them.

C. Counsel

"The right to be heard would be, in many cases, of little avail if it did not comprehend the right to be heard by counsel." Powell v. Alabama, 287 U.S. 45, 68–69, 53 S.Ct. 55, 77 L.Ed. 158 (1932), quoted in *Goldberg, supra*, 397 U.S. at 270, 90 S.Ct. at 1022. Under the present set of rules, prisoners are not entitled to the assistance of retained or appointed counsel or counsel-substitute. Rudimentary principles of due process require the presence of counsel when the rights of an individual are seriously threatened by governmental action. *Cf.* Gideon v. Wainwright, 372 U.S. 335, 83 S.Ct. 792, 9 L.Ed.2d 799 (1963); United States v. Wade, 388 U.S. 218, 87 S.Ct. 1926, 18 L.Ed.2d 1149 (1967); Goldberg v. Kelly, 397 U.S. 254, 90 S.Ct. 1011, 25 L.Ed. 2d 287 (1969). Elements of equal protection demand that when the prisoner is indigent, the state must provide him with counsel. *Cf.*, Douglas v. California, 372 U.S. 353, 83 S.Ct. 814, 9 L.Ed.2d 811 (1963). Recently, the Supreme Court has held that in some instances counsel-substitute will be acceptable. Johnson

v. Avery, 393 U.S. 483, 89 S.Ct. 747, 21 L.Ed.2d 718 (1969). While only counsel is acceptable in the case of an offense which will be referred to the district attorney, in all other cases prison officials should not be precluded from providing an adequate counsel-substitute.

D. Decision Based on the Evidence

[T]he decisionmaker's conclusion as to a recipient's eligibility must rest solely on the legal rules and evidence adduced at the hearing. Ohio Bell Tel. Co. v. P.U.C., 301 U.S. 292, [57 S.Ct. 724, 81 L.Ed. 1093] (1937); United States v. Abilene & S.R. Co., 265 U.S. 274, 288–289, [44 S.Ct. 565, 68 L.Ed. 1016] (1924). To demonstrate compliance with this elementary requirement, the decisionmaker should state the reasons for his determination and indicate the evidence he relied on, cf. Wichita R. & Light Co. v. P.U.C., 260 U.S. 48, 57–59, [43 S.Ct. 51, 54–55, 67 L.Ed. 124] (1922), though his statement need not amount to a full opinion or even formal findings of fact and conclusions of law. Goldberg v. Kelly, *supra* 397 U.S. at 271, 90 S.Ct. at 1022.

Rules of evidence, as a general proposition, do not rise to constitutional levels. Thus, it would be inappropriate for this court to establish a "weight of the evidence" rule more stringent than the due process clause requires. When reviewing a disciplinary committee decision in a suit brought under 42 U.S.C. § 1983, district courts have traditional standards to review decisions for arbitrariness. It is hoped, although not constitutionally compelled, that disciplinary committees will apply a "weight of the evidence" rule somewhat more exacting.

E. Decision by an Unbiased Fact-Finder

[O]f course, an impartial decision maker is essential. Cf. In re Murchison, 349 U.S. 133, [75 S.Ct. 623, 99 L.Ed. 942] (1955); Wong Yang Sung v. McGrath, 339 U.S. 33, 45–46, [70 S.Ct. 445, 94 L.Ed. 616] (1950). We agree with the District Court that prior involvement in some aspects of a case will not necessarily bar a welfare official from acting as a decisionmaker. He should not, however, have participated in making the determination under review. Goldberg v. Kelly, *supra* at 271, 90 S.Ct. at 1022.

Under the present system, there is no prescription against the participation in the decision by one involved in the incident, although such a practice is discouraged. It is difficult in the abstract to establish a fixed rule regarding participation by involved parties, particularly in light of the above-quoted language. But such a rule must be fixed. It follows that if participation by involved parties is, in some instances acceptable, in others it is not. To preclude a multitude of individual challenges, a uniform policy consistent with due process requirements must be established and applied in every case. Such a policy must be framed so as to preclude, in all cases, the participation in any aspect of the decision of the disciplinary committee of anyone charged with a subsequent review of that decision or anyone with personal knowledge of any material fact relevant to the decision. Only through such a policy can complete impartiality be insured in all cases.

F. Right to Appeal

The status of a right to appeal a decision of the disciplinary committee is unclear. It appears that while such a right exists, its existence is not uniformly known, and only irregular, individual efforts to make it known occur.

There is no constitutionally protected right to appeal the decision of a fact-finding tribunal. However, if statutes or regulations provide for an appeal of right, the equal protection clause requires that all those affected be treated alike. See Douglas v. California, 372 U.S. 353, 83 S.Ct. 814, 9 L.Ed.2d 811 (1963). Thus, officials cannot rely on word of mouth to notify prisoners of their right to appeal or the procedures for such an appeal. Nor can they notify some prisoners at the conclusion of disciplinary proceedings and fail to notify others. The equal protection clause contemplates uniform treatment of all prisoners.

Now, therefore, it is ordered, adjudged and decreed that:

1. The above memorandum opinion constitutes the court's findings of fact and conclusions of law pursuant to Fed.R.Civ.P. 52(a);

2. Plaintiffs are hereby granted a declaratory judgment with respect to their first cause of action insofar as this opinion and order declare that the disciplinary procedures employed at San Quentin Prison violate the due process and equal protection clauses of the 14th amendment by failing to provide for adequate notice of charges, the calling of favorable witnesses and cross-examination of accusing witnesses, counsel or counsel-substitute,

a decision by a fact-finder uninvolved with the alleged incident, a written finding of facts, or uniform notice of any right to appeal the decision, when such a disciplinary hearing may result in grievous loss to the prisoner; and that certain disciplinary punishment, including but not necessarily limited to (a) indefinite confinement in the adjustment center or segregation; (b) possible increase in a prisoner's sentence by reason of referral of the disciplinary action to the Adult Authority; (c) a fine or forfeiture of accumulated or future earnings; (d) isolation confinement longer than 10 days; or (e) referral to the district attorney for criminal prosecution, constitute such a grievous loss to the prisoner;

3. Defendants are hereby preliminarily and permanently enjoined from conducting any further disciplinary hearings at San Quentin Prison so long as the procedures employed are constitutionally infirm as set out above;

4. The decisions of the disciplinary committee in the disciplinary hearings of the named plaintiffs, Clutchette and Jackson, are set aside, and said plaintiffs shall be restored to the status of confinement they enjoyed prior to the institution of such proceedings, and such decisions shall be expunged from all their records, and shall not be referred to the Adult Authority;

5. Defendants are ordered to submit a plan for the conduct of disciplinary committee hearings, consistent with the opinion this day entered, to this court within 100 days for approval by this court; 10 days prior to this date of submission, defendants shall serve a copy of said plan to attorneys for plaintiffs;

6. Execution of this order is stayed, insofar as it enjoins any further disciplinary hearings and sets aside the decisions in any disciplinary hearings already held, for 30 days to allow the Attorney General of the State of California to file a notice of appeal, should he so desire. In the event that such a notice is filed, the above-described portion of this order is stayed until further order of this court.

Note 3.

NOLAN V. SCAFATI
430 F.2d 548 (1970)
United States Court of Appeals, First Circuit

COFFIN, Circuit Judge.

On November 22, 1969, state prisoner Daniel Nolan wrote a letter to the Chief Judge of the federal district court in Boston, seeking relief under 42 U.S.C. § 1983 for two alleged violations of his constitutional rights by the prison officials of the Massachusetts Correctional Institution at Walpole. Petitioner claimed that he had been denied procedural due process by the manner in which the prison officials committed him to extended segregated confinement, and that he had been denied access to the courts by the prison officials' refusal to mail his letter to the Massachusetts Civil Liberties Union seeking advice and assistance on his due process claims. On the basis of this letter, the district court took jurisdiction of the matter pursuant to 23 U.S.C. § 1343 and dismissed the complaint on the grounds that petitioner had been accorded due process at the prison hearing in question. Nolan v. Scafati, 306 F.Supp. 1 (D.Mass.1969). No mention was made of petitioner's other objection concerning his letter to the Civil Liberties Union. This appeal followed, and we appointed legal counsel whose brief has been of considerable assistance to us.

Petitioner's letter alleged that, at the time that he wrote, he had been in segregated confinement for almost a month, had been threatened with five more months of such confinement, and might suffer the loss of three days earned good time for every day of confinement. The district court assumed that this confinement was the result of an adverse decision after hearing—and found that such decision was supported by substantial evidence. But petitioner's letter, the only available evidence at this point, suggests that his month's confinement was *not* because of any adverse decision but because his hearing and decision were being delayed until he stopped insisting on legal assistance at the hearing.

The letter, a long and rambling one containing observations general and specific about events past and future, might well have justified summary dismissal but for the combined allegations that petitioner was being subjected to many months of segregated confinement, with multiple loss of good time and consequent delay in time of release from prison, without benefit of any hearing on the charges against him. These allegations were sufficiently serious, we think, that some determination of the underlying facts should have been undertaken before judgment was rendered. So saying, however, we are not to be taken as ruling that petitioner's letter, as it may be rationally although favorably interpreted, necessarily warrants relief. We say merely that, cumulatively, it *may* assert lack of due process. Conversely, we do not hold that every omnibus letter deserves this much attention.

On remand, the district court shall, by affidavit and/or hearing (and we stress that many such claims by prisoners may be satisfactorily resolved by affidavit), ascertain the cause, nature, and duration of petitioner's confinement; the consequent effect, if any, on his earned good time credit; and the nature of the safeguards provided at any prison hearing which may have been accorded petitioner. This having been done, the district court should confront the admittedly difficult—and still largely unexplored—question whether the punishment here proposed or inflicted was sufficiently great to require procedural safeguards, and if it was, whether sufficient safeguards were provided. While all the procedural safeguards provided citizens charged with a crime obviously cannot and need not be provided to prison inmates charged with violation of a prison disciplinary rule, some assurances of elemental fairness are essential when substantial individual interests are at stake....

Note 4.

KRITSKY V. MCGINNIS
313 F. Supp. 1247 (1970)
United States District Court, Northern District of New York

FOLEY, Chief Judge

... I find that the due process of rights of the plaintiff were violated in the type hearing given plaintiff in 1962. The hearing was held a week or ten days after the protest in a room off the segregation area where plaintiff had been confined with only the Principal Keeper, as the disciplinary authority and judge. The plaintiff's testimony is graphic description:

> He (Principal Keeper) advised me that I had been charged with advocating insurrection and a revolution and advocating incendiarism in the prison. He said, "How do you plead?" I said, "Not guilty." He said, "Eighteen months lost time."
> I attempted to speak—
> THE COURT: Wait a minute. He said, "How do you plead?"
> THE WITNESS: I said, "Not guilty."
> THE COURT: All right.
> THE WITNESS: I attempted to speak and he interrupted and said, "That will be all." And I replied, "In other words, I am being summarily dismissed." He said, "Yes".

In my judgment, this hearing, and I accept it as truthfully described by the plaintiff, falls far short of the fundamental fairness expected of due process requirements, no matter the need for summary disposition....

Note 5.

BUNDY V. CANNON
328 F. Supp. 165 (1971)
United States District Court, District of Maryland

THOMSEN, District Judge.

In these cases, which have been consolidated for trial, 82 plaintiffs contend that the procedures under which they were transferred to the Maryland Penitentiary from the Sykesville Laundry Camp and the Maryland House of Correction and were kept in "segregated confinement" and suffered other penalties, do not meet the due process standards guaranteed by the Fourteenth Amendment to the United States Constitution....

In none of the cases was the inmate given written notice of any charges or allegations of misconduct, nor informed that a hearing would be held until just before the hearing. In none of the cases was an inmate given the opportunity for representation or assistance by another inmate or staff member, nor to question the witnesses against him or call witnesses on his behalf....

The procedures followed in the instances where the inmate was charged with an infraction of the rules did not afford him: (1) adequate notice of the alleged misconduct or of the time when the hearing would be held; nor (2) an opportunity to question the person charging him with an offense or to present witnesses on his own behalf; nor (3) an impartial "Adjustment Team", since the correctional officer pressing the charge was a member of the Adjustment Team which heard his case.

Adequate notice of charges in a substantial disciplinary proceeding is necessary to afford a prisoner the opportunity to prepare a defense....

Another basic component of fundamental procedural fairness is a hearing before a relatively objective and impartial tribunal. This principle is violated when the same prison official assumes the dual responsibility of (1) initiating and pressing charges of misconduct, and (2) subsequently determining, as a member of an administrative body, whether misconduct has occurred and assessing appropriate punishment....

Relief

After argument by counsel had been heard, the Court stated that it was prepared to enter an interim opinion and order holding that plaintiffs were entitled to relief in their individual capacities, and to a ruling with respect to the practices generally followed by the Division of Correction.

The amici curiae prepared, submitted to counsel for the respective parties and presented to the Court proposed disciplinary hearing procedures. Counsel for plaintiffs agreed that the disciplinary hearing procedures proposed by the amici curiae met minimum standards of constitutional due process. Counsel for the Division of Correction stated that the proposed procedures appeared practicable, and consented that those procedures be prescribed in an interim order. They assured the Court that the Division would take immediate steps to implement those procedures.

Pursuant to such consent on March 2, 1971, the Court entered an interim order, which: (I, II) granted individual relief to the plaintiffs in the *Bundy* case and in the *Adams* case; and (III) in accordance with the agreement of counsel referred to above, ordered that the Department of Public Safety and Correctional Services of the State of Maryland and its Division of Correction should promptly establish rules and regulations for all future adjustment violations not less favorable to the inmate than the procedures specified in the interim order.

In February 1971, while this case was pending, the Division of Correction issued a new "General Information and Guidance Handbook for Inmates", which included under the heading "General Rules and Regulations", a list of so-called "Adjustment Violations", which could be the basis for disciplinary action.

On March 12, 1971, the Division of Correction adopted "Adjustment Procedures" for dealing with violations of the Rules, which are generally similar to those included in the interim order entered by consent on March 2, 1971. Those procedures, as modified on May 17, 1971, have been filed as an exhibit in this case, and are set out as an appendix to this opinion. The Court is advised that those procedures are being followed, and is assured that they will be followed in the future, with one exception. No funds have yet been provided by the State for the employment of the Hearing Officers in the office of the Commissioner of the Division of Correction, called for by the "Adjustment Procedures". This is unfortunate, because the use of such Hearing Officers from the office of the Commissioner of the Division of Correction, rather than persons employed at the institution, as presiding officers at disciplinary hearings, is a highly desirable feature of those "procedures", analogous to the use of JAG officers in court martial proceedings. The Court has been advised that since March 10, 1971, the Division has been able to provide such a Hearing Officer in some cases, and that they intend to provide such personnel as may be necessary to provide Hearing Officers for major violations.

On March 10, 1971, the Division of Correction adopted an Administrative Directive dealing with non-punitive "Adjustment Transfers to the Maximum Security Institution", which set up reasonable guidelines not required by the interim opinion or order.

For all of the foregoing reasons, the Court does not believe that it is necessary or appropriate to include in the decree to be entered herein any injunctive relief with respect to procedures in future cases. It is not desirable that a federal court should undertake by unjunction or otherwise to supervise the continuous operation of a State correctional system, nor to prescribe rules and regulations governing such operation, although a federal court must in exceptional cases under 42 U.S.C. § 1983 exercise its jurisdiction to prevent deprivation of constitutional rights. . . .

APPENDIX
MARYLAND
Department of Public Safety and
Correctional Services
DIVISION OF CORRECTION
ADJUSTMENT PROCEDURES:

When a written report is submitted to the Classification Department which states that an inmate has committed a violation of the rules, the Adjustment Team will evaluate the report and determine if the alleged violation is a minor or major violation.

MINOR VIOLATION: A minor violation is one that if the inmate is found guilty, the maximum sentence he could receive would not be over fifteen (15) days confinement or the loss of over five (5) days, or both. In minor violations the following procedures shall be followed:

1. The inmate shall be furnished a written statement of the minor violation with which he is charged. The statement should be served not later than forty-eight (48) hours after the alleged violation, and the inmate will appear before the Adjustment Team within seventy-two (72) hours of the alleged infraction, unless prevented by exceptional circumstances.

The inmate will not be given a written statement of the charge until the Adjustment Team has determined that he will have to appear before the Team for a formal hearing.

* * *

4. The inmate will be given a chance to discuss his case when he appears before the Adjustment Team and he may also have the following representation:

(a) Another inmate or staff member to appear before the Adjustment Team with him as his representative. The inmate or staff member must do so on a voluntary basis. . . .

6. If the Adjustment Team determines that the inmate has violated a rule, he may be subjected to one or more of the following actions:

(a) Counselling and/or warning.
(b) Reprimand.
(c) Adjustment release.
(d) Temporary loss of one or more privileges.
(e) Loss of good behavior time (not to exceed five (5) days).
(f) Confinement (not to exceed fifteen (15) days).

The Adjustment Team may recommend a change in housing or job assignment, but said recommendation must be approved by the Classification Team.

7. The Team will make a written summary of its proceeding, including its decision and a brief statement of the reasons for that decision. He shall have the right, at the conclusion of the hearing, to state any objections he may have to the decision of the Team.

8. If the inmate objects to the decision, the Warden or his designated representative shall, within three (3) days after the hearing, review the decision of the Adjustment Team, based upon the record of its proceedings.

9. On review, the Warden may take the following action:

(a) Agree with the decision of the Adjustment Team.
(b) Order further or new proceedings.
(c) Reduce or suspend the decision of the Team.

The Warden cannot increase the sentence handed down by the Adjustment Team, nor can he order new proceedings, charging a major violation in his review of a minor violation.

10. Even if the inmate does not object to his sentence, the Warden will review all cases involving the loss of good behavior time and/or confinement.

11. The inmate will be notified in writing of the result of the review of his case by the Warden.

MAJOR VIOLATIONS: a major violation is one in which the inmate, if found guilty of the violation, could receive a sentence of confinement for more than fifteen (15) days and/or the loss of good behavior time of more than five (5) days). In major violations the following procedures will be followed:

1. The inmate shall be furnished a written statement of the major infraction with which he is charged. The written statement shall be served to the inmate not later than forty-eight (48) hours after the alleged violation, and the inmate will appear before the Adjustment Team within seventy-two (72) hours of the alleged violation unless prevented by exceptional circumstances.

2. The inmate will not be given a written statement of the charge until the Adjustment Team has determined that he will have to appear before the Team for a formal hearing.

* * *

5. The inmate shall appear before the Adjustment Team to discuss his case and he shall be represented by another inmate or a staff member at the hearing, but the inmate or staff member representing the inmate must do so on a voluntary basis.

6. The Adjustment Team shall allow the inmate the opportunity to call one or more witnesses if the Team determines it is practical or relevant to the inmate's case. Such witnesses

may include the accuser and the employee who presented the charges.

7. The Team shall allow the inmate to question any witnesses who testify before the hearing if they deem it relevant to his case.

8. Such rights of the inmate shall not be unreasonably withheld or restricted by the Adjustment Team.

9. The Adjustment Team shall make a written report of all its proceedings to include a summary of the evidence, the Team's evaluation and decision, and the reason for the Team's decision. The decision of the Team must be based on substantial evidence. . . .

11. If the Team determines that the inmate is guilty of the violation, the inmate may receive any one or more of those penalties designated for minor infractions, or he may receive one or both of the following penalties:

(a) Loss of good behavior time to exceed more than five (5) days.

(b) Confinement to exceed more than fifteen (15) days.

The Adjustment Team may also recommend a change in housing or job assignment or a transfer to an institution of greater security, but such recommendations must be approved by the Classification Team.

All cases involving confinement for periods of over thirty (30) days must be reviewed every 30 days by the Classification Team with the idea of determining, if feasible, an alternate to confinement that will be of adjustment value to the inmate. During the period of confinement, the inmate will be seen for counselling on a frequent basis by the psychologist/psychiatrist, and his classification counsellor, and progress reports will be submitted to the Classification Department after each visit. This may include visits from the chaplain and other staff members who may have the ability to communicate with the inmate as long as it does not present a security problem. Deliberate mental or physical abuse of the inmate during his confinement will not be tolerated.

12. The inmate shall be advised of the decision of the Team and the basis for its decision. He shall have the right, at the conclusion of the hearing, to state any objections he may have to the decision of the Team.

13. The Warden will review all cases involving major violations, and upon review may decide on one of the following actions:

(a) Agree with the decision of the Team.
(b) Order further or new proceedings.
(c) Reduce or suspend the sentence.

The Warden cannot increase the sentence determined by the Adjustment Team.

14. The inmate will be notified of the result of the review process.

5. ADMINISTRATIVE SEGREGATION AND DUE PROCESS OF LAW

NOTES

Note 1.

YOUNG v. WAINWRIGHT
449 F.2d 339 (1971)
United States Court of Appeals, Fifth Circuit

PER CURIAM:

Appellant is a Florida state prisoner serving a life sentence for murder. He filed a petition in the court below under 42 U.S.C. § 1983, seeking an injunction to obtain his permanent release from administrative segregation. He alleged that such confinement is unlawful because he has violated no prison regulations. The district court dismissed the petition for failure to state a claim upon which relief may be granted. We affirm. Classification of inmates is a matter of prison administration and management with which federal courts are reluctant to interfere except in extreme circumstances. There being no extreme circumstances present in this case, the judgment below is affirmed.

Affirmed.

Note 2.

URBANO v. McCORKLE
10 Crim. L. Rep. 2201 (1972)
United States District Court, District of New Jersey

In his amended complaint at paragraph 12, Urbano stated: "On November 11, 1968, plaintiff and five others were transferred from

State Hospital to administrative segregation at the New Jersey State Prison Farm at Rahway. None of the six has been given any hearing or advised of any charges or reason for punitive segregation."

Defendant Yeager, the Principal Keeper of the New Jersey State Prison, stated in his affidavit of May 15, 1969, that: "The allegation is false. As indicated previously, the New Jersey State Prison has no 'punitive' segregation. Plaintiff is not in segregation because of any disciplinary charge against him, but is there for the order of the institution in the opinion of the administrative authorities of the State Prison. If he had been charged with a disciplinary infraction then he would have received a hearing." According to this statement, an inmate of the general population may be placed in "administrative" or as Urbano prefers, "punitive" segregation merely by fiat if he is not charged with an infraction of the rules. This would circumvent the requirement of a hearing that exists for cases in which a prisoner is charged with a violation. Consequently, prison officials may segregate any inmate without a hearing merely by stating that it is being done "for the order of the institution in the opinion of the administrative authorities of the State Prison." * * * In "instances [when] . . . state regulations applicable to inmates of prison facilities conflict with federal constitutional rights the regulations may be invalidated." Johnson v. Avery, 393 U.S. 483, 4 CrL 3115 (1968). . . .

This court is of the opinion that prisoners who are confined to administrative segregation for the good of the institution should be entitled to the same minimal due process that is already afforded prisoners who are confined to segregation for disciplinary infractions. Equal protection so requires. Minimal due process in this situation does not mean that a formal hearing or the right to counsel is a requirement. But it does mean that before a prisoner is removed from the general population of an institution and placed in segregation, he should be notified in writing of the charges and nature of the evidence against him and be given a reasonable opportunity to explain away the accusation. We are also of the opinion that in times of emergency situations, such process may be postponed and emergency action taken. But the prisoners affected should thereafter be afforded within a reasonable time the minimal due process that is stated above. For the above reasons, defendants' motion for summary judgment on this issue is denied at this time.

Note 3.

WALKER V. MANCUSI
338 F. Supp. 311 (1971)
United States District Court, Western District of New York

CURTIN, District Judge.

This action was initiated by a pro se complaint submitted to the court by petitioners on October 26, 1971. They alleged that they were being held in A Block, 6 Company, of Attica Correctional Facility under conditions more restrictive than those applied to the general population of the institution without notification that administrative disciplinary charges had been placed against them. They claimed that they were entitled to appearances before the Adjustment Committee of the facility established pursuant to the regulations of the Department of Correctional Services and that the failure of state authorities to provide them such appearances constituted a denial of due process. . . .

[Petitioners] are housed in this area because they were believed to be active participants in the riot situation from September 9 through 13, 1971.

In contrast to the prisoners in general population, the inmates in A Block, 6 Company, are locked in their cells in excess of twenty-three hours a day and are allowed only a brief period of exercise in the yard when prisoners from other areas are not there. They eat in their cells rather than in the mess hall, and they do not work in the jobs they held prior to September 9, although as of November they receive the minimum pay of twenty cents an hour paid to inmates unassigned to jobs through no fault of their own. . . .

The court believes that these facts, while not establishing that the inmates of A Block, 6 Company, have been subjected to cruel and unusual punishment in violation of the Eighth Amendment to the United States Constitution, illustrate that their confinement "involves a harsh reduction of the privileges typically afforded inmates of the general population." Such confinement constitutes punishment sufficiently severe to require minimum due process safeguards. Due process requires at least that the prisoner be confronted with the accusation, informed of the evidence against him and afforded a reasonable opportunity to explain his actions.

6. DAMAGE RECOVERY BY INMATES

NOTES

Note 1.

UNITED STATES v. MUNIZ
374 U.S. 150 (1963)
Supreme Court of the United States

Mr. Chief Justice Warren delivered the opinion of the Court.

The question in this case is whether a person can sue under the Federal Tort Claims Act to recover damages from the United States Government for personal injuries sustained during confinement in a federal prison, by reason of the negligence of a government employee. For reasons to be developed below, we hold that such suits are within the purview of the Act....

Respondent Muniz alleged that he was, in August 1959, a prisoner in a federal correctional institution in Danbury, Connecticut. On the afternoon of August 24, Muniz was outside one of the institution's dormitories when he was struck by an inmate, and then pursued by 12 inmates into another dormitory. A prison guard, apparently choosing to confine the altercation instead of interceding, locked the dormitory. The 12 inmates who had chased Muniz into the dormitory set upon him, beating him with chairs and sticks until he was unconscious. Muniz sustained a fractured skull and ultimately lost the vision of his right eye. He alleged that the prison officials were negligent in failing to provide enough guards to prevent the assaults leading to his injuries and in letting prisoners, some of whom were mentally abnormal, intermingle without adequate supervision.

Whether respondents are entitled to maintain these suits requires us to determine what Congress intended when it passed the Federal Tort Claims Act in 1946. This question would not appear at first glance to pose serious difficulty. Congress used neither intricate nor restrictive language in waiving the Government's sovereign immunity. It gave the District Courts jurisdiction

> of civil actions on claims against the United States, for money damages,... for ... personal injury... caused by the negligent or wrongful act or omission of any employee of the Government while acting within the scope of his office or employment, under circumstances where the United States, if a private person, would be liable to the claimant in accordance with the law of the place where the act or omission occurred. 28 U.S.C. § 1346 (b)....

None of the exceptions precludes suit against the Government by federal prisoners for injuries sustained in prison. So far as it appears from the face of the Act, Congress has clearly consented to suits such as those involved in the case at bar....

An examination of the legislative history of the Act reinforces our conclusion that Congress intended to permit such suits. For a number of reasons, it appears that Congress was well aware of claims by federal prisoners and that its failure to exclude them from the provisions of the Act in 28 U.S.C. § 2680 was deliberate....

The Government argues nevertheless that we should imply an exception to the Federal Tort Claims Act. For one thing, the Government urges that our decision in *Feres* v. *United States,* 340 U.S. 135, controls. For another, it maintains that the impact of liability upon prison discipline would so seriously impair the administration of our prisons that Congress could not have intended such an "extreme" result....

We also are reluctant to believe that the possible abuses stemming from prisoners' suits are so serious that all chance of recovery should be denied. It is possible, as the Government suggests, that frivolous suits will be brought, designed only to harass or, more sinister, discover details of prison security useful in planning an escape. And it is possible that the Government will be subjected to the burden of pretrial preparation, discovery, and trial, even though it prevails on the merits. This seems an inescapable concomitant of any form of liability....

It is also possible that litigation will damage prison discipline, as the Government most vigorously argues. However, we have been shown no evidence that these possibilities have become actualities in the many States allowing suits against jailers, or the smaller number allowing recovery directly against the States themselves....

We are confident that district judges, sitting without a jury as required by 28 U.S.C. § 2402, will be able to dispose of complaints intelligently without undue harm coming to our federal prisons. Federal rules of procedure are not so inflexible that clearly frivolous suits need embarrass prison officials or burden United States Attorneys' offices....

Note 2.

UNITED STATES V. DEMKO
385 U.S. 149 (1966)
Supreme Court of the United States

Mr. Justice Black delivered the opinion of the Court.

The respondent Demko, a federal prisoner, was seriously injured in 1962 in the performance of an assigned prison task in a federal penitentiary. Shortly afterward he filed a claim for compensation benefits under 18 U.S.C. § 4126. That law, first enacted by Congress in 1934, authorized the Federal Prison Industries, Inc., a federal corporation, to use its funds "in paying, under rules and regulations promulgated by the Attorney General, compensation ... to inmates or their dependents for injuries suffered in any industry." Under that law and regulations promulgated under it, respondent was awarded $180 per month which was to start on discharge from prison and continue so long as disability continued. After winning this compensation award, respondent brought this action against the United States in the Federal District Court under the Federal Tort Claims Act, alleging that his injury was due to the Government's negligence for which he was entitled to recover additional damages under that Act. The United States defended on the single ground that respondent's right to recover compensation under 18 U.S.C. § 4126 was his exclusive remedy against the Government barring him from any suit under the Federal Tort Claims Act....

The court below refused to accept the prison compensation law as an exclusive remedy because it was deemed not comprehensive enough. We disagree. That law, as shown by its regulations, its coverage and the amount of its payments to the injured and their dependents, compares favorably with compensation laws all over the country. While there are differences in the way it protects its beneficiaries, these are due in the main to the differing circumstances of prisoners and nonprisoners....

The court below was of the opinion that its holding was required by *United States* v. *Muniz,* 374 U.S. 150. We think not. Whether a prisoner covered by the prison compensation law could also recover under the Federal Tort Claims Act was neither an issue in nor decided by *Muniz.* As our opinion in *Muniz* noted, neither of the two prisoners there was covered by the prison compensation law. What we decided in *Muniz* was that the two prisoners there involved, who were not protected by the prison compensation law, were not barred from seeking relief under the Federal Tort Claims Act. However, that is not this case....

Note 3.

a. SOSTRE V. ROCKEFELLER
312 F. Supp. 863, 885 (1970)
United States District Court, Southern District of New York

The final issue in this case is plaintiff's prayer for $1,200,000 damages. As discussed above, plaintiff's right to recover damages against state officials in their official capacities, who violate rights secured to him by the Fourteenth Amendment, is provided for by 42 U.S.C. § 1983.

The evidence shows that plaintiff was subjected to punitive segregation without due process of law for more than one year under conditions which violate present standards of decency. The court finds that such cruel and unusual punishment over the long period of time involved here resulted in injury to plaintiff as follows: 1) severe physical deprivations, i.e., loss of energy-giving food and loss of exercise, 2) needless degradation, 3) loss of work opportunities of a rehabilitative nature, 4) loss of money which might have been earned by working, 5) loss of schooling and training opportunities, 6) loss of self-improvement through reading books of one's own choice, and 7) great mental anguish.

Therefore, the court awards plaintiff $25.00 per day for every day spent in punitive segregation (372 days), or a total of $9,300 compensatory damages against defendants Follette and McGinnis. "Compensatory damages for deprivation of a federal right are governed by federal standards, as provided by Congress in 42 U.S.C. § 1988, * * *" Sullivan v. Little Hunting Park, Inc., 396 U.S. 229, 239, 90 S.Ct. 400, 406, 24 L.Ed.2d 386 (1969); Basista v. Weir, 340 F.2d 74, 87 (3rd Cir. 1965).

The bad faith and malice toward Sostre (based in large part upon political disagreement with him) that motivated Follette to put plaintiff in punitive segregation and, in effect, to "throw the key away," and McGinnis' failure to act after being notified of Sostre's confinement as early as July 1968, are quite reprehensible; an award of exemplary damages is in order. Basista v. Weir, *supra,* 340 F.2d at 87–88; *accord,* Hague v. Committee for Industrial Organization, 101 F.2d 774, 789 (3rd Cir. 1939), modified on other grounds, 307 U.S. 496, 59 S.Ct. 954, 83 L.Ed. 1423 (1939); Antelope v. George, 211 F.Supp. 657 (D.Idaho 1962); *See also* Comment, Civil Actions for Damages Under the Federal Civil Rights Statutes, 45 Texas L.Rev. 1015 (1967). Otherwise, these malicious acts and acts of studied omission might recur in the future.

The court, therefore, awards the additional sum of $10.00 per day, or a total of $3,720 in punitive damages against defendants Follette and McGinnis. . . .

b. SOSTRE V. MCGINNIS
442 F.2d 178, 204 (1971), *reversing* 312 F. Supp. 863 (1970)
United States Court of Appeals, Second Circuit

All parties seem to agree upon two principles with which we also are in accord. First, Section 1983 authorizes recovery of compensatory, and, in an appropriate case, punitive damages against an individual for the unjustifiable violation of constitutional rights "under color" of state law. Monroe v. Pape, 365 U.S. 167, 81 S.Ct. 473, 5 L.Ed.2d 492 (1961); Basista v. Weir, 340 F.2d 74 (3rd Cir. 1965). This liability, however, is entirely personal in nature intended to be satisfied out of the individual's own pocket. Moreover, the doctrine of sovereign immunity, as codified by the Eleventh Amendment, bars the exaction of a fine from a state treasury without the state's consent, at least on account of tortious actions committed by its agents under the circumstances of this case. Larson v. Domestic & Foreign Corp., 337 U.S. 682, 69 S.Ct. 1457, 93 L.Ed. 1628 (1949); Westberry v. Fisher, 309 F.Supp. 12 (D.Me. 1970).

It follows from these principles[1] that although Sostre was entitled to compensatory damages against Warden Follette,[2] Follette's successor as warden, who had no part whatsoever in Follette's wrongful conduct against Sostre, incurred no personal money responsibility upon Follette's death. We note also that no application was made in the court below to substitute any party who could be held responsible to assume Follette's obligation to Sostre, Rule 25, F.R.Civ.P., if such a party existed. Accordingly, there is no party before us against whom appropriately to award damages.[3]

In any event, we are persuaded to reverse the award of punitive damages. Warden Follette's improper conduct in segregating Sostre so far as appears reflected no pattern of such behavior by himself or by other officials. The deterrent impact of a punitive award would be of minimal use. See Green v. Wolf Corp., 406 F.2d 291, 303 (2d Cir. 1968), cert. denied sub nom. Troster, Singer & Co. v. Green, 395 U.S. 977, 89 S.Ct. 2131, 23 L.Ed.2d 766 (1969).

It is appropriate, lest our action today be misunderstood, that we disclaim any intent by this decision to condone, ignore, or discount the deplorable and counter-productive conditions of many of this country's jails and prisons. We strongly suspect that many traditional and still widespread penal practices, including some which we have touched on in this case, take an enormous toll, not just of the prisoner who must tolerate them at whatever price to his humanity and prospects for a normal future life, but also of the society where prisoners return angry and resentful. Nevertheless, we would forget at our peril and at the peril of our free governmental process, that we are federal judges reviewing decisions made in due course by officers of a sovereign state. We have interpreted and applied the law as it appears to us in light of circumstance and principle. We do not doubt the magnitude of the task ahead before our correctional systems become acceptable and effective from a correctional, social and humane viewpoint, but the proper tools for the job do not lie with a remote federal court. The sensitivity to local nuance, opportunity for daily perseverance, and the human and monetary resources required lie rather with legislators, executives, and citizens in their communities. See, Amsterdam, The Supreme Court and the Rights of Suspects in Criminal Cases, 45 N.Y.U.L.Rev. 785, 810 (1970).

---

[1] As state administrative officials, defendants are not entitled to the protective immunity from a judgment for damages that has been extended to judges, Pierson v. Ray, 386 U.S. 547, 87 S.Ct. 1213, 18 L.Ed.2d 288 (1967), and legislators (Tenney v. Brandhove, 341 U.S. 367, 71 S.Ct. 783, 95 L.Ed. 1019 (7951)). Jobson v. Henne, 355 F.2d 129 (2d Cir. 1966).

[2] Judge Motley awarded $25.00 compensatory damages per day for every day that Sostre spent in segregation (372 days) or a total of $9,300. In view of the conditions of Sostre's segregation, which we have described, this amount is not unreasonable. In addition, she awarded $3,270 in punitive damages.

[3] We do not now decide the question, not passed on below and neither briefed nor argued orally on this appeal, whether plaintiff may yet recover damages against a party not before us.

Note 4.

WRIGHT V. MCMANN
321 F Supp. 127 (1970) *affirmed,* 460 F.2d 136 (1972)
United States District Court, Northern District of New York

FOLEY, J.

The money damages to be awarded Wright as seems prevalent in the application of all legal principles in these claims under the Civil Rights statute enters a complicated phase of judicial writing. Judge Motley covered the leading cases to the date of her decision, May 14, 1970, in Sostre v. Rockefeller et al., supra. Generally, the compensatory damages are to be governed by federal standards. (42 U.S.C.A. § 1983; Sullivan v. Little Hunting Park, Inc., 396 U.S. 229, 239, 90 S.Ct. 400, 24 L.Ed.2d 386; Pierson v. Ray, 386 U.S. 547, 87 S.Ct. 1213, 18 L.Ed.2d 288; Basista v. Weir, 3 Cir., 340 F.2d 74, 87). Supreme Court Justice Brennan expanded upon these writings, concurring in part and dissenting in part in Adickes v. S. H. Kress & Co., 398 U.S. 144, 90 S.Ct. 1598, 26 L.Ed.2d 142, June 1, 1970, stating that the federal courts are duty-bound to enrich the jurisprudence of § 1983 by looking to remedies of the State wherein they sit. The practical guide I think is contained in Monroe v. Pape, 365 U.S. 167, 187, 81 S.Ct. 473, 5 L.Ed.2d 492 to the effect § 1983 should be read against the background of tort liability that makes a man responsible for the natural consequences of his actions. Conventional principles of damages, in my experience never too difficult to apply, fit the situation here. Chief Judge Lumbard recently with ease used the traditional elements of compensatory damage while sitting as a District Judge in Connecticut in Arroyo v. Walsh et al., 317 F.Supp. 869, awarding $2500.00 damages for alleged excessive force by police in making an arrest.

I do not minimize the discomfort Wright had to undergo. However, we do not have the usual propositions of doctor bills, loss of wages, physical injury and possible future physical impairment. Wright is a big, strapping man, and although he testified that under the rigors of his confinement in the cold when nude he lost weight, there is no support for that except his testimony and I refuse to so find. Loss of sleep is believable under the conditions I find existed for periods of the night hours. There are no medical records to substantiate his claims of swollen legs and so forth. (R. 80–87). The doctor did pass his cell daily and there is no record I am aware of with such complaints.

I award no punitive damages because such are justified only as a retributive or deterrent measure. Green v. Wolf Corp., 2 Cir., 406 F.2d 291. Also, to be applied is the statement of Justice Brennan in Adickes, supra, that a defendant, such as the Warden here, must act with actual knowledge he was violating a right secured by the Constitution and laws or acted with reckless disregard of whether he was thus violating such right. Although I do not find sufficient to uphold the good faith or probable cause defense, there is not enough in my judgment to find deliberateness or recklessness on the Warden's part to award punitive damages. Further, because of the examples I have noted of correction and improvement in New York prison conditions that relate to issues of this kind, and the legislative and correctional attitude to update and improve to conform to modern penological surveys and studies, there is no need in my judgment for deterrent measures. The dark cells are changed to such extent that their use although necessary in certain circumstances would be minimal. Neither Wright nor Mosher were ever so confined.

United States Court of Appeals, Second Circuit

LUMBARD, J.

We turn finally to the award by the District Court of $1500.00 damages in Wright's favor against appellant McMann. Reversal is urged on the ground that, although Judge Foley specifically rejected a defense of good faith or probable cause on the part of McMann, he made no finding that McMann personally imposed the deprivations that resulted in the unconstitutional treatment. To find McMann liable when lower prison officials were directly responsible for Wright's treatment, it is argued, is to assess him under a theory of vicarious liability. We disagree.

In the first place, although Judge Foley made no specific findings to this effect, there is indeed evidence in the record from which it could readily be inferred that McMann had definite knowledge of the condition of the "strip cells." As both Judge Foley and this court in the first *Wright* opinion pointed out, McMann's Answer to Wright's complaint acknowledged pointblank that Wright's treatment was commonplace. The Answer states:

> It is the practice at Clinton Prison to place certain inmates in what is known as a strip

cell at the time of their reception in segregation.... A strip cell has only the bare necessities and at times the clothing is taken from the prisoner and at night he is given a blanket to sleep upon the floor.

Also indicative of McMann's actual knowledge is the uncontradicted testimony of Wright that, upon his written complaint, F.B.I. officers interviewed him for several hours in a library behind McMann's office in 1965, and again upon a subsequent complaint from Wright in 1966. During the first interview, according to Wright, the federal officers informed him that they had spoken with McMann as part of their investigation of his complaint.

Wright also testified without contradiction that while he was in segregation his complaints addressed to McMann resulted in his glasses and certain legal materials being restored to him. Furthermore, a letter sent to the commissioner of correction by Wright, in which he thoroughly detailed the conditions he was forced to endure in the "strip cell," passed through McMann's office en route and was read and initialed by him.

Thus there is abundant evidence from which to conclude that McMann must have actually known of the strip cell conditions at the time in question. Furthermore, he was charged with having such knowledge. Ultimate responsibility for the operation of the segregation cells was his, as was made clear from trial testimony, the Employees Rule Book of the New York State Department of Correction then in effect, and section 18, N.Y. Correction Law, McKinney's Consol. Laws c. 43 (1968), as amended L.1970, c. 476, § 4 (1971 Supp.). Furthermore, section 114–a of the New York Correction Law required that the warden

> shall cause to be kept a daily record of the proceedings of the prison, in which shall be entered a note . . . of every punishment inflicted on a prisoner, the nature and amount thereof and by whom it was inflicted, and also a memorandum of every well-founded complaint made by any prisoner of bad or insufficient food, want of clothing, or cruel or unjust treatment by a guard; . . .

As against these directives that the warden exercise responsibility for and be familiar with the treatment of inmates, however, Judge Foley found that "there was a design . . . to avoid written rule-making in the Clinton segregation unit" and that McMann made only "rare" visits to the segregation cells, 321 F. Supp. at 143. In short, applying the common law tort standard appropriate in § 1983 cases, that one is liable for the "natural consequences of his actions," Monroe v. Pape, 365 U.S. 167, 187, 81 S.Ct. 473, 5 L.Ed.2d 492 (1967), we think appellant McMann knew or should have known that Wright was being forced to live under conditions described previously by this court as "foul" and "inhumane," 387 F.2d at 526, and today held unconstitutional.

We think Wright should be properly compensated for the suffering he had to endure, and recovery should not be defeated by an attempt by the warden to shift responsibility to inferiors when there is every reason to believe that he was aware of segregation cell conditions and when responsibility for permitting such conditions to exist was ultimately, in any event, squarely his. We are not moved by the suggestion that if we uphold liability today competent persons tomorrow will refuse to become superintendents, as the title is presently designated. In the unlikely event that a prospective superintendent in fact turns down an offer for fear of personal liability, we think that the position is probably better filled by someone determined to supervise the facility so as to prevent the type of inmate treatment giving rise to this lawsuit.

Note 5.

LILES v. SOUTH CAROLINA DEPARTMENT OF CORRECTIONS
CCH 1969 Trade Cases Par. 72,899 (1969)
United States Court of Appeals, Fourth Circuit

PER CURIAM: Tommy Liles, a South Carolina prisoner, seeks to appeal a denial by the district court (Hemphill, J.) of his "Application for Declaratory Judgment."

In his petition to the district court, Liles complained of the procedures employed by the state prison authorities in the operation of the prison canteen. Alleging that inmates are not allowed to purchase articles from sources other than the canteen, that the prices charged at the canteen include a thirty per cent "administrative duty" added to the normal retail price, and that state sales taxes are imposed on the purchase price *after* the "administrative duty" is added, Liles contends that:

(1) the prices charged constitute monopolistic price fixing in violation of federal law,
(2) the "administrative duty" is imposed in violation of state law,
(3) imposing the tax on the "administrative duty" is in violation of state law, and

(4) the foregoing amount to a denial of equal protection of the laws.

The district court refused relief on the ground that Liles had made no showing that he had exhausted his available state remedies.

After receiving notice of the dismissal of his petition, Liles filed a timely notice of appeal, which the district judge refused to honor. Subsequently, upon Liles' petition to this court that his case be reviewed on appeal, we requested the district court to submit the file to this court for review.

We conclude that the district court erred in refusing relief on the ground of failure to exhaust state remedies. Liberally construing Liles' complaint, he seeks relief under the Sherman Antitrust Act, 15 U.S.C. § 1 et seq., and the Civil Rights Act of 1871, 42 U.S.C. § 1983. Resort to state courts before seeking relief in the federal courts is not required in cases arising under either Act. See *Rivers v. Royster*, 360 F. 2d 592 (4 Cir. 1966); *Cassidy v. Riddles*, No. 11,655 (4 Cir. March 22, 1968) (Mem. Dec.). Therefore, the district court should have considered petitioner's claims on their merits. We remand for such consideration without expressing an opinion on the merit of Liles' contentions. . . .

Note 6.

LOGUE v. UNITED STATES
334 F. Supp. 322 (1971), *reversed,* 459 F.2d 408 (1972)
United States District Court, Southern District of Texas

COX, District Judge.

Reagan Edward Logue, a Federal prisoner, hanged himself in the Nueces County jail. His adoptive father, Orval C. Logue, has brought this suit under the provisions of the Federal Tort Claims Act, 28 U.S.C. § 2671 et seq., to recover damages from the government under the Texas Wrongful Death Act, Article 4671 et seq., Revised Civil Statutes of Texas (1925), as amended, for himself and for Reagan Edward Logue's mother, Alice Maire Logue, now Mrs. Blouin, and on behalf of the Estate of Reagan Edward Logue for the decedent's pain and suffering and for funeral expenses. This Court has full and complete jurisdiction of the subject matter of the parties and venue properly lies.

The Court finds the following facts surrounding the death of Reagan Edward Logue:

1. On May 22, 1968, the deceased, then eighteen years of age, was arrested by Deputy United States Marshal Del W. Bowers in Corpus Christi, Texas, on a bench warrant charging the said Reagan Edward Logue with conspiracy to smuggle 229 pounds of marijuana into the United States, and he was placed in the Nueces County jail as a Federal prisoner.

2. At about 3:00 p. m. the next day, the prisoner attempted suicide by inflicting a serious cut upon his left arm. Thereafter, he was transported from the jail to Memorial Hospital, where he was treated for the laceration and admitted with a diagnosis that he was acutely psychotic.

3. On May 24, 1968, Deputy Marshal Bowers, after conferences with his superiors in the Marshal's Office and with Shannon Gwin, M.D., the prisoner's medical doctor, decided to return the prisoner to the Nueces County jail. Dr. Gwin recommended to the Deputy Marshal that the prisoner remain in the hospital until he could be transferred to another medical facility. At this time, the prisoner had serious suicidal tendencies and his condition was not improved over what it had been when he was admitted to the hospital the day before.

4. At about 3:30 p. m. on the same day, Dr. Gwin, because he thought he had no choice, released the prisoner from the hospital to Deputy Marshal Bowers, who returned him to the Nueces County jail, pending his transfer to a Federal mental institution.

5. Deputy Bowers knew the prisoner had serious suicidal tendencies and should be protected against injuring or killing himself, and at Deputy Bowers' request, the prisoner was put in a cell which had been stripped of everything except the bunk with a mattress, the commode and wash basin. The steel walls and ceiling of the cell were symmetrically perforated with round holes about the size of a half dollar. There was no ceiling light fixture. No specific arrangements were made by the Deputy Marshal for constant surveillance of the prisoner, and this was negligence.

6. The Sheriff's employees in the jail knew the prisoner had serious suicidal tendencies, and they did make precautionary surveillance checks after his return from the hospital, but those surveillance checks were made usually in connection with bringing some other prisoner onto the floor where Reagan Edward Logue was incarcerated. This was inadequate surveillance and was negligence.

7. When the prisoner was returned to the Nueces County jail on May 24, 1968, he had a

long Kerlix bandage on his arm. At about 4:30 p. m. on the afternoon of the next day he removed the bandage and hanged himself with it. Each act of negligence above mentioned was a proximate cause of his death. . . .

The government is not an insurer of the safety of its prisoner; however, once it became aware, through the knowledge of the Deputy Marshals involved, of the psychotic condition and suicidal tendencies of this prisoner, the reasonable care which the government was required to take was that care necessary to make certain the prisoner did not commit suicide while in jail. . . .

It is, therefore, ordered that Orval C. Logue have judgment against the United States of America in the amount of $5,000.00, to be apportioned $3,500.00 to Alice Maire Blouin and $1,500.00 to Orval C. Logue; and the Estate of Reagan Edward Logue, deceased, takes nothing by its suit, except that it shall recover from the United States the funeral expenses in the amount of $1,164.50.

United States Court of Appeals, Fifth Circuit

SIMPSON, Circuit Judge

The United States is subject to suit under the Federal Tort Claims Act for injuries suffered by federal prisoners confined in federal facilities. United States v. Muniz, 1963, 374 U.S. 150, 83 S.Ct. 1850, 10 L.Ed.2d 805. But we agree with the United States that *Muniz* does not extend to the situation now before us, where a federal prisoner is housed in a nonfederal facility pursuant to Title 18, U.S.C., Section 4002. We interpret this section as fixing the status of the Nueces County jail as that of a "contractor". Title 28, U.S.C., Sec. 2671, footnote 2, supra. This insulates the United States from liability under the FTCA for the negligent acts or omissions of the jail's employees. . . .

The judgment of the district court is reversed and the cause is remanded with directions to enter judgment for the United States.

7. PROCEDURE IN PRISONER RIGHTS CASES

NOTES

Note 1.

WILLIAM BENNETT TURNER

Establishing the Rule of Law in Prisons: A Manual for Prisoner's Rights Litigation*

The two principal means of seeking federal judicial review of internal state prison practices are habeas corpus petitions and civil suits under 42 U.S.C. section 1983. In many cases, either route is open.

Habeas corpus may be used even where release is not the remedy sought. Habeas may, therefore, be appropriate to challenge prison conditions or prison administrative decisions which will not, if found unconstitutional, result in the petitioner's release. . . .

Despite the availability of habeas, ordinarily a section 1983 suit will be preferable for a number of reasons. First, exhaustion of state remedies is probably not required, whereas the federal habeas statute requires exhaustion of state remedies. Second, any significant prisoners' rights action will require extensive use of the liberal discovery techniques provided by the Federal Rules of Civil Procedure. These may be resorted to as a matter of course in a civil suit under section 1983. Discovery in a habeas proceeding is a more doubtful matter. In *Harris v. Nelson,* a habeas proceeding, the Supreme Court held that, in certain circumstances, limited discovery may be had upon application to the court. Given judicial reluctance to hear and determine prisoners' rights cases, however, it is advantageous to avoid the necessity of obtaining a court order for routine discovery by using section 1983. Third, maintenance of a class action under rule 23(b)(2) of the Federal Rules of Civil Procedure is possible in a section 1983 suit, assuming that the usual class action requirements can be met. In habeas corpus, however, substantial doubt surrounds the propriety of a class action. Class actions avoid mootness problems if a particular plaintiff is released, and also provide the basis for broad injunctive relief going beyond a particular prisoner's situation. Finally the relief required in a prisoners' rights suit would usually call for exercise of the broad equitable powers of the court. For example, the prison officials may be required to promulgate new rules and regulations, to report to the court, or to file and implement a plan to remedy constitutional deficiencies in the prison system. This kind of injunctive re-

* 23 *Stanford Law Review* 454, 504–07 (1971). Copyright 1971 by the Board of Trustees of the Leland Stanford Junior University. Reprinted with permission of the author and the publisher.

lief, while appropriate in a civil suit, seems inappropriate and would probably be unavailable in a habeas corpus action.

Although there have been uncertainties as to whether exhaustion of state remedies is required in other kinds of civil rights actions, it is clear that no state judicial remedies need be exhausted in prisoners' rights cases under section 1983. In addition, exhaustion of state administrative remedies is not required unless there is an adequate administrative procedure specifically set up to provide a speedy and fair hearing of the prisoner's grievance. In most states there is no formal administrative procedure at all for hearing prisoners' claims.

Further, the doctrine of abstention should not be applied to oust the federal courts of jurisdiction under section 1983. This is certainly true where there is no complex administrative apparatus or other means of hearing and determining the prisoners' complaints and no state statute requiring interpretation by state courts before a federal constitutional question is presented.

In short, neither the exhaustion nor the abstention doctrines present serious problems in a section 1983 suit. Federal jurisdiction is clear, and the court must proceed to determine on the merits whether the prisoners are entitled to relief for violation of federal rights under section 1983.

Where the action seeks an injunction against the enforcement of a state statute or administrative order made under a state statute and the basis of the action is the unconstitutionality of the statute, federal law requires that the case be heard and determined by a three-judge district court. Also, where administrative regulations of statewide applicability are involved, a three-judge court must be convened. Challenges to prison disciplinary rules of statewide applicability would presumably fit the same mold, but general practices not embodied in formal regulations may be considered by a single district judge. Regulations which are not of statewide applicability (for example, regulations governing only one prison in a multi-prison state) do not require a three-judge court even though the regulations are promulgated pursuant to authority conferred by statute and are approved by a state agency. Even where a three-judge court is required, a single judge may grant temporary relief pending the hearing before the full court, at least where preferred constitutional rights are involved.

Note 2.

RONALD GOLDFARB AND LINDA SINGER

Redressing Prisoners' Grievances*

Class actions, in which suits are brought by or against representatives of a class and a decree in favor of or against representatives of a group binds all members of the class, were developed by courts of equity as an answer to the practical problems of multiparty litigation: the unwieldy number of interested parties to the suit, the difficulty of subjecting all the members to service of process, and the likelihood that the membership of so large a group may change during the course of the suit. The nature of actions like this is made to order for litigation by prisoners aimed at general conditions. Judgments in favor of the representatives to a suit would then apply to the entire class and could be enforced by any member of the class. It would be useful, too, for prison administrators who could reduce multiple litigation through precedential test cases.

In *Jordan v. Fitzharris,* a federal district court enjoined California prison authorities from subjecting plaintiff to violations of the Civil Rights Act by confining him in a "strip cell" which lacked the "essentials for survival." The court's opinion was worded in terms that could benefit all inmates of the Soledad prison, or, perhaps of the entire California penal system:

> If the defendants intend to continue with the use of the so-called "strip" or "quiet" cell as device in the general plan of solitary confinement, then its use must be accompanied by supplying the basic requirements which are essential to life, and by providing such essential requirements as may be necessary to maintain a degree of cleanliness compatible with elemental decency in accord with the standards of a civilized community.
>
> * * *
>
> Primitive segregation cells should be so constructed that all parts are visible to the patrolling officer from the corridor. Such cells or at least some of them should be sound proofed....

If the defendants continued using "strip cells" to discipline other prisoners without conforming to the standards set out by the court, the

* 39 *Geo. Wash. L. Rev.* 281, 283–84 (1970). Copyright © The George Washington Law Review 1970.

other affected prisoners probably would have to initiate another lawsuit for their relief, relying on the *Jordan* decision as precedent. If, on the other hand, the *Jordan* suit initially had been a class action, any members of the class included in the decree later could attempt to enforce it by bringing an action for contempt against the prison officials.

Where prisoners are uneducated, unaware of their rights or of the means for implementing them, or unrepresented by counsel, a class suit could provide the only practical means for presenting their grievances to a court. Moreover, class suits are frequently more efficient and economical than individual actions, and save time for the courts, the defending prison officials, and the attorneys. For example, when Georgia prisoners succeeded in a class action in federal court to desegregate all correctional institutions in the state, other prisoners who later sought to block the integration in one prison were precluded from pursuing endless litigation on the ground that they were within the class of plaintiffs represented by the earlier action. . . .

Although class actions are permitted by state statutes, their use has been relatively rare. In fact, there is not a single decision by a state court in which prisoners were allowed to bring a class suit against prison officials.

The adoption of a modified Rule 23 of the Federal Rules of Civil Porcedure in 1966 brought federal class actions into greater prominence than they had enjoyed previously and simplified the requirements surrounding them. Under the new rule there are four requirements for the maintenance of any class action in federal court: (1) The class must be so numerous that it is impractical to bring them all before the court; (2) There must be questions of law or fact common to the class; (3) The claims or defenses of the representative parties must be typical of the claims or defenses of the class; (4) The representative parties must be able to protect the interests of the class fairly and adequately.

In addition to the four general requirements, a class action must fall into one of three categories. First, the prosecution of separate actions must create a risk of inconsistent adjudications or impede the ability of other members of the class to protect their own interests. Second, the party opposing the class must have acted or refused to act on grounds generally applicable to the class. And, third, a court may allow a class action where "the questions of law or fact common to the members of the class predominate over any questions affecting only individual members, and that a class action is superior to other available methods for the fair and efficient adjudication of the controversy."

8. THE INMATE'S RIGHT TO A JUDICIAL HEARING

NOTES

Note 1.

HAINES V. KERNER
404 U.S. 519 (1972)
Supreme Court of the United States

PER CURIAM.

Petitioner, an inmate at the Illinois State Penitentiary, Menard, Illinois, commenced this action against the Governor of Illinois and other state officers and prison officials under the Civil Rights Act of 1871, 42 U.S.C. § 1983, and 28 U.S.C. § 1343 (3), seeking to recover damages for claimed injuries and deprivation of rights while incarcerated under a judgment not challenged here. Petitioner's *pro se* complaint was premised on alleged action of prison officials placing him in solitary confinement as a disciplinary measure after he had struck another inmate on the head with a shovel following a verbal altercation. The assault by petitioner on another inmate is not denied. Petitioner's *pro se* complaint included general allegations of physical injuries suffered while in disciplinary confinement and denial of due process in the steps leading to that confinement. The claimed physical suffering was aggravation of a pre-existing foot injury and a circulatory ailment caused by forcing him to sleep on the floor of his cell with only blankets.

The District Court granted respondents' motion under Rule 12 (b)(6) of the Federal Rules of Civil Procedure to dismiss the complaint for failure to state a claim upon which relief could be granted, suggesting that only under exceptional circumstances should courts inquire into the internal operations of state penitentiaries and concluding that petitioner had failed to show a deprivation of federally protected rights. The Court of Appeals affirmed, emphasizing that prison officials are vested with "wide discretion" in disciplinary matters. We granted certiorari and appointed counsel to represent petitioner. The only issue now before us is petitioner's contention that the District Court erred in dismissing his *pro se* complaint without allowing him to present evidence on his claims.

Whatever may be the limits on the scope of inquiry of courts into the internal administration of prisons, allegations such as those asserted by petitioner, however inartfully pleaded, are sufficient to call for the opportunity to offer supporting evidence. We cannot say with assurance that under the allegations of the *pro se* complaint, which we hold to less stringent standards than formal pleadings drafted by lawyers, it appears "beyond doubt that the plaintiff can prove no set of facts in support of his claim which would entitle him to relief." *Conley* v. *Gibson*, 355 U.S. 41, 45–46 (1957). See *Dioguardi* v. *Durning*, 139 F.2d 774 (CA2 1944).

Accordingly, although we intimate no view whatever on the merits of petitioner's allegations, we conclude that he is entitled to an opportunity to offer proof. The judgment is vacated and the case is remanded for further proceedings consistent herewith.

Reversed and remanded.

Mr. Justice Powell and Mr. Justice Rehnquist took no part in the consideration or decision of this case.

Note 2.

CRUZ V. BETO
405 U.S. 319 (1972)
Supreme Court of the United States

PER CURIAM.

The complaint, alleging a cause of action under 42 U.S.C. Sec. 1983, states that Cruz is a Buddhist, who is in a Texas prison. While prisoners who are members of other religious sects are allowed to use the prison chapel, Cruz is not. He shared his Buddhist religious material with other prisoners and, according to the allegations, in retaliation was placed in solitary confinement on a diet of bread and water for two weeks, without access to newspapers, magazines, and all other sources of news. He also alleged that he was prohibited from corresponding with his religious advisor in the Buddhist sect. Those in the isolation unit spend 22 hours a day in total idleness.

Again, according to the allegations, Texas encourages inmates to participate in other religious programs; providing at the state expense chaplains of the Catholic, Jewish, and Protestant faiths, providing also at state expense copies of the Jewish and Christian Bibles, conducting weekly Sunday school classes and religious services. According to the allegations, points of good merit are given prisoners as a reward for attending orthodox religious services, those points enhancing a prisoner's eligibility for desirable job assignments and early parole consideration. Respondent answered, denying the allegations and moving to dismiss.

The Federal District Court denied relief without a hearing or without any findings, saying the complaint was in an area that should be left "to the sound discretion of prison administration." It went on to say, "Valid disciplinary and security reasons not known to this court may prevent the 'equality' of exercise of religious practices in prisons." The Court of Appeals affirmed. 445 F.2d 801.

Federal courts sit not to supervise prisons but to enforce the constitutional rights of all "persons" which include prisoners. We are not unmindful that prison officials must be accorded latitude in the administration of prison affairs, and that prisoners necessarily are subject to appropriate rules and regulations. But persons in prison, like other individuals, have the right to petition the Government for redress of grievances which, of course, includes "access of prisoners to the courts for the purpose of presenting their complaints." Johnson v. Avery, 393 U.S. 483, 485; Ex parte Hull, 312 U.S. 546, 549. See also Younger v. Gilmore, 404 U.S. 15, aff'g Gilmore v. Lynch, 319 F.Supp. 105 (ND Cal.). Moreover, racial segregation, which is unconstitutional outside prisons, is unconstitutional within prisons, save for "the necessities of prison security and discipline." Lee v. Washington, 390 U.S. 333. Even more closely in point is Cooper v. Pate, 378 U.S. 546, where we reversed a dismissal of a complaint brought under 42 U.S.C. Sec. 1983. We said "Taking as true the allegations of the complaint, as they must be on a motion to dismiss, the complaint stated a cause of action." Ibid. The allegation made by the petitioner was that solely because of his religious beliefs he was denied permission to purchase certain religious publications and denied other privileges enjoyed by other prisoners.

We said in Conley v. Gibson, 355 U.S. 41, 45–46, that "A complaint should not be dismissed for failure to state a claim unless it appears beyond doubt that the plaintiff can prove no set of facts in support of his claim which would entitle him to relief."

If Cruz was a Buddhist and if he was denied

a reasonable opportunity of pursuing his faith comparable to the opportunity afforded fellow prisoners who adhere to conventional religious precepts, then there was palpably discrimination by the State against the Buddhist religion, established 600 B.C., long before the Christian era. The First Amendment applicable to the States by reason of the Fourteenth Amendment, Torcaso v. Watkins, 367 U.S. 488, 492–493, prohibits government from making a law "prohibiting the free exercise of religion." If the allegations of this complaint are assumed to be true, as they must be on the motion to dismiss, Texas has violated the First and Fourteenth Amendments.

The petition for certiorari is granted, the judgment is vacated, and the cause remanded for a hearing and appropriate findings.

So ordered.

Mr. Chief Justice BURGER, joining in the result.

I join in the result reached even though the allegations of the complaint are on the borderline necessary to compel an evidentiary hearing. Some of the claims alleged are frivolous; others do not present justiciable issues. There cannot possibly be any constitutional or legal requirement that the government provide materials for every religion and sect practiced in this diverse country. At most, Buddhist materials cannot be denied to prisoners if someone offers to supply them.

Mr. Justice BLACKMUN concurs in the result.

Mr. Justice REHNQUIST, dissenting.

Unlike the Court, I am not persuaded that petitioner's complaint states a claim under the First Amendment, nor that if the opinion of the Court of Appeals is vacated the trial court must necessarily conduct a trial upon the complaint.

Under the First Amendment, of course, Texas may neither "establish a religion" nor may it "impair the free exercise" thereof. Petitioner alleges that voluntary services are made available at prison facilities so that Protestants, Catholics, and Jews may attend church services of their choice. None of our prior holdings indicates that such a program on the part of prison officials amounts to the establishment of a religion.

Petitioner is a prisoner, serving 15 years for robbery in a Texas penitentiary. He is understandably not as free to practice his religion as if he were outside the prison walls. But there is no intimation in his pleadings that he is being punished for his religious views, as was the case in Cooper v. Pate, 378 U.S. 546 (1964), where a prisoner was denied the receipt of mail about his religion. Cooper presented no question of interference with prison administration of the type which would be involved here in retaining chaplains, scheduling the use of prison facilities, and timing the activities of various prisoners.

None of our holdings under the First Amendment requires that, in addition to being allowed freedom of religious belief, prisoners be allowed freely to evangelize their views among other prisoners. There is no indication in petitioner's complaint that the prison officials have dealt more strictly with his efforts to convert other convicts to Buddhism than with efforts of communicants of other faiths to make similar conversions.

By reason of his status petitioner is obviously limited in the extent to which he may practice his religion. He is assuredly not free to attend the church of his choice outside the prison walls. But the fact that the Texas prison system offers no Buddhist services at this particular prison does not, under the circumstances pleaded in his complaint, demonstrate that his religious freedom is being impaired. Presumably prison officials are not obligated to provide facilities for any particular denominational services within a prison, although once they undertake to provide them for some they must make only such reasonable distinctions as may survive analysis under the Fourteenth Amendment Equal Protection Clause.

What petitioner's basic claim amounts to is that because prison facilities are provided for denominational services for religions with more numerous followers, the failure to provide prison facilities for Buddhist services amounts to a denial of the equal protection of the laws. There is no indication from petitioner's complaint how many practicing Buddhists there are in the particular prison facility in which he is incarcerated, nor is there any indication of the demand upon available facilities for other prisoner activities. Neither the decisions of this Court after full argument, nor those summarily reversing the dismissal of a prisoner's civil rights complaint have ever given full consideration to the proper balance to be struck between prisoners' rights and the extensive administrative discretion which must rest with correction officials. I would apply the rule of deference to administrative discretion which has been overwhelmingly accepted in the courts of appeals. Failing that, I would at least hear argument as to which rule should govern.

A long line of decisions by this Court has recognized that the "equal protection of the laws" guaranteed by the Fourteenth Amendment is not to be applied in a precisely equivalent way in the multitudinous fact situations which may confront the courts. On the one hand, we have held that racial classifications are "invidious" and "suspect." I think it quite consistent with the intent of the framers of the Fourteenth Amendment, many of whom would doubtless be surprised to know that convicts came within its ambit, to treat prisoner claims at the other end of the spectrum from claims of racial discrimination. Absent a complaint alleging facts showing that the difference in treatment between petitioner and his fellow Buddhists and practitioners of more numerous denominations could not reasonably be justified under any rational hypothesis, I would leave the matter in the hands of the prison officials.

It has been assumed that the dismissal by the trial court must be treated as proper only if the standard of Conley v. Gibson, 355 U.S. 41, would permit the grant of a motion under Fed. Rule Civ. Proc. 12 (b) 6. I would not require the District Court to inflexibly apply this general principle to the complaint of every inmate, who is in many respects in a different litigating posture than those who are unconfined. The inmate stands to gain something and lose nothing from a complaint stating facts which he is ultimately unable to prove. Though he may be denied legal relief, he will nonetheless have obtained a short sabbatical in the nearest federal courthouse. To expand the availability of such courtroom appearances by requiring the District Court to construe every inmate's complaint under the liberal rule of Conley v. Gibson, deprives those courts of the latitude necessary to process this ever-increasing species of complaint.

Finally, a factual hearing should not be imperative on remand if dismissal is appropriate on grounds other than failure to state a claim for relief. It is evident from the record before us that the in forma pauperis complaint might well have been dismissed as "frivolous or malicious," under the discretion vested in the trial court in 28 U.S.C. Sec. 1915 (d). This power is not limited or impaired by the strictures of Rule 12 (b). Fletcher v. Young, 222 F.2d 222 (CA 4 1955). Although the trial court based its dismissal on 12 (b) 6 grounds, this record would support a dismissal as frivolous.

The State's answer to the complaint showed that the identical issues of religious freedoms were litigated by another prisoner from the same institution, claiming the same impairment of the practice of the Buddhist religion, which was brought by the attorney employed at the prison to provide legal services for the inmates. It is not clear whether petitioner here was a party to that suit, as he was to many suits filed by his fellow prisoners. If he was, the instant claim may be barred under the doctrine of res judicata. In any event, a prior adjudication of the same claim by another prisoner under identical circumstances would be a substantial factor in a decision to dismiss this claim as frivolous.

In addition, the trial court had before it the dismissal of another of petitioner's cases filed shortly before the instant action, where the trial judge had been exposed to myriad previous actions, and found them to be "voluminous, repetitious, duplicitous and in many instances deceitful." Whether petitioner might have raised his claim in these or several other actions in which he joined other prisoner plaintiffs is also proper foundation for a finding that this complaint is "frivolous or malicious." Whatever might be the posture of this constitutional claim if petitioner had never flooded the courts with repetitive and duplicitous claims, and if it had not recently been adjudicated in an identical proceeding, I believe it can be dismissed as frivolous in the case before us.

9. CORPORAL PUNISHMENT AND THE EIGHTH AMENDMENT

NOTE

JACKSON V. BISHOP
404 F.2d 571 (1968)
United States Court of Appeals, Eighth Circuit

BLACKMUN, Circuit Judge.

The three plaintiffs-appellants, inmates of the Arkansas penitentiary, in separate actions call upon us to direct the entry of an injunction barring the use of the strap as a disciplinary measure in Arkansas' penal institutions. The claim is that the district court

> erred in refusing to hold that corporal punishment of prisoners is cruel and un-

usual punishment within the meaning of the Eighth Amendment to the United States Constitution, and in holding that the whipping of prisoners was not unconstitutional per se....

We conclude that the plaintiffs are correct in their position and that Arkansas' use of the strap, irrespective of safeguards, is to be enjoined. . . .

Corporal punishment in the Arkansas system was authorized formally only in 1962 but evidently it had been employed for many years. At that time the Board, by resolution, authorized such punishment whenever, in the Superintendent's judgment, its infliction was necessary in order to maintain discipline. The resolution did not prescribe form or limit of punishment.

In the *Talley* action, the three petitioning inmates sought injunctive relief with respect to certain prison practices including the infliction of corporal punishment. Chief Judge Henley found that, at that time, there were no written rules as to whipping; that such punishment was administered in the sole discretion of the one inflicting it, subject to an informal requirement that the blows not exceed ten for a single offense; and that two of those three petitioners had been whipped and one beaten by a field-line supervisor-trusty. The judge noted that the Supreme Court of Arkansas, over 80 years ago, deplored the whipping of convicts, Werner v. State, 44 Ark. 122 (1884), and that the Arkansas statutes do not themselves specifically prescribe whipping even as a punishment for crime.[1] He observed, however, that corporal punishment had not been viewed historically as a constitutionally forbidden cruel and unusual punishment. The court concluded that it was not prepared to say that such punishment was unconstitutional per se. Nevertheless, Judge Henley said, 247 F.Supp. at 689, this conclusion presupposes that the infliction of such punishment is surrounded by appropriate safeguards, that is, it must not be excessive, it must be inflicted dispassionately and by responsible people, and it must be applied under recognizable standards so that the convict knows what conduct will cause him to be whipped and how much punishment his conduct will produce. The court found that those safeguards did not exist in the Arkansas system and enjoined further corporal punishment of the petitioners until they were established.

[1] Some state statutes do. See, for example, 11 Delaware Code, §§ 631, 811, 3905, 3906, 3907, and 3908.

The *Talley* opinion was filed on November 15, 1965. As a result, the Board issued written rules and regulations on January 10, 1966. These were in effect until the district court decision in the present case was rendered June 3, 1967. In addition to a number of other provisions, the rules state that certain "major offenses will warrant corporal punishment." The ones listed are homosexuality, agitation, insubordination, making or concealing weapons, refusal to work when medically certified able to work, and participating in or inciting a riot. They further state:

> No inmate shall ever be authorized to inflict any corporal punishment under color of prison authority on another inmate.
> Punishment shall not, in any case, exceed ten lashes with the strap, the number of lashes to be administered shall be determined by a Board of Inquiry, consisting of at least two officials of the Arkansas State Penitentiary, The Superintendent or Assistant Superintendent, and the head Warden or an associate Warden. The Board of Inquiry will request that the accused inmate appear before the Board and speak in his own behalf. No Punishment will be administered in the field.

The straps used in Arkansas vary somewhat but all are similar. Each is of leather and from 3½ to 5½ feet in length, about 4 inches wide, and ¼ inch thick. Each has a wooden handle 8 to 12 inches long.

Since *Talley*, whippings are administered by wardens. The prisoner lies face down and the blows are to his buttocks. Supposedly, they are administered while the prisoner is fully clothed. Petitioners Ernst and Mask, however, testified without contradiction that they were required to lower their trousers and that they received lashes on the bare buttocks. There is corroborating and other evidence to the same effect with respect to other inmates and there was proof, some offered through the State Police, of deep bruises and bleeding.

Whipping is the primary disciplinary measure used in the Arkansas system. Prisoners there have few privileges which can be withheld from them as punishment. Facilities for segregation and solitary confinement are limited.

There is testimony that the strap hurts the inmate's pride, that it has been needed in order to preserve discipline, and that the work level improves after its administration. Contrarily, there is testimony that the whipping generates hate in the inmate who is whipped and that this hate flows toward the whipper, the institution and the system.

The circumstances relative to the punishment administered to the plaintiffs as well as to others and relative to various disciplinary matters are set forth in detail in the district court's opinion. 268 F.Supp. at 809–813. The testimony of James V. Bennett, former Director of the Federal Bureau of Prisons, and that of Fred T. Wilkinson, Director of the Department of Corrections of the State of Missouri (and former Deputy Director of the Federal Bureau of Prisons) are summarized in the district court's opinion. 268 F.Supp. at 813–814. This testimony is to the effect that, among other things, corporal punishment has not been used for disciplinary purposes in federal prisons for years and that only Mississippi, in addition to Arkansas, uses it officially. Testifying as a penologist, it was Mr. Bennett's opinion that the whippings administered to the three plaintiffs were "cruel, degrading and certainly they were unusual in this day and age." Mr. Wilkinson testified that use of the strap "is cruel and unusual and unnecessary."

On July 20, 1966, six months after the issuance of the January 1966 regulations, plaintiff Ernst received two whippings of ten lashes each to the bare buttocks within a period of 45 minutes.

In August 1966 the Superintendent became aware of irregularities. An investigation disclosed violations of serious import. A number of wardens resigned or were discharged. The plaintiffs' cases were filed while this investigation was under way. The present Superintendent candidly does not seek to defend everything which has taken place.

The district judges concluded that the post-*Talley* rules and regulations of January 1966 still did not provide adequate safeguards. The use of the strap was therefore enjoined until further safeguards were provided. The court observed that more than one person's judgment should be required for a decision to administer corporal punishment. . . .

The principal opinion in Trop v. Dulles, supra, 356 U.S. 86, 78 S.Ct. 590, 2 L.Ed.2d 630 (1958), although it commanded the votes of only four justices a decade ago, is, in our view, particularly pertinent. The issue was the validity of a federal statute which would denationalize a native born citizen who deserts the military service in time of war and is convicted thereof by a court-martial and dismissed or dishonorably discharged. The opinion provides guidelines and overtones which we feel safe in regarding as illustrative of the general thinking of a majority of the justices on the subject today. The opinion casts aside the death penalty "as an index of the constitutional limit on punishment," for it "has been employed throughout our history, and, in a day when it is still widely accepted, it cannot be said to violate the constitutional concept of cruelty." 356 U.S. at 99, 78 S.Ct. at 597. The Eighth Amendment's basic concept "is nothing less than the dignity of man" and assures that a state's punishment power "be exercised within the limits of civilized standards." Fines, imprisonment, and even execution may be imposed "but any technique outside the bounds of these traditional penalties is constitutionally suspect." 356 U.S. at 100, 78 S.Ct. at 598. The scope of the Amendment is not "static." It "must draw its meaning from the evolving standards of decency that mark the progress of a maturing society." 356 U.S. at 102, 78 S.Ct. at 598. Virtually all the world's civilized nations refuse to impose statelessness as punishment for crime. 356 U.S. at 102, 78 S.Ct. at 598.

From that opinion we glean a recognition of, and a reliance in part upon, attitudes of contemporary society and comparative law. And the emphasis is on man's basic dignity, on civilized precepts, and on flexibility and improvement in standards of decency as society progresses and matures. Finally, it is "any technique" outside the traditional bounds which "is constitutionally suspect."

In summary, then, so far as the Supreme Court cases are concerned, we have a flat recognition that the limits of the Eighth Amendment's proscription are not easily or exactly defined, and we also have clear indications that the applicable standards are flexible, that disproportion, both among punishments and between punishment and crime, is a factor to be considered, and that broad and idealistic concepts of dignity, civilized standards, humanity, and decency are useful and usable.

With these principles and guidelines before us, we have no difficulty in reaching the conclusion that the use of the strap in the penitentiaries of Arkansas is punishment which, in this last third of the 20th century, runs afoul of the Eighth Amendment; that the strap's use, irrespective of any precautionary conditions which may be imposed, offends contemporary concepts of decency and human dignity and precepts of civilization which we profess to possess; and that it also violates those standards of good conscience and fundamental fairness enunciated by the court in the *Carey* and *Lee* cases.

Our reasons for this conclusion include the following: (1) We are not convinced that any rule or regulation as to the use of the strap, however seriously or sincerely conceived and drawn, will successfully prevent abuse. The present record discloses misinterpretation and obvious overnarrow interpretation even of the newly adopted January 1966 rules. (2) Rules in this area seem often to go unobserved. Despite the January 1966 requirement that no inmate was to inflict punishment on another, the record is replete with instances where this very thing took place. (3) Regulations are easily circumvented. Although it was a long-standing requirement that a whipping was to be administered only when the prisoner was fully clothed, this record discloses instances of whippings upon the bare buttocks, and with consequent injury. (4) Corporal punishment is easily subject to abuse in the hands of the sadistic and the unscrupulous. (5) Where power to punish is granted to persons in lower levels of administrative authority, there is an inherent and natural difficulty in enforcing the limitations of that power. (6) There can be no argument that excessive whipping or an inappropriate manner of whipping or too great frequency of whipping or the use of studded or overlong straps all constitute cruel and unusual punishment. But if whipping were to be authorized, how does one, or any court, ascertain the point which would distinguish the permissible from that which is cruel and unusual? (7) Corporal punishment generates hate toward the keepers who punish and toward the system which permits it. It is degrading to the punisher and to the punished alike. It frustrates correctional and rehabilitative goals. This record cries out with testimony to this effect from the expert penologists, from the inmates and from their keepers. (8) Whipping creates other penological problems and makes adjustment to society more difficult. (9) Public opinion is obviously adverse. Counsel concede that only two states still permit the use of the strap. Thus almost uniformly has it been abolished. It has been expressly outlawed by statute in a number of states. See for example, N.D.Cent. Code § 12–47–26 (1960); S.D.Code § 13.4715 (1939). And 48 states, including Arkansas, have constitutional provisions against cruel or unusual punishment. Ark.Const. art. 2, § 9.

We are not convinced contrarily by any suggestion that the State needs this tool for disciplinary purposes and is too poor to provide other accepted means of prisoner regulation. Humane considerations and constitutional requirements are not, in this day, to be measured or limited by dollar considerations or by the thickness of the prisoner's clothing.

10. PRISON REGULATIONS AND THE VOID FOR VAGUENESS RULE

NOTE

LANDMAN V. ROYSTER
333 F. Supp. 621, 654 (1971)
United States District Court, Eastern District of Virginia

MERHIGE, District Judge

Few of the opinions to date on prison discipline treat in depth the real problem of vagueness in institutional regulations. The evidence, however, shows that the purposes of the constitutional requirement of reasonable specificity—fair warning so that one may conform to the rules, and exactness so that arbitrary penalties or penalties for protected conduct will not be imposed—have been ill-served by the rules enforced against Virginia prisoners. Particularly in a situation where the safeguard of public trial is absent, cf. McKeiver v. Pennsylvania, 403 U.S. 528, 91 S.Ct. 1976, 29 L.Ed.2d 647 (1971) (Brennan, J., concurring and dissenting), and necessarily so, other procedural safeguards against arbitrariness should not be slighted. Morris v. Travisono, *supra*, 310 F.Supp. 861, notes the seriousness of the problem, but does not resolve it. Talley v. Stephens, 247 F.Supp. 683 (E.D. Ark. 1965), required in cases of corporal punishment that recognizable standards of conduct be set. Likewise it is settled that imprisonment does not remove a prisoner's right to be free from arbitrary sanctions. Landman v. Peyton, *supra*. The Constitution requires even of minor criminal laws that they give in advance fair notice of forbidden acts. Palmer v. City of Euclid, 402 U.S. 544, 91 S.Ct. 1563, 29 L.Ed.2d 98 (1971); Bouie v. City of Columbia, 378 U.S. 347, 84 S.Ct. 1697, 12 L.Ed. 2d 894 (1964). Virginia prisoners have been penalized for such ill-defined offenses as "misbehavior" and "agitation." Recent amendments to discipline procedure have not sharpened the outlines of these offenses. On the other hand, existing regulations governing maximum security facilities, which are in the record, demonstrate that the prison authorities are capable of phrasing their requirements with reasonable specificity. The Court does not imply approval of all of those rules; they show, however, that the authorities themselves believe in the practical value and feasibility of rules. See also the disciplinary code reproduced in Bundy v. Cannon, *supra*.

To recanvass the full range of justifications for the vagueness doctrine would unduly prolong this opinion. For useful commentary, see McGautha v. California, 402 U.S. 183, 91 S.Ct. 1454, 28 L.Ed.2d 711 (1971) (Brennan, J., dissenting); Soglin v. Kauffman, 418 F.2d 163 (7th Cir. 1969). In the prison context these considerations argue for application of the requirement:

1. At least in Virginia, where discipline has been used to suppress litigation efforts, the need exists to establish in advance, to avoid a chilling effect, the limits of administrators' power.

2. Like other elements of due process, prior notice of standards of behavior enhances the prisoner's sense of fair treatment and contributes to rehabilitation. See In re Gault, *supra*.

3. Equal treatment of similar conduct—at least to the extent of recording offenses, if not in penalties—will be more certain with fixed rules.

4. The ingredient, in vagueness law, of something like a doctrine forbidding delegation of legislative powers is essential in prison, where the risk of arbitrary action by lower officials is great.

5. The need for judicial review of prison disciplinary actions may greatly decrease in the future if violations of existing rules can be shown.

6. Prison life is highly routine; it therefore ought not to be difficult to establish in advance reasonably clear rules as to expected behavior. Automatic compliance may be expected of many.

7. Specificity has been required in the academic sphere, where administrators likewise are not specialists in legislation.

8. Severe sanctions may result in prison; the greater the individual loss, the higher the requirements of due process.

Countervailing considerations deserve mention:

1. Life is complex in prison as well as outside, and all forms of misbehavior cannot be anticipated. Some may go unpunished for want of a rule.

2. Administrators ought not to be put to the choice of foregoing discipline in such cases or resorting to the ordinary criminal process, for flexibility may work to the benefit of the institution and the inmates as well.

3. Legalistic wrangling over whether a rule was broken may visibly undermine the administration's position of total authority, necessary for security's sake.

4. Prisoners, unlike free men, must well know that they are considered potentially dangerous men and must expect to be highly regimented. In such cases the law requires less in the way of notice, and places a greater burden on the individual to make inquiry or ask permission before acting. Cf. United States v. International Minerals & Chemical Corp., 402 U.S. 558, 91 S.Ct. 1697, 29 L.Ed.2d 178 (1971).

The objections to the applications of some vagueness principle may all be met simply by relaxing the standard somewhat in deference to the state's legitimate needs, rather than by abandoning it. The Court concludes, therefore, that the existence of some reasonably definite rule is a prerequisite to prison discipline of any substantial sort. Regulations must in addition be distributed, posted, or otherwise made available in writing to inmates. Discussion here will be confined to those bases for punishment disclosed in the evidence.

"Misbehavior" or "misconduct," for which, for example, Jefferson and Scott were penalized, offers no reasonable guidance to an inmate, Giaccio v. Pennsylvania, 382 U.S. 399, 86 S.Ct. 518, 15 L.Ed.2d 447 (1966), whereas it leaves the administrator irresponsible to any standard. Penalties may not be imposed on this ground.

"Agitation" appears to encompass discussing litigation with other prisoners, assisting them in litigation, or advising them as to the law. It also includes, as is apparent from Thompson's case, complaining to the authorities, and according to Cunningham, it may include the giving of incorrect legal advice. Prison authorities may legitimately fear the incitement of rule violations and the interruption of orderly activities, and may punish men who engage in such conduct. However, the ban on "agitation" at once gives no fair warning that certain conduct is punishable and, in practice, includes the rendition of legal advice and the preparation of legal pleadings, protected activities.

On the other hand, the Court is not persuaded that the offenses of "insolence," "harassment," and "insubordination," directed against custodial or administrative personnel, are unduly vague. This is not to say, however, that in a given case the imposition of sanctions on such grounds may not be found arbitrary if not based on evidence. . . .

11. JAIL INMATES

NOTES

Note 1.

ON JAILS*

In the vast majority of city and county jails and local short-term institutions, no significant progress has been made in the past 50 years. . . .

In the second decade of this century, Louis Robinson wrote:

> From many points of view, the jail is the most important of all our institutions of imprisonment. The enormous number of jails is alone sufficient . . . to make [one] realize that the jail is, after all, the typical prison in the United States. . . . From two-thirds to three-fourths of all convicted criminals serve out their sentence in jails. But this is not all. The jail is, with small exception, the almost universal detention house for untried prisoners. The great majority, therefore, of penitentiary and reformatory prisoners have been kept for a period varying from a few days to many months within the confines of a county or municipal jail. Then, too, there is the class, not at all unimportant in number, of individuals who, having finally established their innocence, have been set free after spending some time in the jail awaiting trial. Important witnesses also are detained in jail, and it is used at times for still other purposes, even serving occasionally as a temporary asylum for the insane. The part, therefore, which the jail plays in our scheme of punishment cannot be overestimated. Whether for good or for evil, nearly every criminal that has been apprehended is subjected to its influence.

* National Council on Crime and Delinquency, "Survey on Corrections in the United States," The President's Commission on Law Enforcement and Administration of Justice, *Task Force Report: Corrections* 162–65 (1967).

Now, in the seventh decade, this statement by Robinson and his comments on filth, neglect, and maladministration still accurately describe the role and status of jails and short-term institutions in the United States.

These institutions have a long history. As a place of detention for accused persons, the jail traces its lineage back to Biblical times. The workhouse was conceived and developed in the latter half of the 16th century to deal with unemployment, vagrancy, petty thievery, prostitution, and disorderly conduct. So successful was it in clearing the streets and public places of the economically depressed and the socially offensive that Parliament ordained establishment of such an institution for minor offenders in every county in England. The innovation of this type of imprisonment spread during the 17th century to Holland, Belgium, and Germany, and, eventually, to America.

Successful reclamation of vagrants, prostitutes, and disorderly persons through programs of constructive work and training in the houses of correction, combined with concern for the basic dignity inherent in every human being, began to evolve into a new penology in which the focus was on penitence and reform. Punishment as an end in itself was replaced by punishment as a means of deterrence and reform. In the 20th century, the dominant trend in penological thinking—but not, for the most part, in the jail itself—has been toward substitution of constructive treatment programs for mere custody as more promising and more effective controls over offenders.

The deeper the offender has to be plunged into the correctional process and the longer he has to be held under punitive (though humane) restraints, the more difficult is the road back to the point of social restoration. It is logical, then, to conclude that the correctional process ought to concentrate its greatest efforts at those points along the criminal justice continuum where the largest numbers of offenders are involved and the hope of avoiding social segregation is greatest. In a sense, the intensity of the treatment process should be in inverse ratio to the degree of custodial care required. On the correctional continuum, jails are at the beginning of the penal or institutional segment. They are, in fact, the reception units for a greater variety and number of offenders than will be found in any other segment of the correctional process, and it is at this point that the greatest opportunity is offered to make sound decisions on the offender's next step in the correctional process. Indeed, the availability of qualified services at this point could result in promptly removing many from the correctional process who have been swept in unnoticed and undetected and who are more in need of protective, medical, and mental care from welfare and health agencies than they are in need of custodial care in penal and correctional institutions. In a broad sense, the jails and local correctional institutions are reception centers for the major institutions; in effect, they are mausoleums more than first-aid emergency rooms. . . .

Every criminology textbook written within the past 40 years includes a graphic description of the physical and moral decay that grips the majority of jails across the Nation. The indiscriminate mixing of all types of prisoners—the sick and the well, the old and the young, hardened criminals and petty offenders, the mentally defective, the psychotic, the vagrants and alcoholics, the habitual recidivists serving life sentences in short installments—has been recognized for years but, with few exceptions, has remained unchanged. "Fully 50 percent of all commitments . . . are for drunkenness or other offenses directly related to alcohol. Multiple commitments are the rule and not the exception—10, 20, and even 50 commitments of one alcoholic are commonplace." Recordkeeping procedures make it impossible to determine how many persons account for over 1 million commitments a year, but it is safe to estimate that the number of persons is considerably lower than the number of commitments. It is also evident—even though the percentages cannot be computed—that the vast majority of those presently confined in these institutions will return after release for subsequent short terms or will graduate to major institutions as they become more criminally sophisticated.

Note 2. Jail Conditions and the Eighth Amendment

JONES V. WITTENBERG
323 F. Supp. 93 (1971)
United States District Court, Northern District of Ohio

YOUNG, District Judge.

This action was commenced by a number of prisoners in the Lucas County Jail, on behalf of themselves individually and as representing a class of persons who either are or may be confined to this facility. . . .

The trial revealed little dispute about the factual basis of the action.

The evidence disclosed that the Lucas County Jail was originally constructed in the last decade of the Nineteenth Century, and is presently about seventy-six years old. It was designed to hold about one hundred fifty prisoners. The prisoners were to be held in two-man cells each six by nine feet in floor area, equipped with two bunks, toilet, and sink with running cold water. The cells are arranged in one large and two small groups on each of three floors of the jail, and were designed with a remote control locking system so that each individual cell could be locked. This locking system has become badly worn, and functions erratically or not at all. Each group of cells opens into an enclosed area, called a bull-pen. The sizes of the bull-pens vary with the number of cells opening into them. Corridors surround the cell-blocks and bull-pens. There is no ventilation or illumination in either the cells or bull-pens. There is some light in the corridors from electric lights and windows, and some air gets into the corridors when the windows are opened or broken. Some of the windows cannot be opened, and broken windows are not repaired promptly, if at all. In each cell-block, one of the original cells has been converted to a rather primitive shower arrangement, but because of the antiquated plumbing, variations in water pressure make it impossible to control the water temperature in the showers. They sometimes become scalding hot.

Not all of the toilets in the cells work. The soil pipes and waste pipes leak, and the leakage runs upon the floor, which causes problems for those prisoners who, for lack of bunks, are required to sleep on the floor.

Presently the jail holds a population which averages above two hundred prisoners, and has risen at times as high as two hundred seventy-two. About three-quarters of the prisoners are held in pre-trial detention because of their inability to make bond, or because they are held on non-bailable charges. The other prisoners are serving sentences imposed as a result of their convictions for violations of laws, usually misdemeanors.

The prisoners, with the exception of a few trusties, are not furnished with clothing, and there are no facilities for washing their clothing. A few used, and frequently inoperable, washing machines are scattered about the jail, but prisoners have no access to them.

When a prisoner enters the jail he is given a towel, which is replaced by a clean one once a week; a blanket, which may or may not have been washed before it was issued; usually, but not always, a mattress, which often consists of a small piece of foam rubber an inch and a half thick, two feet wide, and from four to six feet long. While bunks have been added so that the cells now hold as many as four bunks, bunks are sometimes placed in the bull-pens, and prisoners frequently sleep on the floor, either in the bull-pens or underneath the bunks in the cells. The prisoners are supposed to be furnished with shaving materials three times a week, but in practice this only happens twice a week, and rarely includes the use of a mirror. The testimony indicated that because of breakage, there were only two mirrors left for the use of the entire population of the jail.

The food for the prisoners is prepared in a kitchen in the basement of the jail. This has recently been improved somewhat by the addition of some donated cooking equipment, but the dishwashing equipment does not meet health standards, as there is no provision for "sanitizing" the dishes after washing and rinsing, which is done by hand. The food storage is not completely adequate or in accordance with health regulations. There is no proper ventilation in the kitchen, and in some of the food handling areas the ceiling is transversed by sewer and water pipes which leak, sweat, or both, onto the floor. The facilities for serving the food are primitive, and result in hot foods cooling and cold foods warming before they are served.

The diet is based on menus which were originally prepared by one of the technical schools in the area, but which are not carefully followed. Because food is not directly purchased by the jail staff, but through the county purchasing department, the planned menus frequently have to be changed because the necessary food supplies were not delivered in time. A study of the meals actually served revealed that they were generally inadequate both in quality and quantity. Certain nutritional elements are seldom provided. On rare occasions, the quantity reaches the minimum level of two thousand calories per day, but it sometimes falls as low as fourteen hundred calories. It never reaches the high edge of average daily requirement for sedentary men, twenty-four hundred calories.

Visitation is very highly limited. Prisoners are permitted visits only on Saturday afternoons from one to four o'clock p. m. Visits by children under eighteen are not permitted. All visits must be conducted by conversing through the heavy screening of the cell-blocks, with both parties standing, usually in groups of as many as three prisoners at a time. There is no semblance of any privacy. Trusties have somewhat greater visiting privileges. The facilities for visitation by attorneys consist of a small cage enclosed by chain link fence, and located adjacent to the guard's desk, on each floor. No privacy of consultation is possible. There are no telephones, and prisoners are permitted to make calls only at the time they first enter the jail, when they are permitted to call family or counsel. However, if they do not succeed in making contact with anyone at this time, they get no further opportunity.

There are few guards. Supposedly a guard is on duty on each floor twenty-four hours a day. Actually, however, due to absence of members of the guard staff, frequently there will be only one or two guards on duty. There are no means for prisoners to summon a guard, except to make a noise which may or may not be heard. From the guard station it is impossible to see into some of the cell-blocks, and, because of the lack of illumination, difficult to see into the others.

There is no attempt to classify or segregate the prisoners in the jail. Trusties, who are selected from among the sentenced prisoners, have separate quarters. Prisoners charged with murder or manslaughter are generally kept in a single cell-block, and there is one cell-block and some slightly better quarters for the women prisoners. Other than this, persons detained waiting trial and convicts serving sentences, old and young, are mingled indiscriminately.

Health facilities are primitive. A nurse is on duty in the daytime, who supervises the prisoners' medication. There is a jail physician who comes two or three afternoons a week, and is on call at other times, but often cannot be reached. A dentist comes sometimes, but only does extractions. There is no infirmary for prisoners who are ill, and only two small offices or examining rooms, with little or no equipment, for use by nurse, doctor and dentist. If a prisoner is ill enough, he may be removed to one of the local hospitals.

There are no facilities or personnel for social services, exercise, recreation, reading, rehabilitation, or any other human resources to meet human needs.

Discipline is enforced by confinement in one of two cells in the basement of the jail. These cells are of masonry construction, totally unfurnished, without drains or sanitary facilities of any kind. One of them is lighted by a single bare bulb. The other is unlighted. Until the preliminary hearing in this case, it was customary to strip any prisoner who was placed in either of these disciplinary cells, although they are below ground level and unheated. Even women prisoners were sometimes stripped before being placed in one of these cells. Since that time, stripping has been discontinued. On occasions, more than one prisoner at a time would be placed in these cells. The high number was sixteen or seventeen men. The length of confinement varies, and the evidence upon it was conflicting. Defendants testified the large group of men was confined less than ten hours. Plaintiffs testified this group was confined there for forty-two hours. The discipline of this confinement is imposed indiscriminately upon convicted prisoners and persons being detained pending trial. It is imposed arbitrarily and without any sort of notice, hearing, or findings, with no right to counsel or assistance in refuting the charges. There was some slight evidence indicating that the decision was supposed to be made after investigation by a different branch of the Sheriff's department, and by a different official than the officer complaining of the offense. It is doubtful at best whether these matters rise to a minimum standard of due process and fair treatment.

The conditions in the Lucas County Jail have been criticized by numerous grand juries, which under Ohio law are required to examine and report on conditions in the jail once during their term. Various civic and professional groups have also criticized the jail from time to time.

The plaintiffs offered expert testimony to show that the Lucas County Jail was outstandingly bad from every standpoint. This expert testimony was not contradicted, and is significant, since local jails appear from the literature to be none too good at best. The Lucas County Jail is a local jail at worst.

It should be pointed out that the responsibility for the operation of county jails is badly fragmented by the law of Ohio. The statutes impose certain duties upon the Board of County Commissioners, certain duties on the County Sheriff, and certain duties on the Court of Common Pleas. These statutes have been pretty much disregarded by all of these officials. One of the requirements is for the Court of Common Pleas to make rules for the operation of the jail, which are to be printed and posted in every cell. The defendant Sheriff took office January 6, 1969, and had difficulty locating a copy of these rules. There is no record of any ever having been posted anywhere. Sometime after the commencement of this action, on or about January 29, 1971, the Court of Common Pleas promulgated new rules, which had not, at the time of the hearing, been printed and posted. . . .

The official policy of the State of Ohio is that the standards of punishment which prevailed in medieval times are to be followed in dealing with those convicted of crimes. Insofar as possible, they are to be removed to remote places, and confined in harsh and forbidding prisons. In constructing its newest prison facility, the State selected one of its most sparsely populated areas as a site, and a medieval French prison as the basic model for building.

We may suppose that the constitutional provision against cruel and unusual punishment was directed against any such activities. In any event, when the total picture of confinement in the Lucas County Jail is examined, what appears is confinement in cramped and overcrowded quarters, lightless, airless, damp and filthy with leaking water and human wastes, slow starvation, deprivation of most human contacts, except with others in the same subhuman state, no exercise or recreation, little if any medical attention, no attempt at rehabilitation, and for those who in despair or frustration lash out at their surroundings, confinement, stripped of clothing and every last vestige of humanity, in a sort of oubliette.

The constitutional prohibition against cruel and unusual punishment "is not fastened to the obsolete, but may acquire meaning as public opinion becomes enlightened by a humane justice." Weems v. United States, 217 U.S. 349, 378, 30 S.Ct. 544, 553, 54 L.Ed. 793 (1910). If the constitutional provision against cruel and unusual punishment has any meaning, the evidence in this case shows that it has been violated. The cruelty is a refined sort, much more comparable to the Chinese water torture than to such crudities as breaking on the wheel. The evidence also shows that in this case at least, the punishment is unusual. The expert testimony, uncontradicted and not successfully challenged, supplies this evidence. Most jails are bad, but this one is unusually bad. Hence both the necessary elements are present in the case of that category of prisoners who are in the jail to serve their sentences, and they are entitled to relief.

Obviously, if confinement in the Lucas County Jail is a cruel and unusual punishment forbidden to be employed against those who are in jail to be punished, it is hard to think of any reason why it should be permitted for those who are only in jail awaiting trial, and are, according to our law, presumed to be innocent of any wrongdoing. For centuries, under our law, punishment before conviction has been forbidden. The Constitution does not authorize the treatment of a pre-trial detainee as a convict. Tyler v. Ciccone, 299 F.Supp. 684 (W.D.Mo.1969).

> Upon the whole, if the offence be not bailable, or the party cannot find bail, he is to be committed to the county gaol by the *mittimus* of the justice * * *; there to abide till delivered by due course of law. * * * But this imprisonment, as has been said, is only for safe custody, and not for punishment: therefore, in this dubious interval between the commitment and trial, a prisoner ought to be used with the utmost humanity, and neither be loaded with needless fetters, or subjected to other hardships than such as are absolutely requisite for the purpose of confinement only: * * *
> 4 W. Blackstone, Commentaries 300.

... Obviously, no person may be punished except by due process of law. Here, the evidence shows that at best, those who are in the Lucas County Jail pending trial of charges against them suffer the same treatment as those who are confined there for punishment. Hence, even if that punishment were not cruel and unusual, it would still be proscribed for them, since it is imposed as a matter of form and routine, and without any semblance of due process or fair treatment.

Since, as pointed out by Blackstone and by the decisions of this Circuit, they are not to be subjected to any hardship except those absolutely requisite for the purpose of confinement only, and they retain all the rights of an ordinary citizen except the right to go and come as they please, their confinement as it is handled in the Lucas County Jail denies them the equal protection of the laws.

This Court therefore finds that the class of plaintiffs have shown themselves, by the evidence, to be deprived of their constitutional rights by state officials acting under color of state law, and to be entitled to relief at the hands of the Court. ...

Note 3. Jail Conditions and the Fourteenth Amendment

HAMILTON V. LOVE
328 F. Supp. 1182 (1971)
United States District Court, Eastern District of Arkansas

With only insignificant exceptions, the Pulaski County jail is an institution used for the purpose of detaining persons who are awaiting trial. The inmates are either being detained because they cannot afford the fee for the bail bond set for them—the usual case—or because they have been accused of a capital or "non-bondable" offense. In all cases, such detainees are presumed innocent, in the eyes of the law, of the crime with which they have been charged. Their actual guilt or innocence remains for future determination.

The complaint alleges that the plaintiffs and the class they represent are being subjected to cruel and unusual punishment and are being denied the equal protection of the law because of certain practices and conditions —20 in number are listed—alleged to obtain at the jail. Illustrative of the charges are the following: all correspondence is censored; there is no ventilation and wholly inadequate bathing and toilet facilities; no provision for minimal medical and dental care; no recreational areas or programs; overcrowded, unsanitary and insecure cells; the presence of rats, roaches and poisonous insects; lack of protection against unprovoked assaults and homosexual attacks because of inadequacy of trained "free world" personnel; no classification system for the detainees or rational separation thereof; absence of or inadequate bedding; and absence of laundry facilities. The plaintiffs contend that these conditions also constitute a denial of due process.

The plaintiffs complain that they are not informed or apprised of the standards of conduct expected of them or of the punishment or discipline which might follow from their departure from such standards. ...

On February 22, 1971, both the plaintiffs and the defendants moved that the Court visit and inspect the Pulaski County jail. The motion was granted and the Court did visit, and make a thorough inspection of, the Pulaski County jail, prior to the hearing.

Early in the hearing, on February 24, 1971, the defendants filed a stipulation, the first paragraph of which reads as follows:

> Defendants stipulate and agree that the general conditions presently existent at the Pulaski County jail (hereinafter referred to as the "jail") taken as a whole do not meet minimum federal constitutional requirements with respect to prisoners' rights to due process of law and to be free from cruel and unusual punishment. ...

The constitutional limitations upon the conditions of pre-trial detention are not as clear as they should be. Since the courts of this country are being forced to deal with such problems more frequently now than ever before, we can expect clearer pronouncements and guidelines from our higher courts over the next few years. Some propositions, however, would seem beyond doubt on the basis of present precedent and the clear language of our constitution.

The inmates of the Pulaski County jail should not be referred to as "convicts" or even "prisoners", considering the usual connotations of such terms. Furthermore, it is not really appropriate to judge the constitutionality of the conditions of their incarceration by referring to the "cruel and unusual punishment" provisions of the Eighth Amendment. Having been convicted of no crime, the detainees should not have to suffer *any* "punishment," as such, whether "cruel and unusual" or not.

As pointed out above, most of the inmates of the Pulaski County jail are there because they do not have the financial resources to pay bondsmen the necessary money to obtain their release. The testimony revealed that there are in excess of 1,300 persons awaiting trial in the state courts of Pulaski County. Some 90 per cent are free and walking the streets of this and other communities. Many of these, who are free upon bond, have criminal records considerably worse than some of those who are presently in the Pulaski County jail. Nevertheless, they are free because they had something else: money.

It is a fundamental constitutional tenet that those similarly classified must be similarly treated, and that the system of classification itself must bear a rational relationship to legitimate state purposes. Under the equal protection clause, it would not seem possible to be able to classify detainees, awaiting trial, in the same group with those persons who have been convicted of crime and sentenced to prison. And, yet, that appears to be what we have been doing as a practical matter, not only locally, but across the nation. Ironically the lot of those detained while awaiting trial appears to be worse than that of those convicted and serving their sentences in the usual penitentiary systems. Indeed there was clear testimony before this court by inmates presently incarcerated at our Arkansas state penitentiaries, who had also previously been incarcerated in the Pulaski County jail, that the conditions in the former institutions were definitely preferable to those obtaining in the Pulaski County jail. They indicated that practically anything was better than "rotting" in a jail cell. In the penitentiaries they have the opportunity of getting out into the fields to work and also the opportunity to engage in sports and other recreational activities, which privileges are denied detainees in the county jail.

It is clear that the conditions for pre-trial detention must not only be equal to, but superior to, those permitted for prisoners serving sentences for the crimes they have committed against society.

The only legitimate state purpose served by holding in jail those who are unable to make bond is to make certain that those detained are present when their cases are finally called for trial. It is simply a means of guaranteeing the appearance of the detainee. *After* trial and conviction, the incarceration of those sentenced to prison may serve other legitimate state purposes, the most obvious of which is punishment itself. . . .

Inadequate resources can never be an adequate justification for the state's depriving any person of his constitutional rights. If the state cannot obtain the resources to detain persons awaiting trial in accordance with minimum constitutional standards, then the state simply will not be permitted to detain such persons. The final decision may, indeed, rest with the qualified voters of the governmental unit involved. This Court, of course, cannot require the voters to make available the resources needed by public officials to meet constitutional standards, but it can and must require the release of persons held under conditions which violate their constitutional rights, at least where the correction of such conditions is not brought about within a reasonable time. . . .

Note 4. Administrative Segregation of Jail Inmates

DAVIS v. LINDSAY
321 F. Supp. 1134 (1970)
United States District Court, Southern District of New York

LASKER, District Judge.

Angela Davis is held in custody in the New York City Women's House of Detention pending the outcome of extradition proceedings brought by the State of California, which has charged her with kidnapping and homicide. She moves for a preliminary injunction restraining the defendants from holding her in solitary facilities, separate and apart from the general inmate population, and for restoration of privileges accorded to inmates at large which she claims have been denied her in part or in whole. Such privileges include, among others, the right to receive and send mail, to receive, read and possess certain newspapers, journals and books, and to receive visitors.

The action is brought under 42 U.S.C. § 1983 and its jurisdictional complement 28 U.S.C. § 1343, and seeks a permanent injunction, declaratory relief and damages.

Plaintiff claims that her being held in solitary facilities and deprived of other privileges violates her rights under the First, Fourth, Sixth, Eighth, Ninth and Fourteenth Amendments to the Constitution.

The relevant facts are not in dispute. On October 13, 1970, plaintiff was received at the Women's House of Detention as a federal stop-over, having been placed under arrest as a fugitive by federal authorities. On October 14 the United States Commissioner issued a warrant for her arrest, charging her with having fled the jurisdiction of the State of California to avoid prosecution. On the same day she was transferred from federal jurisdiction to that of the Criminal Court of the City of New York and held without bail as a fugitive from the State of California.

Upon her first entering the Women's House of Detention she was placed on the fourth floor, a section normally reserved for emotionally and psychologically disturbed inmates. According to the affidavit of Jessie Behagen, Superintendent of the Women's House of Detention, this arrangement was made because the fourth floor is a special security area and it was believed that the nature of the charges against the plaintiff, the substantial amount of publicity she had received, and the fact that she had been the subject of a nationwide search warranted special precautions. When plaintiff's counsel complained of this treatment, the custodial authorities reviewed the case and agreed to a change of housing which, according to the affidavit of Superintendent Behagen, was to have been on an experimental basis. Accordingly the plaintiff was placed on the eleventh floor in a women's dormitory. It is not clear whether or not this transfer placed her in the general inmate population. Plaintiff states that on the eleventh floor "I was allowed to converse and mingle with other inmates." Superintendent Behagen says that at this time plaintiff "remained under 24 hour surveillance and was not in general population." Regardless of this disputed fact, on which no present determination turns, there is no question that on October 23, 1970 plaintiff was moved, without any reason being stated to her, to solitary facilities on the seventh floor.

I have advisedly used the phrase "solitary facilities" in describing the arrangements currently in force because the conditions under which plaintiff is presently housed cannot properly be compared to commonly accepted notions of "solitary confinement." For example, although plaintiff is kept separate and apart from all other prisoners, her room is 12 feet by 10 feet and has two windows overlooking Greenwich Avenue, as compared to the 10 by 6 foot size of the usual cells; her room has hot and cold running water, toilet facilities, table, reasonable lighting, and a radio. She is permitted library privileges for one hour five days a week, allowed to read the Black Panther newspaper, Muslim newspaper and Black World; to take any five books from the library to her room at one time, and, indeed, books which she has requested that were not in the library have been ordered from the publisher for her; her incoming and outgoing mail is opened to be checked solely for contraband, and is not read or censored. She is accorded visiting privileges similar to those of other detention inmates. I find that, in general, with the exception of her being kept separate and apart from other prison inmates, she has been accorded all the privileges granted to the remainder of the population, and indeed, in some respects such as the size of her room and the availability of a radio, the present arrangements are favorable to her.

Plaintiff contends that defendants' course of action deprives her of her rights under the First Amendment freely to associate and communicate with her fellow prisoners, under the Fourth Amendment to be protected against unreasonable searches (her quarters are searched several times daily), under the Sixth Amendment to advice of counsel (she alleges impediments to conferences with counsel), under the Eighth Amendment to be protected from cruel and unusual punishment, under the Ninth Amendment to "the fundamental right of privacy and freedom from gratuitous humiliation at the hands of the state," and under the Fourteenth Amendment to due process and equal protection of the law.

I find that plaintiff's rights to equal protection under the Fourteenth Amendment have been violated and that she should be transferred to quarters shared with the general inmate population and accorded all privileges enjoyed by them. Since no claim is made that the general regulations of the institution violate the Constitution, this disposition of the case renders unnecessary a determination as to the constitutional questions raised other than equal protection.

12. LEGISLATIVE SPECIFICATION OF PRISONER RIGHTS

NOTES

Note 1.

LEONARD ORLAND

*Human Rights for Prisoners**

Hopefully, Tombs, Soledad and Attica will create some pressure for serious public consideration of reform. Pending that, there is an overwhelming need that can be implemented without massive expenditures of money or time —legislative specification of the rights of prisoners.

The Congress, as well as all of the state legislatures, should begin immediately to enact standard minimum rules for the treatment of prisoners. The model for such legislation is available and has had the benefit of four decades of debate and refinement in the international penological community.

I refer to the United Nations standard minimum rules for the treatment of prisoners.

The standard minimum rules are clear, detailed and specific—in effect, a declaration of human rights for prisoners. The rules prohibit racial or religious discrimination, require separation of untried and convicted inmates as well as separating of youthful offenders and hardened criminals. They prohibit corporal punishment as well as punishment by "handcuffs, chains, irons or straitjackets." They declare that no punishment should be imposed unless the inmate has "been informed of the offense alleged against him and given a proper opportunity of presenting his defense." They clearly state that untried prisoners are "presumed to be innocent and should be treated as such."

The legal status of these rules was considered by the fourth United Nations congress on the prevention of crime and treatment of criminal offenders in Kyoto in 1970. The U.S. delegation took the position that the U.N. General Assembly should endorse the rules and "urge member states to take appropriate action toward their implementation."

To date, no nation in the world has enacted the standard minimum rules into positive law. To date, no American state has enacted any code of rights for prisoners.

Note 2.

UNITED NATIONS STANDARD MINIMUM RULES FOR THE TREATMENT OF PRISONERS*

Resolution adopted on 30 August 1955

The First United Nations Congress on the Prevention of Crime and the Treatment of Offenders,

Having adopted the Standard Minimum Rules for the Treatment of Prisoners annexed to the present Resolution,

1. *Requests* the Secretary-General, in accordance with paragraph (*d*) of the annex to resolution 415(V) of the General Assembly of the United Nations, to submit these rules to the Social Commission of the Economic and Social Council for approval;

2. *Expresses* the hope that these rules be approved by the Economic and Social Council and, if deemed appropriate by the Council, by the General Assembly, and that they be transmitted to governments with the recommendation (*a*) that favourable consideration be given to their adoption and application in the administration of penal institutions, and (*b*) that the Secretary-General be informed every three years of the progress made with regard to their application;

3. *Expresses* the wish that, in order to allow governments to keep themselves informed of the progress made in this respect, the Secretary-General be requested to publish in the International Review of Criminal Policy the information sent by governments in pursuance of paragraph 2, and that he be authorized to ask for supplementary information if necessary;

4. *Expresses* also the wish that the Secretary-General be requested to arrange that the widest possible publicity be given to these rules.

---

* *The New York Times*, Sept. 24, 1971, p. 41. Reprinted with permission of the author.

* Adopted by the Economic and Social Council of the United Nations, July 31, 1957.

Annex

Standard Minimum Rules for the Treatment of Prisoners

Preliminary Observations

1. The following rules are not intended to describe in detail a model system of penal institutions. They seek only, on the basis of the general consensus of contemporary thought and the essential elements of the most adequate systems of today, to set out what is generally accepted as being good principle and practice in the treatment of prisoners and the management of institutions.

2. In view of the great variety of legal, social, economic and geographical conditions of the world, it is evident that not all of the rules are capable of application in all places and at all times. They should, however, serve to stimulate a constant endeavour to overcome practical difficulties in the way of their application, in the knowledge that they represent, as a whole, the minimum conditions which are accepted as suitable by the United Nations.

3. On the other hand, the rules cover a field in which thought is constantly developing. They are not intended to preclude experiment and practices, provided these are in harmony with the principles and seek to further the purposes which derive from the text of the rules as a whole. It will always be justifiable for the central prison administration to authorize departures from the rules in this spirit.

4. (1) Part I of the rules covers the general management of institutions, and is applicable to all categories of prisoners, criminal or civil, untried or convicted, including prisoners subject to "security measures" or corrective measures ordered by the judge.

(2) Part II contains rules applicable only to the special categories dealt with in each section. Nevertheless, the rules under section A, applicable to prisoners under sentence, shall be equally applicable to categories of prisoners dealt with in sections B, C and D, provided they do not conflict with the rules governing those categories and are for their benefit.

5. (1) The rules do not seek to regulate the management of institutions set aside for young persons such as Borstal institutions or correctional schools, but in general part I would be equally applicable in such institutions.

(2) The category of young prisoners should include at least all young persons who come within the jurisdiction of juvenile courts. As a rule, such young persons should not be sentenced to imprisonment.

Part I. Rules of General Application

Basic principle

6. (1) The following rules shall be applied impartially. There shall be no discrimination on grounds of race, colour, sex, language, religion, political or other opinion, national or social origin, property, birth or other status.

(2) On the other hand, it is necessary to respect the religious beliefs and moral precepts of the group to which a prisoner belongs.

Register

7. (1) In every place where persons are imprisoned there shall be kept a bound registration book with numbered pages in which shall be entered in respect of each prisoner received:

(*a*) Information concerning his identity;

(*b*) The reasons for his commitment and the authority therefor;

(*c*) The day and hour of his admission and release.

(2) No person shall be received in an institution without a valid commitment order of which the details shall have been previously entered in the register.

Separation of categories

8. The different categories of prisoners shall be kept in separate institutions or parts of institutions taking account of their sex, age, criminal record, the legal reason for their detention and the necessities of their treatment. Thus,

(*a*) Men and women shall so far as possible be detained in separate institutions; in an institution which receives both men and women the whole of the premises allocated to women shall be entirely separate;

(*b*) Untried prisoners shall be kept separate from convicted prisoners;

(*c*) Persons imprisoned for debt and other civil prisoners shall be kept separate from persons imprisoned by reason of a criminal offence;

(d) Young prisoners shall be kept separate from adults.

Accommodation

9. (1) Where sleeping accommodation is in individual cells or rooms, each prisoner shall occupy by night a cell or room by himself. If for special reasons, such as temporary overcrowding, it becomes necessary for the central prison administration to make an exception to this rule, it is not desirable to have two prisoners in a cell or room.

(2) Where dormitories are used, they shall be occupied by prisoners carefully selected as being suitable to associate with one another in those conditions. There shall be regular supervision by night, in keeping with the nature of the institution.

10. All accommodation provided for the use of prisoners and in particular all sleeping accommodation shall meet all requirements of health, due regard being paid to climatic conditions and particularly to cubic content of air, minimum floor space, lighting, heating and ventilation.

11. In all places where prisoners are required to live or work,

(a) The windows shall be large enough to enable the prisoners to read or work by natural light, and shall be so constructed that they can allow the entrance of fresh air whether or not there is artificial ventilation;

(b) Artificial light shall be provided sufficient for the prisoners to read or work without injury to eyesight.

12. The sanitary installations shall be adequate to enable every prisoner to comply with the needs of nature when necessary and in a clean and decent manner.

13. Adequate bathing and shower installations shall be provided so that every prisoner may be enabled and required to have a bath or shower, at a temperature suitable to the climate, as frequently as necessary for general hygiene according to season and geographical region, but at least once a week in a temperate climate.

14. All parts of an institution regularly used by prisoners shall be properly maintained and kept scrupulously clean at all times.

Personal hygiene

15. Prisoners shall be required to keep their persons clean, and to this end they shall be provided with water and with such toilet articles as are necessary for health and cleanliness.

16. In order that prisoners may maintain a good appearance compatible with their self-respect, facilities shall be provided for the proper care of the hair and beard, and men shall be enabled to shave regularly.

Clothing and bedding

17. (1) Every prisoner who is not allowed to wear his own clothing shall be provided with an outfit of clothing suitable for the climate and adequate to keep him in good health. Such clothing shall in no manner be degrading or humiliating.

(2) All clothing shall be clean and kept in proper condition. Underclothing shall be changed and washed as often as necessary for the maintenance of hygiene.

(3) In exceptional circumstances, whenever a prisoner is removed outside the institution for an authorized purpose, he shall be allowed to wear his own clothing or other inconspicuous clothing.

18. If prisoners are allowed to wear their own clothing, arrangements shall be made on their admission to the institution to ensure that it shall be clean and fit for use.

19. Every prisoner shall, in accordance with local or national standards, be provided with a separate bed, and with separate and sufficient bedding which shall be clean when issued, kept in good order and changed often enough to ensure its cleanliness.

Food

20. (1) Every prisoner shall be provided by the administration at the usual hours with food of nutritional value adequate for health and strength, of wholesome quality and well prepared and served.

(2) Drinking water shall be available to every prisoner whenever he needs it.

Exercise and sport

21. (1) Every prisoner who is not employed in out-door work shall have at least one hour of suitable exercise in the open air daily if the weather permits.

(2) Young prisoners, and others of suitable age and physique, shall receive physical and recreational training during the period of exercise. To this end space, installations and equipment should be provided.

Medical services

22. (1) At every institution there shall be available the services of at least one qualified medical officer who should have some knowl-

edge of psychiatry. The medical services should be organized in close relationship to the general health administration of the community or nation. They shall include a psychiatric service for the diagnosis and, in proper cases, the treatment of states of mental abnormality.

(2) Sick prisoners who require specialist treatment shall be transferred to specialized institutions or to civil hospitals. Where hospital facilities are provided in an institution, their equipment, furnishings and pharmaceutical supplies shall be proper for the medical care and treatment of sick prisoners, and there shall be a staff of suitably trained officers.

(3) The services of a qualified dental officer shall be available to every prisoner.

23. (1) In women's institutions there shall be special accommodation for all necessary pre-natal and post-natal care and treatment. Arrangements shall be made whenever practicable for children to be born in a hospital outside the institution. If a child is born in prison, this fact shall not be mentioned in the birth certificate.

(2) Where nursing infants are allowed to remain in the institution with their mothers, provision shall be made for a nursery staffed by qualified persons, where the infants shall be placed when they are not in the care of their mothers.

24. The medical officer shall see and examine every prisoner as soon as possible after his admission and thereafter as necessary, with a view particularly to the discovery of physical or mental illness and the taking of all necessary measures; the segregation of prisioners suspected of infectious or contagious conditions; the noting of physical or mental defects which might hamper rehabilitation, and the determination of the physical capacity of every prisoner for work.

25. (1) The medical officer shall have the care of the physical and mental health of the prisoners and should daily see all sick prisoners, all who complain of illness, and any prisoner to whom his attention is specially directed.

(2) The medical officer shall report to the director whenever he considers that a prisoner's physical or mental health has been or will be injuriously affected by continued imprisonment or by any condition of imprisonment.

26. (1) The medical officer shall regularly inspect and advise the director upon:

(*a*) The quantity, quality, preparation and service of food;

(*b*) The hygiene and cleanliness of the institution and the prisoners;

(*c*) The sanitation, heating, lighting and ventilation of the institution;

(*d*) The suitability and cleanliness of the prisoners' clothing and bedding;

(*e*) The observance of the rules concerning physical education and sports, in cases where there is no technical personnel in charge of these activities.

(2) The director shall take into consideration the reports and advice that the medical officer submits according to rules 25 (2) and 26 and, in case he concurs with the recommendations made, shall take immediate steps to give effect to those recommendations; if they are not within his competence or if he does not concur with them, he shall immediately submit his own report and the advice of the medical officer to higher authority.

Discipline and punishment

27. Discipline and order shall be maintained with firmness, but with no more restriction than is necessary for safe custody and well-ordered community life.

28. (1) No prisoner shall be employed, in the service of the institution, in any disciplinary capacity.

(2) This rule shall not, however, impede the proper functioning of systems based on self-government, under which specified social, educational or sports activities or responsibilities are entrusted, under supervision, to prisoners who are formed into groups for the purposes of treatment.

29. The following shall always be determined by the law or by the regulation of the competent administrative authority:

(*a*) Conduct constituting a disciplinary offence;

(*b*) The types and duration of punishment which may be inflicted;

(*c*) The authority competent to impose such punishment.

30. (1) No prisoner shall be punished except in accordance with the terms of such law or regulation, and never twice for the same offence.

(2) No prisoner shall be punished unless he has been informed of the offence alleged against him and given a proper opportunity of presenting his defence. The competent authority shall conduct a thorough examination of the case.

(3) Where necessary and practicable the prisoner shall be allowed to make his defence through an interpreter.

31. Corporal punishment, punishment by

placing in a dark cell, and all cruel, inhuman or degrading punishments shall be completely prohibited as punishments for disciplinary offences.

32. (1) Punishment by close confinement or reduction of diet shall never be inflicted unless the medical officer has examined the prisoner and certified in writing that he is fit to sustain it.

(2) The same shall apply to any other punishment that may be prejudicial to the physical or mental health of a prisoner. In no case may such punishment be contrary to or depart from the principle stated in rule 31.

(3) The medical officer shall visit daily prisoners undergoing such punishments and shall advise the director if he considers the termination or alteration of the punishment necessary on grounds of physical or mental health.

Instruments of restraint

33. Instruments of restraint, such as handcuffs, chains, irons and strait-jackets, shall never be applied as a punishment. Furthermore, chains or irons shall not be used as restraints. Other instruments of restraint shall not be used except in the following circumstances:

(*a*) As a precaution against escape during a transfer, provided that they shall be removed when the prisoner appears before a judicial or administrative authority;

(*b*) On medical grounds by direction of the medical officer;

(*c*) By order of the director, if other methods of control fail, in order to prevent a prisoner from injuring himself or others or from damaging property; in such instances the director shall at once consult the medical officer and report to the higher administrative authority.

34. The patterns and manner of use of instruments of restraint shall be decided by the central prison administration. Such instruments must not be applied for any longer time than is strictly necessary.

Information to and complaints by prisoners

35. (1) Every prisoner on admission shall be provided with written information about the regulations governing the treatment of prisoners of his category, the disciplinary requirements of the institution, the authorized methods for seeking information and making complaints, and all such other matters as are necessary to enable him to understand both his rights and his obligations and to adapt himself to the life of the institution.

(2) If a prisoner is illiterate, the aforesaid information shall be conveyed to him orally.

36. (1) Every prisoner shall have the opportunity each week day of making requests or complaints to the director of the institution or the officer authorized to represent him.

(2) It shall be possible to make requests or complaints to the inspector of prisons during his inspection. The prisoner shall have the opportunity to talk to the inspector or to any other inspecting officer without the director or other members of the staff being present.

(3) Every prisoner shall be allowed to make a request or complaint, without censorship as to substance but in proper form, to the central prison administration, the judicial authority or other proper authorities through approved channels.

(4) Unless it is evidently frivolous or groundless, every request or complaint shall be promptly dealt with and replied to without undue delay.

Contact with the outside world

37. Prisoners shall be allowed under necessary supervision to communicate with their family and reputable friends at regular intervals, both by correspondence and by receiving visits.

38. (1) Prisoners who are foreign nationals shall be allowed reasonable facilities to communicate with the diplomatic and consular representatives of the State to which they belong.

(2) Prisoners who are nationals of States without diplomatic or consular representation in the country and refugees or stateless persons shall be allowed similar facilities to communicate with the diplomatic representative of the State which takes charge of their interests or any national or international authority whose task it is to protect such persons.

39. Prisoners shall be kept informed regularly of the more important items of news by the reading of newspapers, periodicals or special institutional publications, by hearing wireless transmissions, by lectures or by any similar means as authorized or controlled by the administration.

Books

40. Every institution shall have a library for the use of all categories of prisoners, adequately stocked with both recreational and in-

structional books, and prisoners shall be encouraged to make full use of it.

Religion

41. (1) If the institution contains a sufficient number of prisoners of the same religion, a qualified representative of that religion shall be appointed or approved. If the number of prisoners justifies it and conditions permit, the arrangement should be on a full-time basis.

(2) A qualified representative appointed or approved under paragraph (1) shall be allowed to hold regular services and to pay pastoral visits in private to prisoners of his religion at proper times.

(3) Access to a qualified representative of any religion shall not be refused to any prisoner. On the other hand, if any prisoner should object to a visit of any religious representative, his attitude shall be fully respected.

42. So far as practicable, every prisoner shall be allowed to satisfy the needs of his religious life by attending the services provided in the institution and having in his possession the books of religious observance and instruction of his denomination.

Retention of prisoners' property

43. (1) All money, valuables, clothing and other effects belonging to a prisoner which under the regulations of the institution he is not allowed to retain shall on his admission to the institution be placed in safe custody. An inventory thereof shall be signed by the prisoner. Steps shall be taken to keep them in good condition.

(2) On the release of the prisoner all such articles and money shall be returned to him except in so far as he has been authorized to spend money or send any such property out of the institution, or it has been found necessary on hygienic grounds to destroy any article of clothing. The prisoner shall sign a receipt for the articles and money returned to him.

(3) Any money or effects received for a prisoner from outside shall be treated in the same way.

(4) If a prisoner brings in any drugs or medicine, the medical officer shall decide what use shall be made of them.

Notification of death, illness, transfer, etc.

44. (1) Upon the death or serious illness of, or serious injury to a prisoner, or his removal to an institution for the treatment of mental affections, the director shall at once inform the spouse, if the prisoner is married, or the nearest relative and shall in any event inform any other person previously designated by the prisoner.

(2) A prisoner shall be informed at once of the death or serious illness of any near relative. In case of the critical illness of a near relative, the prisoner should be authorized, whenever circumstances allow, to go to his bedside either under escort or alone.

(3) Every prisoner shall have the right to inform at once his family of his imprisonment or his transfer to another institution.

Removal of prisoners

45. (1) When prisoners are being removed to or from an institution, they shall be exposed to public view as little as possible, and proper safeguards shall be adopted to protect them from insult, curiosity and publicity in any form.

(2) The transport of prisoners in conveyances with inadequate ventilation or light, or in any way which would subject them to unnecessary physical hardship, shall be prohibited.

(3) The transport of prisoners shall be carried out at the expense of the administration and equal conditions shall obtain for all of them.

Institutional personnel

46. (1) The prison administration shall provide for the careful selection of every grade of the personnel, since it is on their integrity, humanity, professional capacity and personal suitability for the work that the proper administration of the institutions depends.

(2) The prison administration shall constantly seek to awaken and maintain in the minds both of the personnel and of the public the conviction that this work is a social service of great importance, and to this end all appropriate means of informing the public should be used.

(3) To secure the foregoing ends, personnel shall be appointed on a full-time basis as professional prison officers and have civil service status with security of tenure subject only to good conduct, efficiency and physical fitness. Salaries shall be adequate to attract and retain suitable men and women; employment benefits and conditions of service shall be favourable in view of the exacting nature of the work.

47. (1) The personnel shall possess an adequate standard of education and intelligence.

(2) Before entering on duty, the personnel shall be given a course of training in their general and specific duties and be required to pass theoretical and practical tests.

(3) After entering on duty and during their career, the personnel shall maintain and improve their knowledge and professional capacity by attending courses of in-service training to be organized at suitable intervals.

48. All members of the personnel shall at all times so conduct themselves and perform their duties as to influence the prisoners for good by their examples and to command their respect.

49. (1) So far as possible, the personnel shall include a sufficient number of specialists such as psychiatrists, psychologists, social workers, teachers and trade instructors.

(2) The services of social workers, teachers and trade instructors shall be secured on a permanent basis, without thereby excluding part-time or voluntary workers.

50. (1) The director of an institution should be adequately qualified for his task by character, administrative ability, suitable training and experience.

(2) He shall devote his entire time to his official duties and shall not be appointed on a part-time basis.

(3) He shall reside on the premises of the institution or in its immediate vicinity.

(4) When two or more institutions are under the authority of one director, he shall visit each of them at frequent intervals. A responsible resident official shall be in charge of each of these institutions.

51. (1) The director, his deputy, and the majority of the other personnel of the institution shall be able to speak the language of the greatest number of prisoners, or a language understood by the greatest number of them.

(2) Whenever necessary, the services of an interpreter shall be used.

52. (1) In institutions which are large enough to require the services of one or more full-time medical officers, at least one of them shall reside on the premises of the institution or in its immediate vicinity.

(2) In other institutions the medical officer shall visit daily and shall reside near enough to be able to attend without delay in cases of urgency.

53. (1) In an institution for both men and women, the part of the institution set aside for women shall be under the authority of a responsible woman officer who shall have the custody of the keys of all that part of the institution.

(2) No male member of the staff shall enter the part of the institution set aside for women unless accompanied by a woman officer.

(3) Women prisoners shall be attended and supervised only by women officers. This does not, however, preclude male members of the staff, particularly doctors and teachers, from carrying out their professional duties in institutions or parts of institutions set aside for women.

54. (1) Officers of the institutions shall not, in their relations with the prisoners, use force except in self-defence or in cases of attempted escape, or active or passive physical resistance to an order based on law or regulations. Officers who have recourse to force must use no more than is strictly necessary and must report the incident immediately to the director of the institution.

(2) Prison officers shall be given special physical training to enable them to restrain aggressive prisoners.

(3) Except in special circumstances, staff performing duties which bring them into direct contact with prisoners should not be armed. Furthermore, staff should in no circumstances be provided with arms unless they have been trained in their use.

Inspection

55. There shall be a regular inspection of penal institutions and services by qualified and experienced inspectors appointed by a competent authority. Their task shall be in particular to ensure that these institutions are administered in accordance with existing laws and regulations and with a view to bringing about the objectives of penal and correctional services.

Part II. Rules Applicable to Special Categories

A. Prisoners Under Sentence

Guiding principles

56. The guiding principles hereafter are intended to show the spirit in which penal institutions should be administered and the purposes at which they should aim, in accord-

ance with the declaration made under Preliminary Observation 1 of the present text.

57. Imprisonment and other measures which result in cutting off an offender from the outside world are afflictive by the very fact of taking from the person the right of self-determination by depriving him of his liberty. Therefore the prison system shall not, except as incidental to justifiable segregation or the maintenance of discipline, aggravate the suffering inherent in such a situation.

58. The purpose and justification of a sentence of imprisonment or a similar measure deprivative of liberty is ultimately to protect society against crime. This end can only be achieved if the period of imprisonment is used to ensure, so far as possible, that upon his return to society the offender is not only willing but able to lead a law-abiding and self-supporting life.

59. To this end, the institution should utilize all the remedial, educational, moral, spiritual and other forces and forms of assistance which are appropriate and available, and should seek to apply them according to the individual treatment needs of the prisoners.

60. (1) The regime of the institution should seek to minimize any differences between prison life and life at liberty which tend to lessen the responsibility of the prisoners or the respect due to their dignity as human beings.

(2) Before the completion of the sentence, it is desirable that the necessary steps be taken to ensure for the prisoner a gradual return to life in society. This aim may be achieved, depending on the case, by a pre-release régime organized in the same institution or in another appropriate institution, or by release on trial under some kind of supervision which must not be entrusted to the police but should be combined with effective social aid.

61. The treatment of prisoners should emphasize not their exclusion from the community, but their continuing part in it. Community agencies should, therefore, be enlisted wherever possible to assist the staff of the institution in the task of social rehabilitation of the prisoners. There should be in connexion with every institution social workers charged with the duty of maintaining and improving all desirable relations of a prisoner with his family and with valuable social agencies. Steps should be taken to safeguard, to the maximum extent compatible with the law and the sentence, the rights relating to civil interests, social security rights and other social benefits of prisoners.

62. The medical services of the institution shall seek to detect and shall treat any physical or mental illnesses or defects which may hamper a prisoner's rehabilitation. All necessary medical, surgical and psychiatric services shall be provided to that end.

63. (1) The fulfillment of these principles requires individualization of treatment and for this purpose a flexible system of classifying prisoners in groups; it is therefore desirable that such groups should be distributed in separate institutions suitable for the treatment of each group.

(2) These institutions need not provide the same degree of security for every group. It is desirable to provide varying degrees of security according to the needs of different groups. Open institutions, by the very fact that they provide no physical security against escape but rely on the self-discipline of the inmates, provide the conditions most favourable to rehabilitation for carefully selected prisoners.

(3) It is desirable that the number of prisoners in closed institutions should not be so large that the individualization of treatment is hindered. In some countries it is considered that the population of such institutions should not exceed five hundred. In open institutions the population should be as small as possible.

(4) On the other hand, it is undesirable to maintain prisons which are so small that proper facilities cannot be provided.

64. The duty of society does not end with a prisoner's release. There should, therefore, be governmental or private agencies capable of lending the released prisoner efficient aftercare directed towards the lessening of prejudice against him and towards his social rehabilitation.

Treatment

65. The treatment of persons sentenced to imprisonment or a similar measure shall have as its purpose, so far as the length of the sentence permits, to establish in them the will to lead law-abiding and self-supporting lives after their release and to fit them to do so. The treatment shall be such as will encourage their self-respect and develop their sense of responsibility.

66. (1) To these ends, all appropriate means shall be used, including religious care in the countries where this is possible, education, vocational guidance and training, social casework, employment counselling, physical development and strengthening of moral char-

acter, in accordance with the individual needs of each prisoner, taking account of his social and criminal history, his physical and mental capacities and aptitudes, his personal temperament, the length of his sentence and his prospects after release.

(2) For every prisoner with a sentence of suitable length, the director shall receive, as soon as possible after his admission, full reports on all the matters referred to in the foregoing paragraph. Such reports shall always include a report by a medical officer, wherever possible qualified in psychiatry, on the physical and mental condition of the prisoner.

(3) The reports and other relevant documents shall be placed in an individual file. This file shall be kept up to date and classified in such a way that it can be consulted by the responsible personnel whenever the need arises.

Classification and individualization

67. The purposes of classification shall be:

(*a*) To separate from others those prisoners who, by reason of their criminal records or bad characters, are likely to exercise a bad influence;

(*b*) To divide the prisoners into classes in order to facilitate their treatment with a view to their social rehabilitation.

68. So far as possible separate institutions or separate sections of an institution shall be used for the treatment of the different classes of prisoners.

69. As soon as possible after admission and after a study of the personality of each prisoner with a sentence of suitable length, a programme of treatment shall be prepared for him in the light of the knowledge obtained about his individual needs, his capacities and dispositions.

Privileges

70. Systems of privileges appropriate for the different classes of prisoners and the different methods of treatment shall be established at every institution, in order to encourage good conduct, develop a sense of responsibility and secure the interest and cooperation of the prisoners in their treatment.

Work

71. (1) Prison labour must not be of an afflictive nature.

(2) All prisoners under sentence shall be required to work, subject to their physical and mental fitness as determined by the medical officer.

(3) Sufficient work of a useful nature shall be provided to keep prisoners actively employed for a normal working day.

(4) So far as possible the work provided shall be such as will maintain or increase the prisoners' ability to earn an honest living after release.

(5) Vocational training in useful trades shall be provided for prisoners able to profit thereby and especially for young prisoners.

(6) Within the limits compatible with proper vocational selection and with the requirements of institutional administration and discipline, the prisoners shall be able to choose the type of work they wish to perform.

72. (1) The organization and methods of work in the institutions shall resemble as closely as possible those of similar work outside institutions, so as to prepare prisoners for the conditions of normal occupational life.

(2) The interests of the prisoners and of their vocational training, however, must not be subordinated to the purpose of making a financial profit from an industry in the institution.

73. (1) Preferably institutional industries and farms should be operated directly by the administration and not by private contractors.

(2) Where prisoners are employed in work not controlled by the administration, they shall always be under the supervision of the institution's personnel. Unless the work is for other departments of the government the full normal wages for such work shall be paid to the administration by the persons to whom the labour is supplied, account being taken of the output of the prisoners.

74. (1) The precautions laid down to protect the safety and health of free workmen shall be equally observed in institutions.

(2) Provision shall be made to indemnify prisoners against industrial injury, including occupational disease, on terms not less favourable than those extended by law to free workmen.

75. (1) The maximum daily and weekly working hours of the prisoners shall be fixed by law or by administrative regulation, taking into account local rules or custom in regard to the employment of free workmen.

(2) The hours so fixed shall leave one rest day a week and sufficient time for education and other activities required as part of the treatment and rehabitation of the prisoners.

76. (1) There shall be a system of equitable remuneration of the work of prisoners.

(2) Under the system prisoners shall be allowed to spend at least a part of their earnings on approved articles for their own use

and to send a part of their earnings to their family.

(3) The system should also provide that a part of the earnings should be set aside by the administration so as to constitute a savings fund to be handed over to the prisoner on his release.

Education and recreation

77. (1) Provision shall be made for the further education of all prisoners capable of profiting thereby, including religious instruction in the countries where this is possible. The education of illiterates and young prisoners shall be compulsory and special attention shall be paid to it by the administration.

(2) So far as practicable, the education of prisoners shall be integrated with the educational system of the country so that after their release they may continue their education without difficulty.

78. Recreational and cultural activities shall be provided in all institutions for the benefit of the mental and physical health of prisoners.

Social relations and after-care

79. Special attention shall be paid to the maintenance and improvement of such relations between a prisoner and his family as are desirable in the best interest of both.

80. From the beginning of a prisoner's sentence consideration shall be given to his future after release and he shall be encouraged and assisted to maintain or establish such relations with persons or agencies outside the institution as may promote the best interests of his family and his own social rehabilitation.

81. (1) Services and agencies, governmental or otherwise, which assist released prisoners to re-establish themselves in society shall ensure, so far as is possible and necessary, that released prisoners be provided with appropriate documents and identification papers, have suitable homes and work to go to, are suitably and adequately clothed having regard to the climate and season, and have sufficient means to reach their destination and maintain themselves in the period immediately following their release.

(2) The approved representatives of such agencies shall have all necessary access to the institution and to prisoners and shall be taken into consultation as to the future of a prisoner from the beginning of his sentence.

(3) It is desirable that the activities of such agencies shall be centralized or co-ordinated as far as possible in order to secure the best use of their efforts.

B. *Insane and Mentally Abnormal Prisoners*

82. (1) Persons who are found to be insane shall not be detained in prisons and arrangements shall be made to remove them to mental institutions as soon as possible.

(2) Prisoners who suffer from other mental diseases or abnormalities shall be observed and treated in specialized institutions under medical management.

(3) During their stay in a prison, such prisoners shall be placed under the special supervision of a medical officer.

(4) The medical or psychiatric service of the penal institutions shall provide for the psychiatric treatment of all other prisoners who are in need of such treatment.

83. It is desirable that steps should be taken, by arrangement with the appropriate agencies, to ensure if necessary the continuation of psychiatric treatment after release and the provision of social-psychiatric after-care.

C. *Prisoners Under Arrest or Awaiting Trial*

84. (1) Persons arrested or imprisoned by reason of a criminal charge against them, who are detained either in police custody or in prison custody (jail) but have not yet been tried and sentenced, will be referred to as "untried prisoners" hereinafter in these rules.

(2) Unconvicted prisoners are presumed to be innocent and shall be treated as such.

(3) Without prejudice to legal rules for the protection of individual liberty or prescribing the procedure to be observed in respect of untried prisoners, these prisoners shall benefit by a special régime which is described in the following rules in its essential requirements only.

85. (1) Untried prisoners shall be kept separate from convicted prisoners.

(2) Young untried prisoners shall be kept separate from adults and shall in principle be detained in separate institutions.

86. Untried prisoners shall sleep singly in separate rooms, with the reservation of different local custom in respect of the climate.

87. Within the limits compatible with the good order of the institution, untried prisoners may, if they so desire, have their food procured at their own expense from the outside, either through the administration or through

their family or friends. Otherwise, the administration shall provide their food.

88. (1) An untried prisoner shall be allowed to wear his own clothing if it is clean and suitable.

(2) If he wears prison dress, it shall be different from that supplied to convicted prisoners.

89. An untried prisoner shall always be offered opportunity to work, but shall not be required to work. If he chooses to work, he shall be paid for it.

90. An untried prisoner shall be allowed to procure at his own expense or at the expense of a third party such books, newspapers, writing materials and other means of occupation as are compatible with the interests of the administration of justice and the security and good order of the institution.

91. An untried prisoner shall be allowed to be visited and treated by his own doctor or dentist if there is reasonable ground for his application and he is able to pay any expenses incurred.

92. An untried prisoner shall be allowed to inform immediately his family of his detention and shall be given all reasonable facilities for communicating with his family and friends, and for receiving visits from them, subject only to such restrictions and supervision as are necessary in the interests of the administration of justice and of the security and good order of the institution.

93. For the purposes of his defence, an untried prisoner shall be allowed to apply for free legal aid where such aid is available, and to receive visits from his legal adviser with a view to his defence and to prepare and hand to him confidential instructions. For these purposes, he shall if he so desires be supplied with writing material. Interviews between the prisoner and his legal adviser may be within sight but not within the hearing of a police or institution official.

D. Civil Prisoners

94. In countries where the law permits imprisonment for debt or by order of a court under any other non-criminal process, persons so imprisoned shall not be subjected to any greater restriction or severity than is necessary to ensure safe custody and good order. Their treatment shall be not less favourable than that of untried prisoners, with the reservation, however, that they may possibly be required to work.

Note 3.

ROBERT COTZBAUER

*Bill of Rights Posted for State Prisoners**

Pennsylvania officials responded this week to the concern for prison reform sweeping the country since Attica by adopting, and posting at all state correctional institutions, a "bill of rights" for prisoners.

It is a copy of the United Nations' "code of standard minimum rules for treatment of prisoners," prepared in 1955 and recommended to all nations and states, but reportedly never adopted anywhere. So Pennsylvania may be the first to do so.

Pennsylvania Attorney General J. Shane Creamer read about the code in an article by a Connecticut law professor, Leonard Orland. He sought out the document and decided to make it official state policy under his administrative powers. Copies were posted Monday.

The code is thousands of words long, and covers the waterfront of real and potential grievances which prisoners like to label "inhumane treatment." One danger in formalizing it and holding it up to inmates as established policy is that it must be followed to the letter or "broken promises" and "lip service to reform" will only be added to the list of complaints.

But Pennsylvania officials don't think this will happen here. They say the state's prison system already meets or exceeds most of the UN standards.

Posting the code, they say, will permit inmates to compare the official standards with the direct and practical effects on their lives, and enable them to bring specific complaints when justified. Also, the code should put institutional officers on their notice to adhere to principles of decent custodial practice. . . .

Note 4.

AN ACT TO PROVIDE FOR MINIMUM STANDARDS FOR THE PROTECTION OF RIGHTS OF PRISONERS**

* *The Philadelphia Evening Bulletin*, Oct. 7, 1971, p. 20. Reprinted with permission of the publisher.

** National Council on Crime and Delinquency, "A Model Act for the Protection of Rights of Prisoners." Reprinted, with permission of the National Council on Crime and Delinquency, from *Crime and Delinquency*, January 1972, pp. 10–14.

§ 1. Declaration of Purpose and Intent

The provisions of this Act shall be liberally construed to promote the intent of the Legislature as follows:

(a) The central principle underlying all rules, regulations, procedures, and practices relating to persons imprisoned in accordance with law shall be that such persons shall retain all rights of an ordinary citizen, except those expressly or by necessary implication taken by law.

(b) Such rights include but are not necessarily limited to nutritious food in adequate quantities; medical care; provision for an acceptable level of sanitation, ventilation, light, and a generally healthful environment; housing, providing for not less than fifty square feet of floor space in any confined sleeping area; reasonable opportunities for physical exercise and recreational activities; and protection against any physical or psychological abuse or unnecessary indignity.

(c) Persons in control of custodial facilities for prisoners shall be held responsible for maintaining minimum standards and shall make use of every resource available to them to prevent inhumane treatment of prisoners by employees, other prisoners, or any other persons.

(d) Measures shall be instituted and maintained within such facilities to protect against suicide or other self-destructive acts.

(e) All reasonable methods shall be used to protect against the theft or destruction of such personal property of prisoners as may be permitted in the institution.

§ 2. Inhumane Treatment Prohibited

Inhumane treatment includes but is not limited to the following acts or activities and is hereby prohibited:

(a) Striking, whipping, or otherwise imposing physical pain upon a prisoner as a measure of punishment.

(b) Any use of physical force by an employee except that which may be necessary for self-defense, to prevent or stop assault by one prisoner upon another person, and for prevention of riot or escape.

(c) Sexual or other assaults, by personnel or inmates.

(d) Any punitive or restrictive measure taken by the management or personnel in retaliation for assertion of rights.

(e) Any measure intended to degrade the prisoner, including insults and verbal abuse.

(f) Any discriminatory treatment based upon the prisoner's race, religion, nationality, or political beliefs.

§ 3. Isolation in Solitary Confinement

A prisoner may be placed in solitary confinement—segregation in a special cell or room—only under the following conditions:

(a) During such confinement, the prisoner shall receive daily at least 2,500 calories of food in the normal diet of prisoners not in isolation.

(b) The cell in which the prisoner is confined in solitary shall be at least as large as other cells in the institution and shall be adequately lighted during daylight hours. All of the necessities of civilized existence, such as a toilet, bedding, and water for drinking and washing, shall be provided. Normal room temperatures for comfortable living shall be maintained. If any of these necessities are removed temporarily, such removal shall be only to prevent suicide or self-destructive acts, or damage to the cell and its equipment.

(c) Under no circumstances shall a prisoner confined in solitary be deprived of normal prison clothing except for his own protection. If any such deprivation is temporarily necessary, he shall be provided with body clothing and bedding adequate to protect his health.

(d) A prisoner may not be confined in a solitary cell for punishment, and may be so confined only under conditions of emergency for his own protection or that of personnel or other prisoners. Confinement under such circumstances shall not be continued for longer than is necessary for the emergency. A prisoner's right to communicate with his attorney or the person or agency provided for in Section 5 to receive complaints shall not be interfered with.

(e) No prisoner shall be kept in a solitary cell for longer than one hour without the approval of the highest ranking officer on duty in the institution at the time.

(f) No prisoner may be kept in a solitary cell for any reason for longer than forty-eight hours without being examined by a medical doctor or other medical personnel under the doctor's direction.

(g) A log in a bound book shall be maintained at or near any solitary cell or cells, and employees in charge of such cell or cells shall be responsible for recording all admissions, releases, visits to the cell, and other events except those of the most routine nature.

§ 4. Disciplinary Procedure

It is the responsibility of any person or persons in charge of the management of an institution for the confinement of prisoners to develop and describe in writing a fair and orderly procedure for processing disciplinary complaints against prisoners and to establish rules, regulations, and procedures to insure the maintenance of a high standard of fairness and equity. The rules shall prescribe offenses and the punishments for them that may be imposed. Any punishment that may affect the sentence or parole eligibility (such as the loss of good-time allowance) shall not be imposed without a hearing at which the prisoner shall have a right to be present and a right to be represented by counsel or some other person of his choice. A permanent record shall be maintained of all disciplinary complaints, the hearings, and the dispositions thereof.

§ 5. Grievance Procedure

The director of the State Department of Correction (or the equivalent official) shall establish a grievance procedure to which all prisoners confined within the system shall have access. Prisoners shall be entitled to report any grievance, whether or not it charges a violation of this Act, and to mail such communication to the head of the department. The grievance procedure established shall provide for an investigation (aside from any investigation made by the institution or department) of all alleged grievances by a person or agency outside of the department, and for a written report of findings to be submitted to the department and the prisoner.

§ 6. Judicial Relief

A prisoner or group of prisoners alleging abuses in violation of this Act may petition [appropriate court] for relief. The court may afford any of the following remedies:

(a) It may make a finding that the allegations are without merit.

(b) It may issue an injunction, prohibitive or mandatory, or utilize any other appropriate remedy in law or equity.

(c) It may prohibit further commitments to the institution.

(d) If the abuses are found to be extensive and persistent, it may order the institution closed subject to a stay of a reasonable period, not to exceed six months, to permit the responsible authorities to correct the abuses. If the abuses are not corrected to the satisfaction of the court, it may order those prisoners who have a history of serious assaultive behavior to be transferred to another facility, and it may order the discharge of other prisoners.

§ 7. Visits to Prisoners and Institutions

The director of a department responsible for the operation of an institution or a system of institutions for the confinement of prisoners shall establish rules and regulations permitting attorneys of record, relatives, and friends to visit and talk in private with any prisoner in an institution at reasonable times and under reasonable limitations. The institution may be visited at any time by members of the state legislature, judges of the criminal or appellate courts, the attorney general, and the governor.

Any other citizen may make application to visit an institution and talk in private with prisoners if the applicant establishes a legitimate reason for such visit and if the visit is not inconsistent with the public welfare and the safety and security of the institution. The director may reject any such application if the visit or any aspect thereof would be disruptive to the program of the institution.

If application for a visit is denied, the person may apply to [court of general jurisdiction] for an order directing the head of the institution to permit the visit. Such order shall be granted after notice and hearing if it is found that (a) the person is a representative of a public concern regarding the conditions of the prison, (b) he is not a mere curiosity seeker, and (c) it is not established by the head of the institution that the visit, or any aspect of it, would disrupt the program of the institution.

E. Judicial Review of Prison Disciplinary Decisions: Loss of Good Time

1. STATUTORY PROVISIONS

NOTES

Note 1.

CONN. GEN. STAT. § 18-7

Any prisoner may, by good conduct and obedience to the rules of said institution, earn a commutation or diminution of his sentence, as follows: Sixty days for each year, and pro rata for a part of a year, of a sentence which is * * * not for more than five years; and ninety days for the sixth and each subsequent year, and pro rata for a part of a year, and, in addition thereto, five days for each month as a meritorious time service award which may be granted in the discretion of the warden and the commissioner for exemplary conduct and meritorious achievement; provided any serious act of misconduct or insubordination or persistent refusal to conform to institution regulations occurring at any time during his confinement in said prison shall subject the prisoner, at the discretion of the warden and the commissioner, to the loss of all or a portion of the time earned....

Note 2.

18 U.S.C. § 4161

Each prisoner convicted of an offense against the United States and confined in a penal or correctional institution for a definite term other than for life, whose record of conduct shows that he has faithfully observed all the rules and has not been subjected to punishment, shall be entitled to a deduction from the term of his sentence beginning with the day on which the sentence commences to run, as follows:

Five days for each month, if the sentence is not less than six months and not more than one year.

Six days for each month, if the sentence is more than one year and less than three years.

Seven days for each month, if the sentence is not less than three years and less than five years.

Eight days for each month, if the sentence is not less than five years and less than ten years.

Ten days for each month, if the sentence is ten years or more.

When two or more consecutive sentences are to be served, the aggregate of the several sentences shall be the basis upon which the deduction shall be computed.

2. ADMINISTRATIVE INTERPRETATION

U.S. BUREAU OF PRISONS

Policy Statement on Withholding, Forfeiture, and Restoration of Good Time*

1. Purpose

To furnish forfeiture, withholding and restoration of good time allowances to be used as case management tools, per guidelines contained in Policy Statement 7400.5A.

2. Directive Affected

Policy Statement 7400.6 is hereby superseded.

3. Withholding Good Time

By statute, 18 U.S.C. 4161, an inmate is entitled to the good conduct allowance when "he has faithfully observed all rules and has not been subjected to punishment." Consonant with that standard, good time may be recommended to be withheld by the Adjustment

* Policy Statement 7400.6A, Aug. 13, 1971.

Committee whenever, upon its investigation of a report of misconduct, it finds that an inmate has violated or failed to comply with institution rules or instructions and that withholding is appropriate. A recommendation for withholding shall be submitted to the Chief Executive Officer for final approval. Withholding should be limited to incidents amounting to misconduct or offenses; it should not be applied as a universal punishment to all persons in segregation status. While the withholding of good time does not require the more detailed procedures of good time forfeiture, withholding shall be limited to the good time creditable for the single month during which the violation occurs. (Some offenses, such as refusal to work at an assignment, may be recurring, and thus may permit consecutive withholding actions.) Offenses which require more than the withholding of good time should be handled by forfeiture proceedings.

While extra good time (e.g., Meritorious, Camp Industrial) is awarded as earned, a termination of these awards need not necessarily follow placement in segregation, if such placement is not based upon misconduct or violation of institution rules.

4. Forfeiture of Good Time

Whenever reported misconduct is of such a nature to warrant consideration of forfeiture action, the committee appointed for such purpose shall conduct a good time forfeiture hearing, observing the following rules:

a. Its Chairman shall make arrangements for conducting the hearing and for the reporting of the hearing.

b. A verbatim transcript need not be made, but the record of the hearing should summarize all aspects of the proceedings and the facts presented before it.

c. The inmate should be called before the committee, and advised of the details of the report of misconduct and of the rules of procedure to be followed by the committee. If it appears at any time to any member of the committee that the inmate may be mentally ill, the Chairman should refer the inmate to the medical staff for a determination of whether the inmate is incompetent, within the meaning of 18 U.S.C. 4244. Good time shall not be forfeited in the case of an inmate who is determined to be incompetent.

d. The inmate should then be asked whether he admits that the report against him is true. If he does, no further evidence need be heard, but the inmate should be permitted to offer any statement he wishes concerning his misconduct, which will be considered by the committee in making its recommendations. The inmate may request a staff member to speak on his behalf at this stage.

e. If the inmate does not admit the misconduct, he shall be advised that he can have a member of the staff to assist him at the hearing. If he wishes a staff representative, the inmate shall be asked to submit the name of a full-time staff member. The Chairman shall, with the consent of the designated staff member, arrange for this person to represent the inmate. If the staff member chosen declines or is not available because of absence from the institution, the inmate should be given the option of choosing another representative or, in the case of an absent designee, of waiting for a reasonable period until his return. The hearing should be recessed by the Chairman to permit the representative to interview the inmate and to prepare the inmate's presentation.

f. Rules of evidence and of trial procedure do not apply to the hearing. The Chairman arranges for the presentation of the evidence to support the misconduct report. Any member of the committee can request that the Chairman arrange for additional investigation or evidence, or for the appearance of additional witnesses, or for the statements of unavailable witnesses. The Chairman may determine that the source of certain information should not be revealed to the inmate, for example when the disclosure may endanger the safety or well-being of another person. In such a case, the report of the committee should summarize the circumstances and the reasons for this determination. Otherwise, all evidence heard or seen by the committee should be made known to the inmate (and his representative).

g. After the evidence supporting the misconduct report is heard, the inmate or his representative shall be permitted to make a statement. The inmate can request witnesses on his behalf. The Chairman will call those witnesses (staff or inmates) who are available, and who are determined by him to be necessary for an appreciation of the circumstances. Repetitive witnesses need not be called. Unavailable witnesses may be asked to submit written statements. The Chairman should note in the committee's report the reasons for declining to call requested witnesses.

h. The inmate (and his representative) shall be permitted to make a final statement on his behalf, and they shall be excused.

i. The members shall discuss the case, deciding upon the findings of fact that are supported by the evidence, and upon the recommendations to be made to the Chief Executive Officer.

j. A written report shall be submitted to the Chief Executive Officer, containing a record of the proceedings and evidence (Paragraph (b) above), and the recommendations of the committee. Any member of the committee can submit a minority report. The recommendations made by the committee members should include reasons, as specific as possible, for the particular recommendations.

The good time available for forfeiture is limited to an amount computed by multiplying the number of months served at the time of the offense for which forfeiture action is taken times the applicable monthly rate specified in 18 U.S.C. 4161 (less any previous forfeiture and withholding outstanding), plus any extra good time which may have been earned to the date of the offense.

The Chief Executive Officer shall review the report of the Good Time Forfeiture Committee, and shall make an endorsement on the report, accepting or rejecting the committee's findings, and ordering a forfeiture if warranted by the evidence and if appropriate under all the circumstances, including the guidelines of Policy Statement 7400.5A.

A copy of the decision by the Chief Executive Officer shall be placed in the inmate's file. The inmate's sentence records shall be changed to reflect any forfeiture ordered. A copy of each forfeiture proceeding and of the Chief Executive Officer's decision should be forwarded to the Office of General Counsel and Review. The Chairman of the Classification Committee, or his designated representative on that Committee, shall inform the inmate of the decision of the Chief Executive Officer, and provide him with a copy of the written report and the decision of the Chief Executive Officer. The inmate shall be advised that this decision can be appealed to the Office of General Counsel and Review through the Prisoners' Mail Box. The inmate should be permitted to confer with the staff member who represented him at the hearing in this regard.

Upon review the following factors will be considered:
Whether or not:
(1) there has been compliance with the procedures set forth in this policy statement;
(2) the determination is founded upon a substantial factual basis;
(3) the amount forfeited is disproportionate to the violation and other circumstances.

4. Exceptional Circumstances

a. When an inmate escapes from custody, good time forfeiture action may be taken in the absence of the inmate by the Adjustment Committee at the institution from which the escape occurred. Such action should be taken, if forfeiture is deemed appropriate, when the inmate is close to his mandatory release date or when it is likely that he will be taken, upon apprehension, to another institution. When the inmate whose good time is forfeited is returned to custody, he should be advised of the forfeiture and given the opportunity to submit a statement in mitigation to the Chief Executive Officer, who may consider it in making a decision as to restoration of good time. If an inmate refuses to appear at such a hearing without the use of force, the hearing, upon full documentation of this, may proceed in his absence. Only in such situations may good time be taken in the absence of the inmate.

b. A noted in Policy Statement 2200.1, when an inmate's misconduct may also be the subject of criminal prosecution, it is not necessary to await the outcome of the criminal trial before disciplinary action, including good time forfeiture, is taken, especially if there is reason to believe there will be a long delay before the trial is held.

5. Restoration of Good Time

Authority to restore all types of forfeited and withheld good time is delegated to the Chief Executive Officer of each institution. The proper administrative form should be used to report restoration action. A copy of the restoration action shall be submitted to the Office of General Counsel and Review. The partial or total restoration of good time is valuable as an instrument of case management.

3. JUDICIAL REVIEW

RODRIGUEZ V. MCGINNIS
451 F.2d 730 (1971)
United States Court of Appeals, Second Circuit

HAYS, Circuit Judge:

This is an appeal from an order of the United States District Court for the Northern District of New York in an action brought by a state prisoner under 28 U.S.C. § 1343 (1964) and 42 U.S.C. § 1983 (1964). After an evidentiary hearing, the district court held that the cancellation by defendants of 120 days of plaintiff's earned good behavior time, was unconstitutionally imposed. The defendant Commissioner of Correction of the State of New York was ordered to restore the remaining period of good behavior time credit to plaintiff. As a consequence of this order plaintiff was released from prison on December 24, 1969, although remaining subject to the supervision of the New York Board of Parole. We reverse the judgment of the district court.

In view of the basis for our disposition, only a brief summary of the facts is necessary. Rodriguez, having been convicted in a New York state court of perjury and attempted grand larceny, was sentenced to imprisonment for an indeterminate term of from one and one-half years to four years. Under New York law, a prisoner serving an indeterminate sentence may elect to participate in a conditional release program by which he may earn up to 10 days per month good behavior time credit toward the reduction of the maximum term of his sentence. Appellee chose to elect this program. Optimally a prisoner so electing may be released under the supervision of the Board of Parole, after having served but two-thirds of his maximum sentence, Correction Law § 803 (McKinney's Consol. Laws, c. 43, 1968), Penal Law §§ 70.30(4) (a), 70.40(1) (a) and (b) (McKinney's Consol. Laws, c. 40, 1967); accrued good behavior allowances so earned, however, may at any time be withdrawn in whole or part for bad behavior or for violation of institutional rules. Correction Law § 803(1) (McKinney 1968).

Appellee was charged in two separate disciplinary action reports dated October 31, 1968, with possession in his cell of five contraband letters written by his wife, and with having six pornographic photographs of his wife in his possession received through illegal channels. The Deputy Warden adjudged that 120 days of the prisoner's earned good behavior time should be cancelled as punishment, "60 days for the letters and 60 days for the pictures." In the "Remarks" action of each judgment was a statement to the effect that appellee had refused to disclose how he had managed to get possession of the uncensored items. The district judge found that this and various other disciplinary actions meted out to Rodriguez (segregation in Sing Sing for a day and a half, segregation in Clinton Prison for several weeks) were really designed to compel these disclosures from appellee. He believed that the imposition of the penalty was a deprivation of Rodriguez' right to due process because the prison regulations prescribed no penalty for refusal to inform. He further found that the Commutation Board at Clinton Prison, which reviews all cases involving forfeiture of good time, failed to comply with a statute directing the Board to forward its reasons for the disallowance of the good behavior time in writing to the Commissioner of Correction and he characterized this failure as the chief basis for his ruling. Correction Law § 236 (McKinney 1968). We cannot agree with the trial judge's view that questions of constitutional significance are involved.

Even if we were inclined to affirm the decision on the merits we would be compelled to reverse on the ground that appellee has failed to exhaust his state remedies. . . .

The "chief basis" of the district court's order is founded on error. The provision of § 236 of the Correction Law under which the prison commutation boards forward their reasons for disallowing good behavior time in writing to the Commissioner of Correction is not constitutionally required. Moreover, a letter from Warden Deegan to Commissioner McGinnis dated November 1, 1968 (Defendant's Exhibit "C") was sufficient to satisfy the statutory requirement, since it contained all the information that would have been included in a letter from the Board to the Commissioner. In any case, even if the requirement of § 236 had federal significance, the most that appellee would be entitled to is a decree ordering the board to forward a report to the Commissioner.

Although punishment for refusing to reveal the sources of his contraband would not reflect any constitutional infirmity, it is quite clear that Rodriguez did not lose his good behavior time for refusal to inform but for possession of the contraband. After the punishment was ordered he was given an opportunity to reduce his lost good time credit by revealing the source of the contraband. This procedure, commonly used in law enforcement efforts, certainly does not violate any constitutional right.

The issue in this case is typical of the increasing number of trivial questions of internal prison discipline now being brought, in the first instance, before the federal courts. If the results were not so serious for the administration of justice through state and federal procedures, the spectacle of a federal court of appeals solemnly deciding on the penalty in terms of good time a state prisoner should receive for having dirty pictures in his cell (or for refusing to be a tattle tale) would be so absurd as to be laughable. But if this court entertains actions of this kind it will encourage state prisoners who have any kind of "beef" to bring such actions and the federal courts will end up sitting as prison boards of discipline in the state prisons.

The federal courts should refuse to interfere with internal state prison administration except in the most extreme cases involving a shocking deprivation of fundamental rights. See, e. g., Church v. Hegstrom, 416 F.2d 449, 450–451 (2d Cir. 1969); Wright v. McMann, 387 F.2d 519, 528 (2d Cir. 1967) (concurring opinion of Lumbard, Ch. J.); Sostre v. McGinnis, 334 F.2d 906 (2d Cir.), cert. denied, 379 U.S. 892, 85 S.Ct. 168, 13 L.Ed.2d 96 (1964); Jackson v. Bishop, 404 F.2d 571, 577 (8th Cir. 1968) (Blackmun, C. J.). A case such as the instant one, which is totally devoid of merit, should be dismissed out of hand.

At a minimum such cases should first be filtered through the state prison administrative process and the state courts. In Wright v. McMann, Chief Judge Lumbard said:

> We are not called upon this time to decide whether Wright would be heard upon his constitutional claims in federal court without first applying for statutory relief in a state court if the New York legislature had given to inmates of its prisons the right to apply for injunctive relief against improper treatment. I would hold that if a state made provision for such relief in its courts the federal courts should abstain for a reasonable period to allow the state courts to hear the complaint and take appropriate action. I do not agree that recent decisions of the Supreme Court mandate or were intended to mandate action by federal courts in all cases involving the treatment of prisoners in state institutions, without a suitable period of abstention where state courts are empowered to hear the case and where there is reason to believe that the state would grant relief if the complaint were well founded. The disciplining of state prisoners is so peculiarly a matter in the discretion of the state, and the possibilities that prisoners will file groundless and numerous complaints in the federal courts are so obvious, that these cases raise 'special circumstances' that make it appropriate to treat them as an exception to the caveat or policy against abstention by federal courts.

The prisoner should be remanded to serve the sixty odd days remaining of his sentence, or, if he chooses, to make an application through state administrative or judicial processes for the relief he seeks.

WATERMAN, Circuit Judge (dissenting):

I respectfully dissent. I would affirm the judgment entered in the Northern District of New York.

In this action brought by a state prisoner under 28 U.S.C. § 1343 and 42 U.S.C. § 1983, Judge James T. Foley, Chief Judge of the United States District Court for the Northern District of New York, after an evidentiary hearing in which the prisoner and the state officer defendants testified and presented exhibits, adjudged that the cancellation by defendants of 120 days of plaintiff's earned good behavior time which, if not canceled, would have reduced his period of incarceration by 120 days was unconstitutionally imposed. The district judge therefore ordered that the defendant Commissioner of Correction of the State of New York restore the remaining period of good behavior time credit to plaintiff. As a consequence of this order plaintiff, although remaining subject to the supervision of the New York State Board of Parole, was entitled to an immediate release from prison, and he was so released on Christmas Eve, 1969.

The facts are fully set forth in the able opinion filed below by Judge Foley in Rodriguez v. McGinnis, 307 F.Supp. 627 (N.D. N.Y.1969), and need to be but briefly reiterated for the purpose of this dissenting opinion.

On February 14, 1967, Rodriguez was sentenced in a New York State court to imprisonment for an indeterminate term of from one and one-half years to four years. According to New York law, a prisoner serving an indeterminate sentence may elect to participate in a conditional release program whereby he may earn up to 10 days per month good behavior time credit toward the reduction of the maximum term of his sentence. Optimally, under this program, a prisoner may be released, under the supervision of the Board of Parole, from prison incarceration after having served but two-thirds of his maximum sentence, Correction Law § 803, Penal Law §§ 70.30(4)(a), 70.40(1) (a) and (b), but accrued good behavior allowances so earned may at any time be withdrawn in whole or in part for bad behavior or for violation of institutional rules. Correction Law § 803(1). Appellee chose to elect the conditional release program.

On October 30, 1968, while he was imprisoned in Sing Sing, Rodriguez was charged in a "disciplinary action" report with having in his possession five uncensored, and therefore contraband, letters written to him by his wife. He was similarly charged on the following day with having in his possession six uncensored pornographic photographs of her. These items were taken from him and turned over to the Deputy Warden. On October 31 it was adjudged by the prisoner's interrogator, the Principal Keeper, the Deputy Warden, that 120 days of the prisoner's earned good behavior time were canceled in order to punish him, "60 days for the letters and 60 days for the pictures." The judgment entered on each of the reports set forth that appellee refused to disclose how he managed to get possession of the uncensored items.[1] Judge Foley, upon hearing appellee's testimony, discredited the "disciplinary action" reports to the following extent, 307 F.Supp. at 631:

> The plaintiff's version given at the trial contradicts these disciplinary reports. He testified he was never confronted with written charges or the contraband. From the beginning, and I so find, the questioning was solely in regard to how he got the uncensored letters and photographs into Sing Sing.

It is clear that, as Judge Foley found, the real motive behind the continuing pattern of punishment, first the cancellation of the 120 days good behavior time earned by a year's good behavior at Sing Sing, second, the immediate incarceration in the "Box" there for a day and a half, and third, the prompt transfer to Clinton Prison following that incarceration, where the confinement in segregation lasted from entry there on November 1 until the first week in December, was not designed to punish Rodriguez for his possession of uncensored mail but rather was designed to compel him to disclose the channel through which he obtained the uncensored items, or, as the majority says, to "tattletale."

Judge Foley also found that the Commutation Board at Clinton Prison, which reviews all cases in which good time has been forfeited by a disciplinary officer, failed to obey the command of the New York statute, and did not forward in writing to the Commissioner of Correction its reasons for withholding appellee's good behavior time. Correction Law §§ 235, 236.

Based on the above, the experienced district judge expressed concern that this pattern of events may well not have comported with "ordinary due process requirements" and stated, "* * * I am not sure the disciplinary officer or an officer of a review board can assume legally the investigative mantle and become prosecutor, judge and jury, and in this instance really the Appellate Court of Review." 307 F.Supp. at 632. I share his concern.

The judge indicated, also, that "the chief basis" for his decision was the failure of the prison commutation board to forward the reasons for its action to the Commissioner and that this failure deprived appellee of due process and equal protection of the law. Id.

Had Judge Foley found that the prison authorities had only proceeded against Rodriguez by confronting him with a charge of violating prison rules in that he possessed uncensored items, had given him a full opportunity to answer only those charges, and then had failed to forward to the Commissioner of Correction the reasons for taking away good behavior time as punishment for the infractions, I would not consider such a statutory violation to constitute such a deprivation of due process as to warrant a federal tribunal in granting relief. However, on the facts found by Judge Foley, it is my belief that this panel has no other valid option but to conclude that the procedures appellee was subjected to in relation to the uncensored mail did not meet the minimum constitutional requirement of "fundamental fairness."

Rodriguez began his drawn out confrontations with prison officials over a simple infraction of prison rules, the possession of uncensored material. Although he was "officially" charged with that simple infraction, official attention soon focused on Rodriguez's refusal to "tattletale" and to incriminate others who

---

[1] The pertinent notations as to the letters follow:

JUDGMENT
60 days. . . .
Remarks: Inmate refuses to disclose who had arranged to get the contraband letters to him.
/s/ R. Treanor
Deputy Warden
letters held in Warden's office.
The pertinent notations as to the photographs follow:
JUDGMENT
60 days. Inmate was adamant in refusal to disclose method by which the pornographic photographs were passed to him.
Remarks:
Pictures held in Warden's office.
/s/ R. Treanor
Asst. Superintendent

might have aided him in receiving the contraband.[2] It is apparent from the severity of his punishment, first, the wiping away of a year's accrued credit for a year's good behavior and the resulting assessment of four months additional incarceration, and second, segregation "in the Boxes" of the two prisons for a total of more than 40 days, that the punitive measures were not inflicted for possession of uncensored letters and photographs but in order to coerce him to tattletale and to divulge information that would inculpate other residents of Sing Sing.

It would seem, then, that the failure of the commutation board to forward its reasons for its actions was merely a part of the pattern of continued procedural dereliction Judge Foley found; and, as the facts he found are not clearly erroneous, and, on the record, I am not convinced that Judge Foley made any mistake in finding the facts as he found them, I approve the conclusion that he necessarily drew from these facts that the coercive procedures adopted by the prison authorities to obtain Rodriguez's confession did not comport with the due process the accused, then a prisoner in custody, was entitled to.

Although not raised before the court below, or considered there, appellee urges us to hold that the imposition of this punishment because he remained silent in the face of interrogation was a violation of his fifth amendment privilege against self-incrimination, citing Spevack v. Klein, 385 U.S. 511, 87 S.Ct. 625, 17 L.Ed.2d 574 (1967). The defendants respond by pointing out that Rodriguez at the hearing before Judge Foley admitted having the uncensored items in his possession and that his refusal to talk was not motivated by any fear of criminal prosecution for possessing the items. This is most assuredly so as to the possession of the contraband, but the prison authorities' questions were not directed at seeking a confession with respect to the contraband; no confession was necessary or needed, he was "caught with the goods." The questions were directed at discovering how the letters and photographs were smuggled past

---

[2] Rodriquez testified as to the initial Sing Sing confrontation as follows:

I was in the visiting room. My wife was visiting me, and an officer came over and told her that the visit was terminated. She left. I was told to remain. A few minutes later, the officer took me to the Warden's office. * * * The Warden said to me "How did you get these uncensored letters into Sing Sing?"

* * * * *

I told him I had nothing to say. He then summoned somebody else and told him "Take him to the box."

Rodriguez testified with reference to the second confrontation at Sing Sing that he was taken from the box to the Deputy Warden's office by a guard. The colloquy follows:

He said to me, the first thing he said to me, is "Look, Gene, I know that it is a waste of time asking you anything, but I want to know how uncensored letters got into Sing Sing." I said, "I have nothing to say." He said—he then said, "If you don't tell me I am going to take sixty days for the letters and sixty days for the pictures, to run consecutively." I didn't say anything. He then said, "I can give you back this lost time, give you back all your lost time." I said, "I have nothing to say."

Q. Now is that the end of the conversation with the P. K.? A. That was it.

Q. And how long were you in this room, total time? A. Oh, wait, there was something else that was said. He said, "You are being transferred to Clinton." He said, "You are being transferred to Clinton, Gene, tomorrow." I said, "Thanks for telling me." Then he said, "Good luck to you." I said, "Good luck to you." We shook hands and I walked out. I was there two minutes or maybe three minutes.

Upon his arrival at Clinton Prison Rodriguez testified that he was immediately taken away to the box there without any further hearing. As to the confrontations at that prison, Rodriguez testified:

While I was in the box on three separate occasions the Warden weekly would have me brought up to his office * * *. The warden would have me brought up to his office and he said to me—what he did was this. He said "Sit down." When I sat down he said, "Look, you are an educated man * * *."

The Court: How often did he do this?
The Witness: He did it three times.
The Court: All right.
The Witness: He did it three consecutive weeks. He said, "Look, you are an educated man." The first time "I want to know how the unauthorized letters got into Sing Sing. I don't like to keep you in the box. You didn't do anything at Clinton but I have to as part of the continuing investigation." I said, "I have nothing to say." He said, "You are going to continue to lose good time and you are going to stay in the box." He said, "We have it narrowed down to two men anyway, so that if you tell us you will save yourself all this aggravation." So I answered him, I said, "Well, if you have it narrowed down to two men, then you don't need me."

So he had me taken out.

prison censors. The obvious import of the interrogation was the discovery of the identity of the "insider" or "insiders" (prison guards, etc.) who must have enabled Rodriguez to receive the uncensored items. Had Rodriguez answered the prison officials and implicated certain persons employed by the prison, he would also, of course, be implicating himself in the conspiracy to circumvent censorship and he could reasonably expect further developments to follow any disclosure he might make. The ramifications of the interrogation were twofold. The information sought would not only open the door for a probable criminal charge against a prison official but also, as Rodriguez would also be a party to the official's criminal act, a possible criminal charge against Rodriguez.

Rodriguez may have been motivated to remain silent solely because of a fear of retaliation by his confederate, whether a prison guard or other prison employee, or even another inmate. But the fifth amendment protection protects irrespective of the subjective motives that prompt one to be silent. If the information sought by officers may tend to incriminate one who is being questioned, he has an absolute right to remain silent. Although "[a]nswers may be compelled regardless of the privilege if there is immunity from federal and state use of the compelled testimony or its fruits in connection with a criminal prosecution against the person testifying," Gardner v. Broderick, 392 U.S. 273, 276, 88 S.Ct. 1913, 1915, 20 L.Ed.2d 1082 (1968), (citing cases), no immunity from prosecution was offered in this case to Rodriguez. Nor is it any answer to say that if Rodriguez had talked under the compulsion of the threats of segregation in the box and the loss of good time credits such compulsion would have rendered his statements or the fruits thereof "coerced" and therefore inadmissible against him in a criminal prosecution. See Garrity v. State of New Jersey, 385 U.S. 493, 87 S.Ct. 616, 17 L.Ed.2d 562 (1967). Absent an assurance that his statements could not be used against him, we cannot assume appellee was aware of any implicit immunity he would enjoy if criminal charges for a complicity in violation of law were brought against him. Cf. Gardner v. Broderick, supra at 278–279, 88 S.Ct. 1913.

I would point out, therefore, that under the circumstances present in this case the fifth amendment privilege against self-incrimination was a bar to the punishment imposed—punishment which obviously was not imposed for the possession of uncensored letters and photographs but imposed solely for the purpose of compelling appellee to divulge incriminating information. However, the pertinence of the fifth amendment's protection was not brought to the attention of the trial court and I find it unnecessary to uphold the decision below by reliance upon it. With reference to the issue that was presented to Judge Foley, his factual findings are not clearly erroneous and his conclusion drawn therefrom that appellee was deprived of due process seems to me to be incontrovertible. I would affirm.

WRIGHT v. MCMANN
460 F.2d 126 (1972)
United States Court of Appeals, Second Circuit

LUMBARD, Circuit Judge:

Lawrence William Wright in March 1966 brought suit under the Civil Rights Act, 42 U.S.C. § 1983, against appellant McMann in the Northern District of New York. . . .

Consolidated with Wright's action was the Civil Rights suit of appellee Robert Mosher, commenced in May 1967 against Warden McMann, for whom appellant LaVallee was substituted when the latter became Superintendent of Clinton in January 1968. . . .

As to Mosher, Judge Foley found that he was confined to segregation for five months in 1967, that two months after his return to general population he was again placed in segregation, where he spent a year, for the same violation which caused him to be sent to segregation the first time, *viz.*, refusal to sign a "safety sheet" detailing safety rules to be observed in prison workshops. Judge Foley found Mosher sincere in his belief that his signature on the sheet would constitute a waiver of prison liability were he to be injured in the shop. . . . Judge Foley . . . ordered restoration of 616 days of Mosher's "good time," 440 of which had been revoked in prison disciplinary proceedings during his confinement to segregation and 176 of which he was prevented from earning because of such confinement.

Mosher's 616 days of "good time" were appropriately restored to him by the district court. He was first confined to segregation in 1967. After five months he was released to the general population, but two months later he was returned upon repeat of the very violation for which he was punished with segregation in the first place. His second stay consumed a year, as he was confined "until further orders" and prolonged matters with various rule infractions while in segregation.

Segregation conditions during Mosher's tenancy, while not ideal according to his testimony, especially in the cells comprising Section 4 (the "strip cells"), were nonetheless considerably improved since Wright's occupancy, and the district court's decision to restore lost "good time" rested on the finding that segregation was "grossly disproportionate for the offense committed" by Mosher. Judge Foley also found "that procedural safeguards * * * in this instance might have averted or corrected this improper punishment," and that the disproportionate initial punishments were "linked clearly to the later violations in segregation." 321 F.Supp. at 145.

Ordinarily we would be most reluctant to find unconstitutionally disproportionate the use of segregated confinement as punishment. Prison officials, not federal judges, are in day to day proximity or contact with the inmates and are consequently better able to determine what punishment might or might not be appropriate to a particular offense commited by a particular inmate. An offense representing another in a series by one inmate might meet a harsher response than the same offense committed by an inmate with a "clean" prison record. Or a prison official might decide that a harsh punishment for a repeatedly disruptive inmate might, under the circumstances, simply reinforce a cycle of offense and punishment which the sagacious employment of leniency might avoid. In short, the inmate alleging disproportionate punishment will ordinarily have a heavy burden.

Here, however, we think that Mosher has successfully met this burden. His offense was his refusal to sign a prison "safety sheet," a single piece of paper with a list of precautions and instructions to be followed by inmates assigned to certain shops in the prison. The following circumstances in combination persuade us that Judge Foley was correct in finding segregation a disproportionate response to Mosher's refusal to sign the sheet:

First, Judge Foley found as a fact, and it is not suggested that this finding be disturbed on appeal, that Mosher believed in good faith that his signature would be the equivalent of a waiver by him of his right to sue the prison in the event he was injured while working in a prison shop due to the negligence of prison officials. This is important inasmuch as it bears on Mosher's attitude and the character of his defiance; that is, Mosher was apparently not making trouble for the sake of being a troublemaker.

Second, testimony by deposition of both Deputy Warden DeLong and Warden McMann indicates that the sole purpose of the safety sheet was simply to assure that inmates were familiar with shop safety regulations. Deputy Warden DeLong, upon whose immediate direction Mosher was sent to segregation, testified that even if an inmate had read and understood the safety sheet he could not work until he signed, and a refusal to sign was tantamount to a refusal to work in his eyes. We have been pointed to no prison manual or rulebook authorizing such an interpretation of a refusal to sign or giving notice to an inmate that such a refusal was a violation or might result in segregation.

Third, and perhaps most important, is Warden McMann's testimony that segregation as punishment for refusal to sign the sheet was inappropriate. Indeed, he testified that no punishment whatsoever was warranted: assignment to "idle" population, where the inmate could not work and earn extra money, was the ordinary consequence of an "offense" such as Mosher's.

In short, for an act which even the warden found deserving of no punishment Mosher was disciplined with the worst punishment the prison had to offer, and it has nowhere been suggested that such a result came about through anything other than the unfettered discretion of the deputy warden. While the area of discretion of prison officials is exceedingly broad, it is not limitless. Appellants urge nothing more specific than that Deputy Warden DeLong's "personal experience" with Mosher somehow justified the use of "his discretion as a disciplinary officer in sending Mosher to segregation." Testimony from the record is no more illuminating: on the day Mosher was punished with segregation he had four previous offenses in prison; that same day another inmate with six offenses refused to work and was punished by DeLong with deprivation of yard privileges for 15 days. When DeLong was asked whether there was any reason for the difference in the punishment, he replied, "I do not recall anything about [the other inmate] nor do I recall anything in particular about Mosher at that particular time. The only thing I can say is that due to the particular circumstances surrounding the case at that time, this was my decision."

The word "discretion" is not talismanic. We think that when an inmate is punished as severely as possible for an act which the warden testifies deserves no sanctions whatsoever it behooves the punishing official to come forth with some justification other than that "the particular circumstances" warranted such discipline.

Sostre is by no means to the contrary. This court there refused to find disproportionate punishment noting its reluctance to "deny to prison authorities the power to use an entirely constitutional means of discipline in response . . . to a prisoner's refusal . . . to obey valid prison regulations." 442 F.2d at 194. In a footnote to that passage, however, we said:

> We stress the seriousness of the multiple offenses charged against Sostre by Warden Follette . . . and express no view as to the constitutionality of such segregated confinement as Sostre experienced if it were imposed for lesser offenses. Specifically, we express no view as to the constitutionality of such segregated confinement if it had been imposed on account of any one or any combination of the offenses charged against Sostre other than all of them.

Id. n. 28.

Thus, although *Sostre* clearly holds that the federal courts should be chary in entertaining inmate petitions claiming unconstitutionally disproportionate punishment, it is equally clear that *Sostre* recognizes that such a constitutional violation might be made out under circumstances more compelling than those present therein.

HAYS, Circuit Judge, dissenting in part:

I dissent from the affirmance of the district court's restoration of good time to Mosher . . .

The restoration of good time to Mosher solely on the grounds of the disproportionate length of his term in segregation is an unwarranted extension of Sostre v. McGinnis, 442 F.2d 178 (2d Cir. 1971), cert. denied, Oswald v. Sostre, 405 U.S. 978, 92 S.Ct. 1190, 30 L.Ed.2d 254, and it violates good sense as well. Unlike Sostre, Mosher was not punished for engaging in constitutionally protected activity, nor did his punishment constitute such extreme physical abuse that the federal court was justified in intervening. *E. g.,* Haines v. Kerner, 404 U.S. 519, 92 S.Ct. 594, 30 L.Ed.2d 652 (1972); Inmates of the Attica Correctional Facility v. Rockefeller, 453 F.2d 12 (2d Cir. 1971); Sostre v. McGinnis, *supra.* When one considers that we are powerless to reduce a prison sentence no matter how "disproportionate" the sentence may be to the offense, see, *e. g.,* X. v. United States, 454 F.2d 255 (2d Cir. 1971) (Hays, Circuit Judge, concurring), there seems to be no adequate ground for our reviewing the loss of good time solely because the punishment appears excessive.

4. GOOD TIME FOR JAIL INMATES

ROYSTER V. MCGINNIS
332 F. SUPP. 973 (1971)
United States District Court, Southern District of New York, *reversed,* 41 U.S.L. Week 4259 (U.S., Feb. 21, 1973)

LASKER, District Judge.

Two New York State prisoners have brought this class action seeking a declaratory judgment that Section 230(3) of the New York Correction Law, McKinney's Consol.Laws, c. 43, under which their "good time" was computed, is unconstitutional and an injunction against the alleged discriminatory practices pursued by defendants in application of that statute.

Plaintiffs attack the constitutionality of the provision in § 230(3) which denies state prisoners good time credit for the period of their pre-sentence incarceration in county jail. They contend that the denial of such good time credit deprives them of equal protection in violation of the Fourteenth Amendment by discriminating against those prisoners who cannot afford or are not granted bail prior to trial and sentencing. . . .

There is no doubt that by its express wording Section 230 mandates the denial of good time credit for the time plaintiffs served in county jail awaiting trial and sentencing. . . .

The burden of plaintiffs' complaint is that Section 230(3) of the Correction Law violates the Fourteenth Amendment because it denies equal protection of the law to those persons who cannot afford to obtain bail (or are not granted bail) between arrest and sentence and so must serve time in jail awaiting judgment. Plaintiffs argue that whereas those fortunate enough to obtain bail prior to sentence are rewarded with a full allowance of good time credit for the entire period which they ultimately spend in custody (in state prison), those defendants (indigents and otherwise) who are jailed between arrest and sentence because of their inability to furnish bail are denied good time credit for the time spent in county jail and must content themselves with the partial measure of credit allotted to them for the period of their state prison confinement alone. Such a difference in treatment between persons sentenced to state prison for like terms of imprisonment smacks of discrimination on its face.

Thus, the real question, and indeed the only question, before the court is whether a rational basis exists for the distinction made by § 230(3) between jail and non-jail defendants in the awarding of good time credit. We find the requisite rationality lacking. . . .

HAYS, Circuit Judge (dissenting):

If a classification made by a state has some reasonable basis it does not violate the equal protection clause. Dandridge v. Williams, 397 U.S. 471, 90 S.Ct. 1153, 25 L.Ed.2d 497 (1970).

There seems to me to be a reasonable ground for distinguishing in the award of good time credit between time spent in state prison under the supervision of the state prison authorities and time spent in county jail under the supervision of local authorities. It was surely not wholly arbitrary for the legislature to provide that the Parole Board should have the power to act upon a prisoner's application only after the prisoner has spent a fixed proportion of his sentence in a place where his conduct has been under the observation of state prison officials rather than in a local jail.

Under the guise of applying constitutional principles federal judges are increasingly taking over from the states the administration of state prison systems. In this case, as in a number of others recently decided, the assumption of these new duties appears to be based rather on the judges' conviction that they can administer state prisons more wisely than can the state authorities, and not on any compelling constitutional considerations.

Supreme Court of the United States

MR. JUSTICE POWELL delivered the opinion of the Court.

The question before us concerns the constitutionality of § 230 (3) of the New York Correction Law which denied appellee state prisoners "good time" credit for their presentence incarceration in county jails. Appellees claim that disallowing such credit to them while permitting credit up to the full period of ultimate incarceration for state prisoners who were released on bail prior to sentencing deprived them of equal protection of the laws. The three-judge District Court, one judge dissenting, upheld their claim, 332 F. Supp. 973 (1971). The State appealed and we noted probable jurisdiction, 405 U.S. 986 (1972). . . .

The State defends the distinction by noting that "state prisons differ from county jails with respect to purpose, usage and availability of facilities." State prisons are "intended to have rehabilitation as a prime purpose and the facilities at these institutions are built and equipped to serve this purpose." The State cites the presence at state prisons of "educational and vocational services such as schools, factories, job training programs and related activities." At argument the State noted: "We have barber shops. We teach trades. We manufacture a lot of goods. . . . Greenhaven State Prison has a textile factory."

We pass no judgment on the success or merits of the State's efforts, but note only that at state prisons a serious rehabilitative program exists. County jails, on the other hand, serve primarily as detention centers. The State asserts they are "neither equipped nor intended to do anything more than detain people awaiting trial and maintain no schools, run no factories and require no work from these inmates. While appellees do point to the existence of some rehabilitative or recreational facilities within some county jails, it is clear that nothing comparable to the State's rehabilitative effort exists.

These significant differences afford the basis for a different treatment within a constitutional framework. We note that the granting of good time credit toward parole eligibility takes into account a prisoner's rehabilitative performance. Section 230 (2) of the New York Correction Law authorizes such credit against the minimum parole date "for good conduct *and efficient and willing performance of duties assigned* [emphasis added]." The regulations of the New York Department of Correction, 7 N.Y.C.R.R. 260.1 (a), state that: "The opportunity to earn good behavior allowances offers inmates a tangible reward for *positive efforts* made during incarceration [emphasis added]." As the statute and regulations contemplate state evaluation of an inmate's progress towards rehabilitation, in awarding good time, it is reasonable not to award such time for pretrial detention in a county jail where no systematic rehabilitative programs exist and where the prisoner's conduct and performance are not even observed and evaluated by the responsible state prison officials. Further, it would hardly be appropriate for the State to undertake in the pretrial detention period programs to rehabilitate a man still clothed with a presumption of innocence. In short, an inmate in county jail is neither under the supervision of the State Correction Department nor participating in the State's rehabilitative programs. Where there is no evaluation by state officials and little or no rehabilitative participation for anyone to evaluate, there is a rational justification for declining to give good time credit. . . .

As the challenged classification here rationally promotes the legitimate desire of the state legislature to afford state prison officials an adequate opportunity to evaluate both an inmate's conduct and his rehabilitative progress before he is eligible for parole, the decision of the District Court is

Reversed.

MR. JUSTICE DOUGLAS, with whom MR. JUSTICE MARSHALL concurs, dissenting.

Under § 230 (3) of the New York Correction Law a prisoner loses "good time" as punishment for offenses against the discipline of the prison. The statutory appearance of inmates before a parole board is computed by allowance of up to 10 days for "good conduct" each month under the law governing appellees. No "good time" credit is allowed, however, for the period of their presentence incarceration in a county jail. Thus two prisoners—one out on bail or personal recognizance pending trial and the other confined in jail while awaiting trial—are treated differently when it comes to parole, though each is convicted of the same crime and receives the identical sentence. The result, as the opinion of the Court makes plain, is that appellees are required to wait some months longer before they may appear before the parole board than do those out on bail or on personal recognizance pending trial but sentenced to the same term for the same crime.

The "good time" deduction is not based on progress toward rehabilitation but as an inducement to inhibit bad conduct. That is what the three-judge court held in 332 F. Supp. 973. That construction accurately reflects New York's interpretation of § 230 (3). The court in *Perez* v. *Follette,* 58 Misc. 2d 319, said:

> "The policy underlying the discretionary grant of good time reductions is clear. The attitude and conduct of prisoners should improve if they are offered an incentive for good and productive behavior while at the same time the fact that reductions can be withheld will inhibit bad conduct." *Id.*, at 321. . . .

The claim that "good time" is correlated to rehabilitative programs that only prisons have is the red herring in this litigation. The District Court exposed the fallacy in that rationale. Since the "good time" credit is to induce good behavior by prisoners while they are confined, the place of their confinement becomes irrelevant. Jail time allowance is allowed those confined in county penitentiaries. § 203 (3). And, as I have said, jail time is credited in computing a prisoner's statutory release date.

It would seem that the "good time" provision in § 230 (3) is used capriciously, since it is allowed in cases not dissimilar to the present one.

After all is said and done, the discrimination in the present case is a statutory one levelled against those too poor to raise bail and unable to obtain release on personal recognizance. See *People* v. *Deegan,* 56 Misc. 2d 567, 289 N.Y.S. 2d 285. That is the real rub in the present case. . . .

If "good time" were related to rehabilitative progress, I would agree that the law passes muster under the Equal Protection Clause of the Fourteenth Amendment. But since "good time" is disallowed only to those who cannot raise bail or obtain release on personal recognizance, the discrimination is plainly invidious. . . .

The present case is on the periphery of one of the most critical problems in criminal law enforcement.

The important issue involved in this case is not when and whether a prisoner is released. It concerns only the time when the parole board may give a hearing. To speed up the time of that hearing for those rich or influential enough to get bail or release on personal recognizance and to delay the time of the hearing for those without the means to buy a bail bond or the influence or prestige that will give release on personal recognizance emphasizes the invidious discrimination at work in § 230 (3).

5. GOOD TIME AND JOB CLASSIFICATION

COLEN V. NORTON
335 F. SUPP. 1316 (1972)
United States District Court, District of Connecticut

ZAMPANO, District Judge.

This petition . . . raises interesting questions with respect to the power of prison officials to remove an inmate from industrial or meritorious good time status.

While it is settled law that the grant or

denial of good time credits rests within the sound discretion of the penal authorities, it also has been emphasized that judicial intervention is warranted if that discretion is abused by a disregard of the rules, regulations and policies of the Bureau of Prisons. . . .

The petitioner is an inmate at the Federal Correctional Institution in Danbury, Connecticut. In October 1970, on the basis of his work in the prison's power plant he was placed on industrial good time status pursuant to 18 U.S.C. § 4162. Sometime prior to May 1971, he was assigned to drive a truck into Danbury daily to deliver and pick up inmates working in the city under the Community Work Release program. On these trips he was permitted to have his evening meal in a local diner.

On May 22, 1971, petitioner completed his afternoon run into Danbury and stopped for dinner at a restaurant. There he met his wife and later was seen to kiss her once in the parking lot of the restaurant. As a result, he was the subject of a disciplinary report on the ground that the visit with his wife was unauthorized and a violation of prison rules.

Four days later the petitioner was presented before an Adjustment Committee composed of three prison officials who convened to consider the charge made in the disciplinary report. At the hearing petitioner denied he violated any prison regulations, requested that certain witnesses be called before the Committee, and sought the assistance of counsel. In short, the petitioner demanded the same rights accorded an inmate whose good conduct time is being considered for forfeiture. These rights include the appearance and cross-examination of witnesses, the reporting of the hearing, and the assistance of a member of the staff to represent the inmate. Policy Statement 7400.6, Bureau of Prisons, § 3 (December 1, 1966).

All the petitioner's requests were denied. The Committee found against the contentions of the petitioner; as a consequence he lost his driving job, six days of statutory good time, the privilege of visiting in the prison's park area for 90 days, and the opportunity to earn industrial good time for the next five months until October 1971. . . .

The only issue that merits attention is whether the prison authorities were empowered under applicable regulations to remove the petitioner from his meritorious good time status prospectively, i.e., for five months following the date of his infraction of the prison rules.

There is no statute or regulation precisely on point. However, 18 U.S.C. § 4162 and two Bureau of Prisons policy statements provide helpful guidelines. Section 4162 states that industrial good time shall be allowed in the discretion of the Attorney General "under the same terms and conditions" as statutory good time under 18 U.S.C. § 4161.

Statutory good time is awarded to a prisoner if he faithfully observes all of the prison rules and has not been subjected to punishment. Misconduct may result in the withholding or forfeiture of good time. . . .

Industrial or meritorious good time is allowed for exceptional work performance as well as productive participation in correctional treatment programs. . . .

Respondent claims that petitioner's loss of good time was neither a forfeiture nor a withholding, but a third form of punishment which is called a "prospective removal from meritorious good time status." It is further argued that an inmate may be so removed without procedural safeguards because there is no statutory mandate compelling prison authorities to grant industrial good time. While submitting that the matter is entirely within the discretion of prison officials, the respondent does concede that this discretion may not be exercised in a capricious or discriminatory manner, or contrary to the policy statements of the Bureau of Prisons.

However, the Court is of the opinion that the forfeiture or withholding of industrial good time should be treated in the same manner procedurally as the methods employed in the forfeiture or withholding of statutory good time. This interpretation has the advantage of having one set of rules governing the loss of the two types of an inmate's good time, and is conducive to promoting stability and fairness in the administration of prison affairs. In addition, it is consistent with the apparent intent of the Bureau of Prisons to limit the removal of a prisoner's name from the meritorious good time status list, Classification Form 13, to one month. See Policy Statement 7600.50A, supra, wherein it is directed that an inmate whose name has been "removed for cause *during the month*" (emphasis supplied) from meritorious good time status shall have an "R" placed next to his name on the classification list. This is not to say, of course, that the Bureau of Prisons may not promulgate separate different regulations solely applicable to industrial good time.

Accordingly, since under the rules statutory good time may not be withheld or removed beyond that time "creditable for the single month during which the violation occurs," it follows that the petitioner's industrial or meritorious good time could not be withheld or removed beyond the month of May, 1971.

Chapter Nine

THE RULE OF LAW AND PRISON LIFE: THE ROLE OF LAWYER AND JUDGE IN INSTITUTIONAL CONTROL OF THE INMATE POPULATION

A. Daily Life

UNITED STATES EX REL POPE v.
WILLIAMS
326 F. SUPP. 279 (1971)
United States District Court, Eastern District of Pennsylvania

LORD, JR., Chief Judge.

Presently before the Court is petitioner's motion to amend, join, revise and correct his complaint. While this action was initially entitled criminal complaint, plaintiff, who is a state court prisoner, has entitled this petition Civil Rights Complaint.

Plaintiff, who has filed with this Court at least fourteen (14) separate actions, may well be the most litigious individual this Court has encountered in over sixteen years on the federal bench. The Court finds this motion, as well as the initial complaint, to be completely without merit and ably demonstrates the increasingly large number of totally frivolous petitions from state court prisoners which are currently burdening the Court and hindering it from effectively performing its other functions. . . .

The substance of the original petition charged the defendant Williams, a guard at the institution, "of maliciously, flagrantly, willfully asserting his own sense of justice * * *" As was the case with the claims against Officer Benedict and the Board of Probation, this claim involves another "reprisal" against him. In this incident plaintiff alleges that the defendant, after excusing him from work for completing the job assignment, "call[ed] me back to work and ordered me to polish the Brass Facing of a door—work in an area not previously assigned to me." In an effort to avoid being repetitious the Court will merely note that this is again exactly that type of problem which relates solely to the internal administration of the state prison. The Court can see no violation of a constitutionally protected right in requiring a prisoner to polish a brass facing plate whether it was originally assigned to him or not. This Court cannot interfere with such internal administrative matters. For this reason the Court will dismiss this action. . . .

RHODES V. SIGLER
448 F.2d 1237 (1971)
United States Court of Appeals, Eighth Circuit

MATTHES, Chief Judge.

In an attempt to resolve a controversy between appellant, a Nebraska state prisoner, and the Nebraska Penal and Correctional Complex over $2.46, appellant filed a complaint in the United States District Court for the District of Nebraska. He alleged jurisdiction under 42 U.S.C. § 1983 and 28 U.S.C. §§ 1331 and 1343(3).

The district court dismissed the complaint with prejudice on the authority of Sigler v. Lowrie, 404 F.2d 659 (8th Cir. 1968). However, the court granted a certificate of probable cause and the matter is here for determination.

Manifestly, the question whether appellant was indebted to the prison complex in the amount of $2.46 is one to be resolved by the prison authorities through appropriate procedures. Certainly, the complaint fails to allege the violation of a federally protected right. It is settled doctrine that except in extreme cases, the courts should not interfere with the internal operations of a prison and with enforcement of reasonable prison rules and regulations.

. . . Respectable authority also teaches that 42 U.S.C. § 1983, the civil rights statute, does not embrace as a civil right the deprivation of a mere property right.

By way of addendum, we take occasion to observe that federal courts stand ready to adjudicate any controversy within their jurisdiction having its roots in the deprivation of a federally protected right. Where, as here, however, it plainly appears from the complaint that the prisoner's claim does not emanate from a violation of a constitutional or other federally protected privilege, the time of the federal courts who are burdened with cases presenting meritorious problems, should not be encroached upon in an attempt to secure an adjudication of matters which best can and should be disposed of through administrative prison procedures.

Furthermore, we observe as we did in United States v. Dennison, 437 F.2d 439 (8th Cir. 1971), that where a prisoner's application for relief is demonstratively devoid of substance so that an appeal would be futile, the district court should exercise restraint in permitting the petitioner to pursue his grievances in the court of appeals. The appeal is dismissed as legally frivolous.

SEALE V. MANSON
326 F. SUPP. 1375 (1971)
United States District Court, District of Connecticut

ZAMPANO, District Judge.

. . . The plaintiff Bobby Seale is incarcerated in the Montville Correctional Center. . . .

The plaintiff Seale challenges the validity of the rule prohibiting beards and goatees. . . .

Of particular significance in this case, and a factor that weighs heavily on the scale, is that the plaintiffs are unconvicted detainees whom the law presumes innocent. Unlike convicted persons, the State's only asserted interest with respect to these inmates is to insure their appearance at trial, Davis v. Lindsay, 321 F. Supp. 1134, 1139 (S.D.N.Y.1970); any limitation on the fundamental rights of unconvicted persons must find justification in the legitimate advancement of that interest. Unconvicted detainees may be treated as convicts only to the extent the security, internal order, health, and discipline of the prison demand; considerations of rehabilitation, deterrence, or punishment are not material.

Prison Directive 2.21 of the Connecticut Department of Corrections reads as follows:

> Inmates may wear sideburns to the bottom of the earlobe. Muttonchops and flares will not be allowed. Hair should be neatly trimmed at all times. Beards and goatees

will not be allowed, but mustaches may be worn if they follow the line of the upper lip and do not extend beyond the corner of the lip.

Upon his refusal to shave off his short ¼" beard and goatee, Seale was placed in administrative segregation in the Connecticut Correctional Institution at Montville. He contends that, as an unconvicted detainee, Directive 2.21 cannot constitutionally be enforced against him. The Court agrees.

The threshold question presented is whether Seale has raised an issue which reaches constitutional dimensions, i. e., whether a citizen who is not incarcerated has a constitutional right to wear a beard and goatee. Most courts which have considered this issue have decided that an individual's head and facial hair style are not sufficiently communicative to warrant protection under the First Amendment, but do constitute a personal liberty which is protected under the Fourteenth Amendment. Since a federally protected right has been established, the remaining issue concerns the reasonableness of a regulation which withdraws that right in the case of a state criminal defendant incarcerated in lieu of bail.

The only justification advanced by the defendants in support of the Directive was that beards and goatees are a potential health hazard in the spread of lice among the prisoners. Medical evidence was submitted in the form of a letter, dated December 4, 1968, from Dr. Franklin M. Foote, Commissioner of Health, which reads as follows:

> Beards and long hair constitute only a potential health hazard but not an actual one except when body lice, head lice or crab lice are present in the institution.
> If either the lice or nits are found on inmates there would be justification to require the man to be clean shaven and have closely trimmed hair because of the possibility that lice might transmit various diseases. However, during periods when no lice or nits are found by the medical personnel I believe it would be difficult to justify requiring all the inmates to be clean shaven.

However, there was no evidence that lice or other body vermin exist as a problem at the Montville jail.

Under these circumstances, it is the opinion of the Court that the Directive prohibiting beards and goatees cannot constitutionally be applied to Seale for the following reasons:

1. Seale has been placed in administrative segregation solely because of his violation of a prison rule which is not reasonably related to his status as an unconvicted detainee;
2. It is clear that Seale's goatee is not a health hazard; it is little more than a fringe around the mouth;
3. No problem of lice, nits, or other body vermin exists at the Montville jail or any other state institution;
4. Dr. Foote's medical opinion states that, absent the presence of lice or nits in the institution, "it would be difficult to justify requiring all of the inmates to be clean shaven;"
5. Former Commissioner MacDougall believed that there should not be a prohibition against all types of beards and goatees and, indeed, urged the Council of Corrections to rescind the present Directive;
6. The defendants make no claim that a beard or goatee is a danger to security or that there exists a nexus between the Directive and the ever present need in a prison to make prompt and accurate identifications of inmates.

This is not to say, however, that the defendants are prohibited from enacting a reasonable directive governing the length, width or style of a beard or goatee to insure desirable health objectives in a prison environment. Present rules regulate the length and shape of hair, sideburns and mustaches, and are unchallenged in these proceedings. It would appear that similar regulations with respect to beards and goatees could be promulgated and enforced by the same methods. Moreover, as Dr. Foote points out, in a situation where lice or other body vermin constitute a health hazard, emergency measures, including clean shaven faces, may well be required.

B. Sexual Relations

PAYNE V. DISTRICT OF COLUMBIA
253 F.2d 867 (1958)
United States Court of Appeals, District of Columbia Circuit

PER CURIAM.

Appellant sued for damages and for injunctive and declarative relief to require appellees to permit conjugal visits to her husband and private accommodations during the time he is lawfully committed to the District of Columbia Jail under a conviction for housebreaking. His incarceration is not challenged. She claims she has been denied rights without due process as to her.

The District Court dismissed the complaint of appellant for failure to state a claim upon which relief could be granted.

We find no error in the dismissal and the judgment of the District Court is therefore Affirmed.

TARLTON V. CLARK
441 F.2d 384 (1971), cert. den., 403 U.S. 934 (1971)
United States Court of Appeals, Fifth Circuit

PER CURIAM.

This appeal is taken from an order of the district court denying the petition for mandamus of a federal prisoner. We affirm for the reasons which are well stated in the order appealed from, which is appended to this opinion.
Affirmed.

Appendix

Petitioner, a federal prisoner confined at the United States Penitentiary, Atlanta, Georgia, has submitted in forma pauperis a petition for writ of mandamus.

Petitioner contends that the United States Bureau of Prisons have denied his Eighth Amendment right under the United States Constitution in that he is not allowed to have sexual relations with his wife during her visit with him at the United States Penitentiary, Atlanta, Georgia.

While other nations have experimented with the idea of "sexual visitations" for prisoners in confinement, the court knows of no case which requires or permits such practices in United States institutions. In any event, such claim would not come up to the level of a federal constitutional right so as to be cognizable as a basis for relief in federal court.

Moreover, such personal grievance is one which would have to be presented, in the first instance, by administrative remedies available to the prisoner with the Bureau of Prisons. The courts have reportedly held that grievances relating to the case and management of prisoners should be presented and processed in such manner.

COLUMBUS B. HOPPER

The Conjugal Visit*

The Mississippi State Penitentiary is located in Sunflower County on the old Parchman plantation. Parchman, as the institution is called, is probably the world's largest penal farm system. Although a state penitentiary, it is essentially a large plantation comprising almost 22,000 acres of rich delta farm land, which the inmates till while repaying a debt to society. After a long period of experimentation in various penal adaptations, Mississippi, during the years from 1895 to 1906, made the

* From Columbus B. Hopper, "The Conjugal Visit at Mississippi State Penitentiary," 53 *Journal of Criminal Law, Criminology and Police Science* 340 (1962). Reprinted by special permission of the *Journal of Criminal Law, Criminology and Police Science*. Copyright © 1962 by Northwestern University School of Law, Vol. 53, No. 3.

transition to the penal plantation system, an adaptation which from all indications has been well-suited to the economy and culture of the state. . . .

The conjugal visit at Parchman is apparently unique in United States penal practice. Although the conjugal visit has been proposed from time to time as a partial solution to the problem of sexual adjustment in prison, it is generally concluded that the conjugal visit would be wholly unrealistic in American culture and that it would have no rehabilitative influence, but would tend instead to heighten rather than relieve tension in the prison. As a consequence of this reasoning, although sexual problems are among the greatest which confront prison administrators, prisons in the United States have been evaluated as having "failed rather signally to develop any satisfactory solution to sex problems and the wardens have believed they were more or less powerless to do anything about such matters." Although deprivation of marital contacts in other countries is less likely to be made a part of punishment than in the United States, with the exception of Mexico, most countries throughout the world do not favor conjugal visits within the prison. Thus conjugal visits have found little favor among prison administrators in general and especially among prison administrators in the United States.

Criticisms of the conjugal visit are in the main well taken. In the United States, the chief objection is that such visits would be incompatible with existing mores, since the visits seem to emphasize only the physical satisfactions of sex. Another objection is that married inmates who could engage in conjugal visits satisfactorily are those who can adjust best to prison life even without sex relations; likewise, those inmates who present the greatest sexual problems, i.e., homosexuals and other sex deviates, are the ones least likely to benefit from conjugal visits. Additional objections are that conjugal visits offer no solution to the sexual tension of either single male prisoners or female prisoners, and that wives may become pregnant, creating further problems for both the state and the prisoners, especially in the case of long-term prisoners. The modern professional consensus in the United States is well stated by Tappan as follows:

> So long as the society requires under its official mores that youths delay heterosexual expression for several years after they reach maturity, we shall probably not provide for normal sexuality in prison. So long as we consider it appropriate to continue numerous forms of deprivation in our correctional institutions, we shall make no exception for sex.

In view of such cogent objections to the conjugal visit, one would expect that it would be practically impossible for such a system to develop in the United States. Nevertheless, the conjugal visit shows considerable evidence of becoming an important and integral part of the Mississippi State Penitentiary.

PIRI THOMAS

Sex in Prison*

Everyone talked about it, most of us indulged in it solo, and some guys took their kicks with each other.

The talk was almost always reminiscences. One of the best of the bullshitters was a big con we called Ching. He had a very vivid memory. "Now dig this," he would say, biting his lower lip and inhaling a long, shuddering breath of jailhouse passion, "this broad's name was Dolores, and she was real fine," and he would paint a dream picture for us. Each of us would get a different picture of Dolores. She would be a blonde, or dark, or Puerto Rican, or whatever we wanted.

But the real action was between men. If you weren't careful, if you didn't stand up for yourself and say, "Hands off, motherfucker," you became a piece of ass. And if you got by this hassle, there always was the temptation of

---

* Piri Thomas, *Down These Mean Streets* 262–63 (1967). Copyright © Alfred A. Knopf, Inc. Reprinted with permission.

wanting to cop some ass. I had a Negro named Claude after me to make him my steady. "Look, why won't you be my man?" he asked me. "I'll give you the moon, the stars, the world, the uni—"

"Shove it," I hissed out. "Cut the shit out. Stop making like you was a for-real broad and get your black ass from here."

"I'll give you cigarettes, anything, baby; I'll keep you real good," he insisted.

I looked past the green bars at Claude and saw a woman's pleading, tormented face. *He wants to buy a daddy-o,* I thought. *But I ain't gonna break. One time. That's all I have to do it. Just one time and it's gone time. I'll be screwing faggots as fast as I can get them. I'm not gonna get institutionalized. I don't want to lose my hatred of this damn place. Once you lose the hatred, then the can's got you. You can do all the time in the world and it doesn't bug you. You go outside and you make it; you return to prison and you make it there, too. No sweat, no pain. No. Outside is real; inside is a lie. Outside is one kind of life, inside is another. And you make them the same if you lose your hate of prison.* "Claude," I said, "if I gotta break your fuckin' jaw, I will. They've put a wall around me for fifteen years, but I've got something real outside, and it makes no difference when I get out, married or not, she's mine, and there'll be no past for the two of us, just a stone present and a cool future. Meanwhile, I'll jack off if I gotta, but I ain't gonna marry you, faggot, no matter what."

C. Medical Treatment

MARTINEZ V. MANCUSI
443 F.2d 921 (1970)
United States Court of Appeals, Second Circuit

LUMBARD, Chief Judge:

This is an action under the Federal Civil Rights Act, 42 U.S.C. § 1983, for willful violation by prison officials of appellant's right to adequate medical care. The District Court for the Western District of New York dismissed appellant's complaint on the ground that the facts alleged were insufficient under the Civil Rights Act to state a cause of action. We reverse the district court's dismissal of the complaint and, without deciding the merits of appellant's complaint, remand for a hearing, at which appellant should be given the opportunity to show the responsibility and liability which his allegations assert....

Appellant Martinez, a young inmate of Attica Prison, suffers from infantile paralysis of the right leg....

Martinez's allegations in this case meet the criteria of *Hegstrum* and *Hyde* for an Eighth Amendment violation and thus a cause of action under the Civil Rights Act. The alleged conduct of the prison authorities in removing him from the hospital before he was ready to be moved, despite the surgeons' orders and without obtaining a discharge, was more than "mere negligence." If proven, it would constitute a deliberate indifference to, and defiance of, the express instructions of the operating surgeons and the hospital attendants. According to the allegations, the guards came to the hospital at the direct order of the prison warden; and in open disobedience of the warnings of the person or persons in charge of appellant, they handcuffed appellant and made him walk....

Once he was returned to Attica, Martinez alleges, he was discharged from the prison hospital by defendant Dr. Williams after only one day, was required to stand, and was not given adequate facilities or the prescribed medication. All this was done despite the surgeons' direct orders to the contrary. Dr. Williams argues that he did not know of those orders and did not know that appellant had not sufficiently recovered to return to prison life, and so his actions were merely negligent. But his alleged refusal to check with Meyer Hospital and with the surgeons who were handling appellant there may be shown to have been a deliberate indifference to appellant's condition and to what the surgeons' orders might have been.

Moreover, the doctor's alleged misconduct in this case is not, as it was in *Hyde*, a matter of medical judgment. Under the allegations here made, his actions were in deliberate disregard of orders and hospital requirements. Obviously, courts cannot go around second-guessing doctors. But neither can they ignore gross misconduct by a doctor, especially when it violates specific orders by the specialists in charge of the case.

Clearly, then, the defendants' conduct, as alleged by Martinez, was more than mere negligence or poor medical judgment; it is charged to have been deliberate indifference to, and defiance of, explicit medical instructions, resulting in serious and obvious injuries. Although we express no opinion on whether appellant should ultimately prevail in his suit, we hold that the facts as alleged are sufficient to constitute a violation of his constitutional rights and thus to state a cause of action under the Civil Rights Act; hence they are sufficient to warrant a hearing on the question. If advised to do so, Martinez should be given leave to file an amended complaint within a reasonable time.

We commend assigned counsel, Herman Schwartz, Esq., for his very able representation of appellant Martinez.

Reversed and remanded.

D. Racial Discrimination

LEE V. WASHINGTON
390 U.S. 333 (1968)
Supreme Court of the United States

PER CURIAM.

This appeal challenges a decree of a three-judge District Court declaring that certain Alabama statutes violate the Fourteenth Amendment to the extent that they require segregation of the races in prisons and jails, and establishing a schedule for desegregation of these institutions. The State's contentions that Rule 23 of the Federal Rules of Civil Procedure, which relates to class actions, was violated in this case and that the challenged statutes are not unconstitutional are without merit. The remaining contention of the State is that the specific orders directing desegregation of prisons and jails make no allowance for the necessities of prison security and discipline, but we do not so read the "Order, Judgment and Decree" of the District Court, which when read as a whole we find unexceptionable.

The judgment is affirmed.

MR. JUSTICE BLACK, MR. JUSTICE HARLAN, and MR. JUSTICE STEWART, concurring.

In joining the opinion of the Court, we wish to make explicit something that is left to be gathered only by implication from the Court's opinion. This is that prison authorities have the right, acting in good faith and in particularized circumstances, to take into account racial tensions in maintaining security, discipline, and good order in prisons and jails. We are unwilling to assume that state or local prison authorities might mistakenly regard such an explicit pronouncement as evincing any dilution of this Court's firm commitment to the Fourteenth Amendment's prohibition of racial discrimination.

E. Religious Freedom

COOPER V. PATE
378 U.S. 546 (1964)
Supreme Court of the United States

PER CURIAM.

The motion for leave to proceed *in forma pauperis* and the petition for a writ of certiorari are granted.

The petitioner, an inmate at the Illinois State Penitentiary, brought an action under 28 U.S.C. § 1343 and 42 U.S.C. § 1983, § 1979 of the Revised Statutes, alleging that solely because of his religious beliefs he was denied permission to purchase certain religious publications and denied other privileges enjoyed by other prisoners. The District Court granted the respondent's motion to dismiss for failure to state a claim on which relief could be granted and the Court of Appeals affirmed. 324 F.2d 165 (C. A. 7th Cir.). We reverse the judgment below. Taking as true the allegations of the complaint, as they must be on a motion to dismiss, the complaint stated a cause of action and it was error to dismiss it. See *Pierce* v. *LaVallee,* 293 F. 2d 233 (C. A. 2d Cir.); *Sewell* v. *Pegelow,* 291 F. 2d 196 (C. A. 4th Cir.).

BARNETT V. RODGERS
410 F.2d 995 (1969)
United States Court of Appeals, District of Columbia Circuit

ROBINSON, III, Circuit Judge:

The basic issue before us is the degree to which officials of the District of Columbia Jail are constitutionally compelled to accommodate the dietary laws of the Muslim faith in the bill of fare afforded Muslim inmates. This question became a matter of judicial concern when appellants, Muslim prisoners in the jail, complained of the menu there in essentially similar *pro se* petitions for writs of habeas corpus filed in the District Court. Citing the doctrinal prohibition of their religion against the consumption of swine, appellants alleged that jail authorities had denied their request to "be fed, at least, one full-course pork-free diet once a day and coffee three times daily." Proceeding obviously on the Free Exercise Clause of the First Amendment, they sought an order directing the superintendent of the jail to respect, to that extent, Muslim dietary tenets in the provision of their meals or, alternatively, directing their release from custody on the ground that continued confinement on existing terms constituted cruel and unusual punishment. . . .

Uncontested evidence at the hearing established the scope and strictness of the Muslim injunction against the eating of swine. A Muslim minister testified that the ban is absolute, and extends to all pork products and to all food prepared with pork derivatives. Another Muslim testified that the interdiction "is a life or death matter." "[I]f our lives depend on it," he explained, "we can't eat pork."

The record discloses, however, sharp conflicts in the evidence as to the board available to prisoners unwilling to partake of pork.

. . . While the District Court made no specific finding in this regard, it is evident that pork and pork derivatives eventuate in some form in a substantial number of the meals provided inmates at the jail. Moreover, appellants complain that they do not eat all of the ostensibly non-pork dishes because they cannot always ascertain that they are pork-free. Many of the dishes contain pork in covert forms, and these the menus do not identify, and even if they did they are not generally posted in areas to which prisoners have access. Not knowing what future servings will bring, they cannot anticipate a meal containing pork items by filling up at a previous all-non-pork meal.

When appellants rested their case-in-chief, the District Court granted a defense motion to dismiss. The court found that "[t]he inmate population of the District of Columbia Jail is fed a well balanced and wholesome diet," and that appellants may "by refraining from eating those things that they consider objectionable practice their religion." The court further found that "[t]he diet provided at the * * * Jail is prepared with no special consideration given to any prisoner or religious denomination." We conclude, however, that this disposition failed to take into account factors of the highest relevance to appellants' constitutional claims. We accordingly reverse the dismissal orders appealed from and remand the cases to the District Court for further proceedings.

Our starting point is the teaching of Cantwell v. Connecticut that the First Amendment

> embraces two concepts,—freedom to believe and freedom to act. The first is absolute but, in the nature of things, the second cannot be. Conduct remains subject to regulation for the protection of society.

Nonetheless, when governmental regulation of action within the reach of the First Amendment is challenged, "[i]t is basic that no showing merely of a rational relationship to some colorable [governmental] interest would suffice." Where governmental activity impairs individual ability to abide religious beliefs, two demonstrations become essential to its validity. The first is a clear showing that "any incidental burden on the free exercise of appellant's religion [is] justified by a 'compelling state interest in the regulation of a subject within the State's constitutional power to regulate * * *;' " on this score, "[o]nly the gravest abuses, endangering paramount interests" can engender permissible limitations on free exercise. The second is an equally convincing showing that "no alternative forms of regulation would combat such abuses without infringing First Amendment rights." For "even though the governmental purpose be legitimate and substantial, that purpose cannot be pursued by means that broadly stifle fundamental personal liberties when the end can be more narrowly achieved." However attractive the end to be achieved, the means employed must hoard First Amendment values.

But appellee would have us believe that he need not make these showings because of appellants' status as his prisoners. Such is not our understanding of the law. It is undoubtedly true that, because the exigencies of governing those in prison are different from and greater than those in governing those without, "[l]awful incarceration brings about the necessary withdrawal or limitation of many privileges and rights, a retraction justified by considerations underlying our penal system." "[B]ut it has never been held that upon entering a prison one is entirely bereft of all his civil rights and forfeits every protection of the law." To say that religious freedom may undergo modification in a prison environment is not to say that it can be suppressed or ignored without adequate reason. And although "within the prison society as well as without, the practice of religious beliefs is subject to reasonable regulations, necessary for the protection and welfare of the community involved," the mere fact that government, as a practical matter, stands a better chance of justifying a curtailment of fundamental liberties where prisoners are involved does not eliminate the need for reasons imperatively justifying the particular retraction of rights challenged at bar. Nor does it lessen governmental responsibility to reduce the resulting impact upon those rights to the fullest extent consistent with the justified objective.

The record supports the District Court's findings so far as they go, but an insuperable difficulty emanates from the absence of findings bearing upon the criteria that are constitutionally crucial. There is no finding as to whether any particular "considerations underlying our penal system" warrant the tax on conscience that the jail's food service policies require appellants to endure. Nor is there a finding as to whether that program could not be administered in such a way as to lighten or eliminate its burden on free religious exercise.

And our own scrutiny of the record has revealed little to legally support the program as it is now conducted.

... That penal as well as judicial authorities respond to constitutional duties is vastly important to society as well as the prisoner. Treatment that degrades the inmate, invades his privacy, and frustrates the ability to choose pursuits through which he can manifest himself and gain self-respect erodes the very foundations upon which he can prepare for a socially useful life. Religion in prison subserves the rehabilitative function by providing an area within which the inmate may reclaim his dignity and reassert his individuality. But, quite ironically, while government provides prisoners with chapels, ministers, free sacred texts and symbols, there subsists a danger that prison personnel will demand from inmates the same obeisance in the religious sphere that more rightfully they may require in other aspects of prison life. This danger is not chimerical. In recent years, against the directives of the District of Columbia Commissioners, Muslim inmates in the custody of the Department of Corrections have been deprived of the most basic religious liberties, which only by court order have been restored.

We do not reach the question whether appellee has violated the Constitution here. We do hold that the District Court erred in dismissing appellants' petitions without determining whether the impediments to appellants' observance of their dietary creed have compelling justifications, and whether the governmental purposes and operations responsible for those impediments could feasibly be "pursued by means that [less] broadly stifle fundamental personal liberties."

We remand these cases to the District Court for further proceedings to determine whether the provision of meals at the District Jail can be squared with constitutional requirements, and to award its decision accordingly. In deference to appellee's admitted authority within the limits set by the Constitution, the court will, as the first step, afford him the opportunity to present a plan which he believes meets constitutional requirements.

Reversed and remanded.

F. Access to Lawyers and Courts

Ex Parte Hull
312 U.S. 546 (1941)
Supreme Court of the United States

MR. JUSTICE MURPHY delivered the opinion of the Court.

In November, 1940, petitioner prepared a petition for writ of habeas corpus and exhibits to file in this Court. He took the papers to a prison official and requested him to notarize them. The official refused and informed petitioner that the papers and a registered letter to the clerk of this Court concerning them would not be accepted for mailing. Although the papers were not notarized, petitioner then delivered them to his father for mailing outside the prison but guards confiscated them. Several days later, petitioner again attempted to mail a letter concerning his case to the clerk of this Court. It was intercepted and sent to the legal investigator for the state parole board.[1] Apparently neither of the letters was returned to the petitioner,[2] and the papers taken from his father were not returned until late in December.

Petitioner then prepared another document which he somehow managed to have his father, as "agent," file with the clerk of this Court on December 26, 1940. In this document petitioner detailed his efforts to file the papers confiscated by prison officials, contended that he was therefore unlawfully restrained, and prayed that he be released.

On January 6, 1941, we issued a rule to show cause why leave to file a petition for writ of habeas corpus should not be granted. The warden filed a return to the rule setting forth the circumstances of the two convictions, the proceedings of the parole board, and numerous exhibits. In justification of the action preventing petitioner from filing his papers or communicating with this Court, the warden alleged that in November, 1940, he had published a regulation providing that: "All legal documents, briefs, petitions, motions, habeas corpus proceedings and appeals will first have to be submitted to the institutional welfare office and if favorably acted upon be then referred to Perry A. Maynard, legal investigator to the Parole Board, Lansing, Michigan. Documents submitted to Perry A. Maynard, if in his opinion are properly drawn, will be directed to the court designated or will be referred back to the inmate."

In answer, petitioner filed a "Response to the Return" which again challenged the validity of this regulation and which contained numerous exhibits. One of the exhibits was the petition for writ of habeas corpus taken from petitioner's father. In brief, this petition assailed the legality of petitioner's imprisonment under the second conviction on the ground that he had been denied procedural due process.

The first question concerns the effect of the regulation quoted in the warden's return.

The regulation is invalid. The considerations that prompted its formulation are not without merit, but the state and its officers may not abridge or impair petitioner's right to apply to a federal court for a writ of habeas corpus. Whether a petition for writ of habeas corpus addressed to a federal court is properly drawn and what allegations it must contain are questions for that court alone to determine. . . .

---

[1] About a week later petitioner received the following reply from the legal investigator: "Your letter of November 18, 1940, addressed to the Clerk of the United States Supreme Court, has been referred to the writer for reply. In the first place your application in its present form would not be acceptable to that court. You must file a petition for whatever relief you are seeking and state your reasons therefor, together with a memorandum brief. Your petition must be verified under oath and supported by proper affidavits, if any you have. Your letter was, no doubt, intercepted for the reason that it was deemed to be inadequate and which undoubtedly accounts for the fact that it found its way to my desk."

Apparently the legal investigator serves as attorney and advisor to the state parole board. His functions with respect to legal documents of prison inmates appear more fully from the prison regulation quoted hereafter.

[2] Neither of the letters reached the clerk of this Court. On December 12, 1940, petitioner requested the prison superintendent of mail to trace the registered letter since he had not received the return receipt which accompanied it. The assistant superintendent replied: "This was mailed thru Perry Maynard by orders from Warden." Apparently the legal investigator made no reply.

JOHNSON V. AVERY
393 U.S. 483 (1969)
Supreme Court of the United States

MR. JUSTICE FORTAS delivered the opinion of the Court.

I

Petitioner is serving a life sentence in the Tennessee State Penitentiary. In February 1965 he was transferred to the maximum security building in the prison for violation of a prison regulation which provides:

> No inmate will advise, assist or otherwise contract to aid another, either with or without a fee, to prepare Writs or other legal matters. It is not intended that an innocent man be punished. When a man believes he is unlawfully held or illegally convicted, he should prepare a brief or state his complaint in letter form and address it to his lawyer or a judge. A formal Writ is not necessary to receive a hearing. False charges or untrue complaints may be punished. Inmates are forbidden to set themselves up as practitioners for the purpose of promoting a business of writing Writs.

In July 1965 petitioner filed in the United States District Court for the Middle District of Tennessee a "motion for law books and a typewriter," in which he sought relief from his confinement in the maximum security building. The District Court treated this motion as a petition for a writ of habeas corpus and, after a hearing, ordered him released from disciplinary confinement and restored to the status of an ordinary prisoner. The District Court held that the regulation was void because it in effect barred illiterate prisoners from access to federal habeas corpus and conflicted with 28 U. S. C. § 2242. 252 F. Supp. 783.

By the time the District Court order was entered, petitioner had been transferred from the maximum security building, but he had been put in a disciplinary cell block in which he was entitled to fewer privileges than were given ordinary prisoners. Only when he promised to refrain from assistance to other inmates was he restored to regular prison conditions and privileges. At a second hearing, held in March 1966, the District Court explored these issues concerning the compliance of the prison officials with its initial order. After the hearing, it reaffirmed its earlier order.

The State appealed. The Court of Appeals for the Sixth Circuit reversed, concluding that the regulation did not unlawfully conflict with the federal right of habeas corpus. According to the Sixth Circuit, the interest of the State in preserving prison discipline and in limiting the practice of law to licensed attorneys justified whatever burden the regulation might place on access to federal habeas corpus. 382 F. 2d 353.

II

This Court has constantly emphasized the fundamental importance of the writ of habeas corpus in our constitutional scheme, and the Congress has demonstrated its solicitude for the vigor of the Great Writ. The Court has steadfastly insisted that "there is no higher duty than to maintain it unimpaired." *Bowen* v. *Johnston,* 306 U. S. 19, 26 (1939).

Since the basic purpose of the writ is to enable those unlawfully incarcerated to obtain their freedom, it is fundamental that access of prisoners to the courts for the purpose of presenting their complaints may not be denied or obstructed. For example, the Court has held that a State may not validly make the writ available only to prisoners who could pay a $4 filing fee. *Smith* v. *Bennett,* 365 U.S. 708 (1961). And it has insisted that, for the indigent as well as for the affluent prisoner, post-conviction proceedings must be more than a formality. For instance, the State is obligated to furnish prisoners not otherwise able to obtain it, with a transcript or equivalent recordation of prior habeas corpus hearings for use in further proceedings. *Long* v. *District Court,* 385 U.S. 192 (1966). Cf. *Griffin* v. *Illinois,* 351 U.S. 12 (1956).

Tennessee urges, however, that the contested regulation in this case is justified as a part of the State's disciplinary administration of the prisons. There is no doubt that discipline and administration of state detention facilities are state functions. They are subject to federal authority only where paramount federal constitutional or statutory rights supervene. It is clear, however, that in instances where state regulations applicable to inmates of prison facilities conflict with such rights, the regulations may be invalidated.

For example, in *Lee* v. *Washington,* 390 U.S. 333 (1968), the practice of racial segregation of prisoners was justified by the State as necessary to maintain good order and discipline. We held, however, that the practice was constitutionally prohibited, although we were careful to point out that the order of the District Court, which we affirmed, made allowance for "the necessities of prison security and discipline." *Id.,* at 334. And in *Ex parte Hull,* 312 U.S. 546 (1941), this Court invalidated a state regulation which required that habeas corpus petitions first be submitted to prison authorities and then approved by the "legal investigator" to the parole board as "properly drawn" before being transmitted to the court. Here again, the State urged that the requirement was necessary to maintain prison discipline. But this Court held that the regulation violated the principle that "the state and its officers may not abridge or impair petitioner's right to apply to a federal court for a writ of habeas corpus." 312 U.S., at 549. Cf. *Cochran* v. *Kansas,* 316 U.S. 255, 257 (1942).

There can be no doubt that Tennessee could not constitutionally adopt and enforce a rule forbidding illiterate or poorly educated prisoners to file habeas corpus petitions. Here Tennessee has adopted a rule which, in the absence of any other source of assistance for such prisoners, effectively does just that. The District Court concluded that "[f]or all practical purposes, if such prisoners cannot have the assistance of a 'jail-house lawyer,' their possibly valid constitutional claims will never be heard in any court." 252 F. Supp., at 784. The record supports this conclusion.

Jails and penitentiaries include among their inmates a high percentage of persons who are totally or functionally illiterate, whose educational attainments are slight, and whose intelligence is limited. This appears to be equally true of Tennessee's prison facilities.

In most federal courts, it is the practice to appoint counsel in post-conviction proceedings only after a petition for post-conviction relief passes initial judicial evaluation and the court has determined that issues are presented calling for an evidentiary hearing. *E. g., Taylor* v. *Pegelow,* 335 F. 2d 147 (C. A. 4th Cir. 1964); *United States ex rel. Marshall* v. *Wilkins,* 338 F. 2d 404 (C. A. 2d Cir. 1964). See 28 U.S. C. § 1915 (d); R. Sokol, A Handbook of Federal Habeas Corpus 71–73 (1965).

It has not been held that there is any general obligation of the courts, state or federal, to appoint counsel for prisoners who indicate, without more, that they wish to seek post-conviction relief. See, *e. g., Barker* v. *Ohio,* 330 F. 2d 594 (C. A. 6th Cir. 1964). Accordingly, the initial burden of presenting a claim to post-conviction relief usually rests upon the indigent prisoner himself with such help as he can obtain within the prison walls or the prison system. In the case of all except those who are able to help themselves—usually a few old hands or exceptionally gifted prisoners—the prisoner is, in effect, denied access to the courts unless such help is available.

It is indisputable that prison "writ writers" like petitioner are sometimes a menace to prison discipline and that their petitions are often so unskillful as to be a burden on the courts which receive them. But, as this Court held in *Ex parte Hull, supra,* in declaring invalid a state prison regulation which required that prisoners' legal pleadings be screened by state officials:

> The considerations that prompted [the regulation's] formulation are not without merit, but the state and its officers may not abridge or impair petitioner's right to apply to a federal court for a writ of habeas corpus. 312 U.S., at 549.

Tennessee does not provide an available alternative to the assistance provided by other inmates. The warden of the prison in which petitioner was confined stated that the prison provided free notarization of prisoners' petitions. That obviously meets only a formal requirement. He also indicated that he sometimes allowed prisoners to examine the listing of attorneys in the Nashville telephone directory so they could select one to write to in an effort to interest him in taking the case, and that "on several occasions" he had contacted the public defender at the request of an inmate. There is no contention, however, that there is any regular system of assistance by public defenders. In its brief the State contends that "[t]here is absolutely no reason to believe that prison officials would fail to notify the court should an inmate advise them of a complete inability, either mental or physical, to prepare a habeas application on his own behalf," but there is no contention that they have in fact ever done so.

This is obviously far short of the showing required to demonstrate that, in depriving prisoners of the assistance of fellow inmates, Tennessee has not, in substance, deprived those unable themselves, with reasonable adequacy, to prepare their petitions, of access to the constitutionally and statutorily protected availability of the writ of habeas corpus. By contrast, in several States, the public defender system supplies trained attorneys, paid from public funds, who are available to consult with prisoners regarding their habeas corpus petitions. At least one State employs senior law students to interview and advise inmates in state prisons. Another State has a voluntary program whereby members of the local bar association make periodic visits to the prison to consult with prisoners concerning their cases. We express no judgment concerning these plans, but their existence indicates that techniques are available to provide alternatives if the State elects to prohibit mutual assistance among inmates.

Even in the absence of such alternatives, the State may impose reasonable restrictions and restraints upon the acknowledged propensity of prisoners to abuse both the giving and the seeking of assistance in the preparation of applications for relief: for example, by limitations on the time and location of such activities and the imposition of punishment for the giving or receipt of consideration in connection with such activities. Cf. *Hatfield* v. *Bailleaux*, 290 F. 2d 632 (C. A. 9th Cir. 1961) (sustaining as reasonable regulations on the time and location of prisoner work on their own petitions). But unless and until the State provides some reasonable alternative to assist inmates in the preparation of petitions for post-conviction relief, it may not validly enforce a regulation such as that here in issue, barring inmates from furnishing such assistance to other prisoners.

The judgment of the Court of Appeals is reversed and the case is remanded for further proceedings consistent with this opinion.

Reversed and remanded.

MR. JUSTICE DOUGLAS, concurring.

The plight of a man in prison may in these respects be even more acute than the plight of a person on the outside. He may need collateral proceedings to test the legality of his detention or relief against management of the parole system or against defective detainers lodged against him which create burdens in the nature of his incarcerated status. He may have grievances of a civil nature against those outside the prison. His imprisonment may give his wife grounds for divorce and be a factor in determining the custody of his children; and he may have pressing social security, workmen's compensation, or veterans' claims.

While the demand for legal counsel in prison is heavy, the supply is light. For private matters of a civil nature, legal counsel for the indigent in prison is almost nonexistent. Even for criminal proceedings, it is sparse. While a few States have post-conviction statutes providing such counsel, most States do not. Some States like California do appoint counsel to represent the indigent prisoner in his collateral hearings, once he succeeds in making out a prima facie case. But as a result, counsel is not on hand for preparation of the papers or for the initial decision that the prisoner's claim has substance.

Many think that the prisoner needs help at an early stage to weed out frivolous claims. Some States have Legal Aid Societies, sponsored in part by the National Legal Aid and Defender Association, that provide post-conviction counsel to prisoners. Most legal aid offices, however, have so many pressing obligations of a civil and criminal nature in their own communities and among freemen, as not to be able to provide any satisfactory assistance to prisoners. The same thing is true of OEO-sponsored Neighborhood Legal Services offices, which see their function as providing legal counsel for a particular community, which a member leaves as soon as he is taken to prison. In some cases, state public defenders will represent a man even after he passes beyond prison walls. But more often, the public defender has no general authorization to process post-conviction matters.

Some States have experimented with programs designed especially for the prison community. The Bureau of Prisons led the way with a program of allowing senior law students to service the federal penitentiary at Leavenworth, Kansas. Since then, it has encouraged similar programs at Lewisburg (University of Pennsylvania Law School) and elsewhere. Emory University School of Law provides free legal assistance to the inmates of Atlanta Federal Penitentiary. The program of the law school at the University of California at Los Angeles is now about to reach inside federal prisons. In describing the University of Kansas Law School program at Leavenworth, legal counsel for the Bureau of Prisons has said:

> The experience at Leavenworth has shown that there have been very few attacks upon the [prison] administration; that prospective frivolous litigation has been screened out and that where the law school felt the prisoner had a good cause of action relief was granted in a great percentage of cases. A large part of the activity was disposing of long outstanding detainers lodged against the inmates. In addition, the program

handles civil matters such as domestic relations problems and compensation claims. Even where there has been no tangible success, the fact that the inmate had someone on the outside listen to him and analyze his problems had a most beneficial effect. ... We think that these programs have been beneficial not only to the inmates but to the students, the staff and the courts.

The difficulty with an *ad hoc* program resting on a shifting law school population is that, worthy though it be, it often cannot meet the daily prison demands. In desperation, at least one State has allowed a selected inmate to act as "jailhouse" counsel for the remaining inmates. The service of legal aid, public defenders, and assigned counsel has been spread too thinly to serve prisons adequately. Some federal courts have begun to provide prisons with standardized habeas corpus forms, in the hope that they can be used by laymen. But the prison population has not found that satisfactory.

Where government fails to provide the prison with the legal counsel it demands, the prison generates its own. In a community where illiteracy and mental deficiency is notoriously high, it is not enough to ask the prisoner to be his own lawyer. Without the assistance of fellow prisoners, some meritorious claims would never see the light of a courtroom. In cases where that assistance succeeds, it speaks for itself. And even in cases where it fails, it may provide a necessary medium of expression:

> It is not unusual, then, in a subculture created by the criminal law, wherein prisoners exist as creatures of the law, that they should use the law to try to reclaim their previously enjoyed status in society. The upheavals occurring in the American social structure are reflected within the prison environment. Prisoners, having real or imagined grievances, cannot demonstrate in protest against them. The right peaceably to assemble is denied to them. The only avenue open to prisoners is taking their case to court. Prison writ-writers would compare themselves to the dissenters outside prison. . . .
>
> Many writ-writers have said that they would be able to make positive plans for the future if they knew when their [indeterminate] sentences would end. They seem to feel that they are living in a vacuum where their fates are determined arbitrarily rather than by rule of law. One writ-writer very aptly summed up the majority's view with these words: 'When I arrived at the prison and discovered that no one, including the prison officials, knew how long my sentence was, I had to resort to fighting my case to keep my sanity.' . . . Psychologically, the writ-writer, in seeking relief from the courts, is pursuing a course of action which relieves the tensions and anxieties created by the [indeterminate] sentence system.

In that view, which many share, the preparation of these endless petitions within the prisons is a useful form of therapy. Apart from that, their preparation must never be considered the exclusive prerogative of the lawyer. Laymen—in and out of prison—should be allowed to act as "next friend" to any person in the preparation of any paper or document or claim, so long as he does not hold himself out as practicing law or as being a member of the Bar.

The cooperation and help of laymen, as well as of lawyers, is necessary if the right of "[r]easonable access to the courts" is to be available to the indigents among us.

MR. JUSTICE WHITE, with whom MR. JUSTICE BLACK joins, dissenting.

It is true, as the majority says, that habeas corpus is the Great Writ, and that access through it to the courts cannot be denied simply because a man is indigent or illiterate. It is also true that the illiterate or poorly educated and inexperienced indigent cannot adequately help himself and that unless he secures aid from some other source he is effectively denied the opportunity to present to the courts what may be valid claims for post-conviction relief.

Having in mind these matters, which seem too clear for argument, the Court rules that unless the State provides a reasonably adequate alternative, it may not enforce its rule against inmates furnishing help to others in preparing post-conviction petitions. The Court does not say so in so many words, but apparently the extent of the State's duty is not to interfere with indigents seeking advice from other prisoners. It seems to me, however, that unless the help the indigent gets from other inmates is reasonably adequate for the task, he will be as surely and effectively barred from the courts as if he were accorded no help at all. It may be that those who could help effectively refuse to do so because the indigent cannot pay, that there is actually no fellow inmate who is competent to help, or that the realities of prison life leave the indigent to the mercies of those who should not be advising others at all. In this event the problem of the incompetent needing help is only exacerbated as is the difficulty of the courts in dealing with a mounting flow of inadequate and misconceived petitions.

The majority admits that it "is indisputable" that jailhouse lawyers like petitioner "are sometimes a menace to prison discipline and that their petitions are often so unskilled as to be a burden on the courts which receive them." That is putting it mildly. The disciplinary problems are severe, the burden on the courts serious, and the disadvantages to prisoner clients of the jailhouse lawyer are unacceptable.

Although some jailhouse lawyers are no doubt very capable, it is not necessarily the best amateur legal minds which are devoted to jailhouse lawyering. Rather, the most aggressive and domineering personalities may predominate. And it may not be those with the best claims to relief who are served as clients, but those who are weaker and more gullible. Many assert that the aim of the jailhouse lawyer is not the service of truth and justice, but rather self-aggrandizement, profit, and power. According to prison officials, whose expertise in such matters should be given some consideration, the jailhouse lawyer often succeeds in establishing his own power structure, quite apart from the formal system of warden, guards, and trusties which the prison seeks to maintain. Those whom the jailhouse lawyer serves may come morally under his sway as the one hope of their release, and repay him not only with obedience but with what minor gifts and other favors are available to them. When a client refuses to pay, violence may result, in which the jailhouse lawyer may be aided by his other clients.

It cannot be expected that the petitions which emerge from such a process will be of the highest quality. Codes of ethics, champerty, and maintenance, frequently have little meaning to the jailhouse lawyer, who solicits business as vigorously as he can. In the petition itself, outright lies may serve the jailhouse lawyer's purpose since by procuring for a prisoner client a short trip out of jail for a hearing on his contentions the petition writer's credibility with the other convicts is improved.

Habeas corpus petitions, as the majority notes, are relatively easy to prepare: they need only set out the facts giving rise to a claim for relief and the judge will apply the law, appointing a lawyer for the prisoner and giving him a hearing when appropriate. This fact does not buttress the unregulated jailhouse lawyer system, but undermines it. To the extent that it is easy to state a claim, any prisoner can do it, and need not submit to the mercies of a jailhouse lawyer. To the extent that it is difficult—and it is necessary to understand what one's rights are before it is possible to set out in a petition the facts which support them—there may be no fellow prisoner adequate to the task. There are some well informed and articulate prisoners and some (not necessarily the same) who give advice and aid out of altruism. When the two qualities are combined in one man, as they sometimes are, he can be a perfectly adequate source of help. But the jails are not characteristically populated with the intelligent or the benign, and capable altruists must be rare indeed. On the other hand, some jailhouse clients are illiterate; and whether illiterate or not, there are others who are unable to prepare their own petitions. They need help, but I doubt that the problem of the indigent convict will be solved by subjecting him to the false hopes, dominance, and inept representation of the average unsupervised jailhouse lawyer.

I cannot say, therefore, that petitioner Johnson, who is a convicted rapist serving a life sentence and whose prison conduct the State has wide discretion in regulating, cannot be disciplined for violating a prison rule against aiding other prisoners in seeking post-conviction relief, particularly when there is no showing that any prisoner in the Tennessee State Penitentiary has been denied access to the courts, that Johnson has confined his services to those who need it, or that Johnson is himself competent to give the advice which he offers. No prisoner testified that Johnson was the only person available who would write out a writ for him or that guards or other prison functionaries would not furnish the necessary help. And it is really the prisoner client's rights, not the jailhouse lawyer's, which are most in need of protection.

If the problem of the indigent and ignorant convict in seeking post-conviction relief is substantial, which I think it is, the better course is not in effect to sanction and encourage spontaneous jailhouse lawyer systems but to decide the matter directly in the case of a man who himself needs help and in that case to rule that the State must provide access to the courts by ensuring that those who cannot help themselves have reasonably adequate assistance in preparing their post-conviction papers. Ideally, perhaps professional help should be furnished and prisoners encouraged to seek it so that any possible claims receive early and complete examination. But I am inclined to agree with MR. JUSTICE DOUGLAS that it is neither practical nor necessary to require the help of lawyers. As the opinions in this case indicate, the alternatives are various and the burden on the States would not be impossible to discharge. This requirement might even be met by the establishment of a system of regulated trusties of the prison who would advise prisoners of their legal rights. Selection of the jailhouse lawyers by the prison officials for scholarship and character might assure that the inmate client received advice which would actually help him, and regulation of the "practice" by the authorities would reduce the likelihood of coerced fees or blackmail. The same legislative judgment which should be sustained in concluding that the evils of jailhouse lawyering justify its proscription might also support a legislative conclusion that jailhouse lawyering under carefully controlled conditions satisfies the prisoner's constitutional right to help.

Regretfully, therefore, I dissent.

NOTES

Note 1. Implementing Johnson v. Avery

CROSS V. POWERS
328 F. Supp. 899 (1971)
United States District Court, District of Wisconsin

The Wisconsin State Prison has promulgated, and at all times relevant to the complaint has enforced, a rule which prohibits inmates in that institution from taking materials, including legal papers, to prison areas shared commonly with other inmates; from passing legal papers to other inmates; from working on other inmates' legal problems; and from preparing legal papers, petitions, and documents on behalf of, or jointly with, other inmates. Violations of this rule are punishable by solitary confinement, loss of good time, or deprivation of certain privileges; plaintiff, who wishes to seek assistance from other inmates to aid him in the preparation of various complaints and petitions, is in jeopardy of being punished for violation of the "no-assistance" rule....

...I now turn to an examination of the record in this case to determine whether the Wisconsin State Prison rule under attack is a barrier to "those unable themselves, with reasonable adequacy, to prepare their petitions [and other initial pleadings]." *Johnson, supra,* at 489, 89 S.Ct. at 751. If the rule does create such a barrier, I must determine whether the prison has provided a "reasonable alternative" to inmate mutual legal assistance. 393 U.S. at 490, 89 S.Ct. 747.

I have already found that many inmates of the Wisconsin State Prison are totally or functionally illiterate, and that the vast majority of the prison's population is indigent. I find further that these illiterate, indigent inmates are unable to adequately prepare their legal pleadings by themselves, and that they are unable to retain counsel to assist them in the preparation of pleadings.

Although the prison rule under consideration herein does not prevent prisoners from verbally discussing legal actions with other inmates, it does prohibit carrying legal papers to prison areas shared commonly with other inmates; passing legal papers to other inmates; possessing legal papers of other inmates; and preparing legal papers on behalf of, or jointly with, other inmates. I find that the verbal discussions allowed are not sufficient to assure effective access to the courts, and that the prison rule under consideration operates as a barrier to illiterate, indigent inmates' effective access to the courts for the purpose of vindicating federal constitutional rights.[1]

Defendants contend that two programs are alternatives to inmate mutual legal assistance: the law student assistance program and the Wisconsin Judicare institutional services program. The law students generally limit their activities to various forms of post-conviction pleadings; Judicare considers itself restricted to civil cases other than habeas corpus petitions and civil rights suits. No other source of assistance is available in such substantial volume as to fulfill the prison population's needs for assistance in the preparation of cases designed to vindicate federal constitutional rights. Therefore, I find that the Wisconsin State Prison has not provided a reasonable alternative to inmate mutual legal assistance. Under these circumstances, the prison "may not validly enforce a regulation such as that here in issue, barring inmates from furnishing such assistance to other prisoners." Johnson v. Avery, supra, at 490, 89 S.Ct. at 751.

---

[1] Defendants have sought to justify the no-assistance rule as part of the prison's disciplinary administration and as an effort to protect inmates and courts from unskilled or dishonest jailhouse lawyers. However, these considerations must give way when the right of access to the courts, a "paramount federal constitutional" right, supervenes. Johnson v. Avery, 393 U.S. 483, 486, 89 S.Ct. 747, 21 L.Ed.2d 718 (1969).

Note 2. Inmate Views of Johnson v. Avery

CHARLES LARSEN

*A Prisoner Looks at Writ Writing**

Why do men in prison write writs if their objective is simply to "escape" from prison? One misconception should be clarified. The old saying that "typewriters have replaced the hacksaw" for breaking out of prison creates a prejudicial conception about writ-writers—more men still escape from prison than gain freedom through writs of habeas corpus! Litigating one's case is certainly much more time consuming than sawing out a heavy steel bar in a prison window and fleeing into the night.

Lawyers generally require at least a fifty dollar fee to travel to the prisons to consult with a prisoner. The ones not able to pay this sum must resort to the next best course of action—act as their own lawyers. The disadvantages to the prisoner are obvious. A lawyer, after examining the prisoner's transcripts or conducting an independent investigation of the facts, could immediately advise him on a course of action. Lacking the money to hire a lawyer, the prisoner must spend considerable time researching the law, preparing the required legal documents, and filing them. Sometimes years pass before the prisoner discovers what a lawyer could have told him in several weeks—that his case either has or lacks merit. The prisoners who have militantly prosecuted frivolous actions have wasted time they could have devoted to preparing themselves for release from prison. The state, by shouldering these indigent prisoners with the responsibility of acting as their own counsel, has dissipated the taxpayers' money in wasted manpower and court costs.

If an analysis were to be made of the reasons prisoners elect to litigate their cases ... against seemingly insurmountable odds, the results would astound judges and lawyers. It is not the rash of decisions such as *People v. Dorado, Escobedo v. Illinois,* and *Gideon v. Wainwright* that send countless writ-writers to read barren case law in the prisons' scanty law libraries and to hover for hours over their typewriters. Three important factors are contributing to the ever-increasing flood of legal actions emanating from the state prisons. They fall into the following loose categories: legal, psychological, and economic.

* "A Prisoner Looks at Writ Writing," by Charles Larsen 56 *California Law Review* 342, 343–49 (1968). Copyright © 1968. California Law Review. Reprinted by permission.

A. Legal Factors

A large percentage of writ-writers are not satisfied that they received due process of law when arrested, tried, and convicted. One common complaint is that they were represented by inadequate counsel. Many were impoverished, living at a bare subsistence level at the time of their arrest. Not having the money to employ private counsel, they were required to accept the services of a court-appointed public defender. Others, not represented by a public defender, employed inexpensive private counsel. Finally, some unsuccessfully defended themselves. In any of the above situations, the state is almost certain to obtain a conviction....

For every one that challenges the adequacy of the court-appointed counsel, there are ten or more writ-writers contesting the infringement of their constitutional and statutory rights. Prisoners today are more literate than their counterparts of twenty or thirty years ago. Today, prisoners have a keener awareness of their rights under the law, and any variance during the criminal proceedings with what they think to be their rights will impel them to seek relief in the courts. Possessing a better fundamental education, the prisoners have been able to penetrate the heretofore impregnable fabric of the law. They have mastered legal semantics and simplified it to their own needs. The law has become the panzer movement they use to strike out toward their elusive goals—to redress the deprivation of their rights.

It is not unusual, then, in a subculture created by the criminal law, wherein prisoners exist as creatures of the law, that they should use the law to try to reclaim their previously enjoyed status in society. The upheavals occurring in the American social structure are reflected within the prison environment. Prisoners, having real or imagined grievances cannot demonstrate in protest against them. The right peaceably to assemble is denied to them. The only avenue open to prisoners is taking their case to court. Prison writ-writers would compare themselves to the dissenters outside prison, with one exception—their grievances are real or they imagine they are real. They are personally involved.

B. Psychological Factors

There are two obvious psychological motives for prosecuting legal actions from prison. The first is an outgrowth of the prison's social environment. Sentenced to serve a term in the state prison under what is termed the "Indeterminate Sentence Law," the prisoner is caught in a dilemma which causes him considerable frustration and despair. He does not know when his sentence will terminate, and must therefore choose between taking his case to court or waiting for the Adult Authority to fix his term of imprisonment. If he chooses to write writs, it is only because the remote possibility of winning his case offers him better odds than waiting for the Adult Authority to set a definite sentence. On the other hand, he may fear that the authorities would disfavor anyone who denies his guilt by continuing to litigate his case. If the prisoner does not write writs, he may never get out; if he does write writs, he may never receive parole.

Many writ-writers have said that they would be able to make positive plans for the future if they knew when their sentences would end. They seem to feel that they are living in a vacuum where their fates are determined arbitrarily rather than by rule of law. One writ-writer very aptly summed up the majority's view with these words: "When I arrived at the prison and discovered that no one, including the prison officials, knew how long my sentence was, I had to resort to fighting my case to keep my sanity." This writ-writer, after twenty years in prison for the offense of robbery, still does not know how much time he will be required to serve. Psychologically, the writ-writer, in seeking relief from the courts, is pursuing a course of action which relieves the tensions and anxieties created by the sentence system.

The second psychological type is the prisoner who writes writs to be "in." He is introduced to writ-writing by acquaintances who are writ-writers. Men falling into this category are not the perennial writ-writers whose names continually appear on documents streaming into the courts. Usually, after a few unsuccessful forays into the legal realm, they stable their white chargers, hang their lances on the wall, and go about the business of serving their sentences.

C. Economic Factors

The last type of writ-writer to be discussed writes writs for economic gain. This group is comprised of a few unscrupulous manipulators who are interested only in acquiring from other prisoners money, cigarettes, or merchandise purchased in the inmate canteen. Once they have a "client's" interest aroused and determine his ability to pay, they must keep him on the "hook." This is commonly done by deliberately mis-stating the facts of his case so that it appears, at least on the surface, that the inmate is entitled to relief. The documents drafted for the client cast the writ-writer in the role of a sympathetic protagonist. After reading them, the inmate is elated that he has found someone able to present his case favorably. He is willing to pay to maintain the lie that has been created for him. After years of futilely applying to the court for various writs, he will leave prison certain that he has not been accorded justice. On the other hand, when a prisoner turns his case over to a writ-writer he is left free to devote his time to serving his sentence. Prisoners who do this maintain an objective outlook. They do not become so emotionally involved with prosecuting their cases that they are unable to take advantage of the prison's self-betterment programs.

HO CHI MINH

Writing a Petition for a Jail-Mate*

Being all in the same boat, we can never refuse
Help to one another. For you I write this petition,
Starting to use expressions considered correct,
Like: "So, in accordance with your sublime
    instructions..."
That kind of phrase I am learning now for the first
    time.
But how you thank me for turning out such a nice job!

* Ho Chi Minh, *The Prison Diary of Ho Chi Minh* 56 (New York: Bantam Books, Bantam Edition, 1971).

G. Inmate Communications

NOLAN V. FITZPATRICK
451 F.2d 545 (1971)
United States Court of Appeals, First Circuit

COFFIN, Circuit Judge.

Plaintiffs Nolan and LeFebvre, two prisoners confined at the Massachusetts Correctional Institution at Walpole, have brought this action to challenge the constitutionality of that prison's total ban on prisoner letters to the news media concerning prison affairs. Plaintiffs have exhausted their administrative remedies under state law and seek a declaratory judgment and injunctive relief, invoking the jurisdictional provisions of 28 U.S.C. § 1343 and the substantive provisions of 42 U.S.C. § 1983.

The district court granted a declaratory judgment and issued an injunction under which prison authorities retain wide discretion. The authorities may refuse to mail a letter if they "have reasonable ground (not necessarily probable cause) to believe that the contents of the letter or the addressee of the letter presents a risk (a) to the security of the public, the prison administration, or the prison population, or (b) to the observance of rules of behavior by prisoners, or (c) to the rehabilitation of prisoners * * *." 326 F.Supp. 209, 217, 218 (D.Mass. 1971). Both parties appeal, the officials contending that the total ban should be upheld and the prisoners contending that restrictions, if any, must be drawn more narrowly.

At the outset, we note that the plaintiffs do not challenge the right of prison authorities to read all letters to the press and to inspect them for contraband or escape plans. Nor do they here assert a right to correspond with the news media about matters of public policy or personal affairs unrelated to the prisons. They claim simply the right to send to the media letters concerning prison management, treatment of offenders, and personal grievances arising within the prison. Plaintiff Nolan wrote seven such letters, and plaintiff LeFebvre wrote one; all were returned by the Walpole censor. The following letter, addressed to the Editor of the Boston Record American, is illustrative:

Dear Sir,
I am writing this letter in regards to an article which I read in your newspaper concerning the work strike at Walpole State Prison. 1/15 [illegible]
I want to thank you for not minimizing our grievances and I would like to point out that the situation in this prison is a great deal more serious than you indicate. Contrary to your statement that 'the Superintendent agreed to discuss our grievances.' This information is incorrect.
The work strike started on Monday afternoon (1/11/71) & continued until late Thursday afternoon 1/14/71.
If you would like to know more about the reasons behind the work strike & other such trouble that has taken place in this prison during these past 10 months, then please contact the above named attorney (482-1390).
Yours,
Dan Nolan /s/
Prisoner, Walpole

Plaintiffs make First Amendment claims under the heads of freedom of speech, freedom of the press, and the right to petition. It is clear that federal courts may no longer refuse to hear such claims. The oft-cited proposition that "Lawful incarceration brings about the necessary withdrawal or limitation of many privileges and rights, a retraction justified by the considerations underlying our penal system", Price v. Johnston, 334 U.S. 266, 285, 68 S.Ct. 1049, 1060, 92 L.Ed. 1356 (1948), must be read in the light of its equally oft-cited contrapositive, that "A prisoner retains all the rights of an ordinary citizen except those expressly, or by necessary implication, taken from him by law," Coffin v. Reichard, 143 F.2d 443, 445 (6th Cir. 1944), cert. denied, 325 U.S. 887, 65 S.Ct. 1568, 89 L.Ed. 2001 (1945).

Since the challenged total ban does deprive prisoners of all opportunity to write letters to the press, we must, as a threshold matter, determine whether one's freedom to write to the press survives his incarceration. While to our knowledge no court has addressed the precise question, many have concluded that various other First Amendment rights survive. The right to free exercise of religion has given rise to most of the litigation. In Cooper v. Pate, 378 U.S. 546, 84 S.Ct. 1733, 12 L.Ed.2d 1030

(1964), the Supreme Court held that a prisoner stated a cause of action in alleging that he was denied permission to purchase certain religious publications and was, because of his religious beliefs, denied other privileges enjoyed by other prisoners. While *Cooper* could conceivably be thought to be grounded in either free exercise of religion or equal protection, it has consistently been intepreted as proceeding on free exercise grounds. *E. g.*, Brown v. Peyton, 437 F.2d 1228, 1230 (4th Cir. 1971); Walker v. Blackwell, 411 F.2d 23, 24 (5th Cir. 1969); Long v. Parker, 390 F.2d 816, 820 n. 17 (3d Cir. 1968). Indeed, the language of these cases suggests the survival of First Amendment rights generally. 437 F.2d at 1231; 411 F.2d at 24. Similar language was used in an opinion holding that prisoners had the right to receive *Fortune News*, a (non-religious) newsletter published by former inmates and often critical of prison authorities. Fortune Society v. McGinnis, 319 F.Supp. 901, 904 (S.D.N.Y.1970).

We need not adopt the broad principle that a prisoner retains all First Amendment rights to conclude, as we do, that he retains the right to send letters to the press concerning prison matters. In so concluding, we rely primarily on the fact that the condition of our prisons is an important matter of public policy as to which prisoners are, with their wardens, peculiarly interested and peculiarly knowledgeable. The argument that the prisoner has the right to communicate his grievances to the press and, through the press, to the public is thus buttressed by the invisibility of prisons to the press and the public: the prisoners' right to speak is enhanced by the right of the public to hear. This does not depend upon a determination that wardens are unsympathetic to the need to improve prison conditions. But even a warden who pushes aggressively for reforms or larger appropriations within his department and before appropriate officials and legislative committees may understandably not feel it prudent to push for more public laundering of institutional linen.

That prisoners themselves have recently begun to realize the importance of a public awareness to any real prospect of change is increasingly demonstrated. The frequency of striking and rioting in the prisons may well derive, at least in part, from this realization. Often, one of the prisoner "demands" in the course of a strike or riot is that press access to the prison be broadened in some respect. Concurrently, the Massachusetts Department of Corrections has taken practical steps which indicate a recognition of the need for more communication between prisoners and the press. By an administrative regulation, the Department now permits newsmen to visit prisoners under most circumstances.

Having concluded that prisoners retain the right to send letters to the news media concerning prison matters, we must still address defendants' argument that state interests unrelated to the suppression of speech justify the restrictions here imposed. The doctrinal framework for our inquiry must come from United States v. O'Brien, 391 U.S. 367, 88 S.Ct. 1673, 20 L.Ed.2d 672 (1968), in which the Supreme Court rationalized the variety of doctrines which it had in the past employed where the government interest was unrelated to the suppression of free expression. Under *O'Brien,* the state's burden in the present case is to establish that the regulation "furthers an important or substantial governmental interest" and that "the incidental restriction on alleged First Amendment freedoms is no greater than is essential to the furtherance of that interest." 391 U.S. at 377, 88 S.Ct. at 1679.

The ban might be thought supportable either as serving the purpose of prison administration or as implementing the purposes of the criminal law generally. Defendants here stress purposes of the first sort. They contend that permitting letters to the press "would be detrimental to the security and good order of the institution" and that "A prison community is not the ideal setting for dispassioned debate. Aggressive feelings and grudges run high not only against society in general and correction personnel, but also between inmates themselves."

Since the state interest in insuring the security of the guards and the prisoners is surely an "important or substantial" one, we must consider whether the ban's restrictive effect on the First Amendment rights of the prisoners and the public "is no greater than is essential to the furtherance of that interest." This entails a closer inspection of the security interest. One aspect of the alleged threat to security is the expectation that prisoners will write inflammatory letters to the press, that these letters will return to the prison as letters to the editor or news stories or editorials, and that, finally, they will cause fellow prisoners to strike or riot. We note first that none of the letters written by the plaintiffs in this case was even arguably of this sort—a total ban is clearly not necessary. Furthermore, prisoners are already entitled to receive newspapers critical of prison authorities. If it be thought that the effect of criticism from within the prison is likely to be greater than that of criticism by outsiders, the short answer is that prisoners are quite well able to proselytize directly. In any event, we have no evidence to the contrary.

The most that can reasonably be said is that, depending upon conditions in the prison when the letter or news story based on it *returns* to the prison, some particularly inflammatory letters may create a "clear and present danger" of violence or breach of security. In that extreme case, prison officials can cope with the situation by refusing to admit the dangerous issue of the newspaper to the prison rather than by refusing to mail the letter in the first instance. The rule against mailing is constitutionally infirm in that it permits officials to withhold letters from the mails on the basis of speculation as to what conditions in the prison will be when and if the letter or article derived from it returns.

The First Amendment prohibition against prior restraints applies with even more than its usual force here. In Cantwell v. Connecticut, 310 U.S. 296, 60 S.Ct. 900, 84 L.Ed. 1213 (1940), the Supreme Court explained that "When clear and present danger of riot, disorder [etc.] appears, the power of the state to prevent or punish is obvious. Equally obvious is it that a State may not unduly suppress free communication of views, religious or other, under the guise of conserving desirable conditions." 310 U.S. at 308, 60 S.Ct. at 905. The truism about an ounce of prevention helps little in this field, for the prior restraint doctrine is customarily invoked despite the fact that the state's bar against expressing views to an audience may well be a more effective way of protecting public order than would subsequent punishment. Here, since the communication which allegedly creates the danger to security does so only when it returns to the prison, the regulation against mailing is, in a sense, prior to a prior restraint in that it cuts off expression even before the tension between free expression and order has come into being. Beyond this, it unnecessarily cuts off prisoner speech to a quite different and larger audience, the public.

The other aspect of the threat to security, the danger that newsmen will participate in escape attempts or assist in transferring contraband from one prisoner to another, is based upon the dubious assumption that newsmen would be willing to cooperate in such projects. Nor has either party suggested that letters involving such threats to security would enjoy First Amendment protection. Defendants' practice of reading outgoing mail, unchallenged here, permits them to thwart these possible breaches of security without imposing a total ban.

Defendant relies as well on the state interest in minimizing the expenses of administration. A flat ban on all letters to the press is obviously inexpensive to administer. It requires little of the censor's time to stamp "Rejected" on a letter, and prison officials need not spend time responding to issues which these letters raise. But on the present facts, the state interest in minimizing expenses does not rise to the level of an "important or substantial" interest. Defendant has made no showing that the costs of censorship would be prohibitively increased by the need to read a moderate number of letters to the press. We grant that an official may feel a need to respond to complaints. If his censor reads the outgoing mail, he will be apprised immediately of any complaint and can attach a response if that is warranted. An editor who reads both the complaint and the response may conclude that the complaint is groundless or that further investigation is necessary. If the mail is not censored, an official can respond when contacted by the editor or reporter who is investigating the matter or, if he is not contacted, when the letter or story based on the letter is published. While these responses may well involve some time and worry, prison officials are, after all, public officials and responsible to the people in that capacity. Nor is the burden new in kind—since newsmen are now permitted to visit the prison, the officials have presumably become accustomed to responding to criticism. . . .

Accordingly, while we are not unmindful of the district court's serious efforts to draw guidelines of operable utility, we conclude that adherence to the constitutional standard is not ensured by broad "reasonable ground" discretionary powers even though these be linked to proper penological objectives. We therefore remand to the district court with directions to enter a judgment declaring that plaintiffs have a right to send letters to the press concerning prison management, treatment of offenders, or personal grievances except those which (a) contain or concern contraband or (b) contain or concern any plan of escape or device for evading prison regulations.

We add this postscript. Subsequent to argument in this case, we have been informed by counsel that defendants have voluntarily adopted new procedures permitting outgoing mail of prisoners to be sent without restriction as to addressees. While such administrative initiative is a welcome constructive step, it does not moot the issue, since the policy can at any time be changed. It does, however, persuade us that injunctive relief is not presently indicated.

Reversed and remanded.

NOTES

Note 1.

SOSTRE V. MCGINNIS
442 F.2d 178 (1971) *cert. den.* 404, U.S. 1039 (1972) United States Court of Appeals, Second Circuit

Correspondence

The distaste with which some observers view prolonged segregated confinement attaches as well to that kind of isolation flowing from restrictions on and censorship of prisoners' correspondence:

> The harm censorship does to rehabilitation cannot be gainsaid. Inmates lose contact with the outside world and become wary of placing intimate thoughts or criticisms of the prison in letters. The artificial increase of alienation from society is ill advised.

The values commonly associated with free expression—an open, democratic marketplace of ideas, the self-development of individuals through self-expression, the alleviation of tensions by their release in harsh words rather than hurled objects—these values that we esteem in a free society do not turn to dross in an unfree one. "Letter writing keeps the inmate in contact with the outside world, helps to hold in check some of the morbidity and hopelessness produced by prison life and isolation, stimulates his more natural and human impulses, and otherwise may make contributions to better mental attitudes and reformation." Palmigiano v. Travisono, 310 F.Supp. 857 (D.R.I. Aug. 24, 1970). Suppression of diversity and dissenting views is probably not less apt in a prison than elsewhere to hasten the stagnation and bureaucratization of the institution that indulges in it. See T. Emerson, Toward a General Theory of the First Amendment 3–15 (1966).

Whatever wisdom there might be in such reflection, we cannot say with requisite certitude that the traditional and common practice of prisons in imposing many kinds of controls on the correspondence of inmates, lacks support in any rational and constitutionally acceptable concept of a prison system. See McCloskey v. Maryland, 337 F.2d 72, 74–75 (4th Cir. 1964) ("Control of the mail to and from inmates is an essential adjunct of prison administration"). See also, Diehl v. Wainwright, 419 F.2d 1309 (5th Cir. 1970); Abernathy v. Cunningham, 393 F.2d 775 (4th Cir. 1968); United States v. Stahl, 393 F.2d 101 (7th Cir.) cert. denied 393 U.S. 879, 89 S.Ct. 181, 21 L.Ed.2d 152 (1968); Carey v. Settle, 351 F.2d 483, 485 (8th Cir. 1965). We note that Sostre did not contest the validity of Warden Follette's action in striking the name of his sister from the list of Sostre's authorized correspondents after it was learned that he was using letters addressed to his sister as vehicles for unauthorized correspondence. *See* fn. 4, *supra.* Discipline and prison order are sufficient interests to justify such regulation incidental to the content of prisoners' speech. See Kovacs v. Cooper, 336 U.S. 77, 69 S.Ct. 448, 93 L.Ed. 513 (1949); Brennan, The Supreme Court and the Meikeljohn Interpretation of the First Amendment, 79 Harv.L.Rev. 1, 11 (1965).

Sui generis in both logic and the case law, however, are letters addressed to courts, public officials, or an attorney when a prisoner challenges the legality of either his criminal conviction or the conditions of his incarceration. See, e. g., Johnson v. Avery, 393 U.S. 483, 89 S.Ct. 747, 21 L.Ed.2d 718 (1969); Cochran v. Kansas, 316 U.S. 255, 62 S.Ct. 1068, 86 L.Ed. 1453 (1942); Ex parte Hull, 312 U.S. 546, 61 S.Ct. 640, 85 L.Ed. 1034 (1941); Coleman v. Peyton, 362 F.2d 905, 907 (4th Cir. 1966) (no censorship permitted of mail between inmate and court with jurisdiction to hear prisoner's complaints); McCloskey v. Maryland, *supra*; Stiltner v. Rhay, 322 F.2d 314, 316 (9th Cir.), cert. denied, 376 U.S. 920, 84 S.Ct. 678, 11 L.Ed.2d 615 (1963) ("reasonable access to the courts is basic to all other rights protected by" the Civil Rights Act). It would be inappropriate on constitutional grounds, ironic, and irrational to permit drastic curtailment of constitutional rights in the name of punishment and rehabilitation, while denying prisoners a full opportunity to pursue their appeals and postconviction remedies. The generous scope of discretion accorded prison authorities also heightens the importance of permitting free and uninhibited access by prisoners to both administrative and judicial forums for the purpose of seeking redress of grievances against state officers. The importance of these rights of access suggests the need for guidelines both generous and specific enough to afford protection against the reality or the chilling threat of administrative infringement.

Thus, we do not believe it would unnecessarily hamper prison administration to forbid prison authorities to delete material from, withhold, or refuse to mail a communication between an inmate and his attorney, see Burns v. Swensen, 430 F.2d 771, (8th Cir., Aug. 31, 1970) (protecting correspondence with the ACLU), or any court, or any public official, unless it can be demonstrated that a prisoner has clearly abused his rights of access. Obviously, the transmittal of contraband or laying plans for some unlawful scheme would constitute such an abuse. In addition, if it were clear that a prisoner's recitation of complaints about his confinement in otherwise protected correspondence were a mere pretext to accomplish his sole motivating purpose of communicating instead about restricted matters, then prison officials may block the inmate's scheme by deleting that portion of such a communication unrelated to the complaints. See Carothers v. Follette, 314 F.Supp. 1014 (S.D.N.Y. filed July 15, 1970); In re Ferguson, 55 Cal. 2d 663, 12 Cal.Rptr. 753, 361 P.2d 417, cert. denied sub nom. Ferguson v. Heinze, 368 U.S. 864, 82 S.Ct. 111, 7 L.Ed.2d 61 (1961). In such a case, the need to restrain the abuse outweighs the danger that prison authorities may by inadvertence or design hamper the prisoner's access.

On the other hand, if a communication is properly intended to advance a prisoner's effort to secure redress for alleged abuses, no interest would justify deleting material thought by prison authorities to be irrelevant to the prisoner's complaint. The danger that an official will improperly substitute his judgment for that of the correspondent's then preponderates. For similar reasons, prison officials may not withhold, refuse to mail, or delete material from otherwise protected communications merely because they believe the allegations to be repetitious, false, or malicious. See Nolan v. Scafati, 430 F.2d 548 (1st Cir. 1970) (absent some countervailing interest other than that prisoner's letter contained "lies," authorities may not prevent inmate from seeking legal assistance); Fulwood v. Clemmer, 206 F.Supp. 370, 377 (D.D.C.1962) (right to seek redress of grievances was abridged by punishment for alleged false accusations about prison conditions in prisoner's letter of complaint to public officials).

Accordingly, we agree with Judge Motley that it was improper for Warden Follette to delete material from correspondence between Sostre and his attorney merely because Follette thought the material irrelevant to Sostre's appeal of his conviction. We believe it was also improper for Follette to refuse to mail a letter of complaint to the Postal Inspector. We leave a more precise delineation of the boundaries of this protection for future cases. We need only add that when we say there may be cases which will present special circumstances that *would* justify deleting material from, withholding, or refusing to mail communications with courts, attorneys, and public officials, we necessarily rule that prison officials may open and read all outgoing and incoming correspondence to and from prisoners....

Possession of Literature and Mere Expression of Beliefs

Our holding that prisoners may not be punished for their beliefs carries the necessary corollary that we may not permit punishment for the mere expression of those beliefs. One can hardly speak of beliefs apart from their expression, cf. Fulwood v. Clemmer, 206 F. Supp. 370 (D.D.C.1962). In the absence of arbitrariness or discrimination, see Jackson v. Godwin, 400 F.2d 529 (5th Cir. 1968); Rivers v. Royster, 360 F.2d 592 (4th Cir. 1966); Sewell v. Pegelow, 291 F.2d 196 (4th Cir. 1961), and Pierce v. LaVallee, 293 F.2d 233 (2d Cir. 1961), we do not say on this record that Warden Follette would have exceeded his legitimate authority if he had confiscated the writings that guards found in Sostre's cell following his release from segregation. Whatever doubts we might have as to the wisdom of seizing an inmate's political writings, we would not lightly overturn a warden's judgment that possession of the writings might subvert prison discipline if there existed the risk of their circulation among other prisoners.

However, Sostre was *punished* simply for putting his thoughts on paper, with no prior warning and no hint that he intended to spirit the writings outside his cell. To sanction such punishment, even though in the judgment of prison officials the writings were "inflammatory" and "racist," as in the instant case, would permit prison authorities to manipulate and crush thoughts under the guise of regulation. The intimidating threat of future similar punishment would chill a wide range of prisoner expression, not limited to that expression which Follette might in fact deem dangerous enough to discipline. The danger of undetected discriminatory punishment of ideas is particularly acute in the absence of statutory standards to guide the exercise of Follette's discretion. See, e. g., Cox v. Louisiana, 379 U.S. 536, 556–557, 85 S.Ct. 453, 13 L.Ed.2d 471 (1965); Schneider v. State, 308 U.S. 147, 60 S.Ct. 146, 84 L.Ed. 155 (1939). Any real threat to prison security that Sostre's possession of his writings might have posed could have been met by confiscation rather than punishment. See Shelton v. Tucker, 364 U.S. 479, 81 S.Ct. 247, 5 L.Ed.2d 231 (1960).

* * *

2. The refusal to mail Sostre's letter to the Post Office Inspector, complaining of prison practices, clearly infringed Sostre's Fourteenth Amendment rights. We also affirm Judge Motley's order insofar as it enjoins defendants Follette and McGinnis, their employees, agents, successors, and all persons in active concert and participation with them, from deleting material from, refusing to mail or refusing to give to Sostre: (1) Any communication between Sostre and the following—(a) any court; (b) any public official or agency; or (c) any lawyer —with respect to either his criminal conviction or any complaint he may have concerning the administration of the prison where he is incarcerated. We reverse, however, insofar as Judge Motley enjoined nonarbitrary restraint of communication between Sostre and his co-defendant in the criminal matter pending against him.

3. There is no cause for an injunction to enforce the principles announced in Johnson v. Avery, *supra,* since no infractions of those principles have been shown. Johnson v. Avery permitted reasonable rules regulating the conduct of inmates in assisting other inmates in legal proceedings. Sostre has not proved that the rules regulating his right to assist other prisoners in their legal affairs were unreasonable and that his punishment was for violating such rules. Therefore, we must reverse the district court insofar as it enjoined interference with Sostre's translation of letters of fellow-inmates since he had failed to comply with the rule requiring that he seek permission of the warden. For the same reason, we reverse the injunction against punishing Sostre for sharing with other inmates his law books, law reviews, and other legal materials, and from refusing to permit Sostre to assist any other inmate in any legal matter.

4. We have held that Sostre was improperly punished for possession of constitutionally protected literature. We perceive no reason, however, to set *political* speech apart from other kinds of constitutionally protected speech. We therefore modify the district court order so as to enjoin defendants Follette and McGinnis, their employees, agents, successors, and all persons in active concert and participation with them, from punishing Sostre for having literature in his possession and for setting forth his views orally or in writing, except for violation of reasonable regulations. We do not hereby enjoin officials from taking reasonable measures to prevent prisoners from inciting disturbances and otherwise to protect the security and order of New York prisons, consistent with prisoners' rights to freedom of expression. Also we do not believe that there is any need for the extraordinary procedure requiring defendants to submit rules and regulations governing the receipt, distribution, discussion and writing of political literature for the approval of the district court.

5. We have no reason to conclude that New York prison officials will not abide by the constitutional rights of prisoners as we define them today. We have refused to set aside Judge Motley's findings that Warden Follette unlawfully committed Sostre to segregated confinement because of his legal activities and beliefs. Warden Follette, however, is deceased and we perceive no threat that others will duplicate his improper conduct. Accordingly, we vacate that portion of the district court order which enjoined defendants and others from returning Sostre to punitive segregation for charges previously preferred against him.

Note 2.

SMITH V. ROBBINS
454 F.2d 696 (1972)
United States Court of Appeals, First Circuit

ALDRICH, Chief Judge.

The primary issue in this case is whether the district court, 328 F.Supp. 162, in a 42 U.S.C. § 1983 suit brought by a state prisoner against his warden, erred in ruling that mail addressed to the prisoner and adequately shown to be from a member of the state bar may not be opened, to see if the envelope contains contraband, in the absence of the prisoner. By contraband is meant some physical object in addition to the attorney's letter; the warden does not complain of that part of the order which forbids the reading of the letter itself. The warden appeals.

The prisoner responds by asking us to

modify the order to bar prison officials from opening attorneys' letters at all unless they have reason to suspect that they contain contraband. If there is merit in this contention, there is certainly not enough to cause us to hold that the district court was obliged to accept it. If the prisoner is present, he can see that the letter is not being read. That is enough.

However strongly the warden may feel about a possible indignity to the prison administration in a suggestion by the court that it is not to be trusted not to read the letter, this misses the point. The court does not suggest that the warden is untrustworthy. Rather, it is that a prisoner, and possibly some attorneys, may feel, if only to a small degree, that someone in the chain of command may not be trusted, and that the resulting fear may chill communications between the prisoner and his counsel. Once it is granted, as the warden now concedes, that the prisoner has a right to have the confidence between himself and his counsel totally respected, the burden must be on the warden to show a need for any act which could produce even a suspicion of intrusion. If a prisoner can see no good reason for opening a letter in his absence, it would not be unnatural for him to suspect a bad one. Inasmuch as the warden has failed to suggest any reason that seems adequate even to us, we see no reason to leave such possible apprehensions on such an important matter as right to counsel in the minds of the prisoner or his attorney. . . .

Note 3.

WASHINGTON POST V. KLEINDIENST
11 Cr. L. 2045 (1972)
United States District Court, District of Columbia

Plaintiffs have a legitimate news interest. The Washington Post has run a comprehensive series on prison conditions, illustrated by articles attached to the complaint. The unsuccessful effort to interview which led to this litigation related to matters of obvious public interest. Recent work stoppages at Lewisburg and Danbury had apparently been satisfactorily resolved without bloodshed through negotiations between the Wardens and inmate representatives. Information subsequently came to the Washington Post that inmate ringleaders had been punished and that this was contrary to assurances given by prison authorities. The newspaper had reason to believe that some members of the inmate negotiating committees may have been placed in solitary, maced, deprived of necessary medical care and otherwise harshly treated.

Defendants contend that the press has no constitutional right of access to inmates for confidential interviews and urge that the same Bureau policy which permits contact between prisoners and the media both through uncensored mail and by casual conversations held in the course of prison tours provides sufficient access and is not arbitrary. * * *

The Washington Post insists that the in-depth individual inmate interviews are essential to adequate, fair reporting. It contends that the limited access afforded under the Bureau's policy is wholly inadequate. Communication by correspondence is said to be too impersonal and time-consuming. In order to write reliable stories, it is suggested, there is a need to observe demeanor, to probe by questioning and to overcome the barrier of semi-illiteracy and suspicion that may inhibit inmates when they write. * * *

Since "[t]he right to speak and publish does not carry with it the unrestrained right to gather information," Zemel v. Rusk, 381 U.S. 1, 17 (1964), the issue here tendered is, nonetheless, whether the interview restraint imposed by the Bureau's policy is unduly restrictive. A continuing flat prohibition against press interviews of any prisoner, at any time, under any circumstances, in any institution, is on its face arbitrary. The burden of justification rests upon the defendants. Cf., Sherbert v. Verner, 374 U.S. 398 (1963); Speiser v. Randall, 357 U.S. 513 (1958). It is not a matter of the Court substituting its judgment for the Bureau's but rather whether, given the breadth of the prohibition, it appears after balancing the considerations pro and con that the justification offered is obviously deficient. In short, are the limitations placed on First Amendment freedoms no greater than is necessary to protect the governmental interests asserted? . . .

Accordingly, it becomes necessary to examine the Bureau's justification for its absolute interview prohibition with care. Several considerations have prompted the Bureau's decision which was reached only after serious deliberation and study: (1) Excessive press attention to a relatively few notorious prisoners has detracted measurably from their rehabilitative treatment and imposed administrative difficulties. (2) When press interviews are held they receive immediate wide attention throughout the prisons and the importance of the prisoner interviewed is exaggerated among other inmates. * * * (3) A few prisoners may use the medium of the press to foster revolt within the walls. All news that goes out comes back in by newspaper, television and radio. Angry words, false accusations and protest geared to violence can light a fuse that erupts the pent-up emotions of inmates who may feel neglected and abused.

These are all real considerations and while somewhat impressionistic, they are supported by experience and advanced in good faith. The Court is satisfied, however, that the interview prohibition is too all-inclusive and that the factors mentioned do not justify a blanket denial of press access to all individual inmates willing to be interviewed. It is possible to prevent the difficulties and excesses feared by far less restrictive measures. Individual interviews may be refused where difficult administrative or disciplinary problems threaten and it goes too far to exclude all inmates from press access through individual interviews. . . .

The rules of the Bureau must be more precisely drawn to prohibit interviews only where it can be clearly established that serious administrative or disciplinary problems are being created. * * * The thrust of new press regulations should be to permit uncensored confidential interviews wherever possible and to withhold permission to interview on an individual basis only where demonstrable administrative or disciplinary considerations dominate. There is no necessity to treat all inmates alike and it will be appropriate to recognize a high degree of discretion in individual prison administrators. * * *

Defendants are directed to issue in thirty days a modified rule governing interviews consistent with this opinion.

Note 4.

CAROTHERS V. FOLLETTE
314 F. Supp. 1014 (1970)
United States District Court, Southern District of New York

It is the prison's practice in handling prisoner's mail, as revealed in depositions and answers to interrogatories, for prison officials to read all correspondence mailed by prisoners, including communications addressed to judges, legislative officials, attorneys, and private parties. Officials also assert the prerogative of deleting any portion of correspondence between an inmate and his attorney which the officials do not consider relevant to the prosecution of the inmate's legal affairs. The deletion is made either by striking the material or cutting off the portion in which the irrelevancy is included. Copies are made of any letters to a judge in which the prisoner complains of treatment or the institution, so that prison officials will have advance warning of any possible litigation that might be instituted against them, and will be able to investigate the complaint and answer inquiries by the court. The officials do not believe that they can refuse to mail correspondence addressed to a court or an attorney, but can if addressed to private parties. . . .

Except for the unsupported statement that "even judges have from time to time fallen by the wayside," (Sattler Aff. at 7), defendants apparently concede that maintenance of prison security does not require them to read a prisoner's letters to the court. Assuming, as we do, that from time to time prisoners misrepresent prison conditions to the court and make unwarranted charges and complaints, we fail to see how such conduct justifies disclosure to prison authorities of their entire correspondence with the court. The desire to be apprised of such matters to facilitate answering inquiries from the court does not, in our view, constitute adequate justification for examination of the prisoner's communication to the court. If the court should decide to follow up any complaint, the prison authorities would then be in a position to obtain the relevant portions of the prisoner's letter from the court so that appropriate investigation might be made.

Regardless of whether the mere reading of a prisoner's letter to the court, standing alone, justifies action on our part, however, we believe that the imposition of punishment or threat of such punishment based upon a prisoner's statements or complaints to the court about prison conditions chills the prisoner's exercise of his First Amendment right to voice legitimate complaints, and thus would amount to a form of deterrent censorship. In the present case, for instance, even if we accept at face value defendants' contention that the prison records are erroneous and that plaintiff was not segregated because of statements made to Judge Supple about harassment, it is undisputed that following transmittal of the letter disciplinary proceedings were instituted against the prisoner on the charge of making false and lying statements to the court about the administration of the prison. That charge (accepting defendants' version of the facts) was dismissed only because plaintiff was "already in segregation," which implies that some punishment, possibly segregation, would otherwise have been imposed. . . .

Note 5.

BERRIGAN V. NORTON
451 F.2d 790 (1971)
United States Court of Appeals, Second Circuit

OAKES, Circuit Judge:

This appeal is taken from the denial by District Judge Clarie of appellants' motion for a preliminary injunction in a suit involving first amendment and prison discipline questions. Appellants are the well-known Roman Catholic priests who in autumn 1970 were confined in the Danbury, Connecticut, Federal Correctional Institution ("Danbury"), following their convictions in connection with the destruction of selective service records in Maryland during 1967 and 1968....

Appellants had apparently drafted a sermon for delivery, but did not seek permission from the warden directly to deliver it in any way or to publish it....

This suit was brought to enjoin Warden Norton from restraining appellants' dissemination of the particular sermon mentioned above, from in any way curtailing the exercise of appellants' first amendment rights, and from enforcing Bureau of Prisons "Policy Memorandum" 7300.14 on the subject of "Inmate Manuscripts," a memorandum which was in the process of revision when suit was brought and which, we are advised by the Government, has since been superseded by "Policy Statement" 7300.7A.

We do not reach the constitutional questions presented in the complaint, nor do we in any way seek to determine what limitations, if any, those in charge of federal correctional facilities properly may place upon inmates' freedom of expression, in the interests of internal prison security or otherwise. Judicial review of issues of as grave importance as these cannot rest upon a record as incomplete as that before us....

There is nothing in this record from which we can conclude with reasonable certainty that the sermon in question would have been rejected had it been submitted, or indeed that any request was made to the caseworkers to submit it to the appropriate prison authority for examination.

This being true, appellants have made an insufficient showing of any infringement of first amendment rights. And, at least from the present state of the record, the appellants do not appear to present a justiciable case or controversy....

Denial of the "extraordinary remedy" of preliminary relief, as a matter of judicial discretion, is not improper where there is no "clear showing of probable success *and* possible irreparable injury."...

Judgment denying preliminary injunction affirmed.

Note 6.

FORTUNE SOCIETY V. MCGINNIS
319 F. Supp. 901 (1970)
United States District Court, Southern District of New York

WEINFELD, District Judge.

This is an action brought under the Civil Rights Act, 28 U.S.C., section 1343, and 42 U.S.C., section 1983, to protect the right of New York State prisoners to receive Fortune News, a newsletter regularly issued by The Fortune Society, Incorporated....

The facts do not appear in dispute. The Fortune Society, Incorporated is a non-profit membership corporation registered as a charitable organization with the New York State Department of Social Services, and is a federally tax exempt organization, which is maintained by contributions from various sources. Its primary purpose is to create a greater public awareness of the prison system in America today. The organization sends out teams of speakers, ex-convicts, who talk to school, church, business and civic groups and also appear on radio and television. The speakers seek to relate their firsthand experience of prison life and to foster a greater awareness of the causes of crime. The organization also seeks to assist ex-convicts, current inmates, and the families of both, by providing counselling, clothing, non-perishable foods, job referrals and other services. The Fortune Store is operated by the organization to provide employment for ex-convicts and as an outlet for ex-convict produced goods and crafts.

The Society publishes a monthly newsletter. The Fortune News, which contains articles and information on prison reform, ex-convicts' rehabilitation and the activities of the organization. This newsletter is widely distributed and is read by inmates in many penal institutions throughout the country....

Significantly, in opposing the plaintiffs' motion for preliminary injunctive relief, the defendants have offered no explanation for their ban of the Fortune News or for their continued refusal to permit its delivery to the two individual plaintiffs or to other prisoners at state institutions under the defendants' control. The sole purported explanation comes from the Executive Secretary of The Fortune Society, who states that the organization was informed by the Deputy Commissioner of Correction that the Fortune News was banned in all facilities under the Department's jurisdiction because the publication and the Society's speakers were not reflecting the truth concerning conditions in the state prison facilities. Also it is alleged that the ban continues in effect. These allegations are not put in issue by the defendants, who also do not deny that other publications are permitted to be delivered to prisoners without restriction or ban. The defendants have referred to no rule or regulation nor set forth any standards governing requests by inmates for publications or their delivery to them. They make no claim that the receipt by the individual plaintiffs or any other prisoners of the Fortune News would interfere with or be disruptive of prison discipline or administration.

The defendants' sole opposition to this motion is that at this juncture of the litigation the plaintiffs have not established they are entitled to preliminary injunctive relief; that they have failed to prove they will probably succeed on the merits, and that without such injunctive relief they will be irreparably damaged. The Court disagrees. To deprive one of his constitutional rights under the First Amendment, his right to read what he will and when he will, is in this Court's view irreparable and immediate injury. Moreover, upon the unchallenged facts here presented, there is indeed likelihood of success upon the trial. . . .

Under the facts as here presented, no compelling state interest has been advanced to justify the ban of the Fortune News. Its repression can be justified only upon a showing of a clear and present danger to prison discipline or security. The defendants have not even presented a pretext for any such claim. In the absence of such compelling justification, the action of the defendants in refusing the individual plaintiffs permission to receive the Fortune News has been arbitrary and is violative of the individual plaintiffs' First Amendment rights. Their arbitrary action is highlighted by the circumstance that New York City correctional authorities (functioning under state authority) have permitted and continue to permit the distribution of the Fortune News, the very newsletter denied to the individual plaintiffs herein. In this circumstance, not only have the plaintiffs' First Amendment rights been violated, but also their right to the equal protection of the laws under the Fourteenth Amendment.

The motion for a preliminary injunction is granted.

Note 7.

SOSTRE V. OTIS
330 F. Supp. 941 (1971)
United States District Court, Southern District of New York

MANSFIELD, Circuit Judge*

The essential question before us is whether any procedural due process safeguards should be afforded as a matter of constitutional right to a prisoner as a means of protecting his exercise of the First Amendment rights to which he is entitled, as so limited by prison conditions. The problem of establishing due process procedures that will be fairly and reasonably suited to prison conditions has only recently been the subject of judicial consideration in other connections. Sostre v. McGinnis, *supra* (prison discipline); Carothers v. Follette, 314 F.Supp. 1014 (S.D.N.Y.1970) (prison discipline); Menechino v. Oswald, *supra* (parole eligibility). This appears to be the first instance where the question has been presented with respect to a prisoner's right to receive and read literature.

It is urged that establishment of any such procedural safeguards is neither mandated nor necessary and that, since the day-to-day power to censor incoming literature (subject to final judicial supervision) is granted prison officials, the procedures followed do not matter: the concern of the courts should be limited to the correctness of the substantive results. This approach has been found unacceptable in the area of prison discipline, Sostre v. McGinnis, *supra*, and we likewise reject it in the equally important area of the prisoner's limited First Amendment rights. Indeed defendants here, by their recent adoption of a procedure having some aspects of due process, apparently recognize the inadequacy of the old approach, which not only has failed to protect such rights as the prisoner does have but has resulted in federal courts being swamped with *pro se* petitions seeking review, on a substantive basis of discipline arising out of exercise of First Amend-

* Was assigned the case as a District Judge and after appointment to the Circuit Court of Appeals was designated to sit on the District Court for the purpose of completing this phase of the case.

ment rights. See, e. g., Fortune Society v. McGinnis, *supra;* Walker v. Blackwell, *supra.* Furthermore, if adequate administrative procedural protection were afforded, federal courts might be relieved of jurisdiction, at least until administrative remedies had been exercised. See Eisen v. Eastment, 421 F.2d 560, 568–569 (2d Cir. 1969); Wright v. McMann, 387 F.2d 519, 527–528 (2d Cir. 1967).

... On the opposite extreme there are those who advocate that there should be no censorship at all, or that the prisoner should have the full panoply of due process rights—i. e., written notice of the proposed censorship, a recorded hearing before a disinterested party where the inmate can cross-examine and call witnesses on his own behalf, representation by retained counsel or a counsel substitute, and a written memorandum of decision setting forth the evidence, the reasons for the decision, and the action taken. The approach was rejected by the court in Sostre v. McGinnis, *supra,* in considering disciplinary procedures. We likewise reject it. As Judge Kaufman stated in *Sostre:*

> If substantial deprivations are to be visited upon a prisoner, it is wise that such action should at least be premised on facts rationally determined. * * * In most cases, it would probably be difficult to find an inquiry minimally fair and rational unless the prisoner were confronted with the accusation, informed of the evidence against him * * * and afforded a reasonable opportunity to explain his actions. Sostre v. McGinnis, 442 F.2d at 198.

We agree, and for the reasons expressed in *Carothers* we believe that a prisoner is entitled as a matter of constitutional right to rudimentary due process under prison conditions including (1) notice; (2) some opportunity to object (either personally or in writing), and (3) a decision by a body that can be expected to act fairly. We see no necessity for detailed rules and procedures on the subject, as long as basic fairness is assured, or for advance court approval of censorship. See Eisner v. Stamford Board of Education, 440 F.2d 803 (2d Cir. 1971) (school officials need not obtain judicial sanction before censoring publications on school property). As the court stated in *Sostre, supra:*

> [W]e do not believe that there is any need for the extraordinary procedure requiring defendants to submit rules and regulations governing the receipt, distribution, discussion and writing of political literature for the approval of the district court (442 F.2d at p. 204.)

... Applying these principles here, defendants appear to have met one of the requirements of due process, i. e., the establishment of a body that will act fairly in deciding censorship disputes. Their recently-adopted procedure represents a step toward eliminating the possibility of arbitrary action which is present when decisions regarding the acceptability of literature for prison inmates are made by a single official acting without the guidance of clearcut standards. The procedure seeks to involve responsible prison officials from a number of fields—including experts in mental hygiene, librarians, and chaplains—in evaluating each piece of literature that is challenged. Such evaluation is to be guided by a presumption that literature should be freely available, and a list of seven specific criteria of non-acceptability is provided. Moreover, the time limits within which decisions must be reached assure the inmate that his right to receive literature not posing a threat to prison order, discipline, and security will not be frustrated by undue administrative delays. In practice, the new procedures appear already to be having a healthy effect, for two publications which had been withheld from Sostre—*Claridad* and the *Guardian*—have now been screened and presented to him.

The foregoing procedure, as far as it goes, is to be commended. However, it does not go far enough. Lacking are the essential elements of notice to the prisoner that literature addressed to him has been censored or withheld and an opportunity to be heard. Notice to the prisoner is needed to inform him of the reason for delays in the receipt of literature, and also to inform him that he may present argument (either orally or in writing) to the committee in favor of a finding that the literature is acceptable. Although in some cases such an opportunity to be heard may have limited utility in that the inmate has no foreknowledge of the material he has ordered, in certain cases the inmate may be able to comment on the basis of knowledge of the material gained from reading it before incarceration, his familiarity with other works by the same author, or other sources such as book reviews, and his views as to the unlikelihood that the literature, however inflammatory, will lead to disruption.

In view of our disposition of this case, it is unnecessary to hold an evidentiary hearing or to review the disputed publications. Cf. Carroll v. President and Commissioners of Princess Anne, *supra,* 393 U.S. at 185, 89 S.Ct. 347, 21 L.Ed.2d 325. We find that the present procedure for screening literature is deficient in the respects indicated and enjoin the defendants from preventing Sostre from receiving literature of any kind, except pursuant to a finding of unacceptability resulting from a screening procedure in which the inmate concerned has notice and an opportunity to be heard.

Sostre's motion for judgment on the pleadings is treated as a motion for summary judgment, Rule 56, F.R.C.P., and is granted to the extent indicated.

We have noted the good faith manifested by the State and its counsel through the adoption of the procedure described above and the approval of much of the literature which Sostre ordered. The State's substantial interests in barring disruptive and inflammatory publications from its penal institutions must also be kept in mind. Therefore, we do not think it unreasonable to require that the publications not yet approved, as well as those previously returned to the publishers, be submitted to procedures complying with minimal due process, if such are adopted by the State. Accordingly, the effectiveness of this order is stayed 40 days from entry so as to permit modification of the recently-developed procedure (1) to require notice to the inmate involved, and (2) to give the inmate involved an opportunity to be heard.

It is so ordered.

Part III

RELEASE FROM PRISON: THE WAY OUT (AND IN AGAIN)

Chapter Ten

PRERELEASE

CONNECTICUT DEPARTMENT OF CORRECTION

Community Release Programs*

1. *PURPOSE*—To establish policies and procedures in accordance with current assessments of operating experience.
2. *POLICY*
    a. Community Release is intended as a correctional tool having many possible applications. While Community Release should be utilized to the fullest extent that circumstances permit, there can be no compromise of essential safeguards, community acceptance and careful selection of inmates. Participation in the Community Release Program may be terminated for willful negligence or misconduct on the part of the inmate involved.
    b. It is imperative that exploitation in any form or to any degree be avoided, either as it might affect the community or community release inmates. Specifically, the compensation of community release inmates will be no less than that of comparable workers, and they shall not be employed under working conditions at less than acceptable minimum standards. Conversely, community release inmates shall not be employed as strike-breakers or in situations that would evoke adverse public reaction directed either at the inmate involved, the Department of Correction, or the State of Connecticut.
    c. All inmates admitted to community release status remain in the custody of the Department of Correction. An inmate who willfully absconds shall be processed as an escapee.
    d. Each job shall be investigated to determine that it is bona fide, is consistent with basic community release policies, and will adequately fulfill the program goals for the inmate involved. In like manner, the Community Release Counselor will investigate each application for Educational Release to determine the suitability of having the inmate pursue further outside study. The Counselor will make known to the head of the educational facility, or his designee, the goals, policies, and operation of the program and as much of the individual's case his-

* Policy Directive dated Sept. 1, 1972.

tory as is necessary to arrive at sound decisions regarding hours and courses of study as well as participation in other related school activities. Case histories will not be discussed with anyone other than the individual responsible for the total daily operation of the facility.

They will further request that absence from classes, failure to absorb specific courses of instruction, or anything else of a detrimental nature be reported by the most expeditious means. While Community Release neither constitutes nor implies a contractual agreement between an employer, or educational facility administrator, and the Department of Correction, it must be recognized that mutual responsibilities exist. These derive from the fact that, though employed or attending school, the inmate is still in custody and his Community Release status is for a specific purpose.

e. Only the Commissioner of Correction, or such person as he designates, is empowered to admit an inmate to community release status or to remove him. Administrative responsibility for managing community release is placed with the Warden or Superintendent of each institution.

3. PROGRAM SUB-DIVISIONS—The various sub-divisions of the Community Release Program at present are: Education Release, Work Release, and the Resources and Opportunities Center. The stated purpose of each is as follows:
   a. *Education Release:* This part of the program provides an opportunity for selected inmates to acquire the benefits of higher education or technical skills for a school or college.
   b. *Work Release:* This portion of the program enables selected inmates confined in a correctional facility to leave the facility daily for employment at a regular job nearby.
   c. *Resources and Opportunities Center:* This Center is established to provide a programmed and supervised transition to productive community living for selected offenders who live within the New Haven area. The Center provides multiple services to its resident population. This program includes a voluntary support program for former residents after release and will continue to provide services for these men when necessary.

4. ADMINISTRATION
   a. *Purpose of Community Release:* Community Release lends itself to multiple uses:
      (1) As a pre-release tool, it provides opportunity to individuals who, in the judgment of the departmental screening committee, need further transitional preparation for community life.
      (2) There are a number of ways in which specific training needs may be met through community release as complements to education and training at the institutions.
      (3) Community Release may be appropriate and useful for certain inmates whose families have economic need.
      (4) It provides an effective way to accumulate savings for release, to make restitution and to pay legitimate debts, especially when such payments will free an inmate from overwhelming financial burden on the day of release.

   For any individual, the "purpose" may be a combination of the foregoing.
   b. *Community Relations:* It is essential that the Wardens, Superintendents and staffs promote public understanding and support for the Community Release Program wherever it exists. In part, this is a matter of developing and maintaining comunications networks for the purpose of imparting basic information, interpreting the aims of community release, and explaining its role in the total correctional process. It is important that institutions take this into account when designing staff training and development programs. Total staff involvement in community release plays a significant role in the professional growth of department employees.

   It is no less important that the official and other important segments of the community be kept advised of progress, modifications, and program innovations. To realize the program's full potential and to guard against any tendency on the part of employers and others to overprotect community release inmates, the understanding and continuing goodwill of community groups must be maintained.

   In line with the requirement that consultations with unions be carried out before inmates are placed in community release positions, it is emphasized that

this requirement applies to state government employee unions as well as those in private industry.
c. *Selection.*
  (1) Application: Any inmate wishing to be considered for any sub-division of the Community Release Program must apply through his institutional counselor on the prescribed form, copies of which are included with this directive. Inmates applying for the various sub-divisions of the program will be considered if they meet the following requirements:
    a. Must have a financial, vocational or educational need.
    b. Must be considered to be normally qualified for minimum custody status.
    c. Must be within one year of parole eligibility or release date.
    d. Must not have a history of serious emotional or psychiatric disorder.
    *e. Must not have a serious background of violent or assaultive behavior.
    *f. Must not have been convicted of a sex crime involving minors or use of force.
    *g. If involved in the use of hard narcotics, i.e., heroin, cocaine, an individual would only be accepted for a Community Release Program if he is involved in a drug treatment modality while in community release.

The Warden or Superintendent will cause the application to be screened by the Classification Committee. If the applicant is not eligible under the criteria established above, the application will be returned to the inmate. When the applicant is approved by the Classification Committee, the Warden or Superintendent will sign two copies of the application and forward them to the Chief of Community Release. If the application is approved, one signed copy will be returned to the institution from which it originated and the inmate may then be placed, or if necessary, transferred to the facility where he will be entered into the program.

  (2) *Custody:* Community Release will not be authorized for offenders identified with large scale organized criminal activity, nor for others whose presence in the community is likely to evoke adverse public reaction toward the inmate or the State of Connecticut.
  (3) *Physical Conditions:* The candidate for Community Release shall be in good health and be physically able to perform the proposed assignments. This requirement should not preclude the use of community release as an unusual opportunity to aid a physically handicapped person in obtaining community employment consistent with his capabilities.
  (4) *Emotional and Behavioral Factors:* Candidates with serious emotional or personality defects and those with histories of violent or assaultive behavior will be excluded. However, community release may be considered, under limited circumstances, for others who are mentally or emotionally handicapped and who are not dangerous to others, when it is apparent that community employment will significantly aid their post-release adjustment.
  (5) *Need:* Community Release is not intended as a program or status to be made available automatically to all who may be technically "eligible." There must be indicated need for the opportunities and responsibilities which community release provides. This is a departmental Screening Committee judgment to be related to the pre-release, family need or other individual circumstances for which community release is particularly appropriate. Further, it must be presupposed that the inmate will benefit from the experience. Decisions in cases of family need, restitution, and debt payment must be based on investigation so that official records will establish the inmate's responsibility and verify that the claimed need exists.
  (6) *Residence:* Preference shall be given candidates whose residence is in the vicinity of the institution or for whom

* Inmates who have unquestionably demonstrated their trustworthiness by a *long* record of stability may be considered for Community Release in some of the above cases, but this must be approved directly by the Deputy Commissioner of Community Services.

release plans in this vicinity are reasonable and appropriate. Although this should not exclude others, a number of factors must be weighed carefully:

(a) It can be expected that many inmates and their employers will want to continue their employment after release from the institution.
(b) No community will tolerate its becoming a "haven" for felony offenders even though they may be under supervision.
(c) There are circumstances in which sound correctional treatment involves relocating an offender from a home or community situation that is untenable or lacking in opportunity. (In this respect, caution is recommended. Experience indicates some strong tie in the new community is needed. Relocating an offender solely because he thinks it's "a good idea" rarely works out, especially in cases of younger offenders.)

(7) *Type of Work:* There need be no general restrictions on the kinds of work release jobs for which candidates may be considered. The expectation is that the job selected will be that which best fulfills the purpose of community release in each case consistent with the fact that the employed inmate is still in custody. Good employment placement will give preference to jobs that are related to prior training, work experience, or institutional training and may be suitable for continuing post-release employment. The "breakeven" point between wages and expenses will tend to eliminate temporary, part-time and intermittent employment.

(8) *Duration:* Placements shall be limited ordinarily to a period of approximately six months immediately preceding the probable release or parole eligibility date. Exceptions can be made when fully justified.

(9) *Transfers:* Inmates shall be recommended for transfer to a specific Community Release function or facility so long as all other eligibility requirements are met.

d. *Transportation:* All transportation arrangements shall be approved by the Chief of Community Release Programs. As a practical matter, little can be accomplished if the travel time between the institution and the job, or place of assignment, exceeds 15 to 30 minutes each way. Within reasonable limits of convenience, Community Release jobs need not be restricted to "normal" work hours. When suitable transportation can be arranged, there should be no objection to shift work or overtime. Community Release inmates may not be permitted to drive personally-owned cars. Community releasees shall pay their share of transportation costs.

5. *FISCAL PROCEDURES*
a. *Receipts:* All funds received are to be deposited intact. All monies are to be transferred to the Work Release Accountant once a week. If mailed, the monies are to be deposited into the Inmates' Fund and a check drawn for the same amount, payable to the Work Release Program. Cash or check payable to inmates are *not* to be sent through the mail. A receipt is given to each inmate every time he turns money into the program. The UARCO Form presently used in the AP Room serves our present needs. The white copy is given to the inmate and the yellow copy, or a photocopy of the yellow copy, is forwarded to Central Office, Hartford, with the monies. The receipt must designate the type of funds that are received on admission; paycheck, visit, etc. Section 432 of the General Statutes states, in part, that, all receipts shall be deposited within 24 hours except that when receipts do not total $100.00, they may not be held in excess of one week. This section of the General Statutes must be complied with.
b. *Weekly Allowance:* Each inmate in the Work Release Program is entitled to a *maximum* of $12.00 per week for personal spending money. No program participant will be allowed to accumulate funds by saving the unspent portion of his weekly allowance. The Community Release Counselor will notify the Work Release Accountant, *in writing,* each week of the amount of the weekly allowance check together with the subsistence deduction.
c. *Subsistence and Transportation:* Each inmate who is employed while on the

Work Release Program will be charged $27.00 per week for subsistence and transportation. The inmate will not be charged for his first week of employment if this is less than three (3) working days. For subsistence portions of weeks (i.e., in situations of less than a 40-hour work week) subsistence and transportation will be based on the following:

	Subsistence Charge
One day	$ 5.40
Two days	10.80
Three days	16.20
Four days	21.60
Five days	27.00

Should an inmate not have enough money on deposit with the program at the time he leaves, he will only be charged an amount equal to his deposit for the last chargeable week.

d. *Special Allowance:* When special funds are needed by the inmate for work clothes, books, tools, court fines, family needs, etc., the Work Release Program "Request for Withdrawal of Funds" form will be completed and submitted to the Deputy Commissioner of Community Services, with a copy forwarded to the Chief of Community Release Programs. This request will be granted only if the inmate has sufficient funds on deposit with the Work Release Program Accountant to comply with a basic reason for this program which is, "to have adequate funds upon release whereby the inmate can maintain himself." It should be noted here that a maximum of $50.00 is allowed for work clothes and this is a one-time allowance.

e. *Payments to Dependents:* The Community Release Counselor will advise the State Welfare Department of all inmates employed on the program. Up to 50% of the inmate's net earnings, after deductions for his weekly allowance and room and board, will be forwarded to the Welfare Department as partial or total reimbursement for his family's support, if any.

f. *Loans:* Loans will be granted to indigent inmates who require funds for work clothes, tools, etc. Loans should be approved by the person in charge of the Community Release Program at the facility and then forwarded to the Chief of Community Release Programs for final approval. Three (3) copies of the Loan Agreement should be completed. The original and one copy retained by the institution.

NOTE: Loans should be repaid from the first paycheck or as soon as possible thereafter and should not be left until the individual is about to be released.

g. *Discharge Allowance:* When an inmate is nearing his release date, the Work Release Accountant is to be notified. Notification should be received *at least* three (3) days in advance to assure that the check will be received in time for the inmate's release.

h. *Guidance and Counseling:* To the fullest extent possible, guidance and counseling services shall be made available to Community Release inmates. Often there will be special and immediate needs for such services arising from problems on the job and working conditions, in addition to the usual range of personal and family matters. Volunteer counselors may assist in this function. However, volunteers must be carefully screened, hours scheduled, and duties clearly defined in a structured program. All such volunteers must receive Central Office clearance over the recommendation of the Warden or Superintendent.

i. *Terminations:* All terminations of community releasees from the program shall be reported on Form COR 107 "Report of Removal from Community Release Program."

1) If the Warden or Superintendent, or person acting in this capacity, or the Community Release Counselor believes that for disciplinary or any other reason, the community releasee should be removed from the program he may restrict the inmate to the work release section or, if he deems it necessary, transfer the inmate to a more secure section of the correctional center and not permit him to go to work, school or other area outside the institution.

2) A report explaining the reasons for recommending the removal of the inmate from the program will then be sent to the Chief of the Community Release Program. If it is believed by the person making the rec-

ommendation for removal that fast action is required, the Chief of Community Release Programs may be notified by phone and if the recommendation for removal is approved, authorization for immediate action may be given with the written report to follow. If the Chief of Community Release Programs is not available, the Deputy Commissioner of Community Services or his delegate should be notified. The above action should be authorized by the Warden or Superintendent.

j. *Clothing:* Clothing may be brought in by authorized persons if the inmate does not have them at the institution. Release clothes may be used when available. If the inmate has not suitable clothes, he may purchase them outside the institution if he has the funds. If the inmate has no funds, he may borrow up to $50.00 for their purchase. The suitability and the cost of the clothes must be approved by the Community Release Counselor who will accompany the inmate while he buys the clothes.

MEDICAL AND DENTAL CARE

a. *Medical Care:* Each correctional facility has its own medical/dental care program which is under the direct control of the Warden or Superintendent. For those Community Release Program sub-divisions which are housed at the various correctional centers, the normal procedure for obtaining treatment or relief is as follows:

1) All medical decisions will be made by approved departmental medical personnel; therefore, an individual requesting medical attention will not report to work but will remain in the Center and the counselor will place his name on the sick call list. At the proper time he will be examined by the physician or medical attendant on duty. Should he require treatment which is not available at the Center, or hospitalization for an extended period, this information must be transmitted through proper channels to the Deputy Commissioner of Community Services who will issue procedural instructions and approve any necessary transfer.

2) *Dental Care:* Dental care will be handled in the same manner.

3) *Injuries:* Should a work releasee be injured while at his place of employment, the employer will be responsible for the emergency medical care required. In the event extended medical care or hospitalization is required, arrangements for such care or hospitalization, at the employer's expense, will be made *only* with the full knowledge of the Warden or Superintendent and the express approval of the physician at the facility and/or the Deputy Commissioner of Community Services.

4) *Medication:* Any form or type of medication received from other than institutional medical facilities will be approved and dispensed in accordance with institutional medical procedures.

5) *Prosthesis:* Eyeglasses, dentures, or any prosthesis that needs repair or replacement will, unless originally provided by the State during a period of incarceration, be paid for by the work releasee; and then only after the Work Release "Request for Withdrawal of Funds" form has been completed and approved by the Deputy Commissioner of Community Services. . . .

NOTES

Note 1. Reducing Isolation from the Community as a Correctional Objective

THE PRESIDENT'S COMMISSION ON LAW ENFORCEMENT AND ADMINISTRATION OF JUSTICE,

Task Force Report: Corrections 56–57 (1967)

With all the innovations and improvements an institution still remains, of course, an institution—isolated from the community where its inmates must eventually make their way. The small-unit, community-oriented model institution based on experience with the special community residential programs attempts to overcome the institution's handicap in promoting reintegration. Its position in the cities from which it draws the bulk of its inmates, its small size and relative informality, would greatly facilitate the use of work- and study-release programs, furloughs and field trips, and the employment of subprofessionals and volunteers in the institution to help overcome the isolation of correctional staff.

But, while aiming for this goal, more traditional institutions can employ many of the same concepts. Doing so will not only help greatly in achieving successful reintegration but also will make it possible for staff to evaluate more accurately the readiness of offenders for release, by noting and discussing their adjustment to the stresses of community life.

For while observations in an institution may add somewhat to the information available on the prospects of an offender's continuation in crime, there are serious inherent limitations on this source of information. Recidivistic offenders who are committed to a life of crime often learn to adjust to imprisonment well and strive to make the most favorable impression possible in order to obtain the earliest opportunity to be free to engage in crime again. And, in many cases, the conditions of imprisonment and the requirements for successful adjustment there differ radically from those prevailing in the free community.

These deficiencies of observation during confinement are diminished greatly in an institution run on the collaborative model, which minimizes the artificialities of prison societies. Nevertheless, the crucial test remains that of observation after release in the community. Parole is supposed to provide observation through its supervision staff, but this usually means brief observation by a parole officer only once in several weeks, and typically in the parole office. A major augmentation to these sources of knowledge about an inmate's readiness to assume responsibility has come from recently developed or expanded procedures for temporary release.

Furloughs from the institution for a few days are one such means of temporary release. These have been most developed in institutions for juveniles, where their use is especially extensive at family occasions such as Christmas, Thanksgiving, weddings, and funerals. Their use for adults is more often to facilitate release arrangements; for example, to contact potential employers. Furloughs from prisons have been most extensive in Mississippi and Michigan, each of which has reported less than 1 percent failure to return.

Liberalization of policies governing visits and letters for inmates is also helpful and can be used even for inmates who cannot be released. A number of volunteer groups, notably the Quakers, visit inmates who desire it, mostly those who have no family visitors. Censoring of inmate mail, except for occasional spot checks, has been abolished in Federal prisons and in several State systems. Classes and lectures bringing in outside leaders or participants are widely used to encourage social contacts among inmates, their families, and groups of citizens who are particularly interested in the field of corrections. Debating societies organized by inmates, discussion groups, bridge and chess clubs, and therapeutic groups such as Alcoholics Anonymous are among the institutional organizations that have frequent contact with counterpart groups in the community.

The corollary to bringing people and programs in from the community is the practice of taking groups of inmates out to participate in a wide variety of recreational and educational activities in the community. Most progressive juvenile institutions use such trips as a reward for good performance. Its value is, of course, substantially curtailed when the institution is in a remote location that offers few of the needed resources.

The most dramatically rapid increase in temporary release from prisons that has occurred in recent years has been in work-release programs. The record with work release has been predominantly favorable, despite some difficulties inherent in the lack of long experience in administering it.

. . . When an individual returns from a temporary release to home, work, or school, his experience can be discussed with him by staff, to try to assess his probable adjustment and to note incipient problems. Many difficulties can be anticipated in this way, the inmate's frustrations can be relieved by discussion, and help can be given him to develop realistic plans and insights for coping with everyday problems. When persistent or serious misbehavior occurs, sanctions are available to staff, ranging from restriction of further leaves or temporary incarceration to renewed institutionalization with a recommendation to the parole board that the date of parole be deferred.

In addition to devices that encourage contact between inmates and the community, there are programs aimed at increasing public interest and participation in institutional management. Private citizens are brought into contact with the institution's programs and policies. Advisory councils are recruited to provide the technical and professional assistance necessary for maintaining adequate standards in institutional education, vocational training, and other specialized operations. They are also effective in educating the public regarding problems and issues. In this way they tend to encourage informed public support of correctional programs.

Note 2. The Frequency of Work-Release

ELMER H. JOHNSON

*Report on an Innovation—State Work-Release Programs**

The work-release approach to penal reform has received remarkable support in the last fifteen years.

... A nationwide survey was made. Each state was asked whether it had passed legislation authorizing work release for inmates of the adult correctional system. If such legislation did exist, a questionnaire was sent to the state correctional agency to determine whether the legislation has resulted in an actual program. Those states where such programs are in effect were asked for information on how certain practical problems are handled. The purpose of the study was to evaluate the progress of such reform in the face of the obstacles confronting it.

Of the fifty states and the District of Columbia, twenty-eight reported existing legislation authorizing a work-release program for the state-operated correctional agency. Seven other states have authorized work release for municipal or county correctional institutions but not for the state agencies. ...

* Reprinted, with permission of the National Council on Crime and Delinquency, from *Crime and Delinquency*, October 1970, pp. 417–19.

TABLE 1.—STATUS OF WORK RELEASE IN STATES WITH LEGISLATION AUTHORIZING PROGRAM (FALL 1968)

State	Year Prison Program Authorized	Year Jail Program Authorized	Prison Program Implemented?	Date Prison Program Implemented	Number of Inmates Now on Program
Alaska	1967	1967	Yes	July 1967	none
Calif.	1965	1957[a]	Yes	Apr. 1966	25
Colo.	1967	1965[a]	Yes	Feb. 1968	4
Conn.	1968	—	In planning stage	—	—
Del.	1958[b]	unreported	No response	1958[b]	unreported
D.C.	1966	1966	Yes	Apr. 1966	117
Fla.	1967	1963[a]	In planning stage	—	—
Ga.	1968	—	In planning stage	—	—
Hawaii	1967	1937	Yes	June 1968	7
Idaho	—	1957	—	—	—
Ill.	1967	—	In planning stage	—	—
Ind.	1967	1963	Yes	Apr. 1968	28
Iowa	1967	1966[a]	Yes	July 1967	7
Me.	1967	1967[a]	Yes	Feb. 1968	22
Md.	1963	1963[a]	Yes	July 1963	207
Mass.	1967	1962[a]	No response	—	—
Mich.	1966	1962[a]	Yes	June 1966	84
Minn.	1967	1959[a]	Yes	Oct. 1967	19
Mont.	—	1968	—	—	—
Neb.	1967	—	Yes	Oct. 1967	11
N.H.	1967	—	Yes	May 1968	11
N.C.	1957	—	Yes	1957	979
N.D.	—	1957	—	—	—
Oreg.	1965	1957[a]	Yes	Mar. 1966	96
Pa.	—	1963	—	—	—
R.I.	1966	1966	Yes	Oct. 1966	13
S.C.	1966	—	Yes	June 1966	42
S.D.	1967	1967[a]	Yes	Jan. 1968	9
Tenn.	—	1967	—	—	—
Utah	1967	1967	Yes	Dec. 1967	30
Vt.	1966	1968	Yes	July 1966	16
Va.	—	1956	—	—	—
Wash.	1967	1961[a]	Yes	Jan. 1968	15
W. Va.	—	1959	—	—	—
Wis.	1965	1913[a]	Yes	Oct. 1965	17

[a] Prison department of the state reports work release has been implemented by some of the local jails.
[b] Source of this information is David A. Bachman, *Work-Release Programs for Adult Felons in the United States: A Descriptive Study*, M.A. thesis, Florida State University, 1968, Table 3.

Note 3. International Perspectives
STANLEY E. GRUPP

Work Release in Other Countries*

A number of countries abroad provide for some form of work release and closely allied procedures. They include Belgium, Denmark, Federal Republic of Germany, France, Great Britain, Italy, New Zealand, Norway, Scotland, Sweden, and The Netherlands. There are probably others. . . .

Inspection of the available information suggests that a number of these programs are comparable to the halfway houses and prerelease guidance centers in this country and therefore depart somewhat from the concept of work release as it is considered in this paper. France is an exception to this generalization for the program includes persons serving short sentences of a year or less.

Sweden may have been the earliest country to experiment with work release. Informal experimentations started there in 1937. Informal work-release procedures seem to have antedated formal inauguration in other countries, too, for example, in Norway and France. And it appears that Germany under the Weimar Republic initiated procedures closely approximating work release.

Sweden formally authorized work release in 1945. Formal inauguration in other countries followed: Scotland in 1947, Norway in 1958, Great Britain in 1953, and France in 1959. Of these countries, it appears that France is currently making the most active use of work release.

---

* Stanley E. Grupp, "Work Release and the Misdemeanant," 29 *Federal Probation* No. 2 at 7 (1965). Reprinted with permission of the author and the publisher.

Chapter Eleven

PAROLE: UNFETTERED POWER AND DISCRETIONARY PREDICTION

A. Historical Perspectives

FREDERICK A. MORAN

The Origins of Parole*

Parole is the conditional release of an individual from a penal or correctional institution, after he has served part of the sentence imposed upon him. Parole did not develop from any specific source of experiment, but is an outgrowth of a number of independent measures, including the conditional pardon, apprenticeship by indenture, the transportation of criminals to America and Australia, the English and Irish experiences with the system of ticket of leave, and the work of American prison reformers during the nineteenth century.

* Reprinted with permission from *1945 Yearbook of the National Probation Association,* pp. 71–82; 84; 87–89; 92–96.

Conditional Pardons and Transportation to America

The transportation of criminals to the American colonies began early in the seventeenth century. . . .

The transportation of criminals to America was backed and supported by the London, Virginia, and Massachusetts companies, and similar organizations. . . . The plan was presented to the King and he approved the proposal to grant reprieves and stays of execution to the convicted felons who were physically able to be employed in service. . . .

In the beginning no specific conditions were imposed upon those receiving these pardons. However, because a number of those pardoned had evaded transportation or had returned to England prior to the expiration of their term, it was found necessary to impose certain restrictions upon the individuals to whom these pardons were granted. It was about 1655 that the form of pardon was amended to include specific conditions and to provide for the nullification of the pardon if the recipient failed to abide by the conditions imposed. . . .

Upon arrival of the pardoned felons in the colonies, their services were sold to the highest bidder and the shipmaster then transferred the "property in service" agreement to the new master. The felon thereupon was no longer referred to as a criminal but became an indentured servant.

The system of indenture dates back to the Statute of Artifices enacted in 1562, and originally it had no relation to persons convicted of crime. Blackstone defined apprentices as "another species of servants who were usually bound out for a term of years by deed indenture." The contract of indenture was written on a large sheet of paper, the halves separated by a wavy or jagged line called an indent. The master and the apprentice or his guardian signed the form, thereby agreeing to conform with the conditions specified. Van Doren in his biography of Benjamin Franklin, quotes the conditions imposed upon Franklin in 1718, when at the age of twelve he became indentured to his brother:

> . . . During which term the said apprentice his master faithfully shall or will serve, his secrets keep, his lawful demands everywhere gladly do. He shall do no damage to his said master nor see it done to others, but to his power shall let or forthwith give notice to his said master of the same. The goods of his said master he shall not waste, nor the same without license of him to give or lend. Hurt to his said master he shall not do, cause or procure to be done. He shall neither buy nor sell without his master's license.
>
> Taverns, inns or alehouses he shall not haunt. At cards or dice tables or any other unlawful game he shall not play. Matrimony he shall not contract nor from the services of his said master day or night absent himself but in all things as an honest faithful apprentice shall and will demean and behave himself toward said master all during said term.

This indenture bears a similarity to the procedure now followed by parole boards in this country. Like the indentured servant, a prisoner conditionally released on parole agrees in writing to accept certain conditions included on the release form which is signed by the members of the parole board and the prisoner. Even some of the conditions imposed today on conditionally released prisoners are similar to those included on the indenture agreement. . . .

The termination of the Revolutionary War ended transportation to America, but England did not repeal her transportation law. Judges continued to impose sentences of transportation and the places of detention for prisoners awaiting transportation soon became overcrowded. Some attempt was made to relieve the situation by granting pardons freely, but when a serious outbreak of crime occurred, the public demanded that the transportation law be enforced. . . .

Australia had been discovered by Captain Cook in 1770 and the government deliberated whether to use this land as a refuge for the thousands of American Royalists who had returned to England and were starving, or to establish Australia as a new colony for the reception of transported felons. In 1787 the King announced that Australia was to be used for convict settlement, and in May 1787 the first fleet sailed, arriving at Botany Bay on January 18, 1788.

A different procedure was followed in dealing with prisoners transported to Australia than had previously been followed in transporting them to America. All the expense incurred was met by the government and the criminals transported did not become indentured servants but remained prisoners under the control of the government which assumed responsibility for their behavior and welfare. . . .

The first governor of Australia received instructions from the government regarding the emancipation and discharge from servitude of prisoners whose conduct and work records indicated they were worthy to receive a grant of land. At first these prisoners received an absolute pardon but later a new form of conditional pardon was instituted which became known as "ticket of leave."

This ticket of leave was merely a declaration signed by the governor or his secretary, dispensing a convict from attendance at government work and enabling him, on condition of supporting himself, to seek employment within a specified district. No provision was made for his supervision by the government. . . . Great stress has been placed upon the experiments of Alexander Maconochie, who was assigned as governor of Norfolk Island in 1840. . . . He proposed that the duration of the sentence be measured by labor and good conduct within a minimum of time; that the labor thus required be represented by marks proportional to the original sentence, the prisoner to earn these marks in penal servitude before discharge. Marks were to be credited day by day to the convict, according to the amount of work accomplished. . . .

In America as early as 1817 provisions had been made for the reduction of sentences by allowance for satisfactory work and conduct. The English Penal Servitude Act of 1853, governing prisoners convicted in England and Ireland, substituted imprisonment for transportation. By this act prisoners who received sentences of fourteen years or less were committed to prison, but the judge was granted permissive power to order the transportation or imprisonment of individuals who had received terms of more than fourteen years. This law also specified the length of time prisoners were required to serve before becoming eligible for conditional release on ticket of leave.

Those who had sentences exceeding seven years but not more than ten years, became eligible for ticket of leave after they had served four years and not more than six years. Prisoners who had sentences of more than ten years but less than fifteen, were required to serve at least six but not more than eight years, and those with sentences of fifteen years or more were required to serve not less than six nor more than ten years. America did not develop the use of the indeterminate sentence until nearly a quarter of a century after the enactment of the English Act in 1853. . . .

Long before the termination of transportation it had been recognized that the experiment followed in Australia of releasing prisoners on ticket of leave without further supervision was a serious mistake. However, this knowledge did not prevent a repetition of the procedure. The public had assumed that the Home Office planned to enforce the conditions imposed upon prisoners released on ticket of leave, but it was discovered later that the Home Office had no such plan and in fact was disinterested.

More than five thousand prisoners were granted tickets of leave during the first two years after the enactment of the Servitude Act of 1853. The outbreak of serious crimes which occurred within the next three years was attributed to the lack of supervision accorded the released prisoners. A campaign of criticism was carried on and ticket of leave men were blamed for most of the crimes committed. The public became convinced that the ticket of leave system was not only a menace to public safety but was an absolute failure. . . .

. . . Sir William Crofton became head of the Irish prison system in 1854, one year after the enactment of the Servitude Act. He accepted the idea that the intent of the law was to make penal institutions something more than places of safe keeping, and that the programs in the prisons should be designed toward reformation and tickets of leave granted only to prisoners who gave visible evidence of definite achievement and change of attitude.

The Irish convict system under Crofton's administration became famous for its three stages of penal servitude, particularly the second stage where classification was governed by marks obtained for good conduct and achievement in education and industry. So-called "indeterminate prisons" were also utilized, where conditions were made as nearly normal as possible and no more restraint was exercised over the inmates than was necessary to maintain order.

The administrators of the Irish system maintained that its success was due to the cooperation extended by the convict toward his own amendment, and his conviction sooner or later that the system, however penal in its character, was designed for his benefit and that stringent regulations imposed for his supervision after release rendered a vocation of crime unprofitable and hazardous to follow. . . .

By 1865 the Crofton system had been widely publicized in America, and prison reformers who were critical of the conditions existing in our prisons suggested the adoption of new methods based on the Crofton plan. Although there were some critics of the Irish system, little attention was given to their opposition and American reformers continuously enunciated the need for new types of prison programs to provide for the grading of criminals according to the degree of their reformation, and the use of the mark system as a check on their progress and restraint against disorder. . . .

At the time the propaganda was being carried on for the adoption of the Crofton plan, the Elmira Reformatory in New York was being constructed. Because of the widespread interest in prison programs, it would logically be assumed that before the new institution was opened, a suitable plan or organization would have been developed and necessary legislation enacted or at least suggested by the board of managers of the state government. Elmira Reformatory was formally opened in July 1876 and had been operating for almost a year before its first superintendent, Z. R. Brockway, drafted a measure establishing a definite policy.

Prior to his appointment to Elmira Reformatory, Mr. Brockway had been head of the House of Correction in Detroit and while there, had drafted an indetermine sentence law. His proposed measure outlined the following special features for the Elmira system: 1) an indeterminate or indefinite sentence, the length of time served to be dependent upon the behavior and capacity of the prisoners, within statutory limitations; 2) the status and privileges accorded to the prisoner, as in the Crofton plan, were to be determined by his behavior and progress; 3) education was to be compulsory; 4) Provision was made for the release on parole of carefully selected prisoners. . . .

The vital principle of the indeterminate sentence was that no prisoner would be paroled until he was fit for freedom. Those who campaigned for the adoption of the indeterminate sentence recognized that in itself it had no mystic power but that its real strength was in the reformatory agencies—labor, education, and religion. It was also recognized that the indeterminate sentence placed in the hands of competent prison officials a tool which could be effectively used. . . .

B. Statutory Structure

AN ILLUSTRATIVE STATUTE: CONNECTICUT*

Sec. 54-124a. Board of Parole

The board of parole shall consist of seven members, including a chairman and two women, all of whom shall be qualified by training and experience for the consideration of matters before them and who shall be appointed by the governor with the advice and consent of either house of the general assembly. The terms of members of the board of parole in office on July 1, 1968, shall terminate on said date. The governor shall appoint the chairman and one other member of said board for terms of four years, two members for a term of three years, two for a term of two years and one for a term of one year from said July 1, 1968, and appointments of members to replace those whose terms expire shall thereafter be for terms of four years. The chairman shall devote his entire time to the performance of his duties hereunder and shall be compensated therefor in such amount as the personnel policy board determines. The other members of said board shall receive seventy-five dollars for each day spent in the performance of their duties and shall be reimbursed for necessary expenses incurred in the performance of such duties. Three members of said board shall constitute a quorum, provided the chairman, or in his absence or inability to act a member designated by him to serve temporarily as chairman, shall be present at all meetings of said board and participate in all decisions thereof.

Sec. 54-125. Parole

Any person confined in the State Prison or the State Prison for Women for an indeterminate sentence, after having been in confinement under such sentence for not less than the minimum term, or, if sentenced for life, after having been in confinement under such sentence for not less than twenty-five years, less such time, not exceeding a total of five years, as may have been earned under the provisions of section 18–7, may be allowed to go at large on parole in the discretion of a quorum of the board of parole, if (1) it appears from all available information, including such reports from the commissioner of correction as the board may require, that there is reasonable probability that such inmate will live and remain at liberty without violating the law and (2) such release is not incompatible with the welfare of society. Such parolee shall be allowed in the discretion of the board to return to his home, or to go elsewhere, upon such terms and conditions, including personal reports from such paroled person, as the board prescribes, and to remain, while on parole, in the legal custody and control of the board until the expiration of the maximum term or terms for which he was sentenced. Each order of parole shall fix the limits of the parolee's

---

* Conn. Gen. Stat. §§ 54–124a *et seq.*

residence, which may be changed in the discretion of the board. Within one week after the commitment of each person sentenced during any criminal term of the superior court, the state's attorney of each country and the state's attorney at Waterbury shall send to the board of parole the record, if any, of each person sentenced to the State Prison or committed to the custody of the commissioner of correction during such term. In the case of an inmate serving an indeterminate sentence at the Connecticut Reformatory or at The Connecticut State Farm for Women, the board of parole shall establish, by rule, the date upon which said board shall notify the inmate that his eligibility for parole will be considered. At any time prior thereto the superintendent may recommend that parole be granted and, under special and unusual circumstances, the superintendent may recommend that an inmate be discharged from the institution.

Sec. 54-126. Rules and Regulations Concerning Parole

Said board of parole may establish such rules and regulations as it deems necessary, upon which such convict may go upon parole, and the commissioner of correction shall enforce such rules and regulations and retake and reimprison any convict upon parole, for any reason that said board, or the commissioner with the approval of the board, deems sufficient; and the commissioner may detain any convict or inmate pending approval by the board of such retaking or reimprisonment.

Sec. 54-127. Rearrest

The request of said commissioner or said board of parole shall be sufficient warrant to authorize any officer of the department of correction, or any officer authorized by law to serve criminal process within this state, to return any convict or inmate on parole into actual custody; and any such officer, police officer, constable or sheriff shall arrest and hold any parolee or inmate when so requested, without any written warrant, and, for the performance of such duty, the officer performing the same, except officers of said department, shall be paid by the state, through the department of correction, such reasonable compensation as is provided by law for similar services in other cases.

Sec. 54-128. Violation of Parole

(a) Any paroled convict or inmate who has been returned to the custody of the commissioner of correction or any institution of the department of correction for violation of his parole may be retained in the institution from which he was paroled for a period equal to the unexpired portion of the term of his sentence at the date of the request or order for his return less any commutation or diminution of his sentence earned except that the board of parole may, in its discretion, determine that he shall forfeit any or all of such earned time, or may be again paroled by said board. (b) Each parolee or inmate, subject to the provisions of section 18–7, shall be subject to loss of all or any portion of time earned.

Sec. 54-129. Discharge of Paroled Prisoner

If it appears to said board of parole that any convict or inmate on parole will continue to lead an orderly life, said board, by a unanimous vote of all the members present at any regular meeting thereof, may declare such convict or inmate discharged from the custody of the commissioner of correction and shall thereupon deliver to him a written certificate to that effect under the seal of the board of parole and signed by its chairman and the commissioner.

NOTES

The Model Penal Code and Prevailing American Statutory Structure

Note 1.

LEONARD ORLAND

On Parole*

The task of Congress in legislating on sentencing is to determine how to direct, control and delegate discretion between the judiciary and parole in determining when incarcerated felons may be released. At one extreme, Congress could, for example, eliminate all judicial discretion at sentencing, either by legislating the mandatory maximum and minimum for

* Statement of Leonard Orland, February 17, 1972, submitted to Subcommittee on Criminal Laws and Procedures of the Senate Judiciary Committee, "The Proposed Federal Penal Code: Some Issues Concerning Sentencing and Parole."

each criminal offense, or by legislatively fixing the maximum incarceration term, but authorizing the parole board, and not the court to determine the "minimum". Alternatively, Congress could circumscribe the authority of the parole decision maker and enlarge the power of the court by authorizing the court, without limitation, to fix the maximum and the minimum.

Existing patterns of sentencing authority vary widely. Several surveys in the 1960's, for example, found fourteen jurisdictions in which the court set both maxima and minima, twelve jurisdictions in which the court fixed the maximum (with the minimum determined by the legislature), eight jurisdictions in which the maximum and minimum was fixed legislatively for each offense, and four jurisdictions, led by California, in which the legislature, not the court, fixed the maximum, and the parole board, not the court, ultimately established maximum and minimum.

The approach of the Model Penal Code is to establish a limited number of felony categories, to mandate a legislatively established maximum within each category, to authorize the court to set the maximum up to that legislatively established, to further authorize the court to set a minimum, but to limit the court's discretion in establishing high minima that began to approach maxima. The consequence of this approach is to severely limit legislative and judicial controls over the actual period of time served and to delegate to the parole board greater authority to determine how much time the offender will actually serve.

The Model Penal Code approach has had great impact on state penal law reform movements and has obvious influence on the proposed federal penal code.

Note 2.

DONALD GLASER, FRED COHEN, AND VINCENT O'LEARY

The Sentencing and Parole Process
[Reprinted *supra*, p. 17.]

Note 3. *Prevailing Parole Patterns*

THE PRESIDENT'S COMMISSION ON LAW ENFORCEMENT AND ADMINISTRATION OF JUSTICE,

Task Force Report: Corrections 60–63 (1967)

The test of the success of institutional corrections programs comes when offenders are released to the community. Whatever rehabilitation they have received, whatever deterrent effect their experience with incarceration has had, must upon release withstand the difficulties of readjustment to life in society and reintegration into employment, family, school, and the rest of community life. This is the time when most of the problems from which offenders were temporarily removed must be faced again and new problems arising from their status as ex-offenders must be confronted.

Many offenders are released outright into the community upon completion of their sentences, but a growing number—now more than 60 percent of adult felons for the Nation as a whole—are released on parole prior to the expiration of the maximum term of their sentences. Parole supervision, which in general resembles probation in methods and purposes, is the basic way—and one of the oldest—of trying to continue in the community the correctional program begun in the institution and help offenders make the difficult adjustment to release without jeopardy to the community. Furloughs, halfway houses, and similar programs are important supplements to effective parole programs, as are prerelease guidance and other social services discussed later in this chapter.

Parole is generally granted by an administrative board or agency on the basis of such factors as an offender's prior history, his readiness for release, and his need for supervision and assistance in the community prior to the expiration of his sentence. The Federal system and those of a few States have a mandatory supervision procedure for offenders not released on parole. Under such a procedure, when an inmate is released for good behavior before serving his maximum term, he is supervised in the community for a period equivalent to his "good time credit."

Table 1 shows the average number of offenders under parole supervision in 1965 and the yearly cost of operations. Data include the small number of offenders released under mandatory supervision but do not include the very limited number of persons on parole from misdemeanant institutions. . . .

The growth of parole services has been continuous, though uneven, the adult field expanding more rapidly than the juvenile. There remain, however, significant gaps in its use. The one of probably most general importance is its infrequent use for misdemeanants sentenced to jail. The National Survey of Corrections found that most misdemeanants are released from local institutions and jails without parole. Information available from a sample of 212 local jails indicates that 131 of them (62 percent) have no parole procedure; in the 81 jails that nominally have parole, only 8 percent of the inmates are released through this procedure. Thus, 92 percent are simply turned loose at the expiration of their sentence.

. . . More exact data can be obtained about use of parole for adult offenders released from prisons. Figure 11–1, adapted from the National Prisoner Statistics of the Federal Bureau of Prisons, discloses sharp variations in the extent of parole use among individual States, from one in which only 9 percent of prisoners were released on parole to others where virtually all were. These reflect in large part differences in sentencing practices as well as parole policies. . . .

While parole has on occasion been attacked as "leniency," it is basically a means of public protection, or at least has a potential to serve this purpose if properly used. Actually prisoners serve as much time in confinement in jurisdictions where parole is widely used as in those where it is not. No consistent or significant relationship exists between the proportion of prisoners who are released on parole in a State and the average time served for felonies before release. The most recent tabulation of median time served for felonies before first release, which was made in 1960, showed that the five States with the longest median time served were Hawaii, Pennsylvania, Illinois, New York, and Indiana. The percentages released by parole in these States in the same year were 99, 89, 47, 87, and 88 respectively. The five States with the shortest median time served for felonies before first release were New Hampshire, Maine, South Dakota, Montana, and Vermont, with percentages of release by parole of 98, 92, 49, 90, and 5 respectively.

Arguments couched in terms of "leniency" deflect attention from a more important problem. The fact is that large numbers of offenders do return to the community from confinement each year. The task is to improve parole programs so that they may contribute to the reintegration of these offenders. The best current estimates indicate that, among adult offenders, 35 to 45 percent of those released on parole are subsequently returned to prison. The large majority of this group are returned for violations of parole regulations; only about one-third of those returned have been convicted of new felonies. Violation rates are higher for juveniles. However, because additional kinds of violations are applicable to them, such as truancy and incorrigibility, precise comparison with adult rates is difficult.

Ideally, the parole process should begin when an offender is first received in an institution. Information should be gathered on his entire background, and skilled staff should plan an institutional program of training and treatment. A continuous evaluation should be made of the offender's progress on the program. At the same time, trained staff should be working in the community with the offender's family and employer to develop a release plan.

Information about the offender, his progress in the institution, and community readiness to receive him would, under such ideal conditions, be brought together periodically and analyzed by expert staff for presentation to a releasing authority whose members were qualified by training and experience. After thoughtful review, including a hearing with the offender present, the releasing authority would decide when and where to release him. On release, he would be under the supervision of a trained parole officer able to work closely with him and the community institutions around him. If there were a violation of parole, a careful investigation would be made and the reasons behind the violation evaluated. A report would be submitted to the releasing authority which, on the basis of careful review of all the evidence and a hearing with the offender, would decide whether to revoke his parole.

Unfortunately, there are wide discrepancies between this description of what parole purports to be and the actual situation in most jurisdictions. . . .

TABLE 1.—AVERAGE NUMBER OF PERSONS ON PAROLE FROM STATE AND FEDERAL CORRECTIONAL INSTITUTIONS, 1965, BY TYPE OF INSTITUTION FROM WHICH RELEASED, AND ANNUAL COSTS OF SUPERVISION

Type of institution	Number on parole[1]	Annual costs of supervision
Prisons	112,142	$35,314,047
Training schools	60,483	18,593,975
Total	172,625	$53,908,022

[1] Includes a small number of persons released under mandatory supervision.

Source: National Survey of Corrections and special tabulations provided by the Federal Bureau of Prisons and the Administrative Office of the U.S. Courts.

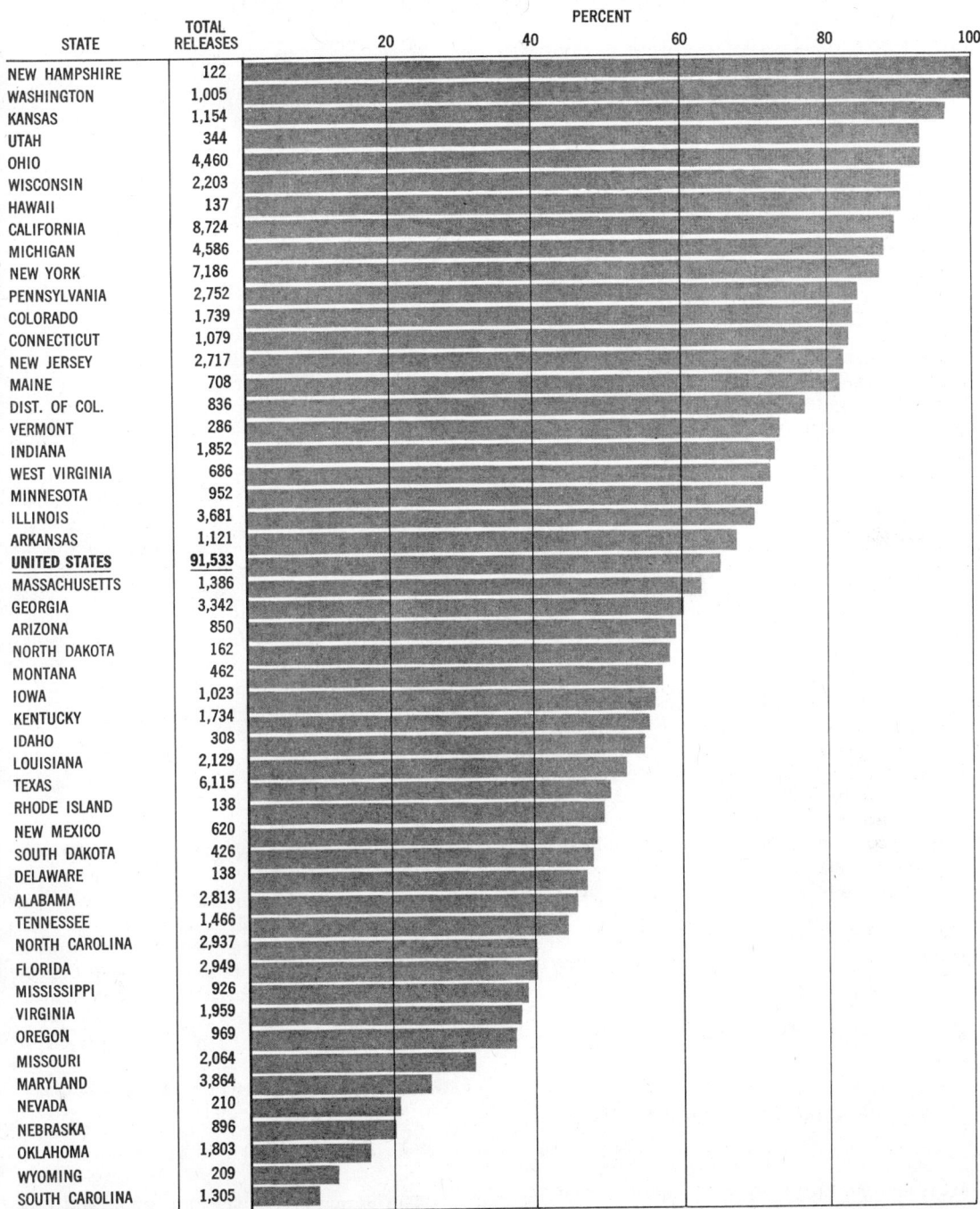

Figure 11-1. INMATES RELASED ON PAROLE[1] AS PERCENTAGE OF ALL PERSONS RELEASED FROM STATE PRISONS, 1964

[1] Includes a small number released under mandatory supervision. Alaska data not available for 1964.

Source: U.S. Department of Justice, Federal Bureau of Prisons, "National Prisoner Statistics: Prisoners in State and Federal Institutions for Adult Felons, 1964," National Prisoner Statistics Bulletin, 38:11 (November 1965).

C. Making Law: Regulations

Connecticut Board of Parole, Statement of Organization and Procedures*

The Parole Decision Process

A. Parole Panels

A three-member panel, including the Chairman, is assigned to each of the correctional institutions and is the paroling authority for the institution to which assigned. When any panel member must be absent, the Chairman may assign a substitute from another panel. Not less than two members must be present at a parole hearing.

B. Notice of Hearings

Parole hearings are held for all inmates on announced dates thirty to sixty days prior to the date of parole eligibility with the exception that at the Correctional Institution, Niantic, each inmate's parole hearing is held during the month in which she becomes eligible for parole consideration. Each inmate is notified of the date of his hearing at least thirty days prior thereto. Inmates may be notified by notices in institutional inmate publications; counselors; institutional parole officers (if the institution staff includes such a position); or other institutional, Division of Parole, or Parole Board staff members.

The Board does not release parole hearing lists to news media. The Board considers this policy to be important to satisfactory community adjustment of inmates released on parole.

C. Attendance at Parole Hearings

Inmates eligible for parole consideration are required to be present at parole hearings unless (1) illness prevents their attendance; (2) they are in punitive segregation; (3) they are confined at a state hospital or receiving treatment at a non-correctional institution hospital; (4) they have been transferred to an institution outside the State of Connecticut; or (5) they waive a hearing before the Board. The Board discourages the waiving of hearings, however, and prefers that all inmates available should be present when their hearings occur.

Attendance at parole hearings is restricted to the members of the Board, the recording secretary, the inmate, and in institutions where they are available, the inmate's institutional counselor. At the discretion of the Board persons with a substantial interest in the administration of criminal justice, and who do not have an interest in a particular case to be considered by the Board, may attend in an observational capacity only. Hearings are not open to the general public since the Board desires to insure the informality of the hearing and to provide each inmate and the Board an opportunity for free discussion of the inmate's case.

Although attorneys, relatives, and other interested persons are not permitted to appear at hearings they may submit to the Board written information pertinent to any case. In addition, such persons are invited to confer with the Chairman or his assistant at the Board's office prior to the parole hearing in which they are interested. The Chairman then provides each member of the hearing panel with a written memorandum concerning the information received at all such conferences. Although the members of the Board prefer that such conferences be held with the Chairman or his assistant, such conferences may also be held with other members of the panel.

D. Procedure at Parole Hearings

The inmate is given an opportunity to make a statement to the panel and to present letters and other documentary information to the panel. Members of the panel may ask questions of the inmate. The hearing is recorded

* Jan. 1, 1972.

except for that portion in which the panel, in executive session, decides the case. (See Section F.)

E. Standards for Granting Parole

The Connecticut General Statutes provide the Board with the authority to release an inmate on parole if it appears that "there is a reasonable probability that such inmate will live and remain at liberty without violating the law and such release is not incompatible with the welfare of society." The Statutes do not provide that upon reaching the date of eligibility the prisoner is granted parole at that time. The Board, therefore, uses its discretion as to if and when in the interest of the prisoner himself and of society an inmate should be paroled.

Parole is not granted merely as a reward for good conduct or efficient performance of duties. There are many factors involved in the decision of the Board as to the "reasonable probability" that an inmate will not violate the law and that his release is compatible with the welfare of society. Most inmates, but not all, are afforded at least one parole prior to the expiration of their sentences.

Among the factors considered by the Board's panels in the parole decision process are:

1. The nature and circumstances of the inmate's offense and his current attitude toward it.
2. The inmate's prior criminal record and his parole adjustment if he has been paroled previously.
3. The inmate's attitude toward family members, the victim, and authority in general.
4. The inmate's institutional adjustment, including his participation and progress in the areas of the institutional program important to his self-improvement.
5. The inmate's employment history, his occupational skills, and his employment stability.
6. The inmate's physical, mental and emotional health.
7. The inmate's insight into the causes of his past criminal conduct.
8. The inmate's efforts to find solutions to his personal problems such as addiction to narcotics, excessive use of alcohol, the need of academic and vocational education, etc., and his use of the available resources related to such problems in the institutional program.
9. The adequacy of the inmate's parole plan. The latter includes the environment to which the inmate plans to return, the character of those with whom he plans to be associated, and the adequacy of his residence and employment program.

F. The Panel's Decision

Following the panel's discussion with the inmate, he is temporarily excused and after careful deliberation and evaluation of all the information obtained from the inmate and the records pertaining to him a decision is made by majority vote of the panel. The panel may decide to parole, deny parole, or continue the inmate's case for further investigation. If parole is granted, the panel will also set the date of release which may be the parole eligibility date or, in appropriate cases, some later date. The inmate is then recalled and is informed of the decision. If the decision is to deny parole, or to continue the case pending further investigation, the inmate is informed of the reasons for the denial or the continuance and the date when he will next be eligible for a parole hearing. Whenever possible the panel will also suggest to the inmate and/or the institutional treatment staff any action it believes may accelerate the inmate's rehabilitation and possible parole. The rehearing date is established for each inmate individually as a result of the panel's judgment of the factors involved in his case.

The panel may parole inmates to programs in Connecticut, to other states under terms of the Interstate Parole Compact, or to warrants. In addition, the Board may grant medical paroles to inmates who have completed their minimum terms, if any, upon the recommendation of the medical staff, to facilitate medical treatment at non-correctional institutional hospitals. Unless otherwise specified all parolees granted medical paroles for this purpose are to be returned immediately to the correctional institution upon being discharged from the hospital. . . .

* * *

Reorientation and Adjustment

The Board recognizes that there are exceptional circumstances in parole supervision when it is advisable to return a parolee to a correctional institution for reorientation and adjustment. Such decisions may be necessary as a result of temporary unemployment; lack of satisfactory residence accommodations; or the inability to arrange a program, which requires special provisions due to physical, mental or emotional disabilities.

The initial decision concerning reorientation and adjustment is the responsibility of the supervising agency, the Department of Correction's Division of Parole. The Board requires, however, that it be notified within forty-eight hours after a parolee is returned to a correctional institution for reorientation and adjustment, and the Chairman shall be provided with a written report concerning such reorientation within five business days. No confinement for reorientation and adjustment shall exceed five days unless so ordered by the Chairman on recommendation of the Commissioner of Correction. The Board authorizes the Chairman to act alone in such cases and to decide if the matter should be referred to the appropriate panel for decision. Confinement for this purpose, after ratification by the Chairman or the panel, shall not exceed a period of sixty days.

Any parolee so returned may appeal his reconfinement for reorientation and adjustment to the Chairman. The Board authorizes the Chairman to act upon such an appeal and to decide if the appeal should be referred to the appropriate panel for decision.

Violation of Parole and Return of Parole Violators

If the Commissioner of Correction or the Chairman of the Board has probable cause to believe the parolee has violated a material condition of his parole, he shall order the parolee to be retaken and to be returned to the custody of the Commissioner of Correction. Such order shall be sufficient warrant to authorize any officer of the Department of Correction, any parole officer or any officer authorized by law to serve criminal process within the State of Connecticut to return the parolee to the custoday of the Commissioner of Correction. Police officers, constables and sheriffs shall arrest and hold any parolee when so requested with or without a warrant.

Revocation of Parole

When a parolee has been returned to a correctional institution as a parole violator, the Division of Parole shall give him timely written notice of the charges against him. The Division of Parole shall also provide the appropriate panel of the Board with a parole violation report to include the charges against the parolee, the current status of his parole, a history of his supervision and adjustment while on parole, and all other information pertinent to the parolee's current status.

The parolee shall be given an opportunity for a revocation hearing before the appropriate Board panel and the Division of Parole shall give the parolee timely written notice of his right to such a hearing. This hearing is normally held in the month following the date when the appropriate panel of the Board receives the complete parole violation report from the Division of Parole and the parolee has been returned to the correctional institution. The parolee may waive such a hearing and, upon receipt of a signed and witnessed waiver of hearing, the panel will make its revocation decision in the parolee's absence.

At the hearing the inmate is given an opportunity to make a statement to the panel and to present letters and other documentary information to the panel. Members of the panel may ask questions of the inmate. The hearing is recorded except for that portion in which the panel, in executive session, decides the case.

Following the hearing, the panel will excuse the parolee temporarily, complete its consideration of all the information obtained at the hearing, from the violation report, and other records pertaining to the parolee, and by majority vote order:

1. That the parolee be continued in parole status. The decision may include (a) a reprimand and warning to the parolee, (b) instructions to the Division of Parole for closer supervision, and (c) additional conditions in the Parole Agreement.
2. That the parole be revoked and the inmate recommitted to the appropriate institution for a period equal to the unexpired portion of the term of his maximum sentence at the date of his violation, as determined by the Board, plus any time earned in diminution of sentence. The decision may, but usually does not, include provision for forfeiture of time previously earned in diminution of sentence.
3. That the parole be revoked but the inmate be reparoled on a date set by the panel. This decision may also include

any of the provisions listed in paragraph No. 1 above.

The panel may order revocation if it is satisfied that:

1. The parolee has failed, without satisfactory excuse, to comply with a substantial requirement imposed as a condition of his parole, and
2. The violation of condition involves
   (a) commission of another crime or
   (b) conduct indicating substantial risk that the parolee will commit another crime or
   (c) conduct indicating that the parolee is unwilling to comply with the proper conditions of parole.

Following the panel's decision, the parolee is immediately recalled and is informed of the decision and the reasons for the decision. If the decision is to revoke parole, the parolee is informed as to the date when he will be eligible for a reparole hearing.

Discharge from Parole

As authorized by the Statute, if it appears to the Board that a parolee has evidenced that he will "continue to lead an orderly life", and that parole supervision is no longer necessary to the welfare of the parolee or of society, the appropriate Board panel by unanimous vote of all the members present at any regular meeting may discharge the parolee from parole. When a parolee is discharged the Board shall deliver to him a written certificate of discharge under the seal of the Board and signed by the Chairman of the Board and the Commissioner of Correction.

Although the Board may grant a discharge from parole at any time, it normally considers a parolee for discharge only after the successful completion on parole of one-half of his maximum parole term. In addition, the Board normally does not consider for discharge a parolee under a life sentence unless he has successfully served a seven-year period under parole supervision. Habitual offenders are normally considered for discharge only following successful completion of a five-year period of parole supervision. In special cases and under special circumstances the Board may grant to an inmate both a parole and a discharge at the same time. . . .

NOTES

Federal Parole

Note 1.

KENNETH CULP DAVIS

Discretion and the U.S. Parole Board*

An outstanding example of completely unstructured discretionary power than can and should be at least partially structured is that of the United States Parole Board. In granting or denying parole, the board makes no attempt to structure its discretionary power through rules, policy statements, or guidelines; it does not structure through statements of findings and reasons; it has no system of precedents; the degree of openness of proceedings and records is about the least possible; and procedural safeguards are almost totally absent. Moreover, checking of discretion is minimal; board members do not check each other by deliberating together about decisions; administrative check of board decisions is almost nonexistent; and judicial review is customarily unavailable.

The board makes about fifteen thousand decisions per year granting or denying parole —an average of about fifty per working day. The board also fixes eligibility dates in some cases, prescribes conditions of parole, issues warrants for retaking parolees, and revokes parole. This discussion is limited to the main function of granting and denying parole.

The board has never announced rules, standards, or guides. The most specific standard is the statutory provision, repeated by the board's regulations, that the board "may in its discretion" release a prisoner on parole if the board finds "a reasonable probability that such prisoner will live and remain at liberty without violating the laws" and that "such release is not incompatible with the welfare of society." The board has never publicly stated any substantive principles that guide it in determining the probability that a prisoner will commit another crime or whether his release will be compatible with the welfare of society. The board has not publicly listed the criteria that are considered. Nor has it even tried to state the characteristics of cases in which parole will obviously be granted or will obviously be denied. It has not indicated its position

* Kenneth Culp Davis, *Discretionary Justice* 126–33 (1969). Reprinted with permission of Louisiana State University Press.

with respect to major patterns of cases that are most frequently recurring.

The board makes no attempt to evolve principles through case-to-case adjudication. It does not select specific cases raising basic questions of policy for especially intensive consideration with a view to creating a useful precedent.

The board's system is the same for easy cases as for hard cases, the same for application of old ideas as for development of new ideas. Each member votes in his own office without discussing the decision with his colleagues. Troublesome problems are never made the subject of board meetings. Board members never deliberate together. They do not write memoranda discussing pros and cons. They think separately. They vote separately. No board member knows the reasons for his colleagues' votes. . . .

If a board member is in such a hurry to get to his golf game that he votes in sixteen cases without looking inside the files, no one under the board's system can ever know the difference, even though the personal liberty of sixteen men may be at stake. How could a board member have less incentive to avoid prejudice or undue haste than by a system in which his decision can never be reviewed and in which no one, not even his colleagues, can ever know why he voted as he did? Even complete irrationality of a vote can never be discovered. Should any men, even good men, be unnecessarily trusted with such uncontrolled discretionary power? . . .

The board in my opinion should (a) develop open standards, as specific as feasible, to guide its decisions, (b) state findings and reasons when parole is denied, and when it is granted on the basis of a policy determination that may have value as a precedent, (c) open proceedings and records to the public except to the extent that confidentiality is essential, (d) develop a system of open precedents, and (e) move toward group decisions made by members who deliberate together. In addition, (f) courts should review parole denials for errors of law, unfair procedure, or abuse of discretion. . . .

Note 2.

UNITED STATES BOARD OF PAROLE, RULES*

In order that each Board member may have an opportunity to review and pass upon

* Effective Jan. 1, 1971, pp. 13–23, 35–36.

each case, a decision regarding parole will not usually be made until a summary of the facts in each case and an opinion or recommendation as to the propriety of granting or withholding parole have been prepared by the interviewing member or examiner. Such decision will also not, as a rule, be made until a quorum of the Board, or the Division, has had an opportunity to review the prisoner's file, the examiner's summary and recommendation, and has indicated concurrence, disapproval, or desire to set some future date for reconsideration.

General Factors in Parole Selection

The grant of parole rests in the discretion of the United States Board of Parole. In general it is granted, when in the judgment of the Board, a prisoner who has made a satisfactory adjustment and is otherwise eligible will avoid further violation of law and when the factors which will affect him and his dependents upon release, assure adequate public security. These factors vary in every case. The Board evaluates each case on its merits and acts as its judgment indicates to grant or to continue the case.

The membership of the Board is composed of individuals who represent various professional disciplines and experiences. From this multi-disciplined background, the individual case is viewed in a manner that will allow all pertinent factors to be considered and evaluated.

The following factors are considered by the Board in its decision making.

A. *Sentence Data*
   (1) Type of sentence
   (2) Length of sentence
   (3) Recommendations of Judge, U.S. Attorney and other responsible officials

B. *Facts and Circumstances of the Offense*
   (1) Mitigating and aggravating factors
   (2) Activities following arrest and prior to confinement, including adjustment on bond or probation, if any

C. *Prior Criminal Record*
   (1) Nature and pattern of offenses
   (2) Adjustment to previous probation, parole, and confinement
   (3) Detainers

D. *Changes in Motivation and Behavior*

(1) Changes in attitude toward self and others
(2) Reasons underlying changes
(3) Personal goals and description of personal strengths or resources available to maintain motivation for law-abiding behavior

E. *Personal and Social History*
   (1) Family and marital
   (2) Intelligence and education
   (3) Employment and military experience
   (4) Leisure time
   (5) Religion
   (6) Physical and emotional health

F. *Institutional Experience*
   (1) *Program goals and accomplishments in areas*:
      (a) Academic
      (b) Vocational education, training or work assignments
      (c) Recreation and leisure time use
      (d) Religion
      (e) Therapy
   (2) *General adjustment*:
      (a) Inter-personal relationships with staff and inmates
      (b) Behavior, including misconduct
   (3) Physical and emotional health, and treatment

G. *Community Resources, Including Release Plans*
   (1) Residence: live alone, with family, or others
   (2) Employment, training, or academic education
   (3) Special needs and resources to meet them

H. *Use of Scientific Data and Tools*
   (1) Psychological and psychiatric evaluations
   (2) Pertinent data from the uniform parole reporting system
   (3) Other statistical data
   (4) Standardized tests

I. *Comments by Hearing Member or Examiner*

> Evaluative comments supporting a recommendation, including his impressions gained from the hearing. . . .

Note 3.

LEONARD ORLAND

The United States Board of Parole*

The United States Board of Parole, created by Congress in 1930, consists of eight members, appointed by the President, subject to Senatorial confirmation, who serve six year overlapping terms.

Last fiscal year, each member of the United States Board of Parole, on the average, made almost 5,000 individual parole decisions. The U.S. Parole Board last fiscal year held 11,784 personal parole hearings at federal correctional institutions.

In an effort to rationalize and expedite the enormous decisional burden on the U.S. Board, a number of procedural innovations have been made, including the appointment of eight hearing examiners, who, it is anticipated, will in the future conduct the initial interviews in two-thirds of all cases. The Board has also come up with a number of other imaginative innovations, including appellate review within the Board of decisions of less than the full Board, en banc full Board consideration of selected cases, and the beginning of articulation of statements of reasons for denial of parole.

The fact remains, however, that the eight members of the Parole Board are required to make crucially important release decisions in well over 17,000 cases a year and it is likely that the decisional caseload of the Board in the future will increase, not decrease. Since the creation of the U.S. Parole Board in 1930, Congress has given no systematic attention to the overwhelming burdens and power resting in the Board.

Note 4. *Relative Responsibility of Prison and Parole Officers to Decide When the Inmate is Eligible for a Parole Hearing*

PEOPLE EX REL ABNER V. KINNEY
30 Ill. 2d 201, 195 N.E.2d 651 (1964)
Supreme Court of Illinois

HERSHEY, Justice.

This is an original petition in this court for writ of *mandamus* directed to respondents Charles F. Kinney, chairman, and Henry S.

---

* Statement of Leonard Orland, February 17, 1972, submitted to Subcommittee on Criminal Laws and Procedures of the Senate Judiciary Committee.

Wise, James C. Craven, Louis Zahn and Douglass R. Turner, associate members of the Parole and Pardon Board of the Department of Public Safety of the State of Illinois, to compel respondents within a reasonable time to grant petitioner, Jess Abner, Jr., a hearing to determine whether he shall be released on parole from the sentence imposed on him in 1954 as required by section 1 of the Sentence and Parole Act. Ill. Rev. Stat. 1961, chap. 38, par. 801.

Petitioner was sentenced to imprisonment for from 10 to 20 years in 1954. He has served the minimum term of his sentence, less good time credit. Section 1 of the Sentence and Parole Act provides: "Every person sentenced and committed to the penitentiary shall, in the discretion of the Parole and Pardon Board, be eligible to parole under rules and regulations adopted therefor by the Parole and Pardon Board, such paroles to be as follows: * * * a person sentenced for an indeterminate term shall not be eligible for parole until he has served the minimum limit fixed by the court, good time being allowed as provided by law."

The "good time" regulations promulgated by the Department of Public Safety provide that a person serving an indeterminate sentence with a minimum of 15 years is eligible to receive a parole hearing after he has served 8 years and 9 months.

Petitioner was eligible to receive a hearing before the Parole Board on April 3, 1963, and he applied for such a hearing. On April 12, 1963, petitioner received a letter from the clerk of the Parole and Pardon Board that his case was continued to make grade. In response to a letter written by petitioner's counsel to the superintendent of the Parole Board he received a letter from such superintendent that under date of January 27, 1955, petitioner was demoted to grade E under the Progressive Merit System and again to Grade E on January 9, 1963, and that he would appear when he regained Grade A for the proper length of time. Petitioner has never had a hearing before the Parole Board.

The refusal to grant petitioner a hearing is based upon Rule 5 of the rules of the Parole and Pardon Board which provides: "Only those prisoners who are in 'Grade A' as determined by the wardens of the respective institutions under the 'Progressive Merit System,' and shall have been in 'Grade A' for three consecutive months, at least ten days prior to the date of the subcommittee sessions at the several institutions, shall be entitled to consideration for parole." This rule was promulgated under section 7 of the Sentence and Parole Act (Ill. Rev. Stat. 1961, chap. 38, par. 807) which authorizes the Board to establish rules and regulations not inconsistent with the act under which prisoners may be allowed to go on parole.

Rule 4 of the rules and regulations of the Parole Board in part reads: "No prisoner will be given a hearing who is out of grade, in isolation or deadlock. His case will be continued until his release from the aforementioned unit or until he is in Grade the proper length of time."

A similar rule has been adopted by the Department of Public Safety which provides in part: "The inmate must be in A grade at least three months and have served his minimum sentence, less 'Good Time', before he will be eligible to a parole hearing by the Parole and Pardon Board."

Petitioner contends respondents have no authority to impose conditions precedent to parole hearings in addition to those established by section 1 of the Sentence and Parole Act, nor to delegate to officials of the several prisons the power to determine that certain prisoners who have served the requisite portions of their sentences shall not be given a parole hearing. The practice of refusing to permit prisoners who are not in Grade A to have parole hearings has been followed by the Parole Board for many years.

The Progressive Merit System is as follows: There are five grades, A through E. Every person sentenced to the penitentiary is automatically placed in Grade C, the neutral grade. If the prisoner's behavior is "satisfactory," he is promoted to Grade B in 3 months, and to Grade A in another 3 months. Thereafter, he may be reduced in grade upon order of the Prison Merit Staff, which at Stateville is composed of the warden, three senior captains, two assistant wardens, and a merit staff clerk. The Merit Staff may, if it chooses, reduce the prisoner to any grade it deems fit. The prisoner has no opportunity to be heard, nor is there any appeal.

Examples of prison rules, a violation of which may result in a disciplinary report and a reduction in grade are: having other than the designated number of blankets in cell, covering of any type on dresser, singing or whistling in cell, talking while bathing, placing shoes on bench while bathing, taking more food than can be eaten (edibles are not to be left on plate), discussion in mail of subjects that are controversial or of the institution or its personnel, and other such rules. . . .

The first Illinois Parole Act was passed in

1895; its constitutionality was upheld several years later in 1897, (George v. People, 167 Ill. 447, 47 N.E. 741). That act and all subsequent parole acts contain provisions relating to procedures before the Board, including the time for eligibility to apply for parole. These provisions have always been viewed as creating mandatory duties on the Board. The Parole Act specifically provides the number of years which a prisoner must serve before he becomes eligible for parole (section 1 of the Sentence and Parole Act). Neither the Parole Board nor the Department of Public Safety can by rules change the statutory provisions of eligibility for parole. When a prisoner becomes eligible for parole, the Parole Board is under a mandatory duty to hear his application for parole.

... The operation of respondents' Rule 5 is an unauthorized delegation of power by the Parole Board to the wardens of the several Illinois State Penitentiaries, since the determination of whether a prisoner is Grade A is made by them and their staff. This in effect makes a condition precedent to the parole and in another aspect gives a veto to the wardens over the discretionary powers of the Parole Board on granting paroles. Section 1 of the Sentence and Parole Act requires that this discretion be exercised by respondents. There is no authorization for the delegation of this discretionary power. ...

D. Applying "Law": The Parole Hearing

1. THE DECISION-MAKING PROCESS

INTRODUCTORY NOTES

Note 1.

LEONARD ORLAND

*Politics and Parole**

Seven out of every ten inmates who leave an American prison do so by virtue of a decision of a parole board. Yet, almost without exception, decisions granting or denying parole are not open to the public and are not subject to judicial review in state or Federal courts. It is apparent that the American system of criminal justice vests enormous power—and concomitant responsibility—in parole boards.

Parole imposes the near-impossible burden of deciding when an inmate can be released without substantial risk that he will commit a new crime. But parole is not simply a matter of choosing the best risks. As a matter of statistical probability, murderers released from prison are far less likely to commit a new crime than any other category of offender. Yet few are prepared to conclude that murderers should be released by parole boards ahead of burglars, thieves or even war resisters.

Parole decision-making requires some judgment concerning the severity of the crime the inmate has committed. It also requires a prediction of the likelihood the inmate will commit a new crime and a judgment concerning the seriousness of that possible new crime.

Note 2.

LEONARD ORLAND

*Parole Board Structure**

In all fifty states, as well as in the Federal system and in the District of Columbia, the decision whether or not to release is made by an administrative agency, the parole board. In the overwhelming majority of jurisdictions, the Governor appoints board members, subject to confirmation by the legislature. In two-thirds of the states, parole boards are composed of three to five members, usually appointed for four year terms. In one-half the states, and in the Federal system, the legislature does not establish minimum qualifications for appointment.

* Statement of Leonard Orland, February 17, 1972, submitted to Subcommittee on Criminal Laws and Procedures of the Senate Judiciary Committee.

* *New York Times,* Jan. 29, 1972, p. 29. Reprinted with permission of the author.

Note 3. The Decision-Making Process

THE PRESIDENT'S COMMISSION ON LAW ENFORCEMENT AND ADMINISTRATION OF JUSTICE,

Task Force Report: Corrections 63–65 (1967)

In the main, releasing authorities must depend on others for information about persons being considered for release. The size and quality of the staff who compile and analyze this information is therefore crucial. They must be able to develop and assemble vital information and present it in such a way as to establish its relevance to the decision.

Far too typically, overworked institutional caseworkers must attempt to gather information on a prisoner from brief interviews with him, meager institutional records, and letters to community officials. This information is often fitted into a highly stereotyped format. Frequently, the sameness of reporting style and jargon makes it very difficult for board members to understand the individual aspects of a given case and assess them wisely. This can lead to decisions which are arbitrary and unfair as well as undesirable from a correctional standpoint. . . .

The data presented to releasing authorities are of many kinds. Assuming that the information is accurate, parole officials must still face the problem of evaluating its meaning. One method, by far the most common, is for the decision-maker to depend basically on his own judgment of the circumstances in an individual case.

Another way of approaching a parole decision is through the use of statistical analyses of the performance of offenders paroled in past years to determine the violation rates of various classifications. Violation rates are related to age, offense, education, work history, prior record, and other factors. The categories are then combined to produce a "probability-of-violation score" for an offender according to his characteristics.

A series of efforts have been made in recent years to develop such procedures. Experiments have also been undertaken to compare the case method and the statistical method. Psychiatrists, psychologists, sociologists, and prison officials have been asked to classify large numbers of cases on the basis of probable success on parole. When statistical prediction methods have been applied to the same group of cases, they have proved better able to determine the probabilities of parole violation for groups of inmates.

Despite the utility of statistical techniques and the potential for increased usefulness with the advance of computer technology, no serious authority has proposed the substitution of the statistical for the case method. Factors unassociated with risk must be considered. Moreover, any individual case may present considerations which are too detailed for statistical analysis or which must be weighed from the standpoint of fairness. Nonetheless, statistical analysis is useful as a general means for educating parole authorities in the significance of various factors in assessment of cases, as a way of evaluating the effectiveness of various treatment alternatives upon parole, and as a check for individual case dispositions. Much further work is needed to develop statistical analysis, particularly to predict the likelihood of violent crimes, as opposed to other offenses, and as a means for determining the optimum time for release. . . .

Releasing authorities can also achieve more rational decision-making by improving their hearing procedures. Improvements must promote both fairness and regularity, as well as effective correctional treatment. In several States there are no hearings at all for adult offenders; decisions are made by parole authorities solely on the basis of written reports. In juvenile programs, hearings are even less common, with reliance again on written reports and also on staff conferences at which the offender may be present.

Procedures for parole hearings are extremely diverse. In many States, especially those with numerous institutions, the parole board is divided into subcommittees, each of which conducts hearings. In some States, one or more board members conduct hearings and report back to the rest of the board. In still other States, boards conduct all hearings *en banc.* . . .

Authorities on parole procedures regard well-conducted hearings as vital to effective decision-making, in terms of expanding the information available to the board as well as for their effect on offenders. Hearings commonly give parole boards an opportunity to identify important points on which information is needed in making their decision. For example, a board may well find from interviewing an inmate that he has several contacts in the community not mentioned in any official report, which later investigation by staff may reveal to have considerable bearing on the place to which he might subsequently be paroled.

The other aim of a hearing is to create

conditions which enhance the treatment goals for an inmate. This does not mean that the hearing should take on the character of a counseling session. The simple opportunity of being given what he perceives to be a fair hearing can be important in creating those conditions. Board members also can often influence the behavior of inmates by encouraging their participation in institutional programs and other self-improvement efforts or by frankly discussing with them, at appropriate times, the probable consequences of failure to participate in programs or of misconduct.

Well-conducted hearings further the trend for parole boards to increase the involvement of inmates in the decisions which affect them and to confront them more directly with the information upon which a decision is being made. Earlier concepts concerning the treatment of offenders placed most emphasis upon the need to resolve their emotional problems. A more recent refinement of this view stresses the need for offenders to be helped to confront and deal with "here and now" issues as a means of strengthening their problem-solving abilities.

An illustration of the trend toward "confrontation" is the way in which inmates are notified of parole decisions. Typically, parole decisions have been communicated in writing or it has been left to others, usually institution staff, to tell inmates if parole was granted or denied. They have had little opportunity to discover the reasons for the decisions and discuss them with parole board members. An increasing number of parole boards have adopted the practice of calling inmates back after a hearing to discuss the decision on their cases. Institution staff and board members in these States—for example, Minnesota and Iowa—report it to be an improvement over prior methods.

Board members are most helpful when they demonstrate a genuine interest in the welfare of an inmate, an ability to withstand manipulation or deception, and a willingness to discuss candidly with an inmate the realities of his case. It is important, however, that board members avoid trying to use the hearing for extensive problem-solving with inmates or as a substitute for work which should be done by staff.

ADVISORY COUNCIL ON PAROLE, NATIONAL COUNCIL
ON CRIME AND DELINQUENCY

Guides for Parole Selection*

Criteria for Decision

Parole board members must have some understanding of the man who will come before them before they can even begin to evaluate his parole potential. As with physical illness, diagnosis and treatment of criminal behavior also require some knowledge of the "patient's" history—especially where the causes of his maladjustment are complex. Information on the inmate's childhood, family, associates, and prior criminal behavior gives the paroling authority a means of gauging changes and improvements under treatment and some inkling of his future behavior.

* Reprinted, with permission of the National Council on Crime and Delinquency, from Council on Parole, National Council on Crime and Delinquency, *Guides for Parole Selection*, 1963, pp. 38; 42; 44; 50–51; 55–57; 59; 61–65.

The parole board, then, should carefully explore the case history of the inmate for evidence of emotional problems or maladjustment and criminal tendencies. They should also look for those elements of his past life, such as indications of close family ties, special aptitudes or interests, self-awareness, and strong motivation for self-improvement, which might point to potentiality for future adjustment. . . .

The most recent offense recorded should be compared with the inmate's total record. What does it tell about the man at the time of his present commitment? If the act was premeditated, for how long was it planned? Did the offense grow out of unusual pressures or did it result from a series of errors in judgment? Was it a situational type of offense? Did the prisoner attempt to escape responsibility for his crime even though his guilt was obvious?

The board should be aware of all these details of the last offense, but should not spend too much time during the hearing discussing them. In fact, with the exception of those cases in which brutal or repeated crimes have aroused hostile public opinion, the last offense may not be very significant in determining readiness for parole. . . .

"There is a close parallel between the part played by experience tables in the parole selection process and the use of life tables in establishing insurance premiums." Although risks for both can be classified on the basis of certain characteristics, it is, of course, impossible to predict the exact degree of parole risk or the date of death for any one person within either group. Formulators of prediction tables have recommended that scores obtained from them should serve only as broad outlines to what has happened in the past and as guidelines for the future. Moreover, statistics collected in one section of the country may not be appropriate for another section. In reviewing tables of successes or failures, the board should bear in mind that a direct relationship may exist between paroling practices for certain types of offenders and their violation rate. . . .

Preparation for parole begins the day the offender enters prison. What happens to the inmate during his confinement and the effect upon his attitude, personality, and capabilities will influence his ability to reestablish himself.

Imprisonment has a powerful impact upon most persons. The results may be beneficial or detrimental, depending upon the institutional climate and program. The inmate's response to correctional treatment depends largely upon the staff, program, and philosophy of the institution. Parole, to be successful, makes demands of both prison and parole agencies in helping the inmate equip himself with skills, reestablish his self-respect, and acquire a healthy regard for the law. Custody with discipline, training, and treatment should be based on a philosophy of rehabilitation and directed toward having the prisoner attain competence in earning a living and in adjusting to family and community life.

On the other hand, the conduct and reaction of a prisoner to a program that is largely punitive and offers little in the way of opportunity for self-improvement can reveal personality qualities also. If a person exposed to unhealthy confinement conditions is able to avoid deterioration and use his time constructively, the outlook is good. In order to make accurate judgments on the effect of the prison experience, the board must have not only full factual information about the inmate's experiences but also the full factual information on the prison's policies, staff, and program. . . .

The inmate's conduct record and his reaction to discipline and supervision should be studied carefully. Paroling authorities should insist on records which give the details of offenses and the corrective action taken. They should also study the periodic evaluations made by the chief custodial officers. A good conduct record in itself does not necessarily indicate that the inmate is a good risk. Major criminals who have become institutionalized through long incarceration are often the best prisoners. On the other hand, a bad record raises serious questions about parolability. Poor conduct in prison is more accurately predictive of poor conduct on parole than good conduct is predictive of good conduct on parole. The parole board must distinguish between conformity to the rules and real change in behavior and attitudes.

Do offenses in prison reflect a behavior pattern, such as resistance to authority or inability to get along with people on a day-to-day basis? How does it compare with conduct patterns prior to confinement? Does prison conduct reveal antisocial tendencies? Does the inmate tend to blame his problems and failures on others? Or are institutional offenses a reflection of an unhealthy prison climate? While misconduct cannot be excused, it should be considered in the institutional setting. Normally, a good conduct and adjustment record for a considerable period prior to the hearing is required. A man's ability to control his emotions under stress or in situations where he believes he has been wronged is one indicator of his maturation. . . .

The overwhelming experience of the correctional field indicates that the institutional staff is not in the best position to make final judgments regarding parole selection because of their closeness to the problem and their great difficulty in maintaining objectivity. Staff observations, however, should not be disregarded. Prison personnel see the man in every aspect of prison life and may note changes which take place within him. Because of their familiarity with the operation of the institution and with the personalities and philosophy of other staff members, they are in a position to evaluate the program.

Paroling authorities pay full attention to the recommendations of key staff members such as the psychiatrist, social workers, vocational and educational supervisors, custodial supervisors, and medical officers as well as to the daily observations of the work supervisors, who know the inmates perhaps more intimately than other staff members.

Institution records provide usable information if they are presented in clear, comprehensive, and nontechnical narrative form. They should cover the programs that have been available to the inmate, the parts of them he has used, and the benefits he has derived from them. The progress report should reflect the prisoner's overall adjustment. . . .

In arriving at its decision, the parole board must consider not only the inmate's institutional adjustment (so often simulated by habitual or professional offenders), but his personality and willingness to lead a decent life. Reviewing his record is not enough. Although the findings and opinions of experts and professional staff are essential to a sound decision, the paroling authority cannot abandon its own responsibility for judging the man's capacity to stay out of trouble in the future. . . .

Selecting persons to be present at the hearing and limiting their number is a delicate question in many jurisdictions where the warden and other custodial and administrative personnel, family members, lawyers, and others have traditionally been allowed to sit in on it. Attendance, which should be controlled by the board, should be restricted to members of the releasing authority, a recorder, the professional staff member responsible for preparing and presenting the case, and the offender himself. Attorneys, the press, and the public should be excluded and the board should not be required to hear testimony or evidence presented by various interested parties at the time of the interview. Instead, it should encourage these persons to submit, in writing and *before the hearing*, whatever information they consider pertinent to the case. Since the effectiveness of the interview depends on the inmate's freedom to discuss his situation and his future frankly and freely, the presence of custodial or administrative personnel causes many prisoners to tighten up to their own disadvantage.

The success of the hearing depends largely on the extent to which members of the board have prepared for it. They should have discussed the case record beforehand or at least be sufficiently acquainted with it to be able to phrase the proper questions for exploration. They may use the case record as a reference during the hearing. In any event, they should avoid retrying the case.

Some provision should have been made for orienting the inmate to the hearing routines before he enters the board room. The parole officer or other institutional staff member who helps prepare the inmate for parole can probably do this best by explaining the board's operating policies and procedures and the general criteria followed in parole selection.

The inmate should be put at ease. A quiet, friendly, man-to-man approach is usually effective. The hearing should be conducted informally, with as little evidence of authority as possible. If the prisoner is tense and frightened, he does not do himself credit.

Questions regarding the circumstances of the offense should be limited to what is necessary to complete the record and to sound out the inmate's feelings about his crime and its effect on his future. Unduly critical comments usually serve only to antagonize the prisoner and cause him to "freeze up." His family situation, prior behavior, and institutional adjustment should be discussed frankly with him. The board should encourage him to talk freely about his future and any special problems which might face him on release. What are his plans for meeting these problems?

Although the board should take care not to give the prisoner false hopes, it should apprise him of the fact that the board's denial may be subject to future review depending on the inmate's development and progress.

The inmate should not be hurried through the interview; he should leave the hearing with the knowledge that sufficient time has been allotted for a thorough consideration of his case—a requisite important to his morale and rehabilitation. For this reason, the board should be careful not to schedule too many cases for one hearing day.

If the board is postponing final decision until other members of the paroling authority can review the case at the executive office, it should make sure that information on any recommended action does not leak out to the inmate, his family, his attorneys, or others. An inmate who is denied parole but knows that a single member of the board had recommended him for it can start a long correspondence or legal inquiry which may further disturb his family and which may work against his morale and ultimate rehabilitation.

The record of every hearing should be made a permanent part of the authority's case history and should form the basis for replies to family or other inquiries and for gauging the need for future review.

As summarized in the Attorney General's Survey of Release Procedures:

1. Adequate time must be allowed to insure careful and objective consideration of each case.

2. The prisoner ought to be present at the hearing, since the main purpose of the hearing is to pass judgment upon the offender as a parole risk. Although a personal interview is sometimes misleading, it is desirable that opportunity be given for personal examination and observation of the prospective parolee.

3. A hearing without an adequate preparole investigation cannot serve any useful purpose. The hearing is meant to complement the preparole investigation, not substitute for it. Before the hearing starts, the parole board members should be thoroughly familiar with the available information in regard to each case scheduled for consideration.

4. Last and most important, the parole board should consist of competent officials with training and experience.

Evaluation of the inmate at the time of the hearing and during the interview should revolve around the inmate's offense, emotional maturity, physical and mental conditions, response to treatment, current attitudes, unsolved problems, occupational potentials, and approach to the future, the board members' observations, and the inmate's own statements on these topics will form part of the basis for the final evaluation.

Because an inmate's insight into his emotional problems can be very revealing of his character, it is perhaps the most important element the board is called upon to evaluate. For this reason, the board must inquire into the inmate's problems as he sees them. If the prisoner thinks that his only problem is getting out or that his only problem is alcohol, he has little or no understanding of his situation. On the other hand, if he is aware of his immaturity, hostility, or insecurity and some of the causes behind them, he is probably making progress. Does he make mention of a broken home or an abusive parent in discussing his background? Is he prepared to do something to resolve some of the problems this background may have caused? Some prisoners do not have the ability to meet their problems; others may have gained confidence through education, religion, vocational training, and the freedom of expression to be achieved in group therapy, group instruction, or group counseling so that they can talk out their frustrations or work them through in acceptable ways. The board members must always be on guard for the glib sociopath who can verbalize freely but has not been able to effect corresponding changes in himself.

Uniform Parole Reports of the National Probation and Parole Institutes*

Basic Data for Parole Prediction

National Tables—1968 Parolees

Parole agencies which submitted 1968 data for the Uniform Parole Reports are listed below. The great majority of these agencies have reported on all their cases which were released to parole supervision by discretionary action

* "You Asked For It—1968 Parolees," *Uniform Parole Reports Newsletter* (Davis, California: National Council on Crime and Delinquency Research Center, November, 1970). Reprinted with permission.

of a parole board. A few of the agencies reported on random samples of various proportions.

Thus, the enclosed tables represent national figures for parole outcomes of all persons released to parole supervision during 1968 and reported to UPR. It should be emphasized that these data do not represent all persons paroled within the United States. As shown below, data for some states are not included, and some states reported only a random sample of their parolees. Data for 1969 parolees, now being routinely reported by all participating agencies, will be more nearly complete.

The enclosed data represent the only available national information on parole outcomes, including a large number of parolees from many agencies, collected in terms of uniform, agreed upon definitions, with both these definitions and the reporting format developed in collaboration with paroling authorities. Fractions of less than ½% are represented by "½%." We believe the data are in a form which is widely useful, while not overly simplified. Your suggestions for improvement are encouraged.

AGENCIES REPRESENTED IN NATIONAL TABLES— 1968 (Percents show proportions of all parolees)

Alabama	25%	Minnesota	100%
Alaska[1]	100%	Missouri	100%
Arizona	100%	Montana	100%
Arkansas[2]	100%	Nebraska	100%
California:		Nevada	100%
CYA Male	15%	New Hampshire	100%
CYA Female	100%	New Jersey	100%
CDC Male	15%	New Mexico	100%
CDC Female	100%		
Colorado	25%	New York	5%
Connecticut Male[3]	50%	North Carolina	100%
Connecticut Female	100%	North Dakota	100%
Delaware	100%	Ohio	10%
District of Columbia[2,4]	100%	Oklahoma	100%
Florida	25%	Oregon	100%
Georgia	100%	Pennsylvania	15%
Hawaii	100%	Puerto Rico	100%
Idaho	100%	Rhode Island	100%
Illinois	100%	South Carolina	100%
Indiana	25%	South Dakota	100%
Iowa	20%	Tennessee	100%
Kansas	100%	Texas	100%
Kentucky	100%	Utah	100%
Louisiana	100%	Vermont	100%
Maine	100%	Virginia	100%
Maryland	25%	Washington[5]	100%
Massachusetts	100%	Wisconsin[2,6]	100%
Michigan	18%	Wyoming	100%

[1] January, February, March parolees only
[2] Added to system in 1968 release year
[3] May, June, July, August parolees only
[4] January, February, March, April parolees only
[5] Limited item reporting due to system translation difficulties
[6] Included in tables I, II and VII only; limited item reporting

UNIFORM PAROLE REPORTS

OBJECTIVES	Reliable nationwide statistical reports on parole based upon (1) uniform definitions of items, and (2) individual persons paroled.
SPONSORS	Association of Paroling Authorities; Interstate Compact Administrators Association for the Council of State Governments; United States Board of Parole; Advisory Council on Parole of the National Council on Crime and Delinquency.
PARTICIPATING AGENCIES	Fifty-five agencies in fifty states, the Federal Government, and Puerto Rico contribute data at their own expense.
DATA	More than 83,000 persons paroled during 1965, 1966, 1967, and 1968 have one year follow-up data in the UPR Data File. Two year follow-up data also are being gathered, beginning with 1968 parolees. Definitions of items are given in the **Coding Manual** available upon request.
RELIABILITY	Reliability studies, which have resulted in the conclusion that the data collected are adequately reliable, are available upon request.

* * * * *

INFORMATION FEEDBACK	Production of yearly statistical tables for all participating agencies has been established. The enclosed tables show the parole outcomes, analyzed by various offender characteristics, for all persons paroled by the agency indicated during the year shown. The parole outcomes are based on one year follow-up study, and persons discharged during that period are included. The percentages given are rounded to the nearest whole percent. The ½% values represent ½% or less.

This investigation is supported by Public Health Service Grant 5 RO1 MH 14798–05 from the National Institute of Mental Health.

Figure 11-2. PAROLE OUTCOME IN FIRST YEAR FOR PERSONS PAROLED IN 1968

Parole Outcome	Commitment Offense								
	Total Part 1 & 2	Willful Homicide	Negligent Manslaughter	Armed Robbery	Unarmed Robbery	Aggravated Assault	Forcible Rape	Statutory Rape	All Other Sex Offenses
CONTINUED ON PAROLE									
No difficulty or sentence less than 60 days	17669 71%	1471 87%	374 87%	1907 73%	618 72%	1029 75%	448 80%	165 79%	620 84%
With new minor conviction(s)	246 1%	12 1%		15 1%	12 1%	13 1%	5 1%	1 ½%	7 1%
New major conviction(s)	133 1%	3 ½%	1 ½%	10 ½%	5 1%	4 ½%	1 ½%	4 2%	1 ½%
Absconder	1755 7%	43 3%	11 3%	168 6%	61 7%	97 7%	19 3%	7 3%	24 3%
RETURN TO PRISON AS TECHNICAL VIOLATOR									
No new conviction(s) and not in lieu of prosecution	2506 10%	88 5%	24 6%	274 10%	82 10%	126 9%	42 8%	10 5%	53 7%
New minor or lesser conviction(s) or in lieu of prosecution	775 3%	40 2%	11 3%	59 2%	27 3%	46 3%	12 2%	9 4%	12 2%
In lieu of prosecution of new major offense(s)	431 2%	7 ½%		41 2%	11 1%	15 1%	11 2%	3 1%	5 1%
Return to prison no violation	28 ½%	2 ½%		2 ½%	2 ½%	1 ½%			1 ½%
RECOMMITTED TO PRISON WITH NEW MAJOR CONVICTION(S)									
Same jurisdiction	1028 4%	13 1%	5 1%	117 4%	39 5%	37 3%	18 3%	8 4%	14 2%
Any other jurisdiction	215 1%	4 ½%	2 ½%	29 1%	3 ½%	7 1%	1 ½%	1 ½%	2 ½%
Total Percentage of Total	24786 100%	1683 7%	428 2%	2622 11%	860 3%	1375 6%	557 2%	208 1%	739 3%

Source: Table 1, Part 1 (1968—National Male—By Commitment Offense), Uniform Parole Reports of the National Probation and Parole Institutes, NCCD Research Center, Brinley Building, Davis, California 95616.

Figure 11-3. PAROLE OUTCOME IN FIRST YEAR FOR PERSONS PAROLED IN 1968

Parole Outcome	Commitment Offense							
	Burglary	Theft or Larceny	Vehicle Theft	Forgery Fraud or Larceny by Check	Other Fraud	Violations of Narcotic Drug Laws	Violations of Alcohol Laws	All Others
CONTINUED ON PAROLE								
No difficulty or sentence less than 60 days	4869 68%	1505 70%	834 63%	1519 62%	157 72%	746 70%	62 86%	1345 73%
With new minor conviction(s)	85 1%	27 1%	14 1%	23 1%	2 1%	17 2%		13 1%
New major conviction(s)	46 1%	14 1%	7 1%	15 1%		14 1%		8 ½%
Absconder	500 7%	186 9%	111 8%	305 13%	25 11%	72 7%	2 3%	124 7%
RETURN TO PRISON AS TECHNICAL VIOLATOR								
No new conviction(s) and not in lieu of prosecution	808 11%	226 10%	148 11%	289 12%	17 8%	122 11%	3 4%	194 11%
New minor or lesser conviction(s) or in lieu of prosecution	245 3%	72 3%	56 4%	86 4%	6 3%	32 3%	2 3%	60 3%
In lieu of prosecution of new major offense(s)	144 2%	47 2%	40 3%	68 3%	1 ½%	6 1%	2 3%	30 2%
Return to prison no violation	13 ½%		1 ½%	2 ½%				4 ½%
RECOMMITTED TO PRISON WITH NEW MAJOR CONVICTION(S)								
Same jurisdiction	410 6%	68 3%	86 6%	98 4%	9 4%	56 5%	1 1%	49 3%
Any other jurisdiction	72 1%	19 1%	29 2%	28 1%	2 1%	7 1%		9 ½%
Total Percentage of Total	7192 29%	2164 9%	1326 5%	2433 10%	219 1%	1072 4%	72 ½%	1836 7%

Source: Table 1, Part 2 (1968—National Male—By Commitment Offense), Uniform Parole Reports of the National Probation and Parole Institutes, NCCD Research Center, Brinley Building, Davis, California 95616.

Figure 11-4. PAROLE OUTCOME IN FIRST YEAR FOR PERSONS PAROLED IN 1968

Parole Outcome	Type of Admission to Prison				
		New Court Not from Probation	Commitment Probation Revoked	Parole Violation Technical	Parole Violation New Conviction
	Total				
CONTINUED ON PAROLE					
No difficulty or sentence less than 60 days	17669	13552	2253	1115	749
	71%	74%	67%	59%	59%
With new minor conviction(s)	246	162	38	23	23
	1%	1%	1%	1%	2%
New major conviction(s)	133	75	11	22	25
	1%	½%	½%	1%	2%
Absconder	1755	1204	208	235	108
	7%	7%	6%	12%	9%
RETURN TO PRISON AS TECHNICAL VIOLATOR					
No new conviction(s) and not in lieu of prosecution	2506	1682	401	282	141
	10%	9%	12%	15%	11%
New minor or lesser conviction(s) or in lieu of prosecution	775	482	147	88	58
	3%	3%	4%	5%	5%
In lieu of prosecution of new major offense(s)	431	267	83	49	32
	2%	1%	2%	3%	3%
Return to prison no violation	28	23		3	2
	½%	½%		½%	½%
RECOMMITTED TO PRISON WITH NEW MAJOR CONVICTION(S)					
Same jurisdiction	1028	685	165	62	116
	4%	4%	5%	3%	9%
Any other jurisdiction	215	158	32	15	10
	1%	1%	1%	1%	1%
Total	24786	18290	3338	1894	1264
Percentage of Total	100%	74%	13%	8%	5%

Source: Table 2 (1968—National Male—By Type of Admission to Prison), Uniform Parole Reports of the National Probation and Parole Institutes, NCCD Research Center, Brinley Building, Davis, California 95616.

Figure 11-5. PAROLE OUTCOME IN FIRST YEAR FOR PERSONS PAROLED IN 1968

Parole Outcome	Prior Prison Sentences								
	Total	None	One	Two	Three	Four	Five	Six	Seven and more
CONTINUED ON PAROLE									
No difficulty or sentence less than 60 days	16882	11333	3058	1359	616	254	131	58	73
	71%	75%	67%	65%	62%	59%	55%	46%	51%
With new minor conviction(s)	246	153	43	26	11	7	4		2
	1%	1%	1%	1%	1%	2%	2%		1%
New major conviction(s)	133	97	18	14		2	1	1	
	1%	1%	½%	1%		½%	½%	1%	
Absconder	1701	813	411	203	126	59	29	26	34
	7%	5%	9%	10%	13%	14%	12%	21%	24%
RETURN TO PRISON AS TECHNICAL VIOLATOR									
No new conviction(s) and not in lieu of prosecution	2394	1390	546	223	111	53	36	17	18
	10%	9%	12%	11%	11%	12%	15%	14%	13%
New minor or lesser conviction(s) or in lieu of prosecution	710	409	144	73	38	21	11	6	8
	3%	3%	3%	4%	4%	5%	5%	5%	6%
In lieu of prosecution of new major offense(s)	412	241	83	38	26	7	4	10	3
	2%	2%	2%	2%	3%	2%	2%	8%	2%
Return to prison no violation	28	9	8	4	3	3	1		
	½%	½%	½%	½%	½%	1%	½%		
RECOMMITTED TO PRISON WITH NEW MAJOR CONVICTION(S)									
Same jurisdiction	1025	606	220	115	42	17	17	4	4
	4%	4%	5%	6%	4%	4%	7%	3%	3%
Any other jurisdiction	215	109	47	27	15	7	5	3	2
	1%	1%	1%	1%	2%	2%	2%	2%	1%
Total	23746	15160	4578	2082	988	430	239	125	144
Percentage of Total	100%	64%	19%	9%	4%	2%	1%	1%	1%

Source: Table 3 (1968—National Male—By Prior Prison Sentences), Uniform Parole Reports of the National Probation and Parole Institutes, NCCD Research Center, Brinley Building, Davis, California 95616.

Figure 11-6. PAROLE OUTCOME IN FIRST YEAR FOR PERSONS PAROLED IN 1968

Parole Outcome		Prior Non-Prison Sentences							
	Total	None	One	Two	Three	Four	Five	Six	Seven and more
CONTINUED ON PAROLE									
No difficulty or sentence less than 60 days	16882 71%	5531 79%	3225 72%	2359 72%	1584 68%	1080 65%	718 60%	538 64%	1847 62%
With new minor conviction(s)	246 1%	51 1%	38 1%	27 1%	31 1%	32 2%	21 2%	7 1%	39 1%
New major conviction(s)	133 1%	27 ½%	16 ½%	19 1%	17 1%	16 1%	6 1%	11 1%	21 1%
Absconder	1701 7%	367 5%	336 8%	227 7%	183 8%	136 8%	115 10%	59 7%	278 9%
RETURN TO PRISON AS TECHNICAL VIOLATOR									
No new conviction(s) and not in lieu of prosecution	2394 10%	495 7%	408 9%	344 10%	260 11%	192 12%	166 14%	118 14%	411 14%
New minor or lesser conviction(s) or in lieu of prosecution	710 3%	141 2%	125 3%	98 3%	69 3%	62 4%	37 3%	44 5%	134 4%
In lieu of prosecution of new major offense(s)	412 2%	120 2%	83 2%	49 1%	37 2%	26 2%	32 3%	11 1%	54 2%
Return to prison no violation	28 ½%	9 ½%	5 ½%		4 ½%	4 ½%	1 ½%		5 ½%
RECOMMITTED TO PRISON WITH NEW MAJOR CONVICTION(S)									
Same jurisdiction	1025 4%	205 3%	181 4%	130 4%	109 5%	86 5%	88 7%	50 6%	176 6%
Any other jurisdiction	215 1%	54 1%	43 1%	36 1%	26 1%	15 1%	13 1%	6 1%	22 1%
Total Percentage of Total	23746 100%	7000 29%	4460 19%	3289 14%	2320 10%	1649 7%	1197 5%	844 4%	2987 13%

Source: Table 4 (1968—National Male—By Prior Non-Prison Sentences), Uniform Parole Reports of the National Probation and Parole Institutes, NCCD Research Center, Brinley Building, Davis, California 95616.

Figure 11-7. PAROLE OUTCOME IN FIRST YEAR FOR PERSONS PAROLED IN 1968

Parole Outcome	Prior Drug Use				Prior Alcohol Use		
	Total	None	Drug Use		Total	None	Alcohol Use
CONTINUED ON PAROLE							
No difficulty or sentence less than 60 days	16882 71%	15112 73%	1770 60%		16882 71%	8443 76%	8439 67%
With new minor conviction(s)	246 1%	189 1%	57 2%		246 1%	121 1%	125 1%
New major conviction(s)	133 1%	83 ½%	50 2%		133 1%	75 1%	58 ½%
Absconder	1701 7%	1452 7%	249 8%		1701 7%	714 6%	987 8%
RETURN TO PRISON AS TECHNICAL VIOLATOR							
No new conviction(s) and not in lieu of prosecution	2394 10%	1989 10%	405 14%		2394 10%	809 7%	1585 13%
New minor or lesser conviction(s) or in lieu of prosecution	710 3%	584 3%	126 4%		710 3%	228 2%	482 4%
In lieu of prosecution of new major offense(s)	412 2%	352 2%	60 2%		412 2%	189 2%	223 2%
Return to prison no violation	28 ½%	27 ½%	1 ½%		28 ½%	13 ½%	15 ½%
RECOMMITTED TO PRISON WITH NEW MAJOR CONVICTION(S)							
Same jurisdiction	1025 4%	807 4%	218 7%		1025 4%	445 4%	580 5%
Any other jurisdiction	215 1%	190 1%	25 1%		215 1%	89 1%	126 1%
Total Percentage of Total	23746 100%	20785 88%	2961 12%		23746 100%	11126 47%	12620 53%

Source: Table 5 and 6 (1968—National Male—By Prior Drug and Alcohol Use), Uniform Parole Reports of the National Probation and Parole Institutes, NCCD Research Center, Brinley Building, Davis, California 95616.

Figure 11-8. NEW MAJOR CONVICTIONS OR ALLEGATIONS WITH PRISON RETURN IN FIRST YEAR FOR PERSONS PAROLED IN 1968

New Offense	Total Part 1 & 2	Willful Homicide	Negligent Manslaughter	Armed Robbery	Unarmed Robbery	Aggravated Assault	Forcible Rape	All Other Sex Offenses
None	23112 / 93%	1659 / 99%	421 / 98%	2435 / 93%	807 / 94%	1316 / 96%	527 / 95%	914 / 97%
Willful Homicide	27 / ½%	7 / ½%		6 / ½%	1 / ½%			
Negligent Manslaughter	6 / ½%				2 / ½%			
Armed Robbery	191 / 1%	2 / ½%		71 / 3%	8 / 1%	8 / 1%	1 / ½%	3 / ½%
Unarmed Robbery	59 / ½%			10 / ½%	10 / 1%	4 / ½%	1 / ½%	
Aggravated Assault	81 / ½%	3 / ½%		10 / ½%	3 / ½%	14 / 1%	2 / ½%	2 / ½%
Forcible Rape	27 / ½%			3 / ½%		1 / ½%	14 / 3%	1 / ½%
All Other Sex Offenses	34 / ½%	1 / ½%		3 / ½%	2 / ½%	1 / ½%	2 / ½%	9 / 1%
Burglary	521 / 2%	4 / ½%	2 / ½%	36 / 1%	13 / 2%	11 / 1%	3 / 1%	4 / ½%
Theft or Larceny	143 / 1%	1 / ½%	1 / ½%	7 / ½%	5 / 1%	4 / ½%	3 / 1%	3 / ½%
Vehicle Theft	153 / 1%	2 / ½%	1 / ½%	7 / ½%	1 / ½%	4 / ½%	1 / ½%	2 / ½%
Forgery Fraud or Larceny by Check	164 / 1%	1 / ½%		9 / ½%	3 / ½%	4 / ½%		2 / ½%
Other Fraud	14 / ½%			3 / ½%			1 / ½%	
Violations of Narcotic Drug Laws	85 / ½%	2 / ½%	2 / ½%	9 / ½%	4 / ½%		1 / ½%	3 / ½%
Violations of Alcohol Laws	7 / ½%							1 / ½%
All Others	105 / ½%	1 / ½%	1 / ½%	8 / ½%	3 / ½%	6 / ½%	1 / ½%	2 / ½%
Total	24729	1683	428	2619	860	1373	557	946

Source: Table 7, Part 1 (1968—National Male), Uniform Parole Reports of the National Probation and Parole Institute, NCCD Research Center, Brinley Building, Davis, California 95616.

Figure 11-9. NEW MAJOR CONVICTIONS OR ALLEGATIONS WITH PRISON RETURN IN FIRST YEAR FOR PERSONS PAROLED IN 1968

New Offense	Burglary	Theft or Larceny	Vehicle Theft	Forgery Fraud or Larceny by Check	Other Fraud	Violations of Narcotic Drug Laws	Violations of Alcohol Laws	All Others
None	6566 / 92%	2030 / 94%	1171 / 89%	2239 / 92%	207 / 95%	1003 / 94%	69 / 96%	1748 / 96%
Willful Homicide	5 / ½%	1 / ½%	2 / ½%	1 / ½%				4 / ½%
Negligent Manslaughter	2 / ½%	1 / ½%	1 / ½%					
Armed Robbery	52 / 1%	14 / 1%	13 / 1%	6 / ½%	1 / ½%	4 / ½%		8 / ½%
Unarmed Robbery	22 / ½%	2 / ½%	4 / ½%	4 / ½%				2 / ½%
Aggravated Assault	19 / ½%	7 / ½%	5 / ½%	7 / ½%		3 / ½%		6 / ½%
Forcible Rape	3 / ½%	2 / ½%	3 / ½%					
All Other Sex Offenses	8 / ½%			3 / ½%		1 / ½%		4 / ½%
Burglary	312 / 4%	38 / 2%	35 / 3%	29 / 1%	2 / 1%	14 / 1%		18 / 1%
Theft or Larceny	57 / 1%	27 / 1%	9 / 1%	13 / 1%	2 / 1%	8 / 1%		3 / ½%
Vehicle Theft	38 / 1%	13 / 1%	58 / 4%	9 / ½%	3 / 1%	3 / ½%	1 / 1%	10 / 1%
Forgery Fraud or Larceny by Check	28 / ½%	6 / ½%	9 / 1%	98 / 4%	2 / 1%			2 / ½%
Other Fraud	3 / ½%		1 / ½%	4 / ½%	2 / 1%			
Violations of Narcotic Drug Laws	19 / ½%	6 / ½%	1 / ½%	6 / ½%		31 / 3%		1 / ½%
Violations of Alcohol Laws	3 / ½%	1 / ½%					2 / 3%	
All Others	31 / ½%	12 / 1%	5 / ½%	8 / ½%		5 / ½%		22 / 1%
Total	7168	2160	1317	2427	219	1072	72	1828

Source: Table 7, Part 2 (1968—National Male), Uniform Parole Reports of the National Probation and Parole Institutes, NCCD Research Center, Brinley Building, Davis, California 95616.

NOTES

Parole Prediction

Note 1.

VICTOR J. EVJEN

*Current Thinking on Parole Prediction Tables**

To learn the extent to which paroling authorities use prediction statistics in parole selection, I sent a form letter, in August, 1961, to the parole boards of the fifty states and several other jurisdictions. The letter asked these two questions:

1. Have prediction statistics (schedules, ratings, etc.) ever been used by your Board in the selection of parolees?
2. Does your paroling authority use prediction devices at the present time? If so, please indicate briefly the manner in which they are used.

Of the forty-eight states responding, forty-four indicated they had never used prediction statistics in parole selection and are not now using them.

The U.S. Board of Parole, the New York City Parole Commission, and the paroling authorities of Puerto Rico, Canada, the U.S. Army, and the District of Columbia also answered "No" to each question.

Illinois has had nearly thirty years of experience with prediction tables. And it is the only state in which a routine system of parole prediction has been established. Since 1933 a sociologist-actuary at each of the major penal institutions has been conducting research in parole prediction and selection and has prepared for the parole board a routine prediction report on each inmate appearing for a parole hearing. He computes the prisoner's statistical chances of making a successful adjustment on parole. The final sentence in the report reads: "This inmate is in a class in which ____ per cent may be expected to violate the parole agreement." Together with sociological, psychiatric, and psychological reports, and interviews by the Board, the probability score is used as an aid in selecting prisoners for parole. The Joliet-Stateville and Menard branches of the Illinois State Penitentiary have one prediction table; the Pontiac branch for "younger improvable offenders" has another. The women's institution at Dwight has none. The tables used at Joliet were originally developed by Burgess (1928) and modified by Ohlin (1951 and 1954). The table now used at Pontiac was developed by Daniel Glaser (1954).

In Ohio a parole prediction index has been developed under the direction of Dr. John Pruski, member of the Pardon and Parole Commission, from a constellation of variables obtained from responses on the Minnesota Multiphasic Personality Inventory (MMPI). Inmate testing under this system began in September, 1961.

In California the Youth Authority and the Department of Corrections have begun an extensive program of establishing "base expectancy" scores, which will be used in parole selection when they become standardized and perfected.

In Colorado the Parole Board, according to Edward W. Grout, Executive Director of the State Department of Parole, is now developing prediction statistics.

In Minnesota, the St. Cloud Reformatory experimented with the Ohlin Prediction Report in the fifties; prediction table are not used in the state at present.

Note 2.

GEORG K. STURUP

*Will This Man Be Dangerous?**

Administrators and theoretical criminologists are involved with principles and systems of decision making. Clinical criminologists, on the other hand, have personal contact with people, be they perpetrators of crimes or their victims. The administrator must rely on reports of people working in the field to build and operate his systems while the clinician, engaged in trying to understand the life careers of his clients, is concerned with how he can use himself and the machinery he controls to make their lives more acceptable to themselves and to society. . . .

After a man has been sentenced, the problem of dangerousness arises again when he is going to leave the prison or specialized treatment institution. I will not comment on the

---

* Reprinted, with permission of the National Council on Crime and Delinquency, from *Crime and Delinquency*, July 1962, pp. 216–17.

* Georg K. Sturup, *Will This Man Be Dangerous?* in A. V. S. deReuck and Ruth Porter, Eds., *The Mentally Abnormal Offender* 5, 11 (1967). CIBA Foundation Symposium. Reprinted with permission of the publisher, Churchill Livingstone, Medical Division of Longman Group Ltd.

problems of evaluating patients about to be released from mental hospitals, but will concentrate my remarks on the pre-parole situation, when a man is going to be paroled after having served a long sentence.

. . . A special problem for the pre-parole adviser is this: if he reports that in his opinion a man is dangerous, or that he behaves so peculiarly that the risk of new dangerous crime seems obvious, the administration will usually not set this man free and the adviser will never know if he was right. The prediction becomes a self-fulfilling prophecy and we gain no experience.

2. EXCERPTS FROM CONNECTICUT PAROLE HEARINGS

The Case of Alex Styer

PAROLE HEARING PROGRESS REPORT

Connecticut Correctional Institution

Date Prepared: 3/2/71
Name   Alex Styer
Number   55394
Age   49 years
Date Received: 5/2/67

Parole Hearing Date: 3/23/71
Offense   Indecent Asslt., 2 cts.
Sentence   5 to 14 yrs.
Parole Elig.   5/30/71
Sentence Exp.   4/13/76

PREVIOUS PAROLE BOARD ACTION
7/14/70—Denied

OTHER BOARD ACTION
None

WARRANTS
None

OTHER SENTENCES
None

LAST CLASSIFICATION COMMITTEE ACTION
10/22/70—Medium (internal)—Data Processing—Annual Review. Approved for 7-day assignment. Not seen by Committee—A special referral.

CUSTODIAL
Subject has received no misconduct reports. He is good in his cell care and personal grooming. His cooperation with housing officers is good as is his attitude toward others and regulations. Quarters officer states that subject is a very good inmate.

WORK AND TRAINING
Subsequent to commitment, subject has worked in the Kitchen; Officers Mess—Days and was assigned to the Data Proc. School on 7/26/68 where he continues to work. He is assigned to the Institution Industries Computer applications in programming capacity. His cooperation is excellent as is his attitude toward everyone. Subject has been a valuable asset to this section and has contributed immeasurably to the success of that section. He has consistently performed above-average and has a very high degree of interest in every phase of the field.

MEDICAL
History of VD—not to handle food; psychiatric pending.

RELIGION

Subject is an occasional chapel attendant. He received his G.E.D. diploma in 1968 and has attended classes given here by Lionelville Community College in the Spring and Summer; also in the Fall. Has a "B" average in the courses he has completed.

SOCIAL

Subject receives no visits. He has twice-monthly correspondence with his mother, Mrs. Judith Styer of Bayer, So. Car. and with a niece, Sherry Stone of So. Car. Institutional acct. balance 1/19/71 $367.62.

ADMISSION SUMMARY

Classif. Hear. Date: 8 June, 1967

Commitment Name	Styer, Alex	Offense	INDECENT ASSAULT, 2 cts.
Number	55394	Sentence	5 to 14 yrs.
True Name	Alexander John Styer	Warrants	None
Alias	None	Other Sent.	None
Birth Date	4 October, 1921	Parole Elig.	11 November, 1970
Birth Place	Boote, S. Car.	Sent. Exp.	16 July, 1976
Race		Plea	Guilty
Military Service	U.S. NAVY	Arrest Date	21 March, 1967
Marital Status	Divorced	Sent. Date	2 May, 1967
Religion	None	Date Rec'd.	2 May, 1967
O.A.S.I. No.	912-62-7777	Judge	J. A. Slocum
F.B.I. No.	42-999 Z	Court	Waterbury—New Haven
D.C.I. No.	08777X	Defense Atty.	Anderson
Co-defendants	None		

5 to 10 yrs. on 1st ct.; 4 years on 2nd ct.—to run consecutive.

SEE PRIOR INSTITUTIONAL ADJUSTMENT ATTACHED ON STYER CSP# 66666.

RELIGION

This subject has been here before, also for an offense in the area of sex perversion. He has no interest or background in religion.

EDUCATION:

The following taken from previous report.

I.Q.: 83		Mathematics:	8.4	Grade Placement:	8.1
Reading: 7.8		Language:	8.3		

MEDICAL

Height: 70"   Weight: 173
Vision: DV L: 20/30   R: 20/40   NV L&R: 20/20
Remarks: None
Work Limitations: None
Housing Limitations: None

PRIOR INSTITUTIONAL ADJUSTMENT AT CONN. STATE PRISON

	NAME & NUMBER:	Alex Styer #55394
PRIOR:	NAME:	Styer, Alex
	NUMBER:	44441
	OFFENSE:	INJURY OR RISK OF INJURY (under 16)
	SENTENCE:	3 to 10 years.
	DATE OF COMMITMENT:	4/26/60

WORK: Subject held work assignments in   Kitchen 5/27/60;
Osborn Div. Kitchen, 6/5/61

His work was considered   outstanding.

CONDUCT: Subject's CONDUCT was considered   Very Good

Subject received the following MISCONDUCT REPORTS   0
how many

Any MISCONDUCTS that should be noted: None

RELEASE DATA: Subject was denied Parole ———— times.

Subject was voted to Parole on   3/6/62   Paroled   6/29/62

Subject was returned for a Parole Violation on ————

Subject Discharged on   3/1/66.

REMARKS:

PRESENTENCE INVESTIGATION REPORT

RE: Alex Styer   STATE NO. 1–6–15015
   Docket No. 2222

SOURCE OF REFERRAL

On April 11, 1967, the Honorable J. A. Slocum referred the case of Alex Styer to the Adult Probation Department for Presentence Investigation. The report is due for sentencing on May 2, 1967.

THE OFFENSES

Styer pleaded guilty in the Superior Court of New Haven County at Waterbury to the offenses of committing (1) an Indecent Assault upon another person at Seaside, on or about the 26th day of February, 1967 and (2) an Indecent Assault upon another person, at Seaside, on or about the 18th day of December, 1966, both counts in violation of Section 53–217 of the General Statutes, maximum penalty ten years each count.

The circumstances surrounding the offenses are as follows:

   3/21/67—Information from Guidance Counsellor of the Seaside School System, Samuel Sanders, that he has sent two mothers to see their family doctors with their ten year old children, Beth Cinderly and Carla Darr, as they had entered a complaint to him that their daughters had been molested by a grown man. Counsellor then told the parents that they were to go to the Police if the story their children told them was true.
   On March 21, 1967, complainants came into the station and said that they had positive proof that the girls were molested, this was verified by a Doctor Bacchus, 45 Apollo Street, Seaside, Connecticut.
   Mrs. Cinderly states that on Sunday March 19, 1967, her daughters, Beth and Sue, both daughters

of the Cinderlys said that a Alex Styer, a friend of the family, asked both girls to give him some pussy. This was asked of the girls while they were riding in the Styer car. The girls came right home and related this to the parents. This happened about dinner time.

Mr. Cinderly then questioned his daughter, Beth again, and she said to him again that Alex wanted some pussy, and Beth said that Alex has asked her about her pussy before. Then Mr. Cinderly told his daughter not to mention that "dirty word" again, and dropped the subject.

Then after dinner, the girls were ready to go to the show, and Carla Darr the girl next door came in, and one of the girls brought up the case again, and Mr. Cinderly heard the girls say that Alex had undressed the Darr girl, and fooled around with her in the bedroom of Alex Styer's home on Main Street, Seaside.

I said to Carla Darr why she did not tell her mother about this, and the girl said that if she did Alex Styer would throw me in the river if she told her mother.

Then at about three P.M. Alex Styer came to the Cinderly home and Mr. Cinderly was going to talk to him about what had happened, but Alex was too drunk and nothing was said at the time. Alex left the Cinderly home about four P.M. and then the girls came home about five from the movies.

Mr. Cinderly then asked his daughter Beth, if Alex had touched her and she said yes he did. I asked her how he did this, and she said with his finger, and with his peter (meaning his private). This Beth said happened about two or three weeks ago.

With this information, Mrs. Cinderly remembered that about two weeks ago that she saw something that looked like blood on the bottom lining of her daughter's coat, and when she asked her about this, her daughter Beth said that this was cherry coke. Mrs. Cinderly let it go at that time as nothing until this information came up and the Cinderly family got worried.

/s/ Lt. Sid Diavolo
Seaside Police Dept.

OFFENDER'S VERSION OF OFFENSE

Defendant admitted his guilt to the offenses as charged. He stated he did not care to go into details of the events.

PREVIOUS RECORD

The Federal Bureau of Investigation and Connecticut State Police were checked on Styer

2/10/59	New London Superior Ct. New London, Conn.	Procuring a Female for the purpose of Prostitution	1 year jail

Involved Styer, his then wife, a 16 and 18-year old girls.

6/29/59	Balance of sentence of 2/10/59 suspended, two years probation.		
4/26/60	New London Superior Ct. New London, Conn.	Risk of Injury	3 to 10 years State Prison

Involved girls under age of 16.

6/29/62 Paroled from State Prison, and discharged from parole on March 1, 1966.

Offender's Personal History

FAMILY BACKGROUND AND EARLY LIFE

Styer was born October 4, 1921, in Boote, South Carolina. He has one brother and sister living in the South.

MARITAL HISTORY

Married a Mary Lambrusco in 1944 while in the Navy. She divorced him in Reno in 1947. There was one child born of this union, a Fred Styer, whose custody was given to his mother.

Defendant married for the second time a Miss Calicid, in Louisiana in 1951. She got a divorce from him in Louisiana as he being in the Navy was away a great deal of the time.

Styer married his third wife, a Patricia Sive, of No. Carolina in Asbury, Connecticut on November 8, 1957. He stated she got a divorce from him while he was in prison. Patricia was arrested in 1959 (when he was) for Procuring Female for Purpose of Prostitution. She received a probation term. There was a child, Janice, born November 26, 1958, of this union, and she is with mother. Styer did not know whereabouts of Patricia at this time.

EDUCATION

Defendant stated he went through the 8th grade, but did complete his high school education equivalency test.

SERVICE RECORD

Entered the U.S. Navy on October 17, 1940, Serial No. 133–6666, and was advanced to Chief Petty Officer October 1, 1945. He was in the Navy at the time of his arrest of February 10, 1959 and was given release because of that conviction. (See addendum to this Presentence Investigation for possible further information on this, if our office receives it on time for court.)

EMPLOYMENT

Defendant was in the U.S. Navy 1940 to 1959. After his release from jail in 1959, he returned to Norfolk, Virginia, and worked in a factory there to 1960.

Returning to Connecticut in 1960, he was sent to prison for the offense already mentioned. After his release from prison in 1962, he worked as a chef for the Hawaiian Room in Seaside, Connecticut, Joel's Restaurant in Delhia, French Arms, in Hartford, and operated with a partner a grill in Bridgeport, Connecticut for a while.

His last employment prior to his current arrest was for Old Bucket Restaurant in Seaside, Connecticut for the past eight months.

ECONOMICS

He has nothing of value, nor does he have many debts.

SUMMARY

Alex Styer, divorced, age 45, white American, pleaded guilty in the Superior Court of New Haven County at Waterbury to the above offenses. He has been confined 42 days since his arrest, in lieu of bond, and is represented by Attorney Samuel Schwartz, of Seaside, Connecticut.

Defendant is before a Superior Court for the third time in recent years, involving most serious offenses against young girls. He has been in jail and State Prison, having been released from parole a little over a year ago.

Styer is originally from South Carolina, and has been married three times. He is a long time Navy man, having been given his discharge because of a felony back in 1959.

He is limited in education, but apparently knows right from wrong, but without much consideration of the wrong involved in his actions.

His employment since leaving service has been mostly as a chef, in Connecticut in various communities.

PERSONAL HISTORY (Pre-Sentence Report)

(Part of the following prepared for the instant case and the balance for Docket No. 5150.)

Subject was born October 4, 1921, in Boote, South Carolina. His father died when he was an infant. His mother still resides on Route 11, Box 82, Bayer, South Carolina. He has one brother, John, age 31, who lives in Richmond, Virginia and a sister, Sandy Slade, who resides with his mother.

Subject married one Mary Lambrusco in 1944. Shortly after the marriage they moved to Oregon, then subject went to the Pacific and remained there for approximately eighteen months before returning to Oregon. His wife returned home as she did not want to move to Oregon nor the Navy way of living, i.e., she would be alone a great deal of the time. Reportedly they never got to see each other enough to actually get to know one another and it has been reported that the wife obtained a divorce in Reno in February of 1947.

One child was born of this union, Fred Styer. The mother was given custody of and an allotment for this child. Subject said he hears from the wife occasionally who is now living in New Jersey with her present husband.

Subject states he married a second time in 1951 in Louisiana to a Miss Calicid. They resided in Louisiana for a short period of time then moved to Norfolk and the subject said he was sent around the world, winding up in Korea, where he remained for about eight months before returning to Norfolk where he remained for some time. Subject said at this time he was going to sea every week and was only home on weekends. He said his wife complained continually about this and when he was later ordered to Europe, where he spent two years, in the interim the wife obtained a divorce in Louisiana.

Subject married his present wife, Patricia Sive, in Asbury, Connecticut, on November 8, 1957. She had met the subject while he was stationed in North Carolina. Her home is in Elma City, South Carolina.

Subject entered the U.S. Navy on October 17, 1940—Serial No. 133–6666. He was advanced to Chief Petty Officer on October 1, 1945, a rating that subject still holds. He was assigned at the Sub Base as Master at Arms at the Galley and under him had many men assigned to handling of the food for the men at the Submarine Base. According to subject's record, he re-enlisted on November 15, 1955 at which time he had fifteen years service. He received average scores on the DCT examination and completed his high school education equivalency test.

Subject stated that at one time he was charged with selling passes at the Submarine Base. After trial, he was acquitted of the charge.

Subject's record would indicate that he was making a career of the Navy in that it has no indication of any former employers. OASI Number: 912–62–7777.

On February 10, 1959 subject was sentenced to one year in the County Jail on a charge of Procuring a Female for the Purpose of Prostitution. On June 27, 1959, the balance of his sentence was suspended and he was placed on probation for two years.

Upon his release from jail he returned to his wife who was then residing in Norwich and who was also on probation in Superior Court for the same charge and was on a suspended sentence to the Connecticut State Farm for Women.

Subject lived with his wife and child for a while in Norwich, obtaining work in various restaurants and stores in the area. He then opened his own business in Bridgeport, Connecticut, which place proved a financial loss and subject gave up the business in January, 1962. Subject then moved to Derby with his family. Shortly after moving to Derby he was arrested on the charges that took place in New London County and he was returned to Norwich and committed to the New London County Jail.

The record informs that subject's plea of guilty on the instant offenses, committed while he was on probation, constitutes a violation of his probation.

EDUCATION

Subject completed the 8th grade at Sweet Seed, South Carolina. He earned and received his high school certificate while in the Navy. On May 5, 1960, subject was tested on the California Achievement BB Inter, and received the following grades:

Grade Placement: 8.1—Reading: 7.8—Language: 8.3—Arithmetic: 8.4. He tested 83 on the Otis IQ Beta.

Subject said while in the U.S. Navy as CPO Commissary Man, he prepared menus, ordered provisions and supervised the cooking and meatcutting. He said he was employed as a meatcutter at Sotten Food Stores in Seaside, Connecticut, when arrested on the present offenses.

Subject said he would like assignment to the Kitchen, Store or Commissary while here. He expressed no dislikes.

MEDICAL

Height: 5'10"
Physical Frame: Good
Orthopedics: None
Hearing: Normal
Venereal Disease: No

Weight: 173
Psychiatric: No psychological done.
Urine: Negative
Vision: R: 20/40   L: 20/30
Narcotic: No   Alcoholic: No

Summary: Regular Duty

RELIGION

Subject is not a Catholic but is interested in becoming one. Prior to coming here he was taking instructions and now desires to continue doing so. He expressed a sincere interest and instructions will be given as requested.

CLASSIFICATION

Close Custody—Assigned to General Maintenance.

Criminal History

2/10/59	New London, Conn.	Procuring Female for purpose of Prostitution	1 year—balance suspended on 6/29/59 2 years probation
4/26/60	" " "	Risk of Injury	3–10 yrs. CSP #44441 Par. 6/29/62 Disc. 3/1/66

PSYCHIATRIC EVALUATIONS

Connecticut Correctional Institution, Somers

March 12, 1971

FROM: Harold Lee, Clinical Psychologist

TO: Board of Parole

SUBJECT: Pre-Parole Psychiatric Evaluation Report on Alex Styer, CCIS 55394, by Hugh Oberdorffer, M.D., on the above date.

Styer is a 49 year old male who has been married three times and has also been divorced three times. Styer is serving 5 to 14 years for two counts of indecent assault committed on two then ten year old girls. Previous criminal history shows a 1960 conviction for risk of injury for which he received a 3 to 10 year sentence in the Connecticut State Prison. This charge according to the admission summary involved girls under the age of 16, which would suggest that there was more than one girl involved. Styer, however, talks in connection with this offense about one 19 year old girl who had been working for him regularly and who had stolen money from his cash register. Styer claims that she had hid the money in her panties and when he asked for it, she challenged him to come and get it, which he subsequently did but apparently as an added fringe benefit, he admitted to touching her genitals in the process. The 1970 pre-parole examination indicates that he admitted that he was accused of providing dates for young girls who had come to his establishment. It is however frustrating not to have the actual details of these crimes available in the admission summary.

As far as the 1959 offense was concerned, both he and his wife were convicted of procuring females for the purpose of prostitution. Styer this time tells me that at the time he was a petty officer and he lived ashore with his wife. He states that one of the men who was working for him was found living with a 19 year old girl. This case was brought to court but he states because his employee and the girl in question claimed to plan to get married, he was given temporary custody of the girl by the court in some fashion until the couple was able to realize their wedding plans. The man in question was subsequently given a two week leave to get married, but he states that because of financial difficulties this girl continued to stay with them after their marriage, presumably for a short time until they could set up housekeeping together. He claimed that somewhat later the police informed him that the couple had not gotten married after all. The police also told him that this girl was apparently circulating nude or semi-nude photographs of herself in the local bar and the police told him to get the pictures from the girl. He states he found out that this girl had been fooling around with some 12 to 15 men and indeed used the pictures to advertise the product that was to provide the services. He admits when questioned that he also had received "a piece of the action" somewhere along the line. Again Styer talks about one girl at the age of 19. The summary speaks about a 16 and a 18 year old girl or girls. Styer was discharged from the Navy as the result of this conviction for which he received a one year jail sentence. The circumstances of the present crime as far as Styer's version is concerned has been, I believe, adequately described in my pre-parole evaluation dated July 9, 1970.

Maybe there is possibly one encouraging factor about this man's offense, and that is possibly the fact that we have no record that he acted out sexually with a girl whom he had never seen before; in other words, so far as he has not been the kind of offender who approaches little girls in parks or invites strange girls into cars or possibly pulls little girls into dark alley-ways. It seemed that in all these situations there was time to develop a certain amount of intimacy before he acted on his impulses. Of course, Styer claims that he has never forced himself on any young girls at any time nor that he ever tried to pick up young girls in parks or other situations where chance meetings with little girls were a possibility.

Styer was questioned about the Parole Board's recommendation that he asked to join Dr. James' sex offenders' therapy group. He stated that he wrote a request in Aug. and did not receive any answer and that subsequently he talked to the clerk in September when he was told that he was placed on the list and that he would be contacted. My question to him was why he did not "pester" Dr. James and the Psychology Department until he had a definite yes or no. He immediately said lamely that he was just waiting and expecting an answer. This man's institutional adjustment of course has been excellent. Matter of fact he has been most valuable as a computer programmer. If he could only be paroled to a young girl-free work and living situation, releasing this man would be much less of an unknown factor. I believe that alcohol has also played a part in lessening self-control as far as his sexual offenses are concerned, and if he would be considered for parole, he should abstain from alcohol. The fact that no real violence has been committed and the fact that these offenses were committed with girls who had regular if not very close contact with the offender before he acted out his sexually immature impulses.

Author: Hugh Oberdorffer, M.D.
Consultant in Psychiatry

Connecticut Correctional Institution, Somers

July 9, 1970

FROM: Harold Lee, Clinical Psychologist

TO: Board of Parole

SUBJECT: Pre-Parole Psychiatric Evaluation Report on Alex Styer, CCIS #55394, on the above date, by Hugh Oberdorffer, M.D., Consulting Psychiatrist.

Styer is a 49 year old three time married and three time divorced individual, who is serving a 5 to 14 year sentence for two counts of indecent assault involving the then two ten year old girls. Previous criminal history shows two previous convictions for or involving sexual offenses. One was for risk of injury, involving at least one girl less than 16 years of age.

Styer in the interview situation is a quiet individual, who relates his story without undue anxiety. When I listen to Styer, as far as the first offense is concerned, he was just trying to help out the police when they requested him to get the nude photographs of the girl in question, of whom he was the guardian in some fashion. However, after he had been able to get these pictures, they mysteriously disappeared and the police then subsequently charged him and his wife with procuring a female. As far as the risk of injury case is concerned; he had a 16 year old girl working for him, who stole money from his cash register, she had hid the money in her panties and he reached in and took the money out. He also states that he was accused of providing dates for young girls who would come to his establishment. The actual details of his crimes is not available in the admission summary.

As far as the present offense is concerned, he states that Mr. and Mrs. Cinderly befriended him. Mr. Cinderly had a night time job and Mrs. Cinderly would ask him to stay over at night. He also claims that the Cinderlys had a car, but neither Mr. or Mrs. Cinderly had a driver's license; so he was frequently asked to drive the children places or to go shopping for the family. Styer then states that Mrs. Cinderly started to send her two daughters to Styer's house for a bath twice a week, because the Cinderlys did not have hot water in their house. He states that the Cinderly girl said "you sleep with mommy, why won't you sleep with me." He then claims that while initially he did not wash them. The mother of the girls had told the girls that "uncle Alex" would wash their backs for them. It was during these activities that he would get a little excited and kiss their budding breasts and while washing them his hand might have passed over their genital areas, but he disclaims that his hand lingered there for any length of time. When asked how this situation came to light? He states that three days before he was arrested, he had told Mrs. Cinderly that as soon as he had enough money to get himself a car, he would be heading out of the State. Mrs. Cinderly did not like this at all and stated that she nor her daughters would see him again.

It appears that Styer has served two sentences innocently; at least this is the implications of his statements and he was practically seduced into the relationship with the mother and both daughters, again this is the implication of his stories.

This kind of rationalization, is of course extremely common among sexual offenders. It also is common that often there is some cooperation from the victim or sometimes from one of the parents of the victims. Styer claims that he will never come near another girl. I recommend that he be considered for treatment in Dr. James' Group Therapy for sex offenders. Styer claims that he had not heard of this group. Whether Dr. James has a place in his group at this point I do not know.

Author: Hugh Oberdorffer, M.D.

PAROLE APPLICATION

From: Alex Styer
Box 100
Somers, Connecticut 06071

March 2, 1971

To Mr. J. B. Glougher, Chairman
State Board of Parole
340 Capitol Avenue
Hartford, Connecticut

Dear Sir,

I have made an effort to compile all the information concerning the educational programs I have participated in as well as my work progress in the Data Processing Department. The supervisors and the director of education were kind enough to sign these papers for me. I hope this will be of help to you in reaching a decision in my case.

In November of 1966 I was involved in an automobile accident which completely demolished my car and cost me all the savings I had. Instead of obtaining a positive mental attitude I resorted to a negative attitude, feeling sorry for myself and began to associate with undesirable people, prostitutes, dope addicts and drunks. Had I known the importance of a positive mental attitude, then this letter would be unnecessary. Shortly after I arrived here on this sentence, I made up my mind that it was time I made an honest effort to better myself and retain all the benefits offered to me through education. I had gone down hill since I was discharged from the U.S. Navy and I decided it was time I changed my attitude. I realized I couldn't change the past, but I sure could do something about my future.

In my three month study of psychology and three month course in 'Guides for Better Living' I learned that the first step toward rehabilitation is for one to realize his own mistakes, admit them to himself and understand the cause of his mistakes, then use them as a stepping stone to guide him into a better and more useful life.

I wrote a request to Dr. Jame about the same time that I wrote the letter to Mr. Stone. After I did not receive a reply to my request. I asked Mr. Jame's clerk to make me an appointment. After a few days the clerk told me that Mr. Jame had my request and would call me. So far my request for an interview has not been granted.

No doubt, you are aware that I suffer from the 'gout'. This means that I can only eat low lipid food, drink no alcoholic beverage, not get excited, or worry if I want to be able to walk. Then on January 8, 1971, I was informed by Doctor Todd that I am a diabetic. If I eat fatty foods, use sugar or drink anything containing sweets I will go into a coma and probably wake up in a hospital.

My sponsor Mr. Daniel Donlevy has letters from two companies that are interested in giving me a job. Forever Life Insurance had promised me a job before I appeared before the Board of Parole last July. According to Mr. Donlevy they are still interested and I am to see the personnel director as soon as I can. The Octogenerian Life Insurance Company has taken my job application and are interested in hiring me in their data processing department. The Squatter's Hill Insurance Company has also sent me a job application. I also have an invitation to see the meat manager of the Goode's Food Company to apply for a job as a meat cutter.

As of October 20, 1970, I have been working from 8:00 a.m. until 6:00 p.m. seven days per week. This is so I can keep the industry work caught up and assist in rewriting the accounting system in upper level language. During the time I am training two men to take over my operation in the event I am granted parole.

Now that I am headed in the direction of a decent education, I intend to make every possible effort to obtain, at least, an associate degree in computer technology. As you can see by the attached letter from Mr. Laffin, he can start me in the summer semester.

In view of the criteria I have presented to you I respectfully ask you to give me the opportunity to take advantage of the education and practical experience I have accumulated since I have been incarcerated in this institution. I sincerely promise the members of the Board of Parole to exert every effort to do my parole, steer clear of trouble and never have to appear before the Board of Parole again.

Very respectfully yours,
Alex Styer

Work Progress of A. Styer

March 2, 1971

I was assigned to the Data Processing Training Program on July 28, 1968. After the initial training period I was assigned to the Accounting System where I have worked through this date. I have worked in all phases of the Accounting Systems using both Basic Assemblers Language and Report Program Generator Language. This includes Accounts Payable, Accounts Receivable, Bookkeeping, Inventory Control, Work Orders, Fixed Assets and the Pay-roll System.

I am capable of setting up an accounting system for a company including all accounting and payroll phases.

I have written programs in 'Basic Assembler Language' (BAL), 'Report Program Generator' (RPG) and Cobol Language.

I have written programs for the Health Department on Air Pollution, O.M.R. Card Layout and Health Needs Survey.

At the present time I am in the process of teaching the accounting system to anyone interested in learning. I have also instructed other programmers in the operation of the various machines used in data processing.

Since Aug. 1969 I have been in charge of the complete industry accounting system for both

Somers and Osborne Prisons. This includes, Accounts Receivable, Accounts Payable, Bookkeeping, Work Order and Fixed Assets. I assisted with the Inventory Control System which was placed into operation July last year. Accounts Receivable and Accounts Payable are run weekly. All programs and systems are run monthly with a special run quarterly and at the end of the fiscal year.

Since August of 1969 I have worked each week end and every day except legal holidays, so as to keep the Accounting System up to date and to be able to present a weekly run to the Industry Supervisor each Monday morning. Since October 20, 1970, I have worked from eight o'clock each morning until six o'clock each night, or ten hours per day, seven days per week. This giving me a total of 6,132 hours of experience in the Data Processing field.

At the present time I am in the process of re-writing and assisting other programmers to re-write all our accounting programs in the Upper Model Bal Language so we can replace the computer with a terminal.

Mr. Bartholomew Butler
Data Processing Supervisor

Very Respectfully,
Alex Styer

Educational Accomplishments of Alex Styer

March 1, 1971

Since I have been in this institution I have accomplished the following educational programs.

Attended the High School Program for one year to gain a High School Diploma. During this time I raised my grade placement average from 8.5 to 11.5.

Participated in the Chef's Program from July of 1967 to July 28, 1968.

Attended Speed Reading classes for approximately 60 hours. Two nights each week, raising my reading ability from 250 words per minute to 894 words per minute with 85% comprehension.

Attended the classes of "Guides for Better Living" and received a mark of excellent in each assignment.

Finished the Data Processing School for the Report Generator Language (RPG). The Basic Assembler Language (BAL) and the Cobol Language.

Finished the Data Processing School for the Teleprocessing System (Faster Language). A minimum training period of at least six months is required to become a efficient programmer in any of these languages.

Assisted in teaching programming. The use of various machines used in Data Processing and the Accounting System to other inmates.

Completed a course in Memory and Concentration Study. This course was presented to me by Mr. Stanley Johnson here at Somers. This course is designed to substitute letters for numbers so numbers can be better remembered.

Completed 21 assignments of an I.C.S. course in Applied Mathematics, Mathematics, Algebra, Equation and Geometry. This course was taken through the Educational Department here at Somers.

Completed 21 courses in accounting with the Morely Technical Institute of Stoneville, Florida. I received an average of 90 on these courses.

As of May 7, 1971, I will have twelve credit courses with the Lionelville Community College. One semester in English Composition, one semester in English Literature, one semester in Psychology and one semester in Biological Science. It is my intention to continue my education with the Lionelville Community College to obtain an associate degree in Computer Technology.

Charles Creon
Vocational Supervisor

J. J. Pinion
Director of Adult Education

A Letter

STATE OF CONNECTICUT
LIONELVILLE COMMUNITY COLLEGE
Lionelville, Connecticut 077364

November 24, 1970

Mr. A. Styer
Box 100
Somers, Connecticut

Dear Mr. Styer:

It is good to hear that you will be employed with Octogenerian Life Insurance Company effective March, 1971.

You will have the opportunity of attending Lionelville Community College since you will be in the area. You have the option of beginning next summer if you wish.

Let me know your plans when you have decided.

Sincerely yours,
Francisco E. Spontaneo

FES/QPD

Note

Mr. Spontaneo was acting from the information he gathered from my application and overlooked the fact that I go to parole in March, 1971. However I am hoping to start college at that time.

A. Styer

Work Progress Report

Inmate Styer has done an outstanding job of absorbing and applying the concepts of computer programming and data processing since his assignment to this section.

His knowledge of data processing as it pertains to accounting procedures and his willingness to conscientiously apply his skills to our internal operation has rendered him a valuable asset to this section. He has exercised a maximum of cooperativeness in voluntary overtime and week-end work.

A most notable facet of his performance has been the commendable manner in which he has approached the job of training his successor. This he has been working at with the same enthusiasm with which he has dealt with all other aspects of his job here.

The Hearing

Alex Styer
  Mr. Styer, my name is Dr. Tunnessey, this is Dean Daley, this is Professor Brock.
  Professor Brock will inquire.
  How are you Mr. Styer?
  Fine thank you.
  Mr. Styer, what offense are you in here for?
  Risk of injury?
  According to our records it was indecent assault.

It was changed.

It was originally risk of injury? What was the problem there?

These people I know—well—we got to be friends where I was working at an apartment and they didn't have any shower and bath at home and they sent the girls down to my place to take a shower.

Whose idea was that?

Well, it was their mother's.

Did you have any sort of relationship with their mother?

Yes sir I did.

Were you sleeping with the mother?

Occasionally, yes.

She had a husband?

Well I never could figure that out. She had a man living with her.

How old were the girls?

10 and 11.

Did you see anything unusual in giving a bath to a 10 year old girl who is not your daughter?

Well I do now yes sir.

At the time?

At the time I did not really think about it much sir.

You had already served a prison sentence for a sexual offense, hadn't you?

Yes sir.

It still didn't occur to you that what you were doing might have got you involved with the law? After you had already served time.

What was the first offense? What was the prior offense? What was the risk of injury one?

This girl was working for me and this night I was counting money you know—in the cash register and she took the money and put it down the front of her pants and I took it away from her and when I got to court she said that I played with her sex organs and all that.

How old was she?

She was 16—going on 16. She won't be 16 until about a month or two.

Did you plead guilty then?

Yes, I did.

Why?

Well I was guilty of what they said—of what she said—that I put my hand in front of her pants and then they put about seven more charges against me and said if I pleaded guilty to this one they would drop all the rest. And so I did.

In 1959 you were found guilty of another sexual offense—is that so?

Oh—why—that was suppose to be for letting this girl go out with men. She was put in my custody and I was told to let her go out—I got the blame for everything.

As a procurer? Procurer for prostitution?

That is what she said, yes sir.

In your own mind as you see things, have you ever committed a crime, a sexual crime? Have you ever done anything wrong?

Well ah—each one of them was wrong—according to the law yes sir.

Well, as you see it?

As I see it—yes sir.

What did you do that was wrong?

Oh—I shouldn't have ever took that girl into my home to begin with.

Which one?

The first one. And the second time I never should of hired that girl to work in the restaurant.

Your mistake was hiring her—that's all?

If I never would of hired her I wouldn't of went around doing anything to her.

The third time?

The third time if I had left and went to St. Louis, Missouri, like I was going to then I wouldn't have gotten mixed up with these people.

Mr. Styer—did you fondle the girls?

Sir?

Did you touch the girls—Beth and Sue?

Well—ah—I washed them—yes.

How many times did you do that?

2—3 times. 3—4 times.

Did they mind?

Evidently their mother told them to let me wash them.

Did—that's not my question. My question is did they mind?

No sir.

Did they enjoy it?

I don't know sir.

Did you like it?

No sir—not especially.

Have you had an opportunity to talk to anyone in this institution about the circumstances under which you came in here—about this offense?

I talked to a psychiatrist two times. He said the only thing I would have to learn was not to even talk to kids.

Do you think you have a problem—with children?

I don't believe so, no sir.

Just a streak of bad luck. Bad luck with the girl who was working for you—bad luck that this woman happened to have 10 year old girls who came to take baths in your place?

No sir, it's not that way I see it is I just

allowed myself to get into these positions which I shouldn't have.

What do you mean allow yourself?

I mean associate with girls—people like that in the first place.

Mr. Styer—if you are paroled—where do you want to go?

Well where I can get a job sir.

Any preference one way or another?

I've got a promise of a job in Bryerton.

How did you happen to get arrested on this most recent offense? Did the girls go to the police?

I don't know exactly how it come about. They just came down while I was working one night and said I was under arrest and I never did find out how it came about. The way I understand from what I can gather that one of them told somebody at the school and then she told someone else. And it went on that way.

I have no more questions.

[Questions by Dean Daley]

You got a general discharge from the Navy, why was that? Because of this offense procuring for prostitution?

Yes sir.

I don't have any other questions.

[Dr. Tunnessey]

I have no questions.

Anything else you want to tell the Board Mr. Styer?

I'd just like to insure you gentlemen that if I'm given a parole I won't mess around with anybody—I will try to get an education to pursue my education and make something out of myself. I've been going down hill ever since I got out of the Navy and I would like to go up hill again for awhile.

We will discuss your case; will you please step outside.

[The inmate leaves the room and the members discuss the case]

[Professor Brock]

This is my case isn't it—and I have a lot of problems here. I find it inherently incredible to believe that someone could serve a 3–10 year prison sentence for risk of injury, get out and then start giving 10 year old girls baths—apparently at least from Dr. Hugh Oberdorffer's psychiatric—deriving sexual gratification from that and not understand in some meaningful sense that he was running grave legal risks. I have also found from my limited experience on the Board that very very frequently with sex offenders in surprising number of cases, and this is where length of time on the Board really does a lot of good there are initial protestations of innocence: I didn't know what happened and then a denial and then you say maybe you better think about it some more and then curiously eight months later when he comes back—well yes—there might have been something to it and then the third time back more insight into the nature of the offense itself. The most common pattern that I've seen again based on very little data is universal denial of the sex offense on the first time up especially with kids under 12.

Dean Daley: What does that prove to you?

Professor Brock: That reinforces my feeling that a denial is in order and that a denial coupled with a suggestion of the desirability of continue looking into this thing professionally—might lead to some additional insight.

Dean Daley: In other words you take seriously the erosion of the innocence statements over a period of time.

Professor Brock: That's right I do. Now maybe I'm wrong.

Dean Daley: Another interpretation would be that they get educated as to what we want to hear.

Professor Brock: Yes unfortunately, unfortunately that's true. On the other hand, with a sex offender, I think that even though they know that's what you want to hear, they're not about to say it. I think it's a very difficult thing for a man to say yes I had sexual relations with this eight year old girl because I'm sick. That's a terrible thing for any man to have to say....

[The inmate returns to the room]

Professor Brock: Mr. Styer, the Board has had a lot of difficulty with your case. Because on the one hand you have done an extraordinary job in terms of your own development in computer programming. I want you to know there is a letter in the file telling of that too. On the other hand, your record particularly with regard to sexual offenses puts us in real doubt. I want to tell you this time we are denying you parole. I'll try to explain why. We're denying parole and will rehear you again in November. It's not because of your efforts with regard to vocational and educational rehabilitation. You've done as much, indeed more, than anyone can be expected to. You are a first rate computer man. But our problem is to determine whether you are going to be a good risk on parole. Frankly, on the basis of the pattern of sexual offenses which you've built up—we see severe problems with regard to that. You're an intelligent man and let me try and be as candid and honest with you as I can. The Board does not see you as someone who goes out and grabs young kids that you've never seen before. That's never happened with you. We frankly don't think that's going to happen in the future. But we do see your problem with going out and getting involved in a social situation or job situation where young girls are present and in which unforeseen complications arise and you find yourself smack in the middle of a sexual problem. Those were 10 year old girls—there was strong sexual overtones to the thing, you served a long prison sentence for a prior sexual offense but that wasn't sufficient to extricate yourself from that very difficult situation and we're afraid of that sort of thing happening again. We urge you as strongly as possible to use every effort you can in this institution to seek help, I'm not saying it's easy, to seek professional help for the problem that brought you in here. Not for a job problem and not for an educational problem. Because that's not the problem the Board has. The problem the Board has is with the probability that when you're released from this institution, through a combination of circumstances, the same sort of thing can happen again. Now I know it's not easy for you, I know you want parole. But I'm trying to be as honest as I can. I welcome any comments that you want to make at this time.

[The inmate]
I believe that right now I'm as ready for parole as I'll ever be and I have too many things going for me now. I've been trying to advance my education where I wouldn't have to work in a restaurant where I'd get involved in situations like this. And also I'm too old to even get involved with a sex situation. I'm going to be 50 years old. And I've even got it out of my head to even think about it.

Professor Brock: You were about 46 when this offense occurred?

Yes, I'm 49 now.

Professor Brock: We'll hear you again in November.

I put in a request right after I been here before and then I never did hear from him then I got a hold of his clerk friend he said that he had my request and he would see me.

Professor Brock: I know. We're not saying it's easy. We're not saying things are just going to walk to you. You're going to reach out for them and you're going to have to push and it's going to be hard and you're going to have to make your voice heard but if you seek hard enough we think that you can get some help.

O.K. Mr. Styer—we'll rehear you in November.

Thank you sir.

3. SOME PROBLEM PAROLE CASES

a. The Case of Jason Tinger

PAROLE HEARING PROGRESS REPORT

Date Prepared: 3/2/71
Name   Jason Tinger
Number   12345
Age   23 years
Date Received   12/4/70

Parole Hearing Date: 3/23/71
Offense   * See Below
Sentence   1-1/2 to 6 yrs.
Parole Elig.   6/6/71
Sentence Exp.   7/3/74

* B & E, 2 cts.; Poss. of Narcotic Drug; Larceny, 2 cts.; Att. to Obt. Money By False Pretenses

PREVIOUS PAROLE BOARD ACTION
None

OTHER BOARD ACTION
None

WARRANTS
None *Disposed of:* On 1/5/71—Wanted—State of Nevada Penitentiary—
     Violation of Parole   —Withdrawn on 1/19/71

OTHER SENTENCES
None

LAST CLASSIFICATION COMMITTEE ACTION
2/10/71—Close Custody—Unas/Seg.—Annual Review. Subject requested to be assigned to Segregation. Fears population assignment. A New Admission.

CUSTODIAL
Subject has received no misconduct reports. He is good in his cell care and personal grooming. His cooperation with housing officers is good as is his attitude toward regulations. His attitude toward other inmates is fair.

WORK AND TRAINING
Subject has had no assignments. Has been unas/seg. since 1/26/71.

MEDICAL
Back trouble; pneumonia, fainting spells; history of hepatitis—not to handle food; drug dependent.

RELIGION
Subject is a Catholic and he has been careless in the practice of his religion. Since coming here, he has made no efforts to attend church services. His biggest problem is with narcotics and he needs help in this area.

SOCIAL
Subject has received four visits in six months from his parents, Mr. & Mrs. Jerome Tinger of Ridgefield. He has weekly correspondence with them and occasional with his sister, Mrs. Phyllis Phanner and his wife, Mrs. Cherle Tinger of Nevada.
Institutional account balance 1/19/71: $6.02

INFORMATION SUMMARY FOR MARCH 23, 1971 HEARING
RE: TINGER, JASON A.   12345

On March 5, 1971, the Board's Chairman held a very lengthy conference with the subject's parents who came from Ridgefield to discuss his possible parole.

Mr. and Mrs. Tinger stated that they were aware of the record which shows that the subject has used narcotics for a number of years probably ever since he was fourteen years old. They stated, however, that in spite of his arrest and convictions for other offenses they never knew he was a narcotic until this arrest. Following his arrest he was sent by the court to Alpha House where he stayed for approximately six months. But he left the program and consequently received this sentence.

Mrs. Tinger stated that she always thought her son had ulcers because he would be very ill and that she gave him medication for ulcers. She now realizes it was a drug problem and that he had not informed her of what was causing his stomach problems.

In this lengthy conference many subjects were discussed including this subject having served time at Cheshire and Nevada. The parents believe, however, that he has changed a great deal during this last period of time even though he did leave Alpha House. They state they are considering moving from Ridgefield to Pardy which is a much smaller community and believe that since he likes to be out of doors moving into a small community may keep him away from drugs. Mr. and Mrs. Tinger were warned that this might not occur since subject is 23 years of age and cannot be treated as a child and if he desires to use drugs will be capable of getting anywhere he wanted to go in order to obtain them.

Mr. and Mrs. Tinger impressed the Chairman very much with their interest in their son and their honesty in discussing his case. They appear to be good middle class people and Mr. Tinger appears to be a hard working man.

The procedures of the Board were explained to subject's parents and they were assured that he would be given careful consideration and the Board would attempt to make the correct decision.

J. B. Glougher, Chairman
State Board of Parole

UNITED STATES DEPARTMENT OF JUSTICE
FEDERAL BUREAU OF INVESTIGATION
WASHINGTON, D.C. 20537

1/7/71
Director

The following FBI record, NUMBER 845 013E, is furnished FOR OFFICIAL USE ONLY

Contributor of Fingerprints	Name and Number	Arrested or Received	Charge	Disposition
SPol Hartford, Conn.	Jason A. Tinger #L-1017-VV174741	8/3/64	B & E with criminal intent L	
SPol Hartford, Conn.	Jason A. Tinger	8/7/64	B & E w/crim/int & L	
Hartford State Jail Hartford, Conn.	Jason A. Tinger #3880	Comm 9/17/64	3 counts of B & E	
Hartford St. Jail Hartford, Conn.	Jason A. Tinger #3880	4/6/65	viol of prob	1 yr in jl
PD Norwich, Conn.	Jason A. Tinger #1014-55	5/1/66	B & E 53-76 larc 53-63	
St. Jail Uncasville, Conn.	Jason A. Tinger #3-461	5/2/66	B & E Larc	bindover
SRef Cheshire, Conn.	Jason A. Tinger #10430	5/24/66	acc to B & E w/criminal intent acc to L of narc 0/$250 b/l/t $2000	Conn Ref Ind
SPol Hartford, Conn.	Jason A. Tinger #0-1671-33	FP 9/27/66	obtaining money under false pretense	
PD Falstaff Nevada	Jason A. Tinger #01205	5/3/68	forg	
PD Falstaff, Nev.	Jason A. Tinger #01205	5/3/68	forgery	

Information shown in this Identification Record represents data furnished FBI by fingerprint contributors. Where final disposition is not shown or further explanation of charge is desired, communicate with agency contributing those fingerprints.

Notations indicated by * are NOT based on fingerprints in FBI files but are listed only as investigative leads as being possibly identical with subject of this record.

The following FBI record, NUMBER 845 013 E, is furnished FOR OFFICIAL USE ONLY. Information shown on this Identification Record represents data furnished FBI by fingerprint contributors, WHERE FINAL DISPOSITION IS NOT SHOWN OR FURTHER EXPLANATION OF CHARGE IS DESIRED, COMMUNICATE WITH AGENCY CONTRIBUTING THOSE FINGERPRINTS.

Contributor of Fingerprints	Name and Number	Arrested or Received	Charge	Disposition
PD Falstaff, Nev.	Jason A. Tinger #01205	5/3/68	forg	1 to 5 yrs in State Pen Drum City Colo
SPen Drum City Nev.	Jason A. Tinger #27876	5/31/68	forg & con com forg	1 to 5 yr & 1-5 yrs CC total 1 to 5 yrs. Paroled 1/13/69
Hartford St. Jail Hartford, Conn.	Jason A. Tinger #0357	1/21/70	ob money false pretense poss cont drugs	
PD Hartford, Conn.	Jason A. Tinger #41301W-14	3/23/70	poss narc para conspr	
Nile St. Jail Hartford, Conn.	Jason A. Tinger #0357	3/31/70	Narc	Cont
SPr Somers, Conn.	Jason A. Tinger #12345	12/4/70	1) B & E 2 cts 2) Larceny 2 cts 3) Poss of Narc drugs 4) Att to obt money by false pretenses	1½ to 6 yrs.

Notations indicated by * are NOT based on fingerprints in FBI files but are listed only as investigative leads as being possibly identical with subject of this record.

John Edgar Hoover
Director

b. The Case of Thomas Mean

PAROLE HEARING PROGRESS REPORT

Date Prepared: 9/25/71
Name Thomas Mean
Number 17623
Age 29 years
Date Received 6/1/68

Parole Hearing Date: 10/13/71
Offense Robbery With Violence
Sentence 2 to 7 yrs.
Parole Elig. 12/15/71
Sentence Exp. 2/16/73

PREVIOUS PAROLE BOARD ACTION
11/19/69—Cont. to Jan. 1970 Inst. Mtg.
 1/14/70—Cont. Indef.
 7/31/70—Votes to Parole
 2/24/71—Denied

OTHER BOARD ACTION
Review Board—12/15/68—Sentence Affirmed.

WARRANTS
None

OTHER SENTENCES
None

LAST CLASSIFICATION COMMITTEE ACTION
9/27/71—Close Custody—No Change—Annual Review. A Counselor referral.

CUSTODIAL
Subject has received misconducts as listed on page two of this report. He is fair in his cell care and in his personal grooming. His attitude in his housing unit is fair. Quarters officer states that subject seems to be a loner and does not bother with any other inmates.

WORK AND TRAINING
Subsequent to commitment, subject was in the Hospital twice for psych. obs. and then in seg., solitary, admin. seg. and unassigned until 5/17/69 when he worked on the Window Washing Detail. He was unassigned on 7/9/69; transferred to Blair Hospital on 1/22/69 and returned to the institution on 7/24/69, and was here in the Hospital-psychiatric. He was assigned to Window Washing on 8/5/70, School on 10/20/70 for four months but made no progress. Was very unstable and next to impossible to teach. He was assigned to the Store on 3/3/71, as Hospital Janitor and to the Corridor on 9/22/71. He has been unassigned since 9/23/71.

MEDICAL
History of VD; otherwise, no major medical findings; psychiatric pending.

RELIGION
Subject is an occasional chapel attendant.

SOCIAL
Subject has no visitors and no correspondence.

MISCONDUCT REPORTS

1. 6/11/68—Disturbing the Block and Insolence. Mental Case. Has been in Hospital and under psychiatric care to 6/12/68. Pun. Seg. Indef. Not earning MGT.
2. 6/18/68—Destroying State Property. Action taken on above report.
3. 6/20/68—Disturbing the Block. Continued stay in pun. seg. Not earning MGT.
4. 6/26/68—Disturbing the Block. Not seen. Continued Isol. Seg. Then back to population.
5. 7/17/68—Disobeying a Direct Order. Isolation seg. indef. Thereafter to Admin. Seg. with referral to Class. Board.
6. 7/17/68—Disobeying a Direct Order; Insolence. Action taken on above report.
7. 7/23/68—Destroying State Property. Extended stay in isolation. Thereafter to Admin. Seg. Not earning M.G.T.
8. 8/22/68—Insolence and refusing a direct order. Removed from Isolation. Time served to 8/30/70. Back to Adm. Seg.
9. 9/12/68—Refusing to Obey a Direct Order and Insolence. On restriction to 9/15/68. Will release from seg. and try again.
10. 3/3/69—Destroying State Property. Mental case. Good Attitude. Lost all recreation priv. thru 3/8/69 incl. Not earning MGT. Lost library priv. for 30 days.
11. 3/12/69—Disobeying a direct order. Lost all recreating priv. thru 3/15/69 incl. Not earning M.G.T.

12. 6/6/69—Viol. of Call House Rules and Creating a Sanitation Problem. Poor attitude. Mental case. Lost all rec. priv. thru 8/11/69, incl. Not earning M.G.T.
13. 8/11/69—Insolence. Isolation seg. indef. Denied M.G.T. Thereafter back to his cell.
14. 11/18/69—Creating a Disturbance and Assaulting An Officer. Inmate was not seen by the Committee. He is already in Isolation. Cont. Isol. Seg. Referred to Psychiatrist.

A PSYCHIATRIC EVALUATION

Connecticut Correctional Institution

October 7, 1971

FROM: William Dixon, Clinical Psychologist

TO: Board of Parole

SUBJECT: Pre-Parole Psychiatric Evaluation Report on Thomas Mean, CCIS #17623 by Maxwell Clark, M.D., on the above date.

Thomas is a 29-year-old single male who is serving a 2 to 7 year term for robbery with violence. This man's adjustment to prison has been less than ideal. From 1968 to November of 1969 he received numerous misconduct reports. Soon thereafter he was transferred to Blair where he stayed six months. Notwithstanding that since his return from Blair Hospital there has been considerable improvement in his behavior, especially the absence of odd and bizarre behavior, he was still not sufficiently stable to carry out even simple assignments such as window washing. Since his return from Blair this man has been practically always unassigned. We have found that this man requires a substantial amount of Thorazine to keep his behavior toned down, otherwise his behavior becomes rather high and because of his limited intelligence his behavior becomes bizarre and annoying. He frequently comes to the psychiatric department asking for help in getting a radio or a new pair of shoes.

Thomas, when seen today, responds to the question of how he feels with the statement that he feels a little slowed down by his medication in the morning. When I comment that he looks quite lively to me at 10:30 in the morning, he states that he has been up for some time. He always talks about how the medication slows him down. We never see any evidence of slowed down behavior. He is usually a little overactive and inappropriately bothering the psychiatric department with requests that absolutely have no relevance to his condition. When he is asked whether he would continue to take the medication when paroled to the streets, he states that he certainly would not because "if I were on the outside, I wouldn't have to take medication; I wouldn't need it." He wants to be paroled to Blair Hospital; "If I go to Blair I would want my suit, my twenty dollars, my shoes and my navy slippers with me." When asked why he wanted to go to Blair rather than directly paroled to the streets, he states that if he were paroled to the streets, he would have to wait a couple of months, but he feels he could be paroled after the parole meeting directly to Blair Hospital.

When I again re-read this man's background and his complete lack of cooperation when on probation, and when I know that this man will not continue to take his Thorazine the moment he leaves prison, I'm only more convinced that he should not be paroled and that he should not be sent to Blair because there is nothing there that can be offered to him which is not available right here except that here there is a better security and he certainly does need controls from time to time. I cannot think of any possible situation where this man would successfully adjust to parole.

I recommend that he stay here until discharge.

Author: Maxwell Clark, M.D.
Consultant in Psychiatry

William Dixon
Clinical Psychologist

c. The Case of John Alling

PAROLE HEARING PROGRESS REPORT

Date Prepared: 9/17/69
Name   John Alling
Number   15219, A. B.
Age   57 years
Date Received 11/7/57

Parole Hearing Date: 10/6/69
Offense   * See Below
Sentence   8 to 30 years
Parole Elig.   12/2/69 on B No.
Sentence Exp. 3/1/78
                 8/20/78 on A No.
                 4/11/73 on B No.

* Larceny: Aggravated Assault (*Habitual Offender*)

PREVIOUS PAROLE BOARD ACTION

8/19/63—Votes to Parole
10/21/63—Parole Susp. until Feb. Inst. Mtg.
3/10/64—Votes to Parole as of 5/10/64
5/10/64—Paroled
6/11/65—Violated Parole
1/16/66—Ret. Parole Violator
1/16/66—Credit 2 days Jail Time

10/18/66—Denied
6/4/67—Voted to Parole
6/12/67—Reparoled
8/6/69—Returned P. V.
9/16/68—Parole Revoked

OTHER BOARD ACTION
None

WARRANTS
None

OTHER SENTENCES
TWO:
    Serving 8–30 yrs. under CCI #15219–A for Statutory Burglary, 3rd Off. running concurrently with present sentence and #15219–B.
    Serving 2 to 7 yrs. under #15219–B for Shoplifting—second off. running concurrently with present sentence and #15219–A.

LAST CLASSIFICATION COMMITTEE ACTION
    4/30/69—Subject's job assignment was changed from Kitchen to Sign Shop. He had requested this change as he was very unhappy with Kitchen work. He will be seen again by the committee in April, 1970.

CUSTODIAL
    Subject has received misconducts as listed on page three of this report. He is good in his cell care and personal grooming. His attitude in his housing unit is good and he appears to be getting along well with everyone.

WORK AND TRAINING
    Subsequent to commitment, subject has had the following assignments: Print Shop, Furniture Factory, Inmate Barber, Garage General Worker, Officers' Barber, Guard Room Corridor Janitor; transferred to Osborn on 3/15/64 and worked there on the Construction Detail until paroled on 5/10/64.
    He was returned as a parole violator on 1/16/66; worked in the Furniture Factory and Industries Office and transferred to Osborn on 10/30/66; worked in the Sign Shop and was reparoled on 8/12/67. Subject was returned as a parole violator on 8/6/68; worked on the Utility Detail and as Officers' Barber; transferred to Osborn on 4/23/69; assigned to the Kitchen on 4/27/69; Sign Shop on 5/1/69 and since 5/21/69, has been working as Officers' Barber.

His cooperation is excellent and his interest in the work is good. Subject works seven days a week cutting officers' hair; keeping barber shop clean and ordering supplies. He is rated as an average worker.

MEDICAL

No major medical or psychiatric findings.

RELIGION

Subject is a Catholic but religion has not played an important part in his life. At times he has shown interest and he does have a very respectful outlook toward the church. He feels it is about time he settled down and appears ready to go back to society.

SOCIAL

Subject has received two visits in six months from his wife, Mrs. Joan Alling of West Haven; five visits from his son, Charles; one from his daughter, Mrs. Mary Worth; and a friend, Michael Spark of Stamford. He has weekly correspondence with his wife and has written once to a son, Charles.

Institutional account balance 8/24/69: $59.78

MISCONDUCT REPORTS

1. 7/23/58—Refusing to Work Where Assigned. Lost all rec. priv. thru July 29. To be unassigned without pay and to lose MGT for the month.
2. 11/17/59—Illegal Possession of a Radio. Radio was confiscated and inmate was denied MGT for November.
3. 8/24/62—Talking from Window of Barber Shop to Visitors. Lost rec. priv., thru 8/30/62 and was denied MGT for August.
4. 10/1/63—Poss. of Contraband (Sex Magazines)—Action taken on following report.
5. 10/1/63—Violation of Trust; lying to an Officer; trafficking in Contraband; Out of Place; Using a Captain's Name to hide Illegal Traffic; Lying to the Deputy Warden. Very uncooperative. Repeated several times under questioning that he had nothing to say. Isol. seg. indef. Denied MGT for Oct. Lost job assignment. Increased to close custody, with referral to the Classification Board for further program.

d. The Case of Ronald Grimes

PSYCHIATRIC EVALUATION

January 12, 1972

FROM: Miles Dawson, Clinical Psychologist

TO: Board of Parole

SUBJECT: Pre-Parole Psychiatric Evaluation Report on Ronald Grimes, CCIS #29075, by Douglas Jackson, M.D., on the above date.

Grimes is a 24-year-old, married male, the father of three stepchildren, ranging from age 8 to 2. Grimes married a 27-year-old divorcee. The marriage is apparently in good shape. There is frequent correspondence between the two, and Grimes' wife visits him weekly. His wife also claims that the children care for their stepfather as they would a natural father. Grimes is serving a 1-to-3-year sentence for escaping from River Valley Hospital. Previous criminal history shows seven convictions; five for B & E, the two others for lesser charges.

Grimes, in the interview situation, looks younger than his stated age of 24. He appears a rather immature, eager to please individual with apparently a passive-aggressive streak in him. Grimes is the oldest of nine children. He never knew his natural father. His stepfather was an alcoholic with a very bad temper whom he was quite afraid of. His parents argued constantly; consequently, he spent much time on the streets, congregating with other unsupervised individuals, leading to delinquency of all kinds, especially burglary for which he was first convicted at age 15. He describes his mother as a big women which is probably meaningful because Grimes himself is of rather small build. He calls his mother good-hearted. He was his mother's favorite. He states that his mother is the kind of woman who wants to keep her children always with her; with other words, a possessive woman who constantly interfered with his relationships with his girlfriends. His mother also doesn't get along with his wife. His wife is the end-all and be-all of his existence. He met her as a friend of his 26-year-old sister when he was paroled from Chatham in 1970. They quickly developed a very close relationship. They lived in a common-law relationship for about a year. Meanwhile he was earning only $45 a week at a restaurant; a job his parole officer had gotten him when he was unable to get himself adequate employment. He asked to be allowed to change his job for a better paying one because he was assuming the obligations of taking care of his common-law wife and three children. He claims that he was not allowed to do so because the owner of the restaurant wanted to keep him on and therefore, the parole officer did not allow him to change. However, he did change his job anyway for one that started off with $80 a week in earnings. Meanwhile his parole officer continuously threatened to bring him back as a parole violator if he didn't return to the restaurant. He became increasingly nervous and fearful to the point that it was finally necessary for his parole officer to admit him to River Valley Hospital, from which institution he escaped when three other individuals overpowered the attendant. He himself was in the bathroom. He claims that he was cleared of all complicity of violence in this escape attempt, and therefore he was only charged with escape. After his escape, he married his common-law wife and worked for a full year before the two of them decided that he turn himself in and face the consequences of his escape. He, during this last year, worked as a painter and according to his employer, did very well. Grimes stated that he had a $100 a week take-home pay from his regular job, and he would have extra income from some jobs on the side. He states that he has not been involved in anything illegal since he met the woman who is now his wife, and that he knows with the utmost certainty that he will never go back to prison again because now he has found a real reason for living, working, and performing.

This man's adjustment in prison has been quite good, and I believe that having a loving and very likely a mothering wife, will very possibly have a continued stabilizing effect on him. On the other hand, if for example, his wife would lose interest in him, I beileve this would very likely cause a severe setback with possible resumption of antisocial behavior. However, considering this stabilizing factor in his life, I would very much like to give this young man the opportunity to prove himself. As far as the above-mentioned parole officer is concerned, Grimes claims that he was fired for forcing another inmate to work under similar circumstances.

Author: Douglas Jackson, M.D.
       Consulting Psychiatrist

Miles Dawson
Clinical Psychologist

e. The Case of Gerald Merrill

PAROLE HEARING PROGRESS REPORT

Date Prepared:

Name	Gerald Merrill	Parole Hearing Date:	2/9/72
Number	43901	Offense	* See Below
Age	25 years	Sentence	2 to 6 years
Date Received	5/15/71	Parole Elig.	4/27/72
		Sentence Exp.	1/17/75

* Violation of State Dep. Producing Drug Law; Theft of M. V. 2 cts.

PREVIOUS PAROLE BOARD ACTION
Note

OTHER BOARD ACTION
None

WARRANTS
None

OTHER SENTENCES
None

LAST CLASSIFICATION COMMITTEE ACTION
6/19/71—Close Custody—Unassigned—Referred for Automotive Apprenticeship. A New Admission. After approval from the commissioner, subject was given an annual review.

CUSTODIAL
Subject has received no misconduct reports. He is good in his cell care and personal grooming. His attitude toward housing officers is good and he appears to be getting along well with everyone and is abiding by regulations.

WORK AND TRAINING
Subject was assigned to the Auto School on 6/27/71 and was put in seg. on 10/9/71. (Subject was in the hospital-med. from 8/4 to 8/10 and Hospital-psych. from 9/12 to 9/15.) He was unas/seg. on 11/15/71; Hospital-psych. on 11/29/71 and since 12/20/71, has been unassigned.

MEDICAL
Subject is on restricted medication; psychiatric pending.

RELIGION
Subject is a rather frequent chapel attendant. Chaplain has no record of subject being enrolled in the drug therapy program, although he desired this therapy when he first came here.

SOCIAL
Subject has received one visit from his father, Norman Merrill of Waterville and he has occasional correspondence with him; a sister, Mrs. Connie Hill of Ga. and his mother, Mrs. Barbara Merrill of Ga. Subject has weekly correspondence with his wife, Mrs. Lynn Merrill of Lexington, Ky. Institutional account balance 12/18/71: $27.53. Bank Balance: $75.28.

DIAGNOSTIC SUMMARY

Name: Merrill, Gerald T.
Number: 43901   D25A
Completion Date: June 10, 1971

T. Blake

1. MEDICAL—DENTAL—This man was examined on 6-15-71 by Dr. Scott, and it is indicated that there are no work limitations, however, it should be noted that he does have low blood pressure and is hyper-sensitive. It should also be noted that he was carried to the hospital on a stretcher because he fainted due to not enough intake of foods. He is obviously underweight. Did have periodic re-examinations at the hospital to check on this particular anemic condition. Extensive drug history.

2. *CUSTODIAL*—Officers Barrows and Mason both see this man as someone who is shy, retiring, avoids attention and generally stays away from others. Gets into games at recreation time only if he is asked. It is further reported that he seems to be afraid of prison life and very unsure of himself and how he will be able to cope with it. Both report that he is rather timid.

3. RELIGIOUS—Chaplain Dix indicates that this man claims that religion has some meaning to him and that he has had frequent religious attendance on the outside.

4. *RECREATION*—No recreation report received, however, it should be noted that he will stay by himself and shy away from getting involved with others unless he is helped into group activities.

5. *SOCIAL*—This man comes from a poor family background that appears to have worsened when he was reaching adolescence. Father was out of the home for most part during this period of his life. This man was married in 1968 to a woman four years older than himself. Both are drug users, and his wife is presently at the Lexington Federal Institution for help with her problem.

6. *VOCATIONAL*—A number of jobs including baking and working for a construction company. Vocational goals reflect poor self-image. Has a hard time seeing himself in any vocation that can make use of what assets he possesses (High School diploma, good math skills, etc.). Am referring for vocational evaluation to Mr. Rudd.

7. *EDUCATIONAL*—This man has completed high school and has an I.Q. slightly above average. Interested in taking the college math course in the Fall when it is available. Scores in the eleventh grade on reading and math, but only in the ninth grade in the California Achievement Test and language ability. Has some educational skills that might be developed further.

8. *PSYCHOLOGICAL*—Very tall, thin, tight and rigid appearing drug addict who talks freely of his problems in many areas. Said he had a problem with his "nerves" at Bridgeport, but he has been O.K. while here, despite the fact that he feels somewhat depressed. He has a very poor self-image and is somewhat afraid of turning out like his father who ended up as mentally disturbed neer-do-well. Somewhat passive and appears to be frightened about being here. Denies any concern about using drugs when he is released, although it is apparent that he is quite frightened of being able to handle the situation.

9. *PSYCHIATRIC*—No reports indicated.

RECEPTION AND DIAGNOSTIC CENTER RECOMMENDATIONS

NAME: Merrill, Gerald T.
NUMBER: 43901   D25A

T. Blake

1. Custody

Mr. Merrill should initially be in close custody because of his extensive drug history. After three or four months when it can be noted how he is adjusting to institutional life and routine, he may then be reviewed for possible transfer to other security designations. He should not pose any particular custody problems, and, if anything, he will be staying by himself and could be helped to get into different activities or engage in conversation by the authority figures. Appears to be very dependent on his wife. Any change in that relationship should be noted to security people because this could result in a depressive and possibly even suicidal situation.

2. Vocation—Educational

In the educational area Mr. Merrill would like to take a college math course in the Fall. Appears to have some potential for development in this area. He has made poor vocational choices that reflect more his poor self-concept than some possibilities and interests that could be developed. Because of this, I have referred him for vocational counseling to Mr. Rudd, whose report will be available to the classification committee.

3. Treatment

This man's counselor should encourage Mr. Merrill to take part in both Mr. Bate's drug group and in the J.C.'s drug group. He states he wants this kind of help but could easily withdraw because of his own fears and shyness. Encouragement and follow-up on a regular basis by the counselor could be helpful to this man.

This man also needs medical follow-up because of his underweight and anemic condition. He appears to have somewhat of a self-destructive trend and also has blood pressure problems as noted above.

4. Special Services

None indicated.

VOCATIONAL EVALUATION

NAME: Merrill, Gerald T.
NUMBER: 43901   D25A

B. Rudd

Inmate Merrill started the vocational evaluation with vocational choices which were very unrealistic and not possible in the near future. He has given some thought to his working future and has made some definite decisions.

His first choice is mechanics. On several occasions he repaired mechanical equipment on combustible engines and pumping machines. He is interested in this area and says he enjoys it. Aptitude testing indicates a mechanical aptitude for the basic mechanical theory involved in advanced training. Merrill wants to enter the auto mechanic school when his custody is reviewed in a few months. He feels he needs the fundamental mechanical theory to make any progress in the field or any specialized area of combustible engines. He started technical school for mechanics but left because of family finances.

In the interim period, he might work on jobs requiring a mechanical aptitude, this includes pipefitter helper, maintenance mechanic helper. He could also use his experience by working as a fork lift truck operator in the warehouse.

When Merrill is released from prison he will seek employment as a mechanic apprentice for an automobile dealer. If this is not possible because of his criminal record, he will work for a construction firm repairing construction equipment.

As an alternate long term choice, inmate would like to join his brother-in-law's flooring business in Georgia.

4. THE PAROLE HEARING AS PERCEIVED BY THE INMATE

ED TROMANHAUSER

Parole*

Parole involves two distinct stages. The first is *selection* of inmates to be paroled, and the second involves the *supervision* of these men once they are released. In this country selection is the province of a board of parole, a quasijudicial function performed as part of the executive arm of the government. Supervision is a bureaucratic function of that same executive arm.

Selection is based on two factors—eligibility and suitability. Usually a minimum amount of time has to be served by a prisoner, as provided by statute, before he is eligible for parole. The date of eligibility is a factor involved in the sentencing procedure and fixed by the courts. There are exceptions to this general rule in a few states.

Suitability is the tricky problem, the horn of the dilemma for both offender and parole board. How do you judge suitability? What factors should be considered, and how much weight should be given to the different factors considered? This is, without any doubt, the hottest issue debated in every yard and cellhouse of every prison in the country.

The prisoners ask themselves such questions as: What does the parole board look for in a man when they consider him for parole? How much weight will be given to my past record? Why do they select Jones and reject Smith when they are both in on the same charge and have almost identical past records?

Many experts in the fields of penology and criminology, both highly educated professionals and those who have come up through the ranks, advocate releasing an offender when he is "ready." That is to say, at the precise moment when he seems most likely never again to commit a crime. As the prison yard scuttlebutt has it, the precise moment is a delicate balance between how many pounds of flesh the society will be satisfied with and the point where the man becomes so embittered that he will be extremely dangerous if *ever* released (although he *must* be released when his sentence expires).

There seems to be a large percentage of experts who believe there is a release time of maximum advantage for both offender and society, a time when the man is psychologically and motivationally ready. This "best time" varies with the individual. To keep a man beyond this "best time" is to reduce his chances of success in proportion to the length of additional time served.

* From H. Jack Griswold, Mike Misenheimer, Art Powers, and Ed Tromanhauser, *An Eye for An Eye* 207–11 (1971). Copyright © 1970 by H. Jack Griswold, Mike Misenheimer, Art Powers, and Ed Tromanhauser. Reprinted with permission of Holt, Rinehart and Winston, Inc. and Curtis Brown Ltd.

Do I believe this? Yes, with additional corollaries. I know that at least 75 per cent of the men in prisons do not have to be there. They are not violence-prone and can be handled in a safer manner, more cheaply, and much much more successfully in the community. I also know that for a lot of men who come to prison, the "best time" to let them go is within a few weeks or months after they arrive (of course this never happens). Because I know what the prison environment does to a man, I take the position that the faster society gets him out of that environment the better, for the man and for the society.

It seems to me that the parole board should be on the side of leniency for the following reason. If a man is held within the degrading, dehumanizing, all-corrupting atmosphere of our nation's prisons any longer than is absolutely necessary, that man is being greatly damaged and so is the society. For he becomes less and less a human being with every dreary day, week, month, and year he is confined.

It never fails to surprise me when I read about some "mad-dog" killer who is terrorizing a community and hear people expressing shock and bewilderment over his actions when it plainly states in the newspaper that the man had just been released from some prison after serving ten or fifteen years. I would venture to say that if you randomly selected a thousand men off the streets of any community in the country and placed them in the nearest state prison for a period of ten years, the following would be the result:

90 per cent of the married men would be divorced by their wives.

75 per cent of the men would find that even their own close relatives—sisters, brothers, sons, daughters—would stop communicating with them.

40 per cent of the men would become so inured to the prison way of life, so indoctrinated by the criminogenic outlook on life, that they would be future serious lawbreakers upon release.

80 per cent of them would become bitter, cynical, vengeful, petty individuals and remain so for the rest of their lives.

25 per cent would become so mentally and emotionally disabled that they would be unable to function as citizens and breadwinners upon return to the community.

This is just the way it is. And it is only an infinitesimal part of what our prisons do to the people in them. This just cannot be a deep, dark secret, known only to a few, any more than Hitler's crematoria and concentration camps were unknown to the people of Nazi Germany. The people know. They just don't give a damn. Or they want it that way.

So you see, it is not the physical isolation from the community, or the deprivation of creature comforts, or even the cruelty and sadism and indifference *per se* that hurt you half as much as the degradation and perpetual dehumanization. Too many men leave prison as zombies, not human beings. That is why I think that the faster you can get a man out, the better for both the man and the society.

Parole boards should not have the power to keep an offender in prison for a disproportionately long period of time beyond his minimum sentence on the highly speculative and purely intuitional ground that he represents a "poor parole risk." Being a "poor parole risk" means being an individual whom the parole board believes will probably either violate the rules of his parole agreement or eventually commit a new crime. OK, so with the mere passage of time, as that same "poor parole risk" remains in prison, does he become a better parole risk? Or release risk? How ridiculous. Maybe, just maybe, it would be different if prisons helped people, but only a liar or a fool or an ignoramus would say that they do.

Some parole board members go along with the concept of readiness, but they immediately pose a difficult question, one which has not been satisfactorily answered by those who advocate the readiness concept. How do you determine *when* a particular individual is ready?

An examination of parole decisions suggests that selection for parole is made in terms of estimations not so much of an offender's "readiness" or chances for success as of his chances for failure. This shift of emphasis from positive to negative considerations suggests that parole decisions relate too often to considerations unrelated to the offender's "readiness," motivational state, or personal adjustment, and clearly states that the basic objective is to minimize risks of failure instead of increasing the number of offenders able to profit.

The easiest way for a parole board to increase its "batting average" is to give paroles only to those who are sure to make good and reject all doubtful cases. But this means rejecting for parole a large amount of cases where the men would make good.

So the parole decision becomes an estimate of the likelihood that a given man will or will not increase the board's failure rate. As such it is a measure of the individual board member's confidence in his own ability to judge and has very little to do with what the prisoner has been trying to do for himself or the circumstances of his case. This is a long way from selecting for parole because of positive value judgments based on the convict's background, ability, and state of mind, or his welfare in general.

This brings us to some very serious gripes concerning variables used in parole decisions. The first concerns the amount of weight given that variable called "past record." The gripe is based on the fact that about three quarters of the men in any prison have a previous record and the parole board considers this *the* most important variable to be considered in granting a parole. What is so frustrating to men who keep getting rejected for parole because of "past record" is that there is obviously nothing that the individual can do about it. It cannot be changed, it cannot be expunged. It therefore generates a feeling of helplessness and frustration, especially in men who take seriously what they are told about rehabilitation and perfect institutional records. These men cannot understand the rationale behind parole denials based on past records if the major goal of the correctional system is rehabilitation and if they have tried to take advantage of every rehabilitation program offered by the institution. The men know that merely serving another two or five years is not going to alter or expunge the past record and it is not going to further the "rehabilitative" process. Their realization must be that rehabilitation is meaningless, and punishment pure and simple is the goal of the parole board.

The second gripe is closely related to the first. It is that both the offender and the parole board know that to turn down parole on the basis of low probability of success is not the way to reduce over-all recidivism rates. For if a man has a low probability of success, he will eventually have an even lower probability of success if *not* paroled. In fact, he may eventually be released with absolutely no supervision or aid, after spending an additional number of years in an environment which is hardly conducive to a healthy mental state.

Parole boards know this, but they usually answer that their principal duty is the protection of society, not the well-being of the offender. Inmates, and a large percentage of penologists and correctional officials, answer in turn that keeping a man in prison is at best only a short-term protection. Many men are much more dangerous to the society when finally released after long years in prison. In reality, parole boards are doing a greater disservice to society by keeping men in prison too long.

A third gripe among prisoners is that parole boards are too easily influenced by pressures put upon them by any number of sources: letters written to the parole board by police and prosecutors in which possible parole for a man is opposed; newspaper editorials and letters to the editor opposing a certain individual's parole or opposing parole in general for all incarcerated men; pressure from victims.

GEORGE JACKSON

Soledad Brother: The Prison Letters of George Jackson*

To be certain that you dig what I'm saying. I'll here admit that most of the people who come through these places are genuinely sick in one way or the other, monsters, totally disorganized, twisted, disgusting epitomes of the

* From *Soledad Brother: The Prison Letters of George Jackson,* pp. 160–61. Published by Coward, McCann & Geoghegan and Bantam Books, Inc. Copyright © 1970 by World Entertainers Limited.

parent monster. Those who aren't so upon their arrival will surely be so when they leave. No one escapes unscathed. An individual leaves his individuality and any pride he may have had behind these walls. When you first enter Chino you're required to write a confession that will be placed right in the front of your jacket under your picture and number. Failure to write this confession means you go to the board. It means that you haven't taken the first step toward rehabilitation. All this is carefully explained to you in Chino. "No confession, no parole." No one walks into the board room with his head up. This just isn't done! Guys lie to each other, but if a man gets a parole from these prisons, Fay, it means that he crawled into that room. Plus it means that he adopted the philosophical attitude toward shit in the face several times since his last board. Of the billions of conflicts and negative exchanges that take place in a year, the pigs choose which ones to pass over. The guy who earns a parole surrendered some face in the course of his stay here prior to board. He walked away from some situation to save his body—at the cost of some part of his face (read mind, or pride, or principle). No black will leave this place if he has any violence in his past, until they see that thing in his eyes. And you can't fake it, resignation—defeat, it must be stamped clearly across the face.

E. The Role of Lawyer and Judge

VINCENT O'LEARY AND JOAN NUFFIELD

Parole Decision-Making Characteristics: Report of a National Survey*

In recent years the former "hands off" position taken by the courts in relation to almost all stages of corrections has in many important respects been modified. . . . A target of increasing attention is the area of parole. Parole boards, which formerly found their operations more or less unrestricted, are now finding themselves under considerable pressure to change. The President's Crime Commission *Task Force Report on Corrections* took the position some four years ago that greater procedural safeguards for the offender would be required for the future of parole. In many quarters this pressure to change is vigorously resisted. A number of correctional authorities—aided by many courts—oppose any proposed alteration in their operations by claiming that parole is an act of grace, and as such is granted under such conditions and procedures as the releasing authority shall see fit. A second defensive rationale argues that a parolee is just a "prisoner without walls," and as such is subject to the same limited rights and freedoms as any confined inmate. The third argument asserts that a parolee freely contracts with the parole board for his release, and thus consents to all the conditions of his release by an open choice. . . .

It is difficult to assess with much accuracy the extent to which parole practices in the United States currently embrace various due process protections because of the lack of reliable data. Reviews of contemporary statutory provisions are of only limited assistance, since in so many jurisdictions actual practice may be poorly portrayed by sparse or generalized statutory language, or board practice may retard or extend a statutory provision. In order to obtain systematic information about the current policies and practices of parole boards in the United States, the writers conducted a survey of all parole authorities in the United States with jurisdiction over criminal offenders committed to imprisonment for a term in excess of one year.

In each state a single agency performs this function, except in California and Indiana, where separate parole boards exist for women. The survey was conducted under the auspices of the National Probation and Parole Institutes —a national organization of parole officials— and was designed to discover the actual operational procedures of each parole board, rather

---

* Vincent O'Leary and Joan Nuffield, *Parole Decision-Making Characteristics-Report of a National Survey*, Vol. 8, No. 8, *Criminal Law Bulletin* (October 1972), pp. 651–59; 661–65; 678. © Warren, Gorham & Lamont, Inc. Boston. Reprinted with permission of the publisher.

than to depend solely on often brief and unclear statutory provisions, or the confusing and flexible court decisions in the area.

A questionnaire was mailed to the fifty adult parole boards for the states, the two state boards responsible for the parole of women, and the two federal parole authorities, the United States Board of Parole and the District of Columbia Parole Board. The questionnaire covered provision for the presence of *counsel,* presentation of *witnesses,* a *record, confrontation* of adverse witnesses, *disclosure* of violation reports, *notice, recording of reasons* for the board's decision, *place of hearing,* and the *manner in which the offender is informed* of the decision in his case. Responses were obtained from all fifty-four jurisdictions. These responses were classified and compared with a survey of relevant parole statutes. A detailed statement describing each system was prepared and returned to each jurisdiction for verification.

Changes are constantly occurring on all levels of each jurisdiction; this survey was designed to reflect the situation in each jurisdiction as of January, 1972. The full results of the survey will be published by the National Probation and Parole Institutes; in the present discussion, the major focus is directed towards the procedural aspects of parole-release and parole-revocation hearings.

Parole-Release Hearing

The parole hearing is the focal point in most parole decision-making. Though a few jurisdictions do not hold parole hearings of any kind, it is usual for the parole authority to conduct at least an interview with the inmate at or before the time he becomes eligible for parole. . . .

In every case, the board which has supervised release jurisdiction over felony offenders is administratively independent of the institution housing the inmates. A few jurisdictions, such as the United States Board of Parole and the California Adult Authority, employ a staff of "hearing representatives" who may hear certain routine cases and report their findings to the parole authority, or share case decision responsibility with the board members. The inmate will usually be heard at this interview in the month preceding eligibility for parole, or in the month during which he becomes eligible. Many parole boards see an inmate several times during the course of his prison sentence; in fact, a number of states provide for at least an annual review of each case, no matter how remote release may be. Hearings may be public or private, and may range anywhere from brief, cursory questioning to a full-blown session with evidence and testimony presented on either side. The latter is a rare occurrence, however, even in jurisdictions which extend fairly comprehensive procedural protections.

The procedures followed at parole hearings are extremely diverse. In some states, each parole applicant is heard by the full board. In others, especially those with numerous correctional institutions, boards split into smaller working panels resembling a panel of a federal court of appeals, each of which conducts hearings on its own and has the power to grant or deny parole. In the case of denial, there often exists the requirement that a case be referred to the full board in the event of a less than unanimous panel vote, or where cases of special interest or sensitivity are heard. In several jurisdictions, a single parole board member may conduct a hearing on his own, and will subsequently submit his findings to his colleagues, at which time a final decision is made.

The time made available for a single parole hearing varies markedly from one jurisdiction to another. Table I displays the number of cases heard in a single day for the fifty-one parole jurisdictions which conduct parole-consideration hearings for felony offenders in the United States.

Further indications of the diversity among parole authorities can be gleaned from a study of Table II, which describes the current practice of parole boards with respect to several dimensions that have been identified by a number of commentators as crucial to effective and fair decision-making.

TABLE I.—AVERAGE NUMBER OF CASES HEARD PER DAY DURING PAROLE-CONSIDERATION HEARINGS: 51 JURISDICTIONS*: FELONY OFFENDERS

Average Number of Cases Heard Per Day	Number of Parole Boards
1-19	11
20-29	15
30-39	15
40 and over	13

* States of Georgia, Hawaii, and Texas not included since no hearings are conducted in these jurisdictions.

TABLE II.—SELECTED PAROLE HEARING PRACTICES OF 51* STATE AND FEDERAL PAROLE BOARDS: FELONY OFENDERS: JANUARY 1972

Selected Practices	No. of Boards Yes	No. of Boards No
Counsel permitted at hearing	21	30
Inmate permitted to present witnesses	17	34
Reasons for decision recorded	11	40
Verbatim record of proceedings made	20	31
Inmate informed of decision directly	22	29

* States of Georgia, Hawaii, and Texas not included, since no hearings are conducted in these jurisdictions.

The table refers to only fifty-one jurisdictions since Georgia, Hawaii, and Texas do not conduct parole-consideration hearings with inmates; they depend instead entirely on a review of the case file for their decision. Alabama, North Carolina, and Mississippi are included in the table although hearings are conducted only in selected cases. Under this scheme, a preliminary review of each case file is conducted by board staff or board members themselves, and on the basis of this review, certain cases are selected for personal interview. The cases usually so selected are the ones which the board feels it is likely to parole at its next meeting; the others are deferred.

Counsel and Witnesses

The assistance of counsel at parole hearings is often characterized as the key to due process protection for the offender seeking release on parole. This is based on the belief that unless some independent agent is present, the typical board's discretion is sufficiently broad to absorb other due process requirements. While the present survey indicates that about 4 percent (twenty-one of fifty-one) of all parole boards having jurisdiction over felony offenders did not prohibit the presence of counsel at hearings, it is rare for any state to provide counsel for indigents at such hearings. Thus, where counsel does appear on behalf of inmates, it is almost invariably true that such an occurrence will be predicated on the ability of the offender to retain his own attorney. The result is that counsel is a rarity at the release hearing even in jurisdictions with no restrictions on counsel's presence. Indeed, the pattern of the granting of counsel in various jurisdictions has changed only slightly in the past fifteen years. . . .

A ranking of jurisdictions according to the percentage of offenders released through parole as opposed to outright discharge can be used as a rough measure of indeterminancy. If the jurisdictions which release more than 70 percent of their inmates by parole—the 1970 national average—are separated from those releasing less than 70 percent, and the two groups are compared on the basis of allowing counsel, as in Table III, which follows, it will be seen that those in the first group are clearly less likely to grant counsel than those in the second. Those jurisdictions granting counsel tend to be smaller states with less full-blown correctional establishments catering to the treatment ideal, in contrast to the states with well-developed departments, such as California and New York. . . .

Witnesses are permitted to appear on behalf of the inmate in almost as many jurisdictions as counsel, but *in no case are witnesses permitted where counsel is not*. It should be noted, however, that in almost all jurisdictions, the board allows the inmate's counsel, family, acquaintances, employer, and others to consult with board members at the central board office or other location at some time prior to the release hearing. At this time, witnesses are

TABLE III.—NUMBER OF PAROLE JURISDICTIONS ALLOWING COUNSEL AT RELEASE HEARINGS ACCORDING TO PERCENT RELEASED ON PAROLE: MALE FELONY OFFENDERS: 1970

	Over 70% Released by Parole	Under 70% Released by Parole
Counsel	6[a]	12[b]
No counsel	16[c]	9[d]

Source: Federal Bureau of Prisons, *National Prisoner Statistics, Prisoners in State and Federal Institutions for Adult Felons, 1968, 1969, 1970*, (Washington, D.C., 1972). Data are not available on Alaska, Arkansas, Maryland, Minnesota, Rhode Island, and the U.S. Board. The data from several states includes conditional releases as well as parolees. Texas, Georgia, and Hawaii do not grant hearings.

[a] Idaho, Illinois, New Hampshire, Oklahoma, Utah, Vermont.

[b] Arizona, Florida, Louisiana, Mississippi, Nebraska, Nevada, North Carolina, North Dakota, South Carolina, South Dakota, Tennessee, Wyoming.

[c] California, Colorado, Indiana, Kansas, Maine, Massachusetts, Michigan, Montana, New Jersey, New Mexico, New York, Ohio, Pennsylvania, Washington, West Virginia, Wisconsin.

[d] Alabama, Connecticut, Delaware, Iowa, Kentucky, Missouri, Oregon, Virginia, Washington, D.C.

SELECTED CHARACTERISTICS OF PAROLE-RELEASE HEARINGS FOR FELONY OFFENDERS IN THE UNITED STATES JANUARY 1972

Jurisdiction	Counsel Permitted at Hearing	Witnesses Permitted at Hearing	How Inmate Informed of Decision	Reasons for Decision Recorded	Verbatim Record of Hearing Made
U.S. Board of Parole	no	no	after hearing[c]	no	yes
Alabama*	no	no	in person[d]	no	no
Alaska	yes	no	after hearing	no	no
Arizona	yes	yes	in person	no	no
Arkansas	yes	yes	after hearing	yes	no
California	no	no	after hearing	no	no
California Women	no	no	in person	no	no
Colorado	no	no	after hearing	no	yes
Connecticut	no	no	in person	no	yes
Delaware	no	no	after hearing	yes	no
District of Columbia	no	no	after hearing	no	yes
Florida	yes	yes	after hearing	no	yes
Georgia	—	—	no hearings	—	—
Hawaii	—	—	no hearings	—	—
Idaho	yes	yes	in person	no	yes
Illinois	yes	no[b]	after hearing	no	yes
Indiana	no	no	in person	no	no
Indiana Women	no	no	in person	no	yes
Iowa	no	no	in person	no	no
Kansas	no	no	after hearing	no	no
Kentucky	no	no	after hearing	yes[e]	no
Louisiana	yes	yes	in person	no	no
Maine	no	no	after hearing	no	no
Maryland	no[a]	no	in person	yes	no
Massachusetts	no	no	in person	no	no
Michigan	no	no	in person	no	no
Minnesota	no	no	in person	no	no
Mississippi*	yes	yes	after hearing	no	yes
Missouri	no	no	after hearing	yes	yes
Montana	no	no	after hearing	no	no
Nebraska	yes	yes	in person	no	yes
Nevada	yes	yes	after hearing	no	no
New Hampshire	yes	yes	in person	no	yes
New Jersey	no	no	after hearing	no	no
New Mexico	no	no	after hearing	yes	no
New York	no	no	after hearing	no	yes
North Carolina*	yes	yes	after hearing	no	yes
North Dakota	yes	yes	after hearing	yes	yes
Ohio	no	no	after hearing	no	no
Oklahoma	yes	yes	after hearing	no	no
Oregon	no	no	in person	no	no
Pennsylvania	no	no	after hearing	yes	no
Rhode Island	yes	no	after hearing	yes	no
South Carolina	yes	yes	in person	no	yes
South Dakota	yes	yes	after hearing	no	no
Tennessee	yes	yes	after hearing	no	no
Texas	—	—	no hearings	—	—
Utah	yes	yes	in person	no	yes
Vermont	yes	no[b]	in person	no	yes
Virginia	no	no	after hearing	no	no
Washington	no	no	in person	yes	no
West Virginia	no	no	in person	yes	yes
Wisconsin	no	no	in person	no	no
Wyoming	yes	yes	after hearing	no	yes

* Selected inmates are chosen for interview.
[a] Law students permitted.
[b] In special cases board may elect to allow specific witnesses.
[c] "After hearing" means notification given by mail or third party.
[d] "In person" means by parole board members at the hearing.
[e] Reasons recorded only if parole denied.

allowed to present their views concerning the inmate's release.

Development of Records and Visibility of Criteria

A significant development in criminal and administrative law in recent years has been the trend towards requiring that a written record be made of the hearing and that reasons be given for discretionary action. Though many parole boards give verbal explanations to the offender for their decisions, as Table II shows, only eleven of the fifty-four jurisdictions keep a written record. About 40 percent maintain verbatim records of all hearings. . . .

There are two considerations which appear to mandate the development of more extensive records in parole. The recording of reasons for the board's decision, in specific and behavioral terms, would allow for substantive review of the board's policy as to release, and the appropriateness in a given case of the application of this policy.

A verbatim record of the proceedings would allow for meaningful appeal of an individual decision on both substantive and procedural grounds by revealing whether a full opportunity was given to the inmate to present his case for release in a manner which satisfied a sense of fairness. It would also give a clearer picture of the factors which were heavily dwelt on and the reliability of the evidence and conclusory statements relied upon. . . .

Dispositional Practices

Only a few years ago, it was by far the most common practice for parole boards to allow the inmate to be informed of the decision in his case either orally or in writing through a clerk or staff member of the institution several days after the hearing. Today, over 40 percent of the parole authorities in this country have adopted the policy of informing the inmate of the decision in person, immediately at the conclusion of the hearing. The potential virtues of the latter method are that it forces the board members to come to grips with their own reasons for their decision-making, eliminates the inevitable vagueness and error which result from the use of a third party to inform the inmate, and gives the inmate a clearer idea of what is expected of him if he is to obtain parole release.

In addition, by directly confronting the inmate with the board's decision and the reasons behind it, one creates a sense of fairness and openness which is essential to promoting a perception of parole as a system which does not make sub rosa judgments based on vague and punitive reasoning. There is a principle in most schools of legal thought which holds that governmental action must not only *be* fair, it must also *appear* to be fair. This critical appearance is especially important in the present correctional climate in this country.

MENECHINO V. OSWALD
430 F2D 403 (1970), CERT. DEN. 400 U.S. 1023
United States Court of Appeals, Second Circuit

MANSFIELD, District Judge.

This appeal by a state prisoner from a judgment of the district court dismissing his complaint under the Federal Civil Rights Law, 42 U.S.C. § 1983, and the Declaratory Judgment Act, 28 U.S.C. § 2201, raises the question of whether a prisoner is entitled under the Fourteenth Amendment to procedural due process rights upon his being interviewed and considered by the New York State Board of Parole for release on parole before the termination of the sentence imposed by the court. For the reasons hereinafter stated we affirm the judgment below.

The essential facts are not in dispute. Appellant is imprisoned in Green Haven Prison, Stormville, N. Y., under a sentence of from 20 years to life imposed on May 6, 1947, by the New York County Court of General Sessions pursuant to his plea of guilty to the charge of murder in the second degree. After having been paroled from Attica Prison on August 14, 1963, he was declared delinquent by the Parole Board on December 31, 1964, and was returned to prison. In May 1965 he appeared without counsel before members of the Parole Board and admitted consorting with individuals having criminal records and giving misleading information to his parole officer.

Following revocation of his parole in May, 1965, appellant appeared on March 16, 1967, at a brief session before three members of the Board of Parole for reconsideration of parole release, which was denied, the Board deciding that his case would be reconsidered in 18 months. . . .

In September, 1968, appellant again appeared before the Board without counsel and was again denied parole with the proviso that his case be considered in another 18 months.

In August 1969, appellant commenced the present action in the district court, invoking its jurisdiction pursuant to 28 U.S.C. §§ 1331, 1343(3), 1361 and 42 U.S.C. § 1983. His complaint alleges that defendants, in violation of his constitutional rights, determined that he is

> Not qualified for release on parole, which, in effect, constitutes a denial of liberty, without adhering to the minimum requirements of procedural due process: (i) notice of charges; (ii) a fair hearing, with the right to counsel, to cross-examination and to present favorable evidence and compel the attendance of favorable witnesses; and (iii) specification of the grounds and underlying facts upon which the determination was based (Complaint ¶13).

The complaint seeks a declaratory judgment to the effect that

> plaintiff is entitled under the Due Process Clause of the Fourteenth Amendment to (i) notice of charges, including a substantial summary of the evidence and reports before the Board, (ii) a fair hearing, including the right of counsel, to cross-examination and confrontation and to present favorable evidence and compel the attendance of favorable witnesses, and (iii) a specification of the grounds and underlying facts upon which the determination is based....

The issue before us is not whether New York, instead of expressly forbidding a prisoner to be represented by counsel or by some other person before the Board of Parole, would have been better advised to adopt statutory measures permitting such representation. The question before us is whether the Constitution mandates the minimum procedural due process demanded by appellant. In resolving that issue we recognize that a fundamental condition for requiring constitutional (as distinguished from statutory) due process is the existence of governmental action which threatens to destroy or impair an existing private interest. Usually such action is accomplished through an adversary proceeding in which a vital issue of fact is resolved against a person without according him the benefit of certain fundamental safeguards. Whether such safeguards are required depends upon the nature of the governmental action and of the private interest affected by that action. The Constitution "does not require a trial-type hearing in every conceivable case of government impairment of private interest," Cafeteria & Restaurant Workers Union, Local 473, A.F.L.-C.I.O. v. McElroy, 367 U.S. 886, 894, 81 S.Ct. 1743, 1748, 6 L.Ed.2d 1230 (1961).

In the present case some of the essential conditions for requiring procedural due process as a matter of constitutional right are missing. In the first place the Board of Parole is not appellant's adversary. On the contrary the Board has an identity of interest with him to the extent that it is seeking to encourage and foster his rehabilitation and readjustment to society. The Board's position was well described by Judge (now Chief Justice) Burger in Hyser v. Reed, 115 U.S.App.D.C. 254, 318 F.2d 225, cert. denied sub nom. Thompson v. United States Board of Parole, 375 U.S. 957, 84 S.Ct. 446, 11 L. Ed.2d 315 (1963), where the court, sitting *en banc,* held that procedural due process was not required by the Constitution in federal parole revocation proceedings:

> The Bureau of Prisons and the Parole Board operate from the basic premise that prisoners placed in their custody are to be rehabilitated and restored to useful lives as soon as in the Board's judgment that transition can be safely made. This is plainly what Congress intends. Thus there is a genuine identity of interest if not purpose in the prisoner's desire to be released and the Board's policy to grant release as soon as possible. Here there is not the attitude of adverse, conflicting objectives as between the parolee and the Board inherent between prosecution and defense in a criminal case. Here we do not have pursuer and quarry but a relationship partaking of parens patriae. In a real sense the Parole Board in revoking parole occupies the role of parent withdrawing a privilege from an errant child not as punishment but for misuse of the privilege. "Probation workers making reports of their investigations have not been trained to prosecute but to aid offenders." Williams v. People of State of New York, 337 U.S. 241, at 249, 69 S.Ct. 1079, at 1084, 93 L.Ed. 1337....
>
> Fundamentally the Parole Board's interest and its objective are to release a prisoner as soon as he is a good parole risk and to allow him to remain at liberty under supervision as long as he is a good risk (318 F.2d at 237, 242).

On the erroneous assumption that the Board's determination of whether the prisoner should be paroled is an adversary proceeding, the complaint alleges that the Board fails to give appellant "notice of charges" against him and demands that such notice be furnished. There are no "charges" or accusations against appellant. Nor is the Board necessarily called upon, in deciding whether he should be released on parole, to resolve disputed issues of fact, which might be the occasion for use of skills associated with lawyers, judges and the judicial process.

The Board's function is a different one. It must make the broad determination of whether rehabilitation of the prisoner and the interests of society generally would best be served by permitting him to serve his sentence beyond the confines of prison walls rather than by being continued in physical confinement. In making that determination the Board is not restricted by rules of evidence or procedures developed for the purpose of determining legal or factual issues. It must consider many factors of a non-legal nature, such as psychiatric reports with respect to the prisoner, his mental and moral attitudes, his vocational education and training, the manner in which he has used his recreation time, his physical and emotional health, his intra-personal relations with prison staff and other inmates, his habits, and the nature and extent of community resources that will be available to him upon his release, including the environment to which he plans to return.

Without suggesting that legal counsel or a social worker could not render any assistance at all with respect to the numerous facets of the picture before the Board, the problem to be resolved is not one which usually demands the traditional skills, training and expertise of legal counsel. Far more important is an understanding of the numerous other factors we have mentioned, which have to do with medicine, psychiatry, criminology, penology, psychology and human relations.

Another essential element missing is the existence of a private interest enjoyed by appellant, or to which he is entitled, of the type qualifying for due process protection. We readily acknowledge, of course, that appellant has an "interest" in being considered by the Board which has the power, in its absolute discretion, to grant him the liberty of serving his sentence outside of prison walls. The type of interest protected by procedural due process, however, is usually one presently enjoyed, e. g., welfare benefits (Goldberg v. Kelly, 397 U.S. 254, 90 S.Ct. 1011, 25 L.Ed.2d 287 (1970)); occupation of premises (Escalera v. New York City Housing Authority, 425 F.2d 853 (2d Cir. April 29, 1970); attendance at school (Dixon v. Alabama State Board of Education, 294 F.2d 150 (5th Cir. 1961)); status as an alien immigrant (Leng May Ma v. Barber, 357 U.S. 185, 78 S.Ct. 1072, 2 L.Ed. 2d 1246 (1958)); employment (Greene v. McElroy, 360 U.S. 474, 79 S.Ct. 1400, 3 L.Ed.2d 1377 (1959)); or existence as a charitable organization (Joint Anti-Fascist Refugee Committee v. McGrath, 341 U.S. 123, 71 S.Ct. 624, 95 L.Ed. 817 (1951)). Appellant, however, does not presently enjoy freedom of movement beyond the prison walls and nothing in the state court's sentence, or in state statutes or rules, entitles him to it, whether it be labeled a "right" or a "privilege." He is entitled only to be released after full service of his sentence less good time earned during incarceration. The Board is given absolute and exclusive discretion to decide whether or not to initiate parole release proceedings and, if so, whether parole should be granted to him. Appellant has been constitutionally deprived of his right to liberty for the period of his sentence. Like an alien seeking entry into the United States (as distinguished from a lawful resident alien) he does not qualify for procedural due process in seeking parole. Shaughnessy v. United States ex rel. Mezei, 345 U.S. 206, 73 S.Ct. 625, 97 L.Ed. 956 (1953); Wong Hing Fun v. Esperdy, 335 F.2d 656 (2d Cir. 1964) (per Judge Marshall), cert. denied sub nom. Ng Sui Sang v. Esperdy, 379 U.S. 970, 85 S.Ct. 667, 13 L.Ed2d 562 (1965).

It is questionable whether a Board of Parole is even required to hold a hearing on the question of whether a prisoner should be released on parole. In this respect the determination to be made differs from revocation of parole, where plausible reasons might be advanced in favor of minimum procedural due process. It may be argued that a parolee, having been released, enjoys a liberty akin to a private interest, and that the Board is seeking to deprive him of that liberty because of his alleged violation of one or more of the conditions of his parole. Upon his denial of the allegation the Board is called upon to resolve the relatively narrow issue thus presented. Under such circumstances, it may further be contended, fundamental fairness dictates that the prisoner be accorded constitutional due process at a trial-type hearing, including the right to legal counsel with traditional skills suited to just such a controversy. Nevertheless, although various jurisdictions by statute permit the parolee to be represented by retained counsel in such a revocation proceeding, all circuit courts of appeal which have passed upon the issue—seven in number—have held that the prisoner is not entitled to due process as a matter of constitutional right.

In accord is the recent unanimous decision of the New York Court of Appeals in Briguglio v. New York State Board of Parole, 24 N.Y. 2d 21, 298 N.Y.S.2d 704 (1969). In view of the unanimous rejection of constitutional due process in parole revocation proceedings, which at least present plausible grounds for such a right, the claim must fail in a release determination, where not even such grounds exist.

A final factor we are entitled to weigh is the burden which minimum due process requirements (advance notice, hearing, provision of counsel, cross-examination and findings) would place upon the State of New York and its parole procedures. Hannah v. Larche, 363 U.S. 420, 442, 80 S.Ct. 1502, 4 L.Ed.2d 1307 (1960). According to the Annual Report of the New York Division of Parole for the year 1967, which has been furnished by counsel, New York holds more than 11,000 parole interviews or hearings annually. From the record of appellant's interviews it appears that while the dossier of written information before the Board may be voluminous, the hearing is usually brief. If, as appellant demands, each prisoner is to appear with counsel we may reasonably anticipate that the administrative burden (including the preparation of advance notice, the subpoenaing and cross-examination of witnesses, arguments of counsel and preparation of written decisions) would be enormously increased, accompanied by the usual delays attendant upon clogged calendars. Initially, of course, there would be the problem of providing competent legal services to the prisoners themselves, most of whom are indigent. It would hardly be fair to provide that the wealthy prisoner should have the right to legal counsel whereas the great majority of prisoners would be denied that right simply because they are too poor. Although the increased administrative burden, standing alone, might not justify denial of the procedural steps demanded by appellant, we believe that when considered with the other relevant factors we have discussed, it militates against such relief.

Urging that parole release represents a form of deferred sentencing, which enables authorities to "tailor a sentence to a particular offender," appellant contends that the situation before us is governed by the Supreme Court's recent decision in Mempa v. Rhay, 389 U.S. 128, 88 S.Ct. 254, 19 L.Ed.2d 336 (1967), which held that a defendant was entitled to be represented by counsel at a deferred sentencing hearing held after revocation of probation. Our attention is particularly directed to the fact that the sentencing court in *Mempa* was required under Washington state law to sentence the defendant to the maximum statutory term and that its function, like that of the Board of Parole here, was limited to making a recommendation to the Board as to the amount of time which the defendant should be required to serve before parole. The Supreme Court noted that aid of counsel was necessary to assist the sentencing judge by marshalling the facts and introducing evidence of mitigating circumstances. Appellant argues that this would be the very function served by counsel in a parole release hearing.

We do not accept appellant's contention that a parole release determination is simply a continuation or deferment of sentencing. The prisoner's sentence has already been finally decreed by the court and cannot be changed. A parole Board's determination as to release, on the other hand, is not final and may be reviewed and changed at any time in the Board's discretion. We recognize that *Mempa* is analogous to our case to the extent that a sentencing hearing is essentially non-adversarial in nature, guilt having been determined, and that legal counsel, among other things, may perform a function similar to that which he might or might not perform at a parole release hearing, i. e., bringing out relevant information and arguing for clemency. However, at a sentencing hearing a lawyer may also be required to perform functions of a *legal* nature not required before the Board of Parole. For one thing he may be called upon to insure that certain legal rights, such as the right of appeal, are not waived. He may well decide at the hearing, depending upon further development of the facts, to advise a client to move to withdraw his plea of guilty or to assert additional grounds for setting aside a guilty verdict or moving in arrest of judgment. These services demand his skill and training as a lawyer, not merely non-legal assistance in pleading for clemency. Thus sentencing represents a defendant's "last clear chance" to protect his legal rights at the trial court level. For this reason it has repeatedly been held that representation by legal counsel is constitutionally required. Townsend v. Burke, 334 U.S. 736, 68 S.Ct. 1252, 92 L.Ed. 1690 (1948).

In the last analysis the Board's determination as to whether a prisoner is a good parole risk represents an aspect of state prison discipline, not an adjudication of rights in an adversary proceeding. Rose v. Haskins, 388 F.2d 91 (6th Cir. 1968). If the federal judiciary, in the name of the Due Process Clause, undertook the supervision of such disciplinary procedures, it would become inextricably involved, upon the suits that would inevitably follow, in non-legal, non-judicial determinations for which it is not equipped by training or experience. Although appellant's counsel, upon oral argument, indicated that initially he seeks only rudimentary due process in the form of providing that counsel be permitted to "assist" the Board, we have no doubt that this would be followed by demands (by appellant or others) for the full panoply of procedural rights demanded in the complaint, including cross-examination of doctors, psychiatrists, case workers, prison officials, and the like. We believe that to embark upon such a course would be unwise.

The judgment of the district court is affirmed.

FEINBERG, Circuit Judge (dissenting):

I respectfully dissent.

The basic issue before us is whether a state prisoner is constitutionally entitled to the services of retained counsel at a parole release hearing. I reject the view that a prisoner has no greater rights than an alien in a foreign land, see pp. 408–409 of the majority opinion. I would hold that the Due Process Clause of the Fourteenth Amendment requires that a prisoner be allowed to have the assistance of retained counsel at his parole release hearing.

I.

Before discussing the applicable law, it is instructive to examine precisely what has happened to appellant in this case. He is now 41 years old and has been in prison continuously since he was 18, with a brief exception from August 1963, when he was released on parole, to March 1965, when he was apprehended pursuant to a parole violation warrant. Appellant is presently serving his original sentence of 20 years to life, imposed in May 1947 upon a plea of guilty to murder in the second degree. Therefore, he will remain in prison for the rest of his life unless the New York State Board of Parole decides to release him. In May 1965, he appeared before the Board of Parole and admitted, *inter alia,* that during his brief return to society he had consorted with individuals having a criminal record and that he had given misleading information to his parole officer. Parole was revoked upon these admissions and appellant was ruled ineligible for reconsideration of his parole qualifications for at least two years. Since then, appellant has received a few interviews with the Board at intervals ranging from one to two years. On each occasion he has been summarily denied release on parole and barred from reconsideration until the next interview. Each interview was quite brief. At no time was appellant given an opportunity to have the assistance of counsel, although recently he has apparently had counsel willing and anxious to assist him. We are told that appellant's next meeting with the Board is scheduled for June 1971.

Appellant sought relief in the state courts and then filed this suit, attacking the procedure before the Board and particularly the prohibition of counsel. Since only declaratory relief was sought, no three-judge court under 28 U.S.C. § 2881 was asked for or required. The district judge felt compelled to grant the State's motion for summary judgment, although indicating that if he "were writing on a *tabula rasa,*" his disposition might not be the same. This appeal followed.

II.

To view the primary issue before us in proper perspective, one must envision a statute which specifically prohibits the assistance of counsel at the sentencing in a criminal case. For that is similar to what New York State has done here. . . .

Thus, we are not dealing with the question whether counsel must be appointed at a parole release hearing. The issue is whether all counsel can be banned. Appellant claims that the quoted Rule denies him procedural due process. His most powerful argument proceeds from two assumptions: that a parole release proceeding is essentially a continuation of sentencing, and that at sentencing he would be entitled to the assistance of retained counsel.

Appellant's basic proposition is that a parole release hearing is part of the entire process of rehabilitation and correction which begins with a finding of guilt, goes on to the fixing of an appropriate sentence, and ends with the expiration of that sentence. Certainly, there is nothing startling about this view. The criminal process does not end abruptly with the clang of the prison gate; society has a pervading interest in what happens to the prisoner thereafter.

Moreover, modern penological attitudes and statutes which reflect them underscore the unbroken nature of the process. It is clearly the trend to divide responsibility for sentencing more and more between the judge who heard the trial or the guilty plea and those persons who thereafter observe the defendant in prison. Thus, in recent decades, Congress and state legislatures have given judges great flexibility in sentencing. A judge can now make merely the initial determination that a defendant should go to prison, fix an outside limit on incarceration and leave the length of custody to be determined by a Parole Board. Also, the judge can instruct the board to consider parole eligibility sooner than it ordinarily would. Moreover, in some situations, a judge may sentence a defendant to prison for an indeterminate period, with a Parole Board later deciding when, if ever, the prisoner's return to society is advisable.

Obviously, then, the responsibility for sentencing is increasingly being shared, with Parole Boards playing a greater and greater part. Moreover, this division of responsibility is explicitly recognized. Thus, the Senate Report on the bill which is now 18 U.S.C. § 4208 stated that the new sentencing procedures "would permit the court, at its discretion, to share with the executive branch the responsibility for determining how long a prisoner should actually serve." Similarly, the Task Force Report on Corrections (1967), prepared for the President's Commission on Law Enforcement and Administration of Justice concluded (at p. 86):

> Parole legislation involves essentially a delegation of sentencing power to the parole board.

For the defendant before a sentencing judge or a prisoner before the Parole Board, the stakes are exactly the same: on the one hand, freedom to remain in or to return to society and on the other, incarceration in prison, in this case possibly for life. In New York, the standards for the judge and the Parole Board in making that determination are remarkably similar. Indeed, the Correction Law of the State of New York refers to the Board's role in a parole release proceeding as a "judicial function." If the functions of judge and Parole Board under these arrangements are viewed objectively, the parole release proceeding in New York, as elsewhere, does seem in practical effect to be an extension of the sentencing process, and I accept that proposition. See Note, Due Process: The Right to Counsel in Parole Release Hearings, 54 Iowa L.Rev. 497, 505 (1968).

This brings us to appellant's second assumption, which concerns those rights guaranteed at sentencing. In Townsend v. Burke, 334 U.S. 736, 741, 68 S.Ct. 1252, 1255, 92 L.Ed. 1690 (1948), the Supreme Court granted a writ of habeas corpus to a state prisoner because of the "requirement of fair play which absence of counsel [at sentencing] withheld from this prisoner." Less than three years ago, the Court unanimously stated in Mempa v. Rhay, 389 U.S. 128, 134, 88 S.Ct. 254, 257, 19 L.Ed.2d 336 (1967):

> In particular, Townsend v. Burke, *supra*, illustrates the critical nature of sentencing in a criminal case and might well be considered to support by itself a holding that the right to counsel applies at sentencing. Many lower courts have concluded that the Sixth Amendment right to counsel extends to sentencing in federal cases.

Thereafter, in McConnell v. Rhay, 393 U.S. 2, 4, 89 S.Ct. 32, 34, 21 L.Ed.2d 2 (1968) (per curiam), the Court made clear that "[t]he right to counsel at sentencing must * * * be treated like the right to counsel at other stages of adjudication." I conclude, therefore, that appellant's minor premise is sound and that at a judicial sentencing the Constitution requires the presence of counsel. See also United States ex rel. Diblin v. Follette, 418 F.2d 408 (2d Cir. 1969).

This, of course, hardly ends the case; it is only the beginning of the necessary inquiry. Appellant in fact claims as a constitutional right more procedural protection than he is now constitutionally entitled to at a judicial sentencing, e. g., confrontation of witnesses. Moreover, even though a parole release proceeding is in practical effect an extension of the sentencing process, it does not follow that it must be treated in exactly the same way. Appellant in effect concedes this by foregoing reliance on the right to counsel guaranteed by the Sixth Amendment as applied to the states through the Due Process Clause of the Fourteenth Amendment. See Gideon v. Wainwright, 372 U.S. 335, 83 S.Ct. 792, 9 L.Ed.2d 799 (1963). He relies instead on the more general requirements of procedural due process, citing principally Goldberg v. Kelly, 397 U.S. 254, 90 S.Ct. 1011, 25 L.Ed.2d 287 (1970); Mempa v. Rhay, *supra*, and In re Gault, 387 U.S. 1, 87 S.Ct. 1428, 18 L.Ed.2d 527 (1967). The Supreme Court has instructed us that in this context due process is an elusive concept. Its exact boundaries are undefinable, and its content varies according to specific factual contexts. * * * Whether the Constitution requires that a particular right obtain in a specific proceeding depends upon a complexity of factors. The nature of the alleged right involved, the nature of the proceeding, and the possible burden on that proceeding, are all considerations which must be taken into account.

Hannah v. Larche, 363 U.S. 420, 442, 80 S.Ct. 1502, 1514, 4 L.Ed.2d 1307 (1960). See also Goldberg v. Kelly, *supra,* 397 U.S. at 263, 90 S.Ct. 1011; Cafeteria & Restaurant Workers Union, Local 473 v. McElroy, 367 U.S. 886, 895, 81 S.Ct. 1743, 6 L.Ed.2d 1230 (1961). Accordingly, I turn to application of these general criteria to a parole release hearing, focusing primarily on the right to assistance of retained counsel.

The most obvious consideration is that for the prisoner the stakes could hardly be higher. Since the Parole Board has the power to determine whether appellant must remain in prison for the rest of his life, he has an obvious interest in having his case for parole presented effectively. Appellant is a man of little education and the transcripts of the parole release proceedings reveal, as might be expected, his inability to express himself clearly and to present his justifications for parole. Apparently the basic reason for the Board's refusal to grant parole release has been appellant's admission of "consorting," which resulted in revocation of parole in 1965. The attempts of appellant, alone in the room with the Board, to persuade its members that he had made a mistake which would not be repeated reflect his own inadequacies and his concern over antagonizing the Board. It requires little imagination to conclude that a trained lawyer could have materially aided both appellant and the Board, unless the inaccurate and unworthy assumption is made that lawyers generally do more harm than good. It makes little difference whether present parole personnel are seen as sincere men earnestly doing the best they can in a difficult job, or are regarded less favorably. On either view, a Parole Board should be interested in such relevant facts as job availability for a prisoner, his family situation, and his progress in self-education. The ability to marshal such facts and to uncover unfairness that a trained lawyer possesses would improve, not injure, the parole release hearing.

The majority opinion suggests that the "administrative burden * * * would be enormously increased" by allowing counsel at a parole release hearing. But some states already do so, and apparently there has been no paralysis of their systems. Nor is it necessary to assume that allowing retained counsel will carry with it an exactly corresponding obligation to appoint counsel for all indigent potential parolees, thus flooding the courts with demands for appointment. While there is force to the equal protection claim, that presents a different question. Thus, the Supreme Court in Chandler v. Fretag, 348 U.S. 3, 9, 75 S.Ct. 1, 5, 99 L.Ed. 4 (1954), which recognized the right to counsel at an "habitual criminal" sentencing, said: "Regardless of whether petitioner would have been entitled to the appointment of counsel, his right to be heard through his own counsel was unqualified." Similarly, the Task Force Report on Corrections, *supra,* at 86, notes this distinction and states that "there seems no legitimate reason for limiting representation by retained counsel at parole hearings." As the Supreme Court observed in Johnson v. Avery, 393 U.S. 483, 489–490, 89 S.Ct. 747, 21 L.Ed.2d 718 (1969), there are a number of less than perfect, but acceptable, solutions to the problem of providing counsel to persons deprived of their liberty, outside the hard core of criminal prosecution itself. One solution, which would go far to ameliorating any fears of enormous administrative burdens, would be to appoint counsel only for those prisoners who have been denied parole at their first opportunity therefore. Finally, allowing retained counsel at a parole release hearing does not mean that he should be allowed to convert it into a trial any more than counsel could achieve such a result at a sentencing in court.

In short, considering the broad discretion wielded by the Parole Board, the virtually unfettered procedure, the gravity of the consequences to the prisoner, his inability to present his case as well as a lawyer could, the sentencing function of the Board, and the possible burdens of allowing the assistance of retained counsel, appellant's legal position is persuasive. I conclude that the traditional procedural due process criteria suggest that a prisoner at a parole release hearing should be entitled to the services of retained counsel.

Turning from these general considerations to the reported cases, so far as I can tell the precedents do not compel us to deny such assistance of counsel. There is authority suggesting that result, which is discussed below, but we are cited to no case in the Supreme Court or in this court which now requires us to take that course. On the other hand, there are recent decisions in the Supreme Court and in the courts of appeals which do lend strong support to appellant's position.

In Mempa v. Rhay, *supra,* the Supreme Court held unanimously that counsel was constitutionally required at a hearing which combined probation revocation and deferred sentencing. . . . I do not suggest that *Mempa* is either controlling or indistinguishable. Obviously, it is neither.

To the extent that *Mempa* emphasized the need for counsel in sentencing by a judge presumably trained in fact-finding and operating within a structure of traditional objectivity and impartiality, one may ask whether counsel is not *a fortiori* required at a sentencing hearing by a Parole Board. Moreover, because the role of the trial judge in *Mempa* was so limited (he could only impose the "maximum term"), the true role of counsel was to produce facts for the future use of the Parole Board. Accordingly, I believe that *Mempa* supports appellant's assertion that he is entitled to the services of counsel before the New York Parole Board for the purpose of "in general aiding and assisting the defendant to present his case as to sentence." *Mempa, supra,* 389 U.S. at 135, 88 S.Ct. at 257. Cf. Hewett v. North Carolina, 415 F.2d 1316, 1322 (4th Cir. 1969), and Ashworth v. United States, 391 F.2d 245 (6th Cir. 1968) (per curiam), both holding that because of *Mempa,* counsel is now required at revocation of probation proceedings. See also Cohen, Sentencing, Probation, and the Rehabilitative Ideal: The View from Mempa v. Rhay, 47 Tex.L.Rev. 1 (1968).

Moreover, there are other recent decisions that support appellant's position. In Johnson v. Avery, 393 U.S. 483, 89 S.Ct. 747, 21 L.Ed.2d 718 (1969), the Court struck down a prison regulation barring inmates from furnishing assistance to other prisoners in the preparation of petitions for post-conviction relief. In Goldberg v. Kelly, 397 U.S. 254, 270, 90 S.Ct. 1011, 25 L.Ed.2d 287 (1970), the Court held that a welfare recipient is entitled to certain due process procedural protections before termination of benefits, including the right to representation by retained counsel at a hearing. Similarly, the meaning of constitutional due process has been expanded in other analogous areas. In re Gault, 387 U.S. 1, 87 S.Ct. 1428, 18 L.Ed.2d 527 (1967), made clear that counsel was required in a juvenile proceeding. Cf. Kent v. United States, 383 U.S. 541, 86 S.Ct. 1045, 16 L.Ed.2d 84 (1966). In Specht v. Patterson, 386 U.S. 605, 87 S.Ct. 1209, 18 L.Ed.2d 326 (1967), the Court held that where the basis for sentencing as a sexual offender was not the finding of guilt, but a new finding of fact, e. g., that the defendant, if at large, constituted a threat of bodily harm to the community, due process required that an adversary hearing be held. In United States ex rel. Schuster v. Herold, 410 F.2d 1071, 1073 (2d Cir. 1969), this court held that before a prisoner may be transferred to a state institution for insane criminals, "he must be afforded substantially the same procedural safeguards as are provided in civil commitment proceedings." In reaching that conclusion, we relied heavily on another recent Supreme Court decision, Baxstrom v. Herold, 383 U.S. 107, 86 S.Ct. 760, 15 L.Ed.2d 620 (1966). In Shone v. Maine, 406 F.2d 844 (1st Cir.), vacated as moot, 396 U.S. 6, 90 S.Ct. 25, 24 L.Ed.2d 6 (1969), the court extended due process procedural protections to juvenile offenders about to be transferred from a boys' training center to a men's correctional center.

Once again, I do not suggest that these decisions are indistinguishable. They did not involve parole release proceedings; moreover, some of them relied in whole or in part on a constitutional theory—denial of equal protection of the laws—which does not so obviously apply here, since the Parole Board regulation bans counsel for rich and poor alike. The majority opinion attempts to distinguish some of these cases on the ground that they involve an "interest * * * presently enjoyed," and appellant does not now "enjoy freedom of movement beyond the prison walls." With all respect, I submit that the distinction is unsound; what is most significant is the type of "interest" involved and the potential effect of the hearing upon it, not whether the "interest" is already held. The decisions discussed above persuade me that when the immediate stakes of a hearing are imprisonment or freedom, due process commands that a prisoner be allowed at least to have the assistance of retained counsel. . . .

In any event, I do not claim that the question before us can be decided by a tally of the cases. I suggest only that the issue whether retained counsel may be banned at a parole release proceeding is at this time an open one in this circuit and in the Supreme Court, and that the most recent decisions of the Court support the view that such a rule offends procedural due process. Accordingly, I would hold that appellant at his next parole release interview cannot be denied such assistance. . . .

Appellant's complaint sought additional relief, including the right "to cross-examination and to present favorable evidence and compel the attendance of favorable witnesses," notice of charges, and specification of grounds upon which the parole release determination was based. At oral argument, most—and perhaps all—of these additional demands were apparently withdrawn or waived. Therefore, extended consideration of these alleged rights is out of place at this time. My basic approach would be to afford appellant no more in the way of these procedural protections than he is constitutionally entitled to at a sentencing proceeding before a judge, and apparently he has received that.

In sum: I conclude that minimum procedural due process requires New York to allow appellant the assistance of retained counsel at a parole release hearing. Because the majority opinion denies that right, I dissent.

Monks v. New Jersey Parole Board
58 N.J. 238, 277, A.2d. 193 (1971)
Supreme Court of New Jersey

JACOBS, J.

The State Parole Board rejected the appellant's request for a statement of its reasons for denial of parole to him. He filed notice of appeal to the Appellate Division which dismissed his appeal as untimely. His petition for certification was granted by this Court.

In 1957 the appellant William Monks, then 15 years of age, was adjudicated a juvenile delinquent for offenses which, if he had been 18 or older, would have constituted murder in the first degree, robbery and atrocious assault and battery. He was committed to the Bordentown Reformatory. His period of confinement was indeterminate, to continue until the appropriate authority decided that he should be paroled though not beyond the maximum provided by law with respect to an adult. . . .

Because of disciplinary problems at Bordentown, Mr. Monks was transferred on May 31, 1967 to the New Jersey State Prison where he is now confined.

Within a four-month period subsequent to the transfer, the Parole Board conducted its initial hearing in Mr. Monks' case and denied parole. It rescheduled the matter for a further hearing in two years. On further hearing, the Board on September 16, 1969 again denied parole and scheduled rehearing for September 1971. The notice to Mr. Monks set forth no reasons for the Board's decision and simply noted that "parole has been denied regardless of the availability of a suitable parole plan." On October 4, 1969 Mr. Monks wrote a letter to the Board in which he said that he would like to know what was necessary to convince the Board that he was "a good parole risk"; that if the Board could be good enough to give him "some idea of the reasons" for its action he would be in a position to behave in any way the Board expected; that he wanted to do whatever he could "to be released at the earliest possible time"; and that if a reconsideration was possible he would like to mention that he had "a very good job waiting" for him and also "a home to live" in with his brother and sister-in-law. In response to this letter the Board notified Mr. Monks on October 21, 1969 that his case had been studied again and that the Board was of the opinion "that there should be no change in the prior determination that parole should be denied and that you should be scheduled for a further hearing in September 1971."

On January 5, 1970, Mr. Amsterdam, an attorney who had been designated by the United States Supreme Court to represent Mr. Monks in a legal proceeding unrelated to the parole matter before us (Monks v. New Jersey, 395 U.S. 942, 89 S.Ct. 2021, 23 L.Ed.2d 461 (1969); 398 U.S. 71, 90 S.Ct. 1563, 26 L.Ed.2d 54 (1970)), wrote a letter to Mr. Harold J. Ashby, Chairman of the Parole Board. In his letter Mr. Amsterdam pointed out that Mr. Monks was unclear as to why he had been denied parole since he felt that his behavior since his transfer to State Prison had been "such as to warrant favorable consideration." Mr. Monks wondered whether there is some damaging information in the Board's files which is "legitimately subject to question or refutation" and whether "there is some way in which his prison behavior should be changed, so as favorably to impress the Board." Mr. Amsterdam renewed Mr. Monks' request "for some explanation of the considerations that moved the Board to deny him parole," pointing out that he could not effectively counsel Mr. Monks and aid in his rehabilitation without knowing "what sorts of considerations" are considered relevant by the Board to the parole determination.

On January 13, 1970 Mr. Ashby replied to Mr. Amsterdam declining to say anything with respect to the reasons for the denial of parole to Mr. Monks. He did however state that "as a matter of policy," the Board does not give reasons, citing New Jersey decisions as holding that it was under no legal obligation to do so. Mr. Ashby's letter closed with a statement that if Mr. Amsterdam desired to discuss the matter further an appointment would be arranged. On March 2, 1970 Mr. Ashby met with Messrs. Newman and Himmelstein, acting as additional counsel for Mr. Monks, and the substance of their meeting was set forth in a letter dated March 23, 1970 to Mr. Ashby which concluded with "a final request" that he furnish the information sought. On March 31, 1970 Mr. Ashby replied, citing N.J.S.A. 30:4–123.14 and repeating his earlier assertion that the reasons for denial of parole "need not be revealed." Mr. Ashby did not suggest that there were circumstances special to Mr. Monks' case which would call for withholding reasons from him, apart from the Board's general policy, and our own examination of the Parole Board's file indicates that there were none....

We granted certification not because of the timeliness question but because we were concerned with whether a parole denial should not in this age be accompanied by a fair statement of reasons. We shall therefore pass the timeliness issue and proceed to the merits, noting however that in any event Mr. Monks has a viable right to seek a declaration as to the validity of the Board's general policy of not stating reasons, a policy which does not rest on any express statutory provision but is embodied in a formal administrative Parole Board rule designated 11:70–54....

The Parole Board has broad but not unlimited discretionary powers. The pertinent legislation (N.J.S.A. 30:4–123.1 et seq.) sets forth guidelines and under our special constitutional structure (N.J.Const. art. VI, sec. 5, para. 4 (1947)) the Board's actions are always judicially reviewable for arbitrariness.... The Legislature has directed the Board not to release on parole merely as a reward for good conduct but only if it is of the opinion that "there is reasonable probability" that the prisoner will assume his proper and rightful place in society, without violation of law, and that his release "is not incompatible with the welfare of society." N.J.S.A. 30:4–123.14. The Department of Institutions and Agencies and the chief executive officers and staffs of the various correctional institutions are directed to cooperate and furnish reports with respect to the prisoner to the Board which, in turn, is directed to receive and maintain records (N.J.S.A. 30:4–123.17, 18) and to "consider the merits of his parole" and make such "investigation as it shall deem necessary and proper." N.J.S.A. 30:1–123.9.

Before reaching a final decision, the Board is directed to have the prisoner appear before it and "personally interview him to consider his ultimate fitness for parole, and verify as far as possible, the information furnished it from other sources." N.J.S.A. 30:4–123.19. There is no legislative provision for counsel at the interview ... although there is legislative provision that when it becomes necessary for the prisoner to appear before the Board "for the purpose of determining his fitness for parole" he "shall have the right to consult legal counsel of his own selection, if he feels that his legal rights are invaded," and subject to the Board's consent "to submit in writing a brief or other legal argument on his behalf."

Professor Kadish has suggested that determinations by the parole board are "in some measure equivalent to the sentencing determinations of the judge" since "decisions on both levels turn on a discretionary assessment of a multiplicity of imponderables, entailing primarily what a man is and what he may become rather than simply what he has done." Kadish, *supra.* 45 Minn.L.Rev. at 812–13. But he quickly acknowledges that under the decided cases the prisoner's constitutional rights at sentencing go far beyond his rights at the parole interview or hearing. *Cf.* Mempa v. Rhay, 389 U.S. 128, 88 S.Ct. 254, 19 L.Ed. 2d 336 (1967); Cohen, "Sentencing, Probation and the Rehabilitative Ideal: The View from Mempa v. Rhay," 47 Texas L. Rev. 1 (1968). Thus we have recognized the prisoner's broad right at sentencing to have counsel who, under State v. Kunz, 55 N.J. 128, 259 A.2d 895 (1969), is afforded fair and timely opportunity of examining a copy of the presentence report on which the sentence is largely based; and we have also recognized that, with the aid of his counsel, the prisoner may readily appeal and pursue an attack on the trial judge's exercise of his sentencing discretion.

In contrast to the foregoing, we have thus far not recognized any right to counsel at the parole interview or hearing. Mr. Monks does not here assert such right to counsel nor does he here question the manner in which his interview or hearing was actually conducted; as already indicated, he merely seeks a statement of reasons so that he may properly be guided in connection with his future conduct and with his forthcoming parole rehearing scheduled for September 1971.

When dealing with administrative agencies generally we have long pointed to the need for suitable expression of the controlling findings or reasons. Thus in Abbotts Dairies v. Armstrong, 14 N.J. 319, 102 A.2d 372 (1954), we stressed that findings were of the utmost importance "not only in insuring a responsible and just determination" by the agency but also "in affording a proper basis for effective judicial review."... See Davis, Administrative Law § 16.12, p. 585 (1970 Supp.): "One of the best procedural protections against arbitrary exercise of discretionary power lies in the requirement of findings and reasons that appear to reviewing judges to be rational."

In Drown v. Portsmouth School District, 435 F.2d 1182 (1 Cir. 1970), the Court of Appeals for the First Circuit recently sustained a request for a statement of reasons though it found no constitutional ground for additional relief. A non-tenure teacher who had not been rehired at the expiration of her annual contract sought but was denied a statement of reasons and a hearing at which she could challenge them. Citing Cafeteria & Restaurant Workers Union, Local 473, A.F.L.–C.I.O v. McElroy, 367 U.S. 886, 81 S.Ct. 1743, 6 L.Ed.2d 1230 (1961) and Goldberg v. Kelly, 397 U.S. 254, 90 S.Ct. 1011, 25 L.Ed.2d 287 (1970), the court noted that in determining what procedures were required, the competing interests of the individual teacher and the school board must be duly balanced. 435 F.2d at 1184. It found that the teacher's interests in knowing the reasons for her nonretention were indeed substantial and that the disadvantages in supplying them were indeed slight; it found further, however, that the full evidentiary hearing sought by the teacher would be unduly burdensome to the school system and was not fairly called for on a weighing of all of the pertinent considerations. It concluded that, while the teacher was not entitled to the hearing she sought, she should nonetheless constitutionally be furnished with a statement of reasons. 435 F.2d at 1185–1188.

The need for fairness is as urgent in the parole process as elsewhere in the law and it is evident to us that, as a general matter, the furnishing of reasons for denial would be the much fairer course; not only much fairer but much better designed towards the goal of rehabilitation. The Corrections Task Force has pointed out that well conducted parole hearings tend desirably to increase "the involvement of inmates in the decisions which affect them and to confront them more directly with the information upon which a decision is being made." President's Commission on Law Enforcement and Administration of Justice, Task Force Report: Corrections, p. 64 (1967). Favorable reference is made to the increasing number of parole boards, including, among others, those in Minnesota and Iowa, which have adopted "the practice of calling inmates back after a hearing to discuss the decision on their cases." Id. at 65. Professor Dawson reports that in Michigan and Wisconsin "the parole boards are careful to explain to the inmate the reason for the decision reached" and "to suggest what, if anything, the inmate can do to improve his chances for parole later." Dawson, "The Decision to Grant or Deny Parole: A Study of Parole Criteria in Law and Practice," 1966 Wash. U.L.Q. 243, 302. He also reports that statements of the reasons are placed in the inmates' files and that although the statements are quite brief, "the necessity for making them requires some reflection on the grounds for the decisions." Id. at 302.

In response to inquiries from our Attorney General, the Parole Board of Pennsylvania has advised that brief written reasons have been furnished by it for the last 15 years to prisoners on denial of parole, and the Parole Board of Connecticut has advised that prior to January 1, 1969 written reasons had been given to prisoners but that a procedural revision took effect as of that date. Under its revised practice the Connecticut Board, at the conclusion of the conference with the inmate, excuses him and then makes its decision in executive session. He is then recalled and is advised of the board's decision, and if there has been a denial, "the reasons for the denial." The board's letter to the Attorney General states that sometimes "it is difficult to explain the reasons for the denial" particularly when the denial is the result of information in the psychiatric evaluation and its disclosure might endanger future psychiatric services; but such special situations could of course be dealt with specially in the formulation of an administrative disclosure rule or policy. See Davis, Discretionary Justice 131 (1969): "I think that justice requires that a prisoner be told the reasons for a denial of parole, with rare exceptions, as when a psychiatric condition otherwise requires. Withholding reasons is likely to harm the rehabilitation process. Statement of findings and reasons will not assure fairness of the decision, but it will pull in that direction."

In his critical discussion of the operations of the United States Parole Board, Professor Davis points to various administrative deficiencies, though our concern here is solely with his comments on the board's policy of not stating reasons for denial of parole. Discretionary

Justice, *supra*, 126 et seq. In that connection he stresses not only that the policy adversely affects the prisoner's rehabilitation (p. 128) but also that it disregards the recognized "advantages of openness" (p. 129) and leads to the likelihood that abuses of discretion will "go uncorrected" (p. 128). Similarly, Professor Dawson in his study of parole law and practice stresses not only the need for legal reviewing mechanisms but, more pointedly, the need for improvement of the board procedures themselves so that society can "be assured that official discretion is being exercised fairly and sensibly." Dawson, *supra*, 1966 Wash.U.L.Q. at 303. Only recently did the English establish a parole system ("Criminal Justice Act," 31 Modern L.Rev. 16, 35 (1968)) and it has understandably brought forth academic comment. See, *e. g.*, Samuels, "Parole: A Critique," 1969 Crim.L.Rev. (Eng.) 456. Mr. Samuels, Senior Lecturer in Law, University of Southampton, points out that a "simple, bald rejection" of parole necessarily increases "uncertainty and frustration and disillusionment and morbid speculation in the prisoner." He recommends that reasons always be given "shortly and simply, except where the Board expressly for good reasons decides otherwise, *e. g.*, where it would manifestly not be in the prisoner's best interests, perhaps because of psychological matters or family matters." Samuels, *supra*, 1969 Crim. L.Rev. (Eng.) at 459.

Our judicial system has historically been vested with the comprehensive prerogative writ jurisdiction which it inherited from the King's Bench; that jurisdiction has been frequently exercised in the supervision of inferior governmental tribunals including administrative agencies. See the very early cases of State v. Justices, &c., of Middlesex, 1 N.J.L. *244 (Sup. Ct. 1794), where Chief Justice Kinsey described the jurisdiction "as unlimited and universal as injustice and wrong can be" (at *248), and Ludlow v. Executors of Ludlow, 4 N.J.L. *387 (Sup.Ct. 1817), where Chief Justice Kirkpatrick described it as "very high and transcendent" (at *389); and also the more recent cases of Fisher v. Twp. of Bedminster, 5 N.J. 534, 76 A.2d 673 (1950), where Justice Heher noted that the "inherent power of superintendence of inferior tribunals" (at 560) was secured by the 1844 Constitution and could not be impaired by the Legislature, and McKenna v. N.J. Highway Authority, *supra*, 19 N.J. 270, 116 A.2d 29, where Justice Burling noted that the prerogative writ jurisdiction included not only the review of "judicial actions" but also the superintendence of civil corporations, magistrates and "other public officers." (at 274, 116 A.2d 29). When our 1947 Constitution was prepared, pains were taken to insure not only that the court's prerogative writ jurisdiction would remain intact, but also that the manner of its exercise would be greatly simplified (art. VI, sec. 5, para. 4). See Ward v. Keenan, 3 N.J. 298, 303–308, 70 A.2d 77 (1949). The implementing court rules now provide an easy mode of review designed to insure procedural fairness in the administrative process and to curb administrative abuses. See In re Masiello, 25 N.J. 590, 603, 138 A.2d 393 (1958); Elizabeth Federal S. & L. Assn. v. Howell, 24 N.J. 488, 499, 132 A.2d 779 (1957).

In White v. Parole Board of State of N.J., 17 N.J.Super. 580, 86 A.2d 422 (App.Div. 1952), a modern counterpart of the ancient writ proceeding, the prisoner's attack on his parole board classification was rejected, but in his opinion for the Appellate Division Justice Brennan suggested that, constitutional compulsions aside, proper procedural safeguards on vital classification issues are called for by "considerations of simple fairness." 17 N.J. Super. at 586, 86 A.2d 422. So here, fairness and rightness clearly dictate the granting of the prisoner's request for a statement of reasons. That course as a general matter would serve the acknowledged interests of procedural fairness and would also serve as a suitable and significant discipline on the Board's exercise of its wide powers. It would in nowise curb the Board's discretion on the grant or denial of parole nor would it impair the scope and effect of its expertise. It is evident to us that such incidental administrative burdens as result would not be undue; the reported experiences in the jurisdictions which have long furnished reasons have given us no grounds for pause.

The Board's rule (11:70–54) states flatly that it will not reveal the basis for a denial either in the notice of denial or otherwise; because of the views expressed earlier in this opinion we find the rule invalid and it is now nullified. It should be replaced at an early date by a carefully prepared rule designed generally towards affording statements of reasons on parole denials, while providing for such reasonable exceptions as may be essential to rehabilitations and the sound administration of the parole system. In the meantime, the Board is directed to grant Mr. Monks' request for a statement of the reasons for the denial of his parole. The judgment of dismissal entered in the Appellate Division is hereby:

Reversed.

SCARPA V. UNITED STATES PAROLE BOARD
11 Cr. L. 2177 (1972)
United States Court of Appeals, Fifth Circuit

TUTTLE, J.

... Essentially, the appellant is here complaining of the fact that, although he was sentenced upon his plea of guilty to one charge of forging a signature on a United States Bond, under the provisions of USCA 18 §4208(a)(2), he has not been afforded the rights which are implicit in the sentencing under this section of the Criminal Code.[1]

It is appellant's contention that this statute, which was passed in 1959, was remedial in nature, to the extent that it modified, in a manner favorable to persons sentenced under it, the provisions of USCA 18 §4202, which restricts the power of the Board of Parole to a release on parole only after serving one-third of the sentence of the court.

The specific complaint made by the appellant was sought to be made by the filing of a suit for declaratory judgment in the district court. It will be noted that he did not file a Petition for Habeas Corpus seeking release or contending that he was entitled to parole. He sought, rather, to assert that under the court's sentence, in keeping with the intent and purpose of the statute, he was entitled to be considered by the Board of Parole for parole eligibility and that, *when so considered*, the Board could not act in a manner that was completely lacking in basic concepts of due process. This, he alleged, the Board had done on the occasion of its first consideration of his request for his parole, and will continue to do whenever it may hereafter consider his case.

As we have stated, Scarpa recognizes that no one is automatically entitled to parole. He knows that the grant or denial of parole is "discretionary." The applicable statute provides that if there is a "reasonable probability that such prisoner will live and remain at liberty without violating the laws, and if in the opinion of the Board such release is not incompatible with the welfare of society, the Board may in its discretion authorize the release of such person on parole." 18 USCA §4203.

What this complainant asks this court to do is to hold that the rubric "discretionary act" does not insulate the one exercising discretion from responding when it is charged that it has abused its discretion. He says that there is no greater immunization of the parole board's abuses of discretion, if they exist, than there is of a court's abuse of discretion. The reviewing of alleged abuses of the discretion of a trial court are a part of the regular grist to our mill as an appellate court.

We have before us purely a legal question, because, having alleged a state of facts which he relied on to entitle him to relief, he was met only with a motion to dismiss for failure to allege facts on which relief could be granted. The trial court granted the government's motion, but in doing so, undertook to make partial findings quite contrary to those alleged, but without any evidence or even denial entered by the government. Of course, such a motion, much like the general demurrer of bygone days, must rest on the proposition that if everything adequately pleaded as fact in the complaint is taken as true, no cause of action has been set out.

What are the facts alleged by Scarpa in his complaint? For this inquiry, of course, we must look to his complaint as amended, and must ignore the elaborate allegations made by him in the "brief" filed by him *pro se* in this court.

Scarpa was sentenced on June 13, 1968, following a plea of guilty, to a term of imprisonment of eight years under the provisions of 18 USCA §4208(a)(2), and he was later incarcerated at the United States Penitentiary in Atlanta. Having made application for parole, the plaintiff appeared before the parole board commissioner on the 13th day of October, 1969. He then alleges the following facts relating to the nature of the proceedings that followed:

> It is a matter of record (See: Parole Boards minutes and records utilized for said hearing, a copy of which is not attached hereto because of plaintiff's inability to acquire possession of same due to parole board rules.) that the consideration afforded

---

[1] "This section, so far as applicable here, provides as follows: "(a) Upon entering a judgment of conviction, the court having jurisdiction to impose sentence, when in its opinion the ends of justice and best interest of the public require that the defendant be sentenced to imprisonment for a term exceeding one year, may ... (2) ... fix the maximum sentence of imprisonment to be served in which event the court may specify that the prisoner *may become eligible for parole at such time as the Board of Parole may determine.*" (Emphasis added.)

the plaintiff for possible release on parole was predicated *solely* upon plaintiff's past criminal record. (Emphasis in original).

Plaintiff was told at said hearing that he (the Parole Commissioner) after having read plaintiff's criminal record, was of the opinion that plaintiff was not ready for parole status in view of his (plaintiff's) past criminal record.

Thereafter plaintiff received further formal denial of parole with a set off date to June 1971 as plaintiff's next scheduled hearing for reconsideration only.

Thereafter plaintiff re-petitioned the defendant parole board for re-consideration as to his possible release on parole, presenting therein the same reasons that presently are argued herein.

Plaintiff was thereafter notified by Parole Executive James R. Pace, that plaintiff's application for re-consideration had been denied. Which therefore had concluded exhaustion of plaintiff's Administrative remedies.

After then outlining his contention that as a matter of law the defendants were mandated "to give plaintiff a fair, full and just hearing; and that they have violated rights to due process," Scarpa outlined what he called "the procedure adopted by the defendants of the United States Penitentiary, Atlanta, Georgia, pertaining to parole hearings on a prisoner committed under 18 USCA §4208(A) (2):"

The inmate is informed by his caseworker that he (the inmate) will be appearing before the defendants shortly and can there appear in person or waive such hearing if he so desires. (Plaintiff in the instant case did not waive.) If the inmate is of the desire to meet the defendants, he is then sent a form and is told that it is necessary for him to fill out said form with the information therein requested. Amongst the demanded information therein requested is such questions as: Are you guilty of this crime. Explain your part in the commission of this crime? Why do you think you should be released on parole? Where will you live if paroled? With whom will you live? Where will you work if paroled? What type of work will you do if paroled? Then a list of all members of the inmate's family who are interested in the inmate's possible release on parole is required. Lastly the inmate is required to obtain a person other than a member of his immediate family to act in the capacity of a parole adviser to the inmate when released on parole.

Thereafter the inmate is called before the board and asked by them the same questions as are set forth in the aforementioned forms and in the case of plaintiff, his name ending in a vowel and being of Italian descent two other questions familiar to all other inmates whose names end similarly, are asked; Are you an Italian? Do you belong to organized crime?

The defendants herein have nothing before them at the time of said hearing other than (a) the standard F.B.I. Report utilized by the sentence court to impose sentence in the first instance, which is a criminal history report, (b) the presentence investigation report utilized also by the court in imposing sentence which is also a criminal history report, (c) a record of the inmates arrest sheet, which was also utilized by the court in their imposition of sentence and which is very clearly a criminal history report. The only other informative report before the defendants is a record of any breach of the prison rules committed by the inmate while in prison, of which plaintiff has none.

The appellant further alleged that:

"Prior to meeting the defendants at said hearing plaintiff consulted with his caseworker, a Mr. Wolfe[2] on the possibility of being recommended and receiving parole. Plaintiff in turn was informed by said caseworker that there was no such possibility, that the purpose of plaintiff meeting the board was "only a get together meeting whereat the board would then set a date approximately two to three years away where at the later date they would decide the possible release date of the inmate on parole." Asked why this was so, the caseworker replied, "The Board doesn't pay any mind to an "A" number as the Judges are giving out too many of them and they don't mean anything any more."

Plaintiff then gave said caseworker the name and address of a person willing to employ plaintiff is paroled and the name and address of a "Parole Adviser" as was required. The caseworker took said information saying, "that the board was not interested in that."

Plaintiff claims that the defendants herein predicated their denial of parole with nothing more before them except reports from various sources belonging to the Federal Government, *solely* pertaining to the Criminal History of plaintiff,

And that although plaintiff was made to

---

[2] It is to be noted that one of the functions of a caseworker is to prepare and present the inmates case to the Board of Parole for their consideration, along with any recommendations that he thinks appropriate.

submit the names and addresses of various members of his family, not a single member of his family was ever interviewed.

Plaintiff further claims that his potential residence if released on parole was not investigated.

Nor was the person interviewed who pledged employment to plaintiff.

Despite the fact that plaintiff was mandated by Rule of the defendants to obtain a person to act in the capacity of "Parole Adviser" to plaintiff before he (plaintiff) could be considered for parole, and the fact that plaintiff succeeded in obtaining the pledge of two highly respectable people, husband and wife; these people were never interviewed in any manner or was there even an attempt to interview them.

Also the defendants herein neither sent for nor requested plaintiff's records from New York's Sing Sing Prison where plaintiff had been incarcerated under a State Rehabilitation Program and from which he had been paroled from but due to the Federal detainer lodged against him for the service of his present Federal sentence, plaintiff was turned over to the custody of the United States Marshalls for commencement of the sentence herein.

It is therefore clearly shown that the defendants herein had no knowledge before them or utilized by them as to plaintiff's employment, residence, family ties, Parole advisers and the rehabilitation report from Sing Sing Prison all of which could have aided plaintiff in his application for parole. . . .

Without requiring a response on the fact issues raised by the complaint, the trial court entered a judgment sustaining the motion to dismiss, saying; "Though the court supports a full, fair hearing and consideration prior to parole decision, it cannot say *on the facts of this case* that petitioner was denied due process. A prisoner's prior criminal record is a legitimate item of consideration in determining whether one is to be released on parole [citing cases]. If, upon petitioner's record, the board determined that petitioner is not a suitable risk for parole, then this court will not interfere with the decision. To require the board to go through a time consuming, expensive investigation, after the board had received sufficient information to conclude that parole would not be appropriate at this time would be a futile exercise and would not enhance due process."

The court then stated: "Petitioner's erroneous perspective on this case apparently stems from his mistaken belief that the parole hearing constituted his entire parole consideration.

Prior to the hearing, reports are compiled. At the hearing the parole applicant is questioned. Subsequently the parole examiner considers the file, prepares a report, including a recommendation, and submits it to the Board of Parole, which takes final action in the case [citing 28 C.F.R. §2.15]."

It must be noted that what the trial court stated to be facts applicable to this case are merely a recitation of what is *required* by the board's regulations. There is no affidavit, or even an answer by the government which sets out the facts which the trial court relied upon in making its judgment. Moreover, the trial court stated, "the action taken by the Board was neither arbitrary nor an abuse of discretion and there has been no deprivation of constitutional rights merely because petitioner did not receive exactly the type of consideration he may have desired."

Thus, the trial court made a finding that the board's action was not arbitrary and was not an abuse of discretion, without having before it any answer to the specific contention that the investigation was based exclusively on reports of Scarpa's criminal activity, and that no consideration was given to other factors or other information, much of which is required by the board's regulations to be supplied by a person seeking parole. . . .

Probably no better discussion of the Parole system can be found than that by the Court of Appeals for the District of Columbia Circuit in the case of *Hyser v. Reed,* 318 F.2d 225 where in an en banc decision by the court an opinion was written by then Circuit Judge, now Chief Justice Burger, reviewing the parole system as it applied both to the opportunity for a prisoner to be granted parole while still incarcerated and the rights of a parolee when the authorities undertook to revoke a parole once afforded him. In discussing the manner in which a parolee gains his initial freedom as a result of an exercise of discretion by the Parole Board, the court says "Each applicant for parole is given a hearing before a member of the Board or an examiner, at the Federal Prison where he is incarcerated. If he is serving a term of more than one year he is entitled to appear at the hearing in person, Parole Board Directive #1, Section 2.15, supra at 8489. The Hearing Officer is required to make a report of the interview under recommendation to the Board. In reaching its decision, the Board *considers the report, the recommendation of the Examiner and all information concerning the prisoner, gathered from recommendations, if any, of the sentencing judge, from the Federal*

Bureau of Investigation, prison and social agencies; Parole Board Board Directive #1, Section 2.14, supra at 8488 (emphasis added). On the basis of this information the Board is empowered to apply a broad congressional standard. The Board may grant parole when it is of the opinion that 'there is a reasonable probability that such prisoner will live and remain at liberty without violating the laws' and upon 'such terms and conditions ... as the Board may prescribe,' 18 U.S.C. Section 4203. Implicit in the term 'reasonable probability' is a recognition that the Board will err sometimes in granting conditional release with the result that the prisoner must be returned to custody to serve his unexpired term. The Board's discretion *to grant, deny or revoke* parole is broad...." 318 F.2d 225, 234. (Emphasis added).

One significant feature of this discussion by the court indicates that the court considered the discretion of the Board to grant parole to be in pari materia with the Board's discretion to revoke. The number of cases in which courts have held that some elements of due process are required with respect to the *revoking* of parole is sufficiently large to permit a strong argument that at least something other than an absolute unbridled exercise of discretion by the Board can be required when the issue at stake is the right of a prisoner to have his request for parole "considered." See, for instance, the case of *Boddie v. Weekly,* 4th Cir., 356 F.2d 242, in which, an opinion written by Chief Judge Haynesworth, the court said, with respect to a revocation proceeding; "It is quite true, as the district court stated, that there is no right of judicial review of a Parole Board's exercise of its discretionary powers. It is also true that we have held that a District of Columbia prisoner is not entitled to the services of appointed counsel in a routine parole revocation hearing. Under Section 24-206 of the D.C. Code, however, he has a statutory right to the assistance of retained counsel, *and there is a judicially enforceable right to fundamental fairness*. The right to fairness includes the right to present the testimony of voluntary witnesses. A colorable claim of deprivation of those rights is justiciable." 356 F.2d 242, 244. (Emphasis added).

The vice of the order here appealed from is that it was summary action based on a motion to dismiss....

This court has very recently dealt directly and plainly with the dismissal on a motion for summary judgment or a motion for judgment on the pleadings in a prisoner application....

Campbell v. Beto, 5 Cir. Dec. April 18, 1972, ―― F.2d ――

We have no doubt that the allegations in this complaint presented serious questions attacking the proceedings before the Parole Board for arbitrariness and lack of fairness, under the regulations issued by the Board itself. We think we ought not at this state of proceedings to attempt to decide to what extent the protections that have now been woven around the somewhat comparable situation in which a parolee is contesting a revocation proceeding ought properly to protect his interest when he comes up for "consideration" of parole by the Board of Paroles.

Nor do we think it necessary to decide whether the fact that this prisoner was sentenced under Subsections A(2) of Section 4208, places any especial gloss on his right to have early "consideration," or whether it merely permits the Board to consider his case at a time less than the normal period of one-third of the sentence.

We think the order dismissing the case for failure to state a claim on which relief could be granted was error, for there is nothing but the government's brief to challenge the assertion by the appellant that he was denied elements of fundamental fairness—not because he was not given a parole, but because when the procedures were invoked his case was not treated with the consideration that was contemplated either by the statute or by the Board's regulations.

The judgment is REVERSED and the case is REMANDED for further proceedings not inconsistent with this opinion.

GEWIN, Circuit Judge, dissenting:

With respectful regard for the views expressed by the majority I am unable to agree with the opinion, and therefore dissent. By equating "some elements of due process" which are required in the revocation of parole with proceedings by the Parole Board to determine whether parole should be granted to an incarcerated prisoner, the opinion opens a vast new area of federal litigation. This case illustrates the truth of the statement of Mr. Justice Douglas "that any principle once announced may in time gain a momentum not warranted by the exigencies of its creation." 397 U.S. 99, 110, 25 L.Ed.2d 146, 155.

In the very beginning it should be noted that this is not a case in which the Board of Parole has failed to give consideration to appellant's eligibility for release on parole. He has not languished in prison without notice or attention by the Board. Indeed the Board has conducted two hearings and Scarpa has twice been considered for parole by the Board within three years after his sentence. See *Scarpa v. U.S. Board of Parole,* 453 F.2d 891. . . .

The doctrine of finality in criminal cases is gasping for life and it may not survive. Under judge-made rules the criminal processes bog down, the courts are crowded with litigation and many criminal cases are never terminated. It is not now enough under the majority decision to have a police investigation, arrest, appearance before a federal magistrate, investigation and indictment by a duly constituted grand jury, arraignment, assurance of counsel, trial, direct appeal, and repeated re-examination by habeas corpus or motions for post-conviction relief. In addition to all of the foregoing procedures the majority concludes that courts should review the actions and conduct of the U.S. Board of Parole, and if I understand the decision, we are to disregard the expertise of the Board and review its actions as though it were a trial court. This is not a proper function of the courts. The routine granting or denial of parole should be left to the Board. Unless there are exceptional circumstances such as fraud, conduct beyond the authority granted by statute, or some other exceptional circumstances, the court should not interfere with the Board. . . .

The appellant contends that there was a lack of minimal standards of due process in hearings before the Parole Board as required by the due process clause of the Fifth Amendment. In his brief on petition for rehearing counsel for appellant contends that appellant is entitled to the following:

1. A hearing before an objective and impartial examiner;
2. adequate notice of that hearing;
3. an opportunity to confront and cross-examine adverse witnesses;
4. a right to retain counsel;
5. a determination stating reasons therefor and an indication of the evidence and rules relied upon. . . .

If the majority opinion becomes the law of this circuit, it is my prediction that in the future there will be cases claiming that the *examiner* was not impartial; that *notice* of the hearing was not sufficient; that the opportunity to *confront* and *cross-examine witnesses* was not sufficiently protected; *counsel* was ineffective; and that the *findings of fact* and *conclusions of law* were not supported by the evidence produced. . . .

F. Parole Supervision

1. PAROLE CONDITIONS

Certificates of Parole

STATE OF CONNECTICUT, BOARD OF PAROLE, PAROLE AND CONDITIONS OF PAROLE

THE BOARD OF PAROLE STATE OF CONNECTICUT, by authority granted to it in Public Act 152, having reviewed and considered your case believes that you will necessarily complete your term outside an institution and whereby grants parole to you, effective on _____ 19____. It is intended that you be released on said date, or as soon thereafter as a satisfactory parole program can be arranged for you and approved by the Commissioner of Correction. This parole is granted to and accepted by you, subject to the following conditions and with the knowledge that the Commissioner of Correction has the authority, at any time, in case of violation of the Conditions of Parole, to cause your detention and return you to his custody pending a review of your case by the Board of Parole, and further, that the Board of Parole has the authority to revoke parole if, in its judgment, you have violated any of the following conditions.

1. Upon release from the institution, you must follow the instructions of the institutional Parole Officer (or other designated authority of the Division of Parole) with regard to reporting to your supervising parole officer, and/or fulfilling any other obligations.

2. You must report to your Parole Officer when instructed to do so and must permit your Parole Officer or any Parole Officer to visit you at your home and place of employment at any time.

3. You must work steadily, and you must secure the permission of your Parole Officer before changing your residence or your employment, and you must report any change of residence or employment to your Parole Officer within twenty-four hours of such change. It is your responsibility to keep your Parole Officer informed at all times concerning your place of residence, your place of employment, and any arrests, convictions, or investigations by law enforcement officials.

4. You must submit written reports as instructed by your Parole Officer.

5. You must not leave the State of Connecticut without first obtaining permission from your Parole Officer.

6. You must not apply for a Motor Vehicle Operator's License, or own, purchase, or operate any motor vehicle without first obtaining permission from your Parole Officer.

7. You must not marry without first obtaining written permission from your Parole Officer.

8. You must not own, possess, use, sell, or have under your control at any time, any deadly weapons or firearms.

9. You must not possess, use, or traffic in any narcotic, hallucinatory, or other harmful drugs in violation of the law.

10. You must support your dependents, if any, and assume toward them all moral and legal obligations.

11. A. You shall not consume alcoholic beverages to excess.
    B. You shall totally abstain from the use of alcoholic beverages or liquors. (Strike out either A or B, leaving whichever clause is applicable.)

12. You are not to correspond, visit or attempt to contact inmates of correctional institutions or their friends and relatives without the permission of your Parole Officer.

13. You must comply with all laws and conduct yourself as a good citizen. You must show by your attitude, cooperation, choice of associates, and places of amusement and recreation that you are a proper person to remain on parole.

Special Conditions

Whenever problems arise or you do not understand what is expected of you, consult with your Parole Officer as it is his responsibility to help you in the interpretation of the conditions of this parole, which can be changed only by the Board of Parole.

STATE OF CONNECTICUT BOARD OF PAROLE

Attest: _____
Chairman

Agreement of Parolee

I have read, or have had read to me, the foregoing conditions of my parole, and I fully understand them and I agree to abide by you and strictly follow them, and I fully understand the penalties involved should I in any manner violate any of the foregoing conditions.

I do hereby waive extradition to the State of Connecticut from any state in the union or the District of Columbia and from any territory, commonwealth or country outside the continental United States, and also agree that I will not contest any effort to return me to the United States or to the State of Connecticut.

_____
Parolee

_____
Date

WITNESS:

_____

Form B.P.1

CERTIFICATE OF PAROLE, UNITED STATES BOARD OF PAROLE

Parole Form H-8
(Rev. Jan. 1967)
(Formerly Parole Form 17)

THE UNITED STATES BOARD OF PAROLE

Washington, D.C. 20537

CERTIFICATE OF PAROLE

Know all Men by these Presents:

It having been made to appear to the United States Board of Parole that ...., Register No. ...., a prisoner in the .... is eligible to be PAROLED, and that there is a reasonable probability that he WILL REMAIN AT LIBERTY WITHOUT VIOLATING THE LAWS, and it being the opinion of the said United States Board of Parole that the release of this person is not incompatible with the welfare of society, it is ORDERED by the said United States Board of Parole that he be PAROLED on ...., 19......, and that he remain within the limits of .... until ...., 19......; or in the event of a committed fine or a committed fine and costs, until the same have been paid or he has been discharged under the provisions of Section 3569, Title 18, U.S. Code, or until other action may be taken by the said United States Board of Parole.

Given under the hands and the seal of the United States Board of Parole this .... day of ...., nineteen hundred and ....

UNITED STATES BOARD OF PAROLE,

By ....
Parole/Youth Division Executive.

[seal]

Adviser ....

Probation Officer ....

This CERTIFICATE OF PAROLE will become effective on the date of release shown on the reverse side. If the parolee's continuance on parole becomes incompatible with the welfare of society, or if he fails to comply with any of the conditions listed on the reverse side, he may be retaken on a warrant issued by a Member of the Board of Parole, and reimprisoned pending a hearing to determine if the parole should be revoked.

Conditions of Parole

1. You shall go directly to the district shown on this CERTIFICATE OF PAROLE (unless released to the custody of other authorities). Within three days after your arrival, you shall report to your parole adviser if you have one, and to the United States Probation Officer whose name appears on this Certificate.

2. If you are released to the custody of other authorities, and after your release from physical custody of such authorities, you are unable to report to the United States Probation Officer to whom you are assigned within three days, you shall report instead to the nearest United States Probation Officer.

3. You shall not leave the limits fixed by this CERTIFICATE OF PAROLE without written permission from the probation officer.

4. You shall notify your probation officer immediately of any change in your place of residence.

5. You shall make a complete and truthful written report (on a form provided for that purpose) to your probation officer between the first and third day of each month, and on the final day of parole. You shall also report to your probation officer at other times as he directs.

6. If in any emergency you are unable to get in touch with your parole adviser, or your probation officer or his office, you shall communicate with the United States Board of Parole, Department of Justice, Washington, D.C. 20537.

7. You shall not violate any law. You shall get in touch immediately with your probation officer or his office if you are arrested or questioned by a law-enforcement officer.

8. You shall not enter into any agreement to act as an "informer" or special agent for any law-enforcement agency.

9. You shall work regularly unless excused by your probation officer, and support your legal dependents, if any, to the best of your ability. You shall report immediately to your probation officer any changes in employment.

10. You shall not drink alcoholic beverages to excess. You shall not purchase, possess, use, or administer marihuana or narcotic or other habit-forming or dangerous drugs, unless prescribed or advised by a physician. You shall not frequent places where such drugs are illegally sold, dispensed, used or given away.

11. You shall not associate with persons who have a criminal record unless you have permission of your probation officer. Nor shall you associate with persons engaged in criminal activity.

12. You shall not have firearms (or other dangerous weapons) in your possession without the written permission of your probation officer, following prior approval of the United States Board of Parole.

I have read, or had read to me, the foregoing conditions of parole. I fully understand them and know that if I violate any of them, I may be recommitted. I also understand that special conditions may be added or modifications of any condition may be made by the Board of Parole at any time.

....
            (Name)   (Register No.)

WITNESSED ....

....
            (Title)   (Date)

UNITED STATES BOARD OF PAROLE:

The above-named person was released on the .... day of ...., 19 ......, with a total of .... remaining to be served.

....
                      (Warden or Superintendent)

UNITED KINGDOM HOME OFFICE, PROBATION AND AFTERCARE DEPARTMENT, LICENCE, CRIMINAL JUSTICE ACT 1967

> Home Office
> Probation and After-Care Department
> Romney House
> Marsham Street
> LONDON S.W.1

The Secretary of State hereby authorises the release on licence of   within fifteen days of the date hereof, who shall on release and during the period of this licence comply with the following conditions or any other conditions which may be substituted from time to time.

1. He shall report to the officer in charge of the probation and after-care office at forthwith.
2. He shall place himself under the supervision of whichever probation officer is nominated for this purpose from time to time.
3. He shall keep in touch with his probation officer in accordance with that officer's instructions.
4. He shall inform his probation officer at once if he changes his address or changes or loses his job.
5. He shall be of good behaviour and lead an industrious life.

This licence expires on   unless previously revoked.

NOTES

The Theory of Imposing Conditions of Parole

Note 1.

LEONARD ORLAND

Politics and Parole*

... If the board member concludes that parole is warranted, he must still wrestle with the problem of what conditions of behavior to impose on the parolee, violation of which may lead to reimprisonment. The theory of imposing conditions is based on the assumption that, given the risk that the parolee may commit a new crime, it is best to closely supervise, control and structure the parolee's behavior and return him to prison if he cannot adjust to these conditions rather than wait for the actual commission of a new crime.

* *The New York Times,* Jan. 29, 1972, p. 29.

Note 2.

LEONARD ORLAND

Conditions of Parole**

Let me briefly mention a couple of problems with parole conditions and parole revocations. Conditions are a hodge-podge. They have historical antecedents directly going back to indentured servitude.

I don't think there is a single parole condition that is common to every state. There is no empirical validation for the assumption that you are going to reduce recidivism rates considerably if you have a lot of conditions than if you have a few conditions.

The English system imposes five simple conditions, including requirements that the parolee be industrious, not violate the law, and report to the parole officer. These conditions come closest, in my view, to what you need.

** Testimony of Leonard Orland before Subcommittee #3, House Judiciary Committee, 92d Cong., 2d Sess., March, 1962.

The concern about parole conditions is the risk of arbitrary power. You don't want in the hands of parole officers the power to call people back to finish a sentence depending on caprice and will, to say you can't associate with undesirable people, the kind of things a parolee will do anyway. To that extent you create some risks of arbitrary action without any real notion that those conditions are really needed.

NOTE

The Prevailing Conditions of Parole

NAT R. ARLUKE

*A Summary of Parole Rules— Thirteen Years Later**

In 1956 a summary was published of the conditions of parole then existing in each of the forty-eight states. The general conclusions reached at that time were that in many states the conditions were entirely too numerous to be of much real value, that some of the statements listed as conditions were actually interpretations of policy or were included in the penal statutes of the state, that many of the regulations were unrealistic and unenforceable, and that the basic rules were not uniform throughout the states. . . .

Currently, as was the case thirteen years ago, no single parole regulation is common to all the states, as evidenced by the chart.

In the states that have added regulations, marked increases occur in the categories of motor vehicle registration and license restrictions; narcotics usage; support of delinquents; the purchase and possession of weapons and the use of hunting licenses; limitations on out-of-state, county, or community travel; compulsory agreements to waive extradition; limitations of indebtedness; and approval of marriage and divorce.

Some states—notably California, Colorado, Mississippi, and Missouri—have decreased the number of conditions; most have increased them. . . .

Some parole conditions are moralistic, most are impractical, others impinge on human rights, and all reflect obsolete criminological conceptions. On the whole they project a percept of a man who does not exist. Nevertheless, prisoners are required to sign the agreement, obviously with many reservations, before being paroled. The most tangible result is the growing number of violations of the conditions imposed.

Conditions should be regarded as aids to successful adjustment rather than as punitive restrictions. Today, courts and paroling authorities are retreating from long lists of specific prohibitions and restrictions. At one time, conditions were predominantly couched in negative terms, and many such prohibitions are still in use: the parolee is required to be in at certain hours and is forbidden to touch intoxicating liquor or to frequent places where it is sold, to own a car, to get married, to leave town, and to participate in a variety of similar activities. The current trend is to frame conditions in positive terms: the parolee is expected to support his dependents, is encouraged to work steadily, is expected to live a law-abiding life and to confer with his parole officer on all basic decisions, etc. A long list of prohibitions was, I believe, characteristic of the era when probation and parole officers were generally untrained, the service was new, and the list was deemed capable of controlling behavior. Courts and paroling authorities have since discovered that improved selection of parole officers makes it possible to place more discretion in their hands and that casework services are more effective than mechanical rules.

Conditions of parole should be realistic and flexible. Each case should be judged separately, taking into consideration the problems, needs, and capacity of the individual offender. Conditions that cannot be enforced invite violations.

* Reprinted, with permission of the National Council on Crime and Delinquency, from *Crime and Delinquency,* April 1969, pp. 267–74.

Figure 11-10. COMPARISON OF PAROLE REGULATIONS

Regulation	Federal Parole	Alabama	Alaska	Arizona	Arkansas	California	Colorado	Connecticut	Delaware	Florida	Georgia	Hawaii	Idaho	Illinois	Indiana	Iowa	Kansas	Kentucky	Louisiana	Maine	Maryland	Massachusetts	Michigan	Minnesota	Mississippi	Missouri	Montana	Nebraska	Nevada	New Hampshire	New Jersey	New Mexico	New York	North Carolina	North Dakota	Ohio	Oklahoma	Oregon	Pennsylvania	Rhode Island	South Carolina	South Dakota	Tennessee	Texas	Utah	Vermont	Virginia	Washington	West Virginia	Wisconsin	Wyoming
1. Liquor usage	4	2	2	2	2	2	2	2	2	2	2	2	2	2	2	2	2	2		2	2	2	2	2			2	2	2	2	4	2	2	2	2	2	2	2	2	2	2	2	2	2	2	2	2	2	2	2	2
2. Change of employment or living quarters	1	1	1		1	1	1	1	1	1	1	1	1	1	1	1	1	1	1	1	1	1	1	1			1	1	1	1		1	1	1	1	1			1	1	1	1	1	1	1	1	1	1		1	
3. Undesirable associations or correspondence	1	2	2	2	2	2	2	2	2	2	2	2	2	2	2	2	2	2		2	2	2	2	1	2	2	2	2	2	2	2	2	2	2	2	2	2	2	2	2	2	1	2	2	2		2	2	2		2
4. Filing written reports	3	3	3	3	3			3		3	3	3	3	3	3	3	3	3		3	3	3	3	3		3	3	3	3	3	3	3	3	3	3	3	3	3	3	3			3	3	3		3	3		3	3
5. Approval of marriage (or of divorce*)	1	1	1		1		1	1	1*	1	1	1	1	1	1	1	1	1		1	1	1	1	1		1	1	1	1	1*	1*	1*	1	1	1	1	1	1	1	1	1	1	1	1	1			1	1	1	1
6. Out-of-state travel	1	1	1		1	1	1	1	1	1	1	1	1	1	1	1	1	1	1	1	1	1	1	1		1	1	1	1	1	1	1	1	1	1	1	1	1	1	1	1	1	1	1	1	1	1	1	1	1	1
7. First arrival report	3	3	3	3	3	3	2	3	1	3	3		3	3	3		3	3	3	3	3	3	3	3				3	3	3	3	3	3	3	3	3	3	3	3	3	3	3	3	3	3			3		3	3
8. Motor vehicle registration and license		1	1		1	1	1	1	1	1	1	1	1	1	1	1	1	1		1	1	1	1	1	1	1	1	1	1	1	1	1	1	1	1	1	1	1	1	1	1	1	1	1	1	1	1	1	1	1	1
9. Narcotics usage	2	2					2	2			2			2		2				2	2									2	2			2		2	2		2		2		2	2							
10. Participation in anti-narcotics program	3		3			3								3											2*	1																		3							
11. Support dependents	3	3	3	3			3	3	3	3	3	3	3	3	3	3	3	3	3	3	3	3	3	3	3	3	3	3		3	3	3	3	3	3	3	3	3	3	3	3			3	3	3	3	3			
12. Weapons; hunting license	1	1	1			2	1	2	1	1	2	2	2	2	2					1	1	1	1	1			2	2		1	1	1	2	1	1	2	2	2	1	1			1	1		1		2	2		
13. Out-of-county or community travel (limited to specific area*)	1	1			1	1	1	1	1	1	1	1	1	1	1		1	1	1	1	1	1	1	1		1	1	1	1	1	1	1	1	1	1	1	1	1	1	1	1	1	1	1	1	1	1	1	1	1	1
14. Waiver of extradition		3	3	3	3		3	3	3	3	3		3	3	3	3	3	3	3	3	3	3	3	3	3	3	3	3	3	3	3	3	3	3	3	3	3	3	3	3	3		3	3	3	3	3	3	3	3	3
15. Indebtedness		1								1		2	1	2	1		a	1		1	1		1	1	1			1	1					1	1	1	1	1		1			1	1	1	1		1			
16. Curfew												b		c									6	6						6					6						6	6	c	6	6						
17. Civil rights; suffrage		7					3*							2															2														2								
18. Gambling					2					2																										1*															
19. Airplane (or power boat*) license	3		3						3	3						1*				3								3			3	3	3	3					1												
20. Report if arrested												5																			5	5		5					3												
21. Treatment for V.D.		3	3			3	3	3	3	7	3		3					3										3			3	3	7						3			6									
22. Credit on return as P.V.		3								3	3									3											3	3	3*						5												
23. Criminal registration	3	3			3	3		3		3	3		3				3					3					3				3	3	3						3			2									
24. Church attendance	3	3																																																	
25. Permit home or job visits (search*)	3	3	3	3	3	3	3	3	3	3	3	3	3	3	3	3	3	3	3	3	3	3	3	3	3	3	3	3	3	3	3	3	3	3	3	3	3	3	3	3	3	3	3	3	3	3	3	3	3	3	3
26. Comply with law	3	3	3	3	3	3	3	3	3	3	3	3	3	3	3	3	3	3	3	3	3	3	3	3	3	3	3	3	3	3	3	3	3	3	3	3	3	3	3	3	3	3	3	3	3	3	3	3	3	3	3
27. Maintain gainful employment (inform employer of parole*)	3	3																															3*					3*													
28. Return to county (or state*) of commitment													1*													1*											1*														
29. Act as informer	2											2																																							

Key: 1. Must have permission. 2. Prohibited. 3. Compulsory. 4. Allowed but not to excess. 5. May receive. 6. Reasonable hour. 7. Advised or recommended.
a. 50 miles. b. 11:00 p.m. c. 10:30 p.m.

Reprinted, with permission of the National Council on Crime and Delinquency, from *Crime and Delinquency*, April 1969, pp. 272–73.

ARCINIEGA V. FREEMAN
404 U.S. 4 (1971)
Supreme Court of the United States

PER CURIAM.

Petitioner's parole was revoked by the Federal Parole Board because of association with other ex-convicts. In a petition for habeas corpus, petitioner contended that the record did not disclose any evidence in support of this conclusion. The Court of Appeals for the Ninth Circuit sustained the revocation on the sole ground that petitioner worked at a restaurant-nightclub that employed other ex-convicts. 439 F. 2d 776.

The Parole Board has wide authority to set conditions, 18 U.S.C. § 4203 (a), and here petitioner was forbidden to "associate" with other ex-convicts. But the Board's own regulations require "satisfactory evidence" of a parole violation to justify an arrest warrant. 28 CFR § 2.35. We do not believe that the parole condition restricting association was intended to apply to incidental contacts between ex-convicts in the course of work on a legitimate job for a common employer. Nor is such occupational association, standing alone, satisfactory evidence of non-business association violative of the parole restriction. To so assume would be to render a parolee vulnerable to imprisonment whenever his employer, willing to hire ex-convicts, hires more than one. Absent a clear Parole Board directive to this effect, we cannot sustain the judgment of the Court of Appeals that on-the-job contact with fellow employees with police records is sufficient evidence of parole violation. If there is in this record other evidence of forbidden association or evidence of other parole violations, neither the Court of Appeals nor the United States has identified it.

The motion for leave to proceed *in forma pauperis* is granted, the petition for a writ of certiorari is granted, and the judgment of the Court of Appeals is

Reversed.

SOBELL V. REID
327 F. Supp. 1294 (1971)
United States District Court, Southern District of New York

FRANKEL, District Judge.

On April 5, 1951, Morton Sobell was given a maximum prison sentence of 30 years for conspiring, between 1944 and 1950, to transmit national defense (atomic bomb) information to the Soviet Union. On January 14, 1969, upon the basis of "good time" earned, 18 U.S.C. § 4161, he was mandatorily released, 18 U.S.C. § 4163. This means that he is now "deemed as if released on parole until the expiration of the maximum term * * * for which he was sentenced less one hundred and eighty days," 18 U.S.C. § 4164, or, specifically, until September 26, 1980. Thus subjected to the continuing jurisdiction of the United States Parole Board, Sobell was presented upon his release with a "Certificate of Mandatory Release," providing that until the end of the period during which he was to remain "as if on parole" he would be governed by the standard "Conditions of Parole" set out on the reverse side of the Certificate. . . . Sobell refused to sign the Certificate, but that appears to be of no consequence for present purposes. The court has proceeded upon the view that the Conditions, to the extent they may validly do so, govern Sobell until 1980.

Of most direct interest in the case now before the court is the third Condition, under which Sobell was not to go outside the limits of the Southern District of New York "without written permission from the probation officer." On a number of occasions after his release, he sought and obtained permission to travel to, and speak at, various places—a Philadelphia television guest appearance, a Cleveland radio and television show, and a speech to students at the Massachusetts Institute of Technology. On other occasions, however, similar requests have been denied:

(1) A request for leave to be in Washington, D. C., for a November 15, 1969, demonstration against the war in Vietnam.

(2) A similar request relating to a demonstration on April 15, 1970.

(3) A request for permission to go to Los Angeles, California, to speak on prison conditions at a banquet sponsored by *People's World*, a newspaper which, as stipulated for purposes of this suit, "is closely identified with the Communist Party * * * and is generally reflective of the positions taken on public issues by the Communist Party."

Early in April of last year Sobell commenced the present suit against the Chairman and Members of the Parole Board in the District Court for the District of Columbia. He charged that defendants' refusal to permit him to travel invaded First Amendment rights. He seeks, to quote the amended complaint now before us, a declaratory judgment and "appropriate equitable relief in the form of injunction or mandamus enforcing plaintiff's rights and defendants' responsibilities under the First and Fifth Amendments to the Constitution of the United States." On defendants' motion the case was transferred to this court. . . . The court is confronted now with what amount to cross-motions for summary judgment. It is agreed all around that the repeated and projected refusals of travel for purposes of speech and assembly present live questions (subject to the dispute considered later as to the court's jurisdiction) and that there is a record of undisputed facts sufficient for decision. Upon a more detailed review of the facts, and for the reasons hereinafter outlined, the court must rule for the plaintiff. . . .

It is not seriously questioned, or questionable, that plaintiff asserts substantial claims (valid ones, as this court holds when the merits are reached) that the Board of Parole has violated his First Amendment rights. It is not suggested that the Board of Parole, whatever its expertise, has credentials qualifying it to rule finally upon such claims. Indeed, it is not indicated that the Board even purported to make a constitutional adjudication in any remotely adequate, adversary fashion. But it is urged that the Board's action is outside the court's power of review. It would be surprising, and gravely questionable, if Congress had meant to confer such final authority upon *any* administrative agency, particularly one that makes no pretense to learning in constitutional law. It would be bizarre to hold, as the Government's position ultimately entails, that assertions of constitutional rights like those made here may be overridden without ever being faced and decided by any tribunal of any kind. But there is no occasion to become upset over such implications. The Government's position is not soundly based. . . .

Broadly speaking, agency action attacked on constitutional grounds "could be immune from judicial review, if ever, only by the plainest manifestation of congressional intent to that effect." Gonzalez v. Freeman, 118 U.S. App.D.C. 180, 334 F.2d 570, 575 (1964) (Burger, J.), and authorities cited.

. . . It flies in the face of that learning to argue, as the Government does, that we should strain now to read into the law some barrier to a judicial hearing of claims that the Parole Board has violated First Amendment rights. The argument is rejected. We proceed to the merits. . . . Whatever may once have been the case, it is not doubtful now that the Constitution, and notably the First Amendment, reaches inside prison walls. The freedoms of conscience, of thought and of expression, like all the rest of life, are cramped and diluted for the inmate. But they exist to the fullest extent consistent with prison discipline, security and "the punitive regimen of a prison * * *." Brown v. Peyton, 437 F.2d 1228, 1231 (4th Cir. 1971).

While there are differences between prisoners and parolees (or released persons like Sobell), there are none that diminish the protections enjoyed by the latter under the First Amendment. So the principles of the foregoing cases apply here. Cf. Hyland v. Procunier, 311 F.Supp. 749 (N.D.Cal.1970); United States ex rel. Sperling v. Fitzpatrick, 426 F.2d 1161, 1164 (2d Cir. 1970). Tested by those principles, the actions of defendants in denying Sobell's requests to speak and assemble with others in public—and denying to others the hearing of his views on prison conditions and other things—violate the First Amendment. . . . If Sobell means to spy, or to do other things comparable to those for which he sojourned so long in prison, there are surely means more potentially effective in the tunnels and warrens of New York City than in the spotlight of a public banquet in Los Angeles. And if he desires to carry on espionage in Los Angeles, he could easily give a reason for travel of which the Board would approve. We may have slipped at times from the heights on which a new nation planted the banner of freedom, risking the dangers of robust, wide-open vituperative, and, let it be faced, potentially subversive speech. But surely the kind of naive and chimerical fear the Parole Board posits cannot be taken as a respectable, let alone "compelling," justification for denying anyone the right to speak or demonstrate. . . .

Finally, there is the shibboleth of "rehabilitation." The word is, of course, from the domain of what ought to be the Parole Board's professional competence. But it has—at best, on the present empty record—no content. Totalitarian ideologies we profess to hate have styled as "rehabilitation" the process of molding the unorthodox mind to the shape of prevailing dogma. Nothing in what the Board submits contains any explicit suggestion of that sort, and the court infers no such alien premise. But there is nothing explicit of any kind. The court, having asked in vain for enlightenment, is left totally in the dark as to what is supposed to have happened thus far to Sobell by way of rehabilitation, and, more importantly, what is happening to him now, that may be diverted or impaired if he speaks or marches as the Board has forbidden him to do.

The court concludes, in sum, that the Parole Board has shown nothing even "reasonable"—certainly, nothing "necessary" or "compelling"—to justify its chilling course. The plaintiff should be freed of restraints like those of which he complains.

2. THE PAROLE OFFICER: COP OR CASEWORKER?

NOTES

Note 1. Introductory Note

*Observations on the Administration of Parole**

The assumption underlying the institution of parole is that a period of guidance and supervision for persons released from prison is useful for helping offenders avoid further criminal activity. Experience has shown, however, that persons once imprisoned will probably again engage in criminal activity, and evaluation of the offender's conduct immediately following release is necessary to determine whether a further period of incarceration is appropriate. The parole system is designed to fulfill the functions of both guidance and evaluation. On the basis of three months of observing parole officers in Connecticut, this Note will examine how the structure of the correctional system, and the assignment of multiple functions to parole officers, limit the officers' ability to accomplish the goal of rehabilitation.

I. The Conditions of Parole

Conditions of parole are imposed on every parolee. They purport to regulate the parolee's behavior extensively, by prohibiting some activities and requiring him to obtain the permission of his officer for others. As tools for control, conditions provide the trigger for initiating revocation: while not all violations lead to revocation, parole is never revoked unless some specific condition is violated. Critics within and outside the field of corrections have argued that conditions of parole are often so broad as to be both meaningless and unenforceable. Many lawyers see such conditions as unbridled license for arbitrary action. Conditions prohibiting association with "undesirable" characters may, for example, be used to invoke sanctions against parolees whom more political agencies wish to punish, such as a Mafia leader against whom no evidence of crime can be found.

Criticism of the breadth of parole conditions has ignored the importance of these conditions in helping the parole officer fulfill his guidance functions. More important to the officer than the use for revocation is his use of conditions to gather information about the parolee. Commentators, while recognizing that the officer has discretion in defining violations, have failed to analyze this use of parole conditions, focusing instead on the general problem of authority in parole supervision. In practice, although conditions may not be a means of building an effective casework relationship, they are nevertheless an important part of parole casework. But this use of the conditions is made less effective by the existence of the threat that the officer will use the information to initiate revocation.

In their initial conversations with newly-paroled men, officers commonly confront a problem: the parolees have learned about parole through a prison communication system which obtains information almost exclusively from prisoners whose parole has been revoked. The parolee's initial expectations, then, are often shaped by "horror stories" about parole officers which have circulated in prison. A large part of the initial interview must therefore be spent trying to dispel the parolee's preconceptions—convincing him, for example, that a violation of his conditions, even an arrest for a misdemeanor, will not automatically result in revocation of his parole. In reviewing the conditions, the officer emphasizes not the pervasive control they authorize but the minimal extent to which they will be used to restrain the parolee's freedom of action.

At the same time, officers stress that the parolee must inform his officer of any violations. The conditions provide that the officer must be informed whenever the parolee contemplates an important change in his life: a switch of residence, a new job, an impending marriage, an intention to purchase a car. Failure to inform the officer never leads to revocation, though it often elicits a reprimand. Officers use the conditions not as tools to control the parolee's behavior, but as devices to legiti-

---

* Reprinted by permission of The Yale Law Journal Company and Fred B. Rothman and Company from *The Yale Law Journal*, Vol. 79, pp. 698–711 (1970).

mize their inquiries into areas of the parolee's life which bear on his rehabilitation. As such, conditions are a tool for casework. But because of the parolee's ineradicable fear that violation may lead to a return to prison, the parolee is never fully candid. He gives some information, retreats, hedges, and must be coaxed into telling a straight story. The officers, recognizing this reluctance, probe cautiously and support the parolee, often by indicating that the officer's intercession with other agencies will help the parolee.

To further a helping relationship with the parolee, the officer must of course elicit information from him. The use of parole conditions to compel disclosure of this information is not, however, necessary for effective casework: once a parolee trusts the officer and sees him as an advocate, information will flow willingly. Eliminating the fear that information will be used as a basis for revocation will facilitate a relationship of trust, and a full and free flow of information will enable the parole officer to be more effective in his guidance function.

II. The Parole Officer As Social Worker

The parole officer functions in much the same way as a social worker. He is instrumental in channeling the parolee to specialized social agencies such as psychiatric clinics and Halfway Houses. The officer attempts to find every parolee an adequate job by developing contacts and cultivating local businessmen. Routinely the officer intercedes with the Motor Vehicles Bureau to restore the parolee's license. When marital difficulties arise, the officer does some counseling, then guides the parolee to a family service agency. . . .

III. Bureaucracy and Professionalism

The parole officer sees himself as a professional in social work and corrections, but his job places him in a bureaucracy whose need for control often conflicts with the professional's desire for autonomy. . . . The parole officer's claim to professionalism is that he does casework, and his professional norms are those of the social worker, not the policeman. Though there are few standard requirements for becoming a parole officer, many have had social work training, and all feel and exhibit a trained sensitivity to the problems of parolees. . . .

IV. The Threat of Role Conflict

The parole officer's authority to invoke sanctions creates conflicts not only with the parolee but also within himself, by forcing him to choose between the goals of rehabilitation and control. Instead of attempting to reconcile these incompatibles, the parole officer unequivocally pursues the former, choosing to be a social worker rather than an adjunct of the police.

Parole officers must go to police headquarters frequently, since parolees are constantly being picked up. Here and at the prison the parole officer talks with men of a different orientation who also have daily contacts with parolees, prisoners, and criminals. And like policemen, urban parole officers develop extensive contacts in the criminal subculture. They take part in the informal criminal communication system to learn what is happening, who is doing it, and why. Information is given by these contacts with the joint understanding that it is not to be used punitively but rather for insight into the parolee's life, to keep him away from activities that will lead to a return to prison.

Observation revealed a striking absence of police ideology among parole officers. For example, revocation was recommended only after a series of events which indicated to the officer that the parolee would not benefit from continued parole. This lack of a punitive orientation is particularly remarkable given the attention paid to the conflict between custodial and treatment goals in the sociology of corrections. . . .

The Department of Corrections shares and reinforces the parole officer's rehabilitative orientation. Promotion of officers with field experience to supervisor, for example, comports with social work ideology, in which supervisors should be sensitive to the problems faced by men in the field. The social agencies and employers whom the officer contacts also view the parole officer as a social worker.

Others, however, expect parole officers to be like policemen. Parolees often cast their officers in this role. But since the parole officer sees these expectations as based on a misconception of his purpose, the expectations cannot define how he ought to behave; they are simply obstacles to be overcome. The police themselves, however, view the parole officer as an ally. Parole revocation is used as an alternative to prosecution for serious offenses, and is seen as an easier method for reincarceration of the offender.

V. Authority and Social Casework

The casework process in parole is distorted at nearly every point by the fact that the parole officer is authorized by the state, not by the parolee, to invoke penal sanctions against the parolee. Parole officers must accommodate themselves to a situation in which they have power to which social work ideology denies legitimacy, that is, where the client's participation in the relationship is compelled rather than voluntary....

In psychological terms the availability of sanctions transforms the parole officer from one who supports the client's ego to one who sits as super-ego on the parolee's shoulder....

If parole officers were deprived of their authority to invoke sanctions, most of the structural obstacles to rehabilitation would disappear. The officers could then pursue more effectively the rehabilitation work they wish to do. Parole revocation could become more judicial, for those who would revoke parole— the Parole Board—would function as decision-makers in an adversary process. Parole officers would represent the state's interest in rehabilitation and the prosecutor and police its interest in deterrence, while the parolee and his lawyer would advocate the parolee's interest.

The alternative system could be instituted without eliminating the functions of parole. Because the parole system would no longer provide penal sanctions, the parole office would become a specialized social agency devoted to the needs of just-released prisoners. It would, of course, provide some rewards, such as job placement and easier access to other agencies, for those parolees who chose to use it. But no parolee would be compelled to report to the parole office; if he came, he would come because he believed the office was designed to help him. Extensive preparation before release would inform prisoners of the help the parole office could give them, but the ultimate decision to use the office would be the parolee's. The parolee's voluntary approach would, in turn, establish the basis for guidance legitimized by the parolee's consent.

In such a system, the police and not the parole officer would invoke the process of summary revocation. If a parolee had used the parole office, it would be informed, and the parole officer would consult with the police and the parolee. At this point, complex issues of confidentiality arise. An absolute privilege for officer-client communications may be necessary to preserve open communication. Even with such a privilege, however, the parole officer may feel a strain between his professional duty to his client and his citizen's duty to the police, as when a parolee tells the officer of a crime the parolee has committed. But such strains inhere in all professions and are resolved by the canons of professional ethics.

Without the risk that the parole officer will invoke penal sanctions, his professional judgment can be trusted during the period of supervision. Vesting the actual responsibility for revoking parole in the Parole Board would bring the revocation process closer to the due process model and, though limiting the parole officer's responsibility, would not diminish his sense of professionalism. The American legal system assumes that lawyers are better able to balance competing considerations of public policy than are other professionals. By assigning single functions to institutions like parole, the legal system would ensure that the balancing be done openly by officials expected to have special abilities.

Any analysis of the operation of parole and of proposals for change must recognize the dual nature of parole. It is a mechanism of control, but it is also an attempt, sincerely and ably implemented, to guide convicted offenders into socially accepted ways of living. Criticism of the parole system, by focusing only on the first purpose, generates understandable resentment from parole officers. Neither an increase in the officers' authority nor a circumscription of that authority by procedural protections can advance the goal of rehabilitation. Criticism of parole is best directed toward those aspects of the system which inhibit rehabilitation. The guidance function of parole officers may best be strengthened by eliminating entirely their authority to invoke sanctions.

Note 2. The Use of Unlawfully Seized Evidence in Parole Revocation Proceedings

UNITED STATES EX. REL. SPERLING V. FITZPATRICK
426 F.2d 1161 (1970)
United States Court of Appeals, Second Circuit

HAYS, J.

Appellant contends that the Board of Parole could not use the fruits of an unlawful search and seizure as evidence to prove a violation of parole. We cannot accede to this contention and affirm the denial of appellant's petition for a writ of habeas corpus on the ground that the exclusionary rule is not applicable in a parole revocation proceeding. . . . Appellant does not dispute that there was reliable evidence that he had possession of a loaded pistol in violation of one of the conditions of his release.

The exclusionary rule is believed to be a necessary restraint on the adversarial zeal of law enforcement officials. "As it serves this function, the rule is a needed, but grudgingly taken, medicament; no more should be swallowed than is needed to combat the disease." Amsterdam, Search, Seizure, and Section 2255: A Comment, 112 U.Pa.L.Rev. 378, 389 (1964).

A parole revocation proceeding is not an adversarial proceeding. A parolee remains, "while on parole, in the legal custody and under the control of the Attorney General." 18 U.S.C. § 4203 (1964); Anderson v. Corall, 263 U.S. 193, 196, 44 S.Ct. 43, 68 L.Ed. 247 (1923). A parole revocation proceeding is concerned not only with protecting society, but also, and most importantly, with rehabilitating and restoring to useful lives those placed in the custody of the Parole Board. To apply the exclusionary rule to parole revocation proceedings would tend to obstruct the parole system in accomplishing its remedial purposes.

There is no need for double application of the exclusionary rule, using it first as it was used here in preventing criminal prosecution of the parolee and a second time at a parole revocation hearing. The deterrent purpose of the exclusionary rule is adequately served by the exclusion of the unlawfully seized evidence in the criminal prosecution.

KAUFMAN, Circuit Judge (concurring in the result).

I concur in the result reached in my brother Hays's opinion, and in much of what my brother Lumbard says in his concurring opinion. I add only a few words to indicate what I believe would be the preferred manner to resolve the conflicts in purpose and means bared by this case.

There is not, I take it, any basic dispute over the proposition that one is not divested of all his constitutional rights once he is sent to prison.

. . . Nor is there any question of the validity of the principle that "[t]he Bureau of Prisons and the Parole Board operate from the basic premise that prisoners placed in their custody are to be rehabilitated and restored to useful lives * * *." Hyser v. Reed, 115 U.S.App.D.C. 254, 318 F.2d 225, 237 (1963) (en banc), cert. denied, Jamison v. Chappell, 375 U.S. 957.

In order to effectuate these purposes, the United States Parole Board is vested with broad discretion to set the terms and conditions on which a parolee may be released. See 18 U.S.C. § 4203 (1964). . . .

Hence if I were presented with a case in which a condition of parole required the parolee to give a satisfactory account of himself to parole officers, or to permit a search of his person by parole officers, I would be inclined to give that determination by the Parole Board considerable weight. . . .

The underlying rationale for excluding evidence seized after an unreasonable search is to impose "a restraint upon the activities of sovereign authority," Burdeau v. McDowell, 256 U.S. 465, 475, 41 S.Ct. 574, 576, 65 L.Ed. 1048 (1921). The interests involved when we balance individual liberty against the aim of reducing crime are difficult enough to define, and are perhaps even less receptive to evaluation and definition when applied to parolees. For that reason, as well as those I have already mentioned, I would prefer to have the Parole Board, the agency Congress has charged with striking that balance in the first instance, spell out in precise terms—before release—its determination that searches like the one to which Sperling was subjected were reasonable in terms of both overall goals of parole and the dangers of harassment or worse. . . .

I am unwilling at this time to say that the Parole Board's failure to set conditions for searches on parolees requires us to order Sperling released. While I am perhaps less inclined than he to believe that there is any considerable likelihood that sporadic searches by police officers have any great effect on the allocation of parole officers' time between supervision and rehabilitation, I would be reluctant at this time in view of the substantial possibility of disruption of the parole system to rule retroactively that the Parole Board may act only through conditions imposed in advance.

Note 3. The Use of Evidence Unlawfully Seized by a Parole Officer in a Subsequent Trial

UNITED STATES EX. REL. SANTOS V. NEW YORK STATE BOARD OF PAROLE
441 F.2d 1216 (1971)
United States Court of Appeals, Second Circuit

The question for review in this case is whether the appellant, a parolee under the custody of the New York State Board of Parole, was deprived of his Fourth Amendment rights by a search of his residence in Hempstead, New York, without a warrant, conducted by his parole officer in the presence of a police officer after which evidence seized was used by the police for purposes of a new prosecution rather than for the revocation of appellant's parole. . . . Appellant contends that the Fourth Amendment bestows on parolees rights coextensive with those guaranteed to ordinary citizens.

Without attempting to define precisely the extent of Fourth Amendment protection against searches and seizures which a parolee might have in the abstract, it is indisputable that the Fourth Amendment affords protection only against unreasonable searches. A search which would be unlawful if directed against an ordinary citizen may be proper if conducted against a parolee. United States ex rel. Randazzo v. Follette, 418 F.2d 1319, 1322, n. 7 (2nd Cir. 1969).

The Board of Parole in New York State is charged with the duty of "* * * supervising all prisoners released on parole * * * and of making such investigations as may be necessary in connection therewith, of determining whether violation of parole conditions exists in specific cases and of deciding the action to be taken with reference thereto." (New York Correction Law, McKinney's Consol. Laws, c. 43, § 210.) In order to discharge its statutory duty, the Board must obtain all the facts and circumstances surrounding a parole violation. This requires that parole officers be vested with authority to search parolees in situations which would be impermissible if directed against ordinary citizens.

Appellant asserts that the search in question cannot be fairly characterized as a mere act of routine parole supervision since the evidence obtained by his parole officer was utilized in a new criminal prosecution rather than to revoke his existing parole. Thus, appellant contends that his parole officer was not merely seeking to ascertain proof of a parole violation but was acting as an agent of the police to enable them to circumvent constitutional requirements that would otherwise be applicable had they investigated Santos without the assistance of the parole officer. This argument overlooks the fact that a parolee is released on the assumption that not only will he meet the conditions of his parole, but that he will "live and remain at liberty without violating the law" (New York Correction Law § 213). A parole officer is charged with the duty of enforcing these conditions. To hold that evidence obtained by a parole officer in the course of carrying out this duty cannot be utilized in a subsequent prosecution because evidence obtained directly by the police in such a manner would be excluded, would unduly immunize parolees from conviction.

The mere fact that the police officer was the first to suspect that appellant was engaged in criminal activity and related this fact to the parole officer and was present at the subsequent investigation in no way alters the legality of the parole officer's presence. It does not require the suppression of the seized evidence from use in a subsequent criminal prosecution. . . .

The order of the district court is affirmed and the petition for a writ of habeas corpus is dismissed.

G. Parole Revocation

1. EXCERPTS FROM CONNECTICUT PAROLE REVOCATION PROCEEDINGS

The Case of Mark Ronald

PAROLE VIOLATION REPORT

Date: August 31, 1970

STATE OF CONNECTICUT
DEPARTMENT OF CORRECTION
DIVISION OF PAROLE

Subject: Ronald, Mark	Institutional No.: CCIS 88801, 75802
Age: 30	Original Offense: Conspiracy to Violate the State Narc. Act; Larceny
Sentence: 2–5 and 1–4	Date of Sentence: 7/27/66 and 7/23/68
Voted to Parole: 1–13/70	Released on Parole: 3/20/70
Months on Parole: less than 5	Parole Warrant Issued: 7/10/70
Expiration of Maximum Sentence when paroled: 7/4/71	Parole Warrant Executed: 7/10/70

This subject was arrested by the Hartford Police as a result of a narcotics raid on July 9, 1970, at 556 Green Mountain Avenue in Hartford, Connecticut. (See Hartford Police Report to the Prosecutor PD Case #70/11046)

This subject was accused of Possession of Narcotics, to wit, heroin, and conspiracy to possess controlled drugs. He was arrested with 7 other individuals, all charged with the same offense. This subject was bound over to the Superior Court for trial on the above mentioned offenses on 7/10/70.

PRESENT STATUS:

This subject is presently awaiting trial and parole revocation consideration at the Community Correctional Center, Hartford Division.

PAROLE EVALUATION:

This subject was originally released to a parole situation with employment at ABC, Inc., Hartford, and to live with his parents. For some unexplained reason, the subject's initial employment situation did not last for the first week that he was on the job. The subject was subsequently, on 3/30/70, referred to Clark, Inc. for work. Subject began work on 4/1/70. He admitted that he has been using drugs on occasion and had been attempting to admit himself to the Green Mountain Clinic, however, there were no openings. The subject was warned that a continuation of his activities could only lead to his being brought back as a parole violator and that he should continue to work with Clark, Inc. and attempts would be made to get him into the Green Mountain Clinic if needed. The subject was adamant in his request to remain on the street and indicated that he would stop using drugs as he was not at that time in physical need of same. On 4/14/70, this subject began making an appearance at the group session in Hartford, and at that time he indicated that all was going well with his drug problem, however, he was not doing well at work, and had requested to leave work. A job check indicated that the subject was sporadic in his attendance and not generally well accepted by the group at Clark, Inc. Apparently there were some mixed feelings between the subject and some of the white personnel that were at Clark, Inc. in regards to a young black female that was working at that time. On June 11, 1970, the subject indicated that he was out of work once again and was not able to find new work. Subject was told that a job still awaited him at Clark, Inc. if he wanted to work there. He said that he would check around and, if need be, he would go back. This subject was arrested by the Hartford Police on 7/9/70 as a result of a narcotics raid and stake-out. The subject is presently awaiting trial on charges of Possession of Narcotics-Heroin and Conspiracy to Possess Controlled Drugs. This subject was informed of the charges against him on July 10, 1970 and he is presently awaiting trial for the above-mentioned offenses.

RECOMMENDATION:

It is recommended that this subject be returned to the Board of Parole for parole revocation consideration on three counts.

1. This subject has admitted to using drugs while in parole status.
2. This subject has failed to maintain employment during his short parole.
3. This subject has been arrested for the crimes of possession of heroin and conspiracy to violate the State Narcotics Act. By the happenstance of his arrest with known drug users and the association with that element of our society, he has shown that he is not prepared at this time to assume a normal role in the community.

It is the recommendation of the undersigned that this subject be found in violation of the conditions of his parole and that his parole be revoked.

Respectfully submitted,

James Smith
Parole Officer

APPROVED:

Mark Dole
Parole Supervisor

POLICE REPORT TO PROSECUTOR

Circuit Court

THIS REPORT IS *CONFIDENTIAL* AND WILL *NOT* BE AVAILABLE
TO DEFENSE COUNSEL

Police Department—	Hartford
Case No.—	70/11046
Date of Offense—	7/9/70
Place of Offense—	556 Green Mountain Ave., Hartford
Date and Time of Arrest—	7/9/70 3:00 p.m.
Place of Arrest—	556 Green Mountain Ave., Hartford

Circumstances of arrest—The undersigned detectives armed with a search warrant for the above address went to this location at approximately 3:00 p.m. Upon our arrival here, accused Jane Folger was walking towards the side rear doorway. Upon seeing the officers exit from their vehicle, she called to the second floor open window saying "the man is here." At this time she was arrested by detectives Brown and Green. As detectives Adams and Smith came to the rear door a man was observed to run from the kitchen to the living room where he was stopped by detectives entering through the front door. The detectives made their way to the second floor and found accused Abbott, Efrem, Wayne, and Ronald. The windows in this room were all open and the accused were all standing around. Being that the officers made a practice of stationing a man outside the building on a raid to watch for items being thrown out, Detective Green saw glassine bags falling from this open window that the accused were standing around. When the glassine bags were recovered, there were five glassine bags containing white powder (heroin). Also recovered from the house were numerous pieces of silver foil, pills found in the living room area. All of the above items have been marked and sent to the State Lab this date. All accused were booked for various narcotics charges.

Signed: Sgt. From

ADDENDUM TO PAROLE VIOLATION REPORT

Date: 9/17/70

Re: Mark Ronald   Institution No: CCI Somers 88801
                                                                    and 75802

This subject appeared in the Hartford Superior Court on 9/17/70 to answer to charges stemming from an arrest of July 9, 1970 by the Hartford Police Department. This subject was charged with the crimes of Possession of Heroin and Conspiracy to Violate the State Narcotics Act. The subject received a nolle (Prosecutorial Dismissal) on all charges this date.

This subject was remanded to the custody of the Community Correctional Center, Hartford Division for further transfer to the Connecticut Correctional Institution, Somers for parole revocation consideration.

Respectfully submitted,

James Smith
Parole Officer

Approved:

Mark Dole
Parole Officer

Subject was returned to CCI, Somers on 9/22/70.
JAM.

PAROLE HEARING PROGRESS REPORT

Date Prepared: 12/9/69
Name   Ronald, Mark
Number   75802
Age   30 years
Date Received 7/23/68

Parole Hearing Date: 1/13/70
Offense   Larceny
Sentence   1 to 4 yrs.
Parole Elig.   3/22/70
Sentence Exp. 4/3/71

PREVIOUS PAROLE BOARD ACTION
5/6/69—Denied

OTHER BOARD ACTION
None

WARRANTS
None

OTHER SENTENCES—ONE—Serving Parole Violation time on Ronald #88801.
Sentence is running concurrently with present sentence. Parole Elig. on 88801 is 3/22/70 while sentence exp. is 9/3/70.

LAST CLASSIFICATION COMMITTEE ACTION
1/30/69—Assigned to Osborn—not seen by Committee—approved for Silk Screen Printer Program—A special referral.

CUSTODIAL
Subject has received no misconduct reports. He is good in his cell care and personal grooming. Quarters officer states that subject is a good inmate who does as he is told; responds well and keeps to himself.

WORK AND TRAINING
Subject was unassigned after admission until transferred to our minimum facility, the Osborn Division, on 9/3/68 and assigned to the Sign Shop. He was approved for Silk Screen printer program on 1/30/69. He is specifically assigned to Layout and drafting dept. as a Film Cutter. His cooperation is excellent and he is interested in his work. Subject is rated as an average worker.

MEDICAL
No psychiatric findings; inactive T. B.

RELIGION
Subject claims a background in the Abbott Baptist Church of Hartford and he is an occasional chapel attendant. He realizes his trouble stems from his drug problem and he is a member of the drug therapy program. He is also interested in the Get Smart Program.

SOCIAL
Subject is visited bi-monthly by his mother and he has monthly correspondence with her. He does not receive any other mail but he has written several letters to friends, Jane Folger, Ruth Gerold and Sue Warren.

Institutional Acct. Balance 11/26/69: $7.31

ADMISSION SUMMARY

Classif. Hear. Date: August 29, 1968

Commitment Name: Ronald, Mark   Offense: LARCENY
Number: 75802   Sentence: 1 to 4 Yrs.

True Name:	Same	Warrants:	None
Alias:	None	Other Sent.	None
Birth Date:	December 25, 1939	Parole Elig.	March 22, 1970
Birth Place:	Hartford, Conn.	Sent. Exp.	April 3, 1971
Race:		Plea:	Guilty
Military Service:	None	Arrest Date:	June 5, 1968
Marital Status:	Single	Sent. Date:	July 23, 1968
Religion:	Prot.	Date Rec'd:	July 23, 1968
O. A. S. I. No.	52–3040–513	Judge:	Howard
F. B. I. No.	367 D–837	Court:	Hartford
D. C. I. No.	Unknown	Defense Atty.	Zale (PD)
Co-Defendants:	None		

RUNNING CONCURRENTLY WITH PV TIME ON #21888 Ronald (Consp. to Viol. Uniform State Narc. Drug Act Parole Elig.: 7/22/69 Sent. Exp.: 9/3/70) SEE INSTITUTIONAL ADJUSTMENT ATTACHED #88801—Ronald

RELIGION:

This newly-admitted subject claims a background in the Abbott Baptist Church of Hartford and while here on a previous sentence was an occasional chapel attendant. He has not been able to control his drug dependency and committed this offense in order to get the funds to keep up his habit. He says he wants to receive treatment for his drug dependency.

EDUCATION:

Subject is eligible for Day School.

I.Q.: 101 Beta   MATHEMATICS: 8.3   GRADE PLACEMENT: 8.6

READING: 9.9   LANGUAGE: 7.6

MEDICAL:

HEIGHT: 5'8-1/2   WEIGHT: 166

VISION: DV 20/30   20/30   NV J–6   J–6

REMARKS: None

WORK LIMITATIONS: None

HOUSING LIMITATIONS: None

8/22/68 add

CSP #463

PRIOR INSTITUTIONAL ADJUSTMENT AT CONN. STATE PRISON

	NAME & NUMBER:	RONALD, Mark #75802
PRIOR:	NAME:	RONALD, Mark
	NUMBER:	#88801
	OFFENSE:	CONSPIRACY TO VIOLATE CT. NARC. ACT.
	SENTENCE:	2–5 Yrs.
	DATE OF COMMITMENT:	7/27/66

This subject has also been previously committed to this institution None times
                                                                    how many
under number (s) _____ .

WORK: Subject held work assignments in Clothing Factory
4/10/67 Trans. to Osborn Division Detail #4 Laundry Pick-up.
_____
_____
_____

His work was considered _____ .

CONDUCT: Subject's CONDUCT was considered Good .
Subject received the following MISCONDUCT REPORTS: None .
                                                   how many

Any Misconducts that should be noted: - - - - - -
_____
_____
_____

RELEASE DATA:
Subject was denied Parole - - - - - - - - - times.

Subject was voted to Parole on 10/4/67   Paroled 1/5/68

Subject was Returned for a Parole Violation V.P.6/10/68   Returned PV 7/23/68

Subject Discharged on _____

REMARKS:
RB/add
8/22/68

CRIMINAL HISTORY

Date	Location	Charge	Disposition
3-18-58	Hartford, Conn.	Theft	60 days, susp., prob. lyr.
5-27-61	New London, Conn.	B & E	90 days, susp., prob. lyr.
1-25-62	Waterbury, Conn.	Shoplifting	15 days, susp.
1-1-63	Hartford, Conn.	Br. of Peace	Nolled
2-26-65	North Haven, Conn.	Rob. W/Viol & Carr. Weap in MV	1 Yr. State Jail
7-27-66	Hartford, Conn.	Consp. to Violate USNDA	CSP #88801 2-5 Yrs. Par. 1-5-68; Ret PV 7-23-68 and Conc. with New Number.

THE REVOCATION HEARING

THE CHAIRMAN: You know Dr. Clark and myself and this is Professor Brock, the other member of the Board. I think you know the purpose of this hearing today before the Board. It's for the Board to make a decision concerning the status of your parole. First you were reported in violation of your parole. Now you requested a hearing. Is this because you don't think you violated your parole or for some other reason?

MR. RONALD: I don't think I violated my parole.

THE CHAIRMAN: Okay. You were charged with admitting using drugs when you were on parole, failing to maintain regular employment while you were on parole, and associating with other drug users while you were on parole. Now you may say what you'd like to say if you want to.

MR. RONALD: The first of the charges is not true. As far as the association is concerned, what happened was a coincidence. I was going to a house—the house where I lived near a police station.

At that time I didn't know that any of these people were using narcotics.

THE CHAIRMAN: Did you know the people?

MR. RONALD: I knew the people. I didn't know they were using narcotics. As a matter of fact, my going into the house was because I was called. I didn't just set out from my house to go to that house. I stopped at the bank to draw out some money. I was walking down Green Mountain Avenue and some fellow called me from his window. I was up about a minute and the police came and arrested everybody in the house for possession of controlled drugs. This was the only association.

THE CHAIRMAN: I thought you worked regularly.

MR. RONALD: I was working for Mr. Jim Brown doing landscape gardening to the middle of June.

THE CHAIRMAN: What did you do after that?

MR. RONALD: Then I couldn't find a job. I've got applications in for about 9 or 10 different things. I wrote several letters for jobs. At about three o'clock, my mother got me up to go to the bank. I withdrew some money and I was walking down the street and I saw this fellow in the window I hadn't seen for a while. I called to him and he told me to come on in. When I went in I didn't know who was in the house.

THE CHAIRMAN: You tried to get in Green Mountain Narcotics Clinic. You were turned down because they didn't have an opening for you?

MR. RONALD: The parole officer told me to go and see the people at Green Mountain Clinic and see if they have an opening. Which I did.

PROFESSOR BROCK: Mr. Ronald, there are just a couple of small things I want to try and clear up. First of all, let me see if I understand correctly that the offense for which you are in here, conspiracy to violate the drug act and larceny, took place while you were on parole from a prior narcotics offense. Is that correct?

MR. RONALD: Yes, and no. I had two prison numbers as you know. First I came in here for conspiracy to violate the narcotic act.

PROFESSOR BROCK: And the other is larceny. But I'm talking about the offense preceding both the narcotics and the larceny. You were paroled and you were returned as a parole violator, you were paroled from your sentence that involved narcotics violation then you violated that with a new offense. What was that new offense?

MR. RONALD: Larceny.

PROFESSOR BROCK: Okay. Was that to support the habit?

MR. RONALD: Yes.

PROFESSOR BROCK: So the background is that you're an addict, you violated your parole by committing larceny to support your habit. And then you were paroled again on March 20. When you were paroled, did you start using drugs in March and April of this year?

MR. RONALD: In March I took one shot and that's all.

PROFESSOR BROCK: In March you took one shot. Just one shot? That's pretty difficult for me to understand. Someone with a history of addiction. How long have you been an addict? Since at least 1966? That's when you were convicted. That someone who has been an addict since 1966 could come out of prison and take one shot and then walk away from it. You must be an extraordinary human being to be able to do that. You had not enough strength to stop taking the one shot but enough to take one and not two?

MR. RONALD: It was like a test.

PROFESSOR BROCK: A test to see if you could take one and walk away from it?

MR. RONALD: Yes.

PROFESSOR BROCK: I see. So it's your position that that's the only time you were out. Did you go to any drug clinic during that time?

MR. RONALD: I went to Green Mountain Clinic. I talked to—I can't remember his name.

PROFESSOR BROCK: It's unimportant.

MR. RONALD: We talked about what he could do for me.

PROFESSOR BROCK: Did you think you needed the clinic?

MR. RONALD: No.

PROFESSOR BROCK: Did you go because you were ordered to?

MR. RONALD: It was suggested to me.

PROFESSOR BROCK: Did you go because you thought it would help you or did you go because you were ordered to?

MR. RONALD: Well I thought. . . .

THE CHAIRMAN: I'd like to point out the fact, Professor, that what Mr. Ronald says is contrary to the parole violation report, which states that he admitted at that time to using drugs and stated that he himself had been to Green Mountain Clinic but that there were no openings. I just point that out.

PROFESSOR BROCK: I want to follow through with regard to your work. You were working at Clark, Inc. You quit that job?

MR. RONALD: Yes, I had to. I was a racial issue, Professor. In this particular job there was one black woman. We had four black men and I think there were 8 or 9 Caucasians. The treatment that this woman got from the Caucasian men was absurd.

PROFESSOR BROCK: I understand that there was an incident. I wasn't sure. So essentially, the incident was your not standing for the putting down of the black woman. Okay. I just wanted to understand that. So you left that job. Did you have any other job?

MR. RONALD: Yes. I started working for Jackson.

PROFESSOR BROCK: And then you left and did you have any other job? Did you attempt to get any other job?

MR. RONALD: Yes.

PROFESSOR BROCK: Did you go to the unemployment office?

MR. RONALD: I went to the unemployment office. I had applications there.

PROFESSOR BROCK: How far did you go in school?

MR. RONALD: I graduated high school.

PROFESSOR BROCK: And were any other jobs offered to you? Through the unemployment office?

MR. RONALD: No sir.

PROFESSOR BROCK: No jobs at all were offered to you? I'm not asking whether they were satisfactory or not.

MR. RONALD: They were talking to me about going to school.

PROFESSOR BROCK: I see. Did you go down to Manpower to get day jobs?

MR. RONALD: No.

PROFESSOR BROCK: The two things that are hardest for me to accept have to do with two extraordinary coincidences that just sort of test my ability to accept things. One of them is that an addict with a history of addiction going back to 1966 admits to taking one shot and walking away from it. And couple that with the extraordinary coincidence of happening to be at a narcotics bust at the precise moment and you were there no more than 60 seconds when the bust takes place. That's extraordinary bad luck. And it's just that I have to reach very hard to accept that. You can see my difficulty?

MR. RONALD: Okay, then again I don't think that you can deem it impossible or highly improbable for a man. . . .

PROFESSOR BROCK: It's theoretically possible. Both of the things you say are theoretically possible. But put them together and it becomes highly improbable.

MR. RONALD: This is true. These things are true.

PROFESSOR BROCK: I see. Do you snort or use dope?

MR. RONALD: If the parole officer thought or knew that I was using narcotics, wouldn't he have given me a urine test?

PROFESSOR BROCK: Not necessarily because it is almost impossible to get them examined in time. This is one of the problems.

MR. RONALD: When I was on parole before I had a urine test.

THE CHAIRMAN: We're not going to turn around, Mr. Ronald, and put the blame on the parole officer. You've tried to turn everything around, everything in the report, you said is not true. Now you say that if he thought you were taking drugs that he would have had you tested. But the fact is he said that you admitted to him that you had taken them so there wasn't any reason to have a test. You admitted it. But he did not say once. You say once.

MR. RONALD: Yes, but if I admitted more than once he would probably take me to the prison.

THE CHAIRMAN: I don't know. The parole officer normally gives every man every chance that he possibly can. It's a last resort when he brings a man back.

MR. RONALD: I'm just trying to be truthful.

THE CHAIRMAN: This will be up to the Board to decide.

MR. RONALD: I mean the only side that I can give is my side. I have a good witness in my mother. She was with me at the time. She hadn't reached her house before she said she heard sirens blowing. The man who let me into the house, he knew that I was only there a minute. There was another fellow that came in behind me. He was coming from the store.

THE CHAIRMAN: Had you ever been there before?

MR. RONALD: No sir.

THE CHAIRMAN: Never been in that house before? Never been with those people before?

MR. RONALD: I'd been with those people before.

PROFESSOR BROCK: Now, you've been an addict on the street a long time and now it's one thing for someone to come in with no history of addiction and say, well, I didn't know this person was an addict or that person was an addict, but I just happened to be around there in a bust, but that again is difficult to accept, given your past history. I'm not talking about whether you did anything wrong, I'm talking about your knowing or not knowing who's on the street and who's on and who's not.

MR. RONALD: It can get complicated. Here is a case where I see one person in the window. He said, hey, what's happened? I never knew this man used narcotics. He says, hey, come on up. I go in the house and there's five other people in the house. I no sooner get to the top of the stairs then the door's busted in. I don't know who's in the house. Was I supposed to ask him, who's in the house man? It's the truth.

THE CHAIRMAN: Anything else you'd like to say Mr. Reeves?

MR. RONALD: No.

THE CHAIRMAN: Okay, you step outside and we'll call you back in a few minutes. [The inmate leaves and the Board members discuss the case; then the inmate is called back.]

THE CHAIRMAN: Mr. Ronald, the Board will continue your case for one month to endeavor to get some information which corroborates your story and/or the violation report. We want to get some further information and confirm some of the information you've given us about violating the use of drugs, and so forth, and we will see you in a month.

[The following month, the inmate's parole was revoked with the provision that the inmate would be reparoled two months thereafter.]

2. SOME PROBLEM PAROLE REVOCATION CASES

The Case of Sherman Leonard

PAROLE VIOLATION REPORT

STATE OF CONNECTICUT
DEPARTMENT OF CORRECTION
DIVISION OF PAROLE

Subject: Sherman Leonard

Age: 25

Sentence: 1–3 years

Votes to Parole: March 3, 1970

Months on Parole: 3

Expiration of Maximum Sentence when paroled: October 3, 1971

Institutional No.: 21213

Original Offense: Obtaining Money Under False Pretenses

Date of Sentence: May 6, 1969

Released on Parole: May 26, 1970

Parole Warrant Issued: 8/27/70

Parole Warrant Executed:

PAROLE VIOLATION REPORT   Date: August 24, 1970

NATURE OF PAROLE VIOLATION

1. By virtue of his arrest in association with James Denny, CCI–S #69122, also on parole.
2. By virtue of his arrest in Waterbury, Connecticut on August 15, 1970 charged with the crime of Attempting to Cash a Stolen and Forged Check.

   1) Eugene was paroled from the Connecticut Correctional Institution on October 31, 1969. On August 15, 1970, Denny was in the Waterbury area, contacted Sherman, associated with him, and was arrested with him, on this date.

   2) On August 15, 1970, Waterbury Police Department received a phone call from the cashier of the Stop & Shop, Waterbury Plaza, Waterbury, Connecticut who stated that a Negro male was attempting to cash a stolen check. After the call was completed, police officers arrived at the Stop & Shop and observed two Negro males fleeing in a Cadillac convertible. The assistant manager told the officers that these were the persons involved in the attempt to cash the stolen and forged check. The officers pursued the vehicle, stopped it at the rear of the shopping plaza, and arrested the two Negro males, later identified as Sherman Leonard, age 25, of 289 North Main Street, Waterbury and Eugene Coleman, age 36, of Orchard Street, Ansonia, Connecticut, both parolees.

   Sherman gave a signed and written statement, that at approximately 7:30 p.m. on August 15, 1970, while walking on Bishop Street in Waterbury, he was approached by James Denny, asked him to get into the car and then opened his wallet and handed Sherman a check. Denny stated that if Sherman would cash the check for him he would buy him a drink. Denny then drove up to the Stop & Shop in the Waterbury area and Sherman went in and attempted to cash the check. The cashier became suspicious and asked the manager to examine the check; when this occurred, Sherman panicked and ran out the door. Sherman further stated that as he got into the automobile owned by Denny, Denny took the check and driver's license which Sherman was using for identification and put them under the seat. He further stated that Denny drove away and told him not to say anything because it was a stolen check. They drove around the plaza and were stopped by police officers. They were then taken into custody.

PRESENT STATUS

On August 17, 1970, Sherman appeared in Circuit Court in Waterbury, Connecticut, and the case was continued until August 20, 1970. A $1000 bond had been set. Subject is presently incarcerated in the Community Correctional Center in New Haven. A Form #58 has been lodged by this Parole Officer. A Warrant was requested on August 20, 1970.

PAROLE EVALUATION

Sherman was paroled on May 26, 1970 to an employment program with the Waterbury Mechanics Co. and would reside at 166 Broad Street, Waterbury, Connecticut. Throughout this man's parole, it was necessary at various times to reprimand him for his drinking habits. Occasionally he would drink too much and not report for work.

On August 3, 1970, subject injured his back at the Waterbury Foundry and was taking treatment at the Waterbury Hospital. While taking treatment, subject "made a pass" at one of the nurses and because of this the doctor in charge refused to treat him any further. The doctor in charge also stated that it was impossible to work with Sherman in regard to his back injury because he always seemed to be recovering from overdrinking. Again Sherman was reprimanded and on August 13, 1970, this Parole Officer contacted Sherman who indicated that he was laid off as of August 12, 1970.

At the time of subject's violation, he was unemployed and was residing at 166 Broad Street, Waterbury, Connecticut. It is this Parole Officer's opinion that Sherman could be considered a young alcoholic; when he begins drinking he cannot stop himself and is unable to maintain steady work habits.

RECOMMENDATION

It is recommended that the parole of Leonard Sherman be revoked and that he be returned to the Connecticut Correctional Institution, Somers, whenever he becomes avaliable.

Respectfully submitted,

Arthur Hill
Parole Officer

Approved:
    James Dugan
    PAROLE SUPERVISOR

JFF/sp

ADDENDUM TO PAROLE VIOLATION REPORT

STATE OF CONNECTICUT
DEPARTMENT OF CORRECTION
DIVISION OF PAROLE
Date: September 16, 1970

Re: Sherman, Leonard   Institution No.: CCI-O #21213

Sherman appeared in Circuit Court in Waterbury, Connecticut on September 2, 1970 and was found guilty of Obtaining Money Under False Pretenses and received a 60 day sentence, execution of sentence suspended. On the charge of Forgery, he received a nolle [Prosecutorial Dismissal] by the Prosecutor.

Although Sherman received a light sentence, it is recommended that his parole be revoked because of his conduct while on parole. He was an habitual drinker and lost his employment because of this. It is felt, at this time, that Sherman needs to be institutionalized for his own good and the good of society. He can be considered an alcoholic and should be treated as such in the institution.

Sherman was transferred to the Connecticut Institution in Somers on September 15, 1970.

Respectfully submitted,

Arthur Hill
Parole Officer

Approved: _____
    James Dugan
    PAROLE SUPERVISOR

JFF/sp

The Case of Charles Golden

PAROLE VIOLATION REPORT

STATE OF CONNECTICUT
DEPARTMENT OF CORRECTION
DIVISION OF PAROLE

Subject: Charles R. Golden

Age: 52

Sentence: 1 yr. 1 day–7 yrs.

Voted to Parole: 11–1–67

Months on Parole: 32

Expiration of
Maximum Sentence
when paroled: 11–26–73

Institutional No.: CCIS #12154

Original Offense: Indecent Assault (5 ct.)

Date of Sentence: 4–18–68

Released on Parole: 1–25–69

Parole Warrant Issued: 8–19–71

Parole Warrant
Executed: 8–19–71

PAROLE VIOLATION REPORT   Date: 9–27–71

NATURE OF PAROLE VIOLATION:

By subject's guilty plea in Mercer County Superior Court to the charge of delivering liquor to a minor on 9–20–71. On same date in Mercer County Superior Court subject was sentenced to 4 months to run concurrently with present prison sentence.

The subject, Golden, was arrested by the W. Haven Police Dept. on July 20, 1971 on a complaint from two 14-year-old boys who he had approached on the street and invited them to his apartment. In subject's apartment it is alleged that the following took place.

   a. Subject did grab each of the boys and grab their genital organs.
   b. Subject did show the boys a deck of colored pornographic playing cards.

Subject was arrested by the W. Haven Police Dept. a short time thereafter and was charged with the following:

1. Breach of Peace
2. Risk of injury or injury to a minor
3. Indecent assault

For further information please refer to the police report which is attached to this Parole Violation report.

PRESENT STATUS:

As of 9–27–71 subject is now incarcerated at Connecticut Correction Institute, Devon, serving his 4 months jail time which he received 9–20–71 on a guilty plea pending from the charge of delivering liquor to a minor.

PAROLE EVALUATION:

Subject was released on 1–25–69 with employment at Main Printing, Main St., Silver Springs, Conn. Subject was at this time a patient at St. Johns Hospital undergoing medical care for heart operation. From notes of his first parole officer it shows that the subject had no real problems except those which stemmed from his poor health. Subject did receive financial help from the Soldier and Sailor Fund and other various social agencies in the state of Connecticut for new job or training.

Subject moved into the Hartford area on or about 7–15–70.

On 8–18–70 subject was transferred to the W. Haven Parole Officer, Mr. Leslie with the job placement at the Acme Wire Works as an oil paint sprayer and the home address of 149 South St. On 9–14–70 til 9–29–71 subject was in the V. A. Hospital with a severe strained back. Subject did return to work and was able to maintain the contacts and hold a responsible job and to live a productive life.

On or about March 9, 1971 subject was admitted to the St. Johns Hospital for a series of operations on his heart. From March 29, 1971 until May 7, 1971 the subject was either in the hospital recovering from his operations or at home recuperating his health.

Subject did return to work shortly after the last Parole Officer visit of May 17, 1971 and was able to continue in his employment until he was arrested by the W. Haven Police Dept. and charged with Breach of Peace, Injury or Risk of Injury to a Minor, and Indecent Assault on 7–20–71.

Subject appeared in Circuit Court #17 on August, 1971 and was bound over to the next general session of the Mercer County Superior Court on Indecent Assault and Injury or Risk of Injury to a Minor.

On 9–20–71 subject appeared in Mercer County Superior Court and did plead guilty to the charge of substitute information delivering liquor to a minor.

On 9–20–71 subject again appeared in Mercer County Superior Court and received a sentence on his guilty plea to delivering liquor to a minor—4 months in the Hartford Community Correctional Center.

On 9–24–71 subject was transferred from the W. Haven Community Correctional Center to CCI Devon to complete his 4 months jail sentence.

RECOMMENDATION:

It is recommended that subject Charles R. Golden's parole be revoked.

Respectfully submitted,

John D. Leslie
Parole Officer

APPROVED:

Michael W. Fox
Parole Supervisor

The Case of Kevin West

PAROLE VIOLATION REPORT

Subject: Kevin West

Age: 26

Sentence: 1 yr. 1 day to 3 yrs.

Votes to Parole: 5–20–68

Months on Parole: 8

Expiration of
Maximum Sentence
when paroled: 4/10/70

Institutional No.: CCI Somers, #14725

Original Offense: Theft of M.V.

Date of Sentence: 2/10/66 began 11/9/67

Released on Parole: 7/30/68

Parole Warrant Issued: 4/3/69

Parole Warrant
Executed: 4/9/69

PAROLE VIOLATION REPORT   Date: 7/16/69

Kevin West is currently in violation of his parole for the following reasons:

1. By moving from his place of residence without the knowledge or permission of his parole officer which is in violation of Condition No. 3 of his Parole Agreement.

2. By failing to notify his parole officer of the fact that he had been arrested on a charge of Robbery with Violence and that he had been bound over to the Superior Court on said charge. This is also in violation of Condition No. 3 of his Parole Agreement.

3. By virtue of his arrest in Rockford, Connecticut on January 6, 1969 on a charge of Robbery with Violence.

Details of Parole Violation:

Kevin West was arrested by Rockford Police on January 6, 1969 on a charge of Robbery with Violence. The offense is alleged to have occurred on January 1, 1969. The subject is alleged to have beaten and robbed $200 from one Robert Downs of Rockford. The victim stated that the accused West held a knife at his throat and threatened to cut him. Sutures were required to close the cuts on the victim's face.

The Division of Parole was not notified of the accused arrest and he was subsequently allowed to make bond. On February 17, 1969 Kevin West was bound over to the Superior Court for Mercer County on the charge of Robbery with Violence. It was not until April 2, 1968 that the information was received that the subject had been arrested and subsequently bound over for the above mentioned offense. During the period intervening between the time of the subject's arrest in January and when we learned of this arrest in April the subject had been seen by this parole officer on 4 separate occasions. On each of these occasions the subject was routinely asked whether he had been involved in any difficulty with the law and on each occasion he stated that he had not been in any difficulty. This was of course untrue. On April 3, 1969 a warrant for the subject's reimprisonment was issued and lodged at the Rockford Police Department whose assistance was requested to apprehend the subject. West was arrested by Rockford Police on our warrant on April 9, 1969.

During our investigation of the subject's activities it was discovered that he was no longer residing in the indicated place of residence at 61 Barnes Street, Rockford but was in fact residing with his girlfriend at 147 Power Street, Rockford. I contacted the subject's girlfriend at that address and she verified the fact that West was living with her permanently and she had been doing so for more than a month. She also volunteered the information that West had been in possession of a .38 caliber revolver and that she had seen this gun in his possession during the last week of March, 1969.

Present Status:

Kevin West was taken into custody by parole officers on April 9, 1969. He was lodged at the Rockford Correctional Center but has subsequently been administratively transferred to the Connecticut Correctional Institution, Devon, where he is now incarcerated.

History of Parole Supervision:

West was released to parole supervision on July 30, 1968. On August 4, 1968 subject was arrested by Rockford Police on a charge of Possession of Narcotics. The subject was arrested on that date after a Rockford Policeman observed one William Day, Edward Price and the subject, all three of whom were on parole at the time, in a motor vehicle on Capitol Street, Rockford. The officer was aware of the fact that Day, driver of the vehicle, did not have an operator's license. He therefore stopped the vehicle. When he stopped the vehicle the officer noticed several glassine bags containing a white powder on the floor of the car. All three individuals were placed under arrest and charged with Possession of Narcotics and Conspiracy to Violate the State Narcotics Law. The subject was confined at the Rockford Correctional Center until December, 1968 when the charges in Circuit Court, Rockford were nolled. Subject was then reinstated on parole.

During December 1968, the subject was employed by the Superior Laundry Company on Stockton Avenue, Rockford. On January 17, 1969, this subject reported to his parole officer that he had left his job at the Superior Laundry Company and that he was then going through the Rockford Community Renewal Team Training Program. He subsequently obtained a job with the Sparks Tool Company in Morgan, Connecticut and later another job with the Regal Tool Company in Rockford.

The subject apparently worked relatively steady during a period from January through March, 1969. As noted above he did report to his parole officer during this period of time.

RECOMMENDATION:

It is recommended that Kevin West's parole be revoked. The fact that the subject reported to his parole officer but in so doing lied to him concerning his activities and his place of residence certainly cannot be condoned. The mere physical act of reporting to his parole officer is meaningless if not accompanied by cooperation and some degree of honesty.

As of this writing the charges of Robbery with Violence are still pending against the subject in Superior Court for Mercer County. However, it is recommended that the subject's parole be revoked regardless of the outcome of that trial.

Respectfully submitted,

Thomas Clancy
Parole Officer

Approved:

Michael W. Fox
Parole Supervisor

3. THE ROLE OF LAWYER AND JUDGE

UNITED STATES EX. REL. BEY V. CONNECTICUT STATE BOARD OF PAROLE
443 F.2d 1079 (1971), *vacated as moot,* 404 U.S. 879 (1971)
United States Court of Appeals, Second Circuit

KAUFMAN, Circuit Judge:

Nearly a century after its inception as one aspect of a reform movement still widely identified as the "new" penology, the device of releasing prisoners from incarceration on a trial basis as parolees has long since gained common acceptance by the penal systems of every state. Unlike most other Circuits, this court until recently has had little occasion to consider constraints that Fourteenth Amendment guarantees may place on the operation of state parole systems. This appeal, however, requires us for the third time within a year to decide whether an important aspect of a state's parole procedures operates to deprive affected prisoners and parolees of due process of law.

Last term we held in Menechino v. Oswald, 430 F.2d 403 (2d Cir. 1970), that due process did not guarantee legal representation to New York State prisoners when they appeared at a hearing to determine whether they would be released on parole. The instant appeal presents the question, expressly reserved for later decision in *Menechino,* but since decided affirmatively by New York's highest court, whether the Constitution nevertheless requires that parolees be afforded legal assistance at a proceeding to determine whether parole status should be *revoked*. We hold that it does, and that Bey, the petitioner and appellant here, was not accorded due process of law when his parole was revoked and he was reimprisoned following a 1960 hearing before the Connecticut Board of Parole where Bey appeared alone, but was not represented by a lawyer.

I

An appreciation of the issue presented to us, and our resolution of it, requires a preliminary understanding of the functioning of the Connecticut parole system as it was constituted in 1960. For purposes of deciding this case, the operation of the system is best described with reference to Bey's own history of brief release and subsequent recommitment to prison more than ten years ago, where he has remained confined since.

Pursuant to state law, Conn.Gen.Stat. §§ 54–125, 54–126, appellant was released as a parolee from the Connecticut State Prison on June 10, 1960, where he had been serving a life term for second degree murder. Bey's release was necessarily premised on a finding by the parole board that there was a "reasonable probability that [he would] live and remain at liberty without violating the law and * * * [that his] release [was] not incompatible with the welfare of society." Id. § 54–125. The board was required to arrive at this finding only after weighing a complex of factors, many intangible and subjective.

Bey was released from prison in the custody of a parole officer under standard conditions stated on a form signed by Bey prior to his release. The restrictions included a requirement that Bey not "own, possess, use, sell, or have under his control any deadly weapons or firearms," and that he not leave Connecticut without prior permission from a parole board staff member.

The events following Bey's provisional release that resulted eventually in his arrest and reimprisonment less than six months later, on November 30, 1960, are known to us only through a report prepared by a parole officer, Earl C. Mercer, after Bey was arrested and in preparation for his revocation hearing. By Mercer's account, Bey appears to have performed the duties required of him by each of three jobs he held while on parole satisfactorily. He, nevertheless, seemed to progressively disappoint, annoy, and disturb his employers and eventually his parole officer.

During the period of his release, Bey was employed successively in unskilled jobs at the Radiant Baseboard Plant in Newington, the Porter School in Farmington, and the Institution of Living in Hartford, a mental institution, all in Connecticut. In each instance minor difficulties developed shortly after Bey assumed each new job. For example, while he was employed at the Newington plant, Bey's parole officer was required to investigate a report by Bey's landlady that he was engaged in a "sex orgy."

Bey later admitted, according to the parole officer, that a friend had arranged to provide him with a girl with whom to have sexual relations. The landlady entered Bey's room to find him on his bed with the girl, a bottle of whiskey on the floor, and his friend in a nearby chair. The parole officer was disturbed not only over the incident but by Bey's apparent "belligerence" at his landlady's and parole officer's interference with his private affairs. The parole officer was also annoyed at Bey's complaints that his job was unsuitable, that he was receiving inadequate medical treatment for boils and a lame shoulder, and that the services provided him by the parole officer were in other ways inadequate.

At the Porter School, the foreman at the school and the parole officer eventually became "very apprehensive" that Bey was becoming too involved with one of the girl students there, whose ages ranged from 13 to 16 years. The bases for their suspicions are not revealed in Mercer's report. Similarly, while Bey was working as a groundsman at the Institute of Living, his parole officer was told by an official at the Porter School that Bey was writing "upsetting" letters to girls and faculty members at Porter and had become "a little too friendly" with two of the girls. Events began to come to a head when the parole officer learned that, contrary to the officer's instructions, Bey had persisted in talking freely about his prison record, and that Bey sometimes bought whiskey which he took to his room but which others consumed there. Finally, on November 29, Bey's parole officer received a call from an unnamed individual "whose word [was] believed to be reliable by the parole officer," reporting that Bey had threatened to leave Connecticut without informing the parole board, had shown a dagger or knife to a fellow-employee, and had bragged that he had killed a policeman before and "could kill again if anyone bothered him." A search of Bey's room was conducted the next morning, after Bey had gone to work, by two parole officers and the Assistant Personnel Director at the Institute. A "new English style hunting knife was found in a paper box under some clean clothing on a shelf in Bey's closet," in the words of Mercer's report. Bey was taken into custody and returned to prison later the same day.

Mercer's report, dated December 14, was addressed to the Executive Secretary of the Parole Board, James I. McIlduff. Notably, Mercer considered the knife incident, although a clear violation of a parole condition (see p. 3006 *supra*), "in itself not of tremendous import." Based on Bey's past record, as well as his record on parole, and on "a number of psychiatric evaluations which have been made," Mercer described Bey as "an extremely unstable individual" and "potentially dangerous." According to Mercer, Bey's parole officer had decided that "it is incompatible with the welfare of society that John Bey be continued on parole." Because he considered Bey to be "mentally incapable of accepting the responsibilities of parole," Mercer recommended that he "should not be re-paroled without extensive psychiatric study."

The procedures to be followed after Bey's arrest and return to prison were prescribed by the parole board Regulation "Revocation of Parole." Bey was to have "reasonable notice of the charges against him" and "an opportunity to appear before the parole board at its next regular meeting at the State Prison to admit, deny, or explain the violation charged." After considering the case, the parole board could select any of five options for disposing of Bey's case. Thus, Bey could be reprimanded; his parole might be continued under more stringent conditions, or closer supervision; time previously earned toward reduction of his term of imprisonment could be withheld or withdrawn; and of course, his parole could simply be revoked.

Following a hearing conducted December 21, 1960, at which Bey appeared *pro se*, the Board chose the last, most severe, alternative. As an automatic consequence of parole revocation, Bey was remanded to prison to serve the unexpired portion of the term of his maximum sentence at the date of his violation of a parole condition. Although he could be reconsidered for parole at any time, he would automatically be heard again for·possible release on parole only after serving another year of imprisonment. Parole Board Regulation X.C, D. Although Bey's arrest was statutorily authorized for any reason "deem[ed] sufficient" by the parole board, a precondition to parole revocation and reincarceration was that Bey had been arrested "for violation of his parole." Conn.Gen.Stat. § 54–128(a).

At the time it revoked Bey's parole, the board had before it Bey's testimony (there is nothing in the record to indicate the nature of the testimony), Mercer's report, and also a much briefer report prepared by the Executive Secretary, James McIlduff. McIlduff's report consisted of a digest of Mercer's report, in the main stressing aspects least favorable to Bey, and miscellaneous representations based on Bey's previous record. For example, McIlduff described Bey as "emotionally unstable" and "somewhat of an agitator" and referred to a period of several years during Bey's earlier incarceration when Bey was confined at the Norwich State Hospital as a mental patient.

We have recounted the facts revealed in this record with somewhat greater detail than necessary to resolve the legal question presented. We have done so to avoid the appearance of resolving the important issue raised on this appeal abstractly or academically. Bey's brief parole history serves better than hypothesis to illustrate concretely the potential importance of a lawyer's presence at a parole revocation hearing.

At the outset, we must note the narrowness of the issue framed by appellant. In 1967 Bey initiated a habeas corpus action in Connecticut state courts by filing a petition which alleged numerous statutory and constitutional deficiencies in the Board's revocation procedure. The Superior Court, Hartford County, denied the petition, Bey v. Reincke, No. 151663 (July 30, 1969). After an application for a certificate of probable cause was denied, Bey proceeded with his present federal application, again raising numerous constitutional challenges. Judge Blumenfeld denied the petition in all respects in a brief opinion filed June 3, 1970. Among the many constitutional issues resolved against him by the district court judge, Bey has chosen to appeal only the holding that he had no right to counsel at the revocation hearing. That is the sole issue briefed and argued before us and it is the only issue we decide today.

II

Precedent on the precise issue before us is conflicting and its significance is difficult to assess. The Tenth Circuit, which has spoken most often and has frequently been followed by other courts, appears to hold that counsel is of sufficient importance that if a parolee is permitted to *retain* counsel to represent him at revocation hearings, then the equal protection and due process guarantees require that counsel also be provided for indigent parolees, Earnest v. Willingham, 406 F.2d 681 (1969), at least when the parolee contests an alleged parole violation, Serviss v. Moseley, 430 F.2d 1287 (1970); Murphy v. Turner, 426 F.2d 422 (1970); but a state may choose to bar counsel from revocation hearings altogether, Firkins v. Colorado, 434 F.2d 1232 (1970) (per curiam); Williams v. Patterson, 389 F.2d 374 (1968). The fount of Tenth Circuit precedent on the latter point seems to be a per curiam opinion in Gonzales v. Patterson, 370 F.2d 94 (1966), relying (as have many courts, including the district court below) on dictum in Escoe v. Zerbst, 295 U.S. 490, 492–493, 55 S.Ct. 818, 79 L.Ed. 1566 (1935) that *probation* is a matter of "grace."

In Williams v. Dunbar, 377 F.2d 505 (1967), the Ninth Circuit rejected a petitioner's claims to various procedural guarantees at a revocation hearing, including a right to compulsory process to summon witnesses and a right to cross-examine and confront adverse witnesses, as well as a right to counsel. Rather than evaluate the merits of each claimed right individually, the *Dunbar* court reasoned broadly that a state required to comply with *all* the procedures sought would abandon its parole system as rigid and unwieldly. See also Mead v. California Adult Auth., 415 F.2d 767 (9th Cir. 1969) (per curiam) (simply citing Williams v. Patterson, *supra*). On the strength of the Escoe v. Zerbst dictum, *supra* (and relying in part also on its earlier decision in Johnson v. Avery, 382 F.2d 353 (6th Cir. 1967), reversed, 393 U.S. 483, 89 S.Ct. 747, 21 L.Ed.2d 718 (1969)), the Sixth Circuit in Rose v. Haskins, 388 F.2d 91, cert. denied, 392 U.S. 946, 88 S.Ct. 2300, 20 L.Ed.2d 1408 (1968) discovered and applied an "axiom" that "the administration of the state's penal system is exclusively a state function under the reserved powers in the Constitution" in finding no right to counsel in state parole revocation proceedings. *Rose* was announced over a scholarly and thorough dissent by Judge Celebrezze, who we believe successfully unravelled the rationale of the majority as well as that of other courts reaching results like that in *Rose*, including those cited above.

The other Circuit to rule on the right to counsel at state parole revocation hearing is the Third. That Court has decided that a state prisoner is not denied due process when revocation is premised on either irrefutable evidence that the parolee violated a condition of his parole, United States ex rel. Halprin v. Parker, 418 F.2d 313, 315 (3d Cir., 1969) (parolee arrested out-of-state; parole revoked because he left the parole board's jurisdiction without permission), or on a criminal act proved after a full trial prior to parole revocation, United States ex rel. Heacock v. Meyers, 367 F.2d 583 (3d Cir., 1966), affirming on opinion below, 251 F.Supp. 773 (E.D.Pa.), cert. denied sub nom. Heacock v. Rundle, 386 U.S. 925, 87 S.Ct. 900, 17 L.Ed.2d 797 (1967). The Third Circuit has not ruled on the right to counsel where the parole violation is less conclusively established prior to revocation. Finally, in other Circuits the precise question before us here as one of first impression appears not to have been squarely decided, although certain views that have been expressed by the Fourth, Fifth, Seventh, Eighth, and District of Columbia Circuits on closely related issues appear to parallel those of the Circuits which have found no right to counsel at state parole revocation hearings. We note, however, that many of the leading cases in other Circuits were decided prior to the landmark Supreme Court decisions in Mempa v. Rhay, 389 U.S. 128, 88 S.Ct. 254, 19 L.Ed.2d 336 (1967) (unanimous) and Goldberg v. Kelly, 397 U.S. 254, 90 S.Ct. 1011, 25 L.Ed.2d 287 (1970), discussed below. Our views coincide with those of courts in Pennsylvania, Michigan and New York, Commonwealth v. Tinson, 433 Pa. 328, 249 A.2d 549 (1969); Warren v. Michigan Parole Board, 23 Mich. App. 754, 179 N.W.2d 664 (Ct.App. 1970), appeal dismissed, Mich., 184 N.W.2d 457 (1971); People ex rel. Menechino v. Warden, 27 N.Y.2d 376, 318 N.Y.S. 2d 449 (1970) and one federal district court, Goolsby v. Gagnon, Civ.No. 70–C–330, 322 F.Supp. 460 (E.D.Wis. 1971), and with the recommendations of several scholars and commentators who have long urged courts to recognize that legal assistance is essential to the fundamental fairness of a parole revocation proceeding.[1]

[1] Standards approved by the House of Delegates of the American Bar Association in February, 1966, recommended that counsel be provided in connection with both probation and parole revocation proceedings. See ABA Project on Minimum Standards for Criminal Justice, Standards Relating to Providing Defense Services 68 (1967). The ABA Project on Minimum Standards of Criminal Justice, Standards Relating to Probation § 5.4(a) (ii) (Approved Draft, 1970) recommends counsel at all probation revocation hearings. The ABA Project on Minimum Standards for Criminal Justice, Standards Relating to Providing Defense Services § 4.2 (Approved Draft, 1968) would require that counsel be provided in all post-conviction proceedings "which are adversary in nature." Both the President's Commission on Law Enforcement and the Administration of Justice, Report: The Challenge of Crime in a Free Society 150 (1967) and its task force reports on The Courts 54 (1967) and Corrections 86–88 (1967), recommended that counsel be provided for probation and parole revocation hearings. The American Law Institute, Model Penal Code § 305.15(1) (Proposed Official Draft 1962) provides that a parolee "shall be permitted to advise with his own legal counsel" in preparing for parole revocation hearings. See also, *id.* § 301.4 (right "to be represented by counsel" at probation revocation hearings). See W. Cohen, Due Process, Equal Protection and State Parole Revocation Hearings, 42 U.Colo.L.Rev. 197 (1970); Note, Constitutional Law, Parole Status and the Privilege Concept, 1969 Duke L.J. 139; Note, Parole Revocation in the Federal System, 56 Geo.L.J. 705, 719–26 (1968). Cf. Comment, Freedom and Rehabilitation in Parole Revocation Hearings, 72 Yale L.J. 368 (1962).

A. The Parolee's Interest in Conditional Freedom

Unlike a prisoner being considered for parole release, a parolee facing reimprisonment stands to lose a "presently enjoyed" interest in his conditional freedom that the *Menechino* panel aptly characterized as "a liberty akin to a private interest." 430 F.2d at 409. It is not sophistic to attach greater importance to a person's justifiable reliance in maintaining his conditional freedom so long as he abides by the conditions of his release, than to his mere anticipation or hope of freedom. In this respect, this case is indistinguishable from Mempa v. Rhay, 389 U.S. 128, 88 S.Ct. 254, 19 L.Ed.2d 336) (1967), establishing the right to legal representation at Washington State's unusual deferred sentencing and probation revocation proceeding. Both the probationer and parolee have "been given a status that is considerably more desirable than that of a prisoner. When revocation is threatened, they all have the same interest in maintaining that status." Rose v. Haskins, 388 F.2d 91, 103 (6th Cir. 1968) (Celebrezze, J., dissenting). The cost to Bey of revocation thus far has been eleven years of imprisonment.

Moreover, we do not doubt that a parole revocation is more likely than a denial of initial release to mar a prisoner's record, perhaps adversely affecting his chances for future parole. Even after release from prison, it is only realistic to assume that a former inmate's job opportunities and standing in the community will also be influenced by his prison record. Parole revocation will inevitably connote wrongdoing and thus the citizen whose parole was once revoked will continue to carry a burden analogous and in addition to his criminal stigma. See Hahn v. Burke, 430 F.2d 100, 102 (7th Cir. 1970). Thus, it seems incontestable to say that "substantial rights" of Bey were "affected" by the revocation proceeding. For that reason as well as those stated below, Bey was entitled to the assistance of a lawyer. Mempa v. Rhay, 389 U.S. 128, 134, 88 S.Ct. 254, 19 L.Ed.2d 336 (1967).

B. The Lawyer's Role in a Parole Revocation Proceeding

A decision to revoke parole, like a parole release determination, inevitably involves the discretionary application of principles and knowledge derived from study and experience in fields such as psychology, sociology, and penology—where ordinarily a lawyer can claim no special expertise. Neither forensic skill, legal training, nor the advocate's role in a decision making process suits a lawyer for effective participation in this judgment phase of the parole process. Unlike a parole release decision, however, a necessary precondition to parole revocation is a finding that events intervening between a prisoner's release and the hearing justify forfeiture of the prisoner's provisional liberty. Thus, in Connecticut, the parole release decision is based on a complex of tangible and intangible, objective and subjective, factors which we have partly enumerated above. By contrast, a necessary precondition to Bey's reincarceration was the finding that Bey had violated a condition of his parole. Whether Bey would lose his conditioned liberty turned on a narrow retrospective determination of a specific factual question. A lawyer's training particularly suits him to analyze and organize for the benefit of an impartial tribunal evidentiary matter bearing on the occurrence or nonoccurrence, as well as the significance, of past events. See Specht v. Patterson, 386 U.S. 605, 87 S.Ct. 1209, 18 L.Ed.2d 326 (1967).

Of course, more complex factual questions than whether Bey had a knife in his closet and why, were also relevant to the disposition of his case by the parole board. Mercer's report reveals the complexity of factual questions that can dispose a parole board or officer to greater or lesser leniency or harshness. None of the incidents that soured Bey's relationship with the parole officer are sharply delineated by Mercer's recitation. McIlduff apparently accepted Mercer's account at face value. A trained lawyer might well have discovered mitigating circumstances and hidden significances not revealed or immediately obvious on the face of Mercer's report. For example, the Board might well have welcomed a suggestion for a fuller investigation of Bey's alleged announced intent to depart the state, or his oblique threat to repeat his past crimes. Perhaps Bey's employers could have supplied useful information as to Bey's dependability and thoroughness on the job. A review of Bey's reported letters to Porter School girl students might have revealed different hues of motivation than found their way into Mercer's report.

Thus, at the least a diligent lawyer representing Bey before the Parole Board might have investigated the decisive events of Bey's brief period of release and in an orderly, disciplined presentation to the Board have attempted to establish facts more favorable to

Bey than those presented by Mercer and McIlduff and have suggested their relevance to the four alternatives less severe than revocation available to the Board in disposing of Bey's case....

The fact that the Board performs a predictive and prognostic function does not depreciate the importance of accurate factual exposition and evaluation. Less educated or intelligent prisoners are particularly likely to suffer from the absence of trained legal assistance. See Johnson v. Avery, *supra*. Bey himself must have been severely handicapped in preparing a case from behind prison walls. Cf. Sostre v. McGinnis, *supra*, 442 F.2d at 196–197. Accordingly, we are compelled to recognize, as did the Court in Mempa v. Rhay, 389 U.S. 128, 135, 88 S.Ct. 254, 256, 19 L. Ed.2d 336 (1967), "the necessity for the aid of counsel in marshalling the facts, introducing evidence of mitigating circumstances and in general aiding and assisting the defendant to present his case."...

For the reasons stated, we hold that parolees are entitled to legal representation at parole revocation hearings that may result in their reincarceration.

We stress once again that the participation of the lawyer at a parole hearing should be limited to investigating and explicating to the board, evidence bearing on the occurrence or non-occurrence of events during the parolee's period of release and their significance, provided these are relevant to the disposition of the prisoner's case. Counsel should not be permitted to employ trial tactics utilized in an adversary context. For example, he should not employ as his forensic text the parolee's entire life history prior to his release on parole. Nor is it counsel's function by cajolery or blandishment or oratory to interfere with the Board's judgment in applying its special expertise to the facts of the case at hand. We emphatically stress that our decision does not detract in the least from the Board's power to limit counsel's participation in revocation proceedings so that parole hearings do not become legal battles. Counsel's proper role is to *assist* the Board, not to impede it, and the Board may take appropriate measures to assure that the counsel appreciates his limited role and presents his client's case accordingly.

Appellant has suggested that the lapse of time and resultant staleness of the evidence bearing on Bey's revocation require that we summarily order his release from prison. But there is no presumption that the Board's initial disposition of Bey's case was erroneous and we will remand the case to the district court for entry of the conditional order usually appropriate in this situation. Bey must be given a new revocation hearing with participation by counsel within the bounds we have defined. He will be released only if such a hearing is not conducted within a reasonable time.

Reversed and remanded.

MORRISSEY V. BREWER
408 U.S. 471 (1972)
Supreme Court of the United States

MR. CHIEF JUSTICE BURGER delivered the opinion of the court.

We granted certiorari in this case to determine whether the Due Process Clause of the Fourteenth Amendment requires that a State afford an individual some opportunity to be heard prior to revoking his parole.

Petitioner Morrissey was convicted of false drawing or uttering of checks in 1967 pursuant to his guilty plea, and was sentenced to not more than seven years' confinement. He was paroled from the Iowa State Penitentiary in June 1968. Seven months later, at the direction of his parole officer, he was arrested in his home town as a parole violator and incarcerated in the county jail. One week later, after review of the parole officer's written report, the Iowa Board of Parole revoked Morrissey's parole and he was returned to the penitentiary located about 100 miles from his home. Petitioner asserts he received no hearing prior to revocation of his parole.

The parole officer's report on which the Board of Parole acted shows that petitioner's parole was revoked on the basis of information that he had violated the conditions of parole by buying a car under an assumed name and operating it without permission, giving false statements to police concerning his address and insurance company after a minor accident, and obtaining credit under an assumed name and failing to report his place of residence to his parole officer. The report states that the officer interviewed Morrissey, and that he could not explain why he did not contact his parole officer despite his effort to excuse this on the ground that he had been sick. Further, the report asserts that Morrissey admitted buying the car and obtaining credit under an assumed name and also admitted being involved in the accident. The parole officer recommended that his parole be revoked because of "his continual violating of his parole rules."

The situation as to petitioner Booher is much the same. Pursuant to his guilty plea, Booher was convicted of forgery in 1966 and sentenced to a maximum term of 10 years. He was paroled November 14, 1968. In August 1969, at his parole officer's direction, he was arrested in his home town for a violation of his parole and confined in the county jail several miles away. On September 13, 1969, on the basis of a written report by his parole officer, the Iowa Board of Parole revoked Booher's parole and Booher was recommitted to the state penitentiary, located about 250 miles from his home, to complete service of his sentence. Petitioner asserts he received no hearing prior to revocation of his parole.

The parole officer's report with respect to Booher recommended that his parole be revoked because he had violated the territorial restrictions of his parole without consent, had obtained a driver's license under an assumed name and operated a motor vehicle without permission, and had violated the employment condition of his parole by failing to keep himself in gainful employment. The report stated that the officer had interviewed Booher and that he had acknowledged to the parole officer that he had left the specified territorial limits and had operated the car and had obtained a license under an assumed name "knowing that it was wrong." The report further noted that Booher had stated that he had not found employment because he could not find work that would pay him what he wanted—he stated he would not work for $2.25 to $2.75 per hour—and that he had left the area to get work in another city.

After exhausting state remedies, both petitioners filed habeas corpus petitions in the United States District Court for the Southern District of Iowa alleging that they had been denied due process because their paroles had been revoked without a hearing. The State responded by arguing that no hearing was required. The District Court held on the basis of controlling authority that the State's failure to accord a hearing prior to parole revocation did not violate due process. On appeal, the two cases were consolidated.

The Court of Appeals, dividing 4 to 3, held that due process does not require a hearing. The majority recognized that the traditional view of parole as a privilege rather than a vested right is no longer dispositive as to whether due process is applicable; however, on a balancing of the competing interests involved, it concluded that no hearing is required. The court reasoned that parole is only "a correctional device authorizing service of sentencing outside the penitentiary"; the parolee is still "in custody." Accordingly, the Court of Appeals was of the view that prison officials must have large discretion in making revocation determinations, and that courts should retain their traditional reluctance to interfere with disciplinary matters properly under the control of state prison authorities. The majority expressed the view that "non-legal, non-adversary considerations" were often the determinative factors in making a parole revocation decision. It expressed concern that if adversary hearings were required for parole revocation, "with the full panoply of rights accorded in criminal proceedings," the function of the parole board as "an administrative body acting in the role of *parens patriae* would be aborted" and the board would be more reluctant to grant parole in the first instance—an apprehension that would not be without some basis if the choice were between a full scale adversary proceeding or no hearing at all. Additionally, the majority reasoned that the parolee has no statutory right to remain on parole. Iowa law provides that a parolee may be returned to the institution at any time. Our holding in *Mempa* v. *Rhay*, 389 U.S. 128 (1967), was distinguished on the ground that it involved deferred sentencing upon probation revocation, and thus involved a stage of the criminal proceeding, whereas parole revocation was not a stage in the criminal proceedings. The Court of Appeals' decision was consistent with many other decisions on parole revocations.

In its brief in this Court, the State asserts for the first time that petitioners were in fact granted hearings after they were returned to the penitentiary. More generally, the State says that within two months after the Board revokes an individual's parole and orders him returned to the penitentiary, on the basis of the parole officer's written report, it grants the individual a hearing before the Board. At that time the Board goes over "each of the alleged parole violations with the returnee, and he is given an opportunity to orally present his side of the story to the Board." If the returnee denies the report, it is the practice of the Board to conduct a further investigation before making a final determination either affirming the initial revocation, modifying it, or reversing it. The State asserts that Morrissey, whose parole was revoked on January 31, 1969, was granted a hearing before the Board on February 12, 1969. Booher's parole was revoked on September 13, 1969, and he was granted a hearing on October 14, 1969. At these hearings, the State tells us—in the briefs—both Morrissey and Booher admitted the violations alleged in the parole violation reports.

Nothing in the record supplied to this Court indicates that the State claimed, either in the District Court or the Court of Appeals, that petitioners had received hearings promptly after their paroles were revoked, or that in such hearing they admitted the violations; that information comes to us only in the State's brief here. Further, even the assertions that the State makes here are not based on any public record but on interviews with two of the members of the parole board. In the interview relied on to show that petitioners admitted their violations, the board member did not assert he could remember that both Morrissey and Booher admitted the parole violations with which they were charged. He stated only that, according to his memory, in the previous several years all but three returnees had admitted commission of the parole infractions alleged and that neither of the petitioners was among the three who denied them.

We must therefore treat this case in the posture and on the record the State elected to rely on in the District Court and the Court of Appeals. If the facts are otherwise, the State may make a showing in the District Court that petitioners in fact have admitted the violations charged before a neutral officer.

I

Before reaching the issue of whether due process applies to the parole system, it is important to recall the function of parole in the correctional process.

During the past 60 years, the practice of releasing prisoners on parole before the end of their sentences has become an integral part of the penological system. Note, Parole Revocation in the Federal System, 56 Geo. L. J. 705 (1968). Rather than being an *ad hoc* exercise of clemency, parole is an established variation on imprisonment of convicted criminals. Its purpose is to help individuals reintegrate into society as constructive individuals as soon as they are able, without being confined for the full term of the sentence imposed. It also serves to alleviate the costs to society of keeping an individual in prison. The essence of parole is release from prison, before the completion of sentence, on the condition that the prisoner abide by certain rules during the balance of the sentence. Under some systems parole is granted automatically after the service of a certain portion of a prison term. Under others, parole is granted by the discretionary action of a board which evaluates an array of information about a prisoner and makes a prediction whether he is ready to reintegrate into society.

To accomplish the purpose of parole, those who are allowed to leave prison early are subjected to specified conditions for the duration of their terms. These conditions restrict their activities substantially beyond the ordinary restrictions imposed by law on an individual citizen. Typically parolees are forbidden to use liquor or to have associations or correspondence with certain categories of undesirable persons. Typically also they must seek permission from their parole officers before engaging in specified activities, such as changing employment or living quarters, marrying, acquiring or operating a motor vehicle, traveling outside the community and incurring substantial indebtedness. Additionally, parolees must regularly report to the parole officer to whom they are assigned and sometimes they must make periodic written reports of their activities. Arluke, A Summary of Parole Rules, 15 Crime and Delinquency 267, 272–273 (1969).

The parole officers are part of the administrative system designed to assist parolees and to offer them guidance. The conditions of parole serve a dual purpose; they prohibit, either absolutely or conditionally, behavior which is deemed dangerous to the restoration of the individual into normal society. And through the requirement of reporting to the parole officer and seeking guidance and permission before doing many things, the officer is provided with information about the parolee and an opportunity to advise him. The combination puts the parole officer into the position in which he can try to guide the parolee into constructive development.

The enforcement leverage which supports the parole conditions derives from the authority to return the parolee to prison to serve out the balance of his sentence if he fails to abide by the rules. In practice not every violation of parole conditions automatically leads to revocation. Typically a parolee will be counseled to abide by the conditions of parole, and the parole officer ordinarily does not take steps to have parole revoked unless he thinks that the violations are serious and continuing so as to indicate that the parolee is not adjusting properly and cannot be counted on to avoid antisocial activity. The broad discretion accorded the parole officer is also inherent in some of the quite vague conditions, such as the typical requirement that the parolee avoid "undesirable" associations or correspondence. Cf. *Arciniega* v. *Freeman*, 404 U.S. 4 (1970). Yet revocation of parole is not an unusual phenomenon, affecting only a few parolees. It has been estimated that 35–45% of all parolees are subjected to revocation and return to prison. Sometimes revocation occurs when the parolee is accused of another crime; it is often preferred to a new prosecution because of the procedural ease of recommitting the individual on the basis of a lesser showing by the State.

Implicit in the system's concern with parole violations is the notion that the parolee is entitled to retain his liberty as long as he substantially abides by the conditions of his parole. The first step in a revocation decision thus involves a wholly retrospective factual question: whether the parolee has in fact acted in violation of one or more conditions of his parole. Only if it is determined that the parolee did violate the conditions does the second question arise: should the parolee be recommitted to prison or should other steps be taken to protect society and improve chances of rehabilitation? The first step is relatively simple; the second is more complex. The second question involves the application of expertise by the parole authority in making a prediction as to the ability of the individual to live in society without committing antisocial acts. This part of the decision, too, depends on facts, and therefore it is important for the Board to know not only that some violation was committed but also to know accurately how many and how serious the violations were. Yet this second step, deciding what to do about the violation once it is identified, is not purely factual but also predictive and discretionary.

If a parolee is returned to prison, he often receives no credit for the time "served" on parole. Thus the returnee may face a potential of substantial imprisonment.

II

We begin with the proposition that the revocation of parole is not part of a criminal prosecution and thus the full panoply of rights due a defendant in such a proceeding does not apply to parole revocations. Cf. *Mempa* v. *Rhay*, 389 U.S. 128 (1967). Parole arises after the end of the criminal prosecution, including imposition of sentence. Supervision is not directly by the court but by an administrative agency, which is sometimes an arm of the court and sometimes of the executive. Revocation deprives an individual not of the absolute liberty to which every citizen is entitled, but only of the conditional liberty properly dependent on observance of special parole restrictions.

We turn therefore to the question whether the requirements of due process in general apply to parole revocations. As Mr. Justice Blackmun has written recently, "This Court has rejected the concept that constitutional rights turn upon whether a governmental benefit is characterized as a 'right' or as a 'privilege.'" *Graham* v. *Richardson*, 403 U.S. 365, 374. Whether any procedural protections are due depends on the extent to which an individual will be "condemned to suffer grievous loss." *Joint Anti-Fascist Refugee Committee* v. *McGrath*, 341 U.S. 123, 168 (1951) (Frankfurter, J., concurring), quoted in *Goldberg* v. *Kelly*, 397 U.S. 154, 163 1970). The question is not merely the "weight" of the individual's interest, but whether the nature of the interest is one within the contemplation of the "liberty or property" language of the Fourteenth Amendment. *Fuentes* v. *Shevin*, ___ U.S. ___ (decided June 12, 1972). Once it is determined that due process applies, the question remains what process is due. It has been said so often by this Court and others as not to require citation of authority that due process is flexible and calls for such procedural protections as the particular situation demands. "[C]onsideration of what procedures due process may require under any given set of circumstances must begin with a determination of the precise nature of the governmental function involved as well as of the private interest that has been affected by governmental action." *Cafeteria & Restaurant Workers Union* v. *McElroy*, 367 U.S. 886, 895 (1961). To say that the concept of due process is flexible does not mean that judges are at large to apply it to any and all relationships. Its flexibility is in its scope once it has been determined that some process is due; it is a recognition that not all situations calling for procedural safeguards call for the same kind of procedure.

We turn to an examination of the nature of the interest of the parole in his continued liberty. The liberty of a parolee enables him to do a wide range of things open to persons who have never been convicted of any crime. The parolee has been released from prison based on an evaluation that he shows reasonable promise of being able to return to society and function as a responsible, self-reliant person. Subject to the conditions of his parole, he can be gainfully employed and is free to be with family and friends and to form the other enduring attachments of normal life. Though the State properly subjects him to many restrictions not applicable to other citizens, his condition is very different from that of confinement in a prison. He may have been on parole for a number of years and may be living a relatively normal life at the time he is faced with revocation. The parolee has relied on at least an implicit promise that parole will be revoked only if he fails to live up to the parole conditions. In many cases the parolee faces lengthy incarceration if his parole is revoked.

We see, therefore, that the liberty of a parolee, although indeterminate, includes many of the core values of unqualified liberty and its termination inflicts a "grievous loss" on the parolee and often on others. It is hardly useful any longer to try to deal with this problem in terms of whether the parolee's liberty is a "right" or a "privilege." By whatever name the liberty is valuable and must be seen as within the protection of the Fourteenth Amendment. Its termination calls for some orderly process, however informal.

Turning to the question what process is due, we find that the State's interests are several. The State has found the parolee guilty of a crime against the people. That finding justifies imposing extensive restrictions on the individual's liberty. Release of the parolee before the end of his prison sentence is made with the recognition that with many prisoners there is a risk that they will not be able to live in society without committing additional antisocial acts. Given the previous conviction and the proper imposition of conditions, the State has an overwhelming interest in being able to return the individual to imprisonment without the burden of a new adversary criminal trial if in fact he has failed to abide by the conditions of his parole.

Yet the State has no interest in revoking parole without some informal procedural guarantees. Although the parolee is often formally described as being "in custody," the argument cannot even be made here that summary treatment is necessary as it may be with respect to controlling a large group of potentially disruptive prisoners in actual custody. Nor are we persuaded by the argument that revocation is so totally a discretionary matter that some form of hearing would be administratively intolerable. A simple factual hearing will not interfere with the exercise of discretion. Serious studies have suggested that fair treatment on parole revocation will not result in fewer grants of parole.

This discretionary aspect of the revocation decision need not be reached unless there is first an appropriate determination that the individual has in fact breached the conditions of parole. The parolee is not the only one who has a stake in his conditional liberty. Society has a stake in whatever may be the chance of restoring him to normal and useful life within the law. Society thus has an interest in not having parole revoked because of erroneous information or because of an erroneous evaluation of the need to revoke parole, given the breach of parole conditions. See *People ex rel. Menechino* v. *Warden,* 27 N.Y. 2d 376, 267 N.E. 2d 238, 239 and n. 2, 318 N.Y.S. 2d 449 (1971) (parole board had less than full picture of facts). And society has a further interest in treating the parolee with basic fairness: fair treatment in parole revocations will enhance the chance of rehabilitation by avoiding reactions to arbitrariness.

Given these factors, most States have recognized that there is no interest on the part of the State in revoking parole without any procedural guarantees at all. What is needed is an informal hearing structured to assure that the finding of a parole violation will be based on verified facts and that the exercise of discretion will be informed by an accurate knowledge of the parolee's behavior.

III

We now turn to the nature of the process that is due, bearing in mind that the interest of both State and parolee will be furthered by an effective but informal hearing. In analyzing what is due, we see two important stages in the typical process of parole revocation.

(a) Arrest of Parolee and Preliminary Hearing. The first stage occurs when the parolee is arrested and detained, usually at the direction of his parole officer. The second occurs when parole is formally revoked. There is typically a substantial time lag between the arrest and the eventual determination by the

parole board whether parole should be revoked. Additionally, it may be that the parolee is arrested at a place distant from the state institution, to which he may be returned before the final decision is made concerning revocation. Given these factors, due process would seem to require that some minimal inquiry be conducted at or reasonably near the place of the alleged parole violation or arrest and as promptly as convenient after arrest while information is fresh and sources are available. Cf. *Hyser* v. *Reed*, 318 F. 2d 225 (CADC 1963). Such an inquiry should be seen as in the nature of a "preliminary hearing" to determine whether there is probable cause or reasonable grounds to believe that the arrested parolee has committed acts which would constitute a violation of parole conditions. Cf *Goldberg* v. *Kelly*, 397 U.S., at 267–271.

In our view due process requires that after the arrest, the determination that reasonable grounds exist for revocation of parole should be made by someone not directly involved in the case. It would be unfair to assume that the supervising parole officer does not conduct an interview with the parolee to confront him with the reasons for revocation before he recommends an arrest. It would also be unfair to assume that the parole officer bears hostility against the parolee which destroys his neutrality; realistically the failure of the parolee is in a sense a failure for his supervising officer. However, we need make no assumptions one way or the other to conclude that there should be an uninvolved person to make this preliminary evaluation of the basis for believing the conditions of parole have been violated. The officer directly involved in making recommendations cannot always have complete objectivity in evaluating them. *Goldberg* v. *Kelly* found it unnecessary to impugn the motives of the caseworker to find a need for an independent decisionmaker to examine the initial decision.

This independent officer need not be a judicial officer. The granting and revocation of parole are matters traditionally handled by administrative officers. In *Goldberg*, the Court pointedly did not require that the hearing on termination of benefits be conducted by a judicial officer or even before the traditional "neutral and detached" officer; it required only that the hearing be conducted by some person *other* than one initially dealing with the case. It will be sufficient, therefore, in the parole revocation context, if an evaluation of whether reasonable cause exists to believe that conditions of parole have been violated is made by someone such as a parole officer other than the one who has made the report of parole violations or has recommended revocation. A State could certainly choose some other independent decisionmaker to perform this preliminary function.

With respect to the preliminary hearing before this officer, the parolee should be given notice that the hearing will take place and that its purpose is to determine whether there is probable cause to believe he has committed a parole violation. The notice should state what parole violations have been alleged. At the hearing the parolee may appear and speak in his own behalf; he may bring letters, documents, or individuals who can give relevant information to the hearing officer. On request of the parolee, persons who have given adverse information on which parole revocation is to be based are to be made available for questioning in his presence. However, if the hearing officer determines that the informant would be subjected to risk of harm if his identity were disclosed, he need not be subjected to confrontation and cross-examination.

The hearing officer shall have the duty of making a summary, or digest, of what transpires at the hearing in terms of the responses of the parolee and the substance of the documents or evidence given in support of parole revocation and of the parolee's position. Based on the information before him, the officer should determine whether there is probable cause to hold the parolee for the final decision of the parole board on revocation. Such a determination would be sufficient to warrant the parolee's continued detention and return to the state correctional institution pending the final decision. As in *Goldberg*, "the decision-maker should state the reasons for his determination and indicate the evidence he relied on . . ." but it should be remembered that this is not a final determination calling for "formal findings of fact or conclusions of law." 397 U.S., at 271. No interest would be served by formalism in this process; informality will not lessen the utility of this inquiry in reducing the risk of error.

(b) The Revocation Hearing. There must also be an opportunity for a hearing, if it is desired by the parolee, prior to the final decision on revocation by the parole authority. This hearing must be the basis for more than determining probable cause; it must lead to a final evaluation of any contested relevant facts and consideration of whether the facts as determined warrant revocation. The parolee must have an opportunity to be heard and to show,

if he can, that he did not violate the conditions, or, if he did, that circumstances in mitigation suggest the violation does not warrant revocation. The revocation hearing must be tendered within a reasonable time after the parolee is taken into custody. A lapse of two months, as the State suggests occurs in some cases, would not appear to be unreasonable.

We cannot write a code of procedure; that is the responsibility of each State. Most States have done so by legislation, others by judicial decision usually on due process grounds. Our task is limited to deciding the minimum requirements of due process. They include (a) written notice of the claimed violations of parole; (b) disclosure to the parolee of evidence against him; (c) opportunity to be heard in person and to present witnesses and documentary evidence; (d) the right to confront and cross-examine adverse witnesses (unless the hearing officer specifically finds good cause for not allowing confrontation); (e) a "neutral and detached" hearing body such as a traditional parole board, members of which need not be judicial officers or lawyers; and (f) a written statement by the factfinders as to the evidence relied on and reasons for revoking parole. We emphasize that there is no thought to equate this second stage of parole revocation to a criminal prosecution in any sense; it is a narrow inquiry; the process should be flexible enough to consider evidence including letters, affidavits, and other material that would not be admissible in an adversary criminal trial.

We do not reach or decide the question whether the parolee is entitled to the assistance of retained counsel or to appointed counsel if he is indigent.

We have no thought to create an inflexible structure for parole revocation procedures. The few basic requirements set out above, which are applicable to future revocations of parole, should not impose a great burden on any State's parole system. Control over the required proceedings by the hearing officers can assure that delaying tactics and other abuses sometimes present in the traditional adversary trial situation do not occur. Obviously a parolee cannot relitigate issues determined against him in other forums, as in the situation presented when the revocation is based on conviction of another crime.

In the peculiar posture of this case, given the absence of an adequate record, we conclude the ends of justice will be served by remanding the case to the Court of Appeals for its return of the two consolidated cases to the District Court with directions to make findings on the procedures actually followed by the Parole Board in these two revocations. If it is determined that petitioners admitted parole violations to the Parole Board, as Iowa contends, and if those violations are found to be reasonable grounds for revoking parole under state standards, that would end the matter. If the procedures followed by the Parole Board are found to meet the standards laid down in this opinion that, too, would dispose of the due process claims for these cases.

We reverse and remand to the Court of Appeals for further proceedings consistent with this opinion.

Reversed and Remanded.

MR. JUSTICE BRENNAN, concurring in the result.

I agree that a parole may not be revoked, consistently with the Due Process Clause, unless the parolee is afforded, first, a preliminary hearing at the time of arrest to determine whether there is probable cause to believe that he has violated his parole conditions and, second, a final hearing within a reasonable time to determine whether he has, in fact, violated those conditions and whether his parole should be revoked. For each hearing the parolee is entitled to notice of the violations alleged and the evidence against him, opportunity to be heard in person and to present witnesses and documentary evidence, and the right to confront and cross-examine adverse witnesses, unless it is specifically found that the witness would thereby be exposed to a significant risk of harm. Moreover, in each case the decisionmaker must be impartial, there must be some record of the proceedings, and the decisionmaker's conclusion must be set forth in written form indicating both the evidence and the reasons relied upon. Because the Due Process Clause requires these procedures, I agree that the case must be remanded as the Court orders.

The Court, however, states that it does not now decide whether the parolee is also entitled at each hearing to the assistance of retained counsel or of appointed counsel if he is indigent. *Goldberg* v. *Kelly,* 397 U.S. 254 (1970), nonetheless plainly dictates that he at least "must be allowed to retain an attorney if he so desires." *Id.,* at 270. As the Court said there, "Counsel can help delineate the issues, present the factual contentions in an orderly manner, conduct cross-examination, and generally safeguard the interests of" his client. *Id.,* at 270–271. The only question open under our precedents is whether counsel must be furnished the parolee if he is indigent.

MR. JUSTICE DOUGLAS, dissenting in part.

Each petitioner was sentenced for a term in an Iowa penitentiary for forgery. Somewhat over a year later each was released on parole. About six months later each was arrested for a parole violation and confined in a local jail. In about a week the Iowa Board of Parole revoked their paroles and each was returned to the penitentiary. At no time during any of the proceedings which led to the parole revocations were they granted a hearing or the opportunity to know, question, or challenge any of the facts which formed the basis of their alleged parole violations. Nor were they given an opportunity to present evidence on their own behalf nor to confront and cross-examine those on whose testimony their paroles were revoked.

Each challenged the revocation in the state courts and, obtaining no relief, filed the present petitions in the Federal District Court which denied relief. Their appeals were consolidated in the Court of Appeals which, sitting *en banc,* in each case affirmed the District Court by a four-to-three vote, 433 F. 2d 1942. The cases are here on a petition for a writ of certiorari, 404 U.S. 999, which we granted because there is a conflict between the decision below and *Hahn* v. *Burke,* 430 F. 2d 100, decided by the Court of Appeals for the Seventh Circuit.

Iowa has a board of parole which determines who shall be paroled. Once paroled a person is under the supervision of the director of the division of corrections of the Department of Social Services who in turn supervises parole agents. Parole agents do not revoke the parole of any person but only recommend that the board of parole revoke it. The Iowa Act provides that each parolee "shall be subject, at any time, to be taken into custody and returned to the institution" from which he was paroled. Thus Iowa requires no notice or hearing to put a parolee back in prison, *Curtis* v. *Bennett,* 256 Iowa 1164, 131 N.W. 2d 1; and it is urged that since parole, like probation, is only a privilege it may be summarily revoked. See *Escoe* v. *Zerbst,* 295 U.S. 490, 492–493; *Ughbanks* v. *Armstrong,* 208 U.S. 481. But we have long discarded the right-privilege distinction. See, *e. g., Graham* v. *Richardson,* 403 U.S. 365, 374; *Bell* v. *Burson,* 402 U.S. 535, 539; *Pickering* v. *Board of Education,* 391 U.S. 563, 568; cf. Van Alstyne, The Demise of the Right-Privilege Distinction in Constitutional Law, 81 Harv. L. Rev. 1439 (1968).

The Court said in *United States* v. *Wilson,* 7 Pet. 150, 161, that a "pardon is a deed." The same can be said of a parole, which when conferred gives the parolee a degree of liberty which is often associated with property interests.

We held in *Goldberg* v. *Kelly,* 397 U.S. 254, that the termination by a State of public assistance payments to a recipient without a prior evidentiary hearing denies him procedural due process in violation of the Fourteenth Amendment. Speaking of the termination of welfare benefits we said:

> Their termination involves state action that adjudicates important rights. The constitutional challenge cannot be answered by an argument that public assistance benefits are 'a privilege' and not a 'right.' " *Shapiro* v. *Thompson,* 394 U.S. 618, 627 n. 6 (1969). Relevant constitutional restraints apply as much to the withdrawal of public assistance benefits as to disqualification for unemployment compensation, *Sherbert* v. *Verner,* 374 U.S. 398 (1963); or to denial of a tax exemption, *Speiser* v. *Randall,* 357 U.S. 513 (1958); or to discharge from public employment, *Slochower* v. *Board of Higher Education,* 350 U.S. 551 (1956). The extent to which procedural due process must be afforded the recipient is influenced by the extent to which he may be "condemned to suffer grievous loss." *Joint Anti-Fascist Refugee Committee* v. *McGrath,* 341 U.S. 123, 168 (1951) (Frankfurter, J., concurring), and depends upon whether the recipient's interest in avoiding that loss outweighs the governmental interest in summary adjudication. Accordingly, as we said in *Cafeteria & Restaurant Workers Union* v. *McElroy,* 367 U.S. 886, 895 (1961), "consideration of what procedures due process may require under any given set of circumstances must begin with a determination of the precise nature of the government function involved as well as of the private interest that has been affected by governmental action." See also *Hannah* v. *Larche,* 363 U.S. 420, 440, 442 (1960). 397 U.S., at 262–263.

Under modern concepts of penology, paroling prisoners is part of the rehabilitory aim of the correctional philosophy. The objective is to return a prisoner to a full family and community life. See generally Note, 56 Geo.

L. J. 705 (1968); Note, 38 N. Y. U. L. Rev. 702 (1963); Comment, 72 Yale L. J. 368 (1962); and see *Baine* v. *Beckstead,* 10 Utah 2d 4, 347 P. 2d 554 (1959). The status he enjoys as a parolee is as important a right as those we reviewed in *Goldberg* v. *Kelly.* That status is conditioned upon not engaging in certain activities and perhaps in not leaving a certain area or locality. Violations of conditions of parole may be technical, they may be done unknowingly, they may be fleeting and of no consequence. See, *e. g., Arciniega* v. *Freeman,* 404 U.S. 4; Cohen, Due Process, Equal Protection and State Parole Revocation Proceedings, 42 U. Colo. L. Rev. 197, 229 (1970). The parolee should in the concept of fairness implicit in due process have a chance to explain. Rather, under Iowa's rule revocation proceeds on the *ipse dixit* of the parole agent; and on his word alone each of these petitioners has already served three additional years in prison. The charges may or may not be true. Words of explanation may be adequate to transform into trivia what looms large in the mind of the parole officer.

> [T]here is no place in our system of law for reaching a result of such tremendous consequences without ceremony—without hearing, without effective assistance of counsel, without a statement of reasons. *Kent* v. *United States,* 383 U.S. 541, 554 (1966).

Parole, while originally conceived as a judicial function, has become largely an administrative matter. The parole boards have broad discretion in formulating and imposing parole conditions. "Often vague and moralistic parole conditions may seem oppressive and unfair to the parolee." Dawson, Sentencing 306 (1969). They are drawn "to cover any contingency that might occur," *id.,* at 307, and are designed to maximize "control over the parolee by his parole officer." *Ibid.*

Parole is commonly revoked on mere suspicion that the parolee may have committed a crime. *Id.,* at 366–367. Such great control over the parolee vests in a parole officer a broad discretion in revoking parole and also in counseling the parolee—referring him for psychiatric treatment or obtaining the use of specialized therapy for narcotic addicts or alcoholics. *Id.,* at 321. Treatment of the parolee, rather than revocation of his parole, is a common course. *Id.,* at 322–323. Counseling may include extending help to a parolee in finding a job. *Id.,* at 324 *et seq.*

A parolee, like a prisoner, is a person entitled to constitutional protection, including procedural due process. At the federal level the construction of Regulations of the Federal Parole Board presents federal questions of which we have taken cognizance. See *Arciniega* v. *Freeman,* 404 U.S. 4. At the state level, the construction of parole statutes and regulations is for the States alone, save as they implicate the Federal Constitution in which event the Supremacy Clause controls.

It is only procedural due process, required by the Fourteenth Amendment, that concerns us in the present cases. Procedural due process requires the following.

If a violation of a condition of parole is involved, rather than the commission of a new offense, there should not be an arrest of the parolee and his return to the prison or to a local jail. Rather, notice of the alleged violation should be given to the parolee and a time set for a hearing. The hearing should not be before the parole officer, as he is the one who is making the charge and "there is inherent danger in combining the functions of the judge and advocate." *Jones* v. *Rivers,* 338 F. 2d 862, 877 (CA4 1964) (Sobeloff, J., concurring). Moreover, the parolee should be entitled to counsel. See *Hewett* v. *North Carolina,* 415 F. 2d 1316, 1322–1325 (CA4 1969); *People ex rel. Combs* v. *LaVallee,* 29 App. Div. 2d 128, 286 N. Y. S. 2d 600 (1968); *Perry* v. *Willard,* 247 Ore. 145, 427 P. 2d 1020 (1967). As the Supreme Court of Oregon said in *Perry* v. *Willard,* "A hearing in which counsel is absent or is present on behalf of one side is inherently unsatisfactory if not unfair. Counsel can see that the relevant facts are brought out, vague and insubstantial allegations discounted, and irrelevancies eliminated." *Id.,* at 148, 427 P. 2d, at 1022. Cf. *Mempa* v. *Rhay,* 389 U.S. 128, 135.

The hearing required is not a grant of the full panoply of rights applicable to a criminal trial. But confrontation with the informer may, as *Roviaro* v. *United States,* 353 U.S. 53, illustrates, be necessary for a fair hearing and the ascertainment of the truth. The hearing is to determine the fact of parole violation. The results of the hearing would go to the parole board—or other authorized state agency—for final action, as would cases which involved voluntary admission of violations.

The rule of law is important in the stability of society. Arbitrary actions in the revocation of paroles can only impede and impair the rehabilitory aspects of modern penology. "Notice and opportunity for hearing appropriate to the case," *Boddie v. Connecticut*, 401 U.S. 371, 378, are the rudiments of due process which restore faith that our society is run for the many, not the few, and that fair dealing rather than caprice will govern the affairs of men.

We do not prescribe the precise formula for the management of the parole problems. We do not sit as an ombudsman, telling the States the precise procedures they must follow. We do say that so far as the due process requirements of parole revocation are concerned:

(1) the parole officer—whatever may be his duties under various state statutes—in Iowa appears to be an agent having some of the functions of a prosecutor and of the police

(2) the parole officer is therefore not qualified as a hearing officer

(3) the parolee is entitled to a due process notice and a due process hearing of the alleged parole violations including, for example, the opportunity to be confronted by his accusers and to present evidence and argument on his own behalf

(4) the parolee is entitled to the freedom granted a parolee until the results of the hearing are known and the parole board—or other authorized state agency—acts. . . .

GAGNON V. SCARPELLI
41 U.S. L. WEEK (1973)
Supreme Court of the United States

MR. JUSTICE POWELL delivered the opinion of the Court.

This case presents the related questions whether a previously sentenced probationer is entitled to a hearing when his probation is revoked and, if so, whether he is entitled to be represented by appointed counsel at such a hearing.

I

Respondent, Gerald Scarpelli, pleaded guilty in July, 1965, to a charge of armed robbery in Wisconsin. The trial judge sentenced him to 15 years imprisonment, but suspended the sentence and placed him on probation for seven years in the custody of the Wisconsin Department of Public Welfare ("the Department")[1] At that time, he signed an agreement specifying the terms of his probation and a "Travel Permit and Agreement to Return" allowing him to reside in Illinois, with supervision there under an interstate compact. On August 5, 1965, he was accepted for supervision by the Adult Probation Department of Cook County, Illinois.

On August 6, respondent was apprehended by Illinois police, who had surprised him and one Fred Kleckner, Jr., in the course of the burglary of a house. After being apprised of his constitutional rights, respondent admitted tht he and Fleckner had broken into the house for the purpose of stealing merchandise or money, although he now asserts that his statement was made under duress and is false. Probation was revoked by the Wisconsin Department on September 1, without a hearing. The stated grounds for revocation were that:

> "1. [Scarpelli] has associated with known criminals, in direct violation of his probation regulations and his supervising agent's instructions;
>
> "2. [Scarpelli] while associating with a known criminal, namely Fred Kleckner, Jr., was involved in, and arrested for, a burglary . . . in Deerfield, Illinois." App., p. 20.

On September 4, 1965, he was incarcerated in the Wisconsin State Reformatory at Green Bay to begin serving the 15 years to which he had been sentenced by the trial judge. At no time was he afforded a hearing.

Some three years later, on December 16, 1968, respondent applied for a writ of habeas corpus. After the petition had been filed, but before it had been acted upon, the Department placed respondent on parole.[2] The District Court found that his status as parolee was sufficient custody to confer jurisdiction on the court and that the petition was not moot be-

---

[1] The Court's order placing respondent on probation provided, among other things, that "[i]n the event of his failure to meet the conditions of his probation he will stand committed under the sentence all ready [*sic*] imposed." App., p. 10. The agreement specifying the conditions of the probation, duly executed by respondent, obligated him to "make a sincere attempt to avoid all acts which are forbidden by law . . . ." App., p. 12.

[2] Respondent was initially paroled to a federal detainer to serve a previously imposed federal sentence arising from another conviction. He was subsequently released from federal custody, but remains a parolee under the supervision of the Department.

cause the revocation carried "collateral consequences," presumably including the restraints imposed by his parole. On the merits, the District Court held that revocation without a hearing and counsel was a denial of due process. 317 F. Supp. 72 (ED Wis. 1970). The Court of Appeals affirmed, *sub nom. Gunsolus* v. *Gagnon*, 454 F. 2d 416 (CA7 1971), and we granted certiorari. 408 U.S. 921 (1972).

II

Two prior decisions set the bounds of our present inquiry. In *Mempa* v. *Rhay*, 389 U.S. 128 (1967), the Court held that a probationer is entitled to be represented by appointed counsel at a combined revocation and sentencing hearing. Reasoning that counsel is required "at every stage of a criminal proceeding where substantial rights of a criminal accused may be affected." 389 U.S., at 134, and that sentencing is one such stage, the Court concluded that counsel must be provided an indigent at sentencing even when it is accomplished as part of a subsequent, probation revocation proceeding. But this line of reasoning does not require a hearing or counsel at the time of probation revocation in a case such as the present one, where the probationer was sentenced at the time of trial.

Of greater relevance is our decision last Term in *Morrissey* v. *Brewer*, 408 U.S. 471 (1972). There we held that the revocation of parole is not a part of a criminal prosecution.

> "Parole arises after the end of the criminal prosecution, including imposition of sentence.... Revocation deprives an individual, not of the absolute liberty to which every citizen is entitled, but only of the conditional liberty properly dependent on observance of special parole restrictions." 40 U.S., at 480.

Even though the revocation of parole is not a part of the criminal prosecution, we held that the loss of liberty entailed is a serious deprivation requiring that the parolee be accorded due process. Specifically, we held that a parolee is entitled to two hearings, one a preliminary hearing at the time of his arrest and detention to determine whether there is probable cause to believe that he has committed a violation of his parole and the other a somewhat more comprehensive hearing prior to the making of the final revocation decision.

Petitioner does not contend that there is any difference relevant to the guarantee of due process between the revocation of parole and the revocation of probation, nor do we perceive one.[3] Probation revocation, like parole revocation, is not a stage of a criminal prosecution, but does result in a loss of liberty.[4] Accordingly, we hold that a probationer, like a parolee, is entitled to a preliminary and a final revocation hearing, under the conditions specified in *Morrissey* v. *Brewer, supra.*[5]

[3] Despite the undoubted minor differences between probation and parole, the commentators have agreed that revocation of probation where sentence has been imposed previously is constitutionally indistinguishable from the revocation of parole. See, *e.g.,* Van Dyke, Parole Revocation Hearings in California: The Right to Counsel, 59 Calif. L. Rev. 1215, 1241–1243 (1971); Sklar, Law and Practice in Probation and Parole Revocation Hearings, 55 J. Crim. L. C. & P. S. 175, 198 n. 182 (1964).

[4] It is clear at least after *Morrissey* v. *Brewer, supra,* that a probationer can no longer be denied due process, in reliance on the dictum in *Escoe* v. *Zerbst,* 295 U.S. 490, 492 (1935), that probation is an "act of grace."

[5] Petitioner argues in addition that the *Morrissey* hearing requirements impose serious practical problems in cases such as the present one in which a probationer or parolee is allowed to leave the convicting State for supervision in another State. Such arrangements are made pursuant to an interstate compact adopted by all of the States, including Wisconsin. Wis. Stat. Ann. § 57.13. Petitioner's brief asserts that as of June 30, 1972, Wisconsin had a total of 642 parolees and probationers under supervision in other States and that incomplete statistics as of June 30, 1971, indicated a national total of 24,693 persons under out-of-state supervision. Petitioner's Brief. pp. 21–22.

Some amount of disruption inevitably attends any new constitutional ruling. We are confident, however, that modification of the interstate compact can remove without undue strain the more serious technical hurdles to compliance with *Morrissey*. An additional comment is warranted with respect to the rights to present witnesses and to confront and cross-examine adverse witnesses. Petitioner's greatest concern is with the difficulty and expense of procuring witnesses from perhaps thousands of miles away. While in some cases there is simply no adequate alternative to live testimony, we emphasize that we did not in *Morrissey* intend to prohibit use where appropriate of the conventional substitutes for live testimony, including affidavits, depositions, and documentary evidence. Nor did we intend to foreclose the States from holding both the preliminary and the final hearings at the place of violation or from developing other creative solutions to the practical difficulties of the *Morrissey* requirements.

III

The second, and more difficult, question posed by this case is whether an indigent probationer or parolee has a due process right to be represented by appointed counsel at these hearings.[6] In answering that question, we draw heavily on the opinion in *Morrissey*. Our first point of reference is the character of probation or parole. As noted in *Morrissey* regarding parole, the "purpose is to help individuals reintegrate into society as constructive individuals as soon as they are able...." 408 U.S., at 477. The duty and attitude of the probation or parole officer reflect this purpose:

> "While the parole or probation officer recognizes his double duty to the welfare of his clients and to the safety of the general community, by and large concern for the client dominates his professional attitude. The parole agent ordinarily defines his role as representing his client's best interests as long as these do not constitute a threat to public safety."[7]

Because the probation or parole officer's function is not so much to compel conformance to a strict code of behavior as to supervise a course of rehabilitation, he has been entrusted traditionally with broad discretion to judge the progress of rehabilitation in individual cases, and has been armed with the power to recommend or even to declare revocation.

In *Morrissey*, we recognized that the revocation decision has two analytically distinct components:

> "The first step in a revocation decision involves a wholly retrospective factual question: whether the parolee has in fact acted in violation of one or more conditions of his parole. Only if it is determined that the parolee did violate the conditions does the second question arise: should the parolee be recommitted to prison or should other steps be taken to protect society and improve chances of rehabilitation?" *Morrissey v. Brewer, supra*, 408 U.S., at 479–480.[8]

The parole officer's attitude toward these decisions reflects the rehabilitative rather than punitive focus of the probation-parole system:

> "Revocation ... is, if anything, commonly treated as a failure of supervision. While presumably it would be inappropriate for a field agent *never* to revoke, the whole thrust of the probation-parole movement is to keep men in the community, working with adjustment problems there, and using revocation only as a last resort when treatment has failed or is about to fail."[9]

But an exclusive focus on the benevolent attitudes of those who administer the probation-parole system when it is working successfully obscures the modification in attitude which is likely to take place once the officer has decided to recommend revocation. Even though the officer is not by this recommendation converted into a prosecutor committed to convict, his role as counsellor to the probationer or parolee is then surely compromised.

When the officer's view of the probationer's or parolee's conduct differs in this fundamental way from the latter's own view, due process requires that the difference be resolved before revocation becomes final. Both the probationer or parolee and the State have interests in the

---

[6] In *Morrissey* v. *Brewer, supra*, we left open the question "whether the parolee is entitled to the assistance of retained counsel or to appointed counsel if he is indigent." 408 U.S., at 489. Since respondent did not attempt to retain counsel but asked only for appointed counsel, we have no occasion to decide in this case whether a probationer or parolee has a right to be represented at a revocation hearing by retained counsel in situations other than those where the State would be obliged to furnish counsel for an indigent.

[7] Remington, Newman, Kimball, Melli & Goldstein, Criminal Justice Administration, Materials and Cases 910–911 (1969).

[8] The factors entering into these decisions relate in major part to a professional evaluation, by trained probation or parole officers, as to the overall social readjustment of the offender in the community, and include consideration of such variables as the offender's relationship toward his family, his attitude toward the fulfillment of financial obligations, the extent of his cooperation with the probation officer assigned to his case, his personal associations, and—of course—whether there have been specific and significant violations of the conditions of the probation. The importance of these considerations, some factual and others entirely judgmental, is illustrated by a Wisconsin empirical study which disclosed that, in the sample studied, probation or parole was revoked in only 34.5% if the cases in which the probationer or parolee violated the terms of his release. S. Hunt, The Revocation Decision: A Study of Probation and Parole Agent's Discretion 10 (unpublished thesis on file at the library of the University of Wisconsin) (1964), cited in Petitioner's Brief, Addendum, p. 106.

[9] Remington, Newman, Kimball, Melli & Goldstein, *supra* n. 7, at 910.

accurate finding of fact and the informed use of discretion, the probationer or parolee to insure that his liberty is not unjustifiably taken away and the State to make certain that it is neither unnecessary interrupting a successful effort at rehabilitation nor imprudently prejudicing the safety of the community.

It was to serve all of these interests that *Morrissey* mandated preliminary and final revocation hearings. At the preliminary hearing, a probationer or parolee is entitled to notice of the alleged violations of probation or parole, an opportunity to appear and to present evidence in his own behalf, a conditional right to confront adverse witnesses, an independent decisionmaker, and a written report of the hearing. *Morrissey* v. *Brewer, supra,* 408 U.S., at 487. The final hearing is a less summary one because the decision under consideration is the ultimate decision to revoke rather than a mere determination of probable cause, but the "minimum requirements of due process" include very similar elements:

> "(a) written notice of the claimed violations of [probation or] parole; (b) disclosure to the [probationer or] parolee of evidence against him; (c) opportunity to be heard in person and to present witnesses and documentary evidence; (d) the right to confront and cross-examine adverse witnesses (unless the hearing officer specifically finds good cause for not allowing confrontation); (e) a 'neutral and detached' hearing body such as a traditional parole board, members of which need not be judicial officers or lawyers; and (f) a written statement by the fact-finders as to the evidence relied on and reasons for revoking [probation or] parole." *Morrissey* v. *Brewer, supra,* 408 U.S., at 489.

These requirements in themselves serve as substantial protection against ill-considered revocation, and petitioner argues that counsel need never be supplied. What this argument overlooks is that the effectiveness of the rights guaranteed by *Morrissey* may in some circumstances depend on the use of skills which the probationer or parolee is unlikely to possess. Despite the informal nature of the proceedings and the absence of technical rules of procedure or evidence, the unskilled or uneducated probationer or parolee may well have difficulty in presenting his version of a disputed set of facts where the presentation requires the examining or cross-examining of witnesses or the offering or dissecting of complex documentary evidence.

By the same token, we think that the Court of Appeals erred in accepting respondent's contention that the State is under a constitutional duty to provide counsel for indigents in all probation or parole revocation cases. While such a rule has the appeal of simplicity, it would impose direct costs and serious collateral disadvantages without regard to the need or the likelihood in a particular case for a constructive contribution by counsel. In most cases, the probationer or parolee has been convicted of committing another crime or has admitted the charges against him.[10] And while in some cases he may have a justifiable excuse for the violation or a convincing reason why revocation is not the appropriate disposition, mitigating evidence of this kind is often not susceptible of proof or is so simple as not to require either investigation or exposition by counsel.

The introduction of counsel into a revocation proceeding will alter significantly the nature of the proceeding. If counsel is provided for the probationer or parolee, the State in turn will normally provide its own counsel; lawyers, by training and disposition, are advocates and bound by professional duty to present all available evidence and arguments in support of their clients' positions and to contest with vigor all adverse evidence and views. The role of the hearing body itself, aptly described in *Morrissey* as being "predictive and discretionary" as well as factfinding, may become more akin to that of a judge at a trial, and less attuned to the rehabilitative needs of the individual probationer or parolee. In the gerater self-consciousness of its quasi-judicial role, the hearing body may be less tolerant of marginal deviant behavior and feel more pressure to reincarcerate rather than continue nonpunitive rehabilitation. Certainly, the decisionmaking process will be prolonged, and the financial cost to the State—for appointed counsel, counsel for the State, a longer record, and the possibility of judicial review—will not be insubstantial.[11]

In some cases, these modifications in the

[10] See Sklar, *supra* n. 3, at 192 (parole), 193 (probation).

[11] The scope of the practical problem which would be occasioned by a requirement of counsel in all revocation cases is suggested by the fact that in the mid-1960's there were an estimated average of 20,000 adult felony parole revocations and 108,000 adult probation revocations each year. President's Commission on Law Enforcement and Administration of Justice, Task Force Report: The Courts 56 n. 28 (1967).

nature of the revocation hearing must be endured and the costs borne because, as we have indicated above, the probationer's or parolee's version of a disputed issue can fairly be represented only by a trained advocate. But due process is not so rigid as to require that the significant interests in informality, flexibility, and economy must always be sacrificed.

In so concluding, we are of course aware that the case-by-case approach to the right to counsel in felony prosecutions adopted in *Betts* v. *Brady*, 316 U.S. 455 (1942), was later rejected in favor of a *per se* rule in *Gideon* v. *Wainwright*, 372 U.S. 335 (1963). See also *Argersinger* v. *Hamlin*, 407 U.S. 25 (1972). We do not, however, draw from *Gideon* and *Argersinger* the conclusion that a case-by-case approach to furnishing counsel is necessarily inadequate to protect constitutional rights asserted in varying types of proceedings: there are critical differences between criminal trials and probation or parole revocation hearings, and both society and the probationer or parolee have stakes in preserving these differences.

In a criminal trial, the State is represented by a prosecutor; formal rules of evidence are in force; a defendant enjoys a number of procedural rights which may be lost if not timely raised; and, in a jury trial, a defendant must make a presentation understandable to untrained jurors. In short, a criminal trial under our system is an adversary proceeding with its own unique characteristics. In a revocation hearing, on the other hand, the State is represented not by a prosecutor but by a parole officer with the orientation described above; formal procedures and rules of evidence are not employed; and the members of the hearing body are familiar with the problems and practice of probation or parole. The need for counsel at revocation hearings derives not from the invariable attributes of those hearings but rather from the peculiarities of particular cases.

The differences between a criminal trial and a revocation hearing do not dispose altogether of the argument that under a case-by-case approach there may be cases in which a lawyer would be useful but in which none would be appointed because an arguable defense would be uncovered only by a lawyer. Without denying that there is some force in this argument, we think it a sufficient answer that we deal here not with the right of an accused to counsel in a criminal prosecution, but with the more limited due process right of one who is a probationer or parolee only because he has been convicted of a crime.

We thus find no justification for a new inflexible constitutional rule with respect to the requirement of counsel. We think, rather, that the decision as to the need for counsel must be made on a case-by-case basis in the exercise of a sound discretion by the state authority charged with responsibility for administering the probation and parole system. Although the presence and participation of counsel will probably be both undesirable and constitutionally unnecessary in most revocation hearings, there will remain certain cases in which fundamental fairness—the touchstone of due process—will require that the State provide at its expense counsel for indigent probationers or parolees.

It is neither possible nor prudent to attempt to formulate a precise and detained set of guidelines to be followed in determining when the providing of counsel is necessary to meet the applicable due process requirements. The facts and circumstances in preliminary and final hearings are susceptible of almost infinite variation, and a considerable discretion must be allowed the responsible agency in making the decision. Presumptively, it may be said that counsel should be provided in cases where, after being informed of his right to request counsel, the probationer or parolee makes such a request, based on a timely and colorable claim (i) that he has not committed the alleged violation of the conditions upon which he is at liberty; or (ii) that, even if the violation is a matter of public record or is uncontested, there are substantial reasons which justified or mitigated the violation and make revocation inappropriate and that the reasons are complex or otherwise difficult to develop or present. In passing on a request for the appointment of counsel, the responsible agency also should consider, especially in doubtful cases, whether the probationer appears to be capable of speaking effectively for himself. In every case in which a request for counsel at a preliminary or final hearing is refused, the grounds for refusal should be stated succinctly in the record.

IV

We return to the facts of the present case. Because respondent was not afforded either a preliminary hearing or a final hearing, the revocation of his probation did not meet the standards of due process prescribed in *Morris-*

sey, which we have here held applicable to probation revocations. Accordingly, respondent was entitled to a writ of habeas corpus. On remand, the District Court should allow the State an opportunity to conduct such a hearing. As to whether the State must provide counsel, respondent's admission to having committed another serious crime creates the very sort of situation in which counsel need not ordinarily be provided. But because of respondent's subsequent assertions regarding that admission, we conclude that the failure of the Department to provide respondent with the assistance of counsel should be re-examined in light of this opinion. The general guidelines outlined above should be applied in the first instance by those charged with conducting the revocation hearing.

Note PREVAILING AMERICAN PAROLE REVOCATION PRACTICES PRIOR TO MORRISSEY V. BREWER*

* Vincent O'Leary and Joan Nuffield, *Parole Decision-Making Characteristics: Report of a National Survey,* Vol. 8, No. 8, *Criminal Law Bulletin* (October 1972), pp. 679–80 (1962). © Warren, Gorham & Lamont, Inc., Boston. Reprinted with permission of the publisher.

SELECTED CHARACTERISTICS OF PAROLE-REVOCATION HEARINGS FOR FELONY OFFENDERS IN THE UNITED STATES: JANUARY 1972 PART ONE

Jurisdiction	Bail Permitted if New Charge Pending	Warrant Needed for Arrest	Written Notice Given to Alleged Violator	Place Where Hearing Held
U.S. Board of Parole	yes	yes	yes	locally[b]
Alabama	no	no	yes	state institution
Alaska	no	no	yes	state institution
Arizona	yes	yes	yes	state institution
Arkansas	yes	yes	no	state institution
California	no	no	yes	state institution
California Women	no	no	yes	state institution
Colorado	no	no	yes	state institution
Connecticut	yes	yes	yes	state institution
Delaware	no	no	yes	state institution
District of Columbia	yes	yes	no	state institution
Florida	yes	no	yes	state institution
Georgia	no	yes	no	locally
Hawaii	no	yes	yes	state institution
Idaho	no	no	yes	locally
Illinois	no[a]	yes	yes	state institution
Indiana	yes	yes	no	state institution
Indiana Women	yes	yes	no	state institution
Iowa	yes	no	no	state institution
Kansas	yes	no	yes	state institution
Kentucky	no	no	yes	state institution
Louisiana	no	no	no	state institution
Maine	no	no	no	state institution
Maryland	yes	yes	yes	state institution
Massachusetts	no[a]	yes	no	state institution
Michigan	no	no	yes	state institution
Minnesota	yes	no	yes	state institution
Missouri	no	no	yes	state institution
Mississippi	no	no	no	state institution
Montana	yes	yes	yes	state institution
Nebraska	yes	no	yes	state institution
Nevada	yes	no	yes	state institution
New Hampshire	no	yes	no	state institution
New Jersey	no[a]	yes	yes	state institution
New Mexico	no	yes	yes	state institution
New York	no	yes	no	state institution
North Carolina	yes	yes	yes	state institution

PAROLE-REVOCATION HEARINGS—PART ONE (Continued)

Jurisdiction	Bail Permitted if New Charge Pending	Warrant Needed for Arrest	Written Notice Given to Alleged Violator	Place Where Hearing Held
North Dakota	yes	no	no	state institution
Ohio	no	no	no	state institution
Oklahoma	no	no	yes	locally
Oregon	yes	yes	no	state institution
Pennsylvania	yes	no	yes	state institution
Rhode Island	no	no	no	state institution
South Carolina	yes	no	yes	state institution
South Dakota	no	no	no	state institution
Tennessee	no	yes	no	state institution
Texas	no[a]	no	no	state institution
Utah	no[a]	no	yes	state institution
Vermont	no	no	yes	state institution
Virginia	no	no	yes	state institution
Washington	no	yes	yes	locally
West Virginia	no	no	yes	locally
Wisconsin	yes	no	yes	locally
Wyoming	no	no	yes	state institution

[a] In special cases parolees facing new charges may be permitted bail.
[b] Locally means at or near the site of the alleged violation.

PAROLE-REVOCATION HEARINGS—PART TWO

Jurisdiction	Counsel Permitted at Hearing	Parolee Allowed to Present Witnesses	Parolee Allowed to Confront Accusers	Parolee Allowed to See Violation Reports	How Parolee Informed of Final Decision	Reasons for Decision Recorded	Verbatim Record Kept of Hearing
U.S. Board of Parole	yes	no	no	no	after hearing[d]	no	yes
Alabama	yes	yes	yes	no	in person[e]	no	no
Alaska	yes	no	yes	yes	after hearing	no	no
Arizona	yes	yes	no[a]	no[c]	after hearing	no	no
Arkansas	yes	yes	no[a]	no[c]	after hearing	yes	no
California	no	no	no	yes	after hearing	no	yes
California Women	no	no	no	yes	in person	no	no
Colorado	no	no	yes	no	in person	no	yes
Connecticut	no	no	no	no	in person	no	yes
Delaware	yes	yes	yes	yes	in person	no	no
District of Columbia	yes	yes	no	no	after hearing	no	yes
Florida	yes	yes	yes	no	after hearing	no	yes
Georgia	yes	yes	yes	no	after hearing	no	no
Hawaii	yes	yes	yes	yes	after hearing	no	yes
Idaho	yes	yes	yes	yes	after hearing	no	yes
Illinois	yes	yes	yes	no	after hearing	no	yes
Indiana	no	no	no	no	after hearing	no	no
Indiana Women	no	no	no	no	in person	no	no
Iowa	no	no	no	yes	after hearing	no	no
Kansas	no	no	no	no	after hearing	no	no
Kentucky	no	no	no	no	in person	no	no
Louisiana	yes	yes	yes	yes	in person	no	no
Maine	no	no	no	no	after hearing	no	no
Maryland	yes	yes	yes	yes	in person	no	yes
Massachusetts	no	no	no	no	after hearing	no	no
Michigan	yes	yes	yes	no	after hearing	no	no
Minnesota	no	no	no	no	after hearing	no	no

PAROLE-REVOCATION HEARINGS—PART TWO (Continued)

Jurisdiction	Counsel Permitted at Hearing	Parolee Allowed to Present Witnesses	Parolee Allowed to Confront Accusers	Parolee Allowed to See Violation Reports	How Parolee Informed of Final Decision	Reasons for Decision Recorded	Verbatim Record Kept of Hearing
Mississippi	yes	yes	no	no	after hearing	no	yes
Missouri	no	no	no	no	after hearing	no	yes
Montana	yes	yes	yes	yes	after hearing	no	no
Nebraska	yes	yes	no	no	in person	no	yes
Nevada	yes	yes	yes	yes	after hearing	no	yes
New Hampshire	yes	yes	yes	yes	after hearing	no	yes
New Jersey	no	no	no	no	after hearing	no	no
New Mexico	no	no	no	no	after hearing	no	no
New York	yes	yes	yes	yes	after hearing	no	yes
North Carolina	yes	yes	yes	no	after hearing	no	no
North Dakota	yes	yes	yes	yes	in person	no	yes
Ohio	no	no	no	no	after hearing	no	no
Oklahoma	yes	yes	yes	yes	after hearing	no	yes[f]
Oregon	no	no	no	no	after hearing	no	yes
Pennsylvania	yes	no	no	no	after hearing	no	no
Rhode Island	yes	no	no	no	after hearing	yes	yes
South Carolina	yes	yes	yes	yes	in person	no	yes
South Dakota	yes	yes	yes	no	after hearing	no	no
Tennessee	yes	yes	no	no	after hearing	no	no
Texas	yes	yes	yes[b]	no	after hearing	no	no
Utah	yes	yes	no	yes	in person	no	yes
Vermont	yes	no	yes[b]	no	in person	no	yes
Virginia	yes	yes	yes	no	after hearing	no	yes
Washington	yes	yes	yes	no	in person	yes	yes
West Virginia	yes	yes	yes	no	after hearing	yes	yes
Wisconsin	yes	yes	yes	yes	after hearing	no	no
Wyoming	yes	yes	yes	yes	in person	no	yes

(a) In rare case confrontation permitted.
(b) Parole officer only.
(c) In rare case disclosure permitted.
(d) "After hearing" means notification given by mail or third party.
(e) "In person" means parole board members at the hearing.
(f) If requested by parolee.

NOTE

The Relationship between Proof of Revocation Charges and Self-Incrimination on New Criminal Charges

MELSON V. SARD
402 F.2d 653 (1968)
United States Court of Appeals, District of Columbia Circuit

PER CURIAM:

This appeal contests the granting of a summary judgment in favor of the appellees, members of the District of Columbia Board of Parole. At issue is the Parole Board's ability, upon the return of a criminal indictment against a parolee, to promptly execute a parole-violator warrant and conduct a revocation hearing, thus requiring the parolee to present some or all of his case in this administrative proceeding prior to his day in court on his criminal charges. Subject to the limitations indicated below, we affirm the District Court's ruling that the Parole Board has authority to retake a parolee upon his indictment for another crime and is not precluded from considering the new criminal charges at its parole revocation hearing. . . .

In his petition for declaratory and injunctive relief appellant contends that he will be denied due process of law if a revocation hearing is held prior to his trial on the murder charges. More specifically, he asserts that his

Fifth Amendment freedom from self-incrimination will be violated if he is forced to face the dilemma of whether to testify at the revocation hearing and seek his release, but risk uttering incriminatory statements that could be used against him at his criminal trial. On the other hand, if he remains silent, he will not fully be able to defend against revocation. Appellant further contends that having to defend against the criminal charges at the revocation hearing will force him to disclose his trial tactics in advance, thus weakening his defense.

Although we fully recognize appellant's dilemma, we are unconvinced that its resolution should be achieved by postponing the revocation hearing....

... We think the solution lies in establishing certain safeguards by which the parolee's dilemma is lessened at the revocation hearing. We feel that the parolee's most significant handicap—the fear of self-incrimination—can readily be eliminated....

If a parolee is not given the full and free ability to testify in his own behalf and present his case against revocation, his right to a hearing before the Board would be meaningless. Furthermore, his Fifth Amendment rights must not be conditioned "by the exaction of a price." Accordingly, we hold that any self-incriminatory statements made in a parole revocation hearing shall not be used affirmatively against the parolee in any subsequent criminal proceeding. . . .

NOTES

"Street Time"

Note 1. Freedom or Incarceration Pending Disposition of Parole Revocation Charges

ROSE V. NICKESON
29 Conn. Supp. 102, 273 A.2d 290 (1970)
Connecticut Superior Court

On November 14, 1961 the petitioner was sentenced in the Superior Court for Fairfield County to a term of not less than twelve nor more than fifteen years at the State Prison for the crime of manslaughter. On July 19, 1969 the petitioner was released on parole. On June 30, 1970 the petitioner was arrested in Bridgeport by federal authorities and charged with violation of the federal narcotic drug laws. The penalties for violation of these laws range from a minimum imprisonment of two years to a maximum imprisonment of twenty years. On August 20, 1970 the petitioner was arrested pursuant to a parole violation warrant issued by the Deputy Commissioner of Corrections and has been detained in custody by the Commissioner of Corrections under this warrant. Since the rearrest of the petitioner and his return to custody the board of parole has neither revoked nor suspended his parole. The petitioner has been admitted to bail in this court in the amount of $5,000 pending the disposition of the present habeas corpus.

The petitioner claims that his parole cannot be revoked without a hearing by the parole board. The respondent agrees. The petitioner claims that no such hearing should be held during the pendency of the federal charges. The respondent agrees. Finally, the petitioner claims that he has a right to remain on parole until the federal charges are resolved. The respondent does not agree. The respondent argues that the effect of the rearrest is to suspend parole while the federal charges are outstanding.

Parole is at the discretion of the board of parole. One of the factors which the parole board must consider in deciding to grant release on parole is whether "there is reasonable probability that such inmate will live and remain at liberty without violating the law." General Statute § 54-125. When a parolee is arrested on another charge the basis for the release is open to question. Under these circumstances the parole board has the discretionary authority to suspend parole or to detain the parolee without bail until the matter is resolved.

At the time of this petition the petitioner was lawfully in custody under a rearrest warrant. Although his detention can be continued only with the approval of the parole board, he can be held in custody under the warrant for a reasonable period of time until the board shall have an opportunity to act.

Accordingly, the petition is dismissed and the petitioner is remanded to the custody of the Commissioner of Corrections.

Note 2. "Credit" for "Clean" Street Time

BONOMO V. NEW JERSEY STATE PAROLE BOARD
104 N.J. Super. 226, 249 A.2d 611 (1969)
New Jersey Superior Court

... Does a convict, paroled during service of his sentence, who commits a crime during parole, but whose parole is revoked for a cause other than commission of crime, forfeit his "street time" (i.e., between date of parole and date of apprehension for delinquency on parole) [?]

In respect of this subject we are controlled by the statute, N.J.S.A. 30:4-123.24, which reads:

> A prisoner, whose parole has been revoked *because of* a violation of a condition of parole or commission of an offense which subsequently results in conviction of a crime committed while on parole, even though such conviction be subsequent to the date of revocation of parole, shall be required, unless said revocation is rescinded, or unless sooner reparoled by the board, to serve the balance of time due on his sentence to be computed from the date of his original release on parole. If parole is revoked *for reasons other than* subsequent conviction for crime while on parole then the parolee, unless said revocation is rescinded, or unless sooner reparoled by the board, shall be required to serve the balance of time due on his sentence to be computed as of the date that he was declared delinquent on parole. (Emphasis added)

It is clear to us that the Legislature has by this language made the consequences of violation of parole, in terms of requirement of service of street time, expressly dependent on the "reasons" for the revocation of parole assigned by the Parole Board. If the parole is revoked "because" of conduct by the parolee during parole which subsequently results in conviction of crime, street time is forfeited. If parole is revoked for any other "reason," it is not, and service of the uncompleted term is required beginning only as of the date of declaration of delinquency on parole. . . .

The Board concedes that Bonomo's conviction of disorderly conduct was not a conviction of a "crime"; and see Sawran v. Lennon, 19 N.J. 606, 611–12, 118 A.2d 10 (1955). It must follow that the Board did not revoke Bonomo's parole because of an offense resulting in conviction of a *crime,* and the second sentence of N.J.S.A. 30:4-123.24 accordingly becomes operative. Defendant can be required to serve only the balance of time due on his sentence to be computed as of the date of declaration of delinquency on parole (subject to our holding in II, hereinafter). . . .

Note 3. Establishing Release Date After Revocation

GIORDANO V. HENDERSON
456 F.2d 1293 (1970)
United States Court of Appeals Second Circuit

PER CURIAM:

The district court denied the petition of this federal prisoner seeking his immediate release. We affirm.

The appellant is serving a ten-year sentence for bank robbery imposed on August 6, 1959, in the Eastern District of New York. After serving five years and eight months, he was released on parole, but was retaken for parole violation on May 19, 1969. Appellant contends that he is entitled to his immediate release because he has served time in excess of his ten-year sentence less good conduct time.

It is settled in this circuit that credit for good time accumulated prior to parole may be revoked after a parole violation. The judgment below is Affirmed.

H. Problems of Federalism: The Parole Compact and Detainers

The Parole Compact*

Sec. 54-133. Interstate Compact for Parolee Supervision

(a) The governor is authorized and directed to execute a compact on behalf of the state of Connecticut with any of the United States legally joining therein in the form substantially as follows: A compact entered into by and among the contracting states, signatories hereto, with the consent of the congress of the United States of America, granted by an act entitled "An act granting the consent of Congress to any two or more states to enter into agreements or compacts for cooperative effort and mutual assistance in the prevention of crime and for other purposes." The contracting states

* Conn. Gen. Stat. §§ 54-133 *et seq.*

solemnly agree: (1) That it shall be competent for the duly constituted judicial and administrative authorities of a state party to this compact (herein called "sending state"), to permit any person convicted of an offense within such state and placed on probation or released on parole to reside in any other state party to this compact (herein called "receiving state"), while on probation or parole, if (a) such person is in fact a resident of, or has his family residing within, and is able to obtain employment within, the receiving state; (b) though such person is not a resident of the receiving state and has no family residing therein, the receiving state consents to allow him to reside therein; provided, before such permission shall be granted, opportunity shall be granted to the receiving state to investigate the home and prospective employment of such person; a resident of the receiving state, within the meaning of this section, being construed to be one who has been an actual inhabitant of such state continuously for more than one year prior to his coming to the sending state and who has not resided within the sending state more than six continuous months immediately preceding the commission of the offense for which he has been convicted; (2) that each receiving state shall assume the duties of visitation of and supervision over probationers or parolees of any sending state and in the exercise of such duties will be governed by the same standards that prevail for its own probationers and parolees; (3) that duly accredited officers of a sending state may, at all times, enter a receiving state and there apprehend and retake any person on probation or parole, and for that purpose no formalities shall be required other than establishing the authority of the officer and the identity of the person to be retaken; all legal requirements to obtain extradition of fugitives from justice are being expressly waived on the part of the states party hereto, as to such persons and the decision of the sending state to retake a person on probation or parole to be conclusive upon and not reviewable within the receiving state; provided, if, at the time when a state shall seek to retake a probationer or parolee, there shall be pending against him within the receiving state any criminal charge, or he shall be suspected of having committed within such state a criminal offense, he shall not be retaken without the consent of the receiving state until discharged from prosecution or from imprisonment for such offense; (4) that the duly accredited officers of the sending state shall be permitted to transport prisoners being retaken through any and all states parties to this compact, without interference; (5) that the governor of each contracting state may designate an officer who, acting jointly with like officers of other contracting states, if and when appointed, shall promulgate such rules and regulations as may be deemed necessary to more effectively carry out the terms of this compact; (6) that this compact shall become operative immediately upon its execution by any state as between it and any other state or states so executing and, when executed, it shall have the full force and effect of law within such state, the form of execution to be in accordance with the laws of the executing state; (7) that this compact shall continue in force and remain binding upon each executing state until renounced by it, that the duties and obligations hereunder of a renouncing state shall continue as to parolees or probationers residing therein at the time of withdrawal until they shall be retaken or finally discharged by the sending state and that renunciation of this compact shall be by the same authority which executed it, by the sending of six months' notice in writing of its intention to withdraw from the compact to each other state party hereto. Whenever the duly constituted judicial and administrative authorities in a sending state shall determine that incarceration of a probationer or reincarceration of a parolee is necessary or desirable, said officials may direct that the incarceration or reincarceration be in a prison or other correctional institution within the territory of the receiving state, such receiving state to act in that regard solely as agent for the sending state. (b) If any section, sentence, subdivision or clause of this section is for any reason held invalid or to be unconstitutional, such decision shall not affect the validity of the remaining portions of this section. (c) Sections 54-132 to 54-138, inclusive, may be cited as the Uniform Act for Out-of-State Parolee Supervision.

Sec. 54-138a. *Retaking of Parolee*

If the parole officer having charge of a paroled prisoner received under the interstate compact authorized under section 54-133 has reasonable cause to believe that he has lapsed, or is probably about to lapse, into criminal ways or company, or has violated the conditions of his parole, such parole officer shall report such fact to the board or agency which is supervising such parolee in Connecticut, or to any officer designated by such board or agency, who thereupon shall issue a warrant for the retaking of such prisoner and for his temporary detention or return to a designated prison. Such warrant shall constitute sufficient authority to the law enforcement officer to whom it is issued and to the superintendent or other person in charge of a jail, lockup or other detention unit to whom it is exhibited to hold in temporary custody the prisoner retaken pursuant thereto. Detention of a parolee under this section shall not continue longer than seventy-two hours unless he has been returned to prison for violation of parole or charged with crime.

NOTE

Implementation of the Parole Compact

RALPH C. BRENDES

Interstate Supervision of Parole and Probation*

Only two juridical documents have formal and practical application throughout all of our fifty states—the Constitution of the United States and the Interstate Compact for the Supervision of Parolees and Probationers.

Unlike the Constitution, little has been written on the Compact; the *Handbook on Interstate Crime Control,* published by the Council of State Governments, which serves as Secretariat to the Parole and Probation Compact Administrators' Association, is the only published source of information on the Compact. This paper will analyze the present operation of the Compact and discuss problems likely to arise in the future.

The states have collaborated in this form of crime control for two reasons: (1) the ever increasing mobility of the American citizen, which frequently results in his conviction away from his home state, although it is in his home state that rehabilitation is more likely to occur because of the positive influences of family and friends; (2) the need to eliminate "sundown probation"—a procedure whereby a criminal sentence would be suspended if the offender left the state by sundown. To improve protection of communities, each state found it mutually advantageous to supervise its resident probationers and parolees who had been convicted in other states. This combination of humanitarianism and local self-interest to avoid unregulated and uncontrolled interstate movement of unsupervised probationers and parolees

* Reprinted with permission of the National Council on Crime and Delinquency, from 14 *Crime and Delinquency,* July 1968, pp. 253–55.

led to the drafting of the Interstate Compact for the Supervision of Parolees and Probationers. . . .

General Provisions

The Compact provides that (1) any state (receiving state) will supervise a parolee or probationer from any other state (sending state) if he is a resident of the receiving state and has employment there; (2) the receiving state will supervise the sending state's parolee by the same standards used for its own parolees; (3) the sending state may revoke parole or probation in any case and retake the parolee or probationer at its discretion and with a minimum of formality.

To be classified a resident of the receiving state, the parolee or probationer must have been an inhabitant of that state for more than a year before he went to the sending state and must have resided within the sending state for less than six months immediately preceding the commission of the crime for which he was convicted. If he fulfills those conditions of residence, the receiving state must accept him, provided his family resides in the state and he is able to find employment there. In all cases the receiving state is given the opportunity, before the parolee or probationer is sent there, to investigate his home and his prospective employment. If he lacks the residence or employment qualifications, he may nevertheless be sent from one state to another if the receiving state consents.

Actual state use of the Compact is impressive. On June 30, 1967, about 10,500 parolees and about 11,000 probationers were under Compact supervision.

States working under the Compact are not bound by any strict rules; they adapt the general terms of the Compact to the specifics of each case. . . .

Administrators' Association

Formed in 1946, the Parole and Probation Compact Administrators' Association meets annually to discuss questions of policy and Compact interpretations and develop necessary administrative regulations. The annual meetings, affording opportunities to solve many operating problems by personal contact among administrators, are a significant factor in the successful operation of the Compact. . . .

NOTES

Detainers

Note 1.

RALPH C. BRENDES

*The Detainer Agreement**

A prisoner who has committed crimes in various jurisdictions before being apprehended will often have a number of detainers placed against him. Until these are resolved, it is difficult for the prisoner and his supervisor to make intelligent decisions concerning his future. To alleviate this problem, the Agreement on Detainers has been promulgated by the Association of Administrators and the Council of State Governments.

> The Agreement on Detainers [says the Council] makes the clearing of detainers possible at the instance of a prisoner. It gives him no greater opportunity to escape just convictions, but it does provide a way for him to test the substantiality of detainers placed against him and to secure final judgment on any indictments, informations, or complaints outstanding against him in the other jurisdiction. The result is to permit the prisoner to secure a greater degree of knowledge of his own future and to make it possible for the prison authorities to provide better plans and programs for his treatment.

Basically, the Agreement provides that a prisoner may, in writing, petition the prosecuting officer for a final disposition of the indictment, information, or complaint which forms the basis of the detainer. In most cases, the prisoner is entitled to a reply, within 180 days after the request, which either initiates a trial or drops the charges. In this way, the prisoner is able to have a clearer view of his future and prison officials have a better chance to bring about his rehabilitation, because definite plans can be made for his eventual release, free from the fear that a trial after his release will result in continued imprisonment.

Drafted in 1957, the Agreement has been passed by twenty states. The intention was to observe its operation in a few states before encouraging uniform ratification, because this Agreement is more complex than the Compact and an experimental period seemed advisable. Experience under the Agreement has been so successful that the Council of State Governments and the Administrators' Association are now actively soliciting all states to join. The Association of Attorneys General has passed a resolution endorsing the Detainer Agreement and urging its enactment.

Note 2.

SMITH V. HOOEY
393 U.S. 374 (1969)
Supreme Court of the United States

MR. JUSTICE STEWART delivered the opinion of the Court.

In *Klopfer* v. *North Carolina,* 386 U.S. 213, this Court held that, by virtue of the Fourteenth Amendment, the Sixth Amendment right to a speedy trial is enforceable against the States as "one of the most basic rights preserved by our Constitution." *Id.,* at 226. The case before us involves the nature and extent of the obligation imposed upon a State by that constitutional guarantee, when the person under the state criminal charge is serving a prison sentence imposed by another jurisdiction....

There can be no doubt that if the petitioner in the present case had been at large for a six-year period following his indictment, and had repeatedly demanded that he be brought to trial, the State would have been under a constitutional duty to try him. *Klopfer* v. *North Carolina, supra,* at 219. And Texas concedes that if during that period he had been confined in a Texas prison for some other state offense, its obligation would have been no less. But the Texas Supreme Court has held that because petitioner is, in fact, confined in a federal prison, the State is totally absolved from any duty at all under the constitutional guarantee. We cannot agree....

At first blush it might appear that a man already in prison under a lawful sentence is hardly in a position to suffer from "undue and oppressive incarceration prior to trial." But the fact is that delay in bringing such a person to trial on a pending charge may ultimately result in as much oppression as is suffered by one who is jailed without bail upon an untried charge. First, the possibility that the defendant already in prison might receive a sentence at least partially concurrent with the one he is serving may be forever lost if trial of the pending charge is postponed. Secondly, under pro-

---

* Reprinted, with permission of the National Council on Crime and Delinquency, from 14 *Crime and Delinquency,* July 1968, pp. 257–60.

cedures now widely practiced, the duration of his present imprisonment may be increased, and the conditions under which he must serve his sentence greatly worsened, by the pendency of another criminal charge outstanding against him.

And while it might be argued that a person already in prison would be less likely than others to be affected by "anxiety and concerns accompanying public accusation," there is reason to believe that an outstanding untried charge (of which even a convict may, of course, be innocent) can have fully as depressive an effect upon a prisoner as upon a person who is at large. Cf. *Klopfer* v. *North Carolina, supra,* at 221–222. In the opinion of the former Director of the Federal Bureau of Prisons,

> [I]t is in their effect upon the prisoner and our attempts to rehabilitate him that detainers are most corrosive. The strain of having to serve a sentence with the uncertain prospect of being taken into the custody of another state at the conclusion interferes with the prisoner's ability to take maximum advantage of his institutional opportunities. His anxiety and depression may leave him with little inclination toward self-improvement.

Finally, it is self-evident that "the possibilities that long delay will impair the ability of an accused to defend himself" are markedly increased when the accused is incarcerated in another jurisdiction. Confined in a prison, perhaps far from the place where the offense covered by the outstanding charge allegedly took place, his ability to confer with potential defense witnesses, or even to keep track of their whereabouts, is obviously impaired. And, while "evidence and witnesses disappear, memories fade, and events lose their perspective," a man isolated in prison is powerless to exert his own investigative efforts to mitigate these erosive effects of the passage of time. . . .

Note 3.

COOKS V. UNITED STATES BOARD OF PAROLE
447 F.2d 63 (1971)
United States Court of Appeals, Fifth Circuit

PER CURIAM:

Cooks' petition for habeas corpus was denied by the court below, without hearing, but after issuance of rule to show cause and filing of a response by the respondent U.S. Board of Parole. The contentions advanced by petitioner-appellant and the district court's reasons for denying relief are fully set forth in that court's unreported order, attached hereto as Appendix "A".

On this appeal Cooks has failed to demonstrate error in the district court's judgment. It is

Affirmed.

Appendix A
Order Denying Petition for Writ of Habeas Corpus

This is a petition for writ of habeas corpus filed by petitioner, a state prisoner, pursuant to the provisions of 28 U.S.C. § 2241 et seq. An order to show cause was issued on July 10, 1970, and a response was received on July 27, 1970.

Petitioner, presently serving a ten year state sentence for breaking and entering, asserts that a detainer placed upon him by the respondent Board for violation of the terms of his federal parole constitutes an unconstitutional restraint upon his liberty. Petitioner was convicted of violations of 26 U.S.C. §§ 4704(a) and 4705(a), and on January 25, 1961, was sentenced to a term of five years imprisonment. On May 24, 1964, petitioner was released on parole until placed in the custody of state officials on September 30, 1965, to begin serving a ten year term for breaking and entering. On June 17, 1965, a parole warrant charging that petitioner violated the terms of his federal parole was issued, but not served, and a detainer was lodged with the warden of the state prison. The petition alleges that the restraint imposed upon the petitioner in the form of the detainer and warrant is violative of the Fourth, Fifth, Sixth, and Eighth Amendments to the United States Constitution in that it denies petitioner equal protection and due process of law, deprives him of his constitutional right of confrontation, and constitutes cruel and unusual punishment. Petitioner's contentions are without merit.

The statute pursuant to which the detainer was issued, 18 U.S.C. § 4205, provides for the issuance of a warrant for parole violation within the maximum term for which he was sentenced, with the unexpired term of imprisonment to begin to run from the date he is returned to the custody of the Attorney General. The period during which a federal parolee is in state custody merely interrupts and suspends the period of parole with the prior obligation being unaffected by the intervening confinement, and therefore there is no danger of imprisonment for a period exceeding the original sentence because of delay in parole revocation. . . .

Additionally, the issuance of a parole warrant may be delayed until the intervening charge is disposed of. Jefferson v. Willingham, supra. Finally, it has been held in several cases that the provision contained in § 4205, i.e., that "the time the prisoner was on parole shall not diminish the time he was sentenced to serve," is not violative of the provisions of the Fifth and Eighth Amendments to the Constitution.

Parole is a matter of grace. It is accepted in the hope that it will discharge the balance of a prison sentence. Had petitioner not violated the conditions of his release it would have done so. . . .

I. Mandatory Release

HANSEN V. SCHMIDT
329 F. SUPP. 141 (1971)
United States District Court,
Eastern District of Wisconsin

GORDON, District Judge.

The petitioner has submitted an application for a writ of habeas corpus in which he alleges that the supervision to which he presently is subject under Wisconsin's mandatory release statute is an abridgement of certain of his constitutional rights. Leave has been granted to proceed in forma pauperis, and the respondent has submitted a response to the petition. On March 24, 1971, in an unpublished opinion, the Wisconsin supreme court denied a similar petition that had been filed by Mr. Hansen. . . .

On December 15, 1970, the petition was released pursuant to the provisions of Wisconsin's mandatory release statute, § 53.11(7) (a), Wis. Stats., which states:

> An inmate or parolee having served the term for which he has been sentenced for a crime committed after May 27, 1951, less good time earned under this chapter and not forfeited as herein provided, shall be released on parole or continued on parole, subject to all provisions of law and department regulations relating to paroled prisoners, *until the expiration of the maximum term for which he was sentenced without deduction of such good time, or until discharged from parole by the department, whichever is sooner.* (Emphasis added)

The petitioner asserts that he is entitled to an absolute discharge from supervision. He alleges that the respondent has granted others an absolute discharge after they had been confined for the period for which they were sentenced, less accumulated "good time," and that the refusal to grant him a similar discharge is discriminatory and violates his constitutional rights. Mr. Hansen also contends that the mandatory release in his case was not voluntarily accepted and that, in addition, his convictions antedated the passage of the mandatory release law. Thus, he argues, "there is no basis [for] such supervision" once he has been released from confinement, and he seeks to remove the "stigma" of such supervision.

Parole under Wisconsin's mandatory release statute initially is a parole of right. Rice v. Schmidt, 277 F.Supp. 811, 813 (E.D.Wis. 1967). However, § 53.11(7), Wis. Stats., makes it clear that the department of health and social services, of which the respondent is director, can discharge an inmate upon mandatory release or can continue to supervise him until the expiration of the maximum term for which he was sentenced. In State ex rel. Stenson v. Schmidt, 22 Wis.2d 314, 316, 125 N.W. 2d 634, 635 (1964), the court stated:

> In the discretion of the State Department of Public Welfare an inmate may be discharged rather than given a conditional release. If he is not discharged, the inmate is paroled or continued on parole to the end of the maximum term of his sentence. Sec. 53.11(7) (a), Stats. If he violates such parole he may be returned to prison to serve out the remainder of his sentence. The remainder of his sentence is deemed to be the amount of good time previously earned. Sec. 53.11(7) (b).

Thus, in effect, the period for which the department can supervise the conduct of a mandatory releasee is equivalent to the amount of good time previously accumulated by the releasee while in confinement.

The principal thrust of Mr. Hansen's petition appears to be that the respondent has abused his discretion in refusing to grant the petitioner an absolute discharge. However, as a mandatory releasee under supervision, the petitioner is on parole and "parole, like probation, is solely a matter of legislative grace and not a constitutional right." . . .

In my opinion, even if Mr. Hansen's allegation that others have been absolutely discharged is taken as true, there is nothing in the petition to indicate that the respondent has abused his discretion by continuing to supervise the conduct of the petitioner. In the absence of a showing that the respondent has exceeded the powers granted to him by law, or that he has in some other way effected an abridgment of the petitioner's federally-protected rights, the arguments in this regard cannot be sustained. . . .

Therefore, it is ordered that Mr. Hansen's petition for a writ of habeas corpus be and hereby is denied.

Chapter Twelve

PARDON: THE INSTITUTIONALIZED APPLICATION OF MERCY

CHRISTEN JENSEN

Pardon*

A pardon is an act of grace which results in the remission of the legal consequences of crime. The term pardon is sometimes used in a generic sense, however, and thus includes all forms of clemency. A pardon is to be distinguished from a reprieve, which is only a suspension of sentence of execution. It is also to be distinguished from an amnesty (*q.v.*), which is rarely if ever invoked in favor of an individual but is commonly employed in favor of classes of persons who are subject to trial but have not yet been convicted. A pardon may be either absolute or conditional.

Evidence of the use of pardons in a crude form extends back to primitive times. The Code of Hammurabi contains no reference to clemency, but it is known that Samsu-iluna, Hummurabi's son, pardoned a slave who had forfeited his life. Although the Mosaic law makes no mention of the subject, King David used the pardoning power, and cities of refuge were provided where fugitives who had innocently shed blood might obtain security from the fury of the avenger. In Athens the assembled people had the right to remit penalties, and the civil law of Rome recognized the right of the emperor as sovereign to grant clemency.

Clemency was practised also among the early Germanic tribes. It was recognized in England in the laws of Aethelberht of Kent, Alfred and Edward the Confessor and later was approved by such early jurists as Glanvill and Bracton. The English conception of clemency was transplanted to the American colonies, where its use by the authorities was regarded as a delegation of the royal prerogative. This view was superseded after American independence by the idea that the power to pardon was a sovereign power inherent in the state, although the principles of English legal construction were retained by American courts.

---

* "Pardon" by Christen Jensen. Reprinted with permission of the Publisher from *Encyclopedia of the Social Sciences,* Edwin R. A. Seligman, Editor in Chief, Volume VI, pages 570–571. Copyright 1931, 1959 by The Macmillan Company.

MARVIN E. WOLFGANG

The Relationship between Judicial and Prosecutorial Recommendations and Pardon Board Action*

Among the states that have established Pardon Boards within constitutional or statutory provisions it is not uncommon practice for these Boards to seek advice and evaluation from Judges and District Attorneys regarding individual applications for pardon or commutation. The purpose of this study is to examine these evaluations among petitions for commutation granted to applicants who had been convicted of first and second degree murder.

The purposes and functions of pardoning power are well known and need not be recounted here. Recorded cases of abuses of this power and recommendations for improving the procedure of granting pardons and commutations have often been made. The composition of Boards of Pardons, types of offenses subject to pardon and commutation, types of hearings, kinds of publicity, and the time when pardon or commutation may be granted vary among the separate states. Whatever procedures are involved, some states assume by law or custom that the Trial Judge and the Prosecuting Attorney should have some voice before the Board of Pardons in aiding the Board to pass final judgment on the application. Unfortunately, there has been little empirical research available that examines in detail the activities of Pardon Boards, or that seeks to investigate the evaluations of Judges and District Attorneys among applications for pardon or commutation of sentence. Particularly if a Board is composed of non-professional personnel, it is important that they have sagacious advice of informed persons to aid in the determination of favorable or unfavorable action on a petition. Such advice should come from the professional staff of the institution where the applicant is incarcerated. In most cases, Judges and District Attorneys are so far removed in time and space from an inmate who applies for commutation that they are unable to evaluate the applicant's socio-psychological condition or his worthiness for executive clemency at the time of his application. Only the institutional staff has extensive data regarding the inmate's vocational, educational, medical, psychological, psychiatric, and other types of personal history that can be used to advise a Pardon Board on the potential capacity of the applicant to benefit from a commutation.

Occasionally, considerable political debate centers around the contention by Judges and other public officials that a Pardon Board has failed to follow the recommendations of Judges and District Attorneys and that a great number of persons were granted commutations despite the opposition of these two groups of advisors. To subject this hypothesis to detailed analysis is the primary purpose of the present study. . . .

Judges and District Attorneys who had originally and respectively tried and prosecuted persons later applying to a Board of Pardons for commutation of sentence were asked to give a positive or negative recommendation to the Board for the latter's guidance. We have examined these recommendations made for 368 petitioners who had been convicted of first and second degree murder and who applied for and received some form of executive clemency in Pennsylvania between 1950 and 1957.

Statistical analysis using standard tests of significance has revealed significant differences of opinion between Judges and District Attorneys for the total 368 cases. These two groups of evaluators disagreed in two-thirds of the cases; Judges, in a significantly higher proportion than District Attorneys, fail to supply the Board with any statement; even in judging the same petitioners there is a low degree of association between the evaluations of Judges and District Attorneys; and in only seven per

---

* From "Murder, The Pardon Board and Recommendations by Judges and District Attorneys." Reprinted by special permission of the *Journal of Criminal Law, Criminology and Police Science*. Copyright © 1959, Vol. 50, No. 4, pp. 338, 345–56.

cent of the total murder cases can it be said that the Pardon Board grants commutation in direct conflict with the combined negative evaluation of Judge and District Attorney.

A Discriminative Index of Support has been established, which considers the combined and variable recommendations which a Pardon Board receives. This Index determines the *degree* of evaluative support (or lack of support) which a Pardon Board has from Judges and District Attorneys in acting favorably on petitions for commutation or pardon. Although in the cases examined the Pardon Board has the positive support of these evaluators, District Attorneys support the Board's decisions in significantly higher proportions than do Judges.

REED COZART

The Benefits of Executive Clemency*

Article II, Section 2, of the Constitution conveys upon the President the power to grant pardons and reprieves of federal offenses, except impeachment. During the past 100 years, the Attorney General has had the responsibility of making recommendations in clemency matters. For approximately 75 years, the Pardon Attorney, on the Attorney General's staff, has made the investigations into all clemency applications and assisted the Attorney General in his recommendations.

The most common form of a clemency application is for a full and unconditional pardon. Approximately 450 such applications are processed each year. During recent years there has been an increasing number of applications filed for a commutation or reduction of sentence. There are occasional requests for remission of fines.

Procedures and Standards

The present rules or regulations governing the exercise of clemency powers of the President are published in the Code of Federal Regulations, Title 28—Judicial Administration (revised January 1, 1968). Generally speaking, it can be said that each seeker of a pardon must make a personal application after a prescribed waiting period after imposition of sentence or release from confinement, and must meet standards of conduct indicating he has been re-established in society over a reasonable period of time. Those seeking a commutation of sentence must show that their sentences are disparate when compared with the average sentence imposed throughout the country under similar conditions or that some exceptional circumstance is present, such as a terminal illness, undue hardship, or that some meritorious situation is present. Those seeking a remission of a fine need usually show inability to pay it.

Policies

Although there always are some variations of viewpoints held by those in the Pardon Attorney's office, in the Attorney General's office, and those on the President's staff that may affect action in some types of cases during changes of administrations or personnel, through the years, there has been no change in approach in the handling of clemency matters. They have always been considered on their merits, without any political or other type of pressure. The writer has been involved in the processing of all clemency cases under the administration of the last three Presidents and five Attorneys General and can testify that any sort of pressure is more likely to cause postponement of favorable action or cause unfavorable action than to cause the desired prompt favorable action. This is as it should be.

Decisions are made in pardon cases after a very careful review of reports submitted by agents of the Federal Bureau of Investigation into the applicant's postconviction conduct, the recommendations of the United States attorney

* 32 *Federal Probation* No. 2, p. 34 (1968). Reprinted with permission.

and the sentencing judge, the facts and circumstances of the offense, the present attitude of the applicant toward his responsibilities, and the possible effect on the public. In the case of applications for a commutation of sentence, careful attention is given to the facts of the case, the nature of the applicant's prison adjustment, and the recommendations of the prison officials, the United States attorney, and the judge as well as to how the sentence imposed compares with other sentences imposed under similar situations.

RICHARD BANBURY

The Pardoning Authority in the Several States: Structures Used and Trends in the Makeup of the Decision-Making Bodies*

The structure of the pardon power in the several states can be conveniently broken down into five categories.

(1) governor alone
(2) advisory board plus governor
(3) authoritative board plus governor
(4) board alone
(5) mixed

(1) *Governor alone.* Eleven states employ a pardon procedure which delegates the full burden and power of granting pardons to the governor....

(2) *Advisory board plus governor.* There are twelve states which use this system....

(3) *Authoritative board plus governor.* Under this procedure the governor's power can be exercised only after favorable action has been taken by an independent board. Analytically this is a two-step process with the positive concurrence of the decision-makers being necessary to effectuate the pardon power. Perhaps it is most easily thought of as a cross-veto system....

Twelve states use this method....

(4) *Board alone.* Six states have a pardon process which involves a board making the final determination....

(5) *Mixed.* There are five states that have hybrid procedures....

* Yale Law School Divisional Research Paper, May 1963, pp. 4–8. Reprinted with permission of the author.

CONN. GEN. STAT. § 18–24a *ET SEQ.*

Sec. 18-24a. Appointment. Term. Compensation. Disqualification.

The Board of pardons shall consist of five members, residents of this state. Biennially, a member or members shall be appointed by the governor, with the advice and consent of either house of the general assembly, to take office the first Monday in June in the year of their appointment for a term of six years to replace those whose terms expire. Two members shall be attorneys, one shall be skilled in one of the social sciences, one shall be a physician and one shall be a judge of the supreme court designated for the purpose by the judges of said court. Not more than three of such members holding office at any one time shall be members of any one political party. The board shall, biennially, elect its chairman. The members of the board shall be paid a per diem fee fixed by the personnel policy board for attendance at each session of the board in lieu of expenses. If the judge member of the board, as a judge of any trial court, tried or heard any case that comes before the board, or if any member has formed an opinion in any matter that comes before it, he shall not act concerning the same, but no member shall be disqualified by reason of having previously heard such case or having formed an opinion thereon at any former application for pardon by the same applicant. When at any session any member is absent or disqualified, the governor may appoint a qualified person to fill the vacancy, and the person so appointed shall have the same power as any other member during such absence or disqualification. The person appointed by the governor to fill a temporary vacancy need not necessarily possess the particular occupational or political qualifications of the member whose place he is temporarily taking.

Sec. 18-26. Jurisdiction.

(a) Jurisdiction over the granting of, and the authority to grant, commutations of punishment or releases, conditioned or absolute, in the case of any person convicted of any offense against the state and commutations from the penalty of death shall be vested in the board of pardons. (b) Said board shall have authority to grant pardons, conditioned or absolute, for any offense against the state at any time after the imposition and before or after the service of any sentence. No pardon shall restore the privileges of an elector to any person who has forfeited the same by reason of conviction of crime.

Sec. 18-27. Sessions, Secretary

Said board shall hold a session when and where occasion requires. Four-fifths of the members of said board shall concur in order to make their judgment operative. Said board shall appoint a secretary trained in the law and fix by rule the mode of procedure before it and the manner in which its judgment shall be carried into effect.

Sec. 18-28. Attendance of Witnesses and Sheriff

Said board shall have all the authority of the superior court to compel the attendance of witnesses summoned by the secretary of said board or other competent authority. The sheriff of Hartford county or his deputy shall attend the sessions of said board and shall receive therefor the fees provided for the sheriff's attendance upon sessions of the superior court.

Sec. 18-29. Prisoners; Attendance; Expenses

The secretary of said board shall have power to issue process under his hand and the seal of said board to the principal officers of the correctional institutions and to the jail administrator, commanding them to have before said board the bodies of the prisoners named in such process who are confined in such institutions or in jail. The sums paid for witnesses and other necessary expenses authorized by said board shall be certified by the chairman of the board, and the comptroller shall draw his order on the treasurer for the same.

Sec. 18-30. Information About Prisoner

Said board may institute inquiries by correspondence or otherwise as to the previous history or character of any prisoner, and each prosecuting officer, judge, police officer or other person shall give said board, upon request, such information as he may possess with reference to the habits, disposition, career and associates of any prisoner.

WILLIAM F. STONE, JR.

Pardons in Virginia: An Empirical Study*

Virginia does not have statutory procedures for informing prisoners of the availability of pardons. Therefore information concerning application for pardons is disseminated on an informal basis and is probably common knowledge within penal institutions.

Unlike many jurisdictions Virgina does not have a requirement of notice on an application for pardon. Other states often do require either the applicant or the governor's representative

---

* 26 *Washington and Lee Law Review* 313–16; 318–19 (1969). Reprinted with permission of Fred B. Rothman & Co. and Washington and Lee Law Review.

to file notice of the application or hearing upon an application with the trial judge and prosecuting attorney or in a newspaper of the county in which the applicant was convicted.

While the governor may grant a pardon on his own initiative, the current Virginia policy is to require a written application by either the prisoner, his counsel, a member of his family, or by any interested person. No more than a simple letter is required, but the application must state facts and circumstances indicating reasons for the governor to consider a pardon. The superintendent of a penal institution would not initiate a pardon application, but he might suggest the possibility of pardon to a prisoner who had spent many years in prison and was either not eligible for parole or had given up attempts to obtain one. In certain unusual circumstances the Probation and Parole Board will initiate a pardon recommendation for a prisoner. This may be done if the prisoner either is not eligible for parole or some factor, such as adverse public opinion, militates against favorable parole consideration.

As a matter of administrative procedure, applications for pardons are referred to the Secretary of the Commonwealth for processing. While the governor could assign this task to another office or administrative assistant, in practice it has remained with the Secretary for a considerable period of time. To avoid the consideration of frivolous and repetitious appeals for pardons, the governor instructs the Secretary to process pardon applications to determine whether certain minimal qualifications have been met. These qualifications may be altered or disregarded by succeeding governors.

If the application is initially accepted for pardon consideration, the governor generally requests the Probation and Parole Board to conduct an investigation of all aspects of the prisoner's personal history, criminal record, prison adjustment and the environment to which he would return upon release from prison. In view of the relatively large number of pardon petitions reaching the governor's office and the Board's accessibility to the petitioner's records, it would seem that the Board is in a better position than other state agencies to handle these investigations.

In making its investigations the Board has at its disposal various sources of information. Its principal source of information is the prisoner's personal file as maintained by the Department of Corrections. This file contains all information available concerning the prisoner, such as his history and environment, criminal record and personal habits in the penal institution. An essential part of this file is the Field Report, which attempts to describe the prisoner's background and home life. The Field Report includes a pre-sentence report, if available, and further investigations by local parole officers on the individual's reputation and the environment in which he was raised. Other information from the prisoner's personal file, such as letters from the trial judge and prosecuting attorney giving their observations of the prisoner, may be forwarded to the governor. According to Mr. Pleasant C. Shields of the Virginia Board of Probation and Parole, the report to the governor is likely to devote more consideration to the nature of the crime than would normally be used by the Board in consideration of parole. The Board may consult with the superintendent of the penal institution or conduct a personal interview with the prisoner himself. However, due to the wealth of information contained in the file, such consultations and interviews are generally not conducted.

Upon receipt of the Board's report and a determination that the petitioner's application is meritorious, the governor usually requests the opinions of the trial judge and the commonwealth's attorney, who were directly involved with the petitioner's trial. If these individuals are not available, the governor is likely to request the opinion of the current judge and the commonwealth's attorney of the jurisdiction of conviction. He may also request the trial record.

These procedures have evolved as a result of the volume of pardon petitions. The governor is free to either fully utilize or totally disregard any or all of them. If the governor possesses personal knowledge of the case, where for example, the petitioner is from the same area of the state as the governor, there would appear to be a diminution of reliance on a Board investigation in reaching a determination. In addition, members of the General Assembly or the public may be questioned as to the level of local feeling. The opinion of the superintendent of the penal institution may be requested. If the prisoner has formally attacked alleged procedural errors in a habeas corpus petition, the governor may request the Assistant Attorney General who represented the Commonwealth in the case to give his observations.

In the Governor's Report to the General Assembly, the governor is required to cite the pertinent factors which he considered in granting a pardon. Of course the governor may not refer to all of his reasons for granting a particular pardon. From these reports the most often cited reason was the prisoner's good record while incarcerated. Five other factors were often cited: the circumstances of the case, the length of time served, the prisoner's prior good record, the favorable environment to which the prisoner would be returning and the prisoner's having received the maximum benefits of imprisonment. The governor frequently includes the opinions of individuals or agencies such as the Probation and Parole Board, the commonwealth's attorney, the trial judge, the superintendent of the prison, the Director of Corrections and interested citizens who have made recommendations on the pardon. It is interesting to note that the trial judges and commonwealth's attorneys prefer to voice no objection to the pardon rather than making favorable recommendations.

The most important factor which enters into consideration is the governor's personal sense of justice. Individuals who have been close to a number of governors, such as Miss Martha Bell Conway, Secretary of the Commonwealth, and Mr. Carter O. Lowance, Commissioner of Administration, agree that Virginia's governors have viewed the power of pardon as one of their most serious and personal responsibilities. While the governor must often depend upon the information gathered by the Board, the ultimate decision rests solely with him. Each governor is likely to have a different view as to the extent as well as to the conditions under which the pardon power should be exercised.

The Role of Counsel in Pardon Proceedings

Petitioner's Brief in Support of Pardon

The Petitioner is requesting a remission of his effective sentence of a minimum of twenty years and a maximum of life, to a minimum of time served (11 years) and a maximum of life, in order to gain eligibility for Parole.

There are as many theories of penology as there are theories of criminal behavior, but one factor is rapidly becoming the ideal. Prisons exist to correct deviant behavior and to mold the inmate into Society's ideal law-abiding citizen. The emphasis is rapidly turning away from punishment and moving toward correction. It is generally agreed that when an inmate is rehabilitated, he should be released. This changing attitude is reflected by recent actions of the General Assembly, which has changed the name of our state penal institutions from "Prisons" to "Correctional Institutions." Since a sentencing Judge is hardly in a position to determine when a violator is corrected, more emphasis is placed on the Boards of Pardon and Parole to perform this function, by the use of indeterminate sentences. To this end, the new Penal Code has provided for a maximum sentence of a minimum of ten years and a maximum of life. (Proposed Conn. Penal Code, §§ 36.2(a), 36.3(a), (1969) Draft). The only problem with this system is the determination of what "correction" means and how a board can tell when an inmate has reached the rehabilitative goal.

The purpose of this Brief is to indicate to the Board that the Petitioner, Robert W. Preston, is, by any definition, rehabilitated and ready to resume his useful place in society. To the extent that prisons punish, the Petitioner has been punished sufficiently by eleven years confinement. Robert Preston's time has come, he has earned it.

I. Background

Until the incident which disrupted his life occurred, the Petitioner was an exemplary citizen. In February, 1942 he enlisted in the U.S. Marine Corps and rose to the rank of Rifle Sergeant. He was involved in four battle campaigns including Iwo Jima, where he was wounded and won the Purple Heart. He was also awarded a Regimental Citation. He married his first wife in May, 1945 and was honorably discharged in September, 1945. He then returned to his old job in a paper mill. During this period he decided to better himself and joined the Carpenters' Union where he became a journeyman and was described as a good worker. He also became a volunteer fireman with the Warrenville Fire Department where he eventually held the rank of Lieutenant. In June, 1946 he became the father of twin boys, both of whom are now firemen, a fact which they attribute to their father's influence. The Petitioner's life was spent in this fashion until late 1957 when his marriage broke up for reasons both he and his ex-wife describe in essence as "just one of those things." They bear each other no enmity.

II. The Crime

Some time after the breakup of his marriage, the Petitioner began to drink and in October, 1959 he remarried. His new wife, a woman older than himself, had three children aged 23, 21, and 14. He admits that this step was a mistake engendered by his confused emotional condition. He left his second wife one month later, in December, 1959, just before Christmas. At the same time, he was laid off from his job and began to drink constantly. He also had a minor brush with the law during this period, which was related to his drinking. After leaving his second wife he moved to a rooming house where he became acquainted with Robert Fletcher, the proprietor, and John Giati, a fellow roomer. On January 19, 1960, this threesome went ice fishing at a local pond. By his own admission, the Petitioner had been drinking steadily for a week. The Petitioner does not remember what happened at the pond that day very clearly. When later interrogated, he told conflicting stories, none of which relate anything useful. What is clear is that Fletcher and Giati were shot to death by Petitioner, and that Petitioner was grossly intoxicated at the time. A blood test performed three hours later indicates his blood level at that time was 0.36% alcohol by weight, a nearly fatal amount. In the opinion of the doctors examining the Petitioner before trial, he had been excessively alcoholic for a long period of time, and there was a serious question of his ability to form intent at the time of the crime. It was said by one of the doctors that Petitioner has always been aggressive and impulsive by nature and extreme intoxication allowed the breakthrough of these impulses. As soon as Petitioner realized what he had done, he turned himself in to the State Police.

Petitioner pleaded guilty to two counts of murder in the second degree and was sentenced on March 23, 1960 to two life sentences, to run concurrently.

III. Prison Record

The most extraordinary factor in Petitioner's record is the fact that he has never had a misconduct report in over eleven years. This is of particular importance since he is confined for a crime of passion, for losing control of his impulses. For eleven years of confinement, Petitioner has never again lost control of his impulses.

For the first six years of his confinement he worked in the Carpenters' Shop, first at Wethersfield, and then at Somers. Since January, 1966, he has been at the minimum security facility at Osborne. Petitioner's record can be described only one way, "a model inmate."

IV. The Future

Petitioner plans upon release on parole to resume his trade as a carpenter. The business agent of the United Brotherhood of Carpenters and Joiners of America, Local 763, New London, Mr. John List, has stated that the Union will accept Petitioner back and attempt to place him with employers. While Petitioner's trade is seasonal in nature, Mr. List believes Petitioner will have no difficulty in supporting himself adequately. Petitioner has saved over $400.00 from his earnings during his confinement and hopes to have in the neighborhood of $600.00 by the time of his parole. His health is excellent and there is no reason to suppose he will not stay active until at least age 65, a fifteen-year period of active contribution to society.

V. Conclusion

This is the story of a man's life which was nearly ruined by alcohol. He has reformed himself to the point where he is clearly ready to rejoin society. He appears highly motivated and has progressed as far as one can go within the correctional system. All this man needs is a chance to prove to society, and more importantly perhaps, to himself, that he can once again be a good citizen. Petitioner prays this Board give him that chance.

Respectfully Submitted,
THE PETITIONER

by _____
Andrew Wittstein
University of Connecticut Law Student
Representative of Petitioner

This is to certify that a copy of the foregoing was mailed, postage prepaid, to the States Attorney.

Chapter Thirteen

AFTER PRISON: THE HARDEST WAY

A. Collateral Consequences of Conviction

THE PRESIDENT'S COMMISSION ON LAW ENFORCEMENT AND ADMINISTRATION OF JUSTICE
Task Force Report: Corrections
88–92 (1967)

Convicted persons are subjected to numerous disabilities and disqualifications quite apart from the sanction imposed in their sentence, and though their sentence may eventually be served, these may never be removed. The inhumanity and irrationality of much of the law in this area has received severe criticism from those who have considered it, but reform has been slow.

Persons convicted of felonies and certain serious misdemeanors have traditionally lost a number of "civil rights"—rights possessed by most citizens, such as the right to vote and hold public office, to serve as a juror or testify in court. In addition a convicted person may be prohibited from participating in numerous activities regulated by the government for the protection of society. He may, for example, be barred from obtaining professional, occupational and business licenses and from certain kinds of employment.

Rights may be suspended for some period of time such as the period of imprisonment or of sentence, or they may be forfeited permanently. Most States have some procedure for the restoration of rights which have been forfeited. Generally restoration statutes have the effect of restoring only certain rights, namely the "civil rights," but they may also remove legal barriers to the restoration of licenses and such, enabling the respective regulating agencies to act as they see fit.

The loss and restoration of rights raise confusing jurisdictional problems. Each jurisdiction generally determines the extent to which convicted persons can exercise various rights and privileges in that jurisdiction, relying as it sees fit on convictions in other jurisdictions. One jurisdiction may remove disabilities and disqualifications resulting from convictions in other jurisdictions through its own procedures. It may on the other hand demand that the convicted person obtain a restoration certificate or pardon in the convicting jurisdiction.

The problem with much of present-day law in this area is not inherent in the concept of imposing various disabilities and disqualifications as consequences of a conviction of crime, but rather results from the misuse of that concept. Many deprivations during imprisonment can be justified on the grounds of administrative convenience or on the grounds that they are appropriate to punitive aims of imprisonment—thus rights to hold public office or to serve as a juror or to carry on one's business, may properly be considered incompatible with the purpose and nature of imprisonment. Further, it is clear that certain deprivations may be useful as independent sanctions for criminal behavior. Thus suspending or revoking a driver's license for a conviction involving dangerous driving might be a far more appropriate sanction than a fine or term of imprisonment. It is likely to be a highly effective deterrent. It protects society from the particular kind of danger this person poses, thus providing almost as effective incapacitation as imprisonment without its costs or harmful side effects.

But little of the present law in this area can be so justified. As a general matter it has simply not been rationally designed to accommodate the varied interests of society and the individual convicted person. There has been little effort to evaluate the whole system of disabilities and disqualifications that has grown up. Little consideration has been given to the need for particular deprivations in particular cases. It is quite common to provide for the blanket loss or suspension of "civil rights" or "civil liberties." And even where rights or privileges are dealt with specifically, it is common to provide that conviction of any felony, or any misdemeanor involving moral turpitude, justifies forfeiture. As a result, convicted persons are generally subjected to numerous disabilities and disqualifications which have little relation to the crime committed, the person committing it or, consequently, the protection of society. They are often harsh out of all proportion to the crime committed. And by cutting the offender off from society, including, perhaps, his chosen occupation, they may impede efforts at rehabilitation.

The law in this area is inordinately complex and confusing. The relevant statutes are hard to locate, even within one jurisdiction. Enacted for various reasons at various times, they are spread throughout the legislative code. Statutes providing for the blanket loss or suspension of civil rights produce great uncertainty as to exactly what rights are lost and for what period of time. Similarly, where provision is made for the restoration of rights, it is often unclear what rights are restored and what disabilities and disqualifications remain.

The legal situation, confusing even to the trained lawyer, is generally quite beyond the understanding of the convicted offender who ordinarily is not advised as to the disabilities and disqualifications accompanying his conviction, nor as to any procedures which may be available for their removal. Such complexity and confusion would seem to detract from whatever deterrent function disabilities might serve. Similarly, restoration procedures cannot accomplish their purpose if convicted offenders are unaware of their availability.

There is a general need to clarify legislation so that offenders are adequately informed of rights lost and of restoration procedures available. But it is of even more basic importance to reevaluate all disabilities and disqualifications to design a system more responsive to the various interests of society as a whole, including the interests of convicted persons themselves. To do this it is necessary to consider each right or privilege individually to determine whether its forfeiture would be appropriate as a deterrent or means of protecting society, and if so what particular crimes should call for forfeiture, and for what period of time. Where practical, cases should be considered individually to determine whether the various applicable disabilities and disqualifications are necessary and appropriate.

Section 306.1[1] of the American Law Institute's Model Penal Code is an example of legislation that would insure that careful consideration be given to the need for particular disqualifications and disabilities:

No person shall suffer any legal disqualification or disability because of his conviction of a crime or his sentence on such conviction, unless the disqualification or disability involves the deprivation of a right or privilege which is:

(a) Necessarily incident to execution of the sentence of the Court; or

(b) provided by the Constitution or the Code; or

(c) provided by a statute other than the Code, when the conviction is of a crime defined by such statute; or

(d) provided by the judgment, order or regulation of a court, agency or official exercising a judisdiction conferred by law, or by the statute defining such jurisdiction, when the commission of the crime or the conviction or the sentence is reasonably related to the competency of the individual to exercise the right or privilege of which he is deprived.

Civil Rights

To a large extent the law in this area represents ar. archaic holdover from the past. At common law, conviction of a felony generally meant death and forfeiture of property. In the United States early statutes provided for "civil death" where the sentence was for death or life imprisonment. Present laws regarding the loss of civil rights, inherited from this era, are simply not appropriate today, when the death penalty is nearly extinct and most offenders given life sentences are eventually released. Similarly, many laws suspending civil rights during sentence date from times when sentence for a period of years meant imprisonment for that full term; the result today is that persons released on probation or parole are subjected to deprivations appropriate only for prisoners. Efforts to improve the situation have generally been piecemeal—elaborate procedures are established to restore rights which should have been removed either not at all or only temporarily.

To give a brief description of the law in this area is difficult because there is such variation between different jurisdictions, and often complexity and confusion within particular jurisdictions. Most of the rights and privileges in this area derive from the States, and it is primarily State statutes and constitutions which provide for their deprivation. Federal law provides for the loss of certain rights such as the right to sit on a Federal jury, the right to hold Federal offices, and to hold union offices. The State statutes which provide for the blanket loss or suspension of "civil rights" are variously interpreted to include rights to sue; to contract; to transfer, devise or inherit property; to vote; to hold public office; to testify; and to serve as a juror. States may, in addition, provide specifically for the loss of other rights. Many States have no such blanket statutes; each deprivation is specified. A few States provide that no civil rights are lost.

State statutes generally do not refer to specific convictions. Ordinarily any felony results in forfeiture; sometimes any misdemeanor involving moral turpitude has the same effect.

Forfeiture of rights may depend on whether conviction results in imprisonment, probation or suspension of sentence—even on whether it was the imposition or the execution of sentence that was suspended. Rights may be merely suspended until discharge from the period of imprisonment or supervision, or until satisfaction of the sentence, or for some other period of time. (This may be termed "automatice restoration.") Often, however, they are forfeited permanently unless restoration is obtained through some formal procedure.

Without attempting to be all-inclusive it is worth discussing some of the more significant disabilities in some detail.

Voting. There may be some justification for suspending the right to vote during imprisonment, on the ground that prisoners as a class have an insufficient interest in the outcome of elections. But there seems no justification for permanently depriving all convicted felons of the vote, as the laws in most States provide. The convicted person may have no strong personal interest in voting, but to be deprived of the right to representation in a democratic society is an important symbol. Moreover, rehabilitation might be furthered by encouraging convicted persons to participate in society by exercising the vote.

Holding Public Office and Positions of Private Trust. Many States deprive convicted felons permanently of the right to hold public office, presumably appointive as well as elective. In some States, provision is merely made for forfeiture of offices held at the time of conviction or suspension of the right to hold office during some period such as the term of imprisonment.

Although certain offenses are clearly related to fitness to hold such positions, it is rarely necessary to provide for automatic disqualification in order to protect society. Instead, where there is someone with authority to appoint or remove, or where the public has such authority through its power to elect, it seems generally preferable to rely on their judgment. The relevance of particular convictions or terms of imprisonment to fitness for the particular position can then be considered. It may however, be necessary to provide for forfeiture of elective office and any appointive office for a term, since there may be no other feasible means of removing an unfit officer.

Jury Service. Suspension of the privilege of serving as a juror may be necessary during imprisonment. But there seems little justification for the laws which exist in a number of States permanently disqualifying all convicted felons from serving as jurors. Reliance should instead be placed primarily on the powers given both parties to challenge jurors; since they and the judge are in a position to consider the relevance of a particular case. The legislature might prescribe certain convictions as grounds for challenges for cause; the judge could allow other convictions to constitute such grounds according to their relevance to the case. In addition, it might be appropriate for the legislature to provide for disqualification in certain cases at least for some period of years.

Testimonial Capacity. The right to testify is commonly suspended during imprisonment. In a few States, persons convicted of perjury are permanently disqualified from being a witness. Such provisions often harm unnecessarily not only the convicted person but others interested in obtaining his testimony.

Certain limits on prisoners' ability to testify in court may be justified during imprisonment but provision should be made for prisoners to give testimony by deposition or in response to interrogatories; and where necessary in the interests of justice to appear in court. No conviction should make a person incompetent to testify. Instead, any convictions particularly relevant to credibility should be admissible to impeach the witness, permitting the finder of fact to weigh the value of the testimony.

Property and Contract Rights; Right to Court Process. In a few States, convicted felons may lose or have suspended during imprisonment, rights to contract and to take or transfer property. Similarly, the right to sue civilly may be lost or suspended during imprisonment.

Since such rights may be essential in order to live a normal life in the community, it is inconsistent with the correctional goal of rehabilitation to impose such restrictions on any persons not actually imprisoned. Moreover, while certain limitations on these rights may be necessary incidents of imprisonment, absolute suspension during imprisonment is inappropriate. Thus it may be proper to restrict prisoners' rights to conduct personal business from within prison or to appear in court to conduct law suits. But if the prisoner is allowed to retain his rights to possess property he should be allowed to inherit property. And rights to transfer property and to contract may be necessary to preserve assets and to support dependents.

Similarly, the right to sue may be necessary to protect assets against third parties and to attack illegal treatment by correctional officials. Allowing suit upon release by tolling the statute of limitations during imprisonment, as many jurisdictions do, is not an adequate substitute for granting the immediate right to sue. Irreparable damage may be done in the meanwhile; and proof may be made impossible by the passage of years. Suit would not necessitate absence from prison. Conduct of the suit could be put in the hands of an attorney; the prisoner's testimony, if needed, could be taken in prison.

Some jurisdictions provide for the appointment of a committee or trustee to manage the affairs of prisoners deprived variously of rights to convey and transfer property, to contract, and to sue in court. But such legislation often is designed primarily to protect rights of creditors and dependents. There seems no reason not to permit the prisoner simply to act through his own agent, when it is impracticable for him to act directly.

Rights to Participate in Activities Regulated by the State

Primarily because of the potential danger—actual or ostensible—to the public welfare posed by a number of private activities, State and local governments frequently limit participation in such activities to those considered qualified. Criminal convictions often result in disqualification either as a direct result of legislation, or because of action taken by a court or, more frequently, an administrative agency entrusted with regulation of the particular activity....

Private employment activities are regulated in this way.... Numerous activities not necessarily involving employment are similarly regulated. Persons may be unable to drive a car, possess a gun, or fish without a license. There are legitimate uses of such disqualifications. Thus it seems appropriate to suspend or revoke licenses for offenses involving dangerous driving, both to remove the unfit driver from the road and to deter such behavior. But to ban convicted persons from numerous activities without regard to the particular conviction's relevance to the particular activity can be expected seriously to impede efforts to rehabilitate offenders by encouraging their participation in society, without any compensating benefit to society.

Most of the law in this area is overly broad. Thus, good character is often made a prerequisite for activities where it is of no particular relevance. It is, for example, a common requirement for obtaining a barber's license. Yet it is doubtful whether good character is of any more importance to exercise of one's duties as a barber than to most other occupations. And regulatory legislation generally makes no effort to define the kind of character, and thus the kind of convictions, relevant to fitness. Instead, where legislatures provide for automatic disqualification, all felonies and sometimes all serious misdemeanors are likely to result in such disqualification. Thus in several jurisdictions any felony will bar a person from the practice of law or medicine. Similarly, where discretionary power is given to regulatory agencies to disqualify on the basis of criminal convictions, there is generally no attempt by the legislature to ensure that only those convictions relevant to fitness for the particular activity be considered. Thus, the California Business and Professions Code makes conviction of any felony or any offense involving moral turpitude grounds for disciplinary action in approximately 40 occupations and professions, including those of physical therapy, nursing, barbering, and guide dog training. Often discretionary power is given to disqualify simply on the basis of lack of good moral character. Most convictions would reflect on one's character, and could thus constitute bars to qualification. Of course, an agency can exercise its discretion and refuse to disqualify on the basis of a conviction it considers irrelevant to fitness. But such general statutes do not invite discrimination among convictions, and the agency's decision to disqualify would be virtually unreviewable.

Most of the disabilities and disqualifications in this area result from the actions of various administrative agencies, rather than directly from the conviction. In the area of individual licenses, professional and occupational groups are often given the power to determine who is initially qualified to receive a license, and to regulate the standards of those licensed by defining rules of conduct and revoking or suspending licenses for breach of those rules. Such groups tend to be primarily concerned with advancing the interests of their own members. Thus, when faced with the problem of whether to license persons with criminal records, they may be unduly concerned with the effect on the status of their professions. Further, to the extent they try to consider the public interest, they are likely to have an unrealistic view of the importance of their own profession or occupation and the potential harm to the public that might be done by unfit persons. They tend to give inadequate weight to the interests of the convicted person, and to those of society as a whole in having the contributions of this person and in not forcing him back into a life of crime.

The need for a thorough overhaul of licensing and regulatory restrictions on exoffenders has been noted.... Criminal convictions should be considered only to the extent actually relevant to fitness to participate in activities posing particular dangers to society. The legislature might specify particular convictions as grounds for disqualification, leaving it to a court or agency to determine the merits of each case. The legislature might mandate disqualification on the basis of selected, particularly relevant convictions. But it would ordinarily be best to provide for discretion so that the relevance of particular convictions could be weighed in light of, for example, the period of time since the criminal offense, the behavior of the individual during that time, and the hardship that disqualification might cause.

The power of excluding offenders from certain activities could be given to the sentencing judge and the correctional system. They could be given the responsibility for deciding the extent to which disqualification is justified for the purposes of public protection and deterrence. This is frequently done today with respect to loss or suspension of driver's licenses for driving offenses.

But where a licensing or other regulatory agency is entrusted with power to determine fitness to pursue a particular activity, that agency would ordinarily be the appropriate body to determine whether an offender should be disqualified. Wherever discretion is confided to a licensing agency, however, and particularly where that agency is associated with the occupation or interests it licenses, care must be taken to guard against the tendency to discriminate against offenders without rational basis that such bodies have commonly exhibited. This should be done by providing explicit legislative guidelines where possible and perhaps by requiring that the agency justify any license denial in terms of a specific danger in an individual case. But irrational discrimination against offenders by regulatory agencies may be inevitable, particularly where such agencies are quasi-private in nature. It may therefore be necessary to provide some procedure whereby decisions regarding the qualification of offenders can be made by a court or an independent board. This is discussed in more detail in the following section.

Assuming that regulatory agencies are given the power to decide, within limits set by the legislature, on the qualifications required for participation in certain activities, there should be some procedure whereby they can obtain relevant information from correctional authorities. Such information would be valuable in deciding whether to license someone with a criminal record, or whether to suspend for some definite or indefinite period of time or to disqualify permanently someone previously licensed, or whether to reinstate someone whose license had been withdrawn.

Restoration of Rights

If rights are "permanently" forfeited, partial or total restoration will often be possible through a variety of procedures, the most common of which is some form of clemency procedure, ordinarily gubernatorial pardon: since this power is generally designed primarily to remedy wrongful convictions and unduly harsh sentences, the result is an erratic and irrational pattern of restoration. In a few States, offenders can apply for restoration to an administrative board or to the warden of their institution. Such procedures ordinarily have the effect only of restoring such civil rights as have been lost. They may, in addition, remove legislative barriers to participation in regulated activities. But where the power of disqualification has been vested in licensing or other agencies, pardons or restoration certificates ordinarily cannot erase the effects of convictions, although agencies will presumably consider their relevance along with that of convictions.

In general, restoration procedures are, for practical reasons, not very effective solutions to the disabilities problem. Offenders often lack the funds, knowledge, or ability to pursue such procedures. And those who have established themselves in a new life are understandably reluctant to request restoration since this usually involves an investigation with all the risks that the past will be brought to light again. Rights should therefore be removed only where there is clear justification and only for the period of time necessary, eliminating the need wherever possible for offenders to pursue formal restoration procedures.

But some restoration procedures will probably nevertheless be necessary. Thus where the legislature considers it necessary for the protection of society to provide for the automatic loss or suspension of certain rights, there should ordinarily be some procedure whereby the offender can obtain relief from the legislative mandate. Such rights could be considered individually, but where many rights are automatically lost by operation of law, the convicted person should probably be able to obtain a general certificate of rehabilitation or restoration. Such procedures may be necessary simply because the offender's rights in other jurisdictions may be unjustly restricted unless he is able to obtain such a certificate in the convicting jurisdiction.

Some such procedure may also be necessary to restore rights to offenders disqualified by licensing or other regulatory agencies. Where authority is vested in such an agency to determine fitness to participate in a particular occupation, it would in general seem irrational to give to the court or another agency power to determine whether convicted offenders should or should not be disqualified. But this may be the only practical way of dealing with the problem of discrimination against offenders by such agencies.

Some authorities have proposed establishment of an annulment procedure, whereby the offender's records would be expunged or sealed, and he would be entitled to say he had never been convicted, or, alternatively, private individuals and official agencies would be prohibited from asking about such convictions. Somewhat the same dilemma is presented in this area. Logically, annulment procedures seem unnecessary to deal with problems of State-imposed disabilities and disqualifications. The convicting jurisdiction can accomplish the same result by simply not depriving the offender of the rights or by restoring them in some appropriate fashion. Actually to expunge records removes all discretion from those legitimately concerned with previous convictions. Thus, while it may not be justifiable to deprive convicted felons of the right to hold public office, those in the position of electing or appointing should presumably know of such convictions. And it would be nearly impossible to determine in one annulment procedure that particular convictions had no relevance for any future decision. In addition to these practical problems, some would question the propriety of government telling an offender that he has a right to deny a prior conviction, and of removing from private individuals or other jurisdictions the right to consider for themselves the relevance of a prior criminal record. But some annulment procedure may be necessary to deal with problems of irrational discrimination against past offenders by licensing agencies, private employers, and society generally.

B. Two Proposals

1. The Criminal Offender, What Should be Done?*

It is pertinent to note that, when it comes to providing jobs 'outside, those very entities that are responsible for rehabilitating prisoners, the states and the Federal government, set a most unedifying example. Most states either are barred by statute or bar themselves by habit from hiring ex-offenders. The Federal government let down its bars somewhat a few years ago; it will now hire ex-offenders on an individual basis, if the agency that wants their services presents a strong brief, and after an elaborate and time-consuming screening by the Civil Service Commission. In other words, it is a great deal more trouble to hire an ex-offender than somebody else and, as a general rule, only agencies with a stake in the matter, the Bureau of Prisons or the Law Enforcement Assistance Administration, for example, are willing to take that much trouble regularly.

Surely the very first step toward improving its correctional process that any government—municipal, state or Federal—should take is to allow ex-offenders to be employed by government. The government is scarcely persuasive when it urges industry to adopt employment policies toward ex-offenders that it itself is unwilling to adopt. We recommend:

> The United States Civil Service Commission should devise and put into operation a plan to stimulate Federal employment of ex-offenders.

We also recommend:

> The National Institute of Law Enforcement and Criminal Justice of the Department of Justice should frame guidelines for state and local governments concerning the employment of ex-offenders.

What is required to make correctional job and job-training programs fruitful is close day-by-day collaboration between correctional agencies on the one hand and industry and labor on the other. The Federal correctional system has been a pioneer in establishing such relationships, and some of the results have been extremely promising, as with the training program for electronic welders operated by Dictograph in the Danbury, Connecticut prison, and a similar program for aircraft sheet-metal workers run by Lockheed in the prison in Lompoc, California.

2. NATIONAL COUNCIL ON CRIME AND DELINQUENCY

Annulment of Conviction of Crime[1]*: A Model Act*†

The 1956 National Conference on Parole, held under the joint auspices of the Attorney

---

* *Report of the President's Task Force on Prisoner Rehabilitation* 10 (1970).

[1] A study published in 1956 by Aaron Nussbaum, assistant district attorney in New York County, comes to the staggering conclusion that in the United States today there are 50 million persons with a criminal record. The computation is based on the municipal police figures collected in the FBI's Uniform Crime Reports. Nussbaum's figures were based on 1953 data, according to which over 6½ million persons were arrested and held for prosecution that year. Of this total, approximately 4½ million were found guilty and were sentenced, and of these it is estimated that a total of 1,600,000 were first offenders. (This does not include minor traffic offenders or those guilty of such violations as disorderly conduct, although even the record of a minor offense takes its toll as a life-long impediment.) In a generation, the total cumulative number of convicted persons is 50 million. If we confine our interest to only those adults and youths convicted of major crimes in one year, Nussbaum points out, the figure is approximately one million, and the total cumulative figure for this group alone is currently over 10 million.

These astonishing figures are based on the best information available on the incidence of crime. But even if the computation, which is somewhat speculative, somehow exaggerates the number of persons with a criminal record, it still seems likely that the true figure is at least somewhere between 10 million and 50 million. About 4 million people are held in local jails every year.

† Reprinted, with permission of the National Council on Crime and Delinquency, from *Crime and Delinquency*, April 1962, pp. 98–100.

General of the United States, the United States Board of Parole, and the National Council on Crime and Delinquency (then the National Probation and Parole Association) . . . declared:

> The present law on deprivation of civil rights of offenders is in most jurisdictions an archaic holdover from early times and is in contradiction to the principles of modern correctional treatment. . . . The law should provide that criminal disposition other than commitment to a penal institution, and such commitments as are revoked by the sentencing court in due course, shall not entail the loss by the defendant of any civil or political rights. If offenders are allowed to retain these rights, their rehabilitation is thereby furthered. Therefore there should be no loss of rights except where protection of the public is involved. The concept of civil death upon life imprisonment existing in certain jurisdictions should be abolished.

A model for such provisions is found in NCCD's Standard Probation and Parole Act, published in 1955:

> Dispositions other than commitment to an institution, and such commitments which are revoked within sixty days, shall not entail the loss by the defendant of any civil rights.
>
> [Discharge of a parolee], and the discharge of a prisoner who has served his term of imprisonment, shall have the effect of restoring all civil rights lost by operation of law upon commitment, and the certification of discharge shall so state.

The parole conference findings went on to say:

> The expunging of a criminal record should be authorized on a discretionary basis. The court of disposition should be empowered to expunge the record of conviction and disposition through an order by which the individual shall be deemed not to have been convicted. Such action may be taken at the point of discharge from suspended sentence, probation, or the institution upon expiration of a term of commitment.

In response to this condition, we have drafted a model statute, set forth below, which provides, in brief, that (a) power to annul the conviction is given to the judge of the court in which the offender was sentenced, and (b) annulment of a conviction is a matter of discretion and not a matter of right. It is preferable to the provision, now found in a number of state laws, which authorizes expunging a record at the discretion of an administrative body, such as a parole board, or in some automatic manner after the expiration of a period of years. The defect of that kind of provision is that the power of the administrative agency is not well known and the agency is ordinarily less accessible than a court. The kind of authority given to the court in the model act should produce wider and more uniform use of the power to expunge the record while allowing for sound discretion to take individual circumstances into account.

Authorized use of such a provision would enable an individual to say, in testifying or in filling out applications of various kinds, that he had not been convicted. If, however, after his conviction has been annulled, he is again convicted, the record of the annulled conviction would be available for consideration by the sentencing court. So long as annulment of the record serves a rehabilitative purpose, the effect of the order continues. If the defendant commits another crime, that purpose has obviously been defeated and the previous record should be available to the sentencing court. The act has been drafted accordingly.

The wording of the model act permits either the offender or the court to initiate consideration of the relief authorized. It is assumed that before issuing the order the court would make any necessary investigation, typically through the resources of the probation department available to it.

The model act follows:

An Act to Authorize Courts to Annul a Record of Conviction for Certain Purposes

Be it enacted [etc.]

The court in which a conviction of crime has been had may, at the time of discharge of a convicted person from its control, or upon his discharge from imprisonment or parole, or at any time thereafter, enter an order annulling, canceling, and rescinding the record of conviction and disposition, when in the opinion of the court the order would assist in rehabilitation and be consistent with the public welfare. Upon the entry of such order the person against whom the conviction had been entered shall be restored to all civil rights lost or suspended by virtue of the arrest, conviction, or sentence, unless otherwise provided in the order, and shall be treated in all respects as not having been convicted, except that upon conviction of any subsequent crime the prior conviction may be considered by the court in determining the sentence to be imposed.

In any application for employment, license, or other civil right or privilege, or any appearance as a witness, a person may be questioned about previous criminal record only in language such as the following: "Have you ever been arrested for or convicted of a crime which has not been annulled by a court?"

Upon entry of the order of annulment of conviction, the court shall issue to the person in whose favor the order has been entered a certificate stating that his behavior after conviction has warranted the issuance of the order, and that its effect is to annul, cancel, and rescind the record of conviction and disposition.

Nothing in this act shall affect any right of the offender to appeal from his conviction or to rely on it in bar of any subsequent proceedings for the same offense.

TABLE OF CASES

Arciniega v. Freeman	492	*Jones v. Wittenberg*	336
Auditor General v. Olezniczak	38	*Kritsky v. McGinnis*	314
Baldwin v. Smith	38	*Landman v. Royster*	294, 333
Barnett v. Rodgers	375	*LaReau v. MacDougall*	292
Berrigan v. Norton	394	*Lee v. Washington*	374
Bonomo v. New Jersey Parole Board	535	*Liles v. South Carolina Department of Correction*	323
Brooks v. Florida	278		
Bundy v. Cannon	314	*Logue v. United States*	324
Carothers v. Follette	393	*McGinnis v. Royster*	38
Chewning v. Cunningham	92	*Martinez v. Mancusi*	373
Clutchette v. Procunier	310	*Melson v. Sard*	534
Colen v. Norton	366	*Mempa v. Rhay*	70
Cooks v. United States Board of Parole	540	*Menechino v. Oswald*	468
Cooper v. Pate	374	*Monks v. New Jersey Parole Board*	477
Cross v. Harris	41	*Morris v. Travisono*	225
Cross v. Powers	383	*Morrissey v. Brewer*	518
Cruz v. Beto	328	*Nolan v. Fitzpatrick*	386
Davis v. Lindsay	340	*Nolan v. Scafati*	313
Ex parte Hull	377	*Oyler v. Boles*	92
Escoe v. Zerbst	73	*Payne v. District of Columbia*	371
Furman v. Georgia	279	*People ex. rel. Abner v. Kinney*	423
Fortune Society v. McGinnis	394	*People v. Mason*	63
Gagnon v. Scarpelli	77, 527	*People v. McAndrew*	51
Giordano v. Henderson	536	*Porth v. United States*	64
Goldberg v. Kelly	75	*Rhodes v. Siegler*	369
Gore v. United States	99	*Rodriguez v. McGinnis*	357
Hahn v. Burke	74	*Rose v. Nickeson*	535
Haines v. Kerner	327	*Royster v. McGinnis*	364
Hamilton v. Love	339	*Scarpa v. United States Parole Board*	481
Hancock v. Avery	291	*Scott v. United States*	81
Hansen v. Schmidt	541	*Seale v. Manson*	369
Irby v. United States	99	*Smith v. Hooey*	539
Jackson v. Bishop	330	*Smith v. Robbins*	391
Johnson v. Avery	378	*Sobell v. Reed*	492

TABLE OF CASES

Sostre v. McGinnis	321, 389
Sostre v. Otis	395
Sostre v. Rockefeller	294, 320
Specht v. Patterson	39
Spencer v. Texas	89
State v. Amiot	104
State v. Kunz	30
State v. Lavelle	37
Tate v. Short	36
Tarlton v. Clark	371
United States Ex. Rel. Bey v. Connecticut State Board of Parole	513
United States v. Daniels	49
United States v. Demko	320
United States v. Dockery	30
United States v. Muniz	319
United States Ex. Rel. Pope v. Williams	368
United States Ex. Rel. Santos v. New York State Board of Parole	497
United States Ex. Rel. Sperling v. Fitzpatrick	496
United States v. Wiley	44, 79
Urbano v. McCorkle	317
Walker v. Mancusi	318
Washington Post v. Kleindienst	392
Watson v. United States	43
Williams v. Illinois	34
Williams v. New York	20
Wilson v. United States	48
Wright v. McMann	290, 309, 322, 362
Young v. Wainwright	317

TABLE OF STATUTES, REGULATIONS, BOOKS, ARTICLES, AND OTHER AUTHORITIES

1. STATUTES

Conn. Gen. Stat. § 18–7 [Good Time]	355
Conn. Gen. Stat. §§ 18–24a *et seq.* [Pardon Board]	546
Conn. Gen. Stat. § 54–109a [Disclosure of presentence reports]	30
Conn. Gen. Stat. §§ 54–124a *et seq.* [Parole]	413
Conn. Gen. Stat. §§ 54–133 *et seq.* [Parole Compact]	536
18 U.S.C.A. §§ 3575 *et seq.* [Organized Crime Control Act of 1970	93
18 U.S.C.A. § 4161 [Good time]	355
21 U.S.C.A. §§ 841 *et seq.* [Comprehensive Drug Abuse Prevention and Control Act of 1970]	95
28 U.S.C.A. § 334 [Sentencing Institutes]	115

2. CORRECTIONAL FILES, TRANSCRIPTS, AND PROCEEDINGS

Presentence Investigation Report	32, 439
Prison Misconduct Hearings	272
Probation Revocation Proceedings	67
Parole Decision Proceedings	437
Parole Revocation Proceedings	499
Pardon Board Proceedings	549
Prison Classification	460

3. CORRECTIONAL POLICY DIRECTIVES AND REGULATIONS

Administrative Office of United States Courts, Conditions of Probation	62
Connecticut Department of Adult Probation, Conditions of Probation	61
Connecticut Board of Parole	
Statement of Organization and Procedures	418
Conditions of Parole	485
Connecticut Department of Correction	
Policy Directive on Discipline Procedures	254
Policy Directive on Use of Force	260
Policy Directive on Community Release Programs	401
Inmate Handbook of Regulations (1970)	270
Rules and Regulations of the Connecticut State Prison (1830)	262
Federal Bureau of Prisons	
Policy Statement on Inmate Discipline	262
Policy Statement on Good Time	355
South Dakota Prison Rules and Regulations	263
United Kingdom Home Office, Probation and Aftercare Department, License	489
United States Board of Parole	
Rules	422
Conditions of Parole	487

4. STANDARDS, GUIDES, AND MODEL ACTS

Administrative Office of the United States Courts, Division of Probation, *The Presentence Investigation Report*   25

Advisory Council on Parole of National Council on Crime and Delinquency, *Guides for Parole Selection*   427

American Bar Association Project on Minimum Standards for Criminal Justice
  Appellate Review of Sentences   112
  Probation   25, 54
  Sentencing Procedures and Alternatives   101

American Correctional Association, *Manual of Correctional Standards*   52, 218, 243

American Law Institute
  Sentencing Provisions of the Model Penal Code   9
  Transcript of Meeting in Connection with Model Penal Code   85

National Council on Crime and Delinquency
  Annulment of Conviction of Crime, A Model Act   557
  An Act to Provide for Minimum Standards for the Protection of Rights of Prisoners   352
  Model Sentencing Act   101

National Probation and Parole Institutes, *Uniform Parole Reports*   430

United Nations, *Standard Minimum Rules for the Treatment of Prisoners*   342

5. FEDERAL GOVERNMENT REPORTS

National Commission on Causes and Prevention of Violence
  Staff Report: Crimes of Violence   88, 215
  Staff Report: Law and Order Reconsidered   139

National Commission on Reform of Federal Criminal Laws
  Consultant's Paper: Low, Peter, "Preliminary Memorandum on Sentencing"   83, 100

The President's Commission on Law Enforcement and Administration of Justice
  Task Force Report: Corrections   24, 53, 207, 406, 426, 551
  Task Force Report: The Courts   13, 23, 78, 110, 118, 119
  Consultant's Report: Conrad, John, *Trends in European Corrections*   178
  Consultant's Report: MacCormick, Austin, *Adult Correctional Institutions in the United States*   133

The President's Task Force on Prisoner Rehabilitation: *The Criminal Offender, What Should be Done?*   557

6. ARTICLES AND BOOKS

Allen, Francis, "Criminal Justice, Legal Values and the Rehabilitative Ideal"   193

American Friends Service Committee, *Struggle for Justice*   197

Arluke, Nat, "A Summary of Parole Rules—Thirteen Years Later"   490

Bailey, Walter, "Correctional Outcome: An Evaluation of 100 Reports"   203

Banbury, Richard, "The Pardoning Authority in the Several States"   546

Barrett, Robert E., "The Role of Fines in the Administration of Criminal Justice in Massachusetts"   38

Best, Judah, and Birzon, Paul, "Conditions of Probation: An Analysis"   58, 65

Brendes, Ralph, "Interstate Supervision of Parole and Probation"   538, 539

Carter, Robert, and Wilkins, Leslie, "Some Factors in Sentencing Policy"   27

Cleaver, Eldridge, *Soul on Ice*   128

Clemmer, Donald, *The Prison Community*   158

Cloward, Richard, *Social Control in the Prison*   167

Cochran, Frank, "The Formal Discipline System in Connecticut Penal Institutions"   272

Conrad, John, *Crime and Its Correction*   4, 189

Cotzbauer, Robert, "Bill of Rights Posted for State Prisoners"   352

Cozard, Reed, "The Benefits of Executive Clemency"   545

Davis, Kenneth Culp, *Discretionary Justice*   421

TABLE OF STATUTES, REGULATIONS, BOOKS, ARTICLES, AND OTHER AUTHORITIES

Evjen, Victor, "Current Thinking on Parole Prediction Tables" 436
Fox, Vernon, "Analysis of Prison Disciplinary Problems" 271
Frankel, Marvin, "Lawlessness in Sentencing" 6, 121, 196
Glaser, Daniel, Cohen, Fred, and O'Leary, Vincent, *The Sentencing and Parole Process* 17, 415
Goffman, Erving, "Characteristics of Total Institutions" 153
Goldfarb, Ronald, and Singer, Linda, "Redressing Prisoner Grievances" 326
Grupp, Stanley, "Work Release and the Misdemeanant" 409
Ho Chi Minh, *The Prison Diary of Ho Chi Minh* 132, 385
Hood, R., "Research on the Effectiveness of Punishments and Treatments" 203
Hoover, J. Edgar, "The Dire Consequences of Premature Release" 55
Hopper, Columbus, "The Conjugal Visit" 371
Jackson, George, "A Letter from Soledad Prison" 130
Jackson, George, *Soledad Brother: The Prison Letters of George Jackson* 464
Jensen, Christen, "Pardon" 543
Johnson, Elmer, "Report on an Innovation—State Work Release Programs" 408
Larsen, Charles, "A Prisoner Looks at Writ Writing" 384
McCleery, Richard, "Authoritarianism and the Belief System of Incorrigibles" 251
Martinez, Joe, "Rehabilitation and Treatment" 225
Misenheimer, Mike, "Classification" 224
Moran, Frederick A., "The Origins of Parole" 410
Morris, Norval, "Lessons from the Adult Correctional System of Sweden" 181
"Note, Pardons in Virginia" 547
"Note, Appellate Review of Primary Sentencing Decisions" 102
"Note, Observations on the Administration of Parole" 494
Ohlin, Lloyd, *Sociology and the Field of Corrections* 168
O'Leary, Vincent and Nuffield, John, "Parole Decision Making Characteristics" 465, 532
Orland, Leonard, "Human Rights for Prisoners" 342
Orland, Leonard, "Politics and Parole" 425, 489
Orland, Leonard, "On Being Incarcerated" 277
Orland, Leonard, Testimony before House Judiciary Committee 489
Orland, Leonard, Statement before Senate Judiciary Committee 414, 423, 425
Packer, Herbert, *The Limits of the Criminal Sanction* 183
Prison Disciplinary Society, *First Annual Report* 241
Rothman, David, "The Invention of the Penitentiary" 141
Schrag, Clarence, "Some Foundations for a Theory of Correction" 169
Schwitzgebel, Ralph, *Development and Legal Regulations of Coercive Modification Techniques with Offenders* 203
Sparks, Richard, "Research on the Use and Effectiveness of Probation" 56
Sturup, Georg, "Will This Man Be Dangerous?" 436
Sykes, Gresham, *The Society of Captives* 160
Sykes, Gresham, and Messinger, Sheldon, "The Inmate Social System" 172
Thomas, Piri, *Down These Mean Streets* 372
Tromanhauser, Ed, "First Day in Prison" 125
Tromanhauser, Ed, "Parole" 462
Turner, William Bennett, "Establishing the Rule of Law in Prisons" 325
Walker, Nigel, *Sentencing in a Rational Society* 5
Wheeler, Stanton, "Socialization in Correctional Institutions" 174
Wilkins, Leslie, "Variety, Conformity, Control and Research" 4, 202
Wittstein, Andrew, "Petitioners Brief in Support of Pardon" 549
Wolfgang, Marvin, "Murder, The Pardon Board and Recommendations by Judges and District Attorneys" 544

INDEX

ALLEN, FRANCIS A.
   Rehabilitation, 193-196
AMERICAN BAR ASSOCIATION
   Guilty pleas, 81
   Minimum term in sentencing, 85
   Standards on probation
      presentence report, 25-27
AMERICAN LAW INSTITUTE, see Model
      penal code
ARKANSAS
   Whipping in prisons, 330-333
   See also Torture
ATTORNEYS
   DA's relationship to pardon boards, 544
   Parole revocation hearing
      lawyer's role, 517-518
      right to counsel
         Supreme Court approach, 518
         Justice Brennan on, 524-525
         Justice Douglas on, 526-527
   Prisoners as laymen lawyers, 377-385
AUSTRALIA
   Parole (ticket of leave) system, 411-412
   See also Parole
AUTHORITARIANISM
   Prison incorrigible units as extreme type,
      253-254
   See also Prisons, Prisoners

BAIL
   Reporting forms, 24
BAILEY, WALTER C.
   Analysis of reports of correctional
      treatment, 203-205
BATES, SANFORD
   Director, U.S. Bureau of Prisons, 133
BEAUMONT, GUSTAVE AUGUSTE de
   Observer of early prison systems, 141,
      143, 150
BLACK MUSLIMS
   Prison menus, 375-376
BORSTAL SYSTEM
   Federal Youth Correction Act modeled
      on, 19
   Influence in America, 180
BOSTON PRISON DISCIPLINE SOCIETY
   Congregate prison systems, 148
   Prison architecture, 142-143
BROCKWAY, ZEBULON R.
   Behavioral view of criminal law, 198

CALIFORNIA SUPERIOR COURT
   Probation system analyzed, 27-30
CAPITAL PUNISHMENT
   Cruel and unusual, 279-290
   Traditional punishment, 286
   See also Eighth Amendment

INDEX

CENSORSHIP
   Prisoner's communications, 386-397
CINCINNATI CONGRESS
   Reformation as objective of imprisonment, 3
CIVIL COMMITMENT
   Alternative to imprisonment, 39-44
   Of drug addicts, 43-44
   Of sexual psychopaths, 40-41
CIVIL RIGHTS ACT (1871) 42 USC 1983
   Judicial review of prison administration, 325-326
   Parole release hearing
      right to counsel, 468-477
   Prisoner's abuse of, 368-369
CLASS ACTIONS
   Judicial review of prison administration, 325-327
CLASSIFICATION, see Prisoners
CLEAVER, ELDRIDGE
   Description of prison, 128-130
CLEMMER, DONALD
   Prisonization, 158-160
      Clemmer's thesis discussed, 174-175
      process of, 158-160
      See also Prisoners
CLOWARD, RICHARD A.
   Status degradation of prisoners, 167
COCHRAN, FRANK B.
   Disciplinary hearings in prison, 272-276
   See also Discipline
COHEN, ALBERT
   Subcultures in working-class juveniles, 170
   See also Juvenile Delinquency
COMMUNITY RELEASE, see Parole, Prisoners
COMPREHENSIVE DRUG ABUSE, PREVENTION AND CONTROL ACT (1970), 95-99
CONNECTICUT
   Connecticut Sentence Review Division, 102-110
   Dept. of Corrections Act, 107
   Indeterminate Sentence Act, 106-107
   Parole statute, 106-107
CONNECTICUT DEPT. OF CORRECTION
   Community release program, 401-406
   Disciplinary hearings
      Cheshire, Conn. reformatory, 272-275
      Somers, Conn. prison, 275-276
   Disciplinary regulations, 254-261
   Haddam training program for correctional personnel, 277-278
   Handbook for inmates, 270-271
CONNECTICUT PAROLE BOARD
   Parole revocation papers, 499-513
   Samples of case records, 437-462
   Statement of procedures, 418-421
   See also Parole

CONRAD, JOHN P.
   Conflicts in correctional practice, 189-192
   European correctional systems, 178-192
   On punishment, 4
CONSCIENTIOUS OBJECTORS
   Religious beliefs, 49-52
CONVICTED PERSONS
   Civil rights lost
      holding public office and positions of private trust, 533
      jury service, 553
      need for reform, 555
      property and contract rights, 554
      restoration of, 555-556
      right to testify, 553-554
      Standard Probation and Parole Act, 558
      voting, 553
   Felony conviction, collateral effects of, 554-555
   Model act to annul a record of conviction for certain purposes, 558-559
CONVICTIONS, see Convicted Persons
CORRECTION, see Punishment
CORRECTIONAL INSTITUTIONS, see Prisons
COURTS
   Bargaining process, 18
   Probational discretion, 16
   Review of sentences
      ABA standards, 112-115
   See also Judges, Appellate
   See also Sentencing (appellate review)
COURTS, FEDERAL
   On prison writ-writers, 377-385
   Presentence reports, 27-30
   Reluctance to interfere with prison administration, 317, 368-369
CRIME
   Annulment of, 557-559
   Rates in Europe, 179
CRIMINAL LAW
   Behavioral view
      aversive suppression, 207
      classical conditioning, 206-207
      crime as individual pathology, 199
      four principal bases, 185
      incapacitation of criminals, 187-188
      individualized treatment model, 197-202
      operant conditioning, 206
      proportioning punishment to offense, 185
      rehabilitation of criminals, 188-189
   Recidivism, 186-187
   Rehabilitative ideal, 193-196
      debasement of, 195
      deterrence, 194
      focus on needs of criminal, 194
      political authority, 195-196
   Retributive view, 183-184, 186

Utilitarian view
  described, 184
  deterrence, 186-187
  recidivism and intimidation, 186-187

CRIMINAL PROCEDURE
  Evidence, see Evidence
  Judicial review of prison administration, 325-327
  Recidivist statutes, 89-91
  See also Habeas Corpus, Prisoners

CRIMINAL THEORY
  Sources, 169-172

CRIMINALS
  Changing criminal values in prison, 168-169
  Dangerous special offenders defined, 93-94
  Detainers, Agreement on, 539
  Ex-offender
    negative attitude of public, 216
  Leasing of convict labor, 151
  Moral rejection of, 162
  Prospects after prison, 557
  Rehabilitation through community based programs, 215-217
  Review of sentence in Conn., 102-104
  Special drug offenders, 95-99
  Treatment in 18 countries, 189-192

CRUEL AND UNUSUAL PUNISHMENT, see Capital Punishment, Punishment, Eighth Amendment

CUSTODY
  Treatment and, compared, 3

DANGEROUS
  Meaning under Sexual Psychopath Act, 40

DANGEROUS OFFENDERS
  Defined, 93-94
  Organized Crime Control Act of 1970, 93-95

DAVIS, ANGELA
  New York City Women's House of Detention, 340-342

DEATH PENALTY, see Capital Punishment

DETAINERS, 539-541
  Adverse to prisoners rehabilitation, 539-540
  Contrary to speedy trial provisions of Sixth Amendment, 539-540

DETAINERS, AGREEMENT ON
  Discussion, 539

DISCIPLINE
  Accepted practices, 245-248
  Connecticut Dept. of Correction definition, 254-255
  Definition and elements of, 243
  Disciplinary report, 255-256
  Disciplinary reports and hearings, 243-245
  Misconduct hearings
    examples of hearings in Connecticut prisons, 272-276
  offenses for which held, 273-276
  Punitive and administrative segregation distinguished, 246-248
  Unaccepted practices, 248-249
  United Nations standards, 345-346
  Who should administer, 249-250
  See also Punishment

DRUG ADDICTION
  Civil commitment of addicts, 43-44

DRUGS
  Consecutive sentences, 99-101
  Continuing criminal enterprise defined, 96
  Dangerous defendant, 98
  Special drug offender defined, 97-98

DUE PROCESS
  Civil Rights Act (1871), 42 USC 1983, 323-324
  Evidentiary hearings, 75
  Grievous loss doctrine, 521-522
  Indeterminate sentences for mentally ill sex offenders, 39-40
  Parole
    statutory limitations on U.S. Parole Board, 481-485
  Parole release hearing
    as continuation of sentencing, 472-474
    right to counsel, 468-477
  Parole revocation hearing
    minimum requirements, 524
    nature of process due, 522-524
    requirements of procedural due process, 526-527
    right to counsel, 513-527
    two-stage process, 522-524
  Presentence reports, 20-23
    disclosure of, 30-32
  Prison disciplinary proceedings, 309-317
    adjustment procedures of Maryland Div. of Correction, 314-317
    administrative segregation, 317-318
    notice of complaint, 311
    right to call witnesses, 311
    right to counsel, 311-312
  Probation revocation hearing, 527-532
  Proceeding to invoke a recidivist statute, 92
  Punitive segregation, 298, 303-305
  Related to exclusion of prejudicial evidence to jury, 89-91
  Right to counsel (6th Amend.), 72
  Termination of public assistance
    post-termination "fair hearing" versus pre-termination review, 75-77
  Vagueness of prison regulations, 333-335
  Withholding literature from prisoner, 395-397

DURKHEIM, EMILE
  Anomie, 169-170

EIGHTH AMENDMENT
Case history, 287-290
Corporal punishment, 330-333
Cruel and unusual punishment
  solitary confinement, 290-309
Jails as cruel and unusual punishment, 336-339
Legislative history, 286-287

EQUAL PROTECTION OF THE LAWS
Extended imprisonment for failure to pay fine, 33-36
Good time for jail inmates, 364-366
Jail conditions, 339-340
Mentally ill sex offenders, 39-40
Proceeding to invoke a recidivist statute, 92

EVIDENCE
Admission of previous crimes, 89
Rules of
  relevance to particular offense, 20-23

FEDERAL CRIMINAL CODE, 8
Consecutive sentences, 100-101

FEDERAL PRISON INDUSTRIES, INC.
Compensation to inmates for injuries, 320

FEDERAL PROBATION ACT
Judicial discretion under, 46-48

FEDERAL TORT CLAIMS ACT
Negligent acts of a "contractor," 324-325
Recovery of damages by prisoners, 319-320

FEDERAL YOUTH CORRECTION ACT, 19

FEDERALISM
Parole compacts and detainers, 536-541

FELONIES
Model penal code on, 9-13

FENCING, 47

FIFTH AMENDMENT
Right to remain silent
  parole revocation hearings and trial on new criminal charges, 534-535

FINES
Alternative to imprisonment, 17, 33-38
Failure to pay, 17
Gt. Britain home office study, 57
Massachusetts practice, 38
Model penal code provisions on, 9-10
Primitive societies, 38
State practices, 38

FINLEY, REV. JAMES B.
Prison society compared to society, 143

FIRST AMENDMENT
Prisoner's rights to literature, 386-397

FORTUNE SOCIETY
Distribution of Fortune News to prisoners, 394-395

FOURTEENTH AMENDMENT, see Due Process

FOX, VERNON
Misconduct in prison, 271

FRANCE
Probation, 179
Work release program, 409

FRANKEL, HON. MARVIN E.
Indeterminate sentence, 196-197
On sentencing, 6-8
On sentencing institutes and councils, 121-122

GAMBLING
Major problem in prison, 271

GOFFMAN, ERVING
On total institutions, 153-158

GOOD TIME, see Prisoners

GROUP COUNSELING
Decision making by group, 208-210
Juvenile delinquents, 208-210

GUARDS, PRISON, see Jailers

GUILT
Plea of guilty
  as affecting sentence, 80-82
  encouraged to save expense of trial, 80-81
  table of, 78

HABEAS CORPUS
Judicial review of prison administrative practices, 325-326
Prison writ-writers, 377-383

HABITUAL CRIMINAL STATUTES, see Recidivism

HEARINGS
Misconduct in prison, 272-276
Prison disciplinary proceedings, 309-317

HETEROSEXUALITY
Deprivation of in prison, 163-164

HO CHI MINH
Description of prison, 132
On prison writ-writing, 385

"HOLE", see Solitary Confinement

HOMOSEXUALITY
Aversive suppression, 207
Classical conditioning, 206-207
Prison, 164

HOOD, R.
Research results on punishment effectiveness, 203

IMPRISONMENT
Alternatives
  civil commitment, 39-44
  fines, 33-38
  probation, 44-48
  suspended sentence, 44-47
Costly nature of, 14
Determination of length, 18-19
Deterrence through isolation, 13-16
For nonpayment of fine, 34
Simulated experience, 277-278

INDEX

State statutes related to failure to pay fine, 36-37
See also Sentencing; Model penal code
INCARCERATION, see Imprisonment
INCORRIGIBLES, see Prisoners
INDETERMINATE SENTENCE
　Basic premises and goals, 8
　Behavioral views of criminal law, 185
　Connecticut Indeterminate Sentence Act, 106-107
　Dangers of, 8
　Defined, 17-18
　Depraving effect, 253
　European practice, 180
　George Jackson on, 132
　Hon. Marvin E. Frankel on, 8
　Origins of parole, 412-413
　Rehabilitation, 196-197
　Related to minimum and maximum sentences, 87
　Sexual psychopath laws, 198
　Sweden, 182
INDIGENTS
　Discriminatory statutes relating to fines and imprisonment, 33-37
INMATES, see Prisoners
INSTITUTIONALIZATION
　Alternatives to for juveniles, 207-215
　Authoritarian qualities of, 252-254
　Classification of inmates, 218-223
　Discipline, 243-250
　Total institutions
　　authority system described, 154-155
　　five groupings, 153
　　forms of adaptation to, 156-158
　　privilege system described, 155-156
　　staff versus inmates, 153-154
INTERSTATE COMPACT FOR THE SUPERVISION OF PAROLEES AND PROBATIONERS
　Parole compacts, 538

JACKSON, GEORGE
　Description of prison, 130-132
　On parole, 464-465
JAILERS
　Description of, 125-130
　George Jackson on, 130-132
　Salaries of, 140
　Tasks described, 160-161
JAILS
　Administrative segregation in, 340-342
　Equal protection of laws in, 339-340
　Good time for inmates, 364-366
　History, 335-336
　Jail-house lawyers, 378-383
　Rights of unconvicted detainees, 369-370

JUDGES
　Discretionary aspects
　　probationary discretion, 16
　　sentencing, 20-23
　　to sentence to maximum term, 83-88
　　to sentence to minimum term, 87-88
　Prejudicial behavior, 49-52
　Reasonable judge test, 103
　Relationship to pardon boards, 544
　Sentencing powers, 7
　Training of
　　sentencing councils, 119-120
　　sentencing institutes, 115-118
JUDGES, APPELLATE
　Review of sentence in Connecticut, 102-104
JUDICIAL REVIEW
　Loss of good time in prison, 357-364
JURIES
　Capital cases, 20-23
JUVENILE DELINQUENCY
　California youth authority community treatment project, 212-214
　Diagnostic parole, 213-214
　Foster and group homes, 210-211
　Guided group interaction program, 208
　Halfway programs, 211
　New Jersey Highfields project, 208-209
　Provo, Utah Pine Hills program, 209

KIDNAPPING
　No probation in New York, 16

LAWYERS, see Attorneys
LEGISLATION
　Prisoner's rights
　　National Council on Crime and Delinquency model act, 352-354
　　United Nations standards, 342-352
　Role of in fixing minimum terms, 84
　Statutory interpretation
　　of cumulative punishment, 99-100
LOW, PETER
　Consecutive sentences, 100-101

MacCORMICK, AUSTIN
　On federal and state prison systems, 133-138
MANDATORY RELEASE
　Parole under, as legal right and as legislative grace, 541-542
McCLEERY, RICHARD H.
　Incorrigible units and authoritarianism, 251-254
MENTAL TREATMENT CENTERS
　Punitive characteristics, 41-43
MESSINGER, SHELDON L.
　Social systems in prison, 172-174
MISDEMEANORS
　Probation reports, 24

INDEX

MISENHEIMER, MIKE
    On classification, 224-225
MISSISSIPPI STATE PENITENTIARY
    Conjugal visits, 371-372
MODEL PENAL CODE
    Alternatives to sentencing, 9-10
    Consecutive sentences, 100-101
    Conviction, collateral consequences, 552
    Fines, provisions on, 9-10
    Legislature's role in fixing minimum terms, 84
    On fines, 17
    On indeterminate sentences, 8
    On presentence reports, 24
    Parole, 414-415
    Probation, criteria in, 10, 16-17
    Sentencing provisions, 9-13
MODEL SENTENCING ACT
    Consecutive sentences, 100-101
    Legislature's role in fixing minimum terms, 84
MULTI-COUNT CONVICTIONS
    With consecutive and concurrent sentences, 99-100

NARCOTIC ADDICT REHABILITATION ACT
    Commitment for treatment under, 43
NARCOTICS, see Drugs
NATIONAL CONFERENCE ON PAROLE (1956)
    Convicted persons and civil rights lost, 557-558
NATIONAL COMMISSION ON CRIME AND DELINQUENCY. ADVISORY COUNCIL OF JUDGES. MODEL SENTENCING ACT. See Model Sentencing Act
NATIONAL COMMISSION ON LAW OBSERVANCE AND ENFORCEMENT
    On fines versus imprisonment, 17
    Presentence reports, 24
NATIONAL COMMISSION ON THE CAUSES AND PREVENTION OF VIOLENCE
    Crimes of violence, 215-217
NATIONAL COUNCIL ON CRIME AND DELINQUENCY
    Model act for protection of rights of prisoners, 352-354
    Model act to authorize courts to annul a record of conviction for certain purposes, 558-559
    Standard probation and parole act, 558
NEW JERSEY
    Highfields project for boys, 208-209
NEW JERSEY STATE PRISON
    Practices of, 160-167

NEW YORK PENAL CODE
    Probation in, 16
NEWSPAPERS
    Interviews with prisoners, 392-393

OHIO
    Lucas County jail described, 336-339
OHLIN, LLOYD
    Changing criminal values, 168-169
ORGANIZED CRIME
    Dangerous offenders, 93-95
    Dangerous special offenders, 93-95
    Special drug offenders, 95-99
ORLAND, LEONARD
    Simulated prison experience, 277-278

PACKER, HERBERT L.
    Justification for punishment, 183-189
PARDON
    Connecticut Board of Pardon, structure, 546-547
    Definition, 543
    Distinguished from reprieve and amnesty, 543
    History of, 543
    Pardon boards
        sources of information about application for pardon, 544
    Role counsel can play, 549-550
    Structure of pardon in the States, 425
    Virginia's policies, 547-549
PAROLE
    As conditioned freedom, 520
    As legal right and as legislative grace, 541-542
    Certificates of parole granted
        Connecticut certificate, 485-486
        United Kingdom Home Office, Probation and Aftercare Dept., certificate, 489
        U.S. Board of Parole certificate, 487-488
    Conditions of, 485-495
        contracts with ex-convicts, 492
        current practice, 490-491
        English system, 489
        excessive number, 489
        freedom to speak and assemble, 492-494
        "rehabilitative" ideal, 493-494
        table of regulations in States, 491
    Connecticut Board of Parole procedures
        discharge, 421
        factors considered in granting, 419
        hearings, 418
        revocation, 420
    Connecticut parole statute, 106-107; 413-414
    Current practices
        dispositional procedures after hearing, 468
        parole-release hearing characteristics, 466-467

INDEX

pressure to change, 465
record keeping, 468
right to counsel and witnesses, 467-468
Function described by U.S. Supreme Court, 520-521
Gt. Britain's prerogative writ jurisdiction, 480
Hearings prior to decision
   aims, 426-427
   Attorney Generals' survey of release procedures, 429-430
   closed nature of, 425; 429
   due process and U.S. Parole Board, 481-485
   excerpts from sample cases, 437-462
   pre-hearing evaluations
      case method, 426-427
      statistical method, 426; 428
   prisoners' right to Board's reasons for denial, 477-480
   Prof. K. Davis on discretionary justice, 479-480
   Prof. Kadish on board determinations, 478
   progress report, 502-503
   right to counsel, 468-477
   structure of board, 425
   structure of hearing, 429
   table of current practices, 469
   transcript of hearing, 448-451
History
   Alexander Maconochie, 412
   Elmira, N.Y. reformatory, 412-413
   English Penal Servitude Act (1853), 412
   indentured servants, 411
   indeterminate sentence, 412-413
   Irish convict system, 412
   Sir William Crofton, 412
   ticket of leave in Australia, 411-412
Ideal process described, 416
Interstate Compact for the Supervision of Parolees and Probationers, 538
Justice Douglas on, 526-527
"leniency" arguments, 416
Model penal code provisions, 11-12; 415
National Conference on Parole (1956)
   convicted persons and civil rights lost, 557-558
National survey of decision-making characteristics, 465-468
New Jersey Supreme Court reforms, 8
Parole boards
   and period of confinement, 18
   role in sentencing, 85-88
Parole officer
   authority of, 496
   compared to social worker, 495-496
Parolee's interest
   in conditional freedom, 517
   in liberty, 521-522

Prediction statistics
   extent of use in North America, 436
   tables, 430-435
Presentence report, 25
Prevailing patterns
   jails, 415-416
   time served before first release, 416
   violation rates, 416
Prisoners' views of process, 462-465
Progressive merit system described, 424
Release and revocation compared, 517
Revocation of
   exclusionary rule of evidence, 496-498
   Fourth Amnedment rights, 497-498
   lawyer's role in proceeding, 517-518
   lawyer's skills with evidence, 518
   not a criminal prosecution, 521
   parole violation reports, 499-501; 507-513
   right to counsel, 513-527
   stigma, 517
   transcript of hearing, 505-507
Revocation hearing
   hearing officers duties, 523-524
   problem of holding hearings prior to trial on new criminal charges, 524-525
   right to counsel, Supreme Court on, 518-527
   status of parolee compared to welfare recipient, 525-526
   tables on, 532-534
   two stage process, 522-524
   who should conduct, 523
Sample case records
   FBI records, 453-454
   parole application, 445-448
   parole hearing progress reports, 437-439; 451-452; 453-456; 457-458; 459-460
   presentence investigation report, 439-443
   psychiatric evaluations, 443-445; 456; 458-459
   transcript of parole hearing, 448-451
Standard Probation and Parole Act (1955), excerpts from, 558
State's interests in parolee, 522
Status of probationer/parolee compared to a prisoner, 517
"Street time," relationship to revocation charges and new offenses, 535-536
Suspended parole, right to of parole board, 535
Uniform Act for Out-of-State Parolee Supervision, 536-538
United States Parole Board
   factors considered in decision making, 422-423
   number of parole decisions, 421; 423
   rationale, 7-8

PAROLE (Continued)
  recommendations for reform, 422
  total discretionary powers, 421-422
  voting procedures, 422
PAROLE AND PROBATION COMPACT ADMINISTRATORS' ASSOCIATION
  Parole compacts, 538
PAVLOV, IVAN
  Classical conditioning, 206-207
PENITENTIARY, see Prisons
PENOLOGY
  Nineteenth century views on, 141-153
  Postulates and conflicts in eighteen countries, 189-192
  Repentance in, 81-82
PLEA BARGAINING
  Differential sentencing, 82
  See also Pleas
PLEAS
  Guilty
    as affecting sentence, 80-82
  Not guilty
    factor in sentencing, 81-82
  Plea bargaining, 78-79
  See also Plea Bargaining
PRESENTENCE INVESTIGATION
  Admissibility questioned, 23
  Aids in trial, 20
  Disclosure problems, 30-32
  Frequency, 23-24
  Function of, 24-25
  Misdemeanor courts, 24
  Reports
    A.B.A. standards, 25-27
    contents, 26
    recommendations and dispositions, 27-30
PRESENTENCE REPORTS
  Dangerous offenders, 93-95
  Special drug offenders, 97
PRESIDENT'S COMMISSION ON LAW ENFORCEMENT AND ADMINISTRATION OF JUSTICE
  Corrections
    convictions, collateral consequences, 551-556
    furloughs from prisons as a correctional device, 406-407
    parole hearing, 426-427
    presentence reports, 24-25
    probation, 53-54
    treatment in community, 207-215
  Courts
    plea bargaining, 78-79
    presentence investigation, frequency, 23-24
    sentence review, frequency, 110-112
    sentencing councils, 119-120
    sentencing in statutes, 13-17
    sentencing institutes, 118-119
PREVENTIVE DETENTION
  Dangers, 41
  Under Sexual Psychopath Act, 41
PRISON DISCIPLINE SOCIETY SURVEY (1826)
  Punishment in prison, 3
  Rationale of whipping, chains and solitary confinement with hunger, 241-242
PRISONERS
  Black Muslims and prison diets, 375-376
  Classification upon imprisonment
    classification defined, 219-220
    features of classification, 218-219
    inmates' view of, 224-225
    reception program, 220-221
    Rhode Island procedures, 225-240
    United Nations standards, 350
  Communications
    correspondence between prisoner and attorney, 389-390; 391-392
    due process in censorship, 395-397
    Fortune Society's Fortune News, 394-395
    letters to news media, 386-389
    literature in cell, 390-391
    newspaper interviews with prisoners, 392-393
    Warden's right to approve, 394
  Community release program
    financial allowances, 404-405
    furloughs, 407
    table of States having, 408
    types of programs, 402
    work release, 407
    work release in other countries, 409
  Compensatory damages for injuries suffered in prison industry, 320
  Conduct of (South Dakota), 263-264
  Damages for cruel and unusual punishment, 320-321
  Deprivations of cataloged, 161-170
  Disciplinary procedures, 243-250
  Disciplinary segregation of, 246-248
  Discipline
    categories of disciplinary action described, 234-235
    review of proceedings, 235-236; 238
  European treatment of, 178-182
  Facilities available for (South Dakota) 264-266
  Good time
    jail inmates distinguished, 364-366
    judicial review of loss of, 357-364
    meritorious distinguished from statutory, 366-367
    statutes, 355; 358
    withholding, forfeiture, restoration, 355-357

INDEX

Handbook of regulations, 270-271
Homosexuality, 164
Incorrigibles
    belief system of, 253, 254
    compared to Plato's allegory of the cave, 251
    environment compared to Nazi concentration camps, 253-254
    leaders described, 253
    solitary confinement of, 251-252
Information withheld from, 165
Inmate social system
    and Weber's theory of bureaucracy, 171
    factors leading to, 172-173
    features of, 175-176
    group cohesion, 173-174
    social rejection coped with, 167
Isolation of in 19th Century prisons, 144; 148
Jails, 335-342
Judicial review of prison administration
    Civil Rights Act (1871), 325-326
    class actions, 325-327
    habeas corpus, 325-326
    religious practices in prison, 328-330
Legal activities, 294-309
Legal aid
    law student programs, 380-381; 383
    negative aspects of prison writ-writers, 381-383
    prison writ-writers, 378-381; 384-385
Loss of societal amenities, 163
Methods of punishment in 1826, 241-242
Misconduct in prison
    major offenses, 271
    percentage figures, 271
Parole decisions
    complaints about, 464
    effects of imprisonment, 462-465
Parole release hearings
    right to board's reasons in denial, 477-480
Political beliefs, 294-309
Prisonization
    compared to assimilation, 158
    criminal and antisocial influences, 159
    Clemmer's hypothesis modified, 175
    Donald Clemmer on, 174-175
    process of, 158-160
    two conflicting views, 176-178
    universal factors of, 159
    Washington State Reformatory survey of, 174-175
Racial segregation unconstitutional, 374
Reactions to rules and regulations, 165
Recovery of damages under Feder Tort Claims Act, 319-320
Security in prison, 166-167
Segregating prisoners with conventional value orientations, 168-169

Sexual relations
    conjugal visits, 371-372
    homosexual, 372-373
Status degradation, 167
Sweden, 181-182
Treatment of, 3
Uniforms first worn, 146
United Nations standards of treatment, 342-352
Visitation, 162
Visitation rights
    National Councils' model act, 354
Visitations, corerspondence, etc. (South Dakota), 267-269
PRISONIZATION, see Prisoners
PRISONS
    Administration of
        changing criminal values, 168-169
        federal courts, 301; 317
        vagueness of regulations, 333-335
    Allocation of funds to, 139
    Architecture of, as moral science, 142
    Attica prison, 295
    Authoritarian qualities, 252-254
    Black Muslims, 294-297
    California system, 133-134
    Classification procedures, 218-240
    Clinton prison, New York, 322-323
    Commission recommendations, 4
    Comparisons to factory in 1820's, 151
    Congregate system, Auburn, New York
        and mid-western states, 149
        described, 142; 144
        origins at Auburn, New York, 141
        Tocqueville on, 148
    Connecticut State Prison regulations (1830) 262
    Corporal punishment in, 330-333
    Description by prisoner, 125-128; 128-130
    Discipline in, 243-250
    1830's compared to 1790's, 142
    Federal Bureau of Prisons regulations on inmate discipline, 262
    Federal system, 133
    Foreign, 3
    Green Haven, N. Y. prison, 294-297
    Ho Chi Minh on, 132
    Inmate social systems, 172-174
    Institutionalization as idea in 1830's, 142
    Labor as rehabilitating device, 146
    Lawyers, courts and "no assistance rule", 378-383
    Libraries in, 346-347
    Local jails and workhouses described, 140
    Military style of, 152
    Misconduct in, 271
    New Jersey State Prison practices, 160-167

PRISONS (Continued)
  Objectives, historical and present-day, 3-4
  Origins of, in America, 141-153
  Post-revolutionary structures to 1830, 145-147
  Prayers in, 142
  Prison buildings described, 139
  Prison canteens, 323-324
  Prison systems evaluated
    good/best systems, 133-136
    mediocre/worst systems, 136-138
  Prisoner-guard system, 136-138
  Psychological effects of, 130-132
  Punishment in (1826), 241-242
  Quakers as reformers, 3
  Ratios of staff to prisoners, 139-140
  San Quentin prison, 310-313
  Security of prisoners in, 166-167
  Separate system, Pittsburgh, Pa.
    described 142-144
    origins at Pittsburgh, Pa., 141
    Tocqueville on, 148
  Socialization in, 174-178
  South Dakota prison rules and regulations, 263-269
  Staff and control of prisoners, 190-191
  Success of correctional methods, 5-6
  Texas system, 134
  "Treatment" versus custody, 3-4
  "Yard" as forum of prison, 251
PRISONS, EUROPEAN
  Correctional work distinguished from American counterpart, 179-180
  Nationally administered, 178
  Personnel characteristics, 178
  Probation, 178-179
  Psychiatry in, 180
  Size of, 178
  Sweden
    labor in prison, 182
    respect for, 181
    women personnel, 181-182
PROBATION
  Administration of, 54
  Alternative to imprisonment, 16
  And A.B.A. standards, 54-55
  And John Augustus, 53
  And research, 56-58
  Appellate review of trial judge's discretionary grant, 44-48
  As matter of "grace", 515
  California Superior Courts system, 27-30
  Circuit courts, 28
  Compared to institutional treatment, 57-58
  Conditions of
    banishment, 60
    bonds posted, 59
    Connecticut form, 61
    contract analogy, 66; 75
    costs imposed, 58
    fines imposed, 59
    imprisonment, 60
    judicial review, 63-67
    legislative control, 66
    restitution, 59
    searches (4th Amendment), 63-64
    support of dependents, 59
    U.S. District Court form, 62
  Cost of supervision, 14
  Defined, 54
  Due process
    Justice Cardozo on, 73-74
  Eligibility, 54-55
  European models, 178-179
  Federal Probation Act, 46-48
  Federal system, 27-30
  French personnel, 179
  Hoover, J. Edgar on, 55-56
  Judicial review of grant or denial, 48-52
  Model penal code criteria, 10; 16-17
  New York laws on, 17
  Origins, 52-53
  Power to revoke, 55
  Presentence reports related to, 23-32
  Revocation hearing, 527-532
    right to counsel, 73-77
    right to counsel not a constitutionally imposed duty, 530
  Right/privilege distinction, 74
  San Francisco project, 27
  Tables on, 54
  Violation of probation and revocation, 67-70
  See also Parole
PROBATION OFFICERS
  Reports as aids in sentencing, 22-23
PUBLIC ASSISTANCE BENEFITS
  Pre-termination hearings, 75-77
  Right/privilege distinction, 76
  Right to counsel, 77
PUNISHMENT
  Analysis of reports of correctional treatment, 203-205
  Classification and disciplinary procedures at Adult Correctional Institution, Rhode Island, 231-240
  Correction
    U.S. compared to U.S.S.R., 190
    postulates of, in 18 countries, 190-191
    conflicts of practice, 191-192
  Cruel and unusual punishment, 279-290
    arbitrarily inflicted punishment, 284
    compensatory damages, 320-323
    constitutional check on congressional representatives, 282
    degrading to human dignity, 283-284
    excessive punishment, 285

INDEX

intent of Framers, 279-282
jail conditions, 336-339
Patrick Henry on, 280; 282
punishment unacceptable to society, 284-285
punitive damages, 320-321
punitive segregation, 297-298
solitary confinement, 290-309
torture as, 281
whipping, 330-333
See also Eighth Amendment
Defined, 4
Deterrent theory, 194-195
Due process in prison disciplinary proceedings
   adjustment procedures of Maryland Division of Correction, 314-317
   rudimentary rights of prisoner, 311-313
   violation requiring due process, 310
Effectiveness, 6
Effectiveness, research results, 203
Fines as, 38
Fines in Connecticut prisons, 257
Force in Connecticut prisons, 260-261
Incorrigibles, 251, 252
Inhuman treatment
   National Council on Crime and Delinquency model act against, 353
Modes of punishment
   in 1826, 3
   in 1970, 3
Rehabilitation, 196-197
Segregation
   administrative and punitive, 258
   facilities, 258-259
   procedures—diet, mail, etc., 259
Solitary confinement
   administrative segregation and due process, 317-318
   administrative segregation in jails, 340-342
   and due process, 313-314
   Dr. Seymour Halleck on, 300-301
   "Hole" described, 277-278
   judicial review, 326
   National Council on Crime and Delinquency model act on, 353-354
   restricted diet, 278-279
   Sol Rubin on, 300-301
South Dakota prison, 269
Stripes (whipping), chains, solitary confinement with hunger (1826), 241-242
"to fit the criminal", 4
United Nations standards on, 345-346
Vengeance or retribution in, 6
Whipping administered by prisoners, 330-331
Whipping as unacceptable practice, 248-249
PSYCHOTHERAPY
   European prisons, 180

QUAKERS
   As reformers, 3

RECIDIVISM
   Deterrent view of criminal law, 186-187
   Related to length of sentence, 88
   Texas statutes on, 89-91
   Research results, 202-203
RECONVICTIONS
   Variables associated with, 5-6
REHABILITATION
   Bentham, Jeremy, 194
   Community based programs, 215-217
   Federal/state prerelease centers, 211-212
   Foster and group homes, 210-211
   Halfway programs, 211
   Juvenile delinquency
      guided group interaction program, 208
      New Jersey Highfields project, 208-209
      Pine Hills (Provo, Utah) program, 209
   Medieval church's position, 193-194
   Modern forms distinguished from earlier forms, 194
   Prison employees engaged in, 139-140
   Treatment in the community, 212-214
RELIGIOUS FREEDOM
   Black Muslims and prison diets, 375-376
RHODE ISLAND
   Classification procedures and regulations at the Adult Correctional Institution, 225-240
RIGHT TO COUNSEL
   and recidivist statutes, 92
RIOTS
   as method of prison reform, 5
ROTHMAN, DAVID
   Origins of American prisons, 141-153
RULES OF EVIDENCE, see Evidence

SCHRAG, CLARENCE
   Sources of modern correctional theory, 169-172
SCHWITZGEBEL, RALPH
   Behavior modification programs, 205-207
SENTENCING
   Administrative sentencing, 19
   Alternatives to, 9-10
   A.B.A. standards on sentencing procedures and alternatives, 101-102
   Appellate review of
      A.B.A. standards, 112-115
      frequency, 110-112
      in the States, 110-111
      objections to, 111-112
   As affected by trial, 80-81
   Consecutive and concurrent sentences, 99-102
   Definite and indeterminate compared, 18

SENTENCING (Continued)
   Deterrent effects of different lengths
      of sentence, 88
   Differential, 81-82
   Discretion in, 6
   Disparity in, 7; 84
   Extended prison terms for dangerous
      offenders, 93-95
   Factors influencing, 6-8
   Guilty pleas, 81
   Indeterminate sentence, see Indeterminate
      sentence
   Judge's authority in, 14
   Judge's discretionary powers, 20-23; 46-48
   Mandatory sentences, 15
   Maximum terms
      A.B.A. report, 83
      discretion to trial judge, 83-84
      discretion to reside in court or
         correctional institution, 85-88
      Prof. Wechsler on, 85-87
   Minimum term
      A.B.A. report, 85
      arguments for, 84-85
      legislative and judicial roles, 84
      statutory controls, 85
      suggested standards in Connecticut,
         108-109
   Model penal code on, 10-11
   Model sentencing act, 16
   Plea bargaining, 78-79
   Presentence investigation
      sample report, 439-443
      under Model penal code, 12-13
   Presentence reports
      dangerous offenders, 93-95
      evidence of repentance, 82
      special drug offenders, 97
   Rationale, 6-8
   Reasonable judge test, 103
   Related to recidivism, 88-89
   Review of sentence
      Connecticut Sentence Review Division, 102
   Sentencing tribunal system, 19
   Statutory framework, 13-17
   Statutory lengths, 15-16
   Structural varieties, 18-19
   Training the judges
      sentencing councils, 119-120
      sentencing institutes, 115-118
   Washington statutes on, 72
   Who decides, 4
   See also Indeterminate Sentence
SEX CRIMES
   In prison, 271
   Indeterminate sentences for mentally ill
      offenders, 39-40
   Sex offenders act (Colorado), 39-40

   Sexual psychopath laws, 40-41
SING-SING
   19th Century practices in, 147; 149-150
SOLITARY CONFINEMENT, see Punishment; Eighth Amendment
SOUTH DAKOTA
   Prison rules and regulations, 263-269
SPEEDY TRIAL
   Detainers and the Sixth Amendment, 539-540
STATUTES
   Probation in, 16
   Statutory controls in sentencing, 85
STATUTES, RECIDIVIST
   Due process clause, 89-92
   Right to counsel, 92
STOLEN MERCHANDISE
   "Chasing" operation, 47
STRIP CELL, see Punishment; Eighth Amendment
SUSPENDED SENTENCE, see Probation
SUTHERLAND, EDWIN H.
   Differential association, 169
SWEDEN
   Correctional system, 181-182
   Work release program, 409
SYKES, GRESHAM M.
   Goals of jailers, 160-167
   Social systems in prison, 172-174

THOMAS, PIRI
   Sex fantasies in prison, 372-373
TOCQUEVILLE, ALEXIS de
   Observer of early prison systems,
      141; 143; 150
TORTURE
   Arkansas prison system, 3
   Flogging in prisons, 137
   Methods of punishment in 1826, 241-242
   Types inflicted in 19th Century, 149-150
TREATMENT, see Rehabilitation
TRIALS
   Defendant's right and guilty pleas, 81
TROMANHAUSER, ED
   Description of prison, 125-128
   On parole, 462-464
TRUSTEES
   Duties described, 128-129

UNIFORM ACT FOR OUT-OF-STATE
      PAROLEE SUPERVISION
   Partial provisions of, 536-538
UNITED NATIONS
   Standard minimum rules for treatment
      of prisoners, 342-352
UNITED STATES BOARD OF PAROLE
   Parole rationale of, 7-8

U.S. BUREAU OF PRISONS
  As an exemplary prison system, 133
  Good time policy, 355-357

VIRGINIA
  Vagueness of prison regulations, 333-335

WALKER, NIGEL
  On reconvictions, 5-6

WEBER, MAX
  Bureaucratic organizations, 170-172

WECHSLER, PROF. HERBERT
  Judge's discretion in sentencing
    to maximum term, 85-86
    to minimum term, 87-88

WHEELER, STANTON
  Socialization in prisons, 174-178

WILKINS, LESLIE T.
  On punishment, 4-5
  "Treatment" of offenders, 202-203

WRIT-WRITING, see Habeas Corpus; Ho Chi Minh; Prisoners

YOUTH CORRECTION ACT, see Federal Youth Correction Act

Soc
HV
9275
O74
cop 2